The Polish Few

The Polish Few

Polish Airmen in the Battle of Britain

Peter Sikora

Pen & Sword
MILITARY

First published in Great Britain in 2018 by
Pen & Sword Military
An imprint of
Pen & Sword Books Ltd
Yorkshire – Philadelphia

ISBN 978 1 52671 485 5

Printed and bound in the UK by TJ International Ltd,
Padstow, Cornwall.

Pen & Sword Books Limited incorporates the imprints of Atlas,
Archaeology, Aviation, Discovery, Family History, Fiction, History,
Maritime, Military, Military Classics, Politics, Select, Transport,
True Crime, Air World, Frontline Publishing, Leo Cooper, Remember
When, Seaforth Publishing, The Praetorian Press, Wharncliffe
Local History, Wharncliffe Transport, Wharncliffe True Crime
and White Owl.

For a complete list of Pen & Sword titles please contact

PEN & SWORD BOOKS LIMITED
47 Church Street, Barnsley, South Yorkshire, S70 2AS, England
E-mail: enquiries@pen-and-sword.co.uk
Website: www.pen-and-sword.co.uk

Or

PEN AND SWORD BOOKS
1950 Lawrence Rd, Havertown, PA 19083, USA
E-mail: Uspen-and-sword@casematepublishers.com
Website: www.penandswordbooks.com

Contents

A coloured vision in a paving-stone
set in this peaceful church within the Strand,
of valiant airmen from another land
who fought beside us when we stood alone;
who kept the faith with all we called our own
this land to cherish like a part of theirs,
as if where courage stands one heartbeat shares;
so much had they believed in, those now gone,
Here lies the memory of those gallant Poles
Who once swept onward in all timeless fight
to deadly target with their warlike goals;
nor shall their image perish from the sight,
but merge as one with all immortal souls
of famous men who flew into the night[1]

Foreword

The Polish Few considers relations between Polish and British aviation since 1915. It includes details of the Polish cadets of the Russian Imperial Air Force, who arrived at Northolt during the Great War, and the purchasing of British aircraft prior to the Second World War. Importantly, and most prevalent to us on modern-day Royal Air Force Northolt, is the narrative regarding the re-forming of the Polish Air Force (PAF) in Great Britain in 1940, the day-by-day operational chronicle of the PAF fighter and bomber squadrons during the Battle of Britain and the biographies of all Polish pilots who flew during the battle. Key for me, and for those of us based at Northolt who are reminded daily of the significant history of this station, are the echoes of the past and voices given to those Polish heroes who contributed so much for our freedoms. For us, we are continually reminded of those Polish air and ground crew who were based here during the war; but most especially the Poles of 303 Squadron who became the highest-scoring squadron of the Battle of Britain.

Group Captain David P. Manning ADC MA CMgr FCMI RAF
Station Commander RAF Northolt

Preface

A few years ago, the world-famous Supermarine Spitfire aircraft, an influential and emotional icon of British history, a magnificent defender of her independence and a perfect symbol of an undefeated nation, was used by one of the United Kingdom's political parties on their leaflets to represent true British traditions and values, and to appeal to the national pride of Britons, but, above all, to show the unfavourable policy of the party (the name of which I am not going to mention, purely because its members are rightfully entitled to have different views and opinions) regarding immigration from certain countries, including Poland. However, someone had not done their homework right.

This particular aircraft, with the code letters RF-D portrayed on the glossy paper, had been regularly flown by Squadron Leader Jan Zumbach, commander of No. 303 Polish Squadron. The distinctive, difficult to misinterpret red and white national emblem of the Polish Air Force was clearly visible on the aircraft's smooth and elegant nose. Oh, yes, someone could claim: these foreigners have used our magnificent aircraft, which we kindly agreed to lend them, to fight not only for our freedom but also for the freedom of their own homeland.

Not a big deal then: they owe us. But is that true, really? When the Second World War ended, the Polish Government in Exile, which had started to be politically inconvenient or even awkward for British Prime Minister Clement Attlee and his team, received a bill for over £107 million, to cover all expenses related to Polish Air Force operations from Britain. Basically, they had to pay back for each bomb they dropped on German targets, each bullet they shot at the common enemy, every single uniform they had worn, every button sewn on it, each slice of bread they ate or every bandage they used to help their wounded. So, was this Spitfire more British or Polish?

When the Battle of Britain Memorial at Capel-le-Ferne near Folkestone had been unveiled in 1993, bizarrely, the badges of Polish Squadrons 302 and 303 were missing from the original design of the monument. Ironically, due to that error and its subsequent corrections, they now have the honourable central position on the memorial, which they deserve. The badges are difficult to miss.

After long consideration, I decided to bring these somewhat controversial examples to readers' attention, not to put a cat among the pigeons, but to illustrate how much still needs to be done to avoid such purposeful wrongdoing or pure ignorance in the future.

It has to be said that the fault lays equally on either side of the barricade. In 2005, the Polish National Tourist Office in London promoted their campaign called 'Londoners, we are with you again!' with the bright poster of an airman standing next to a Hawker Hurricane aircraft with 'artificially' applied PAF emblem, known as the red and white chequerboard. Again, somebody failed to do their homework. They miserably missed the crucial detail that the pilot, who was supposed to be a Pole, was in fact Flight Lieutenant John Kent, a Canadian fighter ace serving with the RAF and consequently in the Polish squadron.

Hawker Hurricane P3939 RF-H, which was transferred from No. 302 Squadron, was the only known 303 aircraft marked with the Polish Air Force chequer used during the Battle of Britain. AC Antoni Głuski is standing on the port wing. The other members of ground crew are standing from left: Cpl Aleksander Leśniewicz (1st), Cpl Mieczysław Kowalski (3rd) and Sgt Karol Błachuta (4th).

Another example? The famous Polish song 'Squadron 303', written after the war, says, 'the Polish signs shine on our wings', ignoring completely the fact that the Polish Air Force flew British aircraft with the RAF roundels on both surfaces. In fact, very little evidence has surfaced so far to prove the presence of Polish marks on 303 Squadron's planes during the Battle of Britain. So much has to be improved here, in Britain just as in Poland. Unfortunately, fifty years of the Iron Curtain, which successfully divided Europe – creating the perception of poor Eastern, second-class neighbours – did its job rather well. Due to the lack of significant information, an average Briton knows very little about the Poles flying operationally from Britain, sailing alongside the Royal Navy on their own warships or fighting with the British Army in Africa, Italy or Western Europe.

How strange it still sounds that the whole impressive 17,000 men and women of the Polish Air Force were serving under British command throughout the war, whilst making the United Kingdom their temporary and only home. On the other hand, the majority of Kowalskis or Nowaks living over 1,000 miles away from here, in Poland, are generally not aware of the scale of the Polish presence amongst the Allied forces in the West. This is a result of communist censorship. They may know the specifically chosen basics about No. 303 Squadron, but only thanks to Arkady Fiedler's 1942 novel *Squadron 303/ Dywizjon 303* being mandatory school reading in Poland.

These people, now the current mature generation of a free Poland, but more worryingly also the country's youth, have no idea about any other wartime Polish participation and achievements. For them, the term 'Battle of Britain' rings a bell, but unfortunately thanks to its name, which suggests the geographical location, it still shockingly reflects all the operations carried out by the Polish Air Force from their bases in the UK between 1940 and 1945, instead of this one specific chapter of the war that significantly affected history.

It would be extremely optimistic to expect the British public to be aware of the Polish involvement in Enigma and the Ultra decoding programme, or the bravery of the soldiers from Polish II Corps, who made the decisive attack on Monte Cassino in Italy in 1944. Who knows that two Polish Army officers invented the mine detector,[1] or that the Polish Home Army captured a long-range V2 flying rocket and sent its parts to Britain? How much do we know about the Polish Independent Carpathian Rifle Brigade's impact during the defence of Tobruk in 1941, or 1 (Polish) Independent Parachute Brigade that saved General Robert Urquhart's British paratroops surrounded in Oosterbeek during the disastrous Operation Market Garden in September 1944? Are we aware of the existence of Roman Czerniawski, a Polish airman, who played a vital role as double agent 'Brutus' and 'Armand' in misleading the Germans where the 1944 Allied invasion of France would take place? How much was said about the Polish squadrons achieving the highest results during the 1942 Dieppe disaster? After the Tehran, Yalta and finally Potsdam conferences, where the fate of Britain's most loyal ally had been sealed, the infamous disappearance of Poland from the map of the modern, post-war world did not help people to keep up with the true facts; therefore all the achievements mentioned above were almost forgotten.

The truth is that in the summer of 1940, Fighter Command and Air Chief Marshal Hugh Dowding, its commanding officer, were struggling to find qualified flying personnel to replace their heavy losses and to face the overwhelming power of the German Luftwaffe.

Having used all their resources, and even employing bomber pilots to fly fighter planes, the RAF was in desperate need of experienced and battle-hardened airmen. Such men had indeed arrived from Poland, having survived two campaigns: the first in their homeland in 1939, and the second in France in 1940. Having experienced terrible scenes in their home skies, the Polish airmen were naturally eager to fight again. Unlike some sources, which make the mistake of claiming that the Polish Campaign was lost within days or even hours of the German invasion, the Poles had fought long and hard enough over Poland to gain a comprehensive understanding of German tactics. They left the enemy aware of the skills and determination of Polish airmen, with the Germans suffering relatively large losses.

These Poles were valuable and highly skilled military personnel who had gained experience of advanced fighting tactics in Poland, including the famous and practical 'four finger' formation, which is often mistakenly associated only with the Germans. Most of them also had an opportunity to fly modern aircraft during their time in France prior to that country's capitulation. The only obstacles that the Poles struggled with were the language barrier and the specific techniques of how British aircraft were operated. Generally speaking, the whole cockpit drill was completely opposite to what they had learnt in Poland and then in France. Also, they were not familiar with Imperial measuring systems; therefore, not knowing gallons, inches, feet, yards and miles, they quite often had to learn the hard way how to recognize the differences, sometimes even by crash-landing. They also hated the British tactic of flying the 'vic' formation because of its vulnerability.

While describing the Polish squadrons' day-by-day activities throughout the Battle of Britain may be easy, but not completely satisfying, if following the obvious sources, it is more difficult when trying to be more precise. The 303 Squadron story, for instance, is considerably easy to track, purely because this unit gained its fame, becoming almost iconic and more popular in Polish

The Polish hatred towards the enemy was fuelled by such scenes. German troops not only were idly watching Cpt Florian Laskowski dying in the wreckage of his aircraft, they also prevented civilians from helping him.

or even British culture and literature. Apart from the Operations Record Book, Monthly Activity Reports or Combat Reports, we have the famous chronicle which started as the personal diary of Mirosław Ferić and then, very smoothly, transferred into an official document. Numerous written memoirs, historical books or often untold stories passed by fathers and grandfathers to their children and grandchildren undoubtedly played a vital role in this case. Photographic coverage of 303's involvement in the Battle of Britain is also wider than the activity of the second Polish squadron or individual pilots during this time, thanks to the popularity that the 303 quickly gained.

The situation with 302 Squadron is imperfect, as a big chunk of their operational data is missing. Photographs showing the unit's pilots or aircraft from that specific chapter of the war are rare, but it could be worse. Thanks to elements of 302's Battle of Britain records published by its pilots, such as Julian Kowalski, Wacław Król or Jan Maliński, we know much more about their duties as a team, but also about personal emotions and brawls involving individuals. Such materials enable authors and researchers to trace the history of both units more precisely.

Poles who flew in the British squadrons, unless they shot down an enemy aircraft or were shot down themselves, captured relatively less attention of the RAF's clerks, who struggled with their foreign names. Their names very often incorrectly appear in the Squadrons' Operations Record Books, so therefore we can establish how frequently they were scrambled or participated in patrols or encounters with the enemy. We know less about their day-to-day whereabouts and personal dilemmas. Those who left behind a legacy in the form of books or even single, loose notes, for many reasons were sporadic. Thanks to their British brothers-in-arms, who kindly mentioned those strange people of Slavic names and adventurous nature in their wartime recollections, we can know more about their feelings, daily language struggle and combat experiences over the skies of Albion.

There is still an immense amount of work ahead, with much research and investigation of events awaiting both British and Polish Air Force historians, researchers or people simply with the desire to find out more. There are only a few dedicated historians, affectionately known as 'maniacs', directly involved in investigation and exploration. As long as they are supported and encouraged by governments and various organizations and private individuals, there will always be light at the end of the tunnel.

In my work, not only on this book but also during my general research, I was kindly supported by many people; not, thanks to God, only by 'the few'. In this case I would like to express my highest admiration and deepest indebtedness to: Dr Bartłomiej Belcarz, the late Stanisław Bochniak, the Borowski family, Nina Britton Boyle, Andrzej Brzezina, Jerzy Butkiewicz, Rodney Byles, the late Stanisław Chałupa, Zbigniew Charytoniuk, Peter Devitt, Mieczysław Dodo, the late Czesława Dombkowska-Wyszyńska, Peter and Tony Drobinski, Janina Dunmil Malinowska, Marek Duryasz, Philip Methuen-Ferić, Brendan Finucane, Stefan Gabszewicz, Gallus family, the late Bolesław Gładych, the late Antoni Głowacki, the late Czesław Główczyński, Zenon Gmur, Stefan Gnyś, Steve Gorzula, Łukasz Gredys, Robert Gretzyngier, Franciszek Grabowski, Adam Jackowski, Jonathan Kellett, Louise Pemberton-Kellett, Alexandra Kent, the late Wojciech Kołaczkowski, Mariusz Konarski, Grzegorz Korcz, the late Franciszek Kornicki, Julian Kowalski junior, the late Tadeusz Kumiega, Jan Łaguna, Krys Lanowski, the late Stanisław Łapka, Łapka family including Josephine Kendrew, Marek Malarowski, Karl and Jack Mierzejewski, Andrew Manning, the late Stanisław Marcisz, Wojtek Matusiak, the late Jerzy Mencel, Teresa Mümler, the late Tom Neil, Sofia Niemiec, the Neyder family, Dorota Nowakowska for Łapkowski family, Stefan Pietrzak, Robert Pliszka, Roman Popławski, Marek Rogusz, Daniel Rolski, Wojciech Sankowski, Alan Scheckenbach, the late Ted Sergison, the late Stanisław Skalski, the late Adolf

Stempkowski, Dr Grzegorz Śliżewski, Topolnicki family, Witold Urbanowicz Jr, Leszek Winiarski, Jan Wojciechowski, the Wójtowicz family, Wydrowski family including Joanna Kieran, Agnieszka Wyszyńska and Kelvin Youngs. Special thanks to my wife Maggie, for her unstinting support and patience. I would like to dedicate this book to the memory of my Mother, my most loyal reader

Introduction

It was Sunday, 1 September 1940, a sunny day from the beginning, with good visibility and little German activity in the morning. The situation changed around 10.30 am, after British Radio Detection Finder stations – later known as radar – discovered a very large enemy formation heading towards Kent. Twelve Hurricanes carrying SD code letters – signifying 501 'County of Gloucester' Squadron – took off at 2.00 pm. Only one section encountered 'Jerry', after identifying twenty-seven twin-engine Messerschmitt Bf 110s of Lehrgeschwader 1 near Maidstone. These Zerstöres, after being attacked from astern, immediately twisted in the direction of Yellow Section and one of them immediately separated from the formation with a disabled engine. A few minutes later, the same Bf 110L1+OH from 13 Staffel LG1, with a crew of Ofw. Rudolf Kobert and Fw. Werner Meining, was finished by Pilot Officer Charles English and Pilot Officer Albert Lewis of 85 Squadron, crashing near Bilsington. This was the only combat success over Tunbridge Wells that was claimed by a young Polish officer known as 'Stan' Skalski, later described by Pilot Officer Kenneth William Mackenzie, a Belfast-born fighter pilot, as, 'a Pole, slightly built, pale-faced, with an emotional hatred of the Germans'.

Twelve aircraft from 501 Squadron safely landed back at Gravesend after a second mission of the day. The battle-hardened Pole was probably disappointed. He already had thirty combat sorties and at least four enemy planes claimed as shot down in Poland under his belt. Skalski, using his poor and basic English, later gave an account of this action:

> 'I was No. 2 in Yellow section when the Squadron was flying at about 18,000ft from Gravesend in the direction of Tunbridge Wells. I saw 9 Me 110s in a defensive circle which was not yet quite complete. I dived down and up again, attacking one of the Me 110s from below. This left the circle and a dog-fight followed. The others attempted to get on my tail. I was forced to break off the engagement. The Me 110 that I attacked was smoking from the port engine and the gunner in the rear ceased fire.'

After providing an Intelligence Officer with the details of this flight, Stanisław Skalski sat down and began dreaming. The Polish pilot, known for his

Stanisław Skalski, 1st from right, was known for his individualism, no surprise then that he graduated in 67th place out of 90 Cadets from Dęblin's AF School. Flying instructor Bronisław Malinowski, 2nd from right, also took part in the Battle of Britain, similarly as Jerzy Czerniak (1st from left).

determination, strong and controversial opinions – but also stubbornness – remembered very well how different everything was back in Poland. Time had gone by very quickly, he thought: the situation had changed yet the enemy remained the same. It was exactly one year earlier that his long journey had started. By then, Skalski was a 24-year-old fighter pilot who had graduated from the prestigious Polish Air Force Cadet Officers College in Dęblin only a year before. With a promising career ahead, holding the rank of podporucznik (Sub-Lieutenant),[1] Skalski was also known as 'Kędzierzawy' (Curly), probably a rather ironic nickname given to him by his friends once the first signs of baldness appeared. Stanisław had been full of dreams and hopes that crashed into pieces within a second when he realized that his beloved PZL P.11 fighter plane was hardly capable of intercepting a German bomber or even a reconnaissance aircraft.

On 1 September 1939 he was pursuing a German Henschel Hs 126 that was eventually shot down by his fellow pilots from 4th Pułk Lotniczy (Air Regiment), Lieutenant Marian Pisarek and Corporal Benedykt Mielczyński (both from 141st Eskadra Myśliwska [Fighter Squadron]).[2] Skalski, who served in the twin 142nd Fighter Squadron, landed near the wreckage to help both wounded enemy airmen, Oblt Siegfried von Heymann and Oblt Friedrich

Wimmer, but also to secure important operational German documentation which he found with them. In this very early stage of the war, the knight's code was still functioning and respected, and he did not know about the Germans targeting Polish airmen baling out from their aircraft.

Skalski quickly realized that the Polish Campaign was spiralling into a one-sided nightmare for his country, despite declarations given publically by government propaganda and his superiors that Poland was 'strong, united and ready'. The Polish Air Force struggled as a result of confusion from pre-war indecision whether it would need more fighters or bombers. The whole Polish defence system was based on obsolete assumptions and relied on its natural, yet easy to cross, borders, of which 85 percent were frontiers with hostile countries. Despite British and French promises of aid, which never materialized, the Poles fought alone against Germany, a country that was allowed to grow back into power by the naive Western governments. The Polish Air Force was badly equipped and logistically weak. Polish Military Aviation, as it was officially called, was definitely not ready for the coming blitzkrieg. But who was ready for it at the time? Not Belgium, Holland, Denmark, France or Britain … even Germany did not then know the true capability of blitzkrieg tactics. No-one really expected such use of air power and fast-advancing tanks.

Chapter One

A Long Way to the 'Island of Last Hopes'

For over 1,000 years of its long history, the Kingdom of Poland always struggled with its neighbours, being forced to defend its borders against a powerful Germany, Prussia, Russia, Sweden, the Ottoman Empire and Tatars. In the sixteenth and seventeenth centuries the Polish-Lithuanian Commonwealth (a union of the Kingdom of Poland and Grand Duchy of Lithuania)[1] was one of the largest countries in Europe, covering nearly a million square kilometres, with its massive territory stretching from the Black Sea to the Baltic Sea.

It was a country of religious tolerance, with a progressive political system, fast-moving scientific and cultural developments, and the first constitution in Europe that consisted of a set of modern, supreme national laws. The Polish cavalry was famous and almost unbeatable, gaining their reputation by destroying the army of German Teutonic Knights in the Battle of Grunwald in 1410; 2,600 eagle-winged hussars also defeated 10,000 Swedish invaders at the Battle of Kircholm in 1605, while eighty years later, a charge by the Polish army led by King Jan III Sobieski saved Vienna from Ottoman oppression.

However, in the second half of the eighteenth century, the situation for this central European country was much more difficult and far from glorious. Politically divided, weak, surrounded by powerful neighbours hungry for her territory and facing her own internal rebellions, Poland eventually fell. After three consecutive territorial partitions, its existence was ended by the Prussian, Austro-Hungarian and Russian empires. The three titans grabbed what was in their reach, aiming to destroy Polish pride, identity, culture and science. The native Polish language was forbidden, Poland was swept from the map of Europe and her citizens had to wait and fight for 123 years to reclaim their independence.

This finally became possible when the guns of the Great War went silent, Poland regaining her place among other nations in November 1918. The country was free, but definitely not safe, and had to reaffirm its freedom by defending its right to exist and making the Polish borders stronger again. New wars started even before Poland returned to the European map. Two weeks prior to the official proclamation of independence, that became a fact on 11 November, conflict began with the West Ukrainian People's Republic and Ukrainian People's Republic (1918-19). This was followed by a decisive war, not fully appreciated by the Western politicians, against Bolshevik Russia (1919-21), when heroic Polish defence crushed the Red Army at the outskirts of Warsaw, and by this act of desperation stopped bloodthirsty communists from marching throughout Europe. While engaged on its eastern flank, the country was invaded by the Czechoslovaks from the south (1919); at the same time, an uprising against German occupation in Greater Poland took place (1918-19), followed by a series of Silesian uprisings (1919-21). Between 1919 and 1920 there was a war against Lithuania, while finally in 1938, Poland was involved in another conflict with Czechoslovakia, both countries claiming their rights to the Zaolzie (trans. Olza Silesia) region.

Years of non-existence as a country or constant movement of its borders made Poland (a ghost country by then) and her citizens a nation of forced travellers. There were several reasons for this. Poles were often obliged to

Since regaining her independence Poland had to fight for survival against neighbouring countries. The Polish Military Aviation was born at the same time, although the first encounters noted by the Polish airmen were recorded prior to independence date. Fokker E.V. CWL001 with personal emblem of compass rose and red and white chequerboard, which belonged to Lt. Stefan Stec. The chequerboard had been adopted as an official badge of the Polish Air Force. During the Great War Stec flew with Flik 3/J and then Flik 9/J, gaining three aerial victories. Flying with 7th Squadron (later 'Tadeusz Kościuszko' Squadron), Stec added two more claims while fighting against Ukrainians.

change their place of residence, either as punishment for illegal independence and liberation activity, or, in many cases, when they were looking for a better life and economic stability within the boundaries of the three governing empires, which split the territory of Poland between themselves. That was why those Poles, including the Polish Battle of Britain pilots, who were born prior to November 1918 consequently grew up as residents of the Austro-Hungarian Empire, Prussian then German Empire and Russian Empire before gaining their own citizenship.

Those who were born within the historical boundaries of the former Kingdom of Poland, or whose parents settled in Russia, Ukraine (a state also ruled by the Tsar) or Germany, were still citizens of those empires but of Polish nationality. This is what mainly causes the numerous mistakes made by Western writers who did not experience the movement of borders, or who never lived in the country that was torn apart. The best example of such confusion, which still exists in non-Polish publications, is Squadron Leader Eugeniusz Horbaczewski, introduced in British literature as a 'Polish-Russian ace' purely because he was born in Kiev.

The birthplaces of those who were born after the date of Polish independence, but were brought up in towns ruled by Poland, like Wilno (Vilnius since 1945) or Lwów (now Lviv), also cause confusion for Western historians. As a result of the Western powers handing over her future to Stalin after the Second World War, Poland, the first country to fight Nazi aggression, lost a massive part of her Eastern territory, and many of her citizens their homes.

It should not, therefore, be unexpected that, due to the historical turbulences of Poland, her political and geographical instability, which all influenced the mixing of cultures, there were Second World War Polish pilots called Ebenrytter, Henneberg, Goettel, Klein, Langhamer, Mümler or Pfeiffer,[2] or, on the opposing side, Germans named Dymek, Guschewski, Kaminski, Kania or Mazurkowski.

During all those struggles, a gradual involvement of the newly born, inexperienced and rather primitive Military Aviation (Lotnictwo Wojskowe) – as officially the future Polish Air Force was called – can be observed. This was a brand new concept and structure that was formed from absolutely nothing. The Polish Military Aviation based its first strength on pioneers, veterans of the Great War who, against their will, served in armies of occupation of the Russian, German and Austro-Hungarian empires, and very often had no other choice than to fight against each other.

These soldiers with no country now gained back their Polish citizenship and learnt how to keep their heads held high. At this point, in utterly new circumstances with limited resources, they had to build a completely new flying arm of the military system, and had to do it quickly, as the enemies of the Second Polish Republic did not want to wait. Like an ancient phoenix rising from the ashes, Poles generated their early air force by using damaged, incomplete or not fully efficient equipment that was left by their former tyrants and oppressors.

Challenges piled up rapidly. Spare parts were desperately needed. Polish industry had been ruined and plundered, and too few skilled personnel were available. There was, however, no lack of enthusiasm or passion. Against all odds, the Polish Air Force was making small steps and getting ready for combat.

Unfortunately, from the moment of its birth the Polish Military Aviation suffered from the Great War syndrome. Veterans of the previous conflict, who remembered flying over the trenches and performing reconnaissance missions, were now in charge. People who did not see how aerial conflict could easily develop, in their minds labelled aircraft as of secondary importance. They were supported in their naivety by the head of the Polish state, Marshal Józef Piłsudski, who strongly believed that in forthcoming conflicts the aviation would only be used over battlefields as a reconnaissance force, in a supporting role to the main power – the army. Piłsudski kept saying that 'aviation is to serve only for reconnaissance purposes and only in this direction should it be used'. Hence, liaison/companion or army co-operation squadrons (Eskadras) were favoured and dominated, and at some point training of military officer pilots had been restricted to only produce more observers. It was like teaching an old dog new tricks, but in this casee the teachers were difficult to find.

An interwar period that Poles themselves rather optimistically called 'twenty years between wars', which was dated from the Armistice of 11 November 1918 that concluded the Great War and ended by German aggression in 1939, had in fact been much shorter, interrupted by the previously mentioned conflicts. Therefore, Polish aviation infrastructure had only very limited time to develop properly before the outbreak of the Second World War. This was not helped by poor budgetary and industrial capability and lack of certainty of the future role of the military aviation, with inadequate plans.

Nevertheless, there was no lack of admiration for this newly born military arm of the Polish defence system. Personnel training expanded rapidly. Thousands of enthusiastic young men joined civilian gliding training, and various air force schools were formed, including the famous Polish Air Force Cadet Officers' School in Dęblin, fairly considered as one of the best aviation academies in the world. Flight Lieutenant Stanisław Bochniak, who earned his wings in Dęblin and later flew operationally in Britain, said:

Albatros D.III of the 7th Fighter Squadron photographed during the Polish – Bolshevik war in 1920. The "Kościuszko" badge designed by Lt Elliot Chess, an American volunteer, can be seen.

'There was a popular saying amongst the aviators that only thanks to us was the Finger Formation called the Polish Formation. [It was a] quite difficult structure, which required a huge amount of skills, which we did not lack by then. This unique aerial arrangement allowed us to watch after each other and to fly safely. English pilots could not understand and adopt such a formation for a very long time. We owed such skills to the Eaglets School at Dęblin, beyond doubt, the best aviation school in the world.'[3]

The 1930s saw an impressive reorganization and intensification of flying training in Poland, while aviation engineering was also improved drastically. In 1939, about 800 pupils were in training in Dęblin and over 300 highly trained cadet officers graduated from this school, 65 per cent of them pilots. Needless to say, Dęblin was only one of the educational elements of the Polish air force chain: there were also Technical and NCO schools.

Although the Polish Military Aviation largely based its strength on French-built or licensed equipment, indigenous technological progress blossomed too. The Polish, or better known as Puławski wing, wing of the gull shape marked a brand new era by boosting Polish industry and outperforming other contemporary fighters across the world. Zygmunt Puławski's design turned into the first totally metal-built fighter aircraft. The P.6 model created an absolute sensation when shown in Paris and then in Ohio, USA, and its successor in 1934, the P.24, was announced as the fastest and best-armed fighter aircraft in the world. Jerzy Rudlicki of the LWS factory in Lublin created a revolutionary Vee-tail unit that was later copied by many other countries.

These are just two out of many examples. All this development was undoubtedly ignited by the success of Captain Stanisław Skarżyński, who made a tour across Africa flying the Polish-built PZL Ł2, and soon after crossed the Atlantic in a RWD-5bis. Poland in the 1930s also blossomed with the success created by the duo of Franciszek Żwirko and Stanisław Wigura who won the Challenge 1932 for domestic production aircraft with the RWD 6, while Captain Jerzy Bajan repeated their success two years later and also flew a Polish aircraft.

Unfortunately, what was considered a great success at the beginning of 1930s was already obsolete just a few years later, lagging far behind the competition. In the mid-1930s, low-wing aircraft with retractable undercarriage, fully enclosed cockpit and metal wings appeared as standard. The British Spitfire

The group of Cadet officers of the 11th class of the Polish Air Force Cadet Officers' School at Dęblin (please note school's badge on their singlets). Amongst them are some future Battle of Britain pilots. Front row, from left to right: Jan Daszewski (1st), Aleksy Żukowski (2nd), Tadeusz Nowak (4th) and Jerzy Czerniak (6th). Back row: Włodzimierz Samoliński (1st).

(despite going into production relatively late), French Morane 406 and German Messerschmitt 109 were not only much faster than Polish planes, but also had an advantage of decisive gun power. Not only was the only Polish front-line fighter and interceptor monoplane, the PZL P.11, with a maximum speed of 233mph and armament of two 7.92mm machine guns, no match for the German Messerschmitt Bf 109 or Bf 110, but its performance also placed this aircraft behind Luftwaffe bombers such as the Dornier Do 17, Heinkel He 111 or Junkers Ju 88.

In 1936, Poland finally began development plans, but the results were not impressive. Due to controversial decisions at various levels and key departments, who were playing a blame game, these plans had no chance of being implemented. The best Polish fighter plane, the PZL P.24, with two Oerlikon 20mm cannons and two machine guns (or four machine guns), were exported to Bulgaria, Turkey and Greece. At the same time, the PZL P.50 'Jastrząb' (Hawk) was still undergoing trials and far from entering final production, similar to the twin-engine PZL P.38 'Wilk' (Wolf), a disappointing interceptor and fighter-bomber. Others, such as the PZL P.45 'Sokół' (Falcon) and PZL P.48 'Lampart' (Leopard), were mostly only on the drawing board or taking shape as prototypes. Sadly, in September 1939, the PZL P.11, the lonely defender of Polish skies, had been left only with its remaining advantages of manoeuvrability, robustness and agility; and of course with highly trained and brave pilots inside their cockpits.

Chapter Two

Myths and Understatements

'I remember 1 September 1939 very clearly, for how could any Polish person ever forget,' wrote Jan Kowalski, instructor of the Air Force NCO School for Minors and future Battle of Britain pilot.

> 'I was asleep and suddenly awoken at 6.30 am by the sound of aircraft approaching. I knew that it was not our aircraft as none went up until after 8 am. Within seconds, the German aircraft were dropping bombs all around us. We quickly ran to the trenches that had only recently been dug out. Three rows of buildings, the mess, living quarters, and hangars were all hit.'[1]

How many times have various books and historical magazines, published in the West, portrayed, unsupported by any facts, the subject of Polish cavalry armed with just lances and swords, but also with romantic heroism yet tremendous stupidity, charging against German tanks?[2] Another myth created by Nazi propaganda that is still widely believed today, without any proof to back it up, is that the Polish Air Force was destroyed almost immediately on the ground, and that the entire Polish Campaign of 1939 lasted only days, followed by the mass escape of Polish forces across the borders into Rumania and Hungary.

Many biographies of the Polish airmen written in English will contain the phrase 'escaped to Britain'. Unfortunate word of 'escape' (in Polish language directly translates to 'running away') thoughtlessly misused so often, makes the Polish military personnel a bunch of deserters, rather than determined airmen, sailors or infantrymen, who left their beloved homeland following specific orders issued by their superiors, to evacuate themselves in a purpose to continue the fight abroad. Although in English 'escape' has more than one meaning, it could be easily misinterpreted by some less experienced history enthusiasts. For many British readers, the story starts in the winter or spring of 1940, when thousands of Polish airmen, defeated twice and after evading captivity, 'fled' Europe and landed in Britain.

It also has to be said that neither the British Government nor the French did anything when Stalin's army attacked the Polish defences from behind two weeks after the German invasion. The eminent British statesman, David Lloyd

George, tried to justify the cowardly Russian move by claiming that the Soviets had freed Polish workers and peasants oppressed by their own regime. First Lord of the Admiralty Winston Churchill, meanwhile, explained that it was actually a strategic move to secure Russia's own safety. Such a closure of the 'Polish problem' provided by such well-respected politicians, not only helped Britons to sleep better, but also ended many people's interest in the war in Poland. For many, this 'foreign war fought far away' ended on 17 September, so therefore even today it is widely thought that the campaign lasted only two weeks.[3]

It has to be said that the Polish defence system was outdated, weak and therefore not ready to face so powerful an enemy as Germany, and that the Polish Air Force was simply unable to last any longer without supplies, new and modern aircraft and Allied support. Poland's borders were far more easy to cross than the English Channel. Needless to say, Luftwaffe bases were deliberately distributed throughout north-east, east and south-east Germany, but also across East Prussia and the newly created pro-fascist Slovak Republic. In fact, the Slovaks (including their air force) are very rarely, if ever, mentioned as the third aggressor against Poland after Nazi Germany and the Soviets.

The geographical location of the 2nd Republic of Poland in the centre of Europe gave her a massive disadvantage.[4] If there wasn't the Channel between France and England, German tanks could have crossed the 20 miles in just an

Zygmunt Puławski's design of a gull shaped wing was innovative and his aircraft was hailed the best fighter machine of the world. In 1939 the time of its glory was long time gone.

hour during the early summer of 1940. Poland did not have the advantage of any natural or man-made obstacles preventing her territory from being invaded. Britain, in 'splendid isolation', was guarded by the sea and the French had their supposedly magnificent Maginot Line, but Poland had no such barriers.

Marshal Herman Göring's Luftwaffe had nearly 2,000 operational aircraft in two Air Fleets (Luftflotten) ready to do their job over Poland. To highlight the disproportionate power on both sides in the 1939 conflict, it should be noted that almost exactly the same number of German aircraft were used in 1941 for the invasion of the much stronger Soviet Russia.

Young Polish front-line pilots awaited the confrontation with high hopes, not yet realizing what was awaiting them. Stanisław Skalski of 142nd Fighter Squadron later said:

> 'I was looking forward to the future. I was ready to face all adversity. What was supposed to happen intrigued me, and excited me, I almost secretly wanted it to occur as soon as possible. I underestimated German power and did not think that the future situation may turn out so tragically. The magnificent fighting spirit of our squadron filled me with confidence.'[5]

The superiority of the Luftwaffe over the Polish Air Force was undoubtedly overwhelming. In fighters there was a ratio of 3.3:1 (523 modern aircraft against 158, the latter number including Poland's obsolete and completely useless PZL P.7s), but the real size of the German advantage can be seen by comparing twin-engine bombers on both sides. The Luftwaffe had 695 of them, while Poland only had thirty-six PZL P.37s 'Łoś' (Elk), the only relatively advanced Polish aircraft with a retractable undercarriage.

Sub-Lieutenant Franciszek Kornicki recalled:

> 'No. 161 Squadron was equipped with P.11 aircraft, while my squadron – No. 162 – had the P.7. This was a disappointment as the P.7 was inferior to the P.11 in every respect and was overdue for replacement. I hoped that we might be re-equipped very soon … It was in this situation that my squadron – 162 – equipped with the outdated P.7, without radios, entered the war.'[6]

'Such a huge difference in the rate of climb has shocked me,' wrote Corporal Michał Cwynar, a pilot of the 113th Fighter Squadron, after an encounter with the German twin-engine Bf 110.[7]

When *Ostmarkflug* – the air attack against Poland – was launched as part of Operation *Fall Weiss*, many peacetime airfields and aircraft factories were immediately badly hit. However, in anticipation of such attack, most operational Polish aircraft had previously been moved to well-hidden advanced landing grounds, from where they operated throughout the campaign. Therefore, the surprise attack only affected unserviceable machines left at principal Polish Air Force bases. Despite this, Poles had very limited chances to survive the onslaught.

Apart from the Luftwaffe, which was equally aiming at military and civilian targets, Polish airmen had to fight a much less official enemy, well hidden in the forests, camouflaged and operating almost under their watchful eyes. Sub-Lieutenant Jan Maliński, a pilot of the 132nd Fighter Squadron, wrote:

'Passing by a single tree I spotted some plates of irregular shape hanging on a branch. I struck it with a stick and the plate disintegrated into small pieces. To my surprise it turned out that they were mirrors. Fifth columnists (a German diversion) surrounded our airfield with the mirrors, to draw the attention of the Luftwaffe crews.'[8]

Fighting alone against three enemies, struggling in isolation for thirty-five days, the Poles naively believed in the materialization of the promised Allied offensive in the West. Although the *Polenfeldzung* – the campaign in Poland – was also called the September Campaign, which suggested it lasted just one month, the battles of the regular units of the Polish Army were fought until 6 October. Their defence lasted almost the same period of time that was needed for Germany to eliminate Belgium, Holland and the major player – France – together with the British Expeditionary Force, in May and June 1940.

Poland was defeated but, unlike other European countries, never surrendered. Polish fighter pilots managed to launch nearly 1,400 sorties and score 107 aerial victories for the price of 120 of their own aircraft lost and fifty pilots killed, missing or wounded. Out of 392 warplanes, plus approximately forty replacements, the Polish Air Force lost 333 machines. By comparison, the victorious Luftwaffe lost 126 of their aircraft during only the first six days of the conflict, and ultimately had 415 aircraft destroyed or damaged due to various causes. It is believed that in fact 230 of them were shot down by Polish fighters.

Sub-Lieutenant Włodzimierz Miksa of 114th Fighter Squadron later wrote. 'It occurred to me that this was the end of the whole show. I felt kind of stupid; I could not accept though that this was the end. Polish aviation was gone, oh beloved God.'[9]

Despite flying aircraft that were no match for the modern, fast and well-armed Luftwaffe machines, Polish pilots gained respect and appreciation from some of their rivals. Oblt Victor Mölders of Zerstörergeschwader 1 praised his opponents:

'Because of their manoeuvrability, Polish fighters were particularly difficult to hit. They have allowed us to chase them, waited until we were ready to shoot, and only then, after performing an Immelman [upwards vertical turn], they were shooting at their rivals from the upside down position. They were magnificent pilots, each of them was an aerobatics champion.'

Poles, on the other hand, were not so generous when describing their adversaries. Stanisław Skalski, the leading ace of the Polish Campaign, said:

'In attempting the task of trying to formulate any just appreciation of the calibre of the German Air Forces, I must confess myself ill-qualified, for eighteen days active contact with them is all too short. Some of the pilots I encountered were obviously first class; others appeared to lack any real flying or fighting technique, the result it would seem, of insufficient instruction. The enemy showed a strange reluctance for combat except when in overwhelming numbers. When engaged they usually resorted to defensive tactics or to escape. If such were their orders, these tactics are excusable, for it should be pointed out that our base was not their objective but merely occurred on their line of flight. They were however, very well informed of our resources in aircraft and war matériel and knew how little opposition they could expect from our small Air Unit, and in view of this, their method of air warfare can only be described as cowardly. The suggestion that they had orders to refrain from any offensive measures I am inclined to question, since I myself have seen them to make callous attacks on peasants working in the fields, people walking in the village streets, refugees etc. What satisfaction such activities can give to any fighting pilot I cannot conceive. The German airmen guilty of such acts stand condemned as an outlaw, betraying the much-vaunted traditions of Richthofen chivalry, and are unworthy of the name so often attributed to the fighting pilot "a noble knight of the air".
'While we were tending their wounded, they were shooting down our airmen attempting to escape by parachute. In fact they seemed to lack any moral scruples. With the scales so heavily weighted in their favour it should surely have been unnecessary to resort to such methods.'[10]

With the Luftwaffe dominating Polish skies, the only hope of the defenders was to see French or British bomber planes targeting the Germans, turning the direction of the war, or to receive the Allied aircraft which – as many Poles naively believed – were on their way. Private First Class Benedykt Dąbrowski of 114th Fighter Squadron was very enthusiastic about the news that Britain and France had declared war on Germany:

'England and France joined the war. We are not alone. These powerful allies will very quickly deal with the aggressive intruder. Our fighting spirit is growing. The newspapers that we are getting, deliver this very important message, which screams by the capital letters of the titles.'[11]

Those innocent hopes were based on initial discussions between Britain and Poland that took place just a few months prior to the outbreak of war. At the beginning of April 1939, Colonel Czesław Filipowicz from the Department of Air Supply visited London, where he met with the Air Ministry to discuss an immediate delivery of British-built aircraft to Poland. On 25 and 26 May, a high-profile conference was held in London, during which both sides discussed the possibility of air support and co-operation. Furthermore, in mid-July the subject arose of using Vickers Wellingtons to attack targets in Germany, operating from bases in England and central Poland.

In June 1939, a Polish Military Mission led by General Ludomił Rayski, former Commander of the Polish Air Force, was sent to Britain, primarily to negotiate purchasing warplanes, engines and spare parts. Lieutenant Colonel Bogdan Kwieciński, Polish Military and Air Attaché in London, was involved

Pilots of 111th and 112th Fighter Squadrons photographed in October 1938 at Aleksandrowice airfield during military operation in Zaolzie, when the Polish army annexed this controversial region, also claimed by Czechoslovakia. Among them are future Battle of Britain pilots, from left to right: Stanisław Karubin (3rd), Arsen Cebrzyński (6th), Eugeniusz Szaposznikow (7th), Wacław Łapkowski (10th), Ludwik Paszkiewicz (19th) and Wojciech Januszewicz (20th).

in the negotiations. This trip was preceded by a loan that Britain offered to its Polish ally. There was an agreement to buy 100 Fairey Battle light bombers, with the possibility of more to follow, but a decision to purchase fighter planes proved more difficult.

Eventually, both sides established that Poland would buy fourteen Hawker Hurricanes, but a decision about purchasing Supermarine Spitfires was far more complicated. The Royal Air Force pointed out that its priority was to send them to British squadrons, as some Fighter Command units were still using rather obsolete equipment.

In late July 1939, the Air Ministry finally allocated just a single Spitfire, L1066, for transport to Poland for trials, along with spare parts. Purchasing Boulton Paul Defiants had also been considered, yet the British said that the development of this aircraft was still at an early stage and the final decision regarding purchasing and delivery could be made no earlier than August 1939, despite personal interest expressed by General Józef Zając, Commander of the Polish Air Force.

It proved much too late when twenty-two Fairey Battle Mk Is, ordered by the Poles, were placed in the holds of the SS *Lassel* and SS *Clan Menzies*. They were accompanied by the fourteen Hurricanes and one Spitfire, plus 500 tons of bombs, followed by the British propellers for the PZL P.50 'Jastrząb' (Hawk) Polish fighter planes that never went further than a prototype. This massive cargo was despatched in early September and initially headed towards the Polish port of Gdynia on the Baltic Sea, but it was soon decided that a safer destination was required, and the ships were redirected to Constanta in Rumania. It was assumed that the embattled Poles could somehow miraculously go that far to collect them.

Unfortunately, in the meantime, Rumania blocked the transportation to Poland of anything that might consist of military equipment, and as a result all the aircraft were offered to Turkey. Up to this point, therefore, Poles could only dream about flying British aircraft: they had to wait several more months before actually doing so.

After Poland was overrun by German and Russian troops, many Polish airmen wanting to continue the fight were faced with a lengthy trek to link up with their allies. Bolesław Drobiński, a future Battle of Britain fighter pilot, recalls his long voyage throughout Europe:

'It was a frightening journey. On the Italian border the carriage was full of drunken Italian Alpine troops. We were huddled in a corner and they were singing songs. We didn't understand Italian but we knew that they were songs against the English and the French.'[12]

After arriving in France, the Poles were astonished by the stagnation, prejudice and complete lack of readiness or willingness to fight. Their French allies often blamed them for 'pulling' France into the war. The French perception of war, however, was much different to the Polish one. The French remembered the Great War as causing the loss of more than a million lives without any significant gains, while for the Poles that conflict, especially its end, brought them their long-awaited freedom. This was the reason why the Poles considered their only option was to continue fighting at any cost to regain their country, regardless of whether the French decided to end the 'Phoney War' and help them achieve that goal. This led to the desperate decision by some less patient Polish airmen to cross the English Channel in the hope of a friendlier reception from the British and the RAF.

'Sikorski's tourists', as they were ironically nicknamed by German propaganda after General Władysław Sikorski (new Commander-in-Chief of the Polish Armed Forces and Prime Minister, who formed the Polish government in

"Sikorski tourists", as they were ironically called by the Nazi propaganda. Indeed, the Polish airmen crossed many borders to reach France. They were pretending to be ordinary civilians and used false names to cover their identity. Amongst this group of escapees, in the first row are two pilots who one year later fought in the Battle of Britain: Julian Kowalski (1st from left) and Stanisław Brzezina (3rd from left).

exile),[13] also had their own issues, mainly internal conflicts and accusations surrounding their recent disastrous defeat. Despite this, Poles endeavoured to preserve their military order, withdrew most of their comrades via the Balkans and Baltic states and eventually were able to recreate and establish an independent air force under the command of the Armée de l'Air (French Air Force).

The Poles' proposal for a Polish-manned fighter brigade with ten squadrons and bomber brigade with another ten squadrons, followed by the organizing of army co-operation and close reconnaissance wings, turned out to be a fantasy. After a long struggle on both sides, only one Polish fighter unit was formed: the 1/145 'City of Warsaw' Squadron was assembled during the 'Phoney War' and designated to support the Fins in their conflict with Russia, the hated enemy of Poland. Nevertheless, after Finland and Russia agreed on a ceasefire, Major Józef Kępinski's pilots stayed in France and were equipped with Caudron-Renault C.714 Cyclones, and 1/145 Squadron became operational in May 1940.

The so-called 'Montpellier Group' was also formed out of Polish fighter pilots. They received Morane MS 406s adorned with the PAF markings, were split into small sections known as 'Patrouille polonaise' and then posted to French squadrons (Groupe de Chasse, or GC). Later, they flew various aircraft such as the Curtiss Hawk H75, Bloch MB 152 or Dewoitine D 520. Other Polish fighter pilots were gathered into so-called 'chimney flights' and dispersed across France to defend factories, bases or industrial centres. These pilots flew MS 406s, MB152s or Koolhoven FK58s.

Embittered Wacław Kól, who flew with GCII/7, had very unpleasant memories of his time in France:

> 'They didn't want this war. They preferred a dolce vita rather than to fight just because Hitler invaded Poland. France is a big country, people lived well and comfortably there, there was plenty of wine and other pleasures.'[14]

Król was supported in his disappointment by fellow pilot Eugeniusz Nowakiewicz:

> 'They only keep drinking and having a good time, and there are so many opportunities for a constant hangover. This bar at the airfield is an idea of Satan, completely unnecessary. They invite you for a cup of coffee, but at the same time they offer a cognac. They are very nice and tender-hearted, but one morning they may be surprised. I feel that the Germans will give them such a slashing that they never received before.'[15]

The disappointment was more than many Poles could cope with. 'How pitiful the French Campaign was,' wrote embittered Jan Falkowski. Falkowski, also known as 'koń' (a horse, due to his long, oval-shaped face), an experienced fighter pilot posted to defend Cognac, continued:

'Us, Poles, who fought so hopelessly against an enemy power that was spreading all over our country, felt this especially hard. La Belle France gave up almost without a fight. The nation had been left without a leader.'[16]

Falkowski had to wait another few months, and only after being posted to No. 32 Squadron, before 'flying with the wind in my face', as he called his wartime memoirs.

The collapse of France was another lost campaign that could have discouraged the willingness and ability of the Polish airmen to fight, as has frequently been mentioned when describing their mood when arriving in Britain. After enduring such a horrible experience not just once but twice in a very short period of time, Poles disembarked in British ports while being suspiciously watched by the natives, yet reservedly welcomed to the 'Island of Last Hope'.

French Morane Saulnier MS 406s from the Polish manned so-called "Montpellier" Group lined up at Lyon. Majority of the Polish pilots, who later fought in the Battle of Britain, flew French aircraft with a retractable undercarriage.

France collapsed, the Polish journey continues.

That island, in the summer of 1940, was literally on its last legs. The British Expeditionary Force had lost all its military equipment on the beaches of Dunkirk and countless sites around France and Belgium. Defending Britain was therefore literally dumped on Fighter Command's shoulders, in the capable hands of Air Chief Marshal Hugh Dowding. Dowding, known as 'Stuffy', was a realistic man. His almost anecdotal lack of humour was substituted by clear vision: the numbers didn't lie. Although shot-down Spitfires and Hurricanes were replaceable, manpower was something that he desperately needed. But at first he was rather reluctant to accept the help of the Polish airmen (and the Czechs who had also followed them to Britain), and admitted:

'I must confess that I had been a little doubtful of the effect which their experience in their own countries and in France might have had upon the Polish and Czech pilots, but my doubts were soon laid to rest, because all three Squadrons swung in the fight with a dash and enthusiasm which is beyond praise. They were inspired by a burning hatred for the Germans which made them very deadly opponents.'

Chapter Three

Getting to Know Each Other

By now Britain and the whole British Empire could hardly have been in a worse position. A giant standing on rather shaking legs was recovering from the shock of the French Campaign and miracle of Operation Dynamo, when hundreds of thousands were saved from the beaches of Dunkirk. British tanks, trucks, guns and even rifles and military boots lay neglected across the Channel, and all that could n ow stop the German army was Fighter Command and the Royal Navy.

One of the fresh Polish newcomers, Jan Zumbach, later wrote of this time:

> 'They knew very well, though, that the Germans in their bases in occupied France were getting ready for the invasion of Great Britain. To be able to face it, islanders needed as many soldiers as possible. I am sure that even if we were hunchbacks, the English still had only one thing in mind: in reach of their hands they had boys, hardened in combat in Poland and France, people who wanted to fight.'[1]

Author Alexander McKee described the state of the hundreds of dedicated Polish compatriots who arrived in Britain:

> 'Most had got out of France without even a toothbrush, in some cases without footwear, but every man had either a rifle, or revolver, or machine gun – and ammunition to go with it. They were fine fighting material and experienced pilots; all they needed was to learn the modern techniques associated with flaps and retractable undercarriages. They had to unlearn almost everything they had been taught about approaches and tended to confront him with a "Me very old pilot" – meaning, what's good for a P.11 is good for a Hurricane.'[2] –

This last opinion is rather unjust because it was purely based on myths used for inspiration, and is perhaps also due to the author's innocent ignorance. In order to clarify this anecdotic misunderstanding, the subject of conversion to British equipment will be covered in a separate chapter of this book.

Witold Urbanowicz remembered:

'The English understood us and our tragedy and tried to make our lives pleasant. They seemed to realise, that we will fight together against the German aggression. They appreciated our combat experience. In their opinion we had some authority as we were part of the nation that first stood against Nazi Germany. Before arriving in England I've heard that English are coldblooded and treat foreigners with distance. Here it was completely different.'[3]

Yet ordinary people, most of whom had never saw a non-English-speaking creature before, who were standing on the streets and curiously watching the 'army' of strange-looking, weirdly dressed foreigners marching throughout their towns, who were singing some odd songs, had to be convinced that this 'invasion' made some sense. R.C. Cobb wrote of those days:

'It would seem that the English public has to "see to believe" and that only the presence of the Poles in our midst could induce our newspapers to pay credit to our first and most courageous Ally. In June and July, to the London editors in search for a "scoop", the men of the Polish Army and Air Force had "news value", and so the public was for a few days reminded of their exploits and of their faith in us.'[4]

There were even isolated unpleasant incidents, or rather acts of ignorance and disrespect shown towards the Poles. Polish sympathizer Professor Peter J. O'Grady wrote:

A comedian at a big show staged at a local theatre facetiously likened the Polish airmen to penguins. The quip stuck. Residents and visitors thereafter, as thoughtlessly as ignorantly, dubbed the Polish pilots as the birds with wings that do not fly. Such manifest injustice to our fearless Polish allies clamours for the veil to be lifted forthwith, and for the public to be enlightened. Daily contact with our Polish Flying Corps at that time placed me in a position of privilege to write this with assurance, and with a proper knowledge of the facts.'[5]

Sometime later, famous British writer Alyse Simpson asked her readers: 'How many of us in this endless hurry of the war had even stolen a few moments to consider what kind of country these young men had come from?'[6]

But what of the Poles and their perception of their new home? Were they more aware of the land they had arrived at; were they less ignorant? It seems that average Kowalski or Nowak[7] knew very little if anything about the country

Some of the Polish airmen after arriving in Britain wearing various uniforms, including long Polish leather flying jacket. Amongst them in the front row from left is Jan Borowski (1st), in the second row is Tadeusz Sawicz (4th).

of William Shakespeare that they had entered, being no better than the statistical Mr Brown or Mrs Smith who only saw Poland as a far-away place. 'Every Englishman is a lord. Every Englishwoman is at least fifty years old, has flat feet and she is ugly like a night,' was the rather ironic and controversial way that Bohdan Arct, a future 306 Squadron pilot, described this brand new situation.

> 'Throughout 362 days in the year, there is a thick fog in England, the remaining days are sunny. A talkative Englishman pronounces three sentences per hour. Less talkative Englishman doesn't talk at all. Every Englishman is wearing a tuxedo for breakfast, and he goes to bed wearing a tail-coat. Shakespeare and Sherlock Holmes are English national heroes. Dog means pies and lady means pani.'[8]

Leaving other unpleasant comments aside, Polish airmen very quickly realized that the picture of female residents of Albion previously painted to them was very much unjust, and wasting no time they decided to show their adoration for them. British women were equally graceful for the Poles' kindness, admiration and courtesy shown when kissing their hands and looking straight into their eyes, and thanks to this simple non-verbal communication the first barriers were quickly broken down. Poles were surprizsed that they had finally found somebody who would show them pure affection and understanding:

> 'English girls were not only far prettier than their reputation but remarkably Polonophile to boot. This later discovery greatly accelerated their linguistic progress, and few had not mastered the phrase, "You very beautiful", within a few days and, "You me go pictures", within a week.'[9]

Pilot Officer Jan Jokiel, who shortly afterwards was posted to No. 302 (Polish) Squadron as an Intelligence Officer, was pleasantly surprised after arriving in Blackpool:

> 'In the period between July and August and also in September 1940, whole trains full of women started to arrive at the aviation centre in Blackpool. For them the main attraction was not always the untidy beach, dull and heatless sun, but rather the possibility to take a close look at the chivalrous Poles, already popular amongst English ladies. Delightfully English women, sometimes spinsters, accustomed to the reserved feelings shown by their boys, plenty of which went away to the Army, Navy and RAF, leaving their sweethearts alone, were looking for compensation. Especially easy-going Polish airmen who very quickly adopted the words "I love you". It must be noted that such avowal from an English gentleman would be treated at least as a formal proposal.'[10]

'I have met my future husband at RAF Northolt,' Constance Blok recalled. Stanislaw 'Charlie' Blok, despite not being with the first group of Poles employed during the Battle of Britain, later became a fighter ace. She continued:

> 'By that time I was a young WAAF stationed at Eastcote. He gave me a quite unusual souvenir – a pair of silk stockings, something that was almost unreal to get those days. No idea where he got those from. Obviously I wasn't allowed to wear them officially, but on the other hand I couldn't resist to put them on. I had to remember to take them off every time I was going back to my unit. "Charlie" was a typical Pole, charming but cheeky. I was walking with him one day, holding hands, when one of his superior officers suddenly appeared in front of us. "Charlie" was an officer, I was not, therefore it was against the regulations to show off

our feelings publically. He chose the best solution, for him of course. He just took off, vanished, leaving me on my own. The other day he arrived wearing his unusually strained battle dress. I was expecting flowers of course, instead a monkey, his squadron mascot, jumped out from his military jacket. I almost had a heart attack. So romantic!'[11]

Despite this occasion, male to female relations went rather smoothly. Zygmunt Jeliński, a 306 Squadron pilot, wrote in his memoirs:

'"The Orchard" was also the place where George [Grzegorz Sołogub, a fighter ace] and Joan (Yanka was the name George immediately bestowed on Joan, which is diminutive of Janina, the Polish equivalent of Joan), met for the first time, and George stole her heart, when at the end of the first evening he carried her all the way to her parked bike. Since that time she became his constant companion, whether in love or in his battles with the opposition – I understand that her handbag was quite a formidable weapon and I would not like to have been at the receiving end.'[12]

Not every Polish airman was so desperately female-orientated though. For Sergeant Stefan Wójtowicz, who was impatiently awaiting his posting to No. 303 Squadron – which had not even been created – the only reason why he travelled to Britain was to face the enemy again. He wrote to a colleague:

'I have some inconvenience with the girl I've met in Blackpool, as she writes letters to me, and I cannot reply, yet my reading is even worse. She was a wife material, but you know what is in my mind … I do not know what should I think about your situation, whether you are happy or not. Anyway, I am sure that flying is something that like in my case, takes priority above all Blackpool's entertainment.'[13]

There were other obstacles too. 'English cooking was radically different from the Polish and French and therefore did not gain even our slightest approval,' complained Wacław Król, who soon joined 302 Squadron.

'The menu was boring and poor. Considering that English people do not fill up their stomachs with bread and potatoes, we had to leave the tables with massive hunger. Various sandwiches containing a thin slice of bread or bread roll with slightly applied margarine surrounded by leaves of some weed did not impress us. Biscuits or cakes, puddings or

What could break the first barriers between these two nations? Football of course! The Polish airmen after arriving in Britain had to learn the new language, King's Regulations and spent some time during sport activities. From left to right are pilots, who soon after were posted to RAF and PAF Squadrons: Zbigniew Nosowicz (1st), Mieczysław Gorzula (2nd), Henryk Szczęsny (3rd), Janusz Żurakowski (7th) and Jerzy Radomski (10th).

dumplings with strange filling did not test well either. There were meat dishes consisting of very thinly sliced uncooked lamb or rarely beef, with no flavour, two watery potatoes and a spoon of carrot, or kohlrabi or blanched cabbage.'[14]

Language was another challenge. 'I had no idea that it was possible to pronounce those three letters [THE] in so many different ways,' Franciszek Kornicki wrote, recalling this huge and unimaginable barrier:

'Apart from ZEE, I also heard DEE, DY, DZE, TZE, TZY and other odd noises in between. By majority of votes we settled for DZY, and borrowed a book which was changing tents every half hour; we copied some words and phrases and tried to learn their meaning and pronunciation. It was hard going.'[15]

However, the language difference, despite seeming overwhelming at the time, was one of the less significant problems for the Poles getting to know each other. Their RAF counterparts were not much more enthusiastic about the new situation. 'It was just about the last straw to find myself after all my efforts posted to a foreign squadron that had not even been formed and I was thoroughly fed up and despondent,' –John Alexander Kent recalled. Kent was given command of 303 Squadron's 'A' Flight, and later wrote:

> 'All I knew about the Polish Air Force was that it had only lasted about three days against the Luftwaffe and I had no reason to suppose that they would shine any more brightly operating from England.'[16]

Ronald Gustave Kellett, soon to be commander of 303 Squadron, had to solve a nuisance of a different nature:

> 'Two O.R.s [other ranks] refused to obey orders of Polish Officers although they expressed willingness to obey English Officers. This was a serious charge but knowing something of their experiences I decided to give them 48 hours in an English flight on the station so that they could reconsider their position. I explained that no differentiation could exist between one officer and another. Next morning we had about 10 men who similarly refused to obey Polish Officers. I had a hurried conference with the Station Commander, Group Captain S. Vincent [Stanley Flamank Vincent], the Polish C.O. and the British Adjutant Upton [David Upton], and the men were paraded and told through the interpreter, "Unless you return to work within 30 seconds it will be my duty to charge you with mutiny and you will be handed over to the Polish Army to meet such punishment as they think fit." Fortunately that was that.'[17]

Initially, even Kellett was not too keen to lead the squadron of foreigners, whose qualities were uncertain. He was happy to admit that openly:

> 'At first, I was quite annoyed at having to lead a Polish squadron; I felt the Polish pilots might be a hindrance more than help to the RAF. I believed the Polish mechanics would not have the skills to work on our aircraft. At first, whenever I spoke to any of them in French, they seemed to almost ignore my instructions. As time passed, I was pleased to admit how wrong I was about the Poles.'[18]

Not every member of his squadron really appreciated his efforts, but Kellett had the advantage of speaking French, a language also used by many Poles. Thomas Neil wrote: 'I remember him calling us in 249 [Squadron] after the Battle of Britain when he had been with 303 for some months, and him speaking of "his Poles" in glowing terms.'[19]

Poles who were arriving in Britain, apart from the traumatic experience of losing their fight and their homeland, brought with them the extra baggage of uncertainty over the safety of their loved ones. Their families had to stay in a country now ruled by two tyrannical enemies. Bohdan Arct wrote in his unpublished diary: 'I was deeply disturbed by the news published by the "Dziennik Polski" [Polish Daily] that on May the 5th Germans took all women and men aged between 18-25 from Warsaw to the labour camps in Germany. It would be horrible if Halina was amongst them.'

German methods applied by the *Generalgouvernment* (Government General) were ruthless and barbarian. In these circumstances of daily horrors experienced by Polish citizens, every sign of life of their husbands, sons or fathers, who were fighting in the West, would prove to be equally miraculous and lethal. German and Russian censorship particularly searched for any clues and words that indicated that the sender was serving with the Allied forces.

For that reason, Polish airmen had to do whatever they could to save these poor people from harm, yet also keep them informed that everything was fine on the other side. To protect their identity, but most importantly to not say officially where they currently lived, they had to use not only fake names and addresses but also to get various middlemen in neutral countries involved in sending letters to and from occupied Poland. Messages from '*ciocia Frania*' (Auntie Frances) and either '*ciocia Aniela*' (Auntie Angela)[20] or '*ciocia Ania*' (Auntie Annie) kept crossing occupied Europe, meaning respectively 'I am safe in France' and 'do not worry, I am in England now'.

'We had no news from my brother since he left Poland,' Mirosław Ferić's brother Zwonimir recorded:

'My brother Mirosław realised that any contact with the West could provoke sanctions (arrest camps) by the Germans. As we learned later, parcels with coffee, which we received from Portugal until the end of the war, were not a sign of life from my brother [he was killed in 1942].'

'Sikorski's tourists' who arrived at, as they were assured, the last rampart of defence against the Nazis, had so many worries to struggle with. Bohdan Arct put another entry in his carefully written and very specific diary:

'Our fate is a big question mark. Military agreement seems likely to be signed with the English soon. Our authorities want to organize an independent air force, but the English tend to put us into the RAF. The political situation is very difficult. England is still fighting alone, there are opinions that Hitler is preparing for the invasion of the Great Britain, which will begin shortly. Hitler has promised the invasion of England within forthcoming days. Night after night Germans are flying above and bombing some facilities nearby.'[21]

Life under such pressure was hard to cope with, yet Polish airmen had to concentrate on their ground training, King's Regulations and getting ready to fly again. 'My beloved sweetheart,' wrote Stanisław Brzezina to his wife. Brzezina was an experienced fighter pilot and commander of the Advanced Flying (Fighter) Course at Ułęż. In Poland, he helplessly looked up at Dorniers and Heinkels which pounded the area of the Dęblin School of Eaglets with bombs, gritting his teeth in disappointment and anger. 'Finally I have moved and I live where Molly lives [this was an encrypted message that he was already in England]. Here I would stay until the sun of the bright Autumn will shine.'[22]

Presumably only lack of trust towards airmen who were involved in two lost campaigns, fuelled by non-existent knowledge about the historical, cultural and geographical background of the Polish contingent, led to some unexpected behaviour that made small scratches on the well-polished lid of diplomacy. 'The English are afraid, especially at the beginning, of all possible complications with the civilian population, suspecting our personnel of being possibly approached by foreign agents,' reported Group Captain Bogdan Kwieciński, the Polish Military and Air Attaché.

A very emotional moment when the Polish Air Force flag was raised at RAF Manston.

On 10 May 1940, a British officer asked Poles to leave a cinema. The very next day, Henryk Szczęsny, who soon after was to join 74 Squadron, was a victim of boorish behaviour during a boxing match. This was followed by a report written by a high-ranking Polish officer stating that, 'Behaviour of English personnel towards Polish enlisted men has become more and more inappropriate.'

The Polish commander of RAF Eastchurch, the first British airbase designated for the new arrivals, had his own headaches to contend with. Group Captain Bolesław Stachoń, an experienced officer who knew how to deal with problems relating to his personnel, had to urgently make some crucial decisions as this initial period had proven to be rather eventful. On a daily basis he had to resolve various troubles of a different nature: 'Sheerness Police reported to us that on 22 of March before noon, a few Polish officers were provoking women on the street in an unacceptable manner that outraged passers-by.' It would be rather difficult to speculate what sort of behaviour aroused this correspondence, but it was soon followed by another report: 'Also Police authorities informed me that during one of the recent nights three Polish officers spent the whole night with two English women in the public room for orchestra.' We can only assume that those officers were teaching them some romantic Slavic tunes! Stachoń finished his report addressed to his superiors with another example of Poles leaving a restaurant with jackets unbuttoned, without hats, but at the same time embracing local women in a gentlemanly manner.

His British counterpart, Group Captain Alexander Davidson (former air attaché in Warsaw and later commander of RAF Bramcote) knew the Poles rather well, but for some reason did not trust their abilities and qualities:

> 'It appears that in the Polish Air Force discipline has never been up to the standards required in the R.A.F. This may be chiefly due to the inherent individualism and egoism of the Poles, neither of which makes co-ordination of effort and team work easy.'[23]

Another of Stachoń's many problems started when a group of Polish cadets arrived at Eastchurch. These boys were at Dęblin Air Force School when the war began and quite a long way from completing their training. After experiencing the national tragedy of Poland's defeat, when all their dreams were crushed, they now felt abandoned by their instructors and superiors, suffering from depression and lack of confidence in authority; but above all they were outraged by the necessity of making an oath of loyalty to the British King George VI, in their opinion the head of a foreign state, which to them had nothing to do with showing patriotism. Some of the most stubborn cadets were sent back to France.

So many Poles' first contacts with the British were rather rough, as Janusz Żurakowski, a future 152, 234 and 609 Squadrons pilot, recalls:

> 'Our arrival destroyed the idyllic peace of this town [Blackpool], which was quiet at that time. For the locals we were the first forerunners of war, the foreign birds, using a strange language. They accommodated us in hotels and B&Bs, where such guests were never seen before.'[24]

Unlike French airmen, who were the only servicemen of the European allied nations permitted to wear their own uniforms, Poles had to strictly follow the RAF's dressing regulations, but with some exceptions. They were allowed to wear their own cap badges with the Polish Air Force (PAF) eagle, although during the very early stages they wore RAF cap badges, having their eagle pinned onto their tunics, below the RAF wings or half brevets. Polish collar rank badges were also worn alongside the British shoulder distinctions, when RAF ranks were higher than the Polish, and only based on the British ranks that Poles were paid by. Polish flying personnel were also entitled to wear their own metal wings, called 'Gapa', which differed only in some details for various specializations such as pilot, navigator (formerly observer), air gunner, wireless operator etc. These were worn above the left pocket of the military tunic. Poles were also allowed to wear their own decorations alongside foreign medals and squadron badges.

Despite all this, it was expected that PAF personnel would follow the King's Regulations and specific dress code. Nevertheless, it wasn't unusual to see some of them wearing French flying leather jackets or even Polish long flying leather jackets instead of the British ones. Even in the later stages of the war, numerous Polish airmen preferred the continental fashion. Particularly during the few months of the Battle of Britain, no one bothered much about such discrepancies.

But was this wave of Polish escapees so strange and foreign at all? Was the aviation of the Central (not Eastern) European country and its achievements so unknown and mysterious for personnel of the RAF? On the other side, how many Poles knew about the RAF? Had they ever met a British aviator before? Perhaps both countries had something in common.

It would be unlikely to expect that either Polish or British airmen knew about Father Jan Łaski, who in the sixteenth century came to Britain, invited by the Archbishop of Canterbury. Łaski was helping to organize the Protestant parishes across the country, and thanks to his dedication his name is still mentioned among other creators of the Anglican Church. In 1835 (four years after the brutally put down November Uprising against Russia of 1830-31), a large group of Polish political ex-fighters, now immigrants, landed in Britain to escape tsarist repressions. London became a temporary home and location of the last performance of Fryderyk Chopin, the world-renowned Polish composer and pianist. Juliusz Słowacki, a Romantic poet, also lived there for some time. Marie Curie Skłodowska, a Polish physicist and chemist and pioneer of research into radioactivity, had visited London in 1930, but being a woman she was prevented from speaking at the Royal Institution. Finally, Joseph Conrad, born in Poland as Józef Konrad Korzeniowski, settled in Britain, where he gained his fame as a great novelist. Those names were not necessarily known to the new generation of Britons. For them, the 1940 newcomers were more or less *tabula rasa* (a clean slate). But airmen from both countries had met before on numerous occasions…

Chapter Four

Encounters with the Past

The Operations Record Book of the newly formed No. 303 (Polish) Squadron said:

> '2.8.40 The nucleus of No. 303 (Polish) Squadron was formed from elements of No. 1 Warsaw Squadron, commanded by Major Zdzislaw Krasnodebski, which had escaped after fighting in Poland and France and collected at Blackpool.'[1]

This was followed by the entry in the Polish diary of 303 Squadron:

> On 2nd August at 8.00 the Warsaw Fighter Squadron left Blackpool by rail to the new base as a combat unit, to Northolt … Arrival at the airfield "R.A.F. Station Northolt" at 15.30.[2]

A brand new chapter of history has been written since the bunch of young men with the Slavic look, tongue-twisting language, unpredictable temperament and eagerness to fight emerged at RAF Northolt in north-west London.

They looked strange, some of them still wearing foreign uniforms, suspiciously watching around and checking their new surroundings, smiling innocently to everyone who dared to start a conversation in English. British personnel found themselves in an uneasy position too. They had to find common ground to live with these characters and to understand this rather eccentric – for British standards – group of people. Some say that this was the moment when the story began, but were they even the first group of Poles to arrive at this RAF Station?

In March 1917, following the February Revolution (or, according to other sources, in December 1916), a group consisting of 112 (or 115) Tsarist officers, air cadets and mechanics, led by Warsaw-born Captain Piotr Abakanowicz (commander of Class No. 1), arrived in England and was posted to Northolt (Ruislip Military School), Upavon (Central Flying School), Catterick Bridge (Military School), Croydon (Beddington), Thetford (Military School), Grantham (Military School) and then to Oxford (Military School) for flying and ground theoretical training. They also participated in theoretical courses

The group of Tsarist airmen at Northolt airfield in 1917. Amongst them are at least two Polish fliers: Piotr Abakanowicz (8th from left leaning on skid) and Witold Piechowski (1st from right). Contacts between Polish and British aviation have a long history, starting twenty four years before the outbreak of World War 2.

at the No. 1 School of Military Aeronautics and School of Technical Training, both at Reading, organized by the Royal Flying Corps. Apart from playing their own night-time version of the infamous Russian Roulette (the majority of them hiding in a completely dark hangar and shouting, whilst one airman aimed at the places where the voices were coming from and shooting; the winner was supposed to be the one with the best wounds),[3] the cadets predominantly flew Maurice Farmans, de Havilland Airco DH6s, R.E.8s and eventually Bristol Fighters.

Although it is difficult to establish just how many Poles were amongst these adventurous people, without doubt we know today that Abakanowicz – or 'Abby' as he was called by the British – was accompanied by at least ten others: Lucjan Biernacki, Eugeniusz Koronowski, Ludwik Pacewicz, Antoni Piątkowski, Witold Piechowski, Jan Pliszke, Stanisław Rymkiewicz, Eugeniusz Sielicki, Mikołaj Sokołowski and Eustachy Wołłowicz.[4] Quite a few of them later joined the Polish Air Force once their country regained its independence.[5] It is worth mentioning that according to Rymkiewicz's report, it was in England where the Polish officers and cadets organized an unofficial patriotic group and discussed the future of the free Polish aviation.[6]

Apparently there were also plans considered by the British to form a unit (either a flight or squadron) consisting of airmen of Polish nationality (presumably former PoWs from the German or Austro-Hungarian armies and volunteers) at Northolt. Rumour has it that only because the Great War ended sooner than expected did this interesting project never materialize. Nevertheless, the Poles had enough time to significantly mark their presence on British soil. Frank Courtney, who was employed as an interpreter, recalled:

'Abby quickly puzzled the officer's mess. Apparently he found scotch whisky to be an acceptable if feeble substitute for his native vodka, and he was frankly disappointed that even the thirstiest British officers could not keep up with his fabulous rate of consumption. Nobody even saw him drunk, and we used to debate whether it was the Russian army or the climate of The Steppes that had provided this priceless training.' [7]

An aviator known as Longin Lipski (later called Lipsky), born in the Russian town of Perm, a close friend and squadron-mate of the Russian fighter ace Ivan Smirnov, and who could be also considered of Polish nationality, by the end of 1917 fled Russia and 19 Corps Aviation Detachment, which had been taken over by the Bolsheviks, and together with Smirnow joined a Suez-based British squadron flying Aircos DH9. Later he was transferred to Britain and posted to the Central Flying School at Upavon in Wiltshire, where Lipski undertook further training on Bristol F2. Fighters, Avro 504Ks and SE.5as, before eventually leaving the RAF. He was naturalized as a British citizen in 1926, and lived in London before emigrating to the United States.

It seems, however, that those Poles were not pioneers.[8] One year before, another officer of the Tsar's aviation visited England. His name was Wiktoryn Kaczyński. On 3 November 1915, Kaczyński, accompanied by a second pilot of the Black Sea Fleet and five other men, went to England to undertake test flights on airships that were used against German U-boats. On 21 January 1916, Kaczyński and his team started training on ordinary balloons. That was followed by a test flight on an airship type B two months later. Thanks to his comments, construction of the B was improved. Later, two British-built airships, Ca and Cc, were delivered to the Crimea. Eventually Kaczyński ended up in Poland, where upon his arrival he took command of the Naval Air Arm.[9]

Eugeniusz Zygmunt Wirpsza, who served in Russian Expeditionary Forces, eventually moved to England, where during the First World War he served in the Machine Gun Corps. When war broke out again in 1939 he joined the Voluntary Reserve of the RAF, and with the rank of Pilot Officer was posted to No. 6 Operational Training Unit in Sutton Bridge, Lincolnshire, as an interpreter. His Polish language proved to be very useful when, in the summer of 1940, Polish fighter pilots started to arrive, before being posted to the front-line squadrons. Later, Virpsha (as he anglicized his name) met Polish airmen again after being attached to No. 307 Polish Night Fighter Squadron 'City of Lwów'. Ian Herman and Noel Grabowsky had Polish ancestors too. Ian served in the Royal Naval Air Service before joining the RAF, while his brother Noel flew airships.[10] There are other names that require further research: Second Lieutenant Alexander Urinowski and his brother William Urinowski, later known as Courtenay, were both sons of Stefan Urinowski, whose first name might suggest having Polish nationality or roots. Alexander was killed on 24 August 1918 while flying as a pilot of No. 48 Squadron RAF, while his brother became a well-known interwar flier.

Two years later, when Poland fought against her Eastern neighbours, two British officers, observers from the RAF, joined the PAF, yet none of them managed to fly operationally. Flight Lieutenant John Tanqueray and Flying Officer Ira Woodhouse were posted on 19 December 1919 to the 1st Air Squadron in Wilno (now Vilnius). Tanqueray left for Britain on 1 March 1920, his colleague following almost two months later (on 29 April 1920). In the meantime, at least two Poles, most probably Eugeniusz Maliszewski and Konstanty Rydzewski, served in either the Slavo-British Aviation Corps formed by the RAF and operating in northern Russia or in one of the RAF squadrons that flew in southern Russia in 1919, during the war against the Bolsheviks.

Although service in the PAF did not go well, Britons increasingly considered Poland as a potential commercial client. In December 1919, a Handley Page 0/400 aircraft with a crew of five British and one Polish airmen flew to Poznań and was displayed at Ławica airfield. Initially, this aircraft received a good report and was discussed as one of the candidates for the new Polish bomber squadron. But the Poles decided that its price was too high and withdrew from buying a further five HPs. The Handley Page company eventually presented one of its aircraft to the Polish government, yet the latter wasn't very enthusiastic about this gift and the HP 0/400 was not used frequently.

There were, however, other British-built aircraft that secured their place in Polish hearts. In September 1919, two PAF officers, Lieutenant Marian Gaweł and Lieutenant Michał Tłuchowski, visited London, where they tested Bristol Fighters, DH9s and SE5as. This soon after resulted in the first order of seventy-five Bristol Fighters placed by the Poles. The British went a step further and offered some DH9s, Sopwith Dolphins and Bristol Fighters free as a goodwill gesture. Eventually, ten Dolphins and twenty DH9s were given to the Polish government, while over 100 F.2Bs were purchased by the Poles, alongside one

British built Handley Page 0/400 at Ławica airfield.

F.4 Buzzard and two SE5as. Forty Bristol Fighters were used operationally against the Bolsheviks soon after being delivered to Nos 1, 9 and 10 Squadrons. They were used in the PAF after the war, gradually changing their role from combat to training aircraft. Quite a few of the future Polish Battle of Britain pilots flew these machines in the early stages of their aviation career. The last F.2Bs were withdrawn from usage in 1932.

Ten Sopwith 5F1 Dolphins had been shipped from Britain and arrived in Poland in April and May 1920. The Poles were not very enthusiastic about them when they discovered that the aircraft were dangerous and unreliable, and had been withdrawn from service. The situation of Poland, however, was not to be envied, and with the Bolsheviks almost at the door of Warsaw, the first Dolphins were sent to the 19th Fighter Squadron. Pilots used them mostly to attack Russian cavalry, infantry and transport.

Poland also got two SE5as, but one of them, after receiving rather positive reports, unfortunately crashed and its pilot was seriously wounded. The second one had a short combat career after being transferred to the famous 7th 'Tadeusz Kościuszko' Fighter Squadron: the same day as it arrived at Hołoby airfield, the SE5a took off on a reconnaissance mission but was shot down by the Bolsheviks. Six years later, two further SE5as were seen over Poland, but they belonged to the Savage Skywriting Co. and were used only for commercial purposes.[11]

Bristol F. 2B Fighter from 1st Reconnaissance Squadron. Picture taken on 16 August 1920 during defence of Warsaw against the Red Army.

James Worledge, owner of the Savage Skywriting Co., whose two SE5as were flown in Poland, held the Polish rank of Captain and between 1922–25 was a flying instructor at the Pilots School in Bydgoszcz. It was not the only Polish episode in his life: during the Second World War, due to his fluent Polish language, he had various duties in some of the Polish squadrons operating from Britain, including as an intelligence officer, before being killed on 9 February 1942.

In the first half of 1920, twenty Airco DH9s and British Siddeley Puma engines reached Polish soil. Some of the DH9s were transported by air to Tarnopol and distributed between 5th and 6th Squadrons. Polish airmen engaged in the conflict with the Red Army complained about their engines and very soon these aircraft were sent back for repairs. When the war ended, some of the DH9s were employed by the 3rd and 4th Air Regiments, while others went to the Officers School for Air Observers.

There were also other British-built planes in Poland. Three Sopwith 1½ – Strutters and one RAF RE8 (the latter previously belonged to the RAF's South Russian Instructional Mission) were war trophies,[12] and there was one Avro 504K (the circumstances of its arrival are not yet known) and Martinsyde F.4 Buzzard. The Buzzard was presented in Warsaw in February 1921, when Flight Lieutenant Percy performed two flights. Despite a rather positive opinion, the

Polish authorities decided not to take the matter further. However, the Buzzard was eventually purchased and used as a personal aircraft of the Commander of the PAF, General Włodzimierz Zagórski.

This was not the only British episode in Zagórski's career. On 26 June 1925, he flew to England, where after landing at Kenley in Surrey, he spent quite a fruitful time. As part of the official visit, he met Secretary of State for Air Samuel Hoare, Chief of the Air Staff Hugh Montague Trenchard and Director of Civil Aviation General William Sefton Brancker (who had previously visited Warsaw). Zagórski was also invited to watch an air competition organized at Hendon, visited the RAF Cadet College in Cranwell and went to the NCOs School in Winterbourne, followed by trips to the Instructor's School in Fileton and the School of Radio Communication in Upavon. He also visited a fighter unit in Winchester and the Armstrong factory in Coventry.

During his trip, an offer had been made by the Armstrong Whitworth factory to deliver twelve of their Siskin I aircraft for the fighter unit of the Polish Naval Air Wing (Morski Dywizjon Lotniczy), but despite the Siskins' attributes being presented to the Polish commander, this proposal had not been considered

DH-60G Gipsy Moth SP-AHD no.1893 purchased in Britain in 1932 as G-ABTW. Owned privately in Poland, then attached to 4th Air Regiment in Toruń and flown until September 1939.

further and was eventually rejected. General Zagórski's opinion about British aviation was very high though; he praised their achievements and placed them far above France, the USA or Spain. He was certainly hoping to get a lucrative contract by securing Poland's key role in air communication to India.

Despite Zagórski soon after being arrested as a result of May 1926's coup d'etat, some delicate marks of his relationship with Britain continued. Twenty of the DH.60s got to Poland, some of them purchased as brand new ones, others bought from previous owners. The PAF expressed interest in light reconnaissance and liaison aircraft, while civilian aviation was keen on leisure planes. Apart from these and thanks to the involvement of Bernard Skórzewski, who was a De Havilland representative to Poland, several other planes arrived: DH.80 Puss Moths, DH.85 Leopard Moths and a single DH.82 Tiger Moth.[13]

Following Zagórski's trip to Britain, Captains Józef Piasecki and Marian Zabłocki went to England for a military internship, which they spent between 26 March and 5 September 1928 at various units and schools, including RAF Digby, Farnborough, Upavon, Weston-Zoyland, Odiham and Milton.

Although in the 1920s and early 1930s the Polish aviation industry and its supply chain were mainly French-orientated and dependent, as were some of the home-grown and foreign yet 'Polonised' strategists, theoreticians looked further, beyond the Channel, to search for inspiration. In 1929, Colonel Stanisław Jasiński, when describing potential future aerial war, referred to the geographical location of the United Kingdom as a crucial part of its defence system. Jasiński also introduced an English example of an independent air force that was so vital in a modern conflict.

The commander of the 6th Air Regiment, Colonel Camilo Perini,[14] suggested in 1928 that Polish air strategy, in any forthcoming conflicts, should rely on co-operation with France, Czechoslovakia, but also with Britain. He had speculated that Britain's RAF bases in Arabia and Persia could be used against one of the biggest enemies of Poland – Russia.[15]

Sub-Colonel Bolesław Stachoń travelled to England, where he undertook training on the Avro-built Cierva C.30A autogyro. After purchasing one plane, he flew it to Poland, where he landed after long and difficult journey at Ławica in July 1934. As previously mentioned, Stachoń visited England six years later when he was appointed Polish commander of RAF Eastchurch, the first British-based gathering point and camp for PAF escapees. His counterpart at that time was Group Captain Alexander Davidson, who previously spent a considerable period of time in Poland as an air attaché.

In 1934, the PAF purchased a licence to produce an Avro 'Tutor' and also bought a single Avro 631. After a series of modifications, the 'Tutor' became a

PWS 18 and its production started in Biała Podlaska's PWS factory. Forty-five of them were built in total and used for training purposes.

Not only aircraft came to the attention of and therefore interested the Polish buyers. In 1926, they were aiming to place an order for Rolls-Royce engines. Although unsuccessful, they finally secured a deal for Bristol Jupiters, Mercurys and Pegasuses. French company Gnome-Rhome, a Bristol main continental dealer, initially helped the Poles to start their own production of the Bristol engines, but after further negotiations, a direct agreement was signed in 1935. Furthermore, de Havilland's Gipsy Major power plants were fitted in Polish-built RWD aircraft, while in some others – also of domestic production – British Cirrus Hermes engines. The PAF widely used Vickers machine guns, and the British manufacturer supplied the Poles with their undercarriage for a 'dream' fighter plane, the P.50 'Jastrząb'.

The British also showed some interest in Polish inventions. Not only was the revolutionary Vee-tail created by Jerzy Rudlicki, chief designer of the LWS factory, copied in many countries, but was also tested in the United Kingdom. Another Polish engineer, Władysław Świątecki, developed a slip bomb device, that was patented in 1926 and some years later used in Lancaster and B-29 bombers.[16] But the most outstanding chapter was written in April 1934, when Air Vice Marshal Edgar Ludlow-Hewitt, Deputy Chief of the Air Staff, received a document which stated:

Martinsyde F.4 Buzzard was another British aircraft used in Poland. This mount H7780 was tested in the air by Lt Stefan Pawlikowski, who almost twenty years later commanded the Polish fighter forces in Britain.

'Further information is now available about the Polish P.Z.24 fighter [in fact the designation was PZL P.24], which you remember Sir John Higgis wanted the Air Ministry to buy to compete with the F.7/30 day and nightfighters which are due shortly at Martlesham … On paper it is fastest of the F.7/30 class now being built . . P.Z.24 is 4 mph [in fact 20 mph] faster than the Supermarine and climbs to 15,000 ft in 2 ½ minutes less. AMSR [Air Marshal Hugh Dowding] and DTD [Directorate of Technical Development] are both opposed to the P.Z.24 being tried out in the day and nightfighter category, but AMSR suggests that it might be of interest as an interceptor (Fury replacement), for which we are issuing a specification this year.'

As history shows, this purchase never materialized and the Hawker Fury was replaced by the Gloster Gladiator, a temporary solution by the RAF. Had the P.24, faster than the Supermarine Type 224 (forefather of the Spitfire), been adopted by the RAF, the story of the most iconic fighter plane of Second World War would have been completely different.

The Poles were not so sceptical when licence production of Leslie Irvin's parachutes was offered to them by the British. Irvin visited Poland to see for himself what sort of clientele he would be dealing with. On 1 June 1928, accompanied by British officer Captain Long, he landed in his de Havilland biplane at Ławica airfield. As part of the agreement, a Polish representative went to Letchworth to learn a new trade under the watchful eye of Mr Irvin and one of his female workers, who – as it turned out – had Polish roots.

Some trips, as mentioned above, were more practical, while others had a more courteous character. For example, on the morning of 24 August 1927, four British hydroplanes – a Saunders A.3 Valkyrie, Short Singapore, Blackburn Iris and Supermarine Southampton[17] – arrived at Pucka Bay with ten officers including Squadron Leader G.L.Scott, who piloted Iris II, and fourteen NCOs[18] on their way from Copenhagen, as a part of what the press at the time called an 'RAF Scandinavian Tour' or 'A Service Flying Boat Cruise'. The crews were welcomed by Colonel Ludomił Rayski, Chief of the PAF, some other notable officers of the Polish Naval Air Arm and the British attaché from Warsaw. After an official ceremony, all four aircraft flew to Gdańsk, from where only three flying boats proceeded to Helsinki at 10 am on 30 August. The Supermarine Southampton had to stay a little longer for some technical repairs. This visit was followed by another, three years later. This time four Supermarine Southampton flying boats from Calshot's No. 201 Squadron Coastal Command visited the Polish Naval Air Wing as a part of another 'Baltic Cruise'. Group Captain Eric Nanson, commander of RAF Calshot, led the group, accompanied by the air

British hydroplanes during their visit to Poland in 1930.

attaché in Berlin (and consequently in Warsaw) Group Captain Ernest Gossage. The Southamptons, piloted by Squadron Leader Edward Turner, commander of No. 201 Squadron, and Flight Lieutenants Alick Stevens, Robert Ragg and G.H. Smith, arrived from the Lithuanian port of Klaipéda, after a trip of 109 nautical miles.[19] On this occasion, their Polish colleagues invited them to a ball that was held on 23 September 1930 at the Zamkowa restaurant in Puck. On 24 September, all the Southamptons left for Sweden, performing an air parade as farewell over the port of Gdynia.[20]

There was yet another British visit, which this time was rather unexpected. In January 1931, Amy Johnson, the pioneering British female aviator nicknamed by the Polish press as the 'Girl from the Sky', flew from Berlin to Warsaw on her way, as the press stated, to Peking, when her plane, 'Jason III', had to land about 90km from the Polish capital due to severe weather. Her surprising arrival at the small village of Krasnosielec became something of a national sensation, followed be a series of pictures that appeared in Światowid magazine. After repairing her DH60 Gipsy Moth, she flew to Warsaw and then continued her trip to the East.

A few months later, on 2 October, a Lublin R.Xa landed at Brooklands, Surrey. The crew of Stanisław Karpiński, future deputy commander of the PAF in the West, and Jerzy Suchodolski completed the next stage of their flight across Europe. The following day, the Polish aviators visited London before leaving Britain to continue their journey. England became a destination for other Polish fliers who were attending various competitions. On many occasions, Poles and Britons competed in international gliding or sport aeroplane tournaments

„Dziewczyna z nieba" w Polsce

BRAWURA i odwaga kobiet angielskich jest rzeczą powszechnie znaną. Po całym świecie napotkać można młode i mniej młode Angielki, które gnane żądzą przygód, popełniają pełne ryzyka treści rozumując, że życie wtedy jest miłe, jeśli ma posmak ryzyka i przygody. To też nikogo nie dziwi, że dwie może najlepsze dziś lotniczki Europy: Miss Amy Johnson oraz Miss Spooner, rekrutują się z kadr młodej Anglji. Miss Spooner brała udział w szeregu długodystansowych raidów, m. in. w rajdzie awionetek w locie dookoła Italji, w których brał udział kwiat lotnictwa europejskiego, a niedawno rozbiła się pod Neapolem w czasie lotu.

Znacznie jednak większe sukcesy odniosła młoda lotniczka Miss Amy Johnson, która oderwawszy się od nudnej maszyny do pisania w zasnutem dymami mieście portowem Hull, zabrała się z pa-

Lądowanie w Krasnosielcu. Aparat Miss Amy Johnson na polach pod Krasnosielcem. Grupa mieszkańców wsi przygląda się ciekawie awionetce.

popularny), przelatuje ponad Morzem Śródziemnem, nad piaskami Arabji, nad burzliwą świecą zatoką. Aby dostać się w pasmo wichrów nad olbrzymiemi połaciami Indyj. Kilkakrotnie zmuszona do nagłego lądowania, kilkakrotnie porwana w ośrodek burzy — wychodzi Miss Amy Johnson zwycięsko z tych zapasów z losem i przyrodą, lądując na ziemi australijskiej. Lot Miss Amy Johnson, finansowany przez wielki dziennik londyński „Daily Mail", rozsławia imię angielskiej lotniczki — za powrotem swojem do Londynu jest „dziewczyna z nieba" (jak nazywają w Anglji Miss Johnson), przedmiotem entuzjastycznego przyjęcia.

Zdawało się, że po wyczerpującej próbie australijskiej, Miss Johnson „uspokoi się" na czas jakiś. Tymczasem w najmniej pomyślnej chwili, startuje na swoim nowym aparacie „Jazon 3" (typu „Moth") z Londynu, ażeby przez Berlin i Warszawę skierować się w stronę bezbrzeżnych pustkowi Rosji, Mongolji i Syberji. Celem jej lotu jest Pekin.

Przedsięwzięcie to skazane było zgóry na pewne niepowodzenia. Przedewszystkiem nie wiadomo było, jak się odniosą władze sowieckie do przelotu nad terytorjum Rosji, potem Miss Johnson miała lecieć nad okolicami, gdzie w razie wypadku, albo przymusowego lądowania, nie miałaby zupełnie pomocy. Następnie ekwipunek jej na tak silne mrozy nie był dostateczny i zachodziła obawa, że w uściskach syberyjskiego mrozu zamarznie oliwa w aparacie śmiałej lotniczki. Płozy, w które zaopatrzony jest aparat Miss Johnson nie gwarantują bynajmniej bezpiecznego lądowania na nierównym śnieżnym terenie.

I oto Miss Amy Johnson, która miała zamiar siąść na lotnisku Mokotowskiem, zmuszona została na skutek warunków atmosferycznych do wylądowania w małej wiosce w powiecie makowskim w dystansie 90 km od Warszawy. Nie wiadomo, czy Miss Johnson będzie kontynuować swój lot,

Autograf lotniczki angielskiej. W czasie swego pobytu w Warszawie Miss Amy Johnson wręczyła przedstawicielom prasy autogram, który w dosłownem tłumaczeniu polskiem brzmi jak następuje: „Wszyscy ludzie w Polsce byli dla mnie niezwykle grzeczni i gościnni. Bardzo się cieszę, że znalazłam się w Polsce. Wszystkim dziękuję za serdeczne przyjęcie. Amy Johnson, Warszawa, 5 stycznia 1931".

Miss Amy Johnson po wylądowaniu w Krasnosielcu, zdjęta przez specjalnego wysłannika „Światowida".

są do lotnictwa. Od początku wykazuje nadzwyczajne uzdolnienie lotnicze, przytomność umysłu, zimną krew i brawurową śmiałość. W roku ubiegłym zdumiewa cały świat fenomenalnym lotem z Londynu do Australji, dokonanym zupełnie samotnie. Na małym aparacie typu „Moth" (t.zn. ćma — typ tego aparatu jest niezwykłe w Anglji

W gościnie u ks. kanonika. Miss Amy Johnson rozmawia z ks. kanonikiem Serejko przed plebanją w Krasnosielcu, gdzie wylądowała przymusowo.

W owalu: „Jazon 3" w Berlinie. Zdjęcie przedstawia odlot śmiałej lotniczki z lotniska Tempelhof w Berlinie do Warszawy, który zakończył się przymusowem lądowaniem w Amelinie. Atlantic-Ph. Berlin.

Samolot przedewszystkiem. Miss Amy Johnson bada w Krasnosielcu uszkodzenie swojego aparatu. Była to pierwsza jej czynność po przymusowem lądowaniu.

chociaż władze sowieckie udzieliły jej wiz. Zorjentowała się ona, że przelot w zimnikach zimowych jest wysoce niebezpieczny i że osiadnięcie na jakimś pustkowiu mongolskiem, czy syberyjskiem grozić może śmiercią.

Jednakże panna Johnson nie należy do kobiet bojaźliwych, gdyż stwierdziła w wywiadzie dziennikarskim w Warszawie, że „my, młode Angielki nie boimy się dziś niczego". Ponieważ zaś panna Johnson przyznaje się, że zapał flirt, zabawę i taniec, ceni sobie przedewszystkiem przygodę, przeto rychło należy się obawiać, że „Jazon 3" poderwie się do lotu w stronę Pekinu...

An article in one of the Polish newspapers describing the unexpected arrival of Amy Johnson, a pioneering British female aviator.

such as the Challenge Internationale des Avions de Tourisme in 1930, when the national teams were represented respectively by twelve (Poland) and seven (United Kingdom) aircraft. One of the Polish contestants was Captain Jerzy Bajan, who four years later won the challenge and during the Second World War served as Polish Liaison Officer with RAF Fighter Command. It is also worth mentioning that Bajan was on a stage placement in Britain in 1935: between 2-5 July he was posted to the Central Flying School in Upavon, from 8-10 July to RAF Tangmere in Sussex and finally, between 23-27 July, to No. 3 Flying Training School in Spitalgate. For this talented and extremely popular pilot, who gained a celebrity status in his own country, visiting the RAF bases proved to be a great learning curve for the future. When he reached Britain again during the war, he could put his observations into practice.

Rivalry betwen both teams continued during first Alpen Flight Contest in 1933, while four years later, Poles and Britons met at the Annual Glider Competition in Wasserkuppe, Germany. Among the Poles who took second place behind the German team was Stanisław Brzezina (future 74 Squadron Battle of Britain pilot), who made an acquaintance with the Wills brothers, Phillip and Richard.[21] Some British glider pilots knew Polish skies rather well, being among 340 foreigners who undertook training in Polish gliding schools. Another interesting chapter of the links between Polish and British aviation involved Squadron Leader William Calder, who went to Poland before the Great War as an English teacher and then worked for the British Consulate in Cracow. Calder was no ordinary clerk; he played for the Cracovia football team as defender and team captain.[22] He was later involved in Polish and British negotiations about re-forming the PAF in Britain.

On 10 October 1934, Group Captain Francis Percival Don OBE was appointed an Air Attaché in Berlin and Warsaw, and on 12 November 1935, Flight Lieutenant William Edwin Coope was made Assistant Air Attaché in both cities. It is believed that Don resided mainly in Berlin, which strategically was more important for Britain, whilst Coope consequently had his office in Warsaw. The latter visited the 2nd Air Regiment in Cracow in 1936. Despite his previous career in diplomacy, Coope returned to operational flying, taking command of No. 87 Squadron in 1939. He flew some missions with No. 17 Squadron during the Battle of Britain, eventually being shot down on 15 April 1941 by the German ace Adolf Galland, while leading Wittering Wing. He was killed south-east of Dover on 4 June 1941 when leading No. 266 Squadron.

Paul Harding, who in the summer of 1940 was appointed an Intelligence Officer of No. 302 (Polish) Squadron, was most probably posted to serve with the Polish airmen due to his knowledge of their language. Before the war, he was employed as a sales representative by the Warsaw-based Schicht-Lever company, a well-known soap and cosmetics manufacturer.

Flt Lt William Edwin Coope, British Assistant Air Attaché accompanied by Lt Wojciech Kołaczkowski at 2nd Air Regiment's airfield in 1936. After arriving in Britain Kołaczkowski commanded No. 303 Squadron between November 1941 and May 1942.

There were also many private visits to both countries. Future No. 308 (Polish) Squadron pilot Andrzej Nahlik went to England in early 1939 to study Shakespeare's language and to gain experience by working in an aircraft factory.

Poland and Great Britain also had other connections. Pilot Officer Ron Landau, an RAF officer who was delegated to work with accommodating the Polish personnel and help organise the structure of the PAF in Britain, had a very interesting background. He was born in Łódź, Poland, in 1899 as Roman Zbigniew Landau, and during the Great War, together with his family, had emigrated to England. He joined the RAF on 28 October 1939, but, strangely, was naturalized as British citizen only on 13 March 1940.

Finally, in June 1939, preceded by negotiations led by General Ludomił Rayski and his official mission to London, a group of four experienced Polish fliers arrived in Britain to perform test flights on Spitfires, Hurricanes and Fairey Battles, which were an object of trade discussions between the Polish and British governments. They were Colonel Jerzy Bajan, Captain Andrzej Włodarkiewicz, both from the PAF, and two test pilots, Bolesław Orliński, representing the PZL factory, accompanied by Roland Kalpas of the Technical Institute. Between 3-14 July, they were attached to the Central Flying School at

RAF Upavon. This trip was soon followed by another visit made on 29 July (and continued for a month until the end of August 1939) by airmen from the 1st Air Regiment in Warsaw. Tactical Officer of the IV/1 Fighter Wing (Dywizjon Myśliwski) Lieutenant Jerzy Jankiewicz, a future Battle of Britain pilot, tested Hawker Hurricanes in the air, his colleague Sub-Lieutenant Michał Liniewski[23] of 222nd Eskadra Bombowa most probably flew Fairey Battles, while Warrant Officer Feliks Świątek[24] – a ground crew member and chief of the radio-communication platoon – was there to learn about the technical details of the British aircraft, in particular RT equipment that was installed in the Fairey Battle. As history was shortly to prove, none of the aircraft mentioned reached Polish soil and all PAF aircrews had to wait a little longer to fly them from British bases. To make this flying possible, however, considerable negotiations, setting conditions and cessations on both sides were needed.

In July 1939, an unsuccessful attempt was made by Captain Stanisław Rymszewicz to forge an agreement with the Royal Navy for the placement of two officers of the PAF Naval Arm, for two weeks' practice in Britain when they would learn about torpedo attacks with the use of hydroplanes.

Chapter Five

English Tea and King's Regulations

On 3 September 1939, the Polish Military Mission arrived in London to negotiate immediate British support for their country, which was already under German attack. Despite Britain doing nothing to fulfil its obligations, General Mieczysław Norwid-Neugebauer, who led the mission, had to play another role in future negotiations. It was he who for the first time mentioned the possibility of re-forming the Polish Air Force by the side of the RAF. This suggestion saw daylight on 20 September. It was followed by a positive opinion from the Air Ministry; however, the way to achieve such plan was to be long and bumpy. The Poles were required to provide their draft proposal. General Józef Zając, commander of the PAF, strongly believed that forming his military aviation under the RAF would be the only option, especially now that his options were limited and hands tied. At that time, the French were rather reluctant to take the matter of a potential ally in their own hands, ironically patronizing and keeping on blaming the Poles for the conflict, which they themselves were involved in against their wish. Seeing the French way of employing the thousands of his airmen who managed to leave Poland as time-consuming, General Zając opted for further conversations with the RAF. In his naivety, Zając also hoped that at the end of the war the British would not ask his government to pay back all costs covering the existence of foreign forces on their soil.[1]

Sub-Colonel Wacław Makowski flew to London, where alongside Sub-Colonel Kwieciński, he participated in a conference when the further fate of the PAF and its units operating from Britain was discussed. Both sides agreed to allocate and create designated places where the Poles would shortly start arriving. They said that written materials were needed to start their ground and then flying training, followed by the necessity of English dictionaries. Another part of the conclusion was that Polish units would consist of Polish personnel who would be treated on the same level as those in the RAF. The recruitment process that involved all 80 per cent of the PAF that escaped to France should have happened immediately. Unfortunately, on 11 October the French unexpectedly expressed their doubts. It is disputable whether they just didn't like the British and tried to make their work more difficult, or they were afraid that after the war the PAF (until 1939 dependent on French equipment) would start ordering British supplies.

On 25 October, another conference was set up in Paris. The British agreed with French terms to split Polish personnel between both countries. The proposal was made that only 300 pilots, followed by 2,000 other air and ground crew, should make their way to Britain to create two medium bomber squadrons. There was no approval for Polish fighter squadrons. The British explained their refusal in a simple way. Tactics and radio contact requires a good communication in English, which was a massive issue at that time. RAF Eastchurch, known better as the Receiving Centre or PAF Centre, with its satellite base in Manston, were appointed as the main and initial gathering points for Polish personnel, while terms of pay were set up as equal to RAF personnel. All this was agreed between the British and French, therefore the Poles had only two options: forget the idea of an independent air force in Britain and agree with this decision or resign from the whole concept and stay in France.

Unhappy with this decision, General Sikorski (who in 1934 had demanded an independent air force) flew to London on 14 November. The British maintained their position that an independent PAF was not possible. They did, however, agree that PAF markings could be applied on their aircraft alongside RAF ones, and that Polish airmen would be allowed to wear RAF uniforms with both RAF and Polish ranks. They expressed the necessity of a double oath of loyalty towards the Polish Government and King George VI. Finally, on 30 November, there was another amendment to the agreement. All British-based Polish personnel would be transferred to the Volunteer Reserve of the Royal Air Force. In short, by this, the chance for independence was lost, at least for the time. It was also stated that no Polish units could be used outside Europe, and that all officers (of trained personnel) would start their service from the bottom, receiving the rank of Pilot Officer, regardless of their previous Polish ones.

Despite this rather unfavourable situation, the first transport of Polish airmen left France on 6 December. Not all was lost, however, as on 19 January the Air Ministry reactivated discussions. Three weeks later, August Zaleski, Polish Minister of Foreign Affairs, arrived in London. Although affiliation to the RAF Volunteer Reserve was still beyond compromise, two bomber and two training squadrons were offered to his countrymen. The idea of setting up a Polish Air Force Inspectorate had been discussed, along with organizational details. Command of each Polish unit had to be divided between PAF and RAF officers, but in the future steeply transferred only to Poles. A few days later, the Poles proposed that more squadrons be formed and suggested the right for the Polish C-in-C and Commander of the PAF to inspect them.

It was slow progress, but the Poles were relatively patient. While Sikorski's countrymen were studying King's Regulations, learning the language, playing football, keeping healthy by swimming or competing in boxing sparring and making themselves familiar with English tea (which was quite unusual to their taste), the Air Ministry agreed on 13 March that the PAF eagle could be worn on hats and the PAF flag could be placed under the RAF one everywhere the Poles operated from. For a long time the Air Ministry was against using Polish fighter pilots, and only in April did this idea start to receive backing. Hugh Dowding, the main opponent of such a concept, argued that the language barrier could create a huge problem, especially in the air. He also looked rather suspiciously at the new arrivals as he believed that they were under surveillance by foreign intelligence services. However, Air Vice Marshal William Sholto Douglas thought that this was nonsense, and that not employing such experienced pilots would be a huge mistake. The Air Ministry ignored Dowding's fears, and on 1 June allowed the first Polish fighter pilots to start their training. Sixteen days later, first group left Eastchurch for 15 Elementary Flying Training School in Carlisle. In the meantime, Polish bomber personnel also started to receive their first postings. On 23 March, the first bunch of them left for No. 18 Operational Training Unit in Hucknall.[2]

Polish consistency in negotiations was eventually rewarded. With France lost, this very rapidly changed everything, especially in British eyes. When the French did absolutely nothing to evacuate Polish personnel, even making such a move very difficult,[3] the British offered their help. Facing a real danger of losing experienced airmen, they completely changed their approach. Prime Minister Winston Churchill said to Sikorski: 'We are now united for better or for worse.' To make the forming of foreign forces in Britain possible, it was necessary to change the law. Up until then, the presence of a foreign army on British soil had never been seen before. In July 1940, Churchill's Government turned to the House of Commons and the law was soon amended.

The situation was rather complicated. The British approved the independence of the Polish Army and Navy, yet they were still struggling with their decision regarding the PAF. Eventually, General Sikorski and Minister Zaleski were invited to visit Churchill's office in Downing Street on Monday 5 August. The Prime Minister, accompanied by Lord Halifax, signed an official agreement which stated among other things that all Polish airmen were obliged to swear loyalty only to their own government, and they would be withdrawn from the RAF Volunteer Rererve and would join the PAF that from this moment woud exist under operational command of the RAF. Four bomber, two fighter and one co-operation squadron would also be formed. Although it was far from perfect, the status of the Polish Air Force in Britain became a little clearer.[4]

Bolesław Drobiński recalled:

'Despite us enquiring, demanding and almost begging to start our fighter pilot's training on English equipment, we kept receiving rather laconic answers, that everything would be sorted in the appropriate time, but for now, above all, we have to learn the English language, the drill, military salutes and English military rules.'[5]

On 6 July, the historic decision was made that the first Polish fighter squadron equipped with Hawker Hurricanes would be formed. Its command was briefly given to Squadron Leader Kazimierz Niedźwiecki and initially this squadron existed only on paper, consisting of seventy-seven very often randomly chosen airmen. Some of them were not even fighter pilots, revealing that its organization was made in a hurry. The list included Pilot Officer Stanisław Skalski, who was quite a character and the most successful Polish pilot of the Polish Campaign, who impatiently awaited his posting to a front-line squadron.

Seeing No. 302 Squadron still under training, this charismatic officer demanded to see action and soon after was posted back and attached to No. 501 Squadron RAF. Shortly after that, the final list of potential pilots was verified and approved.

Although history remembers this squadron as No. 302 'City of Poznań', its first name was rather different. The first Polish fighter unit organized in Britain was actually called after the 'First Polish Combat Units in France'. Many of the Polish pilots of the core squad had served previously in France, therefore the name seemed to be obvious and adequate. On 13 July, Squadron Leader William Satchell was appointed its British commander, with his Polish counterpart Squadron Leader Mieczysław Mümler. The latter was born in 1899 and became the oldest Polish pilot who participated in the

General Józef Zając, the Commander of the Polish Air Force during his visit to RAF Eastchurch. Gpt Cpt Bolesław Stachoń is standing right behind him, whilst Gpt Cpt Davidson is closer to the camera.

Battle of Britain, as well as one of the oldest of 'The Few'.[6] It was decided that the squadron would be formed at RAF Leconfield.

'How enthusiastically all officers, NCOs and enlisted men of the fighter squadrons, who previously fought together in Poland and France and who hoped to beat the Germans again, were welcoming each other,' Mümler recalled. This officer, who lived a Spartan life, drinking only milk and avoiding meat, was a solitary warrior. He was highly respected by his pilots, whom he admired and respected back, despite them occasionally calling him a 'crusader'. Mümler was also known as a bugbear of the young, inexperienced aviators.

On 10 July, another crucial decision was made: a second Polish Hawker Hurricane unit was to be formed at the same airfield. Seven days later, however, Air Vice Marshal Grahame Donald made the famous decisions that in fact the second Polish squadron should be organized at 11 Group's base in Northolt. This was therefore the beginning of the legend of the famous No. 303 Squadron that was now to be given a chance to operate closer to the main theatre of the Battle of Britain. Initially its name was 'IInd Warsaw Fighter Squadron' or 'No. 1 Warsaw Squadron', formed under the command of the charismatic and widely known Squadron Leader Zdzisław Krasnodębski, who later wrote:

General Władysław Kalkus (3rd from left) inspecting the Polish airmen at RAF Eastchurch, accompanied by Gp Cpt Stachoń (1st from left) and Gp Cpt Davidson (2nd). Kalkus was deputy commander of the Polish Air Force, then from June 1940 he led the Polish Air Force Inspectorate until 18 July 1940 when he was replaced by General Stanisław Ujejski.

'In July 1940 in England, whilst in Blackpool, I received orders to organise a Fighter Squadron with my Warsaw crews. This was with the objective to be ready for action as soon as possible. This being in order to assist English fliers, who heroically are worthy of the highest praise, who offered resistance to the German Luftwaffe during the then in progress Battle of Britain.'

This experienced officer was an 'inspirational authority, colleague and friend', as his successor recalled. The core of the future No. 303 'Tadeusz Kościuszko'[8] Squadron left Blackpool (where the Polish Air Force Centre was previously moved from Eastchurch),[9] and arrived at RAF Northolt on 2 August. Its British command was given to Squadron Leader Ronald Gustave Kellett. Entrusting the leading of a foreign squadron to him proved rather a wise move. Kellett's mother, Louise Antoinettte née Monthal, was of French Swiss descent, and thanks to her he learnt to speak French, which eventually allowed him to communicate with his Polish personnel. Such communication sometimes was not as easy as the British commander would have liked it to be. 'I met Squadron Leader Kellett,' Witold Urbanowicz wrote, '[and] we did not like each other from the first moment. An "anti-love" syndrome developed between us.' 'I did often clash with Flying Officer Witold Urbanowicz,' Kellett said. 'Personality wise, we did not always see eye to eye; [but] he was excellent as a pilot and I respected him.'

Chapter Six

Tally-Ho!

Among many myths that arose over the years, the main one was a claim that the Poles, shown as rather romantic and brave barbarians[1] from a country not even known to civilized nations, could not cope with the technologically advanced Hurricanes as they were trained to fly on obsolete and primitive aircraft back in Poland. The most unjust explanation of this thesis would be that they simply couldn't deal with novelties such as the retractable undercarriage that led to many accidents. To understand the situation better, we need to see what one of them had to say on the subject:

> 'The cockpit drill had baffled at first. By comparison with every other type of plane we'd ever flown, everything here was back to front. In Poland and France when you wanted to open the throttle you pulled, here you pushed. We had to reverse all our reflexes.'[2]

British aircraft were completely different from any other Continental fighters that Polish pilots had flown before, and the Poles were no exception and no different from other non-British pilots in this regard in terms of familiarity. Therefore the crucial technical difference that distinguished British planes from other aircraft which were used across the Channel had nothing uniquely to do with either Polish experience or their lack of, and not much to do with flying obsolete aircraft previously in Poland, as many historians try to insist.

As mentioned before, many of the Poles had flown operationally in France and they therefore knew, for example, how retractable undercarriages worked. The main problem was just getting used to British planes:

> 'Making matters worse, the Poles were used to controlling the throttle with their right hand; British aircraft had the throttle on the other side. As a consequence the Poles found themselves having to work opposite to their natural instincts … To complete the Poles' confusion, the Hurricane's flight instruments and pilot's handbook used imperial units to measure speed, altitude and fuel etc. Used to metric measurement (as were other European nations), the Poles initially had no idea what their instruments were telling them. As the instruments were fundamental to the conduct

of a safe flight, not least the landing phase, there were inevitably more than a few hair-rising incidents and a few accidents.'[3]

Not everyone was struggling, though. Wacław Król's account clarifies that some of the pilots, mostly those who experienced flying French aircraft prior to arrival in Britain, found this part of their training rather straightforward:

'There were no problems with pilots' training in the air as all of them flew in France either in Morane MS-406s or Caudron C-714s, Blochs MB-152 or even, such as Pilot Officer Karwowski – on Dewoitine D-520. French fighter planes neither structurally nor by aerial performance characteristics were different than English Hurricanes. We could not speed up the training, however, as Fighter Command imposed a particular training regime, which had to by strictly completed, before allowing our squadron to join the combat. There was a pressure put on the scrupulous following of the regulations, rules and various ordinances in England. This was the rule, and everyone had to follow it.'[4]

By adding language difficulties we can now clearly see the picture of a bunch of pilots determined to fight, yet grounded by other circumstancess. 'Everything is different here,' Bohdan Arct recalled. 'People are polite towards us, despite them not understanding us. Our biggest pain would be learning the language, but so far there are no handbooks nor organised lessons.'[5]

Another story that apparently 'characterizes' their early days in Britain was that for training purposes the Poles used to ride bicycles around the base, to simulate a dog fight and learn how to keep the formation tight. This rather patronizing picture was very often shown by the media as true and was mentioned in many books. Yet there is absolutely no written or photographic evidence of such activities being performed by Polish pilots.

As 'Stuffy' Dowding was rather apprehensive about infiltration of Polish and Czechoslovak pilots into his squadrons, he opted to organize foreign units rather than Poles or Czechs being posted to RAF ones. He recalled after the war:

'I can well remember my thoughts when I was told in the Summer of 1940 that it was proposed to post Polish pilots for service in the Fighter Command. I regarded it as an experiment which might or might not be successful. I knew that the morale of the Polish Air Force was high, but it remained to be seen how that morale had stood the shock of being overwhelmed by superior number and equipment in their own country.

The Polish airmen leaving the train at Blackpool station welcomed by Flg Off Henryk Szczęsny and Flt Lt Stanisław Brzezina. During the early months of 1940 Brzezina was appointed the Polish commanding officer of the Manston receiving centre, which was a satellite base to RAF Eastchurch overcrowded by the Poles.

> There was also the question of language to be considered; and this way by no means a trivial obstacle to be overcome in an organisation which depended so much upon radio telephony for its control.'[6]

Poles, on the other hand, also preferred to fly together. Looking at the structures of 302 and 303 Squadrons, we can see a composition of pilots who not only knew each other rather well, but had flown together in combat either in Poland or France. Most of the essential framework of No. 303 Squadron came from four fighter units of the former 1st Air Regiment in Warsaw (111th, 112th, 113th and 114th Fighter Squadrons), and apart from Flying Officer Marian Pisarek and Sergeants Tadeusz Andruszków, Marian Bełc, Michał Brzezowski, Jan Rogowski and Mirosław Wojciechowski – who were almost outsiders, yet still knew the others – were like the fingers of one hand. Even these outsiders had seen combat while flying with their units across Poland or France.

The final core of No. 302 Squadron was formed from Squadron Leader Mieczysław Mümler's former squadrons of the 3rd Air Regiment in Poznań or pilots who fought together in France. They were equally experienced as their colleagues from 'Tadeusz Kościuszko'[7] group, but less fortunate as they had to remain far from the centre of events.[8] Being in the right place at the right time was a major factor which undoubtably influenced No. 303's success. In both cases, long-lasting friendship and brotherhood that had grown between the Poles throughout their pre-war training and two campaigns was crucial to their discipline, communication, tactics and understanding each other's roles.

There were other aspects that made them more effective and deadly. Back in Poland they flew the most practical formation that was introduced at that date, although now often associated with the Luftwaffe – the Four Finger Formation. Having no radar back in Poland and only few aircraft equipped with radio made them more cautious. They had to trust their own eyes, instead of modern emergency warning systems, therefore spent most of their flying time on constant look-out around 360°. Flying rather obsolete aircraft had also pushed them to engage their more natural, human instincts like perceptivity, followed by the ability to attack from very short range and reliance on themselves. This was what made them so successful and deadly. The Polish fighter boys who made up the core of both squadrons in Britain were old hands, hand-picked by both Polish commanders, who preferred to lead into battle men proven in combat rather than a bunch of novices. This might therefore justify the initial disappointment of the Polish officers and men when three British commanders of No. 303 Squadron arrived with much less combat experience than their subordinates. Apparently they were appointed to guide them.

All that differentiated the Polish squadrons was their location: 302 responded to No. 12 Group orders, whilst 303 Squadron was placed in the centre of the operating area of No. 11 Group. The decisions as to the squadrons' locations profoundly affected which squadron had the greater opportunity for glory in the Battle of Britain. By placing the future 'Tadeusz Kościuszko' Squadron closer to the front line, whilst holding 302 behind, 303 would be constantly in action during the crucial phase of the battle with the Luftwaffe.

Unlike them, other Poles who were about to be posted to RAF squadrons had to face factors such as language difficulties, flying and living away from their countrymen and being forced to follow the RAF 'V' formation – tight and unpractical. 'I was concerned about the squadron's formation,' Witold Urbanowicz wrote.

> 'While facing an enemy they flew like a parade in tight threes, one after another. Such a formation was wrong. Above all for the pilots this was making it difficult to observe air space for the pilots as everyone had to watch his neighbour's plane to avoid collision. Apart from that, a

squadron flying such a tight formation was an easy and compact target for the enemy. Even an ordinary bumbler could shoot down one of the aircraft aiming at the whole group. What is most important, manoeuvring in such a formation was hard as it could lead to a clash between aircraft.'[9]

Karol Pniak complained:

'As a pilot I had by then ten years of experience, a rather high level of training, and about thirty combat sorties during the Polish Campaign. That's why in any way I couldn't agree with my commander's opinion, and tried to explain in my poor English, that their way of flying was basically wrong.'[10]

The group of 145 Polish pilots that eventually officially gained the Battle of Britain's 'The Few' honoured status consisted of various personnel available when needed. As mentioned in the previous chapter, according to the initial plan only two light bomber Polish squadrons were supposed to be created in Britain. Suitable airmen were therefore recruited from the accessible resources and transported from France. They were supplemented by their colleagues, fighter pilots so desperate and frustrated to leave somewhere they did not belong and could not see any future, that they preferred to fly British bombers rather than watch the French enjoying their 'Phoney war'.

This is why Dowding had to deal with different sorts and qualities of Polish airmen who happened to be more or less ready and fit for his Spitfires and Hurricanes. They were boys with a great amount of combat experience from Poland, who had arrived in Britain earlier, followed by the group of fighter pilots who in the summer of 1940 sailed from France (mostly with even more fighting experience). Then there were well-trained personnel who had not seen any combat at all, and finally former bomber or reconnaissance pilots willing to be converted into fighters. This rather diverse mixture of flying personnel had different levels of skills. Quite often, although in not every case, this showed in their efficiency flying over Britain.[11]

Dowding continued:

'It was at first decided to post these pilots in pairs to each of a number of Fighter squadrons, but this scheme was not an unqualified success, since partly from misunderstandings, and partly from excess zeal to get into action against the first German machine which they saw irrespective of the tactical plan of the formation leader, they were sometimes guilty of breaking formation on their own initiative, spoiling the combined attack which was planned. As soon, however, as it was decided to form homogeneous units, these difficulties disappeared.'[12]

Despite these initial flaws that accompanied the first steps made by the reborn PAF and its frustrated airmen, the spirit among the Polish fighter pilots was extremely high.

Polish fighter pilots were not alone in their war preparations. As previously stated, the Air Ministry had also agreed to form light bomber squadrons based on Polish personnel arriving from France, finally settling on four units. They were supposed to be initially equipped with the Fairey Battle single-engine aircraft, then a vague proposal was given to let them fly much bigger twin-engine Vickers Wellingtons. The timing of such a change was uncertain, therefore the issue was left undecided. Despite uncertainty regarding the equipment, the first movement of personnel was made.

On 26 June 1940, the first group of Polish airmen arrived at RAF Bramcote in Warwickshire to form No. 300 Bomber Squadron, later known as 'Mazowian'. On 22 July, at the same Station, another Polish unit was born: No. 301 Bomber Squadron 'Pomeranian', also flying Fairey Battles. Both began intensive training and in August were moved to RAF Swinderby in Lincolnshire. Both squadrons played an important role in an undervalued part of the Battle of Britain – the 'Battle of the Barges'.[13]

Despite previous delays and obstacles, the future of the Polish fighters started to look much more clear and promising. More and more of them were packing their belongings and travelling to No. 15 Elementary Flying Training School, from where they were posted to either No. 5 Operational Training Unit in Aston Down or to No. 6 OTU in Sutton Bridge.

Bolesław Drobiński gave details of his training:

'Our group, which apart from myself, consisted of the pilots: Witold Głowacki, Walenty Krepski, Tadeusz Kumiega, Ludwik Martel, Jerzy Solak, in the second half of July arrived at T.F.S. Old Sarum [near Salisbury]. On July 23rd the first flight with the instructor took place [in a Tiger Moth]. Approximate time on the dual controlled aircraft – 30 minutes single flight altogether 4 hours 55 minutes. Next equipment "Hector", on dual controlled aircraft – 20 minutes, single flights 4 hours 30 minutes. On July 29th, which means 6 days later, we completed this initial course and were posted to 7 OTU Hawarden [near Chester]. He were doing an average ½ hour on dual controlled Fairey Battles and 2 hours solo, after which we went on Hurricanes – each of us flew 18 hours average. The course continued between 2 and 10 August.'[14]

Despite their training, in general, going smoothly, unfortunately accidents started to occur. On 19 July, Leading Aircraftman Zdzisław Urbańczyk damaged his Hurricane while landing. Three days after Urbańczyk's misfortune, Pilot Officer Władysław Różycki experienced the same trouble. Seven days later, Pilot Officer Kazimierz Olewiński, performing a dog-fight exercise, crashed his Hurricane near Wisbech. This Polish Campaign veteran, who flew combat missions with 132nd Eskadra Myśliwska almost a year before, was killed in the impact. The bad luck continued on 8 August. Pilot Officer Dominik Fengler, a former fighter pilot of 142nd and 143rd Eskadras, who received a posting to No. 301 Squadron and was in the process of converting into a bomber pilot, crashed in a Fairey Battle during training, becoming the second fatal victim of this early period. As well as mishaps, however, there were also happy times. A day after Urbańczyk meekly had to listen to a reprimand from his superiors, Flying Officer Antoni Ostowicz, accompanied by Flight Lieutenant Roy Dutton and Pilot Officer Michael Newling, took off for the second time in his front-line career in Britain. His second operational sortie of 19 July proved to be successful and became a historic day for the whole Polish Air Force.

Chapter Seven

First Kills, First Losses

Flying Officer Antoni Ostowicz's military career began as an observer of the 24th Eskadra of 2nd Air Regiment, but deep down he knew that flying fighter planes would be the only love of his life. After completing challenging and intensive training, Antoni achieved what he wanted and in 1936 joined 123rd Fighter Squadron operating from Cracow. Now, after four ears of putting his training into practice and polishing his skills, he had the perfect chance to realise his dreams. Ostowicz was finally able to face the enemy in the air. On 16 July 1940, he was the first Polish pilot posted to a front-line unit of the RAF. At the age of 29, he joined No. 145 Squadron based at RAF Tangmere, commanded by Squadron Leader John Peel, who was only a few months younger than the Pole. On Friday 19 July, three Hurricanes of Red Section climbed into the sky for an afternoon patrol. Ostowicz reported what happened next:

'I was No. 3 Red Section, 145 Sqn. We took off Tangmere at 17.50 with orders to patrol Brighton at 10,000 ft. After one circuit over Brighton above cloud we were ordered to go down to 2,000 ft on a Westerly course along the coast. Shortly afterwards we turned slightly South to sea, and in a few minutes sighted an aircraft flying SSE at approx. 3,000 ft. I followed Red 1 and Red 2 apparently was unable to keep up with us, so I took his place as he fell back behind me. The a/c was identified as a He 111. We closed to within 300 yards of e/a [enemy aircraft] and after Red 1 had fired at him the e/a turned slightly right and I was able to fire a burst at him. Smoke then issued from his starboard engine. I noticed flashes from each side of both engine nacelles below the wings which I took to be two pairs of fixed M.G.s firing backwards. A few moments later I fired another burst and broke away downward to the right. At the same time I looked to see what Red 2 was doing and saw him turning to the north with black smoke coming from his plane. I then saw the e/a turning further to the right and it went into a glide, and subsequently landed on the sea. It sank in about three minutes and I saw four of the crew in the water. I circled for five or ten minutes and was then ordered to pancake.[1] I landed Tangmere 18.40.'

After landing, Ostowicz shared his joy with his friend, 36-year-old Flight Lieutenant Wilhelm Pankratz, another Pole who joined 145 Squadron. Pankratz was selected as 'A' Flight Commander for 303 Squadron when the creation of the new unit had been discussed. However, he never had a chance to serve there. On this afternoon, the list of Polish aerial victories had begun. It turned out that three crew members of the Heinkel He 111 from 7th Staffel of Kampfgeschwader 55,[2] Oblt Westhaus, Uffz. Biskup and Fw. Mäder, were killed, while Fw. Kasten and Gefr. Mansel ended up being taken prisoner. The Hurricane that Ostowicz saw going down was flown by Pilot Officer Newling, who crash-landed at Shoreham. Despite the 'kill' claim only being made by Ostowicz and Dutton, the victory eventually was evenly distributed between the whole section.

Ostowicz had another opportunity to shoot down a Hun on Wednesday, 31st July. He was flying with A Flight, when he spotted the long and thin silhouette of a Dornier Do 17, which was often erroneously interpreted as Do 215. The latter German aircraft was rarely seen over England during the Battle of Britain. 'We followed and I caught sight of him (below cloud). I attacked twice more with short bursts, but after the third attack he disappeared completely in a cloud and I never saw him again,' Ostowicz reported after landing at Tangmere. He was credited with one enemy aircraft damaged.

Meanwhile, more Polish pilots were posted to the front line. Pilot Officers Jan Pfeiffer, Karol Pniak and Bolesław Własnowolski drove to the Biggin Hill-based 32 Squadron. Pfeiffer, who soon after gained the cute name of 'Fifi', was a former fighter pilot of 142nd Fighter Squadron, who before the outbreak of war served as a flying instructor at Air Force NCO Training Centre. The tall Pniak, on the other hand, was both a fighter and aerobatic pilot, who gained fame when flying in the famous 'Cracow Three'. Both Pniak and Własnowolski had combat experience gained over Poland during the 1939 Campaign. Pniak claimed over two kills flying with 142nd Fighter Squadron whilst Własnowolski as 122nd Squadron's pilot on 2nd September scored a shared victory over a Dornier Do 17. During their time with 32 Squadron, Własnowolski and Pniak gained their famous names of 'Vodka' and 'Cognac' respectively, and we can only speculate why these two foreign officers received such a noble reputation!

Flying Officer Witold Urbanowicz, who back in Poland was an instructor with a high reputation amongst Dęblin's 'School of Eaglets' Cadets, and Sergeant Józef Kwieciński joined Ostowicz and Pankratz in 145 Squadron at Westhampnett in Sussex. Urbanowicz had many nicknames given to him by people who either liked him or were afraid of his rather strong opinions: he was known as '*Anglik*' (an Englishman) or '*Mister*' due to his gentlemanly manners, while others called him '*Kobra*' (Cobra) or even '*Le Couteau*' (knife)

Pilots of No. 501 Squadron. Two Poles Flg Off Stefan Witorzeńć and Sgt Antoni Głowacki are standing as 1st and 3rd from left.

as he was always sharp and brutally honest. He was rather impressed by British hospitality:

'Despite being there for the first time, I was treated splendidly. On the whole, British officers were hospitable, friendly and well-mannered. At first glance they made an impression of people behaving with great reserve. Perhaps this is the reason for the opinion that English are cold-hearted. This is not true.'[3]

This was not his first encounter with British planes, having flown Bristol Fighters in 1931 while studying at the Polish Air Force Cadet Officer's School.

Pilot Officer Tadeusz Nowak, known as 'Teddy', and Pilot Officer Włodzimierz Samoliński, both former pilots of III/2 Cracow's Fighter Wing, joined No. 253 'Hyderabad State' Squadron operating from Turnhouse near Edinburgh, while Flying Officer Stefan Witorzeńć and Sergeant Antoni Głowacki, both respected flying instructors, arrived at Gravesend and reported to Squadron Leader Henry Hogan, who commanded No. 501 Squadron 'City of Gloucester'.

Głowacki, known to his Polish chums as '*Głowa*'[4], quickly gained another name: his new British colleagues started calling him 'Toni'.

Poles, although struggling with the English language, made new friends very quickly, gaining high reputation amongst them. An Irishman, Pilot Officer Kenneth Mackenzie, witnessed the arrival of the foreign pilots:

> 'The squadron was made up of regulars and VR pilots, officers and sergeants, with a generous sprinkling of Poles, who were irrepressible, irresponsible in some respects and a laugh a minute at times. We were glad of them as they had mostly received a sound blooding when their country was invaded and had made their way to England by devious ways and means to fight again. Their deep hatred of the Germans was infectious.'[5]

However, not everyone in 501 Squadron was immediately infected by this strong feeling against the enemy. In comparison, British pilots had not suffered such traumatic experiences with the Germans in the past, therefore their minds were only concentrated on defending their country, not on a private vendetta. One of the Battle of Britain's leading aces, Sergeant James 'Ginger' Lacey said:

> 'I didn't go round hating Germans or liking Germans. I had never met a German in my life so I couldn't have any preconceived opinion of what one looked like, acted like or sounded like.'

We have to understand that not everyone felt any bad or good feelings for their Luftwaffe opponents. While Poles hated the Germans with a vengeance, for British pilots their retaliation was yet to come. So far they fought mainly against the aircraft that brought danger to their homeland, not the human beings sitting inside them. German aircrew were the bad guys, but not the embodiment of evil. RAF pilots aimed to eliminate the weapon, not individuals following their orders.

Głowacki's surname was not as challenging to the British as Flight Lieutenant Stanisław Brzezina's and Flying Officer Henryk Szczęsny's of the Hornchurch-based 74 'Tiger' Squadron. When these two former instructors of the Advanced (Fighter) Flying School in Ułęż knocked on Squadron Leader Francis White's door, the immediate problem was what to call them. John Freeborn recalls:

> 'In the first week of August, 74 Squadron received two additional members to their ranks – Flight Lieutenant Stanislaw Brzezina and Flying Officer Henryk Szczęsny, two battle-hardened Polish pilots that were instantly

nicknamed "Breezy" and "Sneezy" by the boys. [I remember them] as possessing a strong hatred towards Germans, a passion which manifested itself in the air. They were both fierce fighter pilots that were more than willing to lend a hand to the British after fleeing from their own country when the Germans invaded Poland.'[6]

Despite the question of what to call these two foreigners finally being resolved, the squadron clerk had many sleepless nights while filling the official reports, and as a result various versions of both names have 'decorated' 74 Squadron's Operations Record Book and survived to this day: Brezezina, Brezczina, Breczina, Brazivi, Brezczini or Brzczina. Szczęsny, also known also as 'Henry the Pole' or '*Hesio*' (the latter given to him by his Polish pupils in Dęblin), had more luck and his family name was only once changed to Szezesny. Putting those difficulties aside, 'they were treated as squadron mascots, and loved it'.[7]

Both Polish pilots were soon put into Spitfire cockpits. 'My knowledge of England – zero,' Szczęsny wrote years later, 'but willingness to fly and murderous vengeance, very high. I did not care about the R/T [radio transmitter], always kept it off, but as soon as I was airborne, I was searching for swastikas.'[8] Soon after, Sergeant Jan Rogowski, veteran of 162nd Fighter Squadron, joined them at Hornchurch.

Flying Officer Władysław Szulkowski (we can only speculate how his name was pronounced by the British!) started his career with No. 65 'East India' Squadron at Hornchurch. This former flying instructor and Brzezina's subordinate started to fly Spitfires and became a close friend of Pilot Officer Brendan 'Paddy' Finucane and Flying Officer Ron Wigg. He was followed by Flying Officer Franciszek Gruszka, a flying instructor of the 6th Air Regiment, who also joined 65 Squadron. Pilot Officer David Glaser remembered the two Poles:

'They were both older than me and had obviously been experienced and respected pilots in their own air force before the war. They were having a hard time coming to terms with the language and so on, and I used to try and teach them English during the time we spent on Readiness. I looked up to them, no question about it.'[9]

Jeffrey Quill recalled:

'In the Mess at Sutton Bridge I had tried to talk to the Poles about their escape, but their English was limited. They had certainly endured a most traumatic time and my heart went out to them, although I was worried about how they would understand orders over the R/T. To be fair, they spent hours studying an English dictionary with David's help.'[10]

In many cases the language difficulties could make a difference between life and death, when commands were not understood correctly, but there were also less serious circumstances that caused laughter with their British colleagues: Poles reporting to their English superiors completion of a task by saying, 'I am Finish', or charming their British sweethearts with their own version of 'Ay lav yu', became almost an anecdotal subject of many conversations across RAF bases around Britain.

Another story, that shows this problem of the very early stage of the relationship between homeboys and foreigners, runs as follows:

'The Polish airman who, on being told by a Station Commander that he is to be remanded for a Court Martial, drops instantly in a dead faint. It is only when the interpreter explains that, at home, this usually means execution by a firing squad within a few hours, that the CO understands why it is that he cannot strike similar terror into the hearts of his British airmen.'[11]

Sergeant Zygmunt Klein, who fought against the Luftwaffe in Poland with 142nd Fighter Squadron, and Sergeant Józef Szlagowski, previously an instructor in Dęblin, were other PAF pilots sent to fly Spitfires. Their destination was No. 234 'City of Durham' Squadron based at St Eval in Cornwall. Flying Officer Michał Stęborowski, again one of the instructors from Ułęż, accompanied by Sergeant Marian Domagała, a former 161st Fighter Squadron pilot, went to No. 238 Squadron flying Hurricanes. Meanwhile, Flying Officer Tadeusz Nowierski, a former 24th Light Bomber Squadron pilot, and Flying Officer Piotr Ostaszewski-Ostoja received their postings to 609 'West Riding' Squadron equipped with Spitfires. Both 238 and 609 Squadrons operated from Middle Wallop, Hampshire. Although Polish colleagues called Nowierski 'Łysek' (bald-headed) due to the first signs of hair loss, his new brothers-in-arms named him 'Novi'. For the second Polish pilot, the soubriquet 'Osti' was an obvious one. This simple way of making life easier for both sides, by using names that everyone could pronounce, worked. Stęborowski, Szczęsny and Ostaszewski-Ostoja had served under Brzezina's command in Ułęż before the war started.

Flight Lieutenant David Crook concluded:

'These two Poles, Novi and Osti, were grand chaps and we were all very fond of them. They had fought in Poland during that desperate month

The Poles of No.609 Squadron. From right are: Plt Off Janusz Żurakowski (1st), Flg Off Tadeusz Nowierski (2nd) and Flg Off Piotr Ostaszewski-Ostoja (4th).

of September 1939, when in spite of inferior equipment and being hopelessly outnumbered, they nevertheless resisted to the bitter end, and then escaped through Rumania to France, where they joined l'Armée de l'Air,[12] and again fought till the French collapse, though they were shabbily treated by the French, who gave them only very obsolete machines to fly … After the French collapse Novi and Osti and several thousand more of their indomitable countrymen escaped once more from a ravaged country and came over to England. It is easy to imagine their pleasure at finding themselves in a really good squadron, efficiently run, and with first-class equipment. They could now fly the finest fighters in the world, and meet their persecutors on equal terms.

'They certainly made the most of their opportunities, and their delight when they shot down a "bloody German" was marvellous to see. They were both very quiet, possessed beautiful manners, were very good pilots, and intensely keen to learn our ways and methods. Their hatred of the Germans was quieter and more deadly than I have ever seen before. They had undergone so much suffering and hardship, and had lost almost everything in life that mattered to them – homes, families, money – that I think the only thing that concerned them now was to get their revenge and kill as many Germans as possible.

'They were certainly two of the bravest people I ever knew, and yet they were not exceptional in this respect when compared with other Poles in the R.A.F. All the squadrons that had Polish pilots posted to them formed an equally high opinion of them, and the feats of the Polish Squadron, who in five days' fighting over London destroyed at least forty-four German machines, as well as probably destroying and damaging many more, must rank as one of the best shows of the whole summer.

'Such indomitable courage and determination cannot go unrewarded, and when this war is won we must see that Poland is again restored to her former liberty and freedom, which her sons fought so valiantly to maintain.'[13]

At the same time, training had been initiated at Northolt. Pilots commanded by Squadron Leader Zdzisław Krasnodębski, better known as '*Król*' ('The King') or '*Knot*' ('Candlewick'), and Squadron Leader Ronald Kellett, rather ironically called '*Psotny Dyzio*',[14] slowly began to overcome technical differences between Hurricanes[15] and the numerous aircraft which they knew and flew before. There were some ups and downs on the way, but the process successfully continued.

Canadian Flight Lieutenant John Kent took command of 'A' Flight, whilst Flight Lieutenant Athol Forbes led 'B' Flight. Ronald Kellett recalled:

'During this time, I and my two flight lieutenants, Kent and Forbes, were busy converting our 20 Polish pilots to Hurricanes. This was going well apart from one or two landings with the undercarriage up. We had all learnt certain Polish words: *Klapy* – flaps, *podwozie* – undercarriage, so that in the air we could remind the pilots of these needs. The rumour got around that the Poles were so keen to land that they failed to put the undercarriage down – typical school-boy humour imparted to high places. I would have none of this as they were being very quickly converted to Hurricanes and had retractable undercarriages for the first time. Certainly both Dowding and Park understood this … We now started Squadron Training and Fighter tactics. It was soon clear however that the four or so attacks laid down by Command were unworkable as the R.T. orders could not be understood and that we would have to perfect one attack only and each battle must be made to fit the attack, i.e. not the method of attack to suit the battle. These matters were discussed with Dowding on his various visits, but above all, he said, "Have you shown them the bloody wall, where we shoot pilots who kill their own side?" I said certainly they practice recognition and I reminded him they had seen the real thing in Poland and France.'[16]

No. 302 Squadron was no different and its pilots – carefully watched by Mümler, also called '*Król Zamczyska*' ('King of the Castle'), Satchell and both Flight Commanders. Flight Lieutenant James Thomson and Flight Lieutenant William Riley – had their own views on the current situation. Wacław Król wrote:

> 'The English took over command of the squadron, and this was what caused disagreements and antipathy from our side towards the English, especially because – apart from Squadron Leader Jack Satchell – the others represented a lower level of experience and aerial training than the Polish commanders. When our squadron went into action during the Battle of Britain, those officers often led pilots into complicated and even disastrous tactical situations. They did not gain our trust, they were inexperienced combat leaders, they could not hold their nerve while facing enemy superiority. There is no surprise that our official and private relationship with the English did not go well. The Commander of the Polish Air Force was aware of the conflict, but preferred to not intervene in order to not upset in any way the hosts.'[17]

Flight Lieutenant Piotr Łaguna and Flight Lieutenant Franciszek Jastrzębski were appointed as Polish counterparts of the flight commanders.[18] Łaguna was called 'Zagłoba' in reference to the ribald character of the fictional seventeenth-century nobleman portrayed in Polish literature. Before the war, he served in both fighter units of the 3rd Air Regiment in Poznań. In France, he was appointed deputy commander and then commander of the Polish 1/145 Squadron. Jastrzębski previously commanded 132nd Fighter Squadron, and during the Polish Campaign achieved three aerial victories. Both Polish officers knew their trade very well.

'The English have enjoyed creating obstacles for us,' Jan Maliński said of 1940:

> 'F/lt Farmer was a leading man in that respect. He didn't like us because we criticized his bitch Peggy. Well, she was extraordinarily odious and unsympathetic, with small eyes and a big muzzle. Everyone treated her with disdain. I do not know whether we didn't like the dog because of the owner, or the other way around. As an act of revenge he kept turning with us upside down in the clouds making deep turns. No one was left behind somehow and all kept the formation until the landing, when we touched down in sections of three aircraft and in very short time spaces. We were benefiting from flying in a blind formation, I suppose. We acquired a

trust towards our leaders; they trusted us because we perfectly polished art of our flying.'[19]

Polish 302 Squadron pilots were upset by the lack of trust. They were equally experienced as their colleagues in No. 303. For example, Mieczysław Mümler was the former commander of the IIIrd Fighter Wing in Poznań, and had four aerial victories gained over Poland under his belt, followed by one more and one shared added in France. Władysław Gnyś was the pilot famous for claiming the destruction of two Dorniers over Żurada, which are considered the first German planes shot down during the Second World War. Wacław Król very often appears to be the main rival of Władysław Gnyś, as he was responsible for the downing of a German reconnaissance aircraft that crash-landed even before Gnyś made his claim. Król was credited with a shared victory in Poland and at least two in France. Stanisław Chałupa, although without success in Poland, shot down more than two German aircraft during the French campaign. Czesław Główczyński came to Britain with three-and-a-half victories achieved in Poland and more than one in France.

Tadeusz Czerwiński shot down two Messerschmitts in France, while Jerzy Czerniak had two victories in Poland and another couple in France. Tadeusz Chłopik, although serving in various fighter units in Poland, distinguished himself as a rigorous flying instructor at the Air Force Training Centre at Dęblin. Similarly Jan Czerny and Antoni Beda, who gained two victories in French skies. Jan Borowski, former deputy commander of the 113th Fighter Squadron, had three enemy planes declared destroyed in Poland, including two shared victories. Antoni Markiewicz twice participated in the destruction of Luftwaffe aircraft in Poland and once again in France, and Eugeniusz Nowakiewicz brought with him to Britain three kills followed by two shared victories that he achieved over France.

Despite the fact that No. 302 Squadron eventually used their raven's motif, an initial attempt was made to standardise their badge and to make its appearance similar to RAF ones.

It was no secret that Squadron Leader Mümler and his Scottish counterpart, Squadron Leader Satchell, did not get on well together at all, having diverse objectives, priorities and views on training and operational readiness. Above all they had dissimilar ambitions and temperaments that eventually led to the disposal of the Polish commander, who in December 1940 left for the Central Flying School at Upavon. He was not the only victim of this 'behind the scenes' disagreement with Jack Satchell: 'King of the Castle' was followed by Flight Lieutenant Jan Czerny and Flying Officer Władysław Goettel.

Rumour had it that both Mümler and Łaguna, due to their quite advanced age for combat pilots, were subjected to endurance tests done by British officers during non-operational flights. Yet after the war, Mümler proved to be a true gentleman by saying very politely:

> 'I have very nice memories from my time at the Leconfield and Duxford stations. With an admiration I think about both teams – Polish and English, with whom I collaborated. How much work and heart Station Commander W/Cdr Nixon, S/Ldr Satchell, F/Lt Farmer, Thomson and Riley put into making the Squadron ready to fight in the shortest possible time.'[20]

At this stage it is worth mentioning a few interesting details about both Polish units. No. 302 (Polish) Squadron was known as '*Poznańskie Kruki*' ('Ravens of Poznań') due to the bird motif that appeared on their badge. This badge was in the shape of a diamond, and alongside other PAF badges was never officially accepted by the RAF, although we do know an attempt was made to create an alternative version of 302 Squadron's badge, similar to that of an edged circle, surmounted by a crown, that was commonly adorned by RAF squadrons.

By adopting the raven's emblem, Poles of 302 Squadron paid tribute to the design used by the former 131st and 132nd Fighter Squadrons of the 3rd Air Regiment (which used red and blue ravens respectively). The 302 emblem also employed French national colours as a reminder of the air battles that many of the pilots participated in over France, and the number 1/145, which symbolized some of 302's airmen who previously served in 1/145 'City of Warsaw' Fighter Squadron across the Channel. Members of No. 302 Squadron were also unofficially called 'Woxhals' due to the code letters WX applied on their aircraft.[21]

Many of the Hawker Hurricanes of No. 303 (Polish) Squadron were adorned with the famous 'Kościuszko' badge that was introduced twenty-one years before by 303's predecessor, 7th Squadron[22] (later called 7th Fighter Squadron), better known as 'Kościuszko Squadron'. This unit was joined by the group of American pilot-volunteers,[23] who came to Poland initially to fight the Ukrainians, but eventually to fly against Bolshevik Russia (1919-20). The Yankees were repaying their debt of gratitude towards Polish national hero Brigadier General Tadeusz Kościuszko, who fought for American independence in the eighteenth century.[24] Ironically, therefore, Kościuszko's name, the man who stood against the British, was reactivated in 1940 as the icon of freedom and Polish-British brotherhood, but was also soon to symbolize the most successful squadron of the whole Fighter Command. Before being reintroduced at Northolt, the 'Kościuszko' emblem was worn proudly by 111th Fighter Squadron (7th Squadron's successor) aircraft until the end of the Polish Campaign in 1939. No. 303 Squadron was given the RF code letters, based on which its members were often called '*Rafałki*'.[25]

Thursday 8 August proved an eventful day. Flying Officer Antoni Ostowicz of 145 Squadron, after taking off from Westhampnett, found himself in action again:

'At about 9.00 I ran into a very large formation of Ju 87 bombers with an escort of Me 109s and a few He 113s[26]. I was attacked by three He 113s which were working to a plan. One was above and the other two worked as a pair. If I attacked the single one the pair attacked me astern, if I turned to attack one of the pair the single one got on my tail. Eventually I damaged the single one severely and he left smoking hard.'

It is extremely difficult to establish who was attacked by the Polish pilot, purely because the Luftwaffe admitted losing only one Ju 87 from the IIIrd Gruppe of Sturzkampfgeschwader 2 '*Immelmann*'.[27] This was not the only encounter by a Polish pilot on that day. Two members of 238 Squadron also had reason to celebrate. Soon after midday, a large German formation was spotted heading towards convoy CW9.

One of the RAF units that were scrambled to engage this formation was 238 Squadron. Flight Lieutenant Michał Stęborowski was amongst those who got close to the raiders. This officer had bad memories of the Luftwaffe, having watched helplessly ass German bombers pounded the airfield of the Polish Air Force College: apart from cursing them from the cockpit of his slow P.7, he could do absolutely nothing about it. Now, finally, he could release his frustration:

'When I recovered I saw a Me 110 and got on his tail and then the rear gunner shot at me with tracer which went over my head. I began to fire at about 250 yards from astern … and I saw the bullets go into the E/A. I think the first burst killed the rear gunner as I received no return fire. After this the E/A turned right and left very slowly and went down in a dive.'

Battle-hardened Sergeant Marian Domagała, who was airborne as well, had his 'five minutes' of combat too. Unlike Stęborowski, he clashed not only with Messerschmitt Bf 110s of Lehrgeschwader 1 (that included fighters, bombers and dive-bombers), but also with their more dangerous cover. He later wrote:

> 'I saw a Me 109 ahead and I went for him but he was very speedy and I could not catch up. I saw another Me 109 which was in a bank and I do not think he saw me and I fired from astern two one-sec. bursts from 50 yards and I broke away to avoid over-shooting. The E/A did a stall turn and went straight down, smoking, and then caught fire. I then saw it go into the sea. I then climbed and I saw many E/A and when I got near I recognised them as 110s. I saw one E/A go away and chased him. I was in very good position almost stern. I got closer and below slightly, and fired from approx. 150 yards one short burst, at slight deflection. I don't think there was a gunner in the Me 110 as I did not see any return fire. I then followed the E/A, which went into a dive doing slight aileron turns. I did not see any smoke or flames, but I saw the bullets [tracer] going into the E/A. I think the gunner must have been killed … I feel sure the E/A was out of control, but did not see it go into the sea.'

In Poland, Domagała had flown operationally and experienced a few encounters with the Luftwaffe after his III/6 Fighter Wing was given an order to support 'Łódź Army', but he had to wait until arriving in Britain to open his score.

Flying Officer Antoni Ostowicz fought again, and this time his luck continued. He took off on an afternoon mission to face a relatively small enemy formation sighted near St Alban's Head in Dorset. Those were heading towards convoy CW9 approaching from Le Havre. Amongst them were Ju 87s with their stridently howling sirens, two-engine Bf 110s and fast and difficult-to-catch Bf 109s. They were flying a few miles south of St Catherine's Point when pilots of 43 and 145 Squadrons saw them. It was 4.05 pm when Ostowicz, flying as Number 3 in Red Section, took his chance once more:

> 'I attacked the second E/A, which turned out to be a Me 109, and gave him one burst at a long range of 300 yards or over. I had hardly started firing when black smoke belched out and he shot straight into the sea. My very first bullets must have got him for I hardly pressed the button for even a full second.'

The Pole most probably met one of the Jagdgeschwader 27 pilots, who apparently did not suffer any losses on this occasion.

Flg Off Antoni Ostowicz (1st from right) during his free time with other 145 Sqn pilots. From left are: Flt Lt Roy Dutton and Sqn Ldr John Peel.

The day after, only one Polish pilot had a chance to intercept enemy machines and take advantage of such an opportunity. Sergeant Józef Szlagowski, surrounded by two RAF pilots of 234 Squadron in the Falmouth area, caught a single Junkers Ju 88 aircraft. The whole section attacked the German plane, giving it a burst from only 50-100 yards. They thought they probably got the rear gunner as he went suspiciously quiet. When the Junkers turned towards the clouds, Pilot Officer Edward Mortimer-Rose and Sergeant Szlagowski fired off another salvo of bullets as a parting gift. The Ju 88 from the 3rd Staffel of Fernauklärungsgruppe 123[28] returned to base with mortally wounded air gunner Uffz. Theodor Bauer. The 234 Squadron pilots were right: they had got him!

The group of Polish pilots being posted to RAF squadrons started to grow even faster. Flying Officer Witorzeńć and Sergeant Głowacki of 501 Squadron welcomed three more colleagues – Flying Officer Kazimierz Łukaszewicz, Pilot Officer Franciszek Kozłowski and Pilot Officer Paweł Zenker – who arrived at Gravesend. Łukaszewicz, aged 27 and called 'Mala' by his friends, was a former pilot of III/5 Fighter Wing in Wilno,[29] and a flying instructor of the Advanced Flying Course at Ułęż. His friend Kozłowski was four years younger, but had some fighting experience from Poland, where he served in 122nd Fighter

Squadron and claimed two shared victories. Born in 1914, Zenker wasn't a greenhorn either; this pilot of 141st Fighter Squadron from Toruń had one shared victory under his belt. At least for the next few days, the Poles felt better flying side-by-side with their countrymen, rather than only alongside people with whom they could barely communicate.

Two Polish pilots received their postings to No. 151 Squadron, which was equipped with Hawker Hurricanes and stationed at North Weald, Essex. They were Pilot Officers Tadeusz Kawalecki and Mieczysław Rozwadowski. The first was a 121st Fighter Squadron veteran, who fought in 1939 defending Poland, while Rozwadowski had also faced the enemy in the air before, being a former pilot of 111th Fighter Squadron. Kawalecki was another good example of how freely Polish names were treated by the squadron clerk: he appeared as 'Kawaliki' in his unit documents.

Another two Poles arrived at Hornchurch, where No. 54 Squadron was based. Sergeant Wojciech Kloziński started his adventure with aviation as a ground crew member, but eventually managed to complete a flying course and became an instructor at the Air Force NCO School for Minors; Sergeant Leon Świtoń was also an instructor before the war.

Sunday 11 August turned out to be another day of Polish successes, but there were also the first painful losses. A huge formation of German aircraft had been spotted heading towards Portland, against which six squadrons were scrambled. No. 145 Squadron with Flying Officers Ostowicz and Urbanowicz and Sergeant Kwieciński flew rapidly to stop the enemy bombers. Urbanowicz reported:

'One section of three Me 109s came in on the beam of my Section, so I headed them off and they left us. Then one smoking enemy aircraft appeared on my left and another Me 109 followed him. I gave chase to the last Me. 109 and he continued to follow the smoking machine towards the south. Soon after I found about 15–17 Me 109s above me: they did not attack me and I dared not disclose my identity by attacking the Me 109 in front of me, so I followed him without firing for 4-5 minutes. Then when I saw it was safe I gained on him and gave him some bursts, upon which he went straight into the sea.'

While Urbanowicz was chasing his victim and contemplating the best tactics, one of his colleagues was in serious trouble. It is believed that one of the Bf 109s that were seen by Witold Urbanowicz actually shot down the Hurricane flown by Ostowicz over Swanage. He thus became the first Polish pilot killed during the Battle of Britain. His aircraft probably crashed into the sea and his body was never found.[30]

No. 238 Squadron was also engaged, especially the Pole Sergeant Marian Domagała, who claimed the destruction of a Bf 109. His encounter, however, ended tragically:

'Just as I opened fire at the enemy aircraft, a Hurricane appeared in my line of sight between the enemy aircraft and myself and got the tail end of the burst, which was a very short burst of 2 secs at a range of 50 yards quarter attack. My burst went into the left wing of the Hurricane, which started smoking and the pilot bailed out. I watched him down and then attacked another Me. After climbing I fired a very short burst at 150 yards from astern but the aircraft dived and I followed it down, and as he weaved I fired each time (about 8 times) from quarter deflection at very close range of about 100 yards. The aircraft climbed slightly and then fell into the sea with a splash.'

It is believed that by this tragic accident Domagała could have hit either Australian pilot Flight Lieutenant Stuart Walch, a 'B' Flight Commander who went down east of Weymouth, or his colleague Flying Officer Michał Stęborowski, as neither returned from this mission. Stęborowski was the second Polish fighter pilot to be killed in the air over Britain that late summer. Domagała was known for his determination in combat and undisputed eagerness to kill every 'Jerry' who came within range. One of the pilots who flew alongside Domagała wrote:

'He can use all his ammo, then land, and without switching off his engine, ask to load more bullets, and then he is back chasing the Germans. All this looks impressive, and he is widely respected here.'[31]

Flying Officer Nowierski of No. 609 Squadron wrote to his friend Flight Lieutenant Stanisław Brzezina:

'Dear Stach – Unfortunately it is one day too late to give your address to Michał – this time they took him off, as you used to say. The whole trio got involved in a big job, as is happening here, and we are only left with memories Domagała is biting back for him; yesterday he fried up a 109 again.'

There were more losses yet to come…

Chapter Eight

First Blood and Sweat

A few days earlier, everywhere you went throughout the airfields occupied by 145 and 501 Squadrons, you would have heard the strange voices of foreign pilots. They were chatting in a tongue-twisting language, rather loudly and in that unusual Slavic manner spontaneously expressing their feelings towards the enemy and sharing their experiences after each sortie. They were commenting on successes and analyzing failures. While 11 August took the lives of two of the newcomers, the following day was even worse. The RAF units, once full of Polish voices, suddenly went quiet.

Soon after 11 am, British radar stations tracked increased German activity across the Channel. Amongst the squadrons sent to face the Luftwaffe and to prevent convoys 'Agent' and 'Arena' from being badly hit was No. 501. Pilot Officer Paweł Zenker, flying as number two of Blue Section, realized that he was about to enter combat with either Ju 87 dive-bombers or their fighter cover of Bf 109s. 'Just as one of the Ju 87s dived to bomb the ship, I followed him down, firing one long burst from 150 yards closing to fifty,' he reported after the flight.

'I then overshot and turned to the right. There I saw 3 Ju 87s low over the sea at 150 yards flying North East in the direction of the Dutch coast and I attacked one on the right and fired three long bursts from 200 to 150 yards, and a third burst caused a fire in the fuselage of the E/A, which turned right and disappeared. Then I caught up with the third, after climbing a little and turning left, and attacked from astern. I was only able to fire a short burst as my ammunition was exhausted. I am not certain whether the third Ju 87 was damaged.'

A little later, 145 clashed with another German formation that was aiming at the Solent, Portsmouth and Ventnor radar station. Red Section pilot Flying Officer Urbanowicz was watching his leader while engaging one of the attackers, when he discovered an opportunity for himself: 'I then saw a Ju 88 by itself at 1,700ft and delivered a beam attack. After this attack the enemy aircraft dived vertically into the sea.' Unfortunately he could only celebrate his victory[1] for a short time: it was a small prize compared to the loss of two dear colleagues. They were chasing a Bf 110 fighter, when three Bf 109s of I Staffel from Jagdgeschwader 53[2] appeared unexpectedly behind their backs. It is believed that the whole section led by Flight Lieutenant Pankratz destroyed an aircraft from I Gruppe of Zerstörergeschwader 2 piloted by Oblt Siegfried Blume, who bailed out. Unfortunately, Flight Lieutenant Pankratz, Sergeant Kwieciński and Pilot Officer John Harrison were so destracted by finishing off their victim, that they did not see the danger coming closer and closer behind their tails. All three Hurricanes were shot down into the sea by two German pilots: Hptm. Hans-Karl Mayer (the Staffel commander) and Uffz. Heinrich Rühl.

Witold Urbanowicz remembered this sad day for a very long time, and wrote:

> 'Evenings at the Officers' Mess usually were noisy. After a day of flying, pilots were telling each other about their dog fights, sharing their impressions and remarks. We lost two fighter pilots on that day and it was them we were talking about the most. They were both lost in the Channel. During my ten years in the air force I got used to such an atmosphere. Every now and then we lost one of our colleagues. And now, when listening to the pilots, I was thinking that the airman's death at such a young age is not bad, as long as there is a benefit to it. Many of my friends died in the English Channel. No funeral, no rules: sudden and mysterious losses.'[3]

On the same day, Pankratz and Kwieciński were replaced by Pilot Off Witold Głowacki and Sergeant Jan Budziński, or 'Budyinski', as his name was misspelt. Both new arrivals had recently completed training at No. 7 Operational Training Unit.

The day's battle was far from over yet. Another group of about sixty raiders had been traced, while passing Cap Gris-Nez near Calais, and the only RAF squadron that was available in this area was 501. Before the RAF pilots were able to catch the German formation of Dornier Do 17s and Bf 110s, the enemy managed to drop their bombs over Manston airfield in Kent. Only Red Section of the 501 Squadron was close enough to get a chance to swipe some 'Jerry' from the air, and Flying Officer Witorzeńć recalled:

> 'I attacked one of them on the south-east side of the aerodrome, opening fire at 150 yards, closing to 100 yards with 2 short bursts from the port side. The E/A emitted white smoke from the port engine and dived into cloud I then turned and attacked another to the left slightly below and

gave it two short bursts from 200 yards. This climbed into clouds to join other German machines.'

As always, the Luftwaffe bombers were protected by the large formation of fighters. One of them skilfully caught in his gunsight the silhouette of the aircraft flown by Flying Officer Kazimierz Łukaszewicz, while the Polish pilot flew over Dover. It was the last mission of the former instructor, who fought in Poland defending the Polish Air Force College. He was lost at sea.

Despite signs of tiredness, in the afternoon three groups of German bombers and fighters flew towards the RAF bases at Hawkinge, Lympne and Manston. It was obvious that they wanted to eliminate RAF fighters from the air by destroying their nests on the ground. When they were over Manston, Spitfires from the Hornchurch-based 54 Squadron stood in their way: Manston was 54's usual forward operating base.

Amongst the pilots who at 5.40 pm met their rivals was Sergeant Wojciech Kloziński, who – as it turned out – was the only lucky pilot of his unit. He wrote:

'I manoeuvred and got on the tail of a Me 109, gave 3 bursts of 3 seconds each and saw it go down in flames. Breaking away, I attacked a second Me 109 and gave two bursts which sent him spinning, and followed him to 1,000ft, when I broke away and returned to base.'

From the left are: Flg Off Witold Urbanowicz (145 Sqn RAF & 303 Sqn PAF), Flg Off Stefan Witorzeńć (501 Sqn RAF) and Flg Off Piotr Ostaszewski-Ostoja (609 Sqn RAF).

But 54 Squadron was not alone when facing the German raiders: 32 Squadron was also on a mission patrolling the Dover area, where its pilots spotted a large formation of Dorniers and Messerschmitt Bf 109s. During a dog-fight, seven Bf 109s were claimed as probably destroyed. One of those was the victim of Pilot Officer Karol Pniak, who initially tried to shoot at a Dornier. 'I then broke away,' he commented later in his poor English, that had to be further polished and adjusted by the Intelligence Officer.

> 'A dog fight with a Me 109 then ensued and I was attacked from above by a Me 109. I turned inside him and got on his tail, he spiralled down and got in 3 or 3½ secs bursts. In a short time I saw much smoke coming from the fuselage. I wanted to make sure of him, so again pressed my m/g [machine gun] trigger but had finished my ammunition.'

By attacking the RAF bases on 12 August, the Luftwaffe was trying to soften Dowding's chain of defence and prepare the battlefield for the following day, which – as Oberkommando der Luftwaffe presumably hoped for – would change the direction of the whole war. The question remained though – for which side of the conflict would the unlucky number thirteen be less favourable?

Many publications that describe the history of No. 303 Polish Squadron during the Battle of Britain erroneously set up 30 August, when Flying Officer Ludwik Paszkiewicz famously claimed the first victory for the whole unit, as the beginning of the operational career of the Slavic formation. Although it has to be admitted that full operational status had only been gained straight after 'Paszka's' claim, his colleagues, the majority busy with training, had been performing patrols since 13 August. Missions had been flown by Squadron Leader Kellett and Flight Lieutenant Kent to intercept enemy aircraft, and consequently patrols by various pilots continued on 24, 26 and 30 August.[4]

Above all, 13 August is mainly remembered as the 'Der Adler Tag' ('Eagle Day'), the first day of the Luftwaffe's Operation '*Adlerangrif*' targeting the RAF, with the aim of eliminating opposition fighters from the skies over Britain. Without such a crucial success –Adolf Hitler believed – the Wehrmacht could not proceed with the invasion of Britain. Fighter Command, the principal target for Göring's fliers and the only hope of the defenders, was far from ready for the latest chapter of the battle. Fighter Command had the aircraft and determination, but was definitely lacking in pilots.

Having firey Poles on board, who had already proved a huge relief for their British brothers-in-arms tired by constant combat, was a valuable advantage. On the morning of Tuesday 13 August, some of the Poles took the first impact of the Luftwaffe's new strategy.

The whole of KG2 '*Holzhammer*' took off from their French base at Arras to attack Eastchurch aerodrome and Chatham dockyard in Kent. They were followed by KG54 targeting the Royal Aircraft Factory at Farnborough and Odiham airfield in Hampshire, while Stukageschwader 77 aimed to divert the RAF's attention by bombing Portland in Dorset. From the beginning, worsening weather and a series of vital misunderstandings led to disaster for the Luftwaffe. Fighter cover, informed of the thick clouds, returned home, leaving the large formation of bombers exposed and without protection. On the opposite side, various squadrons of No. 11 Group were scrambled. When the German formation, personally led by Polish Campaign veteran Generalleutnant Johannes Fink, dropped their first bombs on Eastchurch, only one RAF squadron was there to meet them.

No. 74, known better as 'Tiger' Squadron had no time to waste. Flight Lieutenant Stanisław Brzezina met the foe over Whitstable. He wrote later:

'I attacked No.2 and gave him a long burst, and saw him gliding down towards the sea with smoke coming from the engine. I did not see him go into the water. I then attacked No. 3 of the formation and must have

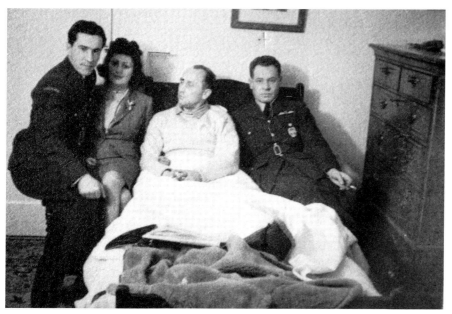

Flying Officers Marian Duryasz (1st from left, 213 Sqn RAF) and Władysław Szulkowski (1st from right, 65 Sqn RAF), both fellow instructors, visiting their former commander at the Advanced Flying Fighter School Flt Lt Stanisław Brzezina. Brzezina (74 Sqn RAF) baled out on 13th August 1940.

got to within fifty yards when there was a sudden explosion in my cockpit and I found myself falling fast.'

'Breezy' already had an allergy towards number thirteen, and he found himself in a life or death situation:[5] 'I managed to get out of the machine at about 2,000ft and made a successful parachute landing.' Not mentioning his injury in his official report, 'Breezy' soon after rejoined his unit.[6]

A second Pole was also airborne. 'Sneezy' remembered this day's combat well for two reasons. He experienced both a victory and a crash-landing followed combat:

> 'I went to attack No. 3 of the formation when he swung round to the right. I broke away to the left and came round behind the Dorniers and on their tails. One of the machines was out of formation and I attacked it from astern. At this point the Do dropped several bombs in the sea. I got a good burst in from very close range and the Do started to dive towards the sea. He tried to land there but as he flattened out he burst into flames and toppled straight into the water.'

Szczęsny, often called 'Hesio',[7] found himself lost after the battle and decided to save his life however, wherever and as soon as possible. He landed at West Malling with the undercarriage up, but shortly after 'Henry the Pole' returned to Hornchurch safe, happy and, most importantly, without injury.

Brzezina's friend, Flight Lieutenant 'Novi' Nowierski, and former subordinate from the Advanced Flying Course in Ułęż, Flying Officer 'Osti' Ostaszewski-Ostoja, also had their say in the battle of 13 August. Both the Polish pilots from 609 Squadron were in the air after 4 pm when their squadron encountered an enemy formation consisting of Ju 87s with their fighter cover that appeared over Portland. 'Osti' followed his leader into attack on a formation of Stukas:

> 'I fired a burst of two seconds at about 400 yards from the beam. No effects were observed. I broke away and turned right and attacked another Ju 87 from astern with a burst of about 3 seconds, opening at 400 yards and closing to 200 yards. No effect was observed and return fire experienced.'

Although it was initially assumed that Ostaszewski-Ostoja, No. 2 of Blue Section, probably destroyed both, eventually none of the StG2 aircraft were credited to the Polish pilot.

His colleague from Green Section had more luck when he spotted an enemy fighter machine 'I climbed up behind him and fired three bursts at fairly close range and dead astern,' 'Novi' reported when on the ground:

'White smoke appeared from his fuselage and he turned over and started to dive. Some large object, probably the cockpit door or roof, flew away and the pilot got out and opened his parachute. I then saw 2 Me 109s behind me and I dived and pulled out in a violent left-hand turn and "blacked out". Ten minutes later I saw another Me 109 ahead and approached him from behind and gave him a good burst at very close range. White smoke appeared from the fuselage and he dived steeply into a cloud and disappeared.'

Nowierski, who previously flew PZL P.23 'Karaś' light bombers, had his first run as a fighter pilot on 13 August. It is believed that he shot down Fw. Hans Heinz Pfannschmidt from 5 Staffel JG53, who was taken prisoner. Despite both Polish pilots finding 609 Squadron a fine establishment, they were not very fond of each other. Nowierski wrote to Flight Lieutenant Brzezina:

'Lack of girls and our time is distracted. Awoken at all times. Only young people are around. The eldest – S/Ldr – is 28 years old; too young for this rank. They all play like children. At the same time they treat their service seriously, but without exaggeration or buffoonery. It is very nice here, but I cannot find a common language with Ostaszewski.'

The morning of 15 August was rather quiet, and only around 11 am did British radar stations start to receive stronger signals from across the Channel: something was building up. No. 501 Squadron, having moved to Hawkinge, was sent to investigate the unclear situation and engage a formation of Ju 87s from IV Gruppe of Stuka Lehrgeschwader 1[8] and II Gruppe StG1 which were heading towards Folkestone.

Flying Officer Stefan Witorzeńć, who flew as No. 2 in Red Section, and Sergeant Antoni Głowacki, No. 2 in Blue Section, were able to claim three Stukas shot down. Witorzeńć said after the combat:

'Red 1 attacked the left aircraft of an enemy section and I attacked one on the right from dead astern, after which the enemy formation broke up. After firing 3 long bursts, I saw the enemy plane diving steeply to the ground with smoke coming out of the fuselage. This was subsequently confirmed. After this I saw a Ju 87 dropping a bomb on the aerodrome and return for home. I followed him and fired two bursts from dead astern after coming up with him over the sea. The rear gunner fired at me but ceased. White smoke came from the enemy plane, which dived at an angle into the sea.'

Although Witorzeńć's Hurricane was damaged in combat, its pilot managed to return safely. His colleague downed another Stuka, as 'Toni' reported: 'I attacked a Ju 87 which was diving and fired one short burst and saw the rear gunner bail out, turning over before my aircraft. I saw the enemy aircraft dive vertically into the sea.' Soon after he tried several times to make his score even better, unfortunately without result:

> 'Then I climbed over Hawkinge and attacked a Ju 87 diving into a hangar from astern, but did not see what happened to it. After this I climbed and attacked an He 113 [*sic*] with a beam attack (90 deg.) deflection and the enemy aircraft climbed quickly out of sight. Then I turned to attack two Ju 87s over Folkestone from astern but my ammunition gave out after firing one short burst at one of them.'

Sergeant Wojciech Kloziński's 54 Squadron was also in action. After a recent move to Manston, they were airborne again and soon caught a second group of Ju 87s supported by Messerschmitt Bf 109s. Kloziński's colleagues claimed one Bf 109 and three Ju 87s destroyed, and two Bf 109s and a further two Ju 87s damaged. Unfortunately, Kloziński was not one of them. He bailed out heavily wounded, and his Spitfire crashed near Hythe. The Pole was taken to Ashford hospital. Despite making slow progress, his condition prevented him from reporting his fight and its result to the Intelligence Officer. His convalescence took two years, after which he did not return to operational flying, becoming a Link Trainer instructor.

Another victory claim had been made during the afternoon's struggles, when several RAF squadrons clashed with the large formation of Junkers Ju 88s, Dornier Do 17s and Messerschmitt Bf 110s and Bf 109s. At 3.30 pm, Pilot Officer Bolesław Własnowolski of 32 Squadron caught Fw. Stiegenberg of 5 Staffel JG51, and said to the Intelligence Officer:

> 'I climbed up and attacked one of the Me 109s from astern, we circled round each other, then the Me 109 dived away. I got in a good burst and the Me 109 burst into flames and dived down towards sea.'

'Vodka' was also in trouble as the temperature of his plane's glycol went up dangerously and he was forced to land in a field near Harwich. Despite his undercarriage being smashed, he left the cockpit unscratched.

No. 151 Squadron, which just a day previously arrived at North Weald, fought in a similar area. At 2.45 pm, the squadron took off from Rochford to intercept an enemy formation and ran into a group of Bf 109s. Amongst victorious pilots was the Pole, Pilot Officer Mieczysław Rozwadowski, who shot down one German fighter that went straight into the sea close to the French coastline. Due to the course of further events, he wasn't able to write a combat report that would provide more details of the fight. When attacking the enemy fighter he was accompanied by Flying Officer Richard Milne.

A very aggressive Sergeant Antoni Głowacki of 501 Squadron was around again to claim another victory. The Pole, flying as Blue 2, and his colleagues were intercepting an enemy raid behind Dover, when they received a message over the radio that German aircraft were recently seen at 5,000ft. 'Toni' described the situation:

> 'Red 1 attacked the second wave of bombers and from astern at the same height I attacked a Do 215 with a beam attack from the third quarter using full deflection. The enemy aircraft dived emitting white smoke and turned over as it dived. I attacked a second aircraft from astern with a long burst, breaking off when my ammunition was finished. I did not see what happened to it.'

In the afternoon, another large bunch of Ju 87s, Bf 110s and Bf 109s, consisting of 200-300 machines, had been observed over the Needles on the Isle of Wight and Selsey Bill in Sussex. Six of the German planes were shot down by 234 Squadron pilots. Pilot Officer Janusz Żurakowski, known as '*Tato*' ('Daddy') or 'Żura', who had recently joined[9] the Middle Wallop-based squadron, remembered this day very well:

> 'On this day I experienced my first air combat and first victory. Our squadron – 234 at Middle Wallop – was taken aback: German planes flew over low and radar did not warn us. A large formation of Messerschmitts started to bomb our airfield. We ran in a hurry to scurry to our aircraft. We took off rapidly, no formation, as each of us could.'[10]

In the air, however, 'Żura' was composed and focused:

> 'I attacked circle of Me 110s from above and behind the last aircraft, and the enemy dived down to the ground. The rear gunner ceased to fire. On the way down a second Spitfire from 609 Squadron [piloted by Flying Officer Piotr Ostaszewski-Ostoja] attacked, but when it broke away I engaged five more times, and the e/a eventually crashed in the Isle of Wight.'

Fw. Jakob Birndorfer, a German pilot from the 6 Staffel of ZG76, lost his life when his Bf 110 crashed to the ground. Rear gunner Uffz. Max Guschewski survived the encounter with the two Polish fighters. Ostaszewski, who equally caused the demise of the two-engine German raider, gave more details of this dog-fight:

> 'I turned inside him and opened fire from the quarter at about 300 yards. I gave him a 2 or 3 second burst and the e/a dived steeply making S turns. I followed him down; we went through the balloon barrage at Southampton. He pulled out just above the ground and started hedge-hopping. I gave him several short bursts closing from 300 yards to 100 yards. The e/a flew low across Southampton Solent and onto the Isle of Wight. I saw another Spitfire, which was chasing him too and firing at him. After several other short bursts I noticed both engines smoking and then stop. The e/a then made a crash landing and burst into flames.'

During this combat 234 Squadron lost three pilots: one of them was killed, and two others ended in German captivity. Sergeant Klein, who took part in this fight, was shot down and crash-landed at Twyford in his badly damaged Spitfire. The Polish pilot was fine and able to rejoin his unit. Klein, unlike his colleague from 151 Squadron, was lucky. Pilot Officer Rozwadowski, who had unfinished business with the Luftwaffe from Poland, was a victim of the combat over Dover. His formation was engaged with a group of enemy bombers surrounded by fighters and lost three of its own Hurricanes. One of them was piloted by 25-year-old Rozwadowski, who probably unconsciously went into the line of fire of one of the Messerschmitts. His plane went straight into the Channel.

The following day brought some successes to the Polish pilots of 65 'East India' Squadron, although the two claims are not easy to find and therefore to confirm. For unknown reasons, no combat reports were written by Flying Officers Franciszek Gruszka and Władysław Szulkowski, and only by reading a document which was drawn up by the Intelligence Officer can we have a hint of the events of 16 August. He wrote:

> '65 Squadron were operating from Manston and at 16.17 hours were detailed to intercept raiders in the Channel. When at 20,000 feet off Deal, they sighted 60 bombers in close formation with 200 escorting fighters about 2,000 feet above .'

Intelligence Officers recorded the individual scores of the pilots involved in this combat, and they included: 'P/O Gruska [*sic*] 200 rounds 1 Me 109 Probable. P/O Shulkouski [*sic*] 400 rounds 1 Me 109 Damaged (NO CLAIM).'

The most important sentence of the whole report can be found at the bottom: 'P/O Gruska has been unable to give a written report as he was missing

Spitfires from No. 65 Squadron. R6712 YT-N was often flown by Flg Off Szulkowski. On 22 August 1940 he claimed his victory flying this mount. This aircraft was also used by Flg Off Gruszka. Both Poles also flew R6714 YT-M, which can be seen in the background.

from the next sortie that evening.'[11] This is incorrect, as Gruszka was reported missing on 18 August, two days later. Why his combat report was not written or requested immediately after his return from Manston, where the Polish pilot landed, or why the lack of such a report had been explained by a lie, remains a mystery. The same question is raised as to why Władysław Szulkowski decided not to follow the procedure of completing the combat report if the initial claim had been made? Perhaps it was another mistake or oversight made by Pilot Officer A. Hardy.

Luckily, Sgt Klein, No. 2 in Red Section of 234 Squadron, had no such difficulties in proving the results of his dog-fight. He was flying towards the Isle of Wight when his colleagues were attacked about fifty Bf 109s that were covering a formation of Ju 87s. Klein wrote:

'I got my sights on one Me. 109 at the top of the loop. I was turning outside or above him. He went straight down. I followed him down to 10,000 feet giving him several short bursts till he went into a cloud. I went round the cloud & below. I saw a man on a parachute & saw nothing more of the machine.'

Chapter Nine

Eager to Fight

'We were eager to start fighting the Germans,' Pilot Officer Bolesław Drobiński said after the Battle of Britain. Known as 'Gandhi' or 'Ski', he was one of the 'Young Guns' of the Polish Air Force. His training at the PAF College had been suddenly cut short by the war, and without the usual grandeur of graduation he had to leave Dęblin.[1] Alongside classmates Stefan Kleczkowski, Walenty Krepski, Jerzy Popławski and Stefan Stegman, he was given an opportunity to fight in the Battle of Britain: 'We didn't want to sit around. We were fighting for the Allies and for Poland.'[2] He was brave, well-skilled, ambitious and hungry for revenge on the Germans. But sometimes he had to deal with disappointment too:

> 'I was devastated to not to get them. I was half a mile behind and maybe 1,000 feet below. I could have hit the last ones, but then realised I was almost out of petrol … You need 10 pairs of eyes to see what is going on in a Spitfire. But once you see the enemy, your fear goes … I have mixture of feelings when I think of the Battle of Britain. I was happy that we got the victory but sad that I lost so many friends.'

To his surprise he was posted to Spitfire squadron:

> 'Three of our group – Krepski, Martel and myself – were posted to English squadrons. Krepski and Martel to 54, and myself to 65 Squadron. Both squadrons were allocated at RAF Station Hornchurch near London. As it turned out, both squadrons were equipped with Spitfires, and none of us had sat in the Spitfire before. At our request, the commander of the 7 OTU agreed for us to perform 3 flights on this machine, altogether 45 minutes.'[3]

Being a young foreign pilot, a new kid on the block, right after joining the squadron in the middle of August he was challenged by his mates and had to prove his qualities. He definitely found his match amongst 65 Squadron's pilots. Brendan Finucane, an Irishman, was two years younger than 'Ski', but he had to show who was the alpha male of the herd:

'Drobinski, aged twenty-one, had escaped through Yugoslavia, Italy and France to fly with the RAF and had done two years' advanced flying at the Polish Air Force Officers School, the equivalent of the RAF's Cranwell. He was no novice and commented: "I don't think Paddy was prepared for my tactics of flying straight at him." Maybe it was the release from tension at Turnhouse or just that he had heard from some of A Flight's pilots about Ski's dogfighting prowess that prompted Finucane to suggest some practice. Whatever it was, Ski was happy to oblige when the self-assured young flying officer, whose briar pipe seemed to be a permanent fixture, came over from B Flight, and twenty minutes later they were at 10,000 feet and turning on reciprocal courses to head back at a closing speed of 700 mph.

'Twice Ski forced Brendan to break away and easily got behind him in a tight turning circle. The third time Ski realised he did not intend to give way and the two Spitfires passed within a wingspan and continued circling with neither able to get the advantage. "It was a hell of a dogfight. We came down to about 1,500 feet and Paddy being in charge had to stop the fight. We were not allowed to do any dogfighting below 5,000 feet and certainly not below 3,000 feet. When we landed my tunic and shirt were soaked with perspiration. My legs were shaking and I was very thirsty. Paddy came over, patted me on the back and said: 'Ski, that was a good fight, but I'll bet you that next time I shall get you twice.' Luckily, perhaps, there was not a second chance for us to meet again in a dogfight."[4]

With their flying ability issue sorted, 'Paddy' Finucane showed his real, caring self. Drobiński, using his basic English, as much as he could told his personal story, mentioning what had happened to his family:

'We talked for about an hour and a half. Speaking slowly to ensure I understood, Paddy said: "Listen, Ski, when this war is over we must make sure there will not be another one. It is a terrible way to settle anything. Until it is won we must shoot every bloody Jerry from the sky," Later that evening at Farrington House, the drinks somehow tasted better.'

The arrival of 'Ski' Drobiński at No. 65 Squadron proved necessary, bringing relief, especially after the tragedy that occurred on 18 August.[5]

Apart from 'Gandhi' and his mates, several more Polish pilots had completed their training and conversion on British equipment. Pilot Officer Franciszek Surma, another battle-hardened fighter pilot who fought in Poland as a member of the 121st Eskadra Myśliwska, was accompanied by Sergeant Feliks Gmur and arrived at the North Weald-based 151 Squadron.[6] Gmur had also flown in combat defending his country as a pilot of 161st Fighter Squadron. Soon after, they were joined by Pilot Officer Franciszek Czajkowski, a 141st Fighter Squadron veteran. All these newcomers flew Hawker Hurricanes. A former instructor of the Advanced Flying School, Flying Officer Marian Duriasz, together with Sergeant Antoni Wójcicki, previously a pilot of the 4th Bomber Squadron – who had just started his journey as a fighter pilot – were attached to No. 213 'Hornet' Squadron, that was also equipped with Hurricanes. This unit operated from Exeter under command of No. 10 Group.

Middle Wallop's 238 Squadron received support too. Pilot Officer Władysław Różycki had experienced combat flying in Poland with 141st Fighter Squadron, so he was warmly welcomed as a new member of the team and a man who knew the reality of aerial warfare. Finally, Flying Officer Jerzy 'Jersey' Jankiewicz – who exactly a year before had visited England to fly Hurricanes – together with Flying Officer Juliusz 'Topola' Topolnicki, a former flying instructor of the Air Force Cadet Officer's School at Dęblin, went to No. 601 'County of London' Auxiliary Air Force Squadron equipped with Hurricanes. Based at Tangmere and commanded by Squadron Leader Edward Ward, they were also known as the 'Millionaires Squadron'.

Despite triumphs for a few Polish Air Force pilots, 18 August marked another sad chapter in the Polish participation in the Battle of Britain. No. 501 Squadron, after taking off from Hawkinge and performing an early morning operational flight, met their opponents over Sandwich. Targeting German bombers, they had to clash with their fighter support provided by Messerschmitt 109s from the IIIrd Gruppe of JG26. The German fighter pilots knew their craft well and didn't want to give way. Pilot Officer Franciszek Kozłowski was successfully attacked by Oblt Gerhard Schöpfel and, badly wounded, crash-landed at Rayhams Farm near Whitstable in Kent. The Polish officer was taken to hospital, where he remained for quite some time, being unable to fly in combat for several months.

His colleague, Pilot Officer Paweł Zenker, flying as No. 2 in Green Section as rear guard, had more luck. While the rest of his squadron was engaged with over twenty Bf 110s and Bf 109s, he saw an opportunity, noticing a single Bf 109 flying below, then three more on his tail. He wrote:

> 'I took evasive action and I attacked one of them with a short burst from quarter at 50 yards range. Then I saw one under me which was diving about 300 yards away. I chased him and from 250 yards I gave him two or three bursts until my ammunition was gone and saw black smoke coming from the side of his fuselage. I did not see what happened to him.'

While 'A' Flight of 65 Squadron was busy chasing a Heinkel He 111 bomber, their colleagues from 'B' Flight apparently had no luck at all in confronting the enemy. So why did they return without one of their Spitfires? Jeffrey Quill explains:

'In 65 squadron we did not fly the useless formation comprising vics of three, but instead flew our four sections of three in line astern. This could be rapidly opened out sideways and, like the German line abreast Schwarm formation, required minimum concentration when flying (unlike the vics, which is what was so dangerous about them). Everyone was therefore able to search the sky for the enemy and I am sure that this increased our chances of survival. Nevertheless we suffered certain causalities, of course. August 18th was a hectic day, and once combat was joined, our two Poles were inclined to go chasing off on their own, so determined were they to get at the enemy. Gruszka sadly failed to return from our lunchtime engagement over Kent, and as we received no reports of any Spitfires having crashed inland, assumed that he must have crashed into the sea. Back at base, Szulkowski was terribly upset but could shed no light on his friend's fate.'[7]

For many years it remained a mystery what had happened to Flying Officer Franciszek Gruszka. Especially after Flying Officer Władysław Szulkowski saw his comrade at 3,000ft flying with no difficulties. Jerzy B. Cynk, a well-known Polish historian, tried to answer this question:

'Gruszka, flying Spitfire R6713, vanished without trace on the 18th at about 13.30 hours over Kent, as did one of the Messerschmitts of 8/JG3 … According to television interviews with local inhabitants, a solitary Spitfire fought a battle with four Messerschmitts at a high altitude on Sunday, 18 August. One German was seen to come down in the Stoodmarsh area and a few minutes later the Spitfire shared the same fate crashing not far from Preston. Gruszka's lonely fight and victory was not listed in any of the official RAF war records.'[8]

When some of the German bombers turned towards Biggin Hill, they were faced by 32 Squadron. Despite some claims, RAF pilots could not stop the Luftwaffe from dropping their bombs. Among the 32 Squadron Hurricanes was one flown by Pilot Officer Bolesław Własnowolski, who, despite not being chosen for this flight, decided to join the rest of his colleagues, showing typical individualism as he ignored orders. Flying Officer R. Leighton, Intelligence Officer of 32 Squadron, described 'Vodka's' experience as follows:

The Polish pilots of No. 32 Squadron. Sitting from the left are: Plt Off Karol Pniak (2nd) and Plt Off Bolesław Własnowolski. (3rd), Plt Off Jan Pfeiffer is standing 1st from left.

'As there was still a Hurricane on the aerodrome when all a/c were ordered off, he took it up and about 2,000 feet he saw three Do.215s in vic formation returning South. Being higher he dived on the starboard e/a, the e/a broke away and zigzagged about, he followed him and got in a 5 or 6 seconds burst, the e/a dived into the ground and burst into flames, near a church about six miles S. of Biggin Hill.'

It is believed that Własnowolski shot down either a Junkers Ju 88 of the 5th Staffel KG76 or a Dornier Do 17 that belonged to the 1st Staffel of the same Geschwader.

In the afternoon, Polish pilots had another opportunity to raise their scores. Quite few of the squadrons were sent to give a warm welcome to another wave of German planes flying from the direction of Saint Omer, Boulogne, Cap Gris-Nez and Lille. Nos. 501 and 32 caught Luftwaffe bombers and their fighter cover north of Margate. Flyingt Officer Stefan Witorzeńć of 501 Squadron flew as Red 2 and sighted a large group of Dorniers and their fighter cover. When his leader, Flight Lieutenant George Stoney, attacked the bombers,[9] the Pole could not wait any longer

'I followed him in but noticed about two Me 109s behind approaching from the third quarter and from above and firing at me. I broke out to the right and engaged the two of them in a dog-fight, diving to 10,000 ft from 14,000 ft. After climbing again I saw 1 Me 109 about 150 yards in front of me and attacked him from the beam with one long burst. The Me 109 turned left and dived with me following him, and I gave him one long burst from dead astern. I saw him catch fire and crash near Wingham and explode.'

Lt Hans-Otto Lessing of the 5th Staffel JG51 lost his life in the encounter.

Another Pole had his chance too. Pilot Officer Paweł Zenker, No. 2 in Green Section, saw a familiar-looking silhouette of Hptm. Horst Tietzen's Messerschmitt through his gunsight. He remembered September 1939, when he so desperately wanted to be able to intercept and destroy one of those, writing:

'He turned back towards France and I chased him as he climbed, firing from 300 yards and closer ranges, and about 10 miles over the sea I saw smoke and fire come from the fuselage and he rapidly lost height. The Me 109 did not adopt evasive action but flew straight on until it crashed into the water somewhere near the North Goodwin Lightship.'

Witorzeńć and Zenker were not the only Polish pilots who were around to score victories that day. No. 32 Squadron was close enough to enter the combat. Pilot Officer Karol Pniak saw two Messerschmitt Bf 109s on his right side and decided to catch them:

'I attacked the one which was nearer me from a distance of 250 yards. I gave him a short burst at first. He was quite surprised; I drew nearer and gave him two (2 sec) bursts and just after I saw an Me 109 in black smoke and flames. He was diving in a SE direction.'

'Cognac', who encountered Major Walter Blume of 7th Staffel JG26, was not done yet. He climbed to 13,000ft, where he noticed two Hurricanes fighting against five Bf 109s.

The Polish pilot chose one of the Germans. Pniak continued his report:

'He saw me because I attacked ¾ from front above. At once he turned in my direction and began to dive. I turned in his direction and after several seconds I was near him. I gave the first burst from 300 yards. After several bursts he was burning.'

Blume, after the action with Pniak and two other pilots, spent the rest of the war in captivity.

Własnowolski was about to claim his second success of the day. After the sortie he reported his attack on a Bf 109 as follows: 'I turned and attacked him, he turned away towards the ground. I followed, firing several short bursts, and he dived into the ground and went up in flames.' Własnowolski noticed that his victim that crashed near Chatham had yellow wingtips: most probably 'Vodka' fought with Lt Gerhard Müller-Dühe, who was killed.

No. 151 Squadron, which received orders to protect the North Weald aerodrome, caught up with a formation of Ju 88s and He 111s flying from the direction of Chelmsford under the protection of Messerschmitt Bf 110s. Pilot Officer Franciszek Czajkowski saw the German bombers approaching his aerodrome, but once the enemy discovered the opposition, they turned back and headed for home. The Pole followed a group of Bf 110s, accompanied by

A group photo of No. 302 Squadron flying personnel taken at RAF Leconfield. In the back row from left to right are: Plt Off Bronisław Bernaś, Plt Off Władysław Gnyś, Plt Off Stanisław Łapka, Plt Off Edward Pilch, Plt Off Wacław Król, Flg Off Jan Czerny, Sgt Antoni Beda, Plt Off Jan Maliński, Sgt Antoni Łysek, Sgt Wilhelm Kosarz, Sgt Marian Wędzik, Plt Off Aleksy Żukowski, Sgt Antoni Markiewicz, Plt Off Stanisław Chałupa, Plt Off Zbigniew Wróblewski, Sgt Eugeniusz Nowakiewicz, Plt Off Włodzimierz Karwowski, Plt Off Stefan Kleczkowski, Sgt Jerzy Załuski. Seated, from the left: Plt Off Jerzy Czerniak, Flt Lt Franciszek Jastrzębski, Plt Off Peter Carter, Flt Lt James Farmer, Flt Lt James Thompson, Flt Lt Piotr Łaguna, Sqn Ldr William Satchell, Sqn Ldr Mieczysław Mümler, Flt Lt William Riley, Flg Off Julian Kowalski, Plt Off Tadeusz Czerwiński and Flt Lt Antoni Wczelik.

the Hurricanes of another squadron. When he was close enough, he decided to take his chances, using his aerial combat skills. He reported to the Intelligence Officer:

'I attacked a 110 and broke away after a short burst. Another Hurricane also fired at this 110 which went down with smoke coming from both engines. I did not see it crash as I was following up the attack of another Hurricane on a 110 and when he broke away I closed with this Me 110 and after a short burst he turned on his back and went down in a spiral and crashed in the sea.'

It is believed that Czajkowski finished off the crew of Uffz. Baar and Fw. Gierga of 4th Staffel ZG26 that was previously attacked by 85 Squadron.

The PAF suffered yet another loss on this day. Squadron Leader Kazimierz Niedźwiecki, in 1936 commander of the III/2 Fighter Wing in Cracow, was chosen three years later to lead a group of airmen travelling to Rumania to pick up the French and British fighter planes which were supposed to arrive there as part of an agreement. Despite being considered the first leader of Polish No. 302 Squadron, he remained as an instructor in No. 6 Operational Training Unit at Sutton Bridge. Niedźwiecki lost his life while performing a training flight in a Hurricane.

At the same time, further north, the first Polish squadron was about to become fully operational. Pilot Officer Władysław Gnyś of 302 Squadron wrote some years later:

'In the middle of August I was transferred together with twelve other officers to 302 squadron which was stationed at Leconfield. This squadron, a Hurricane squadron, was already in the process of training Polish pilots as quickly as possible.'

Gnyś clearly didn't share Jan Maliński's negative opinion on some of their British officers:

'These fine men played a large role in our lives, helping us in every way possible. All were excellent pilots and very likable human beings. We were all very grateful to them for the effort they put forth in helping us during our training and leading us to the first combat … Our group of thirteen pilots from the day of arrival started to train on English aircraft. We found them easy to manoeuvre, dependable and well-armed. Regrettably we had been unable to have this type of plane in Poland.'[10]

Finally, after weeks of internal struggle, 302 Squadron was given the green light and sent for its first operational sortie. On 19 August, at the beginning of the third phase of the Battle of Britain, three of 'City of Poznań' Squadron pilots – Flight Lieutenant Franciszek Jastrzębski, known to his Polish friends as '*Agnieszka*' ('Agnes'), Flight Lieutenant William Riley and Pilot Officer Stanisław Chałupa – performed a patrol over a convoy. Although they did not see anything interesting, they made history by starting a long-lasting operational diary.

The following day brought the first success for the unit. On the Tuesday evening, 20 August, five pilots led by Squadron Leader William Satchell were on patrol over the Leconfield area, when they received an order to extend their mission and continue towards Hull and Spurn Point. Once both sections were on their way, the commander observed a twin-engine aircraft flying in an easterly direction below. When Satchell dived towards the aircraft, he noticed black crosses and identified it as a Junkers Ju 88. The German pilot realized how dangerous the situation was for him and his crew, and immediately tried to find cover in clouds. Satchell climbed above the cloud and eventually found himself in the right position to attack.

Although his bursts went right into the target and silenced the rear gunner, there was also Pilot Officer Stefan Wapniarek very close, who most probably finished off the enemy aircraft. He wrote: 'My bullets were reaching the target as I saw a little sparks jumping on the wings of the enemy aircraft.' The Polish pilot attacked again, right after Satchell completed his second attempt:

'I went to attack again from astern, above, opening fire when my leader broke away. I was shooting from a distance of approximately 200 metres. Flying with high speed and constantly shooting, despite reducing the throttle, in a very short time I found myself at a distance of 80 metres from the target, which started disappearing in a cloud. Visibility inside was good enough, that I was able to follow him still giving a burst. At some point, about 50 metres from me, or even less, I saw a movement on the fuselage of the aircraft – its crew started to bail out.'

Unfortunately, the first victory for 302 Squadron was only given to Satchell, who admitted: 'After I broke away I observed Green 2 on e/a tail for a very short period before the e/a went into clouds.' Regardless of the conflicting reports and opinions on who should get the glory, the Junkers piloted by Uffz. Wilhelm Rautenberg of 8th Staffel KG30 crashed into the ground 5 miles south of Withernsea. The final decision on who was the pilot recorded as successfully attacking the enemy machine only increased the dislike between both Polish and British fliers.

On the day after, two further Ju 88s were probably downed by 302 Squadron pilots, and two Poles were immediately credited with both. Blue Section, led by Flight Lieutenant William Riley, was ordered to patrol Bridlington at 12,000ft. Alongside Riley, Pilot Officer Stanisław Chałupa and Sergeant Edward Paterek were circling for about fifteen minutes, when they sighted a single Ju 88 about 500ft above them, heading west. Once the Germans noticed the presence of the three Hurricanes, the 88's pilot started diving to avoid them. Riley led the attack, opening fire at about 400 yards from the starboard side. The enemy aircraft jettisoned its bombs, yet it was too late as some pieces of the bomber disintegrated from the fuselage. Blue 2 and 3 attacked almost at the same time. Chałupa managed to fire four short bursts before the Junkers disappeared in a cloud, while Paterek fired only one burst.

When Riley and Chałupa continued to chase the enemy, Paterek flew above the cloud, waiting for the aircraft to appear again. His patience paid off as the Junkers left its cover for a while, and the Polish pilot duly sent him another burst of bullets. The Ju 88 began emitting black smoke and went into the clouds for good this time. The former pilot of 132nd Fighter Squadron did not get his chance in Poland serving as flying instructor at the PAF Officer's Training Centre. Flying in combat in France together with the Polish 1/145 'Warsaw' Squadron did not earn him any kills either. Now, at last, he saw some improvement.

Half an hour later, as Blue Section continued their patrol east of Driffield, Chałupa noticed another twin-engine aircraft. This experienced pilot, who fought in Poland with 123rd Fighter Squadron, then in France – where he claimed a few trophies[11] – had a very good hunting instinct. Despite informing his leader over the radio and waggling his wings, his message did not get through and his commander did not intervene, therefore Chałupa decided to take matter into his own hands. He reported:

'Having approached to within 200 yards, I recognised the aircraft as a Ju 88. Having attacked and got in about 3 bursts from about 150 yards, I saw certain objects flying off from the aircraft and a lot of black smoke poured from his port engine. In this state the e/a started to dive and flew into the cloud.'

The Polish pilot could not continue his chase as his engine began to function badly and started developing white smoke from beneath its cowling. Chałupa throttled back and tried to glide towards the aerodrome, but at about 2,000ft the engine began to vibrate. Unable to reach the closest airfield, he went down on its edge without lowering the undercarriage. His Hurricane crash-landed at full impact, although the pilot escaped with only minor scratches on his face. It was a relatively small price for the first 'kill' claim made by a Polish pilot of 302 Squadron. At least Chałupa's comrades had something to celebrate.

Left without his dear companion, Flying Officer Władysław Szulkowski of 65 Squadron had to deal with this loss. During the Battle of Britain there was very little time for mourning after fallen colleagues. Every pilot waiting in readiness knew that the next flight could be the last one. The only way to survive and not allow bad memories to influence their fighting ability was to go back over the Channel and do their best. On 22 August, Szulkowski and ten of his colleagues were directed to fly over the Dover area to intercept a large formation of German bombers surrounded by Messerschmitts.

While 65 Squadron was searching for the bombers, it suddenly became a target for the Luftwaffe fighters. Szulkowski, who flew as Blue 3, was at 20,000ft when he saw a chance to get a score. He said upon returning to base: 'I became separated from my section and attacked one of the stragglers. Before he could attempt evasion I fired several bursts from 350 yards closing to 100 yards and

Flg Off Władysław Szulkowski is sitting first from right on the port wing of No. 65 Sqn Spitfire.

the e/a burst into flames and crashed down into the sea.' The whole fight only lasted a few seconds, and it was 7 pm, when the dog-fight was over.

Pilot Officer Karol Pniak from 32 Squadron received a rather boring order to protect a single Avro Anson. However, when the German formation was observed heading towards Manston and Deal, the Polish pilot wasted no time and joined the rest of his squadron. He connected with them right on time. Together with two other pilots, including Pilot Officer Rupert Smythe, he damaged an aircraft that he recognized as 'Do 215'. The German machine, most probably a Bf 110 rather than a Dornier, left the rest of its formation and, pouring smoke from both its engines, disappeared into clouds.

A very modest yet well-liked former graduate of the National Radio Technical School, short and always smiling, Sergeant Antoni Głowacki from No. 501 Squadron, was about to become the hero of the day. On 24 August, Nos 54 and 501 were posted on patrol over the southern coastline. They had to engage an enemy formation that had already avoided several other squadrons operating in the area. Warsaw-born Głowacki, who flew as No. 2 in Green Section, at 10.30 am sighted around thirty aircraft crossing the shoreline near Hawkinge in Kent and heading north-west. As 501 circled round and 'A' Flight attacked the rear formation of the bombers, the Pole saw some of the German fighters attacking 'B' Flight. 'I had a dog-fight,' he wrote later, 'with an Me 109, which I shot down. The e/a which I followed down hit the ground and exploded.' Unfortunately, while 'Toni' was celebrating his success, a Hurricane with the individual code letter W was hit, presumably by one of the German fighters. The aircraft from 'B' Flight went down straight into the sea with Pilot Officer Paweł Zenker in the cockpit. This talented and brave pilot was lost. Głowacki was overwhelmed with sorrow, but there was no time for emotions as the Battle of Britain continued.

'*Antek*' was airborne again once the British radar stations located a new wave of German machines flying towards RAF aerodromes. One of them was Manston, being attacked by a formation of thirty Ju 88s. No. 501 Squadron immediately turned back from the Dover area and, around 12.45 pm, met the raiders as they were heading back to France. 'I shot down a Ju 88 in flames into the sea,' Głowacki reported briefly, 'and saw a Messerschmitt shoot down either a Hurricane or a Defiant.' The Polish pilot was right, as 264 Squadron lost three of its Defiants. Głowacki was about to claim his third victory of the day: 'I attacked the Me 109 and was able to shoot him down in flames.' Yet for this brave pilot, the battle wasn't yet over.

Another Pole engaged over the Manston airfield was 501 Squadron's Flying Officer Stefan Witorzeńć, who flew as No. 2 in Yellow Section. He was determined to get at least one of the enemies, particularly after noticing

German bombs falling on Manston. When the Junkers turned back after dropping their deadly load, Witorzeńć saw a chance to get a single aircraft that appeared not far from him:

> 'I saw a Ju 88 not in formation and attacked him as he crossed the coast. After firing all my ammunition from astern I saw white smoke come out of him. He turned slowly to the right, gradually losing height.'

Two hours later, another Polish pilot experienced a rather thrilling encounter with the Luftwaffe. Pilot Officer Karol Pniak flew as No. 3 of Blue Section when his 32 Squadron clashed with Messerschmitt Bf 109s north of Dover. As the Germans took them by surprise, two of the squadron's Hurricanes were almost immediately shot. 'Cognac' Pniak remembered quite well the moment when twelve 109s showed up:

> 'They were above us and attacked us. I was attacked by a Me 109 from head on and above. I circled round on his tail, and closing to 150 yards gave him 2 two-seconds bursts. He started to smoke from the engine, I followed him and gave him two more bursts, much black smoke came from the e/a, and he was diving just after this.'

Pniak had no time to follow the Bf 109 of 7th Staffel JG3, as he had a more important problem of his own: 'I felt my machine vibrating and saw smoke coming from the engine and the right wing, and flames also appeared from the right wing.' The former aerobatic pilot knew the drill:

> 'I switched off everything and put my a/c into a dive to land, but when I reached 5,000 ft the flames were so big, that I turned my plane on one side and jumped. I landed very fast because my parachute was not properly open and full of holes. I landed 3 miles NW of Hawkinge, my ankle and knee were injured, and I was taken to hospital.'

Pniak's Hurricane went down at Rhodes Minnis near Lympne. The pilot left hospital on 7 September, and shortly after was posted to No. 257 Squadron.

At 3.40 pm, a very aggressive and success-hungry Antoni Głowacki patrolled again, flying over Hawkinge. In the Lympne area, about thirty Ju 88s were seen, and the whole of 501 Squadron instantly went after them. The enemy aircraft were eventually caught west of Maidstone, despite being protected by a formation of Bf 109s. Głowacki again was very specific and laconic:

'I had a dog-fight with an Me 109 and shot him down in flames. I climbed again and attacked the last aircraft of a formation of bombers from astern and finished my ammunition on it. I saw white smoke come out of him and observers on the aerodrome saw him spinning towards the ground.'

This was Głowacki's fifth victory of the day. Just by shooting the Bf 109 and having already scores from 15 August, gave him the right to be named an ace. However, when his last victim went down, he joined – or rather started – an exclusive group of pilots who achieved five kills within one day and were called 'One-day aces'. Głowacki became the first pilot of the Battle of Britain who gained such a status.

The following day he was recommended to receive the Distinguished Flying Medal. 'Tony Glowacki, a Polish sergeant,' he was remembered by Pilot Officer Mackenzie, 'squat, tough, always laughing no matter what, already experienced from the German invasion of Poland, a smooth pilot and good shot.'[12]

Two days later, another Polish pilot joined Głowacki's squadron: Pilot Officer Stanisław Skalski, who very soon also proved his skills. Mackenzie painted his basic profile: '"Stan" Skalski, a Pole, slightly built, pale-faced with an emotional hatred of the Germans, together with his compatriot Kozlowski, a quiet, unassuming pilot who never showed his feelings.'[13]

The Germans then concentrated their attacks on Hornchurch and North Weald airfields, but were intercepted by 111 and 151 Squadrons. Many bombs did reach their targets, as the Luftwaffe stepped up its plan of eliminating the RAF at its airfields before the Spitfires and Hurricanes could get into the air. Pilot Officer Franciszek Czajkowski, called 'Czajka' (short for his surname, Peewit) by his Polish colleagues, took off from North Weald at 3.30 pm to fight the approaching bombers. He described the action that followed:

'I attacked a He 111 from the beam. After this I was attacked by a Me 110 but not hit. I then got behind the whole formation and saw a single Me 109. I came from the sun onto its tail and opened fire. He took no notice of my first burst. I closed into 60 yds firing all the time and pulled up so as not to collide. At this moment I was attacked by a Me 110 and was therefore unable to see the results of my shooting. I think that the pilot of the Me 109 must have been badly wounded as he did not react when I fired at him, but continued in a gradual turning glide, not fast, and took no evasive action.'

An hour later, the Luftwaffe targeted Portsmouth, and despite strong defence by the RAF, German bombs reached the harbour, port and city itself. One of the squadrons that arrived to fight the raiders was No. 609. Flying Officer

'Novi' Nowierski did not achieve any success, and his Spitfire was damaged in combat. At the same time, his Polish colleague from 234 Squadron had more luck. Pilot Officer Zbigniew Oleński, who arrived at this unit on 11 August,[14] had completed studies at Warsaw Technical University and later worked at the Aviation Technical Institute in Warsaw, being in charge of the fighter performance research. Oleński, a close relative of Marshal Józef Piłsudski's wife, graduated from the Air Force Reserve Cadet Officer's School together with Janusz Żurakowski. On 24 August, Oleński flew as Blue 2 and reported:

> 'Over the interception point I saw 7 Me 109s and was about to attack them when two Me 109s attacked from behind and I saw pairs of Me 109s stepped up 500 feet above each other. I swerved to the right and attacked the last pair from astern, gave a short burst and it dived wildly with smoke coming from its fuselage.'

Żurakowski, meanwhile, had been in serious trouble. The Pole became a target for two of the JG53 pilots, Hptm. Hans-Karl Mayer and Lt Zeiss, who were experienced fliers and attacked Żurakowski. When attacking one of the Messerschmitts, his aircraft received several direct cannon hits, resulting in Żurakowski completely losing control of his Spitfire. Having no other choice, he bailed out and landed about 50ft from where his machine crashed to the ground. Initially, the airman with rather limited English was 'taken prisoner' by an elderly gentleman from the Home Guard, but soon after the Pole was saved by an Army lieutenant. Żurakowski was informed that he had landed on the Isle of Wight.

Before 30 August, the Polish successes in the Battle of Britain were visible, but still rather limited. The tireless Antoni Głowacki, however, claimed another 'Jerry'. On the morning of the 28th, Polish pilots of 501 Squadron had further occasion to celebrate when 'Toni' provided an Intelligence Officer with the following report:

> 'We saw a formation of 17 bombers flying north-west of Canterbury at an altitude of 10,000 feet. While climbing we made a wide circle to attack them. Some twenty Messerschmitt 109s were turning above the bombers and while we were half a mile from the bombers, some Hurricane squadron attacked the bombers, and was itself attacked by the fighters. At this moment we hurried with help to the Hurricane squadron and attacked the Messerschmitts from below at 13,000 feet. I saw a Me 109 on the tail of a Hurricane, and I shot at him from a long distance. When he entered the dive I hit him with two bursts from behind. The Me 109

started to burn, hit in the fuel tank, and the pilot bailed out. The aircraft crashed and exploded in a field south-south-east of Canterbury.'

The Messerschmitt of the Stabstaffel of JG51 piloted by Oblt Kircheis crashed at South Barham Farm in Denton. The wounded pilot bailed out and soon after was taken prisoner.

The last few days had been rather lucky for the Poles, apart for Flying Officer Piotr Ostaszewski-Ostoja being shot down on 25 August. He was amongst 609 Squadron's pilots who were scrambled to face a large German formation heading towards Weymouth Bay. During the dog-fight with the Messerschmitts of JG53, a shell blew off his armour plating, which hit him in the head and arm. Another one went through his Spitfire's engine, and a third slightly damaged the brakes. He managed to return to base and land, but having no brakes ended up with quite a few bruises.

Chapter Ten

For the First Time…

A long time before the Battle of Britain began, Polish Sergeant Leopold Flanek of the Groupe de Chasse III/2, with four victories[1] on his account, met his fate in the skies over Belgium. This experienced veteran of the 121st Fighter Squadron crashed with his Morane 406 at Neuvillete, after being shot down by Obfw. Georg Anthony of the 4th Staffel ZG76. His loss deeply touched his colleagues, who were awaiting an opportunity for revenge. There is a saying in Poland that translates more or less as: the mills of the God grind slowly, yet they grind exceedingly fine. The time for Anthony to pay for this was about to come at the end of August 1940.

In the meantime, at Northolt, events didn't move as quickly as the Polish pilots would have liked. Flight Lieutenant John Kent, so suspicious earlier about the Polish flyers' qualities, finally received their well-deserved respect and trust. His Polish brothers-in-arms showed their sympathy and began to call him 'Kentowski' after Polonising his Canadian name. 'Kentowski' wrote:

'Because of our lack of knowledge of the Poles' experience and their general background we had to be very careful about their training, especially as regards R/T; we could not expect them to remember even what little English we were able to teach them during the excitement of combat. Whereas they could speak to one another, the Controller could neither understand them nor they him. It was necessary, therefore, to have at least one of the British pilots flying with them on all exercises and, later of course, in combat.

'I think perhaps the training period was unnecessarily prolonged and this certainly irked the Poles, who kept remonstrating with us that the best training was over France, but we still had to be quite sure they knew how we operated. This was not always easy to get across as illustrated on one occasion when 'A' Flight was scheduled to act as a formation of 'bombers' while 'B' Flight was to carry out an interception and make dummy attacks on us. I explained this very carefully and impressed upon them that no evasive action was to be taken as we were simulating bombers depending upon crossfire for defence. They all said that they fully understood and off we went.

'I led the flight off to the west and climbed to height, then set course for Northolt. Just east of Reading I saw the other flight diving down to attack, [and] as they completed the attack and started their break away, I was horrified to see my number three, Flying Officer Feric, pull up into a violent barrel-roll and get right on to the tail of one of the attacking Hurricanes. Fortunately he recognised it just in time as he was on the point of shooting it down – he had completely misunderstood what I had said during briefing, even though I had used an interpreter, and thought that we were to be the attacking force.'[2]

Squadron Leader Kellett and both his flight commanders were under immense pressure. They had been given a big task to complete, yet none of them had previous combat experience, unlike many of their untamed and wild Poles.

The first group of pilots, which were posted to the 'Tadeusz Kościuszko' Squadron to create a core of this new unit, had no previous training nor flying experience undertaken in Britain. For most of them, the last time they had flown was in France. Sergeant Eugeniusz Szaposznikow recalled:

'Before becoming operational at Northolt we Poles were anxious to get into battle to blast the Huns from the sky. After our combat experiences in Poland and in France, the wait seemed endless. But we had to follow British regulations that demanded a certain amount of flying hours in their aircraft.'[3]

Unlike their British colleagues, the Poles had left all their old world behind, their lifestyle, peace, familiar places, but most importantly their loved ones, who were over 1,000 miles away, living in country ruled by German and Soviet oppressors. Those Slavic airmen had to reconcile their daily duties with the nightmares of the Polish Campaign and the worry for the safety of their mothers, wives, girlfriends and very often their children. This was something that their British colleagues only barely understood. 'Yesterday, at midnight, a year passed since our farewell with Janeczka in the dark, gloomy Jeziorna gate,' Sergeant Marian Bełc, or *Doktor* ('Doctor'), as he was called by his colleagues, wrote in his personal diary.

'With whom, who was supposed to be my irreplaceable friend, we dreamt about creating our own happiness, not even supposing by then for how long we were saying our goodbyes. Yes, this is a destiny, ah, if I could only know if I return and when.'[4]

Group of No. 303 Sqn pilots. From left to right are: Plt Off Mirosław Ferić, Flg Off Bohdan Grzeszczak, Plt Off Jan Zumbach, Flg Off Zdzisław Henneberg and Flt Lt John Kent.

Not only gauges, levers and instructions were concerning the Poles. They had their own nightmares to live with every day.

But on 30 August, they were briefed to perform yet another training flight. One of these countless ones… However, this time it was supposed to be an interception practice, at least something different and more interesting, after two days of air gunnery exercises at Sutton Bridge.

Before they left Northolt, the other Poles flying in RAF squadrons had already been in action. Pilot Officer Stanisław Skalski from 501 Squqdron, known as 'Skal' by his British friends to make his and their lives easier, was about to claim his first victory since the Polish Campaign at 11.20 am. He flew as Red 2, following the rest of his colleagues towards Dungeness on the Kent coast, where a large German formation had been seen. The RAF pilots saw a big group of bombers consisting of Heinkel He 111s and Dorniers, protected by three waves of dangerous Bf 109s and Bf 110s. The leader of Blue Section attacked the bombers, which immediately turned towards the rest of 501 Squadron. Skalski said:

'After Blue 1 attacked a formation of bombers, which turned towards the squadron, this formation broke and I attacked an He 111 from astern and above. It was attacked at the same time by a Spitfire or Hurricane from below, which was shot by the rear gunner. After I had fired, the Heinkel burst into flames, and I was attacked by 2 Me 109s. I circled round to attack them but they refused combat.'

The Polish officer most probably downed one of the Heinkels from IVth Gruppe KG1 with a crew of Uffz. Emil Burger, Gefr. Walter Feierbend, Gefr. Heinz Hildebrand, Gefr. Willi Klappholz and Gefr. Herbert Roggemann. They were captured soon after landing on British soil.

Skalski was not the only Pole in 501 Squadron who achieved success in this encounter. Sergeant Antoni Głowacki described his role:

'I attacked a Me 110 who was diving upon one of our own aircraft and he broke away from the formation and turned towards the coast. Then I attacked an Me 110 from a defensive circle, and put the rest of my ammunition into him. He dived down emitting white smoke.'

At the same time, No. 253 Squadron was patrolling around Maidstone, but it was near Redhill where the pilots sighted an opportunity to fight. Only Pilot Officer Tadeusz Nowak, who flew as No. 3 in Green Section, went close, writing later:

'I was at 15,000 ft when I attacked number 3 of the leading section of bombers, giving him 3 bursts from astern and beam. I observed incendiary entering the cockpit on my last attack, entering the tanks and wing.'

Although he erroneously thought his target was a Ju 86, he was eventually given credit for damaging a Dornier Do 215. His colleague, Pilot Officer Włodziemierz Samoliński, being the Blue 2, was also in the centre of the combat.He reported:

'My leader attacked the bombers, which were Do 215s and He 111s, and I engaged 3 Me 110s. I attacked the first one from astern, and slightly above, giving a 6 sec burst, silencing the rear gunner, and saw my bullets entering the wings and fuselage. The enemy aircraft dived in a spiral towards the ground. I then engaged a second enemy Me 110 in a similar attack, silencing the rear gunner. I was then attacked by the third Me 110, which dived onto me, and I fired the rest of my ammunition at him in a head-on position but was unable to observe damage.'

Around 4 pm, when 303 Squadron's Hurricanes were taking off for their training flight that was supposed to consist of an attack on six Blenheims pretending to be enemy planes, another large formation of Luftwaffe aircraft were approaching Lympne. More of them were to come. Amongst the RAF squadrons which were scrambled to stop them were eight Hurricanes from the Stapleford based 151 Squadron. Their pilots sighted the enemy approaching from the sea, and all airmen dived at the first bombers in their reach from the beam and then continued down beneath them.

Pilot Officer Franciszek Surma, who was one of them, reported:

'After this attack I saw one He 111 turn away to the right and make for the sea. I was below and chased after him and fired a short burst under him. There was no return fire and I closed in and gave a longer burst from direct astern at about 80 yards. I used all my ammunition and the enemy was then down to about 6,000 ft and continuing in a series of slow turns towards the sea.'

Unfortunately, 151 Squadron returned home with four of its Hurricanes damaged and one pilot killed in combat. His name was Sergeant Feliks Gmur, whose aircraft was shot down by enemy fighters and crashed at Epping Green in Essex. In less than a week he would have been 26 years old.

About twenty minutes later, Pilot Officer Skalski and Sergeant Głowacki from 501 Squadron were able to increase their scores. They were over Chatham when they intercepted a large group of German bombers and fighters flying over the Thames Estuary heading east. It was obvious that this formation was specifically concentrating their attention on Southend and the surrounding areas. The whole of 501 Squadron attacked instantly and simultaneously, and went for a frontal assault. Skalski, flying as Red 2, was about to grab his chance once more:

'I attacked one of the bombers, which turned south back over the Estuary, from astern. The right engine stopped, and the two rear gunners ceased to fire, E/A glided slowly down towards Herne Bay. I returned to base, seeing the E/A last at 4,000 ft, flying on one engine.'

It is possible that the Polish fighter pilot fought with one of the KG3 planes.

Meanwhile, the indefatigable and extremely aggressive Głowacki, No. 2 in Green Section, aimed at another Heinkel:

'We attacked the second "vic" of the bomber formation head-on. This broke up, and I fired at the same aircraft which had turned, and dived down towards the river, jettisoning its bombs. The port engine was emitting white smoke and the enemy aircraft was travelling very slowly.'

The afternoon, in theory, was supposed to go quietly for the boys of 303 Squadron. Six Hurricanes of 'B' Flight took off from Northolt aerodrome at 4.15 pm to perform a mock attack on six Blenheims. Squadronn Leader Kellett was leading the exercise, with five others obediently following him: Flying Officer Wacław Łapkowski, Flying Officer Ludwik Paszkiewicz – known as 'Paszka' – Pilot Officer Jan Daszewski – called *'Długi Joe'* ('Long Joe') or *'Pan Antoś'* ('Mr Tony') – Pilot Officer Witold Łokuciewski ('Tolo') and Sergeant Mirosław Wojciechowski. The main part of the day's training went smoothly, and around 4.35 pm the six machines were leisurely escorting Blenheims over St Albans.

They were not expecting that within a short distance of their path, a combat would took place, and were astonished to see a formation of German planes that were targeting airfields in Kent and across the Thames Eastuary, such as Biggin Hill, Kenley, Luton, North Weald, Oxford and Slough. Kellett, a typically calm Briton, remained composed and knew that the priority for him and his boys was to keep protecting the Blenheims, bring them safely back home and, above all, follow their orders. Years later he recalled:

'On the last training occasion we had 12 Blenheims as targets when we were warned that enemy aircraft were in the vicinity. We were to guard the bombers. I ordered the Squadron to assemble behind and above the bombers and cease attacking.'[5]

However, Paszkiewicz, who had left his wife and daughter in occupied Poland, had had enough. So far he had experienced French listlessness on the continent and what he saw as endless training in England. He wrote:

'After a while I noticed ahead a number of aircraft carrying out various turns. The centre of the commotion seemed to be about 1,000 feet below us to starboard. I reported it to the Officer Commanding, S/Ldr Kellett, by R/T and, as he did not seem to reply, I opened up the throttle and went in the direction of the enemy. I saw the rest of the Flight some 300 yards behind me; below me were the burning suburbs of a town and a Hurricane diving with smoke trailing behind it. Then I noticed, at my own altitude, a bomber with twin rudders – probably a Dornier – turning in my direction. When he noticed me he dived sharply down. I turned over and dived after him. When turning over I noticed

Group photo of 303 Squadron pilots. From the left to right: Sgt Josef František, Sgt Jan Kowalski, Sgt Mirosław Wojciechowski, Flg Off Ludwik Paszkiewicz, Sgt Marian Bełc and Flg Off Walerian Żak.

the black crosses on the wings. Then I aimed at the fuselage and opened fire from about 200 yards, later transferring it to the port engine, which I set on fire. When I drew very close I pressed down under for a new attack and then saw another Hurricane attacking and a German bailing out by parachute. The Dornier went into a steep turn, and I gave him another burst. He dived and then hit the ground without pulling out of the dive and burst into flames.'

Flying Officer Paszkiewicz, who did not fly operationally back in Poland and therefore had less experience than his compatriots, made a schoolboy error in his assessment, confusing the silhouette of a twin-engined Dornier with a Messerschmitt Bf 110. Unaware of this, 'Paszka' flew back to Northolt thrilled to share his success: 'After receiving an order I landed, having made a victory roll, with my joy spoilt by the thought of the Flight fighting somewhere while I had chased a single machine.'

Paszkiewicz, being a typical impatient Pole and wanting to solve problems right away, was rather disappointed by the behaviour of Squadron Leader Kellett: 'Unfortunately, after the Flight returned it turned out the English hero carried on with attacking the Blenheims.' This sad conclusion did not stop him in his excitement, however, as he almost shouted: 'I have been firing at an enemy aircraft for the first time in my life.'

Kellett, the object of his rather unkind comment, was unaware of the Pole's actions and summarized the whole event with equal satisfaction: 'Fortunately the Blenheims were not attacked, and I reported to Group Captain Vincent and A.V.M. Park that we were ready for combat.'[6] Paszkiewicz did not realise that he had actually shot down a Messerschmitt Bf 110 of the 4th Staffel ZG76, piloted by Ofw. Georg Anthony, who a few months previously had killed Polish pilot Leopold Flanek. Uffz. Heinrich Nordmeier, the rear gunner, managed to bail out and with some scars on his forehead and injured spine was taken on a stretcher to Kimpton hospital. Anthony's body was recovered at the crash site at Barley Bins Farm and was initially buried in a private garden. A few days later it was transferred to Hitchin Cemetery. His conqueror outlived him for less than a month…

Flying Officer Jerzy Jankiewicz of 601 Squadron, unlike most of his Polish colleagues, had an advantage of being trained on Hurricanes before the war. Of course others, with some minor problems, learnt to fly this craft very quickly, but to this 27-year-old Polish officer sitting in the cockpit of Sydney Camm's war horse was like meeting an old friend. On Saturday 31 August, he had an opportunity to prove what he had learnt so far, being at the right place when a large German formation of about 100 bombers and Bf 110s was closing on Debden. It was approximately 8.40 am when the Polish pilot, flying as Red 2, saw a defensive circle of about six Bf 109s. Jankiewicz did not wait, and later described his actions:

'I broke away from our formation to observe these e/a and simultaneously one dived down and opened fire head on. He banked steeply to the left and I delivered a beam attack with full deflection. A few seconds after I saw black smoke coming from starboard side of e/a. E/a dived and I followed, firing short bursts continually. The Me 109 drew away from me going SE.'

Jankiewicz was credited with damaging one of the German fighters, which presumably belonged to JG77.

The Luftwaffe continued attacking the RAF, and after 10.20 am another Pole intercepted the enemy aircraft. Pilot Officer Franciszek Czajkowski of 151 Squadron flew alongside seven of his comrades when he sighted twenty-seven Junkers Ju 88s and Dornier Do 17s approaching Chatham, under the watchful eyes of their fighter escort. The Hurricanes went for an immediate clash. 'First attack in formation,' the Polish pilot commented, 'no serious damage observed.' After the bombers jettisoned their deadly load over the Thames, 151 Squadron, being in a rather disadvantaged position, came under attack from above. Czajkowski continued:

'Intercepted by escort 109s, dog-fight ensued with one. Fired 4 sec. burst at 300 yds, closed to 150 yds, fired 6 sec. burst, large volumes of black smoke poured from engine, 109 dived and I followed, firing a 2 sec. burst at 150 yds, more smoke and the 109 went into a spin.'

Czajowski, while desperately chasing his victim, suddenly became the target of another Messerschmitt:

'I turned left to avoid a 109 on my tail, but was attacked from the front. I fired at him but had only 1 sec ammunition left. At this moment I was hit by a cannon shot in the right wing, engine and cockpit, and was wounded. I turned towards the land five miles away. The engine was only running irregularly and petrol and oil fumes poured into the cockpit. I force landed about five miles north of Shoeburyness with dead engine and wheels up. The hydraulics had failed. I was lifted from my machine by a civilian, and a soldier was left guarding the machine.'

Czajkowski, who crash-landed near Foulness on the Essex coast, was seriously injured and taken to St Luke's hospital, where doctors found that he had bullet wounds all over his body, including right arm and shoulder, legs and feet. After convalescence, he returned to operational flying only in February 1941, missing the rest of the Battle of Britain.

The Germans continued attacking British aerodromes for the rest of the day. They sent another raid in the early afternoon to bomb Kenley, Biggin Hill or Croydon. After crossing the coastline near Folkestone, some of the bombers turned in the direction of Croydon and were caught by several RAF squadrons, including No. 253. Its pilots sighted at least twenty bombers flying with the protection of thirty Bf 109s and 110s. Pilot Officer Tadeusz Nowak flew as No. 2 in Red Section on this occasion. The closest target for the 26-year-old Pole was a Heinkel He 111. Nowak wrote later:

'I gave a burst of 1 second on a He 111 flying at 12,000 ft. The enemy aircraft broke away and circled down towards the ground. After my attack two Me 109s were on my tail so I also broke away. I followed the He 111 to the ground where I saw it force land with its undercarriage up in a field.'

A second formation of German bombers attacked Hornchurch, and when all the Luftwaffe planes were heading home with empty bomb bays, they were spotted by the RAF. One of the squadrons closed up very quickly while its rear weaver managed to get close to the bombers. It was again Sergeant 'Toni' Głowacki of 501 Squadron, who was acting as rearguard for his colleagues. Despite being aware of the presence of enemy fighters, he decided to proceed – one 'Hun' less, closer to victory! Głowacki gave a brief description of his actions: 'I attacked the bomber formation which was broken up by very accurate A.A. fire. I saw the last enemy aircraft catch fire and dive. I had attacked it. It was diving down towards Margate.' At this moment, however, Głowacki's luck ran out: 'As he dived the next bomber fired at me and the bullet entered my petrol tank and radiator. On landing my aircraft burst into flames, but I jumped clear, and was only slightly injured.' It is believed that the Polish pilot downed one of the KG3 Dorniers.

Another Pole heavily engaged in the centre of the battle was Pilot Officer Skalski, focused and calm in the air, level-headed on the ground, who wrote:

'I was No. 2 in Red Section, when the squadron was sent to patrol Gravesend at 15,000 ft, and the enemy bombers were flying west along the Thames estuary towards London. We attacked the fighter escort of Me 109s which were very close to the bombers, and a dog-fight developed. I singled out a Me 109 which I attacked from astern, following him as he turned south-west. The plane crashed in a wood near Rochester aerodrome.'

Historians consider a Bf 109 of the 1st Staffel JG77, piloted by Uffz. Franz-Xaver Keck, as Skalski's potential opponent and victim. Keck was badly wounded and bailed out, whilst his machine crashed at Boxley, east of Rochester.

At 5.50 pm, 'A' Flight of 303 Squadron, led by Kellett, left Northolt, followed by 'B' Flight, under the command of Flight Lieutenant Athol Forbes, ten minutes later. They were initially directed towards Croydon, yet eventually found themselves over Biggin Hill. It proved to be right on time, as a formation of sixty Dorniers protected by Bf 109s were closing in. Polish pilots strategically attacking out of the sun, achieved the element of surprise. 'We put on speed and chased them,' Sergeant Stanisław Karubin reported. Karubin knew exactly what to do, as he had flown in Poland as a pilot of 111st Fighter Squadron and had downed one Bf 110 already. He continued:

'Revenge was coming. The three Huns ahead of us split their formation and dived. We dived after them and I gave one of them a burst in the dive. He pulled up – that was what I wanted. A new burst. Fire and smoke broke out in the white belly of the Me 109. It went down like a flaming torch. I fired another burst just in case.'

His 303 comrade from the 111th *Eskadra* and Pursuit Brigade, Sergeant Eugeniusz Szaposznikow, already had one shared victory from France under his belt. 'Szaposzka' got very excited when being debriefed by the Intelligence Officer, Flying Officer Edward Hadwen:

'There was little time to pick one for each of us and I got the left-hand fellow. I sent him a burst just to scare him just as we did it at home. He climbed steeply and in doing so came within my sights, as I was above him. That was the end of him; all I had to do was press the trigger. He turned over and went down followed by a trail of smoke.'

Another veteran of 111th *Eskadra* was 21-year-old Sergeant Kazimierz Wünsche, known by his English colleagues as 'Kaz', who flew as Yellow 2:

'Seeing Huns attacking 'Red' flight I jumped towards one of them as he was going for Sergt Karubin. I wanted to scare him and distract his attention, but he turned over in a flash, showing his black crosses, which made me pretty mad. At the same time another Me 109 jumped up below me on the port side. I instantly fired and saw a wisp of smoke. To make sure I fired again and the Messerschmitt then dived steeply down to the ground.'

It is worth mentioning here that Kellett had well-deserved great admiration towards these three Polish sergeants, calling them 'my three musketeers'. He trusted them completely, always feeling safer when having them around. 'They flew to my aid on many a sortie,' he recollected, 'risking their lives to protect me. I do not believe any other squadron had better maintenance or NCOs than No. 303.'

Half Polish and half Croatian, Pilot Officer Mirosław Ferić,[7] better known as 'Ox', fought side-by-side with Szaposznikow, Karubin and Wünsche in Poland. Despite having two trophies from that period, he also had a debt to pay back: on 3 September 1939 he was shot down. In Poland he had started writing his personal memoirs, which in time became an official diary, or rather a chronicle, of 303 Squadron. Ferić wrote of the action near Biggin Hill:

'Pulling 12lb boost I get on the tail of the other that tried to get to the first section. I close in on him easily, he grows in my sights, his fuselage now fills the entire diameter of the luminous ring. That was the right time to open fire. I strike him completely calmly, somehow without excitement – I feel surprised and puzzled that it is so easy, quite different than in Poland, where one was really tired, sweating, nervous, and eventually got nothing, and was blown away oneself. A short burst of 20 rounds from all guns. The result was immediate and wonderful. The Jerry, hit, literally burns like a candle. With flames the length of the fuselage, he executes a bunt, flashes his white belly and the crosses – and goes down. I follow him. The pilot bails out – his parachute opens. I feel like blowing him away, but there are too many witnesses. There may even be the English – and we have our accounts to settle from Poland. I leave him alone. Anyway, he's going down on land. They'll get him. The hell with you.'

"Three Musketeers" as they were called by Sqn Ldr Kellett: Sergeants Michał Brzezowski, Stefan Wójtowicz and Eugeniusz Szaposznikow.

Ferić's comments may sound extremely vicious, but after experiencing German brutality in Poland, including aiming at defenceless Polish airmen, the only aim that Polish pilots had in mind was to get rid of every 'Hun' possible, no matter how. Having memories of the Luftwaffe ruthlessly butchering innocent civilians, and also purposely and intentionally targeting Polish colleague pilots bailing out – such as Ferić's commander Captain Zdzisław Krasnodębski, Sub-Lieutenant Feliks Szyszka (123rd Fighter Squadron), Corporal Tadeusz Kawałkowski (151st Fighter Squadron) or Sub-Lieutenant Jan Dzwonek (161st Fighter Squadron) – he certainly felt that his intentions were justified.

Ferić knew that soldiers of the German Army were not much better than their flying mates, as they showed with their absolute cruelty by leaving wounded Captain Florian Laskowski (commander of III/4 Fighter Wing) to die in the wreckage of his aircraft, and also murdering Corporal Benedykt Mielczyński (141st Fighter Squadron) after dragging the wounded pilot out of the building where he was kept hidden by locals.[8] These barbaric acts only ignited the spark of revenge and fuelled hatred. Although perhaps not officially accepted, Polish methods were understood by some of the British pilots. Flight Lieutenant Brian Kingcombe of 92 Squadron said:

> 'I know about of more than one Pole who did that – but you could understand it in their case. Some of those Poles had seen their families slaughtered, and they had the most desperate hatred of the Germans.'[9]

This hatred towards the Germans was common and infectious, and seen throughout the forthcoming years of the conflict. We can only speculate what would have happened if by then the Poles were fully aware of all atrocities and cruelty of the Germans, such as the death camps at Oświęcim,[10] Majdanek, Sobibor, Treblinka and many more (not to mention the Soviets, who started the mass murder and deportation of Polish citizens).[11] Another 303 Squadron pilots recalls his temptation to finish off a German airman swinging on a parachute:

> 'I circled round him. He was a live Nazi and I could easily have shot him down. I remembered Warsaw and the Polish women and children, and I would indeed have pressed the button had it not been for the fact that the jam-eaters were all around me and would witness it. Anyway, we were over England and he would not escape, even though execution was justifiable.'

Flight Lieutenant Kent had a long discussion with his Poles about whether it would be correct and desired to shoot enemy flyers dangling beneath a parachute:

'The Poles were fed up with me when I admitted that I could not bring myself to shoot the chap in the parachute and they reminded me of events earlier in the month when we were told that one or two pilots of No. 1 Squadron had bailed out and had then been shot by German fighters. At the time Poles had asked me if it was true that this was happening. I had to tell them that, as far as I knew, it was, at which they asked, "Oh, can we?" I explained that, distasteful as it was, the Germans were within their rights in shooting our pilots over this country and that, if one of us shot down a German aircraft over France and the pilot bailed out, then we were quite entitled to shoot him. But this was not so over England as, aside from anything else, he would be out of the war and might even be a very useful source of information for us. They thought about this for a bit and then said: "Yes, we understand – but what if he is over the Channel?" – to which I had jokingly replied: "Well, you can't let the poor bugger drown, can you?" This remark was quite seriously thrown in my teeth when they heard about the 109 pilot I had just shot down. There was no doubt about it, the Poles were playing the game for keeps far more than we were.'[12]

On 31 August, the last Polish pilot of 303 'Tadeusz Kościuszko' Squadron to claim a victory over a Bf 109 was Flying Officer Zdzisław 'Dzidek' Henneberg, a former 111th Fighter Squadron member and flying instructor at Dęblin's PAF Training Centre. He had some combat experience already, as he fought in France and downed a Heinkel He 111. The 29-year-old Henneberg wrote:

'I went after him, keeping an eye on the others. I had to hurry, as the three Jerries were already behind and above me to the port side. I opened fire at 300 yards. After the first burst he put out smoke. I gave him another two bursts and the Jerry went down with a big trail of grey smoke.'

Kellett, another victorious pilot, impressed by the bravery, aggressiveness and uncompromising attitude of his pilots – and less delighted by the German tactics – concluded his views after the fight:

'The Germans had possibly recruited all their pilots from Railway and Tram drivers as they were at this period flying in very rigid formations, and teutonic like they all had Fuhrers to follow. The first Squadron attack on a German formation showed me that the leaders of the close escort fighters were standing back and above the bombers so that they could see when our fighters were in contact with their bombers, but there was an area of 100 yards in front and 500 behind, below and on the flank, where they could see nothing.'[13]

Despite the commander's rather critical view of the enemy's fighting technique, his Intelligence Officer found Poles very peculiarly prioritizing their targets: 'All six of our pilots destroyed an Enemy fighter, but none of them were able to make contact with the bombers.'

At the same time, the Polish pilots unsympathetically evaluated Kellett's performance: '"Dyzio" full of glory – today brought him a total score of 1 hut and 1 Messerschmitt 109.' This was due to his unfortunate landing after the combat, when Kellett damaged his Hurricane after colliding with the pilots' hut at dispersal.

It is believed that Karubin, who shared his victory with Kellett, destroyed an aircraft from 7th Staffel JG26 piloted by Fw. Martin Klar. Ferić shot down Oblt. Hasso von Perthes of 3rd Staffel LG2, while Henneberg was responsible for the downing of either Oblt. Heinz Ebeling from 9th Staffel JG26 or Uffz. Wilhelm Schaaf from IInd Gruppe JG2.

This was just the beginning: The Polish 303 Squadron had only just started to gain its strength and to build its long-lasting history. The days to come simply proved how eager the 'Kościuszko' boys were to repay the Germans for what they had done a year ago. Air Chief Marshal Sir Hugh Dowding, then commander of RAF Fighter Command, later said:

'No. 303 Squadron operating from Northolt Aerodrome pulled its weight and more than its weight from its first day of operational flying, and I hope that its glorious record of success will never be forgotten, but will become a part of our history.'[14]

While this was a time to fight and claim victories, there was also time for relaxing and celebrations. Flying Officer Geoffrey Marsh, who spoke to the Poles and read their stories, has written a comprehensive history of the Polish pilots:

'In the evening the British Squadron Leader took the pilots to the X Hotel [most probably the Orchard Inn], where writes the chronicler, "our entrance enlivened all the company, especially when it was known that we had shot down six enemy aircraft. They tried to get us into the middle of the room, expressing their appreciation, but we did not wish to be made a spectacle of. Nevertheless, the general atmosphere was very pleasant – we really felt like being at home among our countrymen. We sang English songs and, of course, some of our own."'[15]

In the meantime, a telegram arrived from the Headquarters of No. 11 Group, saying:

> 'Group Commander sends congratulations to No. 303 Squadron on their excellent fighting this afternoon when they destroyed four [actually six] enemy aircraft without casualties to their own pilots or aircraft, which demonstrates good team work and straight shooting.'

This was immediately followed by salutations passed by Group Captain Vincent, commander of RAF Northolt: 'Magnificent fighting 303 Squadron. I am delighted. The enemy has been shown that Polish pilots are definitely on top.'

Despite many accounts claiming Vincent was rather unfavourable and suspicious of the Poles, in fact he loved them, spending his free time surrounded by this foreign legion: Kellett recalled:

> 'Throughout the Battle of Britain, many evenings were spent singing, playing various instruments, and socialising in the mess. Group Captain Stanley Vincent would often join in and a good time was had by all.'

Witold Urbanowicz confirms that the Poles also respected their boss: 'The Northolt Station Commander, Group Captain Stanley Vincent, a man of high culture, became a friend of the 303 crews; he highly valued and loved Poles.'

Chapter Eleven

Bloody September

Pilot Officer Władysław Gnyś, who had been impatiently waiting for his entry into the Battle of Britain at Leconfield, wrote: 'Göring had intensified the raids over England. We were well informed about the gallant fights of pilots of Number 11 Fighter Group and 303 Squadron, and individual Polish pilots in the English squadrons.'[1] But yet another group of Polish fighter pilots had completed their training and were now posted to the front-line airfields. Slim-built Flying Officer Paweł Niemiec, known to his friends as 'Poppet', a former pilot of 132nd Fighter Squadron and flying instructor of the PAF Training Centre, accompanied by Pilot Officer Tadeusz Kumiega, who had flown in Poland with 121st Fighter Squadron and then also joined the PAF Training Centre, were both posted to No. 17 Squadron at Tangmere in Sussex. 'I remember all three Polish officers,' Group Captain Leonard Bartlett wrote in 2006 (during the Battle of Britain he held the rank of Sergeant). In particular he said more about Niemiec: 'My impression was that he was very brave and above all a gentleman.'[2] Pilot Officer Ludwik Martel, better known as 'Zośka' (Sophie), a fighter pilot without combat experience, reported to the Hornchurch-based No. 54 Squadron, which was equipped with Supermarine Spitfires. Martel was given his unusual nickname by his pilot-colleagues after shouting out the name of his pre-war girlfriend while he was sleeping.

One of 54 Squadron's pilots, 22-year-old New Zealander with Irish roots Flying Officer Alan Deere, was there when Martel arrived and said:

> 'During those desperate days of 1940, we fighter pilots were proud of having a group of the Polish airmen attached to our ranks. Those serving in their own squadrons, as well as those individually posted to the British squadrons, did everything that was possible to strengthen the decimated ranks of Fighter Command. Their numerical participation in the Battle of Britain was small, but they compensated for it with their determination and skills, and as fighter pilots they proved themselves to be unrivalled. Great airmen, magnificent colleagues, indeed "some of the Few". Deliberately I do not mention names, as in my view, it would be flagrant to distinguish somebody; however, in my 54 Squadron RAF in the August of 1940 I had two young Poles, and although they were

heavily disabled by the language barrier, that separated them completely, like all other Poles, they never got lost when we "mixed up" with the enemy.'[3]

Pilot Off Marian Chełmecki, who was a pilot of 122nd Fighter Squadron and then an instructor at the Advanced Flying School, and Pilot Officer Zbigniew Nosowicz, a pilot of 131st Fighter Squadron and flying instructor at the PAF Training Centre, arrived at North Weald with their transfer to No. 56 Squadron. Both 17 and 56 Squadron flew Hurricanes. Flying Officer Zbigniew Kustrzyński, previously adjutant of the Pursuit Brigade, and Pilot Officer Janusz Maciński, veteran of 111th Fighter Squadron, travelled to Debden in Essex, where both reported to 111 Squadron flying Hurricanes. No. 111, a few years earlier, was famous for being the first fighter unit in the world flying eight-gun monoplanes. Sergeants Stanisław Duszyński and Józef Jeka joined Sergeant Marian Domagała and Pilot Officer Władysław Różycki at Middle Wallop's 238 Squadron. Duszyński, prior to arrival in Britain, served in 142nd Fighter Squadron before being posted to the Advanced Flying School in Ułęż, while Jeka had been in action in Poland with th 141st Fighter Squadron. Pilot Officer Witold Głowacki and Sergeant Jan Budziński were also moved from No. 145 to 605 'County of Warwick' Squadron flying Hurricanes.

The Polish pilots of No. 501 Sqn at RAF Kenley in October 1940. Seated from the left to right are: Sgt Konrad Muchowski (1st), Sgt Mieczysław Marcinkowski (2nd) and Plt Off Stanisław Skalski (4th). Flg Off Stefan Witorzeńć is standing 2nd from right.

The first day of September proved to be much less successful than the previous day, with only one Polish pilot having reason to celebrate another combat 'kill'. Pilot Officer Stanisław Skalski, the most successful pilot of the Polish Campaign, who had shown that his class and skills could easily be used far from his homeland, flew alongside his 501 colleagues when the squadron intercepted twenty-seven Messerschmitt Bf 110s. At 2.45 pm, the Pole, who was Yellow 2, sighted a group of enemy fighters that formed a defence circle over Tunbridge Wells. 'Skal' explained after his return:

> 'I dived down and up again, attacking one of the Me 110s from below. This left the circle and a dog-fight followed. The others attempted to get on my tail. I was forced to break off the engagement. The Me 110 that I attacked was smoking from the port engine and the gunner in the rear ceased fire.'

The next day was definitely much more eventful for the Poles serving in RAF squadrons and those who operated Hurricanes with the famous 'Kościuszko' badge. Unfortunately, the victor of the previous day's encounter had to taste the flavour of defeat for the first time in his life. In the early morning, 501 Squadron was scrambled and directed to protect the base. The Germans, however, passed them by, and undisturbed they were able to drop their bombs on Gravesend. Two of the Polish pilots were amongst those who engaged enemy bombers from KG3 and their escort consisting of Bf 109s from JG51 and JG53, followed by Bf 110s from ZG26, which showed up over Charing. Skalski, flying in Yellow Section, stated:

> 'I attacked an Me 109 over Ashford from astern, and he crashed near a Do which was shot down by F/O Witorzenc, and had landed in a road near Newchurch. Then I flew west of Lympne and I shot down a Me 109, which was attacking men working in a field. The Me 109 flew out low over the sea, and came down 3 or 4 miles south-east of Hythe. I force-landed near Sellindge with a pierced oil pipe, and my engine had stopped.'

Flying Officer Stefan Witorzeńć, No. 3 in Red Section, delivered a separate report which stated:

> 'I attacked two Me 109s over Charing when the squadron attacked the formation above the formation of bombers. The Me 109s climbed and formed into a defensive circle. Then I saw a Dornier flying SW over Ashford, and I attacked from astern, and finished my ammunition on him at close range. The Dornier emitted black smoke and dived steeply.'

Today, historians consider Lt Herbert Riegel and Obfw. Erich Kühlmann from the 3rd Staffel JG53 as potentially Skalski's victims. Both pilots were amongst those who failed to return from that day's mission.

In 303 Squadron's afternoon operation, four of its fighters, including Czechoslovak pilot Sergeant Josef František, who volunteered to join the Polish Air Force,[4] were successful. Eleven Hurricanes led by Flight Lieutenant Kent were sent up to intercept the Germans, who just bombed Eastchurch and the Short factory in Rochester. When the Hurricanes reached Dover, they were immediately attacked by Messerschmitt Bf 109s. The pair of 303 Squadron weavers, František and Sergeant Jan Rogowski, a Pole who had recently arrived from 74 Squadron, sighted the danger just in time. Rogowski later shared his combat experience:

'I was Green 3, rearguard. I saw 9 Me 109 approaching at 22,000 feet out of the sun to surprise us. I attacked the formation head on. The E/A broke up and scattered and dived towards France. I followed one and after the 4th burst his engine caught fire and he crashed into the sea about 10 miles from France.'

Flying Officer Zdzisław Henneberg, brother of the famous painter Hanna Henneberg – who also happened to be the first woman to obtain a pilot's licence in Warsaw and died in September 1934 after a gliding accident – took part in the fighting in Poland without success. Along with other instructors and pupils, Henneberg desperately tried to defend his beloved Dęblin, the nest of the Polish eaglets. His frustrations were now finally over as he flew an aircraft which was equal to those of the Germans. On 2 September 1940, he experienced an unexpected trip across the Channel, after which he wrote:

'I was Yellow 1. I saw a Me 109 at about 22,500 feet, 3,000 feet above me, near Dover. I climbed and chased one. After two bursts and a dive – I fired at about 150 yards – smoke and fire appeared from the starboard side of his engine. He dived and I again attacked, now eight miles inside France. At 3,000 ft I met heavy m.g. fire and light Flak, so I had to break off the attack and go home and could not see what happened to my enemy, but he was badly damaged.'

Another pilot of 303 Squadron, who as a result of the battle turmoil also ended up over France, was 'A' Flight's Pilot Officer Mirosław Ferić. 'Ox' undoubtedly had some thrilling moments, and told of his experience:

'The Me 109s somehow scattered in escape. And I, having selected one, decided to blow him away. I switched on the "emergency boost" and somehow started to close in on him, perhaps because the Jerry was twisting and turning his machine nervously. He turned his machine on its back and, to my surprise, performed a full roll. All this was happening in dive. At 250 metres I open fire, letting the Jerry know three times that his end is imminent. I repeated all manoeuvres after the Jerry, and since I am better at it, I get closer by 50 metres. From 200 metres I pour another burst over him. In a moment he should start to burn, but somehow he seems very hard – must be well armoured. I am shooting without deflection. We are both over the French coast. We have dived from 20,000 feet to 10,000. Here the Jerry has put his Me on its head, me after him, and I fire a burst. I am quite surprised by the darkness, or rather the eclipse of my windscreen. Needless to say, oil piping has given in and hence the tragedy. I break the chase, make a turn and go back to England.'

Ferić was on his own and almost defenceless, and recognized the real danger he was in when his exhaust started vomiting thick smoke. If this had happened over British soil, perhaps the Polish pilot would feel a little safer. Unfortunately his Hurricane was still far from home, flying over the Channel. He was lucky, though. While crossing the French coast, his altitude was still at 10,000 feet, and two of his colleagues flew from England to protect him: Flying Officer 'Paszka' Paszkiewicz and Pilot Officer 'Tolo' Łokuciewski. Rogowski then joined the team, and 'Ox' was eventually able to see patches of green land below his wings. He selected a large field, opened the undercarriage and with flaps down he landed, ending his very emotional and risky trip to France in English bushes near Dover.

The situation described above was something that kept 303 Squadron so successful yet integrated. Its pilots flew and lived almost like brothers, looking after each other with care and dedication. They celebrated victories together and together contemplated losses, when these eventually started to occur. The best place to release all the tension and emotions was the local Orchard Inn, since 1933 run by the Ansells family in Ruislip. Owned by a Polish-Jewish immigrant and located only a mile from Northolt, this 'heaven on Earth' was regularly visited by the Polish airmen throughout the Battle of Britain and later, as long as Polish fighter squadrons operated from there.[5] Pilot Officer Jan 'Donald' Zumbach wrote after the war:

'Every Pole who was based at Northolt has warm memories of that landlord, who never forgot to send a basket of fruit to the bedside of a wounded comrade. From the day we discovered the Orchard Inn our nervous depressions vanished; the part it played in lifting our spirits has a vital place in any story of the Polish airmen in Britain … Of course, it was the girls who, before anything else, kept us coming back to the Orchard Inn. They were pretty, easy-going and affectionate. They knew us all by our first names and cried real tears when one of us went missing.'[6]

Sergeant Eugeniusz Szaposznikow, known as 'Szaposzka' or 'Gen', also had very fond memories of the Orchard:

'While with 303 during the Battle of Britain we would spend many free evenings in The Orchard public house in Ruislip. They always made us feel so welcome at The Orchard, putting on a good spread for us, which we all appreciated. I spent many enjoyable evenings there with my friends from 303. We used to have our drinks ready for us on the bar as soon as we arrived. When the flight I was in was not on duty until the afternoon, the night before up to ten of us would squash into an old Ford or Squadron Leader Kellett's old Rolls Royce; we were often packed like sardines in a tin but it was worth it. We were told to drink plenty of milk. We had a large milk churn set up on one side of the bar which we would have our whisky topped up with, thus we were often seen to be drinking milk. Often on free evenings spent at The Orchard, by late evening or early morning we would be sleeping on the floor there. But always before 7 am the following morning we would be back at base ready for duty. You needed to have time to relax, as flying in the Battle of Britain was very hectic, and it was nice to have a few hours to chat with your friends socially. I lost many good friends in the Battle of Britain.'[7]

Non-Polish members of 303 Squadron had to prove themselves equal to their Slavic comrades when it came to drinking, which wasn't easy. It appears that only Flight Lieutenant Kent matched or even exceeded these unusual requirements of the Polish, and he evoked memories of fighting a terrible hangover:

'The party was quite fantastic but I managed to hold my own and at three o'clock in the morning the only two left on their feet were Johnny Zumbach, my number two, and myself – and I saw him to bed! This feat boosted my reputation with the Poles quite considerably.'[8]

If they were not in the Orchard, other supplies of alcohol were occasionally available. Surprizingly, this came from the top of the Polish military hierarchy.

303 Squadron's Hawker Hurricane I P3901 RF-E with the personal emblem of Donald Duck, which was usually flown by Plt Off Jan Zumbach. Later this officer used the Donald Duck motif on his personal Spitfires.

When 303 Squadron achieved its 100th victory, apart from greetings, General Sikorski sent a package consisting of ten bottles of whisky for his brave boys. Most probably due to its weight and contents, the airmen had to collect the package themselves.

Apart from the Polish internal hospitality, solidarity and loyalty shown during their time in exile, unlimited friendship, brotherhood and a tendency to celebrate together whatever and whenever possible, there were also some Polish pilots who appreciated the foreign yet somewhat challenging company of their British colleagues. Pilot Officer Ludwik Martel, although communicating only in basic English, found himself warmly treated and very much appreciated after joining an RAF squadron. All this despite his communication issues: 'I felt so happy amongst these comrades, I can honestly say that I never had such a relationship in my life … It is impossible to describe how charming they were, how kind.'[9] Martel was not alone in 54 Squadron. He was joined by Pilot Officer Walenty Krepski, a pre-war skiing enthusiast and graduate of the last entry of the Polish Air Force Officers College.

Sergeant Stefan Wójtowicz, at 21 years of age, was a big young man. Almost 6ft tall, the farmer's son from the small village of Wypnicha near Lublin, chose the love of his youth, flying, over agriculture, which was supposed to be his destiny. Despite his strong build, Wójtowicz was an intellectual type, an independent and rather romantic man of soft nature: he loved books and dreamt about being a pilot. His passion was supported and encouraged by his stepfather, who did whatever he could to help young Stefan pursue a military career. Stefan was a 111th Fighter Squadron veteran, who fought in the Polish Campaign, and after escaping to France he joined the fighter section led by his former chief, Major Zdzisław Krasnodębski. But it was only in England that he felt able to take revenge for the tragedy of 1939. Unfortunately his early days in combat flying, while serving with 303 Squadron, were not easy. On 3 September 1940 he found himself in a life-threatening situation:

'After climbing to 2,500 feet we found ourselves over Dover. We flew along the coast. On my right I noticed two machines that were definitely higher than us, flying towards the English Channel. As the closest, I pulled up my machine to the altitude of the aircraft flying above us and started to cut across their path. At closer distance I recognised the Me 109s. I performed final pre-firing checks, but my opponents must have noticed me too, as the first one executed a bunt, and the other went upwards. I saw F/O Henneberg close to the second one, so without much thought I went back after the first one. I started to fire at a very close distance. My first and second bursts were well aimed. My opponent started to smoke and went starboard into a climbing turn. I put my machine slightly to the starboard and pushed my trigger for the third and last burst of fire in this final attack. The guns fired, but at the same time my machine showered oil and a quite strong wind pushed me "boneshaker" away from its flightpath.'

Wójtowicz regained his nerve, as he realized that there would be another enemy behind him. He could not escape, however, as he noticed flames pouring out of the port side of his engine. His initial thought was to bail out, so he undid his harness and tried to jump out. However, his high speed pushed him back into the seat and held him inside the cockpit. When he finally managed to pull up his aircraft to reduce the speed, Wójtowicz realized that there was a dangerous-looking Channel beneath him. The Pole kept gliding towards land, hoping to reach English soil. Luckily, the flames on the engine went out and finally he was able to land in a fruit orchard near Tenderden in Kent, and was welcomed by soldiers of the army unit based at Woodchurch. His slight wounds excluded him from operational flying for the next three days,[10] during which time he could contemplate how close he had been to death.

'Dzidek' Henneberg, who had been seen by Wójtowicz, had his own troubles to deal with. Fighting with four Messerschmitts, his Hurricane was shot up and damaged in combat over the Channel, yet he managed to fly back to Northolt. Their story was described by the squadron's meticulous chronicler, Ferić, who exactly one year earlier, while fighting over Poland, was shot down himself and therefore knew what it was like to stare death in the face. It was one of the reasons why he documented moments of glory, danger and sadness on each page of his diary.

Also on 3 September, Pilot Officer Jerzy Solak had been posted to No. 151 Squadron at Digby in Lincolnshire. Solak, called 'George', an immediate translation of his Polish name, or 'Jersey' by his English colleagues, had a degree from the Civil Engineering Faculty of Lwów Technical University. Although had no combat experience, he knew the art of flying, as he was active in the local aero club and graduated from the PAF Reserve Cadet Officers School and participated in many flying competitions.

Wednesday 4 September brought more Polish victories, but also another loss. In the early morning, seven Hurricanes of 111 Squadron encountered a large formation of German bombers protected by Bf 109s. Five miles east of Folkestone, Flight Lieutenant Herbert Giddings, who led 'A' Flight, initiated a head-on attack while facing overwhelming air power from the enemy. Although his pilots claimed five victories and a further four enemy planes damaged, 22-year-old Flight Lieutenant David Bruce, 'B' Flight commander, was lost during this combat. Soon after, Pilot Officer Janusz Maciński was also shot down by one of the Messerschmitts. Despite the Polish pilot managing to bail out, he was ruthlessly attacked by a Bf 109 while descending by parachute. Two of his colleagues tried to protect him, but they were not able to save him from the German pilot's brutality. Maciński's body was never found. Such an event only fuelled Polish hatred and led to revenge, whenever possible.

After 1 pm, another combat took place in the area of Hastings and Littlehampton. When the Luftwaffe crossed the Channel, RAF fighters were ready and waiting for them with a welcoming party. Amongst the RAF pilots present at the scene, the Polish flyers distinguished themselves again while fighting Messerschmitt Bf 110s. Sergeant Szlagowski, flying as Red 3 of 234 Squadron, fired a one-second burst from 200 yards at one of the Bf 110s. The Pole did not have to wait long to observe the result of his action: the German dived steeply into the sea, making a spectacular splash. The Polish pilot continued the hunt, and using deflection and supported by a Spitfire from another unit, he shot down a Dornier Do 17 that went into the sea near Hove.

Airmen of No. 234 Squadron photographed at St Eval in August 1940. Two Polish pilots are standing in front of the port wing: Sgt Zygmunt Klein is wearing a forage cap whilst Sgt Józef Szlagowski has a peaked cap.

His colleague Sergeant Klein, who flew as Yellow 3, performed a head-on attack on a Bf 110, whose engine caught fire. The Pole broke away as another unidentified Spitfire attacked his victim from astern, giving his colleague a chance to have his input. When the Spitfire broke away, Klein repeated his action by attacking from astern, and soon after the Messerschmitt crashed to earth.

A third Pole who participated in this combat was Pilot Officer Oleński, who was Green 2. He fired a burst from the beam at 150 yards at a Bf 110, while he was hit himself. Oil poured straight onto his windscreen, causing visibility problems. Despite flying a damaged plane, with his view obscured by the thick patches of engine oil, Oleński noticed fire and smoke in the corner of a small wood that confirmed the fate of his victim. The Polish pilot was lucky not to share the fate of his opponent, landing 15 minutes after his colleagues.

Above Croydon, pilots of 253 Squadron spotted about twenty Zerstőrers when the Germans were bombing Brooklands, and they decided to intervene. Two Polish pilots claimed kills in this encounter. Pilot Officer Samoliński, who was No. 2 in Blue Section, followed his leader: 'I sighted a Me 110 Jaguar from 300-100 yards. I gave two bursts, each about 3 sec. I saw after the bursts a fire in the cockpit and the plane turned left into a dive.' Samoliński wasn't sure what happened to the enemy, as he went up to join the other aircraft of his squadron. Pilot Officer Nowak, flying as Green 3, reported an encounter with another Bf 110: 'I sighted a Me 110 from 200-150 yards. One burst of 3 seconds and later I observed smoke from the fuselage. The Me 110 Jaguar dived down and crashed.'

No. 601 Squadron was scrambled at 1.12 pm from Tangmere to face Luftwaffe aircraft on their way back to France. While over Worthing, Flying Officer Jankiewicz saw his chance:

'I broke away and attacked a Me 110, which climbed and turned. I gave him many bursts at very close range, and saw something fly out of the cockpit. He then turned on his back and dived steeply, upside down, for the sea.'

Unfortunately, Jankiewicz's day was about to turn sour:

'At the same time I received a burst of fire from the starboard side. Glycol and oil filled the cockpit and the gravity tank caught fire. I was then SW of Worthing. After a short time (a few seconds) the fire stopped, and I glided towards land.'

Slightly wounded, Jankiewicz, with his engine off, landed in the safety of Goring by the Sea, just avoiding a high tension transmission cable and telephone lines.

The next day, Krasnodębski's pilots had another opportunity to increase the total score of their squadron, but yet again the Germans proved difficult to fight and to destroy. However, before they took off from Northolt, another Polish pilot was involved in combat. 'Skal' Skalski from 501 Squadron experienced a rather unpleasant rendezvous with Heinkels and their fighter cover. When the 501 pilots tried to get into the bomber formation, Messerschmitts Bf 109s were right on their tails. Skalski, who reported later that he shot down two of the German fighters and one Heinkel He 111, met his match, recalling later:

'We attacked over the Channel, and I saw four Messerschmitts attacking us. I just switched the radio and said: one-oh-nines from back. At this moment I had to turn back to spoil their attack on my squadron. At some moment Messerschmitts climbed in a chandelle, and I do not know how, I found myself on the tail of a Messerschmitt. It was at an altitude of 24,000 feet, 8,000 meters. I gave a short burst, seemingly I hit the tank, because the aircraft immediately went ablaze and spun down.

'Relaxed, I reached for a map, which we tucked in our flying boots, to establish a more exact position of its crash, which I had to provide later in the report. But before I managed to have a look at it, a wall of fire fell on me. In the next split second I noticed a Messerchmitt jumping from below, straight under my nose. I did not know where it came from. He must have caught me from behind and fired a long burst, so it went through the reserve tank, below the seat – bullets bruised the thigh of my right leg – into the instrument panel. The wall of fire which fell on me was the burning fuel from the reserve tank. I was leaving the tank full until the end on purpose, in belief that empty, with petrol vapour only, it was much more dangerous. This time the load of lead pumped by the German into the tank was too big to just cause a small leak. A spark must have appeared somewhere, which turned the fuel into a torch. I flew in short gloves, because the morning was warm, and without goggles, as usual. Eyes and hands were therefore the most vulnerable in the first moments after the explosion. I let go of the controls, covered my eyes with my left hand and unstrapped with the right, wrenched the radio plug, which tied me into the plane, and opened the canopy. The sudden blow of air kindled the raging flames even more. Everything was burning, including my face, hands, clothes. I tried to lift off my seat, but I could not get up more than an inch. The aircraft must have dived down to earth like a stone, as the centrifugal force pressed me into the seat. I grabbed the side of the cockpit, and finally managed to get my head out of the cockpit.

'How I found myself at some point outside the plane – I do not know …Probably with some turn of the aircraft, a slipstream sucked me out of the cockpit, when I was slightly tucked away. I must have hit the fuselage or tail, as it later turned out that I had a bruised right side, especially the elbow and knee.

'The first thing I remember of what happened after bailing out of the plane, was that I was on fire. I did not know at what altitude I was, but I realized that the parachute must not be opened until the flames disappeared. I acted like a robot for some time – I did everything I should, but I do not remember anything. I began to record the full sequence of events only at a height of 200-300 metres above the ground. I was already hanging onto the parachute and there was no fire. I ripped off my face an oxygen mask – along with the skin – because it was quite fried, and I even started to control the parachute by shroud lines. I landed in beets and almost immediately a police patrol car arrived – it was the area of the most frequently conducted dog-fights, so that there was always something falling down on those fields. When they lifted me up … I had no shoes nor socks, and my trousers were only the waist and remains of pantlegs at the top. The uniform was charred, "Mae West" lifejacket burnt, hands – where my gloves ended – burnt, and my face was of the colour of roasted pig, liberally sprinkled with the sauce of my own blood leaking from wounds after the ripped mask.'[11]

After landing in Benenden, he ended up in Herne Bay hospital, where he was taken badly wounded and burnt. According to Skalski's after-war recollections, he was visited there by Sergeant James 'Ginger' Lacey, his squadron mate, to whom he admitted to shooting down two Messerschmitts and one Heinkel, but this message did not go any further and the Polish pilot was eventually credited with just one Bf 109 shot down, probably as it was written in his wartime notes.

It wasn't until 2 pm that the British radar stations started to pick up signals of German planes approaching again. At 2.40 pm, 303 Squadron was airborne, led by its commander, Kellett. One of the Luftwaffe formations, which consisted of Heinkels of KG53 and Messerschmitt 109s from JG54, were spotted by Kellett and his Polish boys over Thameshaven. 'Dyzio' claimed two Messerschmitts: one shot down and another probably destroyed. Flight Lieutenant Forbes also reported the probable destruction of a Junkers Ju 88 that was eventually confirmed as a full victory. Czechoslovakian pilot Sergeant František managed to add one Ju 88 and a Bf 109 to his official score, despite returning to base in a damaged Hurricane.

Meanwhile, Flying Officer Wacław Łapkowski, one of the most experienced pilots of his squadron, who fought in Poland alongside the Pursuit Brigade, found himself in a life-threatening situation. The 26-year-old officer reported later:

'I at once made a second attack, firing at 150 yards and closing from above. Both engines were set on fire, and e/a began to dive. At this time I saw the aircraft at which F/Lt Forbes had fired falling in such a great cloud of smoke that the aircraft became invisible. I am quite certain that this aircraft was destroyed.'

Łapkowski didn't get much time to contemplate the state of the enemy aircraft as he was in trouble himself:

'Then I was shot by a cannon from behind. My engine caught fire. I turned over on to shoulder. I was also burnt in the face and left leg. I came down near Rochford, Southend, and was taken to Rochford Hospital.'

His Hurricane, which he bailed out from, crashed at Bonvills Farm in North Benfleet.[12] 'On this occasion,' he wrote soon after to his colleague while recovering in Torquay Hospital, 'I was burnt a little bit and unpleasantly broke my left arm next to the shoulder joint. Now everything is almost fine. I will probably return to my Flight in the next two weeks.'

Two of the squadron's NCOs had good reason to be happy. Sergeant Stanisław Karubin reported:

> 'I attacked a Me 109 with two short bursts. It went down, burning. I escaped upwards as I was attacked by a Me 109. It was run over by Hurricanes and went down smoking badly – me behind him. We descended to tree-top height. I hit the "boost". I closed onto him, firing several bursts. The Me was still running. This made me nervous and I fired a burst of my last rounds. The Jerry was running. This made me even more angry and I decided to finish him off. I gave a "boost" again, got very close to him and ran a "razor" over him. The Jerry's scared mug flashed before my eyes. This very moment he hit the ground, squirting smoke with lumps of soil.'

Karubin's patience, or rather impatience, eventually paid off with two Bf 109s claimed by him.

His colleague from the same Red Section, Sergeant Kazimierz Wünsche, had similar frustrations and also a lot to say when examined by the squadron chronicler:

> 'One Me 109 immediately got onto the commander's tail. Without thinking I came to the rescue at once. The distance between the commander and me was some 200 metres. Suddenly a Me 109 flew between us. I opened fire. The rounds kept going and going, but resulted in nothing. I moved full ahead, to reduce the distance between us, and made a curtain of rounds in front of the Messerschmitt. I could feel the relief when I saw him going through these rounds. That was a terrible picture.'

Wünsche was credited with the destruction of the Bf 109.

About forty-five minutes later, one more Polish pilot upgraded his combat score. Pilot Officer Janusz Żurakowski was flying as No. 2 in Blue Section of 234 Squadron, which was patrolling over Gravesend. Suspicious enemy activity had been noticed over the Thames Estuary. Before reaching the formation, that was returning to France, 234's Spitfires came under sudden attack from Messerschmitts. Żurakowski, though, from being hunted, very quickly became a hunter and approached one of the German fighters from astern. 'I gave a short burst from 100 yards,' he told his Intelligence Officer.

'He half rolled and dived and flew very low due south. I stayed on his tail firing one 3-seconds burst at 120 yards, and then the rest of my ammunition from very close. He crossed the coast near Hastings. After my first attack he was smoking slightly and later heavily. The enemy pilot pulled open his hood as the machine landed on the sea. The pilot got out and 2 minutes later a/c sank.'

It is believed that it was Fw. Anton Ochsenkühn from 9th Staffel JG53 who was attacked by Żurakowski. The German pilot spent the rest of the war as a PoW.

The following day almost ended in tragedy for the 'Kościuszko' pilots. When the Germans started bombing fuel tanks near Thameshaven in Essex, No. 303 Squadron, which was scrambled at 8.40 am, was still climbing towards the bombers at low speed and altitude, therefore their position was very much disadvantaged. It is disputable now whether it was the late alert that sent 303 Squadron into battle in a hurry, or Squadron Leader Kellett's thoughtless and reckless decision that led to disaster. Nevertheless, Kellett admitted after the fight that it was the biggest formation he had ever seen before. According to Kellett, the wave of enemy machines covered an area of 20 miles by 5 miles. The British commander even reported seeing some 'four-engine aircraft' among the raiders, when the Germans never used any such planes.

The German fighters, which were protecting their bombers, were ready for action and immediately showed their deadly intent and great skills. Over Sevenoaks they fell like a avalanche right onto the 'Kościuszko' boys necks. Kellett, although claiming one bomber shot down, was slightly wounded and, having practically all the fabric shot off the rear of his aircraft, immediately landed at Biggin Hill.

Sergeant Stanisław Karubin, who followed his British commander, also shared his fate. While attacking the bombers, his Hurricane was hit by return fire and crash-landed at Fletchers Farm in Pembury, Kent. Slightly wounded, Karubin was taken to the local hospital. He did claim his victory, though, and was credited with a Heinkel He 111. The third pilot of Kellett's Section was Sergeant Wünsche, who had more luck and showed greater caution before entering the fight. At least he took one more second to look around: watching carefully two Messerschmitts that were attacking a single Hurricane, he decided to attack one of them. 'One broke away and I banked round and gave four bursts at the Me which was firing at the Hurricane,' he wrote.

'The Hurricane went down out of control, and the Messerschmitt went down after it in flames. I turned right, thinking the other Messerschmitt was on my tail but I could not see it. A Messerschmitt then attacked me head-on and we turned round each other. After 1½ turns I was on its tail and gave him two long bursts and ran out of ammunition. I hit the engine, and the Messerschmitt broke off with thick black smoke pouring from the engine. I circled round a British pilot who had bailed out, and saw him land safely.'

Wünsche was credited with one Bf 109 shot down and another probable kill.

This day was a case of déjà vu for the Polish commander. On 3 September 1939, Krasnodębski had been shot down in combat over Poland and bailed out with slight burns. On his way down he was brutally attacked and shot by a German fighter. Despite this, he was able to continue to command his unit. But a year later it was a completely different story, as he wrote:

'Suddenly the glass of the clocks shatters, the tank is riddled with bullets – burning petrol is pouring out. The whole cockpit is filled with fire. I want to bail out as quickly as possible, but cannot unfasten my harness. There's a short moment of surrender. But the will to live wins. Finally I unfasten the belts, open the cockpit, the door and bail out. Remembering the sad experience from Poland, I do not open my parachute to leave the combat area as fast as possible and to not be a target. After a while I decide to open the parachute, but here is another problem: when abandoning the machine my parachute has shifted and I cannot find the ripcord, and the ground is coming fast. At last I find the ripcord and pull. There's a strong jolt – sudden peace and quiet, only the sounds of battle coming from above. After a moment I heard a machine approaching, and thought of history repeating itself. Fortunately it was a Hurricane which protected me down to the ground. I later learned that it was Witek Urbanowicz, who at first took me for a German and intended to reverse the direction of my journey. Coming to the ground I thought that would be the end of my adventures, but it was not, as silhouettes of Homeguardians, with their guns ready to fire, started to emerge out of houses and bushes, looking to have some sport with a German paratrooper, but the calm Englishmen kept their nerves and did not fire. From the place where I landed I was taken to East Grinstead Hospital, where as a patient of famous surgeon McIndoe [Archibald McIndoe, a doctor and pioneer of plastic surgery] and under the solicitous care of nice nurses I returned to health and after less than one year I was able to fly again.'[13]

Flying Officer 'Kobra' Urbanowicz, who didn't yet know that he was about to replace Krasnodębski as squadron commander, was also in the centre of the fight:

Although No. 303 Squadron officially adopted the "Kościuszko" badge, which linked this unit directly to its roots as 7th, 121st and finally 111th Fighter Squadron back in Poland, apparently the artwork shown here may suggest that it was only "A" Flight that adorned this historic symbol, while" B" Flight used a "Salamander" or winged lizard, which previously appeared on some of the 112th Fighter Squadron aircraft. To make the puzzle more complicated, the latter commonly used a "Fighting Cockerel" to distinguish their aircraft. This practice can be confirmed only during the pre-war period, as no such photos taken during the Polish Campaign are known to exist. Instead there are at least three pictures of 112's aircraft taken by the Germans, where a silhouette of a lizard is visible.

'I saw Me 109s and Hurricanes flying across from left to right on each others' tails. One Me 109 then attacked me from starboard. We had a short dog-fight. I fired for 3 or 4 seconds at 200 yards. The engine caught fire and the enemy aircraft fell vertically to earth.'

Although Urbanowicz again had the chance to claim another victory, his encounter with three Bf 109s ended up unresolved.

Not far away, Pilot Officer 'Ox' Ferić, who wasn't happy with the outcome of the morning fight and complained about gaps in RAF tactics and the lack of squadrons that were sent against such a huge formation of German planes, also used his few seconds wisely:

'During the dog-fight that happened over South-East of England, where we could feel the fear, a situation occurred that a plane with the crosses [a German] appeared in a right turn, showing himself. In my gunsight for a split second, I made a correction, gave a relatively short burst and to my surprise Jerry immediately caught fire, gliding in a sad nosedive towards the earth. Its pilot did not bail out.'

While Sergeant František, known for his blusterous character, claimed a Bf 109, B Flight commander Flight Lieutenant Forbes added two Bf 109s to his score (one destroyed and another probably shot down) before he was in trouble himself. His section was unable to reach the bombers, and furthermore he lost contact with Kellett. His Hurricane was successfully targeted by one of the Messerschmitts, whose pilot was aiming at Forbes' fuel tank. The German bullets went straight into his windscreen, and Forbes noticed that the 28 gallon tank received a direct hit, causing an immediate leak: 100 octane aviation spirit started pouring right onto his face. Forbes, despite being wounded, managed to keep decent control of his plane and crash-landed.

His wingman, Sergeant Rogowski, was wounded in the leg during the action and admitted to hospital. This was the first time that 303 Squadron had been under such a disastrous attack and suffered heavy losses. The unit had brave and skilful pilots, yet in the face of a dominating Luftwaffe and tactical mistakes and flaws, they appeared to be only human beings, as vulnerable as their RAF colleagues.

Half an hour later, No. 601 Squadron flew over Redhill where its pilots sighted about fifty Messerschmitt Bf 109s of JG2. They made a similar mistake to the Polish squadron. When 601's Hurricanes started to climb and were unable to engage, they were immediately attacked by another group of German planes. Pilot Officer Juliusz Topolnicki, who flew as Red 3, was one of the victims of this sudden turn of events. He provided the squadron's Intelligence Officer with a detailed report:

'When over Staplehurst at 20,000 ft I sighted 2 Me 109s behind me, flying at 20,000 ft in a westerly direction, in close formation. I informed Red

1 and broke away to attack them from behind. I carried out astern and quarter attacks. Black smoke came from the e/a's engine and he dived steeply with smoke increasing. In the meantime I had been wounded by what appeared to be splinters and therefore did not observe the e/a crash. After making sure that my Hurricane was quite under control, I observed the other Me 109 below and in front. I delivered a beam attack at point blank range after diving down on him, following up with a stern attack and fired many short bursts. I then saw another plane coming up from behind me who also attacked the Me 109. My engine then started to miss and I could not keep up, but almost immediately I saw the e/a climbing and the pilot bailed out. I then turned to fly back to base, but when near Sutton Valence I received what appeared to be a burst of machine-gun fire in the engine and past the cockpit and on looking up saw a/c milling around high overhead. My Hurricane then went out of control and I was obliged to bail out.'

Topolnicki, called 'Julek' by his family, landed on top of a tree near Sutton Valence in Kent and became the subject of intensive interest for local people. After visual assessment followed by verbal investigation, the villagers decided that he was a German. Their suspicions were supported by his rather limited English, and only the intervention of Mrs Sergison, a local housewife, and a forester named Brown saved him from the 'warm hospitality' of angry folk. Topolnicki was taken to hospital at Leeds Castle before returning to his squadron five days later The Hurricane he flew on 6 September crashed at Boycourt Farm. His victim, Lt Max Himmelheber of Stab./JG2, bailed out wounded, while his Messerschmitt plunged into the ground at Plum Tree Farm in Headcorn.[14]

Ten minutes later, No. 234 Squadron was performing a reconnaissance mission vectored east of Brooklands in Surrey, when its pilots noticed at least fifteen Dornier Do 17s with their fighter cover of thirty Messerschmitt Bf 109s. Despite the quantitative advantage of the Germans, 234's pilots flew towards them with the intention to break the approaching group. Pilot Officer Janusz Żurakowski, who flew as No. 2 of Blue Section, was amongst six flyers who returned with at least one Bf 109 destroyed each. In fact, Squadron Leader Joseph O'Brien and Sergeant Alan Harker both claimed a double confirmed victory. Żurakowski, although receiving some German bullets in his wing, shot down Gefr. Biecker of 7th Staffel JG26, whose Messerschmitt crashed at Swamp Farm in Old Romney. The Polish pilot described his combat:

'Attacked a Me 109 in front of the bombers from the front and from a beam. He holed my wing. He went over on his back, dived and I followed him. He climbed and went on his back again: fired second burst, and third burst and he crashed.'

For Żurakowski, the action was not over yet: 'Three Me 109s attacked me at 3,000 ft. I saw close formation of Me 109s in southerly direction, far away.'

To save his life, the Pole spiralled down to pretended that he was already hit and eliminated from combat. Returning to Middle Wallop in one piece but on fuel fumes, 'Zura' could not fully lower the undercarriage and his Spitfire overturned on landing, damaging the machine. After unfastening his harness, he fell from the aircraft, landing on his head, but fortunately his leather flying helmet protected him. 'I looked at the aircraft,' Żurakowski recalled in his memoirs written after the war. 'The wing and undercarriage were damaged by the cannon bullets, and there were a few holes in the wings from small calibre bullets.'[15]

In the afternoon, a formation of Heinkel He 111s bombed fuel tanks at Thameshaven. In response, shortly after 5 pm several RAF squadrons and three aircraft from the Polish No. 303 were sent over the area to intercept the German heavies. Flying Officer Wojciech Januszewicz, who took off late from Northolt, joined No. 1 Canadian Squadron and chased after his colleagues. When over Lenham in Kent, the Canadians caught up with the raiders, and according to Flight Lieutenant Kent's recollections, Januszewicz shot down one Bf 110, although there is no confirmation of such a claim. Januszewicz's aircraft was damaged in combat and he had to force land. The Polish pilot became a local celebrity after being hosted by the Vinson family at Boughton Palace, Boughton Malherbe, and having a few glasses of whisky with them. Knowing the natural ability of Poles to absorb more alcohol without side-effects than other nations, the question 'who gave up first?' remains a mystery.

However, the locals reminisced about that day differently. According to them, the Polish pilot came down at the private tennis club. Their story, that breaks conventions and in a comical way enlightens the etiquette of the time, was told in a typically English manner:

"'Archibald, look, look, one of those Germans is coming down, surely he won't land here, it's private property!" But he did, parachute and all, in a tree by the ladies' dressing-room, where he remained hanging. "Look here, we'll go to the foot of the tree and ask him who he is. If he is a German, we'll leave him up there and phone Police Constable Snotgrass. If he is one of ours, we'll cut him down and give him tea." So they moved over to the tree and shouted up. "Hullo, there! Who are you? Suid sie Allemanish or whatever it is? You know – sie wissen was I mean?

Understanden sie?" "Ask him if he is a Nazi," said the wife triumphantly. "Suid sie Nazi?" "Bloody fools Nazis," came directly from the branches. "Me Polish man!" "Oh, good chap, bloody good chap," said the doggy man, "let him down." Then my sister's father-in-law had an idea and the three whispered together. "But he's not a member," objected the wife. "To hell with that," said her husband vigorously. So they cut him down. "Do you play tennis?" he asked, and the airman replied, "Pardon, yes, thank you. I am quite alright." So they lent some white flannels and took him to the gentleman's dressing-room. When the R.A.F. car came for him, the remaining three staggered to deck chairs. They'd never had such a game. The wife gasped: "Such a nice man, so strong, and how polite!" In the club minutes you can read: "August 23rd [sic],[16] Polish Officer introduced by Mr and Mrs ..." That's how a Pole came to this little town and entered the English Holy of Holies, a lawn tennis club which was strictly closed to all but "nice people". This was the Battle of Britain. "Of course we made him a non-paying member for life, so he's certain to give us another game some day, though between you and me his game's a bit fast for people of my age."[17]

Whether this story of tennis club members being in a quandary by allowing the Pole into the club without being a member, and of being such sticklers for the rules, was true or not, it confirms the short message that was received at Northolt afterwards. It said: 'When Poland is free, come to England and see us. Good luck.' This is how the Vinsons wrote to Januszewicz once he was back at his base. This was followed by another portion of compliments, though not addressed to Januszewicz only, describing more serious matters. Letters from 11 Group, then from Hugh Dowding of Fighter Command himself and eventually from the Air Ministry arrived at Northolt the following day, praising the exploits of the Poles in the air, rather than their achievements on the social scene: 'Great fighting yesterday, with grand results. Yet again well done.'

Chapter Twelve

Turning Point

The pilots of Air Vice Marshal Keith Park, commander of No. 11 Group RAF responsible for fighter defence in south-east England, were truly exhausted, their airfields suffering frequent attacks, badly damaged or destroyed and the whole defence system on its knees and close to breaking point. If only Luftwaffe chief Hermann Göring had realized how little needed to be done to wipe out Fighter Command and smash their capacity of fighting back, he would surely have pushed his airmen, experienced in battles over Spain, Poland and France, for one more decisive push. To do so, he had to convince his boss. The Luftwaffe's superiority at that time was undoubtable, but ironically, Hitler and his commanders did not fully understand this situation or have the right assessment. They made various mistakes, one of which was a lack of appreciation of Fighter Command's determination. Convinced that the British were defenceless, the Germans were astonished by the RAF's ability to fight back. This was despite results of an judgement provided by strategists, who optimistically delivered a verdict that Fighter Command had neither the pilots nor aircraft to continue the battle. Inconclusive reports led to stagnation, and therefore Hitler and Göring wasted time.

The first week of September 1940 could easily have been decisive in securing the German invasion of Britain and then victory, if one silly mistake could have been avoided. German bombers started dropping their deadly loads on London, making Churchill even more determined to stand firm against all odds. The affront of targeting the capital was more than the Prime Minister could tolerate, and eventually turned the whole direction of the conflict. German territory then became an objective too for the RAF's bombers. After Bomber Command took their revenge by striking at targets in his own country, Hitler ordered constant attacks against the British capital, up to now a forbidden aim for his Luftwaffe.

The idea of softening the morale of islanders by bombing was truly a stupid move, based on poor knowledge of the souls of the British people. They were not even close to giving up. Germany's brutal move against civilians, although changing the perception of the war, at the same time gave the RAF a breather, the chance and time to regroup and the possibility of changing its tactics. Fast Messerschmitt Bf 109s on many occasions became largely escort aircraft for bombers heading for London, and as such lost their previous deadly elements of surprise, flexibility and range. Despite the Luftwaffe being far from losing the game, historians consider this point as the beginning of a new phase of the Battle of Britain.

Walenty Krepski, also known as 'Walik', passionately loved climbing the hills in his neighbourhood, and with a rucksack on his back and skis attached to his feet, spent countless hours in beautiful areas near Wilno. When he decided to join the Polish Air Force his mother was very upset; she had already lost her husband, and now her only son had chosen a dangerous life path. When war broke out he was at the Air Force Cadet Officers School in Dęblin, from where he graduated rather more quickly than expected. He missed the opportunity to fight in Poland, so after arriving in Britain Krepski was eager to fly. After his 54 Squadron had been moved from Hornchurch to Catterick and soon after to Hartlepool, County Durham, he was awaiting his chance for his first operational flight.

Such an order came on 7 September, when alongside two of his squadron mates, the Polish pilot took off at 1.20 pm for a short patrol and then, after landing, was quickly airborne again at 1.40 pm. Only Pilot Officers Henry Matthews and John Hart returned, and unfortunately Pilot Officer Walenty Krepski was never seen again. The 54 Squadron Operations Record Book provides some details of this sad day and sheds some light on the last minutes of his life:

> 'P/O Krepski was reported missing during an operational flight in the Whitby area. When his section was vectored home no R/T response could be obtained from him. It is thought that he sighted and followed an enemy aircraft and then lost his way. His very limited English vocabulary was certainly a contributory factor in this unlucky and regretted mishap.'

Some vague details of his death can be obtained from a book written by Air Commodore Alan Deere, who was then a Flying Officer in 54 Squadron, who described the circumstances of Krepski's loss:

> 'I had an odd experience during one of the very few scrambles from Greatham. I intercepted a Junkers 88 near Whitby but before I could fire a shot, and after he had dropped his bomb, the pilot sought the safety of the clouds and headed off eastwards out to sea. There was absolutely no point in trying to ferret him out of the cloud, so I orbited in the vicinity awaiting orders from Control. My number two, a Polish pilot who had but recently joined the squadron and was seeing his first German aircraft

since his arrival in England, had tasted blood and could not be restrained. He shot into cloud after the Hun, despite my orders to the contrary, and was never seen nor heard of again. A plot was followed from the position where they both entered cloud until the track was lost about forty miles off the coast. I suspect the Pole just flew on, further and further out to sea and discovered too late that he was short of petrol and out of R/T range. Perhaps he got the Junkers in the end, but I doubt it. Like many similar incidents during the war, his disappearance remains a mystery.'[1]

Krepski was not the only loss the PAF suffered on this day, but was definitely the most tragic. No. 303 Squadron claimed fourteen enemy aircraft destroyed and a

A group photo of 303 Sqn personnel with their new Polish commander Sqn Ldr Urbanowicz (sitting in the middle in Mae West). Please note that some of the Polish airmen still wore French AF leather jackets. As both Flying Officers Paszkiewicz and Januszewicz are missing from the photo and Sgt František still can be seen, it would be right to assume that the photo was taken after Januszewicz's death (5 October) and before František's tragic accident (8 October). Seated in chairs from left to right: u/i, u/i, Flg Off Hughes (Education Officer), Flg Off Wacław Wiórkiewicz (Engineering Officer), Plt Off Jan Zumbach, Flg Off Dr Zygmunt Wodecki (Medical Officer), Flg Off Marian Pisarek, Flt Lt John Kent, Flg Off Witold Żyborski (Polish Adjutant), Sqn Ldr Ronald Kellett, Sqn Ldr Witold Urbanowicz, Flt Lt Athol Forbes, Flg Off Zdzisław Henneberg, Flg Off David Upton (RAF Adjutant) Flg Off Jarosław Giejsztoft (Polish Intelligence Officer), Plt Off Bogusław Mierzwa, Flg Off Bohdan Grzeszczak, Flg Off Jerzy Palusiński and Plt Off Mirosław Ferić. Sgt Josef František is sitting on the ground between Urbanowicz and Kellett. In the third row standing from the right are: Flg Off Joseph Walters (Interpreter, 2nd), Flg Off Edward Hadwen (RAF Intelligence Officer, 3rd), Sgt Stanisław Karubin (12th), Sgt Marian Bełc (14th), Sgt Eugeniusz Szaposznikow (16th), Sgt Jan Rogowski (17th).

further six probably shot down for the price of two of their own pilots wounded and another shot down. Ten of their Hurricanes plus one borrowed from No. 1 Canadian Squadron took off from Northolt at 4.20 pm. Flight Lieutenant Athol Forbes and Flying Officer Urbanowicz, the new yet temporary Polish commander, were leading them, while Squadron Leader Kellett was recovering from his recent wounds. The Germans crossed the English coast near Dungeness in Kent and Beachy Head in Sussex, and flew on towards London. On their way they were attacked by various RAF squadrons, but the British could not prevent the bombers from a successful attack on factories in Woolwich.

The 'Kościuszko' pilots were much careful than the day before, understanding that it would be impossible to make a successful attack while climbing. When they noticed the German rearguard clashing with Spitfires, they went straight for the bombers: they were 'easy meat', according to Forbes. They were, indeed! Moreover, the Dorniers were making a turn, and therefore even more vulnerable.

Forbes shot down a Dornier Do 17, but shortly after a shell hit his starboard wing root and exploded. Having at least three glycol and hydraulic system leaks and a wounded leg, Forbes returned home. Urbanowicz continued the fight, later writing:

'I attacked one Do-215, which left the formation. I gaive short bursts from a distance of about 100 metres. In my whole body I can feel that my aircraft is slightly slowing down after each burst. I can hear my own shots, they sound like raindrops hitting an umbrella. Both [German] engines caught fire, the bomber crew was bailing out, the aircraft was burning like a torch, without control falling down on its back. Suddenly at my height I noticed two Messerschmitts 109 with white painted muzzles. I attacked the right, closest one. I gave him several bursts before he started emitting smoke. At the same time, another Me 109 with a yellow muzzle jumped at me like thunder from the sky. Bullets traced passed very close to my cockpit. Instinctively I broke out in some weird pirouette, ending on my back. I felt strong tension of my facial muscles, my vision darkened. When I managed to put my plane back to a normal position, the Messerschmitt had disappeared.'[2]

Urbanowicz landed at Detling in Kent, where he refuelled and headed back to Northolt.

Forbes' wingman, Pilot Officer Jan Daszewski, who was Blue 2, had only seconds to celebrate his success after shooting down one Dornier Do 17 and probably another. He was targeted by one of the escort's Messerschmitt Bf 109s, which set his Hurricane on fire. Daszewski was severely wounded in the thigh, but still strong enough and conscious to escape the cockpit. His aircraft crashed at Canterbury Gate near Selsted in Kent, while its pilot landed nearby. Soon after, 'Długi Joe' was admitted to Waldershire Hospital in Kearnsay, and did not return to his squadron until December 1940.

Flying Officer Zdzisław Henneberg, flying as Red 1, scored one Bf 109 destroyed and a second probably shot down, although he had attempted to attack the Dorniers. 'Dzidek' reported:

> 'My engine began to falter and I fell back a little where I was engaged by three Me 109, my engine now working normally. After a few seconds one began to smoke, but I had to break away as I was being attacked from the rear. I climbed and met another formation of Me 109s. I attacked from the rear and after firing two bursts saw the enemy aircraft burst into flames and fall to earth.'

Flying Officer Paszkiewicz also had a lucky day. Flying as Green 1, he shot down one Dornier that crashed to earth in flames. Straight after he went for a second bomber and kept pressing the trigger until he ran out of ammunition. Some of his bullets hit the target as both engines of the enemy aircraft were put out of action. 'Tolo' Łokuciewski could also be proud of his afternoon's work, claiming his first victory in a Hurricane. Green 2 reported to Flying Officer Edward Hadwen, an Intelligence Officer:

> 'Before I had the time to attack mine, Paszka's Dornier was already on fire. Mine started to burn too, and finally burst like a bubble of soap water. After this success I took to another one. I fired a few bursts. He started to smoke, but an Me 109 prevented me from further attacks, so I broke to one side and spotted two Me 109s on my starboard, creeping up to me. I made such a dive that I finished at the aerodrome.'

Flying Officer Marian Pisarek, Green 3, the veteran and last commander of 141st Fighter Squadron, who had at least two aerial victories in Poland under his belt, could not share 'Tolo's' excitement. Despite destroying one enemy plane, he was also involved in a horrific accident, being partially responsible for a tragedy on the ground where innocent people lost their lives. He described later what happened:

> 'Below to our port a battle was going on too. I decided to go there. And suddenly an aeroplane with a swastika on its tail appeared in front of me.

I had advantage of height, so I attacked it with no difficulty from behind and above. I noticed flames bursting from it. This was a Me 109. But after a moment I got a series of strikes from behind myself, and my Hurricane started to smoke heavily and to go into a dive. I unfastened the belts and took off my headgear. At this moment I was thrown out of the cockpit, as the aeroplane was nearly on its back.'

Tragically, Pisarek's Hurricane crashed directly onto an air raid shelter in a garden in Roding Road at Loughton in Essex, killing three civilians inside.[3]

Yellow 2 was Pilot Officer Jan Zumbach, a Pole with strong Swiss roots thanks to his grandfather, a wealthy grain trader, who emigrated to Poland at the end of the nineteenth century. Although Zumbach was born in Poland as a Polish citizen, his connection with the country of his ancestors remained tight throughout his life. His close friends called him 'a larger than life character, a loyal friend who lived life to the full'. On 7 September, 'Johann', as he was known amongst his comrades, claimed his first victories, which eventually led him towards 'ace' status:

'Under me I saw a Do 17, or a Do 215 that had left the formation. I got onto his tail. At this moment the Adolffie squirted a short burst at me. It was short, as apparently with my first rounds his soul was hitting the Land of Eternal Ghosts, into the arms of the good Manitou. The second burst did not bring any results. It took the third, very long one, to leave his starboard engine on fire and the Dornier fell down. I escaped from underneath it and started to close in onto the formation by a left turn. Now I noticed another one slightly above me. He must have left his formation, which had already been broken by ours. I saw Szaposzka's one burn, as did two more enemy aeroplanes, seemingly those of Paszka and Tolo. I also saw three Me 109s that hurried towards Dzidek. I yelled over the radio, but it seems he saw them himself, and broke away. Until my last round I was pounding from 20 metres, with a 3-sec. burst after which his left engine started to burn. I was so close I dropped the aircraft's nose violently. After recovering I 'blackouted' so much that I did not wake up until 10,000 ft below.'

Zumbach's account, apart from the detailed description of his dog-fight, also highlights the subject of the Polish pilots communicating in the air using their native language. Their British commanders and brothers-in-arms did not want or appreciate this. The matter has been raised and discussed many times by Western authors, historians and even filmmakers. Poles are very spontaneous, unlike many other nationalities, including Britons, who are known for their reserve and calmness. The way of expressing their feelings and emotions is more likely to be straightforward, loud and enthusiastic when confronting stress. In the early months of their operational engagement in Britain, their vocabulary and understanding of the technical terms of English were poor.

It was no surprise, therefore, that in face of danger, which often involved life or death situations, to communicate more easily amongst themselves they preferred to use language and terminology they already knew well, rather than struggle with English words they had barely learnt.

Two squadron NCOs also achieved double scores during this encounter. Sergeant Eugeniusz Szaposznikow, who had previous successes, was able to shoot down two aircraft: one Dornier followed by a Bf 109. When the twin-engine bomber was finished, he went for the fighter: 'I dived and having satisfied myself the enemy aircraft was finished I pulled out of the dive and in climbing attacked a Me 109 from forward position. He also burst into flames and fell to earth.'

His much taller colleague Sergeant Stefan Wójtowicz, who had just recovered from the stressful combat in which he participated a few days earlier, also got in on the act. The former 111st Fighter Squadron pilot said:

'I attacked the first on my right. After the third burst the Dornier burst into flames and went down. I did not have to look for another, as it flew into my gunsights. After a small deflection I pushed the trigger, but the Jerry was harder [to hit], his starboard engine started to burn only after six bursts, and then his whole starboard fuselage was on fire.'

Wójtowicz tried to chase other bombers too, but they were impossible to catch.

This was also the day when the British and other English-speaking pilots started to understand the Poles' frustration. Watching massive fires spreading across London, and realizing that it was now the civilian population that was suffering the most, the RAF pilots were angry and frustrated,and their appetite for revenge was aggravated. They knew that there might be their relatives amongst those poor, innocent, vulnerable people being bombed. The British were experiencing the brutality of war and all its consequences, finally starting to appreciate the tragedy of Warsaw and other Polish cities and villages ruthlessly attacked by the Luftwaffe in 1939 despite being non-military targets. Flight Lieutenant Kent recalled:

'On the way home, it was just about dusk, I could see the fires in London that the Luftwaffe had started on this, their first raid on London itself. I don't think I have ever been so angry and I found myself beating my fists against the sides of the cockpit in a fury. It was a strange experience, I had not realised that I could feel so deeply, but at that moment I would have butchered any German I could lay my hands on. That night I looked at the red glow over London and brooded – I was beginning to understand the attitude of the Poles.'[4]

Although 303 Squadron pilots' successes were truly spectacular, they were not the only ones that Polish pilots claimed during the first day of the German offensive against London. Only thirty minutes after the last victim of the 'Kościuszko' boys was shot down, Flying Officer Tadeusz 'Novi' Nowierski scores another. The Pole was flying as Blue 2 of 10 Group's 609 Squadron, which was sent to defend the capital. Nowierski explained to his unit's Intelligence Officer:

'I followed the leader and attacked a big formation of Do 17 (or Me 110), the type of enemy aircraft is not definitely known. A beam attack developed from astern with 2 bursts of 2 seconds, but no results observed. I dived away and then climbed up to 15,000 ft and saw a Me 109. A dog-fight developed but I lost sight of the enemy aircraft. I then saw a Do 17 and attacked from astern at 150 yards range, three bursts of 2 secs, the last burst caused the enemy aircraft to catch fire between the starboard engine and fuselage. A Me 109 then attacked me but I broke away downwards and evaded him.'

Enemy activity was truly intense. Forty-five minutes later, yet another wave of raiders arrived over London. This time there were several other squadrons, including No. 234, forming a welcoming pary for the unwanted guests. This clash proved to be tragic for Squadron Leader Joseph O'Brien and Flight Lieutenant Paterson Hughes, respectively squadron and flight commanders, as both officers, decorated with DFCs, were lost. Sergeant Zygmunt Klein, who flew as No. 2 in Yellow Section, reported his action against a Dornier Do 17:

'I attacked the e/a from astern and put all my ammunition in the fuselage and engines. The port engine started smoking and the rear gunner stopped firing. Then the starboard engine began to smoke and the aircraft began to lose height over the Channel and at 4,000 ft I had to break away owing to lack of fuel. The aircraft was still losing height and smoking from both engines.'

The next few days went rather smoothly for the Polish pilots of Fighter Command, who, apart from one occasion, had very few clashes with enemy planes. However, Pilot Officer 'Donald' Zumbach added to his tally after a nerve-wracking dog-fight. On Monday 9 September both flights of 303 Squadron were in the air just after 5 pm, when their pilots sighted a German formation over the British coast already involved in an aerial battle. The squadron's 'A' Flight commander, Fighlt Lieutenant Johnny Kent, claimed one Bf 109 destroyed and a Ju 88 probably shot down. Czechoslovak maverick Sergeant František, a great fighter although not the best team player – known for his annoying habit of performing solo actions – downed two aircraft, a Bf 109 and He 111, before he was eventually shot down but skilfully landed in a field near Brighton.

Zumbach, initially engaged by only one Messerschmitt Bf 109, that ended up an easy target, soon realized he was flying over enemy territory, and France was not the best place to be alone with a shortage of ammunition and fuel:

'I gave it a two-second burst and from the starboard wing root many pieces fell off and the e/a burst into flames. At this moment I was attacked by an Me 109 on my port side 800 yards away, which missed me from 800/600 yards. I began dog-fighting with him. After a few minutes four more Me 109s appeared, three from below and one from above, and attacked me. Two gained height as I made tight circles and dived on me, giving long bursts. I should not like to have that happen to me again. I continued doing tight circles. One of the Mes came up towards me, and I gave him about 60 rounds from 150 yards. He turned over on his back, smoking and fell into cloud.'

An exhausted Zumbach only then realized where he was, as German anti-aircraft artillery opened fire on his Hurricane. He had to get away from France as quickly as possible.

Sergeant Kazimierz Wünsche had less luck than 'Johann' Zumbach. He was Yellow 3 and flew right into the gunsight of one of the Messerschmitts. When his Hurricane started to burn, the 21-year-old former 111th Fighter Squadron veteran had only one choice, to bail out immediately. He landed in a street near Devil's Dyke in Sussex with a broken leg and burns to his face, back and arm. The Polish pilot was admitted to Hove Hospital, where he spent almost a month, nearly missing the rest of the Battle of Britain. The Hurricane that he leapt from on 9 September crashed at Saddlestone Farm in Poynings.[5]

Unlike the comparatively uneventful 10 September,[6] the following day was one of triumph for the Poles, who claimed at least twenty-one enemy planes destroyed. Unfortunately, this success came at a high price, the PAF losing four

LAC Ryszard Kwiatkowski is cleaning up the fuselage of Hurricane P3700 RF-E. This aircraft was shot down on 9 September 1940, its pilot Sgt Wünsche had to bale out wounded.

of its brave pilots. After a rather quiet morning, coastal British radar stations picked up a large group of German aircraft crossing the Channel at around 3 pm. A significant number of RAF squadrons were directed to engage the Luftwaffe, with Nos 253 and 501 amongst them. Their mission was to patrol Gravesend and Dover (253), and Maidstone and Chatham (501).

No. 253 Squadron tangled with the Dorniers, and at 3.45 pm Pilot Officers Tadeusz Nowak and Włodzimierz Samoliński participated in the joint destruction of one of them. When close to Biggin Hill, Hurricanes with SD code letters came under heavy attack and Sergeant Antoni Głowacki's machine was hit in the wing by a German cannon shell. Despite this, 'Toni' managed to return safely to his aerodrome.

Flying Officer Stefan Witorzeńć, supported by five other pilots, shot down a Dornier Do 17. When over Maidstone, German bombers coming from east of Rochester were engaged by 605 Squadron with its Polish pilots Pilot Officer Witold Głowacki and Sergeant Jan Budziński. Głowacki, known for being the best of his tenth class at the Air Force Cadet Officers School, missed his posting to a front-line unit in Poland, but was shot down by the Soviets while performing an evacuation flight at the end of the Polish Campaign. Over two years younger, Budziński fought over Poland with 141st Fighter Squadron, supporting the 'Pomorze' Army.

In his combat report, which was drawn up after the fight, Głowacki described details of his encounter:

'I attacked the port aircraft of the leading vic of 3 He 111s from the port side with a diving quarters attack from 300 yards, closing to 100 yards with 3 very short bursts, with no visible effect. I then broke under it and circled left and climbed parallel to and above the leading bomber. I again attacked the same He 111 with a diving head-on attack without effect. At that moment I noticed a Me 110 behind me and diving on to me, so I broke away down and to the right. The Me 110 was following me. I then did a climbing turn to the right and saw the Me 110 break away below me to the left, so I continued my turn and dived upon it from astern, firing a five-second burst from 350 to 150 yards when its port engine began to smoke and it turned sharp left and dived into the ground from about 8,000 feet between Rochester and Gravesend. Then I was by myself so I climbed and searched for other enemy aircraft. I saw a He 111 going south-east, being attacked by a Spitfire with a diving attack from astern, so I joined it also with a diving attack from astern, the Spitfire breaking left and I broke right, climbing again to attack. When I made my second attack there were about 7 Hurricanes and Spitfires also attacking it. The He 111 dived from about 8 or 10 miles south-east of Maidstone, three of the crew bailing out; two appeared to land safely but the parachute of the third did not open.'

Budziński also had a successful sortie, explaining:

'I attacked a He 111 in the formation with a beam attack from 400 yards, with a 3-sec burst, with no visible effect. I broke underneath it and saw a Me 109 coming towards me. I made a head-on attack but with no effect. The Me 109 then dived and turned right handed, I turned into him and dived after it to 10,000 ft. I was then in a position to make an astern attack from above. I fired a 5-sec burst from 250 yards, the enemy aircraft broke up and dived down to the ground SE of Gravesend.'

The day was still far from over, and squadrons from No. 12 Group reached London in time to intercept the bombers and their fighter cover. No. 74 Squadron claimed five enemy aircraft destroyed and probably two shot down, with three others damaged. Flying Officer Henryk Szczęsny, Red 3, had some well-deserved luck:

'At 20,000 ft over London I sighted two e/bombers, and delivered astern attack at 100 yards giving 3 x 1 sec burst but observed no apparent damage. I then saw two Me 109s attacking two Spitfires and closed to attack one e/a giving 4 x 1 sec burst at 200 yards range from astern. E/a dived steeply, apparently out of control. I then sighted one lone Mc 110 and closed to attack from astern, giving 5 x 1 sec burst from 300 yards range. E/a dived and crashed on ground in flames.'

Another group of German raiders crossed the Channel and were met by No. 303 Squadron. Flying Officer Paszkiewicz, who led Green Section, was the first pilot to notice the presence of the enemy formation. He informed Flight Lieutenant Forbes over the radio about the location of the approaching planes, but hearing nothing from the British pilot, took matters into his own hands:

'I was drawn into combat with a Me 110 which I set on fire, but I was firing from quite a considerable distance away – about 300 yards – and I used up all my ammunition and had to withdraw from the combat.'

His wingman, 'Tolo' Łokuciewski, also got in on the act:

'We had been attacked head-on from above by a single Me 109. Of course a dog-fight ensued. I thought initially that it was a Hurricane flying straight at me, but I noticed machine-gun trails, so I turned left, until my eyes blacked out, and then I was on his tail. Five short bursts – the one-o-nine is on fire and slides straight into the sea. I gave an additional burst, and some pieces flew away. The pilot did not bail out. In view of the above I gained height and just like Donald I decided to lurk at the coast, waiting for the returning survivors, as I still had some ammo. And I was right! At 8,000 ft – I spotted a Do 215, returning unusually calmly to France. I decided to attack head-on from above for the first time. With a slight advantage of height I attacked, but the result was poor, as he only emitted some smoke and jinked lightly to the left, so then I attacked again from above and behind. I fired bursts up to the last round. He first started to smoke, then to burn, and then in weird manoeuvres, unseen in aerobatics, went to the ground, or more precisely – to the sea.'

This action by Paszkiewicz and his section secured reasonably safe access to the German bombers, and another Northolt-based unit, 229 Squadron, went into the enemy formation amd caused havoc. Unfortunately, Red Section of 303 Squadron was not so successful, being immediately attacked from behind. Flying Officer Arsen Cebrzyński, who led the section during his first operational flight in Britain, was an experienced pilot and then tactical officer of the III/1 Fighter Wing in Poland, where he claimed the joint destruction of a Bf 110. In France he added two more shared kills to his score.

The Operations Record Book rather laconically described what happened to him: 'F/O Cebrzyński jumped and fell near Pembury – his parachute did not open. It is believed that he was wounded if not killed, as he was getting out.' It is now believed that while leaving his Hurricane before the aircraft crashed at Hitchens Farm in Pembury, Cebrzyński was hit by a deadly burst from one of the German pilots. He had bullets all over his body and one of his legs was completely blown off. Another theory suggested he was already dead or possibly unconscious, when his aircraft turned upside down and the Pole fell out. Only two days later, an Intelligence Officer, Flying Officer Hadwen, while visiting a wounded Sergeant Karubin in Pembury Hospital, found Cebrzyński's body.[7]

Flight Lieutenant Kent wrote years later:

'It was strange really, as Cebrzyński knew he would be killed and he told me quite dispassionately only two days before that he would not survive long enough to see the end of the month. He was not morbid about it, he was just stating a fact which he accepted and merely wondered vaguely when it might be.'[8]

Unfortunately, Cebrzyński was not the only victim of that afternoon's combat. The Commander of 303 Squadron received a letter from Westerham Fire Brigade that described the last minutes of Sergeant Stefan Wójtowicz's life. According to them, but also to the local Special Police, the Polish pilot, after being separated from the rest of his squadron, fought bravely with a number of Bf 109s and Bf 110s, and before he was hit in the forehead by a cannon shell, he shot down two enemy planes. Chief Officer F.C. Paige from the Fire Brigade wrote:

'Dear Sir, May I thank you for telling No. 303 Polish Squadron, what little we in Westerham did for their comrade Sergeant pilot Wójtowicz, and if at any time another of them is unfortunate enough to have a mishap in or near our town we will do all in our power to help him. As to your question about Sergeant pilot Wójtowicz putting up a good fight, there is no doubt about his bringing down the two Me.109. As you can see by the enclosed statement which I myself and special Constable have signed, we two stood and watched the fight with other men of the A.R.P.'

Hurricane V7242 RF-B inspected by the ground crew. Wt Off Kazimierz Mozół, chief mechanic, is standing on its port side, watched by Flt Lt Witold Żyborski, Polish Squadron Adjutant. On 11th September 1940 Sgt Wójtowicz was killed while flying this aircraft.

Wójtowicz was the only pilot of Red Section who had flown operationally in England before. His Hurricane, with the young pilot's body still inside its cockpit, crashed in flames at Hogtrough Hill near Westerham at 4.04 pm. After analysis of various reports, Wójtowicz, who left his British fiancée Ruth in tears, was credited with the definite destruction of one Bf 109 and another fighter which was probably shot down. He is linked with the death of Uffz. Albert Heckmeier of the Ist Gruppe LG2. The last words that his mother heard from him, while Wójtowicz was leaving Poland, proved to be prophetic: 'Mother, I must go, you will see, your grandchildren will read about my actions in books.' Yes, he was right and they are!

Meanwhile. Sergeant Michał Brzezowski, the only pilot left from Red Section, was about to score his first 'kill'. He was a 19-year-old veteran of the 151st Fighter Squadron who fought bravely in Poland. It was in France that Brzezowski finally got a chance to see a German aircraft in flames, after being credited with a joint kill of a Henschel Hs 126. By no means the youngest Polish Battle of Britain pilot, he wrote after a fight with a Heinkel He 111:

> 'I engaged one and fired a burst from about 100 yards. Enemy aircraft immediately burst into flames and dived to earth. At that moment I noticed bullets flying past my cockpit. I immediately dived and in pulling out noticed a He 111, which I attacked and fired four bursts at from a distance of about 150 yards. It burst into flames and one of the crew jumped. The enemy aircraft began to dive to earth.'

After this action, the young Pole flew circles around a Hurricane pilot who had parachuted from his burning plane. He knew the danger which this poor chap was facing, therefore decided to protect his brother-in-arms. Then the Pole noticed that his own engine was covered by oil and starting to burn, and having no time to spare, Brzezowski landed at Croydon. He didn't know it then, butt he had only three more days to live…

Yellow Section leader Flying Officer Henneberg, after an unsuccessful clash with the Messerschmitts, went for the bombers. 'I ran into a He 111 returning to France,' 'Dzidek' reported. 'After several bursts stopped both his engines he force landed not far from the sea in a damaged condition.' Pilot Officer Zumbach was also haunting for another trophy. 'Johann' described his fight with a Bf 109:

> 'I easily overtook him and after my firing about 100 rounds he burst into flames and crashed to earth. I then joined two Hurricanes and we attacked five Me 110s. Two Hurricanes broke off the engagement through lack of ammunition. I was left alone and having run out of ammunition and being short of petrol I succeeded in evading the e/a at Biggin Hill to refuel.'

Zumbach was eventually credited with the destruction of one Bf 109 and one He 111.

Sergeant Szaposznikow, affectionately called 'Szaposzka' by his squadron mates, was far from giving up, and achieved a double success. He said of his dog-fight wth a Bf 110:

'I got onto the tail of one and started firing. Since I was quite close, I was rather mightily battered around the sky and my burst moved rather unintentionally to another machine. I take it for a good omen and I start to shoot again and I let go of the machine gun button only after they have gone silent by themselves. Meanwhile the starboard one goes down with a burning engine. After a couple of seconds the same happens to the other one. Both Messies fall to the ground like candles.'

Although a high price was paid by the 'Tadeusz Kościuszko' Squadron by losing two of their valuable and irreplaceable comrades, they also claimed sixteen enemy aircraft, which included victories gained by Flight Lieutenant Forbes and Sergeant František.

At approximately the same time, around Brooklands, 238 Squadron attacked a German formation which consisted of Junkers Ju 88s. Pilot Officer Władysław Różycki of Blue Section explained what happened:

'I fired at a He 111 from 150–200 yards giving a short burst of 2 secs from the front. I saw smoke come from the starboard engine and I then broke away. When I next saw E/A it was in a shallow dive towards the ground. I also saw a Spitfire and other a/c make attack at the same E/A and saw more smoke come from starboard engine. The E/A was at approximately 3,000 ft when I last saw it.'

The bomber from the 3rd Staffel KG26, which the Polish officer was shooting at, crashed at Dormansland near Lingfield in Surrey. Meanwhile, Różycki, after being wounded, had to land at New Alresford.

Despite claiming three bombers destroyed,[9]. 238 Squadron sustained casualties too. One pilot was wounded, while two others lost their lives. Amongst them was 24-year-old Sergeant Stanisław Duszyński, an ex-142nd Fighter Squadron pilot and instructor of the Polish Air Force College who did not have a chance to fly with his squadron for very long: The squadron clerk noted:

'In Sgt. Duszyński the Squadron is robbed all too soon of the services of a Polish pilot. The sergeant had been in the squadron little more than a week and he had had hardly any opportunity to maintain the valour and fortitude in combat of his countrymen.'

His Hawker Hurricane was shot down over Romney Marsh, crashing at Little Scotney Farm in Lydd. For many years, until 1970, when the wreckage was recovered, Duszyński's fate was unproven, leaving his fiancée Czesława Dombkowska in terrible mourning.[10]

Flying Officer Marian Duryasz, flying as Yellow 3, intercepted an enemy formation over Selsey Bill. This pilot was one of the more experienced Poles in the Battle of Britain. He joined the PAF Cadet Officers School in Dęblin in 1932 and subsequently served in the 133rd and 162nd Fighter Squadrons, before being posted back to Dęblin for instructor's duty. During September 1939 he was defending the nest of the Polish Eaglets – Dęblin – flying with an ad-hoc fighter flight. In the middle of August 1940, Duryasz joined No. 213 Squadron. He told his story:

> 'In the August of 1940 I was already in a British squadron. It was 213 Squadron stationed in the area of Exeter. There were two Poles, myself and Sergeant Antoni Wójcicki. And a few Belgians. The English were lacking experienced pilots and were covering the gaps as they could. After the collapse of France, the Polish Air Force was organising again, but before this happened, 85 Polish pilots received their postings to various British squadrons.
>
> 'It was a time when we flew a three-aircraft formation. Flight commander Flight Lieutenant Jack Sink [James Sing] in front, myself on his right … on his left we had a Belgian. My knowledge of English was relatively poor. I could admittedly buy a "Cup of tea" in the Mess, but the lady had to pick the money from my hand. Who could understand, those days, what they were talking to us?'[11]

He could now take revenge for the lost campaign in his homeland, and was about to claim his first aerial victory:

> 'One broke away and I was below it and had a good target to give it five short bursts. The left engine started smoking and it started to dive down in a long left-hand turn. I followed it down to within 1,000 ft of the sea when it burst into flames and dived straight into the water.'

Duryasz's Bf 110 was one of the five machines of this type shot down by 213 Squadron, while two others were damaged. Two of their own Hurricanes were shot down too: one pilot bailed out, but another went into the sea a mile off Selsey Bill. It was soon discovered that this was Sergeant Antoni Wójcicki, who was a freshly converted fighter pilot, with little experience, having previously flown in bombers. During the Polish Campaign, he flew operationally as a pilot of 4th Bomber Squadron. His body was never found.

After an exhausting Wednesday 11 September, the account of successes and losses was calculated and summarized: of eighty-seven victories reported by the whole of Fighter Command, the Polish pilots gained a score of twenty-one enemy planes destroyed for the loss of four of their own pilots pronounced dead.

The following days were rather uneventful, due to poor weather conditions and bad visibility. However, on 13 September Pilot Officer Tadeusz 'Teddy' Nowak provided his 253 Squadron with another success. During an afternoon mission near Hastings, which was targeted to intercept enemy raiders, the Polish pilot, who was Green 2 in a section of two aircraft, lost his leader. Undiscouraged by this mishap, he continued his task until noticing a single Heinkel He 111, which was flying north north-east, just 10 miles west of him:

> 'I got into position and delivered an astern attack on e/a out of the sun and subsequently chased the He 111 in and out of cloud inland to Croydon, where I lost e/a in cloud. I delivered 5 separate attacks, all from astern. After the 2nd attack I received no return fire from the rear gunner and after the 4th attack the port engine of e/a was smoking very badly.'

It is presumed that Nowak was in combat with an He 111 of the 2nd Staffel KG1, that eventually managed to return to Montdidier, where it crashed on landing. Oblt Eisenbrandt and another crew member were killed, while two others sustained injuries.

Plt Off Tadeusz Nowak (3rd from left) together with his colleagues of No. 253 Sqn.

Meanwhile, three PAF Sergeants – Szymon Kita, Konrad Muchowski and Władysław Paleniczek – joined the Church Fenton-based 85 Squadron, whilst Sergeant Wilhelm Szafraniec arrived at 151 Squadron. Pilot Officer Bolesław Własnowolski left 32 Squadron after being posted to 607 Squadron, and finally Flying Officer Zbigniew Kustrzyński was transferred from 111 to 607 Squadron.

Kita was 23 years old at the time, and had plenty of flying experience. Being a pilot of the 56th Army Co-operation Squadron, he participated in the Polish Campaign. On 30 September 1940 he was posted to 253 Squadron. One year younger, Muchowski also had previous experience of combat flying, yet for this pilot of 42nd Reconnaissance Squadron, fighter duties, like for Kita, were relatively new. He was later transferred to 501 Squadron, where he mysteriously appeared as 'Sergeant Konrad'.

Paleniczek, who flew as a pilot of 4th Bomber Squadron back in Poland and was a novice fighter pilot, after a short stay in 85 Squadron had been posted to No. 18 Operational Training Unit. From there he joined No. 300 Polish Squadron and, until his death in June 1941, flew bomber missions. He was the only pilot from this group who did not participate in the Battle of Britain.

Picture of No. 85 Squadron pilots taken on 5 October 1940 at Church Fenton. Two Polish pilots can be seen standing from left to right: Sgt Władysław Paleniczek (5th) and Sgt Konrad Muchowski (6th).

Szafraniec was one of the junior members of this fighting family. After graduating from the PAF Reserve Cadet Officers School, he missed the opportunity of flying operationally in Poland. But he got his chance one year later in Britain.

Further north, crews of both Polish bomber squadrons were progressing with their training, and although not satisfied with the general performance and capability of 'flying coffins', as Fairey Battles were famously described, both units impatiently and anxiously awaited their operational initiation. No. 300 Squadron, named Land of Mazovia, was commanded by 46-year-old Wing Commander Wacław Makowski, a pre-war military pilot and former director of the Polish airline 'LOT'. Makowski took part in the Polish-Bolshevik war, flying, among others, British-built Bristol F.2B Fighters.

On 22 and 23 August 1940, all the personnel and machines of 300 Squadron were moved north-east from Bramcote to Swinderby in Lincolnshire. Five days later, 301 'Pomeranian' Squadron, also equipped with Fairey Battles, under command of Wing Commander Roman Rutkowski, followed their colleagues. Rutkowski was no less experienced than his colleague. He had commanded 141st Fighter Squadron, then 56th and 43rd Army-Co-operation Squadrons and finally IV Army-Co-operation Wing. After both Polish squadrons settled in Swinderby, their crews continued exercises and were looking forward to receiving first combat orders from No. 1 Bomber Group.

On Saturday 14 September 1940, to all the crews' satisfaction, such an operational order finally arrived, and unlike two days previously, this time all looked promising.[12] 'We were so excited,'– Sergeant Władysław Łapot remembered that day with a smile. 'Finally we were about to get to the Germans. We had waited for this for such a long time.'[13] Six crews (three from each squadron) were selected to represent the PAF for the first time. It was decided that they would attack the German invasion fleet at Boulogne, with the reservation that if the attack was not possible, they should drop their bombs on similar targets at Cap Gris-Nez.

All six aircraft left Swinderby at 6.55pm. They were crewed by: Flying Officer Romuald Suliński, Flying Officer Aleksander Bujalski and Sergeant Jan Bieżuński; Flying Officer Jerzy Antonowicz, Pilot Officer Czesław Dej and Sergeant Alfons Kowalski; Pilot Officer Tadeusz Jasiński, Sergeant Bolesław Sobieszczuk and Sergeant Władysław Łapot (all from 300 Squadron); Squadron Leader Stefan Floryanowicz, Flying Officer Antoni Voellnagel and Sergeant Bernard Kowalski; Sergeant Stanisław Jensen, Flying Officer Stanisław Rewkowski and Sergeant Walenty Wasilewski; and Sergeant Kazimierz Lenczowski, Pilot Officer Stefan Hałłas and Sergeant Gustaw Kasianowski (301 Squadron). Weather was on their side, but despite locating the target, they could not see the results of their attack.

'The Battle aircraft, that we had, were poorly equipped,' Łapot recalled:

'They had another fault, that I have found, while being a radio operator. The radio was obsolete and primitive. To change the frequency, I had to change coils, which I kept in the separate pockets of my flying suit, to not misplace them. The Fairey Battle at that time had only one advantage, it was much faster than the Wellingtons that we got later. Swinderby had a grass surface, which would have been dangerous for the Wellingtons with their bomb load.'[14]

The last aircraft dropped their bombs at 8.55 pm. Łapot continued:

'We had to return. I remember that our route led across the Channel and then along the coastline. The problem was that the piece of paper with the codes of our airfields contained mistakes. When we landed at Newton instead of Swinderby, the English were staring at us. They had never seen Polish bomber crews before. They checked that we did not carry bombs, and just in case they removed our machine gun.'[15]

Apart from this inconvenience, all six Fairey Battles safely returned to England, landing between 10.40 and 11.15 pm. A journalist wrote when summarizing the night's events:

'The first raid of the Polish Bomber Squadrons was a complete success, and found its echo in a telegram written in Polish sent by the Officer Commanding their Group: "Well done men of 300 and 301 Squadrons." From that moment events moved rapidly, and the number of raids, the number of aircraft engaged and the weight of bombs dropped increased systematically.'[16]

Chapter Thirteen

The Polish Chapter of Battle of Britain Day

'And now the Battle of Britain is at its height,' wrote an unknown British pilot attached to the Polish unit. 'We have been giving the Huns much to think about during their visits over here and we are still ready to deal with their interference in our daily life. But here they come again!'[1]

On 15 September, the Luftwaffe conducted its largest and so far most concentrated attack against London. All three Air Fleets (Luftflotte 2 with HQ at Brussels and air bases in Belgium, France and Holland; Luftflotte 3 with HQ at Paris and airfields in France, and Luftflotte 5 with its base in Kristiansund and aerodromes spread all over southern Norway) mustered about 1,500 aircraft in the hope of engaging the whole of Fighter Command.

The two Polish squadrons that were sent to fight, and the Poles attached to the RAF units, had gradually gained experience in flying British aircraft and were eager to learn new tactics too. Their combat confidence kept developing, and their ability to achieve results were gradually seen by their colleagues. On 5 September, No. 303 (Polish) Squadron, with nine confirmed kills and one enemy aircraft probably shot down, achieved an amazing result by putting itself in second place of the whole Fighter Command scoreboard. On 7 and 11 September, the 'Kościuszko' boys topped the list with respective scores of fourteen kills and six enemy planes probably shot down and then sixteen kills and one probably destroyed.

On 11 September, the PAF claimed at least twenty-one German aircraft destroyed. It seemed that they did whatever they could, and their results would be almost impossible to beat. Yet 15 September brought even more outstanding results, and despite losing two of their fighter pilots killed and two others shot down, they were able to shine brightly again whilst claiming at least twenty-eight kills, seven planes probably destroyed and three damaged. Nos 303 (No. 11 Group, Northolt Sector) and 302 (No. 12 Group, Church Fenton Sector, Leconfield aerodrome in the East Riding of Yorkshire)[2] respectively took first and third places on the Fighter Command scoreboard.

For a clearer picture we have to bear in mind that for the duration of the first chapters of the Battle of Britain, essentially prior to 15 September, No. 302 was far from the centre of the fight. Furthermore, its command and operational 'freedom' depended on orders coming from Air Vice Marshal Trafford Leigh

Few other 303 Squadron fliers who fought in the Battle of Britain. From the left are: Sgt Stanisław Karubin, Flg Off Wojciech Januszewicz (wearing French uniform), Plt Off Mirosław Ferić, Sgt Stefan Wójtowicz, obscured by Sgt Eugeniusz Szaposznikow. They all flew together in 111th Fighter Squadron back in Poland.

Mallory, who was in command of No. 12 Group, and who literally dragged the Poles into his famous 'Big Wing' concept. Flying in such a formation not only limited their individual abilities, it made the whole Wing less manoeuvrable and difficult to gather before reaching the target, but also made it slow and ineffective. The achievement of more than ten aerial kills on 15 September not only proved that Squadron Leader Mümler's team didn't have any less qualities than their No. 303 colleagues, but also that by entering the conflict in their full strength, they were able to show what they were really capable off. This day was a breaking point and a great day for the 'City of Poznań' pilots. Being at the right place at the right time brought them great success.

As the weather improved, it was only a matter of where and when the Germans would continue their aerial attacks. After a few night missions performed by small groups of Dorniers, Heinkels or Junkers, around 11.30 am on 15 September a much bigger movement of enemy aircraft was spotted over Ramsgate and Dover. These aircraft were 'Jabos', Bf 109s performing bombing missions, soon followed by Dorniers of KG76.

Although unsuccessful in combat, Sergeant Antoni Głowacki from 501 Squadron returned to his aerodrome in his battle-damaged Hurricane. When the Polish pilot was going home, tension was growing. At the same time, the Duxford Wing arrived in the vicinity of south London and its fighters clashed with the Germans.

Flying Officer Julian Kowalski of Red Section, better known as 'Roch', remembered the day as follows:

'Attention, attention. All Hurricane squadrons scramble. Atmosphere has boiled up. The noise of the ignited machine engines and we are taking off in order: Canadians, Poles, Czechs. I fly on the left side of the 302 commander, S/L Satchell, Tadzio Czerwiński on his right. We went through the clouds. I squinted upwards. In the blue sky hundreds of white trails scatter in great disorder, and lines straight, semi-circular and full circles cover the beautiful blue sky; some suddenly break and in a vertical, spiral, blue trail of smoke connect the sky with the ground. Every now and then white balloons open up there; it all looks like a great Christmas decoration, suspended under the dome of sky.

'The combat is already on – I thought, Spitfires are welcoming the Me 109s. Below us, white, neat, puffy clouds, and formations of black German bombers against that background. Some are already scattered by squadrons of Hurricanes and several are heading back south in disorder, but still more and more appear on the horizon. Great noise in my headphones. I am not listening, why would I? I don't understand anything anyway. Suddenly, a voice in Polish, shouting: "Attack! Kill them, bastards!" "That was Northolt," I thought. They were closer, we are flying almost on top of them. Terrible view. I am glad that I am not a German. We carry on. Meanwhile a large formation of Dorniers approached us, and after a moment I can hear the voice of [Douglas] Bader: "Tally-ho!"

'The whole wing almost simultaneously made a sharp turn, and went down at full throttle onto the tight formation of Dorniers. I did not go down to attack. I just got on the tail of one and fired a long burst straight into its fuselage from minimum distance, and the Dornier continued to fly as before. I gave it a thought and shouted loudly – "Roch, aim at the engine!" After a rather short burst from my guns the engine exploded, almost the entire wing fell off and the German disappeared, spinning under the clouds. I was sure that its crew would miss their lunch today. I then aimed at another one. Suddenly a Spitfire falling vertically literally cut a Dornier in half with its wing. The attack of Bader's Wing must have been very effective as after just one kill I could not find another.'[3]

'Roch' Kowalski, a former 123rd Fighter Squadron pilot and flying instructor of the Air Force Cadet Officers School, had an opportunity to fight in France alongside the all-Polish GC1/145. That period left him with a feeling of insufficient resources from the French for their defence and a sense of huge disappointment. Only in Britain did he have a chance to open his personal score: during his first fight on 15 September he was credited with the probable destruction of a Dornier Do 17.

There were more claims to follow. Flight Lieutenant Tadeusz Chłopik, a former 143rd and 141st Fighter Squadrons pilot, was better known for his very strict and adamant way of teaching. Equally to groats (a type of cereal) that was served regularly, Chłopik had become a living legend and nightmare for his pupils at the Dęblin School of Eaglets, where he was an instructor. The leader of Red Section wrote on 15 September:

> 'On seeing the enemy formation breaking up I attacked one Do 215 as it broke away to the left, giving a short burst from the side, then a very long burst from behind until I saw the port engine smoking heavily with black smoke and on fire and the starboard engine emitting blue smoke, and the enemy aircraft dived on its back earthwards. A moment later three of the crew jumped out in parachutes. A moment later I attacked a Do 17 from behind and above. I got in a long burst and saw the port engine emitting smoke.'

His second victim also was attacked by a large number of Hurricanes and two Spitfires. Chłopik's wingman, Flight Lieutenant Franciszek Jastrzębski, was shooting at the same bomber. Almost 35 years old, the former commander of 132nd Fighter Squadron fought in Poland, claiming three aerial victories. After almost a year of waiting, he was about to add another one:

> 'I was in Red Section. Our section attacked the rear of the enemy formation and I got in a burst of 1 sec. at the e/a on the left of the formation. After attacking I made a left turn of 90° and saw only single e/a of the previous formation. I attacked the nearest e/a flying down sun and giving him 3-4

short bursts. The attack was with advantage of height and from the side. The first burst was at 300 and second at about 50 yds. The Do 17 did not fire at me at all but made sharp turns to the left and right. When I had finished my burst the Do was attacked from below by another Hurricane. I turned 180° to the right of the Dornier, which I did not see again, but immediately below on climbing I saw five parachutists.'

Five years younger, Flying Officer Tadeusz Czerwiński flew in Blue Section, which was led by Squadron Leader William Satchell. Czerwiński was also an experienced fighter pilot, whose career included service in 113th Fighter Squadron and instructional duty at the No. 1 Air Force Training Centre. On Sunday 15 September he reported:

'At 12.10 we attacked in section formation with a beam attack the head of the enemy formation with height advantage and at a speed of about 300 m.p.h. I got in two short bursts at 300 yds closing to 100 yds. The result of my bursts I could not see as I broke left immediately after shooting. Climbing again I met a single Do. 17 slightly above and in front of me. I attacked alone from behind and slightly above, getting in three bursts, whereat the E/A left engine caught fire and I broke off to the left and saw the E/A dive steeply. Then I saw three of our a/c attacking this falling E/A. I attacked one more time the E/A but it was already attacked by our a/c and its crew had jumped out.'

Blue 3 was 24-year-old Sergeant Marian Wędzik, a former pilot of 162nd and 121st Fighter Squadron, who in 1939 gained the position of flying instructor in the No. 1 Air Force Training Centre in Dęblin. Both in Poland and France he flew operationally, yet he was still waiting for his first kill. He was now about to get his chance. Flying at 300 mph, Wędzik performed a beam attack:

'I then got on the tail of the E/A which was on the port side of the formation and got in an effective burst at no more than 150 yds, because at the end of my burst I noticed a dense column of black smoke pouring from the port engine and flames from port mainplane. The E/A turned steeply to the left and began to dive.'

Pilot Officer Stanisław Chałupa was appointed to lead Green Section. This 25-years-old Pursuit Brigade veteran flew against the Luftwaffe with 123rd Fighter Squadron in Poland. Angry at the outcome of the campaign, he left for France, where he joined the small Polish Section attached to GCI/2. While in France he gained three aerial victories, two of them shared with other pilots. Chałupa described his encounter on 15 September to the squadron's Intelligence Officer, Flying Officer Paul Harding:[4]

'At 12.10 I noticed a formation of enemy bomber a/c Do 17 or Do 215 through the puffs of our A.A. flying on a course 360°, but which changed quickly to 120° The a/c were a dark colour. I attacked the leader of the second vic in the enemy squadron formation. After getting in three bursts from 250-50 yds I saw smoke coming from the port engine and the E/A dived violently below. After breaking away with a left turn I saw a second Do 17 which I attacked three-quarters from above and slightly to port, getting in two bursts of 3 secs each at about 100 yds. At the end of the burst I noticed smoke and flames coming from the port engine and two airmen jumping out from the burning a/c, which dived to the earth. In the meantime one of our pilots cut the tail off the burning a/c with his wing, tearing his own wing off in the progress. The E/A had fired at me from his top gun turret. The place of attack was South-West London.'

Chałupa's two wingmen were following Green Section leader, and both very quickly discovered an opportunity to meet their hated enemies. Sergeant Edward Paterek, similarly to Jastrzębski, spent part of his career in the 3rd Air Regiment in Poznań, flying in 132nd Fighter Squadron. Later he was transferred to Dęblin, where he held the post of flying instructor. He wrote of the 15 September encounter:

'At 12.10 hrs I noticed E/A flying in formation of 5 close together at a speed of 270 m.p.h. Using beam and No. 1 attack later. After my first attack the enemy rear gunner ceased firing and this enabled me to get in a long burst at very short range, causing the E/A to dive out of control earthwards. There was no smoke and the E/A was at approx 5,000 ft when it started to dive. I did not follow as I considered it to be destroyed.'

Sergeant Jan Palak, straight after completing his flying course, became a flying instructor of the No. 1 Air Force Training Centre. It was only in France that he saw action, being posted to the Polish-manned GC 1/145 with whom he fought the Luftwaffe. Palak said:

'I attacked with the beam attack and got in one burst at about 200 closing to 50 yds. Two other Hurricanes attacked this a/c. I saw black smoke coming from the port engine which was on fire. The E/A dived sharply to the right to earth. Next I climbed again with a right-hand turn and noticed an Me 109 which was diving to attack the Hurricane so I turned towards him, giving him two bursts which were very effective as I noticed bits flying off from the Me 109 which dived vertically into a cloud.'

Sergeant Antoni Siudak, a 31-year-old pilot of Yellow Section, like his comrade Palak, did not fly operationally in Poland, before the outbreak of war being a flying instructor in Dęblin. He also served in GC1/145 whilst in France. The Polish NCO commented on his combat with a Dornier on 15 September:

'Black smoke was pouring from the cockpit and port mainplane. During the first two bursts the rear gunners fired the whole time. My port mainplane lost its machine gun panel and was badly torn. E/A dived into clouds in a spin. Cloud 8/10 thin – sun behind me. A second Hurricane attacked with me at the same time. I fired three short bursts ... I saw the E/A catch fire just before the second Hurricane went into attack and a large piece flew off from underneath the fuselage whereat it disappeared into the clouds.'

The second pilot shooting at this Dornier Do 17 was Yellow Section leader Pilot Officer Stanisław Łapka, a former 113th Fighter Squadron pilot and instructor of the Air Force NCO School for Minors. After returning to Duxford, Satchell, who claimed one Dornier shot down and another probable, Chłopik and Łapka were praised by Squadron Leader Mieczysław Mümler for their leadership skills and bravery that resulted in such a well-performed and successful fight.

Meanwhile, 303 Squadron, led by Flight Lieutenant Kent, took off from Northolt and flew over south-east London. Having failed to intercept the German formation, they noticed a second group of enemy planes that was heading back towards France. The Luftwaffe horde had already dropped their bombs and, protected by Messerschmitts, were returning home at full throttle.

The Poles, unhappy with the way Kent performed the chase, were eventually able to catch the fighters themselves over Folkestone, where individual dog-fights began. Blue Section leader Flying Officer Paszkiewicz reported:

'Kent was leading without any sense – manipulating his throttle and flying blind no-one knows where to. At one point he started to chase a distant formation of Me 109s and 110s. The Squadron broke up. I kept up with the trio of Kent. "Tolo" had already downed an Me 109 that attacked us from one side. I peek upwards, what are the black 109s doing? Kent is firing all his guns like crazy, from a distance of some 1 kilometre.'

Being unhappy with his leader's strange performance did not stop Paszkiewicz from fulfilling his duty:

'The leading A/C of my section attacked the formation, and I followed. Four Me 109s then attacked from the rear. I engaged them and shot down one which fell in flames in the sea, and the other three fled to France.'

His wingman, Pilot Officer 'Tolo' Łokuciewski, Blue 2, had his own story to tell:

'We approached but E/A turned and we attacked them from a deflected angle from the rear and above, but at that moment we ourselves were attacked from the rear by Me 109s. At the same time I noticed another formation of E/A flying towards London, protected by Me 109s &110s. I broke away, and attacked the Me 109s together with another section of Hurricanes. After firing a few bursts a Me 109 began to smoke and eventually burst into flames. I was then hit from the rear by a cannon shell and landed wounded.'

With shell splinters in both legs, Łokuciewski performed a force landing at Northolt and lost consciousness while still in the cockpit. The Polish pilot was pulled out by ground crew and admitted to hospital, where an immediate operation took place, during which numerous pieces of metal were removed from his legs. Over thirty shards were left by the surgeon and stayed with Łokuciewski for the rest of his life. 'I was 23 years old and I really wanted to live,' 'Tolo' concluded.

No. 3 of Blue Section was Sergeant Mirosław Wojciechowski, a 23-year-old 142nd Fighter Squadron veteran, who also completed his combat report:

'I noticed a Me 109 returning towards France. I attacked him from the rear and fired at a very close range, and the Me burst into flames. Climbing to 12,000 ft I met another Me 109 who was smoking slightly and losing height. There was no other machine in the vicinity. I followed him down to the earth, where he crashed, but the pilot stepped out of the plane and was arrested. I again climbed and another machine (from A Flight 'M') joining me, we attacked a Do and firing two bursts, the E/A crashed to earth and burst into flames.'

The Messerschmitt which was observed by Wojciechowski was flown by Uffz. Andreas Walburger of the 2nd Staffel JG27, who landed near Ifield in Sussex.

After returning to Northolt, Wojciechowski was credited with his first victories. It is believed that he shared destruction of the Dornier Do 17 with another Sergeant from 303 Squadron, 19-year-old Tadeusz Andruszków, a pilot who had fought in Poland with 162nd Fighter Squadron and in France under the command of Lieutenant Jan Falkowski. This time Andruszków was Red 2, and he added: 'While returning to Northolt flying as Red 2 with Sergeant Wojciechowski we saw a Do 215 lower and to our right. We both attacked, and watched him fall in flames to the ground.'

John Kent, who commanded Red Section, was not able to catch an enemy plane in his sights for long enough to fire a deadly burst. His No. 2, however, was more successful, and Pilot Officer Mirosław Ferić wrote:

'I was attacked by two Me 109s over the coast at Dungeness. These were reinforced by three other Mes and in the ensuing fight I shot one down, firing a long burst from a distance of 300 yds. Being myself engaged I could not follow the subsequent flight of damaged E/A, but F/Lt Kent who was in the vicinity states that he saw E/A burst into flames and fall to earth.'

Leader of Yellow Section was Flying Officer Zdzisław Henneberg, who achieved great success by shooting down two enemy planes. Henneberg provided Flying Officer Hadwen with the details:

'After a lengthy chase of Me 109s I perceived a formation of about 20 Do 215s flying towards London, protected by a number of Me 109s. I attacked a Do 215, firing a long burst from a distance of 300 yds, decreasing to about 150 yds. Being attacked by three Me 109s, I was forced to break off the engagement with the bombers, but looking round I noticed the right engine and petrol tank of the Do 215 was in flames. Flying south I came across three Me 109s making their way towards the Channel. I gave a chase, and firing from a distance of about 150 yds, I fired a third burst from the rear left side. E/A hit the water at an angle of about 30° and disappeared 10 kilometres from the coast.'

When Henneberg was attacked by the Messerschmitts, it was Pilot Officer Jan Zumbach, Yellow 2, who noticed his colleague in trouble:

'I cut across his path and pumped him a nice burst. He smoked immediately and went spinning down. I followed him and a polka started. Something got into his head, as he was performing fantastic aerobatics, hoping I would let him go. In order to stop his daydream of escaping, or to give him more courage, I fired a little burst every now and then. Since I had spent a lot of ammunition this way, and he just continued to smoke, I decided to wait, until he got fed up with the fun, and started to fly straight. So he did. Being slightly to one side, I turned and hit him from a direct distance. Pieces flew away from him and he started to burn at once. I struggled with him for some minutes. Then I climbed and started to look for another.'

He did not have to wait for very long:

'I then climbed and saw about 12 Dos returning to France without protecting fighters. I signalled another aircraft who joined me, and we attacked, but scarcely had I begun to fire when my ammunition ran out.'

Green 1, Flying Officer Marian Pisarek, after his recent troubles, not only returned to action but struck lucky again. The 28-year-old officer said:

'Flying in a southerly direction, I noticed several Me 109s, and to the right Do 215s. As I approached the Me 109s first, I engaged them, and following on the tail of one I fired several short bursts, but only after falling to about 400 ft did E/A burst into flames, and fall into the sea.'

Pilots of No. 56 Squadron. Plt Off Zbigniew Nosowicz is standing 4th from left while his colleague Plt Gustaw Radwański is kneeling on the right.

Apart from the nine enemy aircraft destroyed by the Polish pilots of 'Tadeusz Kościuszko' Squadron, Czechoslovak Sergeant František, shot down a Bf 110 to add another victory to his impressive score. But the day was far from over, with no time for celebrations.

In the afternoon, the Luftwaffe gathered several more large formations of bombers and, wave by wave, kept sending them across the Channel. At 2.45 pm, twenty Heinkel He 111s from KG53 bombed the West Ham area. They were followed three minutes later by eleven Dorniers from KG3, and twenty-seven Heinkels from KG26 began attacking the Bromley-by-Bow gas works. Five minutes after the Heinkels left their target area, forty-two Dorniers from KG2 swung over south-east London and Kent. Finally, at 3.30 pm, twenty-six Heinkels of KG55 bombed dockyards. Numerous RAF squadrons and both units from the PAF were scrambled and sent to meet such enormous power.

As expected, the German bombers were well protected by their fighter cover, and group after group were passing by the RAF fighters. One of the squadrons that clashed with this giant almost unstoppable force and firepower was No. 17, which took off at about 2 pm from Debden.

Amongst its pilots was Flying Officer Paweł Niemiec, also called 'Poppet', whose surname ironically translates in English to 'German', yet was quite popular in the Cieszyn Silesia region of Poland where the pilot came from. Being a flying instructor in Poland, and having responsibility to look after his pupils, he missed the chance to fight the German invaders in 1939. He could now finally get to grips with them, and wrote in his combat report:

'I was No. 3 in Blue Section when we attacked a formation of 50 or more Dorniers with Me 110s behind and Me 109s above them. There were only two in my section as No 2 did not take off. I made a beam attack on a Do 17 and opened fire at 300 yards closing to 100 yards, giving him a four-second burst. Black smoke started to come from his starboard engine. I broke away under him, and saw another and bigger cloud of black smoke come from an engine which I thought was beginning to catch fire. I then joined up with two of our Hurricanes and coming down through cloud saw another Do 17. I broke away from the Hurricanes and after flying alongside the Do 17 I turned into him in a break in the cloud and gave him a short burst at 150 yards, but observed no result. The Do returned cannon fire, but my aircraft was not hit.'

No. 302 arrived at the scene incomplete. Satchell's and Chałupa's aircraft were both damaged as a result of the previous encounter, and a few other pilots landed on various airfields and, therefore, did not return to Duxford in time for the second mission. Flying Officer Czerwiński's Hurricane also developed engine problems, and consequently its pilot had to return to Duxford. Despite this disadvantage, the Poles sparred with a formation of around 15 bombers using all available Hurricanes. Satchell, who flew a 'borrowed' machine, was credited with one Bf 109 probably shot down. Unfortunately, soon after the Poles suffered their first loss.

Flying Officer Stanisław Łapka, due to being rather short called 'Mały' ('Little') by his friends, was about to score again, when disaster struck. 'Roch' Kowalski reported:

> 'To the starboard and a bit in front I could see Stasio Łapka finish his German, already on fire, and at the same moment I could see a black trial of smoke behind Stasio's Hurricane. I put the transmitter on and shouted: 'Stasiu, jump! Stasiu, jump!' A moment later both the Dornier and Hurricane went behind clouds.'[5]

Luckily Łapka managed to get out of the cockpit and parachute to safety. He was badly wounded, but alive.

His colleague, Pilot Officer Włodzimierz Karwowski, a former 121st Fighter Squadron pilot and flying instructor in Ułęż, who just two days before celebrated his 28th birthday, suffered unfortunate mechanical trouble. When he went in to attack, the port machine-gun panel came loose, causing serious drag, and only his skills and a pinch of luck helped him to land safely.

The leader of Red Section did not know that he was flying his last mission, although everyone who fought in the air realized that sooner or later the end could come. Flightt Lieutenant Tadeusz Chłopik's Hurricane was over North Weald in Essex when the aircraft suddenly came under enemy fire and burst into flames. The pilot, in desperation, pulled up at 10,000ft, opened the canopy and bailed out. Unfortunately, his parachute did not open and Chłopik, watched by RAF personnel based at Southend-on-Sea, fell like a stone. When his body was discovered, no signs of enemy bullets were found.[6]

Flying Officer Julian Kowalski, after entering the formation of Dorniers, earned another score. He recalled:

> 'I was so close behind the tail of a German I could not miss. I aimed at the engines; another one set on fire, the crew bails out. The Dornier spins to hide in the clouds. The third one was lucky: a short burst and I was out of ammo. I shut the throttle a bit, and slowly sink down. I look above. The black band of Dorniers was broken in half.'

Kowalski was credited with two Dorniers: one destroyed and a second one probably shot down. He came back with a hole in his right tyre and an air pipe having been cut.

Pilot Off Edward Pilch was 25 years old and had five years of active flying behind him. During the Polish Campaign he flew in combat with his 122nd Fighter Squadron, and later became Intelligence Officer of the whole III/2 Wing. Until 15 September 1940 he had no luck in aerial combat, but that luck was about to change. 'After our section attacked the E/A broke up formation and disappeared into the clouds,' an excited Pilch told his 302 Squadron mates upon his return.

'I flew below the cloud waiting for them to come out. My first attack was from above and head on. As I flew over him I did not notice any fire from his gunner. At the same time a Spitfire attacked this a/c from behind. My second attack was from behind on his tail and after this attack I noticed black smoke coming from his port engine and the a/c caught fire. It turned towards the coast along the Thames Estuary and dived sharply, burning well. I noticed another Do 215 emerging from the clouds. I attacked at once doing a beam attack. Before the attack I saw the rear gunner taking aim at me but he stopped firing after my first burst, whereas black smoke poured from his port engine. I gave him one more burst from behind but had to break away owing a heavy A.A. fire bursting all around me. I could not finish him off yet but waited for the A.A. fire to stop, which it did and then once more I attacked him over the sea and saw him fall right into the sea near Margate.'

At the same time, 213 Squadron arrived over Edenbridge, where they sighted a relatively large formation of Dornier Do 17s flying without their usual fighter cover. Having no time to lose, pilots decided to perform a head-on attack while another squadron, No. 607, went for the Dorniers from the side. Paweł Niemiec's fellow instructor from the Dęblin Eaglet School, Flying Officer Marian Duryasz, Red 3, was amongst those who managed to get close enough. It was 3.45 pm when he got a Dornier in his gun-sight, aiming at the plane that slightly separated from the group. 'He was attempting to dive down away from into the cloud,' an excited Duryasz said after returning to base. 'I followed, firing all the time. He dropped all his bombs. I watched him blazing on the ground in a small wood.'

Despite the bravery, uncompromising attitude and determination of the RAF pilots, many bombs fell on London. Those German bombers who did survive the bloodbath over the capital and surrounding areas were desperately heading home. One such formation was spotted by seven pilots from 303 Squadron, led by Squadron Leaders Witold Urbanowicz[7] and Ronald Kellett.

They left Northolt at 2.25 pm and reached Gravesend at 18,000ft. According to Kellett, the enemy flew in a huge formation consisting of about 400 planes. They were Dorniers protected by fighters: Bf 109s and 110s. Even though No. 303 appeared in only small number, the decision was made to attack. It was approximately 3 pm when all nine Hurricanes zeroed in on the raiders.

'After a long chase I attacked and fired a burst from a distance of 200 yards,' Urbanowicz wrote. The ambitious officer did not want to be overshadowed by Kellett, a Briton, who had just bagged two Huns: a Bf 110 destroyed and a Bf 109 probably shot down. Urbanowicz continued:

> 'At that exact moment enemy aircraft hid in the clouds. On emerging from the clouds I again attacked from a nearer distance, and in a short while an enemy bomber dived in flames and fell into the sea. I attacked another ¾ from the rear, and after a long burst, one engine stopped working, the aircraft lost speed and began to lose height. Having satisfied myself that no enemy aircraft was on my tail, I again attacked the bomber, and firing from a distance of 150 yards, saw him burst into flames and fall into the sea.'

Urbanowicz thus added two Dorniers to his list of victories.

Flying Officer Walerian Żak,[8] also known as 'Ciotka' ('Aunt'), had served in the Polish Air Force since 1932. After graduating from the PAF College, he flew with the 64th Light Bomber Squadron, then, after conversion, took the role of deputy commander of 112th Fighter Squadron, followed by the position of tactic officer of the III/1 Fighter Wing. When war broke out he was in Dęblin, defending his base together with other instructors and flying obsolete PZL P.7s. Now, he was back in action and full of hope that he could finally get at least one German:

> 'I attacked the first formation which we met south of London, where I was forced into an engagement with Mes who attacked us from the rear. After a few minutes I saw another formation of about 15 Dos without supporting fighters. I attacked the last in the formation several times, firing several bursts. With the last burst the E/A began to pour out clouds of smoke and then both engines were in flames. I had run out of ammunition so I came home.'

Sergeant Wojciechowski, who flew with Żak as part of 'B' Flight, claimed his third victim in one day. It was a Messerschmitt Bf 109, as he explained in his report: 'Being near a Messerschmitt I fired a burst after which he turned and made off towards the sea. I chased him for quite a long time, before I was able to shoot him down. The pilot jumped, and I saw him arrested as he landed.' If Wojciechowski's description is precise, we can assume that he was chasing Uffz. Hermann Streibing from the 1st Staffel LG2, who indeed bailed out, while his aircraft crashed at Rainham.

'Ox' Ferić also added to his tally, being the second pilot of 'A' Flight who scored during this confrontation. Initially he went for the bombers, targeting them with his ammunition, but then he sighted a more challenging target, a Messerschmitt Bf 110: 'Since I had used up half of my ammunition in attacking enemy bombers I approached to about 100 to 80 yards before firing a burst at a Me 110, which immediately burst into flames and fell into the clouds out of control.' Ferić thus added a fifth kill to his total score, and consequently becoming an ace.

Unfortunately, another 'A' Flight pilot was no so lucky, most probably flying straight into an enemy line of fire, and as result failed to return to Northolt. His colleagues could only assume that young Sergeant Michał Brzezowski, who was flying his second mission during the Battle of Britain, together with his Hurricane was lost at sea as his body was never found. His fellow NCO, Sergeant Tadeusz Andruszków, was also shot down, but luckily managed to open the canopy and bailed out. Andruszków landed safely and unhurt near Dartford. It is believed that the Polish Sergeants were shot down by Staffel Commander Oblt Ignaz Prestele and Lt Tone from JG53. Two of the squadron's Hurricanes were damaged, yet Kellett and Ferić, who flew them, returned to Northolt unharmed.

Amongst many squadrons involved in the chase of the fleeing bombers and their protectors was No. 238. While Poles from 'Tadeusz Kościuszko' Squadron were battling them over Gravesend, two of their colleagues left Middle Wallop to patrol over their own airfield. Sergeant Józef Jeka, 23, from the Polish seaside village of Tupadły, remembered his frustration when he was, mostly unsuccessfully, pursuing German aircraft in Poland. Being in the British squadron less than two weeks, he impatiently waited to take advantage of his aircraft's eight machine guns. This time he flew as No. 3 in Yellow Section, and after nearly an hour of searching the sky he saw a potential opponent. When his colleagues also spotted the Germans over Brooklands and Kenley, the Polish Sergeant followed them, flying down close to the rest of his section. Having the sun behind them, they attacked from astern. Jeka wrote in his report:

'I fired at a Me 110 with a burst of 2 secs from 200 yds closing to 50 yds from underneath astern. At first the E/A dived in a corkscrew. I followed and fired several secs' burst from astern. E/A went straight into the ground, either pilot or rear gunner had bailed out. E/A exploded and my last burst went into ground. I circled round and saw someone land by parachute. Then I climbed and attacked another E/A. I fired a very short burst and then found all ammunition gone. The E/A had its starboard engine smoking badly. It was last seen heading south chased by another Hurricane, but I do not know who it was. Most probably this E/A, which I cannot identify, was considerably damaged, and no doubt was finished off by another Hurricane.'

Jeka's colleague, Pilot Officer Władysław Różycki, 33, was also amongst successful pilots of his unit, who altogether claimed six enemy aircraft destroyed, one probably destroyed and three damaged. He was flying as Blue 2 when a large formation of Luftwaffe bombers was spotted. The Pole attacked together with his section, in line astern, firing a two to three seconds burst from astern from a distance of 120-150 yards. He recalled:

'I saw many pieces fly off the wing, but E/A continued in formation. I broke away and attacked a second He 111, firing a long burst of about 3 secs from 50 yds full deflection from below. E/A appeared to go up and then turned over and dived down and I followed him, but was attacked by E/A and made steep turn to avoid. Later I saw other E/A so broke off and returned to base.'

Różycki also remembered that the Heinkel's crew jettisoned their bombs after he opened fire at their aircraft.

When Jeka and Różycki landed at Middle Wallop, another formation of bombers, consisting of 26 Heinkel He 111s from KG55, attacked the dockyards. In this case none of the Polish pilots claimed any victories, yet the end of this confrontation was far from over. At 5.30 pm, more German fighter-bombers arrived over England to bomb the Supermarine factory at Woolston, a suburb of Southampton. Their bombs missed the target, and while on their way back the Messerschmitts from Erprobungs Gruppe 210[9] were intercepted by 607 Squadron.

Only three pilots claimed victories in the area around Poole in Dorset, including one enemy aircraft shot down by Pilot Officers Charles Bowen and John Sulman. Another was added to 'Vodka' Własnowolski's account. Both victims were Dorniers. The Polish pilot, flying as Red 3, sighted a lone Dornier to his right, at 12,000 feet:

'I pursued e/a who tried to escape by taking a zig-zag course above clouds, so fired two bursts from behind and a little below. I saw the engine catch fire and e/a dived below clouds. I followed him down and saw e/a dive into the sea in flames and sink. The enemy pilot sunk with the plane.'

This was the last victory achieved by the Polish pilots on 15 September. Despite losing two of their compatriots, their 'kill' total was amazing and 303 Squadron again was at the top of the daily scoreboard for all Fighter Command, while their colleagues from 302 Squadron were close behind in third place. They could finally show what they were capable of, and prove that only their location had prevented them from achieving more successes in the past.

General Władysław Sikorski, whose name was on the 'most wanted list' prepared prior to the planned invasion of the British Isles by the Oberkommando der Wehrmacht (High Command of the German Armed Forces), praised his fighter boys by complementing their skills, bravery and dedication. Salutations kept arriving. Frederick Ogilvie, Director General of the BBC, admired the great achievements of the 'Tadeusz Kościuszko' Squadron:

'The B.B.C. sends warm greetings to the famous 303 Polish Squadron with lively congratulations upon its magnificent record and all the best wishes for its future. You use the Air for your gallant exploits and we for telling the world of them. Long live Poland!'

Even Squadron Leader Douglas Bader, whose idea of the Big Wing had been questioned by the Poles, showed his adoration towards his 'City of Poznań' Squadron friends, saying:

'My first contact with the pilots of the Polish Air Force was in 12 Group of Fighter Command in September 1940 when I was based at Duxford. 302 Polish Squadron joined us there. At that time I was commanding an RAF Canadian fighter squadron and the Poles and the Canadians found they had much in common. As the years gather memories linger and it is always the gay times that one recalls. So far as we were concerned we love our Polish allies. They were gallant and dedicated to destroying the enemy in the air. On the ground they were gay and amusing, sometimes tragic and forever loyal. It was a privilege to know them, fight with them and live with them. They added lustre to the cause of freedom for which we were all fighting.'

Moreover, Bader enthusiastically participated in operational flying alongside the Poles, when he could assess their skills, usefulness and aptitude, and also spent plenty of time with the Poles between missions. He distributed his happiness widely when 302 Squadron returned from the 15 September mission. According to some of them, 'Dogsbody' – Bader's radio call sign – has been equal to the Poles when drinking and to his Canadians while fighting. Both activities were carried out under his supervision and accompanied by his noisy shouting. Pilot Officer Jan Jokiel, No. 302's Intelligence Officer, recalled:

> 'A magnificent scene took place on the piano, on the top of which a short, dark-haired, fierce as a Gallic rooster, aggressive and fast like a spark Jack Satchell, a Scotsman, boss of 302 Squadron, located himself. In the fighting fervour he was sudddenly swept over from this dominant position by Bader, by one successful push of the piano. The Poles, while saving Satchell, did tear a sleeve off his uniform and slightly damaged his arm.'[10]

Congratulations kept arriving, one after another, and when the flying personnel of both Polish fighter squadrons were resting and recovering, their Intelligence Officers finally summarized lists of victories and losses. At the same time, the almost anonymous second-line warriors, better known as the ground crew, the nearly forgotten heroes of the Battle of Britain, tirelessly worked on their magnificent craft by repairing the damaged, almost unserviceable machines.

Only their precise hands and magical skills gained during pre-war service in various Polish air regiments, long days followed by sleepless nights and endless hours of work, which those men spent in cold and dirty hangars, allowed severely damaged aeroplanes to be ready for combat the very next morning to continue their daily duties. Polish mechanics did not follow the RAF manuals as often as they should, purely because most of the time they improvized to get the job done no matter how, but also because they couldn't read the manuals written in English. Like their more famous fighting colleagues, the mechanics also gained a special places in British hearts. Some of them, like Sergeant Karol Błachuta, were befriended and even almost adopted by local families. Błachuta, in his off-duty time, spent hours looking after his new English family's garden in Ruislip.

Polish pilots completely trusted their ground boys, or 'grey roots of the lush flowers', as fitters, engine mechanics and electricians were poetically labelled.

'It is said that such-and-such squadron is flying, though when you look up in the air and count, only twelve pilots are flying,' said Leading Aircraftman Kazimierz Węgrzecki, No. 303 Squadron HQ clerk, analyzing the underappreciated work of his colleagues.

'So this is only a part of the squadron, as the whole ground personnel that belong to this squadron, stayed down there. But this is how it usually goes, always much more is being said about the airborne squadron, as his work brings more substantial effects, and only incidentally ground crew of the squadron would be mentioned, although without their work it would be difficult to imagine any activity in the air.'[11]

The Engineering Officers of both squadrons – respectively Flight Lieutenant Adam Jaworski and Flying Officer Bartłomiej Popławski (both from 302 Squadron) and Flying Officer Wacław Wiórkiewicz (303 Squadron) – looked after their precious jewels, the Hurricanes, with precise attention to detail. They knew that the lives of the pilots, and therefore the result of the battle, were in their dirty, greasy hands. They were performing their magic.

'The most characteristic attribute of the mechanics' work would be attention to details when it comes to scope of work and specialities,' said Wacław Wiórkiewicz, applauding the involvement of his dedicated team during the Battle of Britain.

'An aircraft is a living creature, that consists of particular systems, blood, nerves, nervous system, gasoline, hydraulics, compressed air, radio, oxygen, armament, aircraft instruments – all this is full of life and works together for the common effort – combat flight. Each of these circuits requires its doctor, when one doctor works on the radio but the fuel system or armament are not his speciality. He does not even touch it as he knows that he could damage it instantly – the modern Hurricane is purebred and requires caring care. In their job, mechanics like their own aircraft. Polish traditions and habits come out. It was tradition that each aircraft had its overseer and assistant – they did not like others and did not want them. Initially, when we blindly followed the English rituals, and did not follow our customs, it was happening that, as in the Bible, various doctors-mechanics argued for a long time on methods of repairing an ill aircraft. Return to the Polish norms left an aircraft with te constant carers, sensitive, tender for the smallest defect of their own aircraft.'[12]

Arkady Fiedler, the famous Polish writer, journalist and traveller, visited 303 Squadron during those extremely daunting days of the Battle of Britain. He paid tribute to the multitude of tireless, unknown soldiers with hands covered in lubricating oil:

'If you open the soul of the Polish fighter pilot and look inside, there would be many feelings, not always for their colleague fighter pilot, although they were connected by their mutual fight and collective fortune – always you would see the best caring love and honest affection to the grey group of little soldiers called the ground crew of the fighter squadron. It was them to whom the fighter pilot dedicated his most secret feelings and to whom he owed almost more then to his colleague-pilot: his life, victories and his glory. And his limitless trust for the aircraft.'[13]

The British also saw and respected the hard work carried out by the Polish ground crew:

'We must never forget how, in the days of the Battle of Britain the ground staff of the Squadron [No. 303] worked strenuously and without a word of

Another Polish victim of the Battle of Britain and the only member of 303's ground crew killed due to enemy action. Aircraftman Antoni Rossochacki (left) was mortally wounded on 27 October 1940, when his squadron was resting at Leconfield. Here he is accompanied by Sgt Stanisław Karubin.

complaint under difficult conditions. There was one period of over three weeks in which work continued for twenty-four hours a day, the airmen sleeping on the floors of the huts, snatching hasty meals between long intervals servicing the machines which did such marvellous damage to the vaunted Luftwaffe. On one occasion three aircraft only out of a flight of twelve returned serviceable from an operation, and by the following morning the nine damaged aircraft were ready once more for another attack. The few English mechanics who worked with the Squadron were amazed at the quickness of the Poles in adopting themselves to English methods and English machines.'[14]

Being overshadowed by their more glorious colleagues – the fighter pilots – it is no surprise that some of the ground crew members decided to follow a dream and pursue a flying career. Both the Guziak brothers, Eugeniusz and Tadeusz, eventually became fighter pilots, as did Jerzy Krzysztofiński, Jerzy Zbrożek and Tadeusz Żurakowski. Meanwhile, Antoni Majcherczyk completed an operational tour as a bomber pilot, and along with Kazimierz Szrajer, who also finished duty as a bomber pilot, went into special operations over occupied Europe in No. 1586 (Polish) Special Duties Flight.

Although the mighty Luftwaffe carried out more and more attacks, which often continued until midnight, only small numbers of their aircraft were involved. It became clear that, although by a narrow margin, the decisive day of 15 September was irrevocably lost, together with the chance for launching the invasion.

The date of 15 September 1940 became a milestone in the history of the Second World War, and in the aftermath of this defeat, Adolf Hitler postponed Operation Sea Lion, which eventually was abandoned altogether. This was a massive blow for the *Herrenvolk* ('Race of Masters') and their leaders.

There were many aspects that lead to this failure, and plenty of them have been analyzed over the years since the Battle of Britain. However, a few should be highlighted. Hermann Göring gained his warfare experience by flying as a front-line fighter pilot and then a flight commander during the Great War. Subsequently, he added two years as a communication pilot in Sweden, before apparently losing all interest in aviation. When he was appointed the commander of the German air force, it was very much a political decision, rather than a practical one. Göring hadn't progressed and evolved since his flying days. In his simple mind, based on experience from over twenty years before, his fighter pilots had to shoot down as many as possible of the opposition planes, while according to the theory of his idole General Giulio Douhet (the Italian air power theorist), 'the bombers will always get through', and the Luftwaffe heavies would carry out their task of destruction. The Reichsmarschall strongly and uncompromisingly believed in the big aerial battle that was very cautiously avoided by the RAF. The latter knew and skilfully used for their benefit the limited range of the German's main fighter planes.

Gőring, in his self-confidence, believed that with victory over the RAF in the air, his Luftwaffe would secure British capitulation, which was quite different to what '*Studie Rot*' ('Red Study') was about – the latter a document that emphasized the difficulties of trying to mount any kind of landing operation against Britain unless the Royal Navy was neutralized. The German air force was supposed to gain and then maintain aerial superiority over the invasion area, then support its troops and armoured vehicles on the ground, but also provide transport for the airborne forces and finally support military action after the landing.

Hitler's impatience did not help either. Due to his military incompetence and lack of vision, on 30 July he issued an order to proceed with the attack, naively expecting that this would happen within twelve hours. Having no clear view on what the invasion should look like, what form it would take, he persuaded Feldmarschalls Albert Kesselring (2 Air Fleet) and Hugo Sperrle (3 Air Fleet) and Generalobest Hans-Jürgen Stumpf (5 Air Fleet) to prepare their personnel for an assault. After that, he made several crucial mistakes, including the wrong assessment of Fighter Command's power, ability and determination, and by switching his aircraft away from the British airfields and engaging them over London instead.

The skirmishes of 15 September were the fiercest engagements for both sides so far, and despite the Battle of Britain being far from over, cracks in the Luftwaffe's unbeaten reputation started to be more visible. Some of them were caused by the brave Polish pilots. So it was perhaps no surprise that not only politicians and high level commanders revealed their admiration for the Polish fliers. The Poles almost instantly became celebrities of British society, called by an American war correspondent 'the real Glamor Boys of England'.

The general public also expressed their indebtedness in the only way they could, with simple gestures of solidarity. Free drinks and meals in bars and restaurants weren't at all rare. Sergeant Marian Bełc wrote in his diary:

> 'Now, wherever we go in the town, everywhere we can hear: "Polish Squadron brave", brilliant. Once we are in the pub, everyone wants to soak us in a beer or other drinks, if they only could. But this is all nothing, if we only could return to our homeland.'

Besides the men of both Polish fighter squadrons, and those who served under immediate British command, RAF Swinderby had another chance to send its Fairey Battles across the Channel. A second order had been received from Bomber Command Headquarters, this time saying that six Polish crews would be required again tonight. Once more, as the night before, their target was specified as German invasion barges in Bolougne harbour. It was decided, however, that on this occasion only 300 Squadron would participate.

At 7 pm, the first Fairey Battle took off, and within fifteen minutes all six bombers were heading to France. Their crews were: Wing Commander Wacław Makowski, Flying Officer Władysław Rogalski and Sergeant Marian Gędziorowski; Flying Officer Mieczysław Kałuża, Flying Officer Tadeusz Chrostowski and Sergeant Władysław Urbanowicz; Flight Lieutenant Stefan Kryński, Pilot Officer Zygmunt Szymański and Sergeant Władysław Graczyk; Flying Officer Jan Gębicki, Sergeant Edward Morawa and Sergeant Tadeusz Egierski; Pilot Officer Kazimierz Kula, Sergeant Marian Przybylski and Sergeant Henryk Kudełko; and Sergeant Józef Kuflik, Pilot Officer Nikodem Koziński and Sergeant Jan Artymiuk.

Despite being fired at by German anti-aircraft artillery, most of the crews managed to drop their bombs (four 250lb bombs each), yet once again they did not see the results. All six aircraft returned home without a scratch.

Fairey Battle L5427 BH-E piloted by Flg Off Antonowicz participated in the first operational mission carried by Polish No. 300 Squadron during the Battle of Britain on 14 September 1940. Antonowicz's crew took part in another sortie on 26 September in the same aircraft, followed by the third action on 13th October, when Sgt Koczwarski flew this machine during the bombing of the German fleet.

Sergeant Władysław Łapot from 300 Squadron, who flew the first historic Fairey Battle mission against the German barges, kept asking until the end of his 100-year-long life:

'I do not understand why crews of both our squadrons are not considered for the Battle of Britain clasp. We flew against the German invasion fleet, that was a real threat for the Britons, and our actions directly prevented their attack. No less than actions of the fighter pilots. Without doubt German soldiers were there for a reason, waiting for the signal. I have asked so many historians and decision makers, but so far no one was able to give me a definite answer.'

'It was terrible, we could feel the tension in the air. The invasion was closer than you could imagine,' his fellow squadron mate, Zygmunt Szymański, recalled. 'I brought a personally made bludgeon with me from France, expecting the worst – a German's visit.'[15]

Chapter Fourteen

The Struggle Continues

During the darkest hours of the Battle of Britain, when the future appeared uncertain and when the next scramble, next fight, next burst of gunfire could have been their last, even the smallest amount of rest, pinch of humanity and dose of humour became a necessity; a few minutes of decency were carved above almost all else. The Polish airmen, known for their cavalier spontaneity, straightforwardness and rectitude, were habitually treated as squadron mascots, due to their lack of English and consequently their bizarre way of expressing themselves and communicating on the ground and in the air. Even their old-fashioned gallantry and the way in which they displayed a Slavic respect to women, including kissing their hands, became a subject of interest from their British counterparts.

Some of the Polish norms of behaviour were questionable, and when pigs, ducks or geese started vanishing from local farms and were transformed into delicious and exotic treats, such as well-smoked sausages, black puddings, head cheese (brawn), lard or bacon on Polish tables, the British began to fear about the future of their flock and how this Polish 'invasion' may end.

Whether it was a drunken fight with the Irish Guards or a shooting competition, with colleagues aiming at a pack of cigarettes placed on the head one of their mates, it only showed the unique Polish method of fighting stress. At one point a plaque with the inscription 'English is also spoken' was fixed next to the door of the Northolt Officers' Mess to send a clear message about who was now in charge there. Various animals, including dogs and a monkey, were, against the will of their Polish owners, forbidden from the base due to their rather unpleasant smell and habits. Poles knew how to assemble their own 'hooch' production line, while the sour odour of homemade sauerkraut or pickled gherkins put off some of the non-Polish crews. All of this caused anxiety and even turbulence among the hosts, despite huge respect towards the (in most cases) vast experience that the Poles brought to the table, the horror they had witnessed before and unlimited hatred towards the enemy.

Wing Commander Tom Neil, who met some of these 'strangers' in 1940, wrote:

'Without in the least belittling their spirited and valiant contribution, there were, in fact, very few non-British subjects involved at the commencement of the Battle and not many more than a few when it ended. Apart from the Polish squadron which fought from Northolt in September and later, small groups of "foreigners" only began to filter into the RAF squadrons stationed around London about halfway through the Battle. Not only did they provide welcome support in terms of numbers and experience, they also provided more than their share of light relief.

'Our first injection of new blood took the form of four Polish and several French officers and NCOs, who arrived during the second week in September. The Poles wore RAF uniform with their own cap badges and wings but the French, in the manner of General de Gaulle, insisted on wearing their blues with gold stripes. They all stood around at dispersal nodding and smiling shyly like new boys at school, conversation being minimal because of the language problem. We welcomed them as cordially as we could, no one particularly keen to practice his schoolboy French and our knowledge of Polish being the cube root of nil. We learned later that a neighbouring station commander had mugged up his rules of etiquette and greeted his Polish contingent with bread and salt, a traditional gesture, and so started off very much on the right foot.

Three Polish pilots of No. 249 Sqn. Standing from left to right: Sgt Michał Maciejowski (previously 111 Sqn RAF), Sgt Mieczysław Popek (non-operational during the Battle of Britain), Wg Cdr Francis Beamish (North Weald Station Commander), Plt Off Jerzy Solak (previously 151 Sqn RAF).

'Our Poles, two officers and two NCOs, were ex-regular members of the Polish Air Force who had escaped through several countries in Europe and North Africa. Their names varied from the simple to the unpronounceable; the Solak's and Popec's[1] we could cope with but the Maciejowski's and the Miedziebrodski's[2] -well, I ask you! Those with the difficult names were assigned others which came more easily to the English tongue and which usually had some bearing on their prowess in the night-spots of London. As habitués of the fleshpots, our Polish colleagues were overshadowed only by the French who turned out to be veritable tigers in the salons of the West End …

'In the air, our "foreigners" quickly proved themselves to be brilliant but unpredictable.

'Our two Polish NCOs were formidable chaps indeed. After his first operational trip, the one we had christened Mickey returned to claim one Dornier 17 destroyed over the Blackwater. An hour later, the Dornier turned out to be an RAF Hampden which, after six dreary hours mine-laying off Norway, had been limping back at dawn only to be set upon when crossing the coast and dumped unceremoniously into an Essex pasture. The crew, not unreasonably, were spitting mad and there were a few tense moments before tempers cooled and order was restored. Then, hardly had the emotion of the occasion evaporated when our second Polish NCO reported shooting down a Focke-Wulf Condor off Cherbourg. Off Cherbourg! 200 miles away! We had barely heard of the place. And as for Condors, they were merely pictures in our recognition handbook.

'The language problem proved to be a sore trial for everyone at first. There was seldom any trouble getting our "foreigners" to the scene of the battle; they simply tagged onto the rest of the squadron and pitched in when the enemy was sighted. Once we had split up, however, the fun began. If the weather was anything other than crystal clear, the business of getting them back to base using ground control became a formidable exercise and there were some dramatic and hysterically funny dialogues over the R/T. Mickey, whose English could only be described as gibberish at the best of times, hit upon a solution almost immediately. After combat, he would put his wheels down and land in the nearest field; whereupon, being unable to express himself, he would be marched off to the nearest police station as a suspected fifth columnist. This meant that one of us would have to trail down to Kent, or wherever, in order to bail him out. Mickey did this twice and only desisted when he was threatened with being grounded if it occurred again.

'Among the many happy recollections of my continental colleagues, however, undoubtedly the most memorable are of one Polish officer I shall call Skalski[3] who, with two Frenchmen, joined the squadron in the late autumn of 1940. The Frenchmen, each of whom sounded like an impersonation of Charles Boyer, were devastatingly handsome. Skalski, on the other hand, being a rather elderly flying officer, seemed a most unlikely fighter pilot and spoke very little English to boot. But, whatever else he lacked, Skalski made up in charm. He was the nicest man imaginable and, having invested heavily in gold teeth, his smile, besides making the heavens rejoice, was like opening the vaults at Fort Knox.

'Shortly after his arrival, I briefed Skalski for his first trip in a Hurricane. He was to carry out a sector reconnaissance, which was really nothing more than a joyride during which time he could familiarise himself with the landmarks in our battle area. After watching him take off and fade into the late afternoon sky, I retired to the Mess – we were not on standby at the time – and I confess, I dismissed him from my mind.

'After tea and a quick look at the *Tatler*, I went to my room to clean up for dinner. I was just about to apply a razor to a well-lathered chin when all the lights went out and there was the usual chorus of protest up and down the corridor. Then, and only then, did I have a terrible thought. Skalski! And, sure enough, it was. Within 15 minutes the police had telephoned to say that one of our Hurricanes had flown through the high tension cables at Chelmsford and had crash-landed in a field. The pilot was damaged, but not seriously.

'Later that night Skalski turned up with the imprint of the gunsight on his forehead and his face looking like a well-wrapped parcel. He explained, with eloquent Polish gestures, that he had been unsure of his position (not lost, mind you) and had taken out his map to check his whereabouts. Then suddenly, Pouff! – Lights! When I enquired at what height he had been flying he replied with injured surprise that he had been at l0ft, as though l0ft was the only height at which to map-read on a sector reconnaissance!

'Skalski was sent immediately on a fortnight's leave and, with a final golden smile between strips of sticking plaster, he disappeared towards London in a haze of blue smoke from the rear end of his ancient Opel. Then, for two glorious weeks, we had only the German Air Force to contend with.

'On his return, I decided to send him off with the two new Frenchmen for formation practice. I explained the purpose of the exercise carefully and in basic English. With Skalski in the lead they were to carry out a series of standard manoeuvres. Then, after 15 min, at a given hand signal, Labouchere would take the lead, and so on. Did they all understand? Three heads went up and clown like yo-yos on a single string and they all departed to their aircraft before taking off in quite a respectable vic formation while I watched with fingers crossed and a prayer on my lips.

'Twenty minutes later, there came a spine-chilling wail which grew like an approaching siren. As we all tumbled out of dispersal to investigate, a Hurricane limped into the circuit with its wheels down and, without preliminaries, dropped on to the grass like a shot grouse. Skalski had returned!

'We ran towards it and almost immediately the engine stopped and the reason for the noise became apparent. The three-bladed Rotol airscrew, normally about 11ft in diameter, was little more than 48in, as a result of which the engine had been revving itself almost into a molten state. Moreover, the bottom engine cowlings were missing together with the oil tank which had been torn out of the port wing root, and the whole of the fuselage was smothered in black goo. Then as we arrived, breathless, the poor maltreated machine sank to its knees like a camel about to rid itself of a particularly unwelcome passenger.

'For a time, Skalski was incoherent with emotion. When I pressed him about the fate of his two companions, all I received were Polish hand signals and the words, "Pouff! Dead! Finis." However, a little later, the story spilled out like a torrent.

'Apparently, Skalski, after about 15 min, had made a hand signal which had been misinterpreted by both Frenchmen, each of whom decided that he was being instructed to take over the lead. The outcome was inevitable. All three met in a jumble of airscrews and wings followed by a flurry of bits, large and small: However, with the luck that seldom attended the British, both Frenchmen managed to reach the ground safely. One, finding his wing and fuselage chewed to pieces, plummeted towards the earth but contrived to round out sufficiently to hit in a reasonably level attitude. He survived the initial thump at more than 200 m.p.h. and the brisk excursion that followed through a series of fields, hedges and ditches. The second, least fortunate (or perhaps more so!) found his aircraft uncontrollable and jumped out at 800ft, striking the ground on the first swing of his parachute. In due course, they both arrived back grinning like chimpanzees and not in the least penitent.

'The passage of time has lent humour to these and a score of other incidents which, had they occurred today, would probably result in a Parliamentary uproar. As it was, they were passed off with many rounds of drinks in the Mess and much riotous laughter. Poles and Frenchmen alike went on to fight gloriously in the months and years ahead although many, ultimately, were killed. Such then was a little of the spirit abroad in the Battle. Overall it was a happy occasion; violent, dangerous, but happy. Ought we not to know more of this and less perhaps of Adolf Galland's cigars?'[4]

Tom Neil's humorous opinion about Flying Officer Henryk Skalski may sound a little harsh, particularly as the Polish pilot was twelve years his senior and much more experienced. Yet it is understandable that both Poles and their British colleagues could have been slightly judgmental. They knew very little about each other, the stigma of their lost campaign was still following the Polish pilots and they had to work even harder to show how good they were. Skalski was formerly a light bomber pilot, who had been converted to a fighter pilot, and had never previously flown operationally against the enemy.

Poles were no less opinionative though. Flying Officer Marian Duryasz of 213 Squadron clearly expressed his likes and dislikes towards some of his colleagues, when describing his time spent in the British squadron:

'After Jack Sink [*sic*], the command of the flight was taken by a cool pilot, an Englishman, Bill Drake [October 1940, 'A' Flight commander]. A chap with much experience gained already on the French front, before Dunkirk. Somebody called MacDonald [Squadron Leader Duncan MacDonald assumed command on 2 September 2 1940] has been appointed the commander, a man who previously served in reconnaissance – bomber squadrons flying Blenheims. Therefore a different scope of experience was gained, not always overlapping with the work of a typical fighter pilot. He wasn't very suitable for the role of commander of our squadron. Personally I would like to see Bill Drake in this position. He wasn't full of himself, he did not favour the English 'la di da', when contacting an ordinary front-line pilot. Especially one who had already chipped his teeth in combat.'[5]

The subsequent two days after the eventful Sunday were determined by the English weather, which deteriorated significantly. It impacted on German activity, although in the early morning of Monday 16 September a considerable formation of enemy planes was sighted. The following day was mostly quiet too, despite another victory for Sergeant Mirosław Wojciechowski from 303 Squadron, who increased his score by adding one Messerschmitt Bf 109.

His squadron took off from Northolt at 3 pm and, together with Canadian No. 1 Squadron, kept patrolling the area north of Biggin Hill. When over the Thames Estuary, they observed numerous Messerschmitts at quite high altitude. The machines from the JG53 '*Pik As*', seeing an easy opportunity, went down to attack the Canadians below them. Wojciechowski saw several Messerschmitts chasing one Hurricane, its Canadian pilot trying to escape by diving away. The Polish Sergeant decided that this poor chap definitely and urgently needed his help:

'I went into attack and engaged the Mes at 17,000 ft. I fired one burst into one of them, which shook and dived towards the earth. The burst was accurate, but I could not follow the enemy aircraft down, as I was engaged with the others. I fired again at another Me and after the second burst his right wing caught fire. I also saw flames inside the cockpit as he fell away from me, but I could not follow him down as I had another of them on my tail. I evaded this one in the cloud and afterwards could not find him.'

The identity of the German pilot whose aircraft went down as result of Wojciechowski's actions is uncertain. As the Pole testified his encounter with two Bf 109s, it seems most likely that it would be either of two 9th Staffel officers, Oblt Herbert Seliger or Oblt Jakob Stoll, both of whom were killed over the sea. Flying Officer Carl Briese, the Hurricane pilot whose life was almost certainly saved by the Polish NCO, force-landed at High Halstow in Kent.

Some of the Polish pilots were moved around between squadrons at this time. Pilot Officers Jan 'Fifi' Pfeiffer and Karol 'Cognac' Pniak left No. 32 Squadron stationed at Acklington in Northumberland, being posted to RAF Martlesham Heath in Suffolk with 257 Squadron, equipped with Hurricanes and commanded by the charismatic Squadron Leader Robert Stanford Tuck. The latter had only recently taken command of this 11 Group unit. The day after, Pilot Officer Marian Chełmecki left No. 17 Squadron at Debden and also travelled to 257 Squadron, where he joined the rest of the Polish team. According to Tuck's recollections, it was rather strange and difficult to manage this unusual foreign establishment. He dealt with them in his own, rather unusual way:

'Tuck liked the Poles. From the start he'd got on well with them, because to their great surprise his knowledge of Russian[6] enabled him to understand almost everything they said to each other. The languages are no more dissimilar than, say, the sort of English spoken by Londoners and the version used in the Scottish Highlands – the swear words are more or less the same! When the Poles got excited in the air and lapsed into their native tongue, their leader would break in and curse them roundly in their accent of a Ukrainian ditch-digger, but after a while even that couldn't hold them in check – they became hurtling bolts of fury, beyond all reason and authority.

'One evening in the mess he turned abruptly to one of them and said, not unpleasantly, "Oh by the way, you and your balmy chums went tearing off on a private war again today. I'm getting thoroughly browned off with these capers. You started it this time – I heard you. So I'm grounding you for twenty four hours. Tomorrow you don't fly." The Pole was aghast. He apologized, he pleaded, but Tuck was adamant. Hopeful till the last, the Pole turned up at dispersal in the morning, wearing his flying gear. Tuck ignored him. When the squadron took off, he was left standing on the tarmac. According to Jeff Myers and Chiefy Tyrer, big tears were rolling down his cheeks. After two or three doses of this medicine, the "Private Polish Air Force" became malleable, and was duly welded into the team.'[7]

Pilot Officer Bolesław 'Vodka' Własnowolski also departed Tangmere's No. 607 Squadron with a posting to 213 Squadron, where he joined Flying Officer Marian Duryasz. His arrival was erroneously described by the latter:

'Two days [actually six days] after Sergeant Wójcicki's death Plt Off Bolesław Własnowolski joined the squadron as an operational pilot. He was an experienced old stager, I must say, because he fought already in 32 fighter squadron.'[8]

The next day, the weather over England eventually improved, leaving its defenders extremely active again. The Germans, though disappointed by the results of their raids on 15 September, once again threw more of their aircraft across the Channel.

It wasn't until the early afternoon that the Polish pilots achieved further successes. They answered a call from the Operations Room that had been notified about a large enemy presence in the area of Calais. It was obvious that something big was building up, and various RAF squadrons were scrambled, accompanied by both Polish units. No. 303 Squadron took off between 12.25-12.30 pm, while their colleagues from No. 302 went up fifteen minutes later. Nine groups of German aircraft crossed the British coastline between Dover and Maidstone. Bombers flew at high altitude, with a large formation of '*Jabos*' shifting beneath. One of the squadrons that went close was No. 501, which was ordered to patrol the West Malling area and keep their height to 20,000ft. They sighted a formation of about twenty bombers heading towards Maidstone, flying around 2,000ft below.

Soon after the Germans started to manoeuvre in the opposite direction, most probably aiming for their bases in France, apparently having completed their mission. Their fighter escort was being engaged by Spitfires, and black puffs of anti-aircraft artillery fire appeared close to the bombers.

There was another traumatic incident when two enemy fighters 'took care' of a parachuting British pilot. Sergeant Antoni Głowacki, who flew as Blue 2, tried to stop them killing this poor chap. He later reported:

> 'I turned and attacked one of them from beam and quarter, and after my second burst he dived vertically from 15,000 ft down to a patch of cloud at 3,000 ft. The last two bursts I fired as he dived astern. When he reached the cloud I went round it, having pulled out of the dive in time. I waited on the side towards the French coast to intercept him but saw no trace of him. At the speed with which the Me 109 was travelling (i.e. 400 mph) it is not possible that he could have pulled out below 3,000 ft. Had he done so, I must have seen him as I placed myself directly on his path home. It is most probable that he went straight in SW of Maidstone.'

When Głowacki's victim was falling from the sky, the Polish team of 303 Squadron, led by Squadron Leader Kellett, after nearly an hour of fruitless patrolling, sighted either a single Dornier (as Pilot Officer Ferić saw it), or one accompanied by a fighter plane (as Kellett recalls). The latter took the credit for sighting the Luftwaffe pair:

> 'On another occasion almost the whole of 11 Group were spread over Kent when I spotted a lone Dornier escorted by one Messerschmitt crossing the Group's front. It passed a number of squadrons unnoticed. 303 bounced the luckless pair. The fighter was disposed of in a second but in line astern one after another we filled the Dornier with lead until it hit the ground in Kent – we circled an oast house [a building for drying hops] until we were certain no one got away and returned to base.'[9]

Although Sergeant František returned to base claiming destruction of the Bf 109, there was not enough evidence to prove that this was in fact the aircraft seen by his commander prior to engagement. Yet such a possibility cannot be ruled out. Furthermore, Ferić rather precisely formulated his opinion on what happened next, saying that the whole squadron saw a reconnaissance Dornier

Do 215 (not even a word about its escort). His version enhances the story with a couple of interesting details:

> 'Paszko is shouting over the radio, but Dyzio cannot hear him. Something terrible, even worse, he could not see, yet Jerry is passing between us and six other Hurricanes. Paszko with the Section separates from the rest, Dyzio is turning left instead of right, I am breaking away and glide.'

The last seconds of the Dornier's journey were accompanied by all the 303 Squadron pilots in action. The victory was shared between Kellett, Flying Officer Ludwik Paszkiewicz, Flying Officer Walerian Żak, Pilot Officer Ferić, Jan Zumbach, Sergeant Marian Bełc, Sergeant Jan Kowalski and Sergeant Mirosław Wojciechowski. Ferić's Hurricane was damaged in this clash, yet its pilot returned home without significant problem, and the ground crew saw his bulletproof glass shattered by enemy bullets. It had saved Ferić's life.

Dornier Do 215s were rarely seen in British skies in those days, so it seems the only such machine from the 4th Staffel Aufklärungsgruppe Oberkommando der Luftwaffe that crashed at Collier Street near Yalding in Kent was most definitely that shot down by the 303 pilots. Fw. Schuetz was killed, while Lt Hans Poser, Uffz. Wiesen and Uffz. Linsner were captured after bailing out.

The Luftwaffe was gathering its planes for the next big wave, so during the following hours activity over England was limited to single missions that did not lead to encounters reported by any of the Polish pilots. It wasn't until 4 pm that the British chain of RDF stations located another large group of aircraft approaching.

The Luftwaffe was ordered to bomb oil tanks at Port Victoria in Kent. Amongst the RAF squadrons that were vectored to 'welcome' the guests were quite a few with the Polish pilots, but also both Polish squadrons led by Squadron Leader Satchell (No. 302) and Flight Lieutenant Kent (No. 303). The whole Duxford Wing consisting of three squadrons was searching for the enemy between Gravesend and Tilbury, when the Poles from 'Poznań' Squadron sighted a group of approximately thirty bombers of KG77 flying at 16,000ft. It was 5.20 pm when the rumpus started.

Satchell, who was also leading Red Section, set a Dornier's engine on fire after two or three attacks. Then Squadron Leader Mümler, who was also in Satchell's section, attacked one of the seven bombers which the Polish officer flew closest to. The oldest Polish Battle of Britain pilot wrote:

> 'I got in one long burst of about 5 secs at 250 yds closing rapidly. At about 100 yds I had to break away and make room for another Hurricane

attacking the same aircraft from the port beam. On breaking away I noticed flames and smoke pouring from the rear top cockpit of the E/A.'

As it turned out, the destruction of the Dornier Do 17 was the first and last victory claimed by this mature fighter pilot during the Battle. Many years later, he recalled that day with a pinch of emotion: 'I am proud that I belonged to this magnificent 302 Fighter Squadron, but also that once, on 18 September 1940, I could participate in combat and shot down one Do 17.'[10] The account written by Mümler is far from being precise, as he participated in twenty-seven operations during the Battle of Britain, four times being engaged in fights.

The third aircraft of Red Section was flown by Flying Officer 'Roch' Kowalski, who gained another kill, stating later:

'I attacked a Do.215 with a right-hand turn from above, getting in 2 bursts of 1 sec., but had to break off very quickly to make way for a Section following me. Next I attacked another Dornier, getting in 3 long burst at 150 yds. After my last burst I noticed a full-sized parachute flying out from the rear gunner's turret, but which became entangled in the tail plane. Bits of the e/a flew off. I could not follow the result of my burst because I received a burst of fire which damaged my rudder and mainplane and I had to adopt evasive tactics. After making sure that my a/c was controllable I attacked another Dornier, getting in two short bursts without visible effect. I had to break off combat owing to lack of ammo. After my second attack I noticed 2 E/A burning but cannot state whether they were the two at which I fired.'

Yellow Section, led by Flight Lieutenant James Farmer, was close behind and swung into action right after the Reds. The leader was credited with one Junkers Ju 88 being damaged, while both his wingmen, Flight Lieutenant Piotr Łaguna and Sergeant Marian Wędzik, were unsuccessful. Green Section, however, had more luck, all three pilots getting the enemy in their gunsight at the right moment. Pilot Officer Edward Pilch, Green 1, saw the results of the previous havoc caused by Red Section, with pieces of aircraft flying around:

'I chose a Ju 88 and attacked, but it defended itself very strongly from the rear upper turret as well as the lower rear turret. I did five attacks on it, and after the first one saw smoke pouring from the port engine. After the 4th attack I saw fierce flames and smoke coming from the port engine. After my 5th attack a very red light shot out of the aircraft. I could no longer follow, having used all my ammo.'

Pilch was credited with the destruction of a Ju 88.

Thirty-year-old Sergeant Edward Paterek was Green 2. When the enemy formation appeared, he was watching his leader charging against them, but he decided to go for the aircraft on the left side, not knowing that this would put him in danger. Paterek reported shortly after returning from this adventurous combat:

'I did No. 1 attack, getting in a short burst which had the effect of setting fire to the port engine which seemed to explode in flame. My second attack was from the quarter and behind, and I got in a short burst where at the crew of the e/a, numbering 3, jumped out and their parachutes opened at once. I gave another burst and pieces of the e/a flew off, one of which hit my propeller, breaking one of the blades, a second piece, or possibly one of the pilots who jumped out, hit my glycol radiator. My aircraft began to flutter violently and the cockpit was filled with petrol from the reserve tank. I switched off and glided from 20,000 feet, landing in a field near Chelmsford without any further damage. Whilst gliding I noticed the e/a diving steeply to earth.'

Thanks to his skills, coolness and composure, Paterek not only avoided enemy planes on his way down, but also did not sustain any wounds while crash-landing at Sandon Lodge Farm near Danbury in Essex. Undaunted, he realized how close he was to being killed and understood the thin line between being a hunter or prey.

Pilot Off Włodzimierz Karwowski, flying as Green 3, also attacked the formation of Junkers, choosing the last aircraft on the starboard side. At the same time he observed a group of aircraft escaping eastwards, therefore he immediately turned and attacked the last machine of that formation. He explained later:

'Having got in two bursts, I suddenly noticed below me, a solitary aircraft, which I then attacked from the beam, getting in three short bursts. I saw something fly out of the aircraft and after a moment saw one of the crew jump out with his parachute, whilst the aircraft simply dived straight into the sea at a place due east of [the] Thames.'

All three pilots from Blue Section could also be proud of their actions that day. Neither Flight Lieutenant William Riley, nor Flight Lieutenant Franciszek Jastrzębski and Pilot Officer Stefan Wapniarek, had any doubts that they made 'Göring's wonderful air force' a little more short of planes and crew. Riley scored a double by shooting down one Ju 88 and adding another as probably destroyed. Jastrzębski (Blue 2) recognized his opponents as Dorniers when he attacked them slightly abeam and getting in a short burst that lasted one second. He reported, with help from an interpreter:

'Next I attacked a single aircraft which had broken away from the rest of the formation, above and abeam down sun. I got in two short bursts from 300–100 yds, but I saw no result. I attacked again, getting in a long burst, and then saw the aircraft go into a dive with black smoke coming from it. I did not see this E/A anymore because I noticed another on my port side, and attacked from above slightly head-on and abeam, but I noticed no effect.'

Jastrzębski, credited with a probable victory, was very evaluative when analyzing the tactical mistakes shown on this occasion by the RAF. He complained about some of their own aircraft waiting above the enemy formation, showing no signs of deciding whether to proceed with the attack or not. He also was disappointed with the way in which the encounter was carried out, as too many aircraft flew very close to each other, the pilots creating a crowd that eventually led to a situation where seven of the German bombers managed to fly away untouched.

The last pilot who earned a success was the 24-year-old Wapniarek, veteran of 132nd Fighter Squadron, who had flown during the Polish Campaign and claimed three aerial victories. He nearly ended his wartime exploits when captured by the Germans, but managed to escape and travelled to France and then to Britain. Wapniarek, who flew as Blue 3, on this occasion decided to attack an enemy bomber which he saw on the left side of the German formation. More details of his encounter can be found in the combat report the squadron's Intelligence Officer, Flying Officer Paul Harding, completed upon his return:

'I attacked from the quarter and slightly above and behind and got in a burst of 3 secs at about 80 yds. My second attack took place after another Hurricane had attacked the Ju 88. I then saw black smoke coming from the aircraft and I got in a short series of 2 secs at about 100 yds and then turned to another Ju 88, having seen the rear gunner of the first Ju 88 jump out at about 10,000 ft over Southend. At this moment I noticed a second Ju 88 trying to escape in the clouds. I turned left at 90° and used No. 1 attack. The rear gunner fired from 3 m.g.s at me. I got in a very long burst at about 50 yds and stopped firing when I noticed my tracer, which meant I only had about 40 rounds per gun left. The fire of the rear gunner was accurate but aimed too high, and after my last bursts he stopped firing. After flying on for a few minutes over the sea I attacked once more at about 30 yds range, firing off the rest of my ammo. The E/A was still gliding and slowly crashed into the sea, breaking up completely.'

By claiming seven enemy aircraft being completely destroyed, three probably shot down and one damaged, No. 302 Polish Squadron reached second position on the Fighter Command scoreboard, only behind 242 Squadron, which gained the amazing result of twelve kills. Whatever is said about Polish determination and bravery, should the contribution not to be ignored of the heroic British and Canadian pilots who flew with them in both Polish units.

Another two operations were carried out by both Polish bomber squadrons on 18 September. As previously, they were scheduled for another mission to destroy German barges across the Channel. For the first operation, performed in the early morning, eight aircraft, including two from 300 Squadron, were to attack targets in the French port of Boulougne, and in case those were obscured or impossible to find, proceed to Cap Gris-Nez and perform a similar activity.

They took off between 2.50-3.15 am, and after over an hour of flying, found themselves over the target. Bombs were observed to hit their targets directly, with numerous explosions seen in the dockyards. All crews, assuming that their mission was successfully accomplished, returned to

301 Squadron's Fairey Battles ready to take off.

Swinderby safely. They were: Wing Commander Roman Rutkowski, Flying Officer Henryk Sawlewicz and Sergeant Franciszek Florczak; Flying Officer Wacław Butkiewicz, Flying Officer Stanisław Starowicz and Sergeant Kazimierz Sawicz; Sergeant Stanisław Kłosowski, Pilot Officer Bolesław Biliński and Sergeant Antoni Lipecki; Sergeant Franciszek Zaremba, Pilot Officer Mariusz Wodzicki and Sergeant Ignacy Bator; Pilot Officer Marian Olszyna, Flying Officer Hieronim Kulbacki and Sergeant Jan Hejnowski; and Sergeant Tadeusz Bojakowski, Flying Officer Józef Koryciński and Sergeant Antoni Dydo (all from 301 Squadron); followed by Flight Lieutenant Stefan Kryński, Pilot Officer Zygmunt Szymański and Sergeant Władysław Graczyk; and Sergeant Józef Kuflik, Pilot Officer Nikodem Koziński and Sergeant Jan Artymiuk (from 300 Squadron).

Orders were received from the Bomber Command via No. 1 Bomber Group to continue destruction of the enemy invasion fleet, so another six crews were chosen for a second mission to France that evening. As previously, Boulogne was the target, but this time only 300 Squadron was to take part. All six Fairey Battles left Swinderby between 7.20-7.40 pm and arrived above the target area after more than an hour. All bombs, except some of those carried by Flying Officer Michałowski's and Sergeant Dziekoński's crews – who struggled to unleash their loads – were skilfully dropped on the mark. The participants on this mission were: Flying Officer Marian Michałowski, Pilot Officer Adam Męciński and Sergeant Tadeusz Świdziński; Sergeant Kazimierz Szymanowski, Pilot Officer Zenon Luba and Sergeant Albin Socha; Sergeant Czesław Dziekoński, Flying Officer Włodzimierz Pęski and Sergeant Tadeusz Bączak; Sergeant Gerhard Goebel, Flying Officer Stanisław Firlej-Bielański and Sergeant Tadeusz Szmajdowicz; Sergeant Marian Kostecki, Flying Officer Jan Piotrowski and Sergeant Feliks Jezierski; and Sergeant Alojzy Ratajczak, Pilot Officer Antoni Pułczyński and Sergeant Tadeusz Egierski.

The following day, unwelcoming English weather dictated the Luftwaffe 'flight plan' and consequently resulted in less British activity. German action over Britain was reduced to single missions by solitary aircraft or small groups of fighters performing sweeps over the south-east. Several RAF squadrons were active throughout the day, including Polish pilots flying within their ranks. Few encounters took place, and only one operation proved to be successful for the Poles.

Six Hurricanes from No. 302 Squadron left Duxford at 10.25 am with the aim of patrolling around London. They split into two separate sections, and only one of them had any success. When over Mildenhall, Blue Section, led by Flight Lieutenant Riley, noticed a suspicious-looking aircraft which appeared to be a Junkers Ju 88 from the 1st Group of KG77. When they confirmed the characteristic silhouette of the enemy machine, pilots of the 'Poznań' Squadron followed directions from the Operations Room.

Riley first took his chances, yet prematurely shooting at the Ju 88 from a distance of 700 yards was not a good decision, and after wasting all his ammo, he had to wait to see what the rest of the Section could achieve. His No. 3, Flying Officer Julian Kowalski, simultaneously went for the kill when the Junkers was at about 16,000ft, getting in two short bursts from a distance of 250 yards. Kowalski reported:

'As the distance between myself and the Ju.88 increased, I pulled the emergency boost and after another minute's flight I was within 80 yrds of the Ju 88. I got in 5 bursts of about half a sec. From the Ju 88 fuel poured out and covered my aircraft. From the upper rear gun turret I encountered very strong M.G. fire. Seeing that my fire hadn't got much effect, I got in two more bursts of half a sec at about 50 yrds. The aircraft caught fire after my second burst and it began to dive steeply through cloud. I followed closely but none of the crew jumped out. After gliding for about 2 minutes it crashed to earth about 4 miles N.E. of Brandon.'

It was quite an impressive result for 'Roch' Kowalski, considering three of his guns did not fire at all. Flight Lieutenant Franciszek Jastrzębski, Blue 2, also fired at the enemy aircraft, but like Riley, he did so rather spontaneously from very long distance. Although Kowalski reported that no evasive action was taken by any of the German crew, in fact Uffz. Ernst Etzold managed to bail out and, after being wounded while landing, was captured by the British. The remaining three – Uffz. Paul Dorawa, Gefr. Erich Schulz and Gefr. Heinz Scholz – weren't so lucky. They went down together with the aeroplane, which crashed at Culford Park in Bury St Edmunds, Suffolk. Despite scoring only one enemy aircraft destroyed, 302 Squadron was just as successful as other units on the day: three other RAF squadrons reported just one kill each.

Friday 20 September did not bring any further successes for the Polish fighter pilots, yet was marked by another tragedy when Pilot Officer Józef Stępień, a former instructor of the Polish Air Force Cadet Officers School, lost his life while performing a training flight in No. 5 Operation Training Unit. The Miles Master which he flew disintegrated in the air whilst over Cherrington in Shropshire. We will never know if he would have completed his preparation for a career as a fighter pilot, and consequently if he could have joined his compatriots in the Battle of Britain.

Another Polish officer, Pilot Officer Witold Głowacki of 605 Squadron, participated in combat with Messerschmitt Bf 109s and his Hurricane was hit by cannon shells and machine-gun bullets, most probably by Obfw. Heinrich Gottlob from 6th Staffel JG26. The Pole returned safely, at least on this occasion, but he would not survive to the end of the month.

Six crews from No. 301 Polish Squadron were debriefed for an operation that was planned for the early hours of the next day. Eventually, the first Fairey Battle took off at 3.25 am on the Saturday, quickly followed by the other five. This time the airmen were told to fly much lower over the target and drop their bombs from 1,000-2,000ft instead of the usual 10,000 ft, quite a risky manoeuvre considering the number of German anti-aircraft artillery nests positioned along the French coast.

Attacking from such a low level most probably scared away all the Germans sleeping beneath, principally because the squadron's mechanics had fitted their Battles with sirens similar to those used by Stuka dive-bombers. The operation went smoothly, apart from the miscalculation of Sergeant Palul and his two crew members who flew in completely the opposite direction, arriving over … Scotland! Their Fairey Battle crash-landed at RAF Annan, although all three Poles escaped unharmed complaining about faulty compass. The crews selected for this mission were: Flight Lieutenant Witold Piotrowski, Flying Officer Julian Pałka and Sergeant Karol Paliwoda; Sergeant Józef Waszak, Flying Officer Jan Kozak and Sergeant Edward Janik; Sergeant Roman Bonkowski, Flying Officer Eugeniusz Domański and Sergeant Zdzisław Pieczyński; Flight Lieutenant Stanisław Brejnak, Flying Officer Antoni Wronka and Sergeant Tadeusz Madejski; Sergeant Antoni Palul, Flying Officer Stanisław Waszkiewicz and Sergeant Konstanty Gołębiowski; and Pilot Officer Bolesław Murawski, Flying Officer Leon Szymkiewicz and Sergeant Czesław Kozłowski.

Saturday 21 September was not much different than the day before. Although German raiders kept visiting southern England, there were only rather small groups of them, which were met by RAF squadrons. Few claims were made throughout the day, without any reported by the Poles. However, the PAF suffered another loss when Flying Officer Juliusz Topolnicki crashed his Hurricane into an anti-aircraft gun post at Exeter airfield. It is assumed that his engine failed right after taking off at 11.25 am to perform a non-operational flight in which he was supposed to practice formation flying. The Polish pilot burned to death in the wreckage. Although shocked by this loss, his Polish squadron mate, Flying Officer Jerzy Jankiewicz, continued aerial training ten minutes later.

A new group of Polish pilots completed their training in No. 6 Operational Training Unit at Sutton Bridge and were posted to various squadrons of the RAF and PAF. Sergeant Maksymilian Frychel and Sergeant Wilhem Sasak arrived at 32 Squadron at Acklington. Twenty-one-year-old Frychel graduated from the

Polish Air Force NCO School for Minors just before the outbreak of war as a bomber pilot, yet did not participate in the Polish Campaign. His posting to 32 Squadron is a mystery, as no flights by this pilot were ever recorded, nor the reason or date of him leaving.[11] Sasak was a graduate of the PAF Reserve Cadet Officers School, similarly to Frychel, without any previous combat experience.

Pilot Officer Edmund Jereczek and Pilot Officer Józef Gil joined No. 43 Squadron at Usworth near Sunderland. Nearly 36 years old, Jereczek, a former flying instructor in Dęblin, took part in the Polish Campaign with the Naval Air Squadron, and like Gil, had never flown fighter aircraft before. Almost ten years younger, Gil, also called '*Zazdrośnik*' ('Jealous'), was commissioned in the 12th class of Cadet Officers School as a bomber pilot. Both undertook fighter conversion in England.

Four others were attached to 302 Squadron: Pilot Officers Bronisław Bernaś and Stefan Kleczkowski, and Sergeants Zbigniew Kleniewski and Jerzy Załuski. Bernaś was 24 and, apart from graduating from the Air Force Reserve Cadet Officers' School and exercises undertaken with the 6th Air Regiment, had little experience as a pilot, especially an operational one. Neither had Kleczkowski, who was one of the Dęblin Eaglets. Despite graduating from this prestigious school, he had no combat experience in Poland.

Unlike the others, Załuski flew in Poland in September 1939, but again, not as a fighter pilot: his duty was with 63rd Reconnaissance Squadron. Kleniewski, after a few years in Switzerland and then studying law in Poland, joined the Training Flight of the 1st Air Regiment in Warsaw in 1939, so when he arrived in Britain did not have much flying experience. No flights with 302 Squadron were ever recorded for this 23-year-old pilot. It can only be assumed that his candidature as a 302 fighter pilot wasn't appreciated by the very strict Mümler.

The changeable English weather again played its hand the next day, decent conditions providing a good opportunity for another raid, with heavy clouds. In the early morning, the Luftwaffe sent reconnaissance aircraft and performed sweeps, but later considerably larger groups of bombers and fighter planes visited England.

Until 26 September the Poles achieved some minor successes in combat, although the scale of these was smaller than before. To cover their recent losses, three Sergeants – Jan Palak, Edward Paterek and Antoni Siudak – were posted from No. 302 to 303 Squadron on 22 September, despite complaints by Squadron Leader Mümler, who was definitely not happy with losing experienced pilots, who had already shared a few victories between themselves.

The day after, a large group of enemy planes was discovered thanks to magnificent work by the RDF, and several RAF squadrons were scrambled to intercept them. One of these squadrons was No. 605 that operated over the

Tunbridge area, when, around 10 am, two Messerschmitt Bf 109s attacked from out of the sun. The squadron was at the point of changing direction to the right, thus flying a bit slower, when a single Bf 109 came between the Hurricanes, shooting at the closest machine. This aircraft was piloted by Pilot Officer Witold Głowacki, who quickly controlled his nerve. He later described the action:

> 'I was then rather higher than the rest of the squadron, and the Me after a short burst over-shot me and I was able to give him a long burst from 300 yards closing to 50 yards. I saw him shudder and try to climb away, but he could not do so and dropped away. This is confirmed by Yellow 1 but neither of us could watch him as another Me 109 was then in position to attack and we had to break away. The second enemy aircraft climbed back to join the rest of the formation alone.'

Głowacki was credited with damaging one Bf 109.

Half an hour later, pilots of 303 Squadron, flying over the Thames Estuary at the head of a larger wing-like formation consisting of aircraft from No. 1 RCAF and 229 Squadrons, spotted the enemy. After a quick count, the Poles, led by

Flt Lt Jerzy Orzechowski (left, 303 Sqn PAF, 607 Sqn RAF & 306 Sqn PAF) during conversation with Sqn Ldr Witold Urbanowicz. Orzechowski arrived at Northolt to take command of 303 Squadron, yet this order never materialised.

'Kentowski', realized that they were facing at least fifteen Messerchmitts flying at 30,000ft, 7,000ft higher than the 303 boys. However, either the Germans did not see them or tried to avoid a fight, as they passed over them flying in the opposite direction.

Soon after, on the far side of the Isle of Sheppey, British, Canadian and Polish pilots were vectored on a south-easterly course, and noticed about twenty contrails above, a sign of the enemy presence. It wasn't long before Flight Lieutenant Kent was warned of another group of 'Bandits' in the area. They were on the starboard side and almost immediately made feint attacks. Kent took the whole formation into the middle of the German circle, which resulted in the enemy fighters breaking off into sections, and began attacking from quite long range. The Canadian officer made two claims on that day, being credited with the destruction of a Bf 109 and then damaging an aircraft classified as a photo reconnaissance or weather research Focke Wulf Fw 58, and not a French-made Potez, as Kent initially thought.

But he was not the only victorious pilot of the 'Tadeusz Kościuszko' Squadron. 'Szaposzka', Sergeant Szaposznikow, flew as No. 2 in Red Section, commanded by Kent. He noticed around eight Bf 109s attacking a single Hurricane, so with no time to spare, the Pole went in for the kill: 'I attacked it from astern and underneath at 300 yards. The Messerschmitt dived down towards the sea. I used up all my ammunition on it, and it crashed into the sea in mid Channel.'

There were many Battle of Britain pilots whose lives were cut short by unclear circumstances, and even today we do not know for certain exactly what happened to them. Their last minutes are secrets taken with them to the grave. One of those pilots was a Polish member of 605 Squadron, Witold Głowacki, who had only recently damaged his latest adversary. Two pilots of the 'County of Warwick' Squadron were scrambled just before 4 pm on 24 September to chase an enemy bomber which was recently seen in the vicinity of Beachy Head. They soon sighted and mistook the Dornier Do 17 as a Do 215, despite the minor difference that this type had in-line engines fitted in contrast to radial engines of a Do 17. Both pilots attacked the German raider repeatedly until the Dornier plunged down near Cap Gris-Nez. However, the triumphant fighters were then intercepted by four fighters of the 3rd Staffel's JG53. Pilot Officer Ian Muirhead, who being born in 1913 was the same age as the Pole, flew inland over France, where he eventually lost his chasers, but Głowacki was shot down by Oblt Michael Sonner and crash-landed near Ambleteuse,[12] north of Wimille.

His Hurricane disintegrated on impact, yet its pilot survived. Photographs taken by German soldiers on the spot show the Polish pilot in relatively good condition, with his head bandaged and a stream of blood on his right check.

It was revealed later that Głowacki was taken to the German field hospital in Guînes, where he died the same day. There was speculation about the cause of Głowacki's death, even suggestions that he was purposely killed, probably as an act of revenge for being born in Berlin. However, the most likely cause of his death was an allergic reaction to an anti-tetanus injection.

There was no rest for the Polish bomber crews, and during the very early hours of Tuesday 24 September, No. 300 'Mazovian' Squadron flew over Bolougne once more. Six Fairey Battles took off from Swinderby between 3.15-3.30 am to attack the German invasion barges and fleet. Heavy cannon fire from German anti-aircraft artillery, the brightness of the searchlights penetrating the sky over the French coast and limited visibility restricted assessment of whether the bombs hit their target or not. Flying Officer Gołko could not find the mark at all, therefore decided to fly to Calais and drop his bombs there. The crews, who all returned safely, were: Flying Officer Jerzy Gołko, Flying Officer Roman Miarczyński and Sergeant Alfons Kowalski; Pilot Officer Marek Rusiecki, Flying Officer Ignacy Szponarowicz and Sergeant Marian Sztul; Sergeant Piotr Nowakowski, Sergeant Tomasz Łubieszko and Sergeant Henryk Kudełko; Sergeant Józef Kazimierczak, Pilot Officer Zygmunt Pluta and Sergeant Jan Bieżuński; Pilot Officer Zdzisław Kurowski, Flying Officer Władysław Rogalski and Sergeant Władysław Łapot; and Flying Officer Jan Konarzewski, Pilot Officer Antoni Pułczyński and Sergeant Feliks Jezierski.

Fairey Battles with the Polish red and white insignia yet again attacked Boulogne the following day, taking off between 3.23-3.40 an. On this occasion, six crews from 301 Squadron were chosen for the raid across the Channel. Their mission ended in tragedy, as only half an hour after leaving the aerodrome, one of the bombers was shot down near Thetford and crashed at Honington in Norfolk, killing all three if its crew.

Pilot Officer Józef Waroński was flying his first mission since being posted to the squadron, although he had a long previous career as a pilot of numerous *Eskadras*, including 31st Reconnaissance Squadron, with which he took part in the Polish Campaign. This graduate of the 11th Class of Dęblin Eaglets School was 33 years old when he lost his life. Pilot Officer Józef Kuliński, a navigator, was seven years younger, although graduated from the Polish Air Force Cadet Officers School one year before Waroński. He also flew operationally in Poland, as a member of 32nd Reconnaissance Squadron. As well as for his older colleague, this was Kuliński's first mission in England. Details of 21-year-old Sergeant Karol Paliwoda are less known: he was trained as a wireless operator and air gunner in No. 18 OTU, and just four days prior to this tragedy he participated in his first mission over France.

The initial theory suggested that the Fairey Battle with the Polish crew had been intercepted and shot down by a German night fighter. Conversely, it is also believed that a British fighter pilot may have been responsible for this tragedy. So far, investigations have found no documented cause of this loss, as no 'kill' claims were made by either side. However, it was reported that on several occasions bomber crews failed to identify themselves when approach by British fighter planes.

The remaining crews performed successful attacks, returning to Swinderby between 6.45-7.23 am. They were: Sergeant Adam Weiss, Flying Officer Henryk Sawlewicz and Sergeant Jan Bujak; Pilot Officer Teofil Pożyczka, Pilot Officer Mieczysław Łapa and Sergeant Ryszard Tydman; Sergeant Zygmunt Popławski, Flying Officer Stanisław Król and Sergeant Bernard Kowalski; Pilot Officer Józef Wójcik, Pilot Off Mariusz Wodzicki and Sergeant Czesław Kozłowski; and Sergeant Antoni Palul, Flying Officer Stanisław Waszkiewicz and Sergeant Konstanty Gołębiowski.

A few hours later, 303 Squadron was airborne again after receiving orders to intercept an enemy formation located around Cherbourg and heading towards Portland. Numerous squadrons that were operating over southern England could not prevent them from bombing the Bristol Aircraft factory at Filton in Gloucestershire. Claiming not even one raider destroyed, the pilots of 'Tadeusz Kościuszko' Squadron landed back at Northolt, where Sergeant Andruszków managed to claim a ground 'victory' after crashing into a car, damaging the undercarriage and propeller of his aircraft. Between 11.40 am and noon, however, three Polish pilots had more luck than Andruszków, destroying actual aerial targets.

Both flights of 609 Squadron were sent into action, at 11.15 am and 11.20 am respectively, with Polish pilots Flying Officer 'Novi' Nowierski and Flying Officer 'Osti' Ostaszewski-Ostoja in 'A' Flight. When patrolling over Portland, the squadron commander received warning that a large pack of enemy planes was expected over Yeovil. Soon after, three large groups of 200 tightly packed Heinkel He 111s and Dornier Do 17s appeared, guarded from above by at least thirty Messerschmitt Bf 110s.

Red Section sighted another bunch of German fighters slightly higher, this time Bf 109s. Ostaszewski, the last pilot of Blue Section, tried to follow his leader when attacking the Dornier that was leading the group. When close to the target, something unexpected happened. A General Report states that Ostaszewski was 'attacking the Leader of the Dornier formation with a four second burst but could not observe results as his hood blew off when he pulled off'. Despite this, Ostaszewski managed to return to Middle Wallop.

Remains of the Fairey Battle L5351 GR-N from No. 301 Squadron that crashed in the early morning of 25 September 1940 near Honington. All three crew members Plt Off Józef Waroński, Plt Off Józef Kuliński and Sgt Karol Paliwoda were killed.

Green Section, in which Nowierski flew, also made several claims. Nowierski, being No. 3, 'also attacked two bombers of which the second was the leader of the whole formation to which he gave a long burst. He claimed no casualty but confirmed landing of a Heinkel at Swanage marked B-H'. Nowierski's recognition of the area where the enemy landed was accurate. The German bomber was actually wearing the marks G1+BH, which helps to identify the Polish pilot's adversary. A Heinkel from 1st Staffel KG55 indeed force-landed at Westfield Farm in Studland, near Swanage, and the crew – Hptm. Karl Kőthke, Fw. Fritz Jürges, Uffz. Josef Altrichter, Gefr. Rudolf Weisbach and Flgr Otto Müller – were taken prisoners. Uffz. Altrichter was seriously wounded and did not survive captivity. Interestingly, after confirming that 609 Squadron pilots shot down eight enemy planes (including two shared with another unit), two probably destroyed and damaged five with no loss of their comrades, Nowierski was eventually credited with the destruction, which apparently was not recognised by the Polish authorities.

No. 238 Squadron, which took off at 11.35 am and flew alongside 609, kept patrolling the Yeovil area, where it was also engaged in combat. Despite noticing two quite large formations of enemy bombers, consisting of forty machines each, protected from above by Messerschmitt Bf 110s, the 238 pilots decided to engage with the Heinkels. Eight claims were made by 238 Squadron airmen, including six aircraft destroyed (of which two were shared with pilots of 609 Squadron) and a further two bombers damaged, with no loss of their own pilots.

One of the victors was Pilot Officer Władysław Różycki, who was No. 2 in Blue Section. Upon returning to Middle Wallop in the afternoon, after a delay due to the necessity of refuelling at Weston Zoyland, he reported to the Intelligence Officer:

'I attacked a He 111 from astern firing 2 sec. burst from about 150 yds. E/A left formation to the right and I attacked again from beam firing about 2 sec. burst at 150 yds. The E/A turned on its back and dived to the ground and burst into flames. I saw parachutes and the crew came down.'

It seems that Różycki was chasing either the aircraft of Staffelkäpitan Hptm. Helmut Brandt from the 6th Staffel that crashed at Church Farm in Woolverton, that of Oblt Gottfried Weigel from 5th Staffel, who went down at Racecourse Farm in Failand, or Oblt Hans Brocker's machine from 7th Staffel which crashed in Branksome Park, Poole.

Other squadrons took part in this battle, but it is No. 601 – with the only remaining Polish pilot, Flying Officer 'Jersey' Jankiewicz -,which is of interest for this book. Jankiewicz, who was also known as 'George', the English equivalent of his native name, was not discouraged after losing his friend, Topolnicki, a few days before. Six Hurricanes took off at 11.20 am, being sent to patrol Portland Bill, then Warmwell and Yeovil. They sighted a formation of bombers flying north by north-west, 10–12 miles west of them, with fighter cover 3,000–4000ft above. When orbiting the Mendips, the six RAF pilots noticed the bombers returning home from a raid. Jankiewicz, who was Red 2, said later:

'We delivered an attack in echelon right on some Me 110s which were wheeling around. I fired 2 short bursts at one e/a then broke away. I then saw an Me 110 which had been attacked by Red 1 with smoke coming from it, then saw some Me 110s below me and attacked a straggler from astern. The rear gunner returned my fire, and I saw black smoke coming from one engine. I broke away and renewed my attack. The rear gunner ceased firing and the other engine started to emit black smoke. By this time I was south of Shaftesbury and my ammunition ran out. I followed the Me 110 south still with smoke coming from both engines and losing height, and 7 miles NW of Bournemouth the e/a was at 6,000-7,000ft. I was then about to be attacked by two other Me 110s and therefore broke away, dived low, and returned to base, landing at Exeter at 12.30.'

It is difficult to say whether Jankiewicz had recognized the German twin-engine aircraft correctly. Misinterpretations of facts or misrecognitions of types happened many times. The local police at Branksome Chine, near Poole, discovered wreckage of a twin-engine Heinkel He 111, which crashed in the location described by the Polish officer. This was an aircraft from 7th Staffel KG55, with a crew consisting of Oblt Hans Brocker, Oblt Heinz Harry Scholz, Uffz. Kurt Schraps, Uffz. Josef Hanft and Uffz. Günter Weidner. Only Schraps survived the crash, becoming another PoW. Or perhaps the Pole was right and he was firing at one of the ZG26 Bf 110 Zerstörers, as a few of them were lost or suffered damage. As Jankiewicz did not see the final stages of his victim's journey, the fate of the aircraft he fought with can only be the subject of discussion and guesswork.

Chapter Fifteen

Mysterious Request from His Majesty

In the early hours of Thursday 26 September 1940, crews of No. 300 (Polish) Squadron were preparing themselves for another mission over France. At their own request, the squadron was allowed to send nine instead of the usual six Fairey Battles, the majority of the aircraft supplied by 1 (Bomber) Group, to bomb the German fleet in the Belgian port of Ostend. Unfortunately, bad weather on the other side of the Channel prevented the Poles from seeing the results of their attacks, and heavy flak had limited their movement over the target.

All nine planes, which performed their mission between 2.45-7.05 am, successfully dropped their bombs and returned with no loss. An order from 1 Group stated that all further operations over France and Belgium should be withheld. It was decided that due to worsening weather and the nights getting longer, the attacks would not be as effective. As it turned out, the next operational flight in which the Polish bombers were involved was on the evening of 9 October.

The nine crews that participated in the operation on 26 September were: Flying Officer Romuald Suliński, Flying Officer Aleksander Bujalski and Sergeant Jan Bieżuński; Pilot Officer Tadeusz Jasiński, Sergeant Bolesław Sobieszczuk and Sergeant Władysław Łapot; Sergeant Marian Kostecki, Flying Officer Jan Piotrowski and Sergeant Feliks Jezierski; Flying Officer Jan Gębicki, Sergeant Edward Morawa and Sergeant Tadeusz Egierski; Flying Officer Mieczysław Kałuża, Flying Officer Tadeusz Chrostowski and Sergeant Władysław Urbanowicz; Flying Officer Jerzy Antonowicz, Pilot Officer Czesław Dej and Sergeant Alfons Kowalski; Flying Officer Marian Michałowski, Flying Officer Adam Męciński and Sergeant Tadeusz Świdziński; Sergeant Józef Kuflik, Pilot Officer Nikodem Koziński and Sergeant Jan Artymiuk; and Sergeant Gerhard Goebel, Flying Officer Stanisław Firlej-Bielański and Sergeant Tadeusz Szmajdowicz.

Just before 11 am on 26 September, German aerial activity increased and several RAF squadrons were scrambled. Two Hurricanes from 253 Squadron took off from Kenley at 10.55 am to intercept them, flown by Squadron Leader Gerald Edge and Pilot Officer Włodzimierz Samoliński. Both pilots were flying over Dungeness when they were attacked by Messerschmitt Bf 109s. The

Operations Record Book of 253 Squadron reveals some details of this fatal operation:

'Acting Squadron Leader G.R. Edge, D.F.C (90249) was shot down in combat and admitted to Willsborough Hospital, Ashford. He abandoned his aircraft and landed in the sea being picked up by motor launch. Flight Lieutenant R.M.B.D. Duke-Woolley[1] (33241) assumed command of this squadron. Pilot Officer W. Samolinski (Polish officer) who was in company with Acting Squadron Leader Edge failed to return and was last seen in combat over the sea.'

Amazingly, Edge claimed that he was shot down by his wingman, but it is extremely difficult to establish what made him think this. Both officers were actually attacked by a pair of Messerschmitts from the 3rd Staffel JG51. Oblt Richard Lappla is considered to be the pilot who shot down Edge, whilst Fw. Walter Meudtner fought with the Pole. Interestingly, the second German attacker failed to return, being seen for the last time over Dungeness.

No. 303 Squadron pilots and ground crew had become accustomed to the frequent visits of various dignitaries, high-ranking military commanders or even heads of states. It was probably due to location of the base, being not far from London and easy to access, making it a model station for such propaganda trips.[2] Yet when the arrival of King George VI was announced, a thrill of excitement passed through the lines of airmen. The purpose of the monarch's early afternoon trip to Northolt was to meet the men of all squadrons stationed there. The king, who was assisted by AVM Keith Park, commander of No. 11 Group, went to 303 Squadron's dispersal where the pilots and ground crew members were introduced to him. Pilot Officer Ferić, known for his relentless determination to gather all battle recollections of his comrades and autographs of their noble visitors, apparently approached His Majesty, asking him to sign his diary that became the unit's official chronicle. It is unclear how an officer with rather limited English achieved this, and presumably some British officers were involved; nevertheless, the king did what he was asked. To complete the usual procedure, Squadron Leader Kellett asked his boys to take off their caps and say 'God save the King'. However, taking into account that most of the squadron did not speak any English, he had no idea what their loyal shouting meant.

When the king was talking to the airmen, at least fifty enemy aircraft were spotted flying towards Britain. They were shortly followed by another two groups of German planes, and the situation appeared to be serious. It was nearly 4 pm when the RDF stations sent the message that something big was

King George VI visiting No.303 Squadron's dispersal on 26 September 1940. From the left to right: Gp Cpt Stanley Vincent, The King, Sqn Ldr Ronald Kellett (obscured), Sqn Ldr Witold Urbanowicz, Flt Lt Athol Forbes, Flg Off Ludwik Paszkiewicz (killed next day), Flg Off Walerian Żak, Flg Off Zdzisław Henneberg (shaking monarch's hand), Flg Off Wojciech Januszewicz, Flg Off Bohdan Grzeszczak, Plt Off Jan Zumbach and Plt Off Mirosław Ferić.

building. Amongst the RAF squadrons that were sent to face the enemy was No. 303 Polish Squadron, which took off from Northolt just prior to the king's departure.

Many publications argue that the monarch left the station, requesting however to be informed of the results of the encounter. Yet both the Operations Record Book of RAF Northolt[3] and Group Captain Vincent's recollections shed some light on the mystery, confirming that events took the opposite direction. 'H.M. The King visited the Station and inspected all Units, watched Squadron in action from Operations Room, and spoke to pilots again after returning from combat,' states the first source. 'He watched the interception from the Sector Operations Room and heard the Leader's "Tally Ho" and subsequent orders etc,' added Vincent, who confirmed that the king 'overstayed his programme time by about two hours'.

It wasn't No. 303 that intercepted the enemy machines as the first line of defence. Both flights of 213 Squadron took off from Exeter between 4.10-4.30 pm, and split up to cover the air space over their own base, while six of them flew to face the Germans. Flying Officer Marian Duryasz, who was No. 3 in Red Section, had to react quickly as his leader's radio did not work, therefore the Pole took command. The pilots were given directions, and after a while they saw anti-aircraft artillery gunfire over Southampton. They knew that this meant trouble.

Duryasz became separated from his comrades and sighted enemy Heinkel He 111s approaching from the south-west. He decided that there was an opportunity to bag some Germans, patiently waiting for them to return from their attack. The Pole climbed, expecting to the see the Germans approximately 1,000 yards to the side. British ground gunners were aiming well, as the enemy formation broke up and one of the bombers left the rest of group. This was the right time for the Pole:

'I carried out a stern attack and after two bursts he started gliding down. I followed, firing all the time. I did not experience any return fire. I ceased attacking when I was out of ammunition. When last seen e/a was still going down and I left him 30 miles from coast 3,000 ft up. Both Sgt [Geoffrey] Stevens who was watching the combat and myself are certain e/a must have landed in the sea.'

Dorniers and Heinkels flew under cover of a fighter escort of Messerschmitt Bf 109s, and over Christchurch were attacked by 609 Squadron. Although its pilots were specifically ordered to engage the bombers, the Messerschmitts made this more complicated. Flying Officer Tadeusz Nowierski, who flew as Green 2, was attacked by one of the fighters, but after shooting one burst could not see any results. Much more was said by Sergeant Józef Jeka, a Polish pilot of 238 Squadron, who also arrived at the scene. Flying over the Isle of Wight, he and his colleagues noticed a large group of Messerschmitt Bf 110s. Jeka was accompanied by another Pole, Pilot Officer Władysław Różycki, who tried to shoot down one of their adversaries with a few long bursts, but it was the NCO, No. 3 of Blue Section, who was successful. He reported:

'I saw He 111s in formation and I attacked last E/A firing 2-3 sec. from quarter about 250 yds long. He broke away and dived in direction of Channel. I made another two attacks, big bursts about 4 sec. each, from

250 yds. The E/A engines smoked and went into sea about 5 miles S of Isle of Wight. I climbed up in a westerly direction into sun. I saw above me (at about 12,000 ft) another He 111 going South. I went over him and attacked, firing 2 bursts of approx. 3-4 sec. each from line astern and quarter respectively, and E/A smoked and I followed him. After 4-5 minutes at about 6,000 ft both engines dropped and he slowly descended and crashed in the sea, and I saw people swimming in sea. Also saw green substance on water. I was at 20 ft off the sea and was then attacked by ME 109 from rear and received bullet in armour plating. The E/A broke off and I came back to base.'

No. 607 Squadron, based at Tangmere, also arrived in time to get involved in the dog-fight. Pilot Officer Franciszek Surma, who had previously scored one He 111 as probably destroyed, was flying as Blue 2 and wisely took his chances when the raiders broke up after the first attempt against the bombers over Southampton was made. Individual dog-fights broke out and the Polish officer, who flew over the Solent, met a formation of about twenty to thirty enemy bombers. They looked to him like Junkers Ju 88s and were at the point of turning from Portsmouth towards the sea. Back at Tangmere, Surma reported:

'At the time I saw a Me 109 gliding down behind and above a Ju 88. I followed e/a for considerable distance and when several miles south of St Catherine's Point I made two or three long bursts from 100 to 150 yds on the tail of e/a, who immediately went into a dive and crashed into the sea.'

Meanwhile, 303 Squadron, led by Squadron Leader Ronald Kellett and followed by 229 Squadron, was ordered to patrol the Guilford area at 12,000ft. The commander wasn't happy with this overcrowded group he had to lead, obviously not being a fan of the 'Big Wing' concept. They were given different directions and when they turned to the west they noticed enemy raiders approaching from the south at a height of 16,000–17,000ft. There were fifty Heinkel He 111s with their fighter escort above them, dropping bombs over Southampton.

Kellett, having two whole squadrons behind, turned towards the enemy and went down at full speed out of the sun. The enemy aircraft were heading towards the French coast, when 'Tadeusz Kościuszko' Squadron's Hurricanes caught their rearguard. Some of the pilots engaged the fighters while the rest took care of the Heinkels. Kellett shot down one Messerschmitt Bf 109, whilst 'B' Flight commander Flight Lieutenant Forbes bagged a He 111. Forbes had a shocking experience when he noticed a trail of white smoke coming from his machine, an explosive bullet having opened up his port wing about a foot from the tip. He was about to bail out when he realized the smoke had stopped. Sergeant Josef František also had some success, destroying two He 111s, while Sergeant Tadeusz Anduszków of Red Section later wrote:

'Following my leader I attacked the last E/A in a formation ¾ from the rear. I then climbed and saw a Do 215 to my left which I attacked. E/A dived and I followed and fired several bursts from a very short distance. E/A continued his dive and crashed into the sea. I was then attacked by a Me 109 which went over me. I followed, but as he continued to draw away I was unable to fire and returned.'

His colleague Sergeant Marian Bełc from Green Section went for the more agile enemy fighters:

'After perceiving an enemy formation of about 40 He 111s I attacked the last machine. I then noticed above me 4 Me 109s flying in twos. I attacked the lower pair and after two short bursts, one burst into flames and fell to earth, falling in the neighbourhood of Portsmouth.'

Bełc then realized that he had gone too far out to sea and turned back from the French coast, quickly heading home. Although his Hurricane had been damaged in combat, the Pole managed to land safely at Biggin Hill.

Flying Officer Bohdan Grzeszczak also intervened and achieved his first enemy machine shot down. The 32-year-old officer was one of those who had recently converted to fighters, and unlike his 303 operational colleagues had never flown a fighter plane in Poland. Although trained as a pilot, he served as an observer in 13th Army Co-operation Squadron and then in 11th Light Bomber Squadron. He underwent fighter conversion in France, managing to fly operationally a Dutch-built Koolhovens FK58.

On 26 September he was eager to shoot down any Luftwaffe aircraft he could:

'From a height of slightly above that of the enemy I attacked a He.111 ¾ from the rear. I fired two long bursts. E/A began to smoke and dived steeply to the sea. At that exact moment my machine was lifted loudly owing to a shell bursting underneath me. I made steep turn to the right, breaking formation, and joined up with aircraft F.R.H [P3544 RF-H flown by Flying Officer Wojciech Januszewicz] which a few moments later let down its undercarriage and landed in a field.'

Grzeszczak noticed a hole in his tail plane. He initially thought the damage was caused by machine-gun fire, but it was more likely from an anti-aircraft shell exploding too close. The aircraft that he saw landed near Fareham, between two farms, Charity and Wyton, but its pilot escaped safely.

Sergeant Jan Kowalski, who flew as Green 3, with help from interpreter Pilot Officer Joseph Walters, provided Flying Officer Hadwen with details of his fight, when he followed his instincts and targeted a fighter aircraft instead of a bomber:

> 'I attacked the bomber from a rear deflected angle, and just on the point of opening fire I noticed a Me above and to the left of me. I broke away from the bombers and attacked the Me, firing two long bursts, after which e/a dived in smoke to earth.'

His leader, Flying Officer 'Paszka' Paszkiewicz, decided to stick to the plan and eliminate a bomber:

> 'I picked out one and fired two bursts. The left engine of e/a stopped. I fired again, and e/a burst into flames. My distance of firing was from 250 to 50 yds. As I had used up all my ammunition I returned to Northolt.'

The Polish commander of 303 Squadron, Acting Squadron Leader Witold Urbanowicz, flew as the leader of Yellow Section and piloted the Hurricane with the code letter 'E', which turned out to be not only the most deadly aircraft of the squadron, but also the most effective one flown by a Polish pilot during the whole war. The total number of enemy aircraft shot down by its eight machine guns was ten. '*Kobra*' Urbanowicz, who claimed nine out of his fifteen Battle of Britain victories whilst sitting in the cockpit of this particular Hurricane,[4] reported:

> 'After breaking up the enemy's last formation I attacked a Vic of the bombers, and firing from a distance of about 400 yds saw E/A begin to smoke and return to its formation. I approached the nearest and fired another burst , after which E/A fell to earth entirely wrapped in thick black smoke.'

Pilot Officer Jan Zumbach, who was his No. 2, had much more to say:

> 'I attacked formation of He 111s and fired a long burst at the last in the formation, which appeared to explode in the region of the cockpit. E/A

fell out of control to earth. I flew towards another formation of E/A and met an Me 109. I fired a burst from a deflected angle from the front, and then another from the rear. The pilot must have been killed as E/A dived into the sea without any visible outward sign of damage. I then chased the rest of the formation but could not catch them up.'

The last successful pilot of 303 Squadron on this occasion was Flying Officer Walerian Żak, who flew in Blue Section of 'B' Flight. Noticing a group of fifty bombers on his left, 'Ciotka' turned towards them:

'I fired a burst at one He 111 from the rear, after which I noticed about 9 Me 109s at my rear. The bombers wheeled to the right and I approached another He 111, and from distance of 50 yds fired a long burst. Both engines began to smoke, and e/a twisting fell towards earth. I did not see him crash, as I attacked another whom I either damaged or destroyed.'

His uncertainty resulted in a score of one He 111 destroyed and another one damaged.

The final score of the squadron was impressive: thirteen enemy aircraft were destroyed – four Bf 109s and nine He 111s – three machines were damaged and two of them were shared between unnamed pilots. No. 303 again positioned itself at the top of the list of best-scoring squadrons, on this occasion being followed by 238 Squadron, which also gained good results with the help of a Polish Sergeant. It is almost certain that the Polish squadron fought with Heinkels from KG55, which were protected by Bf 109s and Bf 110s, the latter from ZG26. Some common mistakes had been made when Zerstörers were misidentified as Junkers Ju 88s and Heinkels as Dorniers. The Germans reported relatively smaller losses in this encounter than claimed by their opponents.

Although the king, awaiting the outcome at the Ops Room, surely did not know all these results, he must have been impressed by the havoc created by the Poles in the enemy raiders.

Time for relaxation was very limited in those days, and the following day was no exception. From the early hours of Friday 27 September, pilots of 303 Squadron were at readiness again. This constant awareness proved necessary as at 8.50 am the first of three large groups of German planes were spotted approaching Dungeness. Several RAF squadrons were scrambled to assess the situation and intercept the enemy, amongst them yet again being No. 303. Unfortunately, on this occasion things turned sour for them. Firstly, Flight Lieutenant Athol Forbes, who led the squadron, lost radio connection with the Canadian Squadron, which this time was leading the whole formation, but also with his own pilots. Then British anti-aircraft artillery fire broke up the lines of the Hurricanes. There were also Messerschmitts hiding above, and when they swung into attack they caused havoc.

When the group of sixty or seventy bombers was seen flying south of Gatwick, the Canadians astonishingly turned left to fly alongside them. Forbes was unable to correct this pointless move as his radio did not work, and flying alone he caught a single Heinkel He 111, which headed towards the coast. After a while the German bomber fell into the sea.

Flying Officer Ludwik Paszkiewicz, who led Green Section and had six kills to his name, apparently assumed command of the remaining eleven Hurricanes to continue the attack, despite Pilot Officer Jan Zumbach's warning of the Messerschmitts waiting above. But it was too late for him. When the Bf 109s came down from the sun, Paszkiewicz was shot down immediately while attempting to destroy one of the bombers, and crashed at Borough Green, Wrotham, in Kent. His badly burned body, with bullet holes in the chest, was later found alongside parts of his Hurricane at Crowhurst Farm. 'Paszka' was presumably killed by the deadly burst while still in the cockpit.

He wasn't the only loss that 303 Squadron suffered that day. Sergeant Tadeusz Andruszków of Red Section soon shared the same fate. He was also a victim of an unexpected attack, and having no chance to shake off several fighters which were seen behind him, the Polish NCO was hit over Horsham and went down in flames, hitting the ground at Holwych Farm near Cowden. When eventually found, he had his chest shot through, and a head injury from a cannon shell.

Flying Officer Walerian Żak from Blue Section managed to shoot down one He 111. But soon after, a German aircraft, which was chasing him sent a deadly burst into the middle of the fuel tank of Żak's Hurricane, which caught fire. The Polish pilot was covered with burning fuel. The only sensible decision that he could have made was to bail out, yet he did not open his parachute until the flames were out. His Hurricane crashed at Blandel Lane, Stoke D'Abernon, near Leatherhead. With burns to his face and hands, but miraculously alive, Żak was admitted to Leatherhead Hospital.

So far on this occasion the German tactics had worked, and the crucial factor of lacking communication amongst themselves proved lethal for the 303 pilots. Some of them, however, were able to take back the initiative. 'Going into the attack I noticed an Me attacking a Hurricane,' reported Jan Zumbach.

> 'I dived onto the Me and firing a long burst set him on fire and saw him go to earth. I did not see him crash as I was myself attacked at that particular moment. I manoeuvred out of range and met a He being attacked by a

From the left to right: Flg Off Marian Pisarek (303 Sqn PAF), Flt Lt Piotr Łaguna, Plt Off Jerzy Czerniak, Flg Off Tadeusz Czerwiński and Plt Off Stanisław Łapka (all four from 302 Sqn PAF).

Hurricane. I joined up with this Hurricane and attacked. A little later three more Hurricanes joined up with us and we five attacked the He. The result of this attack was that one of the enemy crew jumped and the machine crashed into some houses, one of which was set on fire.'

Acting Squadron Leader Witold Urbanowicz, who led Yellow Section, also had some success and reported:

'About 30 miles south of London we intercepted a bombing raid of about 30 He 111s. Over the bombers were about 60 Me 109s which attacked our rear sections. After engaging Me 109s I noticed about 40 Me 110s which were making for London in single line astern. Several Hurricanes cut them off and E/A immediately formed a ring. Seeing one E/A break away from the ring and make as if to return to France I attacked him. I chased him for about seven minutes. During this time I fired several bursts but owing to his continually zig zagging I was unable to score a hit. Approaching however to about 50 yds I fired a last burst. E/A began to smoke and falling on its left side dived, and crashed to earth about 35 miles south of London by the side of some railway lines. One of the crew jumped by parachute. I then began to climb and attacked another Me 110. At the same time I noticed that two Me 109s attacked me, firing from my rear. Engaging them I shot one down. What happened to the other I do not know. E/A shot down burst into flames and fell to earth.'

Some historians consider a Bf 110 from the 15th Staffel of LG1 the potential target of Urbanowicz's attack. This machine went down on Horam Manor Farm, near Horam in Sussex. Uffz. Koch died but his colleague Uffz. Berchtold escaped by parachute and was captured after landing. The Bf 109 that the Polish pilot described downing may haved been flown by Gefr. John of 5th Staffel JG27, who crashed on Lower Mays Farm at Selmeston, Sussex, or another machine from the 3rd Staffel of the same unit which went into the Channel. These two aircraft were also attacked by other pilots, and the participation of Ferić, Grzeszczak, Henneberg and Zumbach in their demise cannot be ruled out.

Sergeant Jan Kowalski, who the day before downed his first German aircraft, was about to add to his tally. Being a wingman of Paszkiewicz, he had more luck than his leader; in fact he only noticed the deadly presence of the Messerschmitts while leaving the battlefield. Kowalski, the only survivor of Green Section, reported:

'On contacting the enemy we attacked ¾ from the rear. I fired two long bursts at an enemy bomber in the last section. E/A broke formation and I again fired a burst from about 200 yds, and starboard motor stopped. E/A began to fly south, losing height. I returned to Northolt through lack of ammunition. Returning, I noticed a number of E/A circling in a ring, and over them Me 109s.'

There is speculation that Kowalski's victims were in fact the crew of a 3rd Staffel KG77 Junkers Ju 88, which was also attacked by various RAF and Polish pilots, including Zumbach and Ferić. This aircraft crashed on to North Edge Lodge at East Grinstead. Fw. Brautigam bailed out, suffered a broken leg and was captured; his colleague Uffz. Winkelmann died from his wounds in hospital, whilst Fw. Precht and Uffz. Kasing were killed.

Flying Officer Zdzisław 'Dzidek' Henneberg, who led Red Section, noticed two types of enemy bombers: He 111s and Do 17s. Initially, as many others, he decided to chase the heavies when they were turning towards London, when he suddenly realized that they were protected by Bf 109s:

'At that moment I noticed on my right two Me 109s. I attacked one, firing from below ¾ from the rear, from a distance of about 200 yds. After the third burst e/a burst into flames and fell to earth.'

Then the real trouble started:

'I then heard three explosions one after the other and smoke began to fill my cockpit. I dived and returned to Northolt. On examination of my aircraft I found that it had been hit by three cannon shells, one of which had punctured the radiator.'

Flying Officer Bohdan Grzeszczak, who flew as No. 3 in Urbanowicz's Yellow Section, said:

'While attacking the bomber formation I noticed four Mes attacking one Hurricane. The Hurricane began to smoke, and turning fell to earth. One of these Mes broke formation and appeared very close to me. I fired a long burst. E/A began to smoke, and crashed to earth.'

He avoided being shot up by two Messerschmitts by taking evasive action after noticing he was out of ammunition.

Pilot Officer Mirosław Ferić claimed a double victory, despite being in serious trouble himself. Once successful, to his consternation the Pole realised that his Hurricane was badly damaged:

'I attacked an Me 109, and after a short burst enemy aircraft exploded into flames and crashed to earth. I then approached the bombers who were already being attacked by some of our aircraft. I attacked a Heinkel and fired three short bursts. The pilot was evidently killed as the machine dived without smoke or flames, and crashed between Croydon and Gatwick. As my aircraft had been hit by machine-gun bullets I returned to Northolt.'

Only then did he see a hole from an armour-piercing bullet only 25cm from where his knees were. It is believed that 'Ox' fought with one of the 2nd Staffel KG 77 Junkers, rather than a Heinkel, as he claimed. Such an aircraft crashed on Folly Farm at South Holmwood in Surrey. Uffz. Wilhelm Menningmann was killed whilst three other members of his crew – Uffz. Rudolf Schumann, Uffz. Hans Tenholt and Uffz. Albert Ackermann – were reported captured.

The final Polish Air Force pilot in this encounter, Sergeant Josef František, once again proved his skills by destroying a Heinkel and Messerschmitt Bf 110.

This day's battle was ferocious, and according to a German airman who participated in it, was the most hectic aerial combat he had experienced. RAF fighters were attacking without a break, and several aircraft were shot down at the same time, trailing black or white smoke like a blazing torch. Although suffering the heavy loss of two experienced pilots killed and one seriously wounded, three aircraft lost plus two others damaged, the total score of at least eleven enemy machines destroyed and one damaged was considered another success for 303 Squadron.

This was also the day when a message arrived signed by General Władysław Sikorski, who complemented his brave boys and congratulated them on achieving such remarkable success. He also appreciated the fantastic achievement of shooting down their 100th enemy aircraft. He concluded by suggesting that they drink to celebrate the health of the talented pilots. A crate of alcohol accompanied his message. But the battle of 27 September was far from over, and the ten bottles sent had to be consumed a little later.

While 303 Squadron was fighting its own battle, Sergeant Jan Budziński from No. 605 was airborne alongside the rest of his squadron. Both flights took off between 9.15-9.20 am, and were patrolling over Croydon when ordered to attack some Messerschmitt Bf 110s spotted south of Kenley in Surrey. German aircraft from LG1 were already engaged in a combat with Spitfires when No. 605 arrived at the scene. The two-engine Zerstőrers were performing their usual tactic of circling, and Budziński and his colleagues had to climb up to get them:

'On my left I saw one Me 110 turning to the left, so I turned left and did a diving quarter astern attack from 250 yards, closing to 30 yards, with a fairly long burst, and I think I killed the rear gunner as he never fired at me. I broke away down and climbed up to the left, and the Me 110 went down a bit and turned to the right. I then did a diving head-on attack at 10,000 ft from 300 yards, closing to 100 yards, and I saw its port engine on fire. The Me 110 went down in flames, fairly gently until quite near the ground, when it dived straight down and exploded on hitting the ground east of Redhill, but north of the railway line.'

The Me 110 belonged to 15th Staffel of LG1 and crashed at Sockett Manor in Oxted. Both members of its crew – Oblt Otto Weckeisser, credited with five victories gained between 15 August and 27 September 1940, and Gefr. Horst Brügow – were captured.

When Fighter Command's Hurricanes and Spitfires returned to their bases to refuel and rearm, the Germans did not rest. Around 11 am, more raiders were sighted approaching from the French coastline and heading towards the Solent. Numerous squadrons were sent there to meet them, but the Luftwaffe, aware of the welcoming party, changed direction and crossed the coast over St Alban's Head. Several 110s left the group and turned back when they were intercepted by 609 Squadron, which had initially been ordered only to patrol over their own base.

Attempts were made to clash with the enemy planes, one of which was interrupted by an attack by two 238 Squadron Hurricanes. Ironically, one of the aircraft was piloted by Sergeant Józef Jeka, who shortly after noticing this obvious mistake attacked the German planes. Luckily none of the 609 Squadron pilots was hurt.

The Operation Record Book of 609 Squadron provides some details of this operation:

> 'The enemy sent a mixed force to bomb Bristol shortly before noon. For the second time in three days No. 10 Group Control positioned the Squadron so badly that they had little or no chance of catching any of the bombers over the coast. Both Flight Commanders' R/T having failed, Yellow Leader, P/O R.C. Miller [Rogers Freeman Garland Miller] led the Squadron into an attack on the escort of fighters that were seen circling over Warmwell, losing his life in a collision with an Me 110, in which both aircraft appeared to explode in mid-air. Deprived of the protection of their escort by 609's demarche, the bomber formation appears to have been broken up effectively by other fighter squadrons.'[5]

Although the squadron documents initially did not take into account Flying Officer Tadeusz Nowierski's participation in the share of claims (seven aircraft destroyed and one probably shot down), the Pole reported damaging one of the Bf 110s by writing:

> 'Over Portland I attacked formation of Me 110s. When one of them was turning I gave him three short bursts in almost head-on attack (each burst from a distance of 300 yards lasted one second). White smoke appeared from his starboard engine. I sighted another Me 110 and tried to catch him when he flew south, towards France. I was unable to intercept him. I was about 1,000 yards behind him, remaining at such a distance for a few minutes. As I was deep over the sea, I decided to leave him and return.'

As it turned out, the two Hurricanes from 238 Squadron which almost clashed with 609's Spitfires had simply tried to make them aware of the German presence. Józef Jeka, flying one of them, was aiming to get another score, following his success the previous day. Blue Section, consisting of the Pole and Canadian Pilot Officer John Urwin-Mann, based at Middle Wallop, took off at 11.01 am with an initial plan to protect their own aerodrome. Soon after they were vectored south of Bristol, where they spotted Heinkels and Bf 110s.

Jeka, Blue 2, explained what happened next:

'I attacked the last formation of He 111s. I gave short 2 sec burst from quarter about 300 yds and broke away because Me 110s from above attacked me. I attacked these Me 110s and fired from below almost astern beginning at 250 yds and closing, about a 4 sec. then I broke away with E/A smoking. 2 Spitfires also attacked and much more smoke came from both engines. The Me 110 dived straight down into the sea. I made an attack on Me 110 when it was diving to the sea, fired a burst of about 2 secs from 100 yds quarter. I saw the 2 Spitfires also make a last attack before E/A crashed into the sea. After this attack an Me 110 was 100 ft above the sea, turned vertically and dived into the sea. I saw a green substance on the water.'

Several other squadrons had attacked the German formation on their way to bomb the Bristol factory in Filton, yet their attempts were not wholly successful. The Luftwaffe managed to break the defensive barrier, but their bombs did not cause any substantial damage and until 2.45 pm there was relative quiet for the Polish airmen. When German activity was noticed once more, several squadrons were sent to meet them. Two groups of enemy planes crossed the coastline between Dover and Dungeness, heading towards Maidstone. After bombing London, they were intercepted by the Northolt Wing, yet only three 303 pilots managed to catch them over Hastings. These men were from Red Section and got close enough to open fire. Flight Lieutenant Kent, who led them, engaged with a Junkers Ju 88. Its air gunner defended his crew by firing fairly accurate bursts, knocked out the Canadian's airscrew and wireless mast. Red 1 eventually shot the German gunner, silenced the starboard engine and finally sent the aircraft down into the sea.

His No. 2, Acting Squadron Leader Urbanowicz, recalled:

'I noticed about 15 bombers, who were being engaged by Hurricanes and Spitfires. The bombers turned tail and we chased them, but owing to their speed did not catch up with them until the coast was reached. I then attacked one and fired from a distance of about 100 yds. E/A smoked for quite a time but did not slacken speed. I fired a longer burst, and the right wing of E/A burst into flames and aircraft crashed into the sea about 300 yds from the shore at Brighton. I then attacked another bomber from the front and beneath and then ¾ from rear and above. I fired for about six seconds. E/A did not catch fire but dived and fell into the sea.'

The KG77 lost several aircraft during the afternoon encounter, but most of these bombers crashed quite far from the location described by the Polish officer. There are, however, two possibilities which could be considered as Urbanowicz's claims. Both aeroplanes belonged to the 5th Staffel: one aircraft that was seen going down south-west of St Leonards-on-Sea in Sussex with a crew of Uffz. Isensee, Gefr. Teichtmayer (the only survivor), Oblt. Ziel and Fw. Niederer; and a second Junkers with a crew of Hptm. Zetsche, Fw. Mahl, Obergefr. Kuhn and Gefr. Burkhardt, which went down in the Channel about 15 miles from Hastings with no survivors.

Sergeant Eugeniusz Szaposznikow, Red 3, unlike Forbes during the early morning encounter, had no reason to complain about his R/T. All seemed to work fine:

'After approaching e/a the chase began. Only at the coast did we catch up with enemy formation. I was left behind alone as I could not keep up the speed of the others, and was attacked by a Me 109 who dived onto me and then rolled. I got onto his tail and fired two bursts. E/A continued its dive and fell into the sea off Brighton.'

To replace the loss of two comrades killed and one badly wounded, the squadron received three officers who had undertakn additional training at No. 5 Operational Training Unit. They were Pilot Officers Bogusław Mierzwa, Jerzy Palusiński and Jerzy Radomski. Mierzwa was an experienced pilot who gained three shared victories in Poland when he flew as a pilot of 114th Fighter Squadron. He was no less skilled than Palusiński, a 111th Fighter Squadron veteran with at least two kills under his belt. Palusiński had been shot down and wounded on the very first day of the war. Radomski was no novice either. The former pilot of 113th Fighter Squadron had reported claims in Poland and then in France. On 2 September 1940, though, it had been decided that all three required some more practice on the new equipment. Sergeant Stanisław Karubin had by now been discharged from hospital, finally recovering from wounds sustained on 6 September. After Paszkiewicz's death, Flying Officer Marian Pisarek was officially appointed the new commander of 'B' Flight.

Chapter Sixteen

Scratches on the Surface

Since Flying Officer Antoni Ostowicz claimed his shared victory of a Heinkel He 111 during an aerial encounter near Shoreham on 19 July 1940, Polish pilots fighting during the Battle of Britain had been credited with the destruction of 157 enemy planes, plus a shared kill. They also probably shot down another thirty of them while damaging a further twenty-four-and-a-half.[1] The victories gained so far were directly related to the percentage of operational use and engagement of the Polish pilots during specific phases of the Battle of Britain. But this was also a direct consequence of their experience and confidence gained throughout the hostilities, based on the strengthening partnership between the Poles and the airmen of other nations.

When the first engagements took place over the Channel between 10 July and 7 August, with the Germans concentrating their attention mostly on British shipping and naval installations, testing the strength of their adversary, only a small number of Poles – just above 20 – were already serving in RAF squadrons. Most of them had only recently arrived, therefore the real Polish impact was yet to emerge.

When the second stage of the air battle began (the period dated between 8–23 August), and despite continuing intensive attacks on British convoys, the Luftwaffe sent their aircraft to attempt to eliminate Fighter Command and dominate British skies; at this time the impact of the Polish fighter pilots significantly improved. During this time they shot down over thirty German aircraft, despite being only a few pilots who flew alone or in small groups in RAF squadrons, with almost no grasp of the English language and only limited knowledge of RAF tactics and procedures.

Both Polish squadrons were under training and only at the stage of starting their operational trials. The time that Poles spent on gaining knowledge and familiarization with new equipment, different from that used on the continent, was also insufficient. The first claims made by Polish pilots of the Polish squadron were also noted,while seven Polish pilots were killed in combat and two others wounded.

The third phase of the Battle of Britain, officially dated between 24 August and 6 September, when the Germans were working hard to damage the defence system of the RAF by attacking its airfields and attempting to destroy the aviation industry, saw the Poles achieving much more success. At least thirty-eight enemy aircraft were shot down by Polish pilots, including fifteen claimed by those who flew with the newly introduced No. 303 Squadron. The latter number shows precisely what Poles were capable off when flying together, understanding the language and integrated with their countrymen. Only three Polish pilots were lost during encounters with the enemy, but eleven of them suffered from various injuries.

The fourth phase of the Battle of Britain started on 7 September, when the Germans unleashed their Blitzkrieg on London as their major target. The Luftwaffe erroneously assumed that they had weakened the RAF enough to secure absolute domination in the air. This gave Fighter Command some time to regroup, take a breath and show the attackers that the narrow margin between losing and surviving made a massive difference and that the enemy's assessment could not be more wrong.

With the great contribution from 303 Squadron, the main Polish unit based closer to London than any other squadron consisting of Poles, and whose Polish pilots shot down over seventy raiders, but also the respectable total

Flg Off Juliusz Topolnicki sitting next to No. 601 Sqn's Hurricane.

of 15 aircraft shot down by its sister 302 Polish squadron, the total score of enemy planes destroyed in the air by the Poles ended up as over 110. At that time, factors such as tiredness, fatigue, stress of being under constant alert and pressure of the importance and decisiveness of the Battle of Britain started to show. Eleven Polish fighter pilots were killed in combat, one in a non-operational flight and another five were wounded.

Up to the end of September, a total of twenty-one Polish pilots were killed in action or, like Witold Głowacki, died as a result of combat injuries. One Polish fighter pilot lost his life in a flying accident prior to a non-operational flight and three members of a Polish bomber crew were shot down and killed on their way to bomb targets in France. Another three perished while undertaking or leading exercises in a fighter Operational Training Unit, plus one in a bomber OTU. One former fighter pilot also lost his life while undertaking conversion to be a bomber pilot.

After the last two days of endless and exhausting combat, neither Polish squadron achieved success on 28 September. Even the Polish pilots dispersed across Fighter Command units and involved in various encounters did not shoot down an enemy plane. This was until 238 Squadron was sent over Southampton and consequently east of the Isle of Wight to intercept an enemy formation consisting of twenty-five Messerschmitt Bf 110s and a group of Bf 109s hiding above.

Twelve Hurricanes of 238 Squadron, which took off at 2.23 pm from their Middle Wallop base, were accompanied by Nos. 56, 213 and 609 Squadrons. When attacking the Zerstőrers, which were flying in a defensive circle, the Hurricanes suddenly came under fire from the Bf 109s diving out of the sun from 300 yards above. Two of their own pilots followed by one from 213 Squadron were lost as result of this surprise attack. Meanwhile, three Bf 110s were shot down by 213 Squadron pilots, and the only victorious pilot from 238 Squadron of this dog-fight over Selsey Bill was the Polish Pilot Officer Władysław Różycki, who flew as Green 2. Różycki reported:

'I attacked one of E/A which was attacking the Squadron formation. I dived from approx. 22,000ft and fired about 4 sec. from line astern about 200 yds. E/A very quickly turned and left circle and flew south. Starboard engine of E/A in flames. I attacked again and fired rest of my ammunition at E/A (very long burst) from 200 closing to 70 yds which went into E/A which then went down very slowly into sea near Isle of Wight (about 5-7 miles south).'

His colleague Sergeant Józef Jeka had been under attack from a few Bf 109s, but managed to outmanoeuvre them and after positioning himself at the right spot, he gave a four-second burst from 400 yards. He was unable to assess whether his action was successful or not, while his potential victim disappeared by gaining speed.

During this relatively quiet time, a few of the Polish pilots received postings to fly with other squadrons: Pilot Officer Ludwik Martel left No. 54 Squadron and transferred to 603; Pilot Officer Jan Pfeiffer arrived at No. 257 Squadron; and Pilot Officer Jerzy Solak, after leaving 151 Squadron, reported to No. 249.

The day after, two aircraft of Blue Section of 234 Squadron took off from their St Eval aerodrome in Cornwall for a reconnaissance patrol when they were vectored to Portsmouth. When Pilot Offficer Kenneth Dewhurst and Pilot Officer Janusz Żurakowski arrived there, they immediately noticed puffs of anti-aircraft artillery smoke, a clear sign of the foe's presence. Both sighted an enemy aircraft which was travelling north-east at 20,000ft. They gave chase, which lasted for about 20 miles, and when their opponent pilot noticed two Spitfires sitting on his tail, he turned south-east and went into a dive. All three aircraft were south of Exmouth, when the dog-fight began.

The Operations Record Book of 234 Squadron gives more details of this encounter:

> 'Blue 2 [Żurakowski] opened fire at 300 yards from starboard beam and from the sun, as e/a was turning and diving Blue 1 and Blue 2 then dived down after e/a. Blue 1 attacked from astern at 200 yards at the same moment as Blue 2 stacked from Starboard Quarter. Both engines of e/a were smoking badly. E/a finally dived into cloud towards sea level with both engines smoking badly. Some rear gun fire was encountered by Blue 1 and he saw tracer coming towards him. The e/a was identified as an Me Jaguar [Bf 110] by its twin rudders, general line of nose as it turned and position of rear gun. Both pilots were impressed by the speed of the e/a which travelled at 320 m.p.h. straight and level. Both pilots consider that the e/a was a reconnaissance plane and that it is a probable casualty. The smoke from the engines [indicated real damage] ... at the same time as the engagement took place group passed report that an e/a had crashed in sea in the same region.'

A few hours later, 23-year-old Sergeant Włodzimierz Mudry from No. 79 Squadron participated in combat and opened fire on the enemy, but the battle, which took place at 6.40 pm near St David's Head in South Wales, proved successful only for his two colleagues. They were credited with the destruction of a Heinkel He 111 and probably another. Mudry, a former pupil of the Polish Air Force NCO School for Minors, flew operationally in Poland as a pilot of the 21st Bomber Squadron. When he arrived in England, he undertook fighter training and since 10 September had flown with 79 Squadron.

Sergeant Wilhelm Szafraniec, who had served in 151 Squadron since 12 September, was posted to 607 Squadron, while Sergeants Paweł Gallus and Józef Biel joined No. 3 Squadron. Gallus was a relatively experienced pilot: having graduated from the Air Force NCO School for Minors, the 20-year-old flew operationally with the 112th Fighter Squadron in Poland. He was also chosen to join the first core group of No. 303 Squadron pilots arriving at Northolt, but had an unfortunate flying accident during the training period and was reposted for further flying experience at 5 OTU. He eventually took part in the Battle of Britain, whilst 23-year-old Biel, a member of the 14th entry of the Polish Air Force Cadet Officers School, whose time at Dęblin was cut short by the outbreak of war, remained a non-operational pilot at this time.

The last day of September proved to be another triumph for the 'Kościuszko' pilots, and once again they topped the Fighter Command scoreboard. When the first warning arrived, they were airborne immediately and between 8.55-10 am flew an unsuccessful patrol to intercept the enemy approaching Slough from the direction of Dungeness. More Luftwaffe formations were then seen, yet no Polish pilot had an opportunity to get close enough to intercept them. It was only when 'B' Flight of 609 Squadron performed an operational patrol over Southampton between 11 am and 12.10 pm that a few of its pilots claimed victories. Flying Officer Nowierski, who was engaged in this battle, gave one long burst towards the enemy, but could not say whether his bullets reached their target.

When No. 303 was sent up for a fourth time, between 1.10-2.45 pm, their luck changed. The whole Northolt Wing was protecting their own base, when a message was received that German planes, after dropping their bombs on London and surrounding areas, were heading home and approaching Dungeness. Once again the concept of the whole wing flying in such ad hoc circumstances, when the situation was almost constantly changing, proved unsatisfactory, and both No. 1 Canadian and 229 Squadron RAF were left behind. Only 303 Squadron caught up with the Germans: at least thirty Dorniers with a strong fighter cover.

Squadron Leader Kellett, who led Red Section, turned towards the Messerschmitts and his wingmen followed. Sergeant Stanisław Karubin, only recently recovered from his wounds, was hungry for more success. He wrote:

'After climbing to 22,000 ft I noticed a formation of enemy bombers in one large formation and Mes in loose formation of 2s. I attacked one

Me from below, firing two short bursts. E/A began to smoke, then burst into flames and fell earthward through the clouds. Next I chased the bomber formation towards the coast, but could not get within reach.'

It is now assumed that Karubin either finished the flying career of Uffz. Karl Vogel from the 4th Staffel JG53,[2] who ended up in captivity, or damaged an engine of Uffz. Marcks' plane, which force-landed north-east of Beachy Head. The latter was a 7th Staffel JG54 pilot, who could not continue his flight to France due to a radiator being hit by enemy bullets.

'*Kobra*' Urbanowicz, who led Yellow Section, was again successful, although his dog-fight nearly ended in disaster. Flying his lucky Hurricane 'E', the Polish officer reported afterwards:

'At about 13.30 I noticed enemy bombers and fighters heading towards the coast. Mes were about 2,000 ft above Dos. Our Squadron attacked the bombers from behind and above. After the second attack two e/a broke away from their formation. One, smoking, fell into the sea. The other was attacked by our fighters and also fell into the sea smoking. Over the Channel I noticed a Do 215 slowly making its way to France. I attacked and fired three bursts from the rear and above from a distance of about 100 yds, but without result, e/a only lost height. Then two fighters appeared above the bomber. Thinking that they were ours, I joined them in order to attack the bomber together. Getting close to them I discovered that they were 2 Me 109s protecting the bomber. From a distance of about 50 yds I fired a burst at one of them. Next I fired a longer burst at the other Me, who did not smoke or burst into flames, but immediately dived headlong into the sea. I again attacked the bomber from a distance of 30 yds to the rear, and fired once more without result. I continued the attack and e/a, which was now over France, made as if to land, hit the ground with its right wing and burst into flames. None of the crew came out.'

It is believed that Witold Urbanowicz was chasing one of the KG2 Dorniers, as one of the 8th Staffel aircraft crashed at Bertincourt near Arras in north-east France, with the crew of Lt Scheffel and three other men being killed. The aircraft which according to Urbanowicz was smoking and fell into the sea could have been a Dornier from the same 8th Staffel that was lost with its crew of Uffz. Schonn, Uffz. Schroff, Fw. Bauer, Fw. Salomo and Fw. Schierling.

Urbanowicz's wingman, Pilot Officer Jerzy Radomski, was another successful pilot in this action, yet he was also very close to not returning from this operation in one piece. His combat report gives more details:

'Yellow section attacked enemy bombers from the rear without result. One e/a broke formation and I fired a short burst at his cockpit, then another at the left motor, which stopped. I again fired several bursts, and after the last the other engine also stopped. Whilst firing a Spitfire joined me, but after the left engine had stopped flew off. E/A fell into the sea about 13 miles from Dungeness. All my attacks were made from the rear side and slightly above.'

Up to this point all seemed to be well for Radomski, who headed back to Northolt excited to share his news with his squadron mates. After combat successes in Poland and then in France, he could add another one, gained in Britain. But Northolt was still very far away:

'Suddenly after what seems to me to be an explosion in the engine, the whole aircraft began to tremble, and smoke and flames issued from the exhausts; so thick was the smoke in the cockpit that I was unable to take any readings from the instruments. As I was over the Channel at a height of about 25,000 ft I decided not to jump. I closed the throttle, turned off the petrol, and switched off the engine and side slipped as smoke was blinding me. I glided and side slipped as far as the coast and landed on shingle without my undercarriage. From the moment of switching off my engine and petrol, smoke and flames continued to issue from the exhaust.'

Radomski was lucky, as he managed to get as far as Lydd beach near Dungeness, where he performed an emergency landing.

No. 303 was back in action two hours later, when both flights took off from Northolt at 4.20 pm and 4.35 pm respectively. Unfortunately, Kellett was in a hurry, deciding not to wait for 'B' Flight and climbing at full throttle; therefore the whole squadron, although being part of the Northolt Wing, flew separately and lost its impact. There were three large groups of German aircraft heading towards London, the Solent and Yeovil. As the formation targeting the capital was the closest one, all three squadrons from Northolt went to intercept it. No. 1 Canadian and No. 229 RAF both clashed with the bombers, but despite losing two aircraft, did not cause any damage to the raiders.

During a combat over Brooklands, Hurricanes with 303 Squadron 'RF' code letters also aimed for the bombers, yet the dangerous Bf 109s were there to protect the Ju 88s. Both Polish flights were involved in individual dog-fights with the German fighters, but only Acting Squadron Leader Urbanowicz and Sergeant František gained convenient positions to give effective and deadly bursts of fire. The Polish commander wrote:

'While climbing, I can clearly see the yellow gobs of Me 109. I cannot get to them, as the formation is turning back, probably after dropping their bombs on the suburbs of London. I am approaching from the sun, getting the advantage of height, and on my way I can see two parachutists hanging below the clouds. I am flying in parallel with the raid which is heading towards the Channel, at a distance of approximately 600 yards. I cannot attack them as I would need to get through the Me 109s, which most definitely will end up with them shooting me and my wingmen. While thinking about it, I am looking back and see that in fact two Me 109s are closing from below and behind at a distance of about 100 yards. I make some sudden overhead turn and am on the Me 109's tail at a distance of 30–50 m, but they still fly in one straight line. I have shot down one of them and I can see that I am on my own. I do not shoot at the second one – as I simply thought that I see the shadow of a Me 109 on my tail. Shame – I thought, but only when in my bed in the evening.'

The aircraft which Urbanowicz shot down was most probably the Messerschmitt Bf 109 flown by Major Walter Kienzle from the Stab JG26, who bailed out and with serious wounds was taken prisoner. His machine crashed at Hides Farm, Roundhurst, near Haslemere in Surrey.

Meanwhile, Sergeant Marian Bełc had a different duty to fulfil. When noticing Pilot Officer Lewis Way from 229 Squadron dangling from the canopy of his parachute, to his horror the Polish NCO also spotted one of the Messerschmitts closing in and presumably aiming at this defenceless pilot. Bełc decided to protect his colleague, and by circling around him eventually scared away the German until Way reached the ground. Being attacked himself, Bełc left the area, heading back to Northolt. Apart from Urbanowicz, only Sergeant František managed to score again, being credited with two Messerschmitts: one destroyed and another probably shot down, and as it turned out, his last kills.

Another group of Germans, which was attacking the Westland aircraft factory in Yeovil, was intercepted by various RAF squadrons, including some Polish pilots. Flying Officer 'Novi' Nowierski from 609 Squadron, also labelled 'Novo' in the Operations Record Book, and Sergeant Józef Jeka, equally known as 'Josef' after someone anglicised his first name, distinguished themselves in combat yet again. No. 609, which took off at 4.15 pm, fought against well-trained fighters of JG2.

'Novi', No. 2 of Green Section, which was ordered to investigate six 'bogeys', reported:

Pilots of No. 74 Squadron with their commander Sqn Ldr "Sailor" Malan, who is standing in the centre. Flg Off Henryk Szczęsny and Flt Lt Stanisław Brzezina are standing right behind Malan in the second row.

'I attacked a Me 109 from astern and gave him a short burst (1 sec. 100–50 yards). I gave him another burst (3 secs) at the same range. White smoke came from the e/a and then very thick black smoke and he started to dive steeply. I noticed another Me 109 on my right and attacked him from astern. I gave him one burst (2 sec. 200–150 yards). White and black smoke came from e/a. I broke away to the left and after a few seconds I saw a man come down in a parachute which did not open. The parachute seemed to be fouled by a cord halfway up the canopy. This was about 10 miles NW of Portland.'

The only detail that was not included in Nowierski's narrative was that several bullets also hit his Spitfire, although the damage was rather minor. The last seconds of life for Gefr. Dollinger from the 5th Staffel JG2, as he was considered as the victim of the Pole, were very dramatic, his aircraft crashing at Sydling St Nicholas in Dorset.

Nowierski's version was later confirmed by his leader, Pilot Officer David Crook:

'Novi and I were the only lucky ones.[3] He had shot down two of the Me 109s, and the pilot got out of the second machine and tried to open his parachute. One of the rigging lines fouled it, however, and it only opened slightly, and the unfortunate German therefore continued his drop with scarcely any reduction in speed, and was killed. Novi, bloodthirsty as ever where Germans are concerned, recounted this story to us with great relish and a wealth of very descriptive gestures.'[4]

Sergeant Józef Jeka from 238 Squadron added another claim to his collection of trophies. After being credited with three enemy planes shot down on his own and a fourth shared with another pilot, all added to his list since 15 September, the former 141st Fighter Squadron pilot was searching the sky for another opportunity:

'I was Green 3 and attacked with formation from line astern. I fired at an Me 110 from astern at a range of 300 yds, giving 4-sec burst after it broke away, then 3 Me 109s attacked me from the rear. The E/A turned to the south with smoke coming from its starboard engine and went into a long glide. I couldn't watch as I had to avoid E/A.'

Although Jeka was able to evade his pursuers, he realized that he was short of fuel, so the best solution was to find the nearest airfield. He was eventually credited with one Bf 110 being damaged.

At the end of September and beginning of October, more Polish pilots were distributed between the RAF and Polish squadrons. After receiving considerable training on British equipment and learning about the RAF's tactics, it was decided that they could support their colleagues fighting in the first line of defence.[5] One of them was Flying Officer Jan Borowski, former deputy commander of the 113th Fighter Squadron in Poland, who joined No. 302 'City of Poznań' Squadron.

A large group of Polish pilots were posted to 607 Squadron stationed at Tangmere and equipped with Hurricanes. They were: Flying Officer Wieńczysław Barański, a very experienced officer with a long and interesting career, whose last posting in Poland was to command the 113th Fighter Squadron; Flight Lieutenant Juliusz Frey, whose career was equal to Barański's, being head of the 114th Fighter Squadron when war broke out; Flying Officer Aleksander Gabszewicz, also known as 'Gabsio' or *Hrabia Oleś* ('Count Oleś'), an Intelligence Officer of the IV/1 Fighter Wing and one of the first scorers of the Polish Campaign; Flight Lieutenant Bronisław Kosiński, famous for flying with the well known acrobatics team 'Bajan's Three', Flight Lieutenant

Adam Kowalczyk, former commander of the 112th Fighter Squadron and IV/1 Fighter Wing; and Flying Officer Wacław Wilczewski, in Poland a pilot of 123rd Fighter Squadron and then commander of the 142nd Fighter Squadron. Kowalczyk and Wilczewski remained non-operational pilots throughout the Battle of Britain.

Pilot Officer Stanisław Czternastek, the pilot who formerly served with the 123rd Fighter Squadron; Flying Officer Jan Falkowski, called '*Koń* '('Horse'), whose career started in the 142nd Fighter Squadron and progressed to flying instructor at Dęblin's School; and Sergeant Antoni Seredyn, who saw combat whilst flying with the 161st Fighter Squadron in Poland, all joined No. 32 Squadron of Hawker Hurricanes at Acklington.

Quite a significant number of Poles, initially posted to 615 Squadron, were transfered to 607 Squadron at Prestwick operating Hurricanes, included the following: Pilot Officer Mieczysław 'Mike' Gorzula, former instructor of the 2nd Air Regiment; Flight Lieutenant Włodzimierz Łazoryk, the last commander of the 152nd Fighter Squadron; Pilot Officer Aleksander Narucki, who flew during the Polish Campaign as a pilot of the ad hoc fighter section formed within the 3rd Air Regiment; Flight Lieutenant Jerzy Orzechowski, previously commanding officer of various units including the 142nd Fighter Squadron and then III/4 Fighter Wing; Flying Officer Henryk Skalski, pilot of the 112th Fighter Squadron and then a flying instructor; and Pilot Officer Bronisław Wydrowski, former pilot of the 3rd Air Regiment but without combat experience.

Sergeant Bronisław Malinowski, veteran of the 63rd Army Co-operation Squadron and a flying instructor, received a posting to the Usworth-based No. 43 Squadron, where he flew Hawker Hurricanes. Pilot Officer Włodzimierz Miksa, who following his graduation from Dęblin School joined the 114th Fighter Squadron and scored several victories during the Polish Campaign, and Sergeant Henryk Skowron, who although serving in the 2nd Air Regiment did not gain any combat experience, were both initially attached to 151 Squadron at Digby, from where they were reposted to No. 303. Both units flew Hawker Hurricanes.

Flying Officer Tadeusz Sawicz, known as 'Szczur' ('Rat'), although it is not known why he had such an unpleasant nickname, was a veteran of the 114th Fighter Squadron with a few claims under his belt, and joined 'Tadeusz Kościuszko' Squadron. Sergeant Szymon Kita, who recently gained experience in the Church Fenton-based 85 Squadron, received a posting to No. 253 at RAF Kenley, while Pilot Officer Gustaw Radwański left 151 Squadron after being posted to Tangmere, where he joined No. 607. Radwański was one of the less experienced Polish pilots, whose pre-war career of reserve cadet officer

Plt Off Mieczysław Gorzula (4th from left) accompanied by his British colleagues. During the Battle of Britain he was initially posted to 303 Sqn PAF, then he served in 615 & 607 Sqns RAF.

led him to fly with an army co-operation squadron. Only when he arrived in Britain did he pursue his dream of being a fighter pilot.

While 1 October was comparatively quiet for the Polish pilots and did not bring any spectacular events, Flight Lieutenant Kent, 'A' Flight commander of 303 Squadron, claimed two Bf 109s, one aircraft being destroyed and another probably shot down. The only Pole who participated in aerial engagement was 238 Squadron's Pilot Officer Władysław Różycki, but he did not open fire. The Polish Air Force suffered two non-operational losses on that day. Thirty-two-year-old Flying Officer Jerzy Sokołowski de Jenko was killed near Checkendon in Oxfordshire in a flying accident while in a Fairey Battle. This officer was initially posted to No. 304 Polish Squadron that was forming at Bramcote, but sent to 12 OTU for further training. Sergeant Stanisław Osmala, a former pilot of the 22nd Light Bomber Squadron in Poland, lost his life during exercises, also flying a Fairey Battle of No. 5 Bombing and Gunnery School. The Pole, together with his British pupil, crashed at Hall Caine, Isle of Man.

The following day, Pilot Officer Ludwik Martel, often called 'Zośka', participated in combat and reported damaging a Messerschmitt Bf 109. His No.

603 Squadron, at full strength, took off at 9.20 am and was sent for a defensive patrol and then to intercept an enemy formation heading for London. Six German aircraft were destroyed or probably destroyed, whilst Pilot Officer Peter Dexter had to bail out, struggling to free his trapped foot and eventually dislocating his knee in order to abandon the aircraft.

Martel, who remembered this day for a less dramatic reason, recalled later:

> 'When on patrol with 603 Squadron I saw one Me 109 coming underneath from the starboard quarter, the squadron being 1,000 ft below me. I dived and made a stern attack and saw glycol smoke came out of the Me 109 which took evasive action. I then saw two Me 109s in my mirror so I half rolled and dived.'

'Zośka', who most probably was shooting at one of JG53's aircraft, was about to score an even better result three days later.[6]

On 5 October, 303 Squadron, alongside the Canadian Squadron of the Northolt Wing, was in action. All twelve Hurricanes left Northolt between 11.05-11.10 am, vectored towards Maidstone, where a German formation was observed. They were then redirected to Rochester in Kent. The Luftwaffe was aiming for Backton and West Malling. When approaching this area, No.1 Squadron Hurricanes were attacked from above, and two pilots of 303 Squadron were able to adds to their successes. Squadron Leader Kellett, who was leading this mission, damaged one Bf 109, which most probably was one of the JG53 machines, whilst Flying Officer Zdzisław Henneberg, commander of Yellow Section, initially aimed at one of the single-engine raiders, but later managed to shoot down a Messerschmitt Bf 110 from ErpGr210. He wrote upon arrival back at base:

> 'I climbed to my former height and after a short while I noticed near the coast a defensive circle of Me 110s. Above them were flying several Me 109s. I attacked a Me 110, but after firing two bursts I observed a Me on my tail. Evading enemy aircraft I chased a Me 110 making towards the coast and began to fire from a distance of 250 yards. After firing two bursts enemy aircraft right engine burst into flames and dived straight for the sea. I was then attacked by three Messerschmitts 109s and evading them returned to Northolt.'

Another group of Luftwaffe raiders were noticed over Lympne in Kent. Sergeant Stanisław Karubin, who flew as Henneberg's No. 3, reported:

'I first noticed a number of Me 109s flying about 5,000 ft above us to our left in the opposite direction. We turned and ran into a number of Me 109s and Me 110s. I attacked one of two Me 109s, firing from the rear and below two short bursts. E/A burst into flames and smoking fell to earth in the region of Kent. I was then attacked by a Me 109, and in the ensuring dog fight fired a short burst. E/A smoking slightly made off.'

Some historians pinpoint Uffz. Wilhelm Gehsla or Lt Zeiss, both from 1st Staffel JG53, as potential targets of Karubin's attack. Fw. von Herwarth-Bittenfeld was the third airman from the same Geschwader shot down in this area.

Kellett's Red 2, Pilot Officer Mirosław Ferić, most probably finished off the aircraft that his colleague 'Dzidek' Henneberg had been attacking. Presumably this machine was flown by a crew consisting of Oblt. Werner Weimann, commander of the Gruppe, with Uffz. Hubner:

'I then noticed an Me 110 break away from the circle, and diving make towards the sea, smoking slightly, but maintaining a very high speed. I chased E/A and catching up with him about seven miles from the coast fired a burst from a distance of about 20 yds into his cockpit. E/A immediately dived into the sea.'

On this occasion, the Polish commander of 'B' Flight was leading Blue Section. Flying Officer Marian Pisarek dived into the battle with typical Polish passion and aggression:

'I attacked a Me 110 and fired three bursts from the front and to the left. The result of this attack I did not see, but according to Sgt Bełc e/a began to smoke, and broke away, probably damaged. I pulled out of my dive and turned and attacked a Me 110 from the rear and above. Firing several short bursts I saw e/a begin to smoke, one engine stopped and e/a fell into the sea.'

His No. 3, Sergeant Marian Bełc, mentioned previously, was also closing on the formation of twin-engine Messerschmitts. As he had spent a relatively long time on sick leave, he was now even more desperate to repay the Germans for what they did to his country. Similarly to Ferić, he did not give much of a chance to his victim, shooting at him from very close range: 'I attacked from the front and below. Me 110 dived. I followed and firing a burst from about 50 yds saw one of the crew jump. E/A crashed to earth near Lympne.' He could theoretically also have been responsible for the loss of the German airmen Weimann and Hubner.

Sergeant Antoni Siudak, No. 2 in Yellow Section, who a week before was transferred from 302 Squadron, had plenty to do when his Hurricane flew into the melee. Keeping a close watch all around, and with a finger attached to the trigger, he joined the mayhem:

> 'I attacked a Me 109 from the rear and slightly to the left, and a Spitfire attacked the same Me from the rear and slightly to the right. I fired two bursts, E/A burst into flames, and fell to earth near Ashford, burning on the ground. I immediately attacked an Me 109 which flew close to me, and fired a long burst. E/A broke up into bits and fell to earth also near Ashford. I then attacked another Me 109 which fled towards the sea. I fired a burst and E/A fell into the sea smoking off Littlestone near a boat.'

Siudak was eventually credited with destroying two Bf 109s, one of which could have been flown by Lt Zeiss, which would also be associated with Karubin's action, and a shared victory against a Bf 110. The latter went down on the Industrial School in Kingsnorth with two crew members, Fw. Fritz Dünsnig and Fw. Krappatch. They were Siudak's first, and unfortunately his last, trophies achieved in 303 Squadron.

Green 3, Sergeant Jan Palak, was the last successful pilot in this combat. Similarly to his mate Antoni Siudak, he joined 'Tadeusz Kościuszko' Squadron only a few days before, previously serving in the 'City of Poznań' unit. Palak described his actions:

> 'I attacked one Me 110 firing a short burst. E/A began to smoke. I did not seen what happened as I was attacked by two Me 109s. I turned and attacked one e/a firing two bursts from the rear. E/a burst into flames and dived to earth in the neighbourhood of Lympne.'

It was also suggested that Palak fought with JG53's Gehsla, as the location given by the Polish pilot resembles the German airman's crash site.

At the time of this merciless battle, no one noticed that the Hurricane flown by Flying Officer Wojciech Januszewicz, an officer who led Green Section, suddenly disappeared. Januszewicz was targeting Zerstőres when one of the Bf 109s from the JG53 went down and swiftly shot up his aircraft. He was hit over Stowting and for some time tried to outmanoeuvre the predator by flying very low. Januszewicz was getting lower and lower, still being chased by the 109. At this point, ground-based anti-aircraft guns, without any visible success, opened fire on the German plane. This was not enough to save the Polish pilot's life, however. The Hurricane, with most probably the severely wounded Pole still inside, crashed in a field and burst into flames close to a tree line, killing the Polish pilot.

There are four possible matches for Januszewicz's conqueror, all pilots from JG53. Lt Erich Schmidt, Oblt Walter Rupp, Hptm. Heinz Bretnütz and Ofw. Werner Kauffmann. Januszewicz, known to his friends as 'Wojtek', distinguished himself during the Polish Campaign not only by commanding the 111th Fighter Squadron, following his superior being wounded in combat, but also by claiming three aerial victories, shooting down one Bf 110 and two Ju 87s. Fighting over France, and then in Britain, was unsuccessful in terms of aerial triumphs, despite him being involved in many missions and fights. This experienced officer rather concentrated on the tactical aspects of the fight, leading his colleagues into the battle and then breaking enemy formations, rather than on individual scoring. It was an attribute of a great commander.

While the Poles fought with determination against both JG53 and Erp. Gr210, Pilot Officer Ludwik Martel from No. 603 Squadron was back in action. He and his colleagues took off at 11.10 am and were sent to patrol over Dover, where they engaged a number of Messerschmitt Bf 109s. Pilot Officer James Morton had to bail out with burns to his body, but other pilots successfully clashed with their adversaries. Martel's companions claimed one Bf 109 probably destroyed and another one damaged, and 'Zośka' proudly gave the following report:

> 'When on patrol with 603 Squadron I saw a circle of Me 109s and one Me 109 left the circle and started to climb and I dived on him and made a beam attack, firing for about three seconds. The Me 109 took evasive action by skidding and I attacked again with slight deflection, firing the reminder of my ammunition from 200 yards. The Messerschmitt went up and then dived gently into the sea. I saw him crash into the sea about 6 miles east of Dover.'

This time there were no doubts about the fate of Martel's opponent and he was given full credit for the kill.

Flight Lieutenant Stanisław Brzezina, one of the two remaining Poles from No. 74 Squadron, was chosen to command the recently created Polish No. 308 'City of Cracow' Squadron, therefore his days with the 'Tigers' theoretically were numbered. As the beginning of the independent PAF's existence in exile was rather stormy, many personnel changes and transfers back and forth happened, and therefore his own posting was postponed and eventually put on hold. Finally Brzezina, while still being assigned to 74 Squadron, due his vast knowledge of human resources and great personal approach and contacts, was given the duty of assisting Group Captain Stefan Pawlikowski. The latter was appointed the chief in command of the Polish fighter force in Britain, and regularly visited all existing as well as new-born fighter units to seek opinions and deal with internal problems.

This was before Brzezina took on the role of Polish Liaison Officer with No. 12 Group. In the meantime, 'Breezy' occasionally flew with 74 Squadron, but no further claims were made by this officer. It was his colleague 'Sneezy' who, after a long break, managed to add to his combat score.

On Saturday 5 October, Flying Officer Henryk Szczęsny, after taking off at 1.20 pm, flew as No. 3 of Green Section, accompanied by Flying Officer Roger Boulding and Pilot Officer Harbourne Stephen, when German activity was spotted 30 miles south of Harwich. It was 2.05 pm when the three Spitfires sighted a single Dornier Do 17 from 2nd Staffel KG 3, mistaken by them as a Do 215, and began their attack, as described by the Pole:

> 'Green Leader and No. 2 attacked e/a first. I attacked him in a dive towards the sea. I opened fire at 250 yards and continued to fire all my ammunition into his engines and fuselage. There was no return fire and e/a was burning from the port engine. I pulled away at 1,000 ft and e/a. was still diving in flames towards the sea at approximately 300 mph. I broke away to port and did not see e/a fall into sea on account of haze at sea level.'

Due to bad weather conditions limiting pilots' visibility, all three were given an equal and shared victory over the attacked aircraft.

When another group of German aircraft was heading towards Poole and Weymouth, several RAF squadrons were sent to intervene and stop them. Amongst the defenders were Nos. 238 and 609, both consisting of Polish pilots. This formation of Spitfires was suddenly attacked over Middle Wallop by fifteen Bf 109s. No. 238 lost one of its pilots, who bailed out, while Pilot Officer Różycki's guns failed to fire: he was deeply disappointed after returning to base at Chilbolton in Hampshire.

This was, however, not the end of Polish bad luck that day. Flying Officer Nowierski from 609 Squadron, finishing the later sortie, experienced difficulties with lowering the Spitfire's undercarriage. Only one of 'Novi's' wheels came down, the second remaining locked. Nowierski had to climb over Salisbury Plain and when reaching a decent height, he attempted to bail out. But the Pole had problems abandoning the Spitfire. Eventually Nowierski turned his aircraft upside down and fell out, landing safely without injury. A crew of Polish No. 307 Squadron experienced a rather unpleasant impact during taxiing at Kirton-in-Lindsey, Lincolnshire, when the Boulton Paul Defiant piloted by Sergeant Jerzy Malinowski was damaged on the runway. This happened when the undercarriage leg failed, and luckily no one was hurt in the incident.

There were further postings that moved some of the Polish pilots between units. Pilot Officers Zbigniew Oleński and Janusz Żurakowski left St Eval's 234 Squadron, being posted to No. 609 stationed at Warmwell in Dorset, where they joined Nowierski and Ostaszewski-Ostoja. Meanwhile, Sergeants Klein and Szlagowski also arrived at Warmwell, reporting to No. 152 'Hyderabad' Squadron. Soon after, Szlagowski was seen as 'very popular with the officers and airmen', and 'thorough both on the ground and in the air'. His skills were highly praised by his commander as 'above average and his flying discipline was excellent'.

The following day, Northolt aerodrome was hit by an unexpected attack carried out by a single Junkers Ju 88, which used thick clouds for cover. Shortly after midday,[7] the Ju 88 from 4th Staffel KG30 suddenly dived down and from a height of 200ft machine-gunned buildings, specifically targeting hangars and 229 Squadron's dispersal. One of the ground crew was killed when two bombs were dropped on the airfield.[8] At the same time, Sergeant Antoni Siudak from 303 Squadron was taxiing his Hurricane, and according to some sources, tried to save the plane by moving it away from the danger zone, or simply taking the Hurricane back to dispersal after its routine maintenance. He was killed when the aircraft received a direct hit from one of the bombs. There are various accounts that his death was caused either by the bomb blast, being hit by the shell or a skull fracture from falling out of the aircraft onto the tarmac.

Three members of the Polish ground crew distinguished themselves during this attack: Flying Officer Wacław Wiórkiewicz, an engineering officer, who commanded the team throughout the bombardment, senior mechanic Warrant Officer Józef Mikołajczyk and Corporal Władysław Roubo. Mikołajczyk was sitting on the wing of Siudak's aircraft, being previously busy with synchronizing the machine guns, and did not leave his post, trying to save the pilot. Meanwhile Roubo, who worked on another Hurricane just 10 metres away from the blast, risked his life by staying with the aircraft and switching off the engine.

Siudak's loss was a shock to the squadron, as only the previous day this brave pilot had achieved great success. The former flying instructor was popular amongst his colleagues, being a 'good pilot; calm and mentally well balanced, extremely tactful, sincere and open'.

Two of 229's Hurricanes, which were already in the air on an earlier defence patrol, intercepted the Junkers and successfully attacked it, which resulted in being credited with causing damage, but in fact the German aircraft was shot down.

Monday 7 October was the day that saw the last combat engagement and therefore the last victories achieved by 303 Squadron during the Battle of Britain. Its pilots were tired, overstretched and required immediate rest. Thus either fresh reinforcements or moving further north from the battlefield was necessary: 'Tadeusz Kościuszko' Squadron soon received both. After a quiet Sunday, on the very next day the weather conditions improved and German activity increased.

Wreckage of Hurricane P3120 RF-A destroyed by a German bomb. Sgt Antoni Siudak lost his life sitting in this aircraft.

From 9.20 am the Luftwaffe started to be spotted by RDF operators, and soon after the first raiders appeared over southern England. It was not until after 1 pm that the Poles had another opportunity to claim more victories. At 1.20 pm, 303 Squadron, led by Kellett, took off from Northolt and together with Canadian No. 1 Squadron were ordered to patrol over Kenley and Brooklands at a height of 20,000ft. Before reaching their designated patrol zone, they were vectored to a new target, a large formation which consisted of at least fifty Messerschmitt Bf 109s. The enemy, who appeared to be ready to fight, initially went for the Canadians, but after their first inefficient attack were unable to confront them again.

Meanwhile, the Poles had noticed another group of fighters, flying to the west, who tried to intervene using their height advantage. This quick attack proved unsuccessful, but the Bf 109s weren't an easy target either, passing by the Polish squadron too quickly. Very few 303 pilots were able to shoot at them, but three of them did so successfully.

'B' Flight commander Flying Officer Marian Pisarek, who flew as Blue 1, was one of these lucky ones. He realized that not all the attackers, after their first attempt, were so eager to continue the fight. 'Flying east I noticed an Me 109 already engaged by other fighters,' he wrote.

'At that exact moment I observed four Me 109s flying underneath me. I attacked and chased one towards the coast, but he evaded me and escaped into the clouds. I turned, and after a while I noticed a Me 109 flying below the clouds towards the sea. I attacked it from beneath, firing a burst of about forty rounds from a distance of fifty yards. E/a dived into the sea, smoking from the port wing and engine.'

Red 3, Sergeant '*Gen*' Szaposznikow, once more witnessed the annoying disadvantage of his Hurricane, being outclassed by the much faster Bf 109, especially when gaining height. It was obvious that the Luftwaffe fighters had adopted new tactics:

'We met a formation of Me 109s flying below us. Then immediately below us I saw 3 Me 109s, followed by two more. I attacked, and after firing one burst, E/a climbed. I followed, and firing two bursts, E/a began to smoke but evaded me. I then met two Me 109s over the coast. I attacked one, and firing a burst saw E/a dive. I fired from a distance of 150 yds, but there was no sign of smoke or flames, although the E/a fell into the sea just off Brighton. I noticed today that, whereas in previous combats E/a dived towards the earth when attacked, they now climbed, easily leaving the Hurricane behind.'

As both Pisarek and Szaposznikow claimed that their adversaries ended up in the sea, they could have been responsible for defeating either Uffz Bley from the 4th Staffel LG2, whose aircraft went down near Greatstone close to Dungeness, or JG51's Lt Erich Meyer, who hit the water off nearby Dymchurch. Both were taken prisoner.

The last pilot of 303 Squadron who managed to score during that afternoon's fight was Sergeant Marian 'Profesor' Bełc, flying as Blue 3:

'Flying S.E. at 18,000 ft I saw several Me 109s flying at 15,000 ft., which we attacked from above. I fired one long burst from a distance of 200 yds. E/a began to circle, and I with it. After the second circle, I fired another burst. Me began to smoke, and the right side of the engine burst into flames. E/a dived straight towards the earth, and disappeared beneath the clouds. The place of its crash would be west of Bedhill.'

Although Bełc is frequently associated with the downing of Oblt Victor Mölders, there is also a strong belief that he rather fought with LG2's Uffz. Morschel. This pilot of the 4th Staffel bailed out and was captured, his aircraft crashing at the Spa Golf Club near Tunbridge Wells.

For the Poles this was again not a victimless encounter, although not so tragic as two days before. Pilot Officer Bogusław Mierzwa, realizing that lack of fuel would not allow him to continue to Northolt, was desperately searching for an alternative landing place. He found such a location at Borstal near Chatham, and after refuelling his Hurricane the Pole tried to take off. Unfortunately the soft ground caught his undercarriage and Mierzwa overturned his aircraft, damaging it slightly.

This was the end of the spectacular Battle of Britain involvement which made 303 Squadron the most successful unit of that period amongst all of Dowding's fighter boys. 'Kościuszko' pilots had to wait another six months to reopen their long list of aerial victories. On 20 April 1941, three pilots from the Battle of Britain-hardened team – Łokuciewski, Daszewski and Palak – respectively shot down one Bf 109, another probably and damaged a third, during the Operation Sphere over Le Touquet in north-east France.

On 7 October, Sergeant Szymon Kita, the Pole who flew with the Kenley-based 253 Squadron, wrote in his flying log book that he shared with Sergeant Kenneth Allen the downing of a Heinkel He 11 during his second sortie. The combat was supposed to have taken place over Tangmere, yet no information of such an engagement could be found. This vague fragment of history remains one of the unsolved Battle of Britain mysteries. Neither of these pilots was credited with an official score. Kita took part in another engagement on that day, but wasn't involved in any dog-fights.

Another NCO of the Polish Air Force fought over Biggin Hill against four Bf 109s, part of a bigger afternoon wave of aircraft which appeared over Britain on 7 October and after 3.30 pm were seen targeting various locations, including London. Sergeant Budziński from Red Section of 605 Squadron was amongst three pilots who clashed with Uffz. Lederer from the 5th Staffel JG27. The Operations Record Book stated:

'During a later patrol the squadron at 27,000 ft again were in position to jump Me 109s. They encountered four of them at 26,000 ft near Biggin Hill, S/L [Archibald] McKellar destroying one and Sgt [Eric]Wright, Sgt Budziński and F/O[Cyril] Passy destroyed another between them.'

According to the pilots involved, their victim turned around, lost its speed and altitude and eventually crashed at a large farm, two miles from a lake in the vicinity of Cranbrook in Kent.

Meanwhile, the pilots of 56 Squadron were ordered to perform an operational patrol to cover their aerodrome at Warmwell in Dorset. Once a message was received that an enemy formation was approaching Yeovil, ten aircraft took off at 3.20 pm and, in fairly good weather, proceeded to search over the town and surrounding areas. Soon after a group of about twenty Ju 88s and Do 17s were spotted approaching, protected by a large bunch of Messerschmitts, which were following them very closely. Two British pilots were awarded the probable destruction of a Bf 110 and Do 17, while one of the defenders was shot down and had to bail out.

'A' Flight's Pilot Officer Zbigniew Nosowicz, a Pole who flew as No. 3 in Blue Section, took part in a combat and reported his claims later:

'At 15.40 saw E/A in mixed formation and made quarter attack from front with a two-second burst, and as enemy rear gunner fired at me I turned slightly and gave a 2-sec. burst. The E/A dived quickly emitting smoke from front and turned seawards, gliding towards sea. Having to meet a second E/A I did not observe whether he crashed. Immediately I attacked another Me 110, the rear gunner of which was firing at me. After I had given a one-second burst the rear gunner ceased fire. Another Me 110 then attacked me and I was obliged to break away. Did not see anyone bale out.'

Twelve Hurricanes from 238 Squadron left their base at Chilbolton, initially only to protect their own airfield, but soon after were redirected towards Bristol, flying west. When over Portland, they were unexpectedly attacked by two Messerschmitt Bf 109s, which resulted in the loss of one of their comrades.

Three Ju 88s were claimed alongside one Bf 110 by 238's pilots in the area between Maiden Newton, Portland and Bridport. Amongst the victorious fighters was Polish Sergeant Józef Jeka, who flew as Green 2. When the Bf 109s attacked his colleagues, the Pole was in trouble himself:

'I was attacked by 2 Mes 109s and the squadron was split up. I evaded these and dived for the bombers which had made a wide circuit, and I came up to them by flying West. I attacked the last Ju 88 in the formation and fired all my ammunition in five separate attacks on this E/A, beginning at 300 yards from quarter and closing to very close (about fifty yards). In fact I was in the slipstream from the E/A which made my machine rock. During two of my attacks the rear gunner shot at me from a cannon firing explosive bullets. After my attacks the Ju's starboard engine went very slowly and the E/A dived towards the sea. I followed it down and saw it crash into the sea about 10 miles due South of Bridport. I flew low, then straight for Portland and Weymouth Bay. I saw a life boat going out to S.E. where I saw a big patch of substance in the water.'

When Jeka was chasing his victim, two other Polish airmen, Sergeants Klein and Szlagowski, were patrolling in the Swanage area. Their 152 Squadron left Warmwell at 3.27 pm, and less than twenty minutes later near Lyme Regis and Exeter clashed with a German formation consisting of thirty Ju 88s, protected by Bf 110s. Although Józef Szlagowski, who was in Blue Section, tried his best to shoot down one of the Messerschmitts, his oxygen supply was causing probleme for the 26-year-old pilot and it was his colleague who had more luck on this day.

Klein, of Green Section, described his combat in the following words:

'I was Green 2 on patrol with the Squadron at 18,000 ft. Enemy sighted NW. We were about to attack the bomber formation when I saw 3 Me 110s about 3 miles behind the bomber formation. I climbed into the sun, and waited until they turned back when I attacked the starboard a/c. I fired 3 bursts at close range, broke way and climbed back into the sun. White smoke was issuing from both engines and e/a was losing height. I attacked again but had to break away before opening fire as there were two 110s on my tail. I did not observe any return fire.'

It is today assumed that Klein was fighting with one of the Bf 110s from the IIIrd Gruppe ZG26, as both Gruppen (II and III) lost seven aircraft during the afternoon engagement.

One more Pole who had an opportunity to claim a successful encounter was Flying Officer 'Jerry' Jankiewicz, Blue 2 in 601 Squadron. The whole unit took off at 3.45 pm from Exeter and climbed in the direction of Yeovil, where they sighted an enemy formation north of Axminster. The Germans were heading south, between Beaminster and Bridport. Twenty bombers flew in sections of either three, two or singly at 11,000 feet, guarded by the same number of fighters, hiding 4,000ft above. Jankiewicz reported upon return to his base:

> 'I saw 2 Me 110s below me and broke away to attack them. I dived down at the near one and carried out a beam attack, firing a short burst with full deflection. The E/A adopted evasive tactics and I made another attack on him from ¾ astern, firing short bursts at ranges from 400 yds closing to 50 yds and finished my ammunition. I saw splinters and pieces flying off the end of his left wing. I broke away, blacking myself out, and on coming out of the turn I saw the E/A well out over the sea.'

The Polish pilot was only credited with damaging the Bf 110.

In the meantime, on the ground, there was further movement of Polish pilots. Pilot Officers Czesław Gauze and Czesław Tarkowski, after finishing their time in the Operational Training Unit, were posted to No. 85 Squadron, where they both remained non-operational pilots throughout the remaining time of the Battle of Britain. Gauze, a 22-year-old son of Polish immigrants, was born in Brazil but moved back to Poland, where he graduated from the Polish Air Force Cadet Officers College together with the one year younger Tarkowski. Soon after they were reposted to 605 Squadron, with whom Gauze lost his life over a month later as a result of a dog-fight over Dover.

Flight Lieutenant Antoni Wczelik left 302 Squadron, where he had served since 20 August (including three weeks which he spent in No. 5 OTU), and joined 'Tadeusz Kościuszko' Squadron. Wczelik was 34 years old at that time and quite experienced. Serving as an observer in the 6th Air Regiment, he completed a flying course and became a pilot in the 2nd Air Regiment, eventually becoming commander of the 122nd and 123rd Fighter Squadrons and finally a flying instructor in Dęblin. Wczelik fought in France, so aircraft with a retractable undercarriage were well known to him.

During the events of the next day, although Polish pilots were kept occupied, the only claim recorded by them was one shared victory for Sergeant Jan Budziński from 605 Squadron, constantly called 'Budyinski' by the unit's clerk. 'A brilliantly fine early morning, deteriorating about 11.15 hours with amazing suddenness,' recorded the squadron's ORB, giving very vague operational details yet providing information about the weather conditions. The squadron's

Flg Off Henryk Szczęsny playing cards with Flg Off John Freeborn, being observed by Flg Off Roger Boulding (with dog).

pilots were sent on patrol at 10.45 am, and 'A' Flight, led by Flight Lieutenant Current, destroyed a single Ju 88 near Gatwick. As no specific names were given, we can assume that all six pilots, including the Pole, participated in this successful action.

It was a very sad day for No. 303 Squadron, which lost one of its most valuable and pugnacious pilots. Sergeant Josef František, known for his individuality, a true maverick who became the most successful pilot of the Battle of Britain, was killed after an uneventful mission when his Hurricane crashed at Ewell in Surrey. Although a non-Polish pilot, he found a very special place in his comrades' hearts, by his own choice becoming a permanent member of the Polish Air Force.

Sgt Mieczysław Marcinkowski, who recently completed his training at an Operational Training Unit, reported to No. 151, from where soon after he was posted to 501 Squadron. Marcinkowski, 21, graduated from the Polish Air Force NCO School for Minors before the outbreak of war, but up to joining 501 had no combat experience.

During the evening of Wednesday 9 October, the Polish bomber squadrons returned to their duties of attacking and harassing the German fleet across the Channel. Eight crews from 301 Squadron were chosen to bomb Le Havre, but shortly after the target area was changed to Calais. The first Fairey Battle took off from Swinderby at 6.23 pm, the last aircraft going up twenty-three minutes later. All Polish airmen reported good visibility over the target. Most of the crews dropped their bombs while dive-bombing at 2,000-3,000ft, while others remained at 6,000ft.

Despite German anti-aircraft artillery and searchlights, all crews returned without a scratch, landing between 9.34 pm and 10.30 pm. During this operation the following crews were used: Squadron Leader Stefan Floryanowicz, Flying Officer Stanisław Rewkowski and Sergeant Ignacy Bator, Sergeant Stanisław Jensen, Flying Officer Leon Szymkiewicz and Sergeant Walenty Wasilewski; Sergeant Stanisław Mierniczek, Flying Officer Hieronim Kulbacki and Sergeant Jan Hejnowski; Sergeant Stanisław Kłosowski, Flying Officer Antoni Wronka and Sergeant Antoni Lipecki; Flight Lieutenant Witold Piotrowski, Flying Officer Julian Pałka and Sergeant Franciszek Florczak; Sergeant Kazimierz Lenczowski, Flying Officer Stefan Hałłas and Sergeant Gustaw Kasianowski; Sergeant Tadeusz Bojakowski, Flying Officer Józef Koryciński and Sergeant Antoni Dydo; and Flying Officer Wacław Butkiewicz, Flying Officer Stanisław Starowicz and Sergeant Kazimierz Sawicz.

On Thursday 10 October, many of the Polish pilots participated in operational flying, while others polished their skills during various flying exercises. Despite increasing German activity, only one Pole had a chance to write a combat report after a clash with the enemy. Around midday, a quite significant raid had been sighted over Dorset, against which several RAF squadrons, including 303 PAF, were sent. However, only 238 Squadron caught up with the raiders, consisting of twenty-five Bf 109s and Bf 110s, flying south of Warmwell. Separate dog-fights broke out and eventually two enemy machines were damaged, whilst one home pilot was wounded and had to bail out.

Pilot Officer Władysław Różycki, Blue 2, being one of the two who got close enough to engage the enemy, wrote:

'I saw several Me 109s to my port, and I went to attack. The E/A were flying from N. to South. I saw a Me 109 dive down and he appeared in front of me, so I gave him a very short burst from behind and below from very close (50 yards), as he could not see me. Whilst giving the burst I turned into him but he quickly turned and went into clouds. I did not see E/A after this. I climbed up and saw what I thought were Hurricanes in formations, but when I got to within 200 yds I saw they were Me 109s which opened fire at me.'

Różycki circled and managed to avoid being hit, eventually escaping inside the clouds.

On this day 1 Bomber Group again requested the Polish presence over the German barges assembled in France. As during the previous night, they were expected to attack the port of Calais. The Fairey Battles from No. 300 Squadron left Swinderby between 6.21 pm and 6.39 pm and flew towards enemy-occupied territory. After completing their task, all eight light bombers turned back. Two of them had some difficulties due to a fuel shortage or engine problems, but eventually every Polish airman returned safely from this mission. The twenty-four Polish airmen involved were: Pilot Officer Kazimierz Kula, Sergeant Marian Przybylski and Sergeant Jan Mieczkowski; Flying Officer Jan Konarzewski, Pilot Officer Antoni Pułczyński and Sergeant Antoni Żychowski; Sergeant Kazimierz Szymanowski, Pilot Officer Zenon Luba and Sergeant Albin Socha; Pilot Officer Zdzisław Kurowski, Flying Officer Władysław Rogalski and Sergeant Oskar Zieliński; Pilot Officer Mieczysław Kałuża, Flying Officer Tadeusz Chrostowski and Sergeant Władysław Urbanowicz; Sergeant Alojzy Ratajczak, Pilot Officer Zygmunt Pluta and Sergeant Marian Gędziorowski; Sergeant Edward Hajdukiewicz, Pilot Officer Czesław Dej and Sergeant Henryk Węgrzyn; and Sergeant Józef Kazimierczak, Sergeant Bolesław Sobieszczuk and Sergeant Tadeusz Szmajdowicz.

The following day marked the end of the spectacular chapter of 303 Squadron's participation in the Battle of Britain. It was finally decided that the pilots and ground crew required some well-deserved time for rest, regeneration and training for the new recruits. Between 11.55 am and 12.45 pm, the squadron completed its last patrol from Northolt, and except one rather unpleasant accident that happened to Pilot Officer Ferić, when the inner tube of one of his Hurricane's tyres burst while landing, everyone was getting ready to move to RAF Leconfield,

Before all eighteen Hurricanes departed from Northolt between 3.40-3.45 pm, the 303 pilots had a chance to say a quick 'hello' to their replacements from 302 Squadron, who landed at their base at 1.30 pm. Friday 11 October also saw Pilot Officer Jerzy Solak from 249 Squadron belly-landing his aircraft after an afternoon mission and Sergeant Michał Maciejowski being posted from No. 111 to 249 Squadron.

Saturday 12 October was again an action-packed day. Despite another mysterious claim made by Sergeant Kita, who wrote in his flying log book that he shot down a Bf 109 near Maidstone, which could not be confirmed elsewhere, there was an uneventful operational initiation of 302 Squadron from Northolt and no spectacular episodes were noted. However, Sergeant Biel of No. 3 Squadron was involved in an accident, damaging his Hurricane at RAF Wick in northern Scotland.

Quite a large group of Polish pilots joined 303 Squadron after leaving 307 Squadron and its infamous Boulton Paul Defiants. These flyers, with experience gained during the war in Poland, wanted to be fighter pilots again, not what they saw as 'unarmed drivers' of the two-seater Defiants, which they didn't like at all. Now they were about to be familiarized with the real war horses of the RAF, Hawker Hurricanes. They were: Flight Lieutenant Władysław Szczęśniewski; Flying Officers Bronisław Mickiewicz and Zdzisław Zadroziński; Pilot Officers Jan Bury-Burzymski, Tadeusz Koc, Franciszek Kornicki, Marian Łukaszewicz and Andrzej Malarowski; and Sergeants Stanisław Brzeski, Wacław Giermer, Bronisław Kościk and Franciszek Prętkiewicz.

A few days later, they were joined by Sergeant Marian Rytka, who soon after was reposted to 302 Squadron. Both Kościk and Łukaszewicz were 151st Fighter Squadron veterans, Burzymski and Brzeski fought in Poland as pilots of the 152nd, and Szczęśniewski commanded the 161st in which Koc, Malarowski and Prętkiewicz had flown. Kornicki and Zadroziński participated in combat with the 162nd Fighter Squadron, while Giermer and Mickiewicz, although both experienced fighter pilots, served as flying instructors when war broke out. Rytka was also a flying instructor, who went into action in France after joining the Polish fighter section attached to GCIII/10.

In the afternoon, No. 301 Polish Squadron dispatched six crews in two groups to bomb two separate targets. Between 6.04-6.18 pm, three Fairey Battles from 'A' Flight took off from Swinderby to attack the Belgian port of Ostend. Their crews were: Flight Lieutenant Stanisław Brejnak, Flying Officer Stanisław Król and Sergeant Tadeusz Madejski; Pilot Officer Michał Liniewski, Flying Officer Antoni Voellnagel and Sergeant Bernard Kowalski; and Sergeant Franciszek Zaremba, Pilot Officer Bolesław Biliński and Sergeant Czesław Kozłowski. Another three Battles from 'B' Flight went up between 6.09-6.19 pm to bomb Boulogne, flown by: Pilot Officer Teofil Pożyczka, Pilot Officer Mieczysław Łapa and Sergeant Ryszard Tydman; Sergeant Józef Waszak, Flying Officer Jan Kozak and Sergeant Edward Janik; and Sergeant Ignacy Radzymiński, Flying Officer Eugeniusz Domański and Sergeant Zdzisław Pieczyński. Each aircraft carried six 250lb bombs, and after a successful mission landed back at Swinderby but also at nearby Grantham and Waddington.

On Sunday 13 October, Pilot Officer Gustaw Radwański and Sergeant Wilhelm Szafraniec left 607 Squadron after being posted to 56 Squadron. Despite a rather quiet day, Bomber Command and 1 Bomber Group ordered another mission for the Polish Battle crews, specifying its target as Boulogne. It would be difficult to establish whether the Polish crews from No. 300 Polish Squadron were superstitious of the 13th while getting ready for their afternoon mission, but unfortunately bad luck was about to show its face in the most tragic way.

Six of the planes, due to their rather infamous operational history known as 'flying coffins', took off from Swinderby between 5.40-6.04 pm. The crews were:

Flying Officer Jan Gębicki, Sergeant Edward Morawa and Sergeant Tadeusz Egierski; Sergeant Wiktor Koczwarski, Flying Officer Ignacy Szponarowicz and Sergeant Marian Sztul; Sergeant Adam Hałabuda, Flying Officer Stanisław Firley-Bielański and Sergeant Tadeusz Szmajdowicz; Sergeant Piotr Nowakowski, Flying Officer Tomasz Łubieszko and Sergeant Henryk Kudełko; Sergeant Marian Kostecki, Flying Officer Jan Piotrowski and Sergeant Feliks Jezierski; and Flying Officer Jerzy Gołko, Flying Officer Włodzimierz Pęski and Sergeant Tadeusz Bączak.

This proved not to be an easy flight at all. Until the order 'bombs away' was given, all was going smoothly, but trouble started on their way back. Visibility worsened rapidly and the crews were flying in a haze, having serious difficulties in steering the right course. Only two aircraft, piloted by Nowakowski and Kostecki, managed to reach Swinderby. Koczwarski's bomber luckily arrived at Hucknall, while Hałabuda and Gołko got as far as Newton, both in Nottinghamshire.

RAF Northolt. Airmen from both Polish bomber squadrons met Sir Archibald Sinclair, Secretary of State for Air and General Władysław Sikorski (both standing in centre). Gp Cpt Bogdan Kwieciński, the Polish military and air attaché in Britain, can be seen standing 2nd from right. Interestingly during the Great War Kwieciński served in the German air force on the Palestinian front and was interned by the British.

There was one aircraft missing. To make the situation even more dramatic, during the crews' absence, at 8.20 pm Swinderby aerodrome was attacked by German aircraft, which dropped ten bombs, damaging two Fairey Battles from No. 300 and one from 301 Squadron. No Polish airmen were hurt. The missing aircraft with the crew of Gębicki, Morawa and Egierski was not heard of until It turned out that the pilot had twice tried to land at Newton. Lacking fuel, the Battle crashed near Oxton, killing all three Polish crew on board. Warsaw-born Gębicki, aged 39, was a test pilot of the RWD aviation factory in Poland, while both his Sergeants were air gunners before the war broke out. Two years younger, Morawa served in the 2nd Air Regiment, while his 22-year-old colleague Egierski, originally from Kielce, took part in the Polish Campaign as an airmen of 12th (212th) Bomber Squadron. The PAF had suffered further Battle of Britain losses.

The following day, Flying Officer Marian Duryasz from No. 213 Squadron damaged his Hurricane at Manston in Kent after returning from an operational mission. The Polish pilot was unhurt.

Chapter Seventeen

Last Kills, Last Losses

So far the Polish pilots of No. 302 Squadron had claimed at least fourteen enemy aircraft destroyed, a further eight probably shot down and one more damaged. By looking at the pure statistics and without understanding the wider context, it would lead us to a rather inequitable assessment of their skills, especially if their achievements were compared to the results gained by their sister squadron, No. 303. Yet the location far from the epicentre of the Battle of Britain resulted in much less engagement than was experienced by their colleagues from 'Tadeusz Kościuszko' Squadron.

Now moved much closer to London, it would seem obvious to expect an increasing involvement in defensive operations and significant participation in losses sustained by the Luftwaffe. But the general situation in October was much different to the previous month. The weather deteriorated and the German bomber force turned their activity towards night attacks, while fighters or fighter-bombers, as they were re-designated, were sweeping across southern England, using the advantage of their high altitude capability. Hence the Messerschmitts were now much more flexible without the heavies to protect.

Although No. 302 had already passed its baptism of fire, the squadron now had to slightly adapt its tactics, operating as a fast response unit rather than long-range cavalry. On Tuesday 15 October, Squadron Leader Mümler's boys underwent their first examination in this role.

When German activity was observed at 9.45 am, two squadrons from Northolt took off to intercept the enemy. No. 302, led by Squadron Leader Satchell, had been ordered to patrol the Biggin Hill area, yet were soon vectored south over Dungeness and the Thames Estuary. Very quickly one of the aircraft was left behind, Pilot Officer Jan Maliński struggling with the engine of his Hurricane. He had to land at West Malling with the undercarriage up. The remaining eleven pilots continued their mission until noticing about forty Messerschmitt Bf 109s flying 3,000ft above them and heading for London.

Once 302 Squadron went for them, another group of raiders suddenly appeared behind them, immediately attacking the Poles. Sergeant Marian Wędzik was hit in the first impact and his Hurricane received a decisive burst into the cockpit and fuel tanks. Wędzik was wounded as the shells went through the fuselage, also sustaining facial burns. Wasting no time, Wędzik bailed out and opened the canopy at a height of 20,000ft. He landed safely at Chatham, not far from the place where his Hurricane crashed, and was admitted to the local hospital. Wędzik knew his war craft well. Before the war he flew in the 162nd and consequently with 121st Fighter Squadrons before being posted to the Air Force Training Centre at Dęblin. After arriving in France, he joined the all-Polish GC1/145.

The first German victim fell to Flight Lieutenant Riley, who was credited with the destruction of a Bf 109. Meanwhile, Satchell's Hurricane came under fire and its pilot had to land in Slough, having no fuel left in his holed tanks. Beforehand he was able to fire at an enemy plane, which was also attacked by Pilot Officer Wacław Król and Sergeant Wilhelm Kosarz. After closer examination, only Król was credited with the destruction of the Bf 109, and he wrote:

'Suddenly I saw a Me 109 attack another Hurricane which was about 300 yards on my port beam slightly below. I did a beam attack on this Messerschmitt, getting in one burst of ½ a second at about 150 to 100 yards range owing to being attacked myself by another Messerschmitt. I had to take evasive action doing steep turns. On orbiting I saw a parachute open. Later I joined up with Celeb leader, S/Ldr Satchell and turning I noticed four Me 109s flying towards us in line astern from above and in front. Each aircraft was about 100 yards behind the other. We were at 20,000 ft while the Mes broke away. After turning I noticed that the pilot had bailed out and that he was not wearing his 'Mae West'. I returned to base with Celeb leader, but owing to lack of fuel I had to land at White Waltham.'

Wacław Król, whose name translates as 'King', was known as '*Monarcha*' ('Monarch') or '*Czarny Wacek*' ('Black Wacek') due to his characteristic dark facial features, hair and eyebrows. This handsome pilot was one of the most experienced members of 302 Squadron. After graduating from the Polish Air Force Officer Cadets School in Dęblin, he was posted to 123rd Fighter Squadron and then reposted to 121st Fighter Squadron as deputy commander. During the Polish Campaign he claimed a shared victory of a Dornier Do 17. According to some historians, Król is considered as the pilot who participated in the first aerial victory of the Second World War. On 8 September 1939, he took command of the 121st Fighter Squadron. Król also fought in France, being posted to GCII/7, with whom he flew Morane MS 406s and Dewoitine D.520s. He was credited with two aircraft being destroyed and one probably destroyed.

Sergeant Kosarz, at 32 years old, also had an interesting military career. The former pilot of 65th Light Bomber Squadron decided to pursue his dream of being a fighter pilot. He not only achieved his goal of completing the required training and then joining the 122nd Fighter Squadron, but also became a member of the famous aerobatic team of Captain Jerzy Bajan known as 'Bajan's Three'. On 15 October 1940, he realized that his remaining fuel would not get him to Northolt, and made an emergency landing at Croydon. After refuelling his Hurricane, the Zaolzie-born Pole took off and struck a balloon cable but miraculously survived.

After returning to Northolt, the Polish pilots blamed Satchell for the irresponsible leading of the whole operation, which almost led to disaster. They also acknowledged their own mistakes, commenting on the fact that no one spotted the Germans approaching from behind. It was another lesson learnt the hard way.

During the afternoon, further waves of German aircraft was seen above Southampton and London. As the signal of their presence arrived very late, some of the squadrons went up while enemy fighters already dominated the airspace. It resulted in surprise attacks against the climbing Hurricanes and Spitfires, one of which was experienced by Polish Pilot Officer Bolesław 'Vodka' Własnowolski of 213 Squadron.

Both flights took off simultaneously at 12.10 pm to patrol around Portsmouth and Swanage. The Polish pilot, repeatedly named by the poor squadron clerk as 'Wlosnowolski', flew as Blue 3 during this mission. His squadron flew over the Isle of Wight when the German attacked from the rear, and he later wrote:

> 'I turned to the right, climbing, and then to the left to get the sun behind me. I saw 2 Me 109s, one a long way off, one below me. I approached the one below me and shot at him about 5 or 6 short bursts from astern and above. I do not think enemy pilot saw me. After my attack he did a stall turn away and then vertically dived to the ground. Smoke was pouring from his engine. I circled looking for him but did not see him again.'

'Vodka' was probably aiming at the aircraft from the Ist Gruppe JG2 flown by Fw. Horst Hellriegel, who crashed at Bowcombe Down on the Isle of Wight.

Another RAF unit which was operating in this area and included Polish pilots was No. 609, which took off at 12.15 pm. Initially its 'A' Flight with Flying Officer Oleński patrolled the Winchester area, while 'B' Flight with Flying Officer Nowierski protected their base. Soon after, ,Novi', Green 3, found himself in a combat situation:

'The squadron was attacked by Me 109s and we split up. A few minutes later I saw an Me 109 slightly above me and opened fire from astern. He went into a left-hand spin and pieces fell off the machine. He disappeared into cloud and I lost him but F/O Oleński followed him down and saw him crash. The pilot did not get out and was lying or sitting with his parachute near the crash (believed between Milton and Lymington).'

It is thought that Nowierski was shooting at Gefr. Alois Pollach of the 2nd Staffel JG2, who was taken prisoner.

The last day of operational use of the Polish bombers during the Battle of Britain was 15 October. This time is was 301 Squadron's turn and six crews were chosen for the mission to the French port of Boulogne. Machines took off between 7.44-8.30 pm. The twenty-four airmen who participated in the raid were: Flight Lieutenant Stanisław Krzystyniak, Flying Officer Bolesław Sadowski and Sergeant Gustaw Kasianowski; Sergeant Roman Bonkowski, Flying Officer Stefan Hałłas and Sergeant Jan Bujak; Sergeant Adam Weiss, Flying Officer Henryk Sawlewicz and Sergeant Hubert Korab-Brzozowski; Sergeant Antoni Palul, Flying Officer Stanisław Rewkowski and Sergeant Ignacy Bator; Pilot Officer Marian Olszyna, Flying Officer Stanisław Waszkiewicz and Sergeant Henryk Choroszewski; and Pilot Officer Józef Wójcik, Pilot Officer Mariusz Wodzicki and Sergeant Antoni Lipecki.

The Polish squadron did not suffer any losses and all crews were back in England between 11.04 pm and 00.15 am. Three days later, both Polish bomber squadrons started to received their Vickers Wellingtons. The weather then drastically worsened, and consequently the operation of 15 October marked the end of this less known and under-appreciated chapter of Polish participation in defending Britain in 1940.

The following two days featured only one successful encounter for the Polish Air Force pilots. This was mainly due to the weather disrupting flying and engagement of enemy raiders. But there were losses, some of them very painful. On 16 October, No. 308 (Polish) Squadron carried out training sorties which ended in tragedy. Squadron Leader John Davies, a former pilot of 604 Squadron, led a section consisting of two Polish pilots, Pilot Officer Erwin Kawnik and Sergeant Władysław Majchrzyk, when he struck some barrage balloons. While both Poles managed to avoid the cables anchored to the ground, Davies went right between them, striking a cable and crashing at Whitley Stadium near Coventry. The British commander, a former Royal Fusiliers member and then Auxiliary pilot, who had many disagreements with his Polish counterpart Squadron Leader Stefan Łaszkiewicz, was killed. This was rather a sad end to the difficult task of beginning to build a relationship between the Poles and

A group of No.501 Sqn's pilots with the tail of a downed Bf 109. Plt Off Franciszek Kozłowski is standing in the doorway, his colleague Plt Off Stanisław Skalski is at lower left.

British, which was most probably due to lack of understanding of each other's nature rather than purposely creating obstacles.

Another member of the British contingent, who also did not gain approval from his fellow Polish pilots and did not get on well with them, was Flight Lieutenant John Young. He also crashed his aircraft during an exercise, although he only damaged his Hawker Hurricane. Young had several ups and downs in his career, having two crash-landings while serving in 249 Squadron. Then he was posted to No. 306 (Polish) Squadron, where he did not make many friends, subsequently being posted to No. 312 (Czechoslovak) and then to No. 308 (Polish) Squadron. In the spring of 1941, Young was posted to the newly formed No. 317 (Polish) Squadron, where his presence and relationship with the Poles again did not go smoothly. He created a very sour atmosphere after making several accusations against his Polish colleagues.

Young was not the only pilot to suffer an accident during this period. Sergeant Władysław Wieraszka, a veteran of the 112th Fighter Squadron in Poland, recently posted to 5 Operational Training Unit, crashed his Hurricane at Chewton Mendip in Somerset and was admitted to the RAF hospital at Locking with minor wounds.

The following day, German movement on the opposite side of the Channel increased again, with 302 Squadron among those units which were sent to intercept Luftwaffe raiders over England. They took off from Northolt at 9.20 am, but were unable to find any targets. On their way back, three pilots lost their way and for one of the Polish pilots his first operational sortie ended in tragedy. Sergeant Jerzy Załuski, noticing that his Hurricane was low of fuel and running on fumes, decided to land at Colliers End in Hertfordshire. Initially his attempt went smoothly, but when he found himself on the top of a hill, the Pole was startled by a flock of sheep that appeared suddenly in front of his aircraft. He braked and turned over his machine. The 24-year-old former pilot of 63rd Reconnaissance Squadron in Poland was found dead with a broken neck.

During a raid that afternoon, numerous RAF squadrons intercepted German formations, yet again no Polish pilot was credited with destruction or even damage of an adversary's plane. Pilot Officer Tadeusz Nowak from 253 Squadron, who experienced engine trouble, tried to land at Grants Hill, where he eventually crashed. Although his Hurricane was badly damaged, he escaped injury.

Around 4 pm, 302 Squadron was back in action, although once more unsuccessfully. Pilot Officer Władysław Gnyś touched down heavily back at Northolt, seriously damaging his Hurricane. Flight Lieutenant Jan Czerny had to force-land on his way back to base and smashed his aircraft while doing so, but was able to take off again and returned to Northolt in one piece. Meanwhile, Pilot Officer Stefan Kleczkowski, who was completing his first operational sortie during the Battle of Britain, was struggling with his oxygen supply. To make the situation worse, he ran out of fuel and had to find a safe place to land. Desperate to save himself and his aircraft, the Pole eventually managed to survive without injury, but his Hurricane was not so lucky after a force-landing near Sittingbourne. Interestingly, this was the place where Kleczkowski settled down after the war and where, allegedly, his English girlfriend lived.

Thursday 17 October witnessed another tragedy for the Polish airmen. Former flying instructor of No. 1 Air Force Training Centre Sergeant Józef Zalewski flew with No. 1 Anti-Aircraft Co-operation Unit to gain more experience on British aircraft. While practicing in the air, piloting a Hawker Henley, Zalewski crashed at Llanaelhaearn in North Wales, killing himself and his British pupil.

On the same day, two pilots joined 302 Squadron after gaining flying experience at No. 5 OTU. They were Flight Lieutenant Władysław Goettel, former deputy commander of the 161st Fighter Squadron, and Flying Officer Jan Borowski. For the latter it was only the beginning of tragedy that was just around the corner rather than a new chapter of his career. At the same time, Pilot Officer Franciszek Surma and Flight Lieutenant Jerzy Orzechowski left 607 Squadron with postings to 47 Squadron and 306 (Polish) Squadron respectively. Orzechowski was appointed to command his new unit, although his position after arrival was rather uncertain and taking charge of the 'City of Toruń' Squadron never actually materialized for him.

Friday 18 October proved a luckless and disastrous day for 302 Squadron. The weather was bad from the early hours, and despite a slight improvement, drizzle continued throughout the day. At 3 pm, the whole squadron was in readiness and six minutes later twelve Hurricanes were breaking up through the curtain of thick clouds. Accompanied by the neighbouring No. 229 Squadron, the Poles were heading towards Maidstone, when at 3.31 pm they were warned over the radio about a German formation approaching from the south. However, they only caught up with a single bomber, recognized as either a Heinkel He 111 or Junkers Ju 88, flying under the watchful eye of a lone Messerschmitt Bf 109.

Flight Lieutenant James Thomson, who led 'B' Flight of the Polish squadron, took the initiative and unleashed an attack. However, he made the unpardonable mistake of not only losing the element of surprise but also, and most importantly, making the whole formation break and proceed with a rather chaotic attempt to engage the enemy. After the attack, Flying Officer Julian Kowalski and Sergeant Eugeniusz Nowakiewicz noticed two German airmen bailing out of their stricken plane.

Nowakiewicz, who was the only pilot credited with the probable destruction of the enemy machine, described this questionable success in the following words:

'I was flying Yellow 2, and after about an hour flying Red 1 attacked a Ju 88, shooting at and receiving very heavy fire from the rear upper gun turret. I attacked after Red 1 from ¾ above and a beam behind. The e/a was painted such a dark green colour that it was scarcely possible to see the black crosses. I was unable to see the effect of Red 1's attack, and with my first attack I got in a burst of two seconds, opening fire at about 250 yards, closing to 100 yards and I did not encounter any fire whatsoever in the e/a either in my first or second attack, and I supposed that the gunner was put out of action by Red 1. I noticed no result at all from my first burst and I attacked a second time from above and behind, opening fire at about 150 yards, closing to about 30 yards, getting in a burst of 3 seconds. I broke away to starboard, climbing, and I noticed two persons from the Ju 88 crew jump out, and their parachutes open.

ARMÉE DE L'AIR   № 279.

D'AVIATION POLONAISE — POLSKIE JEDNOSTKI LOTNICZE

P-0250

Nom :   BOROWSKI
Nazwisko

Prénoms :   JAN
Imiona

Grade :   Lieutenant
Stopien

Né le   31. V. 1912   à Radom (Pologne)
Ur. dn.   w.

Résidant à   Bron / Rhône /.
Zamieszk. w.

Profession :   pilote
Zawod

Fils de Adam   et de Aleksandra
Syn   i   Karasińska

Domiciliés à   Radom
Zamieszk. w.

Situation de famille : / Célibataire, Veuf, Marié /
Stan   / Kawaler,   Wdowiec, Żonaty /

Nombre d'enfants :
Ilość dzieci

Taille : 1 mètre + 1.   centimètres
Wzrost : 1 metr   centymetrow

Marques particulières :
Znaki szczegolne

Fait à Bron   , le 13 mai   1940
Wystawiona. w :   dn :

TES DIGITALES

Palców
Index droit
wskazujacy

Prawy

ATURE DU TITULAIRE :
dpis właściciela dowodu

TESTATION DE L'OFFICIER
RIEUR POLONAIS DÉLÉGUÉ

dczenie starszego polskiego
cera delegowanego :

LE COLONEL COMMANDANT DU DÉPÔT D'INSTRUCTION
DE L'AVIATION POLONAISE

Pulkownik dowodca centrum wyszkolenia
lotnictwa polskiego :

Jan Borowski's French AF service card that was found with the pilot's body.

Once more I noticed no fire from the Ju 88. The e/a continued in a gentle glide earthwards, and after a few seconds disappeared into clouds, lost from view.'

After this action, Thomson led most of 'A' Flight home, while the rest of the squadron, including his own flight, went missing. As it turned out, Flight Lieutenant Jastrzębski, running out of fuel, had to land at Cobham, Flight Lieutenant Wczelik got as far as Heston, while Pilot Officer Bronisław Bernaś desperately landed at Langley. They were the lucky ones. Pilot Officer Stefan Wapniarek crashed at Nutwood Farm in Thames Ditton, Surrey, and was killed in the impact; Pilot Officer Aleksy Żukowski also ran out of fuel and was killed when his Hurricane hit the ground at Harp Farm near Detling in Kent.

Two other Hurricanes went down at the Kempton Park Racecourse in Sunbury, Surrey. They were flown by Flying Officer Jan Borowski and Flying Officer Peter Carter. Carter tried to save his life by evacuating the cockpit, hoping that his parachute would miraculously open on time. Unfortunately, he flew too low before attempting to do so, and falling from a height of just 15 metres had no chance of survival. Approximately 230 metres away, the second pilot hit the ground, still sitting inside the cockpit; the Hurricane immediately exploded, killing the 28-year-old Borowski. The possibility that both planes collided in the air before crashing cannot be definitely ruled out, although another theory suggests that they both hit barrage balloon cables, which caused the double tragedy. An eyewitness, Brenda Telander, who was 10 years old at the time, remembers seeing aircraft pieces flying in the air before Carter's plane hit the ground. This may confirm an aerial collision. She also saw a parachute next to Carter's body, although an official source states that the parachute was found 50 metres from the scene.[1]

Jan Borowski was one of the most experienced Polish combat pilots, having fought in Poland, where he often led 113th Fighter Squadron into battle on behalf of its commander. He was also known for his shooting talent, representing Poland at numerous international competitions, including in Italy in 1935 where he won the first prize.

Twenty-four-year-old Stefan Wapniarek participated in the Polish Campaign, during which he achieved three claims as a 132nd Squadron pilot. In France he flew under Captain Tadeusz Rolski. Aleksy Żukowski, who was 29, was called '*Japończyk*' ('Nipper') by his friends due to his Jujitsu knowledge and skills. Although posted to 151st Fighter Squadron in Poland, he was called back to Dęblin, where he trained his younger colleagues. His combat career started in France, where he joined the all-Polish GC 1/145 and then GCI/1. During fighting in France, Żukowski was credited with two enemy planes destroyed.

The bad luck for the Polish airmen continued, with Pilot Officer Mieczysław Waszkiewicz crashing his aircraft while performing a training flight in No. 58 Operational Training Unit. Luckily he left the crash site unhurt. Meanwhile, Pilot Officers Brunon Kudrewicz, Włodzimierz Miksa and Benedykt Zieliński joined No.151 Squadron. Soon after, Miksa joined the honourable ranks of 'the Polish Few' after being posted to 303 Squadron, with which he flew once operationally during the Battle of Britain. The other two remained non-operational pilots throughout this time.

Flight Lieutenant '*Agnieszka*' Jastrzębski was another victim of the previous day's ill-fortune when he hit a barrage balloon cable on his way back from Cobham and crashed his Hurricane, but fortunately he left the scene in one piece. On 19 October, Sergeant Paleniczek had to leave 85 Squadron after being assessed by its commander. Apparently his skills were not high enough to continue as a fighter pilot, and the Pole was posted to No. 18 OTU to become a bomber pilot.

Bad weather continued throughout the 19th and the following days. Several Polish pilots performed operational sorties, yet no contact was made with the Germans or they were unable to get close enough to open fire. The Luftwaffe, despite poor conditions over England, performed numerous missions, including quite a few large raids.

On 21 October, three pilots – Kudrewicz, Miksa and Zieliński – were transferred to 303 Squadron, while their twin unit at Northolt received two further airmen, Flying Officer Eugeniusz Antolak and Pilot Officer Kazimierz Sporny. Both remained non-operational pilots for the rest of the Battle of Britain. The next day, Pilot Officer Franciszek Surma arrived back at 257 Squadron, having spent a short time with 46 Squadron. Pilot Officer Franciszek Kozłowski was given permission to return to 501 Squadron after recovering from wounds sustained two months earlier. Four days after Paleniczek's departure, three other Polish pilots also left 85 Squadron due to its transformation to become a night fighter unit. Pilot Officers Czesław Gauze and Czesław Tarkowski were posted to 605 Squadron, whilst Sergeant Konrad Muchowski joined No. 501. Only the latter participated in the remainder of the Battle of Britain, flying two operational sorties five days later.

On 23 October, Acting Squadron Leader Witold Urbanowicz was unexpectedly called to Headquarters of No. 11 Group, leaving temporary command of the battle-hardened 303 Squadron in the capable hands of Zdzisław Henneberg. Urbanowicz was given the role of Polish Liaison Officer. For this talented, yet controversial officer, who often expressed loudly in an uncompromising way his opinions and complaints – gaining friends and enemies in equal number   the Battle of Britain was over.

On the same day, two accidents occurred involving one Polish and one British pilot serving in 308 Squadron. Flight Lieutenant Juliusz Frey, while landing after an operational patrol, damaged his Hurricane, and Squadron Leader Brenus Morris, who took command of the 'City of Cracow' Squadron after John Davies' death, touched down at Kinver in Staffordshire with his undercarriage retracted.

Thursday 24 October was marked in Polish chronicles as another day of tragedy, this time for the 'Tadeusz Kościuszko' Squadron. Pilot Officer Jan Bury-Burzymski had only arrived that month, previously flying with No. 307 (Polish) Night Squadron and, like many others, expressing his disappointment with the Boulton Paul Defiants' performance. Burzymski was eager to fight, especially having great experience from Poland, where he fought with 152nd Fighter Squadron and claimed two victories.

During his time with 303 Squadron, he remained a non-operational pilot and his flight on 24 October was a continuation of his aerial training. He took off as part of a section, with Sergeant Bronisław Kościk to practice a dog-fight, when suddenly his Hurricane went into a dive and crashed near Bishop Burton, Beverley, in the East Riding of Yorkshire. It is believed that he lost consciousness, which led to the tragic accident. The remaining pilots continued aerial training and Flying Officer Marian Pisarek damaged his aircraft, although he was unharmed. There was also good news for the Poles of 303 when Flying Officer Jerzy Jankiewicz joined them after leaving 601 Squadron. Many of them knew Jankiewicz well from his time serving in the 1st Air Regiment in Poland, especially when he was appointed as tactics officer of the IV/1 Fighter Wing. However, another tragedy was about to hit 'the Polish Few'.

From the early hours of Friday 25 October, the German aerial presence started to build up across the Channel. Fighter Command realized that Luftwaffe aircraft were bound for Britain, and various RAF squadrons were scrambled to intercept them. Among the squadrons was No. 603 with Pilot Officer Ludwik Martel. They encountered three groups of Bf 109s over Maidstone, and during dog-fights 603 Squadron lost three Spitfires flown by Pilot Officers John Soden, Peter Olver and Ludwik Martel.

Both wounded British pilots bailed out, while the Pole, hit by a cannon shell in the left leg and body, managed to fly as far as Hastings, where he crash-landed. His lack of English led to him being arrested by local Home Guard members. Once his nationality was established, Martel was taken to hospital. His Spitfire, although damaged, proved to be serviceable and survives to this day. Martel was back in action in less than two weeks.

Sergeant Michał Maciejowski, called 'Miki', who flew with 249 Squadron was engaged in combat and having difficulty to reach his base, landed near Colchester.

Just after 9 am, 302 Squadron scrambled from Northolt to intercept Germans approaching from Boulogne and Cap Gris-Nez, but had no luck and, failing to engage, turned back. While returning to Northolt, three Messerschmitt Bf 109 appeared above them. One section led by 'B' Flight commander Flight Lieutenant Franciszek Jastrzębski went after them, yet the chase proved extremely difficult for Pilot Officer Bernaś, who struggled to catch up with the Germans, and for Sergeant Markiewicz, who decided to rejoin his own formation.

Unfortunately Jastrzębski disappeared when chasing the enemy towards the French coast, and never returned. It is believed that his Hurricane was shot down by Maj. Werner Mölders, who commanded the JG51, and the Polish officer died of his wounds in a French hospital. Another theory says that his body was never recovered from the sea.

At 12.50 pm, another German raid was located and several RAF squadrons were sent to intervene. Unfortunately none of the Polish pilots involved went close enough to get a trophy. Pilot Officer Józef Gil, known as '*Zazdrośnik*' ('Jealous'), from 229 Squadron was struggling when approaching Northolt aerodrome, and as a result, after touching down, overturned his Hurricane on the airfield.

Jastrzębski was not the only Polish airman killed on 25 October. Pilot Officer Stanisław Piątkowski, a former glider and Aero Club instructor in Poland, had served with No. 79 Squadron since 11 September 1940. On this day he flew an operational sortie over Linney Head in Pembrokeshire and crashed, coming down near Carew Cheriton. Presumably he knew that due to technical problems he would not be able to reach RAF Pembrey in Carmarthenshire and tried to perform an emergency landing. The 28-year-old Pole was killed instantly. Jastrzębski and Piątkowski were the last two Polish operational fighter pilots killed during the Battle of Britain. But this was not the end of the Poles' bad luck.

The Polish crew of a Fairey Battle from 9 Bombing and Gunnery School was ordered to practice air-to-air firing, when the aircraft rapidly lost height and crashed near Hells Mouth on the Llyn Peninsula in North Wales. Both Pilot Officer Tadeusz Dąbrowski and Sergeant Ładysław Ustyanowski were killed. Dąbrowski, who was 25, flew operationally in Poland as a pilot of 55th Bomber Squadron, whilst Ustyanowski served as a flying instructor of the Air Force Training Centre at Dęblin.

Two other Polish airmen had lucky escapes. Pilot Officer Feliks Szyszka from 308 (Polish) Squadron, stationed at Baginton in Warwickshire, force-landed and damaged his Hurricane. His colleague Sergeant Kazimierz Waśkiewicz from 306 (Polish) Squadron did not lower the undercarriage and belly-landed at Church Fenton. Both pilots were unhurt.

Events on Saturday 26 October started quite early as German activity increased. But it wasn't until 10.25 am that the Polish 302 Squadron was sent into action. Both commanders led their pilots when the enemy presence was spotted. At approximately 11.40 am, Squadron Leader Satchell engaged one of a group of fifteen Messerschmitts which were caught while heading east. Although his opponent escaped into the clouds, the Scotsman noticed debris flying off the Bf 109.

Meanwhile Sergeant Antoni Markiewicz, who flew as Blue 3, spotted the familiar silhouette of a lone Bf 109. He couldn't miss such an opportunity:

'It disappeared into thick cloud, and later came out above it on the port bow. I therefore broke away from my Section and using clouds as cover I went after him, managing to get into an attacking position, slightly above and parallel with the e/a. I opened fire at 200 yards with a beam attack, giving him a burst of 3 seconds. The e/a was taken by surprise and zoomed very steeply. I noticed intense black smoke issuing from the starboard wing centre section. After executing a loop e/a turned on its back and went down out of control. I now gave him another burst of 1 second from 120 yards. The e/a went into cloud. I saw him continuing his dive to earth. I then suddenly noticed two other Me 109s on my port bow about 100 ft below me. In proceeding to attack I became conscious of tracer being fired at me from 3 Me 109s on my starboard bow at about 600 yards distance. I saw the burst which passed my tail unit, took evasive action and escaped into cloud.'

It was time for Markiewicz to head home. He was over enemy territory and had already used most of his ammunition and fuel, and would be very vulnerable if he stayed over France any longer, especially as 229 Squadron, who accompanied the Poles, had left before reaching the French coast. Markiewicz was eventually credited with the unconfirmed destruction of an enemy fighter plane, which was in fact the last probable victory claimed by the Pole during the Battle of Britain. It is believed that the Messerschmitt attacked by the former 122nd Fighter Squadron pilot was flown by Ofw. Werner Kaufmann from the 4th Staffel JG53. The German pilot was later picked up from the sea.

Airmen from No. 301 Squadron including Flg Off Stanisław Król and Flt Lt Witold Piotrowski 2nd and 3rd from left respectively.

Several other Polish pilots were added to the 'unfortunate' list after damaging their aircraft. Pilot Officer Bronisław Skibiński from 308 Squadron had serious problems when landing at Baginton after a non-operational flight. His colleague Sergeant Waśkiewicz, who had struggled the day before, again forgot that the Hurricane had a retractable undercarriage when he attempted to land near Shrewsbury, resulting in his disposal from 306 Squadron. Sergeant Bronisław Kościk, who had recently participated in exercises that led to Bury-Burzymski's death, encountered his own difficulties. His engine started developing problems and he crash-landed at Selby near Leconfield in Yorkshire. Sergeant Władysław Gmitrowicz also gained his British commander's disapproval and was posted away from No. 306.

The next day, an enemy aircraft was reported damaged by a Polish pilot, one of the last PAF claims made during the Battle of Britain. Flying Officer Paweł Niemiec from 17 Squadron was flying between Eastchurch and Sheppey in Kent, when at 10.15 am he spotted a single Dornier Do 17. Supported by Sergeant Glyn Griffiths, 'Poppet' went in to attack:

'I was on patrol with the squadron weaving above when I was given vector 090 degrees and when about 500 yards away from the Squadron following the vector I saw a twin-engine aircraft below me. I dived down, and when above the a/c I circled in and saw the crosses on the fuselage. I attacked him as he went into cloud, diving from above, giving a short burst at about 300 yards. I broke away upwards and saw another Hurricane attacking. I then dived from above astern, firing a 3 to 4-second burst, coming very close, we were then both in cloud and I lost the e/a.'

At about 11.30 am, another wave of German aircraft approached from France, and one section of No. 609 Squadron engaged a two-engine aircraft believed to be either a Junkers Ju 88 or Heinkel He 111, which appeared near Andover in Hampshire. Amongst the pilots was Pilot Officer Piotr Ostaszewski-Ostoja. Although all three airmen attempted to destroy the intruder, the result of their action was uncertain and therefore none of them could be credited with its destruction or damage.

While three pilots from 303 Squadron were on patrol between 5.40-6.35 pm, their own airfield was attacked by the Luftwaffe. At 6 pm, two Heinkels dropped sixteen bombs on the aerodrome in front of the hangars and strafed the aircraft parked within the dispersal area with machine guns. Three Hurricanes from 'A' Flight were damaged and Aircraftman 1st Class Antoni Rossochacki, a ground crew member who was nearby, was badly wounded. Despite the heavy bombardment, Rossochacki was assisting Sergeant Eugeniusz Szaposznikow to start his aircraft.

Only one post of the anti-aircraft artillery fired, causing no damage to the enemy planes, which later attacked a civilian target in Beverley. For his bravery, 26-year-old Rossochacki was awarded the Cross of Valour on 1 November, sadly the day after he died of his wounds, unexpectedly becoming the last of 303's victims of the Battle of Britain. The three pilots who were airborne during this attack returned home after the Germans left, yet Sergeant Marian Bełc damaged his Hurricane while landing when his undercarriage collapsed.

Bełc was not the only Polish pilot who experienced landing problems on this day. Sergeant Markiewicz, who the day before had fought with success, this time had difficulties with finding his airfield and, with no other choice, landed in a field. Both the Hurricane and its pilot survived unscathed.

On Monday 28 October, Flying Officer Franciszek Surma from 257 Squadron reported the last enemy aircraft damaged by the Polish pilot during the Battle of Britain. Surma flew the morning mission as No. 2 in Red Section, when various RAF squadrons were airborne to intercept a German raid over southern England. It was about 10.40 am when he separated from his squadron in the clouds over Ashford and found himself behind the rest of his formation.

Surma began to chase after them, when he noticed a twin-engine aircraft flying in their direction, but below them. He later reported:

'I went to investigate and saw the crosses on the wings so I dived down onto him, but could not attack head-on as it was too late. I zoomed up and made an astern attack. When I was about 300 yards behind the e/a, a He 111, the rear gunner opened fire from below. I gave them one short burst to unnerve them. When I was 150-200 yards behind the e/a's tail on the port side I gave a 3-4 secs. burst at the cockpit. I passed over him and then fired at the starboard engine from about 80 yards. He continued to fly level and I gave him another burst of about 4 secs, from about 100 yards, at the starboard engine. I noticed a small explosion from the engine and saw grey smoke pouring out. At this time, the aircraft lurched to the right, and as I passed him, a piece of the aircraft flew by my plane, almost hitting me. We went into cloud at about 4,500 ft. I levelled out, came out of the layer and searched above and below. As I came below the cloud I saw that I was directly above the coastline. I looked for the e/a without being able to find it.'

Surma had damaged the enemy aircraft, thought to be a Heinkel He 111. What he did not know was that he would soon experience a similar fate himself.

Despite further raids over Britain, no Polish pilot was engaged in combat. In the meantime, No. 306 (Polish) 'City of Toruń' Squadron, which continued its training at Church Fenton, reported reaching the point of being ready for action. On the same day, Sergeant Stanisław Grondowski, a pre-war flying instructor of the No. 1 Air Force Training Centre at Dęblin, crashed in a Boulton Paul Defiant during night exercises, joining the fast-growing group of Polish airmen who disliked this aircraft.

Another British-built plane not popular with the Poles, and often called a 'flying coffin', was the Fairey Battle. As well as being used by both Polish bomber squadrons, this aircraft was also frequently flown by Polish airmen who were undertaking training at various flying schools. Another young life was lost in one of them on 28 October. Sergeant Franciszek Skrzypczak, who prior to the war served in the Training Flight of the 3rd Air Regiment in Poznań, arrived in Britain and was posted to No. 1 Air Armament School. On this day he flew a training mission together with two RAF airmen, Flying Officer Duncan Robertson and Pilot Officer Eric Wright Blackwell, when his aeroplane ditched in the sea 3 miles south of Donna Nook on the Lincolnshire coast. All men on board were killed.

There were several German raids on 29 October, the Luftwaffe targeting London and southern England, but also appearing over the Isle of Wight. None of the Poles participating in the defence at this time had an opportunity to engage. However, Sergeant Mieczysław Marcinkowski from 501 Squadron, described in the Operations Record Book as 'Sergeant Michail', experienced engine trouble and had to perform an emergency landing in a field.

It appears that 'Michail' was not the only Polish airman in difficulty that day. Soon after 3pm, 302 Squadron flew an uneventful patrol over Brooklands; as no German activity was seen, the unit was ordered to return to Northolt. On their way, due to human error, two Hurricanes collided in mid-air. Flight Lieutenant James Thomson had to bail out from his aircraft, which was literally cut in half by the second aircraft, while Flight Lieutenant Jan Czerny struggled to open his canopy. Failing to do so, he realized that his only option was to stay with his machine. The Pole continued to descend, eventually performing an emergency landing at White Waltham in Berkshire. Thomson sustained injuries on landing, whilst his Hurricane crashed at Penny Pot Hill, Chobham, in Surrey. It was a rather unsatisfactory and less-than-heroic ending of the 'City of Poznań' Squadron's operational engagement in the Battle of Britain.

Further German activity was reported at 4pm, and numerous RAF Squadrons were scrambled to meet the raiders. Amongst those was No. 17, operating at 25,000ft above North Weald, with Pilot Officer Tadeusz Kumiega, accompanied by Sergeant Robert Hogg, flying as a weaver, behind the rest of his unit. The remainder of their colleagues did not engage with the attackers, and it was only Kumiega and Hogg who spotted a single Messerschmitt Bf 109 flying below them at 19,000ft just before 5pm. Kumiega had no intentions to wait and let the enemy disappear:

> 'I dived and attacked him from astern quarter, firing a 2-seconds burst at 100 yards range. As I broke away upwards, Sgt Hogg made astern attack at a range of 250 yards, with a burst of 2 seconds. I then made another quarter attack from 300 yards with burst of 1½ seconds. The Me 109 climbed very fast and gained on us. We saw glycol smoke pouring from it. Then the e/a dived and Sgt Hogg caught him just as he went into cloud and fired a 1-second burst at 400 yards. I overtook the e/a turned and made another quarter attack at 80 yards range with a 2-second burst. Sgt Hogg gave several more short bursts. The e/a then turned over on his back and the pilot jumped while his a/c was upside down.'

The Messerschmitt that Kumiega and Hogg were shooting at crashed at March House Farm, Tillingham, in Essex, and its pilot, Fw. Conrad Jäckel from 8th Staffel JG26, was captured.

North Weald aerodrome came under attack and many bombs were dropped by aircraft from II Gruppe of LG2. Both squadrons that were stationed there, 249 and 257, were immediately airborne. Pilot Officer Jerzy Solak, who was amongst the pilots defending their airfield, found himself alone chasing Messerschmitts, several of which were attacking another Hurricane. Solak gave one of them a long burst from his machine guns, losing speed but seeing the attackers scatter. Soon after the Pole neared a German machine flying eastwards. When he gained on him, Solak fired another long burst. The German pilot pulled his aircraft up and then started going down, pouring a black trail of smoke. There was unfortunately no trace on the ground of the aircraft described by the Polish officer, and presumably his 'victim' returned to France damaged but alive.

Sergeant Michał Maciejowski from 249 Squadron had more luck than he had a few days earlier. He pursued one of two enemy aircraft which he found over North Weald. Maciejowski described his actions upon his return:

> 'They dived into cloud and I cut through the cloud and found myself 50 yards behind both of them. I gave one of them a 5-10 seconds burst, astern attack, and it immediately burst into flames and fell to earth about 200 yards from the sea-shore on land, where I saw it burning. I could not tell whether it was by the river Blackwater or river Crouch. There were some small boats nearby. I gave the second one about a 5-seconds burst but then lost it in clouds.'

He shot down a Messerschmitt Bf 109 from the 4th Staffel LG2 piloted by Obfw. Josef Harmeling, who crashed at Langenhoe Wick in Essex. For the wounded German airman, the rest of the war was spent in captivity.

Pilot Officer Franciszek Surma from 257 Squadron, who had recently damaged an enemy plane, found himself in trouble when climbing. He was at 1,000ft when he heard explosions and saw smoke filling the cockpit of his aircraft. He was hit by one of the Messerschmitts which were strafing the aerodrome, and Surma had to bail out, landing with a minor injury in a tree near Matching. His aircraft, shot down by Oblt Gerhard Schöpfel from the IIIrd Gruppe JG26, crashed at nearby Bobbingworth. Franciszek Surma was the last Polish pilot shot down during the Battle of Britain. A rather colourful story of the Polish airman's exploits was written years later:

> 'Franek Surma baled-out at a few hundred feet after a 109 had bounced him on take off. His chute caught in some trees and he finished up dangling ten feet or so above the ground at the back of a local pub. He

had two gorgeous black eyes, and was picking pieces of the instrument panel out of his face. Lunch-time drinkers rushed out and heard him cursing in a strange language. As it happened, Franek always wore a rather flashy Luftwaffe flying jacket which he'd whipped from a wrecked bomber back in the Polish campaign, and he hadn't even bothered to remove the German eagle insignia. Among the people from the pub were a large group of Free French soldiers who wanted to lynch le sale Boche right there in the tree by the simple expedient of climbing up and winding the shroud line once or twice around his neck.

'While the landlord and local people argued with the Frenchmen, somebody had the presence of mind to phone the airfield, which was much closer than the nearest police station. Tuck, Cowboy and 'Buster Brown', the adjutant, drove over at breakneck speed in time to rescue Franek. Once everything had been explained to the French, they poured out apologies, lifted the Pole down tenderly and rained kisses on his blood-streaked cheeks. And when a doctor had been found to dress his wounds, they refused to let his comrades take him back to the drome until everyone concerned had joined them in the salon for several rousing toasts in furtherance of the Allied cause. Franek finished up roaring patriotic songs, passionately embracing the Frenchmen and several pretty girls who chanced to pass near. He seemed to get plastered very quickly, rocking to and from precariously. It wasn't till late that afternoon, when they got him back to sick quarters, that they learned he was suffering from severe concussion. After this incident Tuck prevailed upon him to cut the Nazi badges from his flying clothes.'[2]

There were other squadrons operating at the same time, some of them with Polish pilots. Pilot Officer Tadeusz Nowak from 253 Squadron was flying back alone from the Dover area, after losing contact with his leader and the rest of his unit after they had been involved in a combat. Around 5.20 pm, the Pole noticed a single twin-engine aircraft that appeared to be a German Dornier Do 17.

'I sighted 1 Do 17 at 200 feet with a Spitfire circling at 1,000 feet apparently without ammunition,' Nowak reported.

'I delivered a line astern attack on the enemy aircraft firing a six-second burst, with two further attacks, after which the enemy aircraft went out to sea near Rye. I followed and some 15 miles out when the enemy was losing height I delivered a fourth attack from ¾ to line astern. The enemy aircraft crashed in the sea and I returned to base.'

It is extremely difficult to identify Nowak's victim as no loss of a Dornier was reported at this time by the Luftwaffe, although several of their twin-engine aircraft returned from England badly shot up. This was the last enemy aircraft reported as being destroyed by a Polish pilot during the Battle of Britain.

Despite no more victories claimed by the Poles, some of them experienced rather less prestigious aerial adventures. Squadron Leader Walerian Jasionowski, who commanded No. 308 (Polish) Squadron, had to keep cool when the Hurricane he flew developed severe undercarriage problems. The brakes would not work properly and the Polish officer finished his landing in a brick wall next to Wittering aerodrome. His British counterpart, Squadron Leader Morris, used this accident as one of the reasons to get rid of the Pole from the squadron.

Pilot Officer Włodzimierz Miksa, an experienced combat pilot, also had a very scary moment when landing after an operational patrol. At 6.05 pm, three of 303 Squadron's Hurricanes attempted to land at Leconfield when Miksa's engine stopped. The skilled Miksa did not panic and crash-landed nearby, sustaining a small cut to his face. Flying Officer Zygmunt Kinel from 5 Operational Training Unit at Aston Down in Gloucestershire also damaged a Hurricane during flying exercises on the same day.

This was not the end of the Polish flyers' problems. On this day, three of 300 Squadron's airmen were killed during a non-operational flight. A Fairey Battle piloted by Sergeant Gerhard Goebel lost one of its wings and crashed near Sutton-on-Trent in Nottinghamshire. Goebel and his comrades Flying Officer Stanisław Firlej-Bielański and Sergeant Tadeusz Szmajdowicz were all killed. Silesian-born Goebel, a 26-year-old Bomber Brigade veteran, performed two operational flights during the Battle of Britain, Firlej-Bielański, 33, did three, while the youngest of them, 21-year-old former 217 Bomber Squadron air gunner Szmajdowicz, flew four missions.

Despite German activity over England, only two Polish pilots met their opponents face-to-face. Pilot Officer Jerzy Solak and Sergeant Michał Maciejowski flew an operational sortie between 11.20 am and noon, when 249 Squadron clashed with a group of Bf 109s over Hastings. Recent victor Maciejowski was chasing one of them over the Channel, but on his way back realized that he could not reach the North Weald aerodrome as his fuel was running out. Although he landed at Stoney Field, Blackford Farm, near Herstmonceux in Sussex, in one piece, local policemen initially took him as an enemy pilot before he could convince them otherwise.

Pilot Officer Bolesław Własnowolski from 213 Squadron had less luck. After concluding that he was lost, he decided to land near Amberley in Sussex, where he damaged his Hurricane. Two days later, 'Vodka' Własnowolski was killed in combat over Stoughton in Sussex, ending the promising career of this talented pilot. On Wednesday 30 October, two airmen from No. 307 (Polish) Squadron broke their legs after bailing out from a Fairey Battle which developed cooling system problems. Pilot Officer Kazimierz Kazimierczuk and Sergeant Mieczysław Adamiecki leapt at very low altitude, what caused their injuries.

Between 1.40-2.40 pm, three of 303's pilots performed the unit's last operational made by the Poles during the Battle of Britain. This was a significant moment, ending the commendable period of service for Polish members of 'Tadeusz Kościuszko' Squadron. The flyers engaged during this final mission were Flying Officer Tadeusz Sawicz, Sergeant Henryk Skowron and Sergeant Eugeniusz Szaposznikow. For Sawicz and Skowron, it was their first and last operation during the Battle. Less than two hours later, Flight Lieutenant Jack Adams definitely ended the operational career of 303 Squadron during this significant period, performing a lone patrol. Adams joined 303 Squadron as a replacement for Flight Lieutenant Athol Forbes, yet his role was mainly to train new pilots in night and blind flying.

The last day of October 1940 was foggy, severely limiting activity by the Germans and Fighter Command. Only a few Polish pilots managed to fly operationally, performing patrols with no enemy contact. Almost all these went smoothly, apart from Sergeant Bronisław Malinowski, a Pole serving in 43 Squadron, having to make an emergency early morning landing at Chirnside near Berwick-upon-Tweed in Scotland after the engine of his Hurricane stopped. He left the slightly damaged aircraft without injury.

The well-known saying 'break your leg', which in short means 'good luck', did not work in Sergeant Juliusz Bilau's case. The 307 Squadron airman indeed broke his leg while climbing into the cockpit of a Boulton Paul Defiant, proving that an airman's service could be equally dangerous on the ground as in the skies.

The last operational sortie flown by a Pole during the Battle of Britain was carried out by the very experienced pre-war flying instructor and aerobatic pilot Flight Lieutenant Bronisław Kosiński from 32 Squadron, who on 31 October, between 5.40–6.15 pm, flew a lone patrol over the Berwick area.

Chapter Eighteen

The Aftermath

The situation of the Polish airmen initially stationed only in Britain, and soon after operating from other parts of the Commonwealth, was more complex than we might think. Western media often call them 'the Polish pilots of the RAF' or 'Polish Squadrons of the RAF', without deeper analysis of the key facts. Although very much depending on operational directions by the RAF, which influenced and dictated internal movements of the Polish units, the Polish Air Force fought its own battle to secure independence and sustainable development within the British structure. Unlike the Free French or Czechoslovak airmen, Poles achieved the specific status of a self-contained section of their Armed Forces in exile, which was fighting arm-in-arm with, rather than within, the RAF. Yet their situation was far from ideal, and not as expected by the Poles.

The Polish government, although reborn in exile, could not impact on international politics and trends with the same power as other Allied countries. They had no actual country behind them, as Poland had been occupied and swept off the European map. The situation became even worse on 22 June 1941, when Nazi Germany attacked the Soviet Union. In this fast and dramatic turn of history, a previous enemy became an ally of Britain, and from December 1941 the United States. Stalin, who invaded Poland in September 1939 and sentenced to death hundreds of thousands of Poles, now stood on the same side of the barricade. What did that mean for the Poles, for their future as a part of the anti-Nazi coalition?

During the last stages of the war, the Poles were aware of the political situation whereby their country was a toy in the hands of the world's most influential leaders, and they fought only for their honour and ideals. Having known that Poland, even reborn, would not be the same again, that a massive part of her territory would be handed over to the Russians – who would dominate the rest of the country anyway – the Poles kept their faith and promise to 'fight for their own freedom as well as others'. Called by some the 'biggest illegal army', they were not welcomed to the 'victory parade'. With no free country to return to after the war, they were more or less politely asked to leave.

But the Poles also had loyal friends, who despite political changes, fought for the truth to be known. Ronald Kellett, the former commander of 303 Squadron, wrote:

'I was posted to command 303 Squadron [on] 17.7.1940 and after some days I realised that I had the best of pilots and men in the Squadron. We fought together through the great offensive of 1940 and I then knew that the pilots of 303 were not only of the best but also would see me through any trouble. In the month of September 303 was on top – no Squadron from the Empire could equal the courage and skill of our pilots. Together we have seen good days and bad, but English or Polish we shared them.'

Kellett also assured his pilots and ground crew of his countrymen's loyalty, saying that, 'they have won for Poland a special place in the hearts of people in the British Empire'.[1]

Kellett wrote after the Battle of Britain:

'During the Battle of Britain, my eyes were opened to their outstanding flying skills and bravery. In the air they could sight the enemy when it was but a mere speck in the sky; their eyesight was [acute]. In combat, the pilots of No. 303 Squadron would not hesitate to give their life to save a pilot in distress. Many a time I witnessed this as they would circle around, not leaving until they were sure the danger had passed.'[2]

After the end of hostilities in Europe, some of the Polish airmen went to the newly born Pakistan, where they have helped to create its air force. Amongst the Polish and Pakistani pilots are two Battle of Britain veterans standing from the left: Konrad Muchowski (2nd) and Mieczysław Gorzula (5th).

One of his most trusted men, 'B' Flight commander Athol Forbes, mirrored his words of praise:

'I carry great respect and true affection for the Polish airmen of 303. I was very proud of my time spent with them. Had it not been for some of the pilots of 303 I would not have survived the Battle of Britain. They were gallant and quite fearless when flying to the aid of others in danger. I got on well with them all, they certainly knew how to enjoy themselves when down The Orchard Pub and were popular with the ladies. The ground crew worked tirelessly and nothing was too much trouble. It was a great honour for me when I was awarded the Polish medal, the Virtuti Militari, by General Sikorski at the Rubens Hotel in London.'[3]

John Kent, a Canadian who gained the nickname 'Kentowski', which symbolized his sympathy with and trust of the Polish pilots, also expressed his gratitude with this tribute:

'It was a thrilling experience leading these intensely brave men into action and in fact, the Poles seemed to transport their cavalry tactics, and certainly its elan, it was not difficult to imagine oneself leading a charge of the famed Polish cavalry, from the ground into the air. I cannot say how proud I am to have been privileged to help form, train and lead No. 303 Squadron and later to lead such a magnificent fighting force as the Polish Wing. There formed within me in those days an admiration, respect and genuine affection for these really remarkable men which I have never lost. I formed friendships what are as firm today as they were those twenty-five years ago and this I find most gratifying. We who were privileged to fly and fight with them and will never forget and Britain must never forget how much she owes to the loyalty, indomitable spirit and sacrifice of these Polish fliers. They were our staunchest Allies in our darkest days, may they always be remembered as such!'

But not only the 303 veterans were keen to show their affection when remembering 'the Polish Few'. This mutual friendship and gratitude was also echoed by the pilots who fought alongside the Poles in RAF-manned units during the Battle of Britain. One of them was Alan Deere, who said of them:

'In the desperate days of 1940 we fighter pilots were proud to include in our number Polish airmen who in their own squadrons, and as individuals in British squadrons, did so much to strengthen and stiffen the desperate ranks of Fighter Command. In numbers their contribution in the Battle of Britain was perhaps small but this was more than offset by their guts and fighting ability – as fighter pilots they were second to none. Great aviators; great comrades; truly of "The Few".

Kellett's and Deere's superior officer, Air Chief Marshal Hugh Dowding of Fighter Command, also praised the Poles and their skills, writing in August 1941: 'The first Polish Squadron (No. 303) in No. 11 Group, during the course of a month, shot down more Germans that any British unit in the same period.' 'Stuffy' was the last person who could be accused of being over optimistic about or sympathetic towards the Polish airmen. This document written by Dowding, which was not released to the public until 1946, expressed his respect towards his Polish 'Few' and their influence on the Battle of Britain:

'As the development of the fighting unfolded it became clear that the decisive factor was not going to be the supply of aircraft (thanks to the supreme efforts of Lord Beaverbrook) but that it was going to be the supply of trained pilots.

'There are always armchair critics after a battle who like to say how nearly a battle was lost; how the enemy would have won if he had the endurance to put in just one attack. I have heard this said about the Battle of Britain, and it is not true. But what has to be remembered is that we had no means of knowing at the time how near the enemy had reached to a state of exhaustion. Still, as I say, the critical factor was the supply of trained fighter pilots. The other Commands, the Commonwealth countries and four allies contributed unstintingly to meet the emergency, but if it has not been for the magnificent material contributed by the Polish contingent and their unsurpassed gallantry I hesitate to say that the outcome of the battle would have been the same.

'This is perhaps an idle speculation. What must stand for all time is our appreciation and our gratitude for the help rendered to us in a time of extreme need, and our admiration for the unsurpassed gallantry of those who rendered that help.'

His words were echoed by other high-ranking officers and statesmen. Baron Robert Vansittart, the Under-Secretary for Foreign Affairs, declared:

'We should remember that, during the turning-point of history, Polish airmen were almost the only allies – apart from Commonwealth nations

– who fought in strength at our side. In that battle alone Polish airmen brought down or crippled two hundred enemy aircraft.'

Air Chief Marshal Sir John Grandy added: 'The Royal Air Force was honoured by their presence, inspired by their example and enlivened by their gaiety. We salute a brave band.'

The largely forgotten airmen of the Battle of Britain, the Polish bomber crews, were also highly complemented by the Marshal of the Royal Air Force, Sir Arthur Harris:

'The courage and determination of the Polish crews have always been of the highest order, ably sustained by their tireless and skillful work of the ground staff. Our cause was one and the same and our resolution to fight on until the enemy was defeated was never shaken. May this comradeship always survive.'

This opinion about the Poles was shared by the press, and very often the effectiveness of the first ally was subjected to public scrutiny. An article published in 1941 argued:

'Again, during the Battle of Britain, much was written about the paramount role played by the Polish squadrons in that eventful period; but it was never openly stated that the contribution made by the Poles towards the destruction of the attacking "Luftwaffe", and consequently towards the safeguarding of this Isle from a carefully prepared invasion was proportionally greater than of any other nation represented in the R.A.F., including the British. So it was until October 1940. Then there sat a strange silence, broken only by occasional references to particular feats of Polish airmen and of Polish naval units. The British Press, consequently the reading public, began to forget their debt to the Poles. This was all the more unfortunate as the contribution of the P.A.F. to our war effort continued on a similar scale as in

Shorty after returning to Poland ruled by the communist regime, Stanisław Skalski was arrested, tortured and sentenced to death.

September and October 1940 – their participation in bombing raids, their destruction of German aircraft, and, alas, their losses, remained rather large in proportion to their numbers. All this can be seen at a glance by figures published officially, but not generally included in the public papers. It is necessary that English people should acquaint themselves with these figures, it is right that they should know of the enormous sacrifices made by these men, it is proper that they should learn of the gallant part taken, often at great expense, by the P.A.F.'[4]

One of the propagators of the Polish successes during the Battle of Britain was Professor Peter O'Grady:

'The Polish Air Force holds a record that is a glory in the annals of the epic air battle now being waged against our Nazi adversary. It is imperative that this should be widely known. In the memorable Battle of Britain, as is unstintingly admitted, the Polish squadron was the best squadron in the R.A.F. It shot down 126 enemy planes in the course of that historic event. No other squadron, Allied or British, enjoys so signal a record.' [5]

Professor O'Grady also articulated that the British press generously yet erroneously:

'attributed the desperate dare-devil bravery and dashing recklessness of the Polish airmen to the fact that the Poles had nothing left to live for, whereas the British had still their wives and families to care for. In fact, however, in this battle these daring Polish pilots are fired by the thought of their suffering parents, wives, children and relatives, victims now living under ruthless Nazi rule and foul oppression; their utter disregard of risk is the outcome of that indefinable determination to defeat and destroy the hated Nazi – not in a spirit of unholy hatred – but in a holy élan to hasten to rescue their beloved ones and to reconquer their homes.'[6]

Another example of how enthusiastically the Polish airmen were treated, at least in the first few years of the war, can be found in Anna McLaren's article, which was also written a couple of months after the Battle of Britain:

'Within a few months they were fighting fit, trained to the n-th degree; they had their Spitfires, their Wellingtons, their squadrons and their airfields, and were once more a united fighting force. They waited only the chance to prove their mettle as heroes. From the first take-offs they had proved their splendid quality as pilots. For the fighter pilots this chance came sooner than they had expected – in September 1940, a year after the Polish campaign, with the Battle of Britain. The Polish pilots took their chance with both hands. They stood magnificently by the side of the R.A.F. and played an important part in the destruction of the mighty Luftwaffe's assault on this island and its capital. Since that time Polish pilots have earned for themselves the credit of being responsible for the destruction of hundreds of the enemy airplanes brought down in operations over and around this country.'[7]

But while almost everyone was applauding the skills shown by the Polish pilots in the air, there were some tacticians and military old-stagers still rather reluctant to believe the combat reports provided by the Poles. Group Captain Stanley Vincent at Northolt, despite being respected by his Polish band of pilots, had his doubts regarding their claims. Deputy Chief of the Air Staff, Air Vice Marshal William Sholto Douglas, later known as a big Polish sympathizer, wrote on 26 September 1940 to Hugh Dowding:

'The Polish Squadron seem to be shooting down a terrifying number of Huns. Yesterday 303 Squadron shot down 13 plus one probable in one engagement; they got 15 plus one on 15th September, on which day 302 Squadron got 13 also. I know that everyone has a very high opinion of these Polish squadrons, and that they really are getting right in and shooting down a lot of E.A. but do you think that they are being rather optimistic about their claims? This is always a difficult subject even in the case of British squadrons. Is there anything to be done to check up the Polish claims even more closely then I know you check up our own?'

So what was so unusual and special about this foreign legion? Were they any better than average Royal Air Force pilots? At least they were different. Flying in a group of pilots speaking the same language and remembering similar training that they polished to perfection time after time was a key point. Unlike British pilots, who were there simply defending their country and didn't like the Germans, the Poles were more emotionally attached to the result of each combat. They hated the Germans with a vengeance. For them it was: 'either them or us', 'black or white' with no shades of grey. 'The only good German is a dead German' was what they thought, recalling the picture of their country brutally and ruthlessly invaded (at that point they were not fully aware of

Soviet repressions), therefore every enemy plane shot down made their way back home more real.

They simply flew to eliminate the Germans from the skies. The psychological aspect was no less important. As Britain was the last bastion to defend, there was nowhere else to go. If this battle had also been lost, the only fate for the Poles would be certain death, and automatically also, they strongly believed, for their loved ones some 1,000 miles away. But unlike in Poland, where within hours they realized the overwhelming superiority of the Luftwaffe, or in France, where the fighting spirit evaporated with the first glass of wine – which they believed their hosts preferred to confrontation – Britain and her people had the guts and willingness to survive and, like the Poles, had no place to retreat. According to Churchill's words, surrender was out of the question and losing was not an option.

Group Captain Stanley Vincent recalled:

'The British and Canadians fought well and had grand results against the German Bombers and Fighters, but they had not had their countries overrun by a dirty enemy, vastly superior in numbers and had to leave families and homes behind in order to carry on the fight. 303 went in to attack, and pressed home that attack a hundred yards further in than

Larger than life Jan Zumbach flew as a mercenary in Africa. Here, photographed in August 1967 in Biafra, he is with the local airmen and newly received Douglas RB-26P Invader.

the others – they dived right through Bomber formations, broke them up and clawed the individuals out of the sky remorselessly – they had any number of their aircraft shot down in flames but the pilot would come down by parachute, and report back later clamouring for a new Hurricane – then off again to avenge that insult! The results were that in six weeks they destroyed no less than 126 German aircraft for the loss of only six of their gallant band killed.'

The Poles flying in the Royal Air Force and Auxiliary Air Force squadrons did not have much to say, not only because they spoke very limited English, but more importantly by being in the minority, they had to follow the rules applied to most of His Majesty's flying units. They were required to fly the infamous 'vic' formation, called by the Luftwaffe '*Idiotenreihen*' ('rows of idiots'). They were expected to attack in sections, where the first one was led by the commander and each pilot then had to choose his victim and stick to it until gaining a visible result. Only then were the following sections permitted to strike. This was a challenging system for the Poles, who were known for their individualism.

Although the RAF, and especially Fighter Command, had been recently modernized, mainly by introducing much faster and better-equipped monoplanes such as the Hurricane and Spitfire by the end of 1937 and middle of 1938 respectively, their tactics were still significantly behind the concept of modern aerial warfare. Even in 1938, the thesis of the dog-fight sounded rather foreign and remained misunderstood, while the theory of attacking bombers in principal was completely obsolete and stuck in the Great War era.

The Poles exercised their practical and flexible four-finger formation countless times back in Poland. Flying outdated aircraft made their necks 'elastic' from constantly turning their heads around; their ability to sight the enemy was therefore more natural. As most of their aircraft did not have a radio, the Poles adapted unsurprisingly to this kind of reconnaissance. They were observers, not listeners. Two lost campaigns, although leaving a visible stigma and causing the Poles to question the reason for such disaster and criticizing the abilities of their political and military leaders, did not weaken their combat morale at all, as was initially expected by the British.

The wrong assessment of their skills and previous experience, followed by rather imaginative assumption that the Polish pilots had not flown any modern aircraft before, did not work either. Poles, as much as was possible, developed their own model of tactics. This was mainly possible in the two Polish squadrons where they watched each other's backs, getting much closer to their opponents than their English colleagues when attacking. Maintaining a head-on attack was nothing unusual for the Poles. As long as enemy aircraft caught their fire, all tricks and tactics were acceptable.

All these paid off. Their radio communication was mainly maintained in Polish, for obvious reasons. When they got excited, they simultaneously switched to their native language, which from a psychological point of view is quite understandable. It has to be noted that most of the members of 302 and 303 Squadrons arrived in Britain straight after the French capitulation, and unlike the rest of the Polish contingent pouring in during the winter and spring, they did not have any time to learn new skills such as the English language. This lack of the required form of communication somehow worked to their advantage. They knew within seconds what was going on without thinking: 'Did I understand correctly what was said to me?' And although losing twenty-nine of their colleagues in combat or flying accidents, their final score of 203 enemy aircraft shot down, thirty-five probably destroyed and thirty-six damaged, as officially allocated to the PAF pilots during the Battle of Britain, was and remains very impressive.

When mentioned in various publications, Polish participation in the Battle of Britain has not been precise and is very often associated only with September 1940. This is simply due to the crucial fact of increased influence on German losses and because the great 'shooting contest' began then for the 303's boys, who defended the central and most decisive area of the fight. But the Polish chapter started almost at the beginning of the opening phase of the Battle of Britain, known as 'the Channel Battles', when on 19 July the first claim had been made by Polish flier Flying Officer Antoni Ostowicz. Having only a few pilots in the first line, the score of ½-0–1 (aircraft destroyed, probably destroyed, damaged) seems to be reasonable.

The second phase, called the 'Eagle Attack', saw an increase of Polish presence in British skies, which translated into over thirty aerial victories reported by the Polish fighter pilots and approved by the RAF. During the third phase, a significant improvement can be seen, purely based on engaging 303 Squadron in the epicentre of the battle. Without question the 'Kościuszko' boys did well, and out of forty-three enemy planes downed, nine destroyed probably and seven damaged, only twenty-three were allocated to other Poles serving in RAF units.

The fourth phase, when the 'Blitz' began, brought a further 117 Luftwaffe planes downed by the Poles, with sixteen probably destroyed and ten damaged. This was the last act of desperation shown by Göring and his 'unbeatable eagles', while targeting civilian areas, mostly London. Finally ,the fifth phase, which is notable for the limited number of German bomber raids – carried out instead by fighter-bombers – and the English weather worsening, saw the Poles shooting down over twenty enemy machines, while claiming two as probably destroyed and at least nine damaged.

The total score initially reported by the Poles, or accepted by Fighter Command, was dictated by various factors. These included the relatively limited number of pilots initially accepted into the RAF squadrons during the early stages of the Battle of Britain. This was the result of initial discussions about a very strict number of Polish aircrew permitted to serve under British command. Many experienced fighter pilots remained in France and were on their way while the first fights were beginning. The location of both Polish squadrons also played a vital role, as did the location and movement of the RAF squadrons in which other Polish fliers served. Learning the language, adopting new tactics and understanding British aircraft manuals should also be considered.

Another less known and less significant chapter of the Battle of Britain was written indirectly by three Polish cryptologists: Marian Rejewski, Jerzy Różycki and Henryk Zygalski. In 1932 they decrypted the Enigma code and seven years later handed over their own copy of the German machine to British Intelligence. Although a rather small portion of Luftwaffe messages were sent by Enigma during the Battle of Britain, and their true meaning was known too late, the decoding machine remained useful to understand the general situation across the Channel, rather than keeping Fighter Command informed of each raid.

Out of 145 pilots of Polish nationality who, according to official statistics, took part in the Battle of Britain, twenty-nine were killed during this time, with another thirty-eight losing their lives during the following years of war and a further three in flying accidents after the war. Group Captain Stanisław Brzezina perished in 1946 in a Dakota crash while still serving as a Polish Air Force officer attached to BAFO (the British Air Forces of Occupation), while Józef Jeka and Mirosław Wojciechowski died after being involved in foreign service in the 1950s.

One Polish Battle of Britain veteran received the award of Commander of the Order of the British Empire, and two of 'the Polish Few' were decorated with the Distinguished Service Order, including one with Bar. But the British decorations did not stop there, as thirty-three of them received Distinguished Flying Cross (including one with a single Bar and another with two Bars) and six were awarded the Distinguished Flying Medal. Obviously they were also recognized by the Polish authorities, who decorated seventy-five of them with the Virtuti Militari Cross, the highest Polish military decoration. The Polish Cross of Valour was given to 117 of them, including sixteen with one Bar, forty-one with two Bars and thirty with three Bars.

There were sixty-one Polish survivors from the Battle of Britain fighter family who decided to not to return to communist-ruled Poland, being afraid of the terrible repressions against those who fought in the West. Some of them stayed in the United Kingdom, while others, not feeling welcome there, emigrated to Argentina, Canada, New Zealand or the United States, where they settled for good. A considerable proportion of these well-trained people were able to find

After the 'Polish October 1956' some of the veterans were allowed to join the Polish Peoples' Air Force. Here from the left, standing next to SB Lim-2 aircraft (MiG-15 bis built in Poland under licence), are Stanisław Skalski, Witold Łokuciewski and Wacław Król.

employment within the aviation industry, influencing the new look of modern flying. Bronisław Bernaś worked as an electro-technical engineer at Westlands, being heavily involved in designing helicopters, whereas Jan Budziński, who moved to the USA, found himself a career as an inspector in a jet engine factory. Zbigniew Oleński, after making Britain his new home, was welcomed by the Avro company, where he worked as an aerodynamicist, including involvement in the Vulcan bomber project. Tadeusz Sawicz and Witold Urbanowicz both functioned within the aircraft industry, living in Canada and USA respectively. After the war the world needed skilled and highly qualified pilots elsewhere too. Mieczysław Gorzula, Bronisław Malinowski and Konrad Muchowski were amongst the significant Polish continent of airmen who left Britain to become flying instructors for the newly formed Pakistani Air Force.

Not everyone could or had intentions to continue a military path. Whereas some of 'the Polish Few' remained wearing RAF uniforms, others did not. Antoni Głowacki initially joined the RAF, but eventually moved to New Zealand, where he was an air force pilot. He later got involved in New Zealand's civilian aviation, continuing this adventure to the end of his life. A few other former Polish Battle of Britain pilots joined the RAF, and in most cases were employed as flying personnel, having a chance to fly once more. They were

Michał Maciejowski, Piotr Ostaszewski-Ostoja (also famous as a sports pilot), Jan Palak, Jerzy Radomski (despite receiving a disappointing posting as a catering officer), Henryk Szczęsny and Mirosław Wojciechowski. The latter flew jets before being killed in a flying accident in 1956.

Jan Falkowski, although starting his life in Canada as a farmer, eventually became a flying instructor. Meanwhile, Józef Jeka, who preferred more thrilling and adrenaline-rushing challenges, joined an American air service run by the CIA, before he was killed in 1956 over Indonesia. Jan Maliński secured a few jobs as an airline pilot during the years to come, operating from the UK, Canada and the Bahamas. In his retirement he chose to return to Poland, which by then was free from communist rule.

Ludwik Martel also continued his flying adventure, becoming an agricultural pilot in Africa. Zbigniew Wróblewski, after settling in England, became an airline pilot, whilst Jan Zumbach gained his fame not only as a ladies' man, but also as a smuggler, mercenary pilot in Africa and eventually a nightclub owner in Paris. The last Pole who decided to continue a flying career in the West was Janusz Żurakowski, initially based in Britain as a test pilot, who – after moving to Canada – earned a distinguished role as the Avro Canada chief test pilot and obtained almost legendary status.

Not everyone was able to grasp their chance or allowed to do so. Despite achieving the rank of Wing, Sector and even Station Commander within the Polish Air Force in exile, Aleksander Gabszewicz did not continue flying after the war. He became a family man, being involved in his father-in-law's building materials business in Britain. Gabszewicz, in his free time, became engaged as a social activist. Bolesław Drobiński, Władysław Gnyś, Włodzimierz Karwowski, Egueniusz Nowakiewicz and Jerzy Palusiński became farmers, deciding to live in Canada, New Zealand and the United Kingdom respectively. Their talents were wasted though.

Stefan Kleczkowski ran a B&B business in Kent, Julian Kowalski was employed in the British agricultural machine industry, while Bronisław Malinowski, after returning from Pakistan, opened a garage and then ran a pub. Jerzy Solak started a building company in Britain, renovating houses destroyed during the war, before moving to America, where he became famous for designing some spectacular buildings, including skyscrapers. Jan Palak, after leaving the RAF, worked in a chocolate factory.

For some of the 'Few', their future wasn't so fortunate. Mieczysław Mümler, the former Polish RAF Northolt commander, worked as a baker in London, while Eugeniusz Szaposznikow drove a bus in Nottinghamshire. When interviewed by the local paper, he seemed to enjoy it. Did he have any alternative, after being marked as a 'bloody foreigner' in the country he fought for?

Thanks to British public opinion fanned by some politicians, Poles were only there as potential competitors in the labour market. The imperial economy, stretched by the war effort, was weak, and there were many voices expecting jobs to be offered only to their own boys returning home. It was no surprise then that Bolesław Drobiński, who had been awarded a DFC and given command of 303 Squadron, was told that he had arrived in Britain 'illegally'. He did not complain though, and worked very hard overseas for some time, when employed in the United States, and in England after his return. Still, it could have been worse.

Those who decided to return to Poland, a country then under a government imposed by the Russians, were badly treated by the regime and its political police as an enemy of the state, even if they were briefly admitted to the People's Polish Air Force. Soon after, accused of being a danger to the new democracy, the Polish pilots who had flown in the West were expelled from the armed forces, thereafter having problems finding any employment at all. Marian Duryasz worked as a store keeper in a railway company, whilst Wacław Król, being under constant surveillance, became a driver and then, similarly to Duryasz, a warehouseman. Tadeusz Nowierski eventually found a job as a taxi driver and Karol Pniak was struggling until 1956 to find any employment whatsoever. Stefan Witorzeńć and Kazimierz Wünsche were both sacked from the communist-ruled air force – which by all accounts was deeply loyal to Russia- and, like other colleagues, had to wait until some slight political changes were made in the second half of 1956. Duryasz, Król, Witold Łokuciewski and Witorzeńć were 'mercifully' given the chance to rejoin the Polish communist air force, while Wünsche became a medical service pilot. Some of the former renegades even completed jet flying training, and Łokuciewski surprisingly managed to end his career as military attaché in London. This was all only possible after Josef Stalin's death.

The most drastic fate, however, was that of Stanisław Skalski, who rejected lucrative offers to stay in the West, and after being accepted to the People's Polish Air Force, was soon arrested and sentenced to death for 'espionage' against the system. Skalski, brutally tortured, spent eight long years in Wronki prison, including three years awaiting execution. Eventually released and rehabilitated, Skalski finished his military career in the rank of Brigadier General with ruined health and his dreams of a free Poland crushed to pieces.

While Marian Wędzik flew as a pilot for the Polish LOT Airlines, the rest of his colleagues pursued other ways of life, none of these having anything to do with flying. Jan Czerny worked in education, Szymon Kita found his place and peace in the farming industry and Bronisław Wydrowski found employment with the harbour authorities, trying to escape from his beloved country.

After the war, life for 'the Polish Few' was far from glorious. The heroes of the sky had to adapt to new realities very quickly, losing their celebrity status. They were no longer invited to pubs and given free drinks. 'Work, as for many that had been in the forces, was not easy to find,' wrote Eugeniusz Szaposznikow, who tried his hand at almost everything.

> 'One of my first jobs was sweeping the floor for a little money, this was followed by working for the gas board. Later my wife and I ran a mushroom farm. Later we ran a public house in Matlock for many years.'

Despite being on the winning side, Poland was one of those countries which actually lost the war and its freedom. Jan Kowalski recalls:

> 'I would not return to live in Poland under Communist rule. When the war ended my heart was heavy with sadness for Poland and her people, for what we had lost so much. We had not won the war; politicians had betrayed Poland and given her to the Soviets. England was to become my second home, for it was not the British people who betrayed Poland – they were always loyal. At first, as was the case for many that had been in the forces, work was hard to find. My wife and I settled in Lincolnshire. At first I worked by mending broken furniture and doing a little carpentry.'

Stefanie Palak, Jan's wife, described her husband's great sadness:

> 'The betrayal of Poland meant my husband Jan could never return to live in his beloved country when the war ended. He never attended reunions and rarely spoke about the war, finding it very painful to recount the memories of so many friends lost. His only dream, as for so many from the Polish Air Force, was to one day return when Poland was free and to fly to a free Poland.'

When the long-awaited freedom finally came in 1989 with the end of communist rule, only twenty-nine of the Polish Few were still alive and firmly rooted far away from their homeland. Ten others lived in Poland and could finally take an unfettered breath of fresh air. Was it truly any relief for all these Eagles, who spent most of their lives as forgotten heroes, thousands of miles from their nests, not wanted by the country they fought for? There was perhaps a much stronger feeling of disappointment for those who had returned against all odds to a communist-ruled Poland, which wasn't theirs anymore, only to find that they were not accepted in their homeland. By the time this book was written, all of 'the Polish Few' had passed away, once again flying surrounded by all their friends who lost their lives during the darkest hours of the war. At last the Polish Blue Flight (to which there is a saying that all Polish airmen go after death) is reunited once more …

Table 1: Polish Air Force ranks and their equivalents.

Lotnictwo Wojskowe Polish Air Force	Royal Air Force	Armée de l'Air	USAAF	Luftwaffe
–	Marshal of the RAF	–	–	–
generał broni[8]	Air Chief Marshal	–	General	Generaloberst
generał dywizji	Air Marshal	Général de Division	Major-General	Generalleutnant
generał brygady	Air Vice Marshal	Général de Brigade	Brigadier-General	Generalmajor
–	Air Commodore	–	–	–
pułkownik	Group Captain	Colonel	Colonel	Oberst
podpułkownik	Wing Commander	Lieutenent Colonel	Lieutenant Colonel	Oberstleutnant
major	Squadron Leader	Commendant	Major	Major
kapitan	Flight Lieutenant	Capitane	Captain	Hauptmann
porucznik	Flying Officer	Lieutenent	First Lieutenant	Oberleutnant
podporucznik	Pilot Officer	Sous Lieutenent	Second Lieutenant	Leutnant
–	–	–	Sergeant Major	Hauptfeldwebel
chorąży	Warrant Officer	Adiutant Chef	Master-Sergeant	Stabsfeldwebel
podchorąży[9]	–	Aspirant	–	–
starszy sierżant	Flight Sergeant	Adiutant	Technical Sergeant	Oberfeldwebel
sierżant	Sergeant	Sergant Chef	Staff Sergeant	Feldwebel
–	–	–	–	Unterfeldwebel
plutonowy	Corporal	Sergant	Sergeant	Unteroffizier

Lotnictwo Wojskowe Polish Air Force	Royal Air Force	Armée de l'Air	USAAF	Luftwaffe
kapral	Leading Aircraftman	Caporal Chef	Corporal	Obergefreiter
starszy szeregowy	Aircraftman No.1	Caporal	Private First Class	Gefreiter
szeregowy	Aircraftman No.2	Soldat	–	Flieger

Table 2: Composition of the Polish Air Force and its equivalents.

Lotnictwo Wojskowe Polish Air Force prior to Second World War and during Polish Campaign 1939	Royal Air Force Including PAF under British command	Armée de l'Air Including PAF under French command	Luftwaffe
Klucz or Pluton 3 aircraft	Section 2-4 aircraft	Patruille 3 aircraft	Kette or Schwarm 3-4 aircraft
Eskadra 7-11 aircraft	Flight 4-8 aircraft / Squadron 8-16 aircraft	Escadrille 6-16 aircraft	Staffel 9-12 aircraft
Dywizjon 18-33 aircraft	Wing 32-48 aircraft or from 1½ squadrons and above	Groupe 13-38 aircraft	Gruppe 32-48 aircraft
Brygada 55-86 aircraft	Group 100-300 aircraft	Escadre 28-68 aircraft	Geschwader 75-120 aircraft

Chapter Nineteen

The Polish Few

This list has been compiled according to Polish alphabetical order and shows Battle of Britain ranks of the airmen. The list does not include two Czechoslovak pilots, Sergeant Josef František and Sergeant Jozef Káňa (Slovak). Both, despite voluntarily joining the Polish Air Force respectively in June and July 1939, were not of Polish nationality.

A

TADEUSZ ANDRUSZKÓW, Sergeant, was born on 18 November 1920 in Lwów, Poland (now Lvov, Ukraine). In 1936 he entered the Polish Air Force NCO School for Minors at Bydgoszcz and graduated in 1938 as a fighter pilot from Krosno, where the School was moved in the same year. In the rank of Senior Private, Andruszków was posted to the 162nd Fighter Squadron of the III/6 Fighter Wing of the 6th Air Regiment in Lwów. His unit commanded by Lieutenant Bernard Groszewski was attached to 'Łódź' Army. Andruszków was posted to the section led by Sub-Lieutenant Marian Trzebiński and on the first day of war he damaged his PZL P.7 while landing at Kłoniszewo. After that incident, and due to shortage of aircraft, Andruszków did no fly operationally in Poland. Via Rumania he arrived in France, and after training in the rank of Polish Corporal Anduszków was posted to the Fighter Section of DAT (Territorial Defence Unit) commanded by Lieutenant Jan Falkowski which was stationed at Cognac. The section was later equipped with Morane 406s and Bloch 152s. On 23 June 1940, on board the m/s *Batory*, Andruszków sailed from St Jean de Luz to Britain. There he received service number P-5152 and was posted for conversion training to No. 5 Operational Training Unit at Aston Down. On 21 August 1940 he arrived at Northolt being posted to No. 303 (Polish) 'Tadeusz Kościuszko. City of Warsaw' Squadron. On 15 September Sergeant Andruszków shared in the victory of a Dornier Do 17, but was downed himself. He baled out and landed safely. On 26 September he shot down a Dornier Do 17. The following day he was killed during morning combat over Horsham. He was the twenty-second Polish operational pilot lost during the Battle of Britain. He was buried at Northwood Cemetery, grave H-208, and was posthumously awarded the Polish Cross of Valour and Air Medal. Tadeusz Andruszków is commemorated on the Polish Air Force Memorial at

Sgt Tadeusz Andruszków (3rd from left) with the group of 303 Sqn's ground crew. Flg Off Wacław Wiórkiewicz, Polish Engineering Officer, is standing below the propeller hub.

Northolt and the Polish Air Force Memorial at Warsaw-Mokotów, but also on a memorial plaque at RAF Northolt. He was the second youngest Polish airman who participated in the Battle of Britain. His older brother, Sergeant Marian Julian Andruszków, was killed on 14 November 1943 as wireless operator and air gunner while flying with No. 305 (Polish) 'Wielkopolan. Marshal Józef Piłsudski' Squadron. There was another fighter pilot known as starszy szeregowy Tadeusz Andruszków, who received mortal wounds on 6 September 1939, when the 162nd Squadron's road party was attacked by the Luftwaffe near Brzeziny village. Both Andruszków often confuse historians.

Date & Time	Unit	Aircraft	Score
15.09.1940 12.00	303 Squadron	Hurricane I P3939 RF-H	½-0-0 Do 17 (claimed as Do 215)
26.09.1940 16.30	303 Squadron	Hurricane I V6665 RF-J	1-0-0 Do 17 (claimed as Do 215)

B

WIEŃCZYSŁAW BARAŃSKI, Flying Officer, was born on 19 September 1908 at Solec nad Wisłą into the family of Stanisław and Zofia, within the territory of Poland ruled by the Russian Empire. In 1930 he entered the Polish Air Force College at Dęblin and graduated in 1932 with the 6th class as an observer. Barański was posted to the 13th Light Bomber Squadron of the 1st Air Regiment at Warsaw. To gain a pilot's qualifications he attended a flying training course between May and July 1933, and was then posted to the 114th Fighter Squadron of the same 1st Air Regiment. Between May and July 1934 Barański completed the Advanced Flying Course at Grudziądz and returned to 114th Squadron. Promoted to the rank of Lieutenant, between October 1935 and May 1936 he served as an advanced flying instructor at Grudziądz, after which Barański was a pilot and engineering officer of the 113th Fighter Squadron; in October 1936 he was appointed commander of the III Recruit Flight of the 1st Air Regiment. In November 1936 he became deputy commander of the 113th Squadron, and from December 1938 he commanded the whole squadron. In 1939 he passed exams to study at the Polish Staff Academy, but was unable

Officers of the 1st Air Regiment in Warsaw. Some of them took part in the Battle of Britain. In the back row from left are: Michał Stęborowski (1st), Witold Urbanowicz (2nd) and Wicńczysław Barański (4th). Stefan Pawlikowski (3rd from left in first row) commanded the Polish fighter squadrons in Britain between 1940 and 1943, when he was killed.

to continue due to the outbreak of war. During the Polish Campaign in 1939 Barański led the 113th Fighter Squadron, and on 3 September he claimed two shared victories of a Heinkel He 111 and Junkers Ju 87. He was shot down on 6 September by the air gunner of a He 111 and force landed near Dąbie and Uniejów, and on 9 September returned to his unit. After the collapse of Poland, via Rumania he arrived in France, where he was posted to the Polish Air Force Training Centre at Lyon and then took command of the Polish Fighter Mobile Squadron. From June 1940 he led the Polish section commanded by Captain Mieczysław Sulerzycki and attached to the GCIII/6 at le Luc. On 6 June, while operating from Lyon, he claimed the shared victory of a Heinkel He 111. After the collapse of France he flew to North Africa, from where, via Gibraltar, he travelled to Great Britain. Upon arrival, he received service number P-0249 and was posted to No. 5 Operational Training Unit at Aston Down. Upon completion, on 11 October 1940 he was posted to No. 607 Squadron. In November 1940 Barański was transferred to No. 303 (Polish) 'Tadeusz Kościuszko. City of Warsaw' Squadron, then on 22 February 1941 to No. 316 (Polish) 'City of Warsaw' Squadron, where he was given command of 'A' Flight. From July 1941 he served as a ground control officer in 316's operations room. Then he held similar duties with No. 308 (Polish) 'City of Cracow' Squadron. From 25 August 1942, Barański took command of 'A' Flight of No. 302 (Polish) 'City of Poznań' Squadron, and between 17 May and 17 October 1943 he commanded No. 302 Squadron. He was appointed the Polish Liaison Officer at the headquarters of No. 12 Group, and from 1 April 1944 until November 1944 he studied at the Polish Air Force Academy. After graduation, Barański became a lecturer of fighter tactics. He was demobilized on 20 November 1946 in the rank of Squadron Leader. He was decorated with the Silver Cross of Virtuti Militari no. 8522 and the Cross of Valour with two bars. Wieńczysław Barański did not return to Poland, living in Great Britain. He died on 8 August 1970 in Maidenhead, Berkshire, and was buried at Braywick Cemetery in Maidenhead.

Date & Time	Unit	Aircraft	Score
06.09.1939	113th Squadron	PZL.P.11	⅓-0-0 He 111 ⅕-0-0 Ju 87
01.06.1940	GCMP	Morane Saulnier MS.406	½-0-0 He 111

ANTONI BEDA, Sergeant, was born on 20 May 1912 in Łódź within the territory of Poland, but then ruled by the Russian Empire, into the family of Walenty and Marianna née Ogrodowczyk. As with many of the aviation enthusiasts in Poland, in 1932 he took military flying training at Lublinek aerodrome, then a year later joined the Polish Armed Forces and was posted to the Polish Air Force and the 4th Air Regiment in Toruń. After completion of elementary flying course (between May and July 1933) Beda was transferred to the 42nd Light Bomber Squadron of the 4th Air Regiment. In 1934 he decided to continue his training and joined

the Advanced Flying Course at Grudziądz. As a fighter pilot he was posted to III/4 Fighter Wing at Toruń. When flying with the 141st Fighter Squadron on 2 September 1935 he had an accident in a PZL P.7, but was unhurt. In January 1936 he was posted to No. 1 Polish Air Force Training Centre at Dęblin for instructor's duty. Due to lack of aircraft he did not participate in the Polish Campaign, and on 19 September 1939 Beda crossed the Polish and Rumanian border. On 20 November he arrived in France, less than two months later being attached to the Montpellier Group at Lyon. This was the first group of Polish pilots posted to front-line units. On 26 March 1940 Platoon Commander Beda was assigned to fighter section no. 5 led by Lieutenant Józef Brzeziński and attached to GC I/2 at Xaffevilliers. While flying with this unit Beda claimed one shared victory of a Heinkel He 111 on 2 June and one victory of a Junkers Ju 88 three days later. Beda unofficially is also credited with the damage of a Heinkel He 111 on 10 May and sharing the damage of a Junkers Ju 88 the day after. After the collapse of France, Beda arrived at the port of St Jean de Luz on 21 June, from where he sailed to England. He arrived in Liverpool on 1 July. Antoni Beda received the service number 793548 and was posted for conversion training. On 20 August 1940 he was posted to No. 302 (Polish) 'City of Poznań' Squadron at Leconfield. On 2 September he was reposted to No. 5 Operational Training Unit for further training. Sergeant Beda rejoined 302 Squadron on 26 September. On 29 September 1941 he received a posting to No. 87 Squadron, where he performed night flights in Hawker Hurricanes.

Within less than a month he was involved in a flying accident, when two aircraft collided mid-air. Both pilots, Beda and Sergeant Paweł Gallus, baled out unhurt. On 22 April 1942 Beda arrived at No. 307 (Polish) Night Fighter 'City of Lwów' Squadron at Exeter, which was equipped with Bristol Beaufighters. Antoni Beda was commissioned with the rank of Pilot Officer on 1 June 1942 and received new service number, P-1900. From 7 July 1943 he undertook flying instructor training at No. 3 Flying Instructors School of the RAF, after which he returned to No. 307 Squadron on 15 September 1943. Beda left fighter duties and in January 1944 joined Transport Command. After that he flew with Nos 216 and 167 Squadrons RAF. On 28 April 1945 he was posted to No. 301 (Polish) Squadron and then on 24 January 1946 to No. 304 (Polish) Squadron. Beda was demobilized from the Polish Air Force with the rank of Flight Lieutenant in December 1946. He was decorated with the Polish Cross of Valour and bar and French Croix de Guerre avec Palm. He initially emigrated to the United States, and later lived in Alachua County, Florida. He died in October 1963 in Canada as a result of a car accident, and was buried in Forest Lawn Memory Gardens, Ocala, Marion County, Florida.

Date & Time	Unit	Aircraft	Score
02.06.1940 12.25	GCI/2	Morane Saulnier MS.406	⅓-0-0 He 111
05.06.1940	GCI/2	Morane Saulnier MS.406	1-0-0 Ju 88

MARIAN BEŁC, Sergeant, called 'Doktor' (Doctor), was born on 27 January 1914 in Paplin near Skierniewice within the territory of Poland, then ruled by the Russian Empire, in the family of Jan and Antonina née Trukawka. In 1929 he completed his education at the local primary school in Jeruzal. On 2 November 1934 he volunteered for the Polish Air Force, being posted to the 143rd Fighter Squadron of the 4th Air Regiment in Toruń as a ground crew member. Between 3 January and 15 April 1935 Marian Bełc attended an aircraft maintenance course, after which he served as mechanic assistant, and then from 15 April until 26

August 1935 he took a basic flying course at Radom Sadków. He was then posted to 41st Light Bomber Squadron. From 1 May until 10 July 1936 Bełc completed NCO School within the Air Regiment, and between August and October 1936 the Advanced Flying Course at Grudziądz, after which, on 27 October, he was posted as a fighter pilot to 143rd Fighter Squadron. On 25 November 1936, due to disbandment of his unit, he was transferred to 152nd Fighter Squadron of the 5th Air Regiment at Wilno-Porubanek. Corporal Bełc fought in Poland within the 152nd Fighter Squadron, which operated under command of the 'Modlin' Army. On 3 September 1939 he claimed victory over a Bf 109. On 17 September he crossed the Rumanian border and was interned until 5 November. Via Malta, he then sailed to Marseille where he arrived on 19 November, then three days later was posted to the Polish Air Force Training Centre at Lyon-Bron. Marian Bełc received a posting to the fighter section of DAT at Châteaudun led by Major Zdzisław Krasnodębski, and eventually was attached to GCI/55 at Etampes. After the collapse of France he boarded the Polish ship *Kmicic* and sailed to England, where he arrived on 22 June 1940. On 2 August Sergeant Bełc was posted to No. 303 (Polish) 'Tadeusz Kościuszko. City of Warsaw' Squadron, then six days later lost consciousness and crash-landed in a Hurricane. With the diagnosis of icterus, he was admitted to hospital. He was supposed to be posted to No. 5 Operational Training Unit for further training, however he stayed at Northolt. On 18 September 1940 he flew his first operational sortie during the Battle of Britain. On 26 September he shot down one Bf 109, on 5 October a Bf 110 and then two days later another Bf 109. Bełc claimed further victories after the Battle of Britain, while still flying with No. 303 Squadron: 24 June 1941, one Bf 109; 28 June 1941, another Bf 109; and 24 October 1941, one more Bf 109. Meanwhile, on 15 April 1941 he married Audrey Stephenson, and his son Marian Junior was born on 28 October that year. On 27 May 1942 Bełc was posted to No. 58 Operational Training Unit, and on 1 June he was commissioned, receiving the rank of Pilot Officer. His service number was changed to P1901. On 10 August 1942 Bełc was posted to No. 3 Flying Instructors School at RAF Hullavington, where on 28 August 1942 he was killed in a flying accident. He was on board a Miles Master III and due to pilot error, stalling the aircraft into a steep glide while attempting to land, both men aboard (Bełc and his British instructor) instantly lost their lives in the crash at Babdown Farm airfield, Gloucestershire. Pilot Officer Marian Bełc was buried at Northwood Cemetery, in grave no. H 267. He was decorated with the Silver Cross of Virtuti Militari no. 9177, the Cross of Valour with two bars and the British Distinguished Flying Cross, which after his death was given to his wife and son. He is commemorated on the Polish Air Force Memorial at Northolt, the Polish Air Force Memorial at Warsaw-

Mokotów and by the memorial plaque in Paplin unveiled on 23 September 2012. His personal diary and biography, published by Zbigniew Charytoniuk and Wojciech Zmyślony, were published in Poland in 2012 under the title *P/O Marian Bełc – a Fighter Ace of 303 Squadron 1914 1942*

Date & Time	Unit	Aircraft	Score
03.09.1939	152nd Squadron	PZL.P.11c	1-0-0 Bf 109
26.09.1940 16.30	303 Squadron	Hurricane I V6673 RF-U	1-0-0 Bf 109
05.10.1940 11.40	303 Squadron	Hurricane I V7235 RF-M	1-0-0 Bf 110
07.10.1940 13.50	303 Squadron	Hurricane I L2099 RF-O	1-0-0 Bf 109
24.06.1941 20.45	303 Squadron	Spitfire II P8531 RF-Y	1-0-0 Bf 109
28.06.1941 08.45	303 Squadron	Spitfire II P8531 RF-Y	1-0-0 Bf 109
24.10.1941 15.10	303 Squadron	Spitfire VB AB824 RF-S	1-0-0 Bf 109

BRONISŁAW BERNAŚ, Pilot Officer, was born on 6 August 1906 in Lwów within the territory of Poland, then ruled by the Russian Empire. At a very early age he fought for independence of his home town alongside the 'Lwów Eaglets'. While living in Lwów Bernaś graduated from Mikołaj Kopernik (Nicolaus Copernicus) Mathematical-Biological Secondary School, later obtaining a degree at the Mechanical-Electro-technical Faculty of Lwów Technical University. Between 1931 and 1932 he attended the Air Force Reserve Cadet Officers' School at

Three 302 Squadron pilots, from left to right: Plt Off Marceli Neyder (did not fly operationally during the Battle of Britain), Plt Off Wacław Król and Plt Off Bronisław Bernaś

Dęblin, from which he graduated. While a member of the Lwów Aero-Club and undertaking periodical flying exercises at the 6th Air Regiment based at Lwów, Bernaś worked as an electro-technical engineer with the national railway management. As a reserve pilot he was mobilized on 24 August 1939 and posted to the 6th Air Regiment. After the collapse of Poland he escaped to Rumania and then to France. He decided to travel to Britain, where he arrived in December 1939. Bronisław Bernaś received the rank of Pilot Officer and the service number 76820. To gain fighter pilot skills he was posted to No. 6 Operational Training Unit at Sutton Bridge, and after successful completion on 26 September 1940 Bernaś was posted to No. 302 (Polish) 'City of Poznań' Squadron. He participated in the fatal operation of 18 October 1940, when five aircraft crashed and he was the only survivor. On 14 April 1941 he was posted to No. 57 Operational Training Unit and a week later to No. 58 Operational Training Unit at Grangemouth. In both units he served as an instructor. On 24 November 1941 Bernaś was transferred to No. 288 Squadron, and then in March 1942 was removed from the list of Polish fighter pilots. Soon after, on 28 July, he had a flying accident in a Hawker Hurricane when the engine failed, sustaining serious injuries. In March 1943 he was posted to the Polish Air Force Inspectorate, then served at the Airfield Construction Department. From August 1943 he joined No. 5010 Airfield Construction Squadron, being responsible for electric systems. After leaving the Polish Air Force in late 1946 with the rank of Flight Lieutenant, Bronisław Bernaś decided to settle in Britain. He worked as an electro-technical engineer with the team designing helicopters at Westlands. From 1973 he lived in Folkestone, where he died on 3 September 1980.

Date & Time	Unit	Aircraft	Score
13.03.1941 16.40	302 Squadron	Hurricane II Z2350 WX-W	0-0-1/3 Ju 88

JAN BOROWSKI, Flying Officer, was born on 31 May 1912 at Radom, in part of Poland ruled by Imperial Russia. He was the son of Adam and Aleksandra née Karasińska. Between 1929 and 1933 he studied at the Mechanical Faculty of the Technical University at Warsaw, then graduated from the Air Force Reserve Cadet Officers' School at Dęblin, from which he was transferred to the Air Force Cadet Officers' School, also at Dęblin. Borowski was commission on 15 October 1936 as primus of the whole 9th class. Subsequently he became a pilot and from 1 December 1938 to 1 August 1939 was deputy commander of the 113th Fighter Squadron of the 1st Air Regiment in Warsaw. Meanwhile he participated in various shooting competitions representing Poland, which included winning first place during an international shooting tournament in Italy which took place from 19-29 September 1935. From 1 August 1939 Borowski was employed by the Flight Testing Development as an aircraft manoeuvrability specialist pilot of the Aviation Institute. He was mobilized on 26 August and joined the 113th Fighter Squadron as its deputy commander. He participated in the Polish Campaign as an operational pilot and fought within the Pursuit Brigade, claiming three victories, including two shared. On 18 September he was evacuated to Rumania with the road party of the 113th Squadron. He was interned in Rumania and

then escaped to France, where he arrived on 12 November. From Marseilles, he was transferred to Mions, where he undertook conversion training. Later he joined the Polish fighter section led by Lieutenant Wieńczysław Barański. After the fall of France he travelled to Britain, where he was given the service number P-0250. Borowski was posted to No. 5 Operational Training Unit for training, and then on 17 October 1940 joined No. 302 (Polish) 'City of Poznań' Squadron operating from Northolt. The day after he was performing an operational flight as a member of 'B' Flight to intercept enemy formation. On their way back four Hurricanes crashed as a result of bad weather. It is believed that the Hawker Hurricane I P3930 WX-X, which he flew, hit the cables of barrage balloons or collided with the aircraft piloted by Flying Officer Peter Carter, crashed and exploded at Kempton Racecourse in Sunbury. Borowski was killed, and was buried at Northwood Cemetery in grave no. H 269. He was the twenty-sixth Polish operational pilot killed during the Battle of Britain. He was decorated with the Silver Cross of Virtuti Militari no. 12049. Jan Borowski is commemorated on the Polish Air Force Memorials in Northolt and Warsaw-Mokotów, the memorial plaque at RAF Northolt and also the memorial plaque at Kempton Racecourse, the unveiling of which the author was involved in.

Date & Time	Unit	Aircraft	Score
01.09.1939	113th Squadron	PZL P.11	1-0-0 Bf 109
05.09.1939	113th Squadron	PZL P.11	⅓-0-0 Ju 87
06.09.1939	113th Squadron	PZL P.11	⅕-0-0 Ju 87

STANISŁAW BRZEZINA, Flight Lieutenant, called 'Breezy', was born on 5 March 1904 in Łódź in Poland, which was ruled by the Russian Empire. He was the son of Czech immigrant Václav Březina and Maria née Białecka. His older brother Wacław was also an airman, who was killed in a flying accident in 1926. Together with his family, Stanisław moved to Wilno. He went to a school organized by the Association of Polish Teachers, once Poland regained independence, called Zygmunt August High School. On 25 April 1919, at the age of 15, Brzezina voluntarily

joined the 'City of Wilno' Infantry Regiment which fought against Ukrainians to return Wilno to Poland. In 1920 he fought against the Red Army which invaded Poland. In 1924 he graduated from the Tadeusz Czacki High School in Warsaw, then joined the Infantry Cadet Officers' School in Warsaw. On 2 November 1925 Stanisław Brzezina went to the Air Force Officers' School in Grudziądz (later the Air Force Cadet Officers' School), which eventually was moved to Dęblin. He graduated on 15 September 1927 with the 1st class as an observer (this was the first graduation of the school). He was posted to the 32nd Air Squadron of the 3rd Air Regiment in Poznań. Brzezina was commissioned as a Sub-Lieutenant. From 3 May 1929 he trained as a pilot in Dęblin, and from October flew with the 132nd Fighter Squadron commanded by Lieutenant Mieczysław Mümler. In May and June 1930 Brzezina completed the Advanced Flying Course with the 2nd Air Regiment in Cracow. On 16 April 1931 he was posted to the Air Force Officers' Training Centre at Dęblin for duty as an instructor. On 3 February 1932 he married Bożena Paetz. From October 1933 onwards he regularly flew gliders, participating in numerous competitions and represented Poland abroad. He also commanded the gliding camp at Ustianowa. From 29 November 1935 he served as technical officer of the 142nd Fighter Squadron at Toruń. On 1 April 1936 he was appointed deputy commander of the squadron, and then on 9 October 1936 commander of the 141st Fighter Squadron. Ten day later he started studying at the Polish Air Force Academy in Warsaw. On 25 March 1938 he took command of the Advanced Flying School at Grudziądz, which later was moved to Ułęż. During the Polish Campaign in 1939 Brzezina led a fighter flight consisting of flying instructors which was formed to defend the school. After the collapse of

Poland, on 19 September he was captured by the Soviets, but two days later managed to escape and on the 24th went to Rumania. Initially he was kept in Galati camp, but like many Poles he left and travelled to Balchik port, where he arrived on 4 November. Next day he boarded the ship *Patris* and sailed via Malta to France. On 21 February 1940 he left for England; he was given the service number 76782 and the rank of Acting Flight Lieutenant. From 5 May 1940 he commanded the Polish Training Squadron at RAF Manston, then from 16 July undertook training at the School of Army Cooperation at Old Sarum. On 22 July he was posted to No. 5 Operational Training Unit at Aston Down and on 4 August joined No. 74 Squadron. On 13 August he claimed the destruction of a Dornier Do 215 (actually a Do 17) and damage to another bomber, but his Spitfire was damaged in combat and Brzezina had to bale out. On 25 September he was appointed to command No. 308 (Polish) 'City of Cracow' Squadron, although he kept occasionally flying in 74 Squadron until 21 October. Stanisław Brzezina became Polish Liaison Officer at the HQ of 12 Group RAF. On 4 January 1941 he was appointed Polish Liaison Officer at the HQ of 9 Group RAF. Soon after, on 18 February, he formed and took command of No. 317 (Polish) 'City of Wilno' Squadron. From 10 August he was appointed commander of the 2nd Polish Fighter Wing at Exeter, a position he held until 2 December. Brzezina became Deputy Polish Liaison Officer at the HQ of RAF Fighter Command, and from 5 October 1942 he was Polish Station Commander of RAF Heston. From 1 April 1943 he was a lecturer at the Polish Air Force Staff College, then on 1 October became the Polish Air Force Chief of Staff. Between 19 March and 26 June 1945 Brzezina undertook studies at the US Command and General Staff College at Fort Leavenworth. Upon his return on 19 September 1945 he became the Polish Liaison Officer at the HQ BAFO. He was killed in a flying accident on 13 February 1946 when RCAF No. 435 Squadron's Douglas Dakota III KG397, which flew from Bückeburg in Germany to Croydon, crashed at Warlingham. Group Captain Stanisław Brzezina was buried at St Mary Cray Cemetery at Orpington, Kent, in grave no. E 94. He was decorated with the Silver Cross of Virtuti Militari no. 8991, the Cross of Valour with three bars, the Air Medal and Silver Cross of Merit. A biography of Brzezina entitled *Breezy. A fighter Pilot* was recently written by the author and will be published in Poland.

Date & Time	Unit	Aircraft	Score
13.08.1940 07.00	74 Squadron	Spitfire I N3091	1-0-1 Do 17 (claimed as Do 215)
10.07.1941 12.40	317 Squadron	Hurricane I N3212	1-0-0 Bf 109

MICHAŁ BRZEZOWSKI, Sergeant, who presumably was called 'Miś' (Teddy bear) as this name was painted on his aircraft in France, was born on 26 November 1920 in Dawidogródek, in Solec district, Poleskie Voivodship, in free Poland. In 1936 he entered the Air Force NCO School for Minors at Bydgoszcz, and between April and September 1938 completed an elementary flying course, then from April to June 1939 an Advanced Flying (fighter) Course at Ułęż. Brzezowski graduated at Krosno, where his school was moved, in July 1939 and was posted to the 151st Fighter Squadron of the 5th Air Regiment in Wilno. With this unit he fought during the Polish Campaign as part of the Independent Operational Group 'Narew'. After the fall of Poland he flew to Rumania on 18 September, landing at Cernâuti. He was interned for a short time, after which he sailed to France, where he arrived on 23 January 1940. From Marseilles he was posted for a conversion course, and then with the rank of Corporal joined the Polish fighter section led by Lieutenant Arsen Cebrzyński. This unit was attached to the French GCII/6 at Châteauroux and flew Bloch MB 152s. Brzezowski was shot down in combat on 5 June 1940, but managed to land safely. He was credited with the shared victory of a Henschel Hs 126 reconnaissance aircraft. On 20 June together with his colleagues he was moved to Toulouse, where they were equipped with Dewoitine D.520s. On 24 June at Port Vendres he boarded the ship *Apapa* and sailed to Gibraltar and then to Britain, where he arrived in Glasgow on 7 July. Initially he was posted to Blackpool, from where, after receiving the service number P-5122, he was transferred to No. 5 Operational Training Unit. On 21 August 1940 Sergeant Brzezowski was posted to No. 303 (Polish) 'Tadeusz Kościuszko. City of Warsaw' Squadron at Northolt. He was the youngest Polish airman who participated in the Battle of Britain. On 11 September he shot down two Heinkel He 111s. Four days later he was killed in action when his Hurricane I P3577 RF-E was shot down and crashed into the sea. His body was never found. He was the seventeenth Polish operational pilot lost during the Battle of Britain. Michał Brzezowski was posthumously awarded the Polish Cross of Valour and Air Medal. He is commemorated on the Polish Air Force Memorials at Northolt and Warsaw-Mokotów, and also on the memorial plaque at RAF Northolt.

Date & Time	Unit	Aircraft	Score
15.06.1940 07.00	GCII/6	Bloch MB 152	⅓-0-0 Hs126
11.09.1940 16.00	303 Squadron	Hurricane I V6665 RF-J	2-0-0 He 111

JAN BUDZIŃSKI, Sergeant, was born on 24 June 1916 at Grudziądz in part of Poland ruled by the German Empire, into the family of Julian and Klara. In 1933 he entered the Infantry NCO School for Minors at Nisko nad Sanem, from which he graduated in 1936. Budziński joined the Polish Air Force and was posted to the 4th Air Regiment at Toruń, where he underwent flying training. On 14 October 1936, while flying RWD-8 training aircraft, he had an accident, but he and his instructor from the training flight, Senior Private Leonard Pruski, survived. Budziński successfully completed his training in 1937. On 15 September 1937 he started professional military service and was posted for an Advanced Flying Course at Grudziądz. He joined the 141st Fighter Squadron of the 4th Air Regiment at Toruń. He flew operationally during the Polish Campaign, when his unit was attached to the 'Pomorze' Army. After the fall of Poland he escaped to Rumania, where he was interned in Calafat camp. After escaping he arrived at Bucharest, from where he travelled to the port of Balchik. On board the ship *Patris*, on 15 October 1939 he sailed to France. In January 1940 he sailed to Britain. On arrival he received the service number 780665 and from 11 June he underwent ground training at Blackpool, then – between 22-29 July - completed a pilot's course at No. 1 School of Army Co-operation at Old Sarum. Eventually he was sent for flying training at No. 7 Operational Training Unit at Hawarden. On 12 August 1940, with the rank of Sergeant, he joined No. 145 Squadron. However, on 31 August he left Westhampnett after being reposted to No. 605 Squadron stationed at Drem. During the Battle of Britain he claimed three aerial victories, including one shared. On 27 April 1941 he joined No. 302 (Polish) 'City of Poznań' Squadron, then on 8 August he arrived at No. 2 Air Gunners School at Dalcross. From 28 July 1942 he undertook a course for instructors at No. 2 Flying Instructors School at Montrose, and subsequently from October 1942 served as a flying instructor at No. 16 (Polish) Service Flying Training School at Newton. He left this post on 20 November 1945.

After demobilization with the rank of Warrant Officer, Jan Budziński decided to stay in Britain, but in 1953 he emigrated to Canada. There he was employed in the aviation industry as a jet engine inspector. Five years later he moved to the United States, settling in California, where he died on 26 August 2007, aged 91. In 2012 his ashes were taken to Poland and buried in his hometown of Grudziądz in Farny Cemetery. He was decorated with the Cross of Valour with bar.

Date & Time	Unit	Aircraft	Score
11.09.1940 16.00	605 Squadron	Hurricane I	1-0-0 Bf 109
27.09.1940 09.30	605 Squadron	Hurricane I	1-0-0 Bf 110
07.10.1940 16.30	605 Squadron	Hurricane I	½-0-0 Bf 109

C

ARSEN CEBRZYŃSKI, Flying Officer, was born on 8 March 1912 in Chełm Lubelski in the territory of Poland ruled by the Russian Empire. He grew up in the family of Władysław Cebrzyński and Helena née Obaszydze-Heczynaszwili, a Georgian lady aviator. Arsen's brother Wiktor also became an airman, serving in the 65th Light Bomber Squadron in Poland and then in No. 300 (Polish) 'Mazovian' Squadron in Britain. Arsen's mother was later remarried to Major Stanisław Karpiński, a famous Polish aviator. Arsen graduated from Cadet Corps No. 3 at Rawicz in June 1932, and from July 1932  to January 1933 he continued his education with the infantry course at the Infantry Cadet Officers' School in Różan before joining the Air Force Cadet Officers' School at Dęblin. He graduated on 15 August 1934 with the 8th class as an observer in the rank of Sub-Lieutenant. Cebrzyński was posted to the 13th Army Co-operation Squadron of the 1st Air Regiment in Warsaw. In July 1935 he completed a flying course at the Air Force Training Centre at

Dęblin and was posted to the 11th Light Bomber Squadron. In March 1936 he received a posting to the Training Squadron of the 1st Air Regiment, after which he was sent to the Advanced Flying School at Grudziądz, where he trained between April and June 1936. In September 1936 he joined the 111th Fighter Squadron at Warsaw. In 1937 Arsen Cebrzyński married Jadwiga Kuryluk, an actress known also as 'Kuma', who played roles in theatre and film. The same year his son Jacek Stanisław Cebrzyński (in future also a fighter pilot) was born. On 17 March 1938, in darkness, Arsen Cebrzyński crash landed at Porubanek airfield during the Polish Air Force concentration due to the 'Lithuanian Crisis'. He was seriously injured. In mid-1938 he was accepted for the Polish Staff Academy, but due to the outbreak of war, this path of his life never materialized. In the last days of August 1939 he returned to the 1st Air Regiment, being appointed Tactical Officer of the III/1 Fighter Wing that was part of the Pursuit Brigade. On 3 September 1939 Cebrzyński participated in the shared victory of a Bf 110. He also claimed the shared destruction of a Bf 110 two days later, but his claim was never accepted. On 18 September he crossed the Rumanian border at Śniatyń and for two weeks he worked in the office of the Polish air attaché in Bucharest. Via Yugoslavia and Italy he travelled to France, where he arrived on 12 October. In mid-December 1939 he was posted to Lyon, where he started training, and on 11 March 1940 his aerial training began. On 18 May 1940 he was appointed the commanding officer of the Polish section attached to GCII/6. The Poles joined the 3rd Escadrille 'Cignone' and flew Marcel Bloch MB 152s. His wife's nickname, 'Kuma', was painted on his Bloch MB 152. On 5 June, Cebrzyński was credited with a destruction and a shared victory of a He 111, then on 15 June he participated in the destruction of a Hs 126. After receiving a Dewoitine D.520, he planned to fly to England, but eventually the whole section boarded the ship *Apapa* and sailed to Britain, where they arrived on 7 July. After receiving the serial number P-1416 and the rank of Flying Officer, on 21 August 1940 he was posted to No. 303 (Polish) 'Tadeusz Kościuszko. City of Warsaw' Squadron at Northolt. He was killed during his first operational flight on 11 September. About 16.00 his Hurricane I V6667 RF-K was shot down over Pembury. It is believed that he either fell from his aircraft or was killed when leaving the cockpit, as his body was found with the parachute unopened. Some sources erroneously state that he crash-landed and died of wounds several days later. He was the twelfth Polish operational pilot killed during the Battle of Britain and the first No. 303 Squadron pilot killed during the war. He was buried in Northwood Cemetery, in grave H 187. Arsen Cebrzyński was decorated with the Cross of Valour with two bars. He is commemorated on the Polish Air Force Memorials at Northolt and Warsaw-Mokotów, and also on the memorial plaque at RAF Northolt.

Date & Time	Unit	Aircraft	Score
03.09.1939	III/1 Wing	PZL P.11c	⅓-0-0 Bf 110
05.06.1940	GCII/6	Bloch MB 152	1½-0-0 He 111
15.06.1940	GCII/6	Bloch MB 152	⅓-0-0 Hs 126

STANISŁAW JÓZEF CHAŁUPA, Pilot Officer, was born on 14 January 1914 in Zalas near Chrzanów in the region of Cracow, in part of Poland ruled by the Austro-Hungarian Empire. He grew up in the family of Wincenty and Helena née Małodobra. In 1935 he graduated from high school and joined Polish forces, serving in the Artillery Cadet Officers' School at Włodzimierz Wołyński. He was accepted to the Air Force Cadet Officers' School in Dęblin, where he arrived on 1 January 1936. He graduated on 15 October 1938 (11th class) and in the rank of Sub-Lieutenant was posted to the 123rd Fighter Squadron of the 2nd Air Regiment in Cracow. During the Polish Campaign in 1939 he fought with the 123rd Squadron, attached to the Pursuit Brigade. On 5 September he participated in the shared destruction of a He 111; however this claim was not accepted. After the Soviet attack on Poland's eastern border, he flew a PZL P.7 to the Rumanian airfield of Jassy, where he was arrested. After bribing Rumanian policemen he escaped to Balchik, from where on board the ship *Patris* he sailed to Marseilles. He arrived in France on 27 November. After a stay in Lyon, Chałupa was posted to Montpellier, where he continued training until 15 February 1940. He was moved to Lyon-Bron for further training, which he completed on 29 March. After being attached to the Polish fighter section led by Lieutenant Józef Brzeziński, he was posted to GCI/2 at Xaffévillers, flying Morane MS 406s. Despite being shot down on 11 May by ground fire, he rejoined his unit on 22 May, continued fighting and claimed several victories over France. On 16 June he travelled by train to St Jean de Luz, from where on the 24th he sailed to Britain. Chałupa arrived at Liverpool on 27 June. He received the service number P-1300 and the rank of Pilot Officer, and on 23 July was posted to No. 302 (Polish) 'City of Poznań' Squadron at

Leconfield. On 19 August he participated in the first operational flight of his squadron, and two days later was involved in the probable destruction of a Ju 88. His aircraft was also damaged and he was wounded upon landing. On 15 September he shot down one German bomber and participated in the probable destruction of another. He was hospitalized and underwent a nose operation, which prevented him from operational flying. He served in the Operations Room of No. 302 Squadron, and then in 1943 was sent for similar duty with No. 315 (Polish) 'City of Dęblin' Squadron. On 24 June 1944 Chałupa was posted to No. 16 (Polish) Service Flying Training School for an instructors course, and from September he was there as an instructor. On 30 January 1945 he started a course with the 3 (Pilots) Advanced Flying Unit at South Cerney, then returned to Newton. He left the Polish Air Force in 1946 with the rank of Flight Lieutenant and settled in Britain. He later emigrated to Canada, where he worked in the metallurgical industry. In 1995 Chałupa returned to Poland and lived in Cracow. He died on 24 April 2004 in Katowice, and was buried in Prokocim Cemetery in Cracow. His decorations include the Silver Cross of Virtuti Militari no. 8993, the Cross of Valour and the French Croix de Guerre.

Date & Time	Unit	Aircraft	Score
02.06.1940	GCI/2	Morane MS 406 949/16	⅓-0-0 He 111
08.06.1940 15.30	GCI/2	Morane MS 406 691/12	1-0-0 Bf 109
08.06.1940 19.45	GCI/2	Morane MS 406 691/12	1⅓-0-0 Ju 87
21.08.1940 15.50	302 Squadron	Hurricane I P3934 WX-T	0-1-0 Ju 88
15.09.1940 12.10	302 Squadron	Hurricane I P3923 WX-U	1-1-0 Do 17 (claimed as Do 215)

MARIAN STEFAN CHEŁMECKI, Flying Officer, called 'Maniek', was born on 2 August 1916 in Cracow-Podgórze, into the family of Stanisław and Janina (Aniela). At a young age he moved with his family to Jasło, where he attended Romuald Traugutt Primary School. In 1935 he graduated from Stanisław Leszczyński Secondary School at Jasło, and then from September-December 1935 completed a unitary course at the Infantry Cadet Officers' School in Różan. In January 1936 Chełmecki joined the Air Force Cadet Officers' School at Dęblin, from which he graduated in September 1938 together

Plt Off Marian Chełmecki (17 & 56 Sqns RAF), standing in the middle with Michał Najbicz and Witold Łanowski.

with the 11th Class. After being commissioned and promoted to the rank of Sub-Lieutenant, he was posted to the 123rd Fighter Squadron of the 2nd Air Regiment in Cracow. In October he was posted to the 122nd Fighter Squadron. In August 1939 Chełmecki arrived at the Advanced Flying School at Ułęż as an instructor. During the Polish Campaign in 1939 he was defending Dęblin and Ułęż, together with the ad hoc Instructors' Fighter Flight. After the defeat of Poland he left for Rumania, crossing the border on 17 September. After arriving in Marseilles on 30 October and a short stay in France, he decided to leave for England, where he arrived in the winter of 1939/1940. After receiving the service number 76690 and the rank of Pilot Officer in mid-July, he was posted No. 15 Elementary Flying Training School at Carlisle and in August to No. 6 Operational Training Unit at Sutton Bridge. On 31 August Chełmecki arrived at North Weald, where he joined No. 56 Squadron. On 10 September he was posted to No. 17 Squadron operating from Debden. On 20 March 1941 he was posted to No. 55 Operational Training Unit at Annan, where he served as a flying instructor. Similar duties were given to him in No. 56 and then in No. 60 Operational Training Units. On 5 November 1941 he joined No. 308 (Polish) 'City of Cracow' Squadron, then on 13 June 1942 he took command of B Flight of No. 302 (Polish) 'City of Poznań' Squadron. Between 14 January and 15 February 1943 he led the squadron as acting commander. From 17 May he was posted for staff duty at the HQ of the 2nd Polish Fighter Wing, and then between 21 September 1943 and 26 January 1944 he flew operationally with No. 317 (Polish) 'City of Wilno' Squadron. After leaving this unit he joined the HQ of No. 18 (Polish) Sector RAF, and from 28 August 1944 until 9 May 1945 he commanded No. 317 (Polish) Squadron. Marian Chełmecki then received a posting to the Enemy Aircraft Servicing and Storage Unit at Hamburg-Fühlsbuttel ,and on 8 August 1946 he was released from the Polish Air Force with the rank of Squadron Leader and he decided to return to Poland. He arrived in his home country in 1948 and settled in Zabrze, where he worked as technical specialist for a water supply company. Marian Chełmecki was regularly interrogated by the communist Security Service in connection with his previous service in the West. He retired on 30 June 1979. Chełmecki was married to Janina née Juryś, but the last few years of his life he spent alone. He returned to England for some time, but went back to Poland, where his health deteriorated as he suffered from throat cancer. He died on 28 March 1988 after five months spent in hospital at Gliwice, and was buried at the Roman Catholic City Cemetery in Nowy Sącz. He was decorated with the Silver Cross of Virtuti Militari no. 11089, the Cross of Valour with two bars and the Air Medal.

Date & Time	Unit	Aircraft	Score
08.11.1940 16.00-17.00	17 Squadron	Hurricane I P2794 YB-E	1-0-0 Ju 87
09.11.1940 15.30	17 Squadron	Hurricane I P2794 YB-E	0-0-½ Do 17
11.11.1940	17 Squadron	Hurricane I V6553 YB-J	1-0-0 Bf 109
01.01.1945 09.40-10.20	317 Squadron	Spitfire IX JH-L	1-0-0 Fw 190

TADEUSZ PAWEŁ CHŁOPIK, Flight Lieutenant, was born on 18 June 1908 in Lwów in territory of Poland dominated by the Russian Empire. He went to Cadet Corps No. 1 in Lwów, which he completed in 1927 and then joined the Infantry Cadet Officers' School, from which in 1928 he was transferred to the Air Force Cadet Officers' School at Dęblin. Chłopik graduated in 1930 with 4th class as the seventh best, and after being commissioned in the rank of Sub-Lieutenant was posted to the 42nd Light Bomber Squadron of the 4th Air Regiment in Toruń. Initially he served as an observer, but in August 1933 he completed a flying course at the Air Force Officers' Training Centre at Dęblin.

Upon completion he was attached to the
43rd Army Co-operation Squadron. In July
1934 he completed an Advanced Flying
Course at Grudziądz and joined the 143rd
Fighter Squadron at Toruń. In October
1935 he was sent to Ustianowa, where
he was an instructor with the Military
Gliding Centre. Upon returning to Toruń,
he flew with the 141st Fighter Squadron,
then in November 1936 he was posted to
No. 1 Air Force Training Centre at Dęblin,
as a flying instructor and, between 12
November 1937 and 17 October 1938, the
2nd Training Flight commander. He then
took command of the 3rd Training Flight,
a position he held until the outbreak of
war. During the Polish Campaign in 1939
Chłopik was in charge of a group of cadets,
which he led to Rumania, crossing the

border on 17 September. He was interned there, but managed to escape and
travelled by sea to Marseilles, where he arrived on 29 October. After a short stay
in France, he decided to sail to England, where he arrived on 24 January 1940.
After receiving the service number 76691 and the rank of Flight Lieutenant,
he underwent flying training at No. 6 Operational Training Unit at Sutton
Bridge. In August 1940 he was posted to No. 302 (Polish) 'City of Poznań'
Squadron at Leconfield. On 15 September, during his first mission, Chłopik
shot down one Dornier which he claimed as a Do 215 and participated in the
destruction of a Dornier Do 17. During the second mission he was shot down
himself at 14.45 over North Weald in Hurricane I P2954 WX-E and baled out.
Unfortunately his parachute did not open and he fell to earth at Southend-
on-Sea, Essex. Tadeusz Chłopik was buried at Southend-on-Sea cemetery, in
grave no. 12 238. He was the sixteenth Polish operational pilot killed during
the Battle of Britain and the first No. 302 Squadron pilot killed during the war.
He is also commemorated on the Polish Air Force Memorials at Northolt and
Warsaw-Mokotów. A replica of the Hawker Hurricane I P2954 WX-E in which
he was killed now stands at the entrance to the Imperial War Museum Airfield
at Duxford. Tadeusz Chłopik was posthumously decorated with the Cross of
Valour with bar.

Date & Time	Unit	Aircraft	Score
15.09.1940 12.10	302 Squadron	Hurricane I P2954 WX-E	1-0-0 Do 17 (claimed as Do 215)
15.09.1940 12.10	302 Squadron	Hurricane I P2954 WX-E	½-0-0 Do 17

FRANCISZEK CZAJKOWSKI, Pilot Officer, called 'Czajka', was born on 20 September 1916 in Dzierżno, near Brodnica in Pomerania, which was ruled by the German Empire. He graduated from high school in 1937 and subsequently joined the Air Force Reserve Cadet Officers' School. Upon completion in September 1937, he joined the Air Force Cadet Officers' School at Dęblin. He was commissioned with the 12th class and promoted to the rank of Sub-Lieutenant. In June 1939 Czajkowski was posted to the 141st Fighter Squadron of the 4th Air Regiment at Toruń. During  the Polish Campaign in 1939 he fought with his unit, supporting the 'Pomorze' Army. After the fall of Poland, together with his unit he left on 18 September for Rumania, from where he travelled to France. Czajowski arrived there on 29 October. He decided not to stay there, and volunteered for the Polish Air Force units in Great Britain, where he was sent in January 1940. He received the service number 76692 and the rank of Pilot Officer, and from April started training. In August he was posted to No. 151 Squadron at Martlesham Heath. He claimed three aerial victories while flying with this unit, on 18, 24 and 31 August. On the last day of August he was shot down in a Hurricane I P3301 over the Thames Estuary, and with bullet wounds crash-landed near Foulness. Franciszek Czajkowski was treated at Shoeburyness Hospital, then St Luke's Hospital at Breadford. After a long convalescence, on 16 February 1941 the Polish pilot joined No. 43 Squadron. During an operational mission on 2 June 1941, while chasing a German aircraft, the engine of his Hawker Hurricane II Z2638 developed problems, forcing him to perform a crash-landing near North Berwick. The Pole suffered serious wounds and was taken to hospital in Drem, where a leg had to be amputated. He was sent to the RAF Hospital at Torquay in Devon for further treatment and recovery. On 25 October 1942 the hospital was bombed by a single German aircraft, and as result Franciszek

Czajkowski suffered mortal injuries. He was buried at the Higher Cemetery, Exeter, in grave ZK 90. He is commemorated on the Polish Air Force Memorials at Northolt and Warsaw-Mokotów. He was decorated with the Cross of Valour with bar.

Date & Time	Unit	Aircraft	Score
18.08.1940 17.40	151 Squadron	Hurricane I P3320 DZ-Y	1-0-0 Bf 110
24.08.1940 11.30	151 Squadron	Hurricane I V6537	0-1-0 Bf 109
31.08.1940 10.25	151 Squadron	Hurricane I P3301	0-1-0 Bf 109

JERZY MICHAŁ CZERNIAK, Pilot Officer, was born on 23 January 1913. In 1936 he joined the Air Force Cadet Officers' School at Dęblin and was commissioned in the 11th class on 15 October 1938. Sub-Lieutenant Czerniak was posted to the 123rd Fighter Squadron of the 2nd Air Regiment in Cracow. During the Polish Campaign in 1939 he participated in combat, claiming two aerial victories, including one shared. His unit was attached to the Pursuit Brigade. After the collapse of Poland he left for Rumania, and then travelled to France. Czerniak was posted to the 2nd Flight, Section 4, of the all-Polish 1/145 'City of Warsaw' Squadron, which was formed on 6 April 1940. This unit, also known as GC 1/145, flew Caudron C 714s, with Jerzy Czerniak usually flying an aircraft with the tactical number 6. During hostilities over France he claimed two aerial victories, on 9 and 10 June. On 19 June, together with his comrades, he arrived at the port of La Rochelle, from where he sailed to England the next day, arriving on 21 June. After receiving the service number P-1283 and the rank of Pilot Officer, on 20 August he was posted to No. 302 (Polish) 'City of Poznań' Squadron at Leconfield. He was reposted for further training to No. 5 Operational Training Unit, where between 2-26 September he polished his flying skills. After returning to No. 302 Squadron he participated in the Battle of Britain. On 25 January 1941 he was posted to No. 315 (Polish)

'City of Dęblin' Squadron. On 9 August 1941 he flew an operational sortie over Boulogne when he was shot down by a German fighter. Still in the cockpit of the Spitfire IIB P8506 PK-B, he went down into the sea a few kilometres from the French coast. His body was never found. Jerzy Czerniak is commemorated on the Polish Air Force Memorials at Northolt and Warsaw-Mokotów. His decorations included the Cross of Valour with two bars.

Date & Time	Unit	Aircraft	Score
01.09.1939	123rd Squadron	PZL P.7a	⅓-0-0 He 111
06.09.1939	123rd Squadron	PZL P.7a	1-1-0 Bf 110
09.06.1940	1/145 Squadron	Caudron CR. 714	1-0-0 Bf 109
10.06.1940	1/145 Squadron	Caudron CR. 714	1-0-0 Do 17

JAN TADEUSZ CZERNY, Flight Lieutenant, was born on 2 January 1908 in Strzemieszyce in the Silesian part of Poland ruled then by the Russian Empire. He grew up in the family of Edmund and Maria née Wójcik. He joined No. 1 Cadet Corps at Lwów, from which he graduated in 1926. Next year he was accepted to the Air Force Officers' School at Dęblin (later the Air Force Cadet Officers' School) and commissioned on 15 August 1929 (3rd class) as an observer. In the rank of Sub-Lieutenant, he was posted to the 62nd Light Bomber Squadron of the 6th Air Regiment in Lwów. Between May and August 1931 Czerny completed a flying training course at the Air Force Officer's Training Centre at Dęblin. Later he was posted to the 64th Light Bomber Squadron of the same 6th Air Regiment. From May to July 1932 he undertook training on the Advanced Flying Course at Grudziądz. In September 1932 Czerny was moved to the 121st Fighter Squadron of the 2nd Air Regiment at Cracow, then in April 1934 he completed a flying instructors' course at the Air Force Officers' Training Centre at Dęblin. He was appointed a flying instructor for the Advanced Flying Course at Grudziądz. In September 1934 he was back with the 2nd Air Regiment with a posting to the 121st Fighter Squadron. In May 1936 he was posted to the 123rd Fighter Squadron of the same regiment.

Czerny was posted back to Dęblin, where from November 1936 he served as commander of the No. 3 Flying Training Flight. In September 1939 he was defending the Air Force Cadet Officers' School together with other instructors who formed a fighter flight. He then evacuated some of the school's aircraft, including PZL P.23 'Karaś'. On 17 September he crossed the Rumanian border and was interned. Czerny managed to escape and travelled to France, arriving at Marseilles on 29 October. Almost instantly he volunteered to sail to England to continue the fight. After arriving in Britain in early January 1940, Jan Czerny received the service number 76789 and after a period of training he was posted to No. 302 (Polish) 'City of Poznań' Squadron. He arrived at Leconfield on 20 August; however, on 2 September he was reposted to No. 5 Operational Training Unit for further training. He was back on 26 September and participated in the Battle of Britain. On 29 October Flight Lieutenant James Thomson collided in midair with the Hurricane I V6923 WX-U which was flown by Czerny, and the Polish pilot had to force-land. In December 1940, due to disagreement with British officers, he left the squadron, being posted to No. 1 (Polish) Flying Training School at Hucknall. In June 1941 he was sent for instructors' training at Upavon, and then on 27 October he arrived at No. 25 (Polish) Elementary Flying Training School at Hucknall. Czerny stayed at Hucknall until the Polish school was disbanded in November 1945. He was then posted to No. 16 Service Flying Training School at Newton until September 1946, when he was demobilized with the rank of Flight Lieutenant. Jan Czerny decided to return to Poland, where he arrived in 1947, settling in his hometown of Strzemieszyce. He moved to Gliwice, where he lived and worked in education. He died on 18 February 1991 and was buried in Lipowy Cemetery at Gliwice in the family grave alongside his wife Anna. He was decorated with the Cross of Valour and bar, the Silver Cross of Merit with Swords and the British Air Force Cross. After the war he received the Knight's Cross of Polonia Restituta.

TADEUSZ CZERWIŃSKI, Flying Officer, was born on 17 February 1910 at Grocholica near Lublin, an area of Poland ruled by the Russian Empire. After graduating from high school in 1931 he joined the Infantry Cadet Officers' School. After being commissioned on 15 August 1934 he was posted to the 15th Infantry Regiment. He decided to follow his dream of being a pilot, so from August 1934 until July 1935 he undertook a flying course at No. 1 Air Force Training Centre at Dęblin, after which he was posted to the 1st Air Regiment at Warsaw. In the summer 1936 Czerwiński completed an Advanced Flying Course at Grudziądz, then received a posting to the 113th Fighter Squadron of the 1st Air Regiment at Warsaw. He flew with this unit between August 1936 and January 1938. From September until December

1937 he completed a flying instructor course, and then from January 1938 he served as a flying instructor at No. 1 Air Force Training Centre at Dęblin. From January 1939 he led a platoon of cadet officers. During the Polish Campaign in 1939 he served in an ad hoc instructors' flight that was defending Dęblin, then helped to evacuate cadet officers. His group of cadet officers crossed the Rumanian border on 17 September. After a short internment Czerwiński left Rumania, travelling to France by sea. He arrived at Marseilles on 12 November. He was posted to lead the 3rd Section of the 1st Flight of the all-Polish 1/145 'City of Warsaw' Squadron,

which was formed on 6 April 1940. This unit, also known as GC 1/145, flew Caudron C 714s, with Tadeusz Czerwiński usually flying an aircraft with the tactical number 7. During hostilities over France he claimed two aerial victories on 8 June. On 19 June, together with his comrades, he arrived at La Rochelle port, from where he sailed to England the next day, arriving on 21 June. Upon arrival he received the service number P-1290 and was posted for conversion training. In July 1940 Flying Officer Czerwiński joined No. 302 (Polish) 'City of Poznań' Squadron at Leconfield. During the Battle of Britain he claimed one aerial victory, gained on 15 September. On 13 December he was appointed 'B' Flight commander, then on 3 June 1941 was posted for rest to No. 55 Operational Training Unit at Usworth as an instructor. He was then reposted to No. 58 Operational Training Unit at Grangemouth, where between 19 November 1941 and 8 January 1942 he served as a flying instructor. Then he was posted to No. 306 (Polish) 'City of Toruń' Squadron, where he became 'A' Flight commander. On 15 April 1942 Czerwiński took command of the whole squadron. Soon after, on 26 April, he claimed his last aerial victory. On 22 August 1942 Czerwiński led his squadron in an attack on St Omer aerodrome in France during Operation Rhubarb, when his Spitfire VB EN826 UZ-C was hit by ground fire, alongside three other 306 Squadron aircraft. Squadron Leader Czerwiński was killed, and was buried in Longuennesse Cemetery in France, in grave no. 16, row A, plot 8. He is commemorated on the Polish Air Force Memorials at Northolt and Warsaw-Mokotów. He was decorated with the Cross of Valour with three bars.

Date & Time	Unit	Aircraft	Score
08.06.1940	1/145 Squadron	Caudron CR. 714	2-0-0 Bf 109
15.09.1940 12.10	302 Squadron	Hurricane I V6571 WX-Q	1-0-0 Do 17
26.04.1942 18.00	306 Squadron	Spitfire VB AR346 UZ-J	1-0-0 Fw 190

STANISŁAW JAN CZTERNASTEK, Pilot Officer, was born on 6 May 1916 in Przemyśl, a Polish town within the Austro-Hungarian Empire. He grew up in the family of Jan and Anna née Szymakowska. He was educated at St Jan Kanty Primary School and Kazimierz Morawski Secondary School, both in Przemyśl. After graduation in 1934 he was accepted for the Law Faculty of Jan Kazimierz University in Lwów. In the meantime, Czternastek flew gliders at Bezmiechowa and Ustianowa, obtaining three categories: A, B and C. After one year of studying he decided to join the army. On 1 September 1936 he was accepted to the Infantry Cadet Officers' School at Różan, then from 3 January 1937 he trained at the Air Force Cadet Officers' School at Dęblin. Between 6 April and 10 June 1939 he completed an Advanced Flying Course at Ułęż, and alongside the rest of the 12th class was commissioned without official ceremony. Due to the dangerous political situation, all his colleagues were posted to air regiments on 18 June 1939. He was promoted to the rank of Sub-Lieutenant, serving in the 2nd Air Regiment, and was posted to the 123rd Fighter Squadron. During the Polish Campaign in 1939 he fought with his squadron as part of the Pursuit Brigade. On 1 September he was shot down, but baled out and landed near Nowy Dwór Mazowiecki. After the Soviet attack on Poland, he was evacuated from Petlikowice airfield to Rumania, crossing the border at Kuty on the night 18/19 September. After a short internment he travelled to the port of Balchik, from where he sailed to France, arriving at Marseilles on 30 November. Czternastek decided to go to England, leaving France on 28 December. After arrival in Britain he was sent to RAF Eastchurch. Receiving the service number 76693 and the rank of Pilot Officer, on 2 September 1940 he was sent to No. 15 Elementary Flying Training School at Carlisle and then to No. 6 Operational Training Unit at Sutton Bridge.

On 12 October Czternastek joined No. 32 Squadron, but in December he was transferred to No. 615 Squadron. On 5 February 1941 he participated in an operational flight. While on his way back, in thick fog, he collided with another Polish pilot, Pilot Officer Bronisław Wydrowski, who was badly injured. The Hawker Hurricane I V7598 KW-S flown by Flying Officer Czternastek crashed near Appleton Farm, Marlon, near Dover. Both pilots baled out: Wydrowski's parachute did not open fully, whilst Czternastek's did not open at all and he was killed. He was buried at Hawkinge Cemetery, in grave no. 037. Posthumously promoted to the rank of Lieutenant, he is commemorated on the Polish Air Force Memorials at Northolt and Warsaw-Mokotów.

D

JAN KAZIMIERZ MICHAŁ ANTONI DASZEWSKI, Pilot Officer, called 'Długi Joe' (Long Joe) or 'Pan Antoś' (Mr Tony), was born on 5 April 1916 at Kiev in the Russian Empire. He grew up in the family of Jan Daszewski senior. After returning to Poland, in 1936 he was accepted to the Air Force Cadet Officers' School at Dęblin, from which he graduated on 15 October 1938 with the 11th class. Sub-Lieutenant Daszewski was posted to the 112th Fighter Squadron of the 1st Air Regiment at Warsaw. He took part in the Polish Campaign in 1939, his unit being attached to the Pursuit Brigade. On 1 September Daszewski claimed an aerial victory of a Ju 87. After the fall of Poland he was evacuated and crossed the Rumanian border on 18 September. Travelling to France, he trained at Lyon-Bron. Initially he was chosen to join fighter section DAT led by Lieutenant Wacław Łapkowski, but was eventually posted to a similar unit, also known as 'Chimney Flight', under the command of Captain Tadeusz Opulski. On 17 May 1940 he arrived at Romorantin, where his unit was to defend the factory making Morane aircraft. During the French campaign he claimed one victory of a Heinkel He 111 destroyed on 5 June, although other sources state that on 4 June he also shot down a French Loire-Nieuport 411 by mistake. The Polish pilot thought that he was aiming at a Ju 87. On 18 June he and his colleagues left Romorantin for St Jean de Luz, from where they travelled to England on 21 June on the ship *Arandora Star*. Upon arrival Daszewski was given the service number P-1503 and the rank of Pilot Officer. Initially he was considered for the first basic core of No. 302 (Polish) Squadron, but on 2 August he joined No. 303 (Polish) 'Tadeusz Kościuszko. City of Warsaw' Squadron at Northolt. Despite claiming two victories on 7 September, he was shot down while flying Hurricane I P3890 RF-N over the Thames Estuary. Daszewski was badly wounded, yet managed to bale out. He was taken to Waldershire Hospital at Selstead and was able to rejoin his squadron in December. In September 1941 he was posted to No. 3 Ferry Pilots Pool, but by the end of the same month he was back at No. 303 Squadron. On 22 November he was given command of 'B' Flight, then on 13 December he was wounded again when his Spitfire VB AB936 RF-V was hit over France. The Polish pilot managed to return to base. On 4 April 1942 he flew during Operation Circus 119 in the area of Calais, when his formation was attacked by the I Gruppe of JG26. Although his fate is uncertain, it is believed that he was shot down and went into the sea together with his Spitfire VB AD455 RF-V. His colleagues saw two Spitfires going down. One crashed into the sea 15 miles north-east of Calais; the pilot of the second baled out close to the French coast but was not seen again. Flight Lieutenant Jan Daszewski's body was never found. He is commemorated on the Polish Air Force Memorials at Northolt and Warsaw-Mokotów. He was decorated with the Silver Cross of Virtuti Militari no. 8821, the Cross of Valour and three bars and the Croix de Guerre.

Date & Time	Unit	Aircraft	Score
01.09.1939	112th Squadron	PZL P.11	1-0-0 Ju 87
01.06.1940	Opulski Section	Morane MS 406	1-0-0 He 111
07.09.1940 17.00	303 Squadron	Hurricane I P3890 RF-N	1-1-0 Do 17 (claimed as Do 215)
20.04.1941 11.00	303 Squadron	Spitfire II P8041 RF-E	0-1-0 Bf 109

MARIAN BOGUSŁAW DOMAGAŁA, Sergeant, was born on 23 March 1909 at Lublin, in territory of Poland ruled by the Russian Empire. In 1924 he completed secondary school, then started education at the Teachers' Seminar, where he spent two years. Although being interested in animal breeding, swimming or even working as bar tender, between 15 January 1926 and 10 December 1929 he was employed as an aircraft technician by the Plage and Laśkiewicz aircraft factory at Lublin. While at Lublin he undertook flying training at the local aero club. He joined the military service in 1929, and next year was posted to the Air Force Battalion at Poznań. In 1931 Domagała was posted to the Central NCO

Pilot School at Bydgoszcz, where he completed his pilot's training. After this he was sent to the 6th Air Regiment at Lwów. In 1933 he arrived at Grudziądz, where he completed an Advanced Flying Course and the following year was posted to the 132nd Fighter Squadron of the 3rd Air Regiment at Poznań. Then he was transferred to the 133rd Fighter Squadron and in 1936 to the Air Force Officers' Training Centre at Dęblin for instructor duty. In the spring of 1939, as Platoon Commander, he was posted to the 161st Fighter Squadron of the 6th Air Regiment at Lwów. During the Polish Campaign his III/6 Fighter Wing supported 'Łódź' Army. On 2 September Domagała was shot down while taking off by a Bf 110. Although his aircraft PZL P.11c caught fire, he survived, and after landing jumped into another aircraft and continued the mission. On 12 September he crashed in RWD-8 at Łuck airfield, but survived. After the collapse of Poland, via Rumania he was evacuated to France, where his sister Paulina lived. He arrived in Britain in March 1940, receiving the service number 780671 and the rank of Sergeant. Despite his qualification he was initially considered for the 2nd Polish bomber squadron to be formed in Britain, then his name appeared on the list of airmen who were supposed to join No. 302 Squadron. Others on the list were: Jan Daszewski, Marian Duryasz, Stanisław Duszyński, Jan Falkowski, Mirosław Ferić, Juliusz Frey, Aleksander Gabszewicz, Paweł Gallus, Antoni Głowacki, Feliks Gmur, Bohdan Grzeszczak, Zdzisław Henneberg, Józef Jeka, Stanisław Karubin, Zygmunt Klein, Zdzisław Krasnodębski, Józef Kwieciński, Wacław Łapkowski, Witold Łokuciewski, Kazimierz Łukaszewicz, Tadeusz Nowak, Bolesław Olewiński,

Antoni Ostowicz, Wilhelm Pankratz, Ludwik Paszkiewicz, Marian Pisarek, Karol Pniak, Jan Rogowski, Włodzimierz Samoliński, Stanisław Skalski, Michał Stęborowski, Józef Szlagowski, Leon Świtoń, Stefan Witorzeńć, Stefan Wójtowicz, Kazimierz Wünsche, Jan Zumbach and Walerian Żak. All these pilots were posted either to RAF squadrons or to No. 303 Squadron. After training on Hurricanes, Domagała was posted to No. 238 Squadron at Middle Wallop. He arrived there on 5 August 1940. During the Battle of Britain he claimed three aerial victories, on 8 and 11 August. On 6 April 1941 he was posted to No. 302 (Polish) 'City of Poznań' Squadron, and on 8 May was shot down in combat while flying Hurricane II Z2523 WX-G. On 19 September he was reposted to No. 317 (Polish) 'City of Wilno' Squadron. From 5 February 1942 Domagała served as a flying instructor with No. 58 Operational Training Unit at Grangemouth, then on 1 June 1942 was commissioned, receiving the officer's service number P-1904. At the end of August he attended a flying instructors' course at No. 2 Flying Instructors' School at Montrose. In December he was sent to No. 25 (Polish) Elementary Flying Training School at Hucknall. Upon completing a twin-engine conversion course on 12 March he continued serving as an instructor. Between 1 January 1945 and May 1945 Domagała was an instructor pilot at No. 16 (Polish) Service Flying Training School at Newton. He was demobilized with the rank of Flight Lieutenant in December 1946. After deciding not to return to a Poland ruled by a pro-Soviet regime, he settled in Scotland. He died in Glasgow on 27 January 1991. He was awarded the Cross of Valour and two bars.

Date & Time	Unit	Aircraft	Score
08.08.1940 12.30	238 Squadron	Hurricane I P2989	1-0-0 Bf 109
08.08.1940 12.30	238 Squadron	Hurricane I P2989	1-0-0 Bf 110
11.08.1940 10.45	238 Squadron	Hurricane I P2989	1-0-0 Bf 109

BOLESŁAW HENRYK DROBIŃSKI, Pilot Officer, called 'Ski' or 'Ghandi' (as reference to his slim silhouette that reminded of Mahatma Gandhi, atlhough his nickname was misspelled), was born on 23 October 1918 at Ostroróg nad Horyniem, near Zdołbunów in Wołyń (Volhynia) Voivodship, the son of Felicjan Drobiński and Irena née Bakłanowska. His family moved to Łuck. On 25 May 1937 he graduated from Stanisław Konarski State High School at Dubno. While at school, in 1934 he undertook a gliding course at Goleszów, near Cieszyn. On 21 September 1937 he completed an Infantry Reserve Cadet Officers' Course with the 24th Infantry Regiment at Łuck, and on 1 January 1938 arrived at the Air Force Cadet Officers' School at Dęblin. The education programme for the 13th class had been accelerated due to the political situation, and Drobiński finished school after his second instead of his third year, being promoted to the rank of Sub-Lieutenant on 1 September 1939. He remained at No. 1 Air Force Officers' Training Centre at Dęblin, where he was ordered by Captain Stanisław Brzezina to evacuate to Rumania to collect British aircraft and to return to Poland. After the fall of Poland,

on 17 September Drobiński crossed the Rumanian border at Śniatyń. After a short internment at Slatina camp he escaped to Bucharest. From 6-7 October he stayed in Beograd, Yugoslavia, from where by train he travelled to Modena, Italy, arriving there on 9 October. The day after, Drobiński was in France, reporting to Paris Le Bourget on 10 October. Deciding to travel on to Britain, he arrived there on 27 January 1940, being posted to RAF Eastchurch, where he received the service number 76731 and the rank of Pilot Officer. On 30 May he was moved to the Polish Air Force Wing of No. 3 School of Technical Training at Blackpool, then on 17 July to No. 1 School of Army Co-operation at Old Sarum. On 30 July Drobiński was transferred to No. 7 Operational Training Unit at Hawarden, from where on 12 August 194 he was posted to No. 65 Squadron based at Hornchurch. After the Battle of Britain he remained with No. 65 Squadron, and on 15 February 1941 he had a flying accident in the Spitfire II P7829. On 2 March 1941 he was posted to No. 303 (Polish) 'Tadeusz Kościuszko. City of Warsaw' Squadron. During his service in 303 Squadron he claimed over six aerial victories, achieving the status of an ace. On 18 March 1942 Drobiński was posted for rest as an instructor at No. 58 Operational Training Unit at Grangemouth, returning to his squadron on 10 August 1942. On 15 December he was appointed 'A' Flight commander. On 8 April 1943 he was posted back to No. 58 Operational Training Unit as an instructor, and then on 10 October to No. 61 Operational Training Unit. On 18 October he arrived at No. 317 (Polish) 'City of Wilno' Squadron, taking command of 'B' Flight. The same year he married Marjorie Lewis. In April 1944 Drobiński was appointed Adjutant of the Polish Minister of Defence, then on 28 September he took

command of No. 303 (Polish) Squadron. He left this post on 1 February 1946, being posted to No. 61 Operational Training Unit at Keevil as an instructor, but from 20 March 1946 he served as Polish Liaison Officer at the HQ of No. 11 Group RAF. On 20 January 1947 he was transferred to No. 5 Polish Resettlement Unit. Squadron Leader Bolesław Drobiński was demobilized on 23 January 1947. Together with his wife he emigrated to California in United States, where he worked in the oil company established by his parents in law, but in 1954 he returned to Britain, where he settled at Chiddingfold, Surrey, raising three children. He ran a farm breeding turkeys and cows. During his retirement he was active within the Polish Air Force Association, receiving the rank of Polish Lieutenant Colonel. Together with Ludwik Martel he was also one of the technical advisers for Guy Hamilton's 1969 film, 'Battle of Britain'. He died of cancer on 26 July 1995 and was cremated. His cremation stone can be found at St Teresa of Avila Roman Catholic Church, Chiddingford. He was decorated with the Silver Cross of Virtuti Militari no. 9176, the Cross of Valour and three bars and the British Distinguished Flying Cross. The MiG 29 no.89 of the 23rd Tactical Air Base at Mińsk Mazowiecki has his portrait painted on its tail.

Date & Time	Unit	Aircraft	Score
18.06.1941 18.30	303 Squadron	Spitfire II P8335 RF-R	2-0-0 Bf 109
21.06.1941 12.35	303 Squadron	Spitfire II P8335 RF-R	1-0-0 Bf 109
22.06.1941 16.10	303 Squadron	Spitfire II P8335 RF-R	1-0-0 Bf 109
25.06.1941 12.30	303 Squadron	Spitfire II P8335 RF-R	1-0-0 Bf 109
03.07.1941 16.00	303 Squadron	Spitfire II P8461 RF-R	1-0-0 Bf 109
06.07.1941 09.45	303 Squadron	Spitfire II P8461 RF-R	0-⅓-0 Bf 109
24.10.1941 15.10	303 Squadron	Spitfire VB AB929 RF-R	0-1-0 Bf 109
13.02.1942 15.10	303 Squadron	Spitfire VB AB929 RF-R	1-0-0 Bf 109

MARIAN DURYASZ, Flying Officer, was born on 14 December 1911 at Karolino near Serock in the territory of Poland ruled by the Russian Empire, in the family of Szymon and Wanda née Sujkowska. After graduating from the local secondary school, in 1927 he joined the Cadet Corps at Chełmno and passed A-levels in 1932. He was accepted to the Air Force Cadet Officers' School at Dęblin. Duryasz was commissioned in the 7th class, and on 15 August 1934 in the rank of Sub-Lieutenant was posted to the 62nd Light Bomber Squadron of the 6th Air Regiment in Lwów. In 1935 he returned to Air Force Officers' Training Centre at Dęblin for the flying course for pilots,

and after returning he flew as a pilot of the 65th Light Bomber Squadron. Between April and July 1936 he participated in an Advanced Flying Course at Grudziądz, after which he was back with the 6th Air Regiment. He had a flying accident on 18 July 1936 while flying a Breguet XIX, with instructor Lieutenant Mieczysław Pronaszko. He was then posted to the 66th Army Co-operation Squadron within the same regiment, and during this time he had another accident in a Lublin R XIIID. Both Duryasz and Lieutenant Kazimierz Dobrowolski (observer) were injured. In November 1936 he was posted to the 133rd Fighter Squadron of the 3rd Air Regiment at Poznań, then in November 1937 was transferred back to the 6th Air Regiment, where he served as deputy commander of the 162nd Fighter Squadron. In November 1938 he was posted to Grudziądz, where he served as a flying instructor. In March 1939, together with the school, he was moved to Ułęż. During the Polish Campaign he flew PZL P.7s with the instructors' flight organized to defend Dęblin, and was then sent to Rumania to collect aircraft which were supposed to arrive there from France and Great Britain, and to bring them back to Poland. On 17 September he crossed the Rumanian border but continued his journey to France. Reaching France on 13 October, he was briefly allocated to Le Bourget, Paris. He decided to continue his travels, and on 27 January 1940 he arrived in England at RAF Eastchurch, where he received the service number 76750 and the rank of Flying Officer. On 7 July Duryasz was posted to No. 15 Elementary Flying Training School at Carlisle, then twelve days later to No. 6 Operational Training Unit at Sutton Bridge. Initially he was considered for the first basic core of No. 302 (Polish) Squadron. On 17 August he was posted to No. 213 Squadron stationed at Exeter. During the Battle of Britain he claimed three aerial victories. Due to health problems he was posted to No. 302 (Polish) 'City of Poznań' Squadron, serving as operations room controller. Occasionally he accompanied his colleagues during operational missions. On 23 January 1942 he was posted to No. 317 (Polish) 'City of Wilno' Squadron, where he continued as operations room controller, eventually taking command of 'B' Flight on 16 March. On 1 June he was posted to No. 58 Operational Training Unit at Grangemouth, where he served as flying instructor, then after two weeks he was accepted to the Polish War College. On 14 June 1943 he was posted to No. 316 (Polish) 'City of Warsaw' Squadron, then after six months he started educational duty at the Polish Air Force Staff College. On 14 January 1944 he was posted once more to No. 302 (Polish) Squadron, from where on 23 May he was reposted to No. 308 (Polish) 'City of Cracow' Squadron, where he took command of 'B' Flight. He was back in No. 302 Squadron on 5 July, taking command of the whole squadron. On 22 September he was slightly injured by ground fire while flying Spitfire IX ML136 WX-L (aircraft with the individual 'L' letter were assigned for 302 Squadron commanders). On 30 January 1945 Marian Duryasz was transferred to HQ of the 2nd TAF, which later was changed to BAFO. In February 1946 he took command of the 3rd Polish Fighter Wing, based in Britain. After leaving the Polish Air Force with the rank of Acting Wing Commander, he decided to return to Poland, where he arrived on 30 July 1946. Initially he was accepted to the People's Polish Forces, serving in the communist Air Force. From 25 August 1947 until April 1950 he was assistant section director of the 2nd Department of the General Staff. After being expelled from the forces as a Western Front veteran, he worked as a storekeeper with the Polish National Railway. After political changes in October 1956 he returned to military service. Between November 1963 and November 1964 he was a member of the International Commission of Control and Supervision in Vietnam. Marian Duryasz retired on 24 April 1970, although he continued to work in Polish agricultural aviation in Egypt. He was also an active member of the Aviation Seniors Club at Warsaw. Colonel Marian Duryasz died on 22 March 1993 and was buried in the Powązki Military Cemetery, Warsaw. He was decorated with the Silver Cross of Virtuti Militari no. 10764, the Cross of Valour and two bars, the British Distinguished Flying Cross and Knight's Cross of Polonia Restituta.

Date & Time	Unit	Aircraft	Score
11.09.1940 16.30	213 Squadron	Hurricane I P3780 AK-A	1-0-0 Bf 110
15.09.1940 14.25	213 Squadron	Hurricane I AK-G	1-0-0 Do 17
26.09.1940 16.30	213 Squadron	Hurricane I AK-I	0-1-0 He 111
28.04.1941 11.25	317 Squadron	Spitfire VB AR332 JH-S	1-0-0 Fw 190

STANISŁAW DUSZYŃSKI, Sergeant, was born on 28 October 1915 at Otłoczyn near Toruń in the territory of Poland occupied by the German Empire. He completed his primary education at Aleksandrów Kujawski. In 1931 we was accepted to the Infantry NCO School for Minors, which he completed the following year. Between December 1934 and September 1936 he served in the 71st Infantry Regiment at Zambrów with the rank of Corporal. During the summer 1936 Duszyński undertook a glider course at the Military Gliding Centre at Ustianowa, and from September 1936 he served in 4th Air Regiment at Toruń, where within Training Flight he underwent a basic pilot's course. Between September and

November 1937 he was sent to Grudziądz, where he completed an Advanced Flying Course, and then in November 1937 was posted to the 142nd Fighter Squadron of the 4th Air Regiment at Toruń. During this time he was engaged to Czesława Wyszyńska. In April 1939 he was posted to Ułęż, where he served as a flying instructor at the Advanced Flying Course. In September 1939 he did not participate in combat, but was involved in the evacuation of No. 1 Air Force Training Centre in Dęblin, travelling towards the Rumanian border. He crossed the border at Kuty on 17 September and was interned. After escaping he was kept in the Babadag camp, from which he escaped on 14 October. He left Rumania, travelling to France, and arrived at Marseilles on 12 November. He decided to go on to Britain, seeing no opportunity to continue the fight in France. He arrived in England on 19 February 1940, being posted to RAF

Eastchurch, where he received the service number 780674 and the rank of Sergeant. After conversion to the British aircraft and operational training at No. 6 Operational Training Unit at Sutton Bridge, on 2 September 1940 he was posted to No. 238 Squadron stationed at Middle Wallop. Initially he was considered for the first basic core of No. 302 (Polish) Squadron. On 11 September he flew with his squadron to engage with a German formation over Croydon. His Hurricane I R2682 was shot down over Romney Marsh in Kent, crashing at Little Scotney Farm, Lydd. He was reported missing. He was the fifteenth Polish operational pilot killed during the Battle of Britain. On 13 January 1973 the wreckage of his aircraft was discovered alongside his parachute, shoe, fragments of uniform and personal documents, but the pilot's remains were buried as unknown in an unspecified place. Other sources state that his remains were never found. Stanisław Duszyński is commemorated on the Polish Air Force Memorials at Northolt and Warsaw-Mokotów.

F

JAN PAWEŁ FALKOWSKI, Flying Officer, called 'Koń' (horse), was born on 26 June 1912 at the Polish family estate at Pohulanka near Dyneburg in Latvia. At the age of 2 he went to Siberia with his parents, who organized the repatriation of Poles. They settled at Petropavlovsk. During the revolutionary Bolshevik period his father was shot dead, and his mother died later. Falkowski was taken to the free Poland by a friend, and after a trip lasting 18 months he arrived at Warsaw on 23 September 1922. After finishing primary school he went to a private secondary school, and then studied at the Agricultural Institute at the Stefan  Batory University in Wilno. In the summer of 1932 he went to Lwów, where he participated in a gliding course, after which he completed his studies. In 1934 Falkowski was accepted to the Air Force Cadet Officers' School at Dęblin. He was commissioned on 15 October 1936 alongside the 9th class, and as a Sub-Lieutenant was posted to the 142nd Fighter Squadron of the 4th Air Regiment at Toruń. While flying with this unit he had an accident in a PZL P.7 on 15 November 1937. From 1 January 1939 Falkowski was posted back to Dęblin, where he served as a flying instructor with the Air Force Cadet Officers' School. During the Polish Campaign in 1939 he was responsible for the evacuation of aircraft towards Sokal. During this flight he was attacked by several Bf 109s while sitting in an unarmed PWS-26. He went to Rumania via the Kuty border crossing. Using a stolen car he travelled to Bucharest, where he obtained false documents and continued his trip via Yugoslavia and Italy. On 6 October he arrived in France. After conversion on French fighters at Lyon, he was appointed a flying instructor. On 30 May 1940 Falkowski was posted to Cognac, where he led a Polish Fighter Section of DAT (*Défense Aérien du Territoire*) defending the town. They flew Marcel Bloch MB 152s. On 19 June they were ordered to fly across the Channel, but the state of the aircraft was poor, so Falkowski commanded them to travel by train to Bordeaux, Biarritz and then to St Jean de Luz, from where on 23 June they sailed to England on the Polish ship *Batory*. After receiving the service number P-0493 and the rank of Flying Officer, he was posted for training and on 12 October he joined No. 32 Squadron based at Acklington. Initially he was considered for the first basic core of No. 302 (Polish) Squadron. During a night interception on 16 January 1941 he claimed the destruction of an He 111, but was shot down himself. He baled out and broke a leg. Falkowski returned to No. 32 Squadron on 21 April 1941, then on 29 July he was posted to No. 315 (Polish) 'City of Dęblin' Squadron, where he took command of 'B' Flight. Subsequently, from 22 September he commanded 'A' Flight, then on 12 April 1942 he once more took command of 'B' Flight. On 20 June he left for the Polish Air Force Staff College at Peebles, Scotland. Upon completion he served in the Polish Air Force Inspectorate in London, and in May 1943 he was posted to No. 316 (Polish) 'City of Warsaw' Squadron, where on 11 June he had a landing accident in Spitfire IX BS463 SZ-G. From 4 July 1943 he commanded No. 303 (Polish) 'Tadeusz Kościuszko City of Warsaw' Squadron, then from 22 November Falkowski served at the HQ of No. 11 Group RAF and then at HQ of No. 84 Group RAF. On 30 January 1945 he was appointed commander of the 3rd Polish Fighter Wing at RAF Coltishall. On 9 March 1945 he was shot down by anti-aircraft artillery while flying over The Hague in Spitfire IX BS281 RF-C and baled out. While parachuting he was shot in the leg. After landing he was captured by German soldiers. He was kept in various places, then while being transported by train he escaped at Zwolle railway station and awaited Allied soldiers. Eventually he was rescued by the Canadians and evacuated behind the front line, and on 9 May he returned to England. With the rank of Acting Wing Commander he was released from the Polish Air Force, and in 1948 emigrated to Canada, settling on a farm near Toronto. Later he returned to flying, obtaining work as a flying instructor at a civil school for pilots. On 9 August 1962, while flying a Mooney aircraft, he landed on marshland with his wife, her son and friend on board. He was miraculously found and saved. In 1965 he published his wartime memoirs, *With the Wind in My Face*. At this time he returned to Poland, visiting Warsaw. After retirement he lived at Peterborough, Ontario, where he died on 27 July 2001, holding the Polish rank of Colonel. He was decorated with the Silver Cross of Virtuti Militari no. 9338, the Cross of Valour and three bars and the British Distinguished Flying Cross.

Date & Time	Unit	Aircraft	Score
16.01.1941 19.40	32 Squadron	Hurricane II Z2984	1-0-0 He 111
14.08.1941 17.50	315 Squadron	Spitfire II P8540 PK-K	1-0-0 Bf 109
19.08.1941 1 8.30	315 Squadron	Spitfire II P8540 PK-K	1-0-0 Bf 109
21.08.1941 14.00	315 Squadron	Spitfire II P8648 PK-M	1-0-0 Bf 109
16.09.1941 18.30	315 Squadron	Spitfire VB W3619 PK-F	1-0-0 Bf 109
21.09.1941 15.30	315 Squadron	Spitfire VB W3619 PK-F	1-0-0 Fw 190 (claimed as MC.200)
24.10.1941 15.20	315 Squadron	Spitfire VB W3944 PK-A	1-0-0 Bf 109
22.08.1943 19.10	303 Squadron	Spitfire IX MA304 RF-F	1-0-0 Fw 190
06.09.1943 18.00	303 Squadron	Spitfire IX MA524 RF-F	1-0-0 Fw 190
23.09.1943 16.20	303 Squadron	Spitfire IX MA524 RF-F	1-0-0 Fw 190

MIROSŁAW STANISŁAW FERIĆ, Pilot Officer, called 'Ox' or 'Szkot' (Scotsman), was born on 17 June 1915 at Travnik near Sarajevo in Bosnia-Herzegovina within Austro-Hungarian Empire, the son of Ivan Ferić and Zofia née Babiańska. Both his parents were teachers. He also had a brother, Zwonimir. Ivan Ferić was killed during the First World War, and in 1919 Zofia decided to return with her sons to her native and by then free Poland. They settled at Ostrów Wielkopolski, where Mirosław attended Tadeusz Kościuszko Primary School, then the National High School for Boys. In May 1935 he passed A-level exams and went to the Infantry Cadet Officers' School at Różan, where he underwent a unitary

course. In 1936 he was accepted to the Air
Force Cadet Officers' School at Dęblin, and
after two years, on 15 October 1938, he was
commissioned with the 11th class. In the rank
of Sub-Lieutenant he was posted to the 111th
Fighter Squadron of the 1st Air Regiment at
Warsaw. His unit was attached to the Pursuit
Brigade. Ferić fought during the Polish
Campaign in 1939, claiming two victories
on 1 and 3 September. On 3 September he
was shot down by a Bf 110 over Rembertów-
Warsaw and baled out from his PZL P.11c
no. 4. Wounded, he landed near Okuniewo
and Mnichów. He continued fighting until
the fall of Poland, then flew to Rumania on
17 September, landing at Cernâuti. After a

short internment at Focsani camp, he escaped, travelling to the port of Balcic
on the Black Sea. From there, on 15 October on board the Greek ship *Aghios
Nikolaos* he sailed to Beirut, and from there on the *Ville de Strasbourg* he went
to Marseilles, arriving on 29 October. He was allocated to Salon, then in mid-
December was transferred to the Polish Air Force Centre at Lyon-Bron, where
he started conversion training on French aircraft, flying Morane Saulnier MS
406s fighters. On 11 May 1940 he was posted to No. I Chimney Section under
command of Major Zdzisław Krasnodębski, but on 19 May was ordered back to
Lyon-Bron. Ferić was then posted to No. III Chimney Section commanded by
Captain Kazimierz Kuzian. On 14 June he flew to La Rochelle, from where five
days later he sailed to England, arriving on 23 June at Liverpool. He received
the service number P-1387 and the rank of Pilot Officer. After a short stay at
Blackpool, on 2 August he was posted to No. 303 (Polish) 'Tadeusz Kościuszko.
City of Warsaw' Squadron at RAF Northolt. Initially he was considered for the
first basic core of No. 302 (Polish) Squadron. During the Battle of Britain he
shot down over seven enemy aircraft. He was in trouble on three occasions:
on 2 September he had to force-land in Hurricane I R4178 RF-G, then on 15
and 27 September the Hawker Hurricanes in which he flew were damaged in
combat: R2685 RF-G and V6681 RF-B respectively. On 27 May 1941 he was
invited by BBC Radio to broadcast the achievements of the Polish airmen. In
November 1941 he was appointed commander of 'A' Flight, but soon after was
taken to hospital to recover from a serious illness. In February 1942, on his own
request, he was back in No. 303 Squadron. He was killed in a flying accident on
14 February 1942 over Northolt. At 10.00 am his Spitfire BL432 RF-K dived at an
excessive speed and crashed at Northolt aerodrome. Mirosław Ferić was buried

at Northwood Cemetery, London, in grave no. H 232. He is commemorated on the Polish Air Force Memorials at Northolt and Warsaw-Mokotów, the memorial plaques at RAF Northolt and on the wall of his home in Ostrów Wielkopolski, and on a memorial medal issued by the Polish Archeologic and Numismatic Society. One of the streets at Ostrów Wielkopolski and No. 11 Primary School at Ostrów Wielkopolski are named after him. The MiG 29 no. 111 of the 23rd Tactical Air Base at Mińsk Mazowiecki has his portrait painted on its tail. From the summer of 1939 Mirosław Ferić wrote his memoirs, which in time became an official diary of No. 303 Squadron and is now kept in the Sikorski Institute in London. He was decorated with the Silver Cross of Virtuti Militari no. 8822, the Cross of Valour and bar and the British Distinguished Flying Cross (one of the first five Poles awarded the DFC).

Date & Time	Unit	Aircraft	Score
03.09.1939	111th Squadron	PZL P.11c '4'	⅓-0-0 Bf 110
08.09.1939	111th Squadron	PZL P.11c	1-0-0 Hs 123
31.08.1940 18.25	303 Squadron	Hurricane I P3974 RF-J	1-0-0 Bf 109
02.09.1940 17.50	303 Squadron	Hurricane I R4178 RF-G	0-1-0 Bf 109
06.09.1940 09.00	303 Squadron	Hurricane I P3700 RF-E	1-0-0 Bf 109
15.09.1940 12.00	303 Squadron	Hurricane I R2685 RF-G	1-0-0 Bf 109
15.09.1940 15.00	303 Squadron	Hurricane I R2685 RF-G	1-0-0 Bf 110
27.09.1940 09.20	303 Squadron	Hurricane I V6681 RF-B	1-0-0 Bf 109
27.09.1940 09.20	303 Squadron	Hurricane I V6681 RF-B	1-0-0 He 111
05.10.1940 11.40	303 Squadron	Hurricane I V6681 RF-B	1-0-0 Bf 110
22.06.1941 16.10	303 Squadron	Spitfire II P8385 RF-A	1-0-0 Bf 109
27.06.1941	303 Squadron	Spitfire II P8385 RF-A	0-0-1 Bf 109 (in fact the E/A was damaged on the ground)

JULIUSZ ARTUR FREY, Flight Lieutenant, was born on 14 July 1907 at Opary near Drohobycz, previously part of the Kingdom of Poland, but then ruled by the Austro-Hungarian Empire. He grew up in the family of Juliusz Frey senior. After graduation from a secondary school in 1928, he was accepted to the Air Force Officers' School at Dęblin (which soon after changed its name to the Air Force Cadet Officers' School), and in 1930 was commissioned together with the 4th class. Sub-Lieutenant Frey was posted to the 62nd Light Bomber Squadron of the 6th Air Regiment in Lwów. A year later he completed a flying course at the Air Force Officers' Training Centre at Dęblin, and then

an Advanced Flying Course at Grudziądz. From October 1933 he served at Grudziądz as an advanced flying instructor, then on 1 November 1937 he was posted to the 1st Air Regiment in Warsaw, where he commanded the 114th Fighter Squadron. During the Polish Campaign in 1939 he led the 114th Fighter Squadron, being attached to the Pursuit Brigade, and claimed two victories, including one shared. On 17 September Frey crossed the Rumanian border and travelled to France. After arriving in France, initially he was chosen to be a flight commander for the Polish-manned squadron, equipped with Caudron CR 714s, which was supposed to be sent to Finland, which was being attacked by the Soviet Union (the so-called 'Finnish Squadron'). As the armistice between these countries was signed on 13 March 1940, the Polish airmen were left unused, but out of the personnel destined for Finland the 1/145 Polish 'City of Warsaw' Squadron, also known as GC1/145, was formed and Captain Juliusz Frey took command of 2nd Flight. During the French Campaign he usually flew a Caudron C 714 with the tactical number 1. On 19 June he embarked on a French ship at La Rochelle and sailed to Britain. Upon arrival he received the service number P-0322 and the rank of Flight Commander. On 20 September 1940 he was posted to No. 5 Operational Training Unit, from where on 10 October he was sent to No. 607 Squadron, which at the time operated from Tangmere, but later from Turnhouse. Initially he was considered for the first basic core of No. 302 (Polish) Squadron. On 12 November he was posted to No. 303 (Polish) 'City of Warsaw' Squadron, where he was given command of 'B' Flight. From 20 February 1941 he organized No. 316 (Polish) 'City of Warsaw' Squadron at Pembrey, becoming its first commander. On

10 August 1941 he left for No. 16 (Polish) Service Flying Training School at Newton, where he commanded the training squadron. On 18 March 1943 he joined No. 418 Squadron of the Royal Canadian Air Force and flew night fighter missions. On 11 April he was slightly wounded while flying the Douglas Boston Z2192. On 27 May he was posted to No. 52 Operational Training Unit to train on de Havilland Mosquito planes. On 2 June he was transferred to the Central Gunnery School at Sutton Bridge for gunnery training, and then on 29 June he was back in No. 418 Squadron. Juliusz Frey was posted for rest on 28 December, undertaking staff duties, then in August 1944 he was posted to the HQ of Air Defence of Great Britain (which later reverted to the name Fighter Command). On 18 December 1944 he became 2nd Deputy Polish Liaison Officer at the HQ of Fighter Command. He was demobilized with the rank of Squadron Leader in 1946 and emigrated to Canada. He died on 30 March 1991 at Qualicum Beach. His decorations include the Cross of Valour and two bars.

Date & Time	Unit	Aircraft	Score
01.09.1939	114th Squadron	PZL P.11	1-0-0 He 111
06.09.1939	114th Squadron	PZL P.11	⅓-0-0 Bf 110
24.07.1941 14.25	316 Squadron	Hurricane II Z2805 SZ-E	½-0-0 Bf 109

G

ALEKSANDER KLEMENS GABSZEWICZ, Flying Officer, called 'Hrabia Oleś' (Count Oleś) or 'Gabsio', was born on 6 December 1911 at Szawle, a town previously within the Kingdom of Poland, after the partition of Poland ruled by the Russian Empire, but now in Lithuania. Together with his sister Irena and brother Antoni, he grew up in the family of Piotr Gabszewicz, a general merchant, and Stefania née Tarasiewicz, an opera singer. After moving to a free Poland he attended secondary school for boys and girls at Otwock, from which he graduated in 1931. In 1932 he joined  the Infantry Cadet Officers' School at Ostrowia Mazowiecka, from which he graduated on 15 August 1934 with the rank of Sub-Lieutenant. Meanwhile, he completed a gliding course (between 3-23 September 1933) at Ustianowa as he already planned to join the air force. On 1 September 1934 Gabszewicz was posted to the 30th Kaniów Rifle Regiment in Warsaw, awaiting acceptance for the Air Force Officers' Training Centre at Dęblin. He joined a flying course on 17 September 1934. He had his first flying accident on 11 April 1935, while flying a PWS-12 with instructor Lieutenant Witalis Nikonow. After completion, on 17 September 1935 he was posted for further training to the 1st Air Regiment at Warsaw and flew with the 12th Light Bomber Squadron. He had another flying accident on 1 October 1935, when flying with instructor Sergeant Aleksander Daszkowski. On 20 April 1936 he was sent to Grudziądz, where he completed Advanced Flying Course no. 8 and where on 28 May he had another flying accident in a PWS-10. After completing the course, on 17 July he was posted back to the 12th Light Bomber Squadron, from which on 17 September he was transferred to the 114th Fighter Squadron of the 1st Air Regiment at Warsaw. On 27 April 1937 he had another flying accident, this time while flying a PZL P.11a. From 27 October 1937 he was temporarily assigned deputy commander of the squadron. On 2 May 1938 he was transferred to the 113th Fighter Squadron of the 1st Air Regiment, and from 5 June he was deputy commander. On 1 November Gabszewicz was appointed deputy commander of the 114th Fighter Squadron. Between December 1938 and April 1939 Gabszewicz completed an instructors' course with the 1st Air Regiment. From 6 May until 1 December 1938 he was deputy commander of a fighter section of the Border Defence Corps at Sarny airfield, and from 14 July until 1 August 1939 he commanded a small fighter section preventing German planes from violating Polish airspace, based at Osowiec. In September 1939 he was appointed Tactical Officer of the IV/1 Fighter Wing at Warsaw. He participated in the Polish Campaign of 1939, on 1 September sharing in a victory of a Heinkel He 111, the first German aircraft destroyed around Warsaw. On the same day, in the afternoon, he was shot down, wounded and baled out. After the fall of Poland, on 18 September he crossed the Rumanian border at Śniatyń with the road party of IV/1 Wing. After a short internment he left Rumania and travelled through Yugoslavia and Italy. Gabszewicz arrived in France on 7 October and the next day was sent to Le Bourget, Paris, from where he was posted to the Polish Air Force Training Centre at Lyon Bron. On 1 June 1940 he shot down a Heinkel He 111. Two days later he was posted to lead the Polish section of GCIII/10. The Poles - Lieutenants Tadeusz Sawicz and Bogusław Mierzwa, Sub-Lieutenant Włodzimierz Miksa and Platoon Commander Jan Musiał - flew Bloch MB 152s. After the fall of France Gabszewicz arrived in England on 27 June, and was assigned the service number P-0163 and the rank of Flying Officer.

On 17 July he was sent to Blackpool. Initially he was considerede for the first basic core of No. 302 (Polish) Squadron. On 25 September he was posted to No. 5 Operational Training Unit at Aston Down, which he left on 5 October. On 10 October 1940 he was posted to No. 607 Squadron at Turnhouse. On 12 November he was posted to No. 303 (Polish) 'Tadeusz Kościuszo. City of Warsaw' Squadron, then on 22 February 1941 he joined the newly formed No. 316 (Polish) 'City of Warsaw' Squadron as deputy flight commander. In July 1941 he took command of 'A' Flight, taking command of the whole unit on 14 November. From 5 June 1942 he was appointed Polish Liaison Officer at the HQ of No. 11 Group RAF. On 25 September he took command of the Polish Fighter School at No. 58 Operational Training Unit at Grangemouth. From 25 September until 7 January 1943 he attended a course at the HQ of 1st (Polish) Armoured Brigade and the HQ of the Polish Air Force. Between 27 January and 21 June 1943 he led the 2nd Polish Fighter Wing at Kirton-in-Lindsey, then commanded the 1st Polish Fighter Wing - later called 131 (Polish) Wing - at Northolt. On 2 December 1943 he married Elisabeth Helen Ballimore. On 2 February 1944 he was posted to the 61st Fighter Squadron of the 56th Fighter Group USAAF for flying duties, but on 20 February 1944 took command of No. 18 (Polish) Fighter Sector, then from 12 July commanded No. 131 (Polish) Wing before being posted to the HQ of No. 84 Group. On 17 September 1944 his first son Stefan Aleksander was born. Finally on 21 February 1946 he assumed command of RAF Colitshall, which he left on 21t February 1947, being transferred to No. 5 Polish Resettlement Unit in the rank of Acting Group Captain. After the war he worked with his father-in-law running Roger Constant & Co, a business involved in quarrying and aggregates and on 1 April 1951 was appointed Managing Director. From 1964-1968 and then 1970-1982 he was the Chairman of the Polish Air Force Association. On 1 January 1974 he was promoted to become Brigadier General Gabszewicz. Aleksander Gabszewicz died after a long illness on 10 October 1983 at Henley Swan, Worcestershire. Initially he was buried in Newark Cemetery, but in 1992 his ashes were taken to Poland and scattered over Dęblin and Poniatów, places where he trained as a pilot and was stationed during the Polish Campaign of 1939. He was decorated with the following awards: Golden Cross of Virtuti Militari no.29, Silver Cross of Virtuti Militari no. 9425, Cross of Valour and three bars, Distinguished Service Order and bar, Distinguished Flying Cross, Polonia Restituta, Order of Orange-Nassau and Croix de Guerre avec Palms. A street in Poznań was also named after him. In 2018 the Battle of Britain Memorial Flight introduced their Spitfire XVI TE311, which was painted in the scheme of Gabszewicz's personal aircraft TD240 SZ-G.

Date & Time	Unit	Aircraft	Score
01.09.1939 07.00-07.15	IV/1 Wing/114th Squadron	PZL P.11 '4'	½-0-0 He 111
01.06.1940 1?.?0	PAF Training Centre	Morane MS 406 no 905	1-0-0 He 111
01.04.1941 18.05	316 Squadron	Hurricane I V7000 SZ-S	½-0-0 He 111
24.07.1941 14.25	316 Squadron	Hurricane II Z3573 SZ-D	½-0-0 Bf 109
24.07.1941 14.30	316 Squadron	Hurricane II Z3573 SZ-D	0-0-1 Bf 109
27.03.1942 15.35	316 Squadron	Spitfire VB P8606 SZ-G	0-0-1 Fw 190
10.04.1942 17.40	316 Squadron	Spitfire VB BL901 SZ-G	1-0-0 Fw 190
25.04.1942 10.30	316 Squadron	Spitfire VB W3717 SZ-D	1-0-0 Fw 190
27.04.1942 15.45	316 Squadron	Spitfire VB BL901 SZ-G	1-0-0 Fw 190
05.05.1942 14.40	316 Squadron	Spitfire VB BL901 SZ-G	0-1-0 Fw 190
06.05.1942 18.45	316 Squadron	Spitfire VB BL901 SZ-G	0-1/3-0 Fw 190
04.04.1943 19.30	2nd (P) Wing	Spitfire VB EN865 WX-L	1-0-0 Fw 190
04.07.1943 13.10	1st (P) Wing	Spitfire IX EN526 SZ-G	1-0-0 Fw 190
06.07.1943 10.40	1st (P) Wing	Spitfire IX EN526 SZ-G	1-0-0 Bf 109
19.08.1943 11.20	1st (P) Wing	Spitfire IX EN526 SZ-G	1-0-1 Fw 190

PAWEŁ PIOTR GALLUS, Sergeant, was born on 28 April 1920 at Szczawina, near Gostynin, where in 1934 he completed primary school. In 1936 he joined the Air Force NCO School for Minors at Bydgoszcz, from which he graduated in 1939 after the school was moved to Krosno. He left the school as a fighter pilot, being posted to the 112th Fighter Squadron of the 1st Air Regiment at Warsaw. He fought during the Polish Campaign in 1939, when his unit was attached to the Pursuit Brigade. On 19 September he crossed the Rumanian border, and via Syria travelled to France. Upon arrival on 30 October he was sent for conversion training. In the rank of Corporal he was posted to the Polish fighter section of DAT formed on 12 May 1940 and commanded by Lieutenant Zdzisław Henneberg. Their duty was to defend the SNCASO factory manufacturing Bloch fighter planes. They flew Bloch MB 151s and 152s operating from Châteauroux. On 5 June he participated in combat and attacked and damaged a Heinkel He 111, but his machine guns jammed. Due to the fall of France the

whole unit was evacuated. Gallus, together with the road party, arrived at Bordeaux on 18 June; next day they sailed to England (according to other sources this was on 22 June). He arrived in England on 23 June, receiving the service number 794124 and rank of Sergeant. Initially he was considered for the first basic core of No. 302 (Polish) Squadron. After an initial stay at Blackpool, on 2 August he was posted to No. 303 (Polish) 'Tadeusz Kościuszko. City of Warsaw' Squadron. On 12 August Gallus had a landing accident in the Hurricane I P3890, and on 2 September was sent to No. 5 Operational Training Unit for further training. On 27 September 1940 he was reposted to No. 3 Squadron at Castletown. On 27 March 1941 he was posted to No. 316 (Polish) 'City of Warsaw' Squadron, then on 22 October he was sent to No. 87 Squadron for night flying duties. On 26 October he collided in mid-air with another Polish pilot of this unit, Sergeant Antoni Beda. Both pilots baled out. On 16 March 1942 he was posted to No. 317 (Polish) 'City of Wilno' Squadron, but on 5 April was back at No. 316 (Polish) Squadron. During his time with this unit he claimed at least one aerial victory. On 26 August 1943 he was posted for rest, serving as deputy ground controller at RAF Northolt. On 18 April 1944 he was put back into action and sent to No. 302 (Polish) 'City of Poznań' Squadron. He was wounded while performing an operational mission on 31 December, when German ground fire hit his Spitfire IX MK200 WX-T. On 8 February 1945 he was posted for rest to Blackpool. On 6 April Gallus was posted to No. 70 Group RAF and flew with Nos 639 and 595 Squadrons. Finally he was sent to No. 309 (Polish) 'Czerwieńska Province' Squadron, where he remained until disbandment. Warrant Officer Gallus was demobilized in 1948 and settled in Britain. He worked in the metal industry and at a machine construction factory as an engineer. He was married to Maria Gazda and had two children. Paweł Gallus died aged 90 on 19 April 2011 in Northampton. He was decorated with the Silver Cross of Virtuti Militari no. 10765, the Cross of Valour and two bars and the British Distinguished Flying Cross.

Date & Time	Unit	Aircraft	Score
31.01.1943 15.30	316 Squadron	Spitfire VB BM176 SZ-G	0-1-0 Fw 190
06.07.1943 10.40	316 Squadron	Spitfire IX MA566 2SZ-I	1-0-0 Bf 109

JÓZEF GIL, Pilot Officer, called 'Zazdrośnik' (Jealous) or 'Pedagog' (Pedagogue), was born on 30 January 1914 at Łęg, near Jarocin in Poznań Voivodship, within the territory of Poland ruled by the German Empire. He grew up in the family of Franciszek and Marcela née Barańska. In 1936 he completed a gliding course, category B, and in 1937 was accepted to the Air Force Reserve Cadet Officers' School and then went to the Air Force Cadet Officers' School at Dęblin. On 12 July 1937 he had a flying accident in a Bartel BM-4. In June 1939 he was posted to the 1st Air Regiment for training as a pilot of XX Bomber Squadron. He was commissioned with the 12th class, and on 20 August he was posted as a Sub-Lieutenant to the air base at Małaszewicze, where he was to join the newly formed bomber squadron equipped with PZL P.37 'Łoś' aircraft. He did not fly operationally during the Polish Campaign of 1939, and on 17 September he crossed the Rumanian border and subsequently travelled to France, where he arrived on 29 October. He then decided to go to England in the hope of being able to fight the Germans. He left France with one of the first transports of Polish airmen. He was given the service number 76765 and the rank of Pilot Officer. He was posted to No. 6 Operational Training Unit at Sutton Bridge, where he converted to fighter planes, and on 27 September 1940 was posted to No. 43 Squadron based at Usworth. On 24 October he was posted to No. 229 Squadron and then to No. 145 Squadron. On 29 December Gil was wounded as a result of a flying accident in the Hurricane I V7230. On 12 March 1941 he was posted to No. 53 Operational Training Unit for instructor's duty, and then on 13 April to No. 315 (Polish) 'City of Dęblin' Squadron. On 13 March 1942 he had a taxiing accident when in Spitfire VB AB247 PK-W he collided with another Spitfire. During his time with No. 315 Squadron Józef Gil claimed more than one aerial victory. In June 1942 Gil was appointed commander of 'B' Flight of No. 306 (Polish) 'City of Toruń' Squadron. On 22 August during Operation Rhubarb his Spitfire was damaged by German anti-aircraft artillery. When flying with No. 306 Squadron he achieved at least one more aerial victory. Flight Lieutenant Józef Gil was killed on 31 December 1942 during Operation Rodeo 140 around Le Crotoy and Dunkirk. At 14.45 his Spitfire F IX BS455 UZ-B was shot down by an enemy fighter over Abbeville. He was lost in the sea. Józef Gil is commemorated on the Polish Air Force memorials at Northolt and Warsaw-Mokotów. His decorations included the Silver Cross of Virtuti Militari no. 9688 and the Cross of Valour and two bars.

Date & Time	Unit	Aircraft	Score
09.08.1941 11.30	315 Squadron	Spitfire II P7613 PK-Z	0-1-0 Bf 109
09.08.1941 18.20	315 Squadron	Spitfire II P7434 PK-P	0-0-1 Bf 109
14.08.1941 17.50	315 Squadron	Spitfire II P8588 PK-T	1-0-0 Bf 109
24.10.1941 15.20	315 Squadron	Spitfire VB AB895 PK-X	0-1-0 Bf 109
09.10.1942 10.00	306 Squadron	Spitfire IX BS455 UZ-B	0-0-1 Bf 109
09.10.1942 10.00	306 Squadron	Spitfire IX BS455 UZ-B	1-0-0 Fw 190

ANTONI GŁOWACKI, Sergeant, called 'Głowa' (head) or 'Toni', was born on 10 February 1910 in Warsaw – then part of the Russian Empire - into the family of Antoni and Aurelia. He graduated from the National Radio-Technical School in Warsaw and in 1928 joined an Aero Club based in the Polish capital. In 1928, at Lublinek airfield near Łódź, Głowacki completed a flying training course which was a part of his initial military training. Between 1928 and 1930 he worked as laboratory manager at the Polish Philips factory, then studied at the Wawelberg and Rotwand Machine Construction and Electronics High School. In 1931 he joined the Polish Air Force and was sent for initial flying training to the 1st Air Regiment at Warsaw. He completed the Advanced Flying Course at Grudziądz. From 1935 he served as a regular NCO pilot of the 111th Fighter Squadron at Warsaw. Between 17-20 July 1935, with a delegation from the 1st Air Regiment, he participated in the funeral of Marshal Józef Piłsudski, then in October 1936 he gained joint third place in the fighter pilots' tournament at Grudziądz. In 1938 Głowacki completed a flying instructor's course at the No. 1 Air Force Training Centre at Dęblin. At the beginning of the Polish Campaign in 1939 he served with the instructors flight formed to defend Dęblin's AF School and Ułęż, and was then posted to Captain Julian Łagowski's Reconnaissance (flying) Platoon attached to the Warsaw Armoured-Motorised Brigade. He flew a PZL P.23 Karaś from Kierz airfield. On 17 September he flew to Kuty, where he crossed the Rumanian border. He was interned in Babadag and then Tulcea camps, from where he escaped to Bucharest.

On 5 November he sailed from Balchik to France. Upon arrival he decided to continue fighting from Britain, where he received the service number 780408 and the rank of Sergeant. Initially he was based at RAF Eastchurch, from where he was moved to Blackpool. On 5 July 1940 he was posted to No. 1 School of Army Co-operation at Old Sarum, and on 14 July he was posted to No. 6 Operational Training Unit at Sutton Bridge. Initially he was considered for the first basic core of No. 302 (Polish) Squadron. On 4 August he reported for duty with No. 501 Squadron at Gravesend. During the Battle of Britain Głowacki shot down at least eight enemy aircraft, including five destroyed in one day on 24 August. He was shot down and force-landed in his damaged Hurricane I V6540 SD-P on 31 August, then on 26 September he broke his arm and was hospitalized. Głowacki returned to No. 501 Squadron in January 1941, but on 1 March was posted to No. 55 Operational Training Unit as an instructor. For his wartime achievements he was commissioned on 16 July, receiving the new service number P-1527. On 22 October he was posted to No. 611 Squadron, but soon after, on 7 November, joined No. 303 (Polish) 'Tadeusz Kościuszko. City of Warsaw' Squadron, where he increased his tally of downed German aircraft. On 7 February 1943 he became 'A' Flight commander of No. 308 (Polish) 'City of Cracow' Squadron, where he remained until 22 February 1944. For one month in June 1943 he was transferred to No. 318 (Polish) 'City of Gdańsk' Squadron undergoing training at Detling. On 4 March 1944 he was posted to the 356th Fighter Squadron of 354th Fighter Group USAAF, where he performed non-operational flights only. On 19 May he was appointed a flying instructor at No. 61 Operational Training Unit at Rednal, where he served in

the Polish Fighter School. On 3 September he was posted to No. 309 (Polish) 'Czerwieńska Province' Squadron, whose command he took, being the first officer who started his military wartime career as an NCO to be given such a role. In November 1944 this squadron was converted to a fighter unit. Głowacki left on 16 July 1945 and went to No. 61 Operational Training Unit at Keevil, becoming a chief instructor. He also trained on Gloster Meteor jet planes. On 3 October 1945 he was posted to No. 307 (Polish) 'City of Lwów Night Owls' Squadron, where he flew Mosquitos NF XXX. On 29 November he returned to No. 61 Operational Training Unit. From 1 December he served in the HQ of 13 Group RAF as Polish Liaison Officer, then on 13 May 1946 was transferred to the HQ of 84 Group RAF, BAFO. Acting Squadron Leader Głowacki left the Polish Air Force on 1 September 1948 and joined the RAF. Between 1948 and 1949 he served in No. 57 Squadron, then in July 1949 was posted to No. 264 Squadron. He left the RAF in 1954 and joined the RNZAF, moving with his family to New Zealand. Głowacki retired from the RNZAF in 1960 and started employment in the Department of Civil Aviation at Wellington. He flew his last flight on 22 March 1980 at the age of 70. He passed away on 27 April 1980 and was buried in the Military Karon Cemetery in Wellington. He was decorated with the Silver Cross of Virtuti Militari no. 8814, the Cross of Valour and three bars and the British Distinguished Flying Medal and Distinguished Flying Cross.

Date & Time	Unit	Aircraft	Score
15.08.1940 11.40	501 Squadron	Hurricane I V7234 SD-A	1-0-0 Ju 87
15.08.1940 11.40	501 Squadron	Hurricane I V7234 SD-A	0-0-1 Do 17 (claimed as Do 215)
24.08.1940 10.30	501 Squadron	Hurricane I V7234 SD-A	1-0-0 Bf 109
24.08.1940 13.00	501 Squadron	Hurricane I V7234 SD-A	1-0-0 Bf 109
24.08.1940 13.00	501 Squadron	Hurricane I V7234 SD-A	1-0-0 Ju 88
24.08.1940 15.40	501 Squadron	Hurricane I V7234 SD-A	1-0-0 Bf 109
24.08.1940 15.40	501 Squadron	Hurricane I V7234 SD-A	1-0-0 Ju 88
28.08.1940 09.35	501 Squadron	Hurricane I P5193 SD-O	1-0-0 Bf 109

30.08.1940 11.30	501 Squadron	Hurricane I V7234 SD-A	0-0-1 Bf 110
30.08.1940 16.50	501 Squadron	Hurricane I P3820	0-0-1 He 111
31.08.1940 13.00	501 Squadron	Hurricane I V6540 SD-P	1-0-0 Do 17 (claimed as Do 215)
18.09.1940 13.15	501 Squadron	Hurricane I P5193 SD-O	0-1-0 Bf 109
27.04.1942 15.37	303 Squadron	Spitfire VB AA913 RF-P	0-1-0 Fw 190
19.08.1942 10.35	303 Squadron	Spitfire VC AB174 RF-Q	0-1-0 Fw 190
19.08.1942 16.30	303 Squadron	Spitfire VC AB174 RF-Q	⅓-0-0 He 111
22.09.1943 16.20	308 Squadron	Spitfire VB BL416 ZF-A	0-0-1 Bf 109

WITOLD JÓZEF GŁOWACKI, Pilot Officer, was born on 30 October 1913 in a Polish family living in Berlin, Germany. After moving back to Poland he completed his primary education and enrolled at Karol Marcinkowski High School in Poznań. Meanwhile he participated in the first gliding course organized by the Aero Club in Poznań. After graduation and passing A-level exams, in 1935 he joined the Air Force Reserve Cadet Officers' School at Dęblin. Once he graduated he was accepted to the Air Force Cadet Officer's School at Dęblin. He was

Plt Off Witold Głowacki photographed by the Germans after he crash landed in France. After he was taken to hospital, Głowacki died probably due to an allergic reaction to an anti-tetanus injection.

commissioned as the best in the 10th class on 15 October 1937, and in the rank of Sub-Lieutenant he was posted to the 131st Fighter Squadron of the 3rd Air Regiment at Poznań. In January 1939 Głowacki was appointed commander of the transport platoon of the 3rd Air Regiment, then on 8 July the commander of the airfield maintenance platoon. He was also posted to the HQ of the Polish Air Force. During the Polish Campaign in 1939 he was involved in the evacuation of the 3rd Air Base from Poznań, and on 17 September, while flying an unarmed PWS 26 with observer Lieutenant Stanisław Bielawski, he was shot down by the Soviets. He survived unwounded and joined the road party of the Border Defence Corps battalion from Czortków. On 18 September he crossed the Rumanian border at Śniatyń. Although he was interned, he managed to escape and travelled to France. He arrived at Marseilles on 29 October. After a short stay in France, he decided to join the Polish Air Force in England. Upon arrival he was given the service number 76739 and the rank of Pilot Officer. After a conversion course at No. 7 Operational Training Unit, on 12 August 1940 Witold Głowacki was posted to No. 145 Squadron at Westhampnett. Soon after, on 31 August, he was reposted to No. 605 Squadron operating from Drem. During the Battle of Britain he claimed at least one aerial victory. On 24 September, while flying the Hurricane I P3832 UP-P, he took part in an operation against German raiders over Beachy Head. He chased the enemy to Cap Gris Nez, where his opponent crashed. However, on his way back he was attacked by a formation of Bf 109s and was shot down. He crash-landed in a field near Ambleteuse, north of Wimille, near Boulogne. Wounded, he was taken to the military hospital at Guines, where he died the same day, probably as a result of allergic reaction to an anti-tetanus injection. He was buried in the military plot of the Guines cemetery. He was the nineteenth Polish operational pilot who died during the Battle of Britain. Witold Głowacki was posthumously awarded the Silver Cross of Virtuti Militari no. 8814. He is commemorated on the Polish Air Force Memorials at Northolt and Warsaw-Mokotów.

Date & Time	Unit	Aircraft	Score
11.08.1940 16.00	605 Squadron	Hurricane I	1-0-0 Bf 110
23.09.1940 10.00	605 Squadron	Hurricane I P3583 SD-A	0-0-1 Bf 109
24.09.1940 16.50	605 Squadron	Hurricane I P3832 UP-P	½-0-0 Do 17

FELIKS GMUR, Sergeant, was born on 6 November 1914 at Biniew near Ostrów in Poznań Voivodship, in part of Poland ruled by the German Empire. He grew up together with his ten siblings in the family of Tomasz, a railway worker, and Julianna née Mąka. After the death of his mother on 8 February 1932 he was raised by his father, who remarried. He completed seven classes of basic education and learnt the trade of an ironworker, but on 14 February 1935 he was conscripted and posted to the 25th Light Artillery Regiment at Kalisz. Within this regiment he completed the NCOs course. During the summer of 1936 he was permitted to be transferred to the Polish Air Force, and on 15 July he was sent to the Military Gliding Centre at Ustianowa to undertake the gliding course. A month later he reported to the 4th Air Regiment at Toruń, then completed an aircraft maintenance course. From September 1936 until July 1937 he completed the basic pilot's course with the 4th Air Regiment. On 23 July 1937 he had a flying accident in a Potez XXV during a training flight with instructor Corporal Kazimierz Waśkiewicz. From 10 August 1937 to 28 August 1938 he completed the

Advanced Flying Course at Grudziądz, and was posted to the 142nd Fighter Squadron of the 4th Air Regiment at Toruń. On 24 February 1938 he was involved in a mid-air crash with Corporal Anotni Seredyn; both pilots flew PZL P.11cs and survived. Between April and September 1938 he completed a blind flying course and soon after, on 24 August, he was posted to the 6th Air Regiment at Lwów, in October being transferred to the 161st Fighter Squadron. During the Polish Campaign in 1939 he fought as a pilot of the 161st Squadron, performing several operational missions and participating in combat. His unit supported the 'Modlin' Army. After the fall of Poland, on 17 September he crossed the Rumanian border at Kuty. After a short internment he escaped and travelled to France, where he arrived on 29 October. Gmur decided to join his colleagues undergoing training in Britain, and arrived on 20 February 1940. Receiving the service number 780678 and the rank of Sergeant, he was initially considered for the first basic core of No. 302 (Polish) Squadron. On 3 July 1940 he was posted to No. 15 Elementary Flying Training School at Carlisle and on 17 July for conversion to British fighter planes at No. 6 Operational Training Unit at Sutton Bridge. On 17 August he was posted to No. 151 Squadron at North Weald. He was killed in action on 30 August at 16.00 while flying the Hurricane I R4213 DZ-I, crashing at Jacks Hath, Epping Green, near Epping, Essex. He was found dead in the burning wreckage. He was the ninth Polish operational pilot lost during the Battle of Britain. Feliks Gmur was buried in Epping Cemetery, in grave no. Z-2. He is commemorated on the Polish Air Force Memorials at Northolt and Warsaw-Mokotów.

WŁADYSŁAW GNYŚ, Pilot Officer, was born on 24 August 1910 at Sarnów in the region of Kielce, then ruled by the Russian Empire. He grew up in the family of Jan, who was in the carp breeding and milling business, and Marianna née Burza. In 1915 he started education in the primary school at Sarnów, and in 1919 he continued at the secondary school at Gniewoszów, from where he was transferred to Jan Kochanowski high school at Radom. Unfortunately, due to the family moving to Kawęczyn, he wasn't able to complete his education there. The family's financial situation meant he had to find a job loading wagons. He was influenced by his uncle,

Captain Władysław Gnyś, who was an air force fighter pilot (killed in 1938), to join the Polish Air Force. On 29 October 1931 he was accepted by the service and sent to the 4th Air Regiment at Toruń. Between 2 January and 1 April 1932 he completed a mechanics' course with the regiment, and then on 2 May 1933 he commenced Flying Training School with the 4th Air Regiment. In 1933 he completed a pilot's course at Grudziądz and was posted back to Toruń, where he served in the 42nd Light Bomber Squadron. On 2 May 1934 Gnyś was sent on an Advanced Flying Course at Grudziądz, which he completed, and on 2 October he was posted to the 142nd Fighter Squadron of the 4th Air Regiment. On 11 May 1935 he was involved in a mid-air collision with Lieutenant Dionizy Durko, who was killed, while Gnyś, who flew a PZL P.7, was injured. He had also collided with another fighter aircraft on the ground on 1 August 1934. Between 2 March and 1 May 1936 he undertook an instructor's course at the Air Force Training Centre at Dęblin, and then from 2 May until 29 September he was a flying instructor at the centre. He applied for the Air Force Cadet Officers' School at Dęblin, but to be able to enter was requested to pass A-level exams. Therefore on 1 October he was posted to the Cadet Officers' School for NCOs at Bydgoszcz, where he completed his education, and in August 1938 he joined the 3rd year of the Polish Air Force Cadet Officers' School at Dęblin. While at the Dęblin school he served there as an instructor for his younger colleagues. Prior to official graduation he was posted to the 121st Fighter Flight of the 2nd Air Regiment at Cracow. He was commissioned in the 12th class of the school on 1 August 1939, without the usual ceremony as war was expected. On 1 September he pursued a German formation consisting of Dornier Do 17s, two of which collided in the air and crashed. It is officially assumed that they were lost due to Gnyś' action, and he is considered the first Allied pilot who gained an aerial victory in the Second World War. He was also involved in other combat missions. After the fall of Poland he crossed the Rumanian border at Kuty on 18 September. After a short internment at the Tulcea camp, he travelled towards the port of Balchik, from where on board the SS *Patris* he sailed to France. Gnyś arrived at Marseilles on 19 November. The day after he was transferred to the Polish Air Force Training Centre at Lyon-Bron. On 5 January 1940 he was sent for further training to Montpellier. He undertook initial flying training on 20 January, and then from 3 February continued practicing on Morane Saulnier MS 406s. In the middle of March he joined the fighter section led by Lieutenant Kazimierz Bursztyn, which from 29 March was attached to GCIII/1. The Poles flew MS 406s. During the French Campaign Gnyś participated in three shared aerial victories. On 21 June the Poles left Orange Caritat aerodrome, travelling to Port Vendres, from where they sailed to Oran in Algeria. From Casablanca they sailed to Liverpool, arriving on 12 July. Upon arrival Gnyś received the service number P-1298 and the rank of Pilot Officer. On 20 August he was posted to No. 302 (Polish) 'City of Poznań' Squadron, but on 2 September was reposted to No. 5 Operational Training Unit for further training. He was back at No. 302 Squadron twenty-four days later. On 30 January 1942 he was posted for rest and took up duty in the operations room of No. 302 Squadron, then in December 1942 he flew operationally again with his squadron. On 10 February 1943 he was posted to No. 316 (Polish) 'City of Warsaw' Squadron, where on 15 March he took command of 'A' Flight. From 11 August to 22 October he was posted to No. 309 (Polish) 'Czerwieńska Province' Squadron to help his colleagues undergoing transition from Army Co-operation to fighter duties. Then he reported at the HQ of the 18th Fighter Wing, and then HQ of No. 84 Group RAF where he served as Liaison Officer. On 12 July 1944 he was transferred to the 131st (Polish) Wing, and on 26 August he took command of No. 317 (Polish) 'City of Wilno' Squadron. He was shot down the next day while flying Spitfire LF.IX NH365 JH-A, attacking German infantry around Rouen in France. He was shot on the ground in the chest by Germans and captured. A few days later he managed to escape, and with help from French resistance fighters was handed over to Canadian troops on 3 September. Following convalescence at hospital in Swindon, in January 1945 he joined the Polish Air Force Staff College at Weston-super-Mare, and after graduation in September he received a posting to the HQ of the Polish Air Force. Acting Squadron Leader Gnyś was demobilized in 1948 and emigrated to Canada, where he ran his own farm. In 1953 he sold his farm and started working at an assembly plant. In 1965 he revisited Poland for the first time, then in 1982 his book *First Kill*, largely written by his wife Barbara, was published. He died on 28 February 2000 with the rank of Colonel and was buried at Mount Osborne Cemetery, Beanville, Canada. The Primary School at Żurada in Poland, where he fought on 1 September 1939, was named after him, as well as a street in Cracow. In 2013 a controversial book, *First kill of podchorąży Gnyś. Myth and reality of the first Polish aerial victory in World War II*, was published in Poland, followed in 2017 by another one, *First Kills. The illustrated biography of fighter pilot Władysław Gnyś*, written by his son Stefan. He was decorated with the Bronze Cross of Merit, the Silver Cross of Virtuti Militari no. 10766, the Cross of Valour and two bars, the French Croix de Guerre and the Commander's Cross of Polonia Restituta.

Date & Time	Unit	Aircraft	Score
01.09.1939 06.00	121st Squadron	PZL P.11c '5'	2-0-0 Do 17
12.05.1940	GCIII/1	Morane MS 406 no. 948/III	⅓-0-1 He 111
16.05.1940 13.40	GCIII/1	Morane MS 406 "2"	⅓-0-0 Do 17
25.05.1940 15.30	GCIII/1	Morane MS 406	⅓-0-0 Bf 109
08.06.1940	GCIII/1	Morane MS 406	½-0-0 Ju 87

MIECZYSŁAW STANISŁAW WŁADYSŁAW GORZULA, Pilot Officer, called 'Mike', was born on 1 August 1919 in Cracow-Podgórze into the family of Władysław, a senior guard of the Polish National Railways, and Apolonia. He graduated from the Economic-Trade Secondary School in Cracow, passing A-level exams. In 1936 he attended a gliding course. In 1938 he joined the Air Force Reserve Cadet Officers' School and was commissioned on 15 October 1938. Sub-Lieutenant Gorzula was posted to the 2nd Air Regiment in Cracow. During his service he underwent an instructors' course at Radom (February–April 1939). During the Polish Campaign in 1939 he was posted to the Replacement Flight of the 2nd Air Regiment, and on 17 September he flew to Rumania. Via Syria he travelled to France, where he arrived on 29 October. After a short stay he decided to continue on to Britain, arriving there in January 1940 and being posted to RAF Eastchurch. Upon arrival he was issued with the service number 76695 and the rank of Pilot Officer. On 21 August 1940 he was sent to No. 15 Elementary Flying Training School at Carlisle, which he completed on 3 September. Initially, on 15 September, he received a posting to No. 303 (Polish) 'Tadeusz Kościuszko'.City of Warsaw' Squadron at Northolt, but on 23 September he was reposted for further training to No. 5 Operational Training Unit at Aston Down. From 1 7 October he served in No. 615 Squadron at Prestwick. To his disappointment, from 11 October until 28 November he flew with No. 607 Squadron based at Tangmere, Turnhouse and Drem, being subsequently posted to No. 229 Squadron at Northolt. On his own request, and in answer to his letter to Squadron Leader Joseph Kayll, on 4 December he was reposted to No. 615 Squadron at Northolt, where he remained until 14 May 1941. He received a further posting to No. 302 (Polish) 'City of Poznań' Squadron, but on 4 November he was transferred to No. 87 Squadron, where he undertook night flying training. On 16 March 1942 Gorzula was back with No. 302 Squadron. On 26 April 1943 he was posted for rest, serving as an instructor with No. 58 Operational Training Unit at Ballado Bridge, then he was moved to No. 61 Operational Training Unit. On 10 November he joined No. 315 (Polish) 'City of Dęblin' Squadron, where he was given command of 'A' Flight. On 8 May 1944 he was transferred to No. 84 Group Support Unit, but on 31 July was posted to No. 306 (Polish) 'City of Toruń' Squadron. Almost two months later, on 22 September, he was transferred to the HQ of the Polish Air Force. On 20 November he was posted to No. 309 (Polish) 'Czerwieńska Province' Squadron, where he assumed command of 'A' Flight. On 9 April 1945 he became one of the very few Polish pilots to claim a victory of a German jet plane. In June Gorzula was transferred to the HQ of No. 133 (Polish) Wing as an Intelligence Officer. He was demobilized from the Polish Air Force in the rank of Flight Lieutenant. From 21 December 1948 until 16 February 1950 he served as a flying instructor with the Pakistani Air Force, leaving on his own request. During this time, from 16 February to 5 November 1949, he served at the Royal Pakistani Air Force College at Risalpur. He flew North American Harvards and Hawker Tempests. He then emigrated to Australia, where he worked as an accountant for various building supplies and food wholesale companies; he was also an insurance seller. He moved to Cabramurra. Later he worked as a security guard at the Royal Australian Mint in Canberra, retiring in 2000. Lieutenant Colonel Mieczysław Gorzula passed away, aged 86, on 6 December 2005 at Queanbeyan near Canberra. On 28 November 2015 his ashes were scattered in the Snowy Mountains. He was decorated with the Cross of Valour and two bars.

Date & Time	Unit	Aircraft	Score
09.04.1945 17.55	309 Squadron	Mustang III FZ111 WC-V	1-0-0 Me 262

BERNARD GROSZEWSKI, Flight Lieutenant, called 'Pastor', was born on 9 October 1909 at Grudziądz, a town ruled by the German Empire, into the family of Franciszek and Antonina née Lipertowicz. In 1931 he joined the Air Force Cadet Officers' School at Dęblin and was commissioned with the 7th class on 15 October 1933 as an observer. In the rank of Sub-Lieutenant he was posted to the 6th Air Regiment, where he flew in a light bomber squadron. Then he attended a flying course at the Air Force Officers' Training Centre at Dęblin and the Advanced Flying Course at Grudziądz. He was posted to the 131st Fighter

Squadron of the 3rd Air Regiment at Poznań. On 9 September 1936 he was involved in a flying accident in a PZL P.7. He was transferred to the 133rd Fighter Squadron, but his unit was disbanded by the end of October 1937 and alongside his colleagues Groszewski was transferred to the 6th Air Regiment at Lwów and posted to the newly formed 162nd Fighter Squadron, which he took command of. In September and October 1938 he operated from the Monasterzyska airfield, where his unit was moved due to the annexation of the Zaolzie region. During the Polish Campaign in 1939 he led the 162nd Squadron supporting the 'Łódź' Army. After the fall of Poland he escaped to Rumania and then to France, and in June 1940 he arrived in Britain. He was given the service number P-0544 and the rank of Flight Lieutenant. On 10 September he was posted to No. 307 (Polish) 'City of Lwów' Night Fighter Squadron at Kirton-in-Lindsey. Like many of his colleagues he was disappointed with this posting, and was sent to No. 1 Army Co-operation School at Old Sarum and then to No. 5 Operational Training Unit at Aston Down. On 25 October he was posted to No. 43 Squadron based at Usworth. He joined No. 315 (Polish) 'City of Dęblin' Squadron being formed from 21 January 1941. On 19 August he flew the Spitfire II P8545 PK-F and was shot down over France. Although injured, he managed to force-land near Dover. In September he was posted for rest and served as a flying instructor at No. 61 and then No. 58 Operational Training Units. He returned to No. 315 Squadron in November 1941. During Operation Ramrod 15 on 8 December he was shot down over France while flying the Spitfire VB BL323 PK-W. Groszewski baled out and was seen in the water, but wasn't rescued. He was buried at the Boulogne-sur-Mer Cemetery in France, in plot XII, row D, grave 12. He was decorated with the Cross of Valour. He is commemorated on the Polish Air Force Memorials at Northolt and Warsaw-Mokotów.

FRANCISZEK GRUSZKA, Flying Officer, called 'Frank', was born on 21 January 1910 at Biłka Królewska in Lwów Voivodship, into the wealthy farming family of Piotr and Katarzyna. He graduated from the 7th Tadeusz Kościuszko Secondary School in Lwów, and after passing an A-levels exam on 5 May, in June 1931 he joined the Infantry Reserve Cadet Officers' School at Rawa Ruska. He volunteered for the Polish Air Force and initially on 15 November was posted to the II Observation Balloon Battalion at Toruń, where he remained until 15 August 1932. He was accepted to the Air Force Cadet Officers' School at Dęblin, where he enrolled in 1932. Commissioned with  the 7th class on 15 August 1934 as an observer, Sub-Lieutenant Gruszka was posted to the 64th Light Bomber Squadron of the 6th Air Regiment at Lwów. He decided to be a pilot, undergoing pilot training at the Air Force Officers' Training Centre at Dęblin. After completion in July 1935 he was posted to the 65th Light Bomber Squadron of the 6th Air Regiment. Between April and July 1936 he participated in an Advanced Flying Course at Grudziądz, then was posted to the 66th Army Co-operation Squadron. He had a flying accident on 18 August while flying a Lublin R-XIIID, and was posted to III/6 Fighter Wing. Until August 1937 he was a flying instructor at the Flying School of the 6th Air Regiment. In 1938 he was sent to the Air Force Training Centre at Brzeżany and Łuck. Soon after he was appointed commanding officer of the centre. He did not fly operationally during the Polish Campaign in 1939, and was evacuated alongside the 6th Air Base to Rumania. After obtaining a passport with a false name in Bucharest, he travelled to France via Yugoslavia and Italy, arriving on 7 October. After a short stay Gruszka decided to join his colleagues in Britain, and left France in December. Receiving the service number 76785 and the rank of Flying Officer, he stayed at RAF Eastchurch, where he was responsible for the sporting activities of his colleagues. Gruszka was sent for conversion training at No. 6 Operational Training Unit at Sutton

Bridge. On 7 August 1940 he was posted to No. 65 Squadron at Hornchurch. On 16 August he claimed the probable destruction of a Bf 109. Two days later Gruszka participated in another combat, intercepting a German raid near Canterbury. He did not return from this mission and was reported missing, later being presumed dead on 3 October 1941. Some sources state that he shot down a Bf 109 before he was lost together with the Spitfire I R6713. In March 1971 the unopened parachute of Franciszek Gruszka was found, then on 15 April 1974 the reminder of the Spitfire R6713, the pilot's remains and personal belongings were recovered from Grove Marsh, between Preston Village and Stodmarsh. On 17 July 1975 he was buried in Northwood Cemetery, in grave no. H 202. He is remembered on the Polish Air Force Memorials at Northolt and Warsaw-Mokotów. He was the seventh Polish operational pilot killed during the Battle of Britain.

Date & Time	Unit	Aircraft	Score
16.08.1940 16.30	65 Squadron	Spitfire I X4059	0-1-0 Bf 109
18.08.1940 13.30	65 Squadron	Spitfire I R6713	1-0-0 Bf 109 (unconfirmed)

BOHDAN GRZESZCZAK, Flying Officer, was born on 10 August 1910 at Warsaw within the Russian Empire, into the family of Franciszek and Aleksandra née Tusz. He graduated from St Kazimierz Secondary School in Warsaw, passing his A-level exams. In 1926 he completed a course for aircraft mechanics organized by the Polish Anti-Aircraft and Anti-Gas Defence League. Three years later he also completed a basic flying course run by Initial Military Training in Warsaw Aero Club. Grzeszczak joined the Mechanical Faculty of Warsaw Technical University, but after eighteen months he decided to pursue a military career. In 1930 he was accepted to the Air Force Reserve Cadet Officers' School, which he completed in October 1931 and was posted to the 1st Air Regiment at Warsaw. Soon after he was accepted to the Air Force Cadet Officers' School at Dęblin. He was commissioned with the 7th class on 15 August 1933 as an observer. Sub-Lieutenant Grzeszczak was posted back to the 1st Air Regiment at Warsaw, where he served in the 13th Army Co-operation Squadron. On 20 October 1937 he was transferred to the 11th Light Bomber Squadron. From February 1938 he was appointed a personal record officer of the 1st Air Regiment, then in November 1938 he took on the adjutant's duty. Between June and July 1939 Grzeszczak participated in an aerobatic course organized within the 1st Regiment. During the Polish Campaign in 1939 he did not fly operationally, being appointed adjutant of the 1st Air Base, then from 7 September he served in the 2nd Liaison Platoon of the HQ Air Force and subsequently from 10-17 September at the HQ of Bomber Brigade. He crossed the Rumanian border on 19 September and spent some time in an internment camp. After escaping he travelled to France, arriving at Marseilles on 19 November. After training and conversion to fighter planes, on 29 February 1940 he was posted to Etampes to No. 1 Pilots School. On 5 May he completed training and returned to Lyon-Bron. On 24 May he joined the so-called 'Koolhoven Flight', named after the FK 58 Koolhoven aircraft they were equipped with, commanded by Captain

Walerian Jasionowski, and next day arrived at Salon. From 8 June he operated from Clermont-Ferrand, being appointed commander of the 3rd Section. On 19 June he moved with this unit to Rodez, then via Montpellier and Perpignan travelled to Biarritz, from where on 24 June he sailed to England. Upon arrival he was given the service number P-1391 and the rank of Flying Officer. Initially he was considered for the first squad of No. 302 (Polish) 'City of Poznań' Squadron. In August he was posted to No. 303 (Polish) 'Tadeusz Kościuszko. City of Warsaw' Squadron. During the Battle of Britain he claimed two aerial victories, but he also had to crash-land near Fareham on 26 September after an aerial combat. In April 1941 he was posted for rest and was an instructor at No. 57 Operational Training Unit at Hawarden, from where in June he was transferred to No. 58 Operational Training Unit at Grangemouth. On 28 August he was flying the Miles Master I T8581 with pupil Pilot Officer William MacDonald when the aircraft suddenly spun out of control at 600 metres, crashing near Maddeston. Both airmen were killed. Bohdan Grzeszczak was buried at Northwood Cemetery, in grave no. H 179. He was decorated with the Cross of Valour and bar. He is commemorated on the Polish Air Force Memorials at Northolt and Warsaw-Mokotów.

Date & Time	Unit	Aircraft	Score
26.09.1940 16.40	303 Squadron	Hurricane I P3120 RF-A	1-0-0 He 111
27.09.1940 09.20	303 Squadron	Hurricane I V7244 RF-C	1-0-0 Bf 109

H

ZDZISŁAW KAROL HENNEBERG, Flying Officer, called 'Dzidek' (Polish diminution of his first name), was born on 11 May 1911 in Warsaw, which was ruled by the Russian Empire, into the family of Adolf Romuald and Anna née Mordasiewicz. He completed his primary education and then went to Jan Zamoyski Humanistic Secondary School in Warsaw, passing A-level exams in 1929. He went to the National High School of Mechanical Engineering and Electronics in Warsaw, but decided to follow his dream of being a pilot. In eaerly 1931 he started a unitary course at the Infantry Cadet Officers' School, then was accepted to the Air Force Reserve Cadet Officers' School at

Dęblin. Upon completion on 29 September 1932 he started at the Air Force Cadet Officers' School at Dęblin. Henneberg was commissioned on 15 August 1934 with the 8th class as an observer. With the rank of Sub-Lieutenant, he was posted to the 213th Night Bomber Squadron equipped with Fokker F-VIIB/3ms. In the meantime his sister Hanna Henneberg-Kubicka, a well-known aviator, had a fatal gliding accident in September 1934. By the end of the same month Henneberg was transferred to the 11th Light Bomber Squadron of the 1st Air Regiment. In 1935 he was sent back to Dęblin, where he undertook a flying course, then from 15 April he took the Advanced Flying Course at Grudziądz, which he completed in July. On 1 September that year he joined the 111th Fighter Squadron of the 1st Air Regiment at Warsaw. He then married Krystyna Dydyńska, and on 2 March 1936 he had a flying accident in a PZL P.11a but survived without injury. At this time he was actively participating in civilian aviation, being a sport and glider pilot. He was a member of the Warsaw Aero-Club, and between 4-18 July 1937 he represented Poland in an international gliding competition at Rhön. In July he was also posted to the Air Force Officers' Training Centre at Dęblin, where he served as a flying instructor. He commanded the 2nd Training Squadron, and soon after was appointed to command the 5th Training Squadron. During the Polish Campaign in 1939 he flew operationally, defending Dęblin and Ułęż with a flight formed ad hoc from the instructors. Via Rumania he travelled to France, where initially he was based at Salon, from where in December he was transferred to the Polish Air Force Training Centre at Lyon-Bron. On 12 May 1940 he was appointed commanding officer of the Polish fighter Chimney Section DAT, called IV Patrol Châteauroux. From 20 May his section operated defending the SNCASO factory which manufactured Bloch aircraft, the Poles flying MB 151s and MB 152s. On 5 June Henneberg was credited with the joint destruction of an He 111. Two weeks later his section arrived at Bordeaux. The day after he led two pilots flying to Nantes, from where they flew to Tangmere in England. Henneberg and his pilots left their Bloch aircraft at West Kirby. On 2 August he was posted to No. 303 (Polish) 'Tadeusz Kościuszko. City of Warsaw' Squadron. During the Battle of Britain he claimed the destruction of over eight enemy aircraft. On 7 September he was appointed 'A' Flight commander, being temporarily given command of No. 303 Squadron on 21 October before again taking over 'A' Flight on 6 November. On 20 February 1941 he officially took command of No. 303 Squadron. On 12 April, during combat over France, his Spitfire II P8029 RF-P was damaged by ground fire and Henneberg had to ditch in the English Channel 15 miles from Dungeness. He was lost at sea. He is commemorated on the Polish Air Force Memorials at Northolt and Warsaw-Mokotów, but also on a memorial plaque at RAF Northolt. He was decorated with the Silver Cross of Virtuti Militari no. 8818, the Cross of Valour and two bars, the British Distinguished Flying Cross and French Croix de Guerre. In 2012 the MiG-29 no. 59 from the 23rd Tactical Air Base at Mińsk Mazowiecki was adorned with his portrait.

Date & Time	Unit	Aircraft	Score
05.06.1940 13.00	Henneberg Section DAT	Bloch MB 152	½-0-0 He 111
31.08.1940 18.25	303 Squadron	Hurricane I V7290 RF-H	1-0-0 Bf 109
02.09.1940 17.50	303 Squadron	Hurricane I V7246 RF-D	0-0-1 Bf 109
07.09.1940 17.00	303 Squadron	Hurricane I V6605 YO-N (from No. 1 Sqn RCAF)	1-1-0 Bf 109
11.09.1940 16.00	303 Squadron	Hurricane I P3939 RF-H	1-0-0 Bf 109
11.09.1940 16.00	303 Squadron	Hurricane I P3939 RF-H	1-0-0 He 111
15.09.1940 12.00	303 Squadron	Hurricane I P3120 RF-A	1-0-0 Do 17 (claimed as Do 215)

Date & Time	Unit	Aircraft	Score
15.09.1940 12.00	303 Squadron	Hurricane I P3120 RF-A	1-0-0 Bf 109
27.09.1940 09.20	303 Squadron	Hurricane I V7246 RF-D	1-0-0 Bf 109
05.10.1940 11.40	303 Squadron	Hurricane I V6684 RF-F	1-0-0 Bf 110

J

ZBIGNIEW JANICKI, Pilot Officer, was born into a Polish family on 5 February 1917 in Kursk, Russia. After the family returned to Poland he was educated in a Warsaw secondary school, from where he graduated in 1935, passing A-level exams. Also in 1935 he obtained a 'C' category pass at a gliding course. From autumn 1935 he started compulsory military service, joining the Infantry Reserve Cadet School at Słonim. Upon completion in 1937 he was accepted to the Air Force Cadet Officers' School at Dęblin. Janicki was commissioned with the 12th class on 1 August 1939, although since June he had already served in the 111th  Fighter Squadron of the 1st Air Regiment at Warsaw as the education process was shortened due to the tense political situation. He participated in the 1939 Polish Campaign, flying as a part of the Pursuit Brigade. On 6 September he attacked a Ju 87 near Łubiniec, and by some accounts he was associated with its loss. Two days later he had an accident while riding a motorcycle and received a head injury, which barred him from further flying. Together with a road party he was captured by the Soviets on 18 September near Podhajce when his motorcycle failed. He managed to escape two days later, and on 22 September he crossed the Rumanian border near Zeleszczyki. He sailed to France via Constanta and Beirut, arriving at Marseilles on 29 October. Janicki decided to continue his fight from England, where he arrived in January 1940. He was given the service number 76697 and the rank of Pilot Officer. He was posted to No. 15 Elementary Flying Training School at Carlisle, and on 25

September was sent to No. 5 Operational Training Unit at Aston Down. Upon completion on 12 October he was posted to No. 32 Squadron at Acklington. On 29 November he was transferred to No. 46 Squadron, then on 15 January 1941 to No. 213 Squadron. On 17 April he joined No. 17 Squadron, before being posted to No. 307 (Polish) 'City of Lwów' Night Fighter Squadron on 23 April. Soon after he left, receiving a posting to No. 302 (Polish) 'City of Poznań' Squadron, where he reported on 3 May. During his time with No. 302 Squadron he got married without permission, for which he was sentenced to one month in prison after the war. On 3 November he was involved in a flying accident in the Spitfire II P7610 WX-D. On 14 December he was posted to No. 317 (Polish) 'City of Wilno' Squadron, yet on 12 April 1942 he was temporarily reposted to No. 116 Squadron for radar calibration duties. Janicki was back with No. 317 Squadron on 12 June 1942. In March 1943 he was appointed 'B' Flight commander. In October he was posted for rest to the HQ of No. 9 Group RAF, and was then transferred to No. 61 Operational Training Unit at Rednal for instructor duties. On 3 January 1944 he was posted to No. 2 Tactical Exercise Unit as an instructor. Alongside his Polish colleague pilots he was given permission to fly with the Americans, and on 12 May he joined the 61st Fighter Squadron of 56th Fighter Group, flying operations in P-47 Thunderbolts. Janicki became the only Polish pilot killed while flying with 'Zemke's Woolfpack', as the 56th called itself after its leader Colonel Hubert Zemke. He died whilst flying the P-47D-15-RE 42-76145 (probably HV-Z) on 13 June near La Chantellerie and La Garenne, at Ruille-en-Champagne, about 12 miles from Le Mans in France. He had a problem with jettisoning his fuel tanks and crashed while trying to land at 21.05. He was buried at Le Mans Cemetery, in grave no. 70, plot 21. Survived by his son Piotr Janicki, he is commemorated on the Polish Air Force Memorials at Northolt and Warsaw-Mokotów. A memorial dedicated to Flight Lieutenant Zbigniew Janicki was unveiled at Ruillé-en-Champagne, Sarthe, in June 2015. He was decorated with the Cross of Valour and two bars.

Date & Time	Unit	Aircraft	Score
06.09.1939 05.00	111th Squadron	PZL P.11	½-0-0 Ju 87 (unconfirmed)
18.12.1941 12.45	317 Squadron	Spitfire VB AD269 JH-B	1-0-0 Bf 109
11.09.1943 17.10	317 Squadron	Spitfire VB W3445 JH-Z	½-0-2 Fw 190

JERZY JANKIEWICZ, Flying Officer, called 'Jersey', was born on 14 July 1913 at Kiev, Ukraine, into the Polish family of Stanisław Andrzej and Elżbieta. He graduated from No. 3 Cadet Corps at Rawicz, where he passed A-level exams. On 1 September 1932 he was accepted into the Air Force Cadet Officers' School at Dęblin. Commissioned with the 8th class on 11 August 1934 as an observer, Sub-Lieutenant Jankiewicz was posted to the 11th Light Bomber Squadron of the 1st  Air Regiment at Warsaw. Between 1 June and 1 July 1935 he completed a basic flying course at the Air Force Officers' Training Centre at Dęblin and returned to his squadron. Between 1 April and 1 July 1936 he completed the Advanced Flying Course at Grudziądz and was posted back to the 1st Air Regiment. From 28 August 1937 he flew as a pilot of the 113th Fighter Squadron, then on 1 July 1937 he was appointed deputy commander of the same squadron. On 1 January 1939 he became tactics officer of the IV/1 Fighter Wing. In July and August 1939 he was sent to England, where he underwent training on Hawker Hurricanes, receiving his RAF pilot's wings. On 2 September he was posted to the HQ of the Polish Air Force as an instructor on Hawker Hurricanes, which were expected to arrive. On 11 September he was sent to Rumania to receive delivery of the aircraft, but this plan never materialized. Being aware of the fall of Poland, he travelled via Yugoslavia and Greece to France, where he landed on 23 October. He was sent to Britain to supervise modifications of the Polish Air Lines' Lockheed 14, which was to be used for clandestine flights to occupied Poland. After the project failed, Jankiewicz was transferred to the Polish Air Force, in fact being the last Polish airman joining the RAF Volunteer Reserve, before the Polish Air Force became part of the Polish armed forces in exile. He received the service number 83698 and the rank of Flying Officer. On 18 June 1940 he was sent to Blackpool, then on 17 July was sent to No. 15 Elementary Flying Training School at Carlisle and on 2 August to No. 6 Operational Training Unit at Sutton Bridge. On 17 August he was posted to No. 601 Squadron at Tangmere. During the Battle of Britain Jankiewicz made several claims in aerial combat. On 4 September he was wounded in combat, while flying his Hurricane I R4214. On 29 September he injured his right wrist while flying and was posted sick. On 4 October he was posted to No. 238 Squadron, but on the same day the order was cancelled and he returned to No. 601 Squadron. On 23 October he was posted to No. 303 (Polish) 'Tadeusz Kościuszko. City of Warsaw' Squadron. From February 1941 he served as ground controller of the same unit, becoming 'B' Flight commander on 5 May. On 10 July he was appointed commanding officer of No. 303 Squadron, then on 19 November was posted to HQ Fighter Command, where he served as fighter training officer in the Polish Liaison Officer's office. On 6 May 1942 he went to No. 124 Squadron for flying practice, then on 22 May he took command of No. 222 Squadron. He was the first Polish officer appointed to command an RAF squadron, but soon after was shot down and killed on 25 May while leading the North Weald Wing during an operation over Dunkirk. His Spitfire VB AD233 ZD-F was lost in the sea and Squadron Leader Jankiewicz's body was never found. He is commemorated on the Polish Air Force Memorials at Northolt and Warsaw-Mokotów. In 2016 the MiG-29 no. 54 from the 23rd Tactical Air Base at Mińsk Mazowiecki was adorned with his portrait. He was decorated with the Silver Cross of Virtuti Militari no. 9171, the Cross of Valour and two bars and the British Distinguished Flying Cross.

Date & Time	Unit	Aircraft	Score
31.08.1940 08.40	601 Squadron	Hurricane I R4214	0-0-1 Bf 109
04.09.1940 14.00	601 Squadron	Hurricane I R4214	0-1-0 Bf 110
25.09.1940 12.00	601 Squadron	Hurricane I V6666 UF-J	1-0-0 Bf 110
07.10.1940 14.30	601 Squadron	Hurricane I P3831	0-0-1 Bf 110
15.05.1941 12.45	303 Squadron	Spitfire II P8130 RF-T	½-0-0 Ju 52
22.06.1941 16.10	303 Squadron	Spitfire II P8346 RF-T	1-0-0 Bf 109
06.07.1941 09.45	303 Squadron	Spitfire II P8579 RF-V	0-⅓-0 Bf 109

WOJCIECH JANUSZEWICZ, Flying Officer, called 'Wojtek' (a diminution of his first name), was born on 30 April 1911 at Krzywiec near Słonim within the Russian Empire into the Polish family of Joachim, a farm owner, and Antonina née Minuczyc. Initially he was educated at home, then attended a four-class primary school at Mochnacze. He was a talented musician who played the violin. In 1930 he graduated from the State Teachers College, then worked as a teacher in a local school. On 15 October 1931 he joined the Infantry Cadet Officers' School at Komorowo near Ostrów Mazowiecka, then was posted for a unitary course at Różan. Between 3-28 September 1933 he completed a gliding course at the Military Gliding School at Ustianowa, gaining A and B category. He was commissioned on 15 August 1934, and in the rank of Sub-Lieutenant was posted to the 21st Infantry Regiment at Warsaw. On 17 September he was accepted to attend a flying course at the Air Force Officers' Training Centre at Dęblin, completing in July 1935. On 1 September he joined the 1st Air Regiment at Warsaw, being posted to the 13th Army Co-operation Squadron. On 30 October he was reposted to the 12th Light Bomber Squadron. On 28 February 1936 he was involved in a landing accident when his Breguet XIX crashed into another aircraft. From 20 April he participated in an Advanced Flying Course at Grudziądz, returning to the 12th Squadron on 17

July. On 17 September he was posted to the 111th Fighter Squadron of the 1st Air Regiment at Warsaw. In October 1937 Januszewicz was appointed deputy commander of the 111th Squadron, and in October 1938 alongside his squadron he was sent to Aleksandrowice aerodrome during the annexation of Zaolzie. During the Polish Campaign in 1939 he flew as deputy commander of the 111th Fighter Squadron attached to the Pursuit Brigade, then took command of the squadron after Captain Gustaw Sidorowicz was shot down on 1 September. Januszewicz claimed three aerial victories on 3, 4 and 6 September. On 6 September he was shot down and crash-landed near Zaborowo. After the fall of Poland, on 18 September he crossed the Rumanian border at Śniatyń together with the road party of his unit. He travelled through Rumania, arriving at the port of Balchik, from where on the *Aghios Nikolaos* he sailed to Beirut on 15 October 1939, continuing on board the *Ville de Strasbourg* to France. He arrived at Marseilles on 30 October. Januszewicz was posted for training to the Polish Air Force Training Centre at Lyon-Bron. On 18 May 1940 he was posted to the Polish fighter section commanded by Lieutenant Władysław Goettel and attached to GCII/7. He commanded a smaller section consisting of Sub-Lieutenant Wiktor Strzembosz and Corporal Henryk Szope flying Morane MS 406s and Dewoitine D 520s. After the collapse of France, on 20 June he flew to Algiers and on to Tunis. On 26 June he sailed to Casablanca and Gibraltar, and on board the *Neuralia* arrived at Liverpool on 17 July. He received the service number P-1385 and the rank of Flying Officer. On 22 July it was decided that Januszewicz would join II Fighter Squadron, which later became No. 303 (Polish) 'Tadeusz Kościuszko. City of Warsaw' Squadron. On 2 August he arrived at Northolt. During the Battle of Britain he performed numerous operations, being shot down on 26 September, crash-landing in his Hurricane I P3544 RF-H. He was then shot down and killed on 5 October at 11.40. His Hurricane I P3892 RF-V was hit over Hawkinge and crashed at Stowting, Kent, catching fire with him inside, most probably being wounded. He was buried in Northwood Cemetery, in grave no. H 231. He was the twenty-third Polish operational pilot killed during the Battle of Britain. He is commemorated on the Polish Air Force Memorials at Northolt and Warsaw-Mokotów, but also on the memorial plaque at RAF Northolt. Januszewicz was decorated with the Silver Cross of Virtuti Militari no. 8823 and the Cross of Valour and two bars. In 2013 his biography *A Few Minutes of Life* was published in Poland by Marek Rogusz. The MiG 29 no. 38 of the 23rd Tactical Air Base at Mińsk Mazowiecki has his portrait painted on its tail.

Date & Time	Unit	Aircraft	Score
03.09.1939 09.00	111th Squadron	PZL P.11c	1-0-0 Bf 110
04.09.1939 16.30	111th Squadron	PZL P.11c	1-0-0 Ju 87
05.09.1939	111th Squadron	PZL P.11c	shared victory Ju 87
06.09.1939 05.30	111th Squadron	PZL P.11c	1-0-0 Ju 87

FRANCISZEK JASTRZĘBSKI, Flight Lieutenant, called 'Agnieszka' (Agnes), was born on 10 November 1905 at Zglechów near Sennica in the former territory of Poland ruled by the Russian Empire. He grew up in the family of farmers Karol and Julianna née Osica. In 1926 he graduated from the State Teachers College at Łomża and joined the Infantry Reserve Cadet Officers' School at Ostrów Mazowicka, from where he graduated in 1927. In November of the same year he was accepted to the Air Force Officers' School at Dęblin, which soon after was renamed the Air Force Cadet Officers' School. He was commissioned with the 3rd class on 15 August 1929, and as an observer with the rank of Sub-Lieutenant was posted to the 55th Light Bomber Squadron of the 5th Air Regiment at Lida. Between August and October 1931 he served as adjutant to the commanding officer of the 5th Air Regiment, then from January 1932 to March 1933 he flew in the 51st Light Bomber Squadron. In the middle of 1933 he was sent to the Air Force Officers' Training Centre at Dęblin for the flying course. He was then posted to the 143rd Fighter Squadron of the 4th Air Regiment at Toruń, where he served as technical officer. On 7 August he had a flying accident at Toruń aerodrome. In October he flew to Rumania as part of the Polish team of pilots who presented PZL P.7s to the Rumanian monarch. Then in November 1934 he was posted to Grudziądz, where he served as an instructor on the Advanced Flying Course. Jastrzębski remained at Grudziądz until October 1937, when he was posted to the 3rd Air Regiment at Poznań and took command of the 132nd Fighter Squadron. During the Polish Campaign in 1939 he led his squadron that supported the 'Poznań' Army. He claimed three aerial victories, reported on 2, 8 and 10 September. He was shot down on 10 September and baled out. Later he flew in a single-seater PZL P.11 with III/3 Wing's doctor to the Podlasie region, where he landed at Parczew. Jastrzębski fought with General Franciszek Kleeberg's Army as a cavalryman until 5 October. Then he travelled to Zglechów and then Warsaw. After the fall of Warsaw, accompanied by Captain Jerzy Zaremba, he fled to Hungary via Slovakia, and then via Yugoslavia and Italy travelled to France. He arrived there in January 1940, and soon after was sent to the Polish Air Force Training Centre at Lyon-Bron. On 18 May he was given command of the Polish fighter section attached to GCII/1. They were sent to Buc on 19 May, where they received Bloch MB 152s. After the fall of France Jastrzębski and his pilots travelled to Port Vendres, from where on 23 June he sailed to Oran, then via Casablanca and Gibraltar to Britain. Upon arrival he received the service number P-1296 and the rank of

Flight Lieutenant. He was posted to No. 302 (Polish) 'City of Poznań' Squadron being formed at Leconfield, and on 26 July he took command of 'B' Flight. During the Battle of Britain he claimed a shared victory as well as a probable destruction of an enemy aircraft. On 19 October he hit a barrage balloon cable and crash-landed his Hurricane I P3923 WX U. He was killed on 25 October while patrolling over the English Channel, although the circumstances of his death are not clear. It is believed he was shot down and went into the sea with his Hurricane I V7593 WX-V. He was the twenty-ninth Polish operational pilot killed during the Battle of Britain. His body was later found by the Germans and buried at Westerland, Sylt, in grave no. C.22 on 11 December. After the war he was reburied at Kiel War Cemetery, Germany, in plot IV, row H, grave no. 6. He is commemorated on the Polish Air Force Memorials at Northolt and Warsaw-Mokotów, but also on the memorial plaque at RAF Northolt. He was posthumously decorated with the Silver Cross of Virtuti Militari no. 8985 and the Cross of Valour and three bars.

Date & Time	Unit	Aircraft	Score
02.09.1939	132nd Squadron	PZL P.11c	1-0-0 He 111
08.09.1939	132nd Squadron	PZL P.11c	1-0-0 Bf 110
10.09.1939	132nd Squadron	PZL P.11c	1-0-0 Bf 109
15.09.1940 12.10	302 Squadron	Hurricane I R2684 WX-B	½-0-0 Do 17
18.09.1940 17.20	302 Squadron	Hurricane I P3930 WX-X	0-1-0 Do 17

JÓZEF JEKA, Sergeant, was born on 6 April 1917 at Tupadły near Wejherowo into the Polish family of Antoni and Agata née Mudlaff, settled in a Pomerania ruled by the German Empire. In 1928 he completed primary school at Tupadły and was then accepted to King Jan Sobieski Secondary School at Wejherowo, from where he graduated in 1936. On 1 September 1937 he entered military service and was posted to the 4th Air Regiment at Toruń. Between 3 January and 1 April 1938 he served there as a mechanic's assistant, then completed an aircraft maintenance course. From 1 April until 27 July he undertook a basic flying course with the 4th Regiment.

Between 15 August and 15 November he participated in the Advanced Flying Course at Grudziądz. Upon his return, Jeka was posted to the 141st Fighter Squadron of the 4th Air Regiment at Toruń. Between 1 April and 1 June 1938 he attended the NCOs School within the 4th Regiment. He participated in the Polish Campaign in 1939, flying as a pilot of the 141st Fighter Squadron supporting the 'Pomorze' Army. On 2 September 1939 he took part in a suicidal attack performed by both squadrons of the III/4 Fighter Wing against German tanks, watching four of his colleagues being killed by ground fire. He managed to survive, although his PZL P.11 was damaged. He took part in many combat missions. On 18 September, together with the road party of his unit, he crossed the Rumanian border and was interned in Babadag camp. On 5 October he managed to escape, and travelled via Yugoslavia and Greece to France, arriving at Marseilles on 23 October. After being transferred to Lyon-Bron he decided to pursue his chances of fighting in England. He arrived in Britain on 23 February 1940 and was posted to RAF Eastchurch. He received the service number 780836 and the rank of Leading Aircraftman. On 29 May he was transferred to Blackpool, and on 17 July to No. 15 Elementary Flying Training School at Carlisle. Initially Jeka was considered for the first squad of No. 302 (Polish) 'City of Poznań' Squadron. On 31 July he was posted to No. 6 Operational Training Unit at Sutton Bridge, and on 31 August to No. 238 Squadron at Middle Wallop. Sergeant Jeka, during the Battle of Britain shot down at least four enemy aircraft. He was shot down on 5 November in the Hurricane I V7535, baled out but was wounded. He was taken to Shaftesbury hospital and spent several months recovering. For some time he performed ground duties, until he was operational again. On 15 February 1941 he was posted to No. 306 (Polish) 'City of Toruń' Squadron. During his service with this unit he added at least two victories to his account. On 1 November for his achievements in combat he was commissioned, receiving the new service number P-1654 and the rank of Pilot Officer. On 22 November he was posted for rest as an instructor at No. 58 Operational Training Unit at Grangemouth, where he served until 25 May 1942. On 29 May he was posted back to No. 306 Squadron, but on 3 December he was sent for an officer's course at Cosford. On 24 May 1943 he was posted to No. 308 (Polish) 'City of Kraków' Squadron, and on 11 August reposted to No. 316 (Polish) 'City of Warsaw' Squadron, where he made further claims in aerial combat. On 18 November he was posted to No. 18 Armament Practice Camp at Fairwood Common as an instructor. He returned to combat flying, and on 30 March 1944 took command of 'B' Flight of No. 308 Squadron. He was shot down and reported missing on 21 May during an operational sortie over the Seine in France. After crash-landing at Buchy in his Spitfire IX ML254 ZF-V, he managed to evade capture and on 8 September was back in London. On 24 November he was back with No. 306

Squadron, then for a while was reposted to No. 316 Squadron before returning to No. 306 Squadron, where on 6 December he was appointed commander of 'A' Flight. Jeka was injured in a taxiing accident in the Mustang III KH506. On 25 May 1945 he was appointed commander of No. 306 Squadron, being the second officer who started his military wartime career as an NCO who was given such a command. On 7 April 1946 he was posted to RAF Coltishall, and on 21 January 1948 was transferred to the Polish Resettlement Unit. Acting Squadron Leader Jeka decided to stay in England, and soon after volunteered for a project to drop him into a Poland ruled by the communist regime with the mission of hijacking a MiG-15. This mission was eventually abandoned. He joined American services run by the CIA and performed various clandestine operations. He was killed on 15 April 1958 during the civil war in Indonesia while flying a Douglas B-26. According to his wishes, he was buried at Newark-on-Trent Cemetery, next to the Polish Air Force section. He was decorated with the Silver Cross of Virtuti Militari no. 9166, the Cross of Valour and three bars, the Silver Cross of Merit with Swords and the British Distinguished Flying Medal.

Date & Time	Unit	Aircraft	Score
15.09.1940 15.00	238 Squadron	Hurricane I P3219	1-0-0 Bf 110
26.09.1940 16.30	238 Squadron	Hurricane I L1998	2-0-0 He 111
27.09.1940 11.00	238 Squadron	Hurricane I P3836	½-0-0 Bf 110
30.09.1940 16.20	238 Squadron	Hurricane I P3219	0-0-1 Bf 110
07.10.1940 16.30	238 Squadron	Hurricane I L1889 WX-X	1-0-0 Ju 88
17.06.1941 19.45	306 Squadron	Hurricane II Z3500 UZ-B	1-0-0 Bf 109
27.06.1941 21.50	306 Squadron	Hurricane II Z3438 UZ-C	0-0-1 Bf 109
16.08.1941 12.44	306 Squadron	Spitfire IIB P8325 UZ-B	1-0-0 Bf 109
19.08.1943 11.20	316 Squadron	Spitfire IX LZ989 SZ-J	1-0-1 Fw 190
06.03.1945 14.00	306 Squadron	Mustang III HB861 UZ-B	1-0-0 V1

EDMUND WINCENTY JERECZEK, Pilot Officer, was born on 27 October 1904 at Kościerzyna in Pomerania, which was controlled by the German Empire. After completing his primary education he enrolled at the State Secondary School at Kościerzyna. In 1924 he began education at the Machinery Construction Faculty of the Gdańsk Technical University, but decided not continue and in 1925 started a career in the shipbuilding industry. However, between 1926 and 1927 he was enlisted into the Polish Army. He returned to Gdańsk University between 1931 and 1932, at the same time being an organizer, pilot, technical chief and

secretary of Gdańsk Aero Club at Rumia. Jereczek was accepted to the Air Force Reserve Cadet Officer's School at Dęblin, and then in 1938 completed an instructor's course organized by the Air Force Training Centre at Dęblin. Due to mobilization orders on 24 August 1939 he took command of the newly organized Liaison Platoon (flying) of the HQ Coastal Land Defence. This unit was formed as part of the Naval Air Squadron. During the Polish Campaign in 1939 Jereczek flew over Gdynia and Kępa Oksywska in the civilian aircraft RWD-13 SP-BML that previously belonged to the Gdańsk Aero Club, as well as a Lublin R-XIII and RWD-8. On 13 (or according to other sources on 12 or 14) September, alongside Lieutenant Tadeusz Nowacki, he flew from Kępa Oksywska in an RWD-13 to Gotland, Sweden, landing at Visby. After a short internment he was released, and via Bergen and Newcastle arrived in London on 7 October and was ordered to remain in Britain. He received the service number 76664 and the rank of Pilot Officer and was sent for initial training at No. 1 School of Army Co-operation at Old Sarum and then on 1 September 1940 for conversion to British fighters. He had a flying accident at No. 6 Operational Training Unit at Sutton Bridge while practicing in the Hurricane I P3644, after misjudging his landing approach. On 22 September he was posted to No. 43 Squadron based at Usworth, then in October to No. 229 Squadron at Northolt. On 8 January 1941 Jereczek completed a flying instructors' course and was posted to No. 25 (Polish) Service Flying Training School at Hucknall. From there he was sent to No. 10 Flying Instructors School at Woodley and then to No. 5 Flying Instructors School at Perth. Eventually he returned to Hucknall, where he remained until 13 November 1945, when he was posted to No. 16 (Polish) Service Flying Training School at Newton. He was demobilized in December 1946 with the rank of Squadron Leader and decided to settle in Britain. After the war his whereabouts are not known so far, apart from the fact that he was a member of the Royal Aero Club. He died on 26 August 1984 in Stourbridge and was buried in the Roman Catholic Our Lady and All Saints Church Cemetery at Stourbridge. He was decorated with the British Air Force Cross.

K

STANISŁAW KARUBIN, Sergeant, was born on 29 October 1915 at Woźniki near Świniary in Lublin Voivodship, which was governed by the Russian Empire. He grew up in the family of Wojciech, an estate supervisor, and Sotera née Cibor. After the end of the Great War, when Poland regained its independence, his family moved to Obory near Konstancin Jeziorna. In 1932 he completed seven classes of primary school. As part of the youth military training system he was sent to the 21st Infantry Regiment at Warsaw, where he stayed between September 1932 and June 1933. In September 1933 he was accepted to the Public Trade School no. 32 in

Warsaw. Meanwhile he was sent to the Air Force Officers' Training Centre at Dęblin, where he completed an aircraft maintenance course. Karubin joined the Shooting Association within the 1st Air Regiment at Warsaw. On 2 July 1934 he was enrolled into national military service with a posting to the 1st Air Regiment. From 7 April 1935 he attended the NCOs School at the 1st Regiment, then was sent to the Central NCOs Flying School at Bydgoszcz, from which he graduated on 28 June 1935. On 10 July 1936 he started a basic flying course, which he completed on 27 October. From 4 May to 10 August 1937 he undertook the Advanced Flying Course at Grudziądz. Upon completion he was posted to the 111th Fighter Squadron of the 1st Air Regiment at Warsaw. In October 1938 he was sent with his unit to Aleksandrowice aerodrome due to the Zaolzie crisis. On 28 December Karubin married Janina Chyziak. During the Polish Campaign of 1939 he flew with his unit, being part of the Pursuit Brigade, shooting down a Bf 110 on 3 September . After the fall of Poland, on 17 September he crossed the Rumanian border, travelling via Greece to France. On 21 January 1940 he was sent to the Polish Air Force

Training Centre at Lyon-Bron, then initially was assigned to the 3rd Section of the 1st Polish Fighter Squadron that was intended to be formed. Instead, on 13 May he was posted to the Polish fighter section DAT under the command of Major Zdzisław Krasnodębski at Châteaudun, flying Morane MS 406s, Curtiss H 75As, Koolhoven FK58s, Arsenal VG33s and Bloch MB 152s. From 20 May the Poles were attached to GCI/55. On 3 June he claimed the destruction of a Do 17, yet his claim was rejected. After the collapse of France, on 18 June he sailed on board the Polish ship *Kmicic* from La Rochelle to Britain. Upon arrival on 21 June he received the service number 793420 and the rank of Sergeant. After a short stay at Glasgow and Blackpool he was initially assigned to No. 302 (Polish) 'City of Poznań' Squadron at Leconfield, but he never joined this unit. Instead, on 2 August he was posted to No. 303 (Polish) 'Tadeusz Kościuszko. City of Warsaw' Squadron at Northolt. During the Battle of Britain he shot down six enemy aircraft, being shot down himself on 6 September. Wounded in a leg, he crash-landed in his Hurricane I V7290 RF-H at Fletchers Farm in Pembury, Kent. Karubin spent the following three weeks in hospital. On 7 March 1941 he was posted for rest to No. 57 Operational Training Unit at Hawarden, where he served as an instructor. Then he was reposted to No. 55 Operational Training Unit at Usworth, where he was assigned for similar duty to the Polish Fighter School. On 12 August 1941 he flew the Hurricane I V7742 returning from practice duty, and while descending through clouds he collided with high ground at Horn Cragg near Boot. Karubin was killed, as was another Polish pilot, Flying Officer Zygmunt Hőhne, who flew next to him. Stanisław Karubin was buried at Castletown Cemetery at Hylton, Sunderland, in the War Graves plot, Section D, Row 1, grave no. 722. He is commemorated on the Polish Air Force Memorials at Northolt and Warsaw-Mokotów. He was decorated with the Silver Cross of Virtuti Militari no.8827, the Cross of Valour with two bars and the British Distinguished Flying Medal.

Date & Time	Unit	Aircraft	Score
03.09.1939	111th Squadron	PZL P.11c	1-0-0 Bf 110
03.06.1940	GCI/55	unknown	1-0-0 Do 17 (rejected)
31.08.1940 18.25	303 Squadron	Hurricane I R2688 RF-F	1-0-0 Bf 109
05.09.1940 15.05	303 Squadron	Hurricane I P3975 RF-U	2-0-0 Bf 109
06.09.1940 09.00	303 Squadron	Hurricane I V7290 RF-H	1-0-0 He 111

| 30.09.1940 14.00 | 303 Squadron | Hurricane I V7504 RF-G | 1-0-0 Bf 109 |
| 05.10.1940 11.40 | 303 Squadron | Hurricane I P3901 RF-E | 1-0-0 Bf 109 |

WŁODZIMIERZ EUGENIUSZ KARWOWSKI, Pilot Officer, was born on 13 September 1912 at Kielce, in the part of Poland governed by the Russian Empire. After completing primary school he was accepted to the Stefan Żeromski Secondary School for Boys. In 1934 he graduated, passing A-level exams. He completed the unitary course at the Infantry Cadet Officers' School, then in 1935 was accepted to the Air Force Reserve Cadet Officers' School at Dęblin, later being transferred to the Air Force Cadet Officers' School. Commissioned with the 10th class in 1937, Sub-Lieutenant Karwowski was posted to the 121st Fighter Squadron of the 2nd Air Regiment at Cracow. Between October and December 1938 he completed an instructor's course, and from 1 January 1939 served as a flying instructor at the Advanced Flying Course at Ułęż (moved from Grudziądz). During the Polish Campaign in 1939 he flew with the ad hoc-formed flight of instructors who were defending Ułęż and Dęblin. He crossed the Rumanian border at Kuty on 17 September and was interned. After escaping he travelled via Yugoslavia and Greece, arriving at Marseilles on 29 October. He was sent to Salon, where he remained until December. He was then posted to the Polish Air Force Training Centre at Lyon-Bron. On 7 January 1940 he was sent to Montpellier for training, flying on Morane MS 406s. On 27 March he joined the Polish fighter section under the command of Captain Jan Pentz attached to GCII/6 at Anglure Vonarce. During the French Campaign he claimed two shared victories, on 13 May and 9 June, flying Morane MS 406s. On 20 June he went to Tolouse, from where he collected a Dewoitine D 520. Due to the French capitulation, on 24 June he boarded the *Apapa* at Port Vendres and, via Gibraltar, sailed to England, arriving there ten days later. For his participation in the French campaign Karwowski received a commendation from the French commander. After short stays in Glasgow and Blackpool he received the service number P-1284 and the rank of Pilot Officer, and on 23 July was posted to No. 302 (Polish) 'City of Poznań' Squadron at Leconfield. During the Battle of Britain he shot down one enemy aircraft on 18

September. He was also shot down and crash-landed on 15 September while flying the Hurricane I R4095 WX-M. On 23 November 1941 he was appointed 'B' Flight commander, then on 27 January 1942 'A' Flight commander. In the spring of 1942 he was posted for rest and sent for the instructors' course at the Central Gunnery School at Sutton Bridge. On 26 June he became a flying instructor at No. 58 Operational Training Unit at Ballado Bridge, and on 13 December was posted to No. 316 (Polish) 'City of Warsaw' Squadron, where he took command of 'B' Flight. On 17 March 1943 he was appointed commander of No. 306 (Polish) 'City of Toruń' Squadron, serving until 1 January 1944 when he was transferred to Northolt, where he served as Sector Gunnery Officer at the HQ of No. 18 Wing RAF. Between March and June 1944 he served as Polish Liaison Officer at the HQ of No. 12 Group RAF, from where he was posted to No. 84 Group Support Unit. On 30 January 1945 he became the Chief Flying Instructor at No. 61 Operational Training Unit at Rednal, and on 6 July was posted to the Central Gunnery School RAF at Leconfield. Squadron Leader Karwowski was demobilized from the Polish Air Force and emigrated to New Zealand, where he ran his own farm. Włodzimierz Karwowski died on 29 May 1978 at Auckland and was buried at Purewa Cemetery, Auckland. He was decorated with the Cross of Valour and two bars and the French Croix de Guerre.

Date & Time	Unit	Aircraft	Score
13.05.1940 10.10	GCII/6	Morane MS 406	½-0-0 He 111
09.06.1940	GCII/6	Morane MS 406	½-0-0 Do 17
18.09.1940 17.23	302 Squadron	Hurricane I P3085 WX-A	1-0-0 Ju 88
13.03.1941 15.20	302 Squadron	Hurricane I Z2386 WX-C	0-0-½Ju 88

TADEUSZ WILHELM KAWALECKI, Pilot Officer, was born on 12 March 1915 at Stanisławów within the territory of Poland ruled by the Russian Empire. He grew up in the family of Wilhelm and Kazimiera. After graduating from the secondary school at Stanisławów and passing A-level exams in 1932 he was accepted to Lwów Technical University, completing three years. In 1935 he joined the Air Force Cadet Officers' School at Dęblin. He was commissioned on 15 August 1938 with the 11th class, and in the rank of Sub-Lieutenant was posted to the 121st Fighter Squadron of the 2nd Air Regiment at Cracow. During the Polish Campaign in 1939 he flew operationally from the early hours of 1 September, being the pilot who at 05.29 informed his squadron about German bombers attacking Cracow. While engaging enemy bombers his aircraft was damaged by return fire. Despite this he claimed the destruction of an enemy bomber, probably a Ju 87, that was attacking his aerodrome at Balice, yet this claim was never accepted as the details were not clear enough. The 121st Squadron was supporting the 'Cracow' Army, was then sent to protect Dęblin and surrounding areas and finally attached to the Pursuit Brigade. On 16 September he flew a reconnaissance mission and was shot at by ground fire, then the next day his

aircraft was targeted by Soviet soldiers. The same day he flew to Cernâuti in Rumania, landing at 17.45. He travelled to France, arriving in Marseilles on 29 October. Like many other Polish airmen he decided to continue his fight from England, where he was sent by the end of December 1939 or in January 1940. Upon arrival he was given the service number 76698 and the rank of Pilot Officer. On 1 June 1940 he was posted to No. 3 Training Wing at Blackpool, then was transferred to No. 15 Elementary Flying Training School at Carlisle, and on 15 July to No.7 Operational Training Unit at Hawarden. On 7 August he was posted to No. 151 Squadron at North Weald. On 22 January 1941 he was sent to No. 1 Anti-Aircraft Co-operation Unit at Farnborough, then on 25 October to No. 4 Flying Instructors School at Cambridge. Upon completion he served as an instructor at No. 15 Elementary Flying Training School at Carlisle and No. 25 (Polish) Elementary Flying Training School at Hucknall. He was accepted to the Polish Air Force Staff College on 15 January 1944, and upon completion was posted as an operations officer to No. 84 Group RAF. Squadron Leader Kawalecki returned to the college as a lecturer. While returning from a visit to Polish squadrons based in Holland on 7 April 1945 Kawalecki and Wing Commander Jan Zumbach, piloting two Taylorcraft Austers NX532 and MT440, made navigational errors and force-landed behind enemy lines. Initially both were taken to Arnhem and later kept at Terschelling Island by the Kriegsmarine soldiers. When the war ended he returned to England, being posted once more to the PAF Staff College before being released from service in May 1946. He then emigrated to Canada. Tadeusz Kawalecki died tragically on 19 April 1971 at Stratford, Ontario, and was buried at Avondale Cemetery in Stratford.

Date & Time	Unit	Aircraft	Score
01.09.1939 05.40	121st Squadron	PZL P.11c	1-0-0 Ju 87 (unconfirmed)

SZYMON KITA, Sergeant, was born on 29 October 1916 at Zapusty near Jędrzejów in the territory of Poland ruled by the Russian Empire. He grew up in the family of Władysław and Zuzanna née Kozik. With the family he moved to Stary Sławacinek near Biała Podlaska, where his parents ran their own farm. After completing four classes of primary school he attended Józef Ignacy Kraszewski State Secondary School for Boys. In 1933 he left the school due to the difficult financial situation of his family and decided to help them to run the farm. He voluntarily joined the Polish Army and in September 1934 was sent to the 84th Polesie Fusilier Regiment at Pińsk.

With the regiment he completed the NCOs School. On 1 March 1936 he was transferred to the regiment's administration. On 15 August he started a gliding course at Ustianowa, and then in September was posted to the 5th Air Regiment at Lida. On 15 September he was attached to the Training Flight, where he remained until August 1937. Upon completion of the course he was posted to the 56th Army Co-operation Squadron. While living at Lida he went back to high school to continue his education and finally pass his A-level exams. On 1 March 1939 he was appointed a flying instructor for the Training Flight of the 5th Air Regiment, then on 25 August was posted back to the 56th Squadron, attached to the 'Karpaty' Army. During the Polish Campaign Szymon Kita flew reconnaissance missions in Lublin R-XIIIs or RWD-8s, including over Slovakia, an ally of Germany, mainly with his usual observer Sub-Lieutenant Kazimierz Kucza. On 6 September his aircraft was damaged by German ground fire. On 13 September he flew General Kazimierz Sosnkowski, commander of the Southern Front of Polish forces, to Przemyśl. Four days later, after the Soviet attack, Kita flew RWD-14 'Czapla' to Cernâuti in Rumania, where soon after he was interned and kept in Calafat camp. After escaping he travelled to Bucharest and then to Balchik. In the middle of November he sailed on board the *Patris* to Beirut, arriving on 24 December. A week later he continued on the *Patria* to Marseilles in France. On 18 January 1940 he was posted to the Polish Air Force Training Centre at Lyon-Bron, but unhappy with the situation in France, Kita decided to go to England. On 28

February he arrived at Southampton, the following day being posted to RAF Eastchurch. He received the service number 781003 and the rank of Sergeant. On 12 August he was posted to No. 1 Army Co-operation School at Old Sarum, then on 18 August to No. 5 Operational Training Unit at Aston Down. Upon completion, on 18 September Kita was posted to No. 85 Squadron at Church Fenton, then on 30 September to No. 253 Squadron at Kenley. On 7 October he wrote in his flying log book that he shot down an He 111 together with another pilot; on 12 October that he probably shot down a Bf 109; and on 28 October that he damaged a Bf 109, but these claims were never officially accepted. On 1 December at 11.45 he participated in combat over Brighton and was shot down in his Hurricane I P3678, crashing near Lewes, Kent. Badly wounded, he was pulled from the cockpit of his burning aircraft by civilians. The Pole claimed the destruction of a German plane. Kita spent five months in hospital until 3 May 1941. On 13 June he was posted for rest to Blackpool, then on 9 July to No. 61 Operational Training Unit at Heston. As his previous wounds limited his flying abilities, on 14 July he was posted to No. 11 Group Anti-Aircraft Co-operation Flight at Croydon. On 21 September he was transferred to No. 51 Operational Training Unit at Cranfield, returning to the previous unit at the beginning of October. This flight was soon after converted to No. 287 Squadron. On 10 April 1942 he was posted to No. 1 Flight Ferry Training Unit at Lyneham, and on 15 June he was sent to Africa with a posting to the Polish Ferry Unit at Takoradi in the Gold Coast (modern Ghana). Kita was posted back to England on 19 April 1944, arriving at Whitchurch on 23 April. On 10 June he was sent to No. 25 (Polish) Elementary Flying Training School as an instructor, then on 1 November to No. 16 (Polish) Service Flying Training School at Newton. On 20 March 1945 he joined No. 3 (Pilot) Advanced Flying Unit at South Cerney, being posted to Blackpool on 18 September. Warrant Officer Kita was demobilized in 1947 as he decided to return to Poland. He arrived there on 24 July and settled at Nowogród Bobrzański, then in Zielona Góra, working in the agricultural and building supply industries. He retired on 1 September 1976. Szymon Kita died on 29 September 1980 at Zielona Góra and was buried at the local cemetery in Wrocławska Street. He was decorated with the Cross of Valour and bar.

Date & Time	Unit	Aircraft	Score
07.10.1940 17.00	253 Squadron	Hurricane I P9386	½-0-0 He 111 (unconfirmed)
12.10.1940	253 Squadron	Hurricane I V6815 SW Y	0-1-0 Bf 109 (unconfirmed)

Date & Time	Unit	Aircraft	Score
28.10.1940	253 Squadron	Hurricane I V6815 SW-Y	0-0-1 Bf 109 (unconfirmed)
01.12.1940 11.45	253 Squadron	Hurricane I P3678	1-0-0 Bf 109 (unconfirmed)

STEFAN KLECZKOWSKI, Pilot Officer, was born on 2 September 1917 at Dębowo near Łomża in the territory of Poland ruled by the Russian Empire. He grew up in the noble family of Stanisław and Rozalia née Szulkowska. At the age of 2, he moved with his parents to Kleczkowo near Ostrołęka, a town founded by Stefan's ancestors. In 1924 he was accepted to Tadeusz Kościuszko Primary School at Kleczkowo. Kleczkowski was a great skier, participating in national competitions. He graduated from Stanisław Staszic State Secondary School at Łomża, and was accepted for the gliding course at Ustianowa, which he completed on 8 September 1937. On 21 September he was posted for the unitary course for Infantry Reserve Cadet Officers School to the 18th Infantry Regiment at Zambrów, then on 2 January 1938 he was accepted to the Air Force Cadet Officers' School at Dęblin. Due to the difficult political situation the three-year period (introduced instead of the previously practised two-year period) was shortened, and without official graduation he completed his education alongside his colleagues from the 13th class just before the outbreak of war. Commissioned during the Polish Campaign of 1939, he was evacuated together with a large group of graduates to Rumania and was interned. After escape on 27 September he arrived at Bucharest, where he obtained a false passport. On 15 October he sailed to Beirut, then on 31 October to Marseilles in France. Kleczkowski was temporarily sent to the Polish Air Force Training Centre at Lyon-Bron, but on 28 January 1940 he was sent to Britain. Upon arrival he received the service number 76717 and the rank of Pilot Officer, and was sent to RAF Eastchurch. In May he was sent to Blackpool. On 23 August he was posted to No. 1 Army Co-operation School at Old Sarum, from where on 1 September he was sent to No. 6 Operational Training Unit at Sutton Bridge. On 23 September he joined No. 302 (Polish) 'City of Poznań' Squadron at Leconfield. On 17 October he was wounded during combat while flying the Hurricane I V6735 WX-M and force-landed near Sittingbourne. It was there that he met Betty Margaret Barrow, whom he married on 13 February 1941 and with whom he had two sons. On 28 October 1940 he was posted sick, returning to flying soon after. On 9 February 1941 he was posted to No. 10 Bombing and Gunnery School, from where on 25 May he was reposted to No. 16 (Polish) Service Flying Training School at Newton and then to No. 25 (Polish) Elementary Flying Training School at Hucknall. Between 17 August and 1 September 1942 he stayed at No. 59 Operational Training Unit at Milfield. On 8 October 1944 he was posted to No. 303 (Polish) 'Tadeusz Kościuszko. City of Warsaw' Squadron, but on 15 October was reposted to No. 61 Operational Training Unit for a refreshing course. Kleczkowski reported back to No. 303 Squadron on 23 November and stayed with this unit until it was disbanded. Between 15 February and 25 March 1946 he undertook a navigators course at RAF West Raynham. He was released from the Polish Air Force in December in the rank of Flight Lieutenant. He decided to stay in England, soon after opening a bed and breakfast business in Sittingbourne, which he ran until his death. In 1955 he revisited his beloved Kleczkowo for the first time, accompanied by his wife and two sons, one of whom later became a pilot. Major Stefan Kleczkowski died on 14 February 1992 at Sittingbourne, his remains being taken to Poland and buried in the Parish Cemetery at Kleczkowo. He was decorated with the Cross of Valour.

ZYGMUNT KLEIN, Sergeant, was born on 24 August 1918 at Skórz in Pomerania, part of Poland that was ruled by the German Empire, but grew up at Koronowo, near Bydgoszcz. There he completed primary school and four classes of secondary school. At the age of 18, he voluntarily joined military service and on 2 November 1936 was posted to the 4th Air Regiment at Toruń. From 20 April 1937 he underwent training at the NCOs School of the 4th Regiment. Klein was sent for a gliding course between 4 July and 1 October, then started flying practice in the Training Flight of the 4th Regiment. Upon completion, from 15 August 1938 he began fighter pilot training at the Advanced Flying Course at Grudziądz. On 1 September, after two years of his national service, he decided to stay in the Polish Air Force, and on 16 November was posted to the 142nd Fighter Squadron of the 4th Air Regiment. During the Polish Campaign of 1939 he flew operationally, his

III/4 Fighter Wing supporting the 'Pomorze' Army. On 3 September he claimed a shared victory over a Henschel Hs 126. After the fall of Poland, on 19 September he crossed the Rumanian border, travelling to France, where he arrived on 23 November. He was posted to the Polish Air Force Training Centre at Lyon-Bron. As with many other Poles, Klein did not like the French attitude to the war and decided to continue his fight from England. He arrived there on 19 February 1940, being posted to the Polish Air Force Centre at RAF Eastchurch. He received the service number 780685 and the rank of LAC (Leading Aircraftman). Initially he was considered to join the No. 302 (Polish) 'City of Poznań' Squadron, but instead was sent to No. 5 Operational Training Unit at Aston Down. On 6 August Sergeant Klein joined No. 234 Squadron operating from St Eval in Cornwall. During the Battle of Britain he claimed at least two aerial victories, but was also shot down on 15 August and baled out from his Spitfire I P9363. On 5 October Klein was posted to No. 152 Squadron at Warmwell. On 26 November, due to lack of fuel, he force-landed near Torquay in his Spitfire I L1048. Two days later he fought over the Isle of Wight and was most probably shot down into sea in his Spitfire I P2947. It is believed that before he was killed he shot down Major Helmut Wick, the commander of JG2, although this loss is associated with a well-known RAF pilot. Zygmunt Klein's body was never found. He is commemorated on the Polish Air Force Memorials at Northolt and Warsaw-Mokotów, but also on the memorial in his hometown of Koronowo. He was decorated with the Cross of Valour and bar.

Date & Time	Unit	Aircraft	Score
03.09.1939	142nd Squadron	PZL P.11	¼-0-0 Hs 126
16.08.1940 18.20	234 Squadron	Spitfire I P9466	1-0-0 Bf 109
04.09.1940 13.30	234 Squadron	Spitfire I R6896	1-0-0 Bf 110
07.09.1940 18.15	234 Squadron	Spitfire I R6896	0-1-0 Do 17
07.10.1940 15.45	152 Squadron	Spitfire I P9386	0-0-1 Bf 110
28.11.1940 15.20	152 Squadron	Spitfire I P9427	1-0-0 Bf 109 (unconfirmed)

WOJCIECH KLOZIŃSKI, Sergeant, was born on 26 February 1915 into a Polish family of farmers living at Karnap in Germany's Ruhr district. After moving to a free Poland with his parents and three sisters he completed primary and secondary education. In 1931 he was accepted to the Air Force NCO School for Minors at Bydgoszcz, graduating in 1934 as an aircraft mechanic. He also underwent basic flying training. In 1934 he was sent to the Air Force Officers' Training Centre at Dęblin, where he completed a flying course. Upon completion he was posted to the 1st Air

Regiment at Warsaw, from where he was posted to complete an Advanced Flying Course at Grudziądz. Kloziński was posted to the 132nd Fighter Squadron of the 3rd Air Regiment, but was later posted back to the Air Force NCO School for Minors at Krosno, where he served as a flying instructor. After the fall of Poland, together with a group of pupils he was evacuated to Rumania. On 12 November he arrived in France and was posted to the Polish Air Force Training Centre at Lyon-Bron. Being unhappy with the situation in France he decided to go to England, and after arrival on 9 February 1940 he was sent to the Polish Air Force Centre at RAF Eastchurch, receiving the service number 780465 and the rank of Sergeant. In May he was moved to Blackpool, then to No. 15 Elementary Flying Training School at Carlisle, and eventually on 15 July to No. 7 Operational Training Unit at Hawarden. Initially he was considered for the first group of pilots to form No. 303 (Polish) 'Tadeusz Kościuszko' Squadron, but future events prevented him from taking this post. On 9 August he was posted to No. 54 Squadron at Catterick, and then at Hornchurch. On 12 August Kloziński claimed two enemy aircraft destroyed, including one probable. On 15 August he was shot down in combat over Dover. Badly wounded, he baled out from the Spitfire I R7015. He was hospitalized at Ashford and remained a non-operational member of the Polish Air Force until the end of the war. On 29 October 1941 he was posted to RAF Northolt, where he took up ground duties. On 15 August 1942 he was posted for the Link Trainer instructor's course, and upon completion on 5 November he arrived at No. 58 Operational Training Unit at Grangemouth, serving as a Link Trainer instructor. On 15 October 1943 he was reposted to No. 61 Operational Training Unit, where he held the same post. On 1 September 1944 Kloziński was accepted to the Cadet Officers' School in Scotland, and then on 12 January 1945 arrived at No. 14 Base at Faldingworth as a Link Trainer instructor. On 25 August 1947 he was commissioned, receiving the Polish rank of Sub-Lieutenant. After demobilization he planned to work in agriculture and emigrated to Canada with his wife Emma Stewart, whom he married in June 1946. He sailed from Southampton to Halifax, Canada, on board the ship *Aquitania* on 24 June 1947. Wojciech Klozinski changed his name to V.K. Stewart, and so far his further whereabouts are not known. He was decorated with the Cross of Valour and bar.

Date & Time	Unit	Aircraft	Score
12.08.1940	54 Squadron	Spitfire I L1042	1-1-0 Bf 109

WILHELM KOSARZ, Sergeant, was born on 20 June 1908 at Karwina in Cieszyn Silesia, into the Polish family of Józef and Agnieszka. After the Great War, Karwina was handed over to Czechoslovakia, despite the majority of Poles living there; his name therefore sometimes appears as Vilém Košař. In October 1929 he joined the Polish armed forces and was posted to the 2nd Air Regiment in Cracow. In 1931 he completed a basic flying course organized by the Air Force Training Centre at Bydgoszcz, and on 30 November was posted to the 65th Light Bomber Squadron of the 6th Air Regiment at Lwów. Between July and August 1932 Kosarz successfully completed an Advanced Flying Course at Grudziądz and then returned to the 65th Squadron. On 1 October he was transferred to the 122nd Fighter Squadron of the 2nd Air Regiment at Cracow, where he remained until the end of 1938. He became a member of the famous aerobatic team known as 'Bajan's Three', led by Captain Jerzy Bajan. Kosarz had a flying accident on a PZL P.7 on 24 May 1935, when the engine failed and he had to perform an emergency landing. In January 1938 he was appointed a flying instructor at the Initial Military Training Centre at Cracow. During the Polish Campaign in 1939 he was posted to the Replacement Group of the 2nd Air Regiment at Cracow, then on 2 September was transferred to the No. 1 Air Force Training Centre at Dęblin. As he spoke fluent Czech, he liaised between Captain Zbigniew Osuchowski and the group of Czechoslovak airmen who escaped to Poland and formed the so-called 'Reconnaissance Platoon (flying)'. Osuchowski's unit participated in numerous missions, flying Potez 25s, RWD-8s and PWS-26s. Kosarz was also responsible for training these men. After the fall of Poland on 22 September he flew to Rumania, where he assumed command of the remains of the Czechoslovak unit. In Bucharest, he obtained a Czechoslovak passport and travelled to Constance. From there he sailed to France, arriving at Marseilles on 21 October. Kosarz decided to continue fighting from England, and in early 1940 left France. Upon arrival he received the service number 780828 and the rank of Sergeant. In August he was posted to No. 302 (Polish) 'City of Poznań' Squadron, but on 2 September he was reposted to No. 5 Operational Traning Unit at Aston Down for further training. On 26 September he was back in No. 302 Squadron. On 15 October he force-landed his Hurricane I P3935 WX-D after colliding with a barrage balloon cable near Brooklands. He was killed on 8 November during aerial combat while patrolling over Croydon. It is believed that he baled out from his Hurricane I P3538 WX-J but that his parachute caught fire. The aircraft crashed at Pennybridge Farm, Mayfield Xavierian College, Sussex. Wilhelm Kosarz was buried in Northwood Cemetery, in grave no. H 274. He is commemorated on the Polish Air Force Memorials at Northolt and Warsaw-Mokotów, and the memorial plaque at RAF Northolt. He was decorated with the Bronze Cross of Merit and the Cross of Valour.

BRONISŁAW KAZIMIERZ KOSIŃSKI, Flight Lieutenant, was born on 26 August 1906 at Bolesławice, near Rypin, within the previous territory of Poland by then ruled by the German Empire. He grew up in the family of Kazimierz Konstanty and Zdzisława Zofia née Szramkowska. Upon completion of No. 2 Cadet Corps at Modlin and Chełmno, in 1927 he was accepted to the Air Force Cadet Officers' School at Dęblin. On 15 August 1929 he was commissioned with the 3rd class and in the rank of Sub-Lieutenant was posted to the 54th Light Bomber Squadron of the 5th Air Regiment at Lida, flying as an observer.
In November he was transferred to the Training Flight of the same regiment. In 1930 he was sent to the Air Force Training Centre at Dęblin, where he underwent a flying course. In June and July 1931 he completed an Advanced Flying Course at Grudziądz and by the end of October he was posted to the 2nd Air Regiment at Cracow. He was an aerobatic pilot, flying with the 'Bajan Three'. Posted to the 122nd Fighter Squadron, Kosiński was later sent back to Grudziądz, where he remained as a flying instructor of the Flying School. He had a flying accident on 13 December 1935 in a PZL P.7. During the summer of 1936 he flew gliders

in the Military Gliding Centre at Ustianowa and had an accident while flying a Komar C1-3. In 1938 he was posted to the 4th Air Regiment. During the Polish Campaign of 1939 he did not fly operationally, remaining with the 4th Air Base. After the fall of Poland he travelled to France and was posted to the Polish Air Force Training Centre at Lyon-Bron. On 1 March 1940 he arrived at the Fighter Pilots' School at Avord, where he trained on Morane MS 406s, Morane MS 230s, Dewoitine D 510s and North American A57s. Upon completion, on 15 May he was given command of the Polish Chimney Section, which consisted of the five pilots he trained with, and was posted to Bourges, where they were ordered to defend a factory manufacturing war equipment. The Poles flew Curtiss Hawk H 75s. During the French Campaign Kosiński shared the destruction of an He 111, which was reported on 5 June. After the collapse of France he flew to Algiers, from where he sailed to England, arriving on 7 July. He received the service number P-0298 and the rank of Flight Lieutenant. On 10 September he was posted to No. 307 (Polish) 'City of Lwów' Night Fighter Squadron and was appointed 'A' Flight Commander. Like many other Polish pilots he was unhappy flying Boulton Paul Defiants, deciding to join a day fighter unit, and on 9 October was posted to No. 1 School of Army Co-operation at Old Sarum, from where he was sent to No. 5 Operational Training Unit at Aston Down. On 22 October he reported to No. 32 Squadron at Acklington, then being transferred to No. 229 Squadron. On 22 December he was posted to No. 308 (Polish) 'City of Cracow' Squadron, receiving command of 'B' Flight. He left this unit on 22 June 1941 due to an internal disagreement with the Polish commander, and on 24 July was posted to No. 72 Squadron. Flying with this unit he claimed at least two aerial victories. On 28 November he joined No. 302 (Polish) 'City of Poznań' Squadron, becoming 'A' Flight Commander. He was shot down on 26 January 1942 while patrolling in the Cherbourg area. His Spitfire VB AA747 WX-B was hit over Alderney and Guernsey, and crashed into the sea. Kosiński's body was never found. He is commemorated on the Polish Air Force Memorials at Northolt and Warsaw-Mokotów. He was decorated with the Silver Cross of Virtuti Militari no. 9357, the Cross of Valour and bar and the French Croix de Guerre.

Date & Time	Unit	Aircraft	Score
05.06.1940	DAT Bourges	Curtiss H75	0-0-^{2}/$_5$ He 111
05.06.1940	DAT Bourges	Curtiss H75	^{3}/$_5$-0-0 He 111
29.08.1941 06.35-08.10	72 Squadron	Spitfire V W3511	1-1-0 Bf 109
01.10.1941 11.30-12.40	72 Squadron	Spitfire V P8783	1-1-0 Bf 109

JAN KOWALSKI, Sergeant, was born on 19 November 1916 at Mircze, near Hrubieszów, within the territory of Poland dominated by the Russian Empire. He completed five classes of the secondary school at Włodzimierz Wołyński in 1932 and was accepted to the Air Force NCO School for Minors at Bydgoszcz. He graduated in 1935 as an aircraft mechanic. In 1936 he completed a flying course at the Air Force Officers' Training Centre at Dęblin and was posted to the 12th Light Bomber Squadron of the 1st Air Regiment at Warsaw. Upon completing an Advanced Flying Course at Grudziądz, he was attached to the 112th Fighter Squadron of the 1st Air Regiment.

In 1937 he was posted back to the Air Force NCO School for Minors, this time as a flying instructor. During the Polish Campaign of 1939 he flew PZL P.23 Karaś aircraft with the ad hoc-formed Reserve Reconnaissance Flight; later he was in charge of a group of pupils, whom he led from Krosno to Rumania. After a long journey he arrived in France on 31 October. Initially he was sent to Istres, but later was moved to the Polish Air Force Training Centre at Lyon-Bron. On 4 March 1940 he was posted to the Training Centre at Rennes and became a flying instructor on LeO 20s, Potez 540s and Caudron Goelands. After the collapse of France he travelled to Britain, arriving at Glasgow on 22 June. Kowalski received the service number 793450 and the rank of Sergeant. On 23 August he was posted to No. 303 (Polish) 'Tadeusz Kościuszko. City of Warsaw' Squadron at Northolt. During the Battle of Britain he claimed at least one aerial victory. On 22 January 1941 he was posted to No. 315 (Polish) 'City of Dęblin' Squadron, and on 1 June 1942 commissioned as Pilot Officer with the new service number P-1909. On 5 December he was posted for rest and served at No. 58 Operational Training Unit at Grangemouth as an instructor. At the beginning of February 1943 he was accepted to the team of Polish fighter pilots to form a flight within No. 145 Squadron in North Africa. He flew with so-called 'Polish Fighting Team', better known as 'Skalski's Circus'. In July 1943 Kowalski returned to Britain and on 21 July was posted to No. 316 (Polish) 'City of Warsaw' Squadron. On 20 October he was transferred to the HQ of the No. 1 (soon No. 131) Polish Wing. On 28 April 1944 he joined No. 317 (Polish) 'City of Wilno' Squadron. He was posted for rest on 1 May 1945 and travelled to the Polish Air Force Centre at Blackpool. On 9 November he rejoined

No. 131 (Polish) Fighter Wing in Germany, then on 23 November was posted to the Enemy Aircraft Servicing and Storage Unit at Hamburg. In July 1946 he was back in the United Kingdom with a posting to the Polish Air Force Depot at Dunholme Lodge, completing an air traffic controllers' course at Swinderby and serving as such until demobilization with the rank of Flight Lieutenant. Married to a Polish woman who escaped from Poland during the war, Kowalski ran a workshop mending broken furniture and providing carpentry services. He then opened a small upholstery business before moving to Nottingham in 1955 and worked for Jessops until retirement in 1974. Jan Kowalski died on 15 May 2000 in Nottingham and was buried at St Helen's Churchyard, Burton Joyce. He was decorated with the Cross of Virtuti Militari no. 10789, the Cross of Valour and two bars and the British Distinguished Flying Cross.

Date & Time	Unit	Aircraft	Score
18.09.1940 13.15	303 Squadron	Hurricane I P3089 RF-P	⅛-0-0 'Do 215' distributed between all pilots of No. 303 Sqn
26.09.1940 16.30	303 Squadron	Hurricane I P3089 RF-P	1-0-0 Bf 109
27.09.1940 09.20	303 Squadron	Hurricane I P3089 RF-P	0-0-1 He 111

JULIAN KOWALSKI, Flying Officer, called 'Roch' after the fictitious seventeenth-century ribald nobleman portrayed in Polish literature, was born on 10 July 1910 at Nagórnik, near Kielce, within the former territory of Poland ruled by the Russian Empire. He grew up in the family of Jan and Ewa. In 1924 he completed seven classes of the primary school at Sieciechów, then in 1926 the secondary school in the same town, being accepted to the State Technical Secondary School at Radom and graduating in 1930. He was an apprentice at the Building Transport Company at Stawy (in 1928) and Machinery Factory 'Rudzki' (1929). After graduation he started working as a Road Construction Manager at the Regional Department of Roads at Janów Lubelski (1930-31). He was accepted to the

Air Force Cadet Officers' School at Dęblin and was commissioned with the 8th class on 15 August 1934. As an observer in rank of Sub-Lieutenant he was posted to the 21st Light Bomber Squadron of the 2nd Air Regiment at Cracow. Like many others he decided to pursue a pilot's career and undertook a flying course at the Air Force Officers' Training Centre at Dęblin from April-July 1935. Between May and July 1936 he participated in the Advanced Flying Course at Grudziądz, and upon completion was posted to the 123rd Fighter Squadron of the 2nd Air Regiment at Cracow. He was posted back to Dęblin, where between September 1937 and January 1938 he completed an instructors' course. He remained at Dęblin as a flying instructor. During the Polish Campaign in 1939 Kowalski flew with the ad hoc-formed instructors flight defending the Air Force School. On 19 September he was captured by the Soviets but managed to escape and travelled via Rumania with a group of other Polish airmen. After a short internment he sailed to France, arriving at Marseilles on 12 October. Initially, amongst other volunteers, he was posted to the so-called 'Finnish Squadron', the Polish-manned unit that was planned to be sent to Finland to fight against the Soviets. Training took place in February 1940 at Lyon-Bron. Kowalski remained at Bron after the armistice was announced, and then joined the Polish 1/145 'City of Warsaw' Squadron flying Caudron CR. 714s. He was attached to 1st Flight and appointed Section no. 4 commander. He usually flew Caudron no. 10. On 9 of June he claimed his only aerial victory over France by destroying a Dornier Do 17, together with Captain Antoni Wczelik and Platoon Commander Antoni Markiewicz. During the same combat he was wounded in an arm. On 19 June he embarked on a ship at La Rochelle and sailed to England, where he arrived the next day. Upon arrival he was given the service number P-1400 and the rank of Flying Officer. On 24 July he was posted to No. 302 (Polish) 'City of Poznań' Squadron at Leconfield. During the Battle of Britain he claimed at least two aerial victories and was shot down on 15 September while flying the Hurricane I P3935 WX-D. Kowalski was appointed 'A' Flight commander on 1 January 1941, then in the middle of May he took over 'B' Flight, but on 29 May he returned to his previous post. On 21 November he took command of No. 302 Squadron, then on 18 December was involved in a ground accident, when a ground crew member was killed while Kowalski was taking off in his Spitfire VB AD555. On 25 August 1942 he was appointed Polish Liaison Officer at the HQ of No. 10 Group RAF. On 11 November he was transferred to No. 81 Group RAF. In May 1943 he was posted to the HQ of No. 2 Polish Wing at Church Fenton, and on 20 June took command of the Polish Fighter School within No. 58 Operational Training Unit at Grangemouth. In October 1943 he was transferred to No. 61 Operational

Training Unit. On 2 February 1944 Kowalski was posted to RAF Heston, where on 15 February he took command of No. 133 (Polish) Fighter Wing. On 6 April he was given command of No. 131 (Polish) Fighter Wing, which he led until 10 October. In the meantime he was shot down by 'friendly' fire on 20 June while flying his personal Spitfire IX ML419 JK, and force-landed in France. On 10 October he was posted to the HQ of No.11 Group RAF, then from 25 July 1945 he was the Polish commander of RAF Coltishall Station. On 8 September he was transferred to a similar post at RAF Andrews Field, then on 29 November at Wick and finally on 15 March 1946 at RAF Hethel. As he was married during the war and his son Julian junior was born in 1946, Acting Wing Commander Kowalski and his wife Peggy (former WAAF) decided to stay in Great Britain. After being demobilized in 1947, he started to work in the agricultural and gardening industry, working for Ransomes, Sims and Jefferies as an engineer and innovator and settling in Ipswich. After retiring he moved to Tenerife. Julian Kowalski died on 7 December 1986 in Ipswich and was buried in Lawn Cemetery, Ipswich. He was decorated with the Silver Cross of Virtuti Militari no. 9464, the Cross of Valour and three bars and the British Distinguished Flying Cross.

Date & Time	Unit	Aircraft	Score
09.06.1940 14.30	GC1/145	Caudron CR.714	⅓-0-0 Do 17
15.09.1940 12.10	302 Squadron	Hurricane I P3935 WX-D	0-1-0 Do 17 (claimed as Do 215)
15.09.1940 14.25	302 Squadron	Hurricane I P3935 WX-D	1-1-0 Do 17
18.09.1940 17.15	302 Squadron	Hurricane I P3935 WX-D	0-1-0 Do 17 (claimed as Do 215)
19.09.1940 11.00	302 Squadron	Hurricane I P3935 WX-D	1-0-0 Ju 88
04.03.1941 11.10	302 Squadron	Hurricane I V6744 WX-C	0-0-1 Ju 88
26.04.1942 18.00	302 Squadron	Spitfire VB BL549 WX-L	0-0-1 Fw 190
26.07.1942 13.45	302 Squadron	Spitfire VB EN865 WX-L	1-0-0 Fw 190
20.06.1944	131 Wing	Spitfire IX ML419 JK	0-1-0 Fw 190

FRANCISZEK JAN KOZŁOWSKI, Pilot Officer, was born on 14 April 1917 at Wodzisław near Jędrzejów, within the territory of Poland ruled by the Russian Empire. He grew up in the family of Adam and Eleonora née Ocipska. In 1936 he passed A-level exams at the State Seminar for Teachers at Jędrzejów. He was accepted to the Air Force Reserve Cadet Officers' School at Różan, from where in January 1937 he was transferred to the Air Force Cadet Officers' School at Dęblin. Commissioned with the 12th class, before graduation he was posted to the 122nd Fighter Squadron of the 2nd Air Regiment

at Cracow. Like his colleagues, who were sent to air regiments across Poland in anticipation of imminent German aggression, he received his officer's rank while serving at Cracow. Kozłowski flew operationally during the Polish Campaign of 1939, being involved in the destruction of two Dornier Do 17s on 2 and 3 September, although he is also associated with the loss of a Ju 87 on the 2nd and an He 111 on the 3rd instead of the Do 17s. Both units of the III/2 Fighter Wing with which he flew supported the 'Kraków' Army. On 18 September he crossed the Rumanian border with a road party of the III/2 Wing and travelled to France. After arriving at Marseilles on 30 October he decided that he would get the best opportunity to continue to fight if he was based in England. In December, therefore, he was sent across the Channel to Plymouth and reported to the Polish Air Force Base at RAF Eastchurch. Upon arrival he received the service number 76729 and the rank of Pilot Officer. On 4 July he was posted to No. 5 Operational Training Unit at Aston Down, and on 5 August to No. 501 Squadron at Gravesend. He was shot down on 18 August while flying the Hurricane I P3815. Despite being severely injured and badly burnt, he managed to bale out and was taken to hospital, while his aircraft crashed close to Rayhams Farm, near Whitstable. After recovering from wounds, on 26 February 1941 he was posted to No. 316 (Polish) 'City of Warsaw' Squadron, where in July 1942 he took command of 'A' Flight. During his time with No. 316 Squadron he had a flying accident caused by engine failure; he baled out from his Hurricane II Z2677 on 7 August and landed safely near Ashburton. Between 28 June and 30 July 1942 he served at the HQ of No. 11 Group RAF. He was reported missing in action, most probably shot down by the enemy, on 13 March 1943 while flying Spitfire F.IX EN171

SZ-B over Neufchatel-en-Bray between Rouen and Amiens. Flight Lieutenant Franciszek Kozłowski was later buried in the Canadian Military Cemetery at Hautot-sur-Mer, near Dieppe in France, in grave no. 759. He is commemorated on the Polish Air Force Memorials at Northolt and Warsaw-Mokotów, but also on a symbolic gravestone at the Parish Cemetery at Wodzisław Świętokrzyski. He was decorated with the Cross of Valour and three bars.

Date & Time	Unit	Aircraft	Score
02.09.1939 16.38	122nd Squadron	PZL P.11c	½-0-0 Do 17 (claimed as Ju 87; according to other sources 1/7-0-0)
03.09.1939	122nd Squadron	PZL P.11c	½-0-0 Do 17 (claimed as He 111)

ZDZISŁAW KRASNODĘBSKI, Squadron Leader, called 'Król' (The King) or 'Knot' (Candlewick), was born on 10 July 1904 at Wola Osowińska, near Łuków in Lublin Voivodship, which was ruled by the Russian Empire. He grew up in the family of Zdzisław Jan, a local estate manager, and Maria Wiktoria née Sułkowska. He attended schools at Łomża and Siedlce. After the death of his mother, at the age of 11 he moved to Warsaw. On 20 August 1920, at the age of 16, he volunteered for the Polish Army during the war against Soviet Russia and was posted to the 5th Company of the 201st Infantry Regiment. He was then accepted to No. 1 Cadet  Corps at Lwów and completed A-level exams. On 1 November 1925 he was accepted to the Air Force Officers' School at Grudziądz, which during his stay there was moved to Dęblin and renamed the Air Force Cadet Officers' School. Krasnodębski was commissioned with the 2nd class as an observer, and on 15 August 1928 received the rank of Sub-Lieutenant. On 23 August 1928 he was posted to the 211th Night Bomber Squadron of the 1st Air Regiment at Warsaw. On 4 May 1929 he returned to Dęblin, where he participated in a flying course, and was back in Warsaw on 17 September, posted to the 12th Light Bomber Squadron. On 14 November he was transferred to the 111th Fighter Squadron of the 1st Air Regiment at Warsaw, then on 10 September 1930 was posted to the 2nd Air Regiment at Cracow, where he completed an Advanced Flying Course. He was back at the 111th Squadron on 6 October. Krasnodębski was appointed Acting Technical Officer of the III/1 Fighter

Wing on 18 November 1931, then on 29 January 1932 was posted back to the 111th Squadron. On 7 October 1933 he married Wanda Ciołczyk. On 12 April 1934 he was given a permanent post as the Technical Officer of the III/1 Wing, then on 6 August 1935 was given temporary command of the 111th Squadron, becoming Acting Commander on 26 November. Between 17 August and the middle of November 1936 he operated from Sarny airfield to protect the eastern border of Poland from incursions by Soviet aircraft. From 19 October 1937 he was Acting Commander of the III/1 Fighter Wing at Warsaw, then on 22 November 1938 was appointed permanent commander. In October 1938 he flew with his pilots to Pszczyna, from where they operated during the Zaolzie crisis. During the Polish Campaign of 1939 he commanded III/1 Fighter Wing, which consisted of the 111th and 112th Fighter Squadrons attached to the Pursuit Brigade. On 3 September he claimed the shared destruction of a Bf 110, yet was shot down himself over Rembertów, baling out and being attacked by the German pilot, who eventually was shot down by Arsen Cebrzyński. Krasnodębski landed near Zielonka, suffering hand burns, but despite this he commanded his unit until the end of the campaign. On 18 September, together with the rest of his unit, he crossed the Rumanian border. After obtaining a passport in Bucharest he travelled to France via Yugoslavia and Italy, crossing the border at Modane on 7 October. The next day he was posted to Paris, and on 26 November moved to Le Bourget. Krasnodębski was posted to the Polish Air Force Traning Centre at Lyon-Bron, then in March 1940 was appointed flight commander of the 1st Polish Fighter Squadron, which was never actually formed. Instead he was given command of the Polish section DAT attached on 12 May to GCI/55 at Châteaudun. The Poles flew Morane MS 406s and Bloch MB 152s. Soon after all Poles were moved to Etampes, where they received Koolhoven FK 58s, Curtiss H75s and Arsenal VG 33s. After the fall of France, on 21 June he boarded the Polish ship *Kmicic* at La Rochelle and sailed to Britain, where he arrived on 26 June, and via Glasgow and West Kirby was posted to the Polish Air Force Centre at Blackpool. Krasnodębski received the service number P-1505 and the rank of Acting Squadron Leader. Initially he was considered to join No. 302 (Polish) 'City of Poznań' Squadron, but soon after in July he was appointed commanding officer of No. 303 (Polish) 'Tadeusz Kościuszko. City of Warsaw' Squadron, which was supposed to be formed at Leconfield, but eventually was moved to Northolt. He was shot down on 6 September during a morning operation over Kent. With serious burns he baled out from his Hurricane I P3974 RF-J, and while descending on his parachute was again attacked by a German pilot. Thanks to Witold Urbanowicz, who protected him while descending, he landed safely and was found by the Home Guard. Initially he was taken to hospital at Farnborough.

Later he underwent a long period of treatment, including plastic surgery at the Queen Victoria Hospital in East Grinstead, becoming a member of the 'Guinea Pig Club' for badly injured aircrew. He was unable to continue his operational career. On 1 July 1941 he was appointed to the Polish Military Recruiting Mission in Canada to recruit volunteers of Polish descent to join the Polish Armed Forces. Between 22 March and 3 May he was sent to the United States for a similar role. From 21 October he participated in a flying course at No. 34 Service Flying Training School at Medicine Hat, Alberta. On returning to Britain, on 23 March 1943 he was posted to RAF Heston ,where he was Polish commander of the station. During this time he had several short postings to No. 83 Group RAF, the HQ of No. 122 Airfield and RAF Portreath. On 15 October Krasnodębski was posted to No. 131 (Polish) Airfield 2nd TAF, which he commanded until 17 February 1944. On 25 February he was posted to the Polish Air Force Inspectorate, where he held different posts, including Polish Liaison Officer to the HQ Special Operations. On 2 January 1945 he was sent to the Polish Air Force Staff College at Weston-super-Mare, where he studied until 17 September. On 15 October he was appointed Polish commander of RAF station Newton, where No. 16 (Polish) Service Flying Training School was based. On 18 December 1946 he was sent to the Polish Resettlement Unit at Castle Combe, being demobilized with the rank of Wing Commander on 16 June 1948. Together with his wife, a Home Army soldier who arrived from Poland, he emigrated to South Africa and settled at Cape Town as a taxi driver. In 1951 he moved to Canada, where initially he also worked as a taxi driver. Then he was employed in the aviation industry working for Sanderson Aircraft Ltd, and eventually found employment in the electronics industry working for Motorola Canada Ltd, Addison Industries Ltd and finally Canadian Radio Manufacturing Corporation Ltd. Colonel Zdzisław Krasnodębski died on 3 August 1980 at the Women's College Hospital in Toronto and was buried at the Prospect Cemetery in Sae Town. In 2014 his ashes were transported to Poland, and laid to rest on 14 May at the Powązki Military Cemetery in Warsaw. A primary school in his home town of Wola Osowińska was named after him. The MiG-29 no.15 from the 23rd Tactical Air Base at Mińsk Mazowiecki is adorned with his portrait. He was decorated with the Silver Cross of Virtuti Militari no.8817, the Cross of Valour, the Silver Cross of Merit and, posthumously, the Commander's Cross of Polonia Restituta.

Date & Time	Unit	Aircraft	Score
03.09.1939	III/1 Wing	PZL P.11c	⅓-0-0 Bf 110

WALENTY KREPSKI, Pilot Officer, called 'Walik' (Polish diminution of his first name), was born on 30 July 1917 into a Polish family settled at Chelabinsk in Russia. He was a very fragile and frequently ill child. His parents moved to Wilno in the second half of October 1921. In 1922 he lost his father, which caused him further illness. After fighting his health problems, he became passionate about sport, including ice-skating and skiing. Between 1928 and 1937 he completed Adam Mickiewicz Secondary School at Wilno, passing A-level exams, then was accepted to the 5th Legions Infantry Regiment at Wilno

for the Cadet Officer's Course. On 2 January 1938 Krepski was accepted to the Air Force Cadet Officers' School at Dęblin. After a shortened period of two (instead of three) years he was commissioned with the 13th class as a fighter pilot, receiving the rank of Sub-Lieutenant. He did not participate in combat during the Polish Campaign of 1939 and was evacuated from the No. 1 Air Force Training Centre at Dęblin to Rumania, and eventually to France. With one of the first groups of Poles he was transferred to England and sent to the Polish Air Force Centre at RAF Eastchurch, then in May 1940 moved to Blackpool. Upon arrival he received the service number 76755 and the rank of Pilot Officer. In late July Krepski was sent to No. 15 Elementary Flying Training School at Carlisle, and on 2 August to No. 7 Operational Training Unit at Hawarden, where he remained until 10 August. Upon completion he was posted to No. 54 Squadron at Hornchurch. He was killed on 7 September 1940 while on patrol in the Spitfire I R6901. The Pole left his formation while over Flamborough, Yorkshire, and most probably was lost at sea. He was the eleventh Polish operational pilot lost during the Battle of Britain. In December 1948 his mother received confusing and incorrect information from the Red Cross that her son was buried in Newark Cemetery, in grave no. 306. Walenty Krepski is commemorated on the Polish Air Force Memorials at Northolt and Warsaw-Mokotów.

WACŁAW SZCZEPAN KRÓL, Pilot Officer, called 'Monarcha' (Monarch) or 'Czarny Wacek' (Black Wacek, with Wacek a Polish diminution of his first name), was born on 25 December 1915 at Krakówka, near Sandomierz, within the previous territory of Poland ruled by the Russian Empire. He grew up in the family of farmers Jan and Marianna née Kędziora. He was the youngest brother of Tadeusz Król, who was also an airman and was killed in action on 3 September 1939 while flying in the 21st Bomber Squadron. Wacław Król attended Marshal Józef Piłsudski State Secondary School for Boys and passed A-level exams in 1934. After completing a gliding course at the Military Gliding School at Ustianowa he was accepted to the Infantry Cadet Officers' School at Różan for the unitary course. In 1935 he was accepted to the Air Force Cadet Officers' School at Dęblin and was commissioned as a fighter pilot on 15 October 1937 with the 10th class. He was posted to the 123rd Fighter Squadron of the 2nd Air Regiment at Cracow. In July 1938 he was appointed Technical Officer of his squadron, then in November transferred to the 121st Fighter Squadron of the same regiment. He was appointed deputy commander. By the beginning of August 1939 he was posted to command a forward ambush fighter

Wacław Król, also known as "Black Wacek", in Poland served as deputy commander and then commander of 121st Fighter Squadron. This officer is often considered as the first Allied pilot who participated in successful encounter with an enemy aircraft. In 1940 Król fought over Britain

unit that operated from Wieluń, then on 20 August he commanded a similar unit operating from Aleksandrowice near Bielsko. He fought during the Polish Campaign in 1939. On 1 September soon after 05.00 he damaged a German Henschel He 126, which crash-landed with its observer dying of his wounds. This claim was never accepted, although it could have been Król who gained the first aerial victory during the Second World War. On 3 September he was shot down, baled out and landed near Cikowice and Kłaj. On 5 September he participated in a shared victory of a Dornier Do 17. After the death of Captain Tadeusz Sędzielowski, on 8 September he was appointed commander of the 121st Squadron. After the fall of Poland on 17 September he flew to Cernâuti in Rumania. On 12 October he left for the port of Balchik, from where on 15 October on board the *Aghios Nikolaos* he sailed to Beirut. Upon arrival on 21

October he awaited transport to Marseilles, where he arrived on 29 October. Initially he was sent to Salon, then transferred to the Polish Air Force Training Centre at Lyon-Bron. At the beginning of January 1940 he was posted to Montpellier for fighter training, and on 29 March alongside the Polish section attached to GCII/7 at Luxeuil. Flying Morane MS 406s and Dewoitine D.520s he claimed at least two aerial victories. He was shot down on 5 June and crash-landed. After the collapse of France he flew a Dewoitine D.520 to Algiers, but due to navigational error landed at Bone near the Tunisian border. On 22 June Król flew to Tunis, and the following day performed an operational flight. In Casablanca he boarded the *Neuralia* and via Gibraltar sailed to Britain, arriving at Liverpool on 17 July. He received the service number P-1299 and the rank of Pilot Officer. He was posted to No. 302 (Polish) 'City of Poznań' Squadron at Leconfield, where he reported at the beginning of August. Due to a hand injury he remained a non-operational pilot for some time. On 15 October he claimed his only aerial victory during the Battle of Britain. During his service in No. 302 Squadron he claimed at least one more victory. On 22 November 1941 he was posted on rest for instructor's duty at No. 58 Operational Training Unit at Grangemouth. Król returned to operational flying on 20 May 1942 as 'B' Flight commander of No. 316 (Polish) 'City of Warsaw' Squadron. On 1 December he was posted for rest once more and was operations room controller at No. 315 (Polish) 'City of Dęblin' Squadron. At the beginning of 1943 he was accepted for the 'Polish Fighting Team', better known as 'Skalski's Circus' – a group of Polish pilots attached to No. 145 Squadron in North Africa. During his stay in Africa he claimed three aerial victories. Upon return in July 1943 he was posted to No. 303 (Polish) 'Tadeusz Kościuszko. City of Warsaw' Squadron, then to No. 302 (Polish) 'City of Poznań' Squadron. Król took command of this unit on 18 October. On 5 July 1944 he was sent to the HQ of No. 11 Group RAF, then from 1 October he was a flying instructor in No. 61 Operational Training Unit at Rednal. He was appointed commanding officer of the Polish Fighter School. On 30 January 1945 he reported to the Support Unit of No. 84 Group as the senior Polish officer. On 10 March he became commander of No. 3 Polish Wing, and on 16 July took command of No. 131 (Polish) Wing. Acting Wing Commander Król joined the Polish Resettlement Corps on 9 January 1947 after deciding to return to Poland. He left England on 25 October and settled at Jędrzejów, working as a salesman with a paper company. After moving to Warsaw in the middle of 1948 he was accepted to join the Polish Airlines 'LOT', where he worked as an air traffic controller. He lost this job in September 1949 due to communist persecution against those who served in the West during the war. After that he worked in administration or as a driver. After political changes in 1956, on 19 January 1957 Król joined the People's

Polish Air Force. He held many posts, including Flying Techniques Inspector at the HQ of the Polish Air Force; during this time he flew jet planes such as MiG-15s. He retired on 13 October 1971 in the rank of Colonel. He was married twice, to Leokadia née Pomorska and then Janina née Fiber, and had three children. Based on his wartime recollections he wrote countless articles and thirty-four books which propagated the history of the Polish Air Force in the West as well as his own wartime adventures. Wacław Król died on 15 June 1991 in Warsaw and was buried at the Powązki Military Cemetery in Warsaw. He was decorated with the Silver Cross of Virtuti Militari no. 9543, the Cross of Valour and three bars, the French Croix de Guerre, the British Distinguished Flying Cross and the Commander's Cross of Polonia Restituta. One of the streets in Cracow was named after him.

Date & Time	Unit	Aircraft	Score
01.09.1939 05.00	121st Squadron	PZL P.11c 8.63/2	1-0-0 Hs 126 (not officially accepted)
05.09.1939 12.00	121st Squadron	PZL P.11c	½-0-0 Do 17
24.05.1940	GCII/7	Morane MS 406 N°959	1-1-0 He 111
01.06.1940	GCII/7	Dewoitine D.520 N°241	0-1-0 Do 17
03.06.1940	GCII/7	Dewoitine D.520 N°241	1-0-0 Do 17
15.10.1940 10.15	302 Squadron	Hurricane I P3931 WX-V	1-0-0 Bf 109
13.03.1941 16.40	302 Squadron	Hurricane II Z2485 WX-U	0-0-⅓ Ju 88
08.05.1941 12.15	302 Squadron	Hurricane II WX-M	1-0-0 Bf 109
05.06.1942 15.35	316 Squadron	Spitfire VB AD313 SZ-X	1-0-0 Fw 190
04.04.1943 09.30	PFT	Spitfire IX EN313 ZX-4	1-0-0 Bf 109
20.04.1943 13.00	PFT	Spitfire IX EN313 ZX-4	1-0-0 MC 202
21.04.1943 12.00	PFT	Spitfire IX EN313 ZX-4	1-0-0 Bf 109

TADEUSZ LEON KUMIEGA, Flying Officer, was born on 16th October 1916 at Antoniów near Tarnobrzeg, within the territory of Poland ruled by the Austro-Hungarian Empire. In 1934 he completed eight classes of secondary school and in 1936 was accepted to the Air Force Cadet Officers' School at Dęblin. During his training he suffered a serious accident and broke his left leg while landing by parachute. Commissioned with the 11th class on 15 October 1938, Sub-Lieutenant Kumiega was posted to the 123rd Fighter Squadron of the 2nd Air Regiment at Cracow. Soon after he was transferred to the 121st Fighter Squadron of the same regiment.

At the beginning of August 1939 he was posted to Ułęż, where became a flying instructor of the Advanced Flying Course. During the Polish Campaign in 1939 he joined an ad hoc-formed flight that consisted of instructors, created to defend Dęblin and Ułęż. Later, while evacuating eastwards, on 14 September he joined the Bomber Brigade and performed at least one mission flying a fighter plane with the Fighter Flight within this Brigade. After the fall of Poland he crossed the Rumanian border on 18 September and travelled to France. On 29 October he arrived at Marseilles, and from there was transferred to Salon. He decided to join his colleagues already based in Britain, and on 21 January 1940 reported at the Polish Air Force Centre at RAF Eastchurch. Kumiega was given the service number 76700 and the rank of Pilot Officer. On 1 June he was transferred to Blackpool. On 17 July he was posted to No. 15 Elementary Flying Training School at Carlisle, then on 3 August to No. 6 Operational Training Unit at Sutton Bridge. On 1 September he was posted to No. 17 Squadron at Tangmere. During the Battle of Britain he claimed one shared victory on 29 October. Kumiega was wounded on 11 December in a landing accident in his Hurricane I P3023. On 25 February 1941 he was posted to the newly formed No. 317 (Polish) 'City of Wilno' Squadron. While flying with this unit he claimed at least one aerial victory. On 3 June 1942 he was appointed 'A' Flight commander of No. 306 (Polish) 'City of Toruń' Squadron, but due to poor health this posting was cancelled and Kumiega became a ground controller in the operations room at Northolt. On 15 September he was posted to the HQ of Fighter Command where he undertook administrative duties, including a posting to RAF Matlask as Liaison Officer on 16 September, then from 30 June 1944 he served at the HQ of Air Defence of Great Britain. Finally, on 21 August 1946 he was posted to the Polish Fighter

Station at Coltishall. He was married during the war and a daughter was born in 1946. He was demobilized from the Polish Air Force with the rank of Acting Squadron Leader and joined the Royal Air Force as an administration officer in the Secretarial Branch. Kumiega retired on 1 June 1966. He died on 28 October 1995 in Beverley, Yorkshire, and was buried in the Queensgate Cemetery in Beverley. He was decorated with the Cross of Valour and bar.

Date & Time	Unit	Aircraft	Score
29.10.1940 17.00	17 Squadron	Hurricane I V6743	½-0-0 Bf 109
18.12.1941 12.45	317 Squadron	Spitfire VB AD351 JH-L	1-0-0 Bf 109
26.04.1942 10.50	317 Squadron	Spitfire VB W3424 JH-Q	0-0-½ Fw 190

ZBIGNIEW KUSTRZYŃSKI, Flying Officer, was born on 18 September 1911 in Moscow, Russia, into the Polish family of Jan and Kazimiera. Together with his family he moved back to Poland after the Russian Revolution and settled in Łódź. Kustrzyński completed five years at Mikołaj Kopernik Secondary

Plt Off Zbigniew Kustrzyński flew with Nos. 111 and 607 Squadrons during the Battle of Britain before being posted to 303 Sqn.

School, then attended the State Textile School in Łódź, graduating after four years in 1930. On completion he was employed by a textile company at Łódź and worked as a laboratory apprentice, then moved to Steinert's textile factory in Łódź as an apprentice. Consequently he was accepted to the Karol Buhle textile factory in Łódź, also working as an apprentice, and then employed by Ł.Schmeler Co. as an apprentice and then as the Dyeing Department Manager. He was a very active sportsman, playing tennis, skiing and swimming. He resigned in 1931 and was accepted to the Infantry Cadet Officers' School, from which he graduated in 1934. He was posted to the 27th Infantry Regiment at Częstochowa, but soon after decided to join the Polish Air Force. In September 1934 he was sent to the Air Force Officers' Training Centre at Dęblin, where he participated in a flying course. Upon completion he was posted to the 1st Air Regiment at Warsaw. Between April and July 1936 he completed an Advanced Flying Course at Grudziądz and was reposted back to the 1st Air Regiment. During his service in Warsaw he started studying at the Air Force Staff College, and in 1939 was appointed an Intelligence Officer of the Fighter Group at the 1st Air Regiment. During the Polish Campaign of 1939 he served as adjutant of the Pursuit Brigade. After the fall of Poland he crossed the Rumanian border and then travelled to France. Unhappy with the situation there, he volunteered to join his colleagues in Britain. He was sent to England in January 1940 and reported to the Polish Air Force Centre at RAF Eastchurch. Upon arrival Kustrzyński was given the service number 76718 and the rank of Flying Officer. He was moved to Blackpool, from where on 18 July was posted to No. 15 Elementary Flying Training School at Carlisle, and on 1 August to No. 6 Operational Training Unit at Sutton Bridge. On 1 September he joined No. 111 Squadron at Debden, and on 14 September was moved to No. 607 Squadron at Tangmere. After the Battle of Britain, on 12 November he was posted to No. 303 (Polish) 'Tadeusz Kościuszko. City of Warsaw' Squadron. From February 1941 he was 303 Squadron's ground control officer in the operations room, however occasionally he participated in operational missions. On 4 April 1942 he claimed a double victory over Fw 190s. During the same fight over Saint Omer he was shot down in his Spitfire VB AB824 RF-S and crashlanded in France. He was captured and held at the Stalag Luft III at Żagań (Sagan). On 1 February 1945, during the evacuation of the camp, he escaped, accompanied by Robert Stanford Tuck. Both spent some time fighting alongside Russian troops as they spoke Russian, and were then transported to Moscow, where both obtained documents and sailed to Southampton. He was back in the Polish Air Force in April 1945, and between October and November was posted to the HQ of No. 131 (Polish) Wing as a staff officer. On 20 November he was transferred to the HQ of No. 11 Group

RAF at Uxbridge. Acting Squadron Leader Kustrzyński was demobilized in January 1947, and with his Polish wife Maria née Wiewiórska, a nurse with the 2nd Polish Corps, whom he met while staying in hospital, emigrated to Canada. Despite planning to work in the civil aviation industry, he worked as an executive with the Dominion Textile Company until retirement. Kustrzyński initially lived at Cornwall, Ontario, later moving to Montreal. He died on 4 August 1996 (various sources also state 9 August or 9 September) in Montreal, but was buried at the Roman Catholic Świętego Józefa (St Joseph) Cemetery at Łódź, alongside his wife. He was decorated with the Cross of Valour.

Date & Time	Unit	Aircraft	Score
04.04.1942 10.00	303 Squadron	Spitfire VB AB824 RF-S	2-0-0 Fw 190

JÓZEF KWIECIŃSKI, Sergeant, was born on 4 May 1917. He served in the 4th Air Regiment, where between September 1936 and July 1937 he completed a flying course. He was then posted to Grudziądz, where he participated in an Advanced Flying Course. On 13 October 1937 he had a flying accident in a PZL P.7. In April 1939 he was sent to No. 1 Air Force Training Centre at Dęblin, where he served as an instructor. During the Polish Campaign of 1939 he did not fly operationally, and after the fall of Poland was evacuated to Rumania and then to France. Kwieciński decided to join his colleagues in Britain and sailed across the Channel in December 1940. He was sent to the Polish Air Force Centre at RAF Eastchurch and given the service number 780691. In the rank of LAC he was moved to Blackpool, then posted to No. 1 School of Army Co-operation at Old Sarum. Initially he was considered for the first squad of No. 302 (Polish) 'City of Poznań' Squadron, but on 14 July he arrived at No. 6 Operational Training Unit at Sutton Bridge. Upon completion of his conversion training, on 4 August Sergeant Kwieciński was posted to No. 145 Squadron at Westhampnett. On 12 August he flew on an operational sortie and at 12.20 was shot down in his Hurricane I P3391 over the Isle of Wight. It is believed that during an encounter with Bf 109s and Bf 110s he shot down one of the Bf 110s together with fellow Pole Flight Lieutenant Wilhelm Pankratz and Pilot Officer John Howard Harrison, although none of these pilots survived the sortie to confirm this victory. He most probably crashed into the sea and his body was never found. He was the third operational Polish pilot lost during the Battle of Britain. He was decorated with the Cross of Valour, and is commemorated on the Polish Air Force Memorials at Northolt and Warsaw-Mokotów.

Date & Time	Unit	Aircraft	Score
12.08.1940 12.20	145 Squadron	Hurricane I P3391	¼-0-0 Bf 110 unconfirmed

Ł

PIOTR ŁAGUNA, Flight Lieutenant, called 'Zagłoba' after the seventeenth-century ribald nobleman portrayed in Polish literature, was born on 11 October 1905 at Kędzierowo near Szczurzyn in the Podlasie region, within the territory of Poland ruled by the Russian Empire. He grew up in an old noble family wearing the crest of 'Grzymała'. His father, Piotr, was an estate leaseholder, and mother, Julianna née Chludzińska, was also of noble roots and held the 'Cholewa' family crest. In 1925 he was accepted to the Air Force Officers' School at  Grudziądz, which was moved to Dęblin. He graduated on 15 August 1927 with the 1st class and as an observer was posted to the 32nd Light Bomber Squadron of the 3rd Air Regiment at Poznań. During his time at the Air Force School it was decided that pilot training would be stopped, therefore all graduates would join their regiments as observers. As a result of the cadets' rebellion against this decision, all graduates from the 1st class were punished and left school without commission, but a year later they received the rank of Sub-Lieutenant. In March 1928, already an officer, he was accepted for the flying course at the Air Force Officers' Training Centre at Dęblin and then for the Advanced Flying Course organized by the 2nd Air Regiment at Cracow. Upon his return to the 3rd Regiment he was posted to the 131st Fighter Squadron, soon after being reposted to the 132nd Fighter Squadron. On 11 October 1935 he had a landing accident in a PZL P.7. In 1938 he was sent to the Air Force Staff College at Warsaw, then upon graduation was appointed deputy commander of the 216th Bomber Squadron. Łaguna flew operationally during the Polish Campaign of 1939 with the XV Bomber Squadron as a navigation officer. He also formed a fighter flight to defend Wielick airfield where his squadron was based. This unit consisted of personnel and cadet officers from Ułęż. He also flew defensive missions in a PZL P.11g 'Kobuz'. After the fall of Poland he crossed the Rumanian border and travelled to France. He was sent to the Polish Air Force Training Centre at Lyon-Bron and chosen for the III Polish Fighter Squadron, the so-called 'Finnish Squadron' formed from Polish personnel and to be sent to Finland against Soviet Russia. As an armistice was signed by the adversaries on 12 March 1940, this project never materialized. Instead, in the middle of May, 1/145 Polish 'City of Warsaw' Squadron was created and equipped with Caudron CR.714s. Captain Piotr Łaguna was appointed deputy commander of this unit, which was sent to Villacoublay, then to Dreux and Maison la Blanche. On 10 June Łaguna was appointed commander of GC1/145 as Major Józef Kępiński was shot down and wounded. The same day Łaguna claimed his only victory, shooting down a Bf 109. After the fall of France, on 20 June he sailed to England from La Rochelle. Upon arrival he received the service number P-1287 and the rank of Flight Lieutenant. On 26 July he was appointed 'A' Flight commander of No. 302 (Polish) 'City of Poznań' Squadron at Leconfield. He was involved in a flying accident in a Magister R1918 on 4 or 5 October, force-landing due to engine failure with Flight Lieutenant James Thomson on board. It is thought that both were injured. On 7 December he was appointed commander of No. 302 Squadron, then on 8 May 1941 was shot down during combat while flying the Hurricane II Z3098 WX-A but survived. On 1 June he took command of the 1st Polish Fighter Wing at Northolt. Acting Wing Commander Piotr Łaguna was killed on 27 June 1941 during a mission over France in his Spitfire IIB P8331 RF-B shot down by ground fire at Coquelles, south-west of Calais. He was buried at Pihen-les-Guines Cemetery in France, in grave no. 9, row A, in a military plot. He also has a symbolic grave at the Parish Cemetery at Wąsosz. He is commemorated on the Polish Air Force Memorials at Northolt and Warsaw-Mokotów, and was decorated with the Silver Cross of Virtuti Militari no. 9093 and the Cross of Valour.

Date & Time	Unit	Aircraft	Score
10.06.1940	1/145 Squadron	Caudron CR.714	1-0-0 Bf 109

STANISŁAW ŁAPKA, Pilot Officer, called 'Mały' (Little), was born on 15 August 1915 at Borzymy, near Jadów in the region of Radzymin, within the territory of Poland ruled by the Russian Empire. With his brother he grew up in the farming family of Jan and Marianna. In 1930 he had completed seven classes of primary school at Jadów and was accepted to the Humanistic Secondary School at Świecie, from which he graduated in 1935 and passed A-level exams. After a unitary course with an infantry regiment, in 1936 he was

accepted to the Air Force Cadet Officers' School at Dęblin. Commissioned on 15 October 1938 with the 11th class, Sub-Lieutenant Łapka was posted to the 113th Fighter Squadron of the 1st Air Regiment at Warsaw. On 12 August 1939 he was posted to the Air Force NCO School for Minors at Krosno, where he was a flying instructor and platoon commander. During the Polish Campaign in 1939 he was involved in the evacuation of the school and led a group of his pupils to Rumania, crossing the border at Śniatyń on 17 September. He stayed with the pupils, despite the rest of the officers being separated from the group. He sailed via the Black Sea to France, arriving on 29 October. With one of the first groups of Polish airmen he moved on to Britain, and on 24 January 1940 reported to the Polish Air Force Centre at RAF Eastchurch. He was given the service number 76702 and the rank of Pilot Officer. Alongside bomber crews, in February Łapka was posted to No. 15 Elementary Flying Training School at Redhill, then in March to the Polish Training Unit at Hucknall, which on 15 June became No. 18 Operational Training Unit. On 23 June he was reposted to No. 6 Operational Training Unit at Sutton Bridge. It was decided he would join No. 302 (Polish) 'City of Poznań' Squadron at Leconfield, where he reported on 17 July. On 15 September he claimed the shared destruction of a Dornier Do 17, but was shot down himself and baled out from his Hurricane I V6569 WX-K. Łapka broke a leg on landing and was treated at Ely Hospital, later being transferred to Newquay Hospital on 8 October. He remained in No. 302 Squadron, and on 7 January 1942 was appointed commander of 'B' Flight, then on 21 January of 'A' Flight. He took command of No. 302 Squadron on 25 August. He completed a commanders' course on 14 January 1943, then on 16 May was attached to the HQ of No. 11 Group RAF as Polish Liaison Officer. In late 1943 he was posted to No. 316 (Polish) 'City of Warsaw' Squadron for a short time, then on 1 January 1944 assumed command of No. 306 (Polish) 'City of Toruń' Squadron. He was shot down in combat on 7 June, after destroying a Bf 109 while flying the Mustang III FZ156 UZ-M. Łapka baled out, and with help from French resistance fighters evaded captivity and managed to get to Allied lines, returning to England on 26 August. On 20 October he was posted to the HQ of Air Defence of Great Britain as Squadron Leader Tactics and Organization. On 17 September 1945 he left for the Polish Air Force Staff College at Weston-super-Mare. After completing the 7th course, he remained there as administration officer. In April 1946 he was posted to the HQ of No. 3 Polish Fighter Wing at RAF Hethel. He was demobilized with the rank of Squadron Leader and settled in Britain. On 14 February 1948 Stanisław Łapka married Thelma Vincent, with whom he had two daughters, Maria and Josephine. Known to locals as Stanley Lapka, he was employed at the headquarters of the Eastern Electricity Board at Ipswich, also being an active member of the local choir and the Polish community, leading the local branch of the Polish Air Force Association. He died of cancer in Ipswich on 19 August 1978 and was buried at Ipswich Lawn Cemetery. He was decorated with the Silver Cross of Virtuti Militari no. 8385, the Cross of Valour with two bars and the Silver and Gold Cross of Merit.

Date & Time	Unit	Aircraft	Score
15.09.1940 12.10	302 Squadron	Hurricane I V6569 WX-K	½-0-0 Do 17
07.09.1942 10.20	302 Squadron	Spitfire VB EN865 WX-L	0-1-0 Fw 190
07.06.1944 10.35	306 Squadron	Mustang III FZ156 UZ-M	1-0-0 Bf 109

WACŁAW ŁAPKOWSKI, Flying Officer, was born on 6 November 1913 at Dyneburg in the Russian Empire into the Polish family of Ambroży and Wacława née Stomma-Mirzyńska. His father was killed in 1920 during the Polish – Bolshevik war in rank of Lieutenant. He graduated from No. 2 Cadet Corps at Chełmno and in 1932 was accepted to the Air Force Cadet Officers' School at Dęblin, where he was commissioned with the 8th class on 15 August 1934. As an observer, Sub-Lieutenant Łapkowski was posted to the 212th Night

Bomber Squadron of the 1st Air Regiment in Warsaw. In 1935 he decided to undertake a flying training and was posted back to the Air Force Officers' Training Centre at Dęblin for the flying course, and then between April and July 1936 he participated in the Advanced Flying Course at Grudziądz. Upon completion he was posted back to the 1st Air Regiment, and in November attached to the 112th Fighter Squadron. On 12 January 1937 he was involved in a mid-air flying accident with another PZL P.11c flown by Sub-Lieutenant Henryk Skalski. Łapkowski had another accident on 23 August, again

while flying a PZL P.11c. He was accepted for the Polish War College at Warsaw, but due to the difficult political situation and danger of war, he never started his studies. On 18 March 1938 he flew to Porubanek airfield near Wilno, where his unit was employed during the diplomatic conflict with Lithuania. In October he was sent to Aleksandrowice airfield, where his squadron was stationed during the conflict with Czechoslovakia. He participated in the Polish Campaign of 1939 as a pilot of the 112th Fighter Squadron, defending Warsaw within the III/1 Fighter Wing of the Pursuit Brigade. On 3 September his aircraft was damaged in combat. He claimed a shared kill on 6 September and an individual one on 9 September. On the second occasion his aircraft was damaged in combat. After the death of Lieutenant Stefan Okrzeja on 6 September he took command of the 112th Squadron. On 11 September he damaged his PZL P.11 upon landing at Łuszczów. On 17 September he flew in a PZL P.11c to Cernâuti in Rumania, and then travelled to France. Initially he was chosen for the 1st Fighter Squadron which was supposed to be formed in France. Upon completion of conversion training at the Polish Air Force Training Centre at Lyon-Bron he was appointed commander of the Polish fighter section DAT and sent to defend Bourges. He was posted to Captain Tadeusz Opulski's section, defending the Romorantin area. He was almost killed on 5 June 1940 when a German bomb fell 10 metres from where he was hiding. On 18 June he flew to Bordeaux, and the next day sailed to England from La Rochelle on the *Alderpool*. Upon arrival in Britain he was given the service number P-1506 and the rank of Flying Officer. Initially he was considered for the first squad of No. 302 (Polish) 'City of Poznań' Squadron, but eventually at the beginning of August he was posted to No. 303 (Polish) 'Tadeusz Kościuszko. City of Warsaw' Squadron at Northolt. During the Battle of Britain he claimed an aerial victory on 5 September by shooting down a Ju

88. On the same day he was also shot down in his Hurricane I P2985 RF-Z over Gillingham. Badly wounded, with a broken left hand and burns, he baled out and landed at Hawkwell, while his aircraft crashed at Bonvill's Farm, North Benfleet. He was treated at numerous hospitals including Rochford Hospital and Newquay Hospital and spent several months away from the first line. In January 1941 Łapkowski returned to No. 303 Squadron, and on the 22nd he brought back 25 yards of electric wire that caught on his Hurricane I W9129 RF-W while attacking the German airfield at Crecy in France. On this occasion he destroyed one Bf 109 on the ground. He was appointed 'B' Flight commander on 20 February, and on 13 April took command of No. 303 Squadron after the death of Squadron Leader Zdzisław Henneberg. On the same day he was wounded in the head during combat while flying the Spitfire II P7567 RF-X. He was only able to take command of No. 303 Squadron in early May. In June he claimed four aerial victories. Squadron Leader Łapkowski was killed on 2 July while leading his squadron during Operation Circus 29 escorting Blenheims attacking Lille. He was shot down with his Spitfire IIB P8596 RF-V, crashing into the English Channel. His body was washed ashore and buried at Lombardsije Communal Cemetery in Belgium, in grave no. 224. He left behind his British fiancée, who served in the RAF, and son Wojciech Sylwanowicz, born in Warsaw in 1938. Squadron Leader Łapkowski is commemorated on the Polish Air Force Memorials at Northolt and Warsaw-Mokotów but also he has a symbolic grave in the family tomb at Bartoszyce Cemetery, Kętrzyńska Street. A biographical book about him, *With Great Sacrifice and Bravery. The Career of Polish Ace Waclaw Lapkowski*, was written in 2012 by Glenn Knoblock, with a picture of Edward Paterek mistakenly used on the cover. Łapkowski was decorated with the Silver Cross of Virtuti Militari no. 8819 and the Cross of Valour and three bars.

Date & Time	Unit	Aircraft	Score
06.09.1939	112th Squadron	PZL P.11	⅓-0-0 He 111
09.09.1939	112th Squadron	PZL P.11	1-0-0 He 111
05.09.1940 15.05	303 Squadron	Hurricane I P2985 RF-Z	1-0-0 Ju 88
04.06.1941 17.40	303 Squadron	Spitfire II P8331 RF-M	0-0-1 Bf 109
18.06.1941 18.30	303 Squadron	Spitfire II P8507 RF-V	1-0-0 Bf 109
22.06.1941 16.10	303 Squadron	Spitfire II P8507 RF-V	2-0-0 Bf 109
24.06.1941 20.45	303 Squadron	Spitfire II P8507 RF-V	1-0-0 Bf 109

WŁODZIMIERZ MIKOŁAJ ŁAZORYK, Flight Lieutenant, was born on 27 August 1904 at Kołomyja, within the territory of Poland ruled by the Austro-Hungarian Empire. In 1926 he graduated from the Teachers College at Tarnów and passed A-level exams. In 1927 he was accepted to the Air Force Officers' School at Dęblin. He was commissioned on 15 August 1929 with the 3rd class as an observer. In the rank of Sub-Lieutenant he was posted to the 41st Light Bomber Squadron of the 4th Air Regiment. He decided to complete his flying training, and in 1932 was posted for the flying course to the Air
Force Officer Training Centre at Dęblin. In 1933 he completed an Advanced Flying Course at Grudziądz. The same year Łazoryk was posted to III/4 Fighter Wing at Toruń as a tactical officer. On 27 November 1934 he was appointed commander of the 141st Fighter Squadron, which post he held until 17 January 1935. On 20 September he took command of the 143rd Fighter Squadron, and when this unit was disbanded on 23 November 1937 he was given command of the newly formed 152nd Fighter Squadron that was born out of the previous unit and operated within the 5th Air Regiment at Lida. During the Polish Campaign of 1939 he led the 152nd Squadron, which operated to support the 'Modlin' Army. After the fall of Poland, during the night of 17/18 September he crossed the Rumanian border at Kuty. He travelled to France, where he arrived on 16 October. After initial training at the Polish Air Force Training Centre at Lyon-Bron he was posted to Tours, where he trained on Potez 540 bombers, eventually becoming a flying instructor and officer commanding a group of pupils, being responsible for training air gunners and observers. After the fall of France he was evacuated to Britain, arriving on 23 June 1940. Łazoryk was given the service number P-1000 and the rank of Flight Lieutenant. He was sent to No. 5 Operational Training Unit at Aston Down, then on 3 October he joined No. 615 Squadron at Prestwick and on 10 October No. 607 Squadron at Turnhouse. In December he was reposted to No. 46 Squadron, from which he was transferred to No. 257 Squadron. On 15 February 1941 he was attached to No. 308 (Polish) 'City of Cracow' Squadron as a ground controller serving in the operations room. He remained with this unit until 27 November. As he had decided to fly bomber aircraft, he was posted to No. 3 Service Flying Training School at South Cerney to complete a twin-engine aircraft course. On 9 January 1942 he arrived at No. 18 Operational Training Unit at Bramcote, and then on 15 June he was posted to No. 305 (Polish) 'Wielkopolska Province

Marshal Józef Piłsudski' Squadron. On 22 April 1943 Lazoryk was posted for rest and appointed Polish Liaison Officer with the HQ of No. 9 Group RAF. On 15 September he was transferred to No. 38 Wing RAF as Polish Liaison Officer. The wing consisted of paratrooper carrier units and was transferred to No. 38 Group RAF. From July 1944 he was Polish Liaison Officer at the 9th Troop Career Command USAAF. Upon completion of his service with the Americans, on 1 January 1945 he was sent to the Polish Air Force Staff College at Weston-super-Mare, where he commenced studies. In September he was sent to the HQ of the Polish Air Force. From February 1946 he was back at the Polish Air Force Staff College, this time as a lecturer. Squadron Leader Lazoryk was demobilized in 1946 and emigrated to the United States, where he settled in Chicago. Włodzimierz Lazoryk, who changed his name to Walter Nicolas Lazoryk, died aged 90 on 8 January 1995 and was buried in Our Lady of Czestochowa Cemetery at Doylestown, Bucks County, Pennsylvania. He was decorated with the Silver Cross of Merit, the Silver Cross of Virtuti Militari no. 9681 and the Cross of Valour and two bars.

WITOLD ŁOKUCIEWSKI, Pilot Officer, called 'Tolo' (diminutive of his Polish name), was born on 1 February 1917 at Kamieńskaja Stanica in Russia into the Polish family of Antoni, president of the Wilno Parliament, and Benjamina née Pobiedzińska. His father, a high school principal, was one of the Polish patriots who in 1922 voted for Wilno, where the family moved in 1918, to be part of Poland. After completing primary education, Witold was accepted to Jan Śniadecki High School at Oszmiana, from which he graduated in 1935, passing A-level exams. After the unitary course at the Cavalry Reserve Cadet Officers' School at Grudziądz, in 1936 he was accepted to the Air Force Cadet Officers' School at Dęblin. After being commissioned on 15 October 1938 with the 11th class as a fighter pilot he was posted to the 112th Fighter Squadron of the 1st Air Regiment at Warsaw. During the Polish Campaign in 1939 he fought with his unit as part of the Pursuit Brigade. On 1 September he participated in a shared probable victory of a Junkers Ju 87. He is also associated with the shared victory of a Dornier Do 17 on 6 September. On 18 September he crossed the Rumanian border at Kuty and travelled via Yugoslavia and Italy to France, where he arrived on 7 October. Upon arrival he was posted to the Polish Air Force Training Centre at Lyon-Bron and then to the fighter section DAT led by Captain Tadeusz Opulski, to defend Romorantin. From 17 May 1940 he flew operationally Morane MS 406s. On 25 May he claimed a shared victory of a Heinkel He 111, but this claim was never accepted. On 10 June he shot down a Heinkel He 111. On 21 June he sailed from the French port of St Jean de Luz on board the *Arandora Star*, and upon arrival in Britain was given the service number P-1492 and the rank of Pilot Officer. Initially he was considered for the first squad of No. 302 (Polish) 'City of Poznań', but on 2 August he was posted to No. 303 (Polish) 'Tadeusz Kościuszko. City of Warsaw' Squadron at Northolt. During the Battle of Britain he shot down at least four enemy planes, on 7, 11 and 15 September. On 15 September he was shot down over the Kent coast and wounded in the legs, yet managed to land at Northolt in his Hurricane I P2903 RF-Z. He was admitted to hospital, returning to No. 303 Squadron on 3 October. On 3 April 1941

he was wounded during a flying accident in the Spitfire II P7989 RF-U, then on 20 November he was appointed 'A' Flight commander. On 13 March 1942 Łokuciewski was shot down over Hazebrouck in France and crash-landed in his Spitfire VB BL656 RF-D. He was wounded in a leg. After being captured by the Germans he was held at Stalag Luft III at Sagan (Żagań). He tried to escape on several occasions (including participation in preparations for the Great Escape), even getting as far as Legnica on 15 August 1943, but spent the rest of war in captivity. He was liberated by the British Army in April 1945 and returned to Britain. On 22 September he was posted for administration duty to the HQ of No. 3 Polish Wing at Andrews Field, then on 29 November 1945 arrived back at No. 303 (Polish) Squadron. Łokuciewski took command of the squadron on 1 February 1946. After disbandment of the unit on 9 December he was demobilized with the rank of Squadron Leader. He decided to return to Poland and sailed there on 8 June 1947, initially settling in Lublin. After being employed as a flying instructor at the Lublin Aero Club at Świdnik, in 1949 he lost his job as a result of a communist vendetta against Polish veterans who fought in the West. He had several jobs afterwards, working in a lawyer's chamber and then in a building supplies company. After political changes in 1956, in November of that year he was accepted into the People's Air Force. He flew MiG-15 jet planes, but was also an instructor as well as Inspector of the Staff Service and Inspector of Flying Techniques. Between 1969 and 1972 he was an air attaché in London, retiring in 1974. Colonel Witold Łokuciewski wrote his personal memoirs, *Aviation is my Life*, which were published in 2017; ten years previously the book *Tolo – Musketeer from No.303 Squadron* had been published by his niece. He died on 17 April 1990 in Warsaw and was buried in Powązki Military Cemetery in Warsaw. The MiG-29A no. 83

of the 23rd Tactical Air Base at Mińsk Mazowiecki has his portrait painted on its tail, and a street in Warsaw was named after him. He was decorated with the Silver Cross of Virtuti Militari no. 8824, the Cross of Valour and bar, the British Distinguished Flying Cross, the French Croix de Guerre, and the Commander's and Officer's Cross of Polonia Restituta.

Date & Time	Unit	Aircraft	Score
09.1939 or 06.09.1939	112th Squadron	PZL P.11	0-½-0 Ju 87
25.05.1940	DAT Romorantin	Morane MS 406	½-0-0 He 111 unconfirmed
10.06.1940	DAT Romorantin	Morane MS 406	1-0-0 He 111
07.09.1940 17.00	303 Squadron	Hurricane I P3975 RF-U	1-1-0 Do 17 claimed as 'Do 215'
11.09.1940 16.00	303 Squadron	Hurricane I L2099 RF-O	1-0-0 Do 17 claimed as 'Do 215'
11.09.1940 16.00	303 Squadron	Hurricane I L2099 RF-O	1-0-0 Bf 109
15.09.1940 12.00	303 Squadron	Hurricane I P2903 RF-Z	1-0-0 Bf 109
20.04.1941 11.10	303 Squadron	Spitfire II P7546 RF-T	1-0-0 Bf 109
18.06.1941 18.30	303 Squadron	Spitfire II P8333 RF-S	1-0-0 Bf 109
22.06.1941 16.10	303 Squadron	Spitfire II P8333 RF-S	1-1-0 Bf 109
11.07.1941 11.30	303 Squadron	Spitfire II P8333 RF-S	0-1-0 Bf 109

KAZIMIERZ ŁUKASZEWICZ, Pilot Officer, called 'Mala' (no English equivalent), was born into a Polish family on 25 March 1913 on the Brodziec estate near Ihumeń and Minsk in Russia. After moving to a free Poland he completed primary and secondary education, and in October 1933 he was accepted to the Infantry Cadet Officers' School at Różan, from where in 1934 he was transferred to the Air Force Cadet Officers' School at Dęblin. He was commissioned with the 9th class on 15 October 1936 as a fighter pilot, and with the rank of Sub-Lieutenant was posted to the 141st Fighter Squadron of the 4th Air Regiment at Toruń. Łukaszewicz had a flying accident on 2 July 1937 while in a PZL P.11c. He was transferred to the 143rd Fighter Squadron, and when this unit was disbanded was posted to the 5th Air Regiment at Wilno, where he joined the newly created III/5 Fighter Wing. In November he was attached to the 151st Fighter Squadron, then in December to the 152nd Fighter Squadron. On 15 April 1939 he was posted for instructor's duty to the Advanced Flying Course at Ułęż, which was part of the No. 1 Air Force Training Centre at Dęblin. During the Polish Campaign of 1939 he flew defensive missions, being part of an ad hoc instructors' flight. After the fall of Poland, on 18 September he crossed the Rumanian border, arriving in Marseilles, France, on 29 October. After assessing the situation, he decided to join his colleagues being sent across the English Channel. On 27 January 1940, after arriving at the Polish Air Force Centre at RAF Eastchurch, he received the rank of Flying Officer and the service number 76761. During his stay at Eastchurch his duties included being responsible for swimming exercises. He was posted to No. 6 Operational Training Unit at Sutton Bridge, and on 26 July received a posting to No. 302 (Polish) 'City of Poznań' Squadron, yet soon after it was decided that he would join No. 501 Squadron at Gravesend, where he reported on 7 August. He was lost on 12 August during aerial combat over the English Channel, crashing into the sea in his Hurricane I P3803 SD-Z. His body was never found. Łukaszewicz is commemorated on the Polish Air Force Memorials at Northolt and Warsaw-Mokotów, and was decorated with the Cross of Valour. He was the fifth Polish operational pilot killed during the Battle of Britain.

From the left are: Flg Off Paweł Niemiec (17 Sqn RAF), Flg Off Kazimierz Łukaszewicz (501 Sqn RAF) and Plt Off Stanisław Skalski (501 Sqn RAF). All three are wearing "VR" badges

ANTONI ŁYSEK, Sergeant, was born on 25 January 1917 at Bodziejowice near Włoszczowa in Kielce Voivodship, within the territory of Poland ruled by the Russian Empire. He grew up in the family of Józef and Maria Machelska, who settled at Sitowice near Bydgoszcz. After completing primary education he was accepted to the secondary school at Bydgoszcz and graduated in 1934 after six years. He entered national military service at Bydgoszcz on 1 November 1936 and was posted to the 4th Air Regiment at Toruń. From 1 April until 1 July 1937 he completed the NCOs school within the 4th

Regiment, followed by a gliding course from 4 August, which he completed on 1 October. Between 1 September 1937 and 1 May 1938 he completed a basic flying course, and then between 1 August and 23 October an Advanced Flying Course at Grudziądz. On 16 November he was posted to the 142nd Fighter Squadron of the 4th Air Regiment. During the Polish Campaign of 1939 he flew with his unit, supporting the 'Pomorze' Army. After the fall of Poland, on 19 September he crossed the Rumanian border. He left Rumania on 5 October and was evacuated to France, arriving at Marseilles on 23 October. He was later posted to the Polish Air Force Training Centre at Lyon-Bron. Soon after Łysek decided to travel to England, arriving on 19 February 1940. The following day he was posted to the Polish Air Force Centre at Eastchurch, receiving the service number 780694 and the rank of Sergeant. From 17 July he was training on a flying course at No. 15 Elementary Flying Training School at Carlisle, and on 31 July was sent to No. 3 Polish Wing at Blackpool. On 20 August he was posted to No. 302 (Polish) 'City of Poznań' Squadron at Leconfield, but on 2 September he was reposted to No. 5 Operational Training Unit at Aston Down for further training. Łysek was back with No. 302 Squadron on 26 September. He stayed with this unit throughout the rest of his military career, and in 1941 claimed one enemy aircraft damaged and another destroyed and shared. On 1 June 1942, based on his wartime achievements, he was commissioned as a Pilot Officer and received the new service number P-1911. However, Antoni Łysek was killed on 5 June during Operation Circus 188B over Le Havre while flying his Spitfire VB AD257 WX-D, and was lost at sea. It is believed that the engine of his aircraft was damaged and then failed. He is commemorated on the Polish Air Force Memorials at Northolt and Warsaw-Mokotów, and was decorated with the Cross of Valour and bar.

Date & Time	Unit	Aircraft	Score
04.03.1941 11.10	302 Squadron	Hurricane I P3207 WX-A	0-0-1 Ju 88
28.03.1941 12.33	302 Squadron	Hurricane II Z2806 WX A	½-0-0 Ju 88

M

MICHAŁ MIROSŁAW KAROL MACIEJOWSKI, Sergeant, called 'Miki', 'Mickey' or 'Mickey Mouse', was born on 29 October 1913 at Gródek Jagielloński in Lwów Voivodship, within the previous Kingdom of Poland. After completing primary and secondary education he passed A-level exams, moved with his family to Poznań and was accepted to St Mary Magdalene College Catholic Seminary, but left this path after two years of studying. In 1931 it is thought he enrolled in the Department of Chemistry of the University of Poznań. He also claimed to have completed

two years at the Trade and Business School at Lwów. During his mandatory military service he declared a willingness to join the Polish Air Force, and between August 1936 and August 1937 completed a flying course at the 6th Air Regiment at Lwów, consequently serving as a pilot. Some sources state that he completed two years of the Air Force NCO School for Minors at Bydgoszcz, graduating in 1934 as an air gunner and wireless operator. Between March and July 1939 he served as a flying instructor of the 6th Air Regiment, later being posted to the 3rd Air Regiment at Poznań (where he apparently served from June 1938). He was also a sport pilot and a member of Poznań Aero Club. Maciejowski flew operationally during the Polish Campaign in 1939, from 7 September being posted to the fighter section of the Fighter Unit of Base No. 3 at Świdnik aerodrome. He flew reconnaissance missions for the 'Lublin' Army in an unarmed RWD-8. After the fall of Poland he flew to Rumania. After a short internment he managed to escape and travelled to France via Syria, arriving at Marseilles in February 1940. Having experienced French stagnation, he decided to join his colleagues already stationed in Britain, and upon arrival on 10 February was given the service number 780485 and the rank of Sergeant. After basic training at No. 15 Elementary Flying Training

School at Carlisle (where he practiced from 20 June) and conversion at No. 5 Operational Training Unit at Aston Down on 10 September he was posted to No. 111 Squadron at Drem, being reposted on 26 September to No. 229 Squadron at Northolt. On 11 October he was sent to No. 249 Squadron at North Weald, and on 29 October he shot down a Bf 109. He was also involved in two emergency landings during this time: on 25 October in the Hurricane I V6692 and then on 30 October in the Hurricane I V6685. Maciejowski reported four further aerial victories during his stay with No. 249 Squadron. On 25 February 1941 he was transferred to No. 317 (Polish) 'City of Wilno' Squadron. During Operation Veracity II on 30 December he claimed two Bf 109s. On 1 June 1942 he was commissioned as a Pilot Officer, receiving the new service number P-1912. During Operation Jubilee on 19 August he was responsible for the destruction of one Fw 190, one Ju 88 and the shared destruction of a Do 217. On 25 August he was posted for rest to No. 58 Operational Training Unit at Grangemouth as an instructor. On 23 March 1943 Maciejowski was posted to No. 316 (Polish) 'City of Warsaw' Squadron, where he claimed his last victories. On 9 August during Operation Ramrod 191, around Montreuil in France, he collided in mid-air with another No. 316 pilot, Flying Officer Lech Kondracki. Kondracki was killed, while Maciejowski baled out from his Spitfire F.IX BS302 SZ-E. Upon landing he was captured by the Germans. He was handed over to Gestapo and eventually sent to Stalag Luft III at Żagań (Sagan). He was liberated after almost two years and returned to England on 9 May 1945, and the following month was posted to No. 16 (Polish) Service Training Flying School at Newton for a refresher course. On 11 November he was posted to No. 309 (Polish) 'Czerwieńska Province' Squadron. Flight Lieutenant Maciejowski was demobilized on 6 January 1947, and in 1951 joined the Royal Air Force, where he initially served as a test pilot. Maciejowski changed his name to Michael Manson and later served as a ground officer, from 1958 serving in the Supply Department and eventually in catering. In 1970 he ran the RAF Transit Hotel in Malta. In 1972, at the age of 60, he retired from service and settled in Liverpool. In 1987, after the death of his wife Christine, he moved to Winnipeg in Canada, where he lived with his daughter Karen Schmidt. Maciejowski died on 26 April 2001 in Manitoba. His decorations included the Silver Cross of Virtuti Militari no. 9367, the Cross of Valour and three bars, the British Distinguished Flying Cross and the Distinguished Flying Medal.

Date & Time	Unit	Aircraft	Score
28.10.1940 11.00	249 Squadron	Hurricane I W6693	0-1-0 Bf 109 unconfirmed
29.10.1940 17.00	249 Squadron	Hurricane I P3463 GN-L	1-0-0 Bf 109
07.11.1940 12.45	249 Squadron	Hurricane I V6534 GN-P	1-0-0 Bf 109
28.11.1940 15.00	249 Squadron	Hurricane I V6855	0-1-0 Bf 109 unconfirmed
05.12.1940 11.10	249 Squadron	Hurricane I V6614 GN-B	1-0-0 Bf 109
10.01.1941 13.00	249 Squadron	Hurricane I V6614 GN-B	1-0-0 Bf 109
10.02.1941 12.30	249 Squadron	Hurricane I V6614 GN-B	1-0-0 Bf 109
06.12.1941	317 Squadron	Spitfire VB	1-0-0 Ju 88 unconfirmed
30.12.1941 14.30	317 Squadron	Spitfire VB AA762 JH-W	2-0-0 Bf 109
19.08.1942 10.30	317 Squadron	Spitfire VB AD295 JH-C	1-0-0 Fw 190
19.08.1942 10.30	317 Squadron	Spitfire VB AD295 JH-C	1-0-0 Ju 88
19.08.1942 16.30	317 Squadron	Spitfire VB BL927 JH-L	½-0-0 Do 217
04.05.1943 18.50	316 Squadron	Spitfire IX BS463 SZ-G	0-1-1 Fw 190
11.06.1943	316 Squadron	Spitfire IX BS406 SZ-G	1-0-0 Bf 109

JANUSZ MACIŃSKI, Pilot Officer, was born on 12 June 1916 in Łódź, a Polish town governed by the Russians. After moving to Warsaw, he completed secondary school and passed A-level exams in May 1935. In 1937 he was accepted to the Air Force Cadet Officers' School at Dęblin. He was commissioned with the 12th class earlier than planned, and in June 1939 was posted to the 111th Fighter Squadron of the 1st Air Regiment at Warsaw. He was promoted to the rank of Sub-Lieutenant during the Polish Campaign of

1939, when he fought with the Pursuit Brigade. On 3 September the engine of his PZL P.11 was damaged in combat, and he landed near Sulejówek. As he couldn't use his machine guns, he tried to shoot down an enemy Bf 110 with a revolver. On 6 September he participated in combat with Bf 110s, and made an emergency landing in his damaged PZL P.11 no. 9 near Błonie, where his aircraft overturned. It took him four days to find his squadron, which he rejoined on 10 September near Łuck. Maciński flew reconnaissance missions until the last day of the campaign, and on 17 September he flew a PZL P.11a to Cernâuti in Rumania. The next day he crashed his

aircraft during take-off when his engine failed, and was taken on board a PZL P.23 Karaś by Sub-Lieutenant Józef Waroński from the 31st Reconnaissance Squadron, with whom he flew to Jassy and then to Galati. On 6 October he left for Yugoslavia and Greece, from where he sailed to France, arriving on 16 October. Upon arrival he declared his willingness to continue the fight from Britain, and was sent across the Channel, where on 27 January 1940 he received the service number 76721 and the rank of Pilot Officer. Initially posted to No. 15 Elementary Flying Training School at Carlisle, on 1 August Maciński was posted to No. 6 Operational Training Unit at Sutton Bridge and had two flying accidents: on 20 August he landed in the Fairey Battle L5714 with the undercarriage retracted, then on 23 August he crashed the Hurricane I N2354 at Walpole St Peter, Norfolk, due to a glycol leak. On 31 August he was posted to No. 111 Squadron at Drem. Maciński was shot down on 4th September 1940 at 09.15 while performing an operational mission against a German raid near Folkestone. He was lost at sea, apparently in his Hurricane II Z2309, and his body was never found. Some sources state however that he baled out, but a rescue found no trace of either pilot or the aircraft. Other sources state that he was machine-gunned while descending on his parachute. The remains of Hurricane Z2309 were found in 1976 at Dene Farm, West Stourmouth, 20 miles north of Folkestone, which may confirm the theory that the pilot abandoned his aircraft. He was the tenth Polish operational pilot killed during the Battle of Britain. Janusz Maciński is commemorated on the Polish Air Force Memorials at Northolt and Warsaw-Mokotów. He was posthumously decorated with the Cross of Valour.

ANDRZEJ KAZIMIERZ MALAROWSKI, Pilot Officer, was born on 11 February 1911 in Łódź, in a Poland ruled by the Russian Empire. He grew up in the family of Andrzej and Stanisława née Lipińska. After completing primary education he was accepted to the Trade School, which he graduated from in 1928 as an ironworker mechanic and draughtsman. At the same time he was interested in car mechanics, photography and sport. Between 1928 and 1930 he was employed by the Łódź-based J. Jarich factory manufacturing screws. In 1930 he joined Łódź Aero Club, and in 1931 the Polish Air Force. Malarowski was posted to the 131st Fighter Squadron of the 3rd Air Regiment at Poznań, where he served as ground crew. In the same year he won an inter-regimental boxing competition and was sent for basic flying training to the Air Force NCOs Training Centre at Bydgoszcz. Upon completion he was sent to the 34th Light Bomber Squadron of the 3rd Air Regiment. In 1934

Plt Off Andrzej Malarowski (303 Sqn PAF). This Polish officer was never considered a Battle of Britain pilot, however his flying log book states that he flew one operational mission on 26 October 1940. Malarowski was also awarded the Battle of Britain clasp that survives in his family archive

he had a flying accident, landing in a river in a Potez XXV. He completed an Advanced Flying Course at Grudziądz and was reposted to the 131st Fighter Squadron. On 5 July he was involved in a mid-air crash with Lieutenant Gustaw Langner, who lost his life, while Malarowski baled out from his PZL P.7a. Between 1935 and 1936 he was employed by the Air Force Technical Institute in Warsaw, then in 1936 he was accepted to the Infantry Cadet Officers' School at Bydgoszcz, where he completed his education and passed A-level exams in 1938. He was thus allowed to join the Air Force Cadet Officers' School at Dęblin, and as an experienced airman was attached to the second year of the 12th class. Between 5 April and 10 June 1939 he was at the Advanced Flying Course at Ułęż, then he completed his education earlier than expected due to the dangerous political situation. Before his official promotion as an officer, on 1 August he was posted to the 161st Fighter Squadron of the 6th Air Regiment at Lwów. He was commissioned on 31 August. Malarowski fought during the Polish Campaign of 1939, when his unit was attached to the 'Łódź' Army. On 2 September he participated in the shared destruction of a Dornier Do 17, which was erroneously logged as a Ju 86. Later on the same day he fought against a formation of Bf 110s, when he was wounded in the neck and an enemy bullet lodged very close to his spine and was never removed. After the fall of Poland he travelled via Rumania, Yugoslavia and Italy to France. On 1 March 1940 he was posted to No. 1 Flying School at Etâmpes, where he served as an instructor. Later he returned to the Polish Air Force Training Centre at Lyon-Bron and was given administration duties. On 22 May he was posted to the so-called 'Koolhoven Flight' commanded by Captain Walerian Jasionowski at Salon, flying Koolhoven FK58s. Malarowski was appointed commander of No. 2 Section. After the fall of France, on 24 June he sailed on the *Arandora Star* to England. Upon arrival he was given the service number P-0527 and the rank of Pilot Officer. After a short stay at the Polish Air Force Centre at Blackpool, on 1 September he was posted to No. 307 (Polish) 'City of Lwów' Night Fighter Squadron at Kirton-in-Lindsay. Like many other Polish pilots he expressed disappointment after being ordered to fly Boulton Paul Defiants, and was reposted to No. 5 Operational Training Unit at Aston Down. On 11 October Malarowski joined No. 303 (Polish) 'Tadeusz Kościuszko. City of Warsaw' Squadron at Leconfield. According to his flying log book, during the Battle of Britain he performed one operational flight on 26 October, information which until recent years could not be found in any other documents. Malarowski was awarded the Battle of Britain clasp, which could confirm that he indeed flew operationally. On 8 November he was posted to No. 43 Squadron, where two days later he made an emergency landing on water. On 15 December, engine failure forced him to bale out from his Hurricane I R4227 FT-H, and he spent half an hour in a dinghy a mile from the Isle of May in Scotland. On 25 February 1941 he was posted to No. 317 (Polish) 'City of Wilno' Squadron, then in September to No. 87 Squadron, where on 5 December he attacked a Ju 88, which managed to escape. On 19 August 1942, during an operation covering the Dieppe Raid, he was shot up while flying his Hurricane II LK-J and made an emergency landing at Tangmere. Soon after he was transferred to No. 533 Squadron, where he remained until January 1943 when this unit was disbanded. The next month Malarowski was posted to No. 264 Squadron, where he flew Mosquitos. On 25 May he was posted for rest and served as a flying instructor at No. 16 (Polish) Service Flying Training School at Newton. On 15 September 1944 he was posted to No. 303 (Polish) Squadron, where he took command of 'A' Flight. He remained in No. 303 Squadron until this unit was disbanded. After demobilization with the rank of Flight Lieutenant he decided to stay in the United Kingdom, and in 1948 married Hilda Abbot and they had two sons. He was accepted into the Royal Air Force, where he served as a pilot and instructor until 1956. Later he worked in the construction office of Sigma Instruments at Letchworth. Between 1964 and 1976 Malarowski was employed by Cam Gears as a constructor. After retirement he settled in Hitchin, where he died after a heart attack on 4 October 1985. He was buried at St John's Road Cemetery at Hitchin. He was decorated with the Cross of Valour and bar.

Date & Time	Unit	Aircraft	Score
02.09.1939 10.50	161st Squadron	PZL P.7a	⅓-0-0 Do 17 claimed as Ju 86

BRONISŁAW MALINOWSKI, Sergeant, was born on 12 February 1912 at Lwów, a Polish town ruled by the Russian Empire. Together with his ten brothers and one sister he grew up in the family of Jan, an engineer, and Anna née Popiołek. At a very early age he moved to Salzburg in Austria, where his younger brother Jan, in future also a fighter pilot of Nos 317 and 308 (Polish) Squadrons,  was born. During the independence wars three of his brothers were killed. After completing primary education he was accepted to the State Industrial College at Lwów and graduated after three years as a turner-mechanic. At the age of 17 he volunteered for the Polish Armed Forces and was posted as a ground crew member to the 6th Air Regiment at Lwów. In 1930 he was sent to the Air Force NCOs Training Centre at Bydgoszcz for the flying course, and upon completion joined the Training Flight of the 6th Air Regiment. In 1932 Malinowski completed an Advanced Flying Course at Grudziądz and was then posted to one of the fighter squadrons of the 3rd Air Regiment at Poznań. He returned to the 6th Air Regiment and in 1935 flew with the 63rd Reconnaissance Squadron, before being appointed a flying instructor in 1936 and posted to the Air Force Cadet Officers' School at Dęblin. He joined the instructors flight formed ad hoc to defend Dęblin and Ułęż and flew obsolete PZL P.7s during the Polish Campaign of 1939. In a RWD-8 training aircraft he flew towards the eastern border of Poland, but after the Russian attack he left the aircraft and was evacuated on 17 September by crossing the Rumanian border. He travelled via Yugoslavia to Greece, and in the port of Piraeus boarded a ship and sailed to Marseilles in France. He was posted to the Polish Air Force Training Centre at Lyon-Bron, and soon after joined the 2nd Flight of the 1st Observers Squadron formed at Clermont-Ferrand. As this unit never saw action, on 13 May 1940 Malinowski was posted to the group of ferry pilots commanded by Lieutenant Mieczysław Wolański and stationed at Châteaudun. He flew various aircraft, including Morane MS 406s, Koolhoven FK58s and Bloch MB 152s. On 23 June he flew from Marignane to North Africa, piloting a LeO-451 bomber. Via Algiers he flew to Oran, from where via Casablanca he sailed to Gibraltar, on 13 July arriving at Liverpool. Upon arrival he was given the service number 782059 and the rank of Sergeant. On 10 September he was posted to No. 307 (Polish) 'City of Lwów' Night Fighter Squadron at Kirton-in-Lindsey. Like many others he was unhappy to fly Boulton Paul Defiants, and on 9 October he was reposted to No. 1 School of Army Co-operation at Old Sarum and then to No. 5 Operational Training Unit at Aston Down. On 25 October he was posted to No. 43 Squadron at Usworth. On 31 October engine failure forced him to perform an emergency landing at Chirnside. In December he was posted to No. 501 Squadron, and then on 11 April 1941 to No. 302 (Polish) 'City of Poznań' Squadron. On 30 December he claimed his first victory by probably shooting down a Bf 109. On 27 April 1942 he was sent to No. 58 Operational Training Unit as an instructor and on 19th August 1942 he was wounded as a result of a flying accident in the Miles Master I T7433. On 10 November Malinowski returned to No. 302 Squadron. At the beginning of 1943 he applied and was accepted for a tour in North Africa with the Polish Fighting Team, also known as 'Skalski's Circus'. After arriving in Tunisia the Poles were attached to No. 145 Squadron. On 7 April he shot down a Bf 109. He returned to England on 22 July and once more was posted to No. 302 Squadron. On 8 September during an operational sortie over France he claimed two Bf 109s destroyed, but was also shot down and wounded in his Spitfire VB AA928 WX-U. He landed at Zillebeke near Ypres in Belgium. With the help of locals he avoided captivity and hid under the false name of Jean Nicolas Van de Ven in the local mortuary, where Belgian doctors operated on him. After three weeks he travelled via France to Spain, and from Gibraltar on to England, arriving at Portreath on 13 December. On 25 March 1944 Malinowski was posted to No. 1 Aircraft Delivery Unit, and on 29 June rejoined No. 302 Squadron. On 30 June he was shot down over Normandy by German ground fire and force-landed his Spitfire IX MJ359. With both legs broken he was saved by a Canadian tank crew and taken to hospital. He never flew again. On 18 March 1945 he arrived at the HQ of No. 133 (Polish) Wing, and then on 8 August he was posted to the HQ of the Polish Fighter Station at Coltishall. On 9 June he was commissioned, receiving the rank of Pilot Officer and the new service number P-3036. He was sent to the Polish Resettlement Corps and decided to stay in the United Kingdom with his French wife Jacqueline Leckie, whom he had married on 4 November 1944 at Ruislip. Demobilized with the rank of Flying Officer, he decided to travel to the newly born Pakistan, where he served in the Royal Pakistani Air Force as a flying instructor at the RPAF College at Risalpur. Upon his return to England he ran his own pub and then a car garage. In 1976 he visited Belgium, where he participated in unveiling a memorial plaque dedicated to the four locals who were killed after helping him to escape in 1943. Captain Bronisław Malinowski died on 1 May 1982 in London and his ashes were taken to Poland and laid to rest in the cemetery in Ksawerów. His decorations included the Silver Cross of Virtuti Militari no. 8580, the Cross of Valour and three bars and the British Distinguished Flying Cross.

Date & Time	Unit	Aircraft	Score
30.12.1941 14.00	302 Squadron	Spitfire VB AA752 WX-W	0-1-0 Bf 109
07.04.1943 08.00	Polish Fighting Team	Spitfire IX EN300 ZX-9	1-0-0 Bf 109
08.09.1943 09.20	302 Squadron	Spitfire VB AA928 WX-U	2-0-0 Bf 109

JAN LEONARD MALIŃSKI, Pilot Officer, was born on 1 March 1917 in Berlin, Germany, into the Polish family of Jan and Marianna née Ratajewska. After Poland regained independence, at the age of 3 he returned to Poland with his parents and initially settled in Poznań. Two years later they moved to Swarzędz. In 1924 he was accepted to the primary school at Olszyna and continued his education at Ostrzeszów, where his family finally settled. In 1931 he was accepted to the Salesian Teachers' Seminar at Ostrzeszów, and continued when the school was moved to Krotoszyn. In 1933 and 1934 Maliński undertook gliding training at the Silesian Aero Club, including a gliding  course at Goleszów. In the summer of 1936 he participated in a flying course at Lublinek, where he flew RWD-8s. On 1 September he started a unitary course at the Infantry Cadet Officers' School at Różan, and on 3 January 1937 started at the Air Force Cadet Officers' School at Dęblin. His education was shortened by the dangerous political situation, and he left Dęblin without official graduation, together with the whole 12th class. On 15 June 1939 Maliński was posted to the 132nd Fighter Squadron of the 3rd Air Regiment at Łódź. He was commissioned during the Polish Campaign in 1939. He participated in combat as his unit within III/3 Fighter Wing supported the 'Poznań' Army. On 3 September he helped damage two German bombers, yet he was given only a shared victory over one Do 17 or He 111. On 7 September he claimed the destruction of an He 111 (according to other sources Bf 110), but was shot down himself by a Bf 110. Maliński was wounded and baled out. He was hospitalized at Koło, Kutno and then in Łowicz. Unable to escape from Poland, he returned to Ostrzeszów, where he was arrested by the Germans and held in Stalag XXIA. Due to serious illness he was released, and on 4 April 1940 he escaped from Ostrzeszów, travelling via Hungary and Yugoslavia. On board the *Patris* he sailed from the port of Split, arriving in France. On 6 June he was transferred to the Polish Air Force Training Centre at Lyon-Bron. After the fall of France he sailed to England on the *Arandora Star* from St Jean de Luz on 21 June. Upon arrival he was given the service number P-1286 and the rank of Pilot Officer. After a short stay at Blackpool on 20 August he was posted to No. 302 (Polish) 'City of Poznań' Squadron at Leconfield. However, on 2 September he was reposted for further training to No. 5 Operational Training Unit at Aston Down and returned to No. 302 Squadron on 26 September. On 15 October he performed an emergency landing in his Hurricane I R2684 WX-B with the undercarriage up. On 4 March 1941 he participated in the shared damage of a Ju 88, then on 28 June was transferred at his own request to No. 307 (Polish) 'City of Lwów' Night Fighter Squadron. On 20 May 1942 he was posted for rest and served as Sector operations room controller, from where he was posted to Ground Controlled Interception at Wrafton. In 1943 he served as controller on HMS *Glasgow*. Maliński returned to No. 307 Squadron on 16 September 1944 and flew operationally until the end of war. On 25 July 1945 he was posted to No. 229 Transport Group RAF in South-East Asia, where he served until the end of September 1946. He was demobilized from the Polish Air Force with the rank of Flight Lieutenant. Maliński decided to stay in the West, and initially settled in England. On 9 July 1947 he obtained a civilian pilot's, navigator's and radio operator's licence, working for various companies such as the Lancashire Aircraft Co. and Air Charter. In 1949 and 1950 he participated in the airlift to Berlin during the Russian blockade, then was employed by the CIA performing secret flights to Albania, Bulgaria and Rumania. In 1953 for the second time he took part in the Berlin airlift, and then completed a course at the British Institute of Engineering Technology. In 1956 he emigrated to Canada, where he was employed by Maritime Central Airways flying with supplies for the Distant Early Warning Line. He worked for the Can Car company before being employed by Trans Air Ltd. After losing this job he opened a small manufacturing business in his garage at Montreal. In 1964 Maliński moved to the Bahamas, where two years later took a job with Bahamas Airways, then worked for Grand Bahama Hydroponic Gardens. In 1972 he returned to Poland and settled in Ostrzeszów, where a year before he had sent his children. He worked in his own mushroom business, also as a translator, eventually retiring in 1982. In 2000 his autobiographical book, *An aeroplane has obscured the Sun*, was published. On 7 April 2001 he was made an honorary citizen of Ostrzeszów. Colonel Jan Maliński died aged 88 on 6 February 2006 at Ostrzeszów and was buried there in the Roman Catholic Cemetery. His decorations included the Cross of Valour. He was posthumously awarded the Commander's Cross of Polonia Restituta. One of the streets in Ostrzeszów is named after him.

Date & Time	Unit	Aircraft	Score
03.09.1939	132nd Squadron	PZL P.11c	⅓-0-0 Do 17
07.09.1939	132nd Squadron	PZL P.11c	1-0-0 He 111
04.03.1941 11.10	302 Squadron	Hurricane I V6860 WX-B	0-0-1 Ju 88

MIECZYSŁAW STANISŁAW MARCINKOWSKI, Sergeant, was born on 24 February 1919 at Rytwiany near Sandomierz, Kielce Voivodship, in free Poland. He attended primary school at Rytwiany, but completed his education at Staszów. In the same town he also completed three years of the secondary school. In 1936 he was accepted to the Air Force NCO School for Minors at Bydgoszcz, and in 1939 graduated from the school, which was moved to Krosno. As a bomber pilot he was posted to the Training Flight of the 1st Air Regiment at  Warsaw. During the Polish Campaign in 1939 he was employed evacuating an aircraft. Marcinkowski crossed the Rumanian border on 18 September and travelled to France. He decided to continue to England via Beirut, arriving on 9 February 1940, receiving the service number 780491 and the rank of Sergeant. On 6 August he was sent to No. 1 School of Army Co-operation at Old Sarum, and then on 1 September to No. 6 Operational Training Unit at Sutton Bridge. Upon completion he was posted to No. 151 Squadron at Digby, then in October he was reposted to No. 501 Squadron at Kenley. On 1 November he flew a patrol over the English Channel and was reported missing due to unknown circumstances. He was last seen flying towards the French coast in the Hurricane I V7405, and it is believed that he crashed into the sea due to oxygen failure. His body was never found. He is commemorated on the Polish Air Force Memorials at Northolt and Warsaw-Mokotów.

ANTONI LUCJAN MARKIEWICZ, Sergeant, was born on 13 January 1915 at Sandomierz, in Kielce Voivodship in Poland, governed by the Russian Empire. In Sandomierz he completed primary school and two years of secondary school before he was accepted to the Air Force NCO School for Minors at Bydgoszcz, which he entered in 1931. He graduated in 1934 as an aircraft mechanic with basic flying training, and was posted to the 2nd Air Regiment at Cracow. During his service in the 2nd Regiment he completed further flying training and  was posted to the 22nd Bomber Squadron. He was then sent to Grudziądz, where he completed an Advanced Flying Course. During this time he had a flying accident on 6 April 1937 in a PZL P.7. Upon completion he was reposted to Cracow and attached to the 122nd Fighter Squadron, also serving as a flying instructor of the Training Flight and having an accident in a Potez XXV on 14 July 1937. During his stay in Cracow he completed his secondary education and obtained a Matriculation Certificate. He was posted to Aleksandrowice airfield, where he became a pilot of the ambush section under the command of the 122nd Squadron, which supported the Cracow Army. On 1 September 1939 he participated in shooting down a Henschel Hs 126. On 2 September alongside seven other pilots he participated in the shared destruction of a Ju 87, and was credited with half a victory of a Do 17. On 3 September he participated in the shared destruction of an He 111, but this claim was also never accepted. On 7 September he took part in an aerial combat and claimed damage to a Ju 86. This was in fact a Do 17 and Markiewicz's claim was never accepted. After the fall of Poland, on 17 September he flew to Cérnauti in Rumania, from where on 15 October he sailed to Beirut on the *Aghios Nikolaos*, continuing on the *Ville de Strasbourg* to France, arriving at Marseilles on 29 October. In December he was posted to the Polish Air Force Training Centre at Lyon-Bron. He was then posted to the so-called 'Finish Squadron' which was supposed to be deployed to Finland against the Russian aggressors. After an armistice was signed on the night of 12/13 March 1940 it was decided to form the 1/145 'City of Warsaw' Squadron at Lyon-Bron. Markiewicz was attached to Section 1 of 2nd Flight. The squadron, also known as GC 1/145, was equipped with Caudron CR 714s. On 9 June he was credited with the shared destruction of a Do 17. On 15 June alongside seven pilots of 2nd Flight Markiewicz was dispatched to GCI/1, and on 18 June with two other pilots encountered an He 111, which crashed. The very next day he sailed to England, where he arrived on 21 June. He was given the rank of Sergeant and the service number 793546, and on 6 August was posted to No. 302 (Polish) 'City of Poznań' Squadron at Leconfield. On 26 October he probably shot down a Bf 109. On 2 February 1941, while flying the Hurricane I V6753 WX-Z in mist, he hit a wave and made a crash-landing, sustaining injuries. Upon convalescence Markiewicz was posted to No. 1 Aircraft Delivery Flight, where on 15 May he had another flying accident at Northolt when he was ferrying the Hurricane II Z3154. On 29 July 1942 he was posted to No. 2 Flying Instructors School, and after completion served at No. 16 (Polish) Service Flying Training School at Newton as an instructor. Whilst there, he attended the Cadet Officers' School at Auchtermuchty in Scotland. On 4 August 1943 he was posted to Blackpool, and in 1946 was posted to RAF Hucknall. At the end of 1946 he joined the Polish Resettlement Corps, deciding to stay in Britain with his wife Yvonne Munday and two children. Warrant Officer Markiewicz was demobilized on 9 November 1948, later being commissioned with the Polish rank of Sub-Lieutenant. Initially he lived at Burton Joyce near Nottingham, before moving to Southern England. After naturalization he changed his name to Anthony Martin and worked as a radio and tv technician. Later he ran his own textile business, but was also employed as a business representative. Antoni Markiewicz died aged 90 on 30 April 2005 at Rustington and was buried in the local cemetery. He was decorated with the Cross of Valour and two bars.

Date & Time	Unit	Aircraft	Score
01.09.1939 13.00	122nd Squadron	PZL P.11c	½-0-0 Hs 126
02.09.1939 16.38	122nd Squadron	PZL P.11c	½-0-0 Do 17
03.09.1939 10.00	122nd Squadron	PZL P.11c	¼-0-0 He 111 unconfirmed
07.09.1939 17.00	122nd Squadron	PZL P.11c	0-0-1 Do 17 claimed as Ju 86

Date & Time	Unit	Aircraft	Score
09.06.1940 14.00	1/145 Squadron	Caudron CR 714	⅓-0-0 Do 17
18.06.1940 17.40	GCI/1	Caudron CR 714	⅓-0-0 He 111 unconfirmed
26.10.1940 11.30	302 Squadron	Hurricane I V6942 WX-S	0-1-0 Bf 109

LUDWIK ALFRED MARTEL, Pilot Officer, called 'Zośka' (little Sophie, a nickname given to him after his girlfriend), was born on 5 March 1919 at Piotrków Trybunalski, into the family of Ludwik and Helena née Czeczor. After completing primary school in Sieradz he was accepted to the Technical Textile Secondary School in Łódź, and also completed gliding training. Martel passed A-level exams in 1937 and completed a flying course on RWD-8 aircraft, and then in January 1938 was accepted to the Air Force Reserve Cadet Officers' School in Radom-Sadków. Upon completion on 15 September he was posted

back to civilian life, although assigned to the 3rd Air Regiment at Poznań in case of war. In 1938 and 1939 Martel was employed by Państwowe Zakłady Lotnicze at Mielec, where he was involved in the production of PZL P.37 'Łoś' bombers. During the summer of 1939 he was sent to the 3rd Air Regiment, where he undertook training on PZL P.11 fighters. He was mobilized and attached to the Training Flight of the 3rd Air Regiment, and together with the rest of the staff was evacuated to Rumania, crossing the border on 17 September. After a short internment, he travelled via Yugoslavia and Italy toFrance, arriving on 9 October. Unhappy with the French approach, Martel decided to join his colleagues already stationed in Britain. While in France he was commissioned as a Sub-Lieutenant. He arrived in England, in January 1940 and was posted to the Polish Air Force Centre at Eastchurch, receiving the service number 76812 and the rank of Pilot Officer. On 1 June he was transferred to No. 3 Polish Wing at Blackpool, and from 22-29 July completed a basic flying course at No. 1 School of Army Co-operation at Old Sarum. He was immediately transferred to No. 7 Operational Training Unit at Hawarden, before joining No. 54 Squadron at Hornchurch on 23 August. On 29 September he was transferred to No. 603 Squadron. While flying with this unit he made two claims, on 2 and 5 October. He was shot down and wounded on 25 October over Hastings, while flying the Spitfire II P7325 XT-W. After less than two weeks in hospital, he returned to No. 603 Squadron. On 19 March 1941 Martel was posted to No. 317 (Polish) 'City of Wilno' Squadron, then on 30 January 1942 arrived at No. 58 Operational Training Unit at Grangemouth, where he served as an instructor. He returned to No. 317 Squadron on 25 August. At the beginning of February 1943 Martel was accepted for the 'Polish Fighting Team', better known as 'Skalski's Circus', and sent to North Africa. Flying with No. 145 Squadron he made three claims on 4 and 20 April. After the end of the African Campaign and the disbandment of 'Skalski's Circus' he left for Gibraltar and tried to get on board the Liberator used by General Władysław Sikorski, which later crashed, killing all except the pilot. Martel arrived back in Britain on 5 July, and on 22 July was once more posted to No. 317 Squadron. On 20 August he was posted for rest to No. 16 (Polish) Service Flying Training School at Newton. On 4 November he reported back to No. 317 Squadron, and on 8 April 1944 became 'A' Flight commander. Upon completion of an operational tour on 12 July he was posted to the HQ of Fighter Command, but volunteered for the secret operations as a potential agent to be dropped in occupied Poland. This project never materialized and Martel was posted to the HQ of No. 84 Group as Liaison Officer. Between January and October 1946 he served at the HQ of British Air Forces of Occupation in Germany. He was demobilized in 1947 with the rank of Flight Lieutenant and stayed in Britain with his wife Zofia Suszyńska. Martel once more volunteered for secret operations, this time offering to be part of a team which would steal a MiG-15 from Poland. From 1953 he flew as an agricultural pilot in Africa, and after 1965 set up a sewage business in Britain with another Battle of Britain pilot, John Kent. After retirement Colonel Martel settled in Wimbledon in London. He died aged 91 on 25 April 2010 in London and was buried at Putney Vale Cemetery. His decorations included the Silver Cross of Virtuti Militari no. 8597 and the Cross of Valour and two bars.

Date & Time	Unit	Aircraft	Score
02.10.1940	603 Squadron	Spitfire I X4274 XT-P	0-0-1 Bf 109
05.10.1940 11.50	603 Squadron	Spitfire I X4348 XT-R	1-0-0 Bf 109
04.04.1943 09.30	Polish Fighting Team	Spitfire IX EN361 ZX-3	0-0-1 Fw 190

Date & Time	Unit	Aircraft	Score
20.04.1943 12.35	Polish Fighting Team	Spitfire IX EN261 ZX-10	1-0-0 Bf 109
20.04.1943 12.35	Polish Fighting Team	Spitfire IX EN261 ZX-10	0-1-0 MC.200

BOGUSŁAW LEON MIERZWA, Pilot Officer, was born on 14 March 1918 in German-occupied Warsaw, and grew up in the family of Władysław Mierzwa. He graduated from primary and secondary school in Warsaw and was accepted to the Air Force Cadet Officers' School at Dęblin, starting his education in 1937. Together with the rest of his 12th class he left Dęblin early without official graduation due to the dangerous political situation, and in June 1939 was posted to the 114th Fighter Squadron of the 1st Air Regiment at Warsaw.

Commissioned on 1 August, he received the rank of Sub-Lieutenant. During the Polish Campaign of 1939 he fought with the IV/1 Fighter Wing of the Pursuit Brigade, and on 1 September claimed one shared victory, followed by the shared damage of an enemy aircraft. On 6 September he was involved in the destruction of a Bf 110. After the fall of Poland, on 17 September he was evacuated to Rumania, from where he travelled to France. He was posted to the Polish Air Force Training Centre at Lyon-Bron, where he completed training on French fighter planes. He also flew defensive patrols over the base, including one on 1 June 1940 when his commander, Lieutenant Aleksander Gabszewicz, shot down an He 111. The same day he was posted to the Polish section commanded by Gabszewicz and attached to GCIII/10, and the next day sent to Deauville. During the French Campaign Bogusław Mierzwa flew between ten and fifteen operational sorties. On 21 June he was evacuated to Britain. Upon arrival he received the service number P-1389 and the rank of Pilot Officer, and on 23 August was posted to No. 303 (Polish) 'Tadeusz Kościuszko. City of Warsaw' Squadron at Northolt. On 2 September he was reposted to No. 5 Operational Training Unit at Aston Down for further training. Mierzwa returned to No. 303 Squadron later in September. On 7 October he damaged his Hurricane I P3089 RF-P, while landing in error at a decoy landing ground at Borstal, which was created to mislead the Germans. He remained with No. 303 Squadron, and on 16 April 1941 participated in an operational flight escorting Blenheim bombers attacking Berck-sur-Mer airfield near Boulogne. During their return at about 18.00 the Polish formation was attacked by German fighters, and Flying Officer Mierzwa was shot down into the sea and killed near Dungeness in his Spitfire IIA P7819 RF-S. He was buried at the Polish airmen cemetery at Northwood, London, in grave no. H 290. He is commemorated on the Polish Air Force Memorials at Northolt and Warsaw-Mokotów. A small memorial plaque was placed at Dungeness, near a bird observatory, close to the place where he was killed. He was decorated with the Cross of Valour.

Date & Time	Unit	Aircraft	Score
01.09.1939 08.50	114th Squadron	PZL P.11c	⅓-0-0 He 111
01.09.1939 17.20	114th Squadron	PZL P.11c	0-0-½ Bf 109
06.09.1939 06.00	114th Squadron	PZL P.11c	⅓-0-0 Bf 110

WŁODZIMIERZ JANUSZ MIKSA, Pilot Officer, called 'Pies' (dog), was born on 27 September 1915 at Łódź in part of Poland ruled by the Russian Empire. He grew up in the family of Wawrzyniec and Helena née Antoniewicz,

graduated from primary and then secondary school and passed A-level exams. He was accepted to the Air Force Cadet Officers' School at Dęblin in 1937, and two years later completed his training without official graduation. The whole 12th class was commissioned during the Polish Campaign of 1939. In June 1939 he was posted to the 114th Fighter Squadron of the 1st Air Regiment at Warsaw. During the Polish Campaign he flew operationally with the IV/1 Fighter Wing under the command of the Pursuit Brigade. On 1 September his aeroplane was slightly damaged when he attempted to attack a formation of He 111s. Miksa is officially associated with several claims, including two on 7 September and two the day after. On 6 September he participated in the destruction of a Bf 110, but this claim was erroneously noted as 7 September. He also took part in the damage of a Do 17 and destruction of an Hs 126 on 9 September, but this was added to his account for the 8th. On 17 September he attacked Soviet cavalry forces several times. After the fall of Poland he was evacuated to Rumania and then to France. He was posted to the Polish Air Force Training Centre at Lyon-Bron, where he completed training on French fighter planes. He also flew defensive patrols over the base. On 1 June 1940 he was posted to the Polish section commanded by Lieutenant Aleksander Gabszewicz and attached to GCIII/10, and the next day sent to Deauville. The Poles flew Bloch MB 152s. He was evacuated from France and arrived in Britain on 16 July. Miksa received the service number P-0286 and the rank of Pilot Officer. On 25 September he was posted to No. 5 Operational Training Unit at Aston Down, then on 19 October to No. 151 Squadron at Digby and on 23 October to No. 303 (Polish) 'Tadeusz Kościuszko. City of Warsaw' Squadron. He was wounded on 29 October while landing his Hurricane I P3206 RF-X. On 22 January 1941 he was posted to No. 315 (Polish) 'City of Dęblin' Squadron, and in June 1942 took command of 'B' Flight. During his time with No. 315 Squadron he claimed the destruction, probable destruction and damage of enemy aircraft, all in one day. On 5 April 1943 he was posted for rest as a flying instructor to No. 58 Operational Training Unit at Grangemouth, then from 18 October served in No. 302 (Polish) 'City of Poznań' Squadron. On 1 January 1944 he took command of No. 317 (Polish) 'City of Wilno' Squadron. Upon completion of his operational tour, he was posted to No. 12 Group RAF as Polish Liaison Officer. Between 15 May 1945 and 17 February 1947 he served at the HQ of Fighter Command. Flight Lieutenant Miksa was demobilized and settled in Britain. In 1945 he had married Angela Pilkington, daughter of Geoffrey from the Pilkington Brothers glassmakers; they had five sons. Miksa changed his name to Pilkington-Miksa and ran a successful PVC business, employing many Poles. After divorce in 1970, he married Anna Krawczyk and had two children with her. They lived in Kingston-upon-Thames. Lieutenant

Colonel Włodzimierz Miksa died on 20 August 1999 and was cremated at Putney Vale Crematorium, London. He was decorated with the Silver Cross of Virtuti Militari no. 10295, the Cross of Valour and two bars and the British Distinguished Flying Cross.

Date & Time	Unit	Aircraft	Score
07.09.1939/06.09.1939 05.00	114th Squadron	PZL P.11c	½-0-0 Bf 110
07.09.1939	114th Squadron	PZL P.11c	1-0-0 Ju 86
08.09.1939/09.09.1939 07.30	114th Squadron	PZL P.11c	0-0-½ Do 17/He 111
08.09.1939/09.09.1939 08.00	114th Squadron	PZL P.11c	⅓-0-0 Hs 126
21.10.1941 12.00	315 Squadron	Spitfire VB AB931 PK-C	1-1-1 Bf 109

KONRAD ANTONI MUCHOWSKI, Sergeant, was born on 3 July 1918 at Kościerzyna in Pomeranian Voivodship, in part of Poland ruled by the German Empire. Together with two brothers and three sisters he grew up in the family of Ignacy and Aniela Angelika Warnke. He graduated from secondary school in Kościerzyna, which he attended between 1929 and 1937, and completed a gliding course at Ustianowa. During his military service he was posted to the 4th Air Regiment at Toruń, where in 1937 and 1938 he completed a flying course. Upon completion he was attached to the 42nd Light Bomber Squadron of the 4th Air Regiment. During the Polish Campaign of 1939 he flew as a pilot of the 42nd Reconnaissance Squadron, equipped with PZL P.23 'Karaś' light bombers, supporting the 'Pomerania' Army. He usually flew with the crew of Bohdan Makowski (observer) and Stanisław Pęczak (air gunner). His aircraft was damaged by anti-aircraft artillery and a Bf 110 on 4 September while observing German movements near Bygoszcz and Nakło. Although Muchowski was able to fly back to the airfield, Makowski was wounded in the stomach and died next day in hospital at Żychlin. After the fall of Poland, on 17 September he crossed the Rumanian border at Kuty.

After arriving in France on 11 November he was posted to the Polish Air Force Traning Centre at Lyon-Bron, but soon after he volunteered for the Polish units planning to be organized in Britain. Upon arrival on 26 January 1940 at Eastchurch he received the service number 780531 and the rank of Sergeant. On 30 May 1940 he was posted to the Polish Air Force Centre at Blackpool. On 19 August he was posted for conversion to No. 5 Operational Training Unit, and on 10 September was posted to No. 85 Squadron at Castle Camp and then on 23 October to No. 501 Squadron at Kenley. On 9 March 1941 he was sent to No. 308 (Polish) 'City of Cracow' Squadron, but left on 25 June, and on 4 July he was struck off the list of fighter pilots and moved to training. Muchowski was posted to the Central Gunnery School at Warmwell as a staff pilot, then on 22 July 1943 sent to Flying Instructors School and on 23 October to No. 25 (Polish) Elementary Flying Training School at Hucknall. On 15 July he had been commissioned, receiving the rank of Pilot Officer and the new service number P-2208. On 5 January 1946 he was transferred to No. 16 (Polish) Service Flying Training School at Newton. He was demobilized in November 1946 with the rank of Flight Lieutenant and married Eleanor Hellawell. In 1949 he decided to travel to the newly formed Pakistan, where he served as flying instructor, including at the Royal Pakistani Air Force College at Risalpur. In 1955 he returned to England, where the next year he was naturalized and changed his name to Steven. He worked as a driver for public services and died on 4 May 1988 at Huddersfield in Yorkshire, although some sources state that he died in Pakistan.

WŁODZIMIERZ WŁADYSŁAW MIROSŁAW MUDRY, Sergeant, was born on 29 April 1917 at Grzymałów near Tarnopol, in part of Poland ruled by the Austro-Hungarian Empire, the son of Irena (his father fought during the Great War in the Austro Hungarian Army and was shot by the Russians). In 1931 he was accepted to the Air Force NCO School for Minors at Bydgoszcz, although there is no information about his graduation. Initially he worked as an engine mechanic before completing a flying course. Mudry was posted to the 21st Light Bomber Squadron of the 2nd Air Regiment at Cracow. He completed his education in 1939, graduating from secondary school after six years. During  the Polish Campaign of 1939 he flew as a pilot with the 21st Bomber Squadron (from 1 September named the 1st Bomber Squadron) under the command of

II Bomber Wing which belonged to the Bomber Brigade. He flew PZL P.23 'Karaś' light bombers with the usual crew of Ferdynand Stutzman (observer) and Jan Gwóźdź (air gunner). On 3 September he took part in the bombing of German tanks in the region of Radomsko and Pławno. On 9 September, with his regular crew, he patrolled the region of Kutno-Łowicz-Rawa Mazowiecka, observing movements of the German Army. After the fall of Poland he crossed the Rumanian border on 17 September and travelled to France, from where he was sent to England. Mudry received the service number 780416 and the rank of Sergeant. On 17 August 1940 he was sent to No. 1 School of Army Co-operation at Old Sarum, where he underwent conversion training, and then to No. 5 Operational Training Unit at Aston Down. On 10 September he was sent to No. 79 Squadron at Pembrey. On 1 December Mudry was transferred to No. 87 Squadron, returning to No. 79 Squadron on 20 December. He was posted to No. 316 (Polish) 'City of Warsaw' Squadron on 23 February 1941, from where he was sent to No. 2 Aircraft Delivery Flight. On 4 March 1942 he was posted to Nos 286 and 285 Squadrons, then on 22 June 1944 arrived at No. 16 (Polish) Service Flying Training School at Newton, where he served as an instructor. In January 1945 he was released from the Polish Air Force with the rank of Warrant Officer, and with his wife settled at Radcliffe-on-Trent. Mudry, known by then as 'Willy', joined the Royal Air Force as an instructor, and on 1 August 1948 qualified as a Master Pilot. He was naturalized in 1949 and commissioned in 1951, retiring from the service on 29 April 1967. Later he worked as a branch inspector for Dunlop Tyres. Włodzimierz Mudry died in June 1988 at Grantham, Lincolnshire, but some sources state that he died in 1990.

MIECZYSŁAW MÜMLER, Squadron Leader, known as 'Król zamczyska' (King of the Castle) or 'Miętek' (Minty, a diminutive of his first name), was born on 10 December 1899 in Lwów, a Polish town governed by the Austro-Hungarian Empire. He lost his father Walerian Mümler when he was 3 years old, and his mother Katarzyna née Butz six years later, and therefore grew up with his younger sister Janina. In 1910 he graduated from primary school, then in 1917 from the 5th Humanistic High School at Lwów. Since a very early age he belonged to a Scouting organization at Lwów, also being involved in the Polish independence movement. A member of

'Orlęta Lwowskie' (Lviv's Eaglets), on 1 November 1918 he joined the fight against Ukrainians, being wounded in January 1919. In February he joined the 1st Field Artillery Regiment of Legions and participated in the Greater Poland Uprising. In 1920 he was accepted to the Artillery Cadet Officer's School at Poznań, graduating two years later and with the rank of Sub-Lieutenant being posted to the 6th Field Artillery Regiment at Cracow. In 1926 he showed an interest in joining the Polish Air Force, and on 12 May was posted to the 11th Fighter Regiment at Lida for a flying course. Upon completion on 24 June he remained in the 11th Fighter Regiment ,then on 14 July 1928 was posted to the 3rd Air Regiment at Poznań, in October 1929 becoming commander of 132nd Fighter Squadron. In November 1930 he was temporarily sent to the Air Force Officers' Training Centre at Dęblin for the commanders' course. He completed this course in March 1931, returning to Poznań. In July Mümler was sent for the Advanced Flying Course at Grudziądz, where he stayed as a flying instructor. He returned to the 132nd Squadron in September. On 15 December he married Irena Władysława Hahn at Częstochowa, the couple having two daughters. In October 1937 he left the 132nd Squadron and took command of the whole III/3 Fighter Wing. One year later his wing was placed under the command of Independent Operational Group 'Śląsk' and was sent to resolve the conflict with Czechoslovakia. During the Polish Campaign of 1939 he commanded III/3 Fighter Wing, operating in support of the 'Poznań' Army. On 6 September he participated in shared victory of a Do 17, although the Polish pilots said they saw a Ju 86 and some sources state that this happened on 8 September. On 12 September he claimed the destruction of an He 111 and participation in destroying another bomber, and the next day he shot down an Hs 126, although it is possible that he encountered an Hs 46. After the fall of Poland on 17 September he flew his personal aircraft to Rumania, landing at Cernâuti. After internment he escaped and travelled via Yugoslavia and Greece, arriving in France on 23 October. Initially he was posted to the officers' camp at Salon, from where he was sent to the Polish Air Force Training Centre at Lyon-Bron. By the end of December it was decided that the 2nd Polish Fighter Squadron 'Cracow-Poznań' should be organised, with Mümler taking command. On 7 January 1940 he was sent for training with a group of pilots, yet the squadron was never actually formed. On 5 April he was attached to the Polish section of GCII/7 commanded by Lieutenant Władysław Goettel at Luxeuil. Although he was posted there only for a short time, he flew operationally in Morane MS 406s and Dewoitine D 520s. On 25 May he claimed to have shot down an He 111, but this victory was never officially accepted. On 1 June he destroyed an He 111, and on 15 June participated in the destruction and damaging of two Do 17s. His Dewoitine no. 119, with the personal code letter 'M', was also shot down and he crash-landed near Ouanne.

Mümler was initially captured by French soldiers, but later managed to get to his unit. After the fall of France, on 20 June he flew to Algiers, but had to return due to lack of fuel. Eventually on 22 June he did manage to fly to Algiers, from where he travelled to Morocco. He sailed from Casablanca via Gibraltar to England. Upon arrival he received the service number P-1288 and the rank of Squadron Leader, and was posted to the Polish Air Force Centre at Blackpool. On 23 July he organized and took command of No. 302 (Polish) 'City of Poznań' Squadron at Leconfield. He was the highest-ranking Polish officer (Colonel) who took part in the Battle of Britain, and also the oldest participating Polish pilot. Mümler shot down a Do 17 on 18 September. As result of conflict with his British counterpart, Squadron Leader William Satchell, he left his command on 7 December, being posted for the instructors course at the Central Flying School at Upavon, where he arrived on 15 December. On 24 February 1941 he took on the role of the Polish commander of No. 58 Operational Training Unit at Grangemouth, soon after commanding the Polish Fighter School at No. 5 Operational Training Unit at Usworth. On 25 August 1942 he was posted to No. 306 (Polish) 'City of Toruń' Squadron for refresher training as part of his preparation for taking command of RAF Northolt. On 25 September he became Polish Station Commander of RAF Northolt, occasionally flying operational missions. On 3 February 1943 he claimed to have damaged an Fw 190. From 24 October he served as Polish Liaison Officer at the HQ of No. 84 Group RAF, and in 1945 arrived at Mainland. On 19 June he was transferred to the HQ of Fighter Command, returning to No. 84 Group on 21 February 1946. Acting Group Captain Mümler was demobilized in December 1946 and decided to settle in Britain. After bringing his family from communist-ruled Poland, he lived in London and worked as a baker. His third daughter was born at this time. After retiring he moved to Ealing. He died on 5 September 1985 after a long illness and was buried at Gunnersbury Cemetery, London, in grave no. M/25. Colonel Mümler was awarded the Silver Cross of Merit, the Silver Cross of Virtuti Militari no. 8990, the Cross of Valour and bar, the British Commander, Order of the British Empire, the British Distinguished Flying Cross and the French Croix de Guerre.

Date & Time	Unit	Aircraft	Score
06.09.1939/08.09.1939	III/3 Wing	PZL P.11c no.2	½-0-0 Do 17 claimed as Ju 86
12.09.1939	III/3 Wing	PZL P.11c no.2	1-0-0 He 111
12.09.1939	III/3 Wing	PZL P.11c no.2	⅓-0-0 He 111

Date & Time	Unit	Aircraft	Score
13.09.1939	III/3 Wing	PZL P.11c no.2	1-0-0 Hs 126 or Hs 46
25.05.1940	GCII/7	Morane MS 406	1-0-0 He 111 unconfirmed
01.06.1940	GCII/7	Dewoitine D 520 119/M	1-0-0 He 111
15.06.1940 15.15	GCII/7	Dewoitine D 520 119/M	½-0-0 Do 17
15.06.1940 15.15	GCII/7	Dewoitine D 520 119/M	0-0-½ Do 17
18.09.1940 17.20	302 Squadron	Hurricane I P3588 WX-J	1-0-0 Do 17
03.02.1943 11.10	1 Polish Wing	Spitfire VB	0-0-1 Fw 190

N

ALEKSANDER RYSZARD NARUCKI, Pilot Officer, was born on 1 January 1916 into a Polish family settled at Orenburg in Russia. After completing his primary and secondary education he joined the Polish Forces, and upon completion of flying training was posted to the 3rd Air Regiment at Poznań as a reserve officer. He was mobilized in August 1939 and posted to the fighter section of the 3rd Air Base in Poznań. This unit, commanded by Captain Jerzy Orzechowski, was initially stationed at Świdnik aerodrome and later operated from Kierz near Lublin. On 4 September he participated in a reconnaissance mission near

Kielce and Sandomierz to locate German movements. After the fall of Poland, on 17 September Narucki crossed the Rumanian border at Kuty. He travelled to France and on 1 March 1940 was posted to the Training Centre at Rabat in Morocco. Under the command of Major Wiktor Ryll he served there as a towing target pilot for the air gunners flying Potez 25 and LeO 206 aircraft. After the collapse of France he arrived in Britain on 16 July, receiving the service number

P-0146 and the rank of Pilot Officer. Following conversion to Hurricanes he was posted to No. 607 Squadron at Turnhouse, where he arrived on 9 October. On 7 November he was posted to No. 302 (Polish) 'City of Poznań' Squadron. On 11 May 1941 Narucki performed a training flight, and while landing in his Hurricane IIB Z3435 WX-B at Kenley aerodrome he stopped on the runway due to a mechanical failure. He was then hit by the Hurricane II Z3433 and killed. The pilot of the second aircraft, Pilot Officer Zbigniew Wróblewski, was unhurt. Flying Officer Aleksander Narucki was buried at the Northwood Cemetery, London, in grave no. H 286. He is commemorated on the Polish Air Force Memorials at Northolt and Warsaw-Mokotów.

PAWEŁ NIEMIEC, Flying Officer, called 'Poppet', was born on 25 November 1913 at Cieszyn in the Cieszyn Silesia region, a Polish town ruled by the Austro-Hungarian Empire. He grew up in the family of Paweł, a furniture factory owner, and Anna née Wania. After the death of his father in 1917 he was raised by his mother. In 1925 he completed primary school, and on 1 September 1929 was accepted to the State Mathematic and Natural Sciences High School in Cieszyn, passing A-level exams on 22 June 1933. He was an active ice skater and professional footballer of the local club DSK. Between 1 October 1933 and 28 September 1934 he completed a unitary course at the Infantry Cadet Officers' School

at Różan and went to the Air Force Cadet Officers' School at Dęblin. He was commissioned with the rank of Sub-Lieutenant as a fighter pilot on 15 October 1936 with the 9th class, and posted to the 132nd Fighter Squadron of the 3rd Air Regiment at Poznań. In 1937 Niemiec participated in a Central Fighter Competition organized by the 4th Air Regiment in Toruń and won first prize in the flying category. In the same year he completed his instructor's training at the Air Force Reserve Cadet Officers' School at Radom-Sadków. On 15 January 1938 he was appointed a flying instructor at the No. 1 Air Force Training Centre at Dęblin. On 1 July 1939 he became commander of the 2nd Training Platoon of the 1st Training Flight, then led the 4th Training Platoon of the 5th Training Flight. On 2 September he led a formation of eight PWS-26 training aircraft piloted by pupils to Kierz near Lublin. Later, with the road party of Captain Jan Czerny and still leading the group of cadets, he travelled to Kuty and crossed the Rumanian border during the night of 17/18th September. Via Yugoslavia and Italy Niemiec travelled to France, where he arrived on 10 October. Initially posted to Le Bourget assembly camp, on 8 January 1940 he was transferred to the Polish Air Force Training Centre at Lyon-Bron. Unhappy with the French approach, he decided to continue his journey to England and left on 19 January. On 27 January he was sent to the Polish Air Force Centre at Eastchurch, receiving the service number 76748 and the rank of Flying Officer. He was appointed deputy instructor of sport activities. On 17 July he was posted to No. 15 Elementary Flying Training School at Carlisle, then on 1 August transferred to No. 6 Operational Training Unit at Sutton Bridge. On 1 September he arrived at No. 17 Squadron at Tangmere. During the Battle of Britain he claimed one Do 17 damaged on 15 September and shared damage of a Do 17 on 27 October. He stayed with No. 17 Squadron after the battle, claiming the destruction of a Ju 87 on 8 November and shared destruction of a Bf 110 on 17 November. On 24 February 1941 he was reposted to No. 317 (Polish) 'City of Wilno' Squadron, and on 2 June claimed the first (shared) victory for this unit. On 9 July he had an accident while taking off, damaging his Hurricane I V7123 JH-Z at Exeter. Five days later he damaged another Hurricane, V7223 JH-V, at Friston. On 14 September he was posted for rest to the Unitary Centre at Stanmore, followed by a posting to a flying controllers course at Clamp Hill. From 4 October he served as ground controller of No. 317 Squadron. On 1 March 1942 he was appointed 'A' Flight Commander, then on 15 March he was injured while attempting an emergency landing in mist in his Spitfire VB AD321 JH-A. After convalescence on 23 August he took command of 'B' Flight. On 4 March 1943 he was appointed commander of No. 308 (Polish) 'City of Cracow' Squadron, then on 17 May transferred to the Station HQ of RAF Heston. From 21 June to 5 August he served in No. 309 (Polish) 'Czerwieńska Province' Squadron as a tactics instructor. On 7 August he was posted to No. 316 (Polish) 'City of Warsaw' Squadron, and on 15 September appointed its commander. On 26 June 1944 he took command of No. 306 (Polish) 'City of Toruń' Squadron, and on 26 July he claimed the shooting down of a V1 flying bomb together with another pilot. After leaving No. 306 Squadron Niemiec was posted to the HQ of the Polish Air Force, and subsequently was posted as Polish Liaison Officer to the HQ of No. 13 Group. On 11 March 1945 he was sent for a course at the School of Air Support at Old Sarum, and from 18 April was commander of No. 84 Group Support Unit at Lasham. On 18 May he took command of No. 317 (Polish) 'City of Wilno' Squadron, then on 13 August married Maria Niemiec (her maiden name was also Niemiec). On 12 October he again took command of

No. 316 Squadron, becoming the only Polish officer who led four different squadrons, including one on two occasions. He led No. 316 Squadron until disbandment on 17 December 1946. Squadron Leader Niemiec was released from the Polish Air Force and initially settled in London. He and his wife emigrated to Argentina in October 1948, and he ran a roofing business until retirement. He had one son, Miguel. Lieutenant Colonel Paweł Niemiec died of heart failure on 11 May 1985 at Buenos Aires and was initially buried at Chacarita Cemetery. His ashes were later spread over Nahuel Huapi lake in Bariloche, Rio Negro Province. He was decorated with the Silver Cross of Virtuti Militari no. 11062 and the Cross of Valour and two bars. In 2013 hi, biography, *One of the Few. Paweł Niemiec, a Fighter Pilot from Cieszyn"* was published by this author in Poland. In November 2013 a memorial plaque dedicated to this pilot was placed on the wall of his family home in Cieszyn.

Date & Time	Unit	Aircraft	Score
15.09.1940 14.00	17 Squadron	Hurricane I P3788 YB-X	0-0-1 Do 17
27.10.1940 10.15	17 Squadron	Hurricane I P2794 YB-E	0-0-½ Do 17
08.11.1940 17.00	17 Squadron	Hurricane I V6759	1-0-0 Ju 87
17.11.1940 09.15	17 Squadron	Hurricane I V6759	½-0-0 Bf 110
02.06.1941 22.29	317 Squadron	Hurricane I V7123 JH-Z	½-0-0 Ju 88
26.07.1944 08.05	306 Squadron	Mustang III UZ-X	½-0-0 V1

ZBIGNIEW NOSOWICZ, Pilot Officer, was born on 2 January 1914 at Wilno in Poland, then ruled by the Russian Empire. He graduated from the Adam Mickiewicz Secondary School in the same town. In September 1934 he joined the Infantry Cadet Officers' School at Różan, and in October 1935 was transferred to the Air Force Cadet Officers' School at Dęblin. Commissioned with the 10th class as a Sub-Lieutenant on 15 October 1937, he was posted to the 131st Fighter Squadron of the 3rd Air Regiment at Poznań. He completed an instructors course at the No. 1 Air Force Training Centre at Dęblin, and in January 1939 was posted to the Air Force Cadet Officers' School as an instructor and Flying Platoon commander. His unit belonged to the 2nd Training Flight and operated from Borowina airfield. During the Polish Campaign of

1939 he was in charge of the evacuation PWS-26 aircraft flown eastwards by some of the pupils. On 13 September he had to abandon the aircraft and travelled by road, crossing the Rumanian border at Kuty on 17 September. He sailed from Rumania to France, arriving at Marseilles on 29 October. Nosowicz decided not to stay in France, and in early January 1940 travelled to England. Upon arrival he was posted to the Polish Air Force Centre at Eastchurch, receiving the service number 76703 and the rank of Pilot Officer. He was later moved to No. 3 Polish Wing at Blackpool, and on 15 July
sent to No. 15 Elementary Flying Training School at Redhill. On 1 August he was sent to No. 6 Operational Training Unit at Sutton Bridge, and on 31 August joined No. 56 Squadron at North Weald. During the Battle of Britain Nosowicz claimed two aerial successes, both on 7 October, when he probably destroyed a Do 17 and damaged a Bf 110. He had an accident at Middle Wallop on 12 December when his Hurricane I P3870 collided with another aircraft flown by Pilot Officer Kenneth Marston. The latter was killed while the Pole sustained severe injuries. He finished his convalescence on 23 February 1941 and was posted to the Operations Room of No. 316 (Polish) 'City of Warsaw' Squadron as a ground control officer. From the second half of July he flew as an operational pilot of No. 316 Squadron, and on 12 January 1943 took command of 'B' Flight, but on 10 February it was decided that due to health issues he was unable to continue his flying career. Nosowicz was diagnosed with tuberculosis and sent to Halton hospital. Later he was a flying instructor for No. 16 (Polish) Service Flying Training School at Newton. He was demobilized with the rank of Flight Lieutenant, and with his English wife returned to Poland. Soon after he decided to return to the West, and in 1950 attempted to illegally leave Poland, which was ruled by the communists. His plans were discovered by the secret police, but in 1958 he successfully left for Britain, where in 1963 he was naturalized. His later whereabouts are not known so far; however, it was established that in the 1970s he was living in London. He was decorated with the Cross of Valour.

Date & Time	Unit	Aircraft	Score
07.10.1940 16.00	56 Squadron	Hurricane I V7605	0-1-0 Do 17
07.10.1940 16.00	56 Squadron	Hurricane I V7605	0-0-1 Bf 110

TADEUSZ NOWAK, Pilot Officer, called 'Teddy', was born on 2 June 1914 at Zawiercie near Będzin in a Poland ruled by the Russian Empire. He grew up in the family Walenty and Franciszka née Bielna. He was educated in his hometown, where he completed primary school, and in June 1935 graduated from the Teachers Association's High School for Boys. On 25 October 1935 he joined the 27th Infantry Regiment at Częstochowa, where he participated in a Reserve Cadet Officers' Course. After three months, in January 1936 he was sent to the Air Force Cadet Officers' School at Dęblin. Nowak was commissioned

with the 11th class in the rank of Sub-Lieutenant on 15 October 1938 and posted to the 121st Fighter Squadron of the 2nd Air Regiment at Cracow. In October he operated from Aleksandrowice airfield during the conflict with Czechoslovakia when the Polish Army annexed the Zaolzie region. In August 1939 he operated within the so-called ambush sections from Częstochowa, Wieluń and Aleksandrowice, with orders to intercept German aircraft. On 1 September he operated from Aleksandrowice, but later joined the rest of the 121st Squadron, which operated as part of III/2 Fighter Wing. On 2 September he participated in the destruction of a Ju 87, but this was never officially accepted. On 3 September he took part in an unsuccessful combat with an He 111 and his aircraft was damaged. He was erroneously given a shared victory of an He 111, but there is no confirmation of the presence of the enemy aircraft. On 5 September his aircraft was mistakenly shot up by Polish artillery and Nowak received a minor hand wound. On 12 September he participated in another encounter, and despite claiming shared victory of a Do 17 his claim was not accepted. On 17 September his aircraft was once again damaged by ground fire. On the same day he flew a PZL P.11 to Cernâuti in Rumania, where he left his aircraft. He travelled to the port of Balchik and on 15 October sailed to Beiruit on board the *Aghios Nikolaos*. From there he travelled on the *Ville de Strasbourg*, arriving at Marseilles on 29 October. Like many other Polish airmen Nowak decided to fight from Britain, and in December he left France. Upon arrival at the Polish Air Force Centre at Eastchurch he received the service number 76704 and the rank of Pilot Officer. On 23 June 1940 he was sent to No. 6 Operational Training Unit at Sutton Bridge, and on 16 July joined No. 253 Squadron at Kenley. During the Battle of Britain he claimed one aircraft probably destroyed on 30 August, three destroyed on 31 August,

4 September and 29 October, and one damaged on 13 September. On 17 October the engine of his Hurricane I P3537 failed and Nowak had to crash-land near Yalding. On 13 November he was posted to No. 303 (Polish) 'Tadeusz Kościuszko. City of Warsaw' Squadron, then on 24 January 1941 to No. 315 (Polish) 'City of Dęblin' Squadron. On 19 August he claimed the destruction of a Bf 109. On 21 September he participated in Opertion Circus 101, and on his way back was shot down over the sea. He went down in the Spitfire VB AB927 PK-S near Dover, and despite rescue efforts he drowned. His body was washed ashore near Dieppe and was buried at Quiberville Communal Cemetery, in grave no. 11, military section. Flying Officer Tadeusz Nowak was decorated with the Silver Cross of Virtuti Militari no. 8994 and the Cross of Valour with two bars. He is commemorated on the Polish Air Force Memorials at Northolt and Warsaw-Mokotów.

Date & Time	Unit	Aircraft	Score
02.09.1939 16.20	121st Squadron	PZL P.11c	⅓-0-0 Ju 87 unconfirmed
03.09.1939 10.00	121st Squadron	PZL P.11c	½-0-0 He 111
12.09.1939 11.20	121st Squadron	PZL P.11c	⅓-0-0 Do 17 unconfirmed
30.08.1940 11.10	253 Squadron	Hurricane I P2883	0-1-0 Do 215 claimed as Ju 86 damaged
31.08.1940 13.00	253 Squadron	Hurricane I P2883	1-0-0 He 111
04.09.1940 13.30	253 Squadron	Hurricane I P2883	1-0-0 Bf 110
13.09.1940 16.00	253 Squadron	Hurricane I N2455	0-0-1 He 111
29.10.1940 17.20	253 Squadron	Hurricane I V6637	1-0-0 Do 17
19.08.1941 18.30	315 Squadron	Spitfire II P7839 PK-T	1-0-0 Bf 109

EUGENIUSZ JAN ADAM NOWAKIEWICZ, Sergeant, called 'Gienek' or 'Nowak', was born on 2 January 1919 in Jasło, Cracow Voivodship, in a free Poland, into the family of Jan, a butcher, and Franciszka née Stachowicz. In his home town he completed his primary education, followed by six years at Stanisław Leszczyński High School. In 1936 he was accepted to the Air Force NCO School for Minors at Bydgoszcz and graduated in 1939 at Krosno. On 1 June he was sent on an Advanced Flying Course at Ułęż, followed by a posting to the 123rd Fighter Squadron of the 2nd Air Regiment at Cracow. During the Polish Campaign of 1939 his unit was attached to the Pursuit Brigade. He was shot down on 4 September while attacking a formation of Ju 87s. He left his PZL P.7a and returned to his unit, and the aircraft was repaired. On 17 September he flew a PZL P.7a to Rumania, but due to lack of fuel landed near

Kołomyja. Later he flew across the border and left his aircraft at Cernâuti. After arriving in France he was posted to the Polish Air Force Training Centre at Lyon-Bron, where it was decided that he would join the 2nd Fighter Squadron commanded by Major Mieczysław Mümler. As this unit was never organised, on 7 January 1940 Nowakiewicz was posted to Montpellier. While there he trained on various French aircraft, including the Morane MS 230, Caudron C 635 Simoun, Dewoitine D 501 and Morane MS 406. On 16 February he was sent back to Lyon-Bron, and in the middle of March was attached to the fighter section commanded by Lieutenant Władysław Goettel and attached to GCII/7 at Luxeuil. On 19 April he took part in their first encounter with German aircraft. On 11 May he participated in the shared destruction of an He 111. Due to lack of fuel he had to make an emergency landing and returned to his unit after three days. He was one of the first two Poles who flew a Dewoitine D 520, receiving these aircraft to replace Morane MS 406s. On 1 June he again took part in the shared destruction of an He 111. His next successful fight took place on 4 June when he individually claimed the destruction of an He 111. According to a report provided by his colleague, on 10 June Nowakiewicz took part in the destruction of a Do 215, yet this claim was never officially accepted. On 14 June he shot down a Hs 126 together with his French colleague, although he was credited with the individual victory, and on 15 June together with Major Mümler damaged a Do 17. After the fall of France, on 20 June he flew to Algiers. Via Casablanca and Gibraltar, Nowakiewicz arrived in Britain on 16 July, receiving the service number 793583 and the rank of Sergeant. On 20 August he was posted to No. 302 (Polish) 'City of Poznań' Squadron at Leconfield. On 18 October he claimed the probable destruction of a Ju 88, but on 8 November he was wounded in combat and crash-landed at Detling in his Hurricane I P3935 WX-D. On 13 March he participated in damaging a Ju 88, and on 8 May destroyed a Bf 109. On 1 June he was commissioned, receiving the new service number P-1913 and the rank of Pilot Officer. Nowakiewicz was injured in a flying accident on 8 July 1941 in the Miles Master T9752, the engine of which failed. He was shot down and wounded by ground fire while performing an operational sortie over France on 23 July 1942. He force-landed his Spitfire VB BL549 WX-E at Equihen-Plage, south of Boulogne (not at Pont de Brique as some sources state), at a place known as Noquet. Locals and resistance fighters helped him to evade capture. From Pont de Brique he travelled by train to Paris, where he was captured by the Gestapo as his false documents looked suspicious. He was kept at Fresnes prison, from there sent to a POW camp at Szubin in occupied Poland, and eventually transferred to Stalag Luft III at Sagan (Żagań). He was liberated on 2 May 1945 at Lübeck, and on 9 May was sent to Britain. Upon arrival he was posted to Blackpool, then completed a refresher course at No. 7 Flying Training School in January 1946. He was released from the Polish Air Force with the rank of Flight Lieutenant in 1947 and decided to settle in Britain. Nowakiewicz, who changed his name to Novak, and his wife Rita Jane Moseley, former Miss Nottinghamshire, ran a business as pig farmers and then potato merchants under the name R.J. & E. Novak" in Osgodby village. Later they settled in Manchester. He visited Equihen-Plage in France in 1991 and met with people who helped him in 1942. From the 1970s onward he regularly visited Poland. Captain Eugeniusz Nowakiewicz died on 5 January 1998 at Manchester and was buried at Blackley Cemetery in grave 276.

Date & Time	Unit	Aircraft	Score
11.05.1940 08.00	GCII/7	MS 406 no. 959	1-0-0 He 111 (some sources claim as shared)
01.06.1940	GCII/7	Dewoitine D 520 no. 62	⅓-0-0 He 111
04.06.1940	GCII/7	Dewoitine D 520	1-0-0 He 111
10.06.1940	GCII/7	Dewoitine D 520	shared victory Do 215 unconfirmed
14.06.1940	GCII/7	Dewoitine D 520 no. 62	1-0-0 Hs 126

15.06.1940	GCII/7	Dewoitine D 520 no. 62	½-0-0 He 111/Do 17
15.06.1940	GCII/7	Dewoitine D 520 no. 62	0-0-½ Do 17
18.10.1940 17.05	302 Squadron	Hurricane I P3705 WX-E	0 1 0 Ju 88
13.03.1941 15.20	302 Squadron	Hurricane I Z2523 WX-G	0-0-½ Ju 88
08.05.1941 13.00	302 Squadron	Hurricane II	1-0-0 Bf 109

TADEUSZ NOWIERSKI, Flying Officer, called 'Novi' or 'Łysek' (Bald Headed), was born on 22 June 1907 at Piotrków Trybunalski in part of Poland dominated by the Russian Empire. He grew up in the family of Ludomir, a doctor of the Polish Legions, and Stanisława née Altdorfer. After completing primary school he was accepted to Bolesław Chrobry High School at Piotrków Trybunalski. In 1929 he joined the Polish Army and was sent to the 1st Air Regiment at Warsaw. The same year he completed a flying course at the Air Force NCO Training Centre at Bydgoszcz, and in November 1929 was posted to the 13th Light Bomber Squadron of the 1st Air Regiment. In 1931 Nowierski was posted to the Air Force Officers' Training Centre at Dęblin, then in September 1932 to the NCO Cadet Officers' School at Bydgoszcz. During the autumn of 1934 he completed a gliding course and obtained A and B categories. On 15 October 1935 he was commissioned, receiving the rank of Sub-Lieutenant, and was posted to the 2nd Air Regiment at Cracow. Between April and July 1935 Nowierski completed an Advanced Flying Course at Grudziądz and was sent to the 24th Light Bomber Squadron. During the Polish Campaign of 1939 he flew operational missions in PZL P.23 'Karaś' light bombers, supporting the "Cracow" Army. From 1 September, with the usual crew of Aleksander Bujalski, Adam Gisman, Aleksander Paszkowski or Julian Wojda (observers) and Zygmunt Gaik or Antoni Młodzik (air gunners), he flew reconnaissance missions observing movements of the German Army. On 2 September he successfully bombed German tanks near Częstochowa. On 15 September, under heavy fire, he flew to Warsaw, at the time surrounded by

Germans, and delivered orders. On 16 September he flew an LWS-3 'Mewa' to deliver orders for the HQ of the Polish Army. After the fall of Poland he flew to Rumania. After arriving in France, he decided to join his colleagues being sent to England. Upon arrival on 15 March 1940 he received the service number 76803 and the rank of Flying Officer. Posted to the Polish Air Force Centre at Eatchurch, on 1 June he was sent to No. 3 Polish Wing at Blackpool. In July he completed a conversion course at No. 1 School of Army Co-operation at Old Sarum, and on 22 July was posted to No. 5 Operational Training Unit at Aston Down. On 5 August he was posted to No. 609 Squadron at Middle Wallop. On 13 August he destroyed a Bf 109 and damaged another one. This was followed by the probable destruction of a Bf 109 on 7 September. He made more claims during the Battle of Britain: on 27 September he damaged a Bf 110, on 30 September he destroyed one Bf 109 and damaged another, and on 15 October he destroyed one more Bf 109. He had to abandon his Spitfire I N3223 PR-M due to undercarriage problems and successfully baled out. On 2 December he reported shared damage of a Do 17. He was shot down but unhurt on 13 February 1941 in the Spitfire I X4773 while attacking a Ju 88, which was reported as damaged. On 22 March he was transferred to No. 316 (Polish) 'City of Warsaw' Squadron, and on 10 August was appointed 'B' Flight commander. He had a landing accident on 11 January 1942 at Northolt when he forgot to lower the undercarriage in his Spitfire VB W3230 SZ-O. On 17 January he became commander of No. 308 (Polish) 'City of Cracow' Squadron, and from 9 May served as deputy commander of No. 1 Polish Wing. On 19 August 1942, during the Dieppe Raid, he claimed damage of two Do 217s. He was then appointed Polish Liaison Officer at the HQ of No. 11 Group and served there from 10 December. On 27 January 1943 Nowierski became commander of the Polish Fighter School at No. 58 Operational Training Unit at Grangemouth. He took command of No. 2 Polish Wing on 20 June, then from 20 October he commanded No. 133 Airfield and frequently participated in operations. On 5 August 1944 he destroyed a V1 flying bomb. On 19 March 1945 he was sent to the United States, where he studied at the Command and General Staff College at Fort Leavenworth. He returned to England on 26 June and was posted to the Central Fighter Establishment, and then became a staff officer and finally was appointed Polish Station Commander at Dunholme Lodge. Acting Group Captain Nowierski was then demobilized and returned to Poland on 8 June 1947. Due to his previous service in the West he was not accepted by either the People's Polish Air Force or civilian aviation. He worked as a taxi driver in Warsaw until his arrest on 4 June 1948. After investigation under false charges of conspiracy he was released on 31 May 1950, and worked as a craftsman in his own workshop. Colonel Tadeusz Nowierski died on 2 April 1983 and was buried in the family grave at Old Powązki Cemetery in Warsaw. He was decorated with the Silver Cross of Virtuti Militari no. 9048, the Cross of Valour and three bars and the British Distinguished Flying Cross.

Date & Time	Unit	Aircraft	Score
13.08.1940 16.00	609 Squadron	Spitfire I L1082 PR-A	1-0-1 Bf 109
07.09.1940 18.00	609 Squadron	Spitfire I R6922 PR-T	0-1-0 Do 17
27.09.1940 12.00	609 Squadron	Spitfire I N3223 PR-M	0-0-1 Bf 110
30.09.1940 17.15	609 Squadron	Spitfire I R6961 PR-P	1-0-1 Bf 109
15.10.1940 12.45	609 Squadron	Spitfire I R6961 PR-P	1-0-0 Bf 109
02.12.1940 12.30	609 Squadron	Spitfire I X4471 PR-R	0-0-½ Do 17
13.02.1941 17.30	609 Squadron	Spitfire I X4773	0-0-1 Ju 88
19.08.1942 10.30	1 Wing	Spitfire VB BL860 JH-T	0-0-2 Do 217
05.08.1944	133 Wing	Mustang III HB886 TN	1-0-0 V1

O

ZBIGNIEW OLEŃSKI, Pilot Officer, was born on 13 November 1907 at Żytomierz, a town previously in the Kingdom of Poland but then within the Russian Empire. He was the son of Kazimierz and Maria née Nowicka and was closely related to Marshal Józef Piłsudski's wife. In 1926 he graduated from the State High School in Zamość and was accepted to the Warsaw Technical University, completing studies there. From an early age he was interested in aviation. In September 1929 he completed the 2nd course of the Academic Aero Club. In 1935 he graduated from the Air Force Reserve Cadet Officers' School at Dęblin. He was in the same class as his future squadronmate Janusz Żurakowski. Between April and July 1936 he completed an Advanced Flying

Course at Grudziądz. As a reserve officer he performed flights with various units of the 1st Air Regiment at Warsaw. He was also employed by the Aviation Technical Institute, where he was in charge of fighter performance research, flew as a test pilot and was an active member of Warsaw Aero Club. In September 1938 Oleński participated in a Baltic raid, and on 6 September performed an aerobatic flight from Riga in Estonia in the RWD-10 SP-BLO and crashed into a lake. He lost consciousness and damaged his spine. After being taken from the water and driven to the Central Military Hospital he recovered from his wounds. In September 1939, together with other staff members, he

was evacuated to Lwów, from where he travelled to Zaleszczyki, where on 17 September he crossed the Rumanian border. He travelled via Yugoslavia and Greece to France. Upon arrival he decided to continue his journey and volunteered to be sent to England. He arrived there in December and was posted to the Polish Air Force Centre at Eastchurch. On 16 December he received the service number 76617 and the rank of Pilot Officer. On 1 June 1940 he was transferred to No. 3 Polish Wing at Blackpool, then on 22 July was posted to No. 1 School of Army Co-operation at Old Sarum. Upon completion on 29 July he was sent to No. 7 Operational Training Unit at Hawarden. On 6 August he was posted to No. 152 Squadron at Portreath, and on 11 August transferred to No. 234 Squadron at Middle Wallop. While flying with this unit he made two claims, with one Bf 109 probably destroyed and another destroyed on 24 August and 4 September respectively. On 5 October he was reposted to No. 609 Squadron at Middle Wallop. While serving in this British unit he completed and submitted a report on shortcomings of the Spitfire I and suggested modifications of its design. On 8 November he had a landing accident when returning from an operational mission; after noticing a technical failure, his Spitfire I X4560 PR-H overturned but he escaped unhurt. On 28 March 1941 he was posted to the Aerodynamics Department of the Royal Aircraft Establishment at Farnborough, where he was involved in the process of analyzing the performance and strength of airframes. He was appointed Senior Aerodynamicist. When testing aircraft he occasionally flew with No. 316 (Polish) 'City of Warsaw' Squadron (for two weeks from 1 July 1942) and No. 309 (Polish) 'Czerwieńska Province' Squadron. From 29 October 1945 Oleński worked for the Central Fighter Establishment RAF, and on 4 June 1946 was transferred to the HQ of Fighter Command. He was released from service with the rank of Flight Lieutenant in March 1947. He settled in Britain and was employed by A.V. Roe (Avro) aircraft manufacturers at Manchester, where as an aerodynamicist he worked on several projects, including the Avro Vulcan bomber. Zbigniew Oleński suffered a stroke in 1960 and died on 20 June 1970 at Cheshire. He was decorated with the Silver and Golden Cross of Merit and the Cross of Valour.

Date & Time	Unit	Aircraft	Score
24.08.1940 16.50	234 Squadron	Spitfire I N3279 AZ-Y	0-1-0 Bf 109
04.09.1940 13.20	234 Squadron	Spitfire I X4182	1-0-0 Bf 109

BOLESŁAW CZESŁAW OLEWIŃSKI, Sergeant, was born on 26 October 1919 in Jersey City, United States, into a family of Polish immigrants. He returned to Poland, where he regained Polish citizenship, and in 1936 joined the Air Force NCO School for Minors at Bydgoszcz. He graduated in 1939 from Krosno as a fighter pilot, and on 1 July was posted to the 114th Fighter Squadron of the 1st Air Regiment at Warsaw. During the Polish Campaign in 1939 he fought with the IV/1 Fighter Wing under the command of the Pursuit Brigade. Initially it was decided that Olewiński would join a spare flight as his 114th Squadron  commander did not believe that his flying experience was good enough for combat. On 1 September he was shot down when attempting an attack on three aircraft recognized as 'Ju 86'. He was wounded and baled out, landing near Wyszków. He was found by locals and taken to hospital. After the fall of Poland he was evacuated with other patients to Rumania, from where he travelled to France. Upon arrival he declared that he wanted to be transferred to England. On 20 February 1940 he arrived at the Polish Air Force Centre at Eastchurch and received the service number 780695. Corporal Olewiński was posted for conversion training and then to No. 5 Operational Training Unit at Aston Down. Promoted to Sergeant, he was initially considered for No. 302 (Polish) 'City of Poznań' Squadron. On 10 October he was posted to No. 111 Squadron at Dyce, and was killed on 3 November while patrolling over Peterhead. His Hurricane I V6560 was shot down and went into the sea. His body was never found. He is commemorated on the Polish Air Force Memorials at Northolt and Warsaw-Mokotów. His brother, Pilot Officer Kazimierz Jan Olewiński, a former 132nd Fighter Squadron pilot, was killed in a flying accident while at No. 6 Operational Training Unit at Sutton Bridge on 29 July 1940.

JERZY ORZECHOWSKI, Flight Lieutenant, was born on 12 May 1905 into a Polish family at Jarmolińce, Ukraine. From an early age he was interested in photography and crafts, yet decided to pursue a military career. In 1925 he graduated from Cadet Corps No. 2 at Lwów, where he passed A-level exams. He was accepted to the Air Force Officers' School at Grudziądz (later the Air Force Cadet Officers' School), which eventually was moved to Dęblin. He graduated on 15 September 1927 with the 1st class as an observer. In the rank of Sergeant – Cadet he was posted to  the 42nd and later the 41st Light Bomber Squadron of the 4th Air Regiment at Toruń. In 1928 he was commissioned, receiving the rank of Sub-Lieutenant. In 1930 he went to Air Force Officers' Training Centre at Dęblin and completed flying course, followed by the Advanced Flying Course at Grudziądz, and upon completion returned to the 4th Air Regiment. He was married, and his daughter was born in 1934. In March 1933 he was appointed commander of the 142nd Fighter Squadron, then from November 1937 he led the whole III/4 Fighter Wing. In September 1938 Orzechowski was posted to Warsaw, where he studied at the Polish Air Force Staff College. During the Polish Campaign of 1939 he commanded the Fighter Unit of the 3rd Air Base at Świdnik, later moved to Kierz near Lublin. After the fall of Poland, on 17 September he crossed the Rumanian border with the road party of his unit. After arriving in France on 7 October he decided to continue his journey to England. Before he left France he was posted for administrative duties at the HQ of the Polish Air Force. He sailed to England and reported to the Polish Air Force Centre at Eastchurch on 29 April 1940. Orzechowski received the service number 76825 and the rank of Flight Lieutenant. On 1 June he was transferred to No. 3 Polish Wing at Blackpool, where he was posted to No. 15 Elementary Flying Training School at Carlisle and to No. 6 Operational Training Unit at Sutton Bridge. On 16 September he was appointed commander of No. 303 (Polish) 'Tadeusz Kościuszko. City of Warsaw' Squadron at Northolt. He was supposed to replace Flying Officer Witold Urbanowicz, who temporarily took command after Squadron Leader Zdzisław Krasnodębski was wounded in combat. On 21

September the posting was cancelled and Orzechowski was sent back to No. 6 Operational Training Unit. On 3 October he was attached to No. 615 Squadron at Prestwick, then on 10 October to No. 607 Squadron at Turnhouse. On 22 October he was posted to No. 306 (Polish) 'City of Toruń' Squadron to take command, but after a few days this order was cancelled. On 15 November he was posted to No. 245 Squadron, then on 29 November back to No. 615 Squadron. On 8 December he was appointed commander of No. 308 (Polish) 'City of Cracow' Squadron, a post he held until 22 June 1941. As a result of internal conflict with Flight Lieutenant Bronisław Kosiński ('B' Flight commander) he left, and on 23 June was attached to RAF Middle Wallop. A month later he was transferred to No. 81 Group RAF as Polish Liaison Officer. Between 13 August 1942 and 25 September 1942 he trained at No. 51 Operational Training Unit at Cranfield in night flying, and upon completion was posted to No. 23 Squadron based in Malta. He had a landing accident on 27 September while approaching Luqa airfield when the undercarriage of his Mosquito NFII DD691 did not lock down. Both Orzechowski and Flight Lieutenant Ignacy Szponarowicz were unhurt. He remained with No. 23 Squadron until 1 April 1943, then took command of No. 307 (Polish) 'City of Lwów' Night Fighter Squadron. On 11 September he claimed the probable destruction of one Bf 110 and damage of three others. He left No. 307 Squadron on 8 November after being appointed head of the Fighter Faculty at the Polish Air Force Staff College at Peebles. On 20 October 1944 he was transferred to the HQ of the Polish Air Force as deputy Liaison Officer at the HQ of Fighter Command. Between May and 10 September 1945 he served as Polish air attaché in Paris, returning to his duty as Polish Liaison Officer at Fighter Command HQ. Wing Commander Orzechowski was released from the Polish Air Force in January 1947. Jerzy Orzechowski emigrated to Canada, where he lived until his death aged 82 on 14 January 1988. He was decorated with the Silver Cross of Virtuti Militari no. 8410, the Cross of Valour and two bars and the British Distinguished Flying Cross.

Date & Time	Unit	Aircraft	Score
11.09.1943 14.12	307 Squadron	Mosquito VI HX859 EW-O	0-1-3 Bf 110 with Flight Lieutenant Ignacy Szponarowicz

PIOTR OSTASZEWSKI-OSTOJA, Flying Officer, called 'Osti', was born on 6 May 1910 into a Polish family settled at Sarny in Volhynia, a region that previously belonged to the Kingdom of Poland but by then ruled by the Russian Empire. He grew up in the family of Piotr Ostaszewski-Ostoja. After completing primary school in 1922 and high school, passing A-level exams in 1930, he started studying at the Chemistry Faculty of Lwów University and completed three years of studies followed by a semi-degree in chemistry. On 19 September 1933 he joined the Artillery Reserve Cadet Officers' School at Włodzimierz Wołyński, then on 21 June 1934 was transferred to the Air Force Reserve Cadet Officers' School at Dęblin and on 29 September posted to the 6th Air Regiment at Lwów. On 29 November he was accepted to the Air Force Cadet Officers' School at Dęblin. Between 1 May and 31 July 1936 he completed an Advanced Flying Course at Grudziądz. He

was commissioned on 15 October with the 9th class and received the rank of Sub-Lieutenant. Ostaszewski joined the 133rd Fighter Squadron of the 3rd Air Regiment at Poznań. On 17 September 1937 he was transferred to the 131st Fighter Squadron and on 17 November 1938 to the 132nd Fighter Squadron. He was a section commander, then an engineering officer. On 5 April 1939 he was posted to Ułęż, where he became a fighter specialization instructor of the Advanced Flying Course. During the Polish Campaign of 1939 he was attached to an ad hoc-formed Instructor Flight to protect Ułęż and Dęblin school. Flying PZL P7s he performed two operational flights and was involved in three combats. On 9 September he flew east, evacuating one of the aircraft, and crossed the Rumanian border on 17 September. Ostaszewski arrived at Marseilles in France on 29 October, and on 26 November was posted to the Air Force Centre at Salon, then in January 1940 moved to the Polish Air Force Training Centre at Lyon-Bron. He decided not to stay in France, and on 27 January arrived in England and was sent to the Polish Air Force Centre at Eastchurch. He received the rank of Flying Officer and the service number 76741. On 15 July he was posted to No. 1 School of Army Co-operation at Old Sarum, and on 21 July to No. 5 Operational Training Unit at Aston Down. He was initially considered to join No. 302 (Polish) 'City of Poznań' Squadron at Leconfield, but instead on 4 August joined No. 609 Squadron at Middle Wallop and on 15 August claimed the destruction of a Bf 110. Ten days later he was wounded in combat over Portland while flying the Spitfire I R6986 PR-S. Despite this he managed to successfully perform an emergency landing. On 1 March 1941 he was posted to No. 317 (Polish) 'City of Wilno' Squadron as a ground controller in the operations room. Consequently he kept the same duty in various squadrons: Nos 1 and 41 (between 15 January and 9 April 1942), then

No. 303 (Polish) 'Tadeusz Kościuszko. City of Warsaw' Squadron. On 3 August Ostaszewski was transferred to No. 302 (Polish) 'City of Poznań' Squadron, and on 12 September to No. 308 (Polish) 'City of Cracow' Squadron, where he also flew operationally. From 7-26 January 1943 he completed a course at the Polish Air Force Inspectorate. Between 1 June and 17 August he was a ground controller at No. 306 (Polish) 'City of Toruń' Squadron, then between 17 August and 28 September completed twin-engine aircraft conversion at No. 12 (Pilots) Advanced Flying Unit. Upon completion he took a night flying course at No. 51 Operational Training Unit. During 1942 and 1943 Ostaszewski externally completed studies at London University. On 8 February 1944 he joined No. 85 Squadron and flew with radar operator Sergeant Józef Bachleda. On 30 April he was transferred to No. 125 Squadron, from where on 15 August he was moved to No. 501 Squadron. On 25 September 1944 Ostaszewski joined No. 307 (Polish) 'City of Lwów' Night Fighter Squadron and flew with the same radio operator. He became 'A' Flight commander on 2 December 1945 with the rank of Acting Wing Commander. From 19-23 December he took part in an engine course at the Rolls-Royce factory in Derby. Between 23 April and 25 May 1945 he was appointed a night operations controller of No. 12 Group RAF. On 14 July 1945 at Beirut he married Jadwiga Wieczerzyńska. On 1 August he was moved to No. 11 Group, where as Liaison Officer he remained until 10 September. By then he was attached to No. 229 Group RAF based in South-East Asia and flying from Egypt. From 20 September he served in No. 229 Transport Squadron. On 12 December Ostaszewski joined No. 78 Transport Squadron, then on 10 July 1946 he returned to England and was posted to No. 301 (Polish) 'Pomerania Province' Transport Squadron, where he remained until disbandment on 18 December 1946. Flight Lieutenant Ostaszewski left the Polish Air Force and joined the RAF, receiving the new service number 500064. Apart from military service he participated in sports events as a pilot. During the Daily Express South Coast Race, flying a Miles Hawk Trainer III, he took first place in the 500–1,000 kg aircraft category on 16 September 1950. He changed his name to Peter Raymond, and in 1954 was transferred to reserve. Lieutenant Colonel Piotr Ostaszewski-Ostoja died on 8 May 1965 in London. He was decorated with the Cross of Valour and two bars, the Silver Cross of Merit and the British Distinguished Flying Cross.

Date & Time	Unit	Aircraft	Score
15.08.1940 18.06	609 Squadron	Spitfire I L1065 PR-E	1-0-0 Bf 110

ANTONI OSTOWICZ, Flying Officer, was born on 22 May 1911 at Rożdżałów, near Chełm in Lublin Voivodship, in a Poland ruled by the Russian Empire. He grew up in the family of Ludwik and Zofia née Kamińska. In November 1931 he joined the Air Force Reserve Cadet Officers' School at Dęblin, graduating in August 1932. He was posted to the Training Flight of the 1st Air Regiment at Warsaw. In 1932 he was accepted to the Air Force Cadet Officers' School at Dęblin. Ostowicz was commissioned with the 8th class on 15 August 1934, and with the rank of Sub-Lieutenant was posted to the 22nd Light Bomber Squadron of the 2nd Air Regiment at Cracow as an observer. Between April and June 1935 he completed an Advanced Flying Course at Grudziądz, after which he was posted to the 123rd Fighter Squadron of the 2nd Air Regiment. In April 1936 he was transferred to 121st Fighter Squadron, where he served as a pilot and engineering officer. Between 4-10 October 1937 he represented III/2 Fighter Wing in Cracow during the Central Fighter Competition organized by the 4th Air Regiment in Toruń. He was one of three pilots - with Lieutenant Władysław Nowak and Corporal Jan Kremski - from the 2nd Regiment who jointly won first place. In December 1938 Ostowicz was posted to the Prototype Flight, part of the Independent Experimental Air Squadron. During the Polish Campaign of 1939 he was involved in the evacuation of Independent Experimental Air Squadron aircraft, then from 15 September he led the evacuation of aircraft of the Air Force Cadet Officers' School at Dęblin. According to some sources he was a member of the flight that was formed ad hoc to defend Dęblin. On 18 September he crossed the Rumanian border and travelled by sea to France, arriving at Marseilles on 29 October. He decided to continue his journey to England, and in December was sent across the Channel. Upon arrival he received the service number 76705 and the rank of Flying Officer, and was sent to the Polish Air Force Centre at Eastchurch. He was initially considered for posting to No. 302 (Polish) 'City of Poznań' Squadron. After completing conversion training, on 16 July 1940 he was posted to No. 145 Squadron at Tangmere. Three days later he shared in the destruction of an He 111, which was the first success achieved by a Polish pilot during the Battle of Britain. This was followed by damaging a Do 17, which he claimed as a Do 215, on 31 July, also shooting down a Bf 109 on 8 August and damaging an aircraft which he reported as an He 113 on the same day. He was shot down and killed on 11 August, becoming the first Polish operational pilot fallen in action during the Battle of Britain. He went into the sea near Swanage in his Hurricane I V7294 at 10.35. German reports claim that his body was washed ashore and buried, but there is no evidence of Ostowicz's grave. He is commemorated on the Polish Air Force Memorials at Northolt and Warsaw-Mokotów. He was decorated with the Cross of Valour and bar. On 29 May 2015 the Air Navigation Laboratory of the Engineering Studies Centre at the State School of Higher Education in Chełm was named after him. On 19 July 2015 a memorial plaque to Antoni Ostowicz was also unveiled in his native Rożdżałów.

Date & Time	Unit	Aircraft	Score
19.07.1940 17.55	145 Squadron	Hurricane I N2496	½-0-0 He 111
31.07.1940 08.00	145 Squadron	Hurricane I	0-0-1 Do 17 claimed as Do 215
08.08.1940 09.10	145 Squadron	Hurricane I P3391	0-0-1 'He 113'
08.08.1940 16.20	145 Squadron	Hurricane I N2496	1-0-0 Bf 109

P

JAN PALAK, Sergeant, was born on 12 February 1911 at Kozubszczyzna near Lublin within the territory of Poland ruled by the Russian Empire. In 1926 he completed seven years at primary school in Lublin and later obtained the profession of a fitter mechanic. Between July 1928 and April 1932 he was employed by the Plage and Laśkiewicz aircraft factory in Lublin as a fitter mechanic apprentice. He was interested in motorcycle sport and sailing. In 1931 he was conscripted, and while serving in the Polish Air Force completed pilot training. Palak also completed an Advanced Flying Course at Grudziądz and was posted to the Air
Force Officers' Training Centre at Dęblin, where from 1 January 1939 he was a flying instructor. After the fall of Poland he was evacuated to Rumania

and then to France. On 12 November he was posted to the Polish Air Force Training Centre at Lyon-Bron. He was posted to the so-called 'Finnish Squadron' which was supposed to be deployed to Finland against the Russian aggressors. After an armistice was signed on the night of 12/13 March 1940 it was decided instead to form the 1/145 'City of Warsaw' Squadron at Lyon-Bron. Palak was attached to Section 3 of 2nd Flight. The squadron, also known as GC 1/145, was equipped with Caudron CR 714s, in which Palak participated in operational missions. After the fall of France on 20 June he sailed from La Rochelle to England. Upon arrival he was given the rank of Sergeant and the service number 793341. On 24 July he was posted to No. 302 (Polish) 'City of Poznań' Squadron at Leconfield. On 15 September he reported the probable destruction of a Bf 109 and participated in destroying an aircraft recognized as a Do 215. On 23 September Palak was reposted to No. 303 (Polish) 'Tadeusz Kościuszko. City of Warsaw' Squadron at Northolt, and on 5 October claimed the destruction of a Bf 109 and damage of a Bf 110. He was involved in a collision with Flying Officer Stefan Paderewski on 17 April 1941 while flying his Spitfire IIA P8073 RF-Z: both pilots were unhurt. Three days later he damaged a Ju 88. On 27 January 1942 he was posted for rest as a flying instructor at No. 58 Operational Training Unit at Grangemouth, then on 29 June rejoined No. 303 Squadron. On 18 September 1943 he was once again posted for rest and transferred to No. 303 Squadron's operations room as a deputy controller. On 11 November he was transferred to the operations room of No. 315 (Polish) 'City of Dęblin' Squadron. On 1 April 1944 he was attached to No. 302 Squadron again, and on 18 April reassumed operational flying. On 18 March 1945 Palak was moved to No. 411 Repair and Salvage Unit as a test pilot. While at Quakenbrück in occupied Germany he met his future wife, Stanisława Pala, whom he married in 1946, and later had two sons and a daughter. He left the Polish Air Force with the rank of Warrant Officer and in 1947 joined the RAF, serving as a test pilot. He retired in 1960 and moved with his family to Somerset. Until his civilian retirement he worked for the Cadbury chocolate factory. Later he was commissioned and received the Polish rank of Sub-Lieutenant. Jan Palak died in February 1987 in Bath, England. He was decorated with the Silver Cross of Virtuti Militari no. 10776, the Cross of Valour and two bars and the British Distinguished Flying Cross. His younger brother Wacław Palak was also an airman and served as a ground crew member in the Air Force Officers' Training Centre at Dęblin and then in No. 307 (Polish) 'City of Lwów' Night Fighter Squadron.

Date & Time	Unit	Aircraft	Score
15.09.1940 12.10	302 Squadron	Hurricane I V7417 WX-T	0-1-0 Bf 109
15.09.1940 12.10	302 Squadron	Hurricane I V7417 WX-T	⅓-0-0 Do 17 claimed as Do 215
05.10.1940 11.40	303 Squadron	Hurricane I P3217 RF-S	1-0-0 Bf 109
05.10.1940 11.40	303 Squadron	Hurricane I P3217 RF-S	0-0-1 Bf 110
20.04.1941 11.20	303 Squadron	Spitfire II P8079 RF-M	0-0-1 Ju 88

JERZY HIPOLIT PALUSIŃSKI, Pilot Officer, known as 'Palus', was born on 13 August 1912 in Częstochowa in a Poland governed by the Russian Empire. After completing primary school and then Henryk Sienkiewicz Secondary School in Częstochowa and passing A-level exams, he completed gliding training at Bezmiechowa in the Bieszczady region. Together with Hieronim Dudwał, also a future fighter pilot, he constructed a glider. In 1935 he was accepted to the Air Force Cadet Officers' School at Dęblin. On 15 October 1937 he was commissioned with the 10th class, and as a Sub-Lieutenant was posted to the 111th Fighter Squadron of the 1st
Air Regiment at Warsaw. His unit was attached to the Pursuit Brigade. On 1 September 1939 he fought against twelve enemy aircraft and was credited with the destruction of two Do 17s and probable destruction of another, although it is believed that in fact he fought with Bf 110s. He was shot down himself while flying in the PZL P.11a no. 3 over Marki and Radzymin, and crash-landed near Nadma. His aircraft overturned and the wounded Palusiński was initially taken to Radzymin. Subsequently he was transported to Marshal Józef Piłsuski Hospital in Warsaw, where on 3 September he was visited by journalists and the Polish C-in-C, Marshal Edward Rydz-Śmigły. This led to an article in the *Morning Express* newspaper describing his adventures. On 5 September he was evacuated to Chełm, where on 14 September he left hospital with the aim of rejoining his unit. Palusiński was captured by the Soviets, but managed to escape from a railway wagon. Once more arrested by the Soviets

at Szepietówka, he was sent to hospital at Równe. He escaped again, reaching Lwów and then Zakopane. Via Slovakia he travelled to Hungary, where he arrived on 18 November. From there he continued his journey via Yugoslavia and Italy. After arriving in France he continued his convalescence. After the fall of France he was transported to England and posted to No. 3 Polish Wing at Blackpool. He received the rank of Pilot Officer and the service number P-1388. On 21 August 1940 he was posted to No. 303 (Polish) 'Tadeusz Kościuszko. City of Warsaw' Squadron at Northolt, but on 2 September posted for further training to No. 5 Operational Training Unit at Aston Down. He crashed his Hurricane I L1821 on 21 September, but returned to No. 303 Squadron on 27 September. On 19 February 1941 Palusiński was transferred to RAF Northolt for ground duties in the operations room serving for No. 308 (Polish) 'City of Cracow' Squadron (from 28 February 1942), No. 303 Squadron (from 15 March), No. 306 (Polish) 'City of Toruń' Squadron (from 24 May), once more for No. 303 Squadron (from 12 June) and for No. 316 (Polish) 'City of Warsaw' Squadron (from 21 September 1943). In early November 1943 he was posted to the Administration and Special Duties Department, where he held various administrative posts. On 7 September 1945 he was posted to the HQ of No. 84 Group RAF. He was released from the Polish Air Force in January 1947 with the rank of Flight Lieutenant. He decided to settle in Britain, where he worked on his own pig farm. Major Jerzy Palusiński died on 10 May 1984 at Fordingbridge (some sources state that he died at Frogham, Hampshire). He was decorated with the Silver Cross of Valour no. 12073 and the Cross of Valour. On 25 October 2011 a memorial plaque dedicated to Jerzy Palusiński was unveiled at the No. 4 Henryk Sienkiewicz High School in Częstochowa.

Date & Time	Unit	Aircraft	Score
01.09.1939 09.03	111th Squadron	PZL P.11a no. 3	2-1-0 Do 17

WILHELM PANKRATZ, Flight Lieutenant, was born on 1 October 1903 at Łomianki near Warsaw in a Poland ruled by the Russian Empire. He grew up in the family of Julian and Krystyna née Hekmann. He was born under the name Pankracy, but changed it in the 1930s. He passed A-level exams, graduating from Mikołaj Rej High School in Warsaw. In 1925 he completed the Cavalry Reserve Cadet Officers' School at Grudziądz and served in the 1st Light Cavalry Regiment in Warsaw. In 1926 he joined the Air Force Officers' School at Grudziądz, and was commissioned with 2nd class on 15 August 1928 as an observer when the school was moved to Dęblin. With the rank of Sub-Lieutenant he was posted to the 11th Light Bomber Squadron of the 1st Air Regiment at

Warsaw. Between April and September 1929 he completed a flying course at the Air Force Officers' Training Centre at Dęblin. Upon completion he was posted to the 112th Fighter Squadron of the 1st Air Regiment at Warsaw. In 1930 Pankratz completed an aerobatics course organized by the 2nd Air Regiment at Cracow, followed by an aircraft maintenance commanders' course at the Central School for Air Mechanics at Bydgoszcz. Between June and November 1931 he left the 112th Squadron once more after being posted to the Advanced Flying Course at Grudziądz, where

he served as an aerobatics instructor. From 1932 until 1936 he studied at Warsaw Technical University and obtained a degree in mechanics. After that he served in the Armament Department of the Aviation Technical Institute. He was attached to the Independent Experimental Squadron. After the fall of Poland he crossed the Rumanian border and travelled to France. In December 1939 he was sent to Britain, receiving the service number 76662 and the rank of Flight Lieutenant. He was posted to the Polish Air Force Centre at Eastchurch, in March 1940 to No.15 Elementary Flying Training School at Redhill and then on 23 April to the Polish Training Unit at Hucknall, which on 15 June became No. 18 Operational Training Unit. On 23 June he was transferred to No. 6 Operational Training Unit at Sutton Bridge. He was considered for the first squad of No. 302 (Polish) 'City of Poznań' Squadron being organized at Leconfield, then as the flight commander at No. 303 (Polish) 'Tadeusz Kościuszko. City of Warsaw' Squadron at Northolt. On 16th July 1940 Pankratz joined No. 145 Squadron at Tangmere. On 12 August he participated in an aerial combat and was shot down while flying the Hurricane I R4176 in the Isle of Wight area. He was lost at sea and his body was never found. It is believed that during this encounter with Bf 109s and Bf 110s he shot down one of the Bf 110s, together with Sergeant Józef Kwieciński and Pilot Officer John Howard Harrison, although none of these pilots survived the fight to confirm this victory. Wilhelm Pankratz is commemorated on the Polish Air Force Memorials at Northolt and Warsaw-Mokotów. He was decorated with the Silver Cross of Merit and the Cross of Valour. He was the fourth Polish operational pilot lost during the Battle of Britain.

Date & Time	Unit	Aircraft	Score
12.08.1940 12.20	145 Squadron	Hurricane I R4176	⅓-0-0 Bf 110 unconfirmed

LUDWIK WITOLD PASZKIEWICZ, Flying Officer, called 'Paszka', was born on 21 October 1907 at Wola Gałęzowska in Lublin Voivodship, within territory of Poland ruled by the Russian Empire. He grew up in the family of Ludwik and Janina née Horciak. His surname is commonly and erroneously used by British historians as 'Paskiewicz'. After completing primary education he graduated from high school in Lublin, passing A-level exams in May 1925. He was accepted to the Mechanical Faculty of Warsaw Technical University and later transferred to Lwów Technical University, completing two years of studying. In 1931 he completed a unitary course at the Infantry Cadet Officers' School at  Mołodeczno with the 86th Infantry Regiment. In November 1931 he joined the Air Force Reserve Cadet Officers' School, and upon graduation in October 1932 was transferred to the Air Force Cadet Officers' School at Dęblin. Paszkiewicz was commissioned on 15 October 1934 as second best in the 8th class, and was posted as an observer with the rank of Sub-Lieutenant to the 12th Light Bomber Squadron of the 1st Air Regiment at Warsaw. In December he was transferred to the Staff Training Flight of the 1st Air Regiment, where he also served as an engineering officer. Between April and July 1936 he completed an Advanced Flying Course at Grudziądz and was posted back to the 1st Air Regiment, where he served as an instructor of the Training Flight. In August he joined 112th Fighter Squadron of the 1st Air Regiment. In 1937 he married Maria Piwnicka, and a year later his daughter Marcelina Maria Paszkiewicz was born. In March 1938 he flew with his unit to Porubanek airfield, from where the 112th Squadron flew missions to show Polish strength in the face of possible conflict with Lithuania. On 1 August he was appointed tactical officer of the III/1 Fighter Wing of the 1st Air Regiment. In October he flew to Aleksandrowice airfield during the Zaolzie annexation by Polish Armed Forces. On 27 August 1939 he was sent to France as a member of the Polish Air Force Mission for a Morane MS 406 handling course. Initially he was only an interpreter, but after the death of Captain Andrzej Włodarkiewicz he became a test pilot. Upon completion of the mission he was not able to return to Poland as it was invaded by Germany, so he was sent to Britain, from where he was supposed to fly a Fairey Battle to Poland. This plan never materialized and in November 1939 Paszkiewicz was ordered back to France. Initially he was stationed at d'Argeles sur Mer, then transferred to the Polish Air Force Training Centre at

Lyon-Bron. He was considered for the 1st Polish Fighter Squadron which was supposed to be formed in France, and in theory was attached to no. 6 section. On 18 May 1940 a Polish fighter section under the command of Paszkiewicz was formed and attached to GCII/8 at Amiens. This unit was equipped with Bloch MB 151s and 152s. He performed his first of eighteen operational sorties during the French Campaign on 23 May. On 18 June he performed a strafing attack against German road transport. After the collapse of France he sailed from La Rochelle and arrived in Plymouth on board the *Robur III* (according to other sources the *Alderpool*) on 21 June. Initially he was considered for the first squad of No. 302 (Polish) 'City of Poznań' Squadron at Leconfield. He was given the rank of Flying Officer and the service number P-1293 (there is uncertainty with this number; some authors refer to P-0042, however this number was assigned to Flight Lieutenant Witold Wojciech Paszkiewicz, who was killed on 5/6 January 1944 while flying as a navigator of No. 1586 (Polish) Special Duty Flight). While at the Polish Air Force Centre at Blackpool Ludwik Paszkiewicz was attached to No. 303 (Polish) 'Tadeusz Kościuszko. City of Warsaw' Squadron being formed at Northolt. Paszkiewicz arrived there on 2 August. On 9 August he crashed his Hurricane I P3645 RF-R during a training flight, then on 15 August he was appointed the Polish commander of 'B' Flight. On 30 August during a training sortie he shot down a twin-engine aircraft he identified as a 'Dornier', which in fact was a Bf 110. This was the first kill of No. 303 Squadron, although some sources state that Paszkiewicz was attacking an aircraft which was destroyed by No. 85 Squadron pilots. On 7 September he claimed the destruction of two Do 215s, on 11 September shot down a Bf 110, on 15 September he managed to destroy a Bf 109 and on 26 September he shot down an He 111. He was shot down and killed the next day while performing an intercept mission against a German raid. His Hurricane I L1696 RF-T was hit at 09.20 and crashed at Borough Green, Wrotham. Ludwik Paszkiewicz was buried at Northwood Cemetery, London, in grave no. H 224. He was the twenty-first Polish operational pilot killed during the Battle of Britain. He was decorated with the Silver Cross of Virtuti Militari no. 8831, the Cross of Valour and the British Distinguished Flying Cross. He is commemorated on the Polish Air Force Memorials at Northolt and Warsaw-Mokotów, and also on the memorial plaque at RAF Northolt. His portrait was painted on the tail of the MiG-29 No. 118 of the 23rd Tactical Air Base at Mińsk Mazowiecki. Ludwik Paszkiewicz's memorial stone is going to be unveiled at the crash site at Crowhurst Farm, Plaxtol, Kent on 29 September 2018. Paszkiewicz's only child died in 1941. His widow joined the Polish underground movement and took part in the Warsaw Uprising in 1944. In 1960 she joined a convent, where she remained until her death in 1995, known as sister Augustyna.

Date & Time	Unit	Aircraft	Score
30.08.1940 16.35	303 Squadron	Hurricane I R4217 RF-V	1-0-0 Bf 110 claimed as Do 17; also appears as Do 215
07.09.1940 17.00	303 Squadron	Hurricane I V7235 RF-M	2-0-0 Do 17 claimed as Do 215
11.09.1940 16.00	303 Squadron	Hurricane I V7235 RF-M	1-0-0 Bf 110
15.09.1940 12.00	303 Squadron	Hurricane I V7235 RF-M	1-0-0 Bf 109
26.09.1940 16.30	303 Squadron	Hurricane I V7235 RF-M	1-0-0 He 111

EDWARD PATEREK, Sergeant, was born on 30 May 1910 at Obojna, in the Tarnobrzeg region of Poland ruled by the Austro-Hungarian Empire. He was an ironworker by trade68m ,. In October 1929 he was conscripted into the 6th Air Regiment at Lwów, where between January and April 1930 he completed an aircraft maintenance course. He was attached as an assistant mechanic to the 62nd Light Bomber Squadron of the 6th Air Regiment. Between May and November 1931 he completed flying training at the Air Force NCO Training Centre at Bydgoszcz, returning to the 62 Squadron as a pilot. In June and July 1932 he underwent an Advanced Flying Course at Grudziądz before again returning to his squadron. On 1 October Paterek was transferred to the 132nd Fighter Squadron of the 3rd Air Regiment at Poznań, then in March 1933 was sent for an instructors' course organized by the Air Force Officers' Training Centre at Dęblin. Upon completion he returned to the 132nd Squadron. On 21 April 1936 he was detached to the Air Force Officers' Training Centre at Dęblin as a flying instructor. During the Polish Campaign of 1939 he was involved in the evacuation of training aircraft, and on 18 September crossed the Rumanian border. He sailed to France, where he arrived on 12 November. Initially posted to the Polish Air Force Training Centre in December, he was chosen for the so-called 'Finnish Squadron' to be deployed to Finland against their Russian aggressors. After the armistice was signed on 12/13 March 1940 it was decided to form the 1/145 'City of Warsaw' Squadron at Lyon-Bron. Paterek was attached to Section 2 of 2nd Flight. The squadron, also known as GC 1/145, was equipped with Caudron CR 714s. After the fall of France he sailed from La Rochelle to England on 20 June. He was given the service number 793342 and on 23 July was posted to No. 302 (Polish) 'City of Poznań' Squadron at Leconfield. He claimed his first success on 15 September with the probable destruction of a He 111. Three days later he was shot down while flying the Hurricane I P3086 WX-Z, but before this he managed to shoot down a Ju 88. On 22 September he was transferred to No. 303 (Polish) 'Tadeusz Kościuszko. City of Warsaw' Squadron at Northolt. On 21 January 1941 he joined No. 315 (Polish) 'City of Dęblin' Squadron. He was killed on 27 March 1941 in a mid-air collision. While returning from an operational patrol in his Hurricane I V7187 he crashed with the aircraft piloted by Flight Lieutenant Władysław Szulkowski near the Bar lightship in the Mersey. Both pilots lost their lives, although only Paterek's body was lost at sea. He is commemorated on the Polish Air Force Memorials at Northolt and Warsaw-Mokotów. He was decorated with the Cross of Valour. Edward Paterek is often mistakenly called 'Wacław Łapkowski' in several historical publications.

Date & Time	Unit	Aircraft	Score
15.09.1940 12.10	302 Squadron	Hurricane I P3086 WX-Z	0-1-0 He 111
18.09.1940 17.20	302 Squadron	Hurricane I P3086 WX-Z	1-0-0 Ju 88

JAN PIOTR PFEIFFER, Pilot Officer, called 'Fifi', was born on 25 November 1905 at Łódź in the territory of Poland ruled by the Russian Empire. He grew up in the family of Hugon Pfeiffer. After completing primary and secondary education he was conscripted in September 1928 and served in the 4th Air Regiment at Toruń. He decided to join the flying personnel, and in November 1931 completed a flying course organized at the Air Force NCO Training Centre at Bydgoszcz. Upon completion he was posted to the 41st Light Bomber Squadron of the 4th Air Regiment, where he served as a pilot. Between June and August 1932 he completed an Advanced Flying Course at Grudziądz, and was posted to the 142nd Fighter Squadron of the 4th Air Regiment. In April 1934 Pfeiffer completed an instructors' course and was

detached to the Air Force Officers' Training Centre at Dęblin, where he served as a flying instructor. In September 1935 he was accepted to the Cadet Officers' School for NCOs, and on 15 October 1938 was commissioned. With the rank of Sub-Lieutenant he was posted to the Air Force NCO School for Minors at Bydgoszcz, where he remained as a flying instructor and platoon commander of the 6th Training Flight until the outbreak of war. During the Polish Campaign of 1939 he took part in the evacuation of the school towards the Rumanian border. He crossed the border on 17 September at Śniatyń. In order to stay with his pupils, he changed his officer's uniform to that of an NCO. In October he led the group of ninety pupils to the Black Sea. He sailed to France, arriving on 29 October. Pfeiffer decided not to stay in France, sailing to England in December. He was posted to the Polish Air Force Centre at Eastchurch, receiving the rank of Pilot Officer and the service number 76728. In July 1940 he was attached to No. 1 School of Army Co-operation at Old Sarum, then on 14 July was moved to No. 6 Operational Training Unit at Sutton Bridge. On 4 August he joined No. 32 Squadron at Biggin Hill. He crashed his Hurricane I P3205 at Hawkinge on 22 August, then sustained an injury the next day when landing on one wheel in the Hurricane I P2795, which was damaged in combat. On 16 September he was transferred to No. 257 Squadron at Martlesham Heath, on 28 September was posted to No. 5 Bombing and Gunnery School as a staff pilot and later served as an instructor at No. 16 (Polish) Service Flying Training School at Newton. He was badly injured on 20 August 1941 while flying the Airspeed Oxford N4608, although his pupil Sergeant Henryk Bober was unhurt. After a long convalescence he was posted to No. 12 (Polish) Advanced Flying Unit at Grantham for a refresher course. From 13 July 1943 he took part in twin-engine fighter training at No. 54 Operational Training Unit at Charter Hall, prior to a return to operational flying. On 12 October he was posted to No. 307 (Polish) 'City of Lwów' Night Fighter Squadron. On 20 December he was returning from Sumburgh to Drem after an operational sortie in the de Havilland Mosquito II DD618 EW-X with Pilot Officer Kazimierz Kęsicki when their aircraft, for unknown reason, crashed into the sea. Kęsicki's body was recovered, while Flight Lieutenant Pfeiffer's was lost at sea. It is believed that the crash was due to engine failure. He is commemorated on the Polish Air Force Memorials at Northolt and Warsaw-Mokotów.

STANISŁAW PIĄTKOWSKI, Pilot Officer, was born on 1 May 1912 at Jaroszówka, near Winnica, Podole, within the territory of Poland ruled by the Russian Empire. He grew up in the family of Teofil and Maria née Bichniewicz. After graduating from primary and secondary school, from 1929 he studied at Lwów Technical University, then in 1931 was transferred to Warsaw Technical

University. He graduated in 1937. He was a pilot and glider instructor at Warsaw Aero Club. In 1938 he completed the Air Force Reserve Cadet Officers' School and was a reserve officer of the 5th Air Regiment at Wilno. He was mobilized and in August 1939 attached to the Aviation Technical Institute at Warsaw. After the fall of Poland he was evacuated to Rumania, from where he travelled to France. In December, with one of the first Polish transports, he went to Britain. He received the rank of Pilot Officer and the service number 76618, and was posted to the Polish Air Force Centre at Eastchurch. After conversion training in August 1940 he was posted to No. 5 Operational Training

Unit at Aston Down. On 15 August he crashed at Flax Bourton in Somerset, but was unhurt. On 11 September he joined No. 79 Squadron at Biggin Hill. Stanisław Piątkowski was killed on 25 October after his Hurricane I N2708 overturned during an emergency landing, with an unknown cause, near Carew Chariton. He was the last Polish operational pilot killed during the Battle of Britain. He was buried at St Illtyd's churchyard, Pembrey, Carmarthenshire, Wales, in the RAF Section. He is also commemorated on the Polish Air Force Memorials at Northolt and Warsaw-Mokotów, as well as on the memorial plaque at Powązki Military Cemetery in Warsaw. He was awarded the Cross of Valour.

EDWARD ROMAN PILCH, Pilot Officer, was born on 25 February 1915 at Tanowiec near Jasło in Cracow Voivodship, in part of Poland ruled by the Austro-Hungarian Empire. In Jasło he studied at Romuald Traugutt Primary School and then King Stanisław Leszczyński State Secondary School for Boys. He passed A-level exams in 1934. On 1 October 1934 he joined a unitary course at the Infantry Cadet Officers' School at Różan, then between 15 July and 13 August 1935 completed glider

training at the Military Gliding School at Ustianowa. On 15 September 1935 he was accepted for the second year of the Air Force Cadet Officers' School at Dęblin. He was commissioned on 15 October 1937 with the 10th class, and with the rank of Sub-Lieutenant was posted to the 123rd Fighter Squadron of the 2nd Air Regiment at Cracow. Between 19 October 1938 and 15 July 1939 he commanded the 2nd platoon of the flying course at the Training Flight. In July 1939 he was transferred to the 122nd Fighter Squadron of the 2nd Air Regiment, and was appointed deputy commander. He flew combat missions throughout the Polish Campaign of 1939. On 1 September he was appointed a Tactical Officer of the III/2 Fighter Wing; his squadron was to support the 'Cracow' Army. After the fall of Poland on 17 September he flew a PZL P.11c to Rumania, where he was interned. He escaped from the Foscani camp, and from Balchik sailed to Beirut on 15 October on board the *Aghios Nikolaos*. From there he continued on board the *Ville de Strasbourg*, arriving at Marseilles on 29 October. He was sent to Salon, where he decided to join his colleagues in England. On 24 January 1940 Pilch arrived in Britian, where he received the rank of Pilot Officer and the service number 76706, and was sent to the Polish Air Force Centre at Eastchurch. On 1 March he was posted to No. 15 Elementary Flying Training School at Carlisle, then on 26 March was sent to RAF Hucknall. In July he was sent to No. 6 Operational Training Unit at Sutton Bridge, and upon completion on 16 July was posted to No. 302 (Polish) 'City of Poznań' Squadron at Leconfield. On 15 September he claimed the destruction of a Do 17 and Do 215, although the first claim was not accepted. On 18 September Pilch destroyed Ju 88, and on 16 February 1941 he added a shared victory of a Ju 88. On 20 February he was on training sortie when, at 15,000ft, his Hurricane I R2687 WX-X went into an uncontrolled dive, caught fire and crashed near Arundel, Sussex. Pilot Officer Edward Pilch was killed in the wreckage. He was buried at Chichester Cemetery, Sussex, in plot 42, grave no. 1. His decorations included the Silver Cross of Virtuti Militari no. 9265 and the Cross of Valour and bar. He is commemorated on the Polish Air Force Memorials at Northolt and Warsaw-Mokotów.

Date & Time	Unit	Aircraft	Score
15.09.1940 14.45	302 Squadron	Hurricane I P3086 WX-Z	1-0-0 Do 17 unconfirmed
15.09.1940 14.45	302 Squadron	Hurricane I P3086 WX-Z	1-0-0 Do 17 claimed as Do 215
18.09.1940 17.23	302 Squadron	Hurricane I V7417 WX-T	1-0-0 Ju 88
16.02.1941	302 Squadron	Hurricane I P3877 WX-T	½-0-0 Ju 88

MARIAN PISAREK, Flying Officer, was born on 3 January 1912 at Łosie village near Radzymin in the part of Poland ruled by the Russian Empire. He grew up in the family of Stanisław and Józefa née Oleksiewicz. In 1931 he graduated from No. 2 Cadet Corps at Chełmno, passing A-level exams. On 13 July 1932 he joined the Infantry Cadet Officers' School at Ostrów Mazowiecka Komorowo. While at school he decided to join the Polish Air Force and completed a gliding course at Ustianowa. He was commissioned on 15 August 1934, and with the rank of Sub-Lieutenant was posted to the 4th Regiment of Highland Fusiliers

at Cieszyn, where he took command of the platoon. On 17 September he started a flying course at the Air Force Officers' Training Centre at Dęblin (2nd Applicants' Course). Upon completion in July 1935 he was posted to the 61st Light Bomber Squadron of the 6th Air Regiment in Lwów. From 20 April until 15 July 1936 he completed an Advanced Flying Course at Grudziądz, and was then posted to the 142nd Fighter Squadron of the 4th Air Regiment at Toruń. In June 1937 he was transferred to the 141st Fighter Squadron of the same regiment. He was appointed section commander and on 18 March 1938 deputy commander of the squadron. During the Polish Campaign of 1939 he flew with his unit and the whole III/4 Fighter Wing, supporting the 'Pomorze' Army. On 1 September he shared a victory of an Hs 126, then on 2 September claimed the destruction of another Hs 126 and a Do 17. On the same day, after the death of Captain Florian Laskowski (who commanded the III/4 Wing), Captain Tadeusz Rolski took his place, leaving command of the 141st Squadron to Marian Pisarek. On 3 September by mistake he shot down a Polish PZL P.23 'Karaś' from the 42nd Reconnaissance Squadron, and the two crew members died from their wounds. On 4 September he participated in damaging a Ju 87, but also performed an emergency landing in his damaged aircraft after combat with a Bf 110. After the Soviet invasion he crossed the Rumanian border on 17 September and travelled via Yugoslavia and Italy, arriving in France on 9 October. Initially he was assigned to administrative duties at the HQ of the Polish Air Force. Although he volunteered to travel to England and awaited departure at Le Bourget, on 28 May 1940 he was attached to the group of pilots commanded by Captain Tadeusz Rolski which formed a fighter section and was posted for training to Saint Etiénne, where he flew Romano R.82s. On 13 June, after receiving Morane MS 406s, his unit was sent to Châteauroux to support a French squadron. After the collapse of France he boarded the *Alderpool*, and on 20 June sailed to England. Pisarek received the service number P-1381 and the rank of Flying Officer. On 1 July he was sent to the Polish Air Force Centre at Blackpool and was considered for posting to No. 302 (Polish) 'City of Poznań' Squadron at Leconfield. Instead, on 21 August he was attached to No. 303 (Polish) 'Tadeusz Kościuszko. City of Warsaw' Squadron at Northolt. On 7 September he claimed the destruction of a Bf 109, but was also shot down and baled out from his Hurricane I R4173 RF-T. His abandoned aircraft crashed at 40 Roding Road, Loughton, killing two members of the Bockwell family and a Mrs Gurden. On 15 September Pisarek claimed another Bf 109, followed by shooting down and probably destroying two Bf 110s on 5 October and the destruction of a Bf 109 on 7 October. On 29 September he had been appointed the Polish commander of 'B' Flight, which he handed over on 29 November. On 21 January 1941 he was posted to No. 315 (Polish) 'City of Dęblin' Squadron, and then on 30 March to No. 308 (Polish) 'City of Cracow' Squadron. Pisarek took command of 'A' Flight, then took command of the whole squadron on 23 June. While in No. 308 Squadron he claimed several victories: on 2 July he destroyed a Bf 109, on 17 July he shared the destruction of a Bf 109, on 22 July he claimed the probable destruction of a Bf 109, on 14 August he destroyed another Bf 109, on 20 September he added another Bf 109 shot down, followed by one more on 21 September, and finally on 13 October he claimed destruction of a Bf 109. On 2 July his Spitfire II P7446 ZF-A was badly damaged during Operation Circus 29, then on 24 July Pilot Officer Jan Jakubowski collided with him over France, yet Pisarek managed to return to England in his damaged Spitfire II P8676 ZF-H. On 10 December Pisarek was rested and found himself at the HQ of No. 11 Group RAF as the Polish Liaison Officer. He returned to operational flying after taking command of the 1st Polish Fighter Wing at Northolt on 17 April 1942. On 29 April he participated in Operation Circus 145 when his formation was intercepted by the Luftwaffe over Le Treport. He was shot down and killed in unclear circumstances, flying the Spitfire VB BM307 RF-Q. It is believed that he crashed into the sea. His body was never found. He was decorated with the Golden Cross of Virtuti Militari no. 143, the Silver Cross of Virtuti Militari no. 8830, the Cross of Valour and three bars and the British Distinguished Flying Cross. He is commemorated on the Polish Air Force Memorials at Northolt and Warsaw-Mokotów. Streets at Cracow, Warsaw and Mielec are named after him, as well as No. 1 Primary School at Radzymin. In 2005 a biographical book about Wing Commander Pisarek, *Take-off into Eternity*, by Krzysztof Kubala was published in Poland. The MiG 29 no. 56 of the 23rd Tactical Air Base at Mińsk Mazowiecki has tail art commemorating this brave pilot.

Date & Time	Unit	Aircraft	Score
01.09.1939	141st Squadron	PZL P.11c	½-0-0 Hs 126
02.09.1939	141st Squadron	PZL P.11c	1-0-0 Do 17
02.09.1939	141st Squadron	PZL P.11c	1-0-0 Hs 126
04.09.1939	141st Squadron	PZL P.11c	0-0-1 Ju 87
07.09.1940 17.00	303 Squadron	Hurricane I R4173 RF-T	1 0 0 Bf 109
15.09.1940 12.00	303 Squadron	Hurricane I V7465 RF-V	1-0-0 Bf 109
05.10.1940 11.40	303 Squadron	Hurricane I V7503 RF-U	1-0-1 Bf 110
07.10.1940 13.50	303 Squadron	Hurricane I V7503 RF-U	1-0-0 Bf 109
02.07.1941 12.45	308 Squadron	Spitfire IIB P7446 ZF-A	1-0-0 Bf 109
17.07.1941 20.55	308 Squadron	Spitfire IIB P8676 ZF-H	½-0-0 Bf 109
22.07.1941 13.50	308 Squadron	Spitfire IIB P8341 ZF-A	0-1-0 Bf 109
14.08.1941 17.30	308 Squadron	Spitfire IIB P8318 ZF-P	1-0-0 Bf 109
20.09.1941 16.00	308 Squadron	Spitfire VB W3702	1-0-0 Bf 109
21.09.1941 15.12	308 Squadron	Spitfire VB AB825	1-0-0 Bf 109
13.10.1941 13.20	308 Squadron	Spitfire VB W3798 ZF-Y	1-0-0 Bf 109

KAROL PNIAK, Pilot Officer, called 'Cognac', was born on 26 January 1910 at Jaworzno, Silesia, in the part of Poland ruled by the German Empire. He grew up in the family of Franciszek, a coal miner, and Maria née Wałaga. He completed primary school at Jaworzno and then Stanisław Staszic Secondary School at Chrzanów. His two brothers served in the Polish Navy, and he also decided to join the Polish Armed Forces. He volunteered for the Air Force on 23 October 1928 and was posted to the 2nd Air Regiment at Cracow. In January 1929 he was attached to the Training Squadron, and he completed aerial training in May. The same month he was posted to the Air Force NCO Flying School at

Bydgoszcz, from which he graduated in October 1930. Upon completion he was posted to the 22nd Light Bomber Squadron of the 2nd Air Regiment. In July 1931 he was sent on an Advanced Flying Course at Grudziądz, which he completed in September, and was posted to the 122nd Fighter Squadron of the 2nd Air Regiment. He was a well-known aerobatic pilot and member of the so called 'Bajan's Three'. Together with Captain Jerzy Bajan (often replaced by Lieutenant Bronisław Kosiński or Sub-Lieutenant Antoni Wczelik) and Corporal Stanisław Macek, he participated in various air shows and competitions. In 1932 and 1933 he took first place in air shooting during a national air competition organized at Grudziądz.

On 25 May 1933 he represented his regiment during an air show organized by Warsaw Aero Club. He had a landing accident at Cracow on 5 June 1934, colliding with an aircraft piloted by Corporal Leopold Flanek. On 3 October the same year he made an emergency landing due to technical issues. In 1935 he was a member of the winning team of the III/2 Fighter Wing during the Central Air Competition for fighter units. In September 1936 he was sent to the Air Force Cadet Officers' School for NCOs at Bydgoszcz, completing his secondary education and passing A-level exams. During this time he married Helena Paul. On 17 October 1938 he was transferred to the Air Force Cadet Officers' School at Dęblin and attached to the 3rd term. On 15 June 1939 he was posted to the 142nd Fighter Squadron of the 4th Air Regiment at Toruń. Due to the difficult political situation none of the 12th class cadets had an official graduation, and all were commissioned at various regiments. Sub-Lieutenant Pniak took part in the Polish Campaign in 1939. Although he participated in the destruction of an Hs 126 on 1 September, his claim was not accepted. On 2 September he claimed the destruction of a Do 17 and on 3 September shared in destroying an Hs 126. The day after he shot down one Ju 87 and damaged another. He also shared the damage of a Do 17. During the campaign the whole III/4 Fighter Wing was supporting the 'Pomorze' Army, and Karol Pniak flew twenty-four combat sorties. After the fall of Poland on 18 September he crossed the Rumanian border, from where he travelled to France. He reached Marseilles on 29 October. He decided to continue his fight from England and on 24 January 1940 reported to the Polish Air Force Centre at Eastchurch. He was given the service number 76707 and the rank of Pilot Officer. On 4 July he was sent to No. 1 School of Army Co-operation at Old

Sarum, then on 14 July to No. 6 Operational Training Unit at Sutton Bridge. He was considered for joining No. 302 (Polish) 'City of Poznań' Squadron at Leconfield, but this posting did not materialize. Instead, upon completion on 3 August he was posted to No. 32 Squadron at Biggin Hill. On 12 August he reported the destruction of a Bf 109, followed by the probable destruction of a Bf 109 and damage of a Do 17 on 15 August. On 18 August he shot down two Bf 109s, and on the 22nd participated in damaging a Do 17. He claimed his last trophy during the Battle of Britain on 24 August when he probably shot down a Bf 109. On the same day he was wounded in combat and had to bale out from his Hurricane I V6572, which crashed at Rhodes Minnis in Kent. Pniak returned to No. 32 Squadron on 7 September. On 16 September he was transferred to No. 257 Squadron at Martlesham Heath. He participated in the so-called 'Spaghetti Party' on 11 November when No. 257 Squadron encountered an Italian formation of bombers with fighter cover. Pniak claimed the destruction of a Fiat BR.20. On 25 November he was posted to No. 306 (Polish) 'City of Toruń' Squadron. The Polish pilot sustained an injury after force-landing at Richmond Park on 23 July 1941 in his Hurricane I V6572. On 23 October he returned to No. 306 Squadron, but did not fly operationally. On 18 February 1942 he was transferred to the Air Fighting Development Unit at Duxford. From 9 April he returned to No. 306 Squadron, where he took on the duties of a ground controller officer and was sent on an air controllers' course on 31 May. On 2 July 1942 he resumed operational flying, and on 1 December became 'B' Flight commander. In February 1943 he was accepted for the 'Polish Fighting Team', also known as 'Skalski's Circus', and on 20 February 1943 left for North Africa. After the campaign in Africa Pniak returned to Britain, and on 22 July was attached to the HQ of No. 3 Polish Wing at Perranporth. On 24 September he was posted to No. 58 Operational Training Unit at Grangemouth as a flying instructor, then between 6 October 1943 and 12 March 1944 was a ground controller at RAF Northolt. His next duty was as chief fighter instructor at No. 61 Operational Training Unit, then on 25 September 1944 he was posted to No. 84 Group Support Unit. Karol Pniak was posted to No. 308 (Polish) 'City of Cracow' Squadron on 6 November 1944, and on 28 November assumed its command. He led this squadron until 30 June 1945. On 1 July he was transferred to Blackpool and then served at the HQ of No. 131 (Polish) Wing, then in September 1946 once more assumed command of No. 308 Squadron, which he held until disbandment on 18 December. Squadron Leader Pniak was then demobilized, and on 24 February 1947 returned to Poland. He settled at Szczakowa near Cracow, and until 1956 was unemployed as the communist regime prevented him from taking any jobs as part of the repression against veterans who fought in the West. He was even accused of spying. In 1950 his only son, Karol junior, was born. In 1956 he finally found employment in the building industry and worked in Cracow. However, in 1959 he was diagnosed with tuberculosis and was out of work again, spending time on various medical treatments. He died on 17 October 1980 in Cracow and was buried at the Parish Cemetery at Jaworzno-Szczakowa. He was decorated with the Silver Cross of Virtuti Militari no. 8995, the Cross of Valour and three bars, the Bronze Cross of Merit and the British Distinguished Flying Cross. On 9 May 1998 a memorial plaque dedicated to Major Karol Pniak was unveiled at Jaworzno. There is also an estate and a street in the same town named after him, as well as the Polish Air Force Association of Southern Poland based in Cracow. His biography, *Mjr. pil. Karol Pniak*, by Grzegorz Sojda and Grzegorz Śliżewski was published in Poland in 2015.

Date & Time	Unit	Aircraft	Score
01.09.1939	142nd Squadron	PZL P.11c	⅓-0-0 Hs 126 unconfirmed
02.09.1939 14.30	142nd Squadron	PZL P.11c	1-0-0 Do 17 or Bf 110
03.09.1939	142nd Squadron	PZL P.11c	¼-0-0 Hs 126
04.09.1939	142nd Squadron	PZL P.11c	1-0-1 Ju 87
04.09.1939	142nd Squadron	PZL P.11c	0-0-⅓ Do 17
12.08.1940 17.20	32 Squadron	Hurricane I R4106	1-0-0 Bf 109
15.08.1940 17.48	32 Squadron	Hurricane I N2524	0-1-0 Bf 109
15.08.1940 17.48	32 Squadron	Hurricane I N2524	0-0-1 Do 17
18.08.1940 17.30	32 Squadron	Hurricane I N2524	2-0-0 Bf 109
22.08.1940 19.00	32 Squadron	Hurricane I P6546	0-0-½ Do 17
24.08.1940 15.06	32 Squadron	Hurricane I V6572	0-1-0 Bf 109
11.11.1940 13.30	257 Squadron	Hurricane I V7296 DT-Z	1½ -0-0 BR.20

JERZY POPŁAWSKI, Pilot Officer, was born on 1 October 1919 at Model village near Gostyń and Warsaw in a free Poland. He had two brothers: Tadeusz was killed in a German death camp and Roman served in the Polish Armed Forces in the West. In 1936 Jerzy Popławski passed A-level exams at the Humanistic Secondary School, and on 28 September was sent for the unitary course to the 44th Infantry Regiment at Równe. In January 1937 he started his education at the Air Force Cadet Officers' School at Dęblin, and during the second year completed an Advanced Flying Course at Ułęż. Due to the uncertain political situation the learning programme was shortened to two years and the graduates of the 13th class were commissioned during the Polish Campaign in 1939 while serving in regiments or staying at Dęblin. After the fall of Poland he was evacuated to Rumania, and then from Balchik on the Black Sea he sailed to Beirut on 15 October on the Greek ship *Aghios Nikolaos*. The *Ville de Strasbourg* then took him to Marseilles, arriving on 29 October. Not seeing any possibility for combat in France, he decided to travel further and on 27 January 1940 arrived in England, where he received the service number 76751 and the rank of Pilot Officer. Initially stationed at Eastchurch, in May he was transferred to Blackpool. On 20 June he was posted to No. 15 Elementary Flying Training School at Carlisle, then on 11 August to No. 1 School of Army Co-operation at Old Sarum. On 17 August he arrived at No. 5 Operational Training Unit at Aston Down. Meanwhile on 30 July he was posted to No. 302 (Polish) 'City of Poznań' Squadron at Leconfield, but on 10 September was attached to No. 111 Squadron at Drem and then on 26 September reposted to No. 229 Squadron at Northolt. He was injured during a crash-landing on 6 November at Streatley in Berkshire while in his Hurricane I P3898. He left No. 229 Squadron on 13 November 1940, being posted once more to No. 302 Squadron. On 16 March 1941 he was posted to No. 308 (Polish) 'City of Cracow' Squadron, and from September to November that year claimed most of his kills. On 4 September he shot down a Bf 109, and again on 16 September. He reported the destruction of further Bf 109s on 21 and 27 September, and again on 13 October. On 8 November he damaged another Bf 109. On 30 April 1942 he was appointed 'A' Flight commander, but on 1 September left operational flying, being posted to No. 58 Operational Training Unit at Grangemouth, where he remained until early April 1943 as a flying instructor of the Polish Fighter School. Subsequently

he was appointed commander of No. 315 (Polish) 'City of Dęblin' Squadron. He claimed his last victim on 20 April, damaging a Fw 190. Jerzy Popławski was posted for rest on 16 February 1944 and was sent to the Polish Air Force Inspectorate as a Liaison Officer. From 3 April he studied at the Polish Air Force Staff College at Weston-super-Mare, then on 28 November was posted to the HQ of No. 11 Group. He also served at Fighter Command headquarters at Stanmore. After the war he was demobilized with the rank of Squadron Leader and decided to emigrate to Argentina. He settled in Buenos Aires and worked as a freelance translator, then joined food manufacturer Bunger&Börn. He had a son, Roman, and in his free time he played tennis. Colonel Jerzy Popławski died aged 84 on 21 June 2004 in Buenos Aires and was buried at Parque Memorial Cemetery, Pilar, Buenos Aires. His decorations include the Silver Cross of Virtuti Militari no. 9340 and the Cross of Valour and three bars.

Date & Time	Unit	Aircraft	Score
04.09.1941 16.25	308 Squadron	Spitfire II P8543	1-0-0 Bf 109
16.09.1941 18.30	308 Squadron	Spitfire VB W3230	1-0-0 Bf 109
21.09.1941 15.12	308 Squadron	Spitfire VB W3230	1-0-0 Bf 109
27.09.1941 14.32	308 Squadron	Spitfire VB W3230	1-0-0 Bf 109
13.10.1941 13.20	308 Squadron	Spitfire VB AD119	1-0-0 Bf 109
08.11.1941 11.45	308 Squadron	Spitfire VB W3798 ZF-Y	0-0-1 Bf 109
20.04.1942 19.35	315 Squadron	Spitfire IX EN184 PK-Y	0-0-1 Fw 190

R

JERZY RADOMSKI, Pilot Officer, was born on 18 July 1915 at Czernihów near Desna within the former Kingdom of Poland (there are documents providing 18 July 1918 as an alternative date of birth). He grew up in the family of Aleksander Radomski. After moving with his family to Warsaw at the age of 6, he studied at the State Joachim Lelewel Secondary School and

on 1 September 1930 was accepted to Cadet
Corps No. 2 at Chełmo. He graduated in the
summer of 1936 with high marks, and after
A-level exams in September 1936 he was
accepted to the Air Force Cadet Officers'
School at Dęblin. Like the whole 12th class,
before official graduation he completed his
education and in June 1939 was posted to
the 113th Fighter Squadron of the 1st Air
Regiment at Warsaw, being commissioned
with effect from 1 August. During the
Polish Campaign of 1939 he fought with
the Pursuit Brigade. On 1 September Jerzy
Radomski reported the destruction of a
Bf 109 and damage of a Ju 86, although he
was wounded in a hand. On 4 September he

was involved in the destruction of a Ju 87, although officially this claim appears
under the 5th, and on 6 September he participated in a successful attack on
a Bf 110. After the fall of Poland he was evacuated to Rumania, from where
he travelled to France. Upon arrival he was posted to the Polish Air Force
Training Centre at Lyon-Bron, where he completed training on French fighter
planes. He also flew defensive patrols over the base, including one on 1 June
1940, when together with Aleksander Gabszewicz he claimed the destruction
of a He 111. On the same day he joined the Polish fighter section commanded
by Major Eugeniusz Wyrwicki and attached to GCII/10 at Bernay, where the
Poles flew Bloch MB 152s. He was in the 2nd Flight. After a combat on 7 June
he made an emergency landing on one of the RAF airfields in France. It is
believed that he shared a victory of a Bf 109. Three other Polish pilots, including
Wyrwicki, were killed during this fight, therefore Radomski remained the only
Polish officer in GCII/10. After the fall of France, he flew on board a transport
aircraft from Cazaux to Perpignan de la Salanque on 21 June, and on the 22nd
to Oran. Via Casablanca and Gibraltar he sailed to Britain, where he received
the service number P-1427 and the rank of Pilot Officer. On 21 August he was
posted to No. 303 (Polish) 'Tadeusz Kościuszko. City of Warsaw' Squadron at
Northolt, but on 2 September was reposted to No. 5 Operational Training Unit
at Aston Down for further training. Radomski returned to No. 303 Squadron
on 27 September and three days later shared in a victory of a German bomber
reported as a 'Do 215'. His Hurricane I P3663 RF-H was damaged in combat
and he made a forced landing on the beach near Lydd. On 14 April 1941 he
was posted for rest as a flying instructor to No. 55 Operational Training Unit at

Aston Down, from where on 1 August he was reposted to No. 61 Operational Training Unit and on 14 September transferred to No. 58 Operational Training Unit at Grangemouth. Radomski returned to No. 303 Squadron on 19 November, but on 14 December was reposted to No. 316 (Polish) 'City of Warsaw' Squadron. While flying with this unit he made two claims: on 25 April 1942 he damaged a Fw 190, and on 6 May participated in the probable destruction of a Fw 190. On 27 August he joined No. 72 Squadron, and then No. 222 Squadron. He was back in No. 303 Squadron on 8 December, but on 28 June 1943 he joined No. 317 (Polish) 'City of Wilno' Squadron. Flying with this unit he made two more claims: on 27 July he damaged a Fw 190, and on 8 September shot down one Bf 109 while damaging another. On 2 September he took command of 'A' Flight. After completing his operational tour on 8 April 1944 he was sent to the HQ of the Polish Air Force, and subsequently in January 1945 to the Polish Air Force Staff College. Upon completion he remained there as an instructor, then on 20 September was posted to No. 46 Group RAF as Liaison Officer. He was married in 1946, and on 13 January 1947 his only son, Andrzej, was born. Radomski was demobilized in November 1947 with the rank of Flight Lieutenant. He decided to stay in Britain and was naturalized on 29 December 1949. He joined the RAF in 1951 and served as a flying instructor at No. 6 Flying Training School at Acklington until June 1962. Later he served in the Catering Branch. He retired on 18 July 1973 with the rank of Squadron Leader and settled in Wimbledon. Jerzy Radomski died on 17 December 1978 in London and was buried in Putney Vale Cemetery. He was decorated with the Silver Cross of Virtuti Militari no. 8431, the Cross of Valour and three bars and the French Croix de Guerre.

Date & Time	Unit	Aircraft	Score
01.09.1939 17.20	113th Squadron	PZL P.11	0-0-1 Ju 86
01.09.1939 17.20	113th Squadron	PZL P.11c no.2	1-0-0 Bf 109
04 or 05.09.1939 16.55	113th Squadron	PZL P.11	⅓-0-0 Ju 87
01.06.1940 12.20	PAF Training Centre	Morane Ms 406	½-0-0 He 111
07.06.1940	GCII/10	Bloch MB 152	shared Bf 109 unconfirmed
30.09.1940 14.00	303 Squadron	Hurricane I P3663 RF-H	½-0-0 Do 215

25.04.1942 10.35	316 Squadron	Spitfire VB BL631 SZ-F	0-0-1 Fw 190
06.05.1942 18.45	316 Squadron	Spitfire VB BL631 SZ-F	0-⅓-0 Fw 190
26.07.1943 11.25	317 Squadron	Spitfire VB W3445 JH Z	0-0-1 Fw 190
08.09.1943 09.30	317 Squadron	Spitfire VB AR550 JH-A	1-0-1 Bf 109

GUSTAW MARIAN RADWAŃSKI, Pilot Officer, called 'Gucio' (diminutive of his first name) was born on 2 May 1913 at Warsaw in a Poland ruled by the Russian Empire. He completed primary school, followed by Stanisław Staszic State Secondary School in Warsaw in 1930. He was accepted to the University of Warsaw and in 1934 graduated with a degree in psychology. Between 1937 and 1939 he worked as the head of the Psycho-Technical Laboratory at the Military Engineers Training Centre. After completing a flying course at the Air Force

Reserve Cadet Officers' School at Dęblin he was posted to reserve as a reserve cadet and was assigned to the 1st Air Regiment in Warsaw. Radwański was an active Scouting movement member and commanded 16th 'Zawisza Czarny' Scouting Squad in Warsaw. He also published in *Sulimczyk* scouting magazine. In August 1939 he was mobilized and posted to the 1st Air Regiment at Warsaw, where he joined a training flight. After the fall of Poland he was evacuated to Rumania and then to France, arriving at Marseilles on 29 October. Initially he was posted to Istres-en-Provence, where on 1 November he was commissioned. From there he was posted to the Polish Air Force Training Centre at Lyon-Bron. He decided to pursue his flying career in England, where he arrived in early 1940 and was posted to the Polish Air Force Centre at Eastchurch. On 24 January he received the service number 76708 and the rank of Pilot Officer. In May he was transferred to Blackpool. He completed initial training at No. 15 Elementary Flying Training School at Carlisle, followed by conversion at No. 5 Operational Training Unit at Aston Down. On 12 September Radwański was posted to No. 151 Squadron at Digby, then on 3 October was moved to No. 607 Squadron at Tangmere and on 14th October to No. 56 Squadron at Boscombe Down. On 6 April 1941 he damaged a Do 17. Shortly after, on 21

May, he was transferred to No. 302 (Polish) 'City of Poznań' Squadron. On 16 December he joined No. 316 (Polish) 'City of Warsaw' Squadron. He had a mid-air collision while flying his Spitfire VB AB825 SZ-T on 13 February 1942. Radwański was wounded and the pilot of the second Spitfire, Sergeant Jan Musiał, was killed. He returned to No. 316 Squadron on 9 March, but soon after it was decided further convalescence was needed and he left on 6 April. From 4 July he served as a flying instructor at No. 16 (Polish) Service Flying Training School at Newton, then completed an instructors' course at No. 2 Flying Instructors School at Montrose. From 15 April 1944 he served at the HQ of the Polish Air Forces, from where on 8 January 1945 was posted to No. 61 Operational Training Unit at Rednal for a refresher course. On 28 February he was attached to No. 84 Group Support Unit and eventually on 11 March returned to operational flying with No. 317 (Polish) 'City of Wilno' Squadron. In August 1946 he was again posted to the HQ of the Polish Air Force. He was demobilized in 1946 with the rank of Flight Lieutenant and settled in Britain, where he completed a degree in psychology and worked as a psychologist and teacher. While studying he worked night shifts at Wall's ice-cream factory. During the 1950s and until his death he was a lodger in a house owned by fellow Polish pilot Józef Mierzejewski in Putney, London. He never married. Major Gustaw Radwański died on 10 October 1961 in a hospice in London from pancreatic cancer, and was buried at Streatham Park Cemetery in London. He was decorated with the Cross of Valour and two bars.

Date & Time	Unit	Aircraft	Score
06.04.1941	56 Squadron	Hurricane II Z2636 US-U	0-0-1 Do 17

JAN ROGOWSKI, Sergeant, was born on 16 August 1917 at Jurowce near Białystok in Poland, which was occupied by the German Empire. He grew up in the family of Jan and Paulina née Piesiecka. He completed primary school at Jurowce and was accepted to the State School of Craft and Industry, from which he graduated in 1935 as an ironworker. On 2 November 1936 he volunteered for the 5th Air Regiment at Lida and joined his older brother, Wiktor, who served there as a mechanic in the 55th Bomber Squadron. Between January and April 1937 Jan Rogowski completed an aircraft maintenance

course, then was sent for a gliding course to Ustianowa. In 1937 and 1938 he completed flying training at the Regimental Flying Training School, and in August 1938 was posted to the Advanced Flying Course at Grudziądz. After over two months he was posted to the 151st Fighter Squadron of the 5th Air Regiment at Wilno. At the end of April 1939 he was transferred to the 162nd Fighter Squadron of the 6th Air Regiment at Lwów. During the Polish Campaign of 1939 he flew operationally with his unit, and together with the whole of III/6 Fighter Wing supported the 'Łódź' Army. He operated from an ambush airfield at Kłoniszewo. After crossing the Rumanian border on 18 September he was interned in Celafat camp, but after escaping he travelled to France, arriving at Marseilles on 19 December 1939. From there he was transferred to the Polish Air Force Training Centre at Lyon-Bron. Rogowski arrived in England on 3 March 1940 and received the service number 780965. With the rank of Corporal he was sent to RAF Manston, which was a satellite base for Eastchurch. Between 17 July and 5 August he trained at No. 5 Operational Training Unit at Aston Down. He was considered for No. 302 (Polish) 'City of Poznań' Squadron at Leconfield, then for No. 303 (Polish) 'Tadeusz Kościuszko. City of Warsaw' Squadron even before No. 303 was organized, but instead on 7 August with the rank of Sergeant he joined No. 74 Squadron at Hornchurch. On 19 August he was reposted to No. 303 Squadron at Northolt. On 2 September he claimed the destruction of a Bf 109, but four days later was shot down in his Hurricane I V7243 RF-P. He crash-landed at Biggin Hill and was taken to hospital. Rogowski returned to No. 303 Squadron on 23 October. He was transferred to No. 91 Squadron on 2 February, but a week later was posted back to No. 74 Squadron. On 21 February he was forced to make an emergency landing due to lack of fuel at Langley Green, Eastbourne, in his Spitfire II P7559 and received scalp wounds. While with No. 74 he claimed the destruction of a Bf 109 on 7 April. On 6 August he joined No. 308 (Polish) 'City of Cracow' Squadron, flying operational sorties with this unit until 1 July 1942, when he was posted to No. 1489 Anti-Aircraft Co-operation Flight. On 22 June 1943 he was back in the front line with No. 302 (Polish) 'City of Poznań' Squadron. On 9 January 1944 Rogowski was once more posted for rest and joined No. 16 (Polish) Service Flying Training School at Newton. He resumed operational flying after being posted on 10 June to No. 306 (Polish) 'City of Toruń' Squadron, with whom he claimed the destruction of several V1 flying bombs, including one and another shared on 16 August and two victories on 28 August. He left No. 306 Squadron on 21 August 1945 and was posted to No. 25 (Polish) Elementary Flying Training School, being released from service on 21 December with the rank of Warrant Officer. Rogowski decided to remain in Britain and settled initially in Chelmsford. He moved to Ipswich in 1960, where he worked for Ransomes agricultural machinery manufacturers. He was a frequent customer of the Falcon pub, which was next door to his home. He died on 17 August 1997, the day after his 80th birthday, at Stowmarket Nursing Home and was buried in an unmarked grave in the Catholic section of Ipswich Lawn Cemetery. On 12 September 2002 a headstone with his name, wartime achievements and decorations was unveiled. Jan Rogowski's decorations included the Silver Cross of Virtuti Militari no. 11118, the Cross of Valour and two bars and the Silver Cross of Merit with Swords. He is often confused with Sergeant Jan Aleksander Rogowski, who was killed on 28 May 1943.

Date & Time	Unit	Aircraft	Score
02.09.1940 17.50	303 Squadron	Hurricane I R4217 RF-V	1-0-0 Bf 109
07.04.1941 10.00	74 Squadron	Spitfire II P8199	1-0-0 Bf 109
16.08.1944 17.50	306 Squadron	Mustang III FB358 UZ-C	1-0-0 V1
16.08.1944 19.00	306 Squadron	Mustang III FB358 UZ-C	½-0-0 V1
28.08.1944 14.25	306 Squadron	Mustang III FX979 UZ-I	1-0-0 V1
28.08.1944 14.40	306 Squadron	Mustang III FX979 UZ-I	1-0-0 V1

MIECZYSŁAW ROZWADOWSKI, Pilot Officer, was born on 30 May 1915 into the Polish family of Wacław Jordan-Rozwadowski and Tamara, settled at Petersburg in the Russian Empire. After moving to Poland he graduated from secondary school in Warsaw, and passing A-level exams in 1936 was accepted to the Air Force Reserve Cadet Officers' School at Dęblin, in 1937 transferring to the Air Force Cadet Officers' School at Dęblin. Like all of the 12th class he completed his studies early, and in June 1939, before official graduation, was posted to the 111th Fighter Squadron of the 1st Air Regiment at Warsaw. Along with other 12th class graduates he was commissioned with effect from 1 August. He participated in the Polish Campaign of 1939 when his unit was part of the Pursuit Brigade. On 8 September he protected Mirosław Ferić whilst his leader shot down an Hs 126. On the same day Rozwadowski and Kazimierz Wünsche mistakenly pursued a PZL P.23 Karaś from the 24th Reconnaissance Squadron, but luckily both recognized their mistake, leaving the Karaś with several bullet holes. After the fall of Poland he was evacuated to Rumania, from where he travelled to France. In January 1940 Rozwadowski arrived in Britain and was given the service number 76720 and the rank of Pilot Officer. He was sent to the Polish Air Force Centre at Eastchurch. In May he was transferred to Blackpool. He completed initial training at No. 15 Elementary Flying Training School at Carlisle and No. 6 Operational Training Unit at Sutton Bridge. On 8 August he joined the North Weald-based No. 151 Squadron. He claimed his only victory on 15 August when he shot down a Bf 109. Mieczysław Rozwadowski was killed on the same day while flying his Hurricane I V7410. He was shot down by German fighters and went down into the Channel near Dover. His body was never found. He was the sixth Polish operational pilot lost during the Battle of Britain. He was decorated with the Cross of Valour and bar. He has a symbolic grave in the family tomb at the Parish Cemetery at Skolimów. He is commemorated on the Polish Air Force Memorials at Northolt and Warsaw-Mokotów.

Date & Time	Unit	Aircraft	Score
15.08.1940 15.30	151 Squadron	Hurricane I V7410	1-0-0 Bf 109 or ½-0-0 Bf 109

WŁADYSŁAW RÓŻYCKI, Pilot Officer, was born on 11 August 1907 at Jurkowice near Opatów in Kielce Voivodship, within the territory of Poland ruled by the Russian Empire. He grew up on a farm in the family of Franciszek and Antonia née Kasprzyk. He completed seven years of coeducational primary school, followed by secondary school, and worked on the family farm, that specialized in the cultivation of plants. In 1928 he volunteered for military service and was posted as a ground crew member to the 35th Light Bomber Squadron of the 3rd Air Regiment in Poznań. On 22 September 1930 he decided to permanently stay in the air force and was posted to the Air Force NCO Training Centre

at Bydgoszcz for a flying course. Upon completion he returned to the 35th Squadron. He married Walentyna, whom he met during his short service with the 6th Air Regiment, and had two children: Zofia (born 1936) and Andrzej (1939). Różycki joined the Air Force Cadet Officers' School for NCOs at Bydgoszcz, and was then transferred to the Air Force Cadet Officers' School at Dęblin. He was commissioned with the 11th class on 15 October 1938, and with the rank of Sub-Lieutenant was posted to the 141st Fighter Squadron of the 4th Air Regiment at Toruń. He fought during the Polish Campaign of 1939 when his squadron, alongside the whole III/4 Fighter Wing, supported the 'Pomorze' Army. On 2 September he participated in a suicidal attack on a German armoured column near Gruta that ended in disaster, three pilots being killed. On 3 September he shot down an Hs 126. After the fall of Poland, on 18 September, together with the road party of his squadron, he crossed the Rumanian border at Kuty, travelling to France. He decided to continue his journey to England, and on 13 February 1940 reported to the Polish Air Force Centre at Eastchurch. He received the service number 76762 and the rank of Pilot Officer. On 4 July he was posted to No. 15 Elementary Flying Training School at Carlisle, from where on 18 July he was transferred to No. 6 Operational Training Unit at Sutton Bridge. He crashed his Hurricane I N2354 at the aerodrome on 22 July but was unhurt. On 17 August he joined No. 238 Squadron at St Eval, and on 11 September claimed the destruction of an He 111, but was wounded and made an emergency landing in his Hurricane I P3618. On 15 September he damaged one He 111. This was followed by the destruction of an He 111 on 25 September and shooting down a Bf 110 on 28 September. He reported his last success on 10 October, damaging a Bf 109. On 14 November, while flying his Hurricane I P3618, the engine failed and he crash-landed with the undercarriage up. Seven days later Różycki was transferred to No. 306 (Polish) 'City of Toruń' Squadron, but from 3 May 1941 he flew in No. 23 Night Fighter Squadron. On 23 April 1942 he was transferred to No. 307 (Polish) 'City of Lwów' Night Fighter Squadron, where he was appointed 'A' Flight commander. On 16 November 1942 he was posted for rest, serving as Polish Liaison Officer at No. 10 Group. From 28 May 1943 he served as a flying instructor at No. 54 Operational Training Unit, then on 26 July transferred to No. 60 Operational Training Unit, where he undertook further training before being posted back to No. 23 Squadron on 26 October. He was appointed deputy commander of the flight, operating in Italy. On 14 March 1944 he returned to Britain, being posted to No. 605 Night Fighter Squadron. On 18 September Różycki was transferred to No. 1 Aircraft Delivery Flight, and from 21 July 1945 to No. 5 Aircraft Delivery Flight in Egypt. From 18 March 1946 he served as a pilot at No. 21 Personnel Transit Centre at Kasfareet in the Middle East. The same year he managed to bring his family from Poland, which was occupied by the Soviets. He was released from the Polish Air Force in September 1946 with the rank of Flight Lieutenant. Initially he settled in Melton Mowbray, but in 1948 emigrated to Canada, where he ran the Ontario Bread Ltd bakery. Major Władysław Różycki died in Toronto on 8 August 1970 and was buried at Park Lawn Cemetery at Etobicoke. He was decorated with the Silver Cross of Virtuti Militari no. 9130, the Cross of Valour and three bars and the British Distinguished Flying Cross.

Date & Time	Unit	Aircraft	Score
03.09.1939	141st Squadron	PZL P.11c	1-0-0 Hs 126
11.09.1940 15.45	238 Squadron	Hurricane I P3618	1-0-0 He 111
15.09.1940 15.00	238 Squadron	Hurricane I P3618	0-0-1 He 111
25.09.1940 12.00	238 Squadron	Hurricane I P3618	1-0-0 He 111
28.09.1940 14.40	238 Squadron	Hurricane I P3618	1-0-0 Bf 110
10.10.1940 12.30	238 Squadron	Hurricane I P3618	0-0-1 Bf 109

S

WŁODZIMIERZ MICHAŁ CZECH SAMOLIŃSKI, Pilot Officer, was born on 14 October 1916 at Poznań in Poland, which was then ruled by the German Empire. In 1935 he graduated from Adam Mickiewicz Secondary School, and after passing A-level exams was accepted to the Air Force Cadet Officers' School at Dęblin. Commissioned on 15 October 1938 with the 11th class and with the rank of Sub-Lieutenant, he was posted to the 122nd Fighter Squadron of the 2nd Air Regiment at Cracow. Between July and August 1939 he operated from a small ambush airfield near Zawiercie to intercept

German aircraft violating Polish airspace. During the Polish Campaign of 1939 he flew operationally as his unit supported the 'Cracow' Army. On 3 September he led a section and participated in combat with an enemy raid, and with a desperate attack he prevented the Germans from dropping bombs on their target. His PZL P.11c was damaged during this encounter. After the fall of Poland, on 17 September he flew to Cernâuti in Rumania. He then travelled to France, arriving at Marseilles on 29 October. Samoliński left France with one of the first groups of airmen, and on 24 January 1940 reported at the Polish Air Force Centre at Eastchurch. He received the service number 76709 and the rank of Pilot Officer. He was posted for training on 23 June, and was initially considered for No. 302 (Polish) 'City of Poznań' Squadron at Leconfield. He completed conversion to Hurricanes at No. 6 Operational Training Unit at Sutton Bridge, and on 16 July was posted to No. 253 Squadron at Turnhouse. On 30 August he shot down one Bf 110, and on 4 September added another Bf 110 destroyed. He was shot down over the Channel and killed on 26 September while flying the Hurricane I V7470. His body was lost at sea. He was the twentieth Polish operational pilot killed during the Battle of Britain. He was decorated with the Silver Cross of Virtuti Militari no. 8987 and the Cross of Valour. He is commemorated on the Polish Air Force Memorials at Northolt and Warsaw-Mokotów.

Date & Time	Unit	Aircraft	Score
30.08.1940 11.15	253 Squadron	Hurricane I P3717	1-0-0 Bf 110
04.09.1940 13.20	253 Squadron	Hurricane I	1-0-0 Bf 110

WILHELM WŁADYSŁAW SASAK, Sergeant, called 'Gorol' (Highlander), was born on 11 October 1916 at Nowy Targ in the Tatra Mountains in southern Poland, which was ruled by the Austro-Hungarian Empire. He grew up in the family of Piotr and Wiktoria née Kukulska. He underwent basic education in his hometown, followed by Seweryn Goszczyński State Secondary School in 1934 and passing A-level exams. In 1935 he joined the Polish Armed Forces, and in September was posted to the 4th Regiment of Highland Fusiliers at Cieszyn for the Reserve Cadet Officers' Course. Upon completion in December 1935 he was sent to the Air Force Reserve Cadet Officers' School at Dęblin. From 4 January 1936 he participated in a basic flying course, then on 25 September 1937 was released into civilian life with a mobilization assignment to the 2nd Air Regiment. Some sources state that he remained in the air force and served as a

flying instructor of the Air Force Reserve Cadet
Officers' School. Between 22 July and 31 August
1938, and then from 22 June to 18 July 1939, he
participated in aerial exercises organized by the
2nd Air Regiment. During the Polish Campaign
of 1939 he was attached to the 2nd Air Base at
Cracow, and with all personnel was evacuated
towards south-east Poland. On 17 September he
crossed the Rumanian border. While in France
he volunteered to join the Polish Air Force in
Britain, where he arrived on 14 March 1940.
Sasak received the service number 781267
and the rank of Leading Aircraftman, and was
posted to RAF Manston, a satellite base of the
Polish Air Force Centre at Eastchurch. He was
posted to No. 1 School of Army Co-operation

at Old Sarum, from where on 1 September he was moved to No. 6 Operational
Training Unit at Sutton Bridge. Upon completion, with the rank of Sergeant
he was posted to No. 32 Squadron at Acklington and subsequently to No. 145
Squadron at Westhampnett. On 30 November 1940 he was returning to his
base after completing a patrol when the engine of his Hurricane I V7470 caught
fire. Sergeant Wilhelm Sasak broke out of formation but did not bale out, most
probably being bemused by fumes. The aircraft crashed at Donnington, one mile
south of Chichester and the pilot was killed. He was buried in the Roman Catholic
Cemetery, Chichester, in square 42, R.C. plot, grave no. 40. He is commemorated
on the Polish Air Force Memorials at Northolt and Warsaw-Mokotów.

TADEUSZ WŁADYSŁAW SAWICZ, Pilot Officer, called 'Szczur' (Rat), was
born on 13 February 1914 in Warsaw, in a Poland ruled by the Russian Empire.
He grew up in the family of Włodzimierz Władysław Sawicz, a military doctor
who specialized in aviation medicine and worked at the Polish Air Force Central
Medical Establishment, and Emma Helena née Makowska. As his father was
mobilized to the Tsar's army, Tadeusz spent a few years in Moscow. In 1918
he returned to Poland and attended primary school at Kowel, then the King
Władysław IV State School for Boys in Warsaw and finally the private Secondary
School 'Collegium'. He passed A-level exams in 1933. Between September and
December 1933 he completed a unitary course at the Infantry Cadet Officers'
School at Zambrów, from where on 3 January 1934 he was transferred to the
Air Force Reserve Cadet Officers' School at Dęblin. Upon completion on
20 September he was posted to the 5th Air Regiment at Wilno, but Sawicz

decided to join the Air Force Cadet Officers'
School at Dęblin. Between April and June
1936 he completed an Advanced Flying
Course at Grudziądz, then between July and
August a gliding course at Ustianowa. He
was commissioned with the 9th class on 15
August. Sub-Lieutenant Sawicz was posted
to the 111th Fighter Squadron of the 1st
Air Regiment at Warsaw. On 23 October
1937 he was transferred to the 114th Fighter
Squadron of the same regiment. In the
summer of 1938 he had an accident when
his aircraft turned around while landing.
From 5-9 November he participated in the
Central Fighter Tournament in Toruń and
won the flying competition. During the

Polish Campaign of 1939 he flew operationally as part of the Pursuit Brigade.
On 1 September he destroyed a Bf 109, this claim officially assigned to both
him and Bogusław Mierzwa. The same day Sawicz protected his colleague
Aleksander Gabszewicz, who was shot down and baled out, by scaring away
a Bf 110 which was very close and was shooting at Gabszewicz. During this
encounter Sawicz's aircraft was damaged. On 4 September he was appointed
deputy commander of the 114th Squadron. He also reported destruction
of a Do 17, or most probably a Bf 110, although this claim appears under 5
September. On 6 September he claimed the destruction of an He 111 or Ju
86 and damage of a Ju 86 and a Do 17. On 14 September he flew with orders
to Warsaw, which was surrounded by the Germans. After the fall of Poland,
on 17 September he flew to Rumania. Via Bucharest, and then Yugoslavia
and Italy, he travelled to France, arriving on 7 October. In early 1940 he was
transferred to the Polish Air Force Training Centre at Lyon-Bron, and from 10
May at Lyon-Mions, starting aerial training on 29 February on Romano R.82s,
Caudron C.636 Simounes, Caudron CR.714 Cyclones, Dewoitine D.501s and
Morane MS 406s. On 1 June he joined the Polish fighter section commanded by
Lieutenant Aleksander Gabszewicz and was attached to GCIII/10 at Deauville.
He flew operational missions in Bloch MB 152s. After the collapse of France he
flew to Algiers, from where he travelled to Casablanca and Gibraltar. He sailed
for Britain, arriving on 17 July. Sawicz received the service number P-0596
and the rank of Pilot Officer. After a short stay at the Polish Air Force Centre
at Blackpool, on 22 September he was posted to No. 1 School of Army Co-
operation at Old Sarum. At the beginning of October he was posted to No. 5

Operational Training Unit at Aston Down, and on 19 October joined No. 303 (Polish) 'Tadeusz Kościuszko. City of Warsaw' Squadron at Leconfield. On 22 February 1941 he was posted to No. 316 (Polish) 'City of Warsaw' Squadron. On 9 April he claimed the destruction of an He 111, which was the second victory gained by his unit since it was formed. On 14 November he was appointed 'A' Flight commander. On 4 June 1942 he was transferred to No. 58 Operational Training Unit at Grangemouth, where he stayed as an instructor, then on 25 September he took command of No. 315 (Polish) 'City of Dęblin' Squadron. On 13 March 1943 he probably shot down or damaged a Bf 109, but did not report this claim. However, on 4 April he definitely damaged one Fw 190. On 15 April he was appointed Squadron Leader Tactics of No. 1 Polish Fighter Wing, being deputy commander of the wing. On 4 July he was posted for rest and served as Polish Liaison Officer of No. 12 Group, then from 18 October he was a flying instructor at the Polish Fighter School at No. 61 Operational Training Unit at Rednal. On 3 March 1944 he was posted to the HQ of the 9th United States Air Force, then from 20 April he flew operationally with the 61st Fighter Squadron of 56th Fighter Group USAAF. On 22 May he claimed the damage of a Fw 190, but once more he did not report this claim further. On 15 June he was appointed commander of No. 3 Polish Wing. On 24 August he married Diane Stanley Hughes, then on 14 October took command of No. 131 (Polish) Fighter Wing, but on 21 October was injured in a landing accident in his Spitfire IX MK944 JH-Z and taken to No. 53 Mobile Field Hospital in Ghent. He was able to lead No. 131 Wing into action on 17 December. In the summer of 1945 he learnt that his stepsister Maria Sawicz was killed during the Warsaw Uprising in 1944. On 16 July Sawicz was posted to the HQ of RAF Andrews Field Station, and from 8 August he once more commanded No. 3 Polish Wing. On 17 May 1946 he was posted to the HQ of RAF Coltishall. In February 1947 he was demobilized with the rank of Acting Wing Commander. He decided to settle in Britain, and on 15 August 1952 was naturalized. He ran his own farm near North Bersted, Sussex, and then near Liphook, Hampshire. After divorce, Sawicz married Kazimiera Baczyńska Dekańska. In 1957 he emigrated to Canada and worked for Wheeler Airlines. Between 1970 and 1974 he worked for the Canadian Government as air transport co-ordinator in British Guyana. After the death of his wife, in 1990 he married Jadwiga Dekońska Jaworska. On 3 May 2006 he was promoted to the rank of General Brigadier. He died aged 97 on 19 October 2011 in Toronto, and was buried at Powązki Military Cemetery in Warsaw. He was the last Polish survivor of the Battle of Britain. He was decorated with the Silver Cross of Virtuti Militari no. 8359, the Cross of Valour and three bars, the British Distinguished Flying Cross, the American Distinguished Flying Cross and the Dutch Vliegerkruis.

His biography, *Generał brygady Tadeusz Sawicz 1914-2011*, was published in Poland in 2012 by Wojtek Matusiak. He was the only Allied airman who was in action from the first day of the war (on 1 September 1939 claimed destruction of a Bf 109) until the last (on 8 May 1945 he led Spitfires during a victory air parade over occupied Germany).

Date & Time	Unit	Aircraft	Score
01.09.1939 17.20	114th Squadron	PZL P.11c no.4	0-0-½ Bf 109
04or 05.09.1939 17.10	114th Squadron	PZL P.11	1-0-0 Do 17
06.09.1939 15.10	114th Squadron	PZL P.11	1-0-1 Ju 86 or He 111
06.09.1939 15.10	114th Squadron	PZL P.11	0-0-1 Do 17
09.04.1941 09.50	316 Squadron	Hurricane I P3926 SZ-P	1-0-0 He 111
13.03.1943 15.10	315 Squadron	Spitfire IX EN172 PK-K	0-1-0 or 0-0-1 Fw 190 unconfirmed
04.04.1943 12.30	315 Squadron	Spitfire IX EN172 PK-K	0-0-1 Fw 190
21 or 22.05.1944	61st Fighter Squadron	P.47D-1-RE Thunderbolt 42-7941 HV-R	0-0-1 Fw 190 unconfirmed

ANTONI SEREDYN, Sergeant, called 'Tony', was born on 15 August 1913 at Łoje near Kozienice, in a Poland ruled by the Russian Empire. In 1929, after four years of education, he graduated from the Humanistic Secondary School at Chełmża. He volunteered for the Polish Air Force and was posted to the 4th Air Regiment at Toruń. Between September 1936 and July 1937 he completed a basic flying course at Toruń, then from September-November 1937 an Advanced Flying Course at Grudziądz. Upon completion he flew as a pilot in the 142nd Fighter Squadron of the 4th Air Regiment at Toruń. Seredyn had a flying accident on 24

February 1938 when he collided in mid-air with another PZL P.11c piloted by Corporal Feliks Gmur. Both pilots were unhurt. On 1 October 1938 he decided to permanently stay in the air force. He was transferred to the 161st Fighter Squadron of the 6th Air Regiment at Lwów. During the Polish Campaign of 1939 he flew operationally with his unit supporting the 'Łódź' Army. After the fall of Poland Seredyn flew to Rumania on the morning of 18 September; and his RWD-8 was damaged by Russian ground fire, he was wounded but managed to land in Rumania. From the port of Balchik on board the *Aghios Nikocalos* he sailed to Beirut, and then to Marseilles on the *Ville de Strasbourg*, arriving on 29 October. On 13 January 1940 he was transferred to the Polish Air Force Training Centre at Lyon-Bron, but soon decided to continue his journey to England. On 27 February he reported to the Polish Air Force Centre at Eastchurch, but on 3 April was moved to RAF Manston, a satellite station for the Polish Centre. He received the service number 780958 and the rank of Sergeant. Initially he was transferred to the Polish Wing at No. 3 School of Technical Training Blackpool on 1 June, but due to kidney problems his further posting were delayed. On 12 September Antoni Seredyn went to No. 15 Elementary Flying Training School at Redhill, from where on 25 September he was sent to No. 5 Operational Training Unit at Aston Down, then on 12 October he joined No. 32 Squadron at Acklington. Later in the autumn of 1940 his kidney trouble developed once more, which resulted in three months in hospital, after which he was sent for longer convalescence. On 2 July 1941 he was posted to No. 13 Group Flight at Turnhouse, and then was posted to No. 285 Squadron where he was engaged in anti-aircraft co-operation duties. In September 1943 he joined No. 286 Squadron, and on 9 May 1944 was posted for a refresher course to No. 61 Operational Training Unit and converted to Mustangs at No. 3 Tactical Exercise Unit from 8 September. Seredyn joined No. 315 (Polish) 'City of Dęblin' Squadron on 24 September. On 17 November 1945 he was posted to No. 316 (Polish) 'City of Warsaw' Squadron, but eleven days later transferred to the Polish Air Force Centre at Blackpool. Antoni Seredyn was released from the Polish Air Force on 25 May 1947 with the rank of Warrant Officer. He decided to settle in Britain, and after marrying an English woman lived in Barnsley and then in Blackpool. He was employed as a tourist bus driver. Antoni Seredyn died aged 84 on 8 June 1998 in Blackpool and was cremated at Carleton Crematorium. He was decorated with the Cross of Valour. He is often confused with Mieczysław Antoni Seredyn from No. 305 (Polish) 'Wielkopolan' Squadron.

ANTONI SIUDAK, Sergeant, was born on 1 April 1909 at Imbramowice near Olkusz in Kielce Voivodship, in a part of Poland ruled by the Austro-Hungarian Empire. On 28 October 1930 he joined the Polish Air Force and initially served as mechanic's assistant in the 12th Light Bomber Squadron of the 1st Air Regiment. After completing his national service he decided to stay in the air force permanently, and on 6 May 1932 completed basic flying training at the Elementary Flying School at Bydgoszcz. In November 1932 he was posted to the Training Flight of the 1st Air Regiment, then from 1 August 1933 underwent an Advanced Flying Course at Grudziądz. Upon completion on 21 November he was posted to the 114th Fighter Squadron of the 1st Air

Regiment, then after six months was posted to the 112th Fighter Squadron of the same regiment. Siudak left his unit on 1 January 1936 after being posted for an instructors' course at No. 1 Air Force Training Centre at Dęblin. From 2 April he served there as a flying instructor. During the Polish Campaign of 1939 he was evacuated from Dęblin, and after crossing the Rumanian border on 17 September he sailed from Balchik on 5 November, six days later arriving in France. Upon arrival he was posted to the Polish Air Force Training Centre at Lyon-Bron. Siudak was chosen for the Polish-manned squadron equipped with Caudron CR 714s which was supposed to be send to Finland as it was being attacked by the Soviet Union (the so-called 'Finnish Squadron'). However, an armistice between both countries was signed on 13 March 1940 so the Polish squadron was unused, but out of the personnel destined for Finland 1/145 Polish 'City of Warsaw' Squadron, also known as GC1/145, was formed. Siudak initially joined this unit and served in Section 1 of 1st Flight, but on 22 May he was posted to the Polish fighter section DAT under the command of Lieutenant Robert Janota at Angers, flying Bloch MB151s. After the fall of France he boarded a Czechoslovak ship at Bordeaux on 19 June and sailed to Britain. Upon arrival he received the service number P-5128 and the rank of Sergeant. On 23 July he was posted to No. 302 (Polish) 'City of Poznań' Squadron at Leconfield. On 15 September he claimed the shared destruction of a Do 17. Six days later he was transferred to No. 303 (Polish) 'Tadeusz Kościuszko. City of Warsaw' Squadron at Northolt. On 5 October he reported the shared destruction of a Bf 110, followed by shooting down two Bf 109s. Next day he was killed at 10.30 am while helping ground crew members to synchronize the machine guns of his Hurricane I P3120 RF-S, when a single German bomb dropped by a Ju 88 destroyed his aircraft. There are conflicting reports saying that he was killed while in the cockpit or that he fell to the tarmac and fractured his skull. He was the the twenty-fourth

Polish operational pilot killed during the Battle of Britain. He was buried in Northwood Cemetery, in grave no. H225. Sergeant Siudak was decorated with the Silver Cross of Virtuti Militari no. 8989 and the Cross of Valour. He is commemorated on the Polish Air Force Memorials at Northolt and Warsaw-Mokotów, but also on the memorial plaque at RAF Northolt.

Date & Time	Unit	Aircraft	Score
15.09.1940 12.10	302 Squadron	Hurricane I P3867 WX-F	½-0-0 Do 17
05.10.1940 11.40	303 Squadron	Hurricane I N2460 RF-D	½-0-0 Bf 110
05.10.1940 11.40	303 Squadron	Hurricane I N2460 RF-D	2-0-0 Bf 109

HENRYK SKALSKI, Flying Officer, was born on 21 September 1908 at Łódź in part of Poland ruled by the Russian Empire. In 1929 he graduated from Cadet Corps No.2 at Chełmno and passed A-level exams. On 1 September he joined the Polish Armed Forces and in 1933 completed an Artillery Cadet Officers' School at Toruń. Upon completion Skalski decided to join the Polish Air Force, and between autumn 1933 and summer 1934 completed basic flying training and then further training at the 1st Air Regiment at Warsaw. Between April and June 1935 he completed an Advanced Flying Course at Grudziądz, then was attached to the 11th Light Bomber Squadron of the 1st Air Regiment. He was wounded on 16 January 1936 while making an emergency landing in a Breguet XIX due to engine failure; his observer Sub-Lieutenant Edward Hubicki was also injured. Skalski was transferred to the 112th Fighter Squadron in Warsaw, where on 12 January 1937 he had a mid-air collision with Sub-Lieutenant Wacław Łapkowski. Neither pilots were hurt. Skalski was transferred to the Air Force NCO School for Minors at Bydgoszcz, where as flying instructor and adjutant he remained until the outbreak of war, serving at Krosno airfield. He was then evacuated to Rumania and on to France. His whereabouts in France are not known, apart from that he was stationed at Le Bourget. He arrived in Britain on 27 June 1940 and received the service number P-0156 and the rank of Flying Officer. Initially he was posted to the Polish Air Force Centre at Blackpool, then to No. 1 School of Army Co-operation at Old Sarum and eventually on 18 September to No. 5 Operational Training Unit at Aston Down. On 4 October he joined No. 615 Squadron at Prestwick, from where on 9 October he was transferred to No. 607 Squadron at Tangmere. On 2 December he was moved to No. 46 Squadron at North Weald, then three days later to No. 249 Squadron, also at North Weald. On 24 February 1941 he was posted to No. 306 (Polish) 'City of Toruń' Squadron, where he remained as a ground controller officer. On 3 March Skalski returned to No. 249 Squadron, where on 11 April he sustained injuries from a flying accident in his Hurricane II Z2450. He had another accident on 18 February 1941 when he collided in mid-air with another aircraft; on this occasion he flew the Hurricane II Z2695. At the end of April he went to No. 55 Operational Training Unit, where he had a third flying accident. On this occasion, on 28 April, he flew the Hurricane I L1836. He was posted to No. 11 Group, where he flew in the Army Air Corps Flight, from where on 24 July he was transferred to No. 72 Squadron. During his stay in No. 72 Squadron he had a landing accident on 16 August in his Spitfire VB W3170. He was shot down and wounded on 27 August in his Spitfire VB W3408 while participating in Operation Circus 85. Skalski was captured by the Germans and spent rest of the war in Stalag Luft III at Sagan (Żagań). In May 1945 he returned to Britain and was posted to the Polish Air Force Centre at Blackpool. In April 1946 he was posted to the Polish Fighter Station at Coltishall, but on 23 May transferred to No. 306 (Polish) 'City of Toruń' Squadron. He stayed there until this unit was disbanded on 6 January 1947. Henryk Skalski was released from the Polish Air Force with the rank of Flight Lieutenant and settled in Britain. He died on 23 August 1977 in London and was buried at Acton Park Royal Cemetery. He was decorated with the Cross of Valour.

STANISŁAW SKALSKI, Pilot Officer, called 'Skal' or 'Kędzierzawy' (Curly), was born on 27 November 1915 at Kodyma, near Odessa, close to the Moldavian border in the Russian Empire. He grew up in the Polish family of Szymon, who led an experimental agrarian station, and Józefa née Biernat. In 1916 he moved with his parents to Kharkov. After the Bolshevik Revolution together with his mother he went to Zbaraż, followed by his father, who rejoined his family in 1923. After moving to Dubno Stanisław Skalski completed primary school and in 1925 was accepted to

Stanisław Konarski Secondary School. After graduation in 1933 he attempted to join the Air Force Reserve Cadet Officers' School at Dęblin, but was rejected as he was not yet 18. Instead he studied at the Warsaw University of Technology and then the School of Diplomacy. At the same time he joined Warsaw Aero Club and completed a gliding course at Polichno, obtaining A and B categories. In 1935 he particpated in Military Preparation, and in April and May flew powered aircraft near Łuck. He gave up his studies and on 17 September was accepted to the Infantry Reserve Cadet Officers' School at Zambrów, from where on 4 January 1936 he was transferred to the Air Force Cadet Officers' School at Dęblin. Between April and June 1938 he completed an Advanced Flying Course at Grudziądz. He was commissioned with the 11th class on 15 October, and with the rank of Sub-Lieutenant was posted to the 142nd Fighter Squadron of the 4th Air Regiment at Toruń. In August 1939 Skalski twice intercepted German aircraft violating Polish airspace. During the Polish Campaign of 1939 he flew operationally, his unit and the whole III/4 Fighter Wing were supporting the 'Pomorze' Army. On 1 September he participated in the destruction of an Hs 126, yet his claim was rejected. Skalski landed, captured and bandaged both German airmen, and at the same time obtained secret military documents of great importance. On 2 September he shot down two Do 17s and returned in his damaged PZL P.11c. On the next day he participated in the destruction of an Hs 126 and shot down another one. On 4 September he participated in damaging a Do 17, then he shot down a Ju 87. He flew operationally until the end of the campaign, and on 16 September attacked German cavalry. Skalski became the first Allied ace of the Second World War. Together with the road party of III/4 Wing he crossed the Rumanian border at Śniatyń. He boarded the *Aghios Nikolaos* at Balchik and sailed to Beirut, from where he sailed on the *Ville de Strasbourg*, arriving in Marseilles on 29 October. Initially allocated to the Polish Air Force Training Centre at Lyon-Bron, he was unhappy with the French approach and decided to continue his journey to England. On 27 January 1940 Skalski sailed to Britain and was posted to the Polish Air Force Centre at Eastchurch. Upon arrival he received the service number 76710 and the rank of Pilot Officer. On 5 May he was transferred to Blackpool. On 5 July he was posted to No. 1 School of Army Co-operation at Old Sarum, and ten days later to No. 6 Operational Training Unit at Sutton Bridge. On 3 August he was posted to No. 302 (Polish) 'City of Poznań' Squadron at Leconfield, but was unhappy as this unit was undergoing training, whilst Skalski was eager to fly operationally. On 12 August he was sent back to Blackpool. On 26 August he was posted to No. 501 Squadron at Gravesend. On 30 August he claimed one He 111 and another one shared. On the next day he shot down one Bf 109, followed by damaging a Bf 110 on 1 September and destroying two Bf 109s on 2 September.

He was shot down three days later over Canterbury in his Hurricane I V6644 SD-B, and was seriously wounded in a leg and badly burnt. Skalski baled out and landed at Benenden, and was treated at Herne Bay hospital. Although he claimed destruction of two Bf 109s, this claim was unsubstantiated. He returned to No. 501 Squadron on 16 October. He had an accident in the Hurricane I V7614 SD-E on 5 November, but although his aircraft was damaged Skalski was unhurt. On 8 November he added the shared destruction of a Bf 109. On 1 March 1941 he was transferred to No. 306 (Polish) 'City of Toruń' Squadron. Initially he served in the operations room, then continued operational sorties. On 24 July he destroyed one Bf 109, then on 19 August 1941 one more Bf 109. Two days later he probably destroyed a Bf 109, followed by two Bf 109s shot down on 17 September. On 15 September he had taken command of 'B' Flight. On 1 March 1942 he was posted to No. 316 (Polish) 'City of Warsaw' Squadron, where was appointed 'B' Flight commander. While with No. 316 Squadron Skalski made several more claims. On 10 April he destroyed a Fw 190, on 24 April damaged a Bf 109 and on 3 May probably shot down a Fw 190. Two days later he took command of No. 317 (Polish) 'City of Wilno' Squadron, then on 8 November was posted to No. 58 Operational Training Unit at Balado Bridge as a flying instructor. On 28 January 1943 he was posted to the HQ of No. 1 Polish Wing, but in February was appointed commander of the Polish Fighting Team, better known as 'Skalski's Circus', a group of Polish pilots sent to North Africa and attached to No. 145 Squadron. Between March and June 1943 he claimed several victories over Tunisia. On 28 March he shot down a Ju 88, on 2 April he destroyed a Bf 109, on 4 April he shot down another Bf 109 and on 6 May he damaged a Bf 109. Skalski decided to remain in the Mediterranean, and on 30 June was posted to No. 601 Squadron, which he commanded between 15 July and 20 October. After Jerzy Jankiewicz, he was the second Pole to command an RAF squadron. Returning to England, Skalski was posted to RAF Northolt where he served in the Station's HQ. On 12 December he was appointed commander of No. 131 (Polish) Wing. On 6 April 1944 he took command of No. 133 (Polish) Wing, and on 24 June he claimed his last two victories by destroying Bf 109s. He left his command on 2 August ,and between 6 October and 20 January 1945 he studied at the Command and General Staff College at Fort Leavenworth, USA. From 25 February 1945 he served in No. 11 Group as a staff officer, on 19 March being reposted to No. 133 (Polish) Wing. Skalski was the top-scoring Polish fighter pilot of the Second World War. He volunteered to fight against Japan with the United States Air Force, but before his application was considered the war with Japan had ended. On 1 February 1946 he became a staff officer at the HQ of British Air Forces of Occupation in Germany. Despite offers to remain in the West, Skalski returned to Poland on 8 June 1947, serving as a Piloting Technique

Inspector at the HQ of the Polish People's Air Force. He was arrested on 4 June 1948 under fabricated charges of spying. He was tortured and on 7 April 1950 sentenced to death, spending almost eight years in prison. During his stay in prison he wrote the book *Black Crosses over Poland*. On 11 April 1956 he was released after a decision by the Supreme Military Court, and was also rehabilitated. Skalski returned to the Polish People's Air Force and held various posts, such as Chief of the Testing Department, Piloting Techniques Inspector and Air Training Inspector. He trained and later flew jet fighter aircraft. On 30 June 1959 he married Maria Janina Sobiczewska, but their marriage did not last. Between 1968 and 1970 he was Secretary General of the Aero Club of Poland, and from 1970 until 1972 its Vice-President. He retired in 1972 and was promoted to the rank of General Brigadier in 1988. Skalski was also involved in politics, being a candidate to the Polish Parliament. In 1990 during a visit to Germany he met Fritz Wimmer and the brother of Siegfried von Heymann, two members of the crew of the Hs 126 whom he had helped on 1 September 1939. Stanisław Skalski died aged 88 on 12 November 2004 at the Military Hospital in Warsaw and was buried in Powązki Military Cemetery in Warsaw. There were two books published in Poland about his life - *Stanisław Skalski* by Katarzyna Ochabska in 2007 and *Generał pilot Stanisław Skalski, portet ze światłocieniem* by Grzegorz Sojda and Grzegorz Śliżewski in 2015 - followed by *Skalski Against all Odds: The First Allied Ace of the Second World War* by Franciszek Grabowski, published in 2017 in England. The MiG-29UB no. 4105 from the 22nd Tactical Air Base at Malbork has Skalski's portrait painted on its tail. There are streets in Toruń, Będzin, Gorzów Wielkopolski, Lubsko, Łowicz, Łódź, Pruszcz Gdański and Świdnik named after him, as well as the 22nd Tactical Air Base in Malbork, 32nd Centre of Command and Guidance in Cracow, Pomorze Aero Club, No. 10 High School in Zielona Góra, a bridge at Chełmno, park in Cracow and primary school at Polichno. He was decorated with the Golden Cross of Virtuti Militari no. 32, the Silver Cross of Virtuti Militari no. 8996, the Cross of Valour and three bars, the British Distinguished Service Order and the British Distinguished Flying Cross and two bars.

Date & Time	Unit	Aircraft	Score
01.09.1939 15.30	142nd Squadron	PZL P.11c	⅓-0-0 Hs 126 unconfirmed
02.09.1939	142nd Squadron	PZL P.11c	2-0-0 Do 17
03.09.1939	142nd Squadron	PZL P.11c	1¼-0-0 Hs 126
04.09.1939 07.00	142nd Squadron	PZL P.11c	0-0-⅓ Do 17

Date & Time	Unit	Aircraft	Score
04.09.1939 13.30	142nd Squadron	PZL P.11c	1-0-0 Ju 87
30.08.1940 11.20	501 Squadron	Hurricane I P2760 SD-B	1-0-0 He 111
30.08.1940 16.50	501 Squadron	Hurricane I P2760 SD-B	0-0-1 He 111
31.08.1940 13.15	501 Squadron	Hurricane I P5194 SD-J	1-0-0 Bf 109
01.09.1940 14.45	501 Squadron	Hurricane I N2329 SD-K	0-0-1 Bf 110
02.09.1940 08.50	501 Squadron	Hurricane I V7230 SD-H	2-0-0 Bf 109
05.09.1940 08.50	501 Squadron	Hurricane I V6644 SD-B	2-0-0 Bf 109 unconfirmed
08.11.1940 13.40	501 Squadron	Hurricane I V6723	⅔-0-0 Bf 109
24.07.1941 15.25	306 Squadron	Spitfire IIB P8549 UZ-K	1-0-0 Bf 109
19.08.1941 10.55	306 Squadron	Spitfire IIB P8531 UZ-Y	1-0-0 Bf 109
21.08.1941 14.00	306 Squadron	Spitfire IIB P8531 UZ-Y	0-1-0 Bf 109
17.09.1941 14.35	306 Squadron	Spitfire VB UZ-N	2-0-0 Bf 109
10.04.1942 17.40	316 Squadron	Spitfire VB BL646 SZ-R	1-0-0 Fw 190
25.04.1942 14.30	316 Squadron	Spitfire VB W3718 SZ-S	0-0-1 Bf 109
03.05.1942 16.05	316 Squadron	Spitfire VB BL646 SZ-R	0-1-0 Fw 190
28.03.1943 10.45	PFT	Spitfire IX EN459 ZX-1	1-0-0 Ju 88
02.04.1943 16.00	PFT	Spitfire IX EN459 ZX-1	1-0-0 Bf 109
04.04.1943 09.40	PFT	Spitfire IX EN315 ZX-6	1-0-0 Bf 109

06.05.1943 08.00	PFT	Spitfire IX EN267 ZX-5	0-0-1 Bf 109
24.06.1944 12.05	133 Wing	Mustang III FZ152 SS	2-0-0 Bf 109

HENRYK SKOWRON, Sergeant, was born on 26 May 1916 in Prądnik Czerwony near Cracow, in the part of Poland ruled by the Austro-Hungarian Empire. He grew up in the family of Stanisław and Anna. In September 1926 he began his education at the 4th Henryk Sienkiewicz Secondary School in Cracow, and in 1936 passed A-level exams. On 1 September 1936 he joined the Air Force Cadet Officers' School at Dęblin and was posted for the unitary course to the Infantry Cadet Officers' School at Komorowo. On 4 January 1937  Skowron returned to Dęblin. On 8 March 1938 he became ill and was sent to No. 1 Regional Hospital in Warsaw. Despite returning to Dęblin on 15 April, after being away for a month he was unable to keep up with the rest of his class and on 25 May was released from the school. The next day he joined the 2nd Air Regiment at Cracow and was posted to the Training Flight, but on 1 June he was transferred to the 22nd Light Bomber Squadron. On 25 July he left the 2nd Regiment after completing his compulsory military service, going to work for the Polish National Railways. On 22 June 1939 he was called up for military exercises and attached to the 23rd Accompanying Squadron of the 2nd Air Regiment at Cracow. He completed his training on 1 August, and soon after was mobilized and rejoined the 2nd Air Regiment. After the fall of Poland he travelled to France and then to Britain. On 13 March 1940 he reported at RAF Manston, a satellite base for the Polish Air Force Centre at Eastchurch. He received the service number 781238 and the rank of Sergeant. On 21 October 1940 he was posted to No. 303 (Polish) 'Tadeusz Kościuszko. City of Warsaw' Squadron at Leconfield. Some sources state that he arrived there from No. 151 Squadron, but there is no confirmation of his attachment to this British squadron. On 8 November he was posted for further training to No. 56 Operational Training Unit, then on 9 December returned to No. 303 Squadron. There is again information that on 2 February 1941 Skowron was posted to No. 151 Squadron, but the squadron's documents do not confirm this. It is believed that instead he was posted to the Polish Air Force Centre at Blackpool. On 8 April he went to No. 10 Air Observers

School at Dumfires, and was killed on 18 July at 18.30 during a training flight. The Fairey Battle I L5775 that he piloted crashed into the sea near Blackhaw Bank in the Solway Firth, Scotland ,killing Skowron and Leading Aircraftman William Weatherburn. He was buried in St Andrews Cemetery, Dumfires, in grave no. 240. He is commemorated on the Polish Air Force Memorials at Northolt and Warsaw-Mokotów.

JERZY JAKUB SOLAK, Pilot Officer, called 'Jersey' or 'George', was born on 22 August 1910 at the Reyów estate in Przecław near Mielec, in part of Poland ruled by the Austro-Hungarian Empire. He grew up in the family of Jakub, the estate administrator, and Maria Karolina née Koller. His older brother Bolesław Jan Solak was later a well-known aviation constructor and test pilot. During the war Bolesław served as radio and communication officer of Nos 300 and 301 (Polish) Squadrons, and also worked at the Royal Aircraft Establishment at Farnborough on new methods of bombardment and new radio and radar systems. Jerzy Solak moved with his family to Bukowina, and in 1920 to Lwów. In 1928 he graduated from the 9th Humanistic Secondary School in Lwów, passing A-level exams, and was accepted by Lwów Technical University at the Civil Engineering Faculty & Water Engineering, where he completed studies in 1933. During his studies he joined Lwów Aero Club. He joined the Air Force Reserve Cadet Officers' School at Dęblin and was commissioned in 1934. He was formally attached to the Training Flight of the 6th Air Regiment at Lwów. Together with his brother he regularly participated in various aviation competitions, gaining fourth, third and second places in National Aviation Championships in 1935, 1936 and 1937 respectively. Between September 1937 and September 1938 he was employed as a construction manager at a bishop's estate in Lwów, and from September 1938 until the outbreak of war was the main engineer at Kocimski Ltd. During the summer of 1937 he took part in an Air Meeting in Switzerland, then in 1939, together with his brother Bolesław, in similar competition in England, returning to Poland only a few days before the outbreak of war. He was mobilized to the 6th Air Regiment and posted to the Training Flight, and then to No. 1 Initial Flying School at Brzeżany as an aerobatics instructor. After the fall of Poland, on 17 September he flew in a PWS-26 to Cernâuti in Rumania. He was held in Foscani camp, from where he escaped, and in Bucharest was involved in organizing transports for Polish airmen to France.

After arriving in France he was posted to Le Bourget, but had no further postings, so decided to sail for England on 8 February 1940. After receiving the service number 76766 and the rank of Pilot Officer, he was posted to the Polish Air Force Centre at Eastchurch, being moved to Blackpool on 30 May. After completing elementary training on 22 July he was posted to No. 7 Operational Training Unit at Hawarden. On 28 August Solak was posted to No. 151 Squadron at Digby, then on 27 September to No. 249 Squadron at North Weald. He was known there for processing photographs taken by his colleagues. On 24 February 1941 he was transferred to No. 317 (Polish) 'City of Wilno' Squadron. On 18 December, during take-off in thick fog for an operational mission in Spitfire VB W3425, he crashed with another aircraft. Solak was injured, but Flying Officer Marian Sikorski was killed. On 16 June 1942 he was transferred to No. 164 Squadron, and on 8 August to No. 609 Squadron. On 4 February 1943, at his own request, he was transferred to an Air Fighting Development Unit at Fulbeck. From 9 April he was attached to No. 41 Squadron, and on 4 June claimed the destruction of a Fw 190. On 25 October he was posted to the HQ of Fighter Command as Polish Liaison Officer, then on 4 April 1944 as an operations officer to the 9th Air Force of the United States Army Air Force. He was attached to the 48th Fighter Group, flying operational missions. He was shot down on 10 August by ground fire over Tinchebray in France in the Thunderbolt P-47D-22 42-26334 F4-V from the 492nd Fighter Squadron. With broken ribs and injuries to his arms and legs he was captured by the Germans and admitted to hospital in Paris. Solak managed to escape and reached the Allied lines. On 30 August he was back with the 48th Fighter Group. On 18 December he was transferred to the HQ of the Polish Air Force, and on 24 April 1945 he went to Blackpool. On 7 June he was appointed Polish Liaison Officer at No. 84 Group as part of the British Air Force of Occupation in Germany. He returned to Britain on 6 May 1946 and was posted to the Polish Fighter Station at Coltishal. He was released from the Polish Air Force with the rank of Flight Lieutenant and formed his own company rebuilding private houses in London destroyed during the war. In the spring of 1949 he emigrated to the United States and settled in New York, later moving to San Francisco. He designed many well-known buildings, including the Opera House and the tallest building in San Francisco. After retirement in 1990 he moved to Emeryville, California. Major Jerzy Solak died aged 91 on 5 February 2002 at Emeryville. He was decorated with the Silver Cross of Virtuti Militari no. 11122 and the Cross of Valour and two bars.

Date & Time	Unit	Aircraft	Score
04.06.1943 11.25	41 Squadron	Spitfire XII MB800 EB-B	1-0-0 Fw 190

STEFAN STEGMAN, Pilot Officer, was born on 15 October 1915 into a Polish family at Penza in the Russian Empire. After moving back to an independent Poland he graduated from secondary school in Koło, passing A-level exams in 1933. In 1937 he graduated from the Construction High School at Grudziądz. After completing a unitary course at the Engineering Cadet Officers' School in Warsaw, on 2 January 1938 he joined the Air Force Cadet Officers' School at Dęblin. During the summer of 1939 he completed an Advanced Flying Course at Ułęż, and without official graduation after two years instead of

From left: Plt Off Jerzy Popławski and Plt Off Stefan Stegman.

three was commissioned with the 13th class. He achieved the rank of Sub-Lieutenant in September. He was evacuated to Rumania with the personnel of No. 1 Air Force Training Centre at Dęblin. In Balchik, Stegman and another pilot Konrad Stembrowicz were followed by a German spy. During a fight the German was accidently killed by the Poles. Stegman sailed from Balchik to Beirut on the *Patris*, and then travelled on the *Ville de Strasbourg* to France, arriving in Marseilles on 29 October. He decided to continue his journey, and in January 1940 arrived in England. He received the service number 76711 and the rank of Pilot Officer. Initially he was posted to the Polish Air Force Centre at Eastchurch, and in May transferred to Blackpool. On 25 July he was posted to No. 15 Elementary Flying Training School at Carlisle, then to No. 1 School of Army Co-operation at Old Sarum and finally to No. 5 Operational Training Unit at Aston Down. On 11 September Stegman joined No. 111 Squadron at Croydon, and was then posted to No. 229 Squadron at Northolt on 5 October. He joined No. 316 (Polish) 'City of Warsaw' Squadron on 22 March 1941, and in November was transferred to No. 58 Operational Training Unit at Grangemouth as a flying instructor. On 24 April 1942 he was back with No. 316 Squadron, and in March 1943 was appointed 'B' Flight commander. He was shot down by German fighters and killed over the sea, off Bruges, at 09.45 on 17 June 1943 while flying the Spitfire F.IX BR143 SZ-Q during Operation Circus 311. His body was washed ashore on 3 July and he was buried at the British Military Cemetery in Ostend, Belgium, in grave no. 20, row 5, plot 9B. Flight Lieutenant Stefan Stegman was decorated with the Cross of Valour and bar. He is commemorated on the Polish Air Force Memorials at Northolt and Warsaw-Mokotów.

MICHAŁ JAN STĘBOROWSKI, Flight Lieutenant, was born on 7 June 1909 at Regnów near Rawa Mazowiecka, in part of Poland ruled by the Russian Empire. He grew up in the family of Michał and Julia née Sumińska. He attended the Bolesław Prus State Humanistic Secondary School at Skierniewice, in 1929 passing A-level exams. On 16 October 1929 he joined a unitary course at the 31st Regiment of Kaniów Fusiliers, then on 25 November was transferred to the Infantry Cadet Officers' School at Różan. Upon completion on 27 July 1930 he was posted to the 61st Infantry Regiment at Bydgoszcz, but on 13 October was transferred to the Air Force Cadet

Officers' School at Dęblin. He was commissioned on 15 August 1932 with the 6th class as an observer, and with the rank of Sub-Lieutenant was posted to the 11th Light Bomber Squadron of the 1st Air Regiment at Warsaw. On 2 May 1933 he was posted to the Air Force Training Centre at Dęblin for a flying course. Upon completion on 14 August he returned to the 11th Squadron, but on 1 October 1933 he was transferred to 113th Fighter Squadron of the 1st Air Regiment. On 4th May 1934 posted for an Advanced Flying Course to Grudziądz, from where he returned on 16 July 1934. He was appointed Technical Officer of the 113th Squadron and held this post until 22 November. On 12 March 1936 he was once more sent to Dęblin, where he participated in an instructors' course. Stęborowski returned to the 113th Squadron on 7 April, but on 25 May was appointed as a fighter instructor at the Advanced Flying Course at Grudziądz, where he remained until the outbreak of war (in 1939 the school was moved to Ułęż). During the Polish Campaign of 1939 he joined the ad hoc-formed instructors' flight to defend Dęblin and Ułęż, flying obsolete PZL P.7s. On 8 September he was evacuated to Radziechów and then towards the Rumanian border. He led a group of airmen who were sent to Rumania on 17 September to collect British aircraft which were supposed to be waiting there, but was interned at the Babadag and Tulcea camps. After escaping on 5 October he travelled via Yugoslavia and Greece to Marseilles in France, where he arrived on 16 October. On 18 October he went to Bessieres, and on 26 November to Le Bourget. He volunteered to join the Polish Air Force in Britain, and on 8 March 1940 arrived at the Polish Air Force Centre at Eastchurch. He received the service number 76794 and the rank of Flying Officer. In May he was transferred to Blackpool, then on 4 July to No. 1 School of Army Co-operation at Old Sarum. Subsequently he was posted to No. 5

Operational Training Unit at Aston Down. Initially he was considered for No. 303 (Polish) 'Tadeusz Kościuszko. City of Warsaw' Squadron which was about to be formed at Northolt, and also for No. 302 (Polish) 'City of Poznań' Squadron at Leconfield. Instead, on 5 August he joined No. 238 Squadron at Tangmere. Three days later he claimed his only victory, the destruction of a Bf 110. He was shot down and killed on 11 August at 10.45 in his Hurricane I P3819 during combat over Portland. His body was never found. Michał Stęborowski was the second Polish pilot killed during the Battle of Britain. He was decorated with the Cross of Valour. He is commemorated on the Polish Air Force Memorials at Northolt and Warsaw-Mokotów, but also on the memorial plaque in the Church of Our Lady Mary in Skierniewice. One of the streets in this home town was also named after him.

Date & Time	Unit	Aircraft	Score
08.08.1940 12.30	238 Squadron	Hurricane I P3919	1-0-0 Bf 109

FRANCISZEK SURMA, Pilot Officer, was born on 1 July 1916 at Głębocz village near Jastrzębie Zdrój, Silesia, in part of Poland ruled by the German Empire. He grew up in the family of Franciszek and Tekla née Wodecka. He graduated from the primary school at Gołkowice, and then between 1928 and 1932 completed the Karol Miarka Town Coeducational Secondary School in Żory. In 1932 he was transferred to Cadet Corps No. 3 at Rawicz, and in 1936 passed A-level exams. He volunteered for the Polish Armed Forces and from 1 September 1936 took a unitary course at the Infantry Cadet Officers' School at Różan. On 4 January 1937 he joined the Air Force Cadet Officers' School at Dęblin, and between April and June 1939 undertook an Advanced Flying Course at Ułęż. Before official graduation the whole 12th class completed their training, and due to the dangerous political situation all cadets were sent to various regiments. On 18 June 1939 Surma was posted to the 121st Fighter Squadron of the 2nd Air Regiment at Cracow. He was commissioned during the Polish Campaign of 1939 with effect from 1 August. During the campaign his unit supported the 'Cracow' Army. On 2 September he participated in the destruction of a Ju 87, however his claim was never accepted. Next day he was engaged in combat with an He 111 and his aircraft was damaged. After the fall of Poland, on 18 September he crossed the Rumanian border at Śniatyń and travelled to France, arriving at Marseilles on 29 October. He decided to continue his journey to England, and on 27 January 1940 left France. Upon arrival in England he went to the Polish Air Force Centre at Eastchurch, receiving the service number 76713 and the rank of Pilot Officer. In May he was transferred to Blackpool, and on 3 July to No. 15 Elementary Flying Training School at Carlisle, from where on 18 July he was posted to No. 6 Operational Training Unit at Sutton Bridge. On 5 August he joined No. 151 Squadron at Martlesham Heath, and on 30 August claimed the probable destruction of an He 111. On 11 September Surma was posted to No. 607 Squadron at Tangmere, and on 26 September he destroyed a Bf 109. On 18 October he was posted to No. 46 Squadron at Stapleford, but two days later he went to No. 257 Squadron at North Weald. On 28 October Surma damaged a He 111. The day after he was shot down in combat over North Weald in his Hurricane I P3893, baling out safely. On 6 December he crash-landed in Clacton in his Hurricane I V7052. On 12 December he was transferred to No. 242 Squadron, then on 13 March 1941 he joined No. 308 (Polish) 'City of Cracow' Squadron. On 26 March he reported the shared probable destruction of a Ju 88. Due to engine failure, on 11 May he baled out from his Spitfire I R6644 ZF-H. On 27 June he destroyed one Bf 109 on the ground and another probably. Later he reported several more aerial claims. On 22 July he destroyed a Bf 109, on 16 September he shot down one more Bf 109, followed by another two Bf 109s on 20 September. On 27th September he probably destroyed a further Bf 109, and finally on 12 October he claimed one more Bf 109. On 8 November, during an encounter with enemy fighters, he left his formation in the Spitfire VB AB930 ZF-J off Dunkirk and was never seen again. His body was lost at sea. He is commemorated on the Polish Air Force Memorials at Northolt and Warsaw-Mokotów, and the secondary school at Gołkowice was named after him. Flying Officer Surma was decorated with the Silver Cross of Virtuti Militari no. 9239 and the Cross of Valour and two bars.

Date & Time	Unit	Aircraft	Score
02.09.1939 16.20	121st Squadron	PZL P.11c	1/7-0-0 Ju 87 unconfirmed
30.08.1940 16.20	151 Squadron	Hurricane I	0-1-0 He 111
26.09.1940 16.10	607 Squadron	Hurricane I	1-0-0 Bf 109

Date & Time	Unit	Aircraft	Score
28.10.1940 10.50	257 Squadron	Hurricane I P3893	0-0-1 He 111
26.03.1941 12.00	308 Squadron	Hurricane I V6999	0-⅓-0 Ju 88
22.07.1941 13.50	308 Squadron	Spitfire IIB P8317 ZF-C	1-0-0 Bf 109
16.09.1941 18.30	308 Squadron	Spitfire VB AB930 ZF-J	1-0-0 Bf 109
20.09.1941 16.00	308 Squadron	Spitfire VB AB825	2-0-0 Bf 109 officially 1-1-0 Bf 109
27.09.1941 14.25	308 Squadron	Spitfire VB AB825	0-1-0 Bf 109
12.10.1941 12.35	308 Squadron	Spitfire VB AB825	1-0-0 Bf 109

WILHELM SZAFRANIEC, Sergeant, was born on 1 December 1915 in Cracow, in part of Poland ruled by the Austro-Hungarian Empire. He completed primary education in his home town and started studying at the Jagiellonian University in Cracow. In 1937 he completed the Air Force Reserve Cadet Officers' School in Dęblin. He was mobilized in September 1939 and joined the Reserve Squadron of the 2nd Air Regiment in Cracow. Other sources state that he was mobilized to the 3rd Air Regiment at Poznań and attached to the 3rd Air Base personnel. After the fall of Poland he was evacuated to Rumania, from where he travelled to France. At the beginning of 1940 he went to England, where he received the service number 781312 and the rank of Sergeant. Initially he was stationed at Eastchurch, but in May 1940 was posted to the Polish Air Force Centre at Blackpool. After initial and operational training in early September he joined No. 79 Squadron at Pembrey, then on 12 September he was posted to No. 151 Squadron at Digby. On 29 September Szafraniec was transferred to No. 607 Squadron at Tangmere, and then on 14 October to No. 56 Squadron at Boscombe Down. On 23 November he collided in mid-air with Pilot Officer Thomas Guest and was killed in his Hurricane I V7569, which went down at Andover. Guest escaped unhurt. Szafraniec was buried in Amesbury Cemetery, Wiltshire. He was commissioned posthumously on 15 August 1941. He is commemorated on the Polish Air Force Memorials at Northolt and Warsaw-Mokotów.

EUGENIUSZ MIROSŁAW SZAPOSZNIKOW, Sergeant, called 'Szaposzka' or 'Gen', was born on 17 July 1916 in Warsaw, in part of Poland ruled by the Russian Empire, into the family of Jan Szaposznikow. His mother died when he was aged 6. In 1930 he completed his primary education and for the next two years attended the State Trade School, and during the following two years evening classes at the Industrial School. He was interested in car mechanics, but decided to pursue a military career. On 1 March 1935 he joined the 1st Air Regiment at Warsaw, where between September and November 1936 he completed initial flying training, followed by advanced training  between April and July 1937 at the Advanced Flying Course at Grudziądz. From 1 August 1938 he served in the 111th Fighter Squadron of the 1st Air Regiment at Warsaw. In October he flew with his unit to Aleksandrowice due to the annexation of the Zaolzie region. During the Polish Campaign in 1939 he participated in operational missions, with his unit attached to the Pursuit Brigade. On 1 September he reported the probable destruction of an He 111; however, some sources state that on this day he was involved in the shared destruction of an He 111 and a Do 17. None of these claims were ever accepted. After the fall of Poland, together with the road party of III/1 Wing he crossed the Rumanian border at Śniatyń on 18 September. In his memoirs he claimed that in fact he flew to Rumania. After a short internment in Rumania, on 15 October he arrived in France and was attached to the list of pilots who were supposed to form the 1st Polish Fighter Squadron under the command of Lieutenant Colonel Leopold Pamuła. Szaposznikow was briefly assigned to the 5th Section, commanded by Lieutenant Arsen Cebrzyński. Later he was considered for the Polish fighter section formed to defend Nantes, but eventually joined the Polish fighter section commanded by Cebrzyński and on 18 May 1940 was attached to GCII/6 at Beauvais. Szaposznikow flew Bloch MB 152s, his personal aircraft having the name 'Iraś' painted on its fuselage, which probably referred to his girlfriend Irena who had stayed in Warsaw. On 15 June he participated in the shared destruction of an Hs 126. On 24 June he boarded the *Apapa* at Port-Vendres and sailed to Britain, arriving on 6 July. He received the service number 793414 and the rank of Sergeant. On 2 September he joined No. 303 (Polish) 'Tadeusz Kościuszko. City of Warsaw' Squadron at Northolt. On 31 August he shot down a Bf 109, followed by a double score on 7 September when he claimed the destruction of a Do 215 and a Bf 109. Four days later Szaposznikow added two Bf 110s, on 23 September one Bf 109, another Bf 109 on 27 September and finally on 7 October he claimed one Bf 109 destroyed and another damaged. On 14 May 1941 he was posted to No. 8 Service Flying Training School at Montrose, where he served as a flying instructor. After completing an officers' course he was commissioned on 1 November . On 2 February 1942 he joined No. 2 (Service) Flying Training School, and on 1 April No. 16 (Polish) Service Flying Training School at Newton. He was arrested and imprisoned for a month for not informing the Polish authorities about his marriage to his girlfriend Olive. Later he was posted to No. 2 Advanced Flying Unit, from where on 14 November 1943 he was posted to No. 316 (Polish) 'City of Warsaw' Squadron. On 21 December 1943 he rejoined No. 303 Squadron, with whom on 8 April 1944 he had a take-off accident when his Spitfire VB AD237 RF-W was hit on the ground by another aircraft piloted by Flying Officer Ludwik Kraszewski. Both pilots escaped unhurt. On 6 July Szaposznikow took command of 'A' Flight. He left No. 303 Squadron on 17 October, and on 14 November once again joined No. 16 (Polish) Service Flying Training School at Newton, where he remained as an instructor until September 1946. He commanded a Training Flight there. He was demobilized with the rank of Flight Lieutenant and settled in Britain. After changing his name to Eugene Sharman he lived in Nottingham, where initially he was sweeping floors, then worked for a gas company. Together with his wife he opened a mushroom business and ran a public house in Matlock. Eugeniusz Szaposznikow died on 8 July 1991 in Nottingham. He was decorated with the Silver Cross of Virtuti Militari no. 8828, the Cross of Valour and three bars and the British Distinguished Flying Medal.

Date & Time	Unit	Aircraft	Score
01.09.1939 08.50	111th Squadron	PZL P.11c	0-1-0 or ½-0-0 He 111 unconfirmed
01.09.1939 10.30	111th Squadron	PZL P.11c	⅙-0-0 Do 17 unconfirmed
15.06.1940 19.00	GCII/6	Bloch MB 152 no. 622 '15'	⅓-0-0 Hs 126

Date & Time	Unit	Aircraft	Score
31.08.1940 18.25	303 Squadron	Hurricane I V7242 RF-B	1-0-0 Bf 109
07.09.1940 17.00	303 Squadron	Hurricane I V7244 RF-C	1-0-0 Do 17 claimed as Do 215
07.09.1940 17.00	303 Squadron	Hurricane I V7244 RF-C	1-0-0 Bf 109
11.09.1940 16.00	303 Squadron	Hurricane I V7244 RF-C	2-0-0 Bf 110
23.09.1940 10.00	303 Squadron	Hurricane I V7244 RF-C	1-0-0 Bf 109
27.09.1940 15.25	303 Squadron	Hurricane I V7244 RF-C	1-0-0 Bf 109
07.10.1940 13.50	303 Squadron	Hurricane I V7244 RF-C	1-0-1 Bf 109

HENRYK SZCZĘSNY, Flying Officer, called 'Hesio' (Polish diminutive of his first name), 'Sneezy' or 'Henry the Pole', was born on 27 March 1909 at Ruszkowo village in the Warsaw district, Mazovia, in the part of Poland ruled by the Russian Empire. He grew up in the family of Stanisław and Marianna née Werc. He completed basic education and graduated from the secondary school at Pułtusk, and in 1930 passed A-level exams. In 1930 he joined the Polish Armed Forces and completed a unitary course at the Infantry Cadet Officers' School at Różan. On 5 October 1931 he went to  the Air Force Cadet Officers' School at Dęblin, from which with the 7th class he graduated as an observer on 15 August 1933. After being commissioned, Sub-Lieutenant Szczęsny was posted to the 51st Light Bomber Squadron of the 5th Air Regiment at Lida. In January 1934 he was transferred to the 54th Light Bomber Squadron of the same regiment. In 1934 he also completed a flying course at the Air Force Officers' Training Centre at Dęblin, followed by the Advanced Flying Course at Grudziądz in 1935. In 1936 he was posted to he 133rd Fighter Squadron of the 3rd Air Regiment at Poznań. In August 1938 he took command of the 2nd platoon of the Training Flight. In January 1939 Szczęsny was transferred to an Advanced Flying Course at Grudziądz, where he remained as a flying instructor. Later he moved with the school to Ułęż. During the Polish Campaign of 1939 he served as pilot in the ad hoc-formed instructors flight also known as the 'Dęblin Group' that was defending Ułęż and Dęblin. On 2 September, flying an obsolete PZL P.7a, he probably destroyed one Do 17 and damaged another, then on 3 September he claimed the destruction of a Ju 87 and damage of another 'Stuka'. On 14 September, flying a PZL P.11g Kobuz prototype, he shot down an He 111, followed by another He 111 the next day. At this time he was wounded in a leg. On 17 September he was evacuated by the crew of a PZL P.37 'Łoś' bomber from the 216th Bomber Squadron commanded by Lieutenant Zygmunt Szymański, and was hospitalized in Bucharest. On board the *Patris* he sailed from Balchik, and via Malta arrived at Marseilles on 12 November. He decided to continue his journey and left France, arriving in England in February 1940. He received the service number 76781 and the rank of Flying Officer. Initially he was posted to the Polish Air Force Centre at Eastchurch, and was later transferred to RAF Manston, where he commanded a platoon of cadets. In May he went to Blackpool, then on 15 July was posted to No. 1 School of Army Co-operation at Old Sarum. From there he was posted to No. 5 Operational Training Unit at Aston Down. He was initially considered to join No. 302 (Polish) 'City of Poznań' Squadron at Leconfield, but instead on 5 August he joined No. 74 Squadron at Hornchurch. He claimed several victories while flying with this unit. On 13 August he shot down a Do 17, but while landing at West Malling damaged his Spitfire I K9871 ZP-O. On 11 September he shot down a Bf 110, and on 5 October shared the victory of a Do 215. After the Battle of Britain Szczęsny added several more kills. On 1 December he destroyed a Bf 109, followed by damaging another Bf 109 the next day, and on 5 December he shot down a further Bf 109. On 12 December he was transferred to No. 257 Squadron, but on 19 December joined No. 302 (Polish) 'City of Poznań' Squadron. On 24 February 1941 he was posted to No. 317 (Polish) 'City of Wilno' Squadron, where he took command of 'B' Flight. On 10 July he shared the victory of a Bf 109, and four days later shared another victory, this time of a Ju 88. He was appointed squadron commander on 20 August, and kept this post until 28 February 1942. After leaving No. 317 Squadron, from 7 March he was Polish Liaison Officer at the HQ of No. 10 Group, and on 12 May transferred to the HQ of No. 12 Group. He returned to operational flying on 28 December as Squadron Leader Flying - deputy commander of No. 1 Polish Fighter Wing. On 4 April 1943 he participated in combat over Rouen in his Spitfire IX BS541 PK-U and shot down one Fw 190, but he collided in mid-air with another Fw 190 (which was added to his score). Szczęsny baled out and was captured by the Germans. He was initially held at an airfield near

Dunkirk, and was later transferred to the Dulag Luft at Oberusel Wetzlar and was hospitalized at Hohemark. Eventually he was transported to Stalag Luft 3 at Sagan (Żagań), where he remained until the end of hostilities. On 9 May 1945 he returned to England and was posted to the Polish Air Force Centre at Blackpool. Later he went to No. 12 Group, where he served as Polish Liaison Officer until 1946. He was demobilized with the rank of Squadron Leader and joined the RAF. Szczęsny received the service number 500158 and served in administration at RAF Hereford. He retired on 27 March 1965. His son, an airline pilot, was killed in a flying accident. Lieutenant Colonel Szczęsny died aged 87 on 25 July 1996 in London and was buried in Gunnersbury Cemetery. He was decorated with the Silver Cross of Virtuti Militari no. 9116, the Cross of Valour and three bars and the British Distinguished Flying Cross.

Date & Time	Unit	Aircraft	Score
02.09.1939	Instructors Flight	PZL P.7	0-1-1 Do 17
03.09.1939	Instructors Flight	PZL P.7	1-0-1 Ju 87
14.09.1939	Instructors Flight	PZL P.11g Kobuz	1-0-0 He 111
15.09.1939	Instructors Flight	PZL P.11g Kobuz	1-0-0 He 111
13.08.1940 07.00	74 Squadron	Spitfire I K9871 ZP-O	1-0-0 Do 17
11.09.1940 16.00	74 Squadron	Spitfire I X4167	1-0-0 Bf 110
05.10.1940 14.05	74 Squadron	Spitfire II P7363	⅓-0-0 Do 17 claimed as Do 215
01.12.1940 12.00	74 Squadron	Spitfire II P7363	1-0-0 Bf 109
02.12.1940 11.40	74 Squadron	Spitfire II P7363	0-0-1 Bf 109
05.12.1940 15.30	74 Squadron	Spitfire II P7363	1-0-0 Bf 109
10.07.1941 12.48	317 Squadron	Hurricane I W9272 JH-S	½-0-0 Bf 109

Date & Time	Unit	Aircraft	Score
14.07.1941 16.20	317 Squadron	Hurricane I W9272 JH-S	½-0-0 Ju 88
04.04.1943	1 Wing	Spitfire IX BS514 PK-U	2-0-0 Fw 190

JÓZEF AUGUSTYN SZLAGOWSKI, Sergeant, was born on 5 January 1914 at Kościerzyna in Kashubia, in part of Poland ruled by the German Empire. He grew up in the family of Feliks Teofil, a Polish National Railway Station Manager, and Franciszka. In 1927 he completed seven years of primary education, then in 1930 three years of trade school as an electrician with a specialization of repairing electrical engines. Between 1930 and 1934 he worked at the town's Power Station at Kędzierzyna. Conscripted in 1934, he was sent  to the 4th Air Regiment at Toruń, where between September 1936 and July 1937 he completed a flying course and afterwards was sent to Grudziądz for an Advanced Flying Course. In 1937 he went to the Air Force Cadet Officers' School at Dęblin, where until the outbreak of war he remained as a flying instructor. During the Polish Campaign of 1939 he served as a pilot of the ad hoc-formed instructors flight also known as the 'Dęblin Group' defending Ułęż and Dęblin. After the fall of Poland he was evacuated to Rumania, from where via Beirut he travelled to Marseilles in France. He was stationed at the Polish Air Force Training Centre at Lyon-Bron. Szlagowski volunteered to join the Polish Air Force being re-formed in Britain, and on 9 March 1940 sailed across the Channel. Upon arrival he received the service number 780712 and the rank of Leading Aircraftman. In May he was transferred to Blackpool. In early July he went to No. 15 Elementary Flying Training School at Carlisle, then on 20 July to No. 5 Operational Training Unit at Aston Down. Initially he was considered for a posting to No. 302 (Polish) 'City of Poznań' Squadron at Leconfield, but instead he joined No. 234 Squadron at St Eval on 3 August. On 8 August he crash-landed in his Spitfire I N3278 at Pensilva near Liskeard, but escaped unhurt. Next day he damaged a Do 17, which he reported as a Do 215, then on 4 September shot down a Bf 110 and a Do 17. On 5 October Szlagowski was transferred to No. 152 Squadron at Warmwell. On 4 March 1941 he was transferred to No. 303 (Polish) 'Tadeusz

Kościuszko. City of Warsaw' Squadron, with whom on 15 May he crash-landed his Spitfire IIA P8085 RF-J. On 22 June he was involved in a mid-air collision with a Spitfire piloted by Pilot Officer Maciej Lipiński: both pilots survived and Szlagowski was able to return to base in his Spitfire II P8189 RF-J. The day after he claimed the probable destruction of a Bf 109. On 25 June he went to No. 1 Air Gunners School as a staff pilot, and on 16 July had to make an emergency landing in his Henley L3382 due to engine failure. On 23 December he went on an instructors' course at the Central Flying School at Upavon. On 2 March 1942 he went to No. 16 (Polish) Service Flying Training School at Newton, where he served as a ground controller and later as a flying instructor. Upon completion of a twin-engine course he became an instructor on this type of aircraft. He was married and had a son, followed by a daughter in 1943. On 29 April 1942 he had another flying accident when the engine failed on the Airspeed Oxford X7251. Szlagowski and his pupil, Sergeant Stanisław Piasecki, escaped unhurt. He remained at Newton until demobilization in 1946. He left the service with the rank of Warrant Officer and decided to stay in Britain. Joseph Szlagowski, as he was later known, worked for the Wilkinson Sword company and died on 4 December 1993 in London. He was decorated with the Cross of Valour.

Date & Time	Unit	Aircraft	Score
09.08.1940 14.15	234 Squadron	Spitfire I R6985	0-0-1 Do 215 claimed as Do 17
04.09.1940 13.15	234 Squadron	Spitfire I X4251	1-0-0 Bf 110
04.09.1940 13.30	234 Squadron	Spitfire I X4251	1-0-0 Do 17
23.06.1941 20.30	303 Squadron	Spitfire II P8385 RF-A	0-1-0 Bf 109

WŁADYSŁAW SZULKOWSKI, Flying Officer, was born on 6 November 1909 at Goworowo village, near Ostrołęka, Warsaw Voivodship, in part of Poland ruled by the Russian Empire. He grew up in the family of Roch and Katarzyna née Jarka. After completing basic education he graduated from the secondary school, passing A-level exams. In 1930 and 1931 he completed an infantry cadet officers' course, and in September 1931 was attached to the second term of the Air Force Cadet Officers' School at Dęblin. He was commissioned as an observer with the 7th class, and with the rank of Sub-Lieutenant was posted to the 53rd Light Bomber Squadron of the 5th Air Regiment at Wilno. He decided to pursue a pilot's career, and during the autumn of 1933 completed a gliding course, followed by a flying course which he undertook in spring and summer 1934 at the Air Force Officer's Training Centre at Dęblin. On returning to the 5th Air Regiment in October 1934 he was attached to the 56th Light Bomber Squadron. In 1935 Szulkowski completed an Advanced Flying Course at Grudziądz and was posted to the 55th Light Bomber Squadron of the 5th Air Regiment. In December he received a posting to the 143rd Fighter Squadron of the 4th Air Regiment at Toruń. In 1939 he went to Ułęż, where he was appointed a flying instructor for the Advanced Flying Course. During the Polish

Flg Off Władysław Szulkowski (right) with Flg Off Ron Wigg

Campaign of 1939 he served as a pilot in the ad hoc-formed instructors' flight also known as the 'Dęblin Group' that defended Ułęż and Dęblin. After the fall of Poland he was evacuated to Rumania, and from there to France. He decided to continue his journey to England, and upon arrival received the service number 76747 and the rank of Flying Officer. He was initially posted to the Polish Air Force Centre at Eastchurch, but in May transferred to Blackpool. In early July he started basic training at No. 15 Elementary Flying Training School at Carlisle, from where on 20 July he was transferred to No. 5 Operational Training Unit at Aston Down. Szulkowski joined No. 65 Squadron on 5 August. On 22 August he claimed the destruction of a Bf 109. He suffered injuries after a landing accident in the Spitfire I R6987 on 26 November. On 21 January 1941 he was posted to No. 315 (Polish) 'City of Dęblin' Squadron. On 27 March, while flying in the Hurricane I V7188 PK-X and returning from an operational mission, he collided over the sea with Sergeant Edward Paterek at 25,000ft. Paterek's propeller blade hit Szulkowski's plane's tail and cut it off completely. Both aircraft went down into the sea near the Bar lightship in the River Mersey with the pilots still in their cockpits. Flight Lieutenant Szulkowski's body was washed up on the shore at Freshfield on 20 May. He was buried in West Derby Cemetery in Liverpool, in grave no. 392, row 11, plot RC. He was decorated with the Cross of Valour. He is commemorated on the Polish Air Force Memorials at Northolt and Warsaw-Mokotów. His younger brother, Sergeant Wacław Szulkowski, was a ground crew member of No. 300 (Polish) Mazovian Squadron.

Date & Time	Unit	Aircraft	Score
22.08.1940 17.00	65 Squadron	Spitfire I R6712 YT-N	1-0-0 Bf 109

Ś

LEON ŚWITOŃ, Sergeant, was born on 10 October 1915 at Osiek near Wieluń, in part of Poland ruled by the Russian Empire. He completed primary education followed by trade school, and graduated as a mechanic. He was employed as an aircraft mechanic and obtained his pilot's licence at Łódź Aero Club, where between 1 March 1937 and 1 February 1938 he was a flying instructor. Subsequently he went to No.1 Air Force Training Centre at Dęblin, where he also served as a flying instructor. He was later posted to the Air Force Training Centre at Krosno. He did not fly operationally during the Polish Campaign of 1939 as he was in charge of the evacuation of his  pupils from the Air Force NCO School for Minors at Krosno. He went to Rumania, from where he travelled to France. Świtoń decided to continue his journey to England, and in February 1940 was posted to the Polish Air Force Centre at Eastchurch. He received the service number 780519 and the rank of Leading Aircraftman. After completing initial training he was posted to No. 5 Operational Training Unit at Aston Down. Initially he was considered to be posted to No. 302 (Polish) 'City of Poznań' Squadron at Leconfield, but on 3 August he joined No. 54 Squadron at Hornchurch. On 16 August he was transferred to No. 303 (Polish) 'Tadeusz Kościuszko. City of Warsaw' Squadron at Northolt. On 29 December 1940 he went to No. 1 (Polish) Flying Training School at Hucknall, where as an instructor he served until 3 March 1941. He was then posted to No. 8 Service Flying Training School at Montrose, where he continued service as a flying instructor. On 26 March 1942 he went to Canada and was attached to No. 39 and then No. 34 Service Flying Training Schools at Medicine Hat and Swift Current respectively. On his return to England Świtoń participated in a refresher advanced flying course at No. 60 Operational Training Unit and was posted to No. 16 (Polish) Service Flying Training School at Newton, where as an instructor he remained until demobilization. He left military service in 1946 with the rank of Warrant Officer and emigrated to Argentina, settling in Empalme, Cordoba. He was employed there as a civilian airline pilot. He died at Empalme in Argentina on 13 July 1978 and was buried at Toledo Cemetery near Cordoba.

T

JULIUSZ TOPOLNICKI, Flying Officer, called 'Topola' (diminutive of his surname but also the Polish name for a poplar tree), was born on 7 March 1910 at Kiwerce in the region of Łuck, Volhynia, in part of Poland ruled by the Russian Empire. He grew up in a family of gentry with a long military tradition. His father Władysław was involved in building the Trans-Siberian Railway and subsequently worked as an engineer, then for the Ministry of Military Affairs and later commanding the Sappers School at Piastów. Juliusz completed National Agricultural School at Czernichów, passing A-level exams in 1931. In 1931 and 1932 he  completed course at the Infantry Cadet Officers' School at Śrem. After leaving he was posted to the Armoured Forces Training Centre in Warsaw and sent for training to the 4th Armoured Cars Squadron at Brześć on the Bug. Between 1 October 1932 and 10 August 1934 he attended the Cavalry Cadet Officers' School at Grudziądz, and after being commissioned went to the 3rd Mounted Fusiliers Regiment at Wołkowysk. On 1 September he joined a flying course at the Air Force Officers' Training Centre at Dęblin, and upon completion on 1 August 1935 he was posted to the 3rd Air Regiment at Poznań. Topolnicki joined the 34th Light Bomber Squadron, but on 1 May 1936 was sent on an Advanced Flying Course at Grudziądz. Upon completion he served as a fighter pilot of the 133rd Fighter Squadron of the 3rd Air Regiment. After disbandment of this unit in October 1937 he was posted to the 161st Fighter Squadron of the 6th Air Regiment at Lwów. In November he was appointed deputy commander of the squadron. In November 1938 he was reposted to the Air Force Cadet Officers' School at Dęblin and served as a flying instructor at the Borowina airfield. In 1939 he married Halina Bębenkowska. During the Polish Campaign of 1939 he was responsible of the evacuation of his pupils, although some sources state that he also served as a pilot of the ad hoc instructors' flight also known as the 'Dęblin Group' that was there to defend Ułęż and Dęblin. After an unsuccessful attempt to cross the Rumanian border on 19 September, he travelled via the Yablonitsky Pass to Hungary and was interned in Egër. Topolnicki escaped nine days later and travelled through Yugoslavia and Greece. He arrived at Marseilles in France on 16 October, and two days later was sent to Le Bourget. He decided to continue his journey to England, where he arrived on 27 January

1940. After receiving the service number 76722 and the rank of Flying Officer he was posted to the Polish Air Force Centre at Eastchurch, from where in May he went to Blackpool. On 17 July he joined No. 15 Elementary Flying Training School at Carlisle, then on 1 August went to No. 6 Operational Training Unit at Sutton Bridge. On 18 August he joined No. 601 Squadron at Tangmere. He claimed his only victory on 6 September against a Bf 109, but he was also wounded and shot down. Topolnicki baled out from his Hurricane 1 P3382 and landed in a tree at Staplehurst. His aircraft crashed at Boycourt Farm. The Polish pilot was taken to Leeds Castle hospital. He rejoined the squadron at his own request and flew again from 13 September. On 21 September at 11.25 he was about to take off from Exeter airfield when his Hurricane I L1894 crashed into an anti-aircraft post and exploded. He was killed in the wreckage. Juliusz Topolnicki was buried at the Catholic High Cemetery in Exeter, in section ZK, grave no. 32. He was the eighteenth Polish operational pilot killed during the Battle of Britain. He is commemorated on the Polish Air Force Memorials at Northolt and Warsaw-Mokotów, and was awarded the Cross of Valour.

Date & Time	Unit	Aircraft	Score
06.09.1940 09.30	601 Squadron	Hurricane I P3382	½-1-0 Bf 109

U

WITOLD ALEKSANDER URBANOWICZ, Flying Officer, Acting Squadron Leader, called 'Kobra' (Cobra), 'Le Kuto' (the French le Couteau, Knife), 'Polish Shark', 'Mister' or 'Anglik' (Englishman), was born on 30 March 1908 at Olszanka near Augustów in part of Poland ruled by the Russian Empire. He grew up in the farming family of Antoni and Bronisława née Jurewicz. After completing primary school in 1923 he was accepted to the secondary school

at Suwałki, and in 1925 to No. 2 Cadet Corps at Modlin and later at Chełmno. In 1930 he passed A-level exams and in September joined the Infantry Cadet Officers' School at Komorów. On 16th October 1930 however he was transferred to the Air Force Cadet Officers' School at Dęblin. Urbanowicz was commissioned as an observer on 15 August 1932 with the 7th class, and with the rank of Sub-Lieutenant was posted to the 213th Bomber Squadron of the

1st Air Regiment at Warsaw. Between 2 May and 14 August 1933 he completed a flying course at the Air Force Officers' School at Dęblin, then went to the 113th Fighter Squadron of the 1st Air Regiment. Between May and August 1934 he participated in an Advanced Flying Course at Grudziądz. From 19 March 1935 he was deputy commander of the 111th Fighter Squadron, and in August 1936 was sent to Sarny airfield, from where he claimed the destruction of a Soviet Polikarpow R-5 aircraft which violated Polish air space. On 10 October he had a serious landing accident in a PZL P.11a during the Central Fighter Competition, but escaped unhurt. On 1 November he was transferred to the Air Force Officers' Training Centre at Dęblin, where he remained as a flying instructor. On 12 January 1937 he had another landing accident in a PWS-16. He then served as a flying instructor at the Advanced Flying Course at Grudziądz, and consequently at Ułęż. In January 1939 he passed exams to the Polish Staff Academy in Warsaw. During the Polish Campaign of 1939 he served as a pilot of the ad hoc instructors' flight known as the 'Dęblin Group' to defend Ułęż and Dęblin, performing several operational sorties. Later he participated in the evacuation of the school and led his pupils towards the Rumanian border. Urbanowicz and a few of his pupils were ordered to collect British aircraft which were supposed to be waiting in Rumania. Despite crossing the border on 17 September, Urbanowicz decided to return to Poland and was captured by the Soviets. He managed to escape and was held in a Rumanian camp in Slatina. After escaping he travelled to Balchik, from where on board the *Aghios Nicolaos* he sailed for Beirut on 15 October. Two weeks later, on 29 October, he arrived at Marseilles in France. He was posted to Istres, where he commanded a group of cadets. Later he was transferred to Lyon-Bron, but decided to continue his journey to England. After arrival on 27 January 1940 he received the service number 76735 and the rank of Flying Officer. He was initially posted to the Polish Air Force Centre at Eastchurch, then in May was posted to Blackpool. On 4 July he went to No. 1 School of Army Co-operation at Old Sarum, then to No. 6 Operational Training Unit at Sutton Bridge. According to some sources, on 4 August he joined No. 601 Squadron at Tangmere, where on 8 August he claimed the destruction of a Bf 110. Then he joined No. 145 Squadron at Westhampnett, and on 11 August destroyed a Bf 109, which was eventually recorded as a Bf 110. The next day he shot down a Ju 88. After a brief attachment to No. 253 Squadron, on 21 August he was transferred to No. 303 (Polish) 'Tadeusz Kościuszko. City of Warsaw' Squadron at Northolt. Urbanowicz took command of 'A' Flight. On 6 September he shot down a Bf 109, and on the same day was appointed the Polish commander of No. 303 Squadron after Squadron Leader Zdzisław Krasnodębski was shot down and badly wounded. On 7 September he shot down a Do 17 and probably destroyed a Bf 109. On 15 September he claimed the destruction of two Dorniers, but his Hurricane I V6684 RF-F was damaged in combat. He claimed more victories during the Battle of Britain. On 26 September he destroyed an He 111, next day he claimed the destruction of one Bf 110, a Bf 109 and two Ju 88s, then on 30 September he shot down three Bf 109s and one Do 17. Urbanowicz became the top-scoring pilot of the Polish Air Force during the Battle of Britain and the second most successful Polish fighter pilot of the Second World War. Between 20-23 October he was briefly attached to No. 43 Squadron at Usworth, but on 11 November started duty as Polish Liaison Officer at the HQ of No. 11 Group. On 15 April 1941, as the first Polish officer, he took command of No. 1 Polish Fighter Wing, being heavily involved with its organization. On 1 June Urbanowicz was transferred to the Inspectorate of the Polish Air Force, but on 24 June left for Canada, where he was responsible for recruiting Americans and Canadians of Polish descent to join the Polish Air Force. He returned to England and on 27 July 1942 went to No. 2 Flying Instructors School at Montrose, followed by instructor's duty at No. 16 (Polish) Service Flying Training School at Newton, where he arrived on 25 October. Soon after, on 2 November, he returned to the Polish Inspectorate and was once more sent to North America, being appointed deputy air attaché of the Polish Embassy in Washington. In September 1943 he volunteered to fly at the Chinese-Japanese front, and thanks to General Claire Chennault between 23 October and 15 December flew operational missions with the 16th Fighter Squadron stationed at Chengkung, later being transferred to the 74th Fighter Squadron at Kunming and finally to the 75th Fighter Squadron of the 23rd Fighter Group at Heygyang. On 11 December he shot down two Nakajima K-43s, which were claimed as 'Zeros'. At the beginning of 1944 Urbanowicz returned to Britain, where he was posted to the HQ of the Polish Air Force, but in July he was reposted to Washington, where he took on the duty of air attaché. Despite completing his duty in August 1945 he stayed in the United States, as the British Parliament withdrew recognition of the Polish Government in exile. At his own request he was demobilized on 1 October with the rank of Acting Group Captain. With his wife Jadwiga and son Witold Kazimierz he settled at Queens, New York, and was employed by the American Oversees Airlines. He was also secretary of the YMCA. In 1947 he visited Poland and was arrested by the secret police. Upon his return to USA he worked for Eastern Airlines and the Republic Aircraft Corporation. During his free time he wrote wartime memoirs in the form of four books published in Poland. In 1995 Urbanowicz was promoted to the rank of General Brigadier of the Polish Air Force. He died aged 88 on 17 August 1996 in New York and was buried at Our Lady of Czestochowa Cemetery in Doylestown, Bucks County,

Pennsylvania. His decorations included the Silver Cross of Virtuti Militari no. 8820, the Cross of Valour and three bars and the British Distinguished Flying Cross. His biography by Wojciech Krajewski was published in Poland in 2008 under the title *Witold Urbanowicz - A Legend of Polish Wings*. The MiG-29A no. 40 from the 23rd Tactical Air Base at Mińsk Mazowiecki has his portrait painted on its tail. There are streets in Dęblin and Cracow named after him, as well as a roundabout at Suwałki and Radom and a primary school in his native Olszanka.

Date & Time	Unit	Aircraft	Score
08. or 09.1936	Border Defence Corps	PZL P.11c	1-0-0 R-5 unconfirmed
08.08.1940	601 Squadron	Hurricane I	1-0-0 Bf 109 unconfirmed
11.08.1940 10.30	145 Squadron	Hurricane I P3391	1-0-0 Bf 109 or Bf 110
12.08.1940 12.12	145 Squadron	Hurricane I R4177	1-0-0 Ju 88
06.09.1940 09.00	303 Squadron	Hurricane I V7242 RF-B	1-0-0 Bf 109 or Bf 110
07.09.1940 17.00	303 Squadron	Hurricane I R2685 RF-G	1-0-0 Do 17 claimed as Do 215
07.09.1940 17.00	303 Squadron	Hurricane I R2685 RF-G	0-1-0 Bf 109
15.09.1940 15.00	303 Squadron	Hurricane I V6684 RF-F	2-0-0 Do 17 claimed as Do 215
26.09.1940 16.30	303 Squadron	Hurricane I P3901 RF-E	1-0-0 He 111
27.09.1940 09.20	303 Squadron	Hurricane I P3901 RF-E	1-0-0 Bf 110 or Do 17
27.09.1940 09.20	303 Squadron	Hurricane I P3901 RF-E	1-0-0 Bf 109
27.09.1940 15.25	303 Squadron	Hurricane I P3901 RF-E	2-0-0 Ju 88
30.09.1940 13.35	303 Squadron	Hurricane I P3901 RF-E	2-0-0 Bf 109
30.09.1940 13.35	303 Squadron	Hurricane I P3901 RF-E	1-0-0 Do 17 claimed as Do 215

| 30.09.1940 16.35 | 303 Squadron | Hurricane I P3901 RF-E | 1-0-0 Bf 109 |
| 11.12.1943 | 75th Fighter Squadron | P-40K-1 Warhawk | 2-0-0 Ki-43 claimed as A6M Zero |

W

STEFAN WAPNIAREK, Pilot Officer, was born on 23 February 1916 at Oberhausen into a Polish family settled in Germany (or according to other sources in Poznań, in part of Poland ruled by the German Empire). His parents Walenty and Anna née Kosicka moved back to Poland, where Stefan obtained primary and secondary education. On 4 January 1937 he joined the Air Force Cadet Officers' School at Dęblin, and between April and June 1939 undertook an Advanced Flying Course at Ułęż. Before official graduation the whole 12th class completed their training, and due to the dangerous political situation all cadets were sent to various regiments. In June Wapniarek joined the 132nd Fighter Squadron of the 3rd Air Regiment at Poznań. He was commissioned in September, with effect from 1 August. With his squadron, and supporting the 'Poznań' Army, he took part in the Polish Campaign of 1939. On 11 September he claimed the destruction of a Bf 109, followed by shooting down a Do 17 on 15 September and an Hs 126 on 16 September. Many authors claim that on 18 September he was captured by the Germans but managed to escape. In fact Wapniarek, who commanded the road party of his unit, travelled as far as Iłów, from where he walked towards Bzura river. After noticing German soldiers, he hid from them, then in peasant's clothing returned to his family home in Ponań. Soon after he travelled to Zakopane, from where he managed to cross the Slovakian border. Via Rumania he travelled to France, and in January 1940 was posted to the Polish Air Force Training Centre at Lyon-Bron. On 10 April , together with twenty other pilots commanded by Captain Tadeusz Rolski, he was posted to Saint Etiénne for flying training. A few days later the whole group was moved to Mions aerodrome. After conversion to Caudron CR 714s, Wapniarek flew to Clermont-Ferrand, where from 16 June he flew Morane MS 406s. On board a Caudron Goelland he flew to Oran in

North Africa, landing on 23 June. From there, by sea, he arrived in England, receiving the service number P-1291 and the rank of Pilot Officer. On 30 July he was posted to No. 302 (Polish) 'City of Poznań' Squadron at Leconfield. On 18 September he claimed the destruction of a Ju 88, but exactly one month later was killed while returning from an operational sortie. On 18 October he attempted an emergency landing and crashed at Nutwood Farm, Chobham, Surrey, in his Hurricane I P3872 WX-R due to lack of fuel and bad visibility due to fog. He was buried in Northwood Cemetery, in grave no. H 268. Stefan Wapniarek was the twenty-seventh Polish operational pilot killed during the Battle of Britain. He was decorated with the Silver Cross of Virtuti Militari no. 12083 and the Cross of Valour. He is commemorated on the Polish Air Force Memorials at Northolt and Warsaw-Mokotów, and also by the memorial plaque at RAF Northolt.

Date & Time	Unit	Aircraft	Score
11.09.1939	132nd Squadron	PZL P.11c	1-0-0 Bf 109
15.09.1939	132nd Squadron	PZL P.11c	1-0-0 Do 17
16.09.1939	132nd Squadron	PZL P.11c	1-0-0 Hs 126
18.09.1940 17.20	302 Squadron	Hurricane I P3924 WX-V	1-0-0 Ju 88

ANTONI WCZELIK, Flight Lieutenant, was born on 4 October 1906 at Kalinowszczyzna, near Czortków in the region of Tarnopol, in part of Poland ruled by the Russian Empire. With his five siblings he grew up in the family of Zygmunt and Stanisława née Rodzoniak. After completing primary and secondary education he passed A-level exams in June 1916, and in November 1927 joined the Air Force Officer's School at Dęblin, which during his stay changed its name to Air Force Cadet Officers' School. He was commissioned on 15 August 1929 as an observer with the 3rd class, and with the rank of Sub-Lieutenant was posted to the 61st Light  Bomber Squadron of the 6th Air Regiment at Lwów. In 1931 he returned to Dęblin, where he participated in a flying course organized by the Air Force Officers' Training Centre. This was followed by the Advanced Flying Course at Grudziądz, which he attended in 1932. In January 1932 he joined the 2nd

Air Regiment, where he flew in the 122nd Fighter Squadron but also became a member of the famous aerobatic team known as 'Bajan's Three'. In October 1935 he commanded the team while taking part in the Central Fighters Competition at Grudziądz. Together with Platoon Commanders Karol Pniak and Stanisław Macek he won the competition for the III/2 Fighter Wing. On 1 February 1936 he took command of the 122nd Fighter Squadron, being transferred in the same position to the 123rd Fighter Squadron in November. Wczelik was posted to No. 1 Air Force Training Centre at Dęblin, where until the outbreak of war he held the post of flying instructor and commander of the 3rd Training Flight. During the Polish Campaign of 1939 he served as a pilot of the ad hoc instructors' flight also known as the 'Dęblin Group', defending Ułęż and Dęblin and performing several operational sorties. On 2 September he was credited with damaging two Do 17s. Later he participated in the evacuation of the school and led his pupils towards the Rumanian border. He reached Rumania during the night of 17/18 September, and travelled via Yugoslavia and Greece, arriving at Marseilles in France on 16 October. In December he was posted to the Polish Air Force Training Centre at Lyon-Bron. He was attached to the so-called 'Finish Squadron' which was supposed to be deployed to Finland against the Russian aggressors. Wczelik was to have taken command of one of the flights, but after an armistice was signed on the night of 12/13 March 1940 it was decided to form 1/145 'City of Warsaw' Squadron at Lyon-Bron. He was appointed commander of 1st Flight. On 8 June he shot down a Bf 110, followed by a shared victory of a Do 17 the next day. On 10 June he was appointed deputy commander of 1/145 Squadron, but on 14 June he took command of a small group consisting of seven pilots detached to GCI/1, where they flew Bloch MB 152s. On 18 June he participated in the destruction of an He 111, however this kill was never officially accepted. After the collapse of France he was evacuated from either Bordeaux or St Jean de Luz. Wczelik arrived in Britain on 12 July, receiving the service number P-1419 and the rank of Flight Lieutenant. He was considered for No. 302 (Polish) 'City of Poznań' Squadron at Leconfield, where he reported on 20 August. On 3 September he went for further training at No. 5 Operational Training Unit at Aston Down, and on 26 September returned to No. 302 Squadron. On 7 October 1940 he was transferred to No. 303 (Polish) 'Tadeusz Kościuszko. City of Warsaw' Squadron at Northolt, but later returned to No. 302 Squadron. Wczelik force-landed at Detling on 8 November in his Hurricane I V6860 WX-B after it was damaged in combat, but escaped unhurt. On 6 March 1941 he was posted to No. 317 (Polish) 'City of Wilno' Squadron, where he took command of 'A' Flight. On 1 September he was transferred to No. 306 (Polish) 'City of Toruń' Squadron, taking command of the unit. On 27 September he damaged one Bf 109, then on 30 December claimed another

Bf 109 destroyed. Squadron Leader Wczelik was killed on 14 April 1942 while participating in Operation Circus 123. His Spitfire VC AB182 UZ-C was shot down into the sea and his body was never found. He is commemorated on the Polish Air Force Memorials at Northolt and Warsaw-Mokotów, and has a symbolic grave in the Parish Cemetery at Zakopane, where his wife Jadwiga is buried. He was decorated with the Bronze Cross of Merit and the Cross of Valour and two bars.

Date & Time	Unit	Aircraft	Score
02.09.1939	Instructors Flight	PZL P.7a	0-0-2 Do 17
08.06.1940 16.00	1/145 Squadron	Caudron CR 714 no.3 33 B 3	1-0-0 Bf 110
09.06.1940	1/145 Squadron	Caudron CR 714 no.3 33 B 3	⅓-0-0 Do 17
18.06.1940 17.40	GCI/1	Bloch MB 152	⅓-0-0 He 111 unconfirmed
27.09.1941 14.20	306 Squadron	Spitfire VB UZ-W	0-0-1 Bf 109
30.12.1941 14.13	306 Squadron	Spitfire VB UZ-W	1-0-0 Bf 109

MARIAN WĘDZIK, Sergeant, was born on 3 November 1913 at Gucin near Łask in part of Poland ruled by the Russian Empire. He grew up in the family of Józef and Józefa. After completing basic education in 1931 he joined the Air Force NCO School for Minors at Bydgoszcz, qualifying in 1934 as an aircraft mechanic with basic flying training. He was posted to the Air Force Officers' Training School at Dęblin, where he underwent a flying course. Upon completion he was posted to the 162nd Fighter Squadron  of the 6th Air Regiment at Lwów. In 1936 he was transferred to the 122nd Fighter Squadron of the 2nd Air Regiment at Cracow, where he remained until 1939. Wędzik was posted to No. 1 Air Force Training Centre at Dęblin and served there as a flying instructor. During the Polish Campaign of 1939 he served as a pilot of the ad hoc-formed instructors' flight also known as the 'Dęblin Group' that defended Ułęż and Dęblin, and he performed several operational sorties. During the evacuation of the school, together with Bronisław Malinowski and Edward Paterek he flew in PZL P.7s to Radom. On 11 September all three pilots had to abandon their aircraft due to lack of fuel and returned to Dęblin. After obtaining RWD-8 training aircraft they flew east. After the Soviets invaded eastern Poland, he crossed the Rumanian border on 17 September. He travelled to France, where he was attached to the Polish Air Force Training Centre at Lyon-Bron. He was also attached to the so called 'Finnish Squadron' which was supposed to be deployed to Finland against the Russian aggressors. After an armistice was signed by both sides on the night of 12/13 March 1940 it was decided to form 1/145 'City of Warsaw' Squadron at Lyon-Bron. Initially he joined the 3rd Section of the 1st Flight, but on 25 May he left for Angers, where he flew Bloch MB 151s in the Polish Section commanded by Lieutenant Robert Janota protecting the HQ of the Polish government. On 19 June he boarded a Czechoslovak ship at Bordeaux and sailed to England. Upon arrival he received the service number 793549 and the rank of Sergeant. On 23 July he was posted to No. 302 (Polish) 'City of Poznań' Squadron at Leconfield. Wędzik claimed the destruction of a Do 17 on 15 September, but on 15 October he was shot down and injured over London while flying his Hurricane I P2752 WX-R. He stayed in Chatham Hospital until 25 October, returning to operational flying on 14 November. He claimed a shared victory of a Ju 88 on 16 February 1941, then on 4 May he baled out from his Hurricane II Z2350 WX-W after it caught fire. On 1 June 1942 he was commissioned and received the new service number P-1917. Wędzik added the probable destruction of a Fw 190 on 26 July 1942. On 3 November he went to No. 58 Operational Training Unit as a flying instructor. Wędzik was posted to No. 317 (Polish) 'City of Wilno' Squadron on 12 May 1943, and on 14 July destroyed a Fw 190. On 22 October he became an air traffic controller in the operations room of No. 131 (Polish) Wing. On 28 April 1944 he joined No. 306 (Polish) 'City of Toruń' Squadron, sharing the destruction of two V1 flying bombs on 17 and 18 August. On 30 December he went to No. 316 (Polish) 'City of Warsaw' Squadron as 'B' Flight commander. He was posted to the Polish Air Force Centre at Blackpool on 5 April 1945, but on 25 May he started a flying instructors course at No. 25 (Polish) Elementary Flying Training School, where he remained until 5 January 1946. He was demobilized with the rank of Flight Lieutenant, and on 1 June returned to Poland. Wędzik was employed by LOT Polish Airlines as a civilian pilot until retirement in 1972. He was married with a daughter and son. Captain Marian Wędzik died on 10 October 1977 in Warsaw and was buried in the family grave at North Cemetery, Warsaw, in plot E-VIII-5, row 9, grave no. 3. He was decorated with the Silver Cross of Virtuti Militari no. 8449, the Cross of Valour and three bars, the British Distinguished Flying Cross, the Golden and Silver Cross of Merit and the Knight's Cross of Polonia Restituta.

Date & Time	Unit	Aircraft	Score
15.09.1940 12.10	302 Squadron	Hurricane I P2752 WX-R	1-0-0 Do 17
16.02.1941 12.10	302 Squadron	Hurricane I P2918 WX-Y	½-0-0 Ju 88
26.07.1942 13.45	302 Squadron	Spitfire VB BL235 WX-W	0-1-0 Fw 190
14.07.1943 09.03	317 Squadron	Spitfire VB EP328	1-0-0 Fw 190
17.08.1944 06.30	306 Squadron	Mustang III UZ-V	½-0-0 V1
19.08.1944	306 Squadron	Mustang III	½-0-0 V1

STEFAN WITORZEŃĆ, Flying Officer, was born on 15 January 1908 at Lida, Nowogród Voivodship in part of Poland ruled by the Russian Empire. He grew up in the family of farmers Bolesław and Jadwiga née Brejwo. After graduating from primary school he completed Hetman Karol Chodkiewicz State Secondary School at Lida. On 17 October 1929 he joined the Air Force Reserve Cadet Officers' School at Dęblin, from which on 25 September 1930 he was transferred to the 5th Air Regiment at Lida. He joined Stefan Batory University at Wilno, but decided not to follow this path and left his studies.

On 16 October he was back at Dęblin and joined the Air Force Cadet Officers' School. He was commissioned on 15 August 1932 with the 6th class, and with the rank of Sub-Lieutenant joined the 31st Light Bomber Squadron of the 3rd Air Regiment at Poznań as an observer. In May and June 1933 he completed an Advanced Flying Course at Grudziądz and joined the 132nd Fighter Squadron of the 3rd Air Regiment. Witorzeńć was appointed Technical Officer of this unit on 15 August 1934, and on 15 April 1935 he left for Grudziądz, where he was appointed as a flying instructor and training flight commander of the Advanced Flying Course. In the spring of 1939, together with the school's personnel he was transferred to Ułęż. He was responsible for strategic planning of the defence of

Dęblin. During the Polish Campaign of 1939 he served as a pilot of the ad hoc instructors' flight also known as the 'Dęblin Group', defending Ułęż and Dęblin, and performed several operational sorties. He commanded one of the fighter sections. On 9 September he was evacuated to Sokal, and on 17 September crossed the Rumanian border. Despite being interned, Witorzeńć managed to escape on 15 October and from Balchik sailed to Beirut and then to France, arriving at Marseilles on 29 October. Initially he stayed at Salon, where he reported on 4 November, but declared that he would like to be sent to England. He sailed on 27 January 1940 and was sent to the Polish Air Force Centre at Eastchurch, receiving the service number 76730 and he rank of Flying Officer. In May he went to Blackpool, then in July to No. 1 School of Army Co-operation at Old Sarum. From there on 14 July he was posted to No. 6 Operational Training Unit at Sutton Bridge. He was considered to join No. 302 (Polish) 'City of Poznań' Squadron at Leconfield, but instead joined No. 501 Squadron at Gravesend on 5 August. On 12 August he damaged a Bf 110, then three days later shot down two Ju 87s. On 18 August he added one Bf 109 destroyed and on 24 August a Ju 88 damaged. On 2 September he destroyed a Dornier. His last claim during the Battle of Britain was reported on 11 September, damaging a Do 17, which he reported as a Do 215. Witorzeńć was posted to No. 306 (Polish) 'City of Toruń' Squadron on 22 November and took command of 'A' Flight, then on 14 May 1941 he went to No. 302 (Polish) 'City of Poznań' Squadron, where he also commanded 'A' Flight. A week later he took command of the squadron. On 4 September he claimed his last aerial victory by shooting down a Bf 109. On 25 November he took command of No. 2 (Polish) Wing. From 25 September 1942 he served as Polish Liaison Officer at the HQ of No. 11 Group, and on 18 February 1943 was appointed deputy of the Polish Liaison Officer at Fighter Command. He represented the Polish Air Force on the committee that awarded soldiers of the Polish Armed Forces in the West with the Virtuti Militari Cross. From 24 April 1944 he was Polish deputy commander of No. 61 Operational Training Unit at Rednall and the chief of training at the Polish Fighter School. From July he flew operationally with No. 131 (Polish) Wing, and from 18 August served at the HQ of No. 131 Wing. He returned to No. 61 Operational Training Unit on 18 October , then on 9 January 1945 was appointed commanding officer of No. 25 (Polish) Elementary Training Flying School at Hucknall. From 19 June he commanded No. 131 (Polish) Wing, holding this post until its disbandment. Acting Group Commander Witorzeńć was demobilized and in 1948 returned to Poland. Like many other Polish Air Force veterans who fought in the West he was prevented from joining the People's Polish Air Force, and from 1 August 1954 worked in the office of a clothing manufacturer in Łódź. After some political changes the attitude of the communist regime softened and he was able to join the air force on 27 February 1957. He served at the HQ of the Polish People's Air Force, then from 11 July 1958 commanded the Advanced Air Training Centre at Modlin and the Aerial Training Centre. He retired on 15 June 1967, and in 1991 was elected as Chairman of the Polish Air Force Association in Poland. Colonel Stefan Witorzeńć died aged 86 on 30 December 1994 in Warsaw and was buried in the Military Powązki Cemetery in Warsaw. He was decorated with the Silver Cross of Virtuti Militari no. 8992, the Cross of Valour and two bars, the British Distinguished Flying Cross and the Commander's Cross of Polonia Restituta.

Date & Time	Unit	Aircraft	Score
12.08.1940 12.45	501 Squadron	Hurricane I V7230 SD-H	0-0-1 Bf 110
15.08.1940 11.30	501 Squadron	Hurricane I V7230 SD-H	2-0-0 Ju 87
18.08.1940 17.35	501 Squadron	Hurricane I L1868 SD-D	1-0-0 Bf 109
24.08.1940 13.00	501 Squadron	Hurricane I P3803 SD-Z	0-0-1 Ju 88
02.09.1940 08.10	501 Squadron	Hurricane I L1868 SD-D	1-0-0 Do 17 claimed as Do 215
11.09.1940 16.00	501 Squadron	Hurricane I P5194 SD-J	½-0-0 Do 17 claimed as Do 215
11.09.1940 16.00	501 Squadron	Hurricane I P5194 SD-J	⅕ or ⅙-0-0 Do 215 unconfirmed
04.09.1941 15.00	302 Squadron	Hurricane II Z3425 WX-A	1-0-0 Bf 109

BOLESŁAW ANDRZEJ WŁASNOWOLSKI, Pilot Officer, called 'Vodka', was born on 29 November 1916 in Cracow, in the part of Poland ruled by the Austro-Hungarian Empire. He grew up in the family of Władysław, a railway clerk, and Maria. He completed primary education in his home town, followed by passing A-level exams in 1936 at the Henryk Sienkiewicz State Secondary School in Cracow. On 21 October 1936 he started a Cadet Officers' Course at the 82nd Infantry Regiment at Brześć on Bug, and on 3 February 1937 joined the Air Force Reserve Cadet Officers' School at Radom Sadków. On 28 September he went to the 2nd Air Regiment at Cracow and flew with the Training Flight. On 22 October he was accepted for the second year to the Air Force Cadet Officers' School at Dęblin. On 5 April 1939 he started an Advanced Flying Course at Ułęż. Before official graduation, like many of his 12th classmates, he was posted to a first line unit due to the difficult political situation and the prospect of war. On 16 June he joined the 122nd Fighter Squadron of the 2nd Air Regiment at Cracow. He was commissioned in September, with effect from 1 August. During the Polish Campaign in 1939 he flew operationally, his III/2 Fighter Wing supporting the 'Cracow' Army. On 2 September he shared the destruction of a Ju 87. On 19 September he crossed the Rumanian border with the road party of his unit, and on 15 October sailed from the port of Balchik on board the *Aghios Nikolaos* to Beirut. After a few days he boarded the *Ville*

de Strasbourg, and on 29 October arrived at Marseilles in France. After being posted to Salon, Własnowolski decided to continue his journey and on 27 January 1940 went to England, where he received the service number 76736 and the rank of Pilot Officer. Initially he was stationed at the Polish Air Force Centre at Eastchurch, but in May was transferred to Blackpool. He was sent to No. 1 School of Army Co-operation at Old Sarum and No. 6 Operational Training Unit at Sutton Bridge. He joined No. 32 Squadron at Biggin Hill on 8 August. On 14 August his Hurricane I V7223 was damaged in combat over Dover, but next day he claimed the destruction of a Bf 109. Again his Hurricane I N2671 was damaged and the Pole had to perform an emergency landing. As on the previous occasion he escaped unhurt. On 18 August he shot down a Do 17, which he recognised as a Do 215, then destroyed a Bf 109. On 13 September he went to No.607 Squadron at Tangmere, and on 15 September claimed the destruction of a Do 17. Two days later he joined No. 213 Squadron, also operating from Tangmere. Własnowolski made his last kill on 15th October 1940 when he shot down one Bf 109. On 1 November at 16.00 he flew an operational mission with his squadron and was shot down over Stoughton. His Hurricane I N2608 AK-V crashed near Liphook Game Farm and Własnowolski was killed in the wreckage. He was buried in Chichester Cemetery, in grave no. 45. He is commemorated on the Polish Air Force Memorials at Northolt and Warsaw-Mokotów, and also on a memorial plaque unveiled on 25 July 1997 at Church Farm near Stoughton. He was decorated with the Silver Cross of Virtuti Militari no. 8988 and the Cross of Valour.

Date & Time	Unit	Aircraft	Score
02.09.1939 16.40	121st Squadron	PZL P.11c	½-0-0 Ju 87 or Do 17
15.08.1940 15.30	32 Squadron	Hurricane I N2671	1-0-0 Bf 109
18.08.1940 13.20	32 Squadron	Hurricane I P3679	1-0-0 Do 17 claimed as Do 215
18.08.1940 17.30	32 Squadron	Hurricane I P3679	1-0-0 Bf 109
15.09.1940 15.00	607 Squadron	Hurricane I	1-0-0 Do 17
15.10.1940 12.30	213 Squadron	Hurricane I P3641 AK-P	1-0-0 Bf 109

MIROSŁAW IGNACY WOJCIECHOWSKI, Sergeant, called 'Woj', was born on 6 March 1917 at Sopoty Wolne near Gdańsk in the Pomerania region, in part of Poland ruled by the German Empire. He grew up in the family of Ignacy, a cavalryman, and Wanda Gertruda née Behrendt. In 1928 he completed seven years of primary education, followed by four years of secondary school at Toruń, from where he graduated in 1932. On 4 November 1934 he joined the Air Force NCO School for Minors at Bydgoszcz and graduated in 1937 as an aircraft mechanic. He was posted to the 4th Air Regiment at Toruń. In 1937 and 1938 he participated in a flying course, and during the summer of 1938 completed an Advanced Flying Course at Grudziądz. After returning to the 4th Air Regiment he was posted to the 142nd Fighter Squadron. He flew operationally during the Polish Campaign of 1939, when his unit and the whole III/4 Fighter Wing supported the 'Pomorze' Army. On 18 September he was evacuated to Rumania and travelled to Yugoslavia, where he arrived on 14 October. Three days later he went to Greece, and via Piraeus left for France on 20 October, arriving on 23 October. Wojciechowski was posted to the Polish Air Force Training Centre at Lyon-Bron but decided to continue his journey to England. On 18 February 1940 he reported at the Polish Air Force Centre at Eastchurch, receiving the service number 781062 and the rank of Sergeant. It was decided that he required initial training at No. 1 School of Army Co-operation at Old Sarum, where he went on 22 July, leaving for

No. 7 Operational Training Unit at Hawarden on 29 July. He was posted to
No. 303 (Polish) 'Tadeusz Kościuszko. City of Warsaw' Squadron based at
Northolt on 12 August. On 15 September he claimed the shared destruction
of a Do 17, followed by shooting down two Bf 109s. However, his Hurricane
I V6673 RF-U was damaged in combat. This was followed by another victory
on 17 September, when he claimed one Bf 109. On 25 February 1941 once
more his aircraft suffered combat damage. Despite his Spitfire I N3108 RF-P
being badly shot up over France with a smashed rudder, he managed to return
to Northolt. His last aerial victory was reported on 23 June, when he downed
a Bf 109. Wojciechowski was wounded in combat on 2 July while flying an
operational sortie in the Spitfire P8390 RF-U and landed at Martlesham.
He was treated at East Suffolk Hospital, returning to No. 303 Squadron
in December. He was posted for rest on 11 November 1942, attending an
instructor's course at No. 2 Flying Instructors School at Montrose. In February
1943 he returned to No. 303 Squadron, but on 1 April went to No. 25 (Polish)
Elementary Flying Training School at Hucknall. On 7 February 1946 he was
transferred to No. 16 (Polish) Service Flying Training School, where he served
as an instructor. He was demobilized with the rank of Warrant Officer, and in
November 1948 joined the RAF as a Master Pilot. He was married in 1949 to
an English woman and had two children, Krystyna and Jan. Wojciechowski
was posted to No. 2 Squadron on 1 January 1950 and flew reconnaissance
missions over East Germany and Poland. After conversion to Meteors in 1951,
he flew jets in Nos 2 and 247 Squadron. From June 1955 he flew Hunters, and
in the summer of 1956 was appointed a flying instructor at No. 288 Squadron.
Mirosław Wojciechowski lost his life in a flying accident on 22 October 1956
while being the second pilot of the Boulton Paul Ballilol T.2 WG184. First pilot
Squadron Leader Charles Warren collided with a Chipmunk and baled out,
but Wojciechowski remained in the cockpit and was killed when the aircraft
crashed. His parachute was partially open, which suggests that he had tried to
bale out. The pilot of the Chipmunk, Flying Officer Htay Maung, also survived
the incident. Wojciechowski was buried in Over Wallop St Peter Churchyard.
He was decorated with the Silver Cross of Virtuti Militari no. 9658 and the
Cross of Valour and two bars. His biography is available on the website www.
wojciechowski.freeserve.co.uk, which is maintained by his son Jan.

Date & Time	Unit	Aircraft	Score
15.09.1940 12.00	303 Squadron	Hurricane I V6673 RF-U	½-0-0 Do 17 claimed as Do 215
15.09.1940 12.00	303 Squadron	Hurricane I V6673 RF-U	1-0-0 Bf 109

Date & Time	Unit	Aircraft	Score
15.09.1940 15.00	303 Squadron	Hurricane I V6673 RF-U	1-0-0 Bf 109
17.09.1940 16.00	303 Squadron	Hurricane I P3975 RF-U	1-0-0 Bf 109
23.06.1941 20.30	303 Squadron	Spitfire II P8333 RF-S	1-0-0 Bf 109

ANTONI WÓJCICKI, Sergeant, was born on 1 August 1914 into a Polish family settled in Essen, Germany. Upon the family's return to an independent Poland he completed primary and secondary education, and joined the Polish Air Force. He was posted to the 6th Air Regiment at Lwów, where between August 1936 and August 1937 he completed a flying course. He then served as a pilot in 64th Light Bomber Squadron of the 6th Air Regiment. During the Polish Campaign in 1939 he flew operationally PZL P.23 Karaś light bombers with the 4th (formerly 64th) Bomber Squadron as part of II/6 Bomber  Wing attached to the Bomber Brigade. His unit initially operated from Skniłow airfield, then Nosów, and later was moved south-east. After the fall of Poland, on 18 September he crossed the Rumanian border at Kuty and travelled to France. Wójcicki decided to continue his journey, and in early 1940 went to England, receiving the service number 780525 and the rank of Sergeant. He initially stayed at the Polish Air Force Centre at Eastchurch, and in May was transferred to Blackpool. As he decided to convert to a fighter pilot he was posted to No. 15 Elementary Flying Training School at Carlisle, and on 18 July to No. 6 Operational Training Unit at Sutton Bridge. On 19 August he joined No. 213 Squadron at Exeter. Wójcicki was killed on 11 September, shot down into the sea near Selsey Bill in his Hurricane I W6667 AK-P. His body was never found. The fourteenth Polish operational fighter pilot killed during the Battle of Britain, he is commemorated on the Polish Air Force Memorials at Northolt and Warsaw-Mokotów.

STEFAN WÓJTOWICZ, Sergeant, was born on 19 June 1919 at Wypnicha village in the region of Lubartów, Lublin Voivodship, in a free Poland. He grew up in the family of farmers Stanisław and Weronika née Pejta. After the death of his father, his mother married Ignacy Aftyka, also a farmer, who looked after young Stefan, encouraging him to join the Polish Air Force. He completed four classes of primary school at Wypnicha, and from 1933 continued his education at Michów for the next three years. On 1 September 1936 he joined the Polish Air Force NCO School for Minors at Bydgoszcz. In June and July 1937 he took a gliding course at Ustianowa, then in September and October completed a basic flying cours e in a RWD-8. From May to August 1938 he flew PWS-26s and was selected as a potential fighter pilot. At that time his school was moved to Krosno. Before official graduation, he was posted to

the 111th Fighter Squadron of the 1st Air Regiment at Warsaw. He arrived there on 1 July 1939 due to the dangerous political situation. During the Polish Campaign of 1939 he flew operationally, with his III/1 Fighter Wing absorbed by the Pursuit Brigade. Wójtowicz performed his first operational sortie on 1 September and participated in an unsuccessful attack on a Dornier Do 17. After the fall of Poland, he crossed the Rumanian border on 18 September at Śniatyń. Initially he stayed at Pitesti, but on 15 October he boarded the *Aghios Nikolaos* at Balchik and sailed to Beirut. From there, on the *Ville de Strasbourg*, he travelled to France, arriving at Marseilles on 29 October. He was posted to the Polish Air Force Training Centre at Lyon-Bron and was considered to join the 1st Polish Fighter Squadron which was planned to be formed. Wójtowicz, together with Kazimierz Wünsche, was supposed to join the 7th Section commanded by Sub-Lieutenant Witold Dobrzyński. Instead he joined a group of pilots commanded by Major Zdzisław Krasnodębski, and on 13 May 1940 was sent to Châteaudon to ferry French aircraft. However, two days later his posting was cancelled and Wójtowicz returned to Lyon to join the Polish fighter section known also as 'chimney section', under the command of Captain Kazimierz Kuzian. He was attached to this unit on 19 May and sent to Nantes to defend the SNCAO factory manufacturing LeO 451 aircraft and to fly Morane MS 406s. After performing between twenty and thirty operational sorties he flew to Bordeaux, from where on 19 June he left for England. After arrival at Liverpool on 23 June he was posted to Blackpool, where he received the rank of Sergeant. It is believed that the service number P-5024 was issued after his death. Initially he was considered to be posted to No. 302 (Polish) 'City of Poznań' Squadron at Leconfield, but instead on 2 August he joined No. 303 (Polish) 'Tadeusz Kościuszko. City of Warsaw' Squadron at Northolt. On 3 September he was shot up and slightly wounded in combat, crash-landing his Hurricane I R2688 RF-F at Tenderden near Woodchurch. On 7 September he claimed the destruction of two Do 17s, which he reported as Do 215s. He was killed during aerial combat on 11 September at 16.04 when a single bullet went into his cockpit and shrapnel hit him in the head. His Hurricane I V7242 RF-B crashed at Hogtrough Hill near Westerham. According to witnesses, before he died he fought and shot down two Bf 109s. He was the thirteenth Polish fighter pilot flying operationally to be killed during the Battle of Britain. He was also the second pilot of No. 303 Squadron killed during the war. He was buried in Northwood Cemetery, in grave no. H 209. He is commemorated on the Polish Air Force Memorials at Northolt and Warsaw-Mokotów, on a mamorial plaque at RAF Northolt, but also on a memorial unveiled on 19 July 2016 near the crash site. In his native Wypnicha a memorial plaque commemorating village citizens killed during the Second World War was unveiled, and Wójtowicz's name is among them. He was awarded the Silver Cross of Virtuti Militari no. 8816. His great nephews continued the family tradition, as at the time of publication Robert Wójtowicz works at the Polish Air Force Academy at Dęblin while Grzegorz Wójtowicz flies F-16s in the Polish Air Force.

Date & Time	Unit	Aircraft	Score
07.09.1940 17.00	303 Squadron	Hurricane I P3939 RF-H	2-0-0 Do 17 claimed as Do 215
11.09.1940 16.00	303 Squadron	Hurricane I V7242 RF-B	1-1-0 Bf 109

ZBIGNIEW TADEUSZ ADAM WRÓBLEWSKI, Pilot Officer, called 'Valentino', was born on 25 April 1914 in Warsaw, in part of Poland ruled by the Russian Empire. In 1934 he graduated from Śniadeckich Secondary School and passed A-level exams. Later he settled at Kielce. In the same year he was accepted to the Cavalry Reserve Officers' School at Grudziądz, and upon completion in 1937 joined the Air Force Cadet Officers' School at Dęblin. Before official graduation, like many of his 12th classmates, he was posted to a first line unit due to the worsening political situation and the threat of war. In June 1939 he joined the 114th Fighter Squadron of the 1st Air Regiment at Warsaw ,and was commissioned in September with effect from 1 August. During the Polish Campaign of 1939 he flew operationally, together with the

IV/1 Fighter Wing being attached to the Pursuit Brigade. On 7 September he shared the victory of a Bf 110. After the fall of Poland, on 17 September he flew in a PZL P.11c to Cérnauti in Rumania. He sailed to France, where on 11 November he was posted to the Polish Air Force Training Centre at Lyon-Bron and on 15 May 1940 joined 1/145 Polish 'City of Warsaw' Squadron. He was attached to the 5th Section of the 2nd Flight and flew Caudron C.714 Cyclones. On 19 June at La Rochelle he embarked on a ship and next day sailed to Britain. After arrival on 21 June he received the service number P-1285 and the rank of Pilot Officer. On 23 August he joined No. 302 (Polish) 'City of Poznań' Squadron at Leconfield, but on 2 September went for further training to No. 5 Operational Training Unit at Aston Down. He returned to No. 302 Squadron on 26 September. On 8 May 1941 he claimed the probable destruction of a Bf 109. Wróblewski had a landing accident on 11 May when his Hurricane IIB Z3433 collided with an aircraft piloted by Flying Officer Aleksander Narucki, who was killed. He claimed another Bf 109 probably shot down on 21 May. Wróblewski sustained an injury on 9 January 1942 during a force-landing of his Spitfire VB W3209 WX-F caused by a lack of fuel. He was hospitalized and spent a few months convalescing, returning to No. 302 Squadron in April. On 25 February 1943 he went to No. 317 (Polish) 'City of Wilno' Squadron, where he was appointed 'A' Flight commander. He claimed the destruction of a Fw 190 on 26 July. On 5 September he was sent to the Polish Air Force Staff College. After graduation he served as a lecturer's assistant, and was then

Plt Off Zbigniew Wróblewski

posted to the Polish Air Force Inspectorate. In March 1944 he arrived at No. 16 (Polish) Service Flying Training School at Newton for a refresher course. From 20 December he flew operationally with No. 602 Squadron, and on 9 June 1945 was appointed Station Adjutant at RAF Coltishall, where No. 3 Polish Wing was stationed. He was transferred to RAF Andrews Field in August. Wróblewski was demobilized in December 1945 with the rank of Flight Lieutenant. During his civilian life he was employed as an airline pilot working for British and then Nigerian airlines, retiring in 1980 and moving to Tenerife. He died on 23 April 1995 at Hove, Sussex, and was buried in Wales. He was decorated with the Silver Cross of Virtuti Militari no. 8445, the Cross of Valour and two bars and the French Croix de Guerre.

Date & Time	Unit	Aircraft	Score
07.09.1939	114th Squadron	PZL P.11c	½-0-0 Bf 110
08.05.1941 19.00	302 Squadron	Hurricane II Z2806	0-1-0 Bf 109
21.05.1941 17.35	302 Squadron	Hurricane II	0-1-0 Bf 109
26.07.1943 11.25	317 Squadron	Spitfire VB AR550 JH-A	1-0-0 Fw 190

KAZIMIERZ ROMAN WÜNSCHE, Sergeant, called 'Kaz', was born on 5 June 1919 in Jarosław, Lwów Voivodship, in a free Poland. He grew up in the working-class family of Edward and Stanisława née Talent. He attended primary school at Bydgoszcz, then completed five years of the State Secondary School in Jarosław. In the autumn of 1936 he joined the Air Force NCO School for Minors at Bydgoszcz, graduating in 1939 as a fighter pilot (in the meantime the school was moved to Krosno). In June 1939 he was posted to the 111th Fighter Squadron of the 1st Air Regiment at Warsaw. During the Polish Campaign of 1939 he flew operationally, his unit and the whole III/1 Fighter Wing were  operating within the Pursuit Brigade. He performed sixteen operational sorties, and after the fall of Poland, on 18 September, together with the road party of his unit, crossed the Rumanian border at Śniatyń. Through the Black Sea and via

Malta he sailed to France, where he arrived on 11 November. After completing training at the Polish Air Force Training Centre at Lyon-Bron, in mid-May 1940 he joined the Polish fighter section led by Lieutenant Ludwik Paszkiewicz and attached to GCII/8, and on 19 May was posted to Villacoublay. He performed operational sorties flying Bloch MB 152s. On 19 June he sailed from La Rochelle on the *Alderpool* to Plymouth. Upon arrival in Britain he received the service number 793443 and the rank of Sergeant. Initially considered for No. 302 (Polish) 'City of Poznań' Squadron at Leconfield, instead he went on 2 August to No. 303 (Polish) 'Tadeusz Kościuszko. City of Warsaw' Squadron at Northolt. Wünsche claimed his first victory on 31 August, shooting down a Bf 109. On 5 September he destroyed another Bf 109, followed by one more Bf 109 and another probably destroyed the next day. He was shot down and wounded on 9 September while flying the Hurricane I P3700 RF-E. He suffered burns, baled out and landed at Devil's Dyke, damaging his spine, while his aircraft crashed at Saddlescombe Farm. He was hospitalized at Hove, returning to No. 303 Squadron on 23 October. During his further service with the same unit he made more claims. On 23 June 1941 he shot down a Bf 109, and on 3 July 1942 participated in the destruction of a Ju 88. On 6 September he was posted for rest and joined No. 58 Operational Training Unit at Grangemouth as a flying instructor. He was commissioned on 1 January 1943, receiving the new service number P-2096 and rejoining No. 303 Squadron on 21 March. During this time he was posted for an officers' course at RAF Cosford between 4-29 April. On 1 October he went to Blackpool, but on 18 April 1944 was attached to No. 315 (Polish) 'City of Dęblin' Squadron. On 4 August he claimed the shared destruction of a V1 flying bomb. On 25 October he went for a short rest to Blackpool, returning to No. 315 Squadron on 6 December and taking command of 'B' Flight. On 6 December 1945 he was transferred to No. 309 (Polish) 'Czerwieńska Province' Squadron, where he served as Navigation Officer. He stayed at this post until the disbandment of No. 309 Squadron on 6 January 1947. Wünsche was demobilized with the rank of Flight Lieutenant and returned to Poland. Initially he was employed as a flight commander of the 3rd Fighter Regiment of the People's Polish Air Force. In 1949 he was transferred to the Officers' Air School at Dęblin as a flying instructor. As a veteran who served in the West, he was expelled from service in 1952. Five years later he was able to join the air medical service, including the Voivodship Emergency Rescue Station at Białystok and the Central Emergency Rescue Station in Warsaw, also flying as a sea and mountain rescue pilot. In 1959 he completed helicopter pilot training and worked saving people's lives until early retirement in 1970, which was caused by heart problems. He settled in Warsaw, where he died on 10 July 1980 and was buried in Powązki Cemetery in Warsaw. He was decorated with the Silver Cross of Virtuti Militari no. 9550, the Cross of Valour and three bars, the British Distinguished Flying Medal and the Knight's Cross of Polonia Restituta Oder.

Date & Time	Unit	Aircraft	Score
31.08.1940 18.25	303 Squadron	Hurricane I V7244 RF-C	1-0-0 Bf 109
05.09.1940 15.05	303 Squadron	Hurricane I V7289 RF-S	1-0-0 Bf 109
06.09.1940 09.00	303 Squadron	Hurricane I V7289 RF-S	1-1-0 Bf 109
23.06.1941 20.30	303 Squadron	Spitfire II P8325 RF-B	1-0-0 Bf 109
03.07.1942 20.25	303 Squadron	Spitfire VB AB151 RF-F	½-0-0 Ju 88
04.08.1944 15.50	315 Squadron	Mustang III FB123 PK-W	½-0-0 V1

BRONISŁAW FRANCISZEK WYDROWSKI, Pilot Officer, was born on 1 September 1916 at Mechlin, near Śrem in Greater Poland, ruled then by the German Empire. In Poznań he completed secondary school and passed A-level exams. Between June and September 1934 he completed initial flying training at Łuck, then from September to December 1935 completed the Infantry Reserve Cadet Officers' Course at the 55th Regiment at Leszno. In January 1936 he went to the Air Force Reserve Cadet Officers' School at Dęblin, graduating in September. In June 1937 he was posted to the 3rd Air Regiment at Poznań, and then decided to permanently join the Polish Air Force, remaining at the 3rd Air Regiment. He served in the 35th Light Bomber Squadron until July 1937. Wydrowski was badly injured on 2 September during a flying accident while in a Lublin R-XIII of the Training Flight, the result of a low fly-past over buildings. Zdzisław Radomski, who flew with him on that occasion, was also seriously wounded. In November and December 1938 he served in the 132nd Fighter Squadron of the 3rd Air Regiment. Wydrowski joined the Training Flight as a flying instructor and did not participate in operational flying during the Polish Campaign of 1939. Together with the 3rd Air Base in Poznań he was evacuated to Lublin and then crossed the Rumanian border. He was amongst the Polish airmen ordered to collect aircraft which were supposed to arrive from England. During his stay in France he was posted to the Polish Air Force Training Centre at Lyon-Bron, although some sources claim that he went to Aulnat Sud, where he served at the military repair workshops ARAA. He later commanded a fighter section defending Lyon. Via North Africa he travelled to England, where he arrived on 22 June 1940, receiving the service number P-0316 and the rank of Pilot Officer. After staying at No. 3 Polish Wing at Blackpool, on 5 September he was posted to No. 1 School of Army Co-operation at Old Sarum and then to No. 5 Operational Training Unit at Aston Down, where he reported on 18 September. On 28 September Wydrowski joined No. 615 Squadron at Prestwick, then on 10 October No. 607 Squadron at Turnhouse. On 26 November he was moved to No. 229 Squadron, but returned to No. 615 Squadron on 2 December. He was involved in a mid-air collision with another Hurricane on 5 February 1941. While descending through thick clouds after a combat sortie, his Hurricane I V6618 collided with an aircraft piloted by Flying Officer Stanisław Czternastek. While Wydrowski, who baled out, was seriously injured, Czternastek lost his life. After recovering from wounds, on 16 May he was posted to No. 302 (Polish) 'City of Poznań' Squadron and on 12 December moved to No. 234 Squadron. Flying with this unit he reported his only aerial claim on 17 April 1942, damaging a Bf 109. He was withdrawn from the Polish Air Force fighter pilot's group and on 27 July transferred to No. 2 Aircraft Delivery Unit, but on 15 October he was struck off the list of flying personnel of the Polish Air Force in the rank of Flying Officer and subsequently transferred to the Army. He was married in Scotland, but in 1946 returned to Poland where he married again and settled in Poznań. He later moved to Radom, and then to Szczecin. He tried to escape to the West, but his attempt was unsuccessful. He worked for the Szczecin Harbour Authority, throughout this time being an active pilot of Poznań and Szczecin Aero Clubs. He died on 1 January 1994 at Szczecin and was buried in the Central Cemetery 'Ku Słońcu', Szczecin, in 64B, row 7, grave 14.

Date & Time	Unit	Aircraft	Score
17.04.1942 09.35	234 Squadron	Spitfire VB BL828	0-0-1 Bf 109

Z

JERZY SERGIUSZ ZAŁUSKI, Sergeant, was born on 16 August 1916. In 1932 he joined the Air Force NCO School for Minors at Bydgoszcz, graduating in 1935 as an aircraft mechanic. He was sent to No. 1 Air Force Training Centre at Dęblin, where he completed a flying course, and in May 1939 was posted to the Training Flight of the 1st Air Regiment at Warsaw. Also in May he was transferred to the 63rd Reconnaissance Squadron of the 6th Air Regiment at Lwów. During the Polish Campaign of 1939 he flew operational sorties in RWD-14 'Czapla' aircraft, supporting the 'Łódź' Army. Together with the road party of his unit he crossed the Rumanian border on 18 September. He travelled to France

and then to England, where he arrived in February 1940 and was given the service number 781415 and the rank of Leading Aircraftman. Initially he was posted to No. 1 School of Army Co-operation at Old Sarum, from where on 1 September he went to No. 6 Operational Training Unit at Sutton Bridge. On 9 September he had a landing accident, damaging his Hurricane I L1506. On 21 September he left Sutton Bridge, and two days later was posted to No. 302 (Polish) 'City of Poznań' Squadron at Leconfield. On 29 September he had a taxiing accident when he collided his Hurricane I P3924 with another aircraft. Sergeant Załuski was killed on 16 October 1940. His Hurricane I V7417 WX-T overturned after an emergency landing at Colliers End as a result of lack of fuel caused by the pilot being lost. He was buried in Northwood Cemetery, in grave no. H 252. He was the twenty-fifth operational Polish fighter pilot killed during the Battle of Britain. He is commemorated on the Polish Air Force Memorials at Northolt and Warsaw-Mokotów, but also on the memorial plaque at RAF Northolt. Occasionally his surname is misspelt as 'Załucki'.

ALEXANER ROMAN ZATONSKI, or Aleksander Roman Zatoński, Pilot Officer, called 'Alex', was born on 1 November or 11 January 1915 in Philadelphia, Pennsylvania, USA, into the family of Polish immigrants Józef and Marta. According to other sources he was born in Poland, and at an early age emigrated to North America. Zatonskis settled at Brantford, Ontario, Canada in 1926, where Alexander completed his education, including at Central School. He was an active member of the Skylark Club in Brantford, later attending Brantford Collegiate Institute, where he successfully passed A-level exams. Before the outbreak of war Zatonski travelled to Europe and planned to visit Poland. On 3 September, two days after the war began, he was in England, where he joined the Royal Air Force, on 25 September receiving the service number 43052. He was posted to No. 2 Flying Training School at Brize Norton, where he participated in no. 46 course between 25 March and 11 July 1940. On 13 July he joined No. 79 Squadron at Acklington. He was shot down on 28 August while flying an operational

sortie over Hythe in his Hurricane I P2718. He was badly burnt and wounded in a leg and baled out, landing in the English Channel. Zatonski was taken to Hythe Small Arms School and then to St Athens Hospital for treatment. Following rest at the RAF Convalescent Centre in Torquay, he returned to No. 79 Squadron on 4 December. He was sent back for further treatment on 20 December. While staying in Torquay he met and married Constance Mary Bunce on 21 May 1941. He once more rejoined No. 79 Squadron on 10 March 1941, but nine days later was again posted on non-effective sick. Flying Officer Zatonski was posted to No. 238 Squadron, and in May 1941 sent to the Middle East. He was lost on 6 December after combat with German and Italian fighters over the border of Cyrenaica. There is information that he was buried at El Gubbi in Libya, but his grave was never found and he is commemorated on the Alamein Memorial at Matruh, Egypt, column 241. After his death his son, John Alexander Zatonski, was born. On 29 March 2001 one of the streets in Brantford was named after him.

PAWEŁ ZENKER, Pilot Officer, was born on 25 December 1914 in Chocicza village near Jarocin in Poznań Voivodship, in part of Poland ruled by the German Empire. He grew up in the family of Leon and Emilia née Ruszkiewicz. He completed primary education, and in 1934 graduated from the State Teachers College, passing A-level exams. Between 18 September and 31 December 1934 he completed a unitary course at the Infantry Reserve Cadet Officers' School, and from 1 January to 14 September 1935 the Air Force Reserve Cadet Officers' School at Dęblin. From 19 September 1935 until graduation on 15 October 1937 he attended the Air Force Cadet Officers' School at Dęblin. Between 1 May and 30 July 1937 he completed an

Advanced Flying Course at Grudziądz. He was commissioned with the 10th class, and with the rank of Sub-Lieutenant joined the 142nd Fighter Squadron of the 4th Air Regiment at Toruń. He was appointed Technical Officer on 8 October 1938, and on 5 May 1939 was transferred to No. 1 Air Force Training Centre at Dęblin, where until 26 July he remained as a flying instructor. Then he returned to the 142nd Squadron. He flew operationally during the Polish Campaign of 1939, when his unit was part of the III/4 Fighter Wing supporting the 'Pomorze' Army. On 2 September he  participated in an attack on an Hs 126, but his machine guns jammed. The next day he took part in the shared victory of an Hs 126. On 8 September his PZL P.11c overturned during take-off, but Zenker escaped with no major injuries. Together with the road section of III/4 Fighter Wing he crossed the Rumanian border, and on 15 October sailed from Balchik to Beirut. He arrived at Marseilles in France on 29 October. Initially he stayed at Salon, but soon decided to continue his journey to England, where he arrived on 24 January 1940. After receiving the service number 76714 and the rank of Pilot Officer he went to the Polish Air Force Centre at Eastchurch. He was involved in a road accident on 13 May at 23.15 while driving from Sherness to Eastchurch as a passenger in a military van. Despite multiple injuries, including abrasions to his left cheek, Zenker immediately pulled his fellow airman from under the van. On 3 July he was posted to No. 15 Elementary Flying Training School at Carlisle, then on 27 July to No. 5 Operational Training Unit at Aston Down. On 7 August he joined No. 501 Squadron at Gravesend, and on 12 August claimed the destruction of a Ju 87. On 18 August he damaged a Bf 109 and later shot down another aircraft of the same type. Paweł Zenker was killed on 24 August while flying his Hurricane I P3141 SD-W, pursuing Do 17s and Bf 109s north-west of Dover. He was reported missing, and most probably was shot down into the sea. His body was never found. Zenker was the eighth Polish operational fighter pilot killed during the Battle of Britain. He is commemorated on the Polish Air Force Memorials at Northolt and Warsaw-Mokotów. He was decorated with the Cross of Valour and two bars.

Date & Time	Unit	Aircraft	Score
03.09.1939	142nd Squadron	PZL P.11c	¼-0-0 Hs 126
12.08.1940 11.30	501 Squadron	Hurricane I P3397 SD-M	1-0-0 Ju 87
18.08.1940 13.00	501 Squadron	Hurricane I	0-0-1 Bf 109
18.08.1940 17.40	501 Squadron	Hurricane I R4105 SD-U	1-0-0 Bf 109

JAN EUGENIUSZ LUDWIK ZUMBACH, Pilot Officer, known as 'Kaczor Donald' (Donald Duck), 'Johnny' or 'Johann', was born as a Polish citizen on 14 April 1915 at Ursynów near Warsaw, in part of Poland ruled by the Russian Empire. He grew up in the family of Eugeniusz (Eugene) Zumbach, a Swiss citizen, and Halina née Gorzechowska. His ancestors from his father's side arrived from Switzerland and settled in Poland at the end of the nineteenth century, thanks to which Jan Zumbach had dual citizenship. In 1922 his family moved to Bobrowo near Brodnica, where Jan was educated at home. He then attended secondary school and the Jan Małachowski Secondary School, both at Brodnica. He passed A-level exams in May 1935. On 22 September he started a unitary course at the 27th Infantry Regiment at Częstochowa, and on 13 January 1936 went to the Air Force Cadet Officers' School at Dęblin. Between 3 May and 28 August 1938 he completed an Advanced Flying Course at Grudziądz, and on 15 October was commissioned with the 11th class. Sub-Lieutenant Zumbach joined the 111th Fighter Squadron of the 1st Air Regiment in Warsaw. On 26 May 1939 he had an accident when his PZL P.11c no. 1 collided with an ambulance. Zumbach broke a leg and was taken to the Institute of Surgery in Warsaw, then continued his recovery at a sanatorium in Zaleszczyki. When the war began he tried to find his unit, and on 3 September was allocated to the HQ of the Bomber Brigade as a liaison pilot. Still looking for the 111th Squadron, he flew east in a civilian RWD-13 SP-BMF and on 17 September flew to Rumania, landing at Tulcea. On 15 October he sailed from Balchik on the *Aghios Nicolaos* to Beirut, and from there on the *Ville de Strasbourg* to France, arriving at Marseilles on

29 October. He was initially posted to Salon, then on 16 December went to the Polish Air Force Training Centre at Lyon-Bron, where he trained on Morane MS 406s and Caudron C 714 Cyclones. He was chosen to join the 1st Polish Fighter Squadron which was supposed to be formed in France, but instead, in mid-May 1940, he joined the Polish fighter section of Défense Aérienne du Territoire (DAT) commanded by Major Zdzisław Krasnodębski at Châteaudun and equipped with Bloch MB 152s. On 15 June Zumbach was ordered to form his own section, but due to retreating Allied forces it was too late for this, and on 19 June he boarded the Polish ship *Kmicic* at La Rochelle, sailing to Plymouth. Upon arrival in Britain he received the service number P-1382 and the rank of Pilot Officer. After an initial stay at Blackpool it was decided to send him to No. 302 (Polish) 'City of Poznań' Squadron at Leconfield, but instead on 2 August he joined No. 303 (Polish) 'Tadeusz Kościuszko. City of Warsaw' Squadron at Northolt. On 7 September he claimed the destruction of two bombers reported as Do 215s, followed by shooting down one Bf 109 and another reported as probably destroyed on 9 September. Two days later he added a Bf 109 destroyed, then one more on 15 September. On 26 September Zumbach made two kills of a Bf 109 and a He 111, and the next day he shot down another Bf 109. He had a landing accident at London Colney on 24 February 1941 after his Spitfire I R6977 RF-C ran out of fuel, then two days later he reported the probable destruction of a Bf 109, but this claim was not approved. Zumbach baled out from his Spitfire II P7962 RF-A on 9 May after an aerial combat and was wounded. On 2 July he claimed the destruction and probable destruction of two Bf 109s, then on 9 September went to No. 3 Delivery Flight, returning to No. 303 Squadron on 16 September. On 13 October he destroyed a Bf 109 and damaged a Fw 190, but was slightly wounded and had to bale out from his Spitfire VB AB976 RF-D. On 24 October he added the destruction of another Bf 109. He was posted for rest on 27 November, serving as a flying instructor at No. 58 Operational Training Unit at Grangemouth. Returning to No. 303 Squadron on 20 March 1942, he was appointed 'A' Flight commander. On 27 April he probably destroyed a Fw 190. On 18 May he took command of No. 303 Squadron. During the infamous Operation Jubilee at Dieppe on 18 August he shot down one Fw 190 and claimed another Fw 190 probably destroyed. Later he shared a victory of a He 111. He left No. 303 Squadron on 1 December and went to the Polish Air Force Inspectorate, where he served as a Liaison Officer. On 14 March 1943 he was transferred as Liaison Officer to the HQ of No. 9 Group, then from 15 April studied at the Polish Air Force Staff College at Eddleton. On 16 January 1944 he arrived back at Northolt, but two weeks later, on 1 February, he took command of No. 3 Polish Wing. On 14 June he went to the HQ of No. 18 (Polish) Sector, and from 8 July led

No. 135 Wing, then on 16th July he took command of No. 133 (Polish) Wing. On 25 September he claimed his last aerial success, probably destroying a Fw 190. On 29 January 1945 Zumbach was transferred to the HQ of No. 84 Group as Operations Officer. On 7 April, during an inspection flight from Gilze Rijen to Grave with Flight Lieutenant Tadeusz Kawalecki, who flew another aircraft, he landed by mistake in an Auster MT440 behind enemy lines. Both were captured by the Germans and held at Terschelling. Zumbach returned to England on 12 May and was sent to Blackpool. Later he was an Operations Officer of No. 81 Group, and on 4 September 1946 was posted to RAF Hethel, where No. 3 (Polish) Wing was stationed. He was demobilized on 30 November with the rank of Wing Commander and left Britain for Switzerland. In 1947 he established FlyAway Ltd, a company which officially was an air transport business, but was actually smuggling Swiss gold to Britain or Palestine and cigarettes to Italy. In 1955 he opened a dancing club in Paris, and from 1962 he flew as a mercenary pilot in Katanga, Congo. He was back in Africa in 1967, again as a mercenary, flying over Biafra. In the 1970s he published his autobiography under the title *Mr Brown*, later published as *On the Wings of War*. He was married to Giselle (in 1962) and had one son Hubert, and while living in France was known as Jean Zumbach. The circumstances of his death are not clear, and many myths arose since he died on 3 January 1986 in France. Lieutenant Colonel Jan Zumbach was buried in Powązki Cemetery in Warsaw. The Museum of the Cultural Heritage at Bobrowo is named after him. He was decorated with the Silver Cross of Virtuti Militari no. 7488, the Cross of Valour and three bars and the British Distinguished Cross and bar.

Date & Time	Unit	Aircraft	Score
07.09.1940 17.00	303 Squadron	Hurricane I V7242 RF-B	2-0-0 Do 17 claimed as Do 215s
09.09.1940 18.00	303 Squadron	Hurricane I R2685 RF-G	1-1-0 Bf 109
11.09.1940 16.00	303 Squadron	Hurricane I R2685 RF-G	1-0-0 Bf 109
15.09.1940 12.00	303 Squadron	Hurricane I P3577 RF-E	1-0-0 Bf 109
26.09.1940 16.30	303 Squadron	Hurricane I V6684 RF-F	1-0-0 He 111

Date & Time	Unit	Aircraft	Score
26.09.1940 16.30	303 Squadron	Hurricane I V6684 RF-F	1-0-0 Bf 109
27.09.1940 09.20	303 Squadron	Hurricane I V6684 RF-F	1-0-0 Bf 109
26.02.1941 14.00	303 Squadron	Spitfire I R6763 RF-B	0-1-0 Bf 109 unconfirmed
02.07.1941 12.45	303 Squadron	Spitfire II P8385 RF-A	1-1-0 Bf 109
13.10.1941 13.30	303 Squadron	Spitfire VB AB976 RF-D	1-0-0 Bf 109
13.10.1941 13.30	303 Squadron	Spitfire VB AB976 RF-D	0-0-1 Fw 190
24.10.1941 15.10	303 Squadron	Spitfire VB AB976 RF-D	1-0-0 Bf 109
27.04.1942 15.37	303 Squadron	Spitfire VB BM144 RF-D	0-1-0 Fw 190
19.08.1942 10.30	303 Squadron	Spitfire VB EP594 RF-D	1-1-0 Fw 190
19.08.1942 16.30	303 Squadron	Spitfire VB EP594 RF-D	⅓-0-0 He 111
25.09.1944 17.00	133 Wing	Mustang III HB866 JZ	0-1-0 Fw 190

Ż

WALERIAN ŻAK, Flying Officer, called 'Ciotka' (Aunt), was born on 14 April 1911 at Bóbrka, near Przeworsk in Lwów Voivodship, within the territory of Poland ruled by the Austro-Hungarian Empire. He grew up in the family of Franciszek Żak. After eight years of education he completed the Mathematical and Biological Secondary School at Jarosław, passing A-level exams on 20 May 1931. Between 1 September and 20 November he completed a unitary course at the Artillery Reserve Cadet Officers' School at Włodzimierz Wołyński, and between 20 November 1931 and 15 August 1932 was at the Air Force Reserve Cadet Officers' School at Dęblin. He was posted to the 2nd Air Regiment at

Cracow on 17 August, but on 12 September moved to the reserve. On 29 September he joined the Air Force Cadet Officers' School at Dęblin, and he was commissioned on 15 August 1934 with the 8th class. Sub-Lieutenant Żak was posted as an observer to the 65th Light Bomber Squadron of the 6th Air Regiment at Lwów, but on 10 November transferred to the 64th Light Bomber Squadron. He attended an Advanced Flying Course at Grudziądz on 15 April 1935, and upon completion on 7 July was posted back to the 64th Squadron. On 20 October he went to the 112th Fighter Squadron of the 1st Air Regiment in Warsaw, and

between 1 February and 1 September 1937 served as deputy commander of the squadron. Żak was involved in a mid-air accident and wounded on 15 June while flying a PZL P.11c. On 1 November he was appointed Technical Officer of the III/1 Fighter Wing. Between 20 March 1938 and 1 September 1939 he was a flying instructor at the Advanced Flying Course at Grudziądz, and from April 1939 at Ułęż. He later commanded a fighter training platoon. During the Polish Campaign of 1939 he served as a pilot of the ad hoc instructors' flight known as the 'Dęblin Group' to defend Ułęż and Dęblin, and flew several operational sorties. From 3 September he was involved in the evacuation of the school's aircraft further east. Żak crossed the Rumanian border in the back of a lorry at Kuty on 17 September. After obtaining a passport in Bucharest on 27 September he continued his journey, leaving Rumania on 5 October. Via Yugoslavia and Italy he travelled to France, crossing the border at Modena on 12 October. The next day he was moved to Paris, then on 26 November to Le Bourget. On 20 January 1940 he went to the Polish Air Force Training Centre at Lyon-Bron, and on 1 March started flying training at No. 1 Fighter School at Etampes together with a group of airmen led by Captain Walerian Jasionowski. On 9 May he returned to Lyon, but on 22 May joined the so-called 'Koolhoven Flight' led again by Jasionowski and sent to defend Salon. The Poles flew Dutch Koolhoven FK 58 fighter planes. Żak was appointed commander of the 1st Section. After the collapse of France, on 24 June he boarded the *Arandora Star* at Biarritz and sailed to Liverpool, arriving there on 27 June. He received the service number P-1390 and the rank of Flying Officer. Initially he was considered to join No. 302 (Polish) 'City of Poznań' Squadron at Leconfield, but instead on 21 August joined No. 303 (Polish) 'Tadeusz Kościuszko. City of Warsaw' Squadron at Northolt. On 15 September he claimed the destruction

of a German bomber which he recognized as a Do 215; his Hurricane I L2099
RF-O was damaged in the combat. He shot down one He 111 and damaged
another on 26 September, but the next day he was shot down in the Hurricane
I V7289 RF-S, which crashed near Leatherhead. He was seriously wounded,
including facial burns, but managed to bale out and was taken to hospital.
Żak returned to No. 303 Squadron on 5 May 1941, but was not able to fly
operationally until June. On 9 July he was appointed 'B' Flight commander ,but
on 22 November left for No. 58 Operational Training Unit at Grangemouth,
where he remained as a flying instructor until 7 April 1942. Żak returned to
No. 303 Squadron as 'B' Flight commander, and on 7 May took command of
the whole squadron. Soon after, on 28 May, he was appointed commander of
No. 308 (Polish) 'City of Cracow' Squadron. On 3 February 1943 he probably
shot down one Fw 190, then ten days later left for rest and served as Polish
Liaison Officer at the HQ of No. 12 Group. On 29 June he took command of
No. 3 Polish Wing. From 4 October he led No. 133 (Polish) Wing, and on 26
July he damaged a Fw 190. Between 15 February and 24 April 1944 he served
as Operations Officer at No. 11 Group, and subsequently was appointed Polish
Liaison Officer at the HQ of the Air Defence of Great Britain. On 6 January
1945 he received a posting to No. 61 Operational Training Unit as a flying
instructor, then on 21 June was moved to RAF Andrews Field. On 8 August
he was appointed commander of No. 3 Polish Wing. On 3 August 1946 he
married Jeanne Damson, formerly Alcock, and was demobilized with the rank
of Wing Commander on 15 January 1947. Walerian Żak decided to remain
in the United Kingdom, where he completed technical studies. He lived in
Surbiton, Surrey, until his death on 14 March 1969. This date is engraved on
his head stone, but despite this many publications claim that he died on 13
March 1969. He was buried in Northwood Cemetery, in grave no. B475. He
was decorated with the Silver Cross of Virtuti Militari no. 9616, the Cross of
Valour and two bars and the British Distinguished Flying Cross.

Date & Time	Unit	Aircraft	Score
15.09.1940 15.00	303 Squadron	Hurricane I L2099 RF-O	1-0-0 Do 17 claimed as Do 215
26.09.1940 16.30	303 Squadron	Hurricane I V7289 RF-S	1-0-1 He 111
03.02.1943 11.00	308 Squadron	Spitfire VB BL940 ZF-V	0-1-0 Fw 190
26.07.1943 11.25	3 Wing	Spitfire VB EP227 WX-W	0-0-1 Fw 190

ALEKSY ŻUKOWSKI, Pilot Officer, called 'Alosza' (Russian diminutive of his Polish name) or 'Japończyk' (Japanese, due to his ju jitsu training), was born on 28 March 1911 in Wilno, in part of Poland ruled by the Russian Empire. He graduated from Zygmunt August Secondary School in Wilno, where he passed A-level exams. He also completed a unitary military course. At the same time he obtained gliding and powered aircraft qualifications during initial military training at Wilno Aero Club. In January 1936 he went to the Air Force Reserve Cadet Officers' School at Dęblin, and upon completion in September was transferred to the 2nd term of the Air Force Cadet Officers'

School at Dęblin. Żukowski was commissioned with the 11th class on 15 October 1938, and with the rank of Sub-Lieutenant joined the 151st Fighter Squadron of the 5th Air Regiment at Porubanek airfield near Wilno. In July 1939 he was transferred to No. 1 Air Force Training Centre at Dęblin as a flying instructor. During the Polish Campaign of 1939 he was involved in the evacuation of the school, moving towards the east of Poland. He crossed the Rumanian border on 17 September and travelled to France. In December he was posted to the Polish Air Force Training Centre at Lyon-Bron. He was attached to the so-called 'Finnish Squadron' which was to be deployed to Finland against the Russian aggressors. After an armistice was signed on the night of 12/13 March 1940 it was decided to form 1/145 'City of Warsaw' Squadron at Lyon-Bron out of the former 'Finnish Squadron'. Żukowski was appointed commander of Section 5 of 1st Flight. The squadron, also known as GC 1/145, was equipped with Caudron CR 714s. Żukowski usually flew aircraft with the tail number 13, and between 19 May and 1 June operated from Villacoublay aerodrome. Later they were based at Dreux, Sermaises, Châteauroux and Rochefort. On 8 June he was involved in combat with Bf 110s, and despite it being shared between him and two of his colleagues, officially he claimed a victory. Later he was credited with the destruction of another Bf 110. Two days later he shot down a Do 17. On 19 June he arrived at La Rochelle, embarked on a French ship and next day sailed to Britain. Upon arrival in July he was posted to Blackpool, where he received the service number P-1292 and the rank of Pilot Officer. On 20 August he joined No. 302 (Polish) 'City of Poznań' Squadron at Leconfield, but on 3 September arrived at No. 5 Operational Training Unit at Aston Down to complete further conversion training needed for the pilots who recently arrived from France. He left on 26 September, returning to No. 302 Squadron. He took off from Northolt on 18 October at 15.00 to intercept a German raid, and while returning from the operation in bad weather, limited visibility and due to lack of fuel he force-landed at Harp Farm near Detling in his Hurricane I V6571 WX-Q and was killed in the wreckage. News about his death did not reach Northolt until 23 October. Aleksy Żukowski was the twenty-eighth Polish operational pilot lost during the Battle of Britain and was buried at Northwood Cemetery, in grave no. H 297. He is commemorated on the Polish Air Force Memorials at Northolt and Warsaw-Mokotów, but also on the memorial plaque at RAF Northolt. He was awarded the Cross of Valour. Various publications often erroneously misspell his first name as 'Aleksiej', which is a Russian name.

Date & Time	Unit	Aircraft	Score
08.06.1940 17.00	GC 1/145	Caudron C 714 no. 13	1-0-0 Bf 110 probably He 111
10.06.1940 09.00	GC 1/145	Caudron C 714 no. 13	1-0-0 Do 17

JANUSZ ŻURAKOWSKI, Pilot Officer, called 'Zura', was born on 12 September 1914 at Ryżawka near Humań, Ukraine, into the Polish noble family of Adam Wiktor, a doctor, and Maria Antonina née Szawłowska. In 1921 he moved with his family to Garwolin in free Poland, and in 1926 they settled in Lublin. There he completed Stanisław Staszic Secondary School and passed A-level exams. From an early age he was interested in aviation, and during his stay at school he started constructing models of aircraft and wining local model competitions. He applied for a flying course but was rejected due to intervention by his father. However, in 1933 he started a gliding course at Bezmiechowa, obtaining A and B categories. This was followed by a second gliding course at Pińczów in the summer of 1934, when he obtained C category. His brother Bronisław Żurakowski was also a glider pilot. Upon completion in September 1934, Janusz joined the Infantry Reserve Cadet Officers' School at Tomaszów Mazowiecki, then in January 1935 was transferred to the Air Force Reserve

Cadet Officers' School at Dęblin. One of his classmates was Zbigniew Oleński, with whom Żurakowski later participated in the Battle of Britain in No. 609 Squadron. Żurakowski was moved to the 2nd term of the Air Force Cadet Officer's School at Dęblin. During the spring and summer of 1937 he completed an Advanced Flying Course at Grudziądz. He was commissioned on 15 October 1937 with the 10th class, and with the rank of Sub-Lieutenant was posted to the 161st Fighter Squadron of the 6th Air Regiment at Lwów. During this time he had a gliding accident at Bezmiechowa, and after crash landing was taken to hospital. On 4 April 1939 he went to Ułęż as a flying instructor of the Advanced Flying Course. During the Polish Campaign of 1939 he served as a pilot of the ad hoc-formed instructors flight known as the 'Dęblin Group', defending Ułęż and Dęblin, and performed several operational sorties. According to some sources, including his own memoirs, on 2 September he damaged a Do 17. His aircraft was also damaged in this combat. On 9 September he was ordered to evacuate an obsolete Potez 27 to Sokal, and on 17 September crossed the Rumanian border at Kuty. He was interned at Tulcea but managed to escape, and on 15 October boarded the *Aghios Nicolaos* in Balchik and sailed to Beirut. From there, on board the *Ville de Strasbourg*, he travelled to Marseilles, arriving there on 29 October. Initially posted to Salon, Żurakowski decided not to stay in France and to continue his journey to England. On 17 December 1939 he was transferred to the Polish Air Force Training Centre at Lyon-Bron, but in January 1940 arrived in Britain. After receiving the service number 76715 and the rank of Pilot Officer, he went to the Polish Air Force Centre at Eastchurch. In May he was transferred to Blackpool, and on 17 July to No. 1 School of Army Co-operation at Old Sarum. On 21 July he arrived at No. 5 Operational Training Unit at Aston Down. From there on 5 August he was posted to No. 152 Squadron at Warmwell, and on 12 August to No. 234 Squadron at St Eval. Żurkowski claimed his first official victory on 15 August, destroying a Bf 110. However, he was shot down on 24 August while flying his Spitfire I N3239, baling out over the Isle of Wight. On 6 September he overturned his Spitfire I N3279 while landing at Middle Wallop after a successful sortie when he shot down a Bf 109. Next day he added one more Bf 109 destroyed. This was followed by sharing the probable destruction of a Bf 110 on 29 September. Żurakowski was transferred to No. 609 Squadron, also stationed at Middle Wallop, on 5 October. On 21 March 1941 he was posted for a rest from operational flying as a flying instructor of No. 57 Operational Flying Unit at Hawarden. He subsequently also served as an instructor at Nos 55, 56, again 55 and 61 Operational Training Units, finally being moved to No. 58 Operational Training Unit at Grangemouth. On 9 December he was posted to No. 315 (Polish) 'City of Dęblin' Squadron, but on 6 April 1942 took command of 'B' Flight of No. 306 (Polish) 'City of Toruń' Squadron. He took command of No. 316 (Polish) 'City of Warsaw' Squadron on 5 June and led this unit until 28 December. In January 1943 he was appointed Sector Gunnery Officer at RAF Northolt, still flying operationally. On 17 May he claimed his last trophy, damaging a Bf 109, and on 4 July became Deputy Commander (Squadron Leader Flying) of No. 1 Polish Wing at Northolt. On 30 October he left for the HQ of Fighter Command, where he remained until March 1944. On 17 May he received a posting to the Empire Test Pilot's School, then to the Aeroplane and Armament Experimental Establishment at Boscombe Down, where he reported on 5 January 1945. From there he flew over forty types of aircraft, including Gloster Meteors and Vampires. Acting Squadron Leader Żurakowski was demobilized in 1947 and found employment with Gloster Aircraft as a test pilot. He met and married his pre-war sweetheart Anna Danielska, who studied in France and moved to Prestbury. He held a speed record in 1950 achieved in a Gloster Meteor, when he flew from London to Copenhagen and back. This was followed by his own aerobatic move, known since then as 'Zurabatics'. In 1952 he emigrated to Canada and became chief test pilot of Avro Canada. He baled out from a CF-100 on 23 August 1953. He was the first pilot in Canada performing test flights on Avro CF-105s, and who flew supersonically on 25 March 1958. After the cancellation of the Avro Canada CF-105 Arrow supersonic fighter project he settled near Wadsworth lake and later by Kamaniskeg lake, both in Ontario, where he ran his private resort 'Kartuzy Lodge'. He had two sons, Jerzy and Marek. In 2002 he published his autobiography *Not only about flying*. Lieutenant Colonel Janusz Żurakowski died aged 89 on 9 February 2004 at Barry's Bay, Ontario, and was buried in St Hedwig Cemetery, Barry's Bay. In 2004 a biography was published by Bill Zuk, *Janusz Żurakowski. Legend of the Skies*. He is included in the Canadian Hall of Fame and his portrait was shown on a special $20 coin in 1996. There is a building at Cold Lake named after him, as well as a library at Kartuzy, Modavska Valley Park, and a small memorial in Canada, but also Zura Avenue in Gloucester, England. He was decorated with the Silver Cross of Virtuti Militari no. 8488 and the Cross of Valour and two bars.

Date & Time	Unit	Aircraft	Score
02.09.1939	Instructors Flight	PZL P.7	0-0-1 Do 17 unconfirmed
15.08.1940 18.00	234 Squadron	Spitfire I X4016	1-0-0 Bf 110

05.09.1940 15.38	234 Squadron	Spitfire I N3279 AZ-Y	1-0-0 Bf 109
06.09.1940 09.40	234 Squadron	Spitfire I N3279 AZ-Y	1-0-0 Bf 109
29.09.1940 13.45	234 Squadron	Spitfire I N3191 AZ-F	0-½ 0 Bf 110
17.05.1943 15.20	1 Wing	Spitfire IX BS456 SZ-Z	0-0-1 Bf 109

Notes

1. Edwin Beer, poem written on the Polish Air Force Memorial in the Church of St Clement Danes, London.

Preface
1. Mine Detector (Polish) Mk I – initial research and work was done in Poland before the war, but it was eventually invented by two officers of the Polish Army in the winter of 1941/42.

Introduction
1. For the Polish ranks and their equivalents, see Table 1.
2. The Polish word 'Eskadra' translates into English as 'Flight', yet it rather resembles a 'Squadron'. The Eskadra could have been Myśliwska (if it was a fighter unit), Bombowa (bomber), Liniowa (light bomber unit), Towarzysząca (accompanying or army co-operation unit) or Rozpoznawcza (reconnaissance unit). Eskadra in many respects functioned as an independent military unit, with its own commander, aircraft (numbering six to ten), ground crew and its own badge. Pre-war 'Dywizjon', which translates as 'Squadron', usually consisted of two or three Eskadras and operated similarly to the 'Wing' structure. In England, however, Poles adopted this name and commonly used to call their squadrons 'Dywizjon' instead of 'Eskadra' to raise their profiles. The number of aircraft (eighteen to twenty) in British and therefore PAF squadrons was much bigger than in pre-war Eskadras in their combat strength, but it was the most obvious choice of terminology. For a clearer view of this matter, see Table 2.

Chapter 1
1. Called the Eternal Union. Later known as the Republic of the Two Nations
2. Not to mention Polish fighter pilot Flying Officer Werner Kirchner or ground crew members Sergeant Henryk Messerschmidt and LAC Jan Messerszmidt.
3. Interviewed by the author.

Chapter 2
1. Nina Britton Boyle, *Blood on their Wingtips*, Book Tower Publishing, Redditch, 2016.
2. Italian war correspondent Indro Montanelli, who worked for *Corriere della Sera* magazine in 1939, instead of glorifying German successes in Poland, complemented Polish courage by saying that the Poles were so brave that they would defend their country even by using swords and lances. German propaganda used his words to ridicule the Poles.

3. Despite the British Government ratifying a military alliance with Poland on 25 August 1939, they did absolutely nothing when the Rumanians interned the Polish president, other members of the Polish Government and the heads of the Polish armed forces.
4. In the West, Poland is repeatedly called an Eastern European country. It is believed that this is a reference to her after-war affiliation to the Eastern Bloc (due to the Western Allies' 1945 betrayal), which since 1989 is no longer valid, rather than to the geographical location, although an ignorance of the shape of Europe cannot be definitely ruled out. Geographically, Poland is located in Central Europe; however, the term 'Central' does not appear to be frequently used by Westerners when discussing Europe.
5. Stanisław Skalski, *Czarne krzyże nad Polską* (*Black Crosses over Poland*), MON, Warsaw, 1957.
6. Franciszek Kornicki, *The Struggle. Biography of a Fighter Pilot*, Stratus, Sandomierz 2008
7. Michał Cwynar, *Wartime Recollections*, Warsaw 2004
8. Jan Maliński, *Samolot zakrył słońce* (*An aeroplane has obscured the Sun*), Altair, Warsaw 2000
9. Włodzimierz Miksa, *Ostatnie Rozpoznanie* (*The Last Reconnaisance*), Skrzydła – Wings. Wiadomości ze świata 154/640.
10. Franciszek Grabowski, *Skalski. Against All Odds. The First Allied Ace of the Second World War*, Fonthill, Stroud, 2017.
11. Benedykt Dąbrowski, *114 na Start!* (*114th – Take-off!*), Czytelnik, Warsaw, 1948.
12. 'Boys' own stories', *Sunday Express*, 8 July 1990.
13. General Władysław Sikorski, former Prime Minister and Minister of Military Affairs, was for many years kept away from politics by the Polish 'Sanation' Government.
14. Wacław Król, *Walczyłem pod niebem Francji* (*I Fought under the Sky of France*), LSW, Warsaw, 1984.
15. Ibid.
16. Jan Falkowski, *Z wiatrem w twarz* (With the Wind in My Face), Mon, Warsaw 1969.

Chapter 3

1. Jan Zumbach, *Ostatnia walka* (*The Last Fight*), ECHO, Warsaw, 2000.
2. Alexander McKee, *Strike from the Sky. The Story of the Battle of Britain*, Souvenir Press, London, 1989.
3. Witold Urbanowicz, *Świt zwycięstwa* (*Dawn of the Victory*), Znak, Cracow, 2009.
4. R.C. Cobb, 'The Polish Air Force and English Public Opinion', *Skrzydla* (*Wings*) Polish AF magazine.
5. Professor Peter J. O'Grady, 'The Exploits of the Polish Air Force and the British Press', *Skrzydla* (*Wings*) Polish AF magazine.
6. Alyse Simpson, *Englishwoman looks at the Poles*, 'Skrzydla' ('Wings') Polish AF magazine.

7. Kowalski and Nowak are the most common Polish surnames, similar to Smith or Brown in England.

8. Bohdan Arct, *Polskie skrzydła na Zachodzie* (*Polish Wings in the West*), Interpress, Warsaw, 1970.

9. Stephen Bungay, *The Most Dangerous Enemy. A History of the Battle of Britain*, Aurum Press, London, 2000.

10. Jan Jokiel, *Udział Polaków w Bitwie o Anglię* (*Poles in the Battle of Britain*), PAX, Warsaw, 1972.

11. Conversation with the author.

12. Letter from Zygmunt Jeliński to Joan Sołogub.

13. From the Wójtowicz family archive.

14. Wacław Król, *Walczyłem pod niebem Londynu* (*I Fought Under the Sky of London*), LSW, Warsaw, 1982.

15. Franciszek Kornicki, *The Struggle. Biography of a Fighter Pilot*, Stratus, Sandomierz, 2008.

16. Johnny Kent, *One of the Few*, The History Press, Stroud, 2016.

17. Ronald Gustave Kellett, *303 Squadron Polish Air Force*, Skrzydła Wings. Wiadomości ze świata, 106/592.

18. Nina Britton Boyle, *Blood on their Wingtips*, Book Tower Publishing, Redditch, 2016.

19. Letter to the author.

20. The average Pole, in mentioning Great Britain, would most probably use the colloquial term 'Anglia' (England).

21. Bohdan Arct, unpublished diary.

22. Author's collection.

23. *Gapa* Polish aviation magazine, 14/2015.

24. Janusz Żurakowski, *Nie tylko o lataniu* (*Not Only About Flying*), PFW, Toronto, 2002.

Chapter 4

1. 303 Squadron Operations Record Book, National Archives, Kew, AIR27/1659.

2. Polish Institute and Sikorski Museum (London), LOT A.V.49/6-14.

3. Such an innovative, original and rather dangerous practice was discovered by shocked British officers and stopped immediately.

4. In the RFC documentation entitled 'Visit of Russian Officers and Men to England for training in aeroplane duties', AIR2/10,National Archive, Kew, Piechowski and Wołłowicz appear to be French. There were also others, such as Warsaw-born Armanach Sarkissov, K. de Ladycz (again RFC documents show him as French), M. Yakoubovsky (Jakubowski) or P.E. Voznicsnaky (Woźnicki), although their Polish roots and connections are as yet unconfirmed. There was also a French airman, Georges Richonier (also known as Jerzy Richonier), who completed training in England and later escaped by air from the Bolshevik Air Force accompanied by Juliusz Gilewicz (a Pole who was forced to serve in the enemy's aviation). Richonier got to the Polish lines by flying a British-built Sopwith Struttter and later became a flying instructor in Poland.

5. Piechowski was killed in a flying accident on 21 November 1918 (as the first Polish airman of the independent country).

6. The course lasted until 20 August 1917.

7. Frank T. Courtney, *Flight Path*, William Kimber & Co. Ltd, London, 1973.

8. A Polish independence fighter and veteran of the unsuccessful November Uprising (1830-31) against Russia, called Dunin, emigrated to Scotland, where he purchased land near St Andrews. His estate gained the official name of Dunino, under which it is known to this day. This ground has been used for an airfield, that was opened in 1941. In May 1941, Polish No.309 Army Co-operation Squadron was moved there. Ironically, amongst the Polish airmen who lost their lives whilst operating from Dunino was its first owner's relative, Flight Lieutenant Piotr Dunin, who was killed on 25 February 1942 in a flying accident.

9. After a tragic accident on 15 August 1922, when bombs were dropped on members of the public and resulted in some deaths, Kaczyński was discharged and imprisoned. He eventually emigrated to Belgium and then to the United States.

10. Noel's son, Richard Noel Grabowsky-Atherstone, joined the RAF as a doctor.

11. The British also offered some of their seaplanes, but their proposal was refused by the Poles.

12. See Georges Richonier.

13. In 1931, Polish aviator Kajetan Czarkowski-Golejewski chose a DH60 Gipsy Moth for his (unsuccessful) flight around the world. Five years later, the same pilot, together with three other Poles including Jan Kazimierz Lasocki, flew from Gatwick to Spain. Their mission was to deliver a Fokker F.XII aircraft (some sources state that four aircraft were involved) to General Francisco Franco's air force. This mission failed and Lasocki was killed.

14. An officer of Italian nationality who joined the PAF in 1918. In 1939, he returned to his country and organized the evacuation of Polish soldiers to France. Arrested by the Italian police, he died in 1942.

15. Polska myśl wojskowa 1918-1939. Wybór dokumentów (Polish Military Ideas 1918-1939. Selection of Documents), KAW, Warsaw, 1987.

16. The Air Ministry claimed that this device was invented at Royal Aircraft Establishment, Farnborough, and as a result Świątecki's family received the rather embarrassing reward of just £350.

17. The Southampton was initially supposed to go no further than Copenhagen.

18. Before leaving for Poland, passengers such as Sir Samuel Hoare, Secretary of State and Air Minister, his wife Lady Maud Hoare and Wing Commander R.B. Maycock stayed in Oslo. Major R.E. Penny from the Directorate of Scientific Research and Technical Development was also on board the Valkyrie, but it is not certain if he visited Poland.

19. Before arriving in Puck, they flew a total of 1,705 nautical miles.

20. The next 'visit' paid by RAF aircraft over the Polish coast took place in November 1940, when two Handley Page Hampdens were bombing German targets in Gdańsk. Information obtained from *Flight* journal, 9 January 1931, & Grzegorz Korcz, *Southamptony nad Bałtykiem* (*Southamptons over the Baltic*), Historie Puckie.

21. After the war, Stanisław Brzezina's son met Phillip Wills at the Polish Air Force Association Gliding Club in Lasham. Wills remembered his father very well.
22. Previously he was a Fullham player.
23. Flying Officer Michał Liniewski was killed in action on 8/9 August 1941 while flying with No. 301 Polish Squadron.
24. After arriving in Britain, he joined No.300 Polish Squadron, where he led both the electrical and RT teams.

Chapter 5

1. As the Polish Air Force (similar to the other Polish Armed Forces in the West) was not a mercenary force, it had very few funds at its disposal. By the end of war, the total costs of the PAF to be refunded, when the Lend-Lease principle was adopted for wartime costs, amounted to over £100,000, although some sources state that it was as high as £68,083,723. Basically, they had to pay for every slice of bread, every button and cup of tea, but also for each bullet and aircraft that they used to defend Britain and its allies.
2. Polish mechanics were posted to No. 13 Maintenance Unit in Henlow, Bedfordshire, with observers to No. 1 Air Observer Navigator School at Prestwick in Scotland.
3. As part of the agreement, the French Government has committed not to start any armistice or peace negotiations without discussion with the Polish Government.
4. Ninety per cent of PAF personnel from France were able to get to Britain. Throughout the war, 17,000 men and women served in the PAF under command of the RAF.
5. Bolesław Drobiński, *Polscy lotnicy w Bitwie o Wielką Brytanię* (*Polish Airmen in the Battle of Britian*), Skrzydła, Wings No. 121/607.
6. The oldest operational pilots of the Battle of Britain (apart from Group Captain Stanley Vincent, b. 1897) were two Czechoslovaks, Squadron Leader Alexander Hess (b. 1898) and Squadron Leader Jan Ambrus (b. 1899), and the Pole Squadron Leader Mieczysław Mümler.
7. Letter from Mieczysław Mümler published in Skrzydła, Wings No. 121/607.
8. The squadron continued the traditions of the 7th Fighter Squadron that consisted of American volunteers and took part in the Polish-Bolshevik War. The name was given after the Polish national hero General Tadeusz Kościuszko, who fought for American independence ironically against British. Over the years, Eskadra changed into the 121st and finally the 111th Fighter Squadron. The official name of 'City of Warsaw' 'Tadeusz Kościuszko' was issued for No. 303 Squadron on 17 September 1940, after receiving a formal order from General Władysław Sikorski.
9. The reason for this movement was the close location to the English Channel and the danger of being attacked by the Germans.

Chapter 6

1. Alexander McKee in his book *Strike From the Sky* wrote about Sergeant Stefan Wójtowicz as a 'simple, uneducated man'. Perhaps Wójtowicz did not complete a university education, but he loved reading books and after three years of intense training, he successfully graduated from the Polish Air Force NCOs School for Minors.

2. Jan Zumbach, *Ostatnia walka* (*The Last Fight*), ECHO, Warsaw, 2000.
3. Richard King, *303 (Polish) Squadron, Battle of Britain Diary*, Red Kite, Walton-on-Thames, 2010.
4. Wacław Król, *Walczyłem pod niebem Londynu* (*I Fought Under the Sky of London*), LSW, Warsaw, 1982.
5. Bohdan Arct, unpublished diary.
6. Air Chief Marshal Lord Dowding, *Polish Airmen in the Battle of Britain*, Skrzydła, Wings No. 142/628.
7. No. 303 Squadron was also known as 'Warsaw' Squadron. In the following years, two fighter squadrons of the Polish Air Force had the same name: 303 and 316, both called 'City of Warsaw'.
8. Pilot Officer Stanisław Skalski was initially posted to 302 Squadron. He was unhappy that this unit, being still under construction, had to spend a considerable amount of time on training instead of being sent to fight. Skalski, whose posting was mainly to help his less experienced colleagues, openly criticized his superiors and as a result was posted back. After sorting out this issue with the PAF Inspectorate and Air Ministry, he finally settled in 501 Squadron.
9. Witold Urbanowicz, *Świt zwycięstwa* (*Dawn of the Victory*), Znak, Cracow, 2009.
10. Adam Zamoyski, *Orły nad Europą* (*Eagles over Europe*), Wydawnictwo Literackie, Cracow, 2004.
11. Among the Polish pilots posted to RAF squadrons were twenty-eight airmen converted to fighter pilots after leaving Poland and thirty-eight without any combat experience. Pilot Officer Walenty Krepski, before he was lost in action, only twice flew operationally (both flights in the UK), while Pilot Officer Stanisław Piątkowski managed to fly only once before he was killed. By contrast, Sergeant Antoni Głowacki, a fighter pilot without combat experience, who flew in the Polish Campaign 1939 as a pilot of a communication unit, gained rather good results in England, as did Flying Officer Tadeusz Nowierski, a former bomber pilot of 24th Light Bomber Squadron, who claimed a few kills during the Battle of Britain.
12. Air Chief Marshal Lord Dowding, *Polish Airmen in the Battle of Britain*, Skrzydła, Wings No. 142/628.
13. No. 304 (Polish) Bomber (later Costal Command) Squadron 'Silesian, Prince Józef Poniatowski' was formed on 22 August 1940, becoming operational on 25 April 1941; No. 305 (Polish) Bomber Squadron 'Wielkopolan, Marshal Józef Piłsudski' was formed on 29 August 1940, becoming operational on 25 April 1941; No. 306 (Polish) Fighter Squadron 'City of Toruń' was formed on 28 August 1940, becoming operational from 8 November 1940; No. 307 (Polish) Night Fighter Squadron 'Lwów Eagle Owl' was formed on 24 August 1940, becoming operational on 4 December 1940; No. 308 (Polish) Fighter Squadron 'City of Cracow' was formed on 9 September 1940, becoming operational on 1 December 1940; No. 309 (Polish) Army Co-operation (later Fighter) Squadron 'Czerwińska Province' was formed on 7 October 1940, becoming operational from 11 November 1940. After the Battle of Britain, more squadrons were formed: No. 315 (Polish) Fighter Squadron 'City of Dęblin' was formed on 21 January 1941, becoming operational on 18 March 1941; No. 316 (Polish) Fighter Squadron 'Warsaw' was formed on

23 February 1941, becoming operational from 25 March 1941; No. 317 (Polish) Fighter Squadron 'City of Wilno' was formed on 22 February 1941, becoming operational on 23 March 1941; No. 318 (Polish) Fighter-Reconnaissance Squadron 'City of Gdańsk' was formed on 20 March 1943, becoming operational from 2 May 1944.

14. Bolesław Drobiński, *Polscy lotnicy w Bitwie o Wielką Brytanię* (*Polish Airmen in the Battle of Britain*), Skrzydła, Wings No 121/607.

Chapter 7

1. In RAF terminology, 'pancake' usually means a hard landing without using the undercarriage. It is not clear what Ostowicz meant by this in this instance, but it may just be that he was ordered to return to base.
2. Bomber wing.
3. Witold Urbanowicz, *Świt zwycięstwa* (*Dawn of Victory*), Znak, Cracow, 2009.
4. In Polish, '*głowa*' means 'head'.
5. Kenneth Mackenzie, *Hurricane Combat, The Nine Lives of a Fighter Pilot*, William Kimber, London, 1987.
6. Christopher Yeoman & John Freeborn, *Tiger Club. The story of John Freeborn DFC, a 74 Squadron Fighter Pilot in WWII*, Pen & Sword Books Ltd, Barnsley, 2009.
7. Stephen Bungay, *The Most Dangerous Enemy, A History of the Battle of Britain*, Aurum Press, London, 2001.
8. Mieczysław Jonikas, Hesio, 'Skrzydła' ('Wings') No. 121/607.
9. Dilip Sarkar, *Missing in Action. Resting in Peace?*, Victory Books, Worcester, 2006.
10. Ibid.
11. Richard Townshend Bickers, Ginger Lacey. Fighter Pilot, Uniform Press, London 2015
12. Similarly to the system that was applied in Britain, the PAF was reborn in France and as such operated under command of the Armée de l'Air.
13. Flight Lieutenant David Crook DFC, *Spitfire pilot. A Personal Account of the Battle of Britain*, Greenhill Books, London, 2006. Crook was lost at sea on 18 December 1944, and therefore did not see how less than a year later Poland was handed over by the Allies from one oppressor to another.
14. His Polish personnel were referring to the popular story of a boy who was constantly causing problems – an Enfant Terrible. Poles were initially rather apprehensive about Kellett due to his lack of combat experience, but also because he came from the Auxiliary Air Force, which in their view was more a 'Sunday flying experience' than a serious staff post. His main opponent was his future counterpart Witold Urbanowicz, who criticized his leading and fighting abilities. By comparison, Flight Lieutenant John Kent quickly gained the respect of his Polish pilots and was subsequently nicknamed 'Kentowski' after his surname had been Polonized.
15. No. 303 Squadron's code letters were RF.
16. Ronald Gustave Kellett, 303 Squadron Polish Air Force, Skrzydła Nr 106/592.
17. Wacław Król, *Walczyłem pod niebem Londynu* (*I Fought Under the Sky of London*), LSW, Warsaw, 1982.
18. No. 302 Squadron's code letters were WX.

19. Jan Maliński, *Samolot zakrył słońce* (*An Aircraft Obscured the Sun*), Altair, Warsaw.
20. Mieczysław Mümler's letter published in Skrzydła, Wings No 121/607
21. Until August 1945, when it changed to QH.
22. Originally formed in November 1918 as III Squadron (*Eskadra*).
23. Lieutenant Elliot Chess designed the 'Kościuszko' badge.
24. Alongside General Kazimierz Pułaski, known as the father of American cavalry, who fought and died during the American Revolutionary War against the British,
25. Rafał is the Polish version of the Hebrew name Rafael, *Rafałki* being a plural diminutive (Rafaels); on 2 August 1945, No. 303 Squadron's code letters were changed to PD.
26. The Luftwaffe did not use this type of fighter aircraft operationally.
27. Dive-Bomber Wing.
28. Long Range Reconnaissance Wing.
29. Now Vilnius.
30. According to German documentation, the body of Antoni Ostowicz was washed ashore and buried, but to date no trace in the records of any known burial place can be found (AIR81/1327, NA, Kew).
31. Letter from Flying Officer Tadeusz Nowierski to Flight Lieutenant Stanisław Brzezina.

Chapter 8

1. Most probably he attacked a Ju 88 of KG51.
2. Fighter Wing.
3. Witold Urbanowicz, *Świt zwycięstwa* (*Dawn of Victory*), Znak, Cracow, 2009.
4. The last one was performed prior to the famous Paszkiewicz encounter.
5. Group Captain Stanisław Brzezina was killed on 13 February 1946 in a flying accident.
6. There is a short note about his injury in his flying log book.
7. This nickname appeared painted on some of the aircraft he flew.
8. Demonstration Wing.
9. 12 August 1940.
10. Janusz Żurakowski, *Nie tylko o lataniu* (Not Only About Flying), PFW, Toronto, 2002.
11. Grzegorz Śliżewski, *Zapomniane zwycięstwo por. Gruszki* (*Lt Gruszka's Forgotten Victory*), Gapa 5/2012.

Chapter 9

1. Since 1936, training at the PAF College in Dęblin had been extended from two to three years. However, due to the danger of the outbreak of war, the 12th Class (1937-39) had been posted to front-line units before their official graduation, whilst the 13th Entry (1938-40) left school a year before the end of their education process. Cadets of both classes were promoted to their officer ranks in the field. The last entry of the PAF College (1939-41) was at an early stage of training, but most of these Cadets received promotions in Britain.
2. Bolesław Drobiński, 'Boys' own stories', *Sunday Express*, 8 July 1990.

3. Bolesław Drobiński, *Polscy lotnicy w Bitwie o Wielką Brytanię* (*Polish Airmen in the Battle of Britain*), Skrzydła, Wings No 121/607.

4. Doug Stokes, *Paddy Finucane. Fighter Ace*, Crécy Publishing, Manchester, 2015.

5. Different dates were given, one of them stating that he arrived on 12 August.

6. They were soon moved to Rochford in Essex.

7. Dilip Sarkar, *Missing in Action. Resting in Peace?*, Victory Books, Worcester, 2006.

8. Jerzy B. Cynk, *The Polish Air Force at War. The Official History. 1919-1943*, Shiffer Publishing Ltd, Atglen, 1998. Franciszek Gruszka's remains were recovered on 15 April 1974 from Grove Marsh. No indication of being shot was found.

9. He was killed on that day.

10. Wladek Gnyś, *First Kill. A Fighter Pilot's Autobiography*, William Kimber, London, 1981.

11. He was credited consequently with 1/3 He 111, 1 Bf 109 and 1 & 1/3 Ju 87, when he flew Moranes MS. 406s with the Groupe de Chasse I/2.

12. Kenneth Mackenzie, *Hurricane Combat, The Nine Lives of a Fighter Pilot*, William Kimber, London, 1987.

13. Ibid.

14. Being previously posted to No. 152 Squadron.

Chapter 10

1. Including one shared.

2. Johnny Kent, *One of the Few*, The History Press, Stroud, 2016.

3. Nina Britton Boyle, *Blood on their Wingtips*, Book Tower Publishing, Redditch, 2016.

4. Marian Bełc's diary, copy in author's possession.

5. Ronald Gustave Kellett, *303 Squadron Polish Air Force*, Skrzydła – Wings. Wiadomości ze świata, 106/592.

6. Ronald Gustave Kellett, *303 Squadron Polish Air Force*, Skrzydła – Wings. Wiadomości ze świata, 106/592.

7. His mother Zofia Babińska married Ivan Ferić, but after the First World War (and her husband's death) returned to Poland.

8. Germans also executed a young local boy who had given help to the Polish pilot.

9. John E. Lewis, *Spitfire. The Autobiography. The plane and the men that saved Britain in 1940 – in their own words*, Robinson, London, 2010.

10. Oświęcim is a Polish name of a town in southern Poland; after German annexation in 1939, names were changed by the occupiers, so therefore the term 'Auschwitz' is still in use to this day (mainly in the West), even though the Germans were forced from Poland in 1945. Hopefully this symbolizes the tragedy that was associated with the German name, rather than shows an ignorance of historians.

11. A series of massacres of nearly 22,000 Polish officers, policemen and intelligentsia were conducted by the Soviet NKVD in the spring 1940 in Katyń forest, Kalinin, Kharkiv and elsewhere. They came to light only in 1943, when German troops found Polish remains in mass graves near Smolensk, Russia.

12. Johnny Kent, *One of the Few*, The History Press, Stroud, 2016.

13. Ronald Gustave Kellett, *303 Squadron Polish Air Force*, Skrzydła – Wings. Wiadomości ze świata, 106/592.

14. Air Chief Marshal Lord Dowding, *Polish Airmen in the Battle of Britain*, Skrzydła, Wings No. 142/628.
15. Geoffrey Marsh, *Squadron 303*, Kościuszko, 'Collaboration with the English'.

Chapter 11
1. Wladek Gnyś, *First Kill. A Fighter Pilot's Autobiography*, William Kimber, London, 1981.
2. Letter to author.
3. Jan Jokiel, *Udział Polaków w Bitwie o Anglię* (*Poles in the Battle of Britain*), PAX, Warsaw, 1972.
4. In at least one Combat Report he appears as 'Polish' and his surname is misspelt as 'Franczisek' or 'Franzisek'. František and Sergeant Jozef Káňa (a Slovak), after the Czechoslovak Armed Forces were dissolved, voluntarily and permanently joined the Polish Air Force in June and July 1939 respectively. Despite the fact that Free Czechoslovak Air Force units were formed in Britain, both stayed in the PAF (in the case of František until his death in 1940 and for Káňa until demobilization in 1946). As they were not of Polish nationality, their actions are not described in this book with details.
5. Seven fighter squadrons of the Polish Air Force operated from RAF Northolt between 1940 and 1944, and the last of them to leave the base was No. 308 in April 1944.
6. Jan Zumbach, *Ostatnia walka* (*The Last Fight*), ECHO, Warsaw, 2000.
7. Nina Britton-Boyle, *Blood on their Wingtips. A Second World War Timeline for No. 303 Kościuszko Polish Squadron at RAF Northolt*, Book Tower Publishing, Redditch, 2016.
8. Johnny Kent, *One of the Few*, The History Press, Stroud, 2016.
9. Stephen Bungay, *The Most Dangerous Enemy. A History of the Battle of Britain*, Aurum Press, London, 2000.
10. Peter Sikora, *Kobiece serce jest głębokim oceanem tajemnic* (*Woman's Heart is a Deep Ocean of Secrets, biography of Stefan Wójtowicz*), Gapa 19, August 2016.
11. Franciszek Grabowski, *Skalski. Against All Odds. The First Allied Ace of the Second World War*, Fonthill, Stroud, 2017.
12. The remains of Hurricane P2985 that he flew are exhibited at the Polish Institute and Sikorski Museum in London.
13. Zdzisław Krasnodębski, *Wspomnienia wojenne* (*Wartime Recollections*), Skrzydła – Wings, 1975. Krasnodębski initially was taken to Farnborough Hospital and consequently to the Queen Victoria Hospital at East Grinstead, where McIndoe performed plastic surgery on him. Despite successful operations, 'The King' did not fly operationally again, despite recovering from this terrible experience.
14. Peter Sikora, *Zapomniany epizod bitwy o Anglię* (*Forgotten Episode of the Battle of Britain*), Lotnictwo z Szachownicą 28 (3/2008).
15. Janusz Żurakowski, *Nie tylko o lataniu* (*Not Only About Flying*), PFZ, Toronto, 2002.
16. No Polish pilot bailed out or crash-landed on that day, therefore the circumstances of the event described remain a mystery.
17. Dr Richard Cobb, 'The Tennis Party', letter published in *Skrzydla* (*Wings*) magazine.

Chapter 12

1. Alan C. Deere, *Nine Lives*, Crécy Publishing Ltd, Manchester, 2005.
2. Witold Urbanowicz, *Świt zwycięstwa* (Dawn of Victory), Znak, Cracow, 2009.
3. Many parts of Pisarek's Hurricane were excavated in 1976. His left shoe that was stuck in the cockpit was also found.
4. Johnny Kent, *One of the Few*, The History Press, Stroud, 2016.
5. Remains of Sergeant Wünsche's Hurricane were found in 1979 and 2015.
6. Except that Pilot Officers Jerzy Popławski and Stefan Stegman, followed by Sergeant Michał Maciejowski, joined 111 Squadron. Pilot Officer Franciszek Surma left 151 Squadron, being posted to 607 Squadron.
7. There are repeated untrue stories published in various books, based on the incorrect date of his death that was initially placed on his grave, claiming that Cebrzyński was still alive when taken to hospital and died almost a week later.
8. Johnny Kent, *One of the Few*, The History Press, Stroud, 2016.
9. It is quite possible that all three pilots were claiming the same aircraft.
10. Duszyński's body was exhumed, but soon after buried as unknown in an unspecified place.
11. Bohdan Ejbich, *Gdzie niebo się kończy* (*Where the Sky Ends*), Bellona, Warsaw, 1997.
12. Two days before, the first operational order had been received, but due to bad weather, eventually the operation was cancelled. Nos 300 and 301 were respectively coded BH and GR.
13. Author's interview with Colonel Władysław Łapot.
14. Ibid.
15. Ibid.
16. 'Polish Bomber Squadrons', *Skrzydła* (*Wings*) No. 131/373, October 1941.

Chapter 13

1. Extracts from the 'Diary of a British Pilot with 303 Squadron', *Skrzydła* (*Wings*) No. 128/370, 1–14 September 1941.
2. They also operated from Duxford on a regular basis.
3. Julian Roch Kowalski, *Nad ujściem Tamizy* (*Over the Thames Estuary*), Skrzydła, Wings, No. 120/606.
4. Combat Reports were written in Polish and then translated into English.
5. Julian Roch Kowalski, *Nad ujściem Tamizy* (*Over the Thames Estuary*), Skrzydła, Wings, No. 120/606.
6. The replica of a Hawker Hurricane at the entrance to the Imperial War Museum at Duxford is finished in the colours of Tadeusz Chłopik's aircraft in which he was killed.
7. Acting Squadron Leader.
8. His first name erroneously also appears as 'Walery' in various publications.
9. Test Wing.
10. Jan Jokiel, *Udział Polaków w Bitwie o Anglię* (*Poles in the Battle of Britain*), PAX, Warsaw ,1972.

11. Kazimierz Węgrzecki, *Kosynierzy Warszawscy. Historia 303 Dywizjonu Myśliwskiego Warszawskiego imienia Tadeusza Kościuszki* (*Warsaw Scythemen. History of No. 303 'Warsaw Tadeusz Kościuszko' Fighter Squadron*), Varitas, London, 1968.
12. Ibid.
13. Arkady Fiedler, *Dywizjon 303* (*303 Squadron*), Wydawnictwo Poznańskie, Poznań, 1985.
14. Geoffrey Marsh, *Squadron 303*, Kościuszko, 'The collaboration with the English'.
15. Author's interview with Colonels Władysław Łapot and Zygmunt Szymański.

Chapter 14

1. Sergeant Mieczysław Popek was a non-operational pilot during the Battle of Britain.
2. No fighter pilot of such or similar name ever served in the PAF.
3. Flying Officer Henryk Skalski, one of three Polish fighter pilots with this surname.
4. Wing Commander Tom Neil, 'The Way it Really Was', *Aeroplane Monthly*, September 1984.
5. Bohdan Ejbich, *Gdzie niebo się kończy* (*Where the Sky Ends*), Bellona, Warsaw, 1997.
6. Both languages, although belonging to the same group of Slavic languages, had the same number of similarities as differences. They may sound alike to non-Polish or non-Russian speaking people, but many words in both languages have completely different meanings, therefore author Larry Forrester's theory expressed above had very little to do with reality.
7. Larry Forrester, *Fly for Your Life: The Story of RR Stanford Tuck, DSO, DFC (Fortunes of War)*, Cerberus Publishing Ltd, London, 2005.
8. Bohdan Ejbich, *Gdzie niebo się kończy* (Where the Sky Ends), Bellona, Warsaw, 1997.
9. Ronald Kellett, *303 Squadron Polish Air Force*, Skrzydła Wings, No. 106/592.
10. Mieczysław Mümler's letter published in Skrzydła, Wings No 121/607
11. In November 1940 he joined Polish No. 307 (Night Fighter) Squadron and was killed in a flying accident on 10 April 1941.
12. Quite often his crash site is erroneously spelled as 'Albermuse'.

Chapter 15

1. Raymond Myles Beecham Duke-Woolley.
2. During the two months of summer 1940 when No. 303 Squadron operated from Northolt, and prior to the King's visit, there were numerous VIPs seen at the Station: the Duke of Kent (who visited several times), the Ambassador of the United States, the First Lord of the Admiralty Albert Alexander, Prime Minister Winston Churchill, General Stanisław Ujejski, the Inspector of the PAF, Group Captain Stefan Pawlikowski (who represented the entire Polish fighter force in Britain), Under-Secretary of State Harold Belfour, General Władysław Sikorski and ACM Sir Edgar Ludlow-Hewitt, Inspector General of the RAF.
3. AIR28/601 National Archives, Kew

4. On 5 October 1940, Sergeant Karubin was credited with one Bf 109 destroyed while flying this aircraft, P3901. A replica of a Hurricane that commemorates this particular aircraft was unveiled by Urbanowicz's son on 4 September 2010 at the site of the RAF Bunker and 11 Group Operations Room at Uxbridge.
5. AIR27/2102, National Archive, Kew.

Chapter 16
1. These and following numbers do not include seventeen victories gained by Czechoslovak pilot Sergeant Josef František. Although he was a legitimate member of the Polish Air Force (not a 'guest', as some sources claim), he wasn't of Polish nationality.
2. This loss is also associated with Urbanowicz's action.
3. Pilot Officer Noel Agazarian was also credited with damaging a He 111.
4. Flight Lieutenant David Crook DFC, *Spitfire pilot. A Personal Account of the Battle of Britain*, Greenhill Books, London, 2006.
5. Various dates of arrival are given.
6. Meanwhile on 4 October, 40-year-old Squadron Leader Karol Eberhardt lost his life in a mid-air crash while serving as an instructor in the Signal School at South Carney. The Westland Wallace in which he flew with a pupil collided in the air with an Airspeed Oxford. Eberhardt formerly served as commander of the 13th Air Squadron (later Accompanying Squadron).
7. Other sources suggest 13.15 as the time of the attack
8. Various accounts differ whether there were four, three or two bombs dropped and one of them did not explode

Chapter 17
1. In October 2015, a memorial plaque was unveiled at Kempton Park Racecourse dedicated to both pilots, Flying Officer Borowski and Flying Officer Carter, in which the author of this book had the honour to be involved.
2. Larry Forrester, *Fly for Your Life: The Story of R.R. Stanford Tuck, D.S.O., D.F.C. and Two Bars*, Bantam Books, New York, 1978.

Chapter 18
1. Ronald Kellett also expressed his gratitude towards the first commander of 303 Squadron, Squadron Leader Zdzisław Krasnodębski, and to Squadron Leader Adam Kowalczyk, who took command on 7 November 1940, and about whom he knew considerably less, hence completely ignoring Witold Urbanowicz, with whom he fought side-by-side throughout most of the squadron's hardest days. This only confirms the lack of goodwill between these two officers.
2. Nina Britton Boyle, *Blood on their Wingtips*, Book Tower Publishing, Redditch, 2016.
3. Ibid.
4. R.C. Cobb, 'The Polish Air Force and English Public Opinion', *Skrzydla* (*Wings*) article dated 1941.

5. Professor Peter J. O'Grady, 'The Exploits of the Polish Air Force and the British Press', *Skrzydla* (*Wings*).
6. Ibid.
7. Anna McLaren, 'Free to Fight', *Skrzydla* (*Wings*).
8. In the Polish Air Force all ranks were the same as in the Army, but always accompanied by the specialization of the airman: (for example 'kapitan pilot', 'porucznik obserwator' [observer] or 'plutonowy strzelec samolotowy' [air gunner]). The lowest rank of flying personnel was 'szeregowy'. In pre-war Poland it was always an officer (mostly observer) who commanded the plane. Unless as the first word of a sentence, all Polish (spelled in Polish) ranks appear in lower case.
9. The only equivalent was Cadet. Podchorąży was a title (not rank) given to all students of Polish Officers Schools.

Index

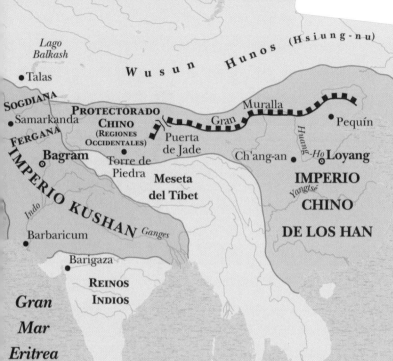

Lago
Balkash

W u s u n   H u n o s   (H s i u n g - n u)

• Talas

SOGDIANA

• Samarkanda

PROTECTORADO
CHINO
(REGIONES
OCCIDENTALES)

Muralla

Gran

Pequín •

FERGANA

Bagram

Torre de
Piedra

Puerta
de Jade

Ch'ang-an •

Huang

-Ho **Loyang**

IMPERIO KUSHAN

Indo

Meseta
del Tíbet

Ganges

IMPERIO

Yangtsé

CHINO

• Barbaricum

DE LOS HAN

• Barigaza

Gran

REINOS
INDIOS

Mar

Eritrea

A E
& I

La legión perdida

Autores Españoles e Iberoamericanos

Santiago Posteguillo

La legión perdida

El sueño inmortal de Trajano

© Santiago Posteguillo, 2016
© Editorial Planeta, S. A., 2016
   Diagonal, 662-664, 08034 Barcelona (España)
   www.editorial.planeta.es
   www.planetadelibros.com

Diseño de la colección: © Compañía
Ilustraciones de guerreros: © Luis Doyague
Ilustraciones de los mapas de interior y de las guardas delanteras: © Gradualmap
Ilustraciones de las guardas traseras: © Alademosca

Primera edición: febrero de 2016
Depósito legal: B. 93-2016
ISBN 978-84-08-15108-1
Composición: Víctor Igual, S. L.
Impresión y encuadernación: Liberdúplex, S. L.
Printed in Spain - Impreso en España

El papel utilizado para la impresión de este libro es cien por cien libre de cloro y
   está calificado como **papel ecológico**

A mi padre
Requiescat in pace in aeternum

AGRADECIMIENTOS

—

La legión perdida ha supuesto el mayor reto narrativo y de documentación al que he hecho frente como novelista. No habría podido terminar este proyecto, que supone el final de la trilogía de Trajano, sin la colaboración y la ayuda de muchas personas. Estoy particularmente agradecido a la doctora Claudia Winterstein, del Departamento de Investigación de Construcciones Históricas del Máster en Conservación de Patrimonio Histórico del Instituto de Arquitectura de la Universidad Técnica de Berlín. La doctora Winterstein hizo su tesis doctoral sobre el monumento funerario a Trajano y me facilitó todo tipo de información relevante sobre éste y otros edificios de la época final del emperador hispano. También he de dar las gracias, una vez más, a la profesora Julita Juan Grau (catedrática de griego clásico en el IES Ribalta de Valencia) por su ayuda con textos latinos, griegos y, muy especialmente, por su trabajo en la elaboración de los glosarios y citas de parto y sánscrito. Pero *La legión perdida* abarca aún más culturas y lugares, de modo que muchas gracias también a la profesora Li Joan Su de la Si Chuan Normal University de China, por tomarse el tiempo de sentarse conmigo a revisar, uno a uno, los textos y citas en chino clásico que aparecen en la novela, para asegurarse de que estén correctamente traducidos o reproducidos en cada momento. Gracias al doctor Lluís Messeguer (catedrático de catalán de la Universitat Jaume I), por ponerme en contacto con la profesora Li Joan Su.

Gracias también a mis compañeros en la Universitat Jaume I, los doctores Jesús Bermúdez (catedrático de latín) y Rubén Montañes (profesor titular de griego clásico), a quienes sigo importunando con preguntas sobre el mundo clásico cada vez que me cruzo con ellos en los pasillos de la universidad.

Por supuesto, cualquier error que pudiera haber en la novela con referencia a estas lenguas u otros ámbitos es responsabilidad únicamente mía.

Gracias al doctor Vicent Climent (rector de la Universitat Jaume I) y su equipo de gobierno y a la doctora Elena Ortells (directora del departamento de Estudios Ingleses), a la doctora Lluïsa Gea (directora de la titulación de Estudios Ingleses) y a la doctora Rosa Agost (decana de la facultad de Ciencias Humanas y Sociales), por facilitar que pueda seguir compatibilizando mi tarea como escritor con la de profesor de lengua y literatura inglesa y americana.

No puedo en modo alguno olvidarme de mi editora, Puri Plaza, de la Editorial Planeta, por su paciencia conmigo y por sus siempre acertadas sugerencias sobre forma y contenido que, con toda seguridad, han mejorado el resultado final del manuscrito. Escribir puede ser difícil, pero con una editora como Puri Plaza todo es mucho más fácil. Gracias también a Consuelo Jiménez por su meticulosa corrección de todo el texto y una mención especial para Ana Jiménez, por estar siempre atenta a tantas palabras extrañas en tantos alfabetos diferentes.

Gracias al resto del equipo editorial de Planeta, en particular a Raquel Gisbert y Belén López, por creer en esta novela tan ambiciosa y permitirme volar con mi imaginación y con mis palabras tanto como he estimado necesario para transmitir a los lectores una amplia recreación del mundo antiguo. Gracias también a Laura Verdura, Carmen Ramírez y Francisco Barrera y a todos los que trabajan en los departamentos de comunicación y comercial de Planeta, que trazan puentes entre escritores y lectores constantemente en tiempos donde ésta es una tarea tan esencial como ardua. Gracias al departamento de diseño gráfico por las ilustraciones y los mapas, que estoy seguro ayudarán a que quienes lean *La legión perdida* puedan hacerse una mejor idea de cómo era aquel mundo antiguo.

Estoy muy agradecido, como siempre, a mi hermano Javier, que hace de primer lector de cuanto escribo. Gracias también a su mujer, Pilar Aznar, por ser también una de las primeras lectoras de la novela y darme su opinión.

Gracias a Lisa, mi mujer, y Elsa, mi hija, por permitirme escribir más horas de las que es sensato y, pese a ello, seguir a mi lado apoyándome en todo momento y con fe ciega en todo lo que hago.

Gracias a los legionarios de la legión perdida de Craso por crear una leyenda tan espectacular que perdura a lo largo de los siglos, y gracias, cómo no, a Trajano, un emperador tan inconmensurable que tres mil páginas de trilogía apenas dan para esbozar una parte de sus méritos, de sus defectos y de sus sueños.

INFORMACIÓN IMPORTANTE PARA EL LECTOR

—

La legión perdida es una novela narrada en dos tiempos: por un lado, la historia del ejército perdido transcurre en el entorno de la segunda mitad del siglo i a. C., mientras que, por otro, la historia de Trajano y su campaña contra los partos tiene lugar aproximadamente ciento cincuenta años después, en el principio del siglo ii d. C.

En la época de la legión perdida, el mundo se dividía en tres grandes imperios: la República de Roma (en transición ya hacia su formato imperial), el Imperio parto y el Imperio han de China. Entre el Imperio parto y el Imperio han estaban los reinos de Sogdiana, Margiana o Fergana, entre otros, que caerán bajo el poder brutal del Imperio huno de los hermanos Zhizhi y Huhanye.

En la época de Trajano, el mundo había cambiado y en lugar de tres había cuatro grandes imperios: el Imperio romano, el Imperio parto, el Imperio kushan del norte de la India y el Imperio han. El territorio de los hunos había pasado a ser controlado por los kushan, y los hunos (o *hsiung-nu*) se desplazaron más al norte.

Los siguientes diagramas resumen los gobernantes más poderosos, las lenguas, las religiones y la población de cada uno de estos territorios en sus respectivos períodos.

Al final de la novela se incluye más información adicional en forma de mapas, apéndices y glosarios sobre la historia de estos territorios que pueden resultar de interés durante la lectura de *La legión perdida*. También hay una nota histórica donde se explica qué hay de realidad y qué de ficción en esta novela, si bien es mejor, para mantener la intriga de ciertos aspectos de la trama, no leerla hasta la conclusión de la obra.

Diagrama I. El mundo a mediados del siglo I a. C.

	EUROPA Y NORTE DE ÁFRICA	ASIA		
	Imperio romano[1]	*Imperio parto* (An-shi)	*Imperio huno* subyugando los reinos de Sogdiana, Margiana y Fergana en Asia central entre otros	*Imperio han del oeste* (China) (Imperio han)
Gobernantes principales	Julio César, Pompeyo y Craso	Orodes	Zhizhi Huhanye	Emperador Yuan

1. Desde un punto de vista técnico el Imperio romano no empieza hasta Augusto, pero en la época de César, Pompeyo y Craso el Estado romano ya funcionaba *de facto* como un imperio.

La legión perdida es la historia de la campaña militar de mayor envergadura que emprendió nunca el Imperio romano, pero también es la historia de las relaciones entre cuatro formas diferentes de gobernar y de entender el mundo. *La legión perdida* es un gran viaje hacia un pasado donde todo, pese a las enormes distancias, estaba mucho más cerca de lo que nos imaginamos.

Diagrama II. El mundo a principios del siglo II d. C.

	EUROPA Y NORTE DE ÁFRICA	ASIA		
	Imperio romano	*Imperio parto*	*Imperio kushan*	*Imperio han del este* (China)
Nombre del imperio para los chinos	Da Qin	An-shi	Yuegzhi	Imperio han
Gobernante principal	Trajano	Osroes	Kadphises y Kanishka	Deng (regente)
Otros gobernantes o líderes de relevancia	Adriano Lucio Quieto	Partamasiris Partamaspates Mitrídates Vologases		Emperador niño An-ti
Población	55-60 millones	10-30 millones	10-30 millones	55-60 millones
Religiones	Politeísmo grecolatino Judaísmo Cristianismo	Zoroastrismo Judaísmo Otras religiones	Budismo Otras religiones	Confucionismo Taoísmo Budismo Otras religiones
Lenguas principales en los círculos de poder	Latín y griego	Parto y griego	Sánscrito	Chino clásico

DRAMATIS PERSONAE
EN TIEMPOS DE CRASO Y LA LEGIÓN PERDIDA
—

Personajes del Imperio romano

Marco Licinio Craso, cónsul al mando del ejército de Oriente
Publio Licinio Craso, tribuno, hijo de Marco Licinio Craso
Casio, *quaestor*
Censorino, tribuno
Megabaco, tribuno
Octavio, tribuno
Petronio, tribuno
Druso, centurión (nacido en Cartago Nova)
Cayo, legionario (nacido en Corduba)
Sexto, legionario (nacido en Corduba)

Personajes del Imperio parto

Orodes, emperador de Partia, rey de reyes
Artavasdes, rey de Armenia
Surena, *spāhbod* o general del ejército parto
Sillaces, oficial del ejército parto
Fraates, hijo de Orodes
Pacoro, hijo de Orodes
Pomaxatres, soldado parto

Personajes del Imperio huno

Zhizhi, líder de los *hsiung-nu* o hunos de Asia central
Huhanye, hermano de Zhizhi enfrentado a éste mortalmente

Personajes del Imperio han

Chen Tang, *chiang-chün* o general del Imperio han
Kan Yen, *shou* o gobernador de Gansu
Ku Chi, embajador han

Personajes de otros reinos o territorios

Ariemnes, mercader árabe
Nanaifarn, comerciante sogdiano

DRAMATIS PERSONAE
EN TIEMPOS DE TRAJANO
—

Personajes del Imperio romano

Familia imperial
Marco Ulpio Trajano, *Imperator Caesar Augustus*
Pompeya Plotina, esposa de Trajano
Publio Elio Adriano, sobrino segundo de Trajano
Vibia Sabina, sobrina nieta de Trajano
Marcia, madre de Trajano
Ulpia Marciana, hermana de Trajano
Matidia mayor, sobrina de Trajano
Matidia menor, sobrina nieta de Trajano
Rupilia Faustina, sobrina nieta de Trajano

Leales a Trajano
Lucio Quieto, *legatus* y jefe de la caballería, amigo de Trajano
Nigrino, *legatus*, amigo de Trajano
Celso, senador y *legatus*
Palma, senador y *legatus*

Amigos de Adriano
Publio Acilio Attiano, antiguo tutor de Adriano
Julio Urso Serviano, cuñado de Adriano
Cayo Fusco Salinator, sobrino político de Adriano
Pompeyo Colega, senador
Cacio Frontón, senador
Salvio Liberal, senador

Otros oficiales
Sexto Attio Suburano, jefe del pretorio

Tiberio Claudio Liviano, jefe del pretorio
Aulo, tribuno pretoriano
Calvencio Victor, jefe de la guardia personal de Nigrino
Julio Alejandro, *legatus*
Julio Máximo, *legatus*
C. Claudio Severo, tribuno al servicio de Palma en Arabia
Tercio Juliano, *legatus* de la VII Claudia en Moesia Superior
Tiberio Claudio Máximo, *oficial* de la caballería romana
Cincinato, tribuno militar en Moesia Superior
Catilio Severo, *legatus* y gobernador de Armenia

Integrantes de una misión secreta
Maes Titianus, comerciante sirio
Marcio (o Senex), gladiador y *lanista* del Anfiteatro Flavio
Alana, guerrera sármata, antigua *gladiatrix*, mujer de Marcio
Tamura, niña sármata, hija de Alana y Marcio
Áyax, gladiador
Arrio, centurión naval
Vibio, soldado pretoriano
Numerio, soldado pretoriano
Servio, soldado pretoriano

Cristianos
Ignacio, obispo de Antioquía
Evaristo, obispo de Roma
Alejandro, asistente del obispo de Roma
Telesforo, asistente del obispo de Roma
Marción, comerciante de Frigia

Otros personajes
Aretas, jefe de la guardia de Petra, al servicio del rey Obodas
Plinio el Joven, senador y abogado
Dión Coceyo, filósofo griego, en la actualidad más conocido
con el sobrenombre de **Dión Crisóstomo**
Fédimo, secretario del emperador Trajano
Critón, médico del emperador Trajano
Cayo Suetonio Tranquilo, escritor romano y *procurator bibliothecae augusti*

Apolodoro de Damasco, arquitecto
Domicia Longina, esposa de Domiciano, retirada de la vida
pública
Menenia, Vestal Máxima
Celer, auriga de la corporación de los rojos

Personajes del Imperio parto

Dinastía arsácida
Osroes, *Šāhān Šāh*, rey de reyes de Partia
Partamaspates, hijo de Osroes
Exedares, sobrino de Osroes, rey de Armenia
Partamasiris, hermano de Osroes, rey de Armenia
Mitrídates, hermano de Osroes
Sanatruces, hijo de Mitrídates
Vologases, noble arsácida que reclama el trono de rey de reyes
de Partia

Séquito de mujeres
Asiabatum, reina de reinas de Partia
Rixnu, reina consorte, favorita de Osroes
Aryazate, princesa parta, hija de Osroes
Kumaramitra, concubina enviada desde el Imperio kushan

Reyes y gobernadores de reinos controlados por Partia
Abgaro, rey de Osroene
Arbandes, hijo del rey de Osroene
Sporaces, rey de Anthemusia
Mebarsapes, rey de Adiabene
Elkud, *mry* o gobernador de Hatra
Nash Rihab, hijo de Elkud

Personajes del Imperio kushan

Kadphises, emperador kushan
Kanishka, hijo de Kadphises, heredero del Imperio kushan

Shaka, embajador y consejero del emperador Kadphises y luego de Kanishka

Buddhamitra, monja budista influyente en la corte kushan

Personajes del Imperio han

Familia imperial

He, emperador del Imperio han, casado con Deng

Deng, viuda del emperador He y regente

An-ti, hijo del emperador He y heredero del trono del Imperio han

Yan Ji, esposa favorita de An-ti

Li, esposa consorte de An-ti, madre del príncipe Liu Bao

Liu Bao, príncipe han hijo del emperador An-ti y de la consorte Li

Funcionarios

Fan Chun, asistente del ministro de Obras Públicas

Kan Ying, funcionario

Militares

Li Kan, oficial de la caballería han

Chi tu-wei, comandante de la caballería han

Otros

Ban Zao, tutora de la emperatriz viuda Deng

Zang Heng, astrónomo y matemático de la corte han

PROOEMIUM

—

Ciudad de Yu-yang
Frontera norte del Imperio han (China),
próxima a la Gran Muralla
Primer año del reinado del emperador An-ti (106 d. C.)

—Te voy a contar, hijo mío, una historia increíble. ¿Me escuchas?

—Sí, padre —respondió el joven que estaba sentado a su lado, junto al lecho de un hombre mayor que hablaba con cierta dificultad, sobreponiéndose al dolor de una larga enfermedad que lo consumía.

—Bien —continuó el anciano—. Atiende entonces, porque esta historia es el origen de tu fuerza. Es un relato, sin embargo, secreto. Nadie lo conoce aquí en la frontera norte del Imperio han. Sólo nosotros sabemos quiénes somos. —Se detuvo un momento. Reunió fuerzas—. Todo empezó hace más de cien años. Bastantes más. Hace... ciento sesenta años,[2] sí. Eran tiempos del emperador Yuan-ti. Hoy día, hijo mío, el mundo está dividido en cuatro imperios: nuestro gran Imperio han, el reino de los Yuegzhi,[3] el Imperio an-shi[4] y finalmente Da Qin.[5] Pero en aquella época los Yuegzhi aún no se habían hecho tan fuertes como ahora y en el lejano Da Qin, esto es lo importante, hijo, el poder estaba dividido entre tres hombres tan fuertes como ambiciosos. No, nadie conoce esta historia, ni los sabios del *Taixue*, la academia imperial, ni los minis-

---

2. Esto es, en 53 a. C.
3. Imperio kushan al norte de la India.
4. Imperio parto.
5. Imperio romano.

tros del emperador niño y de la emperatriz viuda en Loyang, pero nosotros, nuestra familia, siempre la hemos compartido de generación en generación y éste es el momento, muchacho, antes de que yo muera, de que tú la conozcas también.

»Aquellos tres hombres se llamaban César, Pompeyo y Craso. El primero luchaba en el norte de Da Qin o de Roma, como ellos mismos llaman al cuarto imperio; César batallaba para controlar la región y someterla a su mando combatiendo contra unos guerreros que los hombres de Da Qin conocían con el nombre de galos. Pompeyo, el segundo de aquellos gobernantes, dominaba las regiones más remotas de Da Qin, lo que ellos llaman Hispania, allí donde termina el mundo; mientras que el tercero, Craso, que quería igualarlos en poder, se encaminó hacia el oriente de su imperio, hacia la región que llaman Siria, limítrofe con An-shi. Craso era mayor que los otros dos hombres y sentía que se hacía viejo para equipararse en poder con ellos, así que ideó un plan para hacerse más fuerte que sus oponentes en muy poco tiempo: quería lanzarse desde el oriente de Da Qin hacia la conquista del Imperio an-shi o Partia, como Craso y los otros guerreros lo llamaban. Si él conseguía dominar los ríos y montañas de An-shi sería el más poderoso de los tres y luego juntaría a sus dominios el de todo Da Qin, pues estaba seguro de que, una vez sometido el Imperio an-shi, podría derrotar a César y Pompeyo. Así, Craso, con el acuerdo de los otros dos hombres, que absorbidos por sus propios problemas quizá no intuían el plan de su contrincante, reunió un poderoso ejército y cruzó el río que traza la frontera entre Da Qin y An-shi.[6] Ahora te cuento yo esta historia, como hizo antes mi padre y el padre de mi padre al mío y así hasta llegar a tu tatarabuelo, que fue quien vivió en aquel tiempo y fue un importante oficial del ejército de Craso. Aún hoy día, si cierro los ojos, hijo mío, me parece que puedo ver a todos aquellos hombres, a todo aquel inmenso ejército en movimiento, como si lo tuviera ante mí, como si yo mismo hubiera estado allí. Cierra tú ahora los ojos, hijo mío, y escucha mi relato.

6. El Éufrates.

HISTORIA DE LA LEGIÓN PERDIDA

Tiempos de Julio César, Pompeyo y Craso,
mediados del siglo I a. C.

LIBRO I

1
—

LA MALDICIÓN DE ATEYO

Ciudad de Zeugma, junto al Éufrates
Oriente de Siria, frontera entre Roma y Partia
53 a. C.

Druso era un joven centurión de las legiones de Craso desplazadas a Asia para la mayor de las conquistas jamás imaginadas, pero los legionarios bajo su mando no parecían estar tan seguros de que todo fuera a salir bien. Sus hombres hablaban a su espalda mientras él oteaba el horizonte con la mano derecha sobre la frente para protegerse de un sol abrasador.

—Este calor es infernal —empezó Cayo, uno de los soldados más veteranos pese a su juventud, mientras se arrodillaba junto al río Éufrates para echarse algo de agua por el cuello y refrescarse.

—Y no nos toca cruzar hasta el mediodía —añadió Sexto, más joven aún y más inexperto, angustiado por el sudor y la espera interminable—. Aquí no hay sombra donde guarecerse.

Druso pensó en decir algo, en insistir en que eran legionarios de Roma y no niños que tuvieran que estar siempre al abrigo de las inclemencias del tiempo, fueran éstas el gélido frío de las montañas de Helvetia o el asfixiante calor de aquel sol de Siria, pero optó por beber agua y callar. Craso, el cónsul al mando de aquella expedición, había programado aquel cruce del río de forma demasiado lenta; sin duda no parecía el mejor de los líderes posibles. En eso sus hombres llevaban razón y por eso hablaban y se lamentaban.

—Ahora tenemos este sol, sí —continuó Cayo—, pero recordad los truenos y los relámpagos de los días pasados, como venidos de la nada. Y el viento huracanado que hundió varias balsas ayer. Hasta uno de los decuriones se vio arrastrado por las aguas y aún no han encontrado el cuerpo. Y acordaos también de lo que cuentan en la primera legión del estandarte con el águila cuando lo levantaron para empezar a cruzar el río.

—Es cierto: todos son malos augurios —completó Sexto—. El estandarte se giró solo, como si quisiera dirigirse de regreso a Roma.

—Y para colmo ya sabéis qué sacos de comida han abierto los primeros, ¿verdad? —preguntó Cayo, pero feliz al ver que todos negaban con la cabeza se situó en medio del corro de sus compañeros legionarios, que lo escuchaban atentos; le encantaba ser el centro de atención—. Lentejas y sal. Sí, ésos son los sacos que han abierto primero.

Todos negaban con la cabeza como intentando así hacer desaparecer aquella atrocidad. Las lentejas y la sal eran alimento de duelo y se otorgaban como ofrendas a los muertos con frecuencia.

—Es la maldición de Ateyo —añadió Cayo para rematar su perorata desmoralizadora, pero en ese momento Druso intervino al fin y lo interrumpió antes de que siguiera.

—¡Por Hércules! ¡Ya es suficiente! ¡Parecéis viejas a la luz de una hoguera contando historias para asustar a niños cobardes! El tribuno me ha dicho que cruzaremos el río en el siguiente turno por el puente de barcazas, así que recogedlo todo y preparad los pertrechos para llevarlos a la espalda. ¡Trabajad y callad, por Júpiter!

Praetorium *de campaña*

—Alguien tiene que hablar con el ejército e insuflarle valor —dijo Casio, el *quaestor* de las legiones desplazadas a Oriente.

Marco Licinio Craso, el cónsul al mando de aquella gigantesca maquinaria de guerra de más de sesenta mil legionarios, escuchaba sentado en su *sella curulis*.

—Cuando dices alguien, te refieres a mí, ¿no es así, Casio?

El *quaestor* asintió con firmeza.

Craso inspiró profundamente. Los malos augurios los perseguían desde el mismísimo inicio de la campaña y no parecía que hubiera forma de quitar esas ideas absurdas que tenían los legionarios sobre un gran fracaso en aquella guerra de conquista.

—Es la maldición de Ateyo —añadió Casio—. Hay muchos legionarios que parecen incapaces de borrar de su memoria las palabras de ese maldito tribuno de la plebe.

—¡Lo sé, lo sé! ¡Por Marte! —exclamó Craso exasperado al tiempo que se levantaba y empezaba a pasear de un lado a otro de la tienda con las manos en la espalda, como si se hubiera convertido en un león enjaulado que esperara su turno para saltar a la arena—. ¿Han terminado ya de cruzar el río?

—Esta tarde culminaremos la operación —confirmó Casio.

—Sea, entonces ése será un momento bueno para hacer más sacrificios y hablar al ejército. Que se reúnan las tropas junto al río al atardecer.

Craso volvió a sentarse y levantó la mano derecha. Casio comprendió que la conversación había llegado a su fin. El *quaestor* dio entonces media vuelta y salió de la tienda del *praetorium*. No obstante, seguía intranquilo. ¿Era Craso capaz de acometer con éxito la mayor de las conquistas o, por el contrario, era un hombre débil y corrupto que los conduciría a todos al desastre absoluto? Era difícil leer el futuro, por lo que Casio buscó en el pasado algo que le diera esperanzas repasando el historial del cónsul. No lo encontró. Una victoria contra un ejército de esclavos y un enriquecimiento extraño: ése era el dudoso bagaje de Marco Licinio Craso.

Al anochecer
Una tienda de legionarios

Una vez cruzado el río, al abrigo de un brasero, se reunieron Sexto, Cayo y los otros seis legionarios de su *contubernium* o unidad militar dentro de la tienda que acababan de montar. Como el resto de los soldados del ejército, habían asistido al discurso que el cónsul Craso había hecho una vez terminada la operación de cruzar el Éufrates y habían asistido también a los sacrificios. Los ánimos, sin embargo, no habían mejorado.

Cayo habló en voz baja mientras se repartía algo de vino que Craso había ordenado distribuir entre la tropa con el fin de subir la moral de todos y para celebrar que se había entrado en territorio parto sin que el enemigo ocasionase problemas. El centurión Druso, como era oficial, no dormía con ellos, y eso dio a Cayo la posibilidad de retomar sus lúgubres predicciones de la mañana.

—Todo son malos augurios. ¿Habéis visto cómo se le han caído las vísceras a Craso?

Era cierto: al cónsul le había temblado el pulso o había estado torpe al coger una de las vísceras de uno de los animales sacrificados para examinarla y se le había caído al suelo. Craso se dio cuenta de que todos observaron el incidente como un mal augurio, pese a que la víscera no parecía estar en malas condiciones. Intentó solucionar su torpeza con el discurso en el que, entre otras cosas, dijo que aunque se le podía haber caído una víscera nunca se le caería un arma de las manos. Pero dijo más frases, alguna de las cuales resultó también desafortunada, al menos a oídos de quienes lo escuchaban ya de por sí temerosos de emprender aquella campaña.

—Y eso que ha dicho el cónsul luego, lo del puente —añadió Sexto—, ha sonado terrible.

Craso había anunciado que iba a destruir el puente de barcazas porque ninguno de ellos volvería a cruzarlo.

—Imagino que quería decir que lo derribará para que no retrocedamos o algo así —continuó Sexto—, o quizá porque quiere dar a entender que como vamos a ganar nos quedaremos ya como vencedores al otro lado del Éufrates y transformaremos todo el Oriente en una gran provincia romana, pero ha sonado mal; en eso tiene razón Cayo, ¿no creéis?

—A mis oídos —respondió Cayo—, ha sonado como si ninguno fuéramos a regresar vivo de esta campaña. Es la maldición de Ateyo —insistió el legionario, que al ver que todos lo miraban intrigados se sintió espoleado a seguir hablando—. Conocéis esa maldición, ¿verdad? Lo que ocurrió cuando Craso salió de Roma.

Todos negaron con la cabeza. Los compañeros de Cayo se habían unido al ejército expedicionario provenientes de una *vexillatio* de una legión apostada fuera de Italia y no habían presenciado la salida de Craso de la ciudad. El nombre de Ateyo les resultaba familiar por ser un político importante y algo se rumoreaba de una maldición, pero desconocían con exactitud la historia en cuestión.

—¿Qué ocurrió? —preguntó Sexto, que como compartía con Cayo ser de Corduba había trabado más amistad con él—. Todos hemos oído hablar de esa maldición, pero ¿qué es lo que dijo realmente Ateyo, el tribuno de la plebe, cuando Craso salió de Roma?

—Ateyo no veía con buenos ojos que Craso emprendiera esta campaña contra Partia —explicó Cayo con rapidez, siempre en voz baja, como si compartiera con ellos el misterio de un secreto—. Este tribuno de la plebe argumentó para oponerse a esta campaña que los partos no habían atacado ninguna de las poblaciones amigas de Roma en Oriente y que ésta sólo buscaba el enriquecimiento personal de Craso, nuestro cónsul. Ateyo siguió oponiéndose a la salida de Craso al mando del ejército desde la ciudad de Roma. Insistió en que el Senado tenía acuerdos firmados con los partos y que el ataque de Craso iba contra dichas alianzas. No obstante, como el cónsul y sus amigos en el Senado siguieron apoyando la campaña, cuando Craso salía de Roma Ateyo se plantó en una de las puertas de la ciudad y ordenó a algunos de sus asistentes que detuvieran al cónsul, pero se encontró con la oposición de otros tribunos de la plebe. Algunos dicen que éstos habían sido comprados con el oro de Craso, pero esto no lo sabe nadie. El caso es que Craso pudo cruzar la puerta y salir de la ciudad para ponerse al frente de este gran ejército y aquí estamos ahora todos al otro lado del Éufrates.

Aquí Cayo detuvo su relato, entre otras cosas, para coger algo de aliento y echar un trago de vino.

—Pero eso no explica lo de la maldición —dijo entonces Sexto.

—Cierto —convino Cayo—. Ésta es la parte más delicada de todo el asunto: Ateyo tuvo que hacerse a un lado por la presión de los otros tribunos, pero subió a lo alto de la muralla Serviana de Roma, donde tenía un brasero llameante dispuesto para hacer libaciones y sacrificios. Echó incienso por encima de las llamas y profirió la más horrible de las maldiciones, implorando la ayuda de dioses casi olvidados por todos, pues seguía convencido de que incumplir los tratados firmados era una indignidad impropia de Roma. Lo grave es que dicen que, para asegurarse de que su maldición sería efectiva, Ateyo recurrió a la más horrible de todas: aquella en la que quien la profiere se garantiza el éxito de su maldición, a cambio de su propia vida.

—¿Y se sabe algo de cómo está ahora ese Ateyo? —preguntó Sexto.

—Ha desaparecido —respondió Cayo—. Algunos dicen que se oculta por temor a los enemigos de nuestro cónsul. Otros dicen que es seguro que ha muerto. En realidad nadie sabe dónde está.

Un silencio largo.

—¿Y cuál era la maldición exactamente? —preguntó al fin Sexto, poniendo palabras a lo que todos deseaban saber.

Cayo inspiró profundamente antes de responder:

—Ateyo dijo que todos los que siguieran a Craso más allá del Éufrates morirían engullidos por terribles nubes negras.

2

EL REY DE ARMENIA

Cien millas en dirección sureste desde Zeugma
53 a. C.

La arena del desierto se les pegaba al sudor de la piel en los brazos y piernas. El centurión Druso podía ver perfectamente que sus hombres caminaban incómodos por aquella ruta inhóspita, a pesar de que el avance, por el momento, se había hecho en paralelo al Éufrates y se disponía sin dificultad de agua abundante para saciar la sed de todos los legionarios. Lo grave sería si en algún momento el cónsul decidía alejarse del río.

De pronto el ejército detuvo su avance.

—¿Qué ocurre, centurión? —preguntó Sexto, pues era extraña aquella parada nada más empezar la jornada de marcha. Normalmente no se les concedía un descanso hasta el mediodía.

Druso no respondió, sino que se alejó de la centuria unos pasos para encaramarse a lo alto de una duna. Oteó el horizonte y vio un grupo de jinetes que se acercaba a toda velocidad. Y no eran de la caballería romana.

Vanguardia del ejército romano

—¿Son partos? —preguntó Craso.

—No lo creo —respondió Casio—. No parecen venir en busca de batalla. Son pocos. Una treintena quizá. Y se han detenido. Esperan que nos acerquemos. ¿Qué hacemos?

Craso frunció el ceño. El cónsul podía ser un avaricioso y tener también otros defectos, pero no era un cobarde.

—Acudiremos a su encuentro. Ordena que se prepare una *turma* de nuestra caballería para acompañarnos.

Comitiva del rey de Armenia, en medio del desierto

Se acercan, mi señor —dijo uno de los nobles de su guardia.

—Perfecto, para eso hemos venido —respondió el rey de Armenia—, para hablar con los romanos. Dadme la diadema.

Y se la entregaron para que así quedara desvelada su identidad.

Al poco el cónsul de Roma estaba frente a Artavasdes, al que reconoció por la diadema que lucía sobre su cabeza, que había visto en más de una moneda y que muy pocos en aquella parte del mundo podrían exhibir con orgullo.

—Estamos ante el rey de Armenia —dijo Craso en voz baja a Casio, que cabalgaba al paso junto a él.

—Eso parece —confirmó el *quaestor*—. Quizá quiera aliarse con nosotros. De lo contrario no vendría con una pequeña escolta para parlamentar.

Craso no respondió nada.

El rey de Armenia desmontó de su caballo.

Craso lo imitó, al igual que Casio y varios tribunos.

Artavasdes, seguido por un pequeño séquito de nobles, empezó a avanzar para encontrarse con el cónsul cara a cara. Craso, junto con Casio y los tribunos, hizo lo propio. Rey y cónsul se detuvieron apenas a tres pasos el uno del otro.

—Te saludo, cónsul de Roma —dijo el rey de Armenia en griego.

—Y Roma saluda al rey de Armenia —respondió Craso también en esa lengua.

No eran momentos para hablar del tiempo, así que Artavasdes fue directo a aquello que lo había llevado a salir al encuentro de las legiones de Craso.

—Armenia no es enemiga de Roma —empezó el rey.

—No es por Armenia que he cruzado el Éufrates —respondió Craso con la intención de tranquilizar a su interlocutor.

—Lo sé —continuó Artavasdes—. Creo que el cónsul de Roma y el rey de Armenia tenemos un enemigo común, los partos, y a ambos, al cónsul y a mí como rey, nos podría agradar de igual manera que estos enemigos comunes... desapareciesen.

Craso asintió dos veces, lentamente, pero no dijo nada.

—Traigo una propuesta para el cónsul de Roma —prosiguió el rey de Armenia.

—Te escucho —dijo Craso.

Artavasdes miró a sus nobles y éstos afirmaron varias veces con la cabeza. El rey de Armenia se volvió entonces de nuevo hacia el cónsul.

—Mi propuesta es que unamos nuestras fuerzas. Sugiero que el cónsul de Roma, en lugar de seguir la ruta hacia Mesopotamia para enfrentarse directamente con los partos, cambie la dirección de su ejército. Si el cónsul de Roma conduce sus legiones hacia Armenia ayudará a mi pueblo a defenderse de Orodes, el maldito emperador parto que amenaza con destruir mi reino. He venido hasta aquí con un pequeño séquito, pero puedo disponer en poco tiempo de los seis mil jinetes de mi caballería personal, diez mil jinetes más acorazados y hasta treinta mil infantes que se unirían a los legionarios de Craso y su caballería. Con nuestros dos ejércitos juntos derrotaremos primero a los partos en Armenia y luego el cónsul de Roma, si lo desea, podrá lanzarse con mi apoyo hacia el sur, contra el corazón del reino parto. Este plan no sólo tiene la ventaja de unir nuestros ejércitos, sino que además forzaremos a los partos a luchar en nuestras montañas, un terreno irregular donde su caballería de *catafractos* se mueve mal y donde, en consecuencia, podrá ser más sencillo acabar con ellos.

Craso, que había escuchado atentamente la propuesta del rey de Armenia, meditaba sin decir nada. Miró un instante a Casio y a los tribunos que lo acompañaban. Nadie se atrevía a manifestarse en un sentido u otro hasta que el *quaestor* asintió levemente, lo suficiente para transmitirle al cónsul que la idea del rey de Armenia le parecía buena.

Craso miró a Artavasdes.

—El cónsul de Roma ha escuchado al rey de Armenia con

interés y respeto —dijo Craso—, pero he de declinar su propuesta. Mi plan es avanzar hacia el corazón de Mesopotamia directamente y asestar un golpe mortal en la yugular de nuestro enemigo lo antes posible. Avanzar por Armenia retrasa la consecución de este objetivo.

El rey de Armenia miró al cónsul de Roma con los ojos abiertos, sin parpadear, durante un buen rato. No daba crédito a lo que acababa de oír.

Artavasdes miró entonces al suelo. Sacudió la cabeza. No dijo nada y dio media vuelta sin tan siquiera despedirse. Montó sobre su caballo y azuzó al animal para iniciar un rápido trote que al instante transformó en galope. Todos sus nobles lo siguieron y, en poco tiempo, del rey de Armenia sólo quedó una polvareda que se desvanecía en la difusa línea del horizonte de arena.

159 AÑOS DESPUÉS

—

Ciudad de Yu-yang
Frontera norte del Imperio han (China),
próxima a la Gran Muralla
Primer año del reinado del emperador An-ti (106 d. C.)

—Sí, muchacho, aún pienso que los puedo ver a todos como si fueran espíritus que nos han acompañado siempre, pero hoy ya estoy cansado. Te he contado cómo empezó todo y te he explicado algo de cómo era Craso, aunque aún he de contarte más cosas sobre él. Pero para un desastre tan absoluto como el que aconteció no basta con un *chiang-chün*, un líder militar incapaz, torpe y soberbio como era Craso; éste, además, ha de encontrarse con otro *chiang-chün* que sea totalmente opuesto en carácter, un líder astuto e inteligente. Cuando un encuentro así tiene lugar entre dos líderes militares de condiciones tan opuestas, los campos de batalla se convierten en el lugar perfecto para una masacre. Y Craso encontró a Artavasdes, el rey de Armenia, en primer lugar, y lo menospreció. Infravaloró su ayuda y aún más, no calculó bien su reacción al sentirse despreciado; al rechazarlo lo había ofendido y un poderoso que se siente ultrajado es mal enemigo. Pero además, Craso también menospreciaría a otro líder, a Surena, el *chiang-chün* de aquella región de An-shi, el jefe de los partos, como los llamaba el propio Craso y los demás romanos. Ése fue un segundo gran error, porque Surena era un hombre especial, un *spāhbod*, o general en su lengua.

»Pero mañana seguiremos. Hoy déjame dormir. Trae un poco de arroz, hijo mío, y quema algunos trozos de bambú para alejar a los malos espíritus.

35

El hijo salió de la habitación en busca del arroz, pero mientras ajustaba la puerta vio cómo su padre cerraba los ojos. Estaba seguro de que cuando regresara con el cuenco con comida él ya estaría dormido.

Suspiró.

Estaba realmente intrigado por la historia que su padre le estaba contando sobre aquel Craso de Da Qin y su ejército que intentaba conquistar An-shi en el extremo occidental del mundo, pero tendría que esperar al día siguiente para saber más.

HISTORIA DE TRAJANO

Principios del siglo II d. C.

Libro I

MISIONES SECRETAS

3

EL FINAL DE UN GLADIADOR

Roma
107 d. C.

En la arena del Anfiteatro Flavio

—¡Aggggh! —aulló Marcio al caer de espaldas sobre la arena. El otro gladiador, un *retiarius* joven y agresivo, muy veloz de movimientos, había conseguido forzarlo a retroceder demasiado rápido, de forma que Marcio, ya más lento por sus años, trastabilló con el cadáver de un *samnita* a quien los esclavos del anfiteatro aún no habían tenido tiempo de retirar. El *retiarius* no lo dudó y se abalanzó contra el cuerpo de Marcio, esgrimiendo su tridente para acabar con su enemigo. Fue un error. Debería haber echado su red antes y eso habría aprisionado a su oponente, dándole tiempo para herirlo o matarlo luego con el tridente.

Marcio, caído pero no inmovilizado por red alguna, giró como un tronco por la arena y consiguió evitar el ataque mortal del *retiarius*; de inmediato se levantó, apoyándose con la espada en el suelo como si fuera un bastón. Su reincorporación al combate hizo que las gradas vibraran de nuevo.

—¡Senex, Senex, Senex! —bramaba la plebe sin descanso. Ése era ahora su sobrenombre: *Senex.* Marcio sonrió bajo su pesado casco de *mirmillo.* Era como si el pueblo, irónicamente, a la vez que parecía animarlo a seguir en la lucha, se esforzara también en recordarle que era un gladiador viejo, senil; de hecho, así se sentía cada vez más. El *retiarius* se había recuperado también y encaraba de nuevo a Marcio. Éste blandió su espada en el aire cortando el espacio frente a él para que el *retiarius* se lo pensara dos veces antes de iniciar un nuevo ataque. Siete combates. Seis victorias y una *stans missus* en la que el público había perdonado la vida a él y a su contrincante. Eso era lo que había conseguido Marcio en los dos últimos años desde que retornara al Anfiteatro Flavio, y no se sentía capaz de resistir mucho más. Había albergado la esperanza de que el emperador se apiadara de él pronto y le concediera la *rudis*, la espada de madera con la que se obtiene la libertad tras varios combates victoriosos en la arena, pero Trajano, ocupado seguramente con diversos asuntos de mayor relevancia para un César, no había acudido al anfiteatro en bastante tiempo. Marcio miró al palco imperial. Por fin Trajano, sometidos los dacios y resueltos sus asuntos de Estado, había hecho acto de presencia en el palco, pero no parecía prestar demasiada atención a lo que ocurría en la arena, sino que departía con alguno de sus *legati*. Marcio creyó reconocer a aquel alto oficial con el que hablaba el César, pero no tuvo tiempo para más reflexiones. El *retiarius* volvía a atacar. Esta vez había clavado el tridente en el suelo y sacudía su red, asida con ambas manos, por encima de su cabeza, amenazando con arrojarla contra él en cualquier momento...

En el palco imperial

Lucio Quieto, sentado junto al César, escuchaba atento las palabras de Trajano.

—Esta noche va a venir el embajador Shaka de nuevo al palacio, Lucio. Quiero que vengas.

—Sí, augusto —respondió Lucio Quieto en voz no muy alta pese a los gritos de la plebe. Parecía que el emperador le hablara como si no quisiera que su esposa, que estaba sentada al otro lado, se enterara bien de lo que se traían entre manos.

—¿Y hay noticias de Arabia? —preguntó Trajano mirando de reojo hacia la arena donde aquel gladiador, Marcio —o Senex, como parecía preferir llamarlo ahora la plebe— seguía luchando por su vida. Un gladiador que había participado en una conjura para intentar asesinarlo a él, al mismísimo Trajano, pero que, al final, en el último momento, cambió de parecer y en lugar de ayudar a los conjurados se rebeló contra ellos, matando a su jefe justo en el momento en que el traidor iba a asestar un golpe mortal por la espalda a Trajano. Éste había querido liberarlo allí mismo, pero el gladiador había matado ya a algunos pretorianos de su guardia antes de cambiar de bando y eso requería una condena que, en su caso, había sido la arena del anfiteatro. Aquel Marcio, no obstante, era ya un guerrero mayor y no estaba claro que fuera a sobrevivir a esa condena mucho tiempo. De hecho, Trajano se sorprendió al encontrarlo aún vivo cuando regresó al palco del Anfiteatro Flavio después de meses sin acudir a los combates en honor a su victoria absoluta sobre los dacios. Lo que parecía cada vez más improbable, sin embargo, era que Marcio fuera a sobrevivir a aquella tarde. El *retiarius* contra el que luchaba parecía demasiado rápido e inteligente. Sí, estaban ante el fin de un viejo gladiador. Era la última tarde de Senex. De guerrero a guerrero, Trajano podía oler el final de un combatiente como el lobo huele a sus presas desde la distancia. Y le supo mal. En las últimas semanas había imaginado una misión especial para aquel luchador si aún seguía con vida. Perderlo aquella tarde podía obligarlo a alterar sus planes. Y a Trajano no le gustaba cambiar sus propósitos.

—No, no sabemos aún nada de Arabia, pero estoy seguro de que pronto nos llegarán noticias —respondió Lucio volviendo sobre aquel asunto que los tenía a ambos preocupados y entrando en la mente del César.

Sus palabras devolvieron a Trajano al mundo del gobierno del Imperio y dejó de mirar hacia la arena. Había mandado a Palma, uno de los senadores y *legati* de su confianza, a Arabia, con dos legiones y la misión de culminar la anexión de aquella rica región de Oriente. Lucio seguía hablando:

—Se ha adentrado hacia el sur, hacia el desierto. Avanzaba en dirección a Petra, eso es todo cuanto sabemos por el momento. El rey Rabbel II no ha decidido aún cuándo enfrentarse a él, pero aún es pronto para saber cómo acabará la campaña. El desierto es siempre un lugar peligroso para las legiones.

—¿Lo dices por lo de Craso? —preguntó Trajano.

—Por ejemplo —confirmó Quieto—. Aquello fue un desastre absoluto, César.

—Arabia no es Partia —replicó Trajano al comprobar cómo incluso en hombres de la valía de Quieto seguía perviviendo el temor a las arenas de Oriente por causa del tremendo desastre al que el petulante Craso condujo a siete legiones en tiempos de Julio César. El fantasma de la legión perdida seguía vivo en la mente de muchos en Roma.

—Aun así... es el desierto —insistió Lucio Quieto.

Trajano bebió de la copa de vino que sostenía en la mano mientras observaba cómo su esposa, quizá aburrida por el combate que se alargaba en la arena, se levantaba para ir junto a Rupilia y hablar con ella. Adriano y su esposa, Vibia Sabina, no habían acudido aquella tarde al palco imperial. Trajano se dirigió de nuevo a Lucio, una vez más en voz baja para que no le oyera ninguna otra persona, incluida su esposa.

—Quizá algún día no demasiado lejano tengamos que adentrarnos en esos desiertos que tanto temes. ¿Qué me dices a eso, Lucio?

Quieto mantuvo la mirada del emperador mientras pensaba su respuesta, que fue otra pregunta:

—¿Estás considerando de verdad atacar Partia? —En la voz de Quieto había sorpresa y duda y, por qué no decirlo, miedo. Trajano iba a responder, pero en aquel momento se acercó Liviano, el jefe del pretorio, a su espalda.

—El *procurator bibliothecae* está a la entrada del palco —dijo el oficial pretoriano—. Dice que el emperador quería verlo.

—Sí, dile que pase —respondió Trajano y se levantó con la excusa de coger otra copa de vino de una gran mesa donde había frutos secos, queso y copas con el licor de Baco servidas. Las viandas no eran demasiado ostentosas: Trajano no quería exhibiciones de lujo absurdas y menos en público, pero algo de comida y vino siempre estaba disponible. El público también disfrutaba de alimento y bebida si lo deseaba. Lo importante era no hacer alarde de platos refinados de compleja elaboración que claramente indicaran un enorme gasto de dinero por parte de la familia imperial. Trajano observó que la emperatriz miraba a la arena y aprovechó para hacer un gesto a Quieto con la mano y llamarlo junto a él. El *legatus* norteafricano se levantó, fue a la mesa y cogió la copa de vino que el propio emperador le ofrecía.

—¿Crees acaso que conquistar Partia es imposible? —le preguntó Trajano—. ¿Tienes miedo a cruzar el Éufrates y sucumbir como le pasó a Craso? ¿Tienes miedo a la legión perdida?

—El emperador sabe que le seguiré hasta el final del mundo —respondió Lucio con decisión—, pero los legionarios, sin duda, tendrán miedo.

—¿Incluso si van bajo mi mando? —inquirió Trajano.

—Me temo que incluso así, incluso aunque vayan bajo el mando del gran Trajano que nunca ha sido derrotado, muchos tendrán miedo, y el miedo...

—El miedo es un mal soldado —sentenció Trajano interrumpiéndolo.

En ese momento llegó Suetonio. La plebe aulló. Todos miraron hacia la arena. El *retiarius* había lanzado su red con bolas de plomo sobre Senex, pero éste había conseguido zafarse y había respondido con un rápido ataque. Su oponente lo había salvado al recuperar la red con la cuerda que llevaba atada a la mano izquierda y tirar de ella con velocidad. El *mirmillo* había tenido que dar un salto para evitar tropezar con ella y para cuando volvió a encarar a su enemigo, el *retiarius* ya tenía su tridente en la mano. El combate volvió a su principio, sólo que los dos contendientes estaban más cansados. El sudor los cubría. Sus cuerpos brillaban bajo la luz del sol de la larga tarde romana. Trajano se volvió entonces hacia Suetonio, encargado de las bibliotecas de la ciudad, que acababa de incorporarse al palco.

—El emperador deseaba verme —dijo el *procurator bibliothecae*.

—Así es —respondió el César—. Necesito un secretario. Estoy abrumado por el correo que recibo desde todas las provincias. Necesito a alguien de confianza absoluta que organice las cartas que llegan hasta mí por parte de los gobernadores, alguien que pueda leerlas, resumirme sus contenidos y que luego copie mis respuestas al dictado.

—En palacio debe de haber muchos libertos cualificados para semejante tarea, César —respondió Suetonio algo confundido.

Trajano miró su copa vacía antes de responder.

—He dicho que necesito alguien de absoluta confianza y el palacio imperial no es el sitio donde buscar a una persona así. De los únicos que me fío completamente, además de Quieto y otros tres senadores amigos, son Liviano y Aulo, pero son pretorianos, no escribas.

Suetonio parpadeó un par de veces.

—¿Acaso el emperador ha pensado en mí?

Trajano lo miró detenidamente.

—En principio sí, pero, dime, Cayo Suetonio Tranquilo: ¿cuántos años tienes?

—Treinta y siete, augusto.

—Pareces aún mayor —comentó el César—. No te lo tomes a mal, pero no te veo con la fortaleza suficiente para resistir largos viajes, y la persona que sea mi secretario tendrá que venir conmigo en duras campañas. Busco a alguien capacitado para la tarea, pero joven. Además haces un buen trabajo con las bibliotecas y quiero que te encargues de la apertura de las nuevas del foro que Apolodoro está diseñando. No. Tu sitio es el de *procurator bibliothecae*, pero me preguntaba si conoces a alguien que pueda interesarme.

Suetonio asintió varias veces en silencio con la faz muy seria.

—Puede que sí tenga a alguien —respondió.

—Envíamelo. Eso es todo. —Levantó la mano derecha. Suetonio se inclinó, se retiró y salió del palco. Trajano cogió otra copa de vino. Sin mirar hacia atrás sabía que Plotina le estaba observando.

—¿El César no se fía de los que lo atienden en palacio? —inquirió Lucio Quieto.

—No demasiado —dijo Trajano y echó un pequeño trago; luego miró a Quieto—. Adriano va sobornando a cuantos puede.

—¿Qué busca?

—Información.

—¿Qué información, César?

—Quiere saber qué estoy planeando. Necesito un secretario de confianza, alguien que no venga del palacio imperial.

—Quizá una solución —arguyó Quieto— sería enviar lejos a Adriano.

—A su debido tiempo, Lucio. De momento, recuerda que esta noche tenemos la entrevista con el embajador Shaka en la hora duodécima. Te espero en mi cámara. Es una recepción privada. Nadie tiene que saber nada sobre esto, ¿me entiendes? Sobre todo Adriano.

—En algún momento tendrá que saberlo, y el Senado y todos. No se puede invadir Partia en secreto. Necesitaremos al menos cien mil legionarios, César.

—Por supuesto, pero no hay que darse prisa en que lo averigüen. Todo a su tiempo. Ahora me interesa saber cuándo nos llegan noticias de Arabia, de Cornelio Palma y su expedición. El rey nabateo Rabbel II Sóter ha fallecido —reveló Trajano sin dejar de mirar su copa de vino. Podía intuir con el rabillo del ojo la faz de sorpresa de Quieto—. Como ves me llega mucha información, aunque nada de Palma.

Trajano estaba convencido de que el reino era demasiado débil para oponerse a una anexión total, pero la falta de noticias de Palma en los últimos meses lo tenía intranquilo.

—Recuerda la reunión con Shaka —insistió.

—Sí, César —respondió Quieto. Iba a preguntarle al emperador por qué quería invadir Partia, pero éste se alejaba en busca de su asiento presidencial en el gran Anfiteatro Flavio. El norteafricano meditaba: no creía que Trajano quisiera iniciar una guerra tan compleja, por no decir imposible, por simple afán de gloria. Debía de tener otros motivos, pero ¿cuáles?

De pronto se oyó un gran bramido del público. Trajano y Quieto y todos los presentes en el palco imperial miraron hacia la arena. El *mirmillo* yacía en el suelo en medio de un enorme charco de sangre, con el tridente del *retiarius* clavado en su cuerpo. A Trajano no le sorprendió, era una lástima pero era lo más lógico: el *retiarius* era mucho más joven y rápido que el viejo Marcio. El César echó otro trago. Estaba fastidiado: aquello, sin duda, era el fin de Marcio. Tendría que haber intervenido antes, pero ahora no podía inmiscuirse en las reglas del anfiteatro. Definitivamente debería buscar a otro hombre para la misión especial que tenía en mente. El emperador fijó sus ojos en el fin del *mirmillo*. Éste intentaba levantarse con el tridente clavado en una pierna, pero no podía. El *retiarius* se acercaba con el *pugio* del que disponía para cortar la cuerda de la red en caso de necesidad, pero que ahora pensaba usar para rematar a su oponente, obstinado en no darse por derrotado y negándose a pedir clemencia. Trajano apretaba la copa con fuerza. Si Marcio levantara la mano izquierda pidiendo ayuda, quizá el público se apiadaría de él. El viejo gladiador les había dado buenas tardes de lucha y ya había sido salvado en una *stans missus*. En ese caso sí que podría intervenir y darle el perdón. Pero esas heridas... el emperador busca con los ojos a Critón, su médico personal. Suele estar por el palco, pero ahora no acierta a encontrarlo.

Marcio, en la arena, intenta levantarse.

No puede.

Está exhausto.

Sabe que puede pedir clemencia.

Pero no lo hace.

Cualquiera lo haría.

Él no.

4

LA EMPERATRIZ DENG

Loyang, capital del Imperio han (China)
Segundo año del reinado del emperador An-ti (107 d. C.)

Estaba sentada en un trono elevado. Tenía veintiséis años y era mujer, pero las circunstancias o quizá los designios de ese poderoso Buda del que cada vez se hablaba más en su mundo habían querido que fuera ella la que gobernara sobre casi sesenta millones de seres humanos según el último censo. Era la emperatriz Deng desde que el anterior emperador He la había nombrado, tras condenar a su antecesora en el trono, la intrigante Yin, que la precedió en aquel puesto. El emperador He había fallecido sin descendencia y ella, en calidad de emperatriz viuda, ejercía una regencia compleja mientras crecía el pequeño emperador An-ti, sobrino del emperador He, de apenas trece años. El moribundo He sólo le dio a la joven Deng un consejo en su lecho de muerte:

—Sólo puedes fiarte de tu familia y de dos personas más.

—¿Quiénes son esas dos personas? —había preguntado ella en voz baja, hablándole suavemente al oído.

—Tu tutora, Ban Zao y...

—¿Y quién más? —insistió ella cada vez más nerviosa. Ban Zao sería una gran compañía y consuelo, pero también era mujer y, en aquel mundo de hombres, la emperatriz Deng sabía que necesitaba el apoyo de algún hombre fuerte en la corte, o de varios; alguna de las tres excelencias o quizá alguno de los nueve ministros. Sabía que podía contar con la ayuda de su hermano, sin embargo, eso no bastaría... El moribundo emperador volvía a hablar. Ella se agachó aún más y pegó su oído a los labios de su esposo.

—Confía en... Fan Chun —completó al fin el agonizante emperador He en un leve susurro.

Ella, sentada en el trono imperial, lo recordaba todo con la nitidez de la niña que tiene grabados en su memoria instantes que la impactaron para siempre.

—Pero si Fan Chun es sólo un *yu-shih chung-ch'eng*, un asistente personal del ministro de Obras Públicas —dijo ella sin poder evitar que trasluciera su decepción ante aquella supuesta gran revelación.

El emperador He la miró un instante a los ojos y sonrió mientras pronunciaba sus últimas palabras, con las que le explicaba a su esposa por qué Fan Chun ocupaba ese puesto secundario y no otro de más renombre. Ella se agachó de nuevo para poder oírle.

—Recuerda lo que siempre te he... explicado... hermosa Deng... —Y el emperador He murió.

En aquel momento ella no podía recordar aquello a lo que se refirió su esposo, lo que él decía que siempre le había explicado. El emperador He la había instruido con frecuencia en el arte del gobierno, como si intuyera que su enfermedad se lo llevaría pronto y que ella quedaría sola para gobernar un imperio gigantesco. Pero ahora... se sintió casi traicionada: Fan Chun, un asistente de un ministro. Eso era todo de lo que disponía para controlar las intrigas en la corte del Imperio han, con un emperador niño rodeado de consejeros ávidos por poder y dinero, hombres, mujeres y hasta eunucos que parecían olvidar que un imperio podrido en su centro no podría ser capaz de velar por el comercio, la ruta de la seda, las fronteras y, en suma, terminaría sucumbiendo por la ambición desmedida y egoísta de todos.

Sin embargo, para sorpresa de la atribulada emperatriz Deng, Fan Chun se había mostrado como el más eficaz de los consejeros y desde la oscuridad de esa segunda línea de funcionarios del imperio, la estaba ayudando a mantener el orden. Entre las ideas de Fan Chun y los pensamientos de la sabia Ban Zao, la emperatriz había conseguido apaciguar las fronteras del imperio nombrando a buenos oficiales en los lejanos reinos del norte y el oeste, y había fomentado el interés por la educación entre los miembros de la corte, aunque ahí aún quedaba mucho por hacer. Estaba preparando también una nueva ley sobre los juicios con el fin de corregir los cambios recientes, que habían hecho de cada juicio un tormento para los campesinos, quienes se veían obligados a declarar en cualquier momento, desatendiendo las tareas de cultivo, lo que conducía al desastre agrícola en muchas regiones. Lo ideal sería concentrar los juicios en alguna fecha que interfiriera lo mínimo posible con las tareas del campo. Era un asunto serio a estudiar.

—Todo a su tiempo —dijo ella en un suspiro a sus consejeros. Lo de los juicios iba a ser el siguiente punto de las audiencias de aquella jornada, pero antes de iniciar las entrevistas con las tres excelencias y los nueve ministros había requerido la presencia de Fan Chun. Quería hablar con él a solas.

Las puertas de la cámara de audiencias se abrieron y el misterioso asistente del ministro de Obras Públicas apareció con su enjuta figura, caminando despacio y humildemente, siempre mirando al suelo. Ella sabía que Fan Chun anhelaba más que nada convertirse en un eremita, uno de esos filósofos taoístas que buscaban en el retiro la paz y su equilibrio con la naturaleza y el mundo. La emperatriz intuía que era esencialmente por puro afecto al fallecido emperador He que él seguía allí ayudándola. Por supuesto, no podría irse sin su permiso, pero ella lo habría dejado marchar si hubiera sentido que sus consejos carecían de ese intento genuino de contribuir a mejorar el gobierno del imperio.

—Me han dicho que la emperatriz deseaba verme —dijo Fan Chun inclinándose ante ella.

—Te han informado bien —respondió la mujer con voz serena y dulce.

—Siempre es un honor que la emperatriz piense en mí como en alguien que puede ayudar con algún consejo —añadió él alzando levemente la mirada. Había percibido que la emperatriz le permitía ciertas libertades y él las aprovechaba, no por vanidad, sino porque la experiencia le había enseñado que en la mirada de un ser humano estaban las respuestas a todas nuestras preguntas.

—Hemos trabajado sobre la defensa de las fronteras y sobre el asunto de mi seguridad en palacio; tenemos pendiente mejorar la educación en la corte y el espinoso tema de los juicios. Pero hay algo que siempre me ha intrigado de lo que me gustaría tener conocimiento adecuado, aunque antes de preguntarte dime si mis apreciaciones son correctas, en tu opinión.

Fan Chun se inclinó un par de veces, se incorporó un poco y empezó a hablar.

—Los temibles *hsiung-nu* están contenidos en la muralla al norte del imperio, pero preveo problemas en la ruta hacia las regiones occidentales. Intuyo que pronto tendremos que armar de nuevo algún ejército contra los Yuegzhi, pero quizá no sea algo aún extremadamente urgente. He oído que hay agitación en el tercer imperio, mas allá de los Yuegzhi, en el territorio An-shi[7] y eso siempre termina afectándonos de un modo u otro. En cuanto a la seguridad en palacio he hecho traer grandes guerreros de los puestos de frontera, todos hombres valientes y jóvenes que no están contaminados por las ambiciones ni de sus excelencias ni de los ministros. Serán una guardia leal para la emperatriz. Sobre los asuntos de la educación y los juicios, como bien se ha dicho, los tenemos pendientes, pero todo ha de hacerse poco a poco. Creo que la emperatriz está llevando las tremendas tareas de gobierno de este gran imperio con un temple propio del acero de la mejor espada. Y con pulso firme.

—Bien, Fan Chun, me alegra que me contemples con ese optimismo. Hay, no obstante, algo que me perturba hace tiempo.

El asistente la miró de nuevo un instante con ojos inquietos.

—Kan Ying —dijo al fin la emperatriz.

El consejero miró entonces a su alrededor. No había nadie en la sala. La emperatriz, siempre prudente, había tenido la prevención de ordenar que todos los soldados salieran. Algo que él mismo le había aconsejado hacer a la emperatriz sólo

7. Partia.

en su presencia o en la de la tutora Ban Zao, nunca si estaban presentes otras personas, por muy de fiar que éstas pudieran parecer.

—Kan Ying —insistió la líder del Imperio han ante el largo silencio de su consejero.

—No sé exactamente... —empezó Fan Chun, pero la emperatriz lo interrumpió con brusquedad y cierta irritación.

—Me refiero al viaje secreto de Kan Ying —precisó ella para que no hubiera margen de duda alguna—. El emperador He me tenía como confidente en todos los asuntos y en todos los secretos. Sé que hay un hombre a quien se le ordenó viajar más allá de las regiones occidentales bajo nuestro poder, adentrarse en los territorios controlados por los Yuegzhi, seguir avanzando hasta alcanzar y cruzar el Imperio an-shi y no detenerse hasta llegar al mismísimo Da-Qin. Todo eso lo sé. Y me consta que el viaje se hizo, pero el emperador estaba ya bastante enfermo para cuando Kan Ying regresó. Hubo una audiencia con él, en secreto, pero el emperador ya no me comentó más. Estaba más preocupado por su pronto fallecimiento y por mi seguridad que por hablarme de esos antiguos proyectos suyos. Tú mismo, sin embargo, hace un momento has dicho que lo que pase en territorios lejanos al final termina afectándonos, y llevo pensando hace tiempo que quizá, como emperatriz viuda de los Han, sea mi deber conocer bien todo lo que se sabe de esos imperios distantes pero poderosos. Quizá en alguno de ellos esté el enemigo que pueda causarnos daño o el amigo que pueda ayudarnos en tiempos de zozobra.

Fan Chun asintió varias veces durante el discurso de su señora.

—Sí, sin duda, la emperatriz está en lo cierto. Ningún conocimiento sobre otros imperios es desdeñable.

Un nuevo silencio.

—¿Y bien? —preguntó su majestad imperial—. ¿Existió tal viaje? ¿Es ese tal Kan Ying de carne y hueso o acaso el emperador He me contaba mentiras, historias fabulosas para impresionarme?

—No, el emperador He no mentía nunca. Tal viaje, parece ser, tuvo lugar y, desde luego, tal hombre existe. Se celebró una audiencia privada con el emperador en la que nadie más estuvo presente. El emperador, en efecto, estaba ya muy enfermo y tampoco yo tuve oportunidad de departir con él sobre este asunto.

—¿Y sabes dónde está Kan Ying ahora? ¿Puedes encontrar a ese hombre?

Fan Chun se inclinó una vez más mientras respondía.

—Mi misión en esta vida ha sido servir al emperador He primero y ahora a la emperatriz Deng. Encontraré a Kan Ying y lo traeré ante la emperatriz. Será muy interesante, sin duda alguna, saber qué vio en Da-Qin.

LA RETIRADA DE LOS GLADIADORES MUERTOS

Roma
107 d. C.

El *retiarius* se acerca.

Marcio sigue intentando alzarse, pero no puede. La espada, enredada con la red de su enemigo, está inutilizada y ha perdido el escudo al caer. Sólo podrá protegerse con la *manica* de su brazo derecho cuando el *retiarius* se lance sobre él. El público grita.

—¡Senex, Senex, Senex!

Quieren que se levante.

Pero no puede. El *retiarius*, por fin, se lanza; intenta clavarle su *pugio*. Marcio desvía la primera puñalada con las protecciones de su brazo derecho aunque siente que lo han herido también en esa extremidad.

El *retiarius* no cede en su empeño mortal.

Marcio piensa en Alana y Tamura, su esposa y su hija, perdidas en algún rincón desconocido al norte de la Dacia.

—¡Aagggh! —El viejo gladiador ase con las dos manos el tridente y se lo extrae de la pierna. La sangre mana de los tres agujeros de la parte posterior de la espinilla. No puede ponerse en pie ni usando el tridente como bastón, pero el *retiarius*, al ver a su enemigo de nuevo armado, siente pánico y retrocede. Va corriendo a... no sabe dónde: no se puede huir en el Anfiteatro Flavio. Marcio sonríe. No sabe si sobrevivirá o no, tiene muchas heridas y está sangrando más que nunca, intuye que es el fin; pero sí sabe que hay algo que el público no perdona: la cobardía.

Marcio, haciendo un esfuerzo sobrehumano, asistiéndose

con el maldito tridente, se pone en pie. La masa del populacho aúlla con más fuerza que nunca.

—¡Senex, Senex, Senex!

Trajano, sin darse cuenta, se levanta con la copa fuertemente asida. Quieto mira hacia aquel viejo gladiador contra el que se enfrentó en el pasado. Era innegable que tenía un espíritu de combate admirable. Como militar, el norteafricano no podía dejar de reconocer el valor de un guerrero nato.

Marcio avanza cojeando y dejando un reguero de sangre por la arena. El *retiarius* había ido, por puro instinto, en busca de la *porta sanavivaria*, la puerta por donde salen vivos los gladiadores victoriosos. Pero, como todas las puertas del anfiteatro, está cerrada. Su gesto, además, ha irritado al público, que lo abuchea y le escupe y le insulta con tanta brutalidad que el *retiarius* aturdido vuelve hacia el centro de la arena. Recuerda que él también está armado y se aferra a su puñal con rabia.

Marcio lo ve regresar hacia él. Lo ha visto en otras ocasiones. Hay veces en las que un gladiador pierde el valor y piensa en la absurda idea de huir, pero muchos se rehacen y vuelven a intentar combatir. Pero el público ya se ha puesto del lado del que en ningún momento ha mostrado temor, que no es otro que él mismo.

Marcio lo ve acercarse. Sabe que ha de jugar con su miedo.

—¡Ahhh! —grita y levanta el tridente con el brazo derecho herido como si fuera a arrojarlo como un *pilum*. El *retiarius* vuelve a asustarse. Marcio sabe que su oponente, cegado por el miedo, no se da cuenta de que él está herido en el brazo con el que sostiene el tridente y que apenas tiene fuerzas ni para asirlo, y menos aún para arrojarlo, pero al esgrimirlo, amenazar con lanzarlo y gritar, el pavor absoluto se apodera de nuevo del *retiarius* y éste corre hacia otra de las puertas.

Marcio aprovecha el momento. Apenas le quedan fuerzas y levanta los brazos, tridente asido en su mano, y vuelve a gritar justo desde el centro del anfiteatro. Y el pueblo le responde coreando una vez más su sobrenombre:

—¡Senex, Senex, Senex!

La gente lo quiere.

—*Habet, hoc habet!* —grita la plebe de Roma. «¡Lo tiene, lo tiene!» Eso piensa el pueblo. Y todas las miradas se vuelven hacia Trajano.

El emperador hace un gesto. Hay que premiar tanto el valor como castigar la cobardía.

Se abren varias puertas y salen los *confectores*, ejecutores armados con palos gruesos. En un momento rodean al *retiarius*, que se arrodilla aterrado. Ni siquiera esgrime el puñal, sino que lo deja caer.

—¡No, por todos los dioses! ¡No, no, no!

Y se protege con los brazos en un intento inútil de guarecerse de una interminable lluvia de palos. Los esclavos le golpean con una saña bestial, como si fuera un perro rabioso, una alimaña perniciosa que hay que aniquilar con la mayor brutalidad posible. La sangre los salpica mientras siguen asestándole, uno tras otro, golpes salvajes en piernas, espalda, brazos y cabeza. Se oye un «crac» en particular cuando el palo de uno de los *confectores* choca contra la cabeza sin casco del *retiarius*.

Entretanto, un liberto que trabaja para el anfiteatro se acerca hasta el centro de la arena donde, con gran esfuerzo, Marcio sigue en pie. Sabe que la apariencia es fundamental y no debe derrumbarse o perderá el favor del público. El liberto le entrega a Marcio, al que todos siguen aclamando como Senex, la *palma lemniscata* de la victoria y un buen puñado de monedas que le da una a una. A Marcio aquella cuenta lenta de las monedas que se le van entregando se le hace eterna, pero ha de resistir como sea. Al fin, la cuenta termina y el liberto se hace a un lado. Dos esclavos se acercan a Marcio y se ofrecen a ayudarlo para conducirlo hasta la *porta sanavivaria*: él sí se ha ganado el derecho legítimo a salir por ella. A estas alturas, ya le está permitido aceptar la ayuda de los esclavos y se apoya en ellos. Apenas puede caminar, y usa a los dos jóvenes esclavos como si de muletas se tratara, pero el público sigue aclamándolo sin parar. Si la victoria hubiera sido más brillante, quizá el emperador le habría dado la *rudis*, la espada de madera que simboliza la recuperación de la libertad por parte del gladiador. Eso le habría permitido salir de allí y emprender un nuevo viaje al norte en busca de Alana y Tamura.

Ya lo hizo una vez y podría haberlo hecho otra, pero esta

victoria había sido muy ajustada y no muy lucida, basada más que otra cosa en la cobardía de su oponente. Eso, no obstante, le había salvado la vida, pero con aquellas heridas, si sobrevivía, estaba persuadido de que el siguiente combate sería el último y definitivo.

Mientras todos esos pensamientos se agolpaban en la torturada mente de Marcio, lo condujeron por los túneles del anfiteatro hasta llegar a la sala de curas, donde un esclavo que hacía las veces de improvisado médico empezó a examinar las heridas.

Entretanto, en la superficie, en la arena del anfiteatro, otro esclavo disfrazado de Caronte, el barquero del Hades, empuñaba un hierro candente con el que atravesaba el cuerpo del *retiarius* para asegurarse de que estaba completamente muerto. El gladiador permanecía inmóvil y Caronte se apartó para dejar paso a los *libitinarii*, los esclavos encargados de retirar a los gladiadores muertos. Arrastraron el cuerpo mientras los *arenari* empezaban a alisar la arena con rastrillos para dejarlo todo preparado para el siguiente enfrentamiento.

Pero el combate anterior seguía abajo, en los sótanos.

—¡Ahhh! —gritó Marcio tumbado en una especie de mesa de operaciones. Aquel esclavo no parecía saber nada de heridas. Si hubiera tenido su *gladio* de *mirmillo* a mano se lo habría clavado de buen grado en el costado. Sobrevivir a los no muy buenos *medici* del anfiteatro era una segunda audacia para la que Marcio no estaba seguro de disponer de las energías suplementarias necesarias. Suspiró. Estaba demasiado débil.

Se oyeron voces.

—¡Paso al jefe del pretorio! ¡Paso, malditos perros, paso!

Marcio, tumbado, giró el cuello y vio a un montón de pretorianos entrando en la sala subterránea. Todos se apartaban de inmediato. Lo mejor fue que el liberto que hacía de *medicus* también lo dejó en paz.

—¿Es éste el *mirmillo*? —preguntó Liviano con voz rotunda, pues habían retirado el casco y las protecciones al herido y ya no era tan fácil identificarlo. Los esclavos asintieron. El pretoriano se acercó a Marcio y levantó su brazo derecho presentándole una espada de madera. Marcio no podía dar crédito. Era la *rudis*, la espada de la libertad; ya no tendría que luchar más. No podía creerlo. Los esclavos también estaban pasmados. Todos habían oído historias de que la *rudis*, en ocasiones muy especiales, se entregaba no en la arena misma, sino después del combate a un gladiador que el editor de los juegos o el propio emperador deseara liberar por su valor exhibido en la lucha. Todos habían visto el combate y la verdad era que a nadie le pareció que aquella espada fuera entregada de forma impropia: para todos ellos el viejo Senex había luchado de un modo valeroso hasta el final y con energía sorprendente en un gladiador de su edad. Se la merecía.

—Eres libre, gladiador —dijo Liviano—. Ahora levántate y sígueme.

Marcio intentó incorporarse pero no podía. Ni brazos ni piernas parecían responderle ya.

Liviano pareció contrariado. Tenía órdenes precisas del emperador de conducir a aquel gladiador a palacio lo antes posible y Liviano no era oficial que gustara de desatender los deseos imperiales porque alguien tuviera alguna herida que otra. El hecho de que Marcio hubiera matado a pretorianos en el pasado tampoco alimentaba su misericordia.

—¡Levántate, imbécil! —insistió el jefe del pretorio, pero como vio que los gritos no parecían surtir efecto se dirigió a dos de los esclavos que se arracimaban en las paredes de la sala subterránea—. ¡Tú y tú! ¡Levantadlo y seguidme!

Los esclavos no dudaron en acudir prestos a la mesa donde estaba tumbado un Marcio que apenas tenía ya percepción de lo que ocurría a su alrededor. Todo estaba borroso. Pero antes de perder el conocimiento pudo oír otra voz potente.

—¡Dejad a ese hombre donde está!

Liviano se volvió y vio a Critón, el médico del emperador.

El jefe del pretorio no se dejó intimidar por el *medicus* griego. Tenía una orden.

—El César quiere a ese gladiador en palacio lo antes posible.

—¡Y el César me ha ordenado que vele por la salud del gladiador, *vir eminentissimus*! ¡Este hombre está demasiado débil! Es evidente que ha perdido muchísima sangre. Lo sacaremos de aquí cuando detengamos todas las hemorragias. Imagino que el César querrá al gladiador vivo, ¿no crees, *vir eminentissimus?* El emperador te ha ordenado que lo conduzcas a palacio «lo antes posible». Yo me hago responsable de interpretar cuándo es «lo antes posible».

Liviano, muy serio, se hizo a un lado y dejo pasar al *medicus.* Uno de verdad.

6

LA ARENA DE ARABIA

En la ruta entre Bostra y Petra
107 d. C.

Cornelio Palma se sacudió, con un gesto completamente inútil, parte de la arena que tenía pegada a la piel de los brazos. Estaban en un mar de polvo, bajo un sol abrasador en una región perdida del mundo. Pero tenía una misión.

Bebió dos tragos largos de agua del odre que le acercó un legionario.

—¿Qué hacemos? —preguntó Cayo Claudio Severo, uno de los tribunos.

Palma se llevó la mano derecha a la frente para protegerse los ojos.

—Seguiremos avanzando —respondió—. ¡Por Júpiter! ¿Qué otra cosa podemos hacer? ¡El emperador espera noticias de la anexión completa de esta región hace meses y lo único de lo que puedo hablar es de arena!

—Bostra, al norte, está bajo nuestro poder —comentó Severo.

—Sí, eso es cierto —aceptó Palma—, pero apenas hemos encontrado resistencia. Han concentrado sus tropas en el sur, en Petra. Sin tener esa ciudad controlada no podemos escribir al César y decirle que el reino de la Arabia Nabatea es una provincia de Roma, ¿no crees?

El tribuno asintió varias veces con rapidez, como si sintiera que el peso de la ira de Trajano se desplomaba sobre él por no haber conseguido la anhelada victoria en aquellas remotas tierras de Oriente.

—Incluso existe la posibilidad... —Palma se calló. Sí, era

aún posible que fueran derrotados. Apenas disponía de dos legiones no completas llevadas de Siria y Egipto. Si los nabateos se decidían a enfrentárseles con todas sus fuerzas unidas en una gran batalla campal, Palma no las tenía todas consigo. Volvió a repetir el gesto de sacudirse la arena de Arabia de los brazos, pero el sudor de su cuerpo se oponía y los granos de arena, todos y cada uno de ellos, permanecieron donde estaban, pegados a su piel húmeda. Suspiró.

—Vamos allá —dijo al fin Palma—. Hacia Petra.

7

LA CAPITAL DEL MUNDO

Loyang, capital del Imperio han
107 d. C.

«Llegarás a Loyang por el camino del norte», le había dicho a Li Kan su *chi tu-wei*, su comandante en la Gran Muralla. Y es que Li Kan era un joven y valiente guerrero de la gigantesca muralla que el Imperio han había construido hacía décadas al norte para protegerse de los constantes ataques de los *hsiung-nu*.[8] Li Kan se había distinguido por su gran valor y, muertos sus padres, aquel comandante lo había medio adoptado como su pupilo y lo estimaba de verdad. Por eso, cuando llegaron órdenes del nuevo *shou* de la región en las que se indicaba que Fan Chun, uno de los asistentes del ministro de Obras Públicas de la emperatriz Deng, reclamaba guerreros extraordinarios para la corte, el *chi tu-wei* de Li Kan no lo dudó y, en lugar de retener a su joven aprendiz junto a él, decidió enviarlo al sur, a la capital del mundo, para que el joven guerrero prosperara.

«Llegarás a Loyang por el camino del norte.» Eso le había dicho. Y le había proporcionado más indicaciones.

—No darás buena imagen si tienes que preguntar a todo el mundo —le había comentado su comandante—. Así que escúchame: llegarás al gran Altar de la Tierra y enseguida verás el río Ku. Lo cruzarás y entrarás por la puerta Hsia. Con que te asegures de entrar por esa puerta, el resto del camino es sencillo. Una vez cruzadas las murallas por esa puerta, girarás a la derecha siguiendo la propia muralla de la ciudad.

8. Los hunos.

Nada que ver con nuestra Gran Muralla, pero un muro al fin y al cabo. El caso es que pasarás entonces junto a la puerta Shang-shi, dejando el mercado principal de Loyang a tu izquierda. Seguirás en dirección sur y dejarás más puertas ahora a tu derecha: la Yung y luego la Kuang-yang. La muralla girará de nuevo, pues habrás llegado al límite sur del recinto fortificado. En ese momento deberás alcanzar la puerta Hsiao-yuan. Desde allí podrás vislumbrar ya el Gran Palacio Sur. Es ahí donde se encuentran las principales oficinas de los nueve ministros y las tres excelencias que sirven a su majestad imperial. Entregarás esta carta a los guardias de ese palacio y ellos te conducirán hasta el asistente del ministro de Obras Públicas. Memoriza bien todo lo que te he dicho. Un guerrero confuso en la capital no causa buena impresión. Ha de dar siempre la sensación de que sabes lo que haces, incluso si no lo sabes. Las apariencias son siempre importantes, pero en Loyang lo son prácticamente todo.

Y así hizo Li Kan: memorizó bien la ruta y la siguió con minuciosidad. Él nunca había estado en la capital y la extensión de la ciudad, así como el enorme gentío, le impresionaron. No sabía que estaba en una de las tres ciudades más grandes del mundo junto con Ch'ang-an, la antigua capital del Imperio han, y una ciudad que para Li Kan sólo existía en su cabeza como un sueño fruto de las increíbles historias de su difunto padre: la remota capital del cuarto imperio, del desconocido Da Qin, allí donde termina el mundo.

Li Kan desmontó de su caballo en cuanto llegó a la entrada del Gran Palacio Sur y entregó la carta de su comandante a los centinelas, tal y como éste le había instruido. En efecto, al poco tiempo de espera, otro soldado imperial, un oficial, apareció en la puerta y se dirigió a él con aire marcial.

—Sígueme.

Li Kan obedeció.

Pasaron por decenas de oficinas donde centenares de funcionarios se afanaban en escribir cuentas e informes de todo tipo. Li Kan imaginó que todo aquello estaría relacionado con la compleja administración de un imperio de más de sesenta millones de súbditos.

—Es aquí —le dijo el oficial—. Entra cuando te llamen.
—Y desapareció de regreso al exterior.

Li Kan suspiró lentamente. Estaba incómodo. Su ambiente eran las grandes praderas del norte y el combate contra el enemigo. Allí, rodeado de paredes y muros y funcionarios que susurraban por todas partes, se sentía desplazado. Pero su comandante lo había enviado allí y eso sería porque pensaba que era lo conveniente para su futuro en el ejército. De hecho, todos los grandes puestos militares se distribuían desde Loyang, así que, seguramente, aquel viaje debía de ser buena idea.

—Escucha con atención cuando te hablen —le había insistido su comandante— y procura más bien hablar poco. Todo lo que calles queda contigo, pero todo cuanto dices queda en manos de los que te han escuchado. A veces hablar mucho es como entregar espadas al enemigo. Sé cauto. Sé leal.

—¿Leal a quién? —había preguntado a su comandante.

Li Kan repasaba aquella conversación instantes antes de que lo llamaran en un intento por estar concentrado y dar la imagen que de él se esperaba. No quería defraudar a su *chi tuwei* ni mucho menos a sus padres, en especial a su padre, un valerosísimo guerrero del norte con historias extrañas sobre su pasado pero valiente como ningún otro.

—Has de ser leal a la emperatriz viuda regente, que es la que ha reclamado a estos nuevos hombres, estos nuevos guerreros, en la corte, a través del asistente del ministro de Obras Públicas. Y no vaciles nunca en este punto. La lealtad siempre es premiada, pero la traición, al final, siempre es descubierta. Los que creen lo contrario, en Loyang acaban muertos.

De pronto se oyó una voz potente desde el interior de la oficina frente a la que esperaba.

—¡Li Kan!

El joven guerrero dio varios pasos con decisión e irrumpió, con toda probabilidad, con más energía de la que habitualmente empleaban otros en aquella sala, pero ya era tarde para disculparse por aquella entrada como un caballo desbocado. Li Kan optó por el silencio y por mirar al suelo.

Un viejo consejero lo examinó de arriba abajo. Se levantó

de su asiento y caminó alrededor del guerrero observándolo como si de un animal se tratara. Li Kan pensó que era lo mínimo que se merecía, se había comportado como tal. Es terrible: cuando mejor imagen quieres dar de ti mismo es cuando te salen peor las cosas.

—Mi nombre es Fan Chun —dijo el viejo funcionario tomando de nuevo asiento sobre unos almohadones de seda en el suelo—. ¿Sabes quién soy?

—El *yu-shih chung-ch'eng*, el asistente personal del ministro de Obras Públicas —respondió Li Kan sin levantar la mirada.

—Exacto. Eso es correcto —continuó el consejero imperial—. ¿Y sabes por qué estás aquí?

Li Kan dudó y optó por responder con las menos palabras posibles en un intento por reducir el margen de error.

—La emperatriz Deng desea nuevos guerreros en Loyang.

—Correcto también —concedió el funcionario—. ¿Y por qué crees que necesita la emperatriz nuevos guerreros?

Li Kan no había esperado preguntas, sino más bien órdenes. Definitivamente era mucho mejor estar en el norte bajo el mando de su comandante. Con él todo estaba claro: había que matar a los *hsiung-nu* que se acercaran a la Gran Muralla. Si los matabas, nadie hacía preguntas confusas. Pero Li Kan pensó con rapidez: en Loyang había muchos guerreros, los había visto por todas partes, y seguramente habría alguna unidad militar completa, pese a que la mayor parte del ejército estaba en las fronteras del norte, el sur y el occidente. ¿Por qué querían más guerreros en Loyang? Quizá porque necesitaban más. La ciudad había crecido enormemente y debía de tener en torno al millón de habitantes. Desde que el primer emperador de la nueva dinastía Han trasladó la capital de Ch'ang-an a Loyang, la nueva ciudad no había hecho más que crecer y crecer. Quizá ésa fuera la respuesta o quizá...

—Es posible que el gobierno necesite más soldados en Loyang —empezó a decir Li Kan, pero sin acertar a controlar su carácter impulsivo y espontáneo inició la formulación de una segunda hipótesis—, o a lo mejor es que la emperatriz no...

Se detuvo. Era un imbécil. «Habla poco, habla poco», le

había dicho su comandante, y en la primera conversación con un alto funcionario ya estaba hablando de más.

—¿O es que la emperatriz qué? —indagó Fan Chun repitiendo las últimas palabras de su joven interlocutor.

Li Kan se mordió el labio inferior con los dientes.

—Estoy esperando respuesta y no soy hombre habituado a esperar, soldado —añadió Fan Chun con enorme seriedad.

Li Kan suspiró. Pensó en intentar inventar algo con lo que salir del lío en el que sus palabras lo habían metido, pero no valía para eso. Y sólo le faltaba añadir a sus impulsos una mentira. No. Era mejor que lo echaran de allí y lo devolvieran al norte por hablar de más que por mentir. Lo primero sería humillante, lo segundo lo condenaría a tener que abandonar el ejército y el ejército era su vida.

—A lo mejor la emperatriz no confía en los soldados que tiene en Loyang —dijo al fin Li Kan y levantó la mirada para ver cuán mal eran recibidas sus palabras por el funcionario que lo estaba interrogando. Para su sorpresa el consejero imperial sonrió.

—En su carta, tu *chi tu-wei*, tu comandante, dice que además de uno de sus mejores guerreros en el combate eres hombre astuto e inteligente —dijo Fan Chun— y observo con satisfacción que así es. Has dado en lo cierto con tu contestación a mi última pregunta; y con bastante más rapidez que otros con los que he hablado antes. Algunos que ya he devuelto al norte ni siquiera dieron con la respuesta nunca. Pero sí, el caso es que la emperatriz desconfía de gran parte de los guerreros de palacio y estoy encargado de constituir un nuevo cuerpo de guardia. Tenemos un emperador niño y la emperatriz se esfuerza por regir el imperio con rectitud y nobleza a la espera de que el muy joven emperador An-ti esté en circunstancias de gobernar de forma efectiva; pero las regencias, por desgracia, son nidos de conspiraciones. Hay quienes, erróneamente, suponen que es más fácil doblegar a una emperatriz que a un emperador. Es obvio que desconocen la tenacidad y la capacidad de trabajo de nuestra emperatriz. Pero volvamos al asunto: correcto, no nos fiamos de muchos guerreros, pero, y ésta es la cuestión clave: ¿por qué habríamos de fiarnos de ti?

Li Kan no supo bien qué responder ahora.

—No, no digas nada —continuó Fan Chun—. Lo que uno dice sobre uno mismo no es nunca relevante. Es lo que otros dicen de nosotros lo que cuenta, al menos aquí. Los informes de tu comandante son los mejores. Dicen que desciendes de una familia de guerreros brillantes muy distinguidos en la lucha contra los *hsiung-nu*. Dicen también, y esto me llamó la atención, que quizá hay algún secreto relacionado con el origen de las enormes capacidades guerreras de tu familia y que tú pareces haber heredado. Te seré sincero, Li Kan: esta parte no me agrada. No me gustan los secretos. Ya tenemos demasiados en Loyang y no necesito nuevos secretos de los que preocuparme.

Li Kan tragó saliva. No tenía ni idea del modo en que podría concluir aquella enigmática conversación, pero sí sabía que no pensaba desvelar el origen de su familia a nadie que no fuera la propia emperatriz. Ante ella sí desvelaría aquella vieja historia... —¿leyenda?— que le contara su padre en su lecho de muerte, pero ante nadie más. Li Kan temía que la siguiente pregunta del consejero fuera a ponerlo entre la espada y la pared, pero...

—No voy a preguntarte por tu secreto: si es cierto que el origen de tu familia es... especial, pero eres como tu comandante dice que eres, entonces no lo desvelarás; si, por el contrario, tu gran secreto es sólo una leyenda inventada para impresionar a comandantes rústicos del norte, no me interesa. Pero esto me devuelve a la pregunta anterior: ¿por qué hemos de fiarnos de ti? —Hizo una breve pausa que a Li Kan se le antojó eterna—. No tengo más motivos que este informe y esto no es suficiente, pero es cierto que necesitamos guerreros. Así que, ¿sabes cómo sé si un guerrero es de mi confianza o no?

Li Kan volvió a tragar saliva e, instintivamente, miró a su alrededor. Temía un ataque por sorpresa, algo inesperado. Se llevó la mano a la empuñadura de su espada *jian* de doble filo.

—No lo sé, asistente.

—Con una prueba —respondió Fan Chun con serenidad, esbozando una media sonrisa porque eran tan evidentes los nervios de su interlocutor que aquello le divirtió, aparte de que de nuevo le satisfizo lo atento que estaba aquel guerrero del norte: era como hablar con un lobo dispuesto a atacar o defenderse en cualquier momento. Eso era precisamente lo que necesitaban, si pasaba la prueba, claro.

—¿Qué tipo de prueba? —se atrevió a preguntar Li Kan.

—No es siempre la misma —le explicó el funcionario con aire de quien hace algo rutinario—. En tu caso es muy sencilla —y añadió un nombre—: Kan Ying.

—¿Kan Ying? —preguntó Li Kan repitiendo aquel nombre desconocido para él al tiempo que fruncía el ceño confundido.

—Es un antiguo funcionario, un importante antiguo funcionario del Imperio han. Hace unos años se le pidió que hiciera algo para el emperador He. Necesitamos hablar con este Kan Ying, pero no podemos localizarlo. Tu prueba, tu misión, es ir a Ch'ang-an, la antigua capital, donde sabemos que está Kan Ying, pero desde donde no responde a mis cartas, y traerlo aquí ante la emperatriz. Si cumples con esta misión empezaré a pensar que quizá sí seas digno de confianza. ¿Alguna pregunta?

Dejó de mirarlo y pasó a fijar los ojos en un texto escrito en un pesado rollo de bambú.

—Necesitaría saber algo más de este hombre, cómo es físicamente, si tiene familia...

—Se te proporcionará a la salida un informe completo —respondió Fan Chun sin mirarlo—; aquí sabemos hacer informes; también se te hará entrega de un caballo nuevo y cartas para que puedas usar el camino imperial entre Loyang y la antigua capital, con acceso libre a las postas militares donde podrás pernoctar en tu viaje.

Li Kan no preguntó más y se inclinó. Dio media vuelta y empezó a andar en dirección a la puerta cuando oyó, de nuevo, la voz del funcionario.

—Ten cuidado, guerrero del norte: Kan Ying no es de fiar.

Li Kan se volvió pero vio que el funcionario había hablado sin dejar de leer su texto de bambú.

—Sí, asistente —respondió Li Kan y salió. Todo parecía haber salido más o menos bien. Kan Ying. Bien. Lo encontraría y lo llevaría allí. ¿Por qué sería importante aquel hombre?

8

EL PRECIO DE LA LIBERTAD

**Domus Flavia (palacio imperial), Roma
107 d. C.**

Marcio, por segunda vez en su vida, entró en el palacio imperial de Roma. La gran *Domus Flavia* estaba reluciente, limpia, pulcra, pero no había grandes adornos ni telas decorativas por todas partes como en época de Domiciano. Al ahora exgladiador, ya de forma oficial, se le antojaba curioso volver a verse en el interior de aquel gigantesco edificio y, cuando menos, agradecía que esta vez pudiera entrar por la puerta principal, escoltado, que no arrestado, por una docena de pretorianos armados. Además, convaleciente aún de sus numerosas heridas del último combate, no estaba con energías para luchar contra nadie, así que verse protegido y no amenazado por la guardia imperial le resultó un gran alivio. Aun así, aquellas paredes sólo llevaban dolorosos recuerdos a Marcio y, por qué no admitirlo: miedo. Saber a qué temes es lo que te hace capaz de superarlo. Negar que sientes miedo de algo o alguien sólo te hace aún más vulnerable.

Cruzaron la gran *Aula Regia* y los peristilos porticados llenos de columnas que antaño tenían espejos. Ahora relucían blancas como la piedra o el mármol del que estaban hechas.

—Es aquí —dijo Aulo.

Los pretorianos se detuvieron y Marcio miró hacia la gran puerta de bronce que tenía frente a él.

«Sí, aquí era», pensó el antiguo gladiador recordando la galería de cámaras en las que luchó encarnizadamente con los pretorianos de Domiciano. De eso hacía años. Mil cosas habían pasado desde entonces.

Dos guardias abrieron las pesadas hojas de bronce.

—Pasa, gladiador —le dijo Aulo—. El emperador te espera.

Técnicamente Marcio ya no era un gladiador, pero Aulo no estaba para matices, sino para proteger al César.

Marcio entró.

Las puertas se cerraron.

Trajano lo miraba sentado al otro lado de una gran mesa repleta de papiros y mapas.

Marcio dio varios pasos hacia adelante hasta situarse a sólo unos pies de distancia del escritorio del César.

Trajano no habló, sino que se limitó a agacharse un instante y coger algo del suelo que de inmediato puso sobre la mesa. Era un casco de *mirmillo*. Marcio no tardó en reconocer su viejo casco, el que llevaba puesto el día que descendió a las entrañas del Anfiteatro Flavio para ajustar cuentas con Carpophorus. Las fieras habían devorado el cadáver del *bestiarius* y él pensó que con eso quedaba a salvo de su crimen. Luego recordó que había olvidado su casco junto a la pantera negra en aquellos horribles sótanos de la muerte, pero como nadie fue a buscarlo nunca como posible autor de la muerte de Carpophorus, Marcio concluyó que todo aquello estaba olvidado. Era curioso cómo en su vida el pasado volvía siempre de nuevo. La verdad era que ver aquel casco sobre la mesa del emperador lo inquietó. Toda vez que acababa de ser liberado al recibir la *rudis*, Marcio estaba seguro de que ahora podría ir al norte y buscar a Alana y Tamura hasta reencontrarse con ellas. Sin embargo, de nuevo parecía que aquel profundo anhelo podría resultar imposible. Y no tenía sentido negar que aquel casco era el suyo. Si el emperador lo tenía sería, sin duda, porque Trigésimo lo habría recibido de los pretorianos que descendieron a los sótanos del terrible *bestiarius* a ver qué había pasado con Carpophorus cuando no se supo nada de él al día siguiente de su muerte. Trigésimo, el *lanista*, habría reconocido el yelmo de *mirmillo* y se lo habría entregado a alguien, seguramente un oficial pretoriano, puede que incluso al que lo había llevado ese día ante Trajano, y ese pretoriano habría informado al emperador.

—Carpophorus merecía la muerte que tuvo... augusto —dijo Marcio al fin sin negar su participación en el asunto.

—Dicen que fue devorado por sus fieras. Ésa es una muerte bastante horrenda y bastante indigna, incluso si su trabajo era el de *bestiarius* —argumentó Trajano—. Además, mis guardias dicen que encontraron varias celdas de fieras abiertas y eso es raro. No creo que el *bestiarius* fuera un hombre tan descuidado; de lo contrario, no habría durado tantos años en su puesto. Y luego está este casco, tu casco, encontrado justo allí donde apareció Carpophorus muerto. Bueno, lo poco que quedó de él. Las fieras tenían mucha hambre. No hay que ser un dios para imaginar que algo tuviste que ver en la muerte del *bestiarius*.

Se hizo otro silencio. Marcio fruncía el ceño. ¿Tenía sentido defenderse explicando que el *bestiarius* quería su hígado, pues se pensaba que el hígado de un gladiador podía curar algunas enfermedades y que, en consecuencia, había quien estaba dispuesto a comprar las vísceras del mejor de los gladiadores del momento? ¿O que para ello había pactado su muerte con el *bestiarius* y con Trigésimo, el *lanista*? Suponía que no. Asesinar al *bestiarius* de Roma era un crimen grave. El exgladiador bajó la mirada mientras respondía.

—¿El César me ha liberado para volver a condenarme ahora?

—No exactamente —respondió Trajano con rapidez—. Te he liberado de tu servidumbre de gladiador porque te has ganado ese derecho luchando en la arena y te he citado aquí para mostrarte que sería justo volver a condenarte. Incluso si ese miserable *bestiarius* me caía mal, y me consta que sus actividades en los sótanos del Anfiteatro Flavio podrían ser cuestionables, no puedo permitir que un gladiador se tome la justicia por su mano y asesine a quien le parezca, ¿no crees?

—No, imagino que no, augusto.

Marcio suspiró mientras seguía mirando al suelo. En ese momento cayó en la cuenta de que estaban solos, el emperador y él. Aquel César no tenía miedo de quedarse a solas en su cámara imperial con un exgladiador. ¿Podría matar al emperador y buscar el pasadizo secreto que conducía en tiempos pasados a las cloacas de Roma? ¿Seguiría ese pasadizo allí? ¿No lo habrían sellado ya? ¿No habrían puesto verjas de hierro en las cloacas que pasaban por debajo del palacio imperial después de lo que ocurrió con Domiciano? A Marcio le dolía la cabeza y también todo el cuerpo. ¿Tenía él suficiente fuerza para enfrentarse a Trajano? El emperador era mayor que él, pero recio, robusto, y él estaba herido aún... Había pasado de la alegría de la liberación al aturdimiento de verse al borde de la prisión una vez más. No era optimista de natural, pero en algunos momentos desde que recibiera la *rudis*, había pensado que sería posible recuperar su vida con Alana y Tamura, al menos posible... Todo eso suponiendo que ellas también siguieran vivas en el norte, más allá del Danubio, en la lejana Dacia...

—No te he hecho llamar para condenarte de nuevo —continuó Trajano—. Para eso me hubiera bastado con enviar a unos pretorianos. No. Te he mostrado el casco para que veas que sé que deberías ser condenado de nuevo, pero realmente no me importa que mataras a ese Carpophorus asesino de mujeres y quién sabe cuántas cosas más. —Aquí Marcio levantó la cabeza y el emperador asintió mientras continuaba hablando—. No eres el único que tenía conocimiento de las prácticas de ese miserable. Hacía tiempo que estaba considerando sustituirlo, pero he de reconocer que tú fuiste más... expeditivo. Y eso es precisamente lo que me gusta de ti. Cuando te propones algo, lo consigues, por el medio que sea. Hombres así son los que necesita el Imperio. En concreto, tengo una misión para ti.

Marcio se pasó la lengua por los labios resecos. ¿No le iban a condenar?

—¿Qué misión? —preguntó. Sólo quería saber cuánto retrasaría aquello su anhelado intento de reencontrarse con Alana y Tamura. Era todo lo que le interesaba.

—No —respondió Trajano de forma tajante—. Antes de desvelarte la misión he de garantizarme tu lealtad. Y pienso hacerlo de una forma perfecta. No volverás a rebelarte nunca contra mí.

Aquí Marcio empezó a temer de nuevo por Alana y Tamura. ¿No las habrían apresado los romanos?

—Yo sólo soy leal a mí mismo. La vida me ha enseñado

que nadie merece lealtad alguna. Más allá de la familia, nadie —replicó Marcio en un arrebato de sinceridad de cuya utilidad dudó de inmediato.

—La familia, tú mismo lo acabas de decir, es esencial. Pero hay lealtades más allá de la familia. Yo tengo un puñado de hombres capaces de seguirme al fin del mundo. No muchos, pero un pequeño grupo sí. Y esos hombres, a su vez, tienen oficiales que les son fieles y tras esos oficiales hay decenas, centenares de legionarios que obedecen sus órdenes. Así, al final, con lealtad más que con miedo, se consigue gobernar un imperio. Y ahora quiero tu lealtad. ¡Por Júpiter, estuviste a punto de matarme porque tenían presas a tu mujer y a tu hija y cambiaste de opinión porque pensaste que ya habían escapado! Está claro que ése es el único camino para conseguir tu lealtad. —Trajano calló un instante y extrajo de debajo de su túnica un papiro enrollado que depositó en la mesa justo frente al exgladiador—. Ahí tienes: un salvoconducto que te permitirá moverte por todo el Imperio, incluso salir de él y, si quieres, regresar a Roma. Es tuyo. Cógelo. Te será muy útil en ese viaje al norte que debes de estar planeando desde que te condené al Anfiteatro Flavio: eres un hombre libre, Marcio, y puedes usar ese documento para ir en busca de tu mujer y de tu hija. Sólo te pido que si las encuentras, regreses a Roma. Si retornas a mí, te daré trabajo, seguridad para ti y para tu familia siempre y, pasado un tiempo, te reclamaré para esa misión que tengo en mente. Ésta es mi propuesta, ¿qué te parece? También te daré un caballo y dinero para tu viaje al norte. Conmigo a tu lado la búsqueda de tu mujer y tu hija será más fácil. Sin mí te resultará muy difícil, y contra mí imposible. ¿Qué me dices, gladiador?

Marcio tragó saliva mientras miraba fijamente aquel salvoconducto imperial enrollado sobre la mesa del César.

—¿Y si no acepto tu ayuda? ¿Me condenará entonces el emperador por el asesinato de Carpophorus?

Trajano negó con la cabeza.

—No. Que sigas mis órdenes por la fuerza no me sirve. Necesito tu lealtad. Vete sin mi ayuda al norte y que los dioses sean bondadosos contigo, o ve al norte con mi ayuda y deja que el brazo del César te asista en tu búsqueda. Encuentra a quien tanto estimas y sólo entonces decide si merezco tu lealtad o no. Si quiero que me seas fiel no puedo exigirte nada. La fidelidad auténtica la decide el que la entrega, nunca el que la recibe.

Marcio cerró los ojos un momento. Dinero, un salvoconducto y un caballo. Ya no era tan joven. Aquellas herramientas podían ser la mejor de las ayudas para intentar reencontrarse con Alana y Tamura. El exgladiador abrió los ojos, se inclinó levemente hacia adelante alargando el brazo y tomó el salvoconducto con la mano derecha.

—No sé si volveré —dijo. Dio media vuelta con el papiro en la mano y echó a andar hacia la puerta.

—¡Abrid! —gritó Trajano. Y las pesadas hojas de bronce se separaron. Marcio se deslizó entre ellas y desapareció tras una nube de pretorianos.

Aulo entró en la cámara imperial antes de que sus hombres volvieran a cerrar las puertas.

—Dadle todo lo que hemos acordado —dijo Trajano al tribuno pretoriano.

—Sí, augusto —respondió Aulo e iba a marcharse cuando se atrevió a preguntar algo—: ¿Volverá el gladiador, César?

Trajano ladeó la cabeza ligeramente.

—No lo sé, Aulo, pero si vuelve, será nuestro hombre.

UNA PROPUESTA DE LOS KUSHAN

Roma, 107 d. C.

Aulo desapareció con Marcio. Trajano se quedó en silencio mirando al techo pintado con motivos marinos de su cámara imperial. El descanso no le duró demasiado. Llamaron a las puertas de bronce. El emperador se llevó las yemas de los dedos de la mano derecha a la frente. Suspiró. Estaba poniendo en marcha un plan muy ambicioso y tenía que estar concentrado y dispuesto.

—¡Adelante! —dijo Trajano. Liviano entró de inmediato.

—Ya está aquí, augusto —apuntó el jefe del pretorio.

—¿Y Lucio y Dión Coceyo? —inquirió el César.

El pretoriano asintió.

—Entonces vamos allá —respondió Trajano levantándose.

Liviano se hizo a un lado para dejar pasar al emperador y luego lo siguió. Tras ellos una docena de pretorianos los escoltaron mientras cruzaban todas las habitaciones privadas de la familia imperial primero y, a continuación, los grandes peristilos porticados con jardines, hasta que llegaron a la gran *Aula Regia*. Trajano cruzó por el centro de la gigantesca sala de audiencias sin mirar a nadie, absorto en sus pensamientos y con el rostro serio. Sólo había guardias a ambos lados y tres hombres esperando junto al trono imperial: Lucio Quieto, el viejo Dión Coceyo y el embajador Shaka de los kushan.

El emperador tomó asiento y miró a Liviano antes de decir nada. El jefe del pretorio hizo una señal con el brazo y toda la guardia pretoriana salió de la sala, a excepción del tribuno Aulo y del propio jefe del pretorio. Nadie dijo nada mientras los guardias abandonaban el recinto para apostarse en las puertas norte y así vigilar el acceso desde el exterior.

—Ya está, César —dijo Liviano.

Trajano se acomodó en el trono, pero siguió sin decir nada durante unos instantes hasta que por fin se dirigió a Liviano.

—Tú y Aulo también —dijo Trajano, y como vio sorpresa, que no rebeldía, en la faz de su jefe del pretorio, añadió una explicación—: Sabes que tengo absoluta confianza en ti y en tus hombres, pero en estos momentos lo que vamos a hablar es secreto, algo entre el embajador Shaka y el emperador de Roma. Dión Coceyo está presente como intérprete, en caso de que mi griego y el del embajador resulten insuficientes para entendernos. Liviano, más adelante, en su momento, os enteraréis de lo que aquí se hable... y Aulo también... y Roma entera.

El jefe del pretorio, superada la sorpresa inicial, se llevó el puño al pecho y respondió con decisión.

—Siempre al servicio del César. Un jefe del pretorio no debe recibir explicaciones, augusto, sino órdenes.

Trajano asintió y sonrió levemente. No esperaba menos de Liviano, pero estaba bien comprobar de vez en cuando que las personas en las que uno confía reaccionan exactamente como ha previsto. Además, Liviano había evitado hacer la pregunta obvia: ¿y Lucio Quieto? ¿Por qué se le permitía permanecer al *legatus* norteafricano y jefe de la caballería romana? Que Liviano no hubiera hecho la pregunta denotaba, por un lado, que el jefe del pretorio era congruente con su afirmación de no pedir ni esperar explicaciones sobre las acciones del César y, por otro, que entendía bien el mensaje que le estaba mandando: Quieto está por encima de todos los demás, incluido Adriano, que no estaba presente ni se le había llamado.

En cuanto la silueta del jefe del pretorio, seguida de la del tribuno Aulo, se desvaneció por la puerta norte, el emperador, que los seguía con los ojos, se volvió hacia los presentes. La primera mirada con la que se encontró fue con la del propio Quieto, muy serio, como asumiendo la posición que cada vez más claramente parecía indicar Trajano con respecto a él en el entorno imperial. No se dijeron nada. Trajano siguió volviéndose en el trono hasta ver al embajador kushan.

—Una audiencia privada —dijo el César—. Es lo que se me pidió. Una audiencia privada tenemos. Más privada es imposible.

Dión Coceyo tradujo al griego y el embajador se inclinó marcadamente ante el emperador. Luego habló en un latín algo tosco, pero comprensible.

—El César es amable y generoso con un humilde enviado kushan.

Trajano sonrió.

—Veo que hacemos progresos con el latín y agradezco los calificativos sobre mi persona, pero dudo de que el emperador Kadphises del Imperio kushan me haya enviado a alguien humilde como su representante.

Pero el latín de Shaka no daba para tanto y miró a Dión Coceyo. El filósofo tradujo. El embajador volvió a asentir.

—Humilde ante el poder del César, quise decir. De hecho tengo... mandato... creo que me expresaré ya en griego —dijo Shaka. Ante el asentimiento de Trajano, el enviado kushan prosiguió en aquel idioma más conocido de lo que uno imaginaría al norte de la India, herencia de las conquistas del legendario Alejandro Magno—. El asunto es muy sencillo, pero muy ambicioso: entre nuestro imperio y el gran Imperio romano está Partia con su *Šāhān Šāh*, rey de reyes, como los propios partos denominan a su líder, o *Βασιλεύς βασιλέων* [*basileus basileon*] si lo decimos en griego. Un título que de por sí ya denota la endiosada visión que los partos tienen de sí mismos. No les basta con tener un rey o un emperador, sino que el suyo ha de ser rey del resto de los reyes. Esta vanidad incomoda a mi señor, el emperador Kadphises.

Shaka se detuvo, Dión Coceyo tradujo. Trajano entendía bastante griego y podía hablarlo, pero no con soltura suficiente y no quería dar una imagen de desconocimiento o debilidad que podía sugerir un mal uso del lenguaje griego por su parte, de ahí la presencia de Dión Coceyo; además, era prerrogativa suya, como persona de poder, elegir en qué idioma expresarse. También estaba Quieto, cuyo griego era más limitado, y el emperador deseaba que Quieto comprendiera bien todo lo que allí se hablaba. Finalmente, Dión Coceyo sabía algo de sánscrito, una de las lenguas de la corte kushan; si el griego fallaba quizá el embajador quisiera recurrir a ese idioma.

Shaka retomó su discurso.

—El Imperio parto, además, interfiere y dificulta el comercio entre nuestro imperio, las riquezas de la India y otros países más allá de nuestras fronteras orientales, por un lado, y también incomoda los negocios con el propio Imperio romano, por otro. El Imperio parto es, pues, a nuestro entender un... problema.

El filósofo griego volvió a reformular en latín lo expresado por Shaka.

—Un problema difícil de resolver —aceptó Trajano—. Todo esto es muy interesante, pero más importante aún sería para mí confirmar lo que ha llegado hasta mis oídos desde los puestos de frontera de Siria. —Hizo una brevísima pausa y luego lanzó su pregunta, afilada como la más puntiaguda de las flechas—: ¿Es cierto que hay una guerra en el interior de Partia?

Tras la nueva traducción, Shaka asintió varias veces y volvió a hablar en griego.

—Sí, César: hay una guerra civil en ciernes en el Imperio parto: Vonones II dejó el imperio a su hijo Vologases I y éste a su vez a su hijo, que gobernó con el nombre de Vologases II, pero su tío Pacoro II le arrebató el trono por la guerra y gobernó en su lugar. Luego Osroes I, hermano de Pacoro II, continuó en el poder. Los otros hermanos de Osroes I, Partamasiris y Mitrídates, lo apoyan en mayor o menor medida en el gobierno de Partia, pero queda un cabo suelto, por así decirlo.

Dión Coceyo tradujo rápidamente.

—¿Y ese cabo suelto se llama...? —preguntó Trajano.

—Vologases III —respondió Shaka sin esperar una traducción. Entendía bien las preguntas cortas y directas—. Es el hijo del fallecido Vologases II depuesto por Pacoro I y luego por Osroes. Vologases III reclama el trono de Cesifonte y el poder sobre toda Partia y sus reinos vasallos. Y se ha hecho

77

fuerte en la región más oriental, en la frontera con nuestro imperio. Tiene recursos limitados, pero su determinación a luchar contra Osroes parece no admitir que es imposible derrotar a alguien que cuenta con muchos más apoyos.

Tras una nueva traducción del filósofo griego Trajano se levantó del trono imperial, descendió al suelo, en un gesto que sorprendió al embajador, y fue a una mesa que había permanecido semioculta por la falta de iluminación. El emperador se dirigió a Lucio, pues no había pretorianos en la sala para asistir al César.

—Acerca esa antorcha —dijo señalando una de las que se encontraban enganchadas en la pared más próxima. El *legatus* la acercó de inmediato y la luz hizo visible un gran mapa donde se podía ver el mundo entero, desde Roma y el Mediterráneo, pasando por Siria y Partia hasta llegar a la India y, al norte, el Imperio kushan y, más lejos, de forma menos definida por el desconocimiento de quien lo había dibujado, una región amplia marcada con el nombre de Xeres.

—¿Dónde se refugia ese Vologases III de quien hablas? —preguntó Trajano.

El embajador se acercó al mapa. Era parecido a los mapas de los que ellos disponían, sólo que con más detalle en las regiones occidentales y mucho menos acierto a la hora de delimitar los contornos de las regiones orientales como India o el Imperio han. Shaka no hizo comentario alguno a ese respecto. Su misión era conseguir una reacción del César, no informar a los romanos sobre todo aquello que parecían desconocer.

—Aquí —dijo Shaka señalando un punto en el mapa justo donde se encontraba una ciudad. Trajano se acercó para identificarla.

—Merv —dijo el César.

—Es una ciudad muy fortificada —explicó Shaka en latín.

—¿Y cuál es la propuesta que me quieres transmitir del emperador Kadphises? —preguntó Trajano directamente en griego, lo que sorprendió a Shaka, pero se rehízo rápidamente ante aquel descubrimiento y siguió hablando de nuevo en esa lengua.

—Mi señor, el emperador Kadphises piensa que si Roma ataca a Osroes I por el oeste, nosotros atacaremos a Vologases III por el este. La incapacidad de unir sus fuerzas los hace accesibles, vulnerables. Podemos reducir o eliminar el Imperio parto. El comercio entre el Imperio kushan y el Imperio romano se beneficiará notablemente. El César Trajano y mi señor Kadphises salen ganando y con ello sus pueblos. Ésta es la propuesta.

—Traduce lo que ha dicho —dijo Trajano a Dión Coceyo señalando a Quieto para asegurarse de que el norteafricano seguía aquella conversación. El *legatus* escuchaba al filósofo con atención al tiempo que miraba el mapa. Trajano apretaba los labios mientras meditaba.

—Roma no tiene motivos para atacar Partia —dijo el César volviendo al latín—. Los partos no han cruzado el Éufrates en bastante tiempo. Sin *casus belli* no obtendré el apoyo del Senado para una campaña de esta envergadura y hacerlo contra el criterio del Senado en pleno me crearía problemas de gobierno. ¿Por qué no esperar a que Osroes I y Vologases III se enzarcen en una lucha que los destruya por completo?

—Porque Osroes I tiene un plan para cambiar el curso de los acontecimientos, César —añadió Shaka.

—¿Qué plan? —preguntó Trajano volviéndose de nuevo hacia la mesa y mirando el mapa.

—Aryazate —respondió el embajador kushan con rotundidad.

Trajano y Quieto miraron el plano en busca de una ciudad con aquel nombre, pero no acertaron a descubrir su posición.

—Es una mujer —aclaró Shaka.

Trajano y Quieto fijaron los ojos en el embajador.

—¿Una mujer? —repitió de forma inquisitiva el emperador.

—Bueno, realmente es una niña —especificó Shaka—. Es la hija pequeña del emperador parto Osroes, y su plan es casarla pronto, lo antes posible, incluso aunque sea una niña, con Vologases III, en un matrimonio que sellará la paz entre ambos contendientes. Y conseguida la paz entre los dos, Osroes con apoyo de Vologases sería tan fuerte que, sin duda, los límites de su actual imperio le parecerían pequeños y no tardaría en atacar Roma o a los kushan. Mi señor Kadphises piensa que es mejor atacar antes de que esa niña crezca.

Trajano exhaló aire lentamente, abandonó la mesa y retornó dando pequeños pasos al trono, donde volvió a sentarse. Dión Coceyo y el embajador lo siguieron. El *legatus* devolvió la antorcha a su emplazamiento y se situó también junto al César.

—Todo lo que nos cuentas es interesante y agradezco al emperador Kadphises que comparta esta información conmigo. Y entiendo también que la eliminación de los partos de regiones como Mesopotamia y todos los territorios hasta la frontera con los kushan facilitaría las comunicaciones y el comercio entre Roma y Oriente, algo en lo que llevo pensando hace tiempo, pero sin un *casus belli* no puedo emprender una campaña de esta magnitud. Eso sí, en el pasado, los partos han dado motivos para que ataquemos y el emperador Kadphises puede estar bien seguro de que a la más mínima provocación parta mi respuesta será demoledora.

Dión tradujo velozmente.

—¿He de entender, entonces, que el emperador romano puede que ataque Partia, pero no de modo inmediato y no sin un motivo justificado? —preguntó el embajador—. ¿Es ésa la respuesta que he de transmitir a mi señor?

Trajano meditó sobre el tono de decepción con el que se había expresado el embajador mientras Dión Coceyo traducía las palabras que él más o menos ya había comprendido. Las intervenciones de Dión Coceyo le daban tiempo para pensar. Trajano no quería en modo alguno que aquel embajador se fuera desilusionado de allí. La propuesta del emperador kushan era muy tentadora y tener a los partos atacados por dos frentes a un tiempo era interesante. Pero, al mismo tiempo, necesitaba una justificación ante un Senado que tendría miedo a una campaña como aquélla, una campaña que ya se había intentado en el pasado y que había fracasado estrepitosamente; todos los senadores recordarían perfectamente el desastre de Craso y la legión perdida y extenderían su miedo al pueblo. Quieto mismo había manifestado su temor hacía poco sobre el asunto refiriéndose a Craso. No, si quería atacar

80

Partia tendría que andarse con mucho tiento, pero también debía darle algo a aquel embajador: una esperanza.

—No atacaré Partia sin un motivo —repitió Trajano en voz alta—, pero encontraré el motivo.

La sonrisa retornó a la faz del embajador.

—Ésa es, en efecto, una respuesta que resultará del agrado de mi señor —dijo Shaka inclinándose ante el emperador.

—Entretanto, sugiero —continuó Trajano— que te tomes el tiempo que quieras en mi corte antes de retornar a tu patria, o si lo que deseas es partir de inmediato, propongo que en lugar de viajar directamente a Bagram, la capital de vuestro imperio, lo hagas visitando diferentes provincias bajo mi mando para que así, a tu regreso, tengas abundante información que transmitir a tu señor sobre el auténtico poder de Roma.

El filósofo tradujo y ahora fue Shaka quien aprovechó aquel tiempo para meditar su respuesta.

—Creo que el viaje es largo y debo partir cuanto antes. Mi señor espera respuesta lo antes posible, pero me parece muy afortunada la sugerencia del César de que visite diferentes provincias en mi camino de regreso.

Trajano asintió. Miró entonces a Dión Coceyo.

—Gracias por tu ayuda, amigo mío. Acompaña a nuestro invitado a la puerta y que Liviano lo escolte a su residencia. Tú también puedes retirarte y descansar.

El filósofo se inclinó ante Trajano y abandonó la sala junto al embajador.

El emperador descendió del trono y regresó al mapa. Quieto no necesitó que Trajano le dijera nada, recuperó la antorcha de la pared y la acercó de nuevo a la mesa. Los dos hombres contemplaban el mapa del mundo.

—¿Lo ves posible? —preguntó Trajano.

—Necesitaremos al menos dos campañas, como en la Dacia —respondió Quieto con determinación.

—Es mayor. Necesitaremos más de dos campañas, amigo mío. Yo había calculado... tres; puede que cuatro. —Lo miró directamente a los ojos—. Y necesitaremos algo más. Ésta es labor no para uno, sino para dos emperadores.

Tan concentrado como estaba Quieto en asimilar lo que el

César le acababa de decir, y tan absorto como estaba el propio Trajano en calcular el número de legiones que necesitaría para acometer aquella empresa, ambos hombres se olvidaron del nombre de aquella niña que había mencionado el embajador.

En realidad no consideraron que esa niña pudiera ser importante.

10

ARYAZATE

Cesifonte, capital invernal del Imperio parto
107/108 d. C.

Πάλαι μὲν οὖν ἡ Βαβυλὼν ἦν μητρόπολις τῆς Ἀσσυρίας, νῦν δὲ Σελεύκεια ἡ ἐπὶ τῷ Τίγρει λεγομένη. πλησίον δ'ἐστὶ κώμη Κτησιφῶν λεγομένη, μεγάλη· ταύτην δ'ἐποιοῦντο χειμάδιον οἱ τῶν Παρθυαίων βασιλεῖς φεδόμενοι τῶν Σελευκέων, ἵνα μὴ κατασταθμεύοιντο ὑπὸ τοῦ Σκυθικοῦ φύλου καὶ στρατιωτικοῦ· δυνάμει οὖν Παρθική πόλις ἀντὶ κώμης ἐστὶ καὶ τὸ μέγεθος, τοσοῦτόν γε πλῆθος δεχομένη καὶ τὴν κατασκευὴν ὑπ' ἐκείνων αὐτῶν κατεσκευασμένη καὶ τὰ ὤνια τὰς τέχνας προσφόρους ἐκείνοις πεπορισμένη. εἰώθασι γὰρ ἐνταῦθα τοῦ χειμῶνος διάγειν οἱ βασιλεῖς διὰ τὸ εὐάερον· θέρους δὲ ἐν Ἐκβατάνοις καὶ τῇ Ὑρκανίᾳ διὰ τῶν ἐπικράτειαν τῆς παλαιᾶς δόξης.

[En tiempos antiguos, Babilonia era la metrópolis de Asiria, pero ahora Seleucia es la metrópolis; es decir, Seleucia del Tigris, tal y como se la denomina. Allí cerca hay una ciudad llamada Cesifonte. En esta población ubicaron los reyes de Partia su capital de invierno, de forma que los habitantes de Seleucia no se veían obligados a convivir con las tropas escitas de los partos. Debido al poder parto, Cesifonte era una ciudad, más que una pequeña población. Era de tal tamaño que podía albergar a numerosos habitantes y en ella los propios partos habían erigido aún más edificios, con grandes almacenes para el comercio y otras construcciones para las artes que les resultaban placenteras, y es que a los reyes partos les encantaba pasar el invierno allí por la salubridad del aire, pero en verano regresaban a Ecbatana e Hircania por su mayor renombre.][9]

9. Estrabón, XVI 1,16.

Cruzaron el Tigris en una gran barca. Aryazate lo contemplaba todo extasiada: las grandes mansiones de la isla que dejaban atrás, en medio del río, por un lado, y por otro los grandes barcos comerciales que avanzaban hacia los puertos de Seleucia y Cesifonte. Quizá alguno fuera más tarde hasta la remota Carax y de allí a la India, quién sabía si más allá. Los barcos la tenían admirada porque eran tan grandes y viajaban tan lejos... a lugares remotos, cientos de ellos, a los que ella nunca iría. Su sueño era un gran viaje, pero del único gran viaje que se hablaba en relación a ella era uno que la aterrorizaba: ir hacia el este, al final del Imperio parto, cerca de la frontera con los kushan, para desposarse con el sangriento Vologases. Ella sería intercambiada por un pacto de paz entre su padre Osroes y el bandido Vologases, el usurpador, como lo llamaban —entre otras muchas cosas— en la corte de Cesifonte. Ella, que tantos viajes anhelaba, detestaba aquel único que se le ofrecía; pero aquella mañana sus ojos negros, oscuros y grandes, lo miraban todo muy abiertos, con la esperanza inquieta de la inexperiencia.

En realidad ninguna niña debería estar en cubierta, pues la *Bāmbišnān Bāmbišn*, la reina de reinas, era escrupulosa con las normas y no le gustaba que se transgrediera ninguna, pero la pequeña Aryazate gozaba del favor de la joven *Šhar Bāmbišn*, la actual reina consorte, la hermosa Rixnu. Y la *Šhar Bāmbišn* le había permitido subir a cubierta y sentarse a su lado mientras cruzaban el gran río Tigris.

—Será mejor que regreses abajo —le dijo Rixnu con aquella voz dulce con la que había enamorado al propio Osroes.

—Sí, *Šhar Bāmbišn* —respondió la niña de nueve años. Se despidió de la reina consorte inclinándose ante ella y luego corrió rauda hacia el interior del barco. No quería que por una indiscreción suya Rixnu fuera a tener un problema, esto es, otro más, con la seria Asiabatum, la reina de reinas.

La pequeña Aryazate se deslizó entre los eunucos. Alguno vio que la pequeña volvía de cubierta, pero el hombre tuvo el buen criterio de no inmiscuirse en un asunto de las *bānūg*, las jóvenes de la nobleza parta. Si la reina de reinas y la reina consorte tenían formas distintas de educar a las niñas, era mejor no meterse por medio: la furia de Asiabatum era bien conocida por todos los eunucos, mientras que la influencia de la hermosa Rixnu con el *Šāhān Šāh* Osroes era demasiado poderosa como para indisponerse con ella. Mejor que se arreglaran solas.

Aryazate, en su ingenuidad, interpretó como una distracción de los eunucos, aparentemente tan concentrados en las tareas de atraque de la embarcación, el hecho de que no parecieran tener ojos para verla. Así la jovencísima princesa pudo regresar al grupo de niñas del séquito parto sin que nadie la echara de menos en el interior de la nave.

Al poco tiempo se encontró desfilando por los grandes jardines de la bellísima Cesifonte, construida junto al Tigris, a la altura de la vieja Seleucia, como una ciudad independiente diseñada para ser una de las capitales partas: suntuosa, ricamente engalanada no sólo con plantas, sino también con fuentes y estatuas y palacios hermosos fruto de las grandes conquistas y victorias de los partos sobre todos los pueblos de su entorno. Aryazate caminaba encantada. Era la primera vez que pisaba la gran capital. Los *magi*, los sabios que alguna vez habían acudido al séquito de mujeres para enseñarles algo de la historia de Partia, les habían contado que el gran esplendor de Cesifonte, aunque la ciudad fuera más antigua, realmente se inició cuando los partos, bajo el poder del rey de reyes Orodes, consiguieron derrotar a los orgullosos romanos en la lejana batalla de Carrhae, en una guerra que supuso un intento baldío e inútil de la petulante Roma de tratar de hacerse con una Partia demasiado fuerte y demasiado poderosa para aquellos salvajes de Occidente. Un cuadrado. Aryazate recordaba que en aquella batalla alguien había formado un cuadrado y eso había sido un desastre, pero no se acordaba bien de quién ni por qué. Y camellos. Algo de camellos. Pero todo aquello le parecía demasiado distante, como si no tuviera nada que ver con ella. Como si nada de lo que la lejana Roma tramara en el remoto Occidente pudiera, en modo alguno, afectarla nunca. Estaban tan lejos...

Sí, era la primera vez que estaba en Cesifonte, entre los grandes palacios. Del mismo modo que era la primera vez que iba a asistir a un gran banquete en donde vería otra vez no sólo al rey de reyes Osroes, es decir, su padre, sino también a todos sus nobles y consejeros y sabios y, en especial, a los jóvenes príncipes. ¿Por qué no podía encontrar su padre un esposo para ella entre los apuestos príncipes? Eso evitaría que tuviera que desposarse con el malvado Vologases. Todo lo que había oído de aquel bestia que pretendía el trono de su padre era tan terrible que de sólo pensarlo le entraban escalofríos: violaba mujeres y mataba niños y despojaba a todos de todo. Eso sólo para empezar. Cerró los ojos un instante y sacudió la cabeza.

Llegaron al gran palacio y pasaron entre los muros de relieves con escenas de caza hasta entrar en una enorme sala donde habían dispuesto almohadones por el suelo para, al menos, trescientas o cuatrocientas personas. Aryazate vio a muchos consejeros tomando asiento aquí o allá, dirigidos por múltiples asistentes. La niña sabía que todo seguía un protocolo muy estricto, pero le era difícil de comprender cuál porque nadie se lo explicaba. De pronto, un *šabestān*, uno de los eunucos, se aproximó y se inclinó ante ellas al tiempo que les rogaba que se apartaran.

—Por favor, mis *bānūg*, por favor, vienen los príncipes.

Y así era.

Asiabatum miró con desdén a un consejero viejo que estaba en la puerta. Era una mueca que Aryazate conocía bien, pues la había visto en la faz de la reina de reinas muchas veces: era evidente que Asiabatum no estaba contenta con la forma en la que se había organizado la entrada del séquito de mujeres del rey de reyes. Se formó algo de tumulto y mucha confusión. Alguien tocó la espalda de Aryazate. Ella se dio la vuelta sobresaltada, pero cuando iba a gritar vio a Partamaspates sonriendo.

—Hola —dijo el joven de doce años—. ¿Cómo está mi hermanita?

Partamaspates era su hermano mayor. Hacía un par de años que los habían separado. Niños y niñas recibían una educación diferente, pero desde siempre se había sentido muy unida a Partamaspates y su joven hermano la correspondía en su afecto. Así, aprovechaban cualquier ocasión para verse y hablar. Ya no podían jugar, pero, curiosamente, se les permitía hablar entre ellos en público, a fin de cuentas eran príncipe y princesa del gran reino parto; además podían escribirse. Aryazate enviaba algunas cartas muy breves donde hablaba de cosas triviales para Partamaspates, llamado a ser el sucesor de Osroes en el trono y mucho más interesado por las grandes batallas y ejércitos, pero a quien su hermana pequeña despertaba un gran amor fraterno, una especie de instinto natural de protección hacia su misma sangre.

—Estoy bien —dijo ella—. Tú también. Estás más alto.

—Y tú —dijo él.

—¿Sigue el rey de reyes queriéndome casar con ese salvaje? —preguntó ella, pues era el asunto que más la preocupaba últimamente.

—No sé. Un día hablan de lanzar un ejército contra Vologases y otro quieren casarte con él —respondió él.

—¡Que envíen todos los ejércitos de Partia! —dijo ella en voz alta.

—¡Sssh! —exclamó Partamaspates, pero no pasó nada. Asiabatum estaba gritando mucho más fuerte al viejo consejero mientras los príncipes entraban por el pasillo que habían abierto las jóvenes princesas de Partia.

—Si tú comandaras ese ejército —añadió entonces Aryazate, ahora en voz baja— seguro que ganarías todas las batallas y yo no tendría que casarme con ese salvaje de Vologases.

Los jóvenes príncipes partos, desde niños, tenían mucha vanidad. Partamaspates se hinchó como una gran burbuja; hasta pareció crecer de lo recto que se puso ante las palabras de su hermana.

—Bueno —dijo al fin él—. No te preocupes. Creo que padre tiene algún plan para acabar con Vologases sin tener que desposarte con él. Hoy hablarán de ello en el banquete. Estoy seguro, porque han venido todos. Está el tío Partamasiris y el tío Mitrídates. Están organizando un gran ejército.

—Gracias por decírmelo —dijo ella. Él ya se tenía que marchar pues debía incorporarse al final de la larga comitiva de príncipes.

—Siempre te cuidaré —dijo él con una amplia sonrisa.

Y entró en la sala.

El viejo consejero se había arrodillado ante la poderosa Asiabatum disculpándose una y mil veces, pero ésta lo ignoró y entró en la gran sala del banquete. Rixnu, Aryazate y el resto de las princesas la siguieron. Las mujeres de la casa real se dispusieron en sus almohadones, algo alejadas del sitio especial reservado para Osroes, acomodado sobre otros cojines de mucha mayor altura. Aryazate lo observaba todo extasiada: se había percatado, tras asistir ya a varios de aquellos grandes cónclaves partos, de que cuanto más importante era alguien, de más almohadones disponía para sentarse, de la misma forma que la proximidad o lejanía con respecto a su padre Osroes indicaba también el grado de confianza que el rey de reyes tenía en el príncipe o noble en cuestión. Todo parecía algo desordenado y, sin embargo, todo estaba perfectamente calculado.

—Ven conmigo. —Aryazate vio ante ella la mano que le tendía Rixnu. Asiabatum parecía demasiado alterada aún debido al enfado que arrastraba por haberse visto humillada por tener que apartarse cuando llegaron las dos comitivas, la de princesas y la de príncipes al mismo tiempo, y no parecía tener tiempo para supervisar dónde se sentaba cada una de las niñas. Así, Aryazate aceptó encantada la mano de Rixnu y se sentó a su lado.

—Aquí oiremos bien de qué hablan —le explicó ella.

—Pero la música no nos dejará oír nada —dijo Aryazate señalando con el dedo a los músicos que se aprestaban, a su juicio, a preparar sus instrumentos para tocar de inmediato.

—No, pequeña —le explicó Rixnu—. Revisan sus instrumentos. No pueden cometer errores en un gran banquete como éste, pero realmente no tocarán hasta que se hable primero de los asuntos serios. Luego pueden beber tranquilos el rey de reyes y sus hermanos y consejeros. Beber y luego, más tarde... —Pero en ese momento Rixnu pensó en que Aryazate era aún demasiado inocente y no tenía ganas de quebrar aquella inconsciencia antes de hora. Ya se encargarían la vida y los príncipes partos de hacerlo.

Pero la pequeña, que siempre escuchaba muy atenta a Rixnu, la miró curiosa.

—Beben, ¿y más tarde qué?

Rixnu sonrió.

—Beben y luego... hacen otras cosas. Pero mira —Rixnu señaló al rey de reyes—, el gran Osroes va a hablar. Ahora todos callarán. Nosotras también, pequeña.

En efecto, el *Šāhān Šāh* tomó la palabra para dar la bienvenida a sus invitados.

—Os saludo, nobles de las familias arsácida, surena y karina y del resto de las familias nobles de Partia. Saludo a mis leales consejeros y *magi*, y saludo con particular afecto a mis hermanos Partamasiris y Mitrídates. Y también a todos los príncipes, en especial a mi hijo Partamaspates, llamado a sucederme en el futuro como *Šāhān Šāh* al frente de la gran Partia, a la que tanto amamos todos. Saludo, finalmente, a mi *Bāmbišnān Bāmbišn*, mi querida Asiabatum, y al resto de las princesas. —Se tomó un breve respiro tras el largo saludo protocolario antes de seguir hablando, ahora dirigiéndose a Mitrídates—. Nos hemos reunido aquí para que os explique la forma en que he decidido que Partia siga siendo tan grande como hasta ahora, afrontando de una vez por todas el mayor de los problemas que nos acecha en la actualidad y que pone en peligro nuestro imperio y nuestro poder. —Hizo una segunda pausa; siempre le costaba pronunciar en público el nombre de aquel miserable, su maldito sobrino nieto que seguía retándolo desde el extremo más oriental del imperio—. Sí, voy a explicaros hoy cómo acabar con Vologases. Hermano mío —continuó mirando a Mitrídates—, has combatido ferozmente a esa alimaña durante años y, si bien has conseguido mantenerla acorralada en las inmediaciones de Merv, no es menos cierto que no has podido aniquilarla ni aplastarla por completo. —Su hermano fue a hablar, pero Osroes levantó la mano—. No, no hace falta que me des explicaciones. Es evidente que Vologases ha conseguido reunir un número importante de traidores a su alrededor que lo protegen y lo fortalecen. No te he citado aquí para zaherirte, hermano mío, sino para agradecerte el trabajo duro de estos años y para anunciarte que pronto lanzaremos un gran ataque contra Vologases y contra todos y cada uno de los que lo apoyan. —Osroes paseó la mirada por los rostros de todos los nobles, como advirtiéndolos de lo que les esperaba en caso de que alguien pensara en cambiar de bando—. Pero para acabar con Vologases, antes hemos de contar con más recursos: hemos de reunir nuevas tropas de todos los reinos vasallos y, en particular, necesitamos refuerzos de uno de estos reinos más importantes: Armenia.

»Ahora bien, ¿qué ocurre? —En ese instante dejó de mirar a Mitrídates para hacer un nuevo barrido visual con la mirada por toda la gran sala, examinando con atención el rostro, una vez más, de cada uno de los nobles allí reunidos: necesitaba el consenso de todas las familias para poder ejecutar su plan, por eso los había reunido a todos—. Ocurre, amigos míos, que mi sobrino Exedares, rey de Armenia, nos niega repetidamente la asistencia en esta guerra contra Vologases. Arguye toda clase de excusas, pero pregunto yo: ¿cuántas excusas ha de soportar un *Šāhān Šāh* como yo? ¿Es razonable que siga humillándome ante Exedares por la necesidad que tenemos de los ricos recursos de Armenia y que conmigo nos humillemos todos, como si él y no yo fuera el rey de reyes, como si él y no nosotros fuera el que en realidad gobierna Partia y sus reinos vasallos? Yo os digo que mi paciencia ha llegado a su fin. Así que esto es lo que he decidido: Partamasiris, mi otro hermano leal, partirá mañana mismo hacia el norte al frente de mis mejores tropas para someter la insubordinación de Exedares, deponerlo como rey y situarse él en su lugar, como señor de Armenia bajo mi tutela, bajo nuestra tutela. Solucionado el problema de la rebeldía manifiesta de Exedares, Partamasiris enviará los refuerzos que necesitamos a Cesifonte desde una nueva Armenia bien controlada por nosotros. Y desde aquí, junto con mis tropas de élite, enviaremos a todos esos soldados de Armenia y a los nuestros unidos en un gran ejército, nuevo y fortalecido, hacia Oriente para que estas tropas ayuden a mi otro hermano leal, Mitrídates, a masacrar para siempre a Vologases.

Osroes calló y alargó el brazo para coger un vaso de vino de la bandeja que sostenía un esclavo situado cerca de él; el *Šāhān Šāh* bebió un trago, lentamente, para humedecerse la garganta y darse también tiempo para pensar y para que todos pensaran; dejó el vaso sobre la bandeja y volvió a examinar la faz de cada uno de los que lo rodeaban. Asentimientos. Todos se mostraban a favor. Al menos nadie se atrevía a disentir en público. Eso era lo que buscaba. Tenía la esperanza de que el plan pareciera bien a todo el mundo, pero entonces... Mitrídates fruncía el ceño. Algo no le parecía bien. E iba a hablar. Que lo hiciera. Era mejor saber lo que pensaban todos antes de poner en marcha una maquinaria bélica y política de aquella envergadura. Osroes asintió mirando a su hermano, invitándolo a hablar.

—¿Y *Hrōm*?[10] —preguntó Mitrídates sucintamente—. Armenia ha estado bajo su influencia mucho tiempo. ¿No verá el emperador romano, su César, un desafío por nuestra parte si deponemos a Exedares sin consultarlo? Ya tenemos un frente de guerra abierto contra Vologases en Oriente y este plan podría abrirnos un segundo frente de guerra contra el *imperator* de Occidente.

—*Hrōm*, o Roma, como llaman ellos mismos a su imperio, no hará nada, hermano mío —respondió Osroes. Aquella duda que planteaba su hermano era la que otros podían tener y no estaba de más disiparla en público ante todos los nobles—. Nuestro otro hermano, Partamasiris, también me planteó esta cuestión cuando le propuse el plan antes de citaros aquí a todos, pero os responderé lo mismo que le dije a él —y miró hacia Partamasiris, que asintió de forma ostensible para que todos vieran su confirmación con claridad—. El emperador romano Trajano está demasiado ocupado con sus guerras de Occidente.

—Pero, hermano y rey de reyes, hemos de considerar —intervino de nuevo Mitrídates— que el emperador Trajano ha conseguido una gran victoria, o eso dicen todos los mercaderes que vienen de Occidente, contra un pueblo belicoso del norte del Danubio, contra el rey Decébalo. ¿No estará acaso el emperador romano envalentonado y más proclive a emprender alguna acción contra nosotros?

10. Roma.

—No lo creo —se defendió Osroes—. El rebelde Exedares, de hecho, ya está en el trono de Armenia en gran medida por nuestra influencia; no consultamos entonces a Roma y Roma no hizo nada. Tú dices que el emperador romano puede estar envalentonado. Yo te digo que también puede estar cansado. ¿Acaso no lo estamos nosotros de combatir contra Vologases? Trajano luchó contra los dacios por necesidad, porque éstos atacaban sus provincias del norte. De la misma forma, nosotros hacemos lo que hacemos por necesidad: precisamos de una Armenia que coopere para poner fin a Vologases. No creo que Trajano quiera entrar en guerra con nosotros por un reino como Armenia, mucho más próximo a nosotros que a la lejana capital de los romanos. Además, ¿no estarás comparando la gran Partia con cualquiera de esos pueblos nómadas y salvajes del norte del Imperio romano? Y por encima de cualquier otra consideración, no hemos de olvidar que otros líderes romanos atacaron Partia en el pasado y el número de cadáveres de sus legionarios fue incontable. ¡Os juro por Ahura Mazda, y pongo a Zoroastro como testigo, que Roma no se moverá y si lo hace las legiones que crucen el Éufrates seguirán el mismo destino que las tropas de Craso! —Bajó la voz para hablar como quien comparte un gran secreto, una clave especial que conduce a la victoria total—. Este plan, amigos míos, es el camino: primero para subyugar a Armenia; luego, todos juntos acabaremos con Vologases. Después lo que queramos. Puede que Roma, en algún momento, intente hacer algo. No digo que no, pero para entonces seremos los más fuertes del mundo. Nadie podrá detenernos entonces. ¿Qué me decís?

Hubo un instante de silencio, pero, al momento, varios nobles empezaron a alabar al rey de reyes y a secundar en voz alta su plan, hasta que un gran clamor se apoderó de la sala.

—¡Viva nuestro *Šāhān Šāh*! ¡Por Osroes! ¡Por Ahura Mazda! ¡Por Zoroastro!

Osroes invitó a sus hermanos Partamasiris y Mitrídates a beber y, de esa forma, sellar aquel pacto. Mitrídates aceptó de aparente buen grado, aunque en su fuero interno pensaba que el plan tenía demasiados puntos en donde podía fallar; en particular la impredecible reacción de Roma. Sanatruces, su hijo, de eso estaba seguro Mitrídates, compartiría sus dudas, pero no estaba allí para apoyarlo, sino que se había quedado en Oriente al frente de las tropas que contenían las incursiones de Vologases. Mitrídates estaba convencido de que con Sanatruces en aquella reunión el plan de Osroes no habría sido aprobado con tanta facilidad, pero ya estaba hecho. No se podía detener.

En ese instante, la voz de Partamasiris entró en la cabeza de Mitrídates, pues el que parecía destinado a ser futuro rey de Armenia se dirigía ahora a Osroes.

—Esto quiere decir, hermano y *Šāhān Šāh* —dijo Partamasiris en voz baja, pero lo suficientemente audible para el entorno próximo al rey de reyes—, que la idea de casar a la pequeña Aryazate con Vologases queda completamente olvidada.

—Así es —confirmó Osroes y dio un par de sonoras palmadas. Los presentes callaron—. ¡Acércate, princesa Aryazate!

La pequeña se vio sorprendida por aquella petición inesperada de su padre.

—Ve —le dijo Rixnu al oído—. No tengas miedo. Sólo quieren verte. No te harán nada.

Aryazate se levantó, pasó por delante del resto de las princesas, por delante de Asiabatum y luego junto a los príncipes donde vio cómo Partamaspates le sonreía. Eso la animó y le dio fuerzas. La niña se detuvo frente al frente al rey de reyes del mundo.

—Aquí estoy, *Βασιλεύς βασιλέων* [*basileús basiléon*]. —Ella usaba la fórmula griega de respeto para dirigirse a su padre. Muchas de las consortes del séquito del gran rey eran de origen griego y hablaban casi más griego que parto entre las mujeres.

—Date la vuelta despacio y quítate el velo del todo —dijo Osroes.

La niña se descubrió el rostro por completo. Aunque apenas llevaba un fino velo, éste ocultaba algo su faz. Tiró de él hacia arriba, de forma que quedó colgando por encima de su cabello negro y largo. Se volvió despacio. Dio toda una vuelta entera.

—Es de facciones muy suaves —dijo Partamasiris con una amplia sonrisa.

—Ciertamente era una lástima ofrecer algo tan hermoso a un salvaje como Vologases —dijo Mitrídates en un intento por dar a entender que daba por concluidas sus dudas con respecto al plan de Osroes. No era que realmente sus dudas se hubieran disipado, pero estando en franca minoría ante el apoyo general del resto de los nobles, no tenía sentido manifestarse más en contra de la decisión real y despertar sospechas en el rey de reyes.

—Eso pienso yo —confirmó Osroes sonriendo más tranquilo, sin leer entre las líneas de la sonrisa de su hermano Mitrídates la preocupación que el otro mantenía sobre su estrategia.

—Quizá, hermano y gran rey de reyes —dijo Partamasiris abriendo una boca llena de dientes podridos—, Aryazate podría ser un premio a mis esfuerzos por someter a Exedares y deponerlo del trono de Armenia.

Osroes miró a la niña y luego a Partamasiris.

—Me lo pensaré —respondió el rey de reyes. Luego se volvió a la pequeña—. Retírate. Vuelve con el resto de princesas.

Aryazate se puso de nuevo el fino velo y corrió hacia Rixnu. La niña estaba terriblemente asustada. Los dientes podridos de Partamasiris parecían aún más horrendos que la furia salvaje, pero desconocida, de aquel al que todos tanto temían y que llamaban Vologases.

Rixnu la acogió con un suave abrazo. La reina consorte miraba hacia Osroes. El Βασιλεύς βασιλέων de Partia y todos los reinos que la circundaban estaba satisfecho con el apoyo de todos y estaba bebiendo mucho. Rixnu suspiró algo aliviada. Aquella noche el rey no estaría en condiciones de hacer nada. Ella dormiría tranquila. Notó que alguien temblaba a su lado y miró a la pequeña: Aryazate estaba llorando. Era la niña la que no dormiría tranquila. Rixnu la abrazó con más fuerza. La pequeña tenía motivos para su tristeza: si había alguien con quien ninguna mujer del séquito real quería estar casada era con Partamasiris.

11

LOS ESPÍAS

Palacio imperial, Roma
107 d. C.

Se encontraron en uno de los jardines del palacio imperial.

—Quizá no sea buena idea que se nos vea juntos —dijo Atiano en voz baja.

—Muy al contrario —respondió Adriano con seguridad—. Si no tememos que se nos vea hablando es porque no tenemos nada que ocultar, ¿no crees? A fin de cuentas sólo estoy hablando con mi viejo tutor. No veo nada malo en ello. Nadie puede verlo, ni siquiera mí tío, el emperador.

—No estoy seguro de ello, mi señor —insistió Atiano.

—¿Acaso no te ocupaste de hacer desaparecer a aquel hombre? ¿Cómo se llamaba, el que trabajaba con el senador Plinio?

—Atellus.

—Correcto. ¿Acaso no acabaste con él antes de que pudiera comunicar nada a Plinio?

—Así es.

—Entonces no veo de qué forma puede relacionarnos el emperador con..., cómo decirlo... viejos problemas del pasado —argumentó el sobrino del César.

—Aun así, mi señor, tengo la sensación de que el emperador sospecha.

—Puede ser —aceptó Adriano de mala gana—. Pero el motivo por el que te he hecho venir es porque ahora quien sospecha soy yo.

Atiano abrió bien los ojos. No sabía a qué podía referirse su antiguo pupilo.

—No entiendo.

—Por eso tú no estás llamado a ser César y yo sí. Atiano, hace mucho tiempo que yo ya no soy tu alumno, sino tu maestro.

—Cierto, mi señor —y se inclinó levemente sin dejar de andar. Sentía las miradas de muchos pretorianos sobre ellos.

—Trajano ha celebrado una audiencia privada con un embajador extranjero —añadió Adriano— y ésa no es en absoluto su costumbre. He averiguado que el hombre recibido en privado en la mismísima *Aula Regia* fue el embajador Shaka del Imperio kushan.

—¿El reino más allá de Partia?

—En efecto —confirmó Adriano—. Peculiar, ¿no es cierto?

—Es extraño, sí, mi señor —aceptó Atiano.

—La cuestión es: ¿por qué organiza mi tío una reunión en secreto con un embajador de un reino tan distante con el que ni siquiera tenemos frontera?

Atiano guardó silencio mientras ideaba una respuesta.

—Quizá por la ruta comercial con Oriente —se aventuró a sugerir al fin—. Las especias y la seda mueven mucho dinero. Quizá el emperador esté negociando algún acuerdo con los kushan...

—¿En secreto y ocultándolo al Senado? —lo interrumpió Adriano al tiempo que negaba con la cabeza—. No, no es la forma de actuar de mi tío. No, Atiano, si Trajano se esconde es porque trama algo más grande y yo quiero saber qué es. Necesito saber de qué se habló en esa audiencia y quién estuvo presente.

—Sí, por supuesto. Quizá podríamos hablar con el embajador nosotros mismos...

—No, no —volvió a interrumpirlo Adriano—. Ya lo he pensado, pero Trajano ha puesto al lobo de Liviano, al mismísimo jefe del pretorio, de guardaespaldas personal del embajador kushan. Además parece que Shaka no habla latín, sólo sánscrito y griego, y no tenemos a nadie de nuestra absoluta confianza que hable esas lenguas. Más aún, ¿por qué iba ese embajador a revelarnos nada? No, Atiano, lo que tengamos que averiguar lo hemos de hacer desde aquí, desde dentro.

—Lo que no comprendo... —empezó el tutor de nuevo, pero calló. No sabía si su antiguo pupilo estaba interesado en su opinión sobre todo aquello o si sólo lo quería como receptor de órdenes.

—Di, ¿qué piensas? ¿Qué es lo que no entiendes? —inquirió Adriano, no obstante, mirando fijamente a su interlocutor.

—No comprendo que, si el emperador quiere reunirse en secreto con un embajador extranjero, ¿por qué no lo hace en su cámara privada o en otro lugar de Roma, de noche y sin testigos?

—Sí, es una muy buena pregunta —concedió Adriano—, pero ya he dado con la respuesta: Trajano quiso impresionar al embajador con la imponente *Aula Regia*, que incluso medio vacía y sin casi decoración resulta gigantesca. Sí, el emperador quería impresionar a este embajador. Lo lleva haciendo desde que llegó. Por eso lo invitó a que asistiera a las carreras del Circo Máximo. El gran hipódromo repleto de gente es impactante para cualquiera, da igual de qué lejano reino vengas, sobre todo la primera vez que se visita. Por otro lado, verse en secreto con el embajador fuera del *Aula Regia*, en algún lugar oculto o en sus cámaras privadas, podría hacer sospechar al embajador Shaka que el emperador de Roma teme ser espiado o tener enemigos en su propia casa, y eso mandaría un mensaje de debilidad hacia los kushan que, estoy seguro, mi tío nunca se permitiría. Por eso se vio obligado a usar el *Aula Regia*, aun a riesgo de despertar, como es el caso, mis sospechas de que trama algo grande; ha preferido asumir un riesgo con nosotros que con un embajador extranjero. Eso muestra también cómo de fuerte se siente con respecto a sus posibles enemigos en Roma, todos muy debilitados tras las victorias consecutivas sobre la Dacia: Prisco está muerto y Pompeyo Colega y Salvio Liberal han sido enviados como gobernadores a puntos muy distantes del Imperio, Cirene y Chipre, si la memoria no me falla. Y puede ser que, como dices, si Trajano realmente sospecha de nosotros, en algún momento me envíe a mí o a ti o a ambos a alguna remota esquina del Imperio.

—Así es, mi señor; eso es posible —confirmó Atiano ante una rápida mirada del sobrino del César.

—Bien —prosiguió Adriano—. No hemos de perder contacto con Pompeyo Colega y Salvio Liberal. Hemos de mantener los viejos amigos, pero necesitamos nuevos aliados aquí mismo, en Roma. Sólo nos queda el viejo Cacio Frontón. Hemos de ampliar nuestros... —Adriano meditó un momento en busca de la palabra adecuada—... nuestros apoyos en el Senado y nuestros confidentes aquí mismo, en el palacio imperial.

—¿Ha pensado mi señor en alguien?

—Serviano, mi cuñado de Barcino, era una posibilidad, pero ya sabes que la relación entre nosotros es más bien... difícil. He de pensar sobre esto, pero Atiano: en la guardia pretoriana hay más de cinco mil hombres. Sé que primero el viejo Suburano y ahora Liviano se han ocupado de que sean leales a Trajano, pero me parece imposible que hayan podido juntar a cinco mil hombres incorruptibles. Tienes que encontrar a alguien, a varios si es posible, que quieran mirar, digamos, hacia el futuro. Trajano no será siempre emperador.

—Comprendo, mi señor. ¿Qué puedo prometerles como recompensa por su colaboración?

Adriano pensó un rato mientras seguían paseando lentamente por el gran atrio ajardinado del centro del palacio imperial.

—No prometas nada en particular, pero puedes dar a entender que yo nunca olvidaré quién estuvo conmigo en el pasado ni quién en mi contra. Puedes decir que sabré ser generoso. Y juro por los dioses que lo seré. Este camino va a ser más largo de lo que pensábamos, Atiano. Mi tío es tremendamente fuerte políticamente tras la victoria sobre la Dacia, como te he dicho y, a lo que se ve, también físicamente. Necesitamos tiempo, pero también aliados.

—Tendré que ir con sumo cuidado o alguien podría traicionarnos después de haberse negado a colaborar —contraargumentó Atiano.

—Sí, has de ir con tiento —ratificó Adriano—, pero confío en tu natural intuición para detectar las manzanas maduras con tu olfato. ¿Podrás hacerlo?

—Siempre, mi señor.

98

corrupisse eum Traiani libertos, curasse delicatos eosdemque saepe inisse
per ea tempora quibus in aula familiarior fuit, opinio multa firmavit.

[Muchos afirmaban que Adriano estaba sobornando a los libertos de Trajano y cortejando y corrompiendo a sus favoritos durante todo el tiempo que estuvo en la corte imperial]

Historia Augusta, «Vida de Adriano», 4

12

MONTES NIVIUM[11]

Cumidava, nordeste de la Dacia
107 d. C.

Marcio vio aquellas cumbres nevadas y comprendió que el nombre de *Montes Nivium* que le habían dado los romanos era adecuado. Hacía frío, pero se sentía en casa. Llevaba tiempo en la Dacia, reuniendo información sobre el lugar donde poder encontrar a los dacios y los sármatas que no se habían rendido a Roma. No había sido fácil: atravesó el Danubio por el gigantesco puente que el emperador había ordenado construir en Drobeta y de ahí fue hasta Sarmizegetusa Ulpia Traiana, donde esperaba poder presentar su salvoconducto imperial al gobernador de la provincia, pero no tuvo fortuna.

—No está aquí —le dijeron los oficiales romanos, algo petulantes, que lo recibieron en el foro de la nueva capital de la provincia—. Tendrás que buscarlo en el este. Su última carta es de Cumidava.

Los tribunos con los que habló no le proporcionaron más información. Marcio averiguó que el gobernador y *legatus* romano Tercio Juliano, al mando de las legiones allí apostadas, estaba preocupado por las fronteras en diversos puntos de la nueva provincia y andaba inspeccionando las antiguas fortalezas dacias con el fin de reconstruir algunas como bases para las tropas romanas.

Marcio siguió hacia el norte hasta llegar a Apulum, el último bastión romano antes de adentrarse en territorio descono-

---

11. La cordillera de los Cárpatos.

cido, pero allí, pese a su salvoconducto, le denegaron el permiso para cruzar los puestos de guardia de la frontera.

—Has de hablar con el *legatus* imperial —le dijo otro tribuno.

Marcio pensó en atravesar la línea de vigilancia fronteriza por la noche, pero varios comerciantes le informaron de que los sármatas libres, aquellos que no se habían sometido al gobierno de Roma, se habían desplazado a la zona de Cumidava. Por eso estaba allí el *legatus* Tercio Juliano. Quizá, después de todo, lo mejor sería ir.

Eso hizo. Y allí estaba ahora, admirando aquellas cumbres nevadas de los imponentes *Montes Nivium.*

A los pies de la antigua fortaleza de Cumidava había centenares de tiendas de legionarios. Una vez más lo interrogaron en el puesto de guardia, pero, como siempre, ante el salvoconducto del emperador los centuriones buscaron con rapidez a un tribuno y éste, al fin, le dijo que lo llevaría ante el *legatus* y gobernador.

Ascendieron por un camino tortuoso que serpeaba alrededor de la ladera del pétreo cerro sobre el que los dacios habían construido en el pasado una poderosa fortaleza. Había que estar en forma para no quedarse sin aliento en la subida. Cruzaron una, dos y hasta tres puertas protegidas por torres recién reparadas por las legiones. Recorrieron un amplio espacio entre la primera y la segunda puerta y bastante menos entre la segunda y la tercera. Había legionarios por todas partes, inmersos en la tarea de llevar piedras para reconstruir aquellas secciones de las murallas que habían sido destrozadas en la guerra contra Decébalo.

Marcio seguía a aquel tribuno de cerca, rodeado por media docena de legionarios armados que lo miraban con recelo. Seguían ascendiendo. Por fin llegaron al punto más alto de la fortificación, donde un militar de mayor edad, robusto pese a los años, con mirada entre fiera y cansada, oteaba el paisaje que podía vislumbrarse desde aquella posición privilegiada.

—Los dacios sabían dónde construir fortificaciones —dijo aquel hombre sin tan siquiera volverse para mirar a Marcio.

El antiguo gladiador miró a su alrededor: se veían las imponentes montañas nevadas de los *Montes Nivium*, los bosques frondosos y el valle que se adentraba en ellos, perfectamente visible desde aquel enclave privilegiado. Nadie podría pasar de un lugar a otro en aquella zona sin ser descubierto desde allí. Muy costoso debió de ser rendir aquella fortaleza.

—Si no es porque se suicidó Decébalo —continuó el militar sin mirar aún a Marcio, dándose así él mismo respuestas a sus pensamientos—, los defensores no se habrían rendido y aún estaríamos asediando este lugar. Pero bueno... —El hombre se volvió y encaró al antiguo gladiador—. Me dicen que traes un salvoconducto imperial. Yo soy Tercio Juliano, *legatus* de la Dacia. A ver ese documento.

Y extendió el brazo con la palma de la mano derecha hacia arriba.

Marcio le entregó el papiro.

Tercio Juliano lo desenrolló despacio y lo leyó de principio a fin, sin prisa. Luego volvió a enrollarlo y se lo devolvió a Marcio. El *legatus* suspiró.

—No me gustan los salvoconductos imperiales —dijo Tercio Juliano—. Nunca me han gustado, pero eso no cambia el hecho de que he de aceptarlos y colaborar con quienes los exhiben. Cómo alguien como tú puede tener uno de ellos me resulta extraño, pero mientras no me pidas nada que me haga preocuparme por las fronteras no solicitaré confirmación alguna a Roma. ¿Qué es lo que quieres?

—Cruzar al norte.

—¿Por qué?

—Busco a una mujer y a una niña sármatas —respondió Marcio sin rodeos—. Me han dicho que por esta zona hay sármatas que no se han rendido a Roma. He de encontrar a esas mujeres. Es importante para mí.

—Y tienes un salvoconducto imperial, el permiso del emperador para cruzar la frontera del Imperio.

—Así es —confirmó Marcio.

Tercio Juliano inspiró profundamente y luego exhaló el aire de sus pulmones con mucha lentitud. Al fin asintió. Se volvió y señaló un punto al norte.

—Allí hemos avistado sármatas a caballo —explicó el *lega-*

tus—. Mis hombres te acompañarán hasta ese lugar. ¿Quieres disponer de escolta?

—No. Me será más fácil contactar con los sármatas si voy solo.

—O te matarán antes —replicó Tercio Juliano—, pero eso no es asunto mío. Si no me pides protección no seré yo quien insista. No me gusta arriesgar a buenos legionarios de forma inútil. —Miró al tribuno por encima del hombro de Marcio—. Ya habéis oído: escoltadlo hasta la frontera y dejadlo marchar.

Marcio, a modo de agradecimiento, asintió un par de veces. Acto seguido dio la vuelta y emprendió el descenso de la fortaleza de Cumidava junto con el tribuno y los legionarios que lo habían acompañado en el ascenso.

Tercio Juliano se pasó la lengua por los labios resecos. De nuevo salvoconductos imperiales. Así había empezado la guerra contra los dacios. ¿Anunciaba este hombre extraño con otro salvoconducto del emperador el inicio de una nueva confrontación? La Dacia, no obstante, parecía tranquila. ¿Qué estaría planeando el emperador y qué misión tendría destinada en las futuras acciones del César aquel hombre que buscaba a dos mujeres sármatas? Quizá todo lo que se estaba preparando terminara pasando muy lejos de allí. O no. Difícil saberlo. Tercio Juliano escupió en el suelo y se encogió de hombros.

—Vamos a comer algo —dijo el *legatus* a los oficiales que estaban junto a él. Pasara lo que pasase, prefería que le pillara con el estómago lleno.

13

EL CUADRADO MORTAL

**En las proximidades de Petra, Arabia
107 d. C.**

Habían avanzado demasiado aquel día, más de lo prudente, y no habían encontrado ningún oasis nuevo. El *legatus* Palma meditaba mientras examinaba desde lo alto de un promontorio el territorio desértico que los rodeaba: varios grupos de mercaderes con los que se habían cruzado en su avance hacia Petra habían confirmado que el rey Rabbel II Sóter había fallecido y que su joven hijo Obodas le había sucedido en el poder. A partir de ahí ya no sabían nada. Sólo habían encontrado más arena y más desierto y el sonido del viento por las noches.

—La muerte de su rey nos favorece —dijo el tribuno Severo.

Palma, no obstante, negó con la cabeza.

—No estoy tan seguro de ello —argumentó el *legatus*—. Quizá la falta de oposición de los nabateos hasta el momento se debía precisamente a la enfermedad de su rey, pero ahora con un nuevo gobernante joven cualquier reacción es posible.

—¿Incluso un ataque? —indagó Severo con tono de incredulidad.

—Obodas. Ese nombre es clave —apuntó Palma.

—¿Por qué, *legatus*? Un nombre es sólo un nombre —replicó Severo con seguridad.

Palma comprendió entonces que Severo no sabía nada de la historia del reino nabateo al que intentaban someter.

—No, un nombre a veces es mucho más —explicó el *legatus* de Trajano—. Hace años, doscientos años, quizá, no lo recuerdo con exactitud, pero hace tiempo, los nabateos tuvieron un rey de nombre Obodas. Este rey heredó el trono del reino nabateo en medio de una guerra contra la dinastía smoena, que controlaba Judea en aquel período. Luchó contra su enemigo y los derrotó en repetidas ocasiones hasta recuperar parte de los territorios del norte, hasta las montañas del Palus Alphaltites.[12] Todo parecía marchar bien para Obodas, pero a los pocos años el rey seleúcida Antíoco XII lanzó un gran ataque para anexionarse el reino nabateo. Obodas no se rindió, sino que salió a combatir con todo su ejército y se enfrentó a los seleúcidas, más numerosos y más fuertes, según creían todos.

—¿Y qué ocurrió? —preguntó Severo; su curiosidad militar se había despertado ante aquel relato bélico del pasado de la región.

—Tanto el rey Antíoco XII de los seleúcidas como el propio rey Obodas perecieron en la batalla, pero los nabateos consiguieron la victoria y mantuvieron su reino. Desde entonces en esta tierra el nombre de Obodas es adorado casi como un dios. El hecho de que el hijo del recién fallecido rey Rabbel Sóter haya adoptado el nombre de aquel rey guerrero y mítico de los nabateos no es algo que augure nada bueno. ¿Comprendes ahora, Severo, por qué un nombre, a veces, no es sólo un nombre?

El tribuno asintió.

Mientras hablaban habían dejado de observar el atardecer y no se percataron de que algunas nubes de polvo se levantaban en lontananza. Y no había viento ni tormenta.

—Acampemos aquí esta noche —dijo Palma, al fin, con los brazos en jarra, mirando al suelo—. Que se monten las guardias habituales y que salgan patrullas de caballería. No quiero que nos sorprendan, y menos en medio de la noche.

Faltaba una hora para el alba cuando el tribuno Severo irrumpió en la tienda de Cornelio Palma.

12. El mar Muerto.

—¡Han atacado a las patrullas!

No hubo ni saludos ni preguntas absurdas. Palma y Severo se sabían militares en aquel momento y en territorio hostil a Roma, así que no era momento de formalismos inútiles.

—¿A cuántas patrullas han atacado? —preguntó el *legatus* mientras, asistido por un *calon*, se vestía rápidamente con el uniforme y se ajustaba la *spatha*.

—A las cuatro. Ordené que salieran grupos de diez jinetes en cada una de las cuatro direcciones.

—¿Y han atacado a las cuatro patrullas?

—En efecto, *legatus*.

—¿Cuántos supervivientes tenemos?

—Unos cuatro o cinco en cada caso —respondió Severo.

—Es como si quisieran asegurarse de que nos llegaba el mensaje —comentó Palma en voz baja.

—¿Qué mensaje, *legatus*?

—Que estamos rodeados.

Los dos hombres salieron de la tienda. Severo había dado orden a las tropas para que se armaran y estuvieran dispuestas para maniobrar según las instrucciones que diera el *legatus*.

—¿Qué hacemos?

Palma respiraba aceleradamente. Tenía que tomar las decisiones correctas o toda la misión de conquistar Arabia podía terminar en un absoluto desastre. Estaban rodeados y lo lógico era formar un cuadrado defensivo, pero el *legatus* sabía del pánico que todos sus oficiales y hasta muchos legionarios sentirían si daba esa orden. El cuadrado sólo traía a la memoria de las legiones de Roma el desastre de Craso en el desierto de Carrhae y la leyenda de la legión perdida.

—Lo sensato será que dispongamos las legiones de forma defensiva hasta el amanecer, con diferentes cohortes encarando cada uno de los cuatro puntos cardinales —explicó Palma.

—Eso es un cuadrado, *legatus* —respondió Severo con un tinte de temor en la voz.

—¡Ya lo sé, tribuno! Pero ¿qué otra cosa podemos hacer?

Se hizo un silencio. Había más tribunos alrededor del *legatus* junto a una hoguera que ardía en el exterior, frente a la tienda del *praetorium*. Ninguno tuvo las agallas de plantear al *legatus* que la otra opción sensata era retirarse, todos unidos en una sola dirección, y abrirse paso como fuera, seguramente hacia Occidente, con la esperanza de que los nabateos, conseguido el objetivo de forzar el repliegue romano, no atacaran de forma indiscriminada iniciando una batalla de desenlace incierto. Pero el cuadrado que quería Palma, por el contrario, implicaba quedarse allí a la espera de acontecimientos y resultaba inquietante para todos.

Las órdenes del *legatus*, no obstante, se cumplieron con la absoluta disciplina de las legiones de Roma. Lo que Palma no pudo evitar fue el creciente temor de sus legionarios, quienes nada más salir el sol sudaban profusamente y no precisamente por el calor, pues el fresco de la recién terminada noche aún estaba presente en el desierto.

—Lo que no entiendo es cómo han podido rodearnos en tan poco tiempo —comentó Severo mientras acompañaba al *legatus* a lo alto del promontorio para otear de nuevo el entorno en el que se encontraban.

—Ahí tienes la respuesta —dijo Palma señalando hacia el sur, el norte y el oeste. En esos tres frentes se veían las siluetas inconfundibles de la legendaria caballería de camellos de los nabateos. Y al este, en dirección a Petra, la infantería enemiga estaba ya en formación, esperando la orden de su rey.

—Camellos y un cuadrado —pronunció Severo como el augur que vaticina la repetición de un fracaso. También hubo camellos rodeando el cuadrado del ejército de Craso y eso fue el principio del desastre. Todo volvía a pasar. Severo también empezó a sudar, pues en el caso de Craso, al menos, los romanos tenían siete legiones, mientras que ellos sólo disponían de dos.

—¡Envían emisarios! —exclamó otro de los oficiales romanos señalando hacia la infantería enemiga: un grupo de jinetes nabateos a caballo se adelantaban por la inmensa llanura aproximándose hacia la vanguardia romana oriental.

—Bajemos de aquí y escuchemos qué es lo que quieren —ordenó Palma; luego se vovió hacia Severo y le habló en voz baja—: pero en ningún caso nos rendiremos. Antes la muerte.

Severo se llevó el puño al pecho.

No hubo más palabras.

En poco tiempo el *legatus*, acompañado por Severo y un pequeño grupo de jinetes de las *turmae* romanas, avanzaba por la llanura desértica para entrevistarse con los emisarios del ejército nabateo.

En cuanto se encontraron, Palma vio cómo uno de los jinetes enemigos desmontaba y avanzaba en solitario unos pasos. Lo imitó y acudió al encuentro de aquel hombre. El nabateo saludó en griego.

—Mi nombre es Aretas y soy el jefe de la guardia de Petra. Me envía Obodas, rey y señor de los nabateos.

Palma miró a su alrededor: el ejército enemigo estaba desafiante frente a él y a ambos lados, y sabía que en la retaguardia también se encontraba la caballería de camellos preparada para un ataque mortal. Deberían haberse retirado. Eso era lo que debería haber ordenado en cuanto supo lo de las patrullas atacadas, pero ahora ya era tarde para eso.

—Mi nombre es Cornelio Palma y soy *legatus* de Marco Ulpio Trajano, emperador de Roma, señor de todos los territorios desde Hispania hasta Siria, desde la Dacia al norte del Danubio hasta África y Egipto. —Aquello no pareció impresionar lo más mínimo al enviado nabateo, de modo que Palma fue al asunto de la reunión—. ¿Qué quiere vuestro rey?

Arates sonrió de forma enigmática y se permitió mirar también a su alrededor, pero en lugar de con preocupación, como acababa de hacer el *legatus* romano, lo hizo con orgullo y satisfacción mientras paseaba sus ojos sobre cada uno de los inmensos escuadrones de camellos de Petra emplazados en los flancos y la retaguardia romana o sobre el brillo de las armas nabateas de la infantería. Al fin, detuvo la mirada sobre el enviado romano.

—El rey Obodas piensa que la mejor solución, romano, es la rendición.

Cornelio Palma tragó saliva.

Un cuadrado y un ejército que los rodeaba en medio del desierto.

La historia se repetía.

HISTORIA DE LA LEGIÓN PERDIDA

Tiempos de Julio César, Pompeyo y Craso,
mediados del siglo I a. C.

LIBRO II

14

EL PASADO DE CRASO

En ruta hacia el interior de Mesopotamia
53 a. C.

—¿Por qué no hemos aceptado la ayuda del rey de Armenia? —preguntó Casio una vez se quedó a solas con Craso en el *praetorium* de campaña. El *quaestor* estaba iracundo y aunque estuviera ante uno de los cónsules de Roma, apenas podía reprimir su rabia: Craso había dicho que no al rey de Armenia, que le ofrecía caballería, infantería y apoyo logístico. No, Casio no podía entender que un líder romano despreciara semejante ayuda. Habían cruzado el Éufrates con siete legiones, pero estaban solos. ¿Se podía conquistar Partia sin la colaboración de Armenia, sin la colaboración de nadie? El *quaestor* volvió a manifestar su disconformidad al cónsul Craso—. El rey de Armenia venía con seis mil jinetes y ha prometido diez mil jinetes más y treinta mil soldados. Con esas tropas podríamos doblegar a los partos con seguridad. Sin riesgos.

Craso se servía una copa de vino.

—La gloria requiere riesgos, Casio —respondió el cónsul.

—¿Es por eso por lo que estamos aquí? ¿Para conseguir gloria personal? —contrapuso Casio—. Yo creía que estábamos aquí para resolver el problema de la frontera con los belicosos partos.

Craso dejó la copa de golpe sobre la pequeña mesita.

—¡Gloria para la República de Roma! ¡Eso es lo que quiero decir! —exclamó Craso con severidad y rabia; Casio lo sacaba de sus casillas—. ¿No te das cuenta de que si aceptamos la ayuda del rey de Armenia, toda la presencia de Roma en Oriente queda supeditada a su apoyo? Eso sería solucionar un problema creándonos otro. ¿Cuánto tiempo crees que ese rey armenio buscará nuestra amistad? En cuanto terminemos con los partos se rebelará contra nosotros. No, Casio, si Artavasdes tiene problemas con Partia, que se los resuelva él. No necesitamos sus jinetes. Mi hijo va a llegar con un importante regimiento de caballería, hombres valientes que han luchado en la Galia.

Craso evitó mencionar el nombre de Julio César, porque si bien su hijo había combatido con éxito en la Galia, eso era cierto, siempre lo había hecho bajo el mando de César. Aunque nadie ponía en duda el valor del hijo de Craso, ni siquiera el propio Julio César, que hablaba siempre bien de aquel joven en el foro y en el Senado.

Casio decidió no discutir más y salió del *praetorium*. Necesitaba algo de aire fresco. Craso era un hombre capaz, como Pompeyo o el propio Julio César, pero en su opinión tanto César, como Pompeyo o el propio Craso estaban cegados por una ambición sin medida. Casio se preguntaba adónde iban a conducir aquellos hombres a la República de Roma cuando estaban siempre movidos por el afán de obtener poder sin límites. ¿No se tendría que hacer algo para impedirles que cada vez fueran más y más poderosos y que cada vez tomaran las decisiones que afectaban a Roma sin tener ya en cuenta a nadie, como Craso acababa de hacer ahora desechando la ayuda del rey de Armenia sin consultar ni a tribunos ni a otros oficiales? Craso había argumentado que no quería depender de Artavasdes, pero Casio tenía sus dudas: ¿no sería que Craso quería toda la gloria de una posible victoria contra los partos para él solo?

Casio meditaba mientras miraba las tiendas de las legiones: Craso ya había sufrido tener que compartir la gloria de una victoria con otro cónsul y aquello no le debió de gustar nada. Fue durante la guerra servil contra Espartaco, aquel gladiador que se había levantado en armas contra Roma y creado un ejército de esclavos. El Senado concedió el mando de la guerra contra Espartaco a Craso y éste consiguió arrinconarlo al sur de Italia, pero no fue hasta que llegó Pompeyo con tropas adicionales que se logró la derrota absoluta del gladiador rebelde. Eso hizo que Craso no pudiera pedir no ya un triunfo, sino ni siquiera una *ovatio*, por aquella victoria. Pompeyo le privó de aquella gloria y Casio estaba convencido de que ahora Craso quería asegurarse de que nadie ensombreciera su dominio absoluto en aquella nueva campaña: el cónsul no quería que ningún senador pudiera argumentar en el Senado que la victoria contra Partia se debía más a los armenios que a las legiones del propio Craso.

Casio permanecía en pie frente al *praetorium*. Craso, sin embargo, no salía. Mejor. No tenía ganas de verlo en un tiempo. ¿Sería cierto todo lo que se contaba de él, aquello de que era un avaricioso sin control? Casio fruncía el ceño mientras consideraba aquel turbio asunto: se había acusado a Craso en el pasado reciente de acosar a una vestal para conseguir que ésta le vendiera unas tierras; incluso se llegó a hablar de una acusación de *crimen incesti* contra el cónsul, pero la mejor defensa a la que recurrieron los abogados de Craso fue su propia avaricia para certificar que nunca hubo interés carnal en la vestal, sino sólo en su dinero. El asunto era oscuro, confuso. Sin embargo, de lo que nadie dudaba era de que la riqueza inicial de Craso se forjó en los tiempos de Sila, cuando éste asesinaba a sus enemigos y les arrebataba todo en sus famosas *conscriptiones*. Luego el dictador repartía lo robado entre los que estaban con él y allí, dispuesto a lo que hiciera falta, estaba Craso. Pero nadie quería remover aquello; ¿quién estaba libre de culpa, y de sangre, en la época de los enfrentamientos entre Sila y Mario? Sea como fuere, las circunstancias habían encumbrado a Craso, pero al parecer no lo suficiente para él mismo. Quería más. Julio César tenía la Galia, Pompeyo Hispania y el mar y Craso quería Oriente. ¿Un nuevo Alejandro Magno? Eso era, con toda seguridad, lo que anhelaba el cónsul.

Casio vio al oficial Druso, que se le acercaba.

—Los hombres se preguntan, *quaestor*, si hemos aceptado la ayuda del rey de Armenia —dijo el centurión.

Casio inspiró por la nariz, aunque sorbiendo mocos. Estaba resfriado desde hacía días.

—No, Druso. Estamos solos en esto.

El centurión no dijo nada.

No había nada que pudiera decir que pudiera cambiar las cosas y cuando no hay nada que decir, un militar calla.

Otra cosa eran los pensamientos.

15

LAS ÓRDENES DEL REY DE PARTIA

Hatra, Mesopotamia
53 a. C.

Orodes había citado a Surena, su mejor *spāhbod*, su más valiente general, en su tienda de residencia en la ciudad fortificada de Hatra. Los imponentes muros que la rodeaban la hacían inexpugnable contra cualquier ataque del exterior y el oasis permanente en el centro de la fortificación la hacía invencible ante un asedio que buscara rendir aquella imponente plaza por sed. La única forma sería matar de hambre a la población, pero los ciudadanos de Hatra se aseguraban de tener siempre los almacenes repletos de grano, por lo que pudiera ocurrir.

Las puertas de la ciudad se abrieron para Surena y éste accedió al interior de sus murallas, transitó por las principales calles y llegó al palacio donde se alojaba el *Šāhān Šāh*, el rey de reyes, el *basileús basiléon* de los partos, el gran Orodes.

—¿Has venido con todos los hombres que te pedí? —preguntó el rey.

—Arqueros, soldados, *catafractos* y jinetes con camellos —respondió Surena con satisfacción—. Más de diez mil hombres.

El *Šāhān Šāh* asintió.

—Es un esfuerzo notable el que has hecho, Surena, y me siento complacido. No obstante, puede no ser suficiente para la tarea que quiero encomendarte, por eso he de saber si crees que estás a la altura de acometer la ejecución de mi plan para defender nuestro poder.

—Surena escucha y obedece al *Šāhān Šāh*. Su plan será el mío. —Y se inclinó ante el rey.

El *basileús basiléon* de los partos sonrió. Surena siempre hacía muestras públicas de sumisión y disciplina ante él, pero en el fondo Orodes intuía una ambición sin límite oculta en el pecho de aquel bravo *spāhbod*. Por eso había diseñado una estrategia con la que pensaba eliminarlo de Partia para siempre: le encomendaría un imposible y su general, o bien se negaría a hacerlo, con lo que podría relevarlo de su puesto de mando y relegarlo a un segundo plano de la nobleza parta, o bien moriría en el intento de conseguir aquel imposible. Parecía que esto último era lo que iba a acontecer. Mejor aún. Los romanos le iban a ayudar en el trabajo sucio.

—Verás, Surena, como sabrás tenemos no uno, sino dos problemas a la vez: Armenia se ha rebelado y, al mismo tiempo, nos atacan los romanos. No pienso ceder ni ante la rebelión de Artavasdes y mucho menos pienso regalar una sola ciudad a los malditos romanos. Ese orgulloso cónsul de *Hrōm* ha de regresar a Roma, ha de retirarse de nuestras tierras derrotado y humillado, de forma que los romanos nunca más se atrevan a volver a cruzar el Éufrates. Y si conseguimos matar al cónsul Craso, aún mejor; eso sería definitivo: ningún otro romano osará invadirnos. Lógicamente no puedo atender personalmente estos dos problemas al mismo tiempo, Armenia y Roma: he de dividir mi ejército, pero necesito un *spāhbod* que comande las tropas en uno de los dos frentes mientras yo me ocupo del otro. Yo acudiré con el grueso de las tropas a Armenia y resolveré la rebelión de ese miserable de Artavasdes. Entretanto, tú, con los hombres que has reunido, saldrás al encuentro de ese cónsul romano y lo detendrás antes de que llegue al Tigris. No es necesario que te enfrentes a él. Me basta con que lo entretengas hasta que yo regrese victorioso de Armenia y, con nuestros ejércitos reunidos, nos lanzaremos sobre los romanos y los expulsaremos hasta Siria o hasta el mismísimo mar. Pero en este plan que he diseñado, tú dispondrás de un número de hombres muy inferior al que poseen los romanos, que han cruzado el Éufrates con más de setenta mil legionarios. ¿Qué piensas de todo esto? ¿Te ves capaz de lo que te pido?

Surena meditó un momento. Sabía que se le estaba tendiendo una trampa, pero también era consciente de que no tenía mucho margen. En medio de aquella reunión, de aquel consejo de sabios, *magi*, grandes sacerdotes de Zoroastro y todos los nobles no podía titubear o perdería la influencia y el respeto que le tenían unos y otros. Además, Surena sentía, en particular, la mirada atenta de Kari, el líder de la otra gran familia arsácida de Partia, siempre dispuesto a postularse como posible sustituto al mando de la caballería.

—Saldré al encuentro de ese cónsul romano y lo detendré hasta que el *Šāhān Šāh* pueda regresar desde Armenia y solucionar esta invasión romana personalmente.

Orodes sonrió.

—Entonces está todo acordado —dijo el rey de reyes—. Es hora de que nos relajemos un poco. Que empiece la música.

Fraates, un hijo de Orodes que competía con su hermano Pacoro para ocupar el trono en el futuro, se dirigió a su padre en voz baja mientras los músicos empezaban a tocar, al tiempo que una docena de bailarinas entraba en medio del cónclave para deleite de los allí congregados.

—¿No teme el *Šāhān Šāh* que Surena pueda derrotar a los romanos y que eso lo anime a desear más... poder?

—Es posible, pero lo tengo todo pensado, hijo —respondió Orodes con una amplia sonrisa en los labios mientras bebía vino y perseguía con la mirada los movimientos insinuantes de la bailarina que le parecía más hermosa.

Fraates no se quedó satisfecho con aquellas palabras de su padre, pero, por el momento, no podía hacer nada más que esperar y ver cómo se desarrollaban los acontecimientos. Quizá aquella guerra deparara sorpresas que le acortaran la espera para heredar el trono de su padre. A Fraates esperar le resultaba tan irritante...

Hatra, fuera de las murallas

Horas más tarde, en el exterior de Hatra, Surena se reunía con los miembros de su familia, muchos de ellos comandantes de su ejército, en una de las tiendas de campaña levantadas junto a las murallas de Hatra. Surena había aludido al cansancio por el largo viaje para poder retirarse pronto de la fiesta y Orodes le había concedido permiso para regresar con sus hombres.

—Es un encargo imposible —dijo Sillaces, uno de los oficiales de Surena—. Los romanos avanzarán próximos al río para mantener su abastecimiento y así no tendremos ninguna posibilidad.

Surena negó con la cabeza.

—No. Los romanos abandonarán el río y se adentrarán en el desierto —opuso Surena—. Acudirán a una gran llanura y allí nos enfrentaremos a ellos. En esas condiciones no importará que nos superen en número.

—¿Y por qué harán tal cosa? —preguntó Sillaces verbalizando las dudas de todos los que rodeaban a Surena.

—Por la avaricia, siempre la avaricia. —Aquí se permitió una leve sonrisa enigmática—. Orodes quiere enviarnos a nuestra destrucción. Nos teme, y sabe que anhelamos hacernos con el poder en toda Partia. Quiere usar a los romanos para destruirnos, pero yo también he hecho mis planes y en ellos la única destrucción que contemplo es primero la de los romanos y después la de Orodes. Ahora, lo único que necesitamos es a alguien que despierte el ansia de oro del líder de los romanos.

16

ARIEMNES

Norte de Mesopotamia
53 a. C.

El viejo árabe se inclinó ante Craso y luego, tras incorporarse, iluminó su rostro con la más amplia de las sonrisas. Era un hombre afable, casi un mago a la hora de agradar, algo que lo había ayudado inmensamente en su vida como mercader en medio del desierto. Además tenía facilidad para hablar tantas lenguas como fuera menester para entenderse con los unos y los otros: parto, griego, latín... siempre con pronunciación equivocada pero con suficientes palabras para saber halagar a todos según soplara el viento de la guerra, la paz o el poder, de modo que su mal acento era pronto olvidado por aquellos que departían con él.

—Sé que ayudaste en el pasado a Roma —dijo Craso en latín sentado en su *sella curulis*— y que la serviste bien. Así que si tienes algo que decir éste es el momento de hablar. Craso, cónsul *cum imperio* sobre el ejército romano en Oriente, te escucha.

—Oh, sí, mi señor. En el pasado tuve la fortuna de servir al noble Pompeyo y para mí no habría nada que me hiciera más feliz que ayudar ahora al engrandecimiento del famoso Marco Licinio Craso. Me explicaré bien para que se entienda que, además de por amistad con Roma, obro movido por proteger mi vida y mi negocio, lo que estoy seguro que motivará aún mayor confianza en mis consejos: los partos han quebrado muchas de las rutas con Xeres y es difícil conseguir el permiso del rey de reyes, como se hace llamar ese miserable de Orodes, para enviar mis caravanas hacia el este. Estoy seguro de que bajo el gobierno de Roma, el comercio, la paz y la prosperidad para todos será la norma y no la excepción, por eso deseo ayudar al buen y poderoso Craso a que cuanto antes doblegue al rey parto y borre de la faz de la tierra toda prueba de que alguna vez existieron los arsácidas. Éstos controlan Partia y toda la tierra que bañan el Éufrates y el Tigris y, además, aterrorizan y someten a tantos reyes vecinos como pueden.

Y aquí detuvo su discurso un momento. Craso interpretó correctamente que el viejo Ariemnes buscaba confirmación a sus suposiciones.

—Te garantizo que cuando estas tierras estén bajo mi control... bajo el control de Roma, quiero decir, el comercio y aquellos que como tú viven de él, florecerán y, de forma especial, aquellos que como tú nos ayuden en estos momentos de incertidumbre. A los dioses pongo por testigo de mi promesa. Te puedo asegurar que no soy hombre ingrato y sabré recompensarte.

—¿Qué mejor recompensa puede desear alguien que disponer de la amistad de un hombre tan poderoso como Marco Licinio Craso? —dijo el árabe y volvió a inclinarse ante el cónsul.

Casio, que estaba entre los presentes, tuvo que inspirar profundamente para no interrumpir aquella conversación. Aquel árabe no le ofrecía la más mínima confianza, pero cuando miraba al resto de los oficiales, entre los que estaba ya incorporado Publio Licinio Craso, el hijo del cónsul que acababa de llegar con sus jinetes desde la lejana Galia, no veía muestras de dudas en sus ojos, sino de interés y curiosidad por lo que fuera a proponer el viejo árabe. Muchos tribunos y centuriones llevaban mal el calor de la región, el sol y los mosquitos y anhelaban un rápido término de aquella compleja campaña. Si alguien llegaba con una fórmula para acortarla, era bienvenido por ellos. Casio, no obstante, era de la opinión de que los atajos están llenos de trampas.

—He observado —continuó Ariemnes— que el *imperator* Craso avanza siempre próximo al río, pero su enemigo está alejado del cauce del Éufrates y así nunca lo encontrará...

Casio no pudo contenerse e interrumpió al árabe.

—Junto al río tenemos agua abundante y una ruta de aprovisionamiento constantemente abierta con nuestra retaguardia. Alejarnos de él es un error que debemos evitar... —Calló. Craso había levantado la mano derecha y lo miraba molesto por la interrupción.

—Escucharemos primero todo lo que este hombre tiene que decirnos y luego decidiremos —dijo el cónsul y se volvió hacia el árabe, a quien habló con tono afable—. Continúa.

—Como decía, cónsul e *imperator*, los partos están alejados del río. ¿Por qué? Muy sencillo: porque os temen. ¿Dónde está su rey Orodes? Nadie lo sabe. Se oculta por miedo, estoy seguro de ello. Tiene pánico a las siete bravas legiones de Roma que han cruzado el Éufrates en Zeugma. ¿Qué ha hecho? Huir y esconderse, pero para que su pueblo no se rebele ha hecho como si se preocupara de mantener sus dominios y ha enviado a uno de sus generales, su fiel siervo Surena, con un pequeño ejército, mucho menor en número que las legiones de las que dispone Craso. Imagino que Surena tampoco desea entrar en combate y por eso se mantiene alejado del río. La situación puede alargarse durante meses, pero ¿qué ocurre entretanto? Todo el mundo ha sido presa del mismo pánico que atenaza a Orodes y todos huyen. Pero eso no es lo peor para mi señor Craso: la gente se lleva consigo esclavos, víveres, cosechas enteras de grano, oro, plata, incienso, especias, joyas, cualquier cosa de valor es cargada en carros o camellos y alejada de la ruta de Craso. Cada día que pasa, las tierras que Craso quiere someter se empobrecen y pierden valor. No dudo de que el cónsul conseguirá la victoria absoluta, eso es sólo cuestión de tiempo, pues el enemigo es inferior y temeroso, pero para cuando esa victoria llegue quizá Craso sólo obtenga granos de arena del desierto como todo botín de una larga guerra. Una pobre recompensa después de tanto esfuerzo y valor.

Craso se movía incómodo en su *sella curulis*.

—¿Y qué sugieres? —preguntó el cónsul.

—Ah, toda esta campaña puede acortarse. Si el cónsul se aleja del río. —Miró a Casio un instante, pero el *quaestor* se mantenía en silencio ante la mano levantada de su superior—. Si las legiones se alejan del río, en pocos días, por una ruta llana, segura y sin inconvenientes para hombres entrenados como los legionarios de Roma, llegaremos al lugar donde sé que se esconde el ejército de Surena. Un ataque por sorpresa, una victoria rápida sobre este *spāhbod*, sobre este general parto, y todas las ciudades y reyezuelos se rendirán a Craso. Y si el cónsul sabe administrar estas rendiciones con clemencia, verá cómo en poco tiempo toda Partia estará en sus manos: la gente no quiere huir, sino seguir en sus casas, en sus ciudades y tener paz y prosperidad. Para cuando Orodes quiera reaccionar, si es que se atreve alguna vez, Partia será romana.

Se hizo un silencio intenso que duró un rato.

—Espera fuera —dijo al fin Craso. Ariemnes, tras una nueva y larga reverencia, salió de la tienda del *praetorium*.

—¡Por Marte, no me fío de ese hombre! —exclamó Casio en cuanto el árabe los dejó.

—Eso ha quedado claro desde el principio, *quaestor* —replicó Craso con cierta rabia—. Pero ayudó a Pompeyo en el pasado en la guerra contra Mitrídates del Ponto, cuando ese miserable se ocultó en Armenia. ¿Por qué no he de aprovecharme yo ahora de quien antaño favoreció a Pompeyo?

—Su ayuda a Pompeyo fue en asuntos menores —argumentó Casio—. Todo lo que sabemos es que les proporcionó algunas provisiones y algo de información, pero aquí se trata de la ruta a seguir por un ejército de siete legiones. Es algo demasiado importante para depender de la palabra de un mercader de dudosa lealtad.

—Ya te dije que en esta campaña tendríamos que asumir riesgos y éste va a ser uno de ellos —sentenció Craso—. Pero... —y miró a su alrededor en busca del apoyo de su hijo y de los otros tribunos presentes—; pero es razonable ser cautos. Estableceremos un campamento en este lugar, donde estamos ahora, que servirá de punto de abastecimiento. Cogeremos, no obstante, raciones de agua y comida para veinte días. —Alguno de los tribunos ladeó la cabeza hacia un lado—. Sí, lo sé —continuó Craso con rapidez—. Sé que es mucha agua y mucha comida y que eso supone un exceso de peso para cada legionario, pero en esta campaña todos tendremos que esforzarnos. Disponer de provisiones para veinte días nos da un margen de diez días de marcha de ida y diez de vuelta. Si cada día somos capaces de andar unas veinticinco millas, eso nos da un alcance de doscientas cincuenta millas[13] para explorar. Si en esa distancia damos con el ejército de Surena tendremos la oportunidad que buscamos de acabar con esta campaña mucho más rápido de lo inicialmente pensado. Si no, siempre podemos retornar a este punto y seguir por el río. ¿Qué me decís?

Como temía Casio, el ansia por una rápida conclusión de la campaña inclinó la balanza a favor de seguir la ruta propuesta por el viejo árabe. El *quaestor* salió de la tienda del *praeotrium* solo y solo miró hacia el cielo.

—¡Que los dioses estén con nosotros! —exclamó con fuerza, como si quisiera despertar de su sueño divino a Júpiter, Marte y las demás deidades que los protegían.

13. Unos cuatrocientos kilómetros.

MARCHAS FORZADAS

**Unas millas al norte de Carrhae
53 a. C., cinco días después de la conversación entre Ariemnes
y Craso**

Vanguardia del ejército parto al norte de Mesopotamia

Surena oteaba el paisaje desde lo alto de una colina. Ante él el desierto inclemente.

—Acamparemos aquí.

Sus hombres asintieron. A todos les parecía el lugar perfecto para ocultarse.

Unas 125 millas al sur de Carrhae

Vanguardia del ejército romano en Mesopotamia

Cayo se quitó las *caligae* y mostró a todos sus pies llenos de callos.

—Quita eso de ahí, imbécil —le espetó Sexto—. ¿Acaso crees que eres el único que sufre este maldito avance de locos?

Los dos eran de Corduba, de la lejana Hispania. Habían pasado ya mucho juntos y por eso Cayo sabía que su compañero no estaba realmente enfadado con él y volvió a exhibir sus pies malolientes entre carcajadas. Todos rieron y eso les vino bien hasta que apareció la figura de Druso, el centurión de la unidad. Cayo se sentó bien en el suelo y volvió a abrocharse las sandalias militares a toda velocidad.

—El descanso ha terminado —comentó el centurión. Luego sintió que tenía que compartir algo con sus hombres—. Sé que esta marcha es desagradable e interminable. Comeos primero el *caseus* y el *lardum*; el queso y la grasa es lo que peor resiste este calor y también lo que más pesa. Y guardaos para el final el cereal y todas las *buccellata* que tengáis aún. Las galletas pesan poco y aguantan bien este sol.

Luego se alejó en busca de la cabecera de la centuria a su mando.

—Esto no me gusta nada —susurró Cayo—. Cuando el centurión se preocupa porque economicemos en las provisiones es que se ven venir problemas.

—Maldita sea, por Júpiter, ¿y por qué no ha hablado el centurión antes de esto? —preguntó Sexto enfurruñado—. Yo ya me he comido todas las galletas.

En el praetorium

Llegaron emisarios de Artavasdes, el rey de Armenia. Querían hablar con el cónsul de Roma en Oriente y se los condujo a la tienda del jefe de la expedición.

—Mi señor Artavasdes ruega una vez más al cónsul Marco Licinio Craso que acuda en su ayuda a Armenia —dijo uno de los emisarios, el más veterano, con tono serio en un griego suficientemente comprensible para ser entendido sin esfuerzos por Craso—. El rey Orodes ha entrado en nuestro reino y está atacando nuestras ciudades. Artavasdes, señor de Armenia, reitera su deseo de alianza con Roma y su promesa de proporcionar tropas al cónsul Marco Licinio Craso, pero ahora es crucial que el cónsul cambie su ruta y se dirija a Armenia para ayudarnos en nuestra lucha contra el invasor Orodes. Luego uniremos fuerzas y asolaremos Mesopotamia y Partia entera quedará en manos de Roma.

Pocos tribunos entendían griego lo suficientemente bien como para comprender lo que acababa de decir aquel hombre, pero Casio sí lo entendía y apeló en favor de aquellos mensajeros.

—Es la segunda vez que el rey de Armenia se ofrece para unir fuerzas contra Orodes y los partos. Deberíamos aceptar la propuesta y acudir en su ayuda. Este otro camino que seguimos es cada vez más desértico e incierto.

Pero Craso seguía convencido de que debía conseguir sus objetivos sin la ayuda de Armenia, sin la ayuda de ningún rey. Así, el cónsul evitó responder a Casio, lo ignoró y se limitó a hablar en griego con aquellos mensajeros.

—Decid a vuestro rey que la invasión parta de Armenia es asunto que no me concierne. Deseo que los dioses lo ayuden, pero yo rendiré a los partos a mi manera.

El emisario tuvo que hacer esfuerzos para contener su rabia ante tanta arrogancia. Se inclinó y salió del *praetorium* sin decir nada más.

Casio lo siguió.

—¿Cuántos hombres tiene Orodes en Armenia? —preguntó el *quaestor*, pero el emisario armenio lo miró con desprecio, cogió su caballo y junto con su compañero se alejó cabalgando sin mirar atrás.

Casio se quedó en silencio viendo cómo se alejaba aquel jinete en el horizonte infinito de Mesopotamia.

6 de mayo de 53 a. C., apenas a unas veinte millas de Carrhae

Centro del ejército romano

Hacía tres días que no se veían árboles ni tierra que no fuera la arena del desierto. Casio, en calidad de *quaestor*, teniendo en cuenta lo árido del territorio que cruzaban, dio orden de que se racionaran las provisiones y el agua. Se encontró con la agradable sorpresa de que algunos centuriones ya habían dado esas instrucciones a sus legionarios hacía días, en previsión de que el terreno se fuera convirtiendo, como en efecto había pasado, en más hostil y seco.

—¿Dónde está ese maldito árabe? —preguntó Casio al tribuno encargado de custodiar a aquel guía que los estaba conduciendo por terrenos cada vez más inhóspitos. Quería interrogarlo personalmente, sin Craso delante, sobre la ruta que les estaba haciendo seguir.

—Se ha marchado —dijo el tribuno con tranquilidad.

—¿Cómo que se ha marchado? —Casio no daba crédito a lo que oía—. ¿Se os ha escapado?

—No. Se ha marchado con el permiso del cónsul —completó el tribuno y lo miró con fastidio, como quien quería decir que si no le gustaba lo que oía, que fuera a hablar él directamente con el jefe supremo de aquel ejército.

Casio, por supuesto, no lo dudó y al instante se presentó frente a Marco Licinio Craso en la vanguardia de las legiones. El cónsul estaba bebiendo algo de agua, rodeado por varios tribunos que también bebían de un odre que les acercaba un *calon* para que pudieran servirse con comodidad en sus cazos de campaña.

—¿Por qué se ha permitido que el árabe se vaya? —preguntó Casio directamente sin rodeo alguno, sin tan siquiera saludar al cónsul.

Craso terminó de beber despacio. Luego entregó el cazo al esclavo y se encaró con su *quaestor*.

—Porque ha cumplido con su misión —dijo el cónsul y, ante la mirada de extrañeza de Casio, añadió la información relevante para que éste lo entendiera—. Hemos entrado en contacto con el enemigo. Esta mañana han regresado las patrullas de caballería que ordené que fueran por delante del ejército, como avanzadilla, para evitar un ataque por sorpresa de los partos. Varias de las patrullas han sido interceptadas y hemos perdido unos cuantos jinetes, pero lo importante es que sabemos dónde está ese general parto que llaman Surena. Ariemnes, el árabe, como tú lo llamas, ha cumplido su misión de llevarnos hasta el enemigo en diez días. Me ha solicitado retirarse y no me ha parecido mal. Su compromiso con nosotros era conducirnos hasta los partos lo más rápidamente posible. Acabar con el enemigo es asunto nuestro.

Casio se mordía la lengua. Él nunca habría permitido que Ariemnes los dejara. Si tan seguro estaba aquel mercader árabe de que todo iba a salir a la perfección para las legiones romanas, ¿por qué marcharse? El *quaestor* estaba persuadido de que el mercader escondía algo, pero ahora todo lo referente a ese hombre parecía secundario.

—¿Cuántos son los partos? —preguntó al fin Casio.

—No lo sabemos, pero desde luego, según lo que dicen los jinetes supervivientes de las patrullas, por lo que han podido vislumbrar del ejército enemigo, son muchos menos que nosotros. Parece que solo unos pocos miles.

—Cinco mil, cónsul —completó un tribuno.

—Es cierto, esa cifra la ha dado uno de los jinetes —confirmó Craso—. Como verás, la idea de este avance rápido ha sido muy buena. —Miró entonces hacia el horizonte—. Vamos a asestarles una derrota brutal. No quiero prisioneros. Sólo dejaremos escapar a unos pocos para que cuenten al resto de los partos cuál es la auténtica fuerza de Roma. Pronto toda Mesopotamia será nuestra y luego descenderemos por el Tigris hasta llegar a Cesifonte, su capital.

Casio no dijo nada, pero, en su opinión, el cónsul estaba haciendo cálculos y proyectos con demasiada rapidez.

Vanguardia del ejército parto en las proximidades de Carrhae

Ariemnes se inclinó ante Surena.

—Has cumplido con tu palabra, mercader —dijo el líder de los partos—. Es justo que yo cumpla con la mía. —Miró a uno de sus oficiales, el cual rápidamente desapareció un instante para regresar de inmediato con un pequeño cofre que dejó a los pies del árabe. Ariemnes se agachó, cogió el cofre y lo abrió: estaba lleno de monedas de oro. Los ojos de Ariemnes brillaban.

—Surena, cierto es, cumple con lo acordado —dijo el árabe y dejó de mirar las monedas, cerró el cofre y se dirigió de nuevo al jefe de los partos—; he de advertir, no obstante, que los romanos son mucho más numerosos. Quizá unos cincuenta mil.

Surena no pareció preocuparse.

—Eso es asunto mío, mercader. Los has traído al punto acordado e imagino que lo has hecho con rapidez, sin dejarles tiempo para descansar, ¿no es así?

—Con el de hoy los romanos llevan diez días a marchas

forzadas, a razón de veinticinco millas por día. Han de estar agotados, especialmente con todo el peso con el que carga cada uno de sus soldados.

—Perfecto —dijo Surena—. Puedes marcharte. —Ariemnes empezó a volverse, pero Surena añadió unas palabras—: Márchate en paz, pero no olvides nunca quién es el señor de estas tierras.

El mercader árabe se inclinó una vez más ante Surena.

—No lo olvidaré, mi señor —dijo, dio media vuelta y desapareció con su oro como empujado por el viento. Iba a correr mucha sangre. Estar cerca de Carrhae en los próximos días no era buena idea.

Surena se dirigió entonces a Sillaces.

—¿Habéis reunido todas las telas, mantos y capas que os pedí?

—Sí, Surena —respondió su oficial de más confianza.

—Bien, por Ahura Mazda y por Zoroastro —dijo su líder satisfecho y se volvió hacia el oeste, hacia las dunas del desierto por donde debían aparecer los romanos en poco tiempo—. Pues ya sabes lo que hay que hacer. Prepáralo todo.

Vanguardia romana, a cinco millas de Carrhae

Avanzaron todo el día sin descanso. Estaban exhaustos.

—Ni siquiera nos ha dejado... detenernos para comer o... beber agua... —dijo Sexto.

Druso escuchaba a sus hombres quejarse. En otro momento los habría reprendido, pero tras diez días de marchas forzadas, el propio centurión compartía el punto de vista de sus hombres. De hecho, él mismo echaba de menos la paz y el sosiego de su tierra, la tranquila bahía de Cartago Nova. Desde aquel desierto, su ciudad natal parecía el mejor de los paraísos. La vieja Cartago Nova, la Qart Hadsht fundada por los cartagineses. Sus padres le habían dicho que la sangre de los mismísimos Barca, mezclada con la de los Escipiones, corría por sus venas. Druso sonrió en silencio; delirios de grandeza de su familia. Lo único cierto era que él desde legionario había conseguido abrirse camino hasta llegar a ser centurión gracias a su bravura en la lucha. Pero no había tiempo para distraerse con recuerdos nostálgicos. Druso sabía, como todos los oficiales, que el cónsul no quería dejar escapar al enemigo ni darle tiempo para que se retirase, pero, por otro lado, no le parecía buena estrategia llegar a establecer combate sin haber permitido a los hombres descansar un poco y reponerse por el esfuerzo realizado todos aquellos penosos días de marcha bajo el sol abrasador de aquel desierto infinito.

—Hay malos augurios... —comentó entonces Cayo, que, como siempre, parecía deleitarse con aquellas historias sobre vaticinios de mala fortuna—: los estandartes no querían ser desclavados de la tierra este amanecer y el cónsul se equivocó y se puso un manto negro en lugar del púrpura y no se lo cambió hasta que uno de los oficiales se lo indicó. Lo que yo os diga: malos augurios...

—Cayo, pierdes toda fuerza por la boca —lo interrumpió Druso siempre en marcha, sin detenerse—. El día que hables de un buen vaticinio los caballos volarán.

Sexto y los legionarios alrededor de Cayo se echaron a reír. Aquello pareció calmar un poco los ánimos, pero Druso, pese a la broma lanzada por él mismo, no rio demasiado.

18

EL CUADRADO

Junto a Carrhae
6 de mayo de 53 a. C.

Vanguardia del ejército romano

—¡Por Marte! ¡Un río! —exclamó uno de los tribunos.

Llamar al Balissus río era un poco excesivo, pero en cualquier caso aquel pequeño riachuelo se antojaba un auténtico oasis después de diez días sin otra agua que la recalentada por el sol en los odres que transportaban desde el ya lejano Éufrates.

Druso, como el resto de los centuriones, esperaba que Craso diera orden de detener el ejército para que hombres y bestias pudieran beber con sosiego y recargar todos los odres medio vacíos con agua nueva y fresca.

Craso, en efecto, dio la anhelada orden.

Las sonrisas estaban regresando a la faz de los legionarios.

—¿Es este río también un mal augurio? —le espetó Sexto a Cayo mientras se remojaba la frente después de haber bebido varios tragos a manos llenas. Tenían la fortuna de ser los primeros en llegar al arroyo. Era una de las pocas ventajas de estar en vanguardia. De hecho era la única ventaja. Los primeros en beber. Los primeros en luchar. Los primeros en morir.

Druso había saciado también su sed con rapidez, pero no se entretuvo en remojarse la cabeza.

—¡Bebed rápido y rellenar los odres de agua! ¡No estamos en unos baños en el centro de Roma sino en territorio enemigo...!

Aún no había terminado de pronunciar sus instrucciones cuando varios legionarios de vanguardia dieron la voz de alarma.

—¡Están ahí! ¡Por Hércules!

—¡Los partos!

—¡Nos atacan!

Druso miró hacia donde señalaban: centenares de jinetes enemigos descendían desde unas grandes dunas. Estaban aún a un par de millas. Tenían poco tiempo para maniobrar.

Centro del ejército romano

Craso examinaba el avance de la columna de jinetes partos.

—¿Por qué se lanzan contra nosotros si somos mucho más numerosos? —preguntó el cónsul. Ni su hijo ni ninguno de los tribunos tuvo respuesta para aquella pregunta. Sin embargo, para el *quaestor* el porqué de aquel repentino ataque enemigo era evidente.

—No quieren darnos tiempo a beber agua —dijo Casio.

Craso hizo como que no lo había oído. En todo caso, lo esencial era ver de qué forma maniobrar para repeler el ataque parto y luego contraatacar, pero no decía nada. Pensaba.

Demasiado lento para Casio.

—Lo mejor sería distribuir las legiones en un largo frente, una al lado de la otra —propuso el *quaestor*—, de forma que les resulte imposible rodearnos al no poder rebasar nuestra posición en varias millas.

Craso observó la reacción del resto de los tribunos a la sugerencia de Casio. Varios asintieron. Otros no sabían bien qué decir. Publio Craso hijo habló por todos.

—Parece buena idea, padre.

Craso la asumió, al fin, como una idea suya.

—¡Dad las órdenes! —exclamó y pidió que le llevaran su casco. Entonces empezó aquel rugido que estremecía al desierto.

Vanguardia romana

—¿Qué es ese ruido? —preguntó Cayo.

Un enorme estruendo parecía estar apoderándose de toda la llanura. Era un gran clamor, pero rítmico, profundo, gutural, tenebroso e intenso que penetraba en los oídos y perturbaba las mentes.

—¡Son sus tambores de guerra! —gritó el centurión Druso para hacerse oír por encima de aquel tumulto ensordecedor—. ¡Tambores! ¡Es sólo ruido! ¡Eso no mata! ¡No seáis cobardes! ¡Lo que hemos de temer es si carga esa caballería o si nos arrojan flechas!

Para Druso, curtido en mil batallas contra los bárbaros, no era aquélla la primera vez que oía a un enemigo aproximándose con tambores, pero era cierto que un estruendo como aquél no lo había oído nunca y comprendía que sus hombres, muchos de ellos jóvenes e inexpertos, se sintieran empequeñecidos ante la fiereza de *aquel sonido grave y lúgubre, una mezcla del rugido de las bestias salvajes y el estallido estridente del trueno.*[14]

Centro del ejército romano

Los tambores perturbaron también a Craso. No se veía más que aquella columna de jinetes cubiertos de mantos y telas. Por su aspecto desaliñado no parecían muy temibles, pero el resonar de los instrumentos de guerra era extrañamente poderoso. Ni él ni ningún romano sabía que cada tambor de piel estaba rodeado por decenas de grandes cascabeles de bronce que aumentaban el sonido de cada golpe, haciéndolo diez veces más potente a la par que fúnebre. Craso, de pronto, tuvo miedo. ¿Y si la columna de caballería enemiga rompía la formación de las legiones en un punto? Entonces, los jinetes que rebasaran las líneas defensivas romanas podrían revolverse y atacar por la retaguardia.

Marco Licinio Craso pensó en una solución. Además le desagradaba tanto haber ordenado que las legiones formaran según lo especificado por Casio... ¿acaso si se conseguía la esperada victoria, no reclamaría para sí Casio parte del mérito, como hizo Pompeyo en la campaña contra Espartaco? No, eso no podía ser. Tenía que ser él, Marco Licinio Craso, quien

---

14. Literal de *La vida de Craso* de Plutarco.

dictara la estrategia a seguir. Y el peligro de que se quebraran las líneas en un ataque de aquella caballería era una posibilidad devastadora para él. Era como si se hubiera olvidado de que él mismo disponía de sus propios escuadrones de caballería, además de los más de mil jinetes galos llevados por su hijo desde las campañas de la lejana Galia. No, Craso se olvidó de todos esos recursos y dio una contraorden.

—¡En cuadrado! ¡Formad un cuadrado con las cohortes! —gritó mirando a los tribunos más próximos y llamó a su hijo. A Casio no lo tuvo que llamar. En cuanto las legiones de los extremos detuvieron su avance para quedarse en los flancos, al tiempo que los centuriones detenían a su vez parte de las cohortes de vanguardia para que se posicionaran en la zona posterior del cuadrado, el *quaestor* apareció en el improvisado nuevo cónclave del Estado Mayor de Marco Licinio Craso en el centro del ejército romano.

—¿Por qué hemos cambiado la formación? —preguntó Casio.

—Pueden quebrar la línea que estábamos formando y luego atacarnos por la retaguardia. Estamos en una gran llanura, por si no te has dado cuenta, y pueden querer rodearnos, pero si formamos un gran cuadrado hueco —se puso a dibujar la nueva formación en la arena con su propia *spatha* desenfundada—, donde pondremos un escuadrón de caballería detrás de cada uno de los lados del cuadrado, como apoyo a las cohortes, estamos en una posición completamente segura. Mi hijo se hará cargo del flanco derecho; tú, Casio, del izquierdo y yo me situaré en el centro.

En medio del estruendo de los tambores enemigos, conmovidos por aquel rugido desconocido que parecía hacer temblar la arena del desierto, aquella posición más defensiva parecía una buena opción para la mayor parte de los tribunos. Casio no dijo nada. A punto de entrar en combate, no era operativo iniciar un conflicto con la persona al mando, incluso si estaba en desacuerdo con aquella formación. En cualquier caso, seguían siendo mucho más numerosos que la columna de jinetes que se les echaba encima. La victoria sería de Roma. Para Casio habría sido más sencillo avanzar en una larga línea cuyos flancos se cerraran luego sobre la caballería enemiga en una maniobra envolvente como había hecho Aníbal en Cannae, pero si todos preferían una estrategia más defensiva y lenta, tendrían que hacerlo así. Pese a que Craso ejecutaba un plan que lo incomodaba, ni tan siquiera Casio, en aquel momento, contemplaba otra posibilidad que una victoria. Para el *quaestor* la diferente estrategia simplemente comportaría una batalla innecesariamente más larga con más víctimas entre los legionarios, pero nada más.

Vanguardia parta

—¡Que se quiten las telas! —gritó Surena a Sillaces, su lugarteniente—. ¡Quiero que nos vean! ¡Ha llegado la hora de *nabardādan*, la hora de combatir!

Y su instrucción se repitió a lo largo de toda la columna de jinetes partos. *De pronto se quitaron aquellos mantos de sus armaduras y se los vio brillando con sus cascos y cotas de malla, con su acero margiano resplandeciente y cegador, y los caballos con armaduras de bronce y loricas de acero. El propio Surena era el más alto y hermoso de todos, aunque su belleza afeminada no se correspondía con su reputado valor; pero él estaba vestido más al modo de Media, con el rostro pintado y el cabello peinado en dos mitades, mientras que el resto de los partos aún llevaban el pelo largo peinado sobre la frente, según el uso escita, de forma que parecieran formidables.*[15]

Vanguardia romana

—¡Por Hércules! —exclamó Druso poniendo voz a la sorpresa y al pavor que sentían todos sus hombres al ver a aquellos jinetes perfectamente cubiertos de acero y bronce, inexpugnables, muy diferentes a como se habían hecho visibles en un principio, todos cabalgando hacia ellos como si se tratara de semidioses invencibles.

15. Literal de *La vida de Craso* de Plutarco.

—¡Mantened la posición! —repitió Druso apoyando las órdenes que daban sus superiores, pero añadió algo más a sus hombres—: ¡Preparad los escudos, por Marte! ¡Preparadlos!

Cayo y Sexto y todos los demás legionarios de la centuria asieron con fuerza los escudos militares, dispuestos a alzarlos en cuanto recibieran la orden.

Centro del ejército romano

—¿Qué hacen? —preguntó Craso a sus oficiales, dejando de lado ya el efecto sorpresa que había causado que aquellos enemigos no fueran salvajes cubiertos de pieles o telas, sino *catafractos* perfectamente acorazados y armados, temidos en medio mundo.

—¡No cargan contra nuestra vanguardia! —respondió uno de los tribunos.

—¡Eso ya lo sé, imbécil! —replicó Craso con desprecio en medio del ruido de los tambores partos y ante la confusión que le generaba ver que los jinetes *catafractos* partos, en lugar de arremeter contra las cohortes de vanguardia, parecían evitarlas y se diseminaban por todas partes.

Vanguardia romana

—¿Por qué no atacan, señor? —preguntó Sexto a su centurión.

Druso miraba atento la maniobra del enemigo: los jinetes *catafractos* se iban separando unos de otros sin entrar en combate. La columna enemiga se había partido en dos bloques: uno cabalgaba hacia un extremo del cuadrado y el otro bloque hacia el otro extremo.

—Nos rodean —respondió Druso sin levantar la voz, pues estaba aún digiriendo su propia interpretación de la maniobra.

Flanco izquierdo romano

Varias líneas de hombres más atrás, Casio había llegado a la misma conclusión.

—Los partos van a rodear toda nuestra formación —comentó a uno de los oficiales que tenía junto a él.

—Pero no van a encontrar fisuras en nuestro cuadrado —apuntó el oficial—. Tenemos cohortes en los cuatro lados.

Casio asentía. Era cierto. Aquélla era la única ventaja del cuadrado. Entonces ¿por qué los rodeaban? No había puntos débiles. Estaban todas las cohortes muy juntas, ¿demasiado juntas en medio de una llanura?

Centro del ejército romano

—¡Acabemos con esta estupidez de una vez! —gritó Craso—. ¡Que avancen las cohortes de vanguardia y que acaben con esos malditos ahora mismo!

Y las tubas y trompetas romanas sonaron por doquier para transmitir la orden del cónsul.

Vanguardia romana

—¡Adelante! —ordenó Druso a sus hombres.

—¡Marchad!

—¡Al ataque!

Todos los centuriones de las legiones de vanguardia alentaron a los legionarios de las primeras cohortes para lanzarse contra los jinetes partos que tenían más próximos.

Cayo y Sexto iban el uno al lado del otro. No decían nada. Sudaban enormemente, por el calor del sol, por los nervios, por el miedo.

—¡Agh!

—¡Dioses!

Varios de sus compañeros cayeron desplomados.

—¡Escudos en alto! —Era la voz del centurión.

Cayo y Sexto los levantaron de inmediato. La rapidez de su centurión y su pronta respuesta a la hora de obedecer la instrucción los salvó a ellos y a muchos de su centuria, pero en las unidades contiguas los legionarios aún no habían levantado bien los escudos y la lluvia de flechas partas acabó con muchos y a otros los dejó con heridas en piernas, brazos y hasta en el pecho. La sangre de Roma empezó a regar la arena del desierto.

Flanco izquierdo

—¡Atrás, atrás! —ordenó el *quaestor* Casio a las legiones que habían avanzado. Lo mismo hacían en otros puntos de la formación romana.

Centro del ejército romano

—¿Por qué retroceden? —preguntaba ahora Craso.

—¡Los han acribillado, mi cónsul! ¡En cuanto nuestros hombres se les acercan, los partos disparan flechas desde los caballos sin siquiera detenerse!

Craso no dijo nada. Estaba pensando.

El cielo se oscureció.

Craso miró a lo alto extrañado, pues no había visto nube alguna en el horizonte. Y, en efecto, no era una nube normal. Era una nube negra.

Las flechas cayeron por todas partes. El oficial que acababa de hablar con el cónsul cayó atravesado por dos flechas partas a los pies del propio Craso, que lo miró caer muerto con la boca abierta y escupiendo sangre. El cónsul no reaccionaba.

Vanguardia del ejército romano

Los centuriones de todas las cohortes tomaron por cuenta propia la única decisión sensata ante aquella lluvia infinita de dardos mortíferos que les arrojaba el enemigo.

—¡Testudo! ¡Formad en testudo! —gritaban al unísono todos los oficiales romanos de vanguardia.

Retaguardia parta

Surena se había replegado junto con parte de su Estado Mayor para observar el desarrollo de la batalla desde lo alto de una pequeña colina de arena.

—Son muchos —dijo Sillaces—. Incluso si conseguimos que no puedan entrar en lucha cuerpo a cuerpo, nos costará mantenerlos bajo una lluvia de flechas constante.

—Sí podemos conseguirlo —contrapuso Surena—. Usad todos los camellos de retaguardia y organizad una *kārwān*, una gran caravana militar en la que los camellos sólo transportarán una cosa.

—¿El qué? —preguntó Sillaces.

Surena sonrió antes de responder.

—Flechas.

Centro del ejército romano

Casio avanzó entre las confusas filas del corazón del cuadrado del ejército romano. Iba protegido por los escudos de varios legionarios que actuaban a modo de escolta improvisada del *quaestor*. Casio había enviado mensajes a Craso solicitándole algún tipo de acción, pero no había obtenido respuesta o los mensajeros de uno y otro habían caído atravesados por las flechas enemigas. Aquélla no era una posibilidad a desestimar. Por eso decidió ir él mismo a hablar con Craso. Al fin, alcanzó la posición del cónsul.

—¡Hemos de hacer algo como sea! —gritó Craso, pues el rugido de los tambores partos no había cesado desde el comienzo de la batalla y los alaridos de los que caían bajo los dardos enemigos eran cada vez más frecuentes—. ¡Sus flechas atraviesan incluso los escudos! ¡No sé que arcos usan, pero los dardos caen con una fuerza infernal! ¡Hay que lanzar la caballería en bloque contra las filas enemigas!

—¡Ya he lanzado varias cohortes y todas se han replegado por las flechas! —se defendió Craso.

Y era verdad. El cónsul no había estado inactivo del todo. Tras la sorpresa inicial, al fin había ordenado varios contraataques de las cohortes de vanguardia, e incluso había reemplazado algunas por tropas de refresco de retaguardia para intentar entrar en combate cuerpo a cuerpo con el enemigo, pero en cuanto los legionarios avanzaban, los jinetes partos se retiraban, eso sí, siempre lanzando flechas mientras huían, en particular los jinetes de la caballería ligera. Y si en alguna ocasión alguna cohorte había llegado a las posiciones partas, los *catafractos* de la caballería pesada, protegidos con las corazas de bronce y acero, los habían atacado matando e hiriendo a los soldados romanos. Al final, en cada ataque romano las cohortes lanzadas contra el enemigo habían tenido que replegarse. Y seguía la lluvia de flechas interminable. Eso no se detenía nunca. Los partos, además, usaban arcos con listones rígidos y puntas rectas de hueso que actuaban de palanca aumentando la fuerza con la que salía cada flecha en busca de la sangre romana. Disponían, en suma, de arcos mucho mejores y más mortíferos que los de los legendarios escitas.

Los dardos continuaban cayendo por todas partes. Casio seguía frente a Craso.

—¿Qué esperamos para hacer algo, cónsul? —preguntó el *quaestor*.

Impotente, Craso respondió lo único que había podido imaginar como estrategia.

—¡Esperaremos a que se les terminen las flechas!

Casio inspiró aire y negó con la cabeza una y otra vez.

—¡Eso no pasará nunca! —gritó el *quaestor*—. ¡Los hombres de vanguardia dicen que los partos han organizado una columna de camellos que los abastecen de flechas constantemente! ¡Hay que intentarlo con la caballería! —insistió Casio—. ¡Son más rápidos y quizá puedan desbaratar las líneas de los jinetes partos! ¡Luego se puede volver a atacar con las cohortes legionarias, pero apoyadas por un ataque de caballería!

Craso miró hacia el enemigo. Estaban en un promontorio en el centro de la posición del ejército romano, pero aun así era difícil vislumbrar bien los movimientos partos por la arena que levantaban unos y otros en el combate o, para ser más precisos, en los intentos por entablar combate directo. En ese momento, no obstante, en un breve intermedio de la fatídica lluvia de flechas, Craso divisó una larga hilera de camellos que se movía de un lado a otro en la retaguardia enemiga.

—¿Es cierto que los camellos llevan flechas? —preguntó el cónsul con voz vibrante.

—¡Es lo que me ha dicho un centurión de vanguardia! ¡Un veterano de Cartago Nova, hombre de fiar! —certificó Casio.

Craso asintió.

—¡Entonces no podemos esperar! ¡Usaremos la caballería! ¡Pero no enviaremos a cualquiera! —El cónsul se dirigió a uno de los tribunos que estaban al otro lado—. ¡Enviaremos un mensajero a mi hijo con las órdenes! ¿Cuántas cohortes y cuántos jinetes? —preguntó Craso mirando a Casio.

—Mil jinetes, se necesita una fuerza importante de caballería para obligar a esos malditos a alejarse de nuestro ejército y quizá... cuatro cohortes... o incluso menos...

Craso dudaba al final, pues no estaba seguro de cómo podría salir aquella maniobra y no le parecía prudente arriesgar muchos hombres. Pero iba a enviar a su hijo y no quería que fuera sin el apoyo necesario y suficiente para aquel ataque... desesperado.

El mensajero estaba preparado junto al cónsul y el *quaestor*. Craso se volvió hacia él y le dio las instrucciones.

—Dile a mi hijo que salga con, al menos, mil jinetes de su confianza y que se lleve arqueros también y que tome... seis cohortes... no, mejor que lleve ocho cohortes.

EL CONTRAATAQUE DE PUBLIO LICINIO CRASO

Junto a Carrhae, 6 de mayo de 53 a. C.

Retaguardia del ejército parto

—¿Qué hacen? —preguntó Sillaces.

—Están abriendo las líneas de vanguardia —dijo otro de los oficiales partos.

—Van a atacar con la caballería y la infantería a la vez —precisó Surena, que había esperado aquella maniobra hacía rato—. Van a lanzarnos su caballería para alejarnos de su ejército. Se trata de una partición de sus tropas a gran escala. La lluvia de flechas los está obligando a actuar de forma diferente a lo que tenían planeado. O sea, que están haciendo ahora exactamente lo que yo quería.

Luego un breve silencio.

—¿Y qué hacemos? —volvió a preguntar Sillaces—. ¿Les arrojamos a todos los *catafractos*? Eso quizá los detenga.

—Es posible —dijo Surena—, pero por Ahura Mazda que eso no es bastante para mí. No, en esta llanura hemos de conseguir algo más que detener a los romanos, por no decir que si los *catafractos* fallaran, entonces no tendríamos ya nada con que defendernos y ellos aún tienen gran parte de su enorme ejército operativo. Pese al daño que les estamos infligiendo son tan numerosos que aún tienen opciones de destrozarnos —y se volvió hacia Sillaces—. Cogerás a parte de la caballería ligera con sus arqueros y actuarás exactamente como te voy a explicar. Exactamente, ¿me entiendes?

Sillaces, muy serio, asintió y escuchó con atención a su líder. Surena sólo le dijo una palabra en parto:

—*Mig* [nube].

Sillaces no necesitó más.

Flanco derecho del ejército romano

Publio Craso recibió las órdenes de su padre y al momento organizó una importante fuerza militar de ataque: mil trescientos jinetes, entre los que estaban sus mil caballeros galos trasladados desde las lejanas nuevas provincias occidentales, excombatientes de la conquista de aquel territorio bajo el mando de Julio César, y trescientos jinetes más de las cohortes de apoyo; los cuatro mil hombres de infantería que su padre había ordenado que llevara consigo y quinientos arqueros con los que poder responder con la misma moneda a las flechas que les arrojaban los partos.

Censorino y Megabaco, los tribunos al mando de aquellas cohortes, se aproximaron a Craso hijo.

—¡Esto no va a ser fácil! —dijo Censorino gritando para hacerse oír por encima de los tambores partos, que no cesaban nunca en su rítmico canto de terror; Censorino era joven, como el hijo de Craso, y también osado y valiente, pero consciente de que la salida organizada no iba a ser una aventura sencilla.

—¡Saldremos con la caballería por delante, bajo mi mando! —se explicaba Publio Craso dando también grandes voces—. ¡Vosotros me seguiréis! ¡Iremos actuando según encontremos oposición o no del enemigo!

—¡Cualquier cosa será mejor que permanecer aquí bajo esta lluvia de flechas! —sentenció Megabaco.

Vanguardia parta

—Ahí vienen —dijo Sillaces en voz baja, como si hablara para sí mismo. La caballería romana avanzaba al trote hacia ellos. Seguramente no lo hacían al galope para no dejar atrás a los legionarios que los seguían. Parecían unos mil jinetes, quizá alguno más, y varios miles de legionarios. Más de los que habían pensado. Las cosas podían complicarse. ¿Se habría equivocado Surena con aquel plan?

Caballería de Publio Craso

—¡Al ataque! ¡Por Roma, por el cónsul, por todos los dioses!

Y aceleró el ritmo del trote de su caballo hasta iniciar un galope al que se unieron el resto de los jinetes galos y que pareció pillar por sorpresa a los partos, que, en lugar de plantarles cara, iniciaron un repliegue desordenado retrocediendo sobre sus pasos y alejándose del campo de batalla.

—¡Seguidlos! ¡El enemigo nos teme! ¡Por Roma! —aullaba Craso hijo con toda la energía de sus pulmones henchidos de ansia de victoria.

Así galoparon durante un rato hasta que, al fin, los partos se reagruparon y opusieron una pequeña línea de *catafractos*, demasiado pesados para poder alejarse de la caballería romana que los perseguía, menos protegida por no llevar corazas pero mucho más veloz.

—Bien, quieren combate —comentó Craso hijo a los que tenía más próximos a él—. A eso hemos venido. No a luchar contra el polvo y las flechas, sino contra hombres.

Centro del ejército romano, centro del cuadrado

—¿Los ves? —preguntó Craso padre a Casio.

—No los diviso bien —respondió el *quaestor*—. Pero parece como si los partos se hubieran replegado. Desde luego la lluvia de flechas aquí ha disminuido.

—Sabía que mi hijo podría conseguirlo —dijo Craso padre exultante—. Es un valiente. Todo esto es como Alejandro Magno en Gaugamela.

Casio no dijo nada mientras intentaba seguir oteando el horizonte por donde se habían ido las tropas de Craso hijo, pero lo único que acertaba a ver era una gran polvareda que a cada momento se hacía más y más grande.

Craso hijo ordenó una primera carga contra aquellos *catafractos*. Éstos no rehuyeron el enfrentamiento y el choque de las armas resonó con furia. Muchos jinetes partos fueron duramente golpeados por los bravos caballeros galos, pero muy pocos fueron heridos, pues sus poderosas corazas los protegían, mientras que, por el contrario, varias decenas de galos y de romanos caían con heridas brutales en sus costados, brazos o piernas descubiertos y sin armaduras de bronce o acero que guarnecieran sus cuerpos.

—¡Replegaos! —ordenó Craso hijo. Quería reevaluar la situación. No estaba desanimado ni mucho menos. Sabía que en un primer combate contra aquellos jinetes acorazados el asunto no les iba a resultar ventajoso, pero estaba animado porque había contribuido a desviar muchos recursos partos que protegían a los arqueros que estaban acribillando al grueso del ejército de su padre. Además aquel enfrentamiento entre una caballería y otra, aunque desigual, había dado tiempo para que las ocho cohortes que los seguían los alcanzaran. Ahora podía volver a atacar a aquellos *catafractos* combinando el lanzamiento de los *pila* de los legionarios con el combate cuerpo a cuerpo luego de los galos a caballo. Poco a poco, pero se conseguiría acabar con todos aquellos malditos. La victoria era posible y estaba cerca.

—¡Mirad! —exclamó entonces Censorino desde las cohortes que acababan de alcanzar la posición de la caballería romana.

Aparecían decenas, centenares más de partos por todas partes.

—¡Nos han rodeado! —gritó Megabaco.

Craso hijo no decía nada, pero miró a un lado y a otro desde lo alto de su caballo y comprobó que era cierto. Por eso se habían alejado los partos. No huían ni los temían. Sólo había sido una burda estratagema: fingir una huida para distanciarlos del grueso del ejército romano. Tenían ocho cohortes, quinientos arqueros y mil trescientos jinetes, algunos menos tras el primer combate contra los *catafractos*. Pero la fuerza principal de las siete legiones estaba lejos. Y antes de que Craso hijo pudiera dar orden alguna, los *catafractos* y los nuevos jinetes partos de su caballería más ligera que se les habían unido, en lugar de lanzarse contra ellos, empezaron a trotar primero y luego a galopar alrededor de las tropas hasta levantar una inmensa polvareda de arena que se vino sobre ellos.

—¡Dagh! —aulló Censorino comiendo polvo y arena a partes iguales y llevándose, como todos, las manos a los ojos para intentar protegerlos. No se veía nada. Sólo una gigantesca nube que lo envolvía todo.

Entonces cayó sobre ellos una andanada de flechas y luego otra y otra. Una lluvia inclemente de dardos mortíferos que los acribillaban sin piedad alguna.

—¡Que disparen... nuestros... arqueros...! —aulló Craso hijo como pudo, y algunos intentaron obedecerlo, pero cegados por el polvo no sabían hacia dónde disparar. De igual forma, confundidos y aterrados, algunos legionarios que habían desenfundado sus espadas y que estaban en vanguardia de aquellas tropas blandían sus *gladios* también a ciegas, como gladiadores *andabatae* que estuvieran forzados a combatir sin ver al enemigo, hasta el punto de que, como si se encontraran en el terrible Anfiteatro Flavio, los propios legionarios llegaban a herirse entre sí pensando que luchaban contra aquel enemigo tan devastador como invisible que los había atrapado en aquella nube de muerte.

Craso hijo comprendió que los arqueros romanos no sabían contra quién apuntar y que la confusión total se había apoderado de los legionarios. Cualquier otro habría dado por perdido aquel enfrentamiento, pero Craso hijo era hombre de pundonor extremo y de intuición militar. Había caído en una trampa, pero incluso de la peor de las emboscadas se puede intentar salir. Más de una vez, en medio de una gran cacería, había visto a un oso escapar de las redes de sus captores cuando la bestia parecía ya atrapada.

—¡Censorino, Megabaco! —gritó solicitando la presencia de sus tribunos de más confianza. Éstos acudieron como pudieron, casi a gatas, pero cuando llegaron junto a Craso hijo éste les habló con tal energía que les transmitió el valor suficiente para el contraataque—. ¡Nos lanzamos con toda la caballería contra los *catafractos* partos y que los dioses nos protejan! ¡Así detendremos la nube que levantan con su constante galope y los legionarios y nuestros arqueros podrán ver de nuevo contra quién luchamos!

Y no dijo más ni esperó respuesta, sino que rodeado por un nutrido grupo de jinetes galos se arrojó con ellos contra lo más denso de la nube oscura.

En medio de la polvareda más absoluta, Craso hijo cabalgó hasta que su caballo chocó contra uno de los *catafractos* acorazados. Los caballos relincharon de puro terror, pero tanto Craso hijo como el jinete parto, ambos expertos combatientes, se mantuvieron a lomos de sus animales. Craso hijo, advertido ya de que golpear con el *gladio* a aquellos *catafractos* protegidos por férreas armaduras no era lo más eficaz, asió con ambas manos, muy fuertemente, la lanza del parto y tirando de ella con rapidez consiguió desequilibrar a su enemigo y derribarlo. Luego cogió una de sus lanzas del lomo de su montura y la arrojó contra la cabeza del enemigo abatido consiguiendo que la punta del asta entrara por la visera parta. El aullido de dolor del parto muerto le supo a esperanza y más cuando comprobó que muchos de los jinetes galos bajo su mando lo imitaban y usando la misma estrategia conseguían derribar a otros tantos *catafractos*. Pero no todos lo lograban: otros muchos galos y caballeros romanos que intentaban asir las lanzas partas no eran tan hábiles como su líder y eran atravesados por las astas enemigas. Cuando no, las lanzas partas herían mortalmente a sus caballos, de forma que los jinetes galos y romanos quedaban sin montura arrastrándose por el suelo. Aun así, éstos no se daban por vencidos, sino que desenfundaban las espadas y, casi arrastrándose, se introducían por entre las patas de los caballos acorazados hasta situarse justo debajo, el único punto que los caballos partos no llevaban protegido por completo, y entonces clavaban sus armas en el vientre de los animales. Los caballos mortalmente heridos relinchaban con pánico, se ponían a dos patas algunos o caían a plomo sobre la tierra, a veces atrapando al galo o al romano que los había herido, pero siempre arrastrando en la caída a su jinete acorazado.

Craso hijo y sus jinetes lucharon con la bravura de los romanos que habían conquistado Sicilia, Cerdeña, Hispania, derrotado a Aníbal y Cartago y anexionado la Galia e infinidad de ciudades y pueblos por todo el Mediterráneo, pero los partos parecían llegar de todas partes y pese a que habían derribado a muchos, otros tantos seguían combatiendo y pisoteando a unos galos y romanos exhaustos por el combate sin cuartel, la lluvia incesante de flechas, la sed y aquel calor mortal al que no estaban acostumbrados. Si hubieran llegado a la batalla tras un día de descanso, bien alimentados y habiendo bebido buenas cantidades de agua, quizá habrían conseguido revertir el curso de aquella emboscada, pero agotados como estaban, sólo consiguieron encontrar una muerte valerosa y épica, pero nada más.

Entretanto, los arqueros partos habían seguido acribillando a las ocho cohortes romanas de Craso hijo y abatido a miles de legionarios. El desastre en la unidad militar del joven tribuno era completo. Publio Licinio Craso, herido en una mano por una flecha, se replegó junto con Censorino y Megabaco a un promontorio en el centro de su posición. Todo era muerte y sangre y heridos agonizantes. Dos griegos que estaban integrados en las cohortes de Craso en calidad de guías se presentaron ante el propio Craso hijo, se identificaron como naturales de Carrhae y se ofrecieron a llevar al tribuno, junto a sus oficiales, aprovechando la confusión, hacia aquella ciudad, pues el retorno al grueso del ejército romano parecía imposible. Craso hijo se negó.

—¡Marchad y poneos a salvo, pero yo no abandonaré mis tropas!

Los griegos se alejaron entre el mar de heridos en busca de una huida incierta, dejando a Craso hijo con sus oficiales.

El tribuno miró a su alrededor. Era una matanza absoluta. Había conducido a sus hombres a una trampa mortal. Había intentado salvarlos lanzándose en un ataque desesperado contra los *catafractos*, pero éstos lo habían derrotado. Craso hijo cogió su espada con la mano izquierda, pero no podía clavársela con suficiente fuerza con una mano. En la otra, la derecha, seguía clavada aquella flecha parta, sangraba cada vez más y apenas le valía ya para nada que no fuera sufrir. Se dirigió al *signifer*, el portaestandarte que mantenía la insignia de la legión asida con fuerza aún en medio de la debacle absoluta.

—¡Clava la insignia en la tierra! —le ordenó Craso hijo y el portaestandarte obedeció al instante—. ¡Ahora coge tu espada y húndela con fuerza en mi pecho!

El *signifer* dudó.

—¡No puedo, tribuno, no puedo hacerlo! —gritó abrumado por la orden recibida.

—¡No importa! ¡Sostenla con fuerza, recta, con la punta hacía mí! —ordenó entonces Craso hijo. Antes de que el portaestandarte pudiera pensar bien lo que hacía, Craso se arrojó con todas sus fuerzas contra la punta de aquel *gladio* al tiempo que se abrazaba al *signifer* para apretarse aún con más fuerza contra el arma despiadada que sin alma ni remordimiento alguno atravesó la piel y las venas y el corazón de Publio Licinio Craso.

Censorino, herido también en los brazos, recurrió a su vez a otro oficial para realizar la *devotio*, el sacrificio último de quitarse la vida por haber sido incapaz de conseguir una victoria, mientras que Megabaco, que no estaba herido, se suicidó él solo viendo cómo más oficiales los imitaban.

Los partos acribillaron al resto de los romanos de las cohortes de Craso hijo hasta que Sillaces ordenó que detuvieran la matanza. Sólo cogieron a quinientos prisioneros de una fuerza total de más de cinco mil hombres.

El líder parto caminaba por encima de los cadáveres legionarios pisándolos con saña hasta que llegó justo a donde quería, junto al cuerpo de Craso hijo. Hincó una rodilla en tierra y con la espada rebanó el cuello del tribuno romano hasta arrancarle la cabeza de cuajo y despegarla del cuerpo, tirando del pelo enrojecido por la sangre. La levantó en alto y los partos aullaron como lobos tras haber abatido su presa.

El cónsul Craso se sentía más seguro: la salida de su hijo parecía haber forzado a los partos a conducir gran parte de sus tropas contra la caballería galorromana y las ocho cohortes que los habían acompañado; esto había conllevado una reducción de la lluvia de flechas notable y había permitido un repliegue razonablemente organizado del ejército romano hacia la ladera de una montaña, donde la estrategia parta de rodearlos resultaba más compleja, por no decir casi inviable. Todo parecía estar mejor cuando un nuevo acontecimiento inquietó a los romanos: una especie de aullido infernal.

—¿Por qué aúllan ahora? —pregunto el cónsul Marco Licinio Craso.

—No lo sé —respondió Casio arrugando la frente y hablando en voz baja, casi inaudible—, pero los tambores han dejado de sonar...

El *quaestor* intentaba divisar a las cohortes y la caballería del hijo de Craso pero no alcanzaba a verlas. Se habían alejado demasiado. Algo le decía que aquel aullido y el silencio de los tambores no presagiaba nada bueno.

HISTORIA DE TRAJANO

Principios del siglo II d.C.

Libro II

CASUS BELLI

20

LA CARTA DE PALMA

Domus Flavia (palacio imperial), Roma
Finales de 107 d. C.

Lucio Quieto llegó al palacio imperial casi corriendo. Había recibido un mensaje urgente del emperador que lo citaba en su cámara personal. Parecía que al fin había noticias sobre la campaña de Arabia.

Los pretorianos abrían las puertas de cada una de las salas de la *Domus Flavia* ante la llegada del *legatus* norteafricano. Nadie osaba interponerse en su camino. Todos sabían que, poco a poco, aquel jefe de la caballería gozaba de una mayor confianza por parte del emperador. Quizá más confianza de la que tenía en Adriano, pero aquél era un tema del que nadie se atrevía a hablar ni en susurros, en particular ante la faz de rabia contenida que el sobrino segundo del César ponía cuando veía a Quieto en palacio.

Lucio Quieto llegó a la cámara imperial. Liviano, el jefe del pretorio, y Aulo, el tribuno de la guardia imperial, abrieron las puertas personalmente para dejar el paso franco a Quieto y las cerraron en cuanto las flanqueó. El emperador no estaba solo: los senadores Celso y Nigrino estaban junto a él, en pie, a ambos lados de la mesa, sobre la que había una carta. También había un joven de unos veinte años que Quieto no tenía identificado.

—Has llegado, ya era hora —dijo Trajano, sentado en una *cathedra*.

—He venido lo más rápido que he podido —se explicó ante la aparente muestra de irritación del César, que parecía contrariado por su supuesta tardanza.

Trajano levantó la mano como para dejar aquel asunto.

—Eso no es importante ahora. Todos estamos nerviosos, pero he querido que seamos los cuatro juntos los que sepamos del contenido de esta carta. Palma, al fin, ha escrito. Has venido rápido, pero la tensión nos atenaza a todos. —Y se dirigió a sus tres hombres de confianza señalando al joven que estaba en una esquina, con aire algo tímido, mirando al suelo—. Éste es Fédimo, mi nuevo secretario personal. Necesito a alguien de confianza absoluta que me ayude con todo el correo. Lleva ya unos días conmigo y parece eficaz. Pero ahora debemos ocuparnos de esta carta. —Y apuntó entonces con el índice hacia la mesa donde estaba la misiva.

Todos la miraban pero nadie se ofrecía a cogerla y darle lectura. Ni siquiera Trajano.

—He observado que el César —empezó Quieto— se ha ocupado de que hasta los pretorianos que están en la puerta de la cámara imperial sean Liviano y Aulo. No hay nadie de más confianza, pero eso me hace ver que el emperador teme ser espiado.

—Nunca me he sentido seguro en palacio, ya lo sabéis —confirmó Trajano—. No hay lugar más seguro para mí que en medio de un campo de batalla rodeado por los enemigos. Al menos allí sabes a qué atenerte.

—Precisamente, César —continuó Lucio Quieto—, por eso me sorprende que entre nosotros, ahora, para leer esta carta de Palma, esté presente alguien que apenas conocemos —y señaló al joven Fédimo.

Trajano asintió.

—Es de total confianza —apuntó el César—. Le pedí a Suetonio que me enviara a alguien de quien pudiera fiarme por completo, en particular con todo el correo imperial, como decía antes, y el *procurator bibliothecae* me envió a este hombre. Cuando me dijo que se trataba de alguien joven hasta me ilusioné. Tenía la esperanza de que fuera hermoso, pero Suetonio parece que ha visto en Fédimo otras virtudes que no son precisamente su belleza.

Celso, Nigrino y Quieto no pudieron evitar una sonrisa. Todos sabían de los gustos del emperador y no había nadie más distante de ellos que Fédimo: el joven secretario era enjuto, muy delgado, con un rostro algo cadavérico, huesudo, ojos saltones y los dientes superiores prominentes. Fédimo quizá fuera buen secretario, pero nunca sería amante del César. Eso era evidente. La broma imperial pareció relajarlos a todos un poco. Y también tranquilizó a Quieto que el nuevo joven secretario estuviera recomendado por Suetonio, hombre a quien tenía como sumamente leal y discreto. Era obvio que Trajano necesitaba a alguien de confianza que lo asistiera con la creciente burocracia de un imperio que no hacía más que aumentar en territorios con nuevas provincias, más gobernadores y más reinos fronterizos sujetos a los dictados de Roma.

—Además es hispano, como yo —apostilló Trajano con relación a Fédimo—. Me he entendido bien con él desde el principio. De hecho he pensado que, si no os ofrecéis ninguno, puede ser él mismo el que lea la carta de Palma.

Ante la mirada de Trajano, Celso, Nigrino y Quieto, uno a uno, fueron asintiendo. El emperador clavó los ojos entonces en Fédimo, que permanecía callado en la esquina a la espera de instrucciones. El joven, en efecto, llevaba poco tiempo con Trajano, pero había aprendido ya a interpretar sus miradas. Dio unos pasos, llegó hasta la mesa, tomó la carta, la desplegó con tiento y empezó a leer:

Al emperador Marco Ulpio Trajano de parte del legatus *Cornelio Palma, al mando de las legiones desplazadas a Arabia*

Mi señor, escribo para reconocer mi incapacidad y mis errores en esta campaña. Siento no haber estado a la altura de la confianza depositada por el César en mi humilde persona.

Fédimo calló nada más leer ese inquietante inicio. Trajano se pasaba la punta de la lengua por los labios. Celso y Nigrino negaban con la cabeza. Quieto permanecía inmóvil, con los ojos muy abiertos. Parecía contener la respiración. Fédimo no sabía lo mucho que se jugaba allí aquella jornada, pero intuía que si el emperador y tres hombres de su máxima confianza estaban así de nerviosos era porque aquella carta era clave para el futuro de Roma. El César hizo una pequeña indicación con la mano derecha. Fédimo asintió y continuó leyendo:

Mi señor, he obrado llevado de una absurda seguridad al presuponer que podría derrotar a los nabateos emulando las épicas victorias de mi maestro en la guerra, el emperador Trajano, pero en esta campaña he descubierto mis enormes limitaciones y lo importante que es para Roma que quien esté al mando de sus legiones sea, en efecto, alguien que nunca se deje sorprender por el enemigo, como fue mi caso. Pero sé que el César no es hombre de circunloquios, así que iré al grano: avanzamos y nos adentramos en gran parte de Arabia sin encontrar demasiada resistencia. Unos mercaderes nos informaron de la muerte del rey Rabbel Sóter II, dato que seguramente ya habrá llegado a Roma, y de que éste había sido reemplazado en el poder de Arabia por un hijo que había elegido el sobrenombre de Obodas. El recuerdo del antiguo rey Obodas que tan valientemente luchó contra Antíoco XII en el pasado debería haberme puesto más en guardia de lo que en realidad estuve. Es cierto, no obstante, que tomé medidas de precaución y que la noche previa al encuentro con el enemigo ordené que salieran patrullas de jinetes para asegurarnos de que no nos atacarían al abrigo de la oscuridad. Enviamos jinetes hacia el norte, el sur, el este y el oeste. Las cuatro patrullas fueron atacadas. Fue entonces cuando empecé a intuir el nivel de mi torpeza: sin tener un claro conocimiento del territorio, me había adentrado demasiado en el desierto, sin asegurar posiciones de fuerza en retaguardia, de modo que nos vimos rodeados con una rapidez inesperada.

Fédimo detuvo un instante la lectura para tomar aliento. Volvió a observar de reojo a los presentes: los hombres de confianza del César miraban al suelo; el emperador, por su parte, había cerrado directamente los ojos. El secretario siguió leyendo.

Los nabateos cuentan con un importante contingente de jinetes que usan camellos para sus veloces desplazamientos. Los camellos, además, resisten mejor que los caballos la falta de agua y pueden ser tan veloces como éstos. Estos jinetes eran los que habían atacado las patrullas y los que luego nos habían rodeado. Al amanecer ya era tarde para un repliegue sin iniciar una confrontación en toda regla. Opté entonces por algo que sé que no es de grato recuerdo para nadie, pero al verme rodeado por enemigos que podían sobrevenirnos por cualquier flanco, o por vanguar-

dia o por retaguardia, no encontré alternativa mejor, pese a la cara de temor de mis oficiales, que ordenar que las legiones a mi mando formaran un cuadrado.

—¡Maldita sea! —interrumpió Lucio Quieto—. ¡Por Júpiter, otro cuadrado en el desierto, de nuevo, otro no...!

—Deja que termine de leer la carta —intervino Trajano con el tono gélido de su habitual serenidad en tiempos de crisis, como cuando Decébalo contraatacó en la primera campaña dacia y Trajano buscó la forma de rehacerse con el mando de la guerra—. Que lea la maldita carta y luego hablaremos sobre qué debe hacerse.

El César miró de nuevo a Fédimo. Éste, muy rápidamente, reinició la lectura de aquella misiva.

Sí, César, ahondando en mi torpeza ordené la formación de un cuadrado, cuando quizá debería haber optado por un repliegue hacia el oeste luchando contra cualquier cosa que nos fuéramos a encontrar. En ese momento, los nabateos enviaron emisarios y salí a entrevistarme con ellos. Sé que con eso repetía posibles errores, pero pensé que ya en poco podía empeorar nuestra situación. Por todos los dioses que estaba dispuesto a morir en el empeño por no desmerecer la confianza del emperador, pero también estaba en mi ánimo intentar salvar las dos legiones que el César había puesto bajo mi mando y que son una fuerza importante del Imperio, que no conviene malgastar en manos torpes como las mías. El líder de los emisarios nabateos tenía por nombre Aretas y se identificó como el jefe de la guardia de Petra bajo el mando del nuevo rey Obodas. Este emisario planteó como única forma de evitar la batalla una rendición pactada.

—¡No puedo creer que Palma haya aceptado rendir dos legiones a los nabateos! —intervino ahora Nigrino indignado—. Puede que Palma sea más o menos capaz militarmente, pero no lo veo con ánimo de aceptar una rendición humillante de ese tipo. ¡Por Júpiter, eso no lo creo...!

—Quizá acordó una rendición parcial... —apuntó Celso.

—¡Callad los dos! —exclamó Trajano poniéndose un instante en pie.

Se hizo el silencio.

El emperador tomó asiento lentamente. Fédimo no necesitó ni que lo miraran. Siguió con la lectura de aquella misiva de inmediato.

Enseguida asumí que se trataba de nuestra rendición, y ya había ordenado al tribuno Severo que se preparara todo para morir luchando o conseguir la victoria, pero, oh César, aquí me rindo ante el poder del emperador Marco Ulpio Trajano, pues he de confesar que no he sido consciente de bajo las órdenes de quién estoy actuando hasta haber escuchado a aquel emisario nabateo. Intentaré transmitir con precisión las palabras de aquel líder enemigo.

Aretas dijo que el rey Obodas era valiente y estaba dispuesto a morir como sus antepasados en la defensa de la independencia de su reino, pero que el mismo rey Obodas sabía perfectamente que el emperador Trajano no era como los seleúcidas de antaño, sino inmensamente más poderoso. Aretas dijo que el rey Obodas se sentía lo suficientemente fuerte como para derrotarme, a mí y a las dos legiones bajo mi mando, pero que el mismo rey Obodas era consciente de que cuando la determinación del emperador Trajano se pone en marcha ésta ya no se detiene nunca. Obodas, continuó su emisario, era de la opinión de que una vez el emperador Trajano se ha decidido a apropiarse de los territorios de Arabia, nada podrá ya detener al César de Roma. Pero el rey nabateo pensaba también que el emperador Trajano era hombre de nobleza y de quien se podía ser amigo y no sólo enemigo, y por eso estaba dispuesto a proponer una rendición de las tropas nabateas y no atacar a mis legiones, y también estaba dispuesto a rendir Arabia, admitiendo su transformación en provincia romana, si con ello obtenía del emperador la promesa de que los bienes, las costumbres y las creencias de sus súbditos serían respetados por Roma. Cuando escuché todo esto, volví a dirigirme al tribuno Severo para que no se diera la orden de ataque. Llegados a este punto quería oír bien todo lo que el emisario nabateo tenía que decirme.

Fédimo volvió a detenerse. Observó que los tres hombres de confianza del César y también el propio Trajano escuchaban con la boca abierta. Siguió leyendo.

El rey Obodas era de la opinión, según su emisario, de que con un pacto en estos términos, Arabia podría seguir siendo un lugar próspero para todos, donde Roma se beneficiaría del control de esa parte de la ruta comercial con Oriente, pero donde los nabateos podrían también seguir

viviendo en un mismo grado de libertad. Aceptaba pactar unos impues-
tos a Roma que habría que negociar en la confianza de que el César se
mostraría generoso por la predisposición del rey a aquel pacto.

La alternativa, según dijo el emisario, sería que el rey Obodas ani-
quilaría primero las dos legiones a mi mando y luego seguramente pere-
cería combatiendo contra otra fuerza mucho mayor de legiones que Tra-
jano enviaría, como hizo con la Dacia más allá del Danubio; pero no sin
antes haber causado un enorme daño a la fuerza militar de Roma. Un
pacto podía ahorrar sufrimientos a ambas partes. Es aquí donde yo deci-
dí, no sé si excediéndome en mi imperium, *aceptar estas condiciones si*
era el rey quien personalmente me ofrecía este acuerdo. No pasaron ni dos
días cuando tuve delante de mí al propio rey certificando todo lo expresa-
do por sus emisarios. Convine entonces que intercedería ante el César
para que este pacto se aceptara y se certificara en términos razonables
para Arabia en nuestro Senado.

Y es así como doy término a la campaña encomendada por el empe-
rador a mi persona. No es el final que yo habría imaginado nunca, pero
es un desenlace que creo que puede ser óptimo para los intereses de Roma.
No obstante, sólo el emperador sabrá dilucidar si en efecto es así o si, por
el contrario, he obrado incorrectamente y merezco castigo. La región está
en paz. Mis legiones permanecen acantonadas en las proximidades de
Petra. Los nabateos nos vigilan, pero hemos acordado que no habrá ata-
ques ni de unos ni de otros a la espera de recibir respuesta a esta carta.
El rey Obodas me ha ofrecido en varias ocasiones que acuda a su palacio
para agasajarme, pero he declinado estas invitaciones a la espera de co-
nocer el parecer de mi emperador sobre estas negociaciones.

Cornelio Palma
legatus de las legiones desplazadas a Arabia

—Aquí termina la carta, César —dijo Fédimo.

Ni Trajano ni ninguno de los otros hombres decían nada.

El joven secretario se acercó a la mesa, dejó la carta allí desplegada, con cuidado, y se retiró de regreso a su esquina.

—Palma ha conseguido la anexión de Arabia sin perder ni un hombre —dijo al fin Celso.

—No, no es así —interpuso Nigrino—. El miedo que tienen a Trajano es lo que ha hecho que propongan ese pacto. Aunque Palma ha gestionado bien la situación.

El emperador miró a Quieto.

—¿Qué piensas tú de todo esto, Lucio?

—Pienso que si el emperador Trajano es capaz de subyugar una región como Arabia sólo con el miedo que todos le tienen, ¿qué podría conquistar Trajano si decide, en efecto, ponerse de nuevo personalmente al mando de un gran ejército y avanzar hacia Oriente?

Todos callaron durante un rato hasta que el propio emperador decidió dar respuesta a la pregunta.

—No lo sé, Quieto, pero quizá es aún prematuro para averiguarlo. Por de pronto, escribiremos a Palma diciendo que aceptamos los términos del pacto y confirmamos que seremos generosos con los nabateos. —Trajano se reclinó en el respaldo de su *cathedra* y juntó las yemas de los dedos de las manos—. Igual que otros reinos han aprendido mi manera de reaccionar cuando me traicionan, como hizo Decébalo, es importante que demos ejemplo con Arabia de lo generosos que podemos ser con los que aceptan el poder de Roma sin ofrecer resistencia —y miró a Nigrino y a Celso—. Cuento con vosotros para que esto sea refrendado en el Senado.

Ambos asintieron con seguridad.

21

EL SILBIDO DE LA MUERTE

Ciento cincuenta millas al norte de Cumidava
Territorio no controlado por Roma
108 d. C.

Marcio estaba más allá de las fronteras de la nueva provincia romana de la Dacia. Había partido de Cumidava, una de las colonias más septentrionales de todo el Imperio, y se había adentrado en los bosques que las patrullas legionarias sólo osaban pisar en caso de emergencia. De natural, las tropas romanas se limitaban a asegurarse de que ningún bárbaro, dacio, sármata, roxolano o de cualquier otra tribu se atreviera a avanzar hacia el sur.

—Es un territorio peligroso. —Eso le habían dicho los oficiales del último puesto de guardia, pero ante su salvoconducto y las órdenes del gobernador Tercio Juliano se encogieron de hombros. Si aquel hombre quería morir quiénes eran ellos para impedírselo a alguien que tenía el permiso del emperador, confirmado por el gobernador, para ir a donde quisiera.

De aquello hacía meses. Marcio se había cruzado, en efecto, con pequeños grupos de dacios, pero no con sármatas. Intercambió algo de oro por información con unos jinetes que, estaba seguro, pensaron en robarle todo lo que llevaba, pero que ante su mirada indómita, fuera porque le tuvieron miedo o porque no tenían ganas de luchar, lo dejaron en paz y hasta le indicaron en qué dirección podría encontrar sármatas que no se habían rendido a Roma. Pero llevaba semanas en aquella zona y no había encontrado rastro de los sármatas libres, sólo algunos poblados deshabitados desde la guerra.

Marcio empezó a pensar en abandonar la búsqueda de

Alana y Tamura. O quizá debía intentarlo de otra forma. Pero ¿cómo?

Se detuvo en un remanso de un río. Su caballo tenía sed. Él también.

Dejó que el animal se saciara primero mientras miraba a su alrededor.

No se veía el más mínimo movimiento ni de personas ni de animales.

Se arrodilló para beber con más comodidad.

Hundió una mano en el agua fresca del riachuelo mientras que con la otra mantenía bien cogidas las riendas del caballo.

Demasiado silencio.

Bebía despacio atento al bosque que lo rodeaba.

Era extraño que no se oyera ni el canto de un pájaro.

Su instinto guerrero le hizo ponerse en guardia, pero ¿ante qué?, ¿contra qué? Fue entonces cuando oyó el silbido inconfundible de la muerte.

—¡Agh! —No tuvo tiempo de esquivar la flecha.

En los bosques más allá de la Dacia

La mujer caminaba con cuidado de no pisar ramas que pudieran hacer ruido. La niña que iba por delante de ella, como un perro de presa, también hollaba la tierra con tiento. Nadie tenía que decirle a la pequeña qué debía hacer. Lo llevaba en la sangre. De pronto, la niña se detuvo y señaló hacia un punto no muy lejano, justo donde el río del que se nutrían regularmente para saciar la sed, hacía un remanso. Era un buen lugar para cazar, pues muchos animales se acercaban allí para abrevar. Sólo que ahora no se trataba de un animal, sino de un jinete que acababa de desmontar.

Las dos lo vieron arrodillarse y llevarse agua a la boca con una mano.

La niña cogió una flecha y la dispuso con presteza en el arco.

Tensó la cuerda.

Más.

Más aún.

Cuanto más tensa mejor se apuntaba. Había que tirar de la cuerda del arco hasta que te dolieran los dedos. Sólo entonces la pequeña estaba segura de no fallar.

La mujer que estaba su lado no tenía la vista de antaño y había delegado en la niña el lanzamiento de flechas, pero desenfundó muy lentamente, sin hacer ruido, su espada sármata, aunque sabía que no tendría que utilizarla. La niña no erraba nunca. Quizá no tenían por qué actuar así, pero solas en medio de aquellos bosques, preguntar y luego defenderse era inseguro; matar y no hacer pregunta alguna era totalmente seguro. Las dos habían sufrido mucho y no estaban para dudas ni vacilaciones. Súbitamente, la mujer tuvo un destello de intuición y fue a decir algo, fue a pronunciar aquellas palabras...

—No dispares...

Pero la niña acababa de soltar la cuerda del arco.

En el remanso del río, unos instantes después

—¿Dónde... es... tá...? —dijo Marcio y luego gritó cuando Alana le extrajo la flecha—. ¡Por Némesis y todos los dioses!

—Está escondida —respondió la mujer arrojando la flecha a un lado—. Está asustada por lo que ha hecho.

—No le voy a... hacer nada... pero... —continuó Marcio con esfuerzo—. ¡Sólo me han herido dos veces con una flecha y las dos veces ha tenido que ser... mi hija!

—Es una guerrera, ya lo sabes —dijo Alana y sonrió—. Además ha sido sólo en la parte baja de la pierna. No sangra demasiado. Te curarás.

—Ya sé que me curaré, pero duele, como duelen todas las malditas heridas —continuó Marcio—. Menos mal que ha fallado.

Alana se levantó y lo miró fijamente.

—No ha fallado —precisó—, no lo hace nunca. Pero pude empujarla en el último momento, cuando ya había soltado la cuerda del arco, y por eso sólo te ha herido en la pierna. Ella siempre apunta al cuello, así no se puede gritar y dar la voz de alarma —y se volvió hacia el bosque—. ¡Tamura, ven!

Una niña de ocho años apareció entre los arbustos.

—¡Ven! —insistió su madre—. ¡Le duele, pero no te va hacer daño! Nunca lo haría.

La niña se acercó lentamente.

—Ven acá —dijo Marcio y la abrazó con fuerza cuando estuvo cerca de él. La niña se puso a llorar.

Por la noche

Se oía el agua del río y se veían las estrellas del cielo.

La niña dormía.

Alana había hecho un fuego.

—¿Es seguro? —preguntó él.

—Los romanos nunca se adentran en estos bosques de noche —respondió Alana—. Sólo los locos como tú —dijo sonriendo—. Los dacios libres, por el momento, se mantienen más al norte, igual que los roxolanos.

—Yo me crucé con dacios.

—Sería hace tiempo.

—Sí —confirmó Marcio.

—Nosotras también los vimos, pero se han ido.

Pasó un rato en el que nadie dijo nada.

—En Roma el emperador me ofrece protección para los tres —dijo Marcio al fin.

—Quizá sea buena idea —admitió ella—. Aquí es Tamura la que caza. Ella no se da cuenta aún, pero como mi vista no es la de antes, le dejo que sea ella la que mate a los animales de los que hemos vivido. Creo que aún piensa que lo hago para que siga entrenándose, pero no es por eso. Más tarde o más temprano moriré, moriremos los dos, Marcio. Sé que ella podrá sobrevivir aquí sola un tiempo, pero en cualquier momento la pueden atrapar los dacios. Y están sin control. De nuestra gente sármata no queda nadie. Nuestro mundo ha desaparecido.

—¿Por qué no habéis ido más al norte, con otros sármatas? —preguntó él.

—Las cosas también están mal allí. Las tribus germanas nos atacan y no podemos ir al sur porque lo controlan los romanos. Y hacia Oriente están los roxolanos y los escitas. Estoy segura de que me matarían, y a ella, con suerte, la esclavizarían, o algo peor. Ella no querrá yacer con un hombre si no es por su propia voluntad y eso la conduce a la muerte en estas tierras. Si el emperador te ofrece protección para los tres, quizá sea la mejor opción. No me gusta Roma, pero no siempre podemos hacer lo que nos gusta.

Marcio estaba confuso. Había pensado que Alana no querría abandonar nunca los bosques del norte, pero ahora veía que regresar al sur, al Imperio romano, podía ser un plan que ella estaba dispuesta a aceptar.

—Lo que me preocupa de Roma es que Tamura... —continuó Alana señalando a la niña dormida junto al fuego—. Ella es... una guerrera de los bosques. No sé cómo sobrellevará vivir allí.

Se hizo otro silencio. La leña crepitaba en la hoguera. Marcio se llevó una mano a la herida.

—¿Te sigue doliendo? —preguntó ella.

—Bastante, pero como dijiste, me repondré, aunque cada vez me cuesta más recuperarme. Yo también me he hecho viejo. Si el emperador no me hubiera liberado no creo que hubiera podido sobrevivir mucho más en la arena del Anfiteatro Flavio.

—Pero te liberó —dijo ella.

—Sí.

—Y te ofreció protección.

—Sí.

—Será a cambio de algo.

—Sí.

—¿A cambio de qué?

—Dijo que un día me daría una misión y que esperaba lealtad por mi parte, en agradecimiento por haberme dejado recuperaros —se explicó él.

—¿Y qué harás cuando el emperador te dé esa misión?

—Cumplirla. He dado mi palabra.

—¿Nos separarán de nuevo? —preguntó Alana.

—No —respondió Marcio categórico—. Sea lo que sea que me pida el César, lo haremos juntos. Ya solo nos separará la muerte. Eso te lo prometo.

22

LA VIEJA CIUDAD

Ch'ang-an, antigua capital del Imperio han, China
Tercer año del reinado del emperador An-ti
108 d. C.

Eran muchos *li* los que había que recorrer entre Loyang y Ch'ang-an.

Li Kan no se demoró, pero aun así tuvo que pernoctar en varias ocasiones en las diferentes postas del camino imperial que unía la nueva capital con la vetusta ciudad, antiguo centro del poder han. En cualquier caso, llegó a la gran urbe en pocas jornadas, pues la carta del asistente del ministro de Obras Públicas de la emperatriz parecía abrirle las mejores habitaciones en las hospederías militares a lo largo de la ruta y otorgarle el derecho a recibir siempre el mejor caballo disponible. Para Li Kan resultaba evidente que aquel asistente contaba con mucha confianza no sólo de los ministros sino de la propia emperatriz Deng. Lo que no terminaba de entender bien era aquel aviso final de Fan Chun con relación al hombre que debía encontrar en Ch'ang-an. «No es de fiar», había dicho el asistente, pero lo que había leído Li Kan en el informe que se le proporcionó sobre Kan Ying no resultaba amenazador: en tiempos del anterior emperador, el fallecido He, quien fue marido de la actual emperatriz viuda, se le encomendó a Ying alguna misión de relevancia que, al parecer, había satisfecho correctamente. Desde entonces se le había emplazado en la vieja capital como funcionario en el Palacio Kuei, desde donde trabajaba gestionando parte de los suministros de los grandes mercados de la ciudad.

Hasta ahí todo bien.

El problema era que se le habían enviado varias misivas para que se presentara en Loyang a las que Ying, sencillamente, no había respondido, aunque había constancia de que seguía haciendo su trabajo en Ch'ang-an por los informes recabados por Fan Chun a altos funcionarios de la vieja capital. ¿Por qué ignoraba Kan Ying las cartas y las instrucciones que se le enviaban desde Loyang? Li Kan se encogió de hombros. Eso no era asunto suyo. Él sólo debía ocuparse de su misión: llevar a aquel escurridizo funcionario a la nueva capital.

Sus reflexiones lo acompañaron hasta que las gigantescas murallas de Ch'ang-an aparecieron ante sus ojos. Eran imponentes, incluso para alguien como él que estaba acostumbrado a las inmensas fortificaciones de la Gran Muralla. Y es que los muros de la vieja capital han eran enormes, y pese a que habían sido construidos por más de ciento cincuenta mil obreros hacía ya decenios, seguían en buen estado de conservación gracias a las numerosas reparaciones. Aunque estaba el ejército del norte y la Gran Muralla, el temor a una incursión de los *hsiung-nu* permanecía en aquella urbe y las fortificaciones no se habían descuidado nunca.

Li Kan entró por la puerta Pa-ch'eng y cruzó entre los palacios Ming-Kuang y Ch'ang-lo. Giró entonces hacia el sur, siempre siguiendo las indicaciones que se le habían proporcionado en Loyang por escrito, y llegó al centro mismo de la urbe más grande del imperio. Allí encontró la armería central de la ciudad. Tomó entonces una calle que lo conduciría entre el Palacio Wei-Yang y el Palacio Norte, para girar y llegar, por fin, al Palacio Kuei. Preguntó entonces por la oficina de gestión de los mercados y una vez allí preguntó por Kan Ying.

Todos lo miraban con respeto y temor.

Su aire marcial y su uniforme militar, junto con la carta de Loyang firmada por el asistente del ministro de Obras Públicas, infundían miedo entre los funcionarios. Todos intuían que su presencia indicaba que algo no andaba bien, pues la capital nueva no enviaba a un oficial militar en busca de alguien para darte una recompensa; eso se anunciaba por carta. La presencia de un oficial armado era signo de algo negativo.

—El oficial Li Kan puede esperar aquí, por favor —dijo un

funcionario inclinándose y desapareciendo tras un panel de madera. Li Kan podía escuchar la conversación en el interior.

—Te buscan —dijo la voz del funcionario que le había pedido que esperara.

—¿Quién es? —preguntó alguien en un tono irritado—. ¿No ves que estoy trabajando? Faltan verduras en los mercados. Habrá quejas y esto nos traerá problemas.

—Lo siento, pero se trata de un oficial armado venido desde Loyang y pregunta por ti.

Li Kan percibió un silencio tenso.

El joven guerrero han se preguntó si habría otra salida por la que aquel funcionario pudiera intentar escapar, pero cuando empezaba a inquietarse un hombre pequeño, delgado en extremo, con la faz preocupada pero sin llegar a mostrar temor como el resto de los otros funcionarios, salió y se inclinó ante él.

—Yo soy Kan Ying.

—Perfecto —respondió Li Kan—. Tengo órdenes de llevarte a Loyang. Has de acompañarme.

—Sí, claro —aceptó el funcionario—, pero desearía pasar primero por mi casa, coger algunas cosas, hablar con mi familia, despedirme.

Li Kan pensó que lo que planteaba el funcionario era razonable, pero la advertencia de Fan Chun estaba grabada en su mente como si la hubieran tallado en piedra: «No es de fiar».

—Lo siento, pero salimos inmediatamente de Ch'ang-an. Desde alguna de las postas de la ruta imperial podrás enviar una carta a tu familia. Que este hombre u otro funcionario les avise de tu partida...

—Pero necesito ropa... el viaje es largo... —contrapuso Kan Ying.

Li Kan sólo tenía en mente cumplir con su misión. Estaba ante alguien que había ignorado cartas imperiales, no ante quien podría considerarse un servidor ejemplar del imperio. El guerrero han se llevó la mano a la empuñadura de su espada.

No hizo falta más.

Kan Ying tragó saliva, se inclinó varias veces con rapidez y siguió al oficial sin oponer resistencia ni plantear ningún otro requerimiento, pero pese a su aparente sumisión había algo en su mirada que incomodaba a Li Kan.

En un par de horas estuvieron fuera de Ch'ang-an cabalgando en sendos caballos en dirección a Loyang. En la primera posta militar, tal y como había prometido Li Kan, permitió que su «escoltado» escribiera a su familia y remitió la carta junto con el correo imperial que acababa de llegar desde la capital.

Salieron temprano al día siguiente. Todo había sido fácil. Quizá Kan Ying había querido escurrir el bulto pero no había opuesto resistencia física alguna. De pronto, algo extraño ocurrió. Al girar un recodo del camino, apareció un grupo de hombres a pie sin uniforme militar. Aún estaban a cierta distancia como para oír lo que Li Kan o su escoltado pudieran decir. Los hombres iban armados con espadas de un filo y estacas. No llevaban armadura.

—Es muy raro —dijo Kan Ying—. No parecen soldados.

—Muy raro, sí —dijo Li Kan apretando las riendas de su caballo con ambas manos. El camino imperial, como todos los demás caminos importantes del Imperio han, era sólo de uso militar. Los campesinos, comerciantes o cualquier otro que transitara de una población a otra tenían que hacerlo por senderos que discurrían en paralelo a estas grandes rutas imperiales. Trasladarse por un camino militar sin permiso era un crimen, pero, sorprendentemente, tenían delante a una docena de hombres sin uniforme en medio del camino entre Ch'ang-an y Loyang.

Li Kan evaluó la situación con la velocidad del guerrero: los hombres estaban armados, pero no eran soldados, invadían la ruta imperial cometiendo un delito y no parecían preocupados por ello. Había habido muchos desastres naturales en los últimos meses. El hambre se había extendido por la región que atravesaban y como los *hsiung-nu* habían vuelto a atacar la Gran Muralla, muchas tropas habían sido enviadas desde el centro del imperio hacia el norte para asegurar la frontera. Faltaban soldados en la región y el hambre fuerza a la gente a emprender aventuras desesperadas. Li Kan habló a Kan Ying sin mirar atrás. No quería perder de vista a aquella docena de hombres.

—Son bandidos —dijo el guerrero han—. Yo me ocuparé de esto.

El guerrero han consideró diversas opciones con la serenidad de la experiencia militar de quien, aunque joven, lleva en combate toda su vida. Y no luchando contra cualquiera en algún remoto lugar, sino en el centro mismo de la Gran Muralla, contra los brutales jinetes *hsiung-nu*. Ahora tenía a doce hombres a pie. Habían cortado el camino con una especie de barricada formada por ramas de árboles donde sobresalían algunas estacas. El grupo se había apostado justo tras un recodo del camino imperial, de forma que podían sorprender a cualquier correo antes de que éste tuviera tiempo de reaccionar y retroceder en busca de refuerzos en alguna de las postas militares próximas que, por cierto, no estaban tan cercanas sino a muchos *li* de distancia unas de otras. Además era justo un paso estrecho excavado en la ladera de un monte: no se podía escalar hacia arriba, sino con mucha dificultad, y hacia el otro lado, a la derecha de Li Kan, había un gran precipicio. Los bandidos tenían bien pensada su estrategia.

Li Kan miró entonces un instante hacia atrás. Kan Ying estaba sudando profusamente sobre su montura. El guerrero han volvió a mirar hacia el frente. Detuvo su caballo y sintió cómo Kan Ying hacía lo propio. Lo razonable era dar media vuelta, pero de pronto se oyeron gritos a su espalda. Otra docena de bandidos había aparecido por la curva. Por eso se sentían valientes. Eran muchos. Li Kan no se puso nervioso. Su *chi tu-wei* y su propio padre le habían adiestrado bien: «Los nervios no valen de nada y menos ante la muerte», eso le habían dicho los dos siempre.

Li Kan se pasó el dorso de la mano derecha por la barbilla. Él también tenía la piel húmeda. Bueno: no todo se podía controlar. El sudor era peligroso, pero su espada tenía la empuñadura de madera reforzada con escamas y piel de pez raya para, precisamente, evitar que pudiera resbalarse en una circunstancia de tremenda tensión como un combate.

Los hombres se acercaban.

Sonreían.

Li Kan tragó saliva. No había tenido tiempo de observar bien a los bandidos que habían llegado por la espalda, pero con los de delante estaba seguro: no tenían ballestas. Disparar flechas requiere entrenamiento, práctica, disciplina; virtudes de las que carecían aquellos hombres. Si no había ballestas, tenían, al menos, una posibilidad.

Estaba considerando lanzarse al galope, pero el caballo no llevaba protecciones y lo herirían con facilidad. Los bandidos estaban ya muy cerca. Ya no sonreían: ahora se reían a grandes carcajadas. Li Kan hizo entonces algo inesperado: desmontó de su caballo.

—No te muevas —le dijo a Kan Ying.

Li Kan se separó un poco de su propio caballo hasta quedar a apenas cuatro o cinco pasos de distancia de sus oponentes.

Los bandidos iban a hablar. Habían dejado de reír al ver al guerrero imperial desmontar, pero las sonrisas seguían en sus rostros.

—Despejad el camino y retiraos —dijo Li Kan con serenidad helada.

Uno de los bandidos, el más alto, dio un paso al frente y volvió a sonreír abiertamente al tiempo que esgrimía una poderosa espada *dao* de un filo, con toda seguridad arrebatada a algún soldado desafortunado. Había habido informes de ataques a correos imperiales hacía unos meses, pero no recientemente. Eso, al menos, le habían dicho en la última posta militar. Las cosas estaban cambiando de nuevo.

—No veo que estés en situación de dar muchas órdenes —dijo el bandido que se había adelantado y se volvió hacia sus amigos riéndose; sin embargo la risa se vio rápidamente entrecortada porque vio que los otros ladrones de caminos no se reían, sino que daban un par de pasos hacia atrás con cara de asombro. Para cuando el líder de los bandidos quiso volverse su cabeza ya se había separado de su cuerpo y rodaba por el suelo con una estúpida mueca de incredulidad. El cuerpo del ladrón se derrumbó de golpe y empezó a teñir todo el camino con sangre espesa.

Li Kan blandía la espada *jian* de doble filo que acababa de desenfundar con la velocidad del rayo y avanzaba hacia el resto de los bandidos que retrocedían hacia la barricada. Un par de ellos intentaron abalanzarse sobre él, uno con una estaca y otro con un segundo sable *dao*. Li Kan arremetió primero contra el de la espada, por ser el que poseía el arma más peligrosa. El *dao* detuvo el golpe inicial de la espada *jian*, pero la acometida de Li Kan frenó el empuje del bandido, lo que le dio el tiempo suficiente para volverse y cortar como si de un bambú fino se tratara la estaca del otro bandido y, siguiendo el empuje de su ataque, conseguir que el filo de su *jian* se clavara lo suficiente en el cuello del ladrón como para cortarle la yugular. El bandido, herido de muerte, salió despavorido hacia un lado del camino, no se percató del precipicio y cayó al abismo. El forajido de la espada *dao* se había rehecho, pero Li Kan lo ignoró y siguió su avance hacia la barricada donde se habían situado los otros nueve bandidos blandiendo más estacas y, sólo uno de ellos, otra espada. Todos miraban con terror hacia el doble filo de su espada *jian* de acero, no de hierro, como las suyas, que silbaba en el aire al ser blandida con rapidez por Li Kan. Aquella arma, pese a su extensión, apenas pesaba nada, de forma que el guerrero han la esgrimía con gran agilidad y con la destreza de muchos combates a sus espaldas.

—¡Agggh!

Hirió a uno más de los bandidos y a otro y a otro. El resto se refugió muy pegado a la barricada. Entretanto, el bandido con la espada *dao* que había dejado a su espalda avanzaba hacia Kan Ying.

—¡Yo no tengo dinero! ¡No tengo nada! —dijo el viejo Ying—. ¡Es el guerrero han el que lo tiene todo! ¡A mí me lleva preso! ¡Matadlo y me uniré a vosotros y os diré dónde hay más monedas de las que hayáis podido imaginar!

Li Kan se volvió.

«No es hombre de fiar», eso le había dicho el asistente del ministro de Obras Públicas. Parece que llevaba razón. Bien. Que Kan Ying negociara sobre su vida le dejaba las manos libres para seguir atacando al resto de los bandidos que permanecían en la barricada. Porque si había algo que Li Kan había decidido era matar a todos los que pudiera. No eran luchadores. Eran pobres miserables, pero se habían atrevido a atacar a un guerrero han del emperador. El orden debía permanecer o no tendrían nada. Destrozó varias estacas y desarmó al de la espada *dao*. El filo de la *jian* rebañó dos brazos enteros, un muslo y dos cabezas más rodaron por el suelo. Los bandidos supervivientes escalaron la barricada que ellos mismos habían levantado y salieron huyendo a toda velocidad, dejando algunos de ellos largos regueros de sangre.

Li Kan volvió sobre sus pasos. Kan Ying estaba en el caballo. Seguía negociando por su vida.

—¡Sólo tenéis que matarlo y tendréis muchas monedas!

El bandido que blandía la última espada *dao* que les quedaba miró a Kan Ying y luego a Li Kan y finalmente al otro grupo de ladrones que habían aparecido por el otro lado del camino y que, atemorizados por la ferocidad del guerrero han, permanecían inmóviles, sin saber bien qué hacer.

Li Kan avanzaba hacia el bandido sin el más mínimo atisbo de pensar en detenerse o tomarse un respiro. De hecho, el soldado han se estaba sintiendo particularmente cómodo. Había temido que hubiera alguien que sí supiera manejar una espada pero aquellos hombres sólo habían tenido éxito a base de dar miedo. En la lucha no valían nada. Ni siquiera sabían usar los pocos sables que habían sustraído a reclutas inexpertos. El bandido soltó su espada *dao*, que hizo un sonoro clang al caer al suelo de grava triturada y prensada del camino imperial, y echó a correr en dirección al otro grupo de ladrones. Todos desaparecieron por la curva como la tormenta de verano que se desvanece y da espacio al sol con enorme rapidez.

Li Kan cogió la espada *dao* y la introdujo en una de las alforjas que llevaba su montura. Luego miró a Kan Ying con rabia.

—¡Sólo he dicho lo que he dicho para que tuvieras tiempo de luchar mientras este otro grupo estaba distraído conmigo! —exclamó con rapidez el viejo funcionario, pero no observó que estuviera resultando demasiado convincente así que sumó más palabras a sus dudosos argumentos—. Recuerda que has de llevarme vivo a Loyang.

Eso era cierto.

Li Kan llegó junto al funcionario y tiró de él para derribarlo del caballo. Luego, una vez que Kan Ying estuvo sobre la grava del camino, le propinó tres puntapiés en el vientre y uno en la cara. El viejo funcionario empezó a sangrar. Tenía un labio partido. Li Kan se contuvo al fin, se tragó el resto de la rabia, no toda, pero sí una parte sustancial y retornó a la barricada. A su espalda el viejo funcionario gimoteaba encogido en posición fetal. Li Kan se enfundó su espada *jian* y con ambos brazos deshizo parte de la barricada hasta dejar un espacio suficiente para que los caballos, uno detrás de otro, pudieran cruzarla. Ya informaría en la próxima posta militar y mandarían una patrulla para solucionar lo de la barricada y, sobre todo, para castigar como se merecían a los bandidos que habían huido. A continuación regresó junto a Kan Ying, que seguía hecho un ovillo en el suelo sin atreverse a moverse, dolorido y aterrado. El guerrero han se agachó para hablarle.

—Vivo, sí. Te entregaré vivo en Loyang, pero con cuánta sangre dentro o fuera de tu cuerpo es cosa tuya —le advirtió en un susurro—. No vuelvas a intentar nada de aquí hasta nuestro destino o sufrirás como no has sufrido en tu vida.

Lo cogió entonces por debajo de los hombros y lo incorporó hasta conseguir que volviera a montar sobre el caballo. Li Kan retornó seguidamente junto a su propia montura, se subió con agilidad sobre el animal y tiró de las riendas. Kan Ying lo siguió abrazado al cuello de su caballo para no caerse. Aún sangraba profusamente. Se alejaron al paso del lugar. Detrás dejaban varios bandidos decapitados y unos cuantos miembros amputados en diferentes charcos de sangre.

KANISHKA

**Bagram, norte de la India, capital del Imperio kushan
109 d. C.**

El consejero Shaka miraba a su alrededor con la sensación de que, por primera vez en mucho tiempo, no tenía controlada la situación. El viejo Vima Kadphises, el emperador kushan a quien había servido durante años y que lo había enviado a parlamentar con el César Trajano en Roma, estaba enfermo. Unas fiebres lo habían debilitado enormemente meses atrás, durante su larga ausencia en el Imperio romano, y ahora no se le permitía hablar con él. Esto es: Kanishka, el hijo de Kadphises y con toda seguridad el futuro líder del Imperio kushan de Asia Central, no dejaba que nadie que no fuera él mismo accediera al anciano emperador. Shaka lo tenía muy claro: desde su marcha a Roma las cosas habían cambiado y el poder, quizá no nominalmente aún, pero sí de forma efectiva, había pasado de manos. ¿Qué significaría eso con respecto a él? Difícil saberlo.

Las puertas del gran salón del palacio de Bagram se abrieron y el joven Kanishka entró con paso decidido hasta detenerse junto al trono de su padre, ahora vacío por la enfermedad. No había guardias. Kanishka era joven y fuerte e iba armado con espada y daga en la cintura. Un hombre de acción. Shaka comprendió que el joven hijo del emperador Kadphises no lo temía pero, quizá... ¿necesitaría aún los consejos de un viejo pero experimentado consejero?

—Sé que has solicitado ver a mi padre —empezó Kanishka apoyando una de sus manos en el reposabrazos del trono kushan—, pero ya sabes que está muy débil.

—Rezo por la recuperación de mi señor Kadphises —respondió Shaka a la vez que se inclinaba a modo de reverencia.

—Yo también, pero los médicos creen que esta vez las plegarias pueden no ser suficientes. Pero no te he hecho llamar para debatir sobre la salud de mi padre, sino sobre la misión que te encomendó. ¿La cumpliste?

Shaka meditó unos instantes antes de responder.

—En gran medida sí, mi señor —dijo el viejo consejero.

—Eso no es una respuesta sino una evasiva, Shaka. Mi padre siempre te consideró alguien inteligente. ¿Te parezco yo hombre que acepta respuestas como la que me acabas de dar? —dijo Kanishka y se quedó quieto, justo detrás del trono, con ambas manos puestas sobre el respaldo.

—No, mi señor —añadió Shaka y siguió hablando con rapidez—. He cumplido fielmente la parte de saludar al emperador romano Trajano y transmitirle el mensaje de amistad del Imperio kushan. De igual forma he cumplido con la orden de proponerle al César romano que se lance contra nuestros incómodos vecinos partos, al tiempo que nosotros generamos problemas en la frontera parta oriental para facilitarles el avance. Sin embargo, tengo la sensación de que el emperador romano es muy cauto y pese a sus recientes victorias en la Dacia y en Arabia aún duda sobre la conveniencia de cruzar el Éufrates con sus legiones. Siguen teniendo miedo a aquella legión perdida, la que sus antepasados perdieron en los confines del Imperio parto y de la que ya nunca supieron nada. O muy poco. Sólo relatos extraños que no hacen sino incrementar su temor.

—Pero ese Trajano es poderoso, ¿cierto?

—Sin duda, mi señor. De eso no cabe duda: he visto su palacio imperial en Roma, y he asistido a carreras en el estadio que llaman Circo Máximo, el mayor hipódromo del mundo, con capacidad para más de doscientos cincuenta mil espectadores. Tiene además un enorme anfiteatro en donde miles de personas pueden ver combates de luchadores llegados de todo el mundo o cacerías de fieras llevados de todos los rincones de su inmenso imperio. Y luego, al regresar, se me permitió hacerlo pasando por sus nuevas posesiones en el Danubio, el río más caudaloso que he visto nunca. Allí Trajano ha hecho construir un puente tan largo que parece obra de dioses. Si mi señor Kanishka pregunta si el César Trajano es poderoso, la respuesta es que sí, enormemente.

El joven hijo de Kadphises, aún con sus manos apoyadas en el respaldo del trono de los kushan, miraba al suelo en silencio. Luego dirigió sus ojos de nuevo hacia el consejero de su padre.

—Y sin embargo —añadió Kanishka—, pese a todo ese poder, dices que no está decidido a atacar Partia, aun sabiendo que puede contar con nuestro apoyo.

—Aun así lo medita con mucho tiento, sí, mi señor.

—Eso no tiene sentido. Sus conquistas, sus victorias no parecen las de un cobarde. ¿Qué hay al otro lado del Éufrates que teme tanto ese emperador romano? —insistió Kanishka.

—La legión perdida a la que me he referido antes, mi señor —respondió entonces Shaka con voz solemne y observó que Kanishka lo miraba intrigado. El joven hijo de Kadphises despegó sus manos del respaldo del trono, lo rodeó y se sentó en él. Con aquel gesto todo estaba dicho con relación a quién mandaba en el Imperio kushan. Shaka sabía que sólo le quedaba mostrarse realmente útil. De lo contrario pronto pasaría a resultar prescindible, y de ser prescindible en una corte imperial a ser condenado por algún motivo real o inventado hay poco camino que recorrer.

—¿No conoce mi señor la historia de la legión perdida? —preguntó Shaka.

—No, pero tú me la vas a contar.

—Sí, mi señor. —Shaka refirió con rapidez lo que sabía del ejército que el cónsul romano Craso envió contra Partia y cómo aquellas tropas fueron brutalmente derrotadas por los partos, cómo apresaron además a diez mil de aquellos legionarios y cómo su rastro se perdió en el horizonte del tiempo.

—¿Y no se sabe qué paso con aquellos prisioneros?

—No —confirmó Shaka—. Los kushan aún no gobernaban en esta región y no tenemos datos sobre estos detalles de las guerras pasadas entre partos y romanos. Sólo sé que luego otro general romano, un tal Marco Antonio, también intentó invadir Partia y fracasó de nuevo. Los romanos, desde entonces, sólo han conseguido algunas victorias parciales sobre los partos, pero nunca se han atrevido a lanzarse en bloque contra su imperio. La historia de la legión perdida, sea cierta o falsa, de eso no estoy seguro, está en la mente de todos los romanos, ya sean legionarios o senadores, y el César Trajano lo sabe. Eso lo detiene, mi señor.

—¿Un hombre poderoso y decenas de miles de soldados frenados por una vieja batalla, por una derrota del pasado? —preguntó Kanishka incrédulo enarcando las cejas.

—Quizá el César Trajano se decida en algún momento y, pese a esos temores que atenazan a los romanos, termine atacando Partia —aventuró Shaka con tono esperanzado—, aunque... no lo veo probable a corto plazo —matizó.

—Sí, es posible que actúe... —admitió Kanishka—, pero entretanto nuestros enemigos siguen activos. ¿Le comentaste al César Trajano lo de Aryazate?

—Sí, mi señor.

—¿Le dijiste que si Osroes casa a su hija con Vologases y los partos sellan la paz entre ellos serán tan fuertes que no se conformarán ya con su territorio, que querrán más?

—Pongo a la diosa de la verdad Asha como testigo de que así lo hice.

Kanishka lo miró nuevamente un rato sin decir nada.

—Hemos de reevaluar en quién creemos y en quién no —empezó el hijo de Kadphises desde el trono con tono solemne—. Has de saber que he dado orden de que se reúna un nuevo concilio, el cuarto será, de todos los budistas. Ésa es la religión que debemos seguir todos ahora.

Shaka tragó saliva antes de volver a hablar.

—Me parece una sabia decisión de mi señor.

—Ha sido decisión de mi padre. Ha convocado ese gran concilio porque quiere que se recopilen todos los libros que hablan de Buda y que recuperen los textos más relevantes para que se difundan por todo el mundo. Y yo creo que es buena idea.

—Buda es el camino. Pido perdón por mi alusión a creencias antiguas.

Se hizo un nuevo silencio.

—Entonces pese a que le dijiste lo de Aryazate, ¿el César Trajano no parecía decidirse a actuar? —dijo Kanishka volviendo sobre el punto anterior.

—Dijo que lo tendría en cuenta —respondió Shaka aliviado de que se abandonara el asunto de su desliz al referirse a una antigua diosa.

—Pero no crees que actúe, al menos, pronto.

—No, no lo creo, mi señor.

—Y todo por esa legión perdida... por un fantasma... Entonces tendremos que actuar nosotros —afirmó Kanishka con rotundidad.

—¿Qué sugiere mi señor? ¿Atacar a los partos?

Kanishka sonrió. Se levantó y bajó del trono. Dio unos pasos y se situó delante del viejo consejero. Le habló en voz baja.

—No me está permitido aún tomar decisiones. Formalmente es mi padre quien decide todavía las cosas, pero pronto eso cambiará. Por eso te lo advierto ahora, para que tengas tiempo de reflexionar y dar con algún plan que satisfaga mis deseos.

—¿En qué podría ayudar yo a mi señor Kanishka?

El hijo de Kadphises siguió hablando en voz aún más baja.

—Atacar es una opción, pero antes de arriesgar la vida de miles de hombres, prefiero que se intente impedir la reconciliación entre Osroes y Vologases eliminando sólo una vida. Es menos... esfuerzo.

—No entiendo, mi señor. ¿A quién tendríamos que matar para impedir ese plan de Osroes?

Kanishka se acercó aún más y le habló al oído.

—Si matamos a Aryazate, el tema de la reconciliación se dificulta.

—Pero hay otras hijas de Osroes.

—Ninguna de tan alto linaje. Ninguna que pudiera aceptar Vologases.

—¿Ordena entonces mi señor Kanishka que busque la forma de asesinar a la princesa Aryazate de los partos?

Kanishka se alejó entonces de Shaka y volvió a hablar en voz alta mientras caminaba hacia la puerta principal de la sala.

—Te he dicho que no estoy en posición de dar órdenes

aún, consejero. Pero mi padre siempre pensó que eras inteligente.

Y el joven Kanishka salió por la puerta de la sala del trono del palacio kushan de Bagram. El viejo consejero Shaka se quedó solo, mirando a un trono vacío que pronto tendría dueño.

24

LA BATALLA NAVAL

Imperio romano
Sobre el agua
11 de noviembre de 109 d. C.

—¡Remad, remad, remad! —Arrio se desgañitaba dando las órdenes. Iba de un lado a otro de cubierta como trastornado, pero sus hombres, por fin, parecían haber entendido que se la jugaban a una sola apuesta. Si fallaban morirían todos.

—¡Si nos acercamos tanto nos acribillarán con sus flechas! —contrapuso uno de los marineros ante la sorpresa del resto.

—¡Aquí no hay flechas que valgan, imbécil! —rebatió Arrio con rabia ante aquel estúpido comentario—. ¿Te has olvidado acaso de dónde estamos? ¿Cómo van a disponer de arcos aquí? ¡Puede que nos arrojen otras cosas desde el barco, pero nada puede ser peor que dejarlos virar! ¡Si los dejamos girar terminarán embistiéndonos con su espolón, nos abordarán y será el final! ¡Por lo menos nos doblan en número! —insistió Arrio y luego volvió a dirigirse a todos los remeros—. ¡Remad más rápido, por Marte!

La velocidad era su única arma. El *trirreme* contra el que combatían era más grande y más fuerte, con muchos más marineros y más pesado, pero también más lento en sus maniobras. El enfrentamiento tenía lugar en un angosto espacio de no más de 300 pies[16] de ancho, lo que dificultaba las maniobras. Cualquier error y podrían chocar contra las paredes de roca donde se estrellaba el agua agitada por los barcos. La pequeña nave de Arrio, una *liburna birreme*, más pequeña y li-

16. Un pie romano equivalía aproximadamente a 0,3 metros.

gera, alcanzó con rapidez el *trirreme* que, con mucha lentitud, había estado intentando virar para embestirlos lateralmente.

—¡Ya estamos ahí, ya los tenemos! —siguió gritando Arrio—. ¡Marineros, escudos en alto! ¡Remeros, remad! ¡Piloto, más cerca de ellos, más cerca! ¡Quiero todos sus remos en una pasada, todos, que no quede ni uno, por Marte!

El mensaje era claro. Era una locura, era arriesgado, pero les iba la vida en aquel empeño. Si daban tiempo al *trirreme* para virar y poder enfilarlos con la fuerza de todos sus remeros hundiría su barco. Muchos ni siquiera sabían nadar. Y los supervivientes serían masacrados desde el *trirreme* victorioso. Les arrojarían de todo o los golpearían con los remos hasta hundirlos en el agua para siempre.

—¡Ahí los tenemos, son nuestros! —exclamó Arrio y, muy rápidamente, añadió la instrucción clave—: ¡Remos de estribor dentro! ¡Dentro! ¡Ya!

Los remeros de la *liburna* obedecieron y tiraron de sus remos lo más rápidamente que pudieron, introduciéndolos por completo en el casco de su embarcación. La nave, no obstante, por la inercia, siguió su curso sin detenerse.

Todos en el barco contuvieron la respiración.

Se oyó un gran crujido de decenas de maderas quebrándose.

—¡Los tenemos! —aulló Arrio con júbilo mientras la *liburna* navegaba en paralelo al *trirreme* e iba quebrando todos sus remos de estribor.

—¡Cuidado! —advirtió uno de los marineros. Arrio se echó al suelo. Los enemigos arrojaban barriles, sacos, hasta algún remo quebrado. Todo lo que tenían a su alcance, pero no disponían de flechas, como muy bien había predicho Arrio, y apenas causaron más que algunas contusiones entre los tripulantes de la *liburna*.

—¡Rápido, hemos de girar! —dijo Arrio levantándose de nuevo—. ¡Remeros de estribor, quietos; remad los de babor, todos, ahora mismo, por Marte!

Arrio no tenía que explicarse más. Toda la tripulación eran bandidos, truhanes de mil lugares y miserables de toda condición, pero estaba claro que se trataba de repetir la misma operación por el otro lado del *trirreme*. Arrio era, de todos ellos, el único marinero profesional. Había servido en la flota imperial de Miseno y hasta había llegado a mandar un barco como centurión naval, pero primero el juego y luego la bebida lo trastornaron. Faltó al respeto a sus superiores y acabó allí, en medio de aquella estúpida simulación de batalla, jugándose la vida.

Se oyó un nuevo crujir de maderas quebradas.

El público jaleó la acción esta vez, pues era definitiva y admiraban el valor de la tripulación de la pequeña *liburna* frente a la falta de reacción de los ocupantes del *trirreme*, mejor armado y más preparado que sus contrarios para el combate, pero que, sin embargo, se estaba mostrando mucho peor gobernado en el enfrentamiento.

—Los hemos dejado a la deriva —dijo Arrio entre dientes. Realmente habían sido muy lentos en el *trirreme*, pero no debían confiarse. Ellos apenas eran 60 hombres frente a los más de 200 del otro barco, pues la *liburna* se manejaba con 50 remeros y apenas una quincena entre marineros, oficiales e infantes. El *trirreme*, por el contrario, como barco de tres líneas de remos, contaba con 60 tranitas y 50 ziguitas, remeros de los pisos superiores y 50 talamitas más para el piso inferior, además de 30 marineros adicionales.

—¿Y qué hacemos ahora?

—El público quiere ver sangre —respondió Arrio.

Y así era. Las gradas de la gran naumaquia construida por Trajano al norte de la ciudad, al otro lado del Tíber, eran un gran clamor. Estaban satisfechos con aquellas hábiles maniobras de la *liburna* en un pequeño espacio de 300 pies de ancho por casi 1.000 de largo que proporcionaba aquella gigantesca piscina, pero que pese a sus grandes dimensiones, se quedaba pequeña para maniobrar bien aquellas embarcaciones de 90 pies de eslora en el caso del *trirreme* y de 60 pies en el de la *liburna*.

—Necesitamos sangre —repitió Arrio.

Trajano lo contemplaba todo sin hablar con nadie. Estaba solo en el palco, rodeado por la guardia imperial. Plotina había esgrimido un incómodo dolor de cabeza para no acudir con él aquella mañana. El emperador intuía que era una excusa como otra cualquiera para poder quedarse en el palacio y verse con alguien. ¿Adriano? Seguramente. Si confirmaba que eso era lo que estaba ocurriendo, la única solución sería separarlos. A Plotina no podía expulsarla sin crear una crisis en la familia imperial, como hizo Domiciano cuando desterró a Domicia Longina. No. Ése no era el camino. Tenía que apartar a Adriano, pero no de cualquier modo, sino encomendándole alguna misión relevante, algo en lo que no se sintiera humillado. Sí. Tenía que hacerle creer que no había perdido el apoyo del César. Luego ya se vería. Un enemigo desprevenido es siempre mucho más vulnerable.

Lucio Quieto tampoco lo acompañaba aquella mañana. Trajano había decidido reducir sus apariciones en público junto a él. Era otra forma de disminuir las sospechas de Adriano.

Podría hacerse acompañar por Pylades, pero aquel actor le aburría ya. Era tan engreído que hasta su hermosura se diluía en medio de tanta vanidad. Y como amante no era nada del otro mundo. Tenía otros con quien entretenerse, sin duda, pero echaba de menos ese afecto pasional, esa intensidad y, por qué no decirlo, la belleza de un hombre entregado. Pylades, además, se hacía mayor. Trajano miró un momento al suelo. ¿No sería posible volver a encontrar a alguien como Longino y que, además, le correspondiera en el afecto íntimo? ¿No sería posible que él, el hombre más poderoso del mundo, pudiera enamorarse y que su amado le respondiera sin recato ni control sino con la pasión desaforada de los amantes?

Suspiró.

¿Se hacía viejo? ¿Débil?

El público bramó.

Trajano levantó la mirada y sonrió. A falta de compañía tenía los gritos de júbilo de la plebe. Ciertamente quien estuviera al mando de la ligera *liburna* sabía lo que se hacía. El emperador tomó nota. Siempre le hacían falta hombres valientes, hombres que lo hubieran perdido todo, a los que perdonar para conseguir un grupo de leales. Tenía muchos planes. Para los que haría públicos en poco tiempo disponía de Quieto, Celso, Nigrino y Palma, pero para los planes secretos necesitaba de otros hombres.

El joven secretario del emperador, ayudado por la presencia siempre vigilante de Aulo, cruzó la férrea línea de pretorianos, que ante una señal de su tribuno se hicieron a un lado.

—Está aquí, augusto —dijo Fédimo al oído del emperador.

—Muy bien, muy bien —respondió Trajano—, que lo dejen pasar.

Trajano sonrió para sí. Era como si Fédimo hubiera estado leyendo sus pensamientos, y es que al instante el veterano Marcio se encontró junto al César. El exgladiador, nada más regresar a Roma unas semanas atrás, había enviado un mensaje al emperador informando de su llegada, misiva que, acompañada del salvoconducto imperial, llegó sin obstáculos hasta el secretario. Fédimo había comunicado el contenido de la carta y Trajano le había ordenado que llevara al exgladiador a su presencia.

El César se volvió hacia Marcio. Lo miró de arriba abajo.

—Te veo rejuvenecido —dijo el emperador.

—He encontrado a mi mujer y a mi hija. Eso me da fuerzas, augusto.

—Bien, por todos los dioses, me alegro. Cuídalas bien. No quiero que nadie pueda usarlas para que te vuelvan de nuevo contra mí.

Marcio parpadeó varias veces. Nunca había pensado en ello.

—Estamos en Roma y Roma es un lugar seguro —respondió Marcio.

Trajano se le acercó y le habló al oído.

—No creas en todo lo que se dice desde el Senado. Roma puede ser también un lugar peligroso. —Pero enseguida se separó del antiguo gladiador, sonrió, le puso la mano en el hombro y le habló como si fueran amigos de toda la vida—.

Me alegro de que hayas regresado. Podrías no haberlo hecho, pero has vuelto.

—Cumplo mi palabra.

—Cierto, cierto —confirmó Trajano—, y eso está bien. Ahora es hora de que yo cumpla con la mía. Te dije que hasta que encontrara una misión para ti, me ocuparía de tu familia, ¿no es así?

—Eso dijo el emperador.

—Bien, pues...

Pero el griterío del público que bramaba desde todas las graderías que rodeaban la naumaquia se volvió ensordecedor. La *liburna*, después de inutilizar los remos del *trirreme*, había arremetido contra él con su espolón, aprovechando que la otra embarcación no podía maniobrar ya, y había abierto una gran vía de agua. Los marineros del *trirreme* habían intentado abordar la nave enemiga a través de su *corvus*, o gran plataforma de madera, que habían tratado de poner para pasar de un barco a otro, pero quien comandaba la nave más pequeña había hecho que los remeros de la *liburna* bogasen hacia atrás y había separado la embarcación ligera antes de que pudieran abordarlos. Sólo habían saltado unos pocos tripulantes del *trirreme* a la *liburna* y éstos estaban siendo arrojados al agua por los defensores de la nave ligera. El *trirreme*, entretanto, empezaba a hundirse.

Trajano se volvió de nuevo hacia Marcio, sobre cuyo hombro derecho mantenía la mano puesta.

—¿Qué te parecería ser *lanista*? No me gusta cómo hace las cosas el actual. Creo que ha llegado la hora de poner a un veterano al mando del *Ludus Magnus*. Volverás de nuevo al anfiteatro, pero ahora sin nadie que mande sobre ti, ni en tierra ni debajo de ella; de eso último ya te encargaste tú. El nuevo *bestiarius* sólo se ocupa de las fieras. No está loco como Carpophorus. ¿Qué me dices?

Marcio no dudó en su respuesta. Necesitaba un medio de vida para cuidar de Alana y Tamura y la propuesta era muy tentadora. Ser *lanista* del *Ludus Magnus* era una posición muy segura y próspera, y más aún si se contaba con la confianza del emperador.

—El César es muy generoso.

—Bien, eso es todo... por el momento. —Trajano retiró la mano del hombro de Marcio y centró de nuevo la atención, al menos aparentemente, en lo que ocurría en la naumaquia.

Marcio retrocedió con rapidez, dio media vuelta y se marchó.

Fédimo reapareció.

—No sé si el César desea algo más —comentó el secretario en voz baja.

—Sí —respondió Trajano sin dejar de mirar hacia el *trirreme* que se hundía lentamente en el agua entre los gritos de júbilo de la plebe y los aullidos de terror de sus ocupantes—. Dión Coceyo. Lo he visto en las gradas, a mi derecha. Me ha sorprendido su presencia.

—Nadie quería estar ausente en esta inauguración, augusto —respondió Fédimo.

Trajano sonrió. Decidió no mencionar las ausencias de Plotina o Adriano. El resto, era cierto, había acudido. Quieto, Celso, Nigrino y Palma lo habían saludado al entrar en el palco, aunque ocupaban lugares diferentes, con sus familias. También estaban las jóvenes vestales y Menenia, la Vestal Máxima, todos los sacerdotes de Roma, hasta el *flamen dialis* con los ojos vendados para no ver las armas que portaban los pretorianos, por un lado, y los tripulantes de las embarcaciones que luchaban en el centro del agua.

—¿Puedes traerme al viejo filósofo?

—Sí, César —respondió Fédimo, que había aprendido que era importante tener localizadas a las personas de confianza del emperador en todo momento.

—Eres un buen secretario, Fédimo. Dile que venga.

Fédimo se inclinó y salió en busca de Dión Coceyo.

En el centro de la naumaquia

Los hombres de la *liburna* cantaban victoria dando saltos en lo alto de la embarcación.

—¡Coged los malditos remos, imbéciles! —exclamó

Arrio—. ¡Y golpead a todos los tripulantes de la *trirreme* que se acerquen!

Arrio sabía que el público no se conformaría con ver cómo se hundía un barco. Querrían más sangre. Él mismo cogió uno de los remos y, ayudado, por otro marinero para esgrimirlo con más destreza, golpearon en la cabeza a uno de los supervivientes del naufragio de la embarcación enemiga que se aproximaba a la *liburna* nadando. Le abrieron la cabeza y la sangre empezó a rodearlo por todas partes. Arrio sonrió. Todo iba bien.

—¡Centurión! —dijo otro de los marineros—. ¡Se ha abierto una vía de agua en proa!

Arrio se volvió hacia el tripulante.

—¿Estás seguro?

—¡Sí, por todos los dioses! ¡Embestimos con demasiada fuerza al *trirreme*! ¡Nos hundimos también! —A punto estaba de romper a llorar aquel bandido reconvertido en marinero por necesidad.

Arrio pensaba. Podía ocurrir y había pasado: al embestir al *trirreme*, mucho más pesado, el casco de la *liburna* no había resistido y se había abierto al maniobrar hacia atrás, pues el espolón estaba enganchado con el otro barco. En circunstancias normales no tendría por qué haber ocurrido, pero ¿por qué les iban a proporcionar una embarcación en perfectas condiciones? Era mucho más entretenido para la plebe que todos los barcos tuvieran problemas, incluso los que habían vencido.

—¿Qué pasa en el agua? —preguntó el tripulante que había ayudado a Arrio a matar con un golpe de remo al pobre miserable que había intentado acercarse a la *liburna*. Arrio miró al agua. Alrededor del marinero muerto del *trirreme* el agua parecía sacudirse bestialmente y todo se había convertido en una mancha enorme de sangre. Era como si el cuerpo del marinero muerto estuviera siendo desgarrado en mil pedazos debajo de la superficie. Y lo mismo pasaba con otros infelices alrededor de toda la nave.

—Tiburones —masculló Arrio mordiéndose la rabia y el miedo—. Han llenado toda la naumaquia de tiburones.

En el palco imperial

Trajano volvía a estar solo en el palco. Era una lástima que el viejo Licinio Sura hubiera fallecido. Se podía hacer acompañar por él sin despertar la rabia de Adriano, pues al ser tan mayor ya no lo habría visto como un competidor. Trajano echaba de menos, además, sus sabios consejos. Le habría venido bien en estos momentos de duda. Dión Coceyo era sabio, pero demasiado recto. Sura era hábil y se movía entre los senadores y las tensiones y conjuras de Roma como una anguila, pero esa anguila había muerto. Había ordenado construir el *Balneum Surae,* un complejo de baños públicos en su honor, en recuerdo permanente del gran senador que lo ayudó a ser emperador; era lo menos que podía hacer. Y había ordenado también que construyeran aquella gran naumaquia, igual que había ampliado el pomerio sagrado de la ciudad, porque con él Roma estaba creciendo como nunca y ni los límites sagrados de antaño eran suficientes para sus planes de agrandar la urbe. ¿Entenderían los romanos que igual que se cambiaban los límites del pomerio, se podían cambiar también las fronteras, como había hecho con la Dacia y el Danubio o con la anexión de Arabia en Oriente? ¿Estaban preparados para cambios mayores y más ambiciosos o les sobrevendría el miedo? Entretanto, él les seguía regalando más y más edificios y espectáculos: además del *Balneum Surae* y la gigantesca naumaquia había ordenado levantar unas nuevas termas en el centro de la ciudad y unos mercados ciclópeos junto a la explanada que estaba preparando como nuevo foro. Había dado instrucciones también para que se construyera un nuevo teatro, un Odeón, un *Gymnasium* y hasta un nuevo acueducto, el Aqua Marcia, con el que resolvía de una vez el abastecimiento de agua a las termas nuevas y, al tiempo, solucionaba la falta de suministro del preciado líquido al centro de la ciudad. Así había dado cumplimiento a una de las necesidades planteadas por el viejo Frontino en su informe sobre la falta de agua. Todo eso les había proporcionado a los ciudadanos de Roma, gestionando con honestidad los recursos del Estado, pero no parecía ser suficiente para que se decidieran a acompañarlo en cualquier nuevo proyecto que quisiera emprender. ¿O sí? Los gritos de la plebe lo devolvieron a la naumaquia y su espectáculo. Los tiburones empezaban a devorar a los supervivientes del naufragio y, además, parecía que la *liburna* también tenía algún problema, pues se veía a sus tripulantes correr de un lado a otro sin celebrar ya su victoria. ¿Era justo que murieran todos?

Miró a su espalda y encontró a Aulo. Le hizo una seña. El tribuno asintió. En unos instantes el griterío del público empezó a calmarse. Aulo acababa de dar la orden a los pretorianos que vigilaban en los muros de la gigantesca piscina de que liberaran los botes con los que poder acercarse a los tripulantes de la *liburna* y salvarlos de un naufragio que los convertiría a todos en pasto de los tiburones.

—Me dice Fédimo que el emperador deseaba verme —dijo el viejo Dión.

—Ah, sí —respondió Trajano volviéndose hacia el filósofo, al que no había visto llegar pues se había acercado por el lado opuesto a Aulo. La aparición de Dión Coceyo alejó la mente del emperador de la decepción del público que, seguramente, preferiría haber visto morir a todos devorados por los tiburones, aunque algunos tímidos gritos de «César, César, César» empezaban a abrirse camino en el gran estadio acuático.

—Es justo salvar a los que han luchado bien y más aún cuando lo han hecho en inferioridad de condiciones, ¿no crees? —preguntó Trajano al filósofo.

—Es además un mensaje educativo para el pueblo —respondió con seguridad Dión Coceyo—: recompensa para los valientes, muerte para los que no han sabido luchar. El público está reconociéndolo. —Y señaló a las gradas, desde donde cada vez se oía con más claridad un clamor en favor del emperador.

—¡César, César, César!

—Les cuesta reconocerlo —dijo Trajano.

—La sangre los ciega.

—Eso debe de ser, pero no te he hecho venir por esto —añadió el emperador—. Quiero pedirte una cosa.

—Siempre estoy a las órdenes del César.

En el agua

Los botes llegaron junto a la *liburna* y los tripulantes fueron pasando a ellos con rapidez. Alguno, torpe, tropezó y cayó al agua, donde los tiburones dieron buena cuenta de él con una brutalidad pasmosa, más aun cuando uno habría pensado que ya deberían estar razonablemente saciados después de devorar a más de un centenar de infelices o más, pero parecía que su instinto mortal se había desatado y no era fácil de calmar. Sólo los cuidadores de la naumaquia sabían que los escualos llevaban semanas sin alimento para hacerlos más voraces el día del combate naval.

Arrio subió al último bote que se acercó a la *liburna*. En cuanto se alejaron vieron cómo el resto de la embarcación se hundía en las profundidades de la gran piscina de la naumaquia. Arrio no daba crédito a lo que veía. Del *trirreme* hundido apenas asomaba el mástil de la vela. Aquel lago artificial tenía, al menos, 25 pies de profundidad.

—Nos hemos salvado por muy poco —dijo Arrio secándose el sudor de la frente con la palma de una mano ensangrentada.

En el palco

—Verás, hay un hombre, un antiguo gladiador —dijo Trajano continuando su conversación con el viejo filósofo.

—Sí, César.

—Va a ser el nuevo *lanista* —siguió Trajano.

—Un nuevo *lanista*, sí, César —repitió el filósofo.

—Tiene una hija pequeña, de ocho o nueve años o algo así. No estoy seguro.

—Una niña pequeña, sí, augusto.

—Quiero que te ocupes de su educación. Te presentarás ante el nuevo *lanista* en el *Ludus Magnus* de mi parte y te ofrecerás como *paedagogus* de su hija.

—Por supuesto, César, pero creía que el emperador prefería que me ocupara de ayudar a Suetonio Tranquilo con la reorganización de las bibliotecas de Roma —respondió el filósofo con tiento. No le hacía ninguna gracia tener que ocuparse de la educación de una niña y menos a sus años—. Hay tutores más acostumbrados a tratar con niños pequeños que, sin duda, harían una mejor labor...

—Pero no saben sánscrito —lo interrumpió Trajano.

Dión Coceyo guardó un momento de silencio.

—No, no conozco a nadie más que sepa sánscrito en Roma, eso es así, César, pero no entiendo bien...

—Esa niña es importante, aunque ni ella misma lo sepa aún —lo interrumpió Trajano por segunda vez—. Y es aún más importante que esa niña aprenda sánscrito.

El emperador se levantó, saludó al pueblo y éste volvió a aclamarlo mientras se retiraba del palco imperial rodeado por la guardia pretoriana liderada por Aulo.

El viejo filósofo se quedó en el palco imperial vacío. A sus años no era fácil sorprenderse con nada, pero en aquella ocasión el César lo había conseguido. Con el ceño fruncido, Dión Coceyo repitió, de forma interrogativa, una palabra entre las gradas gigantescas de la naumaquia.

—¿Sánscrito?

25

LA CARNE DE LOS SACRIFICIOS

Nicomedia, Bitinia
111 d. C.

Los miraba con rabia y seguía gritándoles a todos.

—¡Os consideráis seguidores de Cristo y coméis esta carne corrupta! ¿Es así como respetáis la venida de Jesús al mundo, traicionándolo a cada momento, en cada comida?

El grupo de hombres y mujeres que se había arremolinado ante el mercader que comercializaba la carne de los sacrificios oficiales se fue alejando del lugar. En Bitinia la religión oficial era, como en todo el Imperio, la romana, aunque había amplia tolerancia con otros credos. Últimamente, no obstante, el cristianismo, en sus múltiples formas, había arraigado con fuerza en toda Asia Menor y en particular en Bitinia y el Ponto, junto a las costas del mar Negro.

Marción seguía preparando su gran viaje a Occidente, a Roma, para entrevistarse con el obispo de la capital del mundo, tal y como había acordado con Ignacio, pero no desaprovechaba ninguna ocasión para mantener el mensaje de Cristo vivo y fuerte en su país. De hecho, había retrasado su anhelado viaje a la capital del Imperio para hacerse más conocido y popular en Asia. Estaba convencido de que sólo así lo tomaría en serio el obispo de Roma.

Aquella mañana, como tantas otras, había acudido a uno de los grandes mercados de Nicomedia para poner en venta sus propios productos cuando, una vez más, se había encontrado con un gran puesto de venta de carne procedente de las bestias que habían sido sacrificadas en los altares de los dioses romanos. El nuevo gobernador de la provincia enviado por Trajano, Plinio, parecía haber querido celebrar con sacrificios extraordinarios el sexto consulado del emperador y por eso había dado orden de sacrificar a más animales de lo acostumbrado. Pero toda aquella carne había sido ofrendada a dioses que renegaban de Cristo; ¿cómo no entendían aquellos que se consideraban cristianos que no podían, que no debían tomar semejante alimento si querían seguir a Cristo y sus enseñanzas?

—¿No lo entendéis? —se dirigió de nuevo a la gente que se aproximaba al puesto, muchos de ellos cristianos que Marción reconocía de diferentes encuentros en los días anteriores al mercado.

Continuó hablándoles, ahora empleando un tono más conciliador, más acorde con su propia visión de Cristo como emisario de la bondad de Dios.

—Jesús, Dios, nos ama y nos quiere, pero no hemos de pagar ese amor que nos profesa insultando su memoria al comer esta carne ofrendada a los dioses del Imperio romano...

Seguía hablando y los compradores, unos por miedo, otros por vergüenza y muchos por pura incomodidad, se alejaban del puesto de venta. El mercader que tenía la carne, y que había pagado sus buenos sestercios por ella, no aguantó más. Si no la vendía estaba arruinado.

—Llamad a los legionarios —le dijo en voz baja a uno de los libertos que trabajaban con él.

Marción siguió predicando y la gente lo escuchaba. Les hablaba de Pablo y sus cartas y sus enseñanzas, de cómo él también estuvo equivocado un tiempo pero al fin supo ver el camino. Lo mismo debían hacer todos ellos y así dar inicio a ese nuevo camino que los condujera directamente a Cristo, alejándose de aquel puesto de venta de carne sacrificada a los dioses equivocados.

—¡Eh, tú!

Marción se volvió. No tuvo ocasión de explicarse. Un puñetazo lo derribó. Lo sacaron a rastras del mercado. Su detención fue una auténtica conmoción, pues Marción era hijo del obispo de Sinope, en el Ponto, la región contigua a Bitinia, y además era de una familia adinerada.

—¡Carne, carne bendecida! —gritaba ahora el mercader—. ¡Carne fresca y sabrosa para todos! ¡Y a buen precio!

Pero con la llegada de los legionarios muchos se fueron con rapidez. Si los soldados se atrevían a detener a Marción, cualquier cristiano estaba en peligro. Y no se equivocaban. Plinio, en efecto, en calidad de nuevo gobernador, había dado orden de detener a todos los que públicamente se confesaran y actuaran como cristianos.

En la prisión

Marción tuvo tiempo de reponerse del golpe propinado. Pasaron varios días antes de que lo juzgaran. De hecho tampoco se encontró con un juicio propiamente dicho, sino ante la presencia del mismísimo Plinio, que lo miró a él y al resto de los detenidos directamente a los ojos mientras les hablaba desde lo alto de un pedestal improvisado en el atrio principal de la residencia del gobernador.

Marción observó que habían seleccionado a los presos de mayor alcurnia y más adinerados. Eso significaba que les iban a dar alguna oportunidad; de lo contrario, no tenía sentido haberlos separado de los cristianos más pobres. Sin embargo, no había ningún ciudadano romano entre ellos. Lógico. A ésos sólo los podrían juzgar en Roma. No, en aquel grupo estaban los hombres de mejor condición que eran cristianos reconocidos en Nicomedia. Marción sabía que todos estaban atentos a él, que lo consideraban su líder natural, casi su profeta. Tenía que estar a la altura de las circunstancias.

—Todos vosotros os confesáis y hasta os jactáis de ser cristianos —empezó el gobernador—. He llegado a la conclusión de que la exhibición pública de esta religión es ofensiva para Roma y para el emperador. No sé aún de qué forma desea el César Marco Ulpio Trajano que se os trate, ni si considera que debéis ser castigados mortalmente o de otra forma. He enviado una carta a Roma a tal efecto, para averiguar cuál es el criterio del César sobre todos vosotros. Pero el enorme número de seguidores de Cristo en esta provincia me incomoda. Tengo infinidad de denuncias, muchas anónimas porque, a lo que se ve, os temen. No sé exactamente qué hacer con vosotros, pero, a la espera de recibir respuesta del emperador, os ofrezco la posibilidad de retractaros ante mí. Veis que he traído una estatua del César Trajano, además de las imágenes de diversos dioses romanos que están a mi derecha. Los que renunciéis aquí y ahora, públicamente, al cristianismo, los que reneguéis de sus prácticas oscuras y hagáis ante mí una ofrenda de pan, vino y otros manjares que se os entregarán, a los dioses romanos y al emperador, seréis perdonados y quedaréis en libertad. Los que os mantengáis sin retractaros, permaneceréis en prisión y será el emperador y su justicia los que decidan en cuanto reciba carta desde Roma con su respuesta oficial. Vosotros veréis. Espero que recapacitéis y que, al menos, unos cuantos de vosotros entréis en razón.

Silencio.

Se podía oír la respiración entrecortada de muchos de los acusados. Todos miraban a Marción. Éste se pasaba la lengua por el interior de los labios. Se sabía su líder, su ministro más escuchado, pese a no superar los treinta años. Todos esperaban su reacción. Él marcaría el ejemplo a seguir. Retractarse era renunciar a Cristo y a Dios, renunciar a su mundo, al perdón del Espíritu. Era absurdo y era cobarde. Y mezquino. Él, más que ningún otro, debía mostrar el camino recto a los demás, igual que había hecho aquellos días en el mercado predicando en contra de consumir la carne de los sacrificios a los dioses romanos. ¿Cómo iba él ahora a adorar a esos mismos dioses, a hacerles ofrendas y, en suma, a retractarse de todo?

Marción dio un paso adelante.

Plinio lo observó atento. Sabía que era su líder. Imaginaba que se mantendría firme en sus sacrilegios a Roma, pero el gobernador aún albergaba la esperanza de que algún otro se retractara y que al ser magnánimo con él pudiera arrastrar a otros que se mostraban temerosos de los castigos que podían imponérseles, ya fuera por orden suya o por orden del propio Trajano cuando llegara su respuesta desde la capital del Imperio. Plinio pensó entonces que se había equivocado. No debería haberse dirigido a todos los acusados en conjunto, sino uno por uno o en pequeños grupos, separando a su líder y a otros que como aquél parecían más firmes en sus convicciones cristianas. Eso habría facilitado que, al menos, algunos se hubieran retractado, pero dejar que ese Marción hablara primero era un error que debía impedir.

Plinio también dio unos pasos adelante e iba a ordenar a Marción que callara, pero llegaba tarde: el mercader ministro de los cristianos ya estaba hablando...

—¡Me retracto! ¡Me retracto! —gritó Marción.

Nada más pronunciar aquellas palabras pasaron muchas cosas al tiempo: Plinio, perplejo, parpadeó hasta que sonrió satisfecho. El resto de los cristianos miraron al que hasta ese momento había sido su líder con sorpresa, decepción y rabia. Algunos empezaron a increparle.

—¡Traidor! ¡Maldito y mil veces maldito!

—¡Traidor a Cristo!

Se organizó un tumulto alrededor de Marción mientras éste se arrodillaba y se protegía la cabeza por si le llovían golpes, pero los que no se retractaban eran demasiado fieles seguidores de Cristo y no pensaban patearlo aunque lo desearan. Incluso algunos empezaban a sustituir los gritos que habían lanzado por lágrimas de pura rabia y decepción. Le habían insultado llevados por la sorpresa, por lo inesperado de la reacción de Marción. Hasta ese momento, todos los cristianos allí presentes lo habían admirado enormemente. Ahora, de pronto, no tenían referente, no sabían bien qué pensar de nada, de nadie.

—¡Proteged a ese hombre! —ordenó Plinio señalando a un atemorizado Marción que se alejaba gateando, como un perro, de los que hasta hacía sólo un momento habían sido sus hermanos. Equivocadamente, temía que le pegaran puntapiés. Seguramente porque él, si la situación hubiera sido la inversa, lo habría hecho.

Separado del resto, Marción se levantó para arrodillarse finalmente ante la estatua del emperador Trajano y ante las imágenes de los dioses romanos contra los que había predicado. Y les ofreció sacrificios entre el silencio cargado de desprecio del resto de los acusados.

Plinio aprovechó el instante.

—Eres un hombre libre de toda acusación —dijo el gobernador—. Puedes marcharte.

Y Marción, sin mirar atrás, salió de aquel atrio tras su nefanda negación a Cristo y, siguiendo a varios legionarios, llegó a la salida de la residencia del gobernador de Bitinia y se adentró por las calles de Nicomedia.

Entretanto, Plinio, en el interior, seguía recibiendo algunas retractaciones más. No tantas como habría esperado tras el arrepentimiento del líder de aquellos cristianos, pero sí unas cuantas. Estaba satisfecho. Sabía que, cuando menos, estaba reduciendo el problema por el que había consultado al emperador. Así, disminuida la cuestión a una dimensión manejable, junto con la respuesta que recibiera, podría dejar el asunto zanjado durante mucho tiempo. Sí, estaba contento.

Entretanto, Marción caminaba por las calles de Nicomedia en busca de un lugar donde esconderse. En cuanto corriera la voz de que se había retractado y que había adorado a dioses romanos, sus amigos le volverían la espalda. Estaba solo. Sabía que había obrado mal, pero dentro de sí hervía la sangre de quien no se rinde. No serían capaces de entenderlo nunca. Daba igual. Lo importante era salvarse. Él tenía la estrategia perfecta para preservar el mensaje de Cristo, mientras que el resto de los cristianos no sabían cómo hacerlo. Ni siquiera los obispos, y menos que todos, el de Roma. Por eso él debía seguir vivo. No estaba dispuesto a permanecer arrestado aguardando la respuesta de un emperador de Roma sobre qué hacer con ellos. Las persecuciones y ejecuciones ordenadas por Nerón o Domiciano estaban frescas aún en el recuerdo de los cristianos de todo el Imperio y también en la mente de Marción. Estaba convencido de que Trajano actuaría igual. No, había que buscar una alternativa diferente. Los caminos de Dios son extraños. Él había obrado seguro de que negando a Cristo aquella mañana salvaría su mensaje. ¿Acaso Pedro no negó a Jesús tres veces y luego fue quien impulsó la Iglesia y su sagrado ministerio? Él sólo lo había negado una vez. Una sola vez. Y sobre esa negación, sin embargo, resucitaría el mensaje que Pedro rescató y que estaba a punto de perderse. Ya verían cómo.

Y su figura, que avanzaba cabizbaja pero con ambos puños bien cerrados y muy prietos, se desvaneció entre la multitud de las calles de Nicomedia.

26

UN NUEVO REY

Artaxata
111 d. C.

Partamasiris ascendió por las calles exteriores de Artaxata. La vieja capital de Armenia había caído al fin tras un largo asedio. El hambre, sólo el hambre había doblegado la terquedad de su sobrino Exedares. Eso y tres años de enfrentamientos por toda Armenia.

Pero todo había terminado.

Partamasiris cruzó el puente que salvaba el río Araxes y llegó hasta las murallas levantadas bajo la supervisión del mítico Aníbal, en los lejanos tiempos en los que el legendario general cartaginés buscó refugio de los romanos que lo perseguían sirviendo a Artaxias I, el entonces rey de Armenia. Partamasiris no pudo dejar de admirar los imponentes muros. Sin duda, sin el hambre no habría conseguido nunca rendir aquella fortificación. Qué bueno que su sobrino Exedares no fuera, en absoluto, alguien parecido a Aníbal, quien con toda seguridad se habría preocupado de abastecerse bien en previsión de un asedio. Pero Exedares no.

Partamasiris seguía paseando por su ciudad recién conquistada. A los muros que había construido el líder cartaginés se unieron luego los nuevos edificios levantados por los arquitectos que el propio Nerón financió cuando Corbulón se hizo con el control de Armenia y entronó a Tiridates I como nuevo rey. Se trataba de construcciones hermosas todas ellas: templos, villas, baños... hablaban del poder comercial de la ciudad y de los doscientos millones de sestercios que Nerón envió a Tiridates para financiar todo aquel renacer de Artaxata.

Sí, estaban bien aquellos nuevos edificios, pero eso de que los romanos, pagaran o no el renacer de Armenia, decidieran quién era el rey de aquella región, se había acabado.

Partamasiris sonreía desde lo alto de su caballo. Por delante, los soldados partos de su guardia iban abriéndose camino entre la gente que se arrodillaba ante él implorando perdón y comida. Artaxata estaba repleta de judíos, griegos, sirios y, por supuesto, armenios. La mayoría eran comerciantes y artesanos que se habían beneficiado durante años del flujo de mercancías entre Oriente y Occidente, pero la guerra los había empobrecido y el asedio los había reducido a su condición actual de miserables. Partamasiris no sentía lástima por ellos. Si hubieran aconsejado y presionado a Exedares para que enviara recursos a Osroes y de esa forma el rey de reyes hubiera podido luchar contra Vologases, todo ese sufrimiento no habría recaído sobre ellos. Se habían buscado lo que tenían. Mejor dicho, lo que no tenían. Partamasiris a punto estuvo de reírse solo, pero se contuvo. Tampoco quería excederse. De hecho, había dado orden de distribuir algo de comida como muestra de que el nuevo gobernante de Armenia, es decir, él, sería generoso con sus nuevos súbditos.

Llegaron al palacio imperial dentro de la ciudadela de Artaxata, en lo alto de la colina. Partamasiris desmontó de su caballo y, siempre rodeado por su guardia, irrumpió en el edificio, cruzando jardines y patios hasta entrar en la sala del *parwāngāh*, el trono, donde un derrotado Exedares lo esperaba.

—He rendido la ciudad según mi *padistud*, según mi promesa —dijo el joven rey que iba a ser depuesto en un instante por su tío—. Espero que a cambio de dar término a este asedio que tanto sufrimiento ha causado a los ciudadanos de Artaxata y que tantas energías consumía a tu ejército, mi tío cumplirá su propia *padistud* y en pago por mi rendición respetará mi vida y la de mis familiares y más fieles servidores. Eso es lo acordado.

Partamasiris volvió a sonreír.

—Es cierto que la palabra dada, que una *padistud*, es para cumplirla —dijo y desenfundó su espada al tiempo que se acercaba a su sobrino.

Exedares frunció el ceño. Sus guardias estaban ya todos desarmados por los soldados de su tío. De pronto el arma de Partamasiris le atravesó el vientre hasta emerger por detrás y clavarse en la madera del asiento real.

—Sí, una promesa es para cumplirla, querido sobrino, pero tú no cumpliste la tuya, la de ser leal a Osroes y ayudarlo en tiempos de zozobra. —Partamasiris empezó a extraer la espada del vientre de su sobrino con lentitud extrema, recreándose en ver la faz de dolor total del moribundo rey de Armenia.

—¡Agghhh! —exclamó Exedares a la vez que se llevaba las manos a un vientre abierto por donde se le salían los intestinos una vez que su tío extrajo su arma por completo.

—Tú no cumpliste tu promesa con Osroes —continuó Partamasiris con cierto tono de indiferencia ante el dolor de su sobrino agonizante—, así que no veo por qué yo ahora habría de ser fiel a mi *padistud* contigo.

Exedares se dobló por completo y cayó de costado sobre el suelo. Dos soldados partos, ante una mirada de su líder, lo cogieron por los pies y lo arrastraron a un lado de la sala. Partamasiris se sentó entonces en el trono de Armenia. El hecho de que estuviera encharcado con la sangre de sus sobrino no pareció incomodarle lo más mínimo.

—Acabad con todos los miembros de su familia y sus consejeros —dijo el nuevo rey de Armenia—. Ah, y dadme esa diadema —añadió señalando en el suelo la corona que hasta hacía unos instantes había lucido Exedares sobre su cabeza.

Un soldado la cogió con cuidado y se la entregó a su líder. Partamasiris no dudó un instante en ponérsela sobre la cabeza. Le había costado tres años conseguirla, pero ya era suya.

—¿A las mujeres del séquito de Exedares las matamos también? —preguntó un oficial.

—A las mujeres las primeras. Cualquiera de ellas podría querer vengarse. Además —prosiguió Partamasiris—, ya nos traeremos aquí nuevas esposas y concubinas desde Partia. Seguro que mi hermano Osroes se mostrará generoso en ese punto en cuanto sepa que toda Armenia está de nuevo bajo el mando del rey de reyes.

Los soldados salieron para cumplir con las órdenes. Pronto todo el palacio se llenó de alaridos de terror y muerte. Partamasiris apoyó la barbilla en la mano derecha y el codo sobre uno de los reposabrazos del trono de Armenia. Era un *parwāngāh* cómodo. Su cabeza no escuchaba los gritos: su mente estaba imaginándose allí, en alguna de las lujosas cámaras reales de Artaxata, en compañía de la hermosa Aryazate completamente desnuda. Habían pasado ya tres años desde que la vio por última vez y ahora tendría ya... ¿once, doce años? Una edad perfecta en cualquier caso. Osroes no podría negarle ahora ese pequeño capricho. Sobre todo pequeño. Y se echó a reír.

27

LA EDUCACIÓN DE TAMURA

Roma, 112 d. C.

Tamura tenía sensaciones contrapuestas en su relación con Roma. Por un lado, en la parte positiva estaba la seguridad en aquella ciudad donde su padre era el entrenador de los gladiadores en la escuela de lucha más importante del Imperio romano. La incertidumbre por si serían atacadas en medio de la noche, violadas o asesinadas había desaparecido en su vida. Y había comida abundante sin tener por qué preocuparse de si los animales se acercaban al río a beber o si escasearían los alimentos en función de la estación del año. En la parte negativa, sin embargo, estaba la ausencia de los bosques del norte. Los echaba de menos cada día y tenía el convencimiento de que ya nunca volvería a esas sombras frondosas que ella siempre consideraba su casa. En Roma había algunos parques y arboledas próximos, pero nada comparable a los ríos, montañas y bosques de los sármatas, más allá del Danubio, en la Dacia.

—Éste es nuestro hogar ahora —le decía su madre cuando ella rogaba por regresar al norte, aunque sólo fuera una temporada.

Pero había más cosas en la vida de la joven adolescente sármata. Aspectos nuevos que ella no tenía claro si ubicar en lo bueno o en lo malo. Un día, al poco de llegar a Roma, un anciano se había presentado a su padre en el *Ludus Magnus*. Se identificó como un *paedagogus*, una especie de instructor en palabras e historia y otros asuntos que poco o nada tenían que ver con la lucha. Y es que si había algo que le había gustado a Tamura de Roma, además de perder la incertidumbre sobre su día a día, era poder asistir a los entrenamientos de los gladiadores. Bueno, para ser precisos, le encantaba en particular asistir a los entrenamientos de Áyax, el mejor gladiador de la escuela. También el más alto y el de cuerpo más hermoso. Era griego y por eso aquel nombre. El anciano tutor, a una pregunta suya —que para eso sí servía lo de tener un instructor de palabras e historia—, le había explicado que hubo un Áyax heroico y valeroso entre los griegos que atacaron Troya, junto con otros guerreros famosos de antaño como Aquiles, Agamenón u Odiseo. Pero ella ya no prestó mucha atención. Tamura admiraba a su padre, pero intuía que pese a toda su experiencia en combate, si éste y Áyax lucharan estaba convencida de que ganaría el segundo. Era más joven y más fuerte y más ágil. Y más guapo. Su padre debió de ser guapo de joven, al menos eso le había dicho su madre, pero las canas y las arrugas en el rostro y las manos... Áyax, en cambio, tenía una piel tersa y fuerte, brillante cuando sudaba luchando bajo el sol de Roma. Lo que Tamura lamentaba infinitamente hasta quitarle el sueño era que ella sólo tenía doce años, de forma que él cuando la miraba sólo veía a una niña, no a una mujer, ni, mucho menos a una guerrera.

—Es la hora.

Tamura tuvo que dejar de mirar a la arena y no pudo admirar por más rato cómo seguía entrenándose su idolatrado Áyax. ¿Conseguiría que se fijara en ella de verdad? El anciano *paedagogus*, el viejo Dión Coceyo, había vuelto y la llamaba. Acudía todos los días. Sin falta, todas las mañanas desde que hablara con su padre. No lo odiaba, pero le restaba tiempo en el colegio de gladiadores y eso la irritaba.

—¿Por qué he de aprender todas esas cosas de las que habla el anciano *paedagogus*? —le había preguntado una y otra vez a su madre.

—Porque estamos ahora en otro mundo y aquí tu arco y las flechas no te asegurarán la supervivencia —le respondía Alana—. Has de aprender cómo viven los romanos. Has de saber su lengua...

—Ya sé su lengua —la interrumpió Tamura.

—Pero no sabes leerla —interpuso su madre.

—¿Y de qué sirve leer?

—Los romanos leen, hablan latín, escriben y gobiernan el mundo —insistía su madre—. De algo valdrá cuando son los más poderosos. Vivimos entre ellos y aprenderás de ellos. Y no se hable más de este asunto porque soy tu madre y te digo que escuches a ese anciano y aprendas de él todo lo que puedas. Quizá un día echarás a faltar sus enseñanzas o lamentarás no haberlo escuchado lo suficiente, así que ahora que tienes la oportunidad, aprovéchala.

Tamura bajó la mirada, enfurruñada, pero era disciplinada y no discutía con su madre.

—Escúchame, hija —continuó Alana—. Vivimos en un mundo que cambia constantemente. Cuantas más cosas sepas, mejor. No te pido que olvides que eres sármata como yo y guerrera, no te pido que olvides cómo usar el arco y cómo luchar. Por eso me parece bien, y a tu padre también, que vayas al colegio de gladiadores y luches con sus armas por las tardes, que te ejercites como guerrera, pero también es importante, y tu padre también lo piensa, que aprendas de ese hombre. A ese anciano, como lo llamas, lo ha enviado el emperador. Todo el mundo respeta a ese viejo aquí. Por algo será.

Tamura dejó de recordar. El anciano en cuestión estaba de nuevo ante ella.

—Es la hora —repitió Dión Coceyo.

Ella asintió y lo siguió a una estancia dentro del mismo *Ludus Magnus* que habían habilitado para sus encuentros diarios. Era una vieja celda de gladiador, pero con una amplia ventana por donde entraba la luz del sol. Ella se sentó en una *sella*, tomó un estilete y una hoja de papiro. Él dictó unas frases en latín y una en griego y ella anotó las palabras con cuidado. Más allá de que le gustara o no hacer las cosas, quería hacerlas siempre bien. Además, el griego podía valerle para hablar algún día con Áyax sin que sus padres los entendieran. Eso la animaba en secreto.

El filósofo la miraba por encima del hombro.

—Eso está... correcto —dijo—. Has practicado. Eso me alegra, aunque soy consciente de que me costará, al menos, una historia más.

La muchacha se volvió hacia el filósofo sonriendo. De todas las cosas de las que le hablaba el anciano, había algo que sí le interesaba: los relatos sobre antiguos guerreros poderosos de Roma. El *paedagogus* le había hablado de Escipión el Africano y su lucha contra el cartaginés Aníbal. Los cuentos de guerra, como ella los llamaba, las estrategias de los militares de antaño, eso sí interesaba a Tamura. Ahora el anciano había empezado con la historia de la lucha por el poder en Roma entre tres hombres: Craso, Pompeyo y César. El filósofo le había prometido que si se aplicaba en aprender bien las lenguas que le enseñaba, él le contaría muchas más historias sobre esos guerreros. Ese día tocaba el relato de cómo Craso fue derrotado por los partos en Oriente. Una narración brutal, le había anticipado el filósofo. Eso le encantaba; cuanto más violento más le gustaba. Luego tendría que venir la historia de la guerra entre Pompeyo y César. Pero antes debía aprender a escribir muchas palabras.

—Sí —dijo Tamura—. He practicado. Hoy terminarás la historia de Craso y la batalla de Carrhae, ¿verdad?

—Puede ser —respondió Dión Coceyo—, aunque es un relato que da para varios días; pero antes has de demostrarme que también has trabajado de verdad —bajó la voz y se acercó al oído de la pequeña—, y que has practicado con la lengua secreta.

—Lo he hecho —confirmó Tamura.

—Veámoslo. Escríbeme algo.

La niña volvió a trazar líneas finas con cuidado sobre el papiro hasta escribir unas palabras, lentamente pero con seguridad:

Adhīśvaras āhvāyaka

Dión Coceyo la observaba con atención mientras la muchacha se esforzaba en escribir bien aquellas palabras sánscritas con los caracteres del alfabeto latino, tal y como le había enseñado él. Cuando el emperador le había encomendado encargarse de la educación de aquella niña, de eso hacía ya un tiempo, nunca pensó que le fuera a tomar cariño a la muchacha. Y menos cuando al verla por primera vez comprendió que estaba ante una bárbara, hija de una guerrera sármata y nada más y nada menos que un gladiador. ¿Qué podía esperarse de semejante alumna? Sin embargo, para sorpresa del filósofo, la muchacha había dado muestras, desde un principio, de una extraña destreza natural para aprender idiomas. En poco tiempo supo leer en latín y al año de trabajar con ella ya podía escribir bien en latín y empezaba con el griego. El sánscrito tenía que ser el siguiente paso, pero Dión Coceyo, sabedor de que aquél era el objetivo auténtico del César —no sabía bien por qué pero así era—, decidió no llevar a la niña al conocimiento del sánscrito como con las otras lenguas, sino que pensó en acercarla a esa forma de expresarse del modo más hábil que pudo imaginar para que nunca quisiera dejar de aprender: meses atrás, uno de los días de clase, mientras ella escribía en latín, él empezó a escribir palabras en sánscrito en un papiro. La niña lo vio y le preguntó qué significaban aquellos términos desconocidos para ella.

—Es una lengua secreta —le había dicho con la voz más grave y misteriosa que pudo.

Aquella respuesta, tal y como esperaba el filósofo, encendió la llama incandescente de la curiosidad de Tamura.

—¿Qué has escrito en esa lengua secreta? —le había preguntado entonces Tamura.

—No puedo decírtelo —había respondido él—. Nadie debe conocer esta lengua y menos una niña. Sólo los muy sabios tienen derecho a conocerla. Y los muy valientes.

—Soy una guerrera sármata y muy valiente —se defendió ella.

—Aun así, esto no puedo enseñártelo.

Y la tuvo así unas semanas hasta que, al fin, ante los ruegos constantes de Tamura, el filósofo aparentó ceder.

—Pero no se lo digas a nadie —le había ordenado el anciano.

—No lo haré —prometió ella.

—De acuerdo. —Entonces, seguro ya de que la niña nunca olvidaría nada de lo que le enseñara de aquella peculiar forma de expresión de Oriente, empezó a hablarle del sánscrito, una lengua hablada más allá del Imperio parto, en una región remota donde gobernaban los emperadores kushan.

—Una lengua que usan sus sacerdotes y monjes para explicar una nueva religión que ha surgido en los confines del mundo —había continuado explicando el filósofo ante los ojos cada vez más abiertos de Tamura—. Eso sí, ellos la escriben con otras letras, pero yo la transcribo de esta forma, con las nuestras, para saber cómo se pronuncian sus palabras

—¿Y qué religión es ésa? —preguntó la niña.

—Está basada en las enseñanzas de un monje antiguo al que llaman Buda.

Pero Tamura no parecía estar demasiado interesada en religiones extranjeras y, para ser precisos, tampoco sabía Dión Coceyo demasiado sobre aquel profeta de remotos territorios. Así que el filósofo, desde aquel ya lejano día, se centró en enseñarle a la muchacha palabras que le resultaban mucho más atractivas.

Ahora repasaban parte de lo que la niña debía haber aprendido.

—*Aśva* —dijo él a la espera de que Tamura le respondiera con la traducción correcta.

—Caballo —dijo ella.

Y siguieron.

—*Matṛ*.

—Madre.

—*Jana*.

—Gente.

—*Hṛd*.

—Corazón.

—Bien. Lo recuerdas todo. Veamos ahora algunos números: ¿*Saptam*?

—Siete —respondió ella con orgullo.

—*Navan*.

—Nueve.

—*Catur*.

—Cuatro.

—*Tri*.

—Tres.

Y así estuvieron un buen rato; sin embargo, el filósofo nunca le desvelaba el significado de las dos palabras sánscritas que la niña escribía siempre al principio de cada clase.

—¿Cuándo sabré qué significan esas dos palabras: *Adhīśvaras āhvāyaka?* —preguntaba ella siempre al final de cada sesión.

Y el filósofo siempre respondía lo mismo:

—Cuando estés preparada. —La niña protestaba, pero Dión ya había aprendido a manejar los sentimientos de la muchacha con cierta habilidad—. Además ahora es el momento de narrarte la batalla de Carrhae.

La niña calló y se dispuso a escuchar. La batalla, tal y como había anticipado el filósofo, daba para un relato largo y el anciano se había detenido la última clase cuando el hijo de Craso se suicidaba junto con sus oficiales. Tamura iba a reclamar que siguiera pero Dión Coceyo, que no había olvidado lo que era ser joven, señaló la arena del *Ludus Magnus*: Áyax volvía a entrenarse. La muchacha salió al exterior de inmediato y el viejo sonrió. El relato sobre Carrhae tendría que esperar.

28

UNA CARTA DE PLINIO

Domus Flavia (palacio imperial)
Roma, 112 d. C.

El emperador estaba revisando los planos que Apolodoro le había presentado sobre las últimas modificaciones en el gran complejo del nuevo foro que estaba levantando en el centro de Roma. Trajano asentía satisfecho mientras analizaba con atención cada pequeño detalle. Apolodoro era, sin duda, vanidoso, algo de lo que se le quejaban a menudo cuantos tenían que colaborar con el arquitecto, pero era, también con toda seguridad, un genio.

—Augusto... Fédimo, el secretario, quiere ver al emperador —dijo un pretoriano con voz tímida entreabriendo levemente la puerta de la cámara imperial.

—Que pase —respondió Trajano sin dejar de mirar los planos del gran nuevo foro. Estaba absorbido por las amplias dimensiones que iba a tener al final la parte dedicada a los mercados. Un enorme espacio de uso público, en parte techado y en parte con calles descubiertas pero donde la entrada a los carros estaría vedada. Un lugar de negocio y esparcimiento al mismo tiempo. Una gran idea, otra más, de su arquitecto.

Fédimo entró en la cámara imperial y se situó frente a la mesa del César, pero guardó un respetuoso silencio hasta que el emperador decidió dedicarle su atención.

—¿Y bien? —dijo al fin Trajano levantando la mirada de la mesa y reclinando la espalda en el respaldo de su *cathedra*.

—Se trata del correo, augusto. Acabo de recibirlo y como el César siempre desea estar informado de su llegada...

—Bien, sí, has hecho bien. —Pero no parecía demasiado

interesado por las cartas que se hubiera podido recibir en aquel momento y volvió a inclinarse sobre los planos—. Ya las veremos más tarde. Mañana.

Fédimo, no obstante, no se movió.

Trajano detectó con el rabillo del ojo que la sombra de su asistente personal seguía inmóvil y levantó de nuevo la mirada. No dijo nada, sino que se limitó a observar fijamente la faz de Fédimo.

—Hay una carta... —inició dudoso el joven secretario—, una misiva que creo que merece la pronta atención del emperador. Hay vidas en juego. Sólo por eso he interrumpido al César.

Trajano asintió con seriedad. Fédimo, pese a su juventud, se había mostrado diligente y con criterio adecuado en asuntos de diferente índole. La recomendación de Suetonio de emplearlo como asistente personal había sido acertada.

—¿Quién la remite? —preguntó el emperador con su tendencia militar a evitar cualquier tipo de rodeo absurdo.

—La envía el senador Plinio, gobernador de Bitinia.

—¿Y qué preocupa al bueno de Plinio en esta ocasión?

—El gobernador, augusto, parece preocupado por el asunto de los cristianos. —Fédimo tenía la potestad de revisar las cartas que recibía el César, decenas al día, en ocasiones más, y seleccionar de todas ellas aquellas que eran, a su juicio, relevantes para su señor—. Parece ser que ha habido muchas denuncias recientes en su provincia y tiene a muchos detenidos. Ha juzgado a algunos según los antiguos edictos imperiales de Nerón, pero tiene dudas sobre cómo continuar procediendo en este tema y desea el consejo del César. Argumenta que el emperador no le dejó instrucciones precisas en el libro de órdenes que le entregó cuando marchó a Bitinia.

—Eso es cierto —confirmó Trajano—. No consideré entonces que el asunto fuera importante, pero si a Plinio le preocupa, escuchémoslo. —Extendió la mano derecha hacia arriba invitando a su secretario a leer el contenido de la misiva del gobernador de Bitinia.

—Sí, por supuesto, César —respondió el asistente y extrajo de debajo de su túnica un papiro enrollado que desplegó con rapidez para proceder a su lectura—: «*C. Plinius Traiano Imperatori. Sollemne est mihi, domine, omnia de quibus dubito ad te referre. Quis enim potest melius...*» [*Mi señor, tengo por costumbre hacerte llegar todas aquellas dudas que me asaltan en cumplimiento de mi cargo. ¿Quién mejor, en efecto, para encauzar mis vacilaciones...?*].[17]

—Sáltate los halagos, Fédimo, y ve directamente al asunto — lo interrumpió el emperador.

—Sí, Cesar, por supuesto. En el siguiente párrafo entra de lleno en el tema: «*Nunca participé en Roma en ningún proceso contra cristianos. Desconozco por ello cuál es el crimen del que se los acusa, qué penas merecen, qué procedimiento debe regular la encuesta judicial y qué límites debe ponerse a ésta. Así, he tenido las más serias dudas sobre si deben establecerse diferencias entre las edades de los reos o si, por el contrario, los más jóvenes, por muy tierna que sea su edad, en nada se distinguen de los mayores...*».

El emperador se levantó al tiempo que alzaba levemente la mano derecha como quien da el alto. Fédimo calló de inmediato mientras observó como el César se desplazaba de la mesa a la ventana de la cámara imperial y miraba hacia el exterior. El secretario respetó las meditaciones de su señor.

Trajano vio una bandada de gaviotas que cruzaba el cielo de Roma. Irían seguramente hacia el vertedero de la ciudad junto al puerto fluvial, allí donde quebraban millares de ánforas cada día y se acumulaban otros desperdicios de los que aquellos animales vivían. El emperador suspiró. Sí, seguramente habría niños y ancianos y mujeres implicados en aquellos juicios contra cristianos. Desde Nerón no había sido habitual hacer distinción en las edades si el delito era ser cristiano. ¿Hasta qué punto era todo aquello justo?

—Sigue leyendo —ordenó Trajano sin dejar de mirar por la ventana.

Fédimo prosiguió con la carta de Plinio.

—«*He tenido dudas sobre si debe concederse el perdón al arrepen-*

---

17. Texto literal de la carta 96, libro X (en esta sección y en las siguientes marcadas en cursiva) que Plinio envió a Trajano entre 111 y 112. Traducción, para esta carta y la respuesta de Trajano, según la versión de José Carlos Martín publicada por Cátedra en 2007 (ver bibliografía).

timiento, o por el contrario, a aquel que haya sido cristiano en nada le beneficia renunciar a serlo; sobre si se castiga el nombre mismo de cristiano, incluso en ausencia de cualquier tipo de crímenes, o lo que se castiga son los crímenes implícitos en dicho nombre.»

Trajano se volvió y miró a su secretario.

—Interesante disyuntiva, ¿no crees, Fédimo? ¿Son los cristianos un peligro para el Estado por el hecho de ser cristianos si no han cometido otro crimen?

El asistente se sintió incómodo. No sabía bien qué responder. No estaba seguro ni siquiera de si el emperador esperaba una respuesta.

—No sé bien qué decir, augusto.

Trajano sonrió.

—Eres discreto, Fédimo, y aprecio esa discreción tuya. Cuando no se sabe algo lo más sensato es callar. Nos vendría bien aquí el consejo de Sura, pero ya no está entre nosotros.

—El emperador tiene a los senadores Celso, Palma o Nigrino en el *consilium augusti* —se atrevió a aventurar Fédimo.

Trajano negó con la cabeza.

—No, no. Es una sugerencia pertinente por tu parte, Fédimo, pero aunque son senadores hábiles en la política de Roma y hombres leales, aquí hay que hilar muy fino. Celso y los otros me valen cuando se trata de decidir sobre el Senado, pero aquí andan tan perdidos como yo.

—Está Lucio Quieto o... —el asistente dudó antes de decir el último nombre—, Adriano.

—No. Quieto es un militar. Cierto es, no obstante, que tendremos que ir probando en algún momento su capacidad para tareas de gobierno más delicadas, pero aún no ha llegado su momento. Y en cuanto a Adriano... —el emperador volvió a mirar por la ventana mientras hablaba—, sí, sería interesante saber qué piensa Adriano sobre los cristianos, pero imagino que si le pregunto, como siempre, no sabré si dice lo que realmente piensa o lo que cree que yo deseo oír. —Suspiró.

—¿Y Dión Coceyo, César? —sugirió entonces el asistente.

—Interesante opción. Pero es demasiado filósofo, poco práctico en asuntos de Estado. Y el tema de los cristianos es ya algo que afecta al Imperio entero. Debe decidir un César. No,

Fédimo, aquí estoy solo. Sigue con la carta. Veamos qué acciones ha emprendido Plinio hasta la fecha.

—Sí, César. —El secretario continuó leyendo—: «*He aquí de qué modo me he comportado por el momento con aquellos que han sido conducidos ante mí acusados de ser cristianos: Les he preguntado directamente a ellos si son cristianos. Al decirme que sí, se lo he preguntado de nuevo una segunda vez y hasta una tercera vez, advirtiéndoles de que su reconocimiento de algo semejante los supondría la muerte. A los que han mantenido su declaración he ordenado ajusticiarlos. La razón de ello fue que no me cabe duda de que, cualquiera que fuese la naturaleza del crimen que confesaban, ciertamente ese fanatismo y esa intransigente obstinación merecían la muerte. Ha habido otros a los que, pese a haber mostrado una irracionalidad semejante, al ser ciudadanos romanos, los he incluido en las listas de aquellos que deben ser enviados a ser juzgados en Roma...*».

Aquí fue Fédimo el que interrumpió la lectura.

—El envío de estas personas, augusto, generará inconvenientes al emperador en Roma.

Trajano asintió mientras seguía observando el ir y venir de las gaviotas.

—Sin duda juzgar aquí a esos acusados puede crearnos incomodidades, pero son ciudadanos romanos y la ley exige que sea cual sea su crimen tienen que ser juzgados en Roma y sólo en Roma. No puedo exigir a los cristianos que cumplan con las leyes, por un lado, y luego no dar yo mismo ejemplo saltándomelas.

—El emperador está en lo cierto, sin duda. Perdón, augusto. —La confianza con la que Trajano lo trataba impulsaba a Fédimo, en ocasiones como ésa, a dar su opinión sobre el correo imperial, pero rápidamente se dio cuenta de cuánta razón tenía el César en lo que acababa de decir: ninguna autoridad puede exigir el cumplimiento de las leyes si esa autoridad es la primera en no cumplirlas.

—Sigue leyendo —dijo el emperador desde la ventana, mirando al cielo de Roma.

Fédimo siguió con la carta.

—«*Ha aparecido, fijada en un lugar público, una denuncia anónima dando a conocer un gran número de nombres. A los que han negado ser o haber sido en algún momento cristianos, los he dejado en libertad, pues han invocado a nuestros dioses de acuerdo con una fórmula dictada por mí en la que se les requería que hicieran una ofrenda de incienso y vino ante tu imagen, que con este propósito yo había ordenado traer junto a las estatuas de los númenes. Además, les he exigido que maldijeran el nombre de Cristo, algo a lo que según se dice, no se puede forzar en modo alguno a los que son verdaderamente cristianos...»*

—Plinio, Plinio, Plinio —dijo el emperador suspirando largamente y apoyando las manos en el alféizar interior de la ventana abierta; luego habló mirando al cielo—: Llevo años intentando separarme de la imagen de Domiciano que se hacía adorar y llamar *Dominus et Deus* y ahora vas tú y haces que me adoren. ¡Por Cástor y Pólux! —Y negó con la cabeza varias veces.

El secretario esperó hasta que el emperador dejó de lamentarse.

—¿Sigo leyendo, augusto?

—Sí.

Fédimo continuó: Plinio seguía exponiendo más detalles relacionados con los juicios contra los cristianos, incluido que había no sólo sacerdotes o ministros entre las gentes de aquella religión, sino también diaconisas o ministras, y así más detalles hasta llegar al momento en que volvía a dirigirse directamente al emperador:

—*«Por todo ello, posponiendo de momento la instrucción de la causa, me he apresurado a consultarte. En efecto, me ha parecido que el asunto merecía que consultase tu parecer, en especial por el número de los acusados, pues muchas personas de todas las edades, de toda condición y tanto de uno como de otro sexo han sido ya procesadas, y muchas otras lo serán igualmente. Y el contagio de esta superstición no se ha extendido únicamente por las ciudades, sino que se ha propagado también por los pueblos y el campo. Creo, no obstante, que la enfermedad puede ser detenida y curada. Ciertamente, es un hecho que los templos, que ya se encontraban prácticamente abandonados, han comenzado a ser frecuentados de nuevo, que las ceremonias sagradas interrumpidas durante largo tiempo vuelven a ser celebradas. Y que por todas partes se vende la carne de las víctimas sacrificiales, para la que hasta hace muy poco se encontraban muy escasos compradores. De ello se deduce fácilmente que gran cantidad de personas podrían ser alejadas de esa superstición si se les ofreciese el perdón en el caso de que se arrepintiesen».* Firma Cayo Plinio, gobernador de Bitinia.

—De acuerdo —respondió Trajano y abandonó la ventana para retornar a su asiento frente a la mesa. Había otro escritorio más pequeño próximo a la ventana, con tinta, papiro y todo lo necesario para escribir. Trajano lo señaló y Fédimo, de inmediato, se sentó en una pequeña *sella* dispuesto a tomar nota de las palabras de su amo.

—Veamos... —dijo Trajano, reclinando la espalda mientras pensaba—. Sí. Anota: «*De Trajano, imperator Caesar augustus, et cetera, et cetera... Actum quem debuisti, mi Secunde, in excutiendis causis eorum, qui Christiani ad te delati fuerant, secutus es. Neque enim in universum aliquid, quod quasi certam formam habeat, constitui potest...*»[18] «*Mi querido Segundo, has seguido el procedimiento que debías en la instrucción de los procesos de aquellos que fueron denunciados ante ti como cristianos. En efecto, no puede establecerse una norma general que imponga, por así decirlo, unos criterios absolutamente rígidos. Los cristianos no deben ser perseguidos de oficio. Si son denunciados y se prueba su culpabilidad, deben ser castigados. No obstante, aquel que niegue ser cristiano y lo demuestre de hecho, esto es venerando a nuestros dioses y al emperador...*»* No. Me he dejado llevar por Plinio. Reescribe esa última frase: *No obstante, aquel que niegue ser cristiano y lo demuestre de hecho, esto es venerando a nuestros dioses, aunque resulte sospechoso de haber sido cristiano en el pasado, debe obtener el perdón por su arrepentimiento.*» ¿Lo has anotado bien, Fédimo?

—Sí, Cesar. He omitido la referencia a lo de adorar al emperador. —Leyó la frase de nuevo. Trajano cabeceó un par de veces.

—Bien —continuó entonces el César—: «*Por lo que se refiere a las denuncias anónimas que puedan aparecer fijadas en lugares*

18. Literal, ésta y las secciones que siguen en cursiva, de la carta 97, Libro X del *Epistolario* de Plinio que Trajano escribió como respuesta a las preguntas del gobernador de Bitinia.

públicos, no deben dar lugar a ningún tipo de acusación, pues es una práctica detestable e impropia de nuestro tiempo». Y firmas con mi nombre, etcétera, etcétera.

Trajano esperó un rato mientras daba tiempo a que su asistente terminara la carta, pero luego volvió a preguntar al secretario imperial.

—Dime, Fédimo, ¿qué piensas de mi respuesta?

El joven asistente dudaba.

—Di lo que piensas —insistió el emperador.

—Creo, augusto, que el César muestra equilibrio en sus palabras: castiga la obstinación de los que al manifestarse pública y reiteradamente cristianos eluden aceptar la forma de vida romana, pero, por otro lado, se niega a escuchar acusaciones anónimas que abrirían el camino a que envidias particulares se mezclaran en este asunto y a que se castigara a muchos inocentes. Aunque...

—Te escucho, Fédimo.

—Como el César me ha preguntado... no sé hasta qué punto es justo condenar a alguien por el hecho de creer en un dios diferente si no han cometido otro crimen. ¿Es realmente un crimen ser cristiano?

—El problema, Fédimo, estriba en que muchos cristianos no quieren reconocer la autoridad imperial, ésa es la cuestión clave. Eso es lo que no puedo permitir. Sólo pido que no hagan exhibición pública de sus creencias. No los quiero buscar pero no puedo tolerar que haciendo exhibición pública de unas creencias que muchos temen desafíen de forma notoria mi autoridad. ¡Por todos los dioses, sólo les pido discreción! La obstinación que han mostrado aquéllos a los que Plinio les ofreció retractarse en público es fanatismo puro y los fanáticos, Fédimo, siempre están mejor muertos. En este punto, Plinio ha obrado correctamente. El día que el fanatismo llegue al poder de Roma, será el fin del Imperio. Y me da igual si esos fanáticos se hacen llamar cristianos o judíos o romanos puros. El fanatismo, venga de donde venga, termina con todo.

—Entiendo, augusto.

Se hizo un silencio algo más largo de lo normal mientras

Trajano miraba fijamente a su joven secretario hasta que el emperador volvió a hablar.

—Dime, Fédimo... ¿eres cristiano?

El secretario vaciló un instante apenas perceptible, pero el César lo detectó.

—No, augusto.

—Pero... ¿has pensado en serlo alguna vez?

—Sí, César. Hubo momentos, cuando era esclavo en Hispania y mis amos no eran tan generosos conmigo como lo fue el *procurator bibliothecae* o el mismísimo emperador ahora, en que pensar en una vida donde los... miserables seríamos bien tratados, tal y como difunden los cristianos, resultaba una idea atractiva, César. Pero no, no soy cristiano.

—Y si te hicieras cristiano... ¿me lo confesarías?

Hubo un nuevo y más largo silencio. El emperador acababa de ordenar al gobernador de Bitinia que condenara a muerte a los que admitieran públicamente ser cristianos. Fédimo tragaba saliva. ¿Era aquella conversación con el César pública o privada?

—No lo sé, César.

Trajano lo miró con seriedad un rato y, al fin, sonrió.

—Desde luego, como me dijo Suetonio, no eres hombre que tienda a la mentira. Ésa es una virtud importante. Ésa y la lealtad.

—El César sabe que tiene mi fidelidad absoluta.

Trajano asintió.

—Lo sé, pero ten cuidado. Ahora envía esa carta, mi respuesta, a Plinio. Como bien has dicho, hay vidas en juego y no debemos retrasar mi mensaje.

Fédimo se dio la vuelta y echó a andar hacia la puerta de bronce, pero antes de llegar a ella, se volvió de nuevo y miró al emperador, que retornaba a su asiento para estudiar de nuevo los planos de Apolodoro de Damasco y el nuevo gran foro de Roma.

—¿De qué he de tener miedo exactamente, César?

Trajano lo miró y respondió con seriedad de forma enigmática.

—A veces la lealtad absoluta conduce a la muerte. Tengo

enemigos poderosos, cualquier emperador los tiene. Algún día, Fédimo, te intentarán comprar. Siempre pasa. Ese día tendrás que decidir entre seguir siéndome leal o salvar tu vida.

Fédimo miraba al emperador sin parpadear.

—Puedes retirarte —dijo Trajano.

El joven secretario se mantuvo en silencio, dio media vuelta, tocó en las puertas de bronce, éstas se abrieron y salió sin mirar atrás.

29

LA INTUICIÓN DE RIXNU

Palacio imperial de Cesifonte, Partia
112 d. C.

Él seguía resoplando encima de ella. La hermosa Rixnu lo sobrellevaba cerrando los ojos y pensando en mil cosas distintas. De esa forma los bufidos del *Šāhān Šāh* de Partia mientras se movía encima de su cuerpo parecían provenir de más lejos, de otro mundo, de un lugar en el que ella no estaba. A Rixnu le preocupaba mucho últimamente la pequeña Aryazate. La niña nunca había estado enferma y, de pronto, llevaba un par de semanas con una fiebre que no terminaba de irse nunca. Era extraño. Aryazate tenía ya doce años. Las niñas más débiles, las que solían morir por enfermedad, fallecían antes. Pasados los doce años las muertes eran por quedarse embarazadas cuando el parto resultaba difícil. Y sin embargo, Aryazate había enfermado ahora. La pequeña era muy importante para todos: para ella misma por puro afecto, y para la corte de Partia porque era clave para pactar con el rebelde Vologases o para premiar al leal Partamasiris. Ninguno parecía un buen futuro para la muchacha pero el destino de una hija de un rey de reyes era el que era. Sí, la pequeña, sin quererlo, era esencial en la política de Partia y parecía, sin embargo, estar muriendo...

—Aaaahhh —exhaló Osroes y se dejó caer de costado liberando a Rixnu de su peso y su sudor y su mal aliento.

La joven *Šhar Bāmbišn*, la reina consorte Rixnu, pudo sentarse entonces en la cama. Lo hizo como si tuviera un resorte en la espalda que la incorporara de golpe.

—La están envenenando —dijo Rixnu en voz alta mientras

se cubría el cuerpo con rapidez con su fina túnica de seda blanca.

—¿Qué dices? —preguntó confuso el rey de reyes Osroes, todavía no repuesto de su placer y del ejercicio para obtenerlo.

La muchacha se volvió y vio a su esposo con los ojos cerrados y algo de baba en la boca, desnudo, boca arriba. Rixnu pensó que no había tiempo para explicaciones. No había un instante que perder.

—¿Mi esposo ha terminado? —preguntó ella con el tono más dócil que pudo emplear.

Osroes no era hombre de gran capacidad física ni en el campo de batalla ni en el lecho.

—Sí.

—Entonces he de regresar junto a Aryazate —continuó ella y se ajustó bien la túnica mientras se levantaba. No quería entretenerse llamando a las esclavas.

—¿Sigue... enferma? —preguntó Osroes y bostezó.

—Sí —confirmó ella ya desde la puerta y salió de la cámara del emperador de Partia. Osroes no se levantó ni dijo nada más. Se había quedado dormido.

Rixnu corrió por todas las estancias del palacio hasta conseguir llegar a la pequeña habitación donde Aryazate continuaba en cama, con fiebre. Como durante los últimos días, la hermosa *Šhar Bāmbišn* encontró al lado de la pequeña a una de las dos mujeres kushan que el nuevo emperador Kanishka del imperio vecino había enviado recientemente como regalo a Osroes para ampliar su séquito de mujeres.

—¿Cómo está? —preguntó Rixnu.

Kumaramitra, la joven kushan, de rodillas junto a la niña, la miró con tristeza.

—Sigue mal.

Kumaramitra era mujer de pocas palabras. Apenas entendía el griego. Eso sí, era bella y dócil y había agradado a Osroes. Un regalo extraño aquel, una especie de envío para que el nuevo emperador kushan se reconciliase con el rey de reyes de Partia tras las diferencias y los conflictos del pasado, cuando el emperador kushan anterior, el viejo Kadphises, había estado ayudando al rebelde parto Vologases en su guerra contra Osroes. Pero Kumaramitra y la otra mujer eran tan hermosas que Osroes y sus consejeros no pensaron en nada más. En ese momento entró también en la sala la veterana Asiabatum. Rixnu no se lo pensó dos veces.

—La están envenenando —dijo ésta a la poderosa reina de reinas.

Asiabatum la miró confusa, pero Rixnu dirigió la mirada a Kumaramitra y la vieja reina de reinas empezó a asentir despacio mientras en su cabeza se formaban las mismas ideas que había tenido Rixnu apenas unos instantes antes: Kumaramitra había llegado hacía unas semanas a la corte de Cesifonte; la pequeña Aryazate, tan dulce y tan extrovertida como siempre, había hecho amistad enseguida con ella y la otra mujer kushan. De hecho, Kumaramitra parecía haber buscado la complicidad de Aryazate antes que la de ninguna otra princesa del séquito real; hasta el punto de que la pequeña estaba enseñando griego a las recién llegadas. Justo a la semana siguiente de la aparición de esas mujeres en la corte de Partia, Aryazate, que nunca había estado enferma, tenía fiebres que no la abandonaban. Tanto aprecio parecían haberle cogido las mujeres kushan que Asiabatum había permitido que la cuidaran ellas mismas. Al lado del lecho de Aryazate había un caldo caliente y Kumaramitra aún tenía la cuchara en la mano. Asiabatum llegó a las mismas conclusiones que Rixnu.

Cualquier otra mujer del séquito de esposas del emperador Osroes habría preguntado antes, pero Asiabatum no. Advertida por Rixnu, de pronto lo vio todo tan claro que sin dudarlo se acercó a Kumaramitra y le propinó una sonora bofetada que la tumbó.

—¿Por qué? —preguntó la reina de reinas mientras le propinaba una segunda y una tercera bofetadas que hicieron que la joven kushan rodara por toda la habitación. Rixnu se acercó, entretanto, al lecho de la pequeña enferma. Aryazate ni siquiera se movía. Debería haberse despertado por el tumulto, pero no reaccionaba.

»¿Por qué? —insistía Asiabatum mientras lanzaba más golpes sobre la mujer kushan, que se protegía la cabeza con las manos como podía.

—¡Tienen a mis hijos! ¡Tienen a mis hijos! —acertó a decir al fin Kumaramitra a modo de confesión y defensa.

Asiabatum dejó de golpearla. No por falta de ganas, sino porque lo esencial ahora era salvar a Aryazate.

—No se mueve —dijo Rixnu en medio de un sollozo ahogado—. La han matado.

30

LA COLUMNA TRAJANA

Roma, 112 d. C.

—Por aquí, César —dijo Apolodoro de Damasco—; por aquí.

El arquitecto le estaba mostrando al emperador de Roma lo que para él era, junto con el gran puente sobre el Danubio en Drobeta, su gran obra maestra, al menos, hasta la fecha: el nuevo foro de Roma. Trajano, mientras seguía meditando en su cabeza que necesitaba un motivo, una justificación para su proyecto de cruzar el Éufrates, oía al arquitecto sirio hablando a su lado. Hasta él mismo, el propio César, pese a sus preocupaciones sobre Oriente, estaba admirado de lo que veía. Y si él estaba impresionado cuánto más lo estaría el pueblo de Roma cuando se abrieran al público todos aquellos edificios. Y es que, a la espera de poder emprender una nueva gran campaña militar, Trajano había seguido con su plan de levantar grandes construcciones públicas en la capital del Imperio y en muchas ciudades provinciales. De hecho, Apolodoro acababa de regresar de supervisar la finalización de las obras del nuevo Portus Traiani Felicis en Ostia, una ampliación de las instalaciones portuarias de Claudio, que habían quedado pequeñas para recibir todo el tráfico de navíos comerciales que llegaban a Italia desde cualquier rincón del mundo. Y Trajano tenía aún más encargos que hacerle a su genial arquitecto, pero, en ese momento, decidió dejarlo hablar. El hombre se había ganado a pulso ser escuchado aquella jornada, así que Trajano decidió olvidarse, aunque sólo fuera por un rato, de sus planes sobre Partia.

—Como verá el César —explicaba Apolodoro—, hemos dejado al sur los antiguos foros de Julio César y Augusto; foros, por otro lado, que ni siquiera juntos alcanzan las dimensiones de este nuevo complejo. El foro del emperador Trajano será mayor que ningún otro, pero no sólo en extensión, César, sino también en alturas. Este complejo tiene varias plantas y he utilizado no sólo columnas, sino también numerosas cariátides para embellecer los puntos de apoyo sobre los que elevo un piso sobre otro. Tenemos entonces una enorme plaza, a modo de un ágora griega, para disfrute de todos los que paseen por este nuevo foro, o como un posible nuevo lugar de reunión y debate. Sé que esto es más griego que romano, César, soy consciente de ello, por eso, nada más atravesar aquella columnata el edificio de la basílica resalta enormemente, devolviéndonos a un complejo más puramente romano. —Caminaron a paso rápido para cruzar aquella gran nueva plaza en el centro de Roma, seguidos de cerca por la guardia imperial y por un Lucio Quieto a quien Trajano había pedido que lo acompañara en aquella visita privada.

Llegaron rápidamente a la columnata en cuestión, pero el emperador se detuvo y con él el resto de la comitiva. Trajano se volvió para admirar de nuevo aquel amplio espacio plano, enmarcado por esbeltas columnas y cariátides.

—¡Por Júpiter! —dijo el César y luego miró a Quieto—. ¿Qué te parece?

—Es inmenso, César —afirmó Lucio Quieto con aplomo—. Una gran obra —añadió mirando al arquitecto.

Apolodoro no estaba acostumbrado a recibir elogios de militares y se inclinó ante el *legatus* de confianza del emperador.

—¿Cruzamos, César? —preguntó entonces el arquitecto señalando hacia la columnata.

—Sí, quiero verlo todo —aceptó Trajano.

Pasaron por entre aquellas columnas que separaban la plaza del ágora de otra segunda plaza en cuyo centro se levantaba la gigantesca basílica Ulpia, llamada a convertirse en el centro de la justicia civil de Roma.

—La idea, César —proseguía Apolodoro mientras rodeaban la nueva basílica— es que al combinar el ágora con una nueva basílica contigua, y todo rodeado por espacios cubiertos, porticados, soportados por columnas, los hombres de leyes y los comerciantes de la ciudad disponen de un gran centro donde departir de sus asuntos al aire libre en primavera y otoño o a cubierto, protegidos del tórrido sol del verano o de la incómoda humedad del invierno.

—Parece que has pensado en todo.

—Es mi obligación, César.

—Cierto —admitió Trajano—, pero no es frecuente que todos cumplan con sus obligaciones, por eso cuando encuentro a alguien que como tú siempre lo hace no puedo evitar sorprenderme. Creo que no necesito más que los dedos de las manos para contar el número de hombres que no me han defraudado. Y aun así, creo que soy afortunado. A más de un emperador le habría bastado con una sola mano —y se permitió una carcajada a la que se unió Quieto y la mayor parte de los pretorianos, empezando por Liviano, el jefe del pretorio. Apolodoro sonrió, asintió y aguardó a que la comitiva se decidiera a seguirlo. Todavía quedaba mucho por ver, pero en ese momento apareció otro pretoriano que cruzaba en diagonal el espacio entre la columnata del ágora y la basílica Ulpia. Debía de tratarse de algo urgente, porque si no los pretorianos que custodiaban todo el complejo, a la espera de ser abierto tras su inauguración por Trajano, no lo habrían dejado entrar.

—Es Aulo —dijo Quieto, que aún conservaba muy bien su vista, mucho mejor que la del César.

—Traigo un mensaje de Siria, César —dijo el tribuno pretoriano en cuanto llegó a la altura de la comitiva imperial.

Trajano alargó el brazo y Aulo le entregó un papiro enrollado que el César desplegó de inmediato. Para leerlo tuvo que dar la espalda al resto para poder disponer de toda la luz del sol de invierno. El mensaje era breve. El emperador leyó en silencio pero sonrió al final. Se volvió hacia Aulo y le devolvió el mensaje.

—Siempre me has traído buenas noticias, Aulo. Eres el mejor Mercurio de que dispongo —dijo Trajano, recordando así que Aulo, hacía ya años, le había llevado el mensaje de su adopción por el divino Nerva, en otros tiempos, cuando Trajano custodiaba la peligrosa frontera del Rin.

Sin embargo, el emperador no desveló a nadie el contenido del papiro que acababa de recibir enviado desde la lejana Siria, sino que se dirigió de nuevo a Apolodoro.

—¿Qué más hay que ver, arquitecto?

Apolodoro los condujo entonces al otro lado de la basílica Ulpia, donde había otro amplio espacio flanqueado por dos edificios de dos plantas cada uno y un amplio patio central con una enorme columna levantándose hacia el cielo orgullosa y completamente decorada con relieves en espiral, que llamaban la atención aún más por los vivos colores —rojos, amarillos, azules— con los que estaban pintados.

—¡Has acabado la columna! —dijo Trajano.

—Por completo, César. Bueno, aún hay algunos operarios terminando algunos detalles —precisó el arquitecto señalando a unos artesanos que aún repasaban con pintura azul, subidos a un andamio, un relieve donde se representaba el Danubio y el imponente puente que Trajano había ordenado construir al propio Apolodoro en aquella parte del mundo.

Todos se quedaron admirados observando aquella columna de más de cien pies de altura[19] que se erigía en el centro del nuevo patio, en la que se veían escenas bélicas de las dos campañas de la Dacia. En la amplia base de piedra y mármol había una inscripción a la que Trajano se acercó y la leyó en voz alta.

SENATVS·POPVLVSQVE·ROMANVS
IMP·CAESARI·DIVI·NERVAE·F·NERVAE
TRAIANO·AVG·GERM·DACICO·PONTIF
MAXIMO·TRIB·POT·XVII·IMP·VI·COS·VI·P·P
AD·DECLARANDVM·QVANTAE·ALTITVDINIS
MONS·ET·LOCVS·TANT<IS·OPER>IBVS·SIT·EGESTVS

[El Senado y el pueblo de Roma (dedican esto) al emperador y César, hijo del divino Nerva, Trajano Augusto Germánico Dácico, pontífice máximo, en su decimoséptimo año como tribuno, habiendo sido aclamado seis veces como *imperator*, seis veces

---

19. Unos treinta y cinco metros si tenemos en cuenta el pedestal.

como cónsul, padre de la patria, para demostrar cómo de alta era la gran colina y el terreno que ha sido excavado para estas grandes obras]

—¿Realmente, Apolodoro, toda la altura de la columna es la que se ha excavado en la colina para poder levantar todos estos edificios? —preguntó Trajano cuando terminó de leer la inscripción..

—Así es, augusto. El César me pidió un monumento que recordara su gran victoria sobre los dacios, algo diferente a un arco de triunfo, algo diferente al arco de Tito, y aquí tiene el César esta columna, donde escena a escena se puede ver recreado todo lo que aconteció contra los dacios. Además, en efecto, marca la altura de la colina que había aquí antes y que hemos excavado para hacer la gran explanada sobre la que construir el ágora, las bibliotecas, la basílica y el nuevo templo.

Trajano fue rodeando la columna impresionado por la altura y por el perfecto detalle de los relieves. Había un hombre esperando a la puerta de una de las dos bibliotecas, pero el emperador no había reparado en él y nadie quería interrumpir al César mientras rodeaba y miraba la columna que rememoraba sus victorias al norte del Danubio.

—Observo —dijo Trajano con tono irónico— que te has permitido recrear también la construcción de tu puente sobre el Danubio... allí y allí. —Señaló un par de relieves donde se veía a las legiones de Roma cruzando el Danubio sobre lo que sin duda era una reproducción en relieve del puente, justo donde los operarios seguían repasando la pintura.

El arquitecto no sabía bien qué decir. Quizá se había dejado llevar por su vanidad, pero, de alguna forma, había querido dejar constancia de la construcción de su puente en otro lugar; ¿quién podía asegurarle que nadie destruyera su gran obra en la Dacia o que los textos escritos que hablaban de ella no se perdieran? Si lo plasmaba en aquella columna, sería otra forma más de preservar la memoria de su obra maestra de ingeniería.

—Pensé que la construcción del puente fue parte de las

campañas de la Dacia, César —argumentó el arquitecto al fin, inseguro de la reacción del emperador.

—¡Por Júpiter, pues claro que lo fue! —confirmó Trajano para alivio del arquitecto y tranquilidad de todos—. Claro que lo fue, una gran obra que merece ser recordada, sin duda, en esta columna... —Fue entonces cuando vio al hombre que esperaba frente a una de las bibliotecas.

—Es Suetonio, César —dijo el arquitecto—. Le he invitado a venir esta mañana para que nos mostrara las bibliotecas por dentro.

—Parece razonable que el *procurator bibliothecae augusti* sea quien me enseñe las nuevas bibliotecas —confirmó el emperador.

Cayo Suetonio Tranquilo saludó al César, al arquitecto y al resto de los miembros de la comitiva imperial y los invitó a entrar en la biblioteca.

—Tenemos esta entrada con cuatro columnas, augusto —empezó a explicar Suetonio—, pero hemos instalado mamparas de bronce entre las columnas de forma que podamos cerrar el acceso a la biblioteca por la noche o según el horario de apertura que estipulemos. Pero pasemos adentro. Aquí, en la gran sala central, hemos distribuido estas grandes mesas para las consultas o lecturas que se hagan en la propia biblioteca. En este edificio tenemos los textos latinos, mientras que en la otra biblioteca, al otro lado de la gran columna, están los textos griegos...

Pero cuando Suetonio se volvió un momento se percató de que los miembros de la comitiva imperial, incluido el César, miraban a lo alto. Y es que el interior de la biblioteca era imponente, con dos alturas con sendas columnatas que ascendían hacia el cielo hasta elevarse casi noventa pies[20] de altura.

—El techo son bóvedas de aristas, César —intervino Apolodoro al constatar, como Suetonio, que todos parecían más interesados por el edificio que por lo que éste podía llegar a contener—. Bóvedas con dos grandes ventanales en ambos extremos para facilitar el acceso de mucha luz al interior. En el

---

20. Concretamente veintisiete metros de altura.

ábside de esta biblioteca y de su gemela he ubicado una gran estatua del emperador. Y el suelo es muy sólido, de bloques de piedra de granito traídos de Egipto pero recubiertos con mármol multicolor proveniente de Asia. Las paredes son de hormigón y ladrillo para evitar la humedad; el *procurator* me insistió enormemente en la necesidad de evitar la humedad en el edificio...

Suetonio, aprovechando el comentario, interrumpió al arquitecto y tomó la palabra de nuevo:

—Sí, augusto, es fundamental mantener la humedad fuera del edificio o, de lo contrario, todos los papiros sufren y se deterioran con rapidez. He ordenado hacer copias de aquellos textos antiguos y modernos más relevantes, pero aun así es imposible copiarlo todo constantemente. Una buena preservación de los documentos es la opción más barata a largo plazo. Quizá en un principio representa un mayor esfuerzo económico y de ingeniería, pero a la larga dará sus frutos. Con estas dos bibliotecas nuevas Roma se podrá comparar pronto con la mismísima Alejandría o con Pérgamo.

Apolodoro enarcó las cejas. Aquello le parecía una exageración, pero era incuestionable que las nuevas bibliotecas engrandecían mucho la capacidad de almacenamiento de papiros en la ciudad de Roma.

—Además —continuó Suetonio—, si me sigue la comitiva imperial, por favor, por aquí —los condujo a los *armaria* de madera donde se guardaban los rollos de papiro en los nichos de las paredes del edificio—, en esta biblioteca la profundidad de los huecos donde hemos puesto los *armaria* es superior a la normal: en lugar de que tengan la misma profundidad que los propios armarios de madera, aproximadamente un pie y medio, el fondo de cada hueco es de dos pies. Esto es muy importante, porque entre el fondo del propio armario de madera y la pared misma del edificio queda un espacio vacío. Así la humedad de las paredes, que siempre se acumula con el tiempo, no toca los *armaria* sino que se queda en ese espacio vacío, evitando así que afecte a los papiros del interior. Sé que esto ha supuesto un esfuerzo adicional a nuestro arquitecto, pero quiero subrayar su importancia y agradecer también la atención que Apolodoro de Damasco ha puesto en este punto, César.

—Hemos dejado aquí, augusto —dijo entonces el arquitecto, feliz de recuperar el turno de palabra—, un hueco donde todavía no están instalados los *armaria* al completo. Así el César puede comprobar cómo, en efecto, los compartimentos de madera no llegan hasta el fondo, que no tocan la pared.

Trajano introdujo la cabeza en el hueco que se le indicaba y pudo apreciar el espacio vacío que haría de cámara de aire protectora y antihumedad.

—Me alegra comprobar que los hombres inteligentes a mi servicio, al servicio de Roma —respondió Trajano satisfecho—, saben colaborar en beneficio del bien común. ¿Lo ves, Quieto? Nuestro bibliotecario y nuestro arquitecto son como los *legati* en campaña militar. Si actúan coordinados son capaces de conseguirlo todo.

La visita condujo entonces a la comitiva imperial de regreso al exterior de la biblioteca, al pórtico en cuyo centro se levantaba la gran columna en memoria de las campañas de la Dacia.

—Le he reservado una sorpresa final al César —dijo Apolodoro con cierto misterio.

—Imagino que te refieres al templo que has levantado allí, entre las dos bibliotecas, ¿no es así? —comentó el emperador bastante persuadido de estar desentrañando la supuesta sorpresa del arquitecto.

—Oh, no. El César ya vio el templo hace unas semanas y no hay nada nuevo añadido en él, salvo los trabajos de limpieza que se han hecho para la próxima inauguración. No, la sorpresa la tiene el César junto a él, sólo que no lo sabe.

—¿Junto a mí? —preguntó Trajano en voz alta y miró a su alrededor—. Lo único que tengo a mi lado es la columna.

—Precisamente, César —confirmó el arquitecto. Como vio que el emperador fruncía el ceño en señal de no comprender, Apolodoro, con una amplia sonrisa, le hizo una invitación—: ¿Le gustaría al emperador subir a lo alto de la columna? La vista es magnífica.

Trajano miró a la columna y parpadeó varias veces.

—¿Es hueca? ¿Se puede subir?

—Es hueca, César, y se puede subir a lo alto —confirmó Apolodoro abriendo una puerta de bronce en la amplia base de la columna. Trajano se asomó y vio que al fondo se veía una escalinata en caracol que ascendía.

—¡Magnífico, por Cástor y Pólux! —exclamó Trajano admirado—. Esto no me lo comentaste nunca cuando me enseñabas los planos.

—Quería dejar algo con lo que sorprender al emperador.

—Vamos allá —dijo Trajano lleno de curiosidad, pero Liviano se interpuso en su camino.

—Es una escalera angosta, César, y con el permiso del emperador, aunque no preveo ningún ataque contra su vida aquí y ahora, preferiría que alguno de los pretorianos abriera la marcha, no fuera a ser que...

—¿No sea que hubiera alguien escondido y armado en el interior de la escalera de la columna? —preguntó Trajano divertido, pero sin hacer mofa del comentario de su jefe del pretorio quien, a fin de cuentas, sólo estaba haciendo su trabajo con celo: velar por la seguridad del emperador.

Trajano se hizo a un lado y asintió.

De inmediato Aulo, a una mirada de Liviano, entró en la base de la columna, desenfundó su *gladio* y empezó a ascender seguido por otros dos pretorianos a los que había señalado Liviano.

—Ahora el arquitecto y el César —dijo Liviano mirando siempre a Trajano en busca de aprobación. El emperador movió la cabeza afirmativamente, pero antes de seguir a Apolodoro se dirigió a Quieto.

—Lucio, tú sígueme.

Liviano no puso reparo alguno a que Lucio Quieto, el hombre en el que más confiaban todos los pretorianos, junto con lo senadores Nigrino, Celso y Palma, siguiera al emperador. A Liviano le pareció que no podía haber mejor guardaespaldas que el *legatus* norteafricano. Quieto era para Trajano lo que Marco Antonio fue para Julio César. De hecho, sólo pudieron acabar con éste al separarlo de Marco Antonio. «Ojalá Trajano tuviera siempre la habilidad de no separarse demasiado de Lucio Quieto», pensó Liviano.

Ascendieron rápidamente al principio, pero pronto fueron perdiendo energía.

—¿Cuántos escalones hay? —preguntó Trajano.

—Ciento ochenta y cinco, César —respondió el arquitecto.

Nadie dijo nada en un rato. Se podía ver perfectamente en el interior de la columna porque Apolodoro había tenido la genial idea, otra más, de abrir pequeñas ranuras por las que se filtraba la suficiente luz a intervalos regulares, de forma que se veían cada uno de los escalones sin que las ranuras fueran visibles desde el exterior. No, al menos, si no sabías de su existencia.

—¿Y cuántas... de estas... pequeñas ventanas... hay? —preguntó Trajano, tomando aire casi entre palabra y palabra.

—Cuarenta... y tres... César —dijo Apolodoro.

—¿Lo tienes todo... contabilizado... calculado? —añadió el emperador.

—Todo... César... la columna mide cien pies... de alto... hay ciento ochenta y cinco escalones... las cuarenta y tres ventanas... todo hecho con veintinueve grandes bloques de mármol... Cada catorce escalones damos una vuelta completa, César... es decir... que necesitaremos trece vueltas completas para llegar a lo alto más tres escalones más...

—En efecto... lo tienes todo... calculado...

Al fin llegaron arriba.

Trajano pudo ver ahora de cerca la estatua a imagen y semejanza suya que coronaba el monumento, así como la magnífica vista que había anticipado el arquitecto.

—Ésos son los miradores que he abierto en las bibliotecas —dijo Apolodoro señalando hacia un lado y al contrario—, de forma que todo el mundo podrá admirar los relieves de la columna desde diferentes alturas, no sólo desde la lejanía del suelo.

—Bien pensado, por Júpiter. Y allí veo los mercados —añadió Trajano señalando hacia la estructura de varias plantas de altura de la gran zona comercial que Apolodoro había construido contigua al nuevo foro. Entre la basílica, las bibliotecas, la columna, el ágora, el nuevo templo y los mercados, aquél era uno de los mayores complejos arquitectónicos de la ciudad, comparable sólo al Circo Máximo o al Anfiteatro Flavio. Y todo en el nuevo foro eran edificios civiles de uso público, para la justicia, para la cultura o el comercio. Nerón o Domiciano se construyeron grandes palacios, pero él, Trajano, había preferido obras para el beneficio y el uso de todos.

—He acabado, César, los trabajos que el César me encargó —concluyó Apolodoro,

—Ya veo —respondió Trajano—. Te has superado, arquitecto. Además has dado término a las reformas del puerto de Ostia.

—Sí, César.

—Es decir, que te veo aburrido, sin proyectos —dijo el emperador bromeando.

—Estoy seguro de que el César ya tiene pensado algo en lo que deba trabajar.

—En efecto.

—¿Dónde, augusto? ¿Aquí en Roma?

Trajano se acercó y le habló al oído como si le fuera decir un secreto.

—No, esta vez es bastante lejos, pero tranquilo, no te voy a pedir un puente. Ni siquiera te voy a pedir algo que no se haya hecho.

—Pero si el emperador ha pensado en mí es que no será una empresa fácil.

—Eso dependerá, como siempre, de tu capacidad. —Trajano recuperó el tono normal mientras seguía admirando el nuevo foro—. Quiero que vayas a Alejandría. En tiempos, parece ser, hubo un canal construido por los faraones que unía la Mar Eritrea con el Mediterráneo. No sé si eso es cierto del todo o no, pero creo que facilitaría mucho el comercio con Oriente si los barcos pudieran cruzar de un mar a otro sin problemas, sin tener que trasladar por tierra las mercancías, ¿no crees?

Apolodoro inspiró profundamente. Algo había oído sobre ese canal de tiempos remotos, pero no como un canal directo entre los dos mares, sino empleando parte del curso natural del Nilo para unir las dos costas.

—Saldré para Alejandría de inmediato, César.

—Perfecto —respondió Trajano—, pero después de que inauguremos el foro. Tú, más que ningún otro, tienes derecho a ver las caras llenas de admiración hacia tu obra del pueblo romano. Pero bajemos, tengo más asuntos que requieren mi atención. —Y miró a Quieto—. Ven conmigo de nuevo, Lucio.

Liviano, Aulo y dos pretorianos abrieron la marcha del descenso, seguidos por el arquitecto, Trajano y Quieto. La bajada era mucho más rápida, pero justo a la mitad, el emperador se detuvo un instante y se volvió hacia el *legatus* norteafricano.

—El mensaje que ha traído Aulo es de Siria —dijo Trajano en un susurro.

—Sí, César —respondió Quieto en voz baja.

—Los partos han matado a Exedares. Osroes ha puesto a Partamasiris, su hermano, en el trono de Armenia.

—Eso es que quieren asegurarse la retaguardia si está preparando un ataque contra el rebelde Vologases en el este de su imperio —comentó Quieto, siempre en susurros.

—Sin duda —aceptó Trajano—, pero eso no es lo esencial. ¿Sabes qué es lo importante de todo esto?

—No, César.

Trajano sonrió.

—Han depuesto a un rey de Armenia y entronado a otro sin consultar a Roma y eso rompe nuestro tratado con Partia. Ya tenemos *casus belli*, ya tenemos una excusa que presentar al Senado para entrar en guerra con Partia.

31

LOS PLANES DE OSROES

Cesifonte, 112 d. C.

Osroes caminaba junto a los estanques del palacio acompañado por su hermano Mitrídates. Los guardias partos vigilaban atentos. Pese al sol, el aire era fresco al lado del agua y las fuentes. El *Šāhān Šāh* de Partia quería saber de primera mano cómo iba la guerra que dirigía su hermano Mitrídates y el hijo de éste, Sanatruces, contra Vologases en el extremo oriental de los territorios bajo su poder.

—¿Cómo van las cosas, hermano? —preguntó Osroes.

—Resistimos, pero necesitamos refuerzos —respondió Mitrídates—. Mi hijo Sanatruces dice que cada día que pasa Vologases parece hacerse más fuerte. Nos hacen falta más tropas.

—Ahora las tendrás —replicó el *Šāhān Šāh* exultante—. Partamasiris ha depuesto a nuestro rebelde sobrino Exedares y se ha hecho con el control efectivo de Armenia. Pronto llegarán a Cesifonte recursos, víveres y soldados desde Armenia y tu hijo tendrá las tropas que reclamas.

—Por Zoroastro, eso es una gran noticia, *Šāhān Šāh*, pero la vida me ha hecho ver que toda buena noticia viene acompañada de algo no tan bueno.

Osroes se detuvo y borró la sonrisa que tenía en el rostro. Estaba sorprendido por la sagacidad de Mitrídates. Se apuntó mentalmente la capacidad de discernimiento de su hermano.

—Es cierto —admitió al fin Osroes y volvió a andar junto a los estanques—. Partamasiris me ha pedido a Aryazate para desposarse con ella.

Mitrídates inclinó la cabeza.

—Ahora que tenemos Armenia quizá ya no la necesitamos

para ofrecérsela a Vologases y pactar con él —argumentó en voz alta aunque con tiento; ni él mismo estaba convencido de lo que decía—. Por otro lado...

—Por otro lado ese matrimonio haría a nuestro muy ambicioso hermano Partamasiris demasiado fuerte ante los Consejos —interpuso Osroes interpretando correctamente las dudas de Mitrídates—. Casado con mi hija, Partamasiris, cuyas ansias de poder me consta que no tienen límites, puede estar tentado de postularse como *Šāhān Šāh*. Y ya sabes que siempre hay quien está descontento y dispuesto a apoyar una rebelión. Por eso quiero que mande tropas, para quitárselas de Armenia y hacerlo más débil.

—¿Y Aryazate se ha recuperado por completo del envenenamiento de las mujeres kushan? —inquirió Mitrídates.

—Sí. Es una niña fuerte. En su momento me alegré, pero ahora que la pretende Partamasiris no sé si habría sido mejor que la niña hubiera muerto.

—Ciertamente es un problema —aceptó Mitrídates—. ¿Qué vas a hacer?

—De momento le diré a Partamasiris que quiero esperar a que la niña sea un poco mayor, pero que tomo nota de su petición —se explicó Osroes.

—Eso nos da algo de tiempo.

—Y eso lo obliga a enviarme las tropas que le pedimos —completó el rey de reyes—. Aunque si cumple fielmente con lo que le exigimos tendré que darle a Aryazate, pero entonces...

—Pero entonces ya no tendrá casi ejército con el que rebelarse porque esas tropas estarán aquí, en Cesifonte, o en Oriente luchando contra Vologases —completó ahora Mitrídates, satisfecho de haber intuido adónde quería llegar su hermano.

—Exacto —certificó Osroes.

Hubo un silencio largo. Mitrídates se acordó de algo y volvió a hablar.

—Por cierto, ¿qué hiciste con las mujeres kushan que intentaron envenenar a Aryazate?

—Ejecutarlas.

—Bien —admitió Mitrídates—. ¿Y vas a tomar represalias contra Kadphises y los kushan?

—Sus consejeros niegan tener conocimiento del plan para asesinar a mi hija. En cualquier caso, de momento no podemos. Hemos de solucionar primero la rebelión de Vologases. Entonces seremos lo que los kushan no querían: fuertes. Será cuando nos venguemos de ellos. Por otro lado, tengo la idea de que lo del intento de envenenamiento no ha sido cosa de Kadphises, que está muy enfermo: ha sido su hijo Kanishka.

Por fin, sólo quedaba un asunto que incomodaba a Mitrídates.

—¿Y Roma? —preguntó.

—Roma siempre es lenta en reaccionar —respondió Osroes con aplomo—. Para cuando quieran hacer algo sobre Armenia, ya seremos... invencibles.

Palacio de las mujeres, Cesifonte

—¿Por qué me quisieron matar esas mujeres, Rixnu? —preguntó Aryazate abrazada a la hermosa *Šhar Bāmbišn*, la reina consorte y favorita de Osroes.

—Porque querían evitar que el rey de reyes te ofreciera en matrimonio a Vologases para terminar con la guerra que desangra Partia. A los kushan les interesa que luchemos entre nosotros.

—Entonces ¿tendré que casarme con ese salvaje de Vologases? —preguntó la pequeña Aryazate aterrorizada, pues todos insistían en que Vologases era vil y cruel, un brutal asesino de mujeres y niños y de todo lo que fuera civilizado y ordenado.

—No, mi pequeña —respondió Rixnu, y la abrazó con fuerza—. Parece que tu padre Osroes ha conseguido que Partamasiris se haga con Armenia. Eso nos hace más fuertes y seguramente ahora no querrán pactar con Vologases, sino derrotarlo con nuevos ejércitos traídos de Occidente y del norte.

—Eso es genial —respondió la niña sonriente y apretando su pequeño puño con fuerza. Le parecía justo que un ser cruel como Vologases acabara muerto en medio de un campo de batalla atravesado por decenas de flechas partas.

—Ajá —dijo Rixnu y la meció como si aún fuera un bebé. La reina consorte pensó que no era momento de desvelarle a Aryazate que si no era ofrecida en matrimonio a Vologases, sería, muy probablemente, desposada con el deleznable Partamasiris. Pero la pequeña estaba aún recuperándose del envenenamiento. Con esa excusa, Rixnu se sintió justificada para guardar silencio.

32

UNA REUNIÓN EXTRAÑA

Roma, 112 d. C.

Domus Flavia *(palacio imperial)*, prima vigilia

Marcio los observaba a todos con curiosidad. Esta vez no era la cámara del emperador, sino alguna sala contigua, no muy grande, donde se había congregado una serie extraña de personas. Intuía que el hecho de que el emperador lo hubiera vuelto a llamar al palacio no se debía a nada relacionado con el *Ludus Magnus*, sino con aquella misión que años atrás le anunciara. Trajano había sido, a su manera, generoso con él: le había otorgado la *rudis* de la libertad casi *in extremis*, cuando ya empezaba a ser demasiado viejo para luchar en la arena, y luego le había permitido ir en busca de Alana y Tamura. Finalmente les había proporcionado una vida cómoda y fácil en Roma al darle el puesto de *lanista*. Hasta había enviado el César a uno de sus viejos consejeros, el filósofo Dión Coceyo, para que educara a Tamura. Mucha generosidad. Marcio sabía que la deuda acumulada con el emperador era grande y estaba convencido de que aquella noche era el momento en que el César querría cobrar.

Marcio permanecía en pie en una esquina. En el centro, sentado junto a la mesa que había en la sala, se veía a un hombre de bastante edad con aire de mercader y, quizá por sus muchos años, muy seguro de sí mismo. No parecía guerrero, sino más bien un rico comerciante o artesano, aunque todo lo que imaginaba eran conjeturas. En otra esquina estaba un hombre alto, moreno y con el rostro ajado por el sol. Podría haber sido un campesino de no ser por aquella mirada feroz. Era un luchador nato que había combatido bajo el sol mucho tiempo. ¿En algún desierto de Oriente? A Marcio no se le ocurría otro lugar donde uno pudiera recibir tanto sol.

El preparador de gladiadores siguió mirando: había también media docena de pretorianos. Marcio elucubraba sobre todos aquellos hombres cuando el emperador entró junto con el jefe del pretorio y el tribuno Aulo.

—Que salgan todos —dijo Trajano. De inmediato los pretorianos abandonaron la sala. Sólo se quedó Liviano y el tribuno, junto con el César y sus tres invitados, esto es, Marcio y aquellos dos desconocidos.

El emperador se sentó junto a la mesa, en la misma *sella* en la que había estado el que Marcio consideraba mercader, pues éste se había levantado nada más ver entrar al César.

—Bien —empezó Trajano mirando al que se acababa de poner en pie—; no tengo tiempo que perder pues he de ocuparme de asuntos importantes mañana al amanecer y ya es muy tarde. Yo haré las presentaciones. —Señaló con el dedo índice de su mano derecha primero al que Marcio había imaginado comerciante o artesano—: Tú eres Maes Titianus, mercader de Siria, tú —y el César apuntó con el dedo al propio Marcio— un antiguo gladiador y actualmente el *lanista* del *Ludus Magnus* y, por último —Trajano bajó la mano pero miró al tercer hombre, el de aspecto feroz y la tez muy morena—, tú eres Arrio, oficial de la marina imperial con tantos problemas con la justicia que has terminado luchando en *naumaquias* y jugándote la vida para el deleite de la plebe, pero digamos que esta misión va a darte la oportunidad de redimirte.

Marcio asintió para sí mismo: marino, por eso el rostro ajado por el sol, nada que ver con el desierto. El emperador seguía hablando.

—Los tres, junto con algunos pretorianos que seleccionaré, partiréis hacia Oriente con una misión: llevar una respuesta mía a una pregunta del emperador Vima Kadphises del Imperio kushan, al norte de la India. Por motivos de seguridad hay que evitar que esta misión pase por Partia, así que tendréis que ir desde Roma hasta Alejandría y desde Egipto surcar toda la mar Eritrea[21] hasta alcanzar las costas de la India. Una vez allí tendréis que ir al norte hasta llegar a Bagram, la capital de los kushan, y entregar mi mensaje. Luego el regreso. Maes Titianus conoce la ruta porque la ha realizado en más de una ocasión. Arrio se incorpora a la misión como marino de la flota imperial para pilotar el barco, o los barcos, que os conducirán hasta la India. Es buen piloto y sabe cómo gobernar un navío, será una gran ayuda si surgen problemas en el tránsito hacia Oriente. Y en cuanto a ti, Marcio, tu obligación es preservar la vida de Titianus a toda costa, pues él es quien llevará el mensaje y quien debe hablar con el emperador Kadphises en mi nombre. —Trajano entregó un papiro enrollado a Titianus, que lo cogió con cuidado y lo guardó bajo su túnica sin ni siquiera abrirlo. El emperador continuó explicándose—: Podría enviar un nutrido número de navíos para esta misión, pero tengo mis motivos para mantener este contacto entre Kadphises y yo en secreto y cuento con vuestra discreción para que esto siga siendo así. —El emperador hizo una breve pausa; luego miró fijamente a los ojos a cada uno y preguntó—: ¿Alguna duda?

Ninguno de los tres dijo nada.

—Pues ya está dicho todo —concluyó Trajano—. Próximamente os haré saber cuándo partís y adónde debéis acudir para iniciar el viaje. Ahora marchad y seguid con vuestra vida en Roma como si esta reunión nunca hubiera tenido lugar.

—De acuerdo, César —dijo Titianus y se inclinó ante el emperador antes de salir. Arrio lo siguió. El marino se limitó a saludar militarmente al emperador sin decir palabra alguna. Aquello le gustó a Marcio: Arrio era hombre callado. Eso estaba bien. Sin embargo, el preparador de gladiadores no salió de la sala, sino que después de saludar al César, se quedó frente a él en silencio.

—Creía que no había dudas —dijo Trajano algo molesto.

—No quería hablar delante de los otros, César —arguyó Marcio en su defensa.

—¿Qué quieres? —preguntó Trajano.

21. La mar Eritrea englobaba el mar Rojo y el océano Índico.

—Proteger a ese hombre yo solo en un viaje tan largo no será fácil.

—Os acompañarán algunos pretorianos —replicó el César con cierta frialdad.

—Aun así, con el debido respeto, augusto, me gustaría que me acompañara alguien más, gente de mi absoluta confianza.

—¿Quién?

—Algún gladiador del *Ludus Magnus.*

Trajano meditó un instante.

—Si crees que puede ser de ayuda, de acuerdo —aceptó el emperador—, pero sé cuidadoso con quién seleccionas.

—Sí, César —respondió Marcio, pero seguía sin emprender la marcha.

—¿Algo más? —inquirió Trajano con el ceño fruncido.

—No me gustaría separarme de nuevo de mi mujer y mi hija —dijo Marcio con tiento.

Trajano lo observó con seriedad.

—Ni yo quiero que las vuelvan a utilizar para manipular tus acciones —dijo el emperador—. Quizá sea mejor que te acompañen.

—Gracias, César —dijo entonces Marcio con alivio—. El emperador puede estar seguro de que protegeré a ese hombre con mi vida.

—No lo dudo, gladiador, no lo dudo.

No hubo más palabras.

Marcio salió.

Trajano se quedó en silencio. Todo estaba en marcha. *Alea iacta est,* como habría dicho el mismísimo Julio César, aunque... El emperador apretó los labios. Quedaban algunos cabos sueltos.

33

EL NOMBRAMIENTO DE ADRIANO

Ἡ Πλωτῖνα ἐξ ἐρωτικῆς φιλίας.

Plotina (...) estaba enamorada de él [de Adriano]

Dión Casio, Libro LXIX, 1

usus Plotinae quoque favore, cuius studio etiam legatus expeditio-
nis Parthicae tempore destinatus est

Disfrutaba [Adriano] de los favores de Plotina.
Y fue por el interés que ella tenía en él que luego,
en los tiempos de la campaña de Partia, [Adriano]
fue designado como legado del emperador.

Historia Augusta, «Vida de Adriano», 4

Cerca de Roma, pero fuera de la ciudad
112 d. C.

—Nos vemos mucho menos de lo que me gustaría —dijo ella
y se volvió en la cama y quedó desnuda, sin la sábana, recosta-
da de lado, dándole la espalda, mirando las pinturas de las
paredes decoradas con motivos de peces y algas marinas.

—No nos vemos más porque tú dices que sospecha —respondió él con aire distraído. Tenía sueño. Siempre tenía sueño después.

Plotina se sentó en la cama.

—Sé que sospecha desde el día en que celebró su triunfo
sobre los dacios —continuó ella sin mirarlo, como extasiada
por los peces pintados—. No sé cómo ni quién, pero alguien

lo puso sobre aviso y desde entonces está infinitamente más distante conmigo. Trajano nunca fue afectuoso en el sentido literal de la palabra, pero había un respeto de él hacia mí que se ha perdido.

—Hace poco ordenó que se levantara el *Ara pudicitia* en tu honor, para que ofrezcas sacrificios en público —contrapuso él—. Es un gran honor.

—Eso sólo demuestra que le preocupa nuestra imagen con relación a la plebe, pero en cualquier caso —y se volvió hacia él—, a ti no parece molestarte que nos veamos menos.

Adriano suspiró. Las discusiones con Plotina lo agotaban, pero sabía que si había alguien con quien no debía discutir era con ella. Cada vez que veía a Lucio Quieto más próximo a su tío, el emperador, estaba seguro de que su mejor aliada para alcanzar el poder era la mujer con la que acababa de hacer el amor. No debía ponerla nerviosa. Debía ser paciente. Y hábil. Pero a veces le costaba tanto...

—Yo te echo de menos siempre —dijo él en un intento por asegurar la complicidad de Plotina.

Ella sonrió, pero era una sonrisa sin convencimiento.

—Mientes mal, Adriano —dijo ella acariciando su poderoso torso desnudo—. Espero que eso sólo te pase conmigo o no conseguirás nunca lo que tanto deseas. Aunque como mientes a hombres sobre todo es muy posible que ellos no se den cuenta.

Él guardó silencio.

Se oían los pájaros en el exterior. Estaban en el campo. Una villa a las afueras de Roma. Siempre buscaban sitios diferentes.

—Te va a mandar a Siria —dijo ella mientras seguía acariciando su pecho.

—¿Siria?

—Como gobernador —señaló ella sin dejar de acariciarlo—. Me lo dijo ayer en la cena. Sé que lo hizo porque quería ver mi reacción. Evidentemente le dije que me parecía buena idea. De hecho le había sugerido ya varias veces que te enviara allí. Siria es una provincia importante. Aunque yo sí te echaré de menos.

—Pero me aleja de Roma —respondió él.

—De eso se trata. —Se dirigía a él como quien habla con un niño que no entiende—. Tenía que demostrarle a Trajano que no me importa separarme de ti. Eso lo tranquilizará, su mente se ocupará de otros asuntos. Además, como te decía, Siria es una provincia importante y algo me dice que Roma entera irá pronto a Siria, como tú sabes. El emperador lleva tiempo con los ojos puestos en Oriente. Sólo está esperando una excusa para lanzarse contra Partia. Muchos senadores lo comentan, en voz baja, eso es cierto, pero hablan de ello constantemente. Y esa excusa acabará llegando. En el fondo es una buena oportunidad para ti.

—Para Trajano sólo valgo para prepararlo todo —contraargumentó Adriano—. Incluso si es cierto todo lo que piensas, incluso si Trajano concentra tropas allí bajo mi mando, ninguna legión se moverá de allí hasta que llegue él y su maldito perro de presa, Lucio Quieto.

—Incluso así, mejor que te mande a ti a concentrar tropas que a otro. —Le dio una pequeña palmada final en el torso. Era la señal de que iba a marcharse. Adriano se volvió hacia la pared mientras ella se vestía.

—Es posible que no volvamos a vernos hasta tu partida —continuó ella mientras se ponía la túnica sola; no quería esclavas alrededor cuando estaba con Adriano—. Y haz el favor de ser amable con Vibia Sabina. Que la sobrina del emperador esté constantemente triste y se queje de ti, su esposo, no te ayuda en absoluto.

Adriano se volvió con mirada intrigante.

—¿Quieres que sea muy amable con ella?

Ella sonrió.

—Los celos no funcionan conmigo; creía que eso ya lo sabías. Consigue que ella deje de quejarse, cómo lo hagas me da igual. Pero si quieres tener a Trajano de tu parte has de lograr que piense que casar a Vibia contigo no fue un error. Haz que terminen las quejas al César de su parte y todo irá bien. Podré hablar al emperador mejor de ti. —Se acercó y le dio un beso en la boca—. Cuando quieres sabes ser muy persuasivo. —Se separó de él—. Feliz viaje a Siria.

Dio media vuelta y salió.

Adriano se quedó en la cama un buen rato.

Se durmió.

Cuando despertó la noche ya había llegado a Roma.

Tenía hambre. Se levantó y fue al atrio, donde pidió que le sirvieran algo de comida y bebida. Un esclavo entró con la comida, otro con el vino y un tercero, el *atriense* de aquella villa, se le acercó y le habló al oído.

—Está aquí —dijo el sirviente.

—Que pase —respondió Adriano mientras pegaba un buen trago a su copa y la apuraba hasta el final—. Más.

El esclavo que sostenía una jarra escanció más vino. Atiano apareció en el atrio. Adriano miró a los esclavos y éstos desaparecieron. A Atiano le habría gustado que su antiguo pupilo le hubiera ofrecido algo de comida o bebida, pero ya sabía que la generosidad no era uno de sus fuertes y menos cuando esperaba noticias.

—¿Qué has averiguado? —preguntó el sobrino segundo del emperador.

—En efecto, como imaginabas, el César trama algo en secreto, pero no sabemos exactamente de qué se trata.

Adriano lo miró exasperado.

—No estás a mi servicio, Atiano, para decirme lo que ya sé. Creía que habías conseguido la complicidad para nuestra causa de algunos de los pretorianos.

—Así es y he averiguado que Trajano va a mandar a un pequeño grupo de hombres hacia Oriente, parece que al Imperio kushan. No sé si eso tiene o no alguna relación con la campaña que todos pensamos que quiere emprender el emperador contra los partos.

—¡Por Júpiter, nunca sabemos nada!

Arrojó la copa de oro contra la pared. No apareció nadie para recogerla o limpiar el suelo. Atiano no se movió, pero apuntó un último dato.

—Los partos han depuesto a Exedares como rey de Armenia y Osroes ha coronado a su hermano Partamasiris como monarca en el trono de Artaxata. Armenia está bajo su control y lo ha hecho sin consultar a Roma.

Adriano suspiró varias veces hasta recuperar un mínimo de control sobre sí mismo. Sólo entonces volvió a hablar.

—O sea, que mi querido tío ya tiene lo que quería: una excusa para atacar Partia. Bien. Veamos, por todos los dioses, yo he de partir a Siria. —Como vio la cara de sorpresa de Atiano, Adriano se permitió el lujo de sonreír mientras se seguía explicando—. Yo también tengo mis fuentes en palacio. Como te decía, el emperador me mandará a Siria próximamente. Ahora ya está claro que todo esto de Oriente va en serio. Cuento contigo para que mantengas vigilado el Senado. La campaña puede ir bien o mal. Si va mal, todo será más sencillo.

—¿Y si va bien? —se atrevió a preguntar Atiano.

—¿Sinceramente crees que se puede conquistar Partia? ¿De verdad crees que no terminarán las legiones que Trajano lance contra Partia igual que la legión perdida de Craso? —preguntó Adriano con auténtico interés por la opinión de su antiguo tutor.

—No lo sé, pero Arabia Félix se rindió ante las legiones enviadas por el emperador bajo el mando de Palma sin ni siquiera combatir. Desde lo de Dacia, Trajano es temido por todos nuestros vecinos. Pero es cierto que Partia es inmensa y también es fácil que esta campaña termine siendo una repetición del error de Craso.

—Puedes estar seguro de ello —afirmó Adriano con rotundidad—, pero en todo caso, mantenme informado de las opiniones del Senado. Cualquier disenso entre los aliados de mi tío nos interesa. Los senadores son temerosos por condición natural. Si mi tío empieza a desabastecer de legiones el Rin y el Danubio para llevarlas a Oriente, a muchos les entrará el miedo. Ésa puede ser nuestra oportunidad, ¿me entiendes?

—Sí, mi señor.

—Bien. ¿Mantenemos contacto con Pompeyo Colega y con Salvio Liberal?

—Sí, mi señor. Siguen como gobernadores en Cirenaica y Chipre, creo recordar.

—Bien, mantén la comunicación con ellos.

Hubo un breve silencio. Adriano lamentó haber tirado la copa. Quería más vino, pero no iba a llamar a los esclavos, no hasta que su antiguo tutor se marchara. La voz de Atiano fue la que volvió a oírse en el atrio de aquella villa.

—¿Y si la campaña sale bien? —insistió el veterano tutor—. Sé que es algo en lo que no quieres pensar, pero hemos de tenerlo todo calculado.

—Si la campaña de Partia sale bien, cosa que veo imposible —se reafirmó Adriano—, ya pensaremos en algo. Ahora me preocupan otros asuntos, como esa maldita misión secreta de la que me has hablado. Quiero que la impidas.

Atiano miró con atención al sobrino del emperador.

—¿Cómo exactamente?

Adriano se levantó. Tenía ganas de beber y para eso hacía falta que Atiano se marchara de una vez. No quería nunca testigos de sus conversaciones privadas con su antiguo tutor.

—Eres un hombre imaginativo —dijo Adriano—, pero por si la imaginación te falla, digamos que esos mensajeros que mi tío quiere mandar a los kushan, no sé para qué ni por qué, son parte de una larga cadena de acontecimientos que mi tío controla, o quiere controlar, para algún fin oculto, y yo quiero que esa cadena se rompa. Las cadenas, Atiano, tienen eslabones y siempre hay alguno que es el más débil. Averigua cuál es el eslabón más frágil de esa cadena y rómpelo. Y si no puedes, al menos infiltra a uno de los nuestros, o a varios, entre los miembros de esa misión para que la entorpezcan y la hagan fracasar. Pero lo primero es intentar romper la cadena. ¿Crees que podrás hacerlo?

Atiano sabía cuándo no había margen para el debate. Asintió al tiempo respondía.

—Mi señor, encontraré el eslabón más frágil de esa cadena. Y lo haré pedazos.

34

EL SECUESTRO

Roma
112 d. C.

Tamura había empezado a hacer cosas que no debía. No sabía bien por qué, pero necesitaba realizar alguna de las acciones que sus padres le tenían prohibidas. Una de ellas era salir sola por Roma. Tamura, aprovechando que su padre estaba casi siempre en el *Ludus Magnus* y que su madre con frecuencia lo acompañaba, decía que se quedaba en la *domus* que Marcio había comprado en el centro de la Subura y que, custodiada por los sirvientes, se quedaría leyendo papiros llevados por el *paedagogus* Dión Coceyo. Sin embargo la muchacha, ante el más mínimo descuido de los esclavos, salía de la casa. Si los sirvientes la descubrían guardaban silencio, pues no sabían qué podía ser peor: que la niña se les hubiera escapado o que se enterara el poderoso *lanista* del *Ludus Magnus* y tomara represalias contra ellos, castigándolos sólo los dioses sabían con qué crueldad. No era que los hubiera maltratado, pero la figura imponente del exgladiador les resultaba siempre amenazadora. No, el silencio para todos ellos parecía una mejor estrategia. Así, los esclavos, cuando detectaron alguna de las fugas de Tamura, intentaron asegurar la puerta y las ventanas de la *domus* para evitar nuevas escapadas, pero no era fácil retener a una hija de una guerrera sármata y un veterano exgladiador si ésta no quería permanecer en aquella casa que para ella se había transformado en una especie de jaula de oro. Si todo estaba cerrado, Tamura escapaba por el tejado trepando por las columnas del atrio. Además, la joven se sentía muy segura, pues había visitado ya el foro Boario o el foro Holitorio y ni en el mercado de la carne o de las verduras, ni en el gran *Mace-*

llum central de la ciudad había tenido problema alguno. Si alguien se quedaba observándola más de la cuenta, la muchacha se desvanecía con rapidez entre la multitud.

No pasaba nada por salir sola.

Nada.

Roma no parecía peligrosa.

La niña de doce años estaba persuadida de que los bosques del norte eran un lugar con muchos más peligros que la capital del Imperio. Por eso decidió atreverse a más. ¿Y si salía por la noche? Ella anhelaba hacer algo audaz, algo que quizá podría compartir en secreto con Áyax y así impresionar al joven gladiador griego.

Todos dormían.

Era ya la *secunda vigilia*. Su padre roncaba. Podía oírlo desde su habitación. Salió descalza porque sabía del sueño ligero de su madre, pero Tamura era como una gata deslizándose sigilosa por las sombras.

Llegó al atrio y escaló de nuevo al tejado. Se descolgó por el muro exterior y decidió adentrarse por las calles oscuras de la ciudad. ¿Qué podría pasarle? Era rápida, astuta y silenciosa. Se sentía tan libre, caminando por entre aquellas calles angostas.

¿Por qué negarse aquel placer?

Tan satisfecha estaba de su audacia que pese a su natural instinto de guerrera no vio a los hombres que la seguían ocultándose en la penumbra de los muros. Tan confiada estaba que para cuando se dio cuenta ya la habían rodeado. Iba armada y fue a desenfundar una daga, pero uno de aquellos hombres ya la había cogido por la espalda. Fue a gritar, pero otro le tapó la boca. Eran hombres muy fuertes.

—¿Qué hacemos? —preguntó uno de aquellos malditos.

—La llevaremos para que la vea. Él decidirá —respondió otro.

Tamura se revolvía con todas sus fuerzas, pero no había calculado que ella era una niña de doce años y aquéllos eran hombres maduros, rudos y entrenados. Algo tan simple había escapado a su pensamiento. La vida, muy velozmente, le estaba enseñando lo estúpido que uno podía llegar a ser por creerse mejor que el resto.

—¡Atadla! ¡Y ponedle una mordaza! No quiero que despierte a toda Roma con gritos.

Tamura intentó evitarlo, pero llevaban todo lo necesario con ellos. Era gente de pocas palabras. Aquellos hombres le recordaron de inmediato a los guardias pretorianos que había visto a menudo en el *Ludus Magnus*, pero ¿por qué la iban a atacar guardias imperiales cuando el emperador parecía proteger a su padre? ¿Tenía realmente el emperador bajo su control a toda la guardia pretoriana?

Intentó revolverse pese a que estaba amordazada y atada. Uno de los hombres la cogió con ambos brazos y la miró muy fijamente mientras la sacudía un momento para que lo escuchara.

—No tengo orden de pegarte, pero si es necesario hacerlo para que te estés quieta, no dudes ni por un momento que lo haré. ¿Me has entendido?

Tamura sabía cuándo alguien no estaba de broma. Asintió.

La condujeron por toda la Subura en silencio.

Hubo un momento en que se cruzaron con un grupo de hombres armados que no eran soldados. Parecían bandidos. Los dos grupos se miraron con recelo mutuo. El soldado que le había hablado a Tamura no se arredró ante los otros hombres, pese a que era un grupo más numeroso, y se dirigió a ellos con resolución.

—Somos pretorianos. Si queréis luchar por nuestro oro, adelante. Hace tiempo que no matamos a nadie y no es bueno perder la costumbre.

Ni siquiera tuvo que desenfundar. Los bandidos se esfumaron tan rápido que a Tamura le quedó hasta la duda de si realmente habían llegado a cruzarse con ellos en algún momento, pero ya tenía claro que la noche romana sí era muy peligrosa. Lástima que lo hubiera aprendido de la peor forma posible.

—Sigamos —dijo el jefe de aquellos pretorianos y añadió unas palabras más con relación a ella—. Véndale los ojos.

Ella no opuso resistencia. ¿Miedo? No, no tenía miedo. En cuanto se descuidaran, y estaba segura de que en algún momento lo harían, se escaparía, y si se descuidaban más de la cuenta, se escaparía después de rebañarle el cuello a más de uno. Había cometido el error de confiarse, eso era cierto, pero ellos también la subestimaban, de eso estaba bien segura. De hecho, las cuerdas con las que la habían atado no estaban muy fuertes. Si la dejaban sola un rato estaba convencida de que podría desatarse.

La venda en los ojos.

Ya no veía.

Sólo podía orientarse por los sonidos o el olfato y ninguno de los dos sentidos, pese a que los tenía bien desarrollados, le dio información suficiente como para saber hacia dónde la conducían. Sólo intuía que debía de ser hacia una zona de templos alejada de la Subura, pues apenas se oían borrachos ni prostitutas ni hombres jóvenes ofreciendo sus servicios a los guardias.

—Esperad aquí —ordenó el líder del grupo al tiempo que la asía con fuerza de un brazo, como el águila cuando levanta el vuelo con su presa en las garras.

La condujo rápidamente por un suelo diferente. Ya no sentía piedras bajo sus pies sino una superficie lisa. ¿Mármol? Y el silencio era penetrante. Debían de estar en un templo... De pronto le retiraron la venda de los ojos.

Tamura se encontró en una sala no muy grande con mármol en el suelo, una ventana pequeña en un extremo y un *cubiculum* en un lado. También había una *sella*. Todo estaba muy limpio.

—Siéntate ahí y no te muevas —dijo aquel soldado que, no obstante, no salió, sino que se quedó en una esquina como si esperara a alguien. Aquello la desanimó un poco. Había visto la ventana y pensaba que ahora tendría su oportunidad, pero no. Si la hubieran dejado sola podría haberse desatado y luego escapar por la ventana. Tendría, no obstante, que esperar un poco más. Curiosamente, pese a su situación lo que más la incomodaba por el momento era que su padre y su madre pudieran enterarse de su escapada nocturna. Aquello sí la preocupaba mucho.

Un hombre mayor entró en la sala. Iba vestido con una túnica de lana blanca y también era alto y fuerte como los pretorianos que la habían atrapado. El soldado iba a decir algo, pero el recién llegado levantó levemente la mano derecha y el pretoriano se mantuvo en silencio. Estaba claro que aquel hombre era muy respetado, o muy temido, por los pretorianos. Quizá ambas cosas.

El hombre mayor se sentó en un extremo del *cubiculum*, en la penumbra, donde no se le veía el rostro, y se quedó mirándola. Hizo otra seña y el pretoriano se acercó a ella y le quitó la mordaza que le habían puesto en la boca. Aquello fue un alivio. Pensó que la iban a desatar, pero no.

—¿Tienes miedo? —le preguntó el hombre mayor que, extrañamente, le recordaba a alguien, pero Tamura no estaba segura de a quién.

—Soy una guerrera sármata y las guerreras sármatas no tenemos miedo.

—Pues deberías —respondió el hombre sentado con seriedad.

Ella no supo entonces qué decir, pero empezó a pensar que su situación quizá fuera grave y que, después de todo, el hecho de que sus padres se enteraran o no de su escapada podría no ser lo peor de aquella noche. El hombre misterioso volvió a hablar.

—Desátala —dijo.

El pretoriano cumplió la orden y retomó su lugar junto a la puerta y la antorcha de la habitación.

—¿Sabes quién soy? —preguntó el hombre, que daba todas las órdenes después de una pausa tensa.

—No estoy segura —dijo mientras se masajeaba la muñeca derecha con la mano izquierda para aliviarse del escozor que le habían dejado las ligaduras, pese a que no estaban muy prietas.

—¿Quién crees que soy?

Tamura había estado confusa por todo lo que le había pasado aquella noche, pero ahora estaba bastante convencida de haber reconocido al hombre que la miraba sentado y serio, pues se había inclinado hacia adelante y la luz de la antorcha que iluminaba la sala dio de pleno en su faz.

—Creo que eres el emperador.

Trajano asintió.

—Correcto. ¿Sabes por qué estás aquí?

Ella miró hacia atrás. El pretoriano permanecía en silencio, de pie, firme, con la mano derecha en la empuñadura de su espada.

—No lo sé —respondió la muchacha.

El emperador miró a Aulo y éste, de inmediato, sin que se le dijera nada, salió de la habitación. Trajano y Tamura se quedaron a solas.

—Ya llevas días escapándote de casa de tus padres, niña —empezó el César—. No te ha pasado nada y crees que es porque eres valiente, pero no te ha pasado nada porque mis hombres te vigilan. A ti y a tu madre.

Tamura recordó vagamente que alguna vez había tenido la sensación de que la miraban con atención, pero nunca imaginó que la estuvieran siguiendo de forma sistemática.

—¿Por qué me vigilan?

—Porque eres hija de un hombre que una vez intentó asesinarme y parece que lo hizo por salvaros la vida a ti y a tu madre. ¿Crees que voy a permitir que eso vuelva a repetirse?

Tamura negó con la cabeza. Empezó a pensar que ante el emperador sería inteligente decir pocas palabras.

—Bien —continuó Trajano—, ¿quieres saber por qué estás aquí?

Tamura asintió. Estaba sudando, y era raro porque ella no sudaba nunca.

Marco Ulpio Trajano se levantó despacio, cogió otra *sella* que estaba en una esquina, oculta por las sombras, la puso justo delante de la niña y se sentó frente a la muchacha.

—Te voy a contar algo y no se lo contarás nunca a nadie. Sólo hablarás de esto con la persona que te voy a decir y no será hasta de aquí un tiempo.

La niña asintió de nuevo.

Marco Ulpio Trajano inspiró profundamente. Luego habló durante un rato. Tamura no lo interrumpió en ningún momento. Tal fue el silencio con el que la niña lo había escuchado que el emperador no estaba seguro de que hubiera comprendido algo.

—¿Has entendido bien lo que te he explicado? —inquirió Trajano.

Tamura cabeceó afirmativamente una vez más.

—No, no me vale un gesto. Si me has entendido quiero oírlo de tus labios.

—Sí, he comprendido todo lo que me ha dicho el emperador —respondió entonces ella, en lo que intentó que fuera una respuesta firme

—Entonces, repítemelo —demando el César.

Y la niña recontó todo lo que se le había dicho de forma clara y precisa.

Trajano se levantó entonces, dio media vuelta y se dirigió a la puerta, pero antes de salir se detuvo un instante y volvió a mirar a Tamura.

—Tienes buena memoria, pero que sepas que no eres valiente.

Tamura lo miró sorprendida y con rabia, pero antes de que pudiera decir nada, el emperador continuó hablando.

—No tener miedo no hace a alguien valiente. Uno es valiente de verdad cuando conoce el miedo y es capaz de enfrentarse a él y superarlo. Eso es valor. Lo demás es imprudencia, locura. Pero no te preocupes. Un día conocerás el miedo, cuando menos lo esperes y de la forma más brutal e imprevista éste te encontrará. Nos encuentra a todos. Ése será el día en el que averiguarás si realmente eres valiente.

Tamura lo miraba en silencio y con los ojos muy abiertos. No era capaz de decir nada.

—Entretanto, te entrego esta estatuilla del dios Júpiter para que vele por ti, hasta que reúnas las fuerzas necesarias para ser realmente valiente.

Trajano le entregó una pequeña figura que tenía al pie de su asiento y en la que Tamura no había reparado hasta ese momento. La cogió con cuidado, pero con dudas.

—Júpiter no es mi dios... —se atrevió a decir.

El emperador no se molestó.

—En este viaje necesitarás la ayuda de muchos dioses. Uno más no te perjudicará y, además, este dios ayudará a que se te escuche allí cuando todos duden de ti.

Tamura miraba la estatuilla de Júpiter sin entender.

Trajano le habló en un susurro.

La muchacha abrió la boca, pero ante la mirada seria del César que señaló a la puerta donde estaban los pretorianos de guardia, la joven, con la frente arrugada, asintiendo levemente, calló. Nadie debía enterarse de aquello.

—Guárdala bien —añadió Trajano.

Acto seguido, el César se levantó, dio media vuelta y desapareció.

El pretoriano entró de nuevo en la habitación, la cogió por el brazo y la puso en pie. No tuvo que decirle que no corriera o que no gritara. La conversación con el emperador parecía haberla tranquilizado, pero sólo en el exterior. En su interior hervían un tumulto de ideas y sentimientos que tardaría años en comprender.

La sacaron del *Atrium Vestae* por la salida del foro.

Trajano se quedó dentro del edificio mirando por una ventana. No estaba seguro de que su plan fuera a resultar exitoso. De hecho era un poco descabellado, al menos en todo lo relacionado con aquel viaje. No, en realidad se trataba de una misión imposible, pero por el momento aquella niña era mucho más segura que un papiro.

—¿Ha conseguido el emperador lo que deseaba?

Trajano se volvió y vio a la Vestal Máxima junto a él. Menenia lo miraba fijamente.

—No lo sé —dijo el César.

—Hay muchas cosas que desconocemos —dijo la Vestal.

—Así es —respondió Trajano—. Me he quedado porque quiero despedirme de ti. Eres lo más próximo que he tenido a una hija. Tú y Vibia Sabina, pero a Vibia es posible que la vuelva a ver, pues lo más seguro es que acompañe a su esposo a Oriente. En tu caso es diferente.

—Es cierto —confirmó Menenia—. Las vestales no podemos alejarnos demasiado de la llama sagrada, pero ¿acaso el emperador no piensa regresar ya a Roma?

—Mi intención es hacerlo y con una nueva victoria. Con la victoria más grande que Roma haya podido celebrar nunca. Una conquista que nos hará más fuertes, pero el camino estará plagado de obstáculos y ya no soy un hombre en la plenitud. Dependeré de otros en mi empeño. No sé cómo terminará todo.

—El César tiene amigos fuertes y leales a su lado, como Quieto, Nigrino, Celso y Palma, por ejemplo.

—Sin duda, pero por Júpiter, estoy seguro de que también van a surgir los que se opongan a mi plan. ¿Crees realmente, Menenia, que soy invencible?

—No soy augur, César.

—Lo sé, pero tu intuición con lo que podía pasar conmigo en el pasado siempre se probó cierta. Me interesa saber tu opinión. ¿Crees que mis enemigos me derribarán?

Menenia se lo pensó unos instantes antes de responder.

—Creo, César, que el emperador sólo podrá ser derribado desde dentro. Así es como lo siento, pero no sé si mis palabras tienen sentido.

Trajano pensó en Adriano.

—Sí, claro que tienen sentido —admitió con cierto aire melancólico—. Cuídate, Vestal Máxima, y cuida de Roma y su llama sagrada.

—Así lo haré, augusto —respondió ella.

—Por último, ¿has traído lo que te pedí? —preguntó Trajano.

La sacerdotisa sacó un papiro de debajo de su túnica blanca inmaculada y lo entregó al emperador.

—Aquí está lo que el César me pidió que custodiara.

Trajano cogió el papiro con sumo cuidado.

—Es un plan perfecto para conquistar el mundo —le dijo.

La Vestal Máxima lo miró sin saber bien qué pensar. Ella nunca había abierto el papiro.

—Si el emperador piensa eso, así debe ser.

—Así es —confirmó Trajano, pero ya no dijo más, se volvió y echó a andar.

En ese momento Menenia dijo algo más.

—El César no debe dejarse llevar por mis palabras con relación al futuro. He dicho lo que siento, pero quizá lo que he dicho pueda tener más de un sentido.

Trajano se detuvo. Asintió sin mirar atrás y reemprendió la marcha, siempre con aquel papiro misterioso en la mano.

Nunca más volvería al *Atrium Vestae* y la próxima vez que Menenia viera el cuerpo del César sólo sería cenizas. No lo sabían, pero era como si sus corazones lo intuyeran.

En las calles oscuras de Roma

Aulo la escoltó hasta la puerta de casa de sus padres.

—¿Llamamos? —preguntó el tribuno.

—No —dijo Tamura—. Treparé. Mis padres no tienen por qué saber de todo esto.

El pretoriano no dijo nada, pero se quedó allí quieto.

La niña se introdujo entonces la estatuilla que le había dado el César en una pequeña bolsa que siempre llevaba consigo, la cerró bien y escaló por la pared de la *domus*.

Aulo la perdió de vista cuando ascendía por el tejado.

El pretoriano miró a ambos lados. No se veía a nadie. Había algo de luna. Dio un paso atrás hasta quedar totalmente oculto en el dintel sombrío de otra puerta.

Hizo guardia hasta el amanecer.

35

EL VIAJE DE KAN YING

Loyang, capital del Imperio han
Séptimo año del reinado del emperador An-ti
112 d. C.

En la sala del trono imperial del palacio de la dinastía han en Loyang estaban presentes cuatro personas y, a su alrededor, varios guardias de la vigilancia personal creada por el consejero Fan Chun. Junto al trono, vacío porque el joven emperador An-ti no había sido convocado por la regente para esa reunión, estaba, sentada en una gran butaca dorada, la emperatriz Deng; frente a ella, arrodillado, el viejo funcionario y embajador Kang Ying y, junto a él, en pie, pero siempre con la cabeza inclinada, el *yu-shih chung-ch'eng* o asistente del ministro de Obras Públicas, Fan Chun. Finalmente, por detrás del humillado Kang Ying, en pie, muy firme y en silencio, tan tieso que parecía una estatua de terracota de un guerrero imperial, estaba Li Kan, quien recordaba muy bien el consejo que Fan Chun le había dado unos días atrás.

—Asistirás a la audiencia especial de la emperatriz Deng con Kan Ying; lo mereces porque has servido bien al imperio estos años y, además, fuiste tú quien trajo a Kan Ying en el pasado, pero permanecerás en perfecto silencio: no dirás nada, no hablarás, no harás gestos, no mirarás a la emperatriz y, si fuera posible, no respiraría.

Fan Chun apreciaba al joven guerrero han, pero temía que una palabra inconveniente pudiera alejarlo de la capital, donde el funcionario pensaba que el valeroso oficial debía permanecer para mantener el estado actual de las cosas. Y es que Li Kan, si bien había ascendido enormemente en poder dentro de la guardia imperial de Loyang y del ejército del Norte, como se denominaba a las tropas establecidas en la capital, estaba en medio de un tremendo avispero: el joven emperador An-ti tenía dieciocho años, pero la regente Deng lo consideraba aún demasiado joven y, sobre todo, influenciable e impetuoso en extremo, por lo que la emperatriz no había dejado el poder, sino que seguía gobernando aconsejada por Fan Chun y otros altos funcionarios, con eficacia, justicia y una firme mano de hierro cuando ésta era necesaria. Para Fan Chun el peligro estaba en la siempre intrigante Yan Ji, la hermosa nueva favorita del joven emperador An-ti, enfrentada a muerte con la consorte Li, joven quizá menos hermosa pero más humilde de carácter y no tan ambiciosa, en consecuencia apreciada por la emperatriz regente Deng y sus consejeros. El enfrentamiento larvado entre la regente Deng apoyando a la joven esposa imperial Li por un lado y el emperador An-ti y su intrigante favorita Yan Ji, seguía intensificándose.

Entre esas tensiones palaciegas, operaciones militares para detener las incursiones de los *hsiung-nu* en el norte y atender a una población sacudida por algunos desastres naturales habían transcurrido cuatro años desde que Li Kan llevara a Kan Ying a la capital, tiempo que este último había pasado en prisión por su negativa a acudir a Loyang por voluntad propia cuando había sido requerido. Los años habían pasado, pero el interés y la curiosidad de la emperatriz regente Deng por aquel misterioso viaje de Ying hacia Occidente retornó, y por eso se celebraba ahora aquella peculiar audiencia. Fan Chun, además, estaba persuadido, y así se lo había transmitido a la emperatriz viuda, de que los años de cárcel habrían facilitado que Kan Ying resultara más proclive a compartir lo que averiguó en aquel viaje, aunque sólo fuera por ver si así se le conmutaba la pena de cadena perpetua a la que había sido condenado por otra más suave con un final próximo.

La emperatriz rompió el silencio dirigiéndose al arrodillado Ying.

—Kan Ying, en los primeros años del gobierno de mi esposo, el emperador He, te fue encomendada la misión de viajar hasta alcanzar el reino de Da Qin.[22] En aquellos años no recibí información precisa sobre el viaje, pero ahora que estoy en la obligación de llevar la carga del gobierno de los territorios del Imperio han, creo que es mi deber saber todo lo posible sobre todos los reinos del mundo y, en particular, tengo interés por saber qué ocurre más allá de nuestras fronteras. Todo cuanto sabemos de Da Qin es que nos compran seda, laca y otros productos que viajan en caravanas y barcos por los imperios de los Yuegzhi y An-shi hasta llegar a sus tierras. Pero ¿es cierto que tú estuviste allí, en el mismísimo Da Qin? Espero que la cárcel te haya hecho ver que sincerarte conmigo es mejor camino para ti que esconderte o mentirme. De tus respuestas depende que te deje en libertad o que retornes a prisión por haberte negado a venir antes. De hecho no entiendo por qué te negaste a acudir, pero ese asunto después. Lo primero es lo primero, como diría Confucio. ¿Realmente llegaste a Da Qin?

Kan Ying asintió.

—Sí, majestad imperial —dijo con voz trémula y de forma casi inaudible. La emperatriz se inclinó en su gran butaca para intentar oír mejor.

—Habla con claridad para que la emperatriz pueda oírte bien, Kan Ying —apostilló Fan Chun en voz muy alta.

—Sí, así es, majestad imperial —repitió el aludido con más volumen y rotundidad.

—¿Y bien? —preguntó la emperatriz.

—El viaje es largo, mi señora. Hay que cruzar los territorios enemigos de los Yuegzhi y el imperio de An-shi, como muy bien ha dicho la emperatriz, algo que conseguí al ir en calidad de embajador del emperador He. El nombre del esposo de mi señora abría las puertas de los palacios más lejanos y se me trató siempre con respeto. Todo fue bien en el viaje, majestad, pero Da Qin, impresionante como pueda ser, está tan lejos que no creo que resulte de interés para la majestad imperial de los han.

22. Recordamos que Da Qin es el nombre que el Imperio han daba al Imperio romano, An-shi se refiere a Partia y los Yuegzhi son los kushan del norte de la India y Afganistán.

—Lo que es de interés o no para mí lo he de decidir yo, ¿no crees? —interpuso la emperatriz.

—Por supuesto, majestad, por supuesto.

Kan Ying se humilló varias veces hasta casi besar el suelo con sus labios resecos y recortados por los años de encierro.

—Cuéntame lo que viste en Da Qin —insistió la emperatriz.

—Sí, majestad, desde luego. Todo lo que vi... Da Qin es... un reino grande, un imperio extenso, el cuarto imperio, sí. Quizá tan grande como el imperio de su excelsa majestad, pero situado en el extremo más occidental del mundo, allí donde todo acaba. *Su territorio abarca varios miles de* li *tienen más de cuatrocientas ciudades y de estados vasallos poseen varias veces diez. Las murallas de las ciudades están hechas de piedra... hay pinos y cipreses y todo tipo de árboles y plantas... la gente se corta el cabello y llevan vestidos con brocados y conducen pequeños carruajes... el espacio que ocupa una ciudad amurallada es de más de cien* li *en una circunferencia. En la ciudad hay cinco palacios, cada uno separado del otro por una distancia de diez* li. *Y en los palacios hay columnas de cristal... El rey acude a uno de los palacios cada día para escuchar reclamaciones. Después de cinco días ha completado su trabajo. Suelen permitir que un hombre con una bolsa siga el carruaje del rey. Aquellos que tienen algo que reclamar, introducen su petición en la bolsa. Cuando el rey llega al palacio pondera sobre lo incorrecto o correcto de cada petición. Los documentos oficiales están controlados por 36* chiang *o generales... sus reyes no son gobernantes permanentes, sino que eligen a hombres de mérito. Cuando acontece un gran desastre o lluvias torrenciales, el rey es depuesto y reemplazado por otro. El que ha sido reemplazado acepta su sustitución sin murmurar siquiera. Los habitantes de aquel país son altos y bien proporcionados...*[23]

Y Kan Ying siguió refiriendo algunos otros fabulosos datos sobre aquel lejano y remoto imperio. La emperatriz escuchaba fascinada y, de igual forma, Li Kan debía esforzarse por no

23. El texto en cursiva es literal de la descripción de Roma hecha en el *Hou-Han-Shu* o *Libro de la dinastía han tardía* de Fan Yen, escrito en el siglo v, sobre los conocimientos que los han tenían en el siglo ii acerca de la Roma del período que abarca del año 6 al 189 d. C.

quedarse con la boca abierta ante los fantásticos sucesos que Kan Ying contaba; sin embargo, Fan Chun miraba muy fijamente y muy serio al viejo embajador mientras éste hablaba sin detenerse. Hasta que, de pronto, calló, casi exhausto. El asistente del ministro de Obras Públicas observó cómo Kan Ying sudaba profusamente, no sólo en el rostro, sino también en las manos, que no dejaba de frotarse una y otra vez. Fan Chun aprovechó aquella pausa en el relato de Kan Ying para intervenir.

—En realidad nunca has estado en Da Qin, ¿verdad? —dijo el asistente del ministro de Obras Públicas.

La pregunta sorprendió a la emperatriz tanto como a Li Kan. Ninguno de ellos dos había considerado la posibilidad de que aquel viejo se atreviera a inventarse una historia tan disparatada. Mentir a la emperatriz viuda podía conllevar la muerte. ¿Por qué arriesgarse?

Kan Ying, ante la interrogante planteada, levantó la cabeza y miró a Fan Chun con auténtico terror.

—¿Por qué crees que miente? —preguntó la emperatriz.

Fan Chun suspiró. Explicar lo evidente lo agotaba, pero la emperatriz intentaba mantener el Imperio han resistiendo frente a los numerosos enemigos interiores y exteriores. No era la más sagaz de las mujeres, pero tampoco una ingenua. Intentaba ser ecuánime en su forma de regir el imperio y se esforzaba por aprender para, así, predicando con el ejemplo, poder exigir a sus funcionarios que aprendieran también tanto como pudieran. Se merecía ayuda cuando la necesitaba, y más si se tenía en cuenta que la alternativa era el muy joven emperador An-ti controlado por la intrigante Yan Ji. Fan Chun se inclinó ante la emperatriz viuda al tiempo que hablaba.

—Majestad: nadie construye palacios con columnas de cristal. Sencillamente, no lo creo. No digo que no sea posible, pero todo el relato me parece demasiado absurdo y, desde luego, no me creo que un emperador se deje sustituir por otro sin oponer resistencia. Ésa ha sido la gota que ha colmado el vaso, majestad. Esta descripción de Da Qin ha de ser... —y buscó bien las palabras precisas—, falsa o, cuando menos, distorsionada. —Se volvió de nuevo hacia Kan Ying—. Dinos la verdad, viejo embajador, ¿realmente has visto con tus ojos eso que nos describes? Si has mentido, porque, según intuyo, tienes miedo de ser castigado por no haber conseguido lo que se te encomendó antaño, es decir, llegar a Da Qin, mereces la muerte, pero si confiesas ahora cuál es la verdad de tu viaje, yo me permito sugerir a la emperatriz que se te perdone y se te deje marchar en libertad. El miedo, Kan Ying, es el peor de los consejeros. La confianza en la magnanimidad de su majestad imperial es un camino más fiable. Tú mismo. Si mientes, te aseguro que lo averiguaré e informaré a su majestad. ¿Qué has de decir ahora?

El silencio que siguió era aún, si cabía, más intenso que en el momento de la entrada de Kan Ying a la sala imperial de Loyang. Sus gotas de sudor caían sobre el suelo de la estancia. El viejo se llevó las manos temblorosas a la boca. Se humilló de nuevo y, con la cabeza escondida bajo unos brazos arrugados, habló entre sollozos.

—Lo siento, majestad. El consejero de la emperatriz tiene la sabiduría de Confucio. Mi incapacidad ha sido descubierta y casi he de admitir que me... sí, me alegro de terminar con esta mentira. Realmente nunca llegue hasta Da Qin. No, no lo hice.

—¿Fue eso lo que contaste al emperador He en el pasado? —insistió Fan Chun.

El interpelado alzó el rostro del suelo y miró al asistente del ministro al tiempo que hablaba con gran rapidez.

—Cuando el emperador me recibió estaba muy enfermo. Sólo me preguntó si el viaje había ido bien y le dije que sí, pero su majestad He estaba demasiado cansado y dijo que hablaríamos en otro momento. Sólo le relaté algunos detalles del viaje, pero antes de que preguntara sobre el cuarto imperio, sobre Da Qin, se quedó dormido. Yo guardé silencio hasta que uno de los guardias que velaban por él me ordenó salir de allí. Eso es todo. Nunca mentí al emperador He. Ahora lo he hecho por temor, sí. En efecto, temía que si se descubría que nunca llegué a cumplir lo que se me encomendó, llegar a Da Qin, entonces la ira de la emperatriz caería sobre mí y me fulminaría. He obrado, como bien dice el *yu-shih chung-ch'eng*, movido por el terror más pernicioso. Ha sido una locura y una falta de respeto —y se volvió a humillar por completo ante la emperatriz—. Sólo merezco morir.

Aquí Fan Chun guardó silencio.

—El miedo, como ha dicho mi sabio consejero, nos hace hacer cosas estúpidas —comentó entonces la emperatriz—. Tu resolución de admitir tu mentira antes de que ésta crezca es muestra de que no eres de espíritu completamente miserable. Te dejaré marchar en libertad si a partir de ahora respondes a las preguntas con sinceridad.

—Sólo la verdad saldrá de mi boca, majestad —respondió Kan Ying sin atreverse a despegar el rostro del suelo.

Aquí la emperatriz se volvió hacia su asistente.

—Haz tú las preguntas. Sé que no sé hacer muchas cosas, pero intento elegir bien quién debe hacer qué en cada momento. Sin duda, tú eres quién sabe qué preguntas hay que plantear en este caso —dijo la emperatriz.

Fan Chun asintió lentamente. Quizá, después de todo, había juzgado mal a la emperatriz y ésta era más inteligente y astuta de lo que imaginaba. Saber delegar era una virtud tan escasa como eficaz en la vida.

—Bien, Kan Ying —empezó Fan Chun—. La pregunta clave es muy sencilla: ¿por qué no cumpliste tu cometido de llegar hasta Da Qin?

—No me dejaron, *yu-shih chung-ch'eng*.

—¿Es por eso, porque temías que se descubriera tu mentira, por lo que no volviste a Loyang cuando se te reclamaba en la corte imperial y por lo que intentaste confabularte con los bandidos que os atacaron cuando Li Kan te traía hasta aquí prisionero?

—Sí, mi señor.

—¿Eras tan ingenuo que pensabas que nunca enviaríamos a por ti y conseguiríamos juzgarte por tu rebeldía? —continuó preguntando Fan Chun.

—Fui un ingenuo, sí, y un estúpido, mi señor.

El asistente asintió una vez. Decidió dejar aquel asunto y volver a centrarse en lo esencial.

—¿Quién no te dejó llegar hasta Da Qin? Sé preciso en tu respuesta.

—La guardia del emperador de An-shi. Pude cruzar el país de los Yuegzhi como legado comercial y embajador del emperador He, pero una vez que llegué a An-shi no se me permitió cruzar todo su territorio siguiendo la ruta terrestre que atraviesa aquel imperio con las caravanas de seda y otros productos. Me vigilaban constantemente. Consideré entonces la posibilidad de intentar embarcarme en alguno de los puertos del sur, como Badis, Harmocia o Carax, pero sólo me permitieron visitar aquellas ciudades marítimas, sin poder subir nunca a barco alguno. Comprendí entonces que aquellos guardias tenían la instrucción muy concreta del emperador de An-shi de no permitirme llegar más allá en mi viaje. Adopté entonces una nueva estrategia. En mi ánimo siempre estuvo intentar cumplir mi misión hasta el final y regresar con informes reales de Da Qin: agradecí a los guerreros de An-shi su escolta y sus servicios y les anuncié mi intención de regresar al Imperio han llevando noticias de lo bien que había sido tratado allí. La guardia imperial me escoltó, es decir, me vigiló, hasta ver cómo entraba de nuevo en territorio Yuegzhi desde la ciudad de Merv en dirección a Samarkanda. En realidad, tenía planeado desviarme hacia el sur una vez estuviera en territorio Yuegzhi, pues éstos también dominan varios puertos de los que me consta que parten barcos hacia Da Qin. Pero una vez en Samarkanda ocurrió algo curioso. Los Yuegzhi ya no se mostraron tan colaboradores como cuando había cruzado su territorio unos años antes, sino que actuaban con hostilidad e impertinencia y se rieron ante mis pretensiones de viajar hacia el sur; así, al igual que habían hecho en An-shi, se me impidió toda posibilidad de embarcarme en dirección a Da Qin. Fue en ese momento cuando comprendí que todo lo que podría contar en la corte del emperador He o, ahora, en la corte de la emperatriz Deng, sería lo que me contaron de Da Qin los marineros que conocí en Carax, uno de aquellos puertos controlados por An-shi y que he mencionado antes: algunos de aquellos marineros hablaban sánscrito, la lengua de algunos Yuegzhi, que conozco lo suficiente para comunicarme rudimentariamente. Había en el puerto de Carax un gran muelle y hasta allí caminé, siempre vigilado por los guardias del emperador de An-shi, pero a cierta distancia. En el centro del muelle hay un altar en el que hacen ofrendas los capitanes de los barcos que van a salir hacia Da Qin, imagino que buscando que sus dioses sean benévolos con ellos y los ayuden a cruzar el gran mar que separa An-shi de Da Qin. Me senté junto a unos fardos amontonados a la sombra de aquel gran altar y allí hablé con dos de esos capitanes de barco. Ellos decían haber llegado hasta en tres ocasiones a Da Qin y fueron los que me refirieron lo que he contado sobre aquel lejano cuarto imperio. Si lo que me contaron era cierto o falso o exageraciones, lo desconozco. Llegar desde el Imperio han hasta Da Qin o viceversa, majestad, es sencillamente imposible. Esto es cuanto sé.

—Lo que te contaron dos capitanes de barco junto a un altar en el puerto de Carax —repitió Fan Chun en busca de confirmación—. ¿Eso es lo que sabes?

—Así es —admitió Kan Ying sin atreverse a despegar la cara del suelo.

Fan Chun se volvió hacia la emperatriz.

—Creo que este hombre ya no tiene nada más que contarnos, majestad.

—Que se lo lleven entonces —dijo Deng mirando a Li Kan—. Ya decidiré luego si debe ser liberado o no.

El guerrero han cogió a Kan Ying del suelo, tirando de su andrajosa ropa por la espalda, y lo levantó como si fuera tan ligero como un junco de bambú.

—Sígueme —le dijo Li Kan.

Los dos desaparecieron de la sala.

El viejo asistente se había quedado mirando al suelo, meditando.

—Me ha sorprendido la rapidez con la que te has percatado de que Kan Ying mentía —dijo la emperatriz—. ¿Eres realmente tan inteligente? ¿No me estará ocultando algo mi más preciado consejero?

Esta vez la pregunta de su majestad sí cogió por sorpresa a Fan Chun. El asistente, que estaba a punto de marcharse, se volvió hacia su majestad para responder a la emperatriz, a la que miró un instante con un brillo especial en los ojos.

—Aunque pueda ser castigado, he de reconocer que me ilusiona ver que su majestad es cada vez más aguda en sus conclusiones. Es cierto que no habría podido intuir que Kan Ying mentía si no hubiera dispuesto de una información que recientemente ha llegado a mi poder. —La emperatriz lo miraba con intensidad—. Me explicaré: hemos estado reorganizando los archivos imperiales para ver qué documentos hay que preservar y cuáles no, ya sabe la emperatriz el tremendo espacio que ocupan los textos en bambú, y entre los documentos apareció el informe que en su momento Kan Ying remitió al emperador He sobre su supuesto viaje a Da Qin. Vuestro esposo debió de considerar que aquél no era un texto muy relevante y lo dejó de lado junto con otros documentos para destruir. Soy meticuloso y antes de quemar algo prefiero leerlo. Lo estudié con atención y concluí en su momento que algunos de los pasajes, como el de que el rey o emperador de Da Qin se dejaban reemplazar sin oponer resistencia, describían imposibles. Luego, ver que Kan Ying refería todo esto entre grandes sudores me reafirmó en que todo o gran parte de su informe era mentira. Ése es mi secreto, que la emperatriz, ante la que me inclino, ha intuido. Debería haber mencionado la existencia de ese informe antes, pero...

—Pero como no sabías si darle credibilidad o no, no lo hiciste, ¿correcto? —dijo la emperatriz interrumpiéndolo y dándole una salida honrosa ante aquella... falta.

—Así es, majestad.

—Bien —continuó la regente Deng—. Quizá, ahora que sabemos que ese informe no es cierto del todo, deberíamos destruirlo.

Aquí Fan Chun se mostró dubitativo.

—Bueno, majestad, no estoy seguro: yo esperaría a disponer de informaciones más precisas. Entretanto archivaría el documento hasta que nosotros u otros en el futuro podamos confirmar qué hay de cierto o de falso en todo lo que allí se cuenta. Aunque... —el viejo consejero bajó la mirada y continuó hablando pero como si pensara en voz alta—; aunque realmente tenemos un problema grave con los archivos. Hemos de encontrar una forma mejor de guardar los textos antiguos, quizá un material diferente al bambú para escribir. He de pensar en ello con detenimiento...

Se hizo un silencio largo.

Fan Chun permaneció en pie, sin decir nada, frente a la emperatriz. Era ahora ella la que meditaba, y no hay que impacientarse nunca con un emperador o una emperatriz. Su majestad volvió a dirigirse a él.

—Es una pena que no hayamos averiguado nada.

—Oh, pero sí hemos averiguado mucho, majestad.

—No te entiendo; ¿qué hemos aprendido hoy? —preguntó Deng arrugando levemente su frente pálida.

Fan Chun se mostró contundente en su respuesta:

—Ahora sabemos que ni los Yuegzhi ni el Imperio an-shi quieren que contactemos con Da Qin. Y siempre es muy interesante saber lo que tus vecinos no desean que consigas nunca.

—¿Crees entonces que deberíamos volver a enviar a alguien hacia Da Qin? Kan Ying dice que es un viaje imposible. ¿Crees que tienes a alguien capaz de hacerlo?

Fan Chun enseguida pensó en Li Kan, pero, una vez más, pesó más en su ánimo la importancia de tener a aquel guerrero en palacio.

—No, majestad. No se me ocurre nadie —mintió, pero lo hizo para tener a su mejor hombre cerca de la emperatriz y protegerla: la joven Ja Yin y su influencia sobre el emperador An-ti eran una fuerza creciente en palacio y temible. No obstante decidió dar una alternativa a la emperatriz Deng—: Pero quizá no tengamos que enviar nosotros a nadie. Quizá el emperador de Da Qin sea quien nos envíe alguna vez a alguien hasta el Imperio han.

—Pero si Kan Ying ha dicho algo de verdad hoy, hemos de entender que ni el Imperio an-shi ni los Yuegzhi dejarán pasar a ningún mensajero de Da Qin. Antes los matarán.

—Seguramente —confirmó Fan Chun—. Si yo fuera el emperador de Da Qin y quisiera enviar a alguien a un viaje tan imposible, encomendaría la misión a alguien sorprendente. Si alguna vez llega hasta Loyang algún mensajero de Da Qin, estoy convencido de que será quien menos imaginemos.

«Los emperadores de Da Qin (Roma) siempre desearon enviar embajadas a China, pero los partos querían controlar el comercio de la seda con China y por eso siempre impidieron esta comunicación.»

Del *Hou Han Shu (Historia de la dinastía Han tardía)* de Fan Ye (y otros autores), escrito en China en el siglo v.

36

LA ÚLTIMA LECCIÓN

Puerto de Ostia, 112 d. C.

En el muelle

Tamura miraba al barco que debía llevarlos muy lejos de Roma.

¿Regresarían alguna vez?

La adolescente lo miraba con ojos grandes, muy abiertos, mientras pensaba en ser fuerte y así hacerse notar, por fin, ante Áyax. Ese viaje le daría la oportunidad que había estado buscando para que el joven gladiador se fijara en ella y dejara de verla como una niña.

En la entrada del puerto

Dión Coceyo no se imaginó nunca haciendo aquello que estaba haciendo y, sin embargo, allí estaba, en el puerto de Ostia, buscando a su pequeña alumna para despedirse de ella antes de que se marchara con su padre y su madre.

El filósofo acababa de llegar a la ciudad portuaria y pudo comprobar que, como siempre, allí la actividad era febril. Por algo era aquella población la receptora de grano —trigo sobre todo, pero también otros cereales—, vino y aceite en millones de ánforas, junto con más recipientes repletos de la salsa *garum* llevada de Hispania, y especias, sedas y hasta muebles lacados desde los más lejanos confines de Oriente, desde el Imperio kushan, las costas de la India o incluso la remota y enigmática Xeres.

A toda esta tumultuosa actividad había que añadir las imponentes obras de ampliación del puerto ejecutadas por Apolodoro de Damasco por orden directa del emperador Trajano. Era cierto que el divino Claudio ya había ampliado aquel puerto en el pasado y que se pensó en su momento que con aquellas obras se terminarían los naufragios de barcos por las tormentas o las avenidas de agua en Roma, cuando el Tíber revertía su curso y dejaba llegar el agua del mar hasta la mismísima urbe. Pero la confianza en las remodelaciones ordenadas por el divino Claudio se probó excesiva: al poco de terminar aquella obra una tormenta hundió más de doscientos barcos amarrados en el puerto de Ostia y apenas unos años después, durante la guerra civil entre Galba, Otón, Vitelio y Vespasiano,[24] el Tíber volvió a inundar Roma, revirtiendo una vez más su curso y dejando que el agua del mar bañara hasta el mismísimo foro. Aquellos dos desastres fueron la prueba evidente de que un nuevo puerto, más protegido, y nuevas obras de encauzamiento del Tíber eran más que necesarias. Pero Nerón tuvo otros intereses, luego llegó la guerra civil y cuando Vespasiano y Tito tuvieron el oro necesario para acometer aquella magna obra, prefirieron invertirlo en la construcción del Anfiteatro Flavio, menos útil para la gente pero más vistoso. Nerva apenas tuvo tiempo de hacer nada. La obra, eternamente pospuesta, quedó, al fin, para Trajano, que al contrario que sus antecesores, no la rehuyó, sino que puso a su mejor arquitecto al mando de la misma: el denominado *Portus Traiani Felicis*, en honor a su promotor, se excavó al sureste de la bahía acondicionada por el emperador Claudio.

La pieza central del nuevo puerto era una gigantesca nueva bahía hexagonal de más de ciento veinte *iugera*[25] de extensión de agua en perfecta calma, al estar protegida por la primera bahía de Claudio. Construir este gran lago artificial más al interior aseguraba una paz total a los barcos allí anclados frente a las tormentas del mar, pero, indudablemente, fue un empeño mucho más costoso en tiempo y dinero. Era, no obstante,

24. 69 d. C.
25. Unas treinta hectáreas.

esta vez sí, la solución definitiva para asegurar todos los barcos comerciales que atracaran en cualquiera de sus veinticuatro estaciones de anclaje, distribuidas por cada uno de los cinco lados del hexágono, cada lado de más de trescientos cincuenta pasos de longitud. El sexto lado, por supuesto, debía quedar abierto justo en el centro para que los barcos tuvieran acceso a la bahía exterior del César Claudio y de ahí al mar abierto.

El filósofo había oído una vez en una conversación en el Circo Máximo entre Apolodoro y el emperador Trajano que había sido necesario extraer más de mil ochocientos millones de libras[26] de tierra para construir aquella nueva bahía artificial.

En cuatro de los lados del hexágono se levantaron también gigantescos *horrea* donde almacenar todas las mercancías desembarcadas. Aquellos almacenes eran estructuras ciclópeas a las que se accedía a través de un peristilo con columnas que daba acceso a un interior de varias alturas. En la planta baja almacenaban el grano y los mármoles llevados desde África, Asia y Egipto, mientras que en los pisos superiores podían acumular mercancías más ligeras como la seda o las especias.

Dión Coceyo se detuvo frente a un barco, un *birreme* militar de la flota imperial, anclado frente a uno de los grandes *horrea*. No tuvo que esperar mucho para descubrir al *lanista*, acompañado de su mujer y su hija, discutiendo con algunos marineros sobre algún asunto relacionado con algo que estaban embarcando. En cuanto la joven Tamura vio a su *paedagogus* se separó del grupo sin pedir permiso a sus padres y se acercó a él. Dión Coceyo no pudo evitar conmoverse por aquel gesto de la niña. Para él seguía siendo una niña, aunque era cada vez más evidente que a sus trece años, Tamura tenía ya más forma de mujer en todo su cuerpo que de niña. Y seguramente sus pensamientos estaban cambiando de igual manera.

—Has venido —dijo Tamura al llegar junto al anciano.

—Prometí que lo haría y las promesas deben cumplirse siempre —respondió el filósofo—, pero estoy cansado. —Miró a su alrededor—. Sentémonos allí.

El anciano y la adolescente se acercaron a otro barco que

26. Unas seiscientas mil toneladas.

desembarcaba grano y caminaron hasta donde se habían acumulado algunos sacos desechados por los comerciantes, porque se habían humedecido y estropeado durante la ruta desde Sicilia o quién sabía si desde Egipto. El filósofo se sentó en uno de aquellos fardos.

—Te he traído tres libros —dijo.

—¿Por qué tres? —inquirió ella curiosa.

Al filósofo la pregunta le pareció correcta: podrían haber sido cuatro o cinco o dos o ninguno.

—Un libro por cada una de las lenguas que has estudiado conmigo —y sacó de debajo de su túnica tres pequeños códices—. Son de pergamino, escrito por ambos lados para que ocupe menos espacio el texto. Los he copiado yo mismo. No me fío de los escribas y menos con estos idiomas. Aquí tienes una copia del libro en sánscrito que hemos estado estudiando.

—¿El de ese profeta del Imperio kushan?

—El de ese profeta, sí —confirmó Dión Coceyo, pero luego la corrigió—, un profeta al que siguen los kushan, pero no sabemos con seguridad que sea de su imperio, quizá naciera en otro lugar. Bien, con él espero que no olvides todo lo que te he enseñado sobre esa lengua.

La niña lo cogió con curiosidad, pero el filósofo sabía que no había sido un gran regalo para ella.

—Gracias —dijo Tamura, no obstante.

—Te he traído otro en griego que te interesará más: *La vida de Craso*. Aquí tienes el final de la historia que empecé a contarte sobre este guerrero que tan mal terminó al cruzar el Éufrates. Y luego tienes este otro códice en latín: hacia donde vas, cada vez que te vayas alejando de Roma, el latín te será menos útil, pero es bueno no olvidar aquello que aprendió uno en el pasado. Quien sabe, quizá alguna vez el latín pueda serte necesario más allá del mundo romano y ni tú ni yo lo sepamos aún. Este último libro lo escribió el mayor guerrero de Roma, al menos, por el momento.

—Julio César —dijo ella con seguridad.

—En efecto. El mejor guerrero de Roma, como te decía, a falta de lo que el emperador Trajano decida hacer. Esperemos que los dioses le ayuden y no cometa los mismos errores que Craso en un nuevo intento de igualarse o superar al divino Julio César. En este libro que te entrego, el divino Julio te explica qué pasó entre él y Pompeyo una vez que Craso fracasó en Partia.

—¿Por qué no me lee mi maestro algo más de la vida de Craso? —preguntó ella—. Tengo mucha curiosidad por conocer el desenlace de su historia.

—¿Leer? ¿Aquí? —preguntó Dión algo incómodo, mirando a su alrededor, viendo a centenares de esclavos, libertos, marineros, mercaderes y legionarios cargando y descargando decenas de barcos.

—Mi maestro siempre me ha dicho que cualquier lugar y cualquier momento eran buenos para leer —replicó ella.

Él sonrió.

—Eso es cierto. Lo dije. Pero antes una última lección.

—Oh, no. No es justo —se quejó la joven sármata.

—Puede que alguna vez eches de menos mis lecciones —respondió él sonriendo—. Además es una lección muy corta. ¿Me escuchas?

—Escucho —respondió ella con un largo suspiro. ¿Qué otra opción le quedaba?

—Bien. Esta lección es breve: cuando tengas problemas graves, usa todo lo que creas que pueda ser útil para encontrar la solución, pero cuando nada haya hecho efecto, entonces usa también todo lo que creas inútil, pues el mundo está lleno de sorpresas —dijo el filósofo y calló.

Tamura asintió, aunque como en tantas otras ocasiones, le parecía que el *paedagogus* griego hablaba con acertijos.

—De acuerdo —dijo la niña, que sabía que hasta que no repitiera el mensaje recibido el filósofo no leería nada, así que así lo hizo—: Si alguna vez estoy en medio de un grave problema, primero usaré todo lo que crea útil para resolverlo y luego, si nada ha surtido efecto, emplearé otras cosas aunque me parezcan inútiles.

—Perfecto —confirmó Dión Coceyo—. Una cosa más —añadió el filósofo y la niña resopló—. Oh, vaya, pensé que mostrarías más interés por que te dijera qué significan aquellas dos palabras sánscritas que te enseñé a escribir y pronunciar pero cuyo significado nunca te expliqué. ¿Recuerdas: «*Adhīśvaras āhvāyaka*»?

Tamura asintió. El brillo de sus ojos informaba al filósofo que sí sentía curiosidad por conocer el significado de aquellos términos secretos.

Dión Coceyo se lo explicó.

Tamura parpadeó un par de veces. No era decepción, era simplemente que no veía con claridad la relevancia de aquellas palabras, pero antes de que pudiera pensar en decir nada, el filósofo volvió a hablar al tiempo que abría el códice de la vida de Craso.

—Veamos, por Zeus, ¿dónde nos quedamos?

Tamura dejó de pensar en las palabras sánscritas y respondió con enorme aplomo y seguridad:

—Craso había cruzado el Éufrates después de rechazar la ayuda del rey de Armenia, algo que había hecho contra la opinión de Casio, el *quaestor* y su segundo en el mando. Cruzó el Éufrates con sus siete legiones para enfrentarse a los partos él solo; bueno, con la ayuda de su hijo Publio Craso, que había venido desde la Galia con mil jinetes. Su hijo era muy valiente y había conseguido varios premios a su valor luchando bajo el mando del mismísimo Julio César... el divino Julio César. Entretanto, el rey de los partos, Orodes, se había lanzado contra el rey de Armenia a la vez que había ordenado a Surena, uno de sus mejores hombres, que contuviera el avance de Craso. Surena era muy inteligente. Craso no. Los romanos cruzaron el desierto y encontraron por fin las tropas de Surena. Éste ocultó las protecciones de sus *catafractos* con telas para que los enemigos no supieran que tenía jinetes acorazados y, además, se presentó ante los romanos poniendo a su ejército en columna, de forma que de frente no era posible saber bien cuál era su auténtico número. Casio le había pedido a Craso que formaran en una gran línea para evitar ser rodeados, y Craso lo hizo al principio, pero en cuanto vio que los partos desplegaban sus jinetes por varios puntos, decidió, siempre contra el criterio de Casio, formar un cuadrado con las legiones. Los partos los rodearon y les lanzaron flechas durante horas. Craso ordenó a su hijo que usara a sus jinetes para intentar desbaratar el ataque constante de los arqueros partos. Publio salió del cuadrado. Los partos huyeron, pero sólo fingían para alejarlo de las tropas de su padre. Una vez distanciado, lo rodearon y acabaron con él. Bueno, Craso hijo y sus oficiales se suicidaron en una *devotio* en la que mostraron gran valor y honor, pero sus cohortes estaban aniquiladas. Pero Craso padre aún no sabía nada de todo esto. Ahí nos quedamos.

Dión Coceyo la miraba perplejo. La muchacha había recitado todo aquello con la velocidad del rayo.

—Por todos los dioses, es un resumen perfecto. Me alegra ver que estos años, en efecto, me has estado escuchando. Al menos cuando se trataba de batallas. Bien, veamos. Craso hijo ha muerto, pero su padre, como bien dices, aún no lo sabe... Sí, aquí. —Abrió el códice y rebuscó unos instantes entre sus páginas hasta que empezó a leer—. *Veamos, Craso padre conduce a las tropas hacia una ladera, donde espera recibir noticias del pronto retorno de su hijo de regreso de la lucha. Pero de los mensajeros enviados por Publio a su padre, cuando empezó a estar en peligro, el primero cayó en manos de los partos y fue asesinado; el siguiente consiguió cruzar las líneas enemigas con dificultad e informó de que Publio estaba perdido a no ser que recibiera ayuda rápida y abundante de su padre. Y ahora Craso era presa de numerosas emociones contradictorias y no consideraba nada de forma sosegada. El temor que tenía de poner en peligro de nuevo todo el ejército le hacía más proclive a no proporcionar esa ayuda, pero, al mismo tiempo, su gran amor por su hijo lo empujaba a enviar esos refuerzos; al final, se decidió por hacer avanzar de nuevo todo su ejército.*[27]

27. Toda la sección en cursiva es literal de *La vida de Craso* de Plutarco.

HISTORIA DE LA LEGIÓN PERDIDA

Tiempos de Julio César, Pompeyo y Craso,
mediados del siglo I a. C.

LIBRO III

37

EL SILENCIO DE LOS TAMBORES

En las proximidades de Carrhae
53 a. C.

—Se han detenido los tambores —dijo Casio.

En ese momento llevaron a un legionario con graves heridas a presencia del cónsul, el *quaestor* y los tribunos de las legiones. Se trataba de un mensajero de Craso hijo, el único que había conseguido cruzar las líneas enemigas para informar de lo que había ocurrido a la caballería y las cohortes de Publio.

—El hijo del cónsul... está rodeado... —dijo como pudo, mientras lo sostenían otros dos legionarios para que no cayera derrumbado, exhausto como estaba por las heridas y el esfuerzo supremo realizado para llegar allí.

Craso se acercó al mensajero.

—Pero podrá salir de allí, ¿no es cierto? —preguntó el cónsul.

—No sin ayuda... no sin ayuda... y rápido... —No pudo decir más.

Craso se dio la vuelta y empezó a caminar de un lado a otro con ambas manos en la nuca. Casio callaba. Retornar a la llanura era una locura: sólo podría implicar volver a ser rodeados y masacrados por las flechas.

—Hemos de volver —dijo al fin Craso mirando a los tribunos. Nadie decía nada. Nadie quería volver—. ¡Por todos los dioses, nos hemos puesto a salvo gracias a mi hijo y su valor!

Los tribunos miraban al suelo. En lo de la valentía de su hijo el cónsul llevaba razón, pero seguían sin hablar, mudos.

—¿Os gustaría que os abandonase si se tratara de uno de vosotros? —les preguntó Craso deteniéndose ante cada uno de los tribunos un instante, aunque se saltó la posición de Casio, intuyendo una negativa por su parte. De hecho, el *quaestor* estaba a punto de hablar y oponerse a las órdenes del cónsul para evitar una nueva masacre cuando, de súbito, un extraño clamor de asombro y miedo llegó hasta ellos. Eran miles de gargantas que suspiraban al unísono, como un largo lamento.

—¿Qué ocurre ahora? —preguntó iracundo Craso mirando a su alrededor, pero sin atisbar a entender a qué venían aquellos suspiros de los legionarios de vanguardia. Un centurión llegó en ese instante desde las posiciones más adelantadas del ejército romano—. ¡Por Júpiter! ¿Qué ocurre? —insistió el cónsul, pero el centurión no dijo nada sino que dobló las piernas y cayó de rodillas ante Craso.

—Lo siento, mi cónsul, lo siento... —No fue capaz de decir nada más.

Craso lo apartó de su lado con un violento manotazo que hizo que el centurión arrodillado cayera de lado y diera con sus huesos en el suelo. El cónsul avanzó entonces hacia la vanguardia seguido por Casio y los tribunos de las legiones. El murmullo de suspiros era incesante y cuando los legionarios veían al cónsul cuchicheaban mascullando palabras que apenas podían entenderse.

—¡Abrid paso! ¡Retiraos! —ordenó uno de los tribunos, adelantándose para ir despejando el camino al cónsul en su rápido avance hacia la vanguardia.

Sólo se veían centenares, miles de legionarios a ambos lados, muchos con heridas en brazos y piernas por las flechas de los partos, hasta que, al fin, se abrió la última cohorte de primera línea y los oficiales de máximo rango del ejército de Roma en Oriente pudieron ver lo que había generado la congoja y la depresión de sus hombres: en medio de la llanura, allí donde se acumulaban muchos muertos romanos acribillados por los dardos mortales del enemigo, cabalgaban los *catafractos* de Partia desafiantes y orgullosos. Surena, su líder, portaba una lanza particularmente larga y en lo alto de la misma, clavada en su punta repleta de sangre, estaba la cabeza de un romano. No había que ser un augur para intuir que se trataba de la cabeza del hijo de Craso.

El cónsul se quedó con la boca abierta.

Alrededor de Craso se hizo un silencio espeso y horrible.

Casio bajó la mirada. Ahora ya sabían todos por qué habían parado los malditos tambores.

38

LA SEGUNDA BATALLA

En las proximidades de Carrhae
53 a. C.

Marco Licinio Craso se pasó el dorso de la mano por la frente primero, luego por los ojos. Unos miraban al líder de los partos cabalgando por el valle con la cabeza de su hijo en la punta de aquella maldita lanza; otros observaban con atención al cónsul.

Craso bajó la mirada al suelo. Puso los brazos en jarras. Se volvió hacia los tribunos.

—Dadme un caballo —dijo sin levantar la voz, pero con una frialdad que hizo temer cualquier locura; sin embargo, el cónsul se limitó a montar sobre el animal en cuanto éste se le dispuso a su lado y luego se dirigió a los allí presentes—. Esto no va a quedar así. ¡Formación de ataque!

Y se lanzó al galope hacia la vanguardia.

Casio no veía nada claro lo de volver a entrar en combate con los partos en la misma llanura donde habían sido acribillados durante horas. Mismas fuerzas y mismo emplazamiento sólo podían conducir a un desenlace similar, pero el cónsul ya hablaba a los legionarios de vanguardia a voz en grito, arengándolos para la nueva batalla.

—¡Han matado a mi hijo y ultrajado su cuerpo, pero *mía, es, romanos, esta pena; y sólo mía; sin embargo, la gran fortuna y la gloria de Roma permanecen inquebrantables e invencibles en vosotros, que estáis vivos y seguros. Y ahora, si sentís algo de lástima por mí, a quien de este modo se le ha arrebatado el más noble de los hijos, mostradla con vuestra ira contra el enemigo! ¡Robadles la felicidad! ¡Vengaos de su crueldad! ¡No os desaniméis por lo que ha ocurrido, pues es necesario que aquellos que intentan conseguir grandes logros deben también sufrir enormemente!*[28]

Craso cabalgaba de un lado a otro de la vanguardia romana, con su *spatha* desenvainada hablando sin cesar a todos los legionarios, que lo escuchaban entre compungidos por lo ocurrido y enardecidos por la fuerza de sus palabras. A ninguno le gustaba la derrota ni la humillación ni los amigos muertos en la llanura ni las heridas que muchos tenían por la lluvia de flechas. Escuchando al cónsul la mecha de la rabia y la cólera prendía en los corazones de las legiones romanas.

—*¡No fue sin sangrientas pérdidas que Lúculo consiguió derrotar a Tigranes o Escipión a Antíoco! ¡Y nuestros más viejos antepasados perdieron mil barcos en Sicilia, y en Italia a muchos imperatores y generales (...)! ¡No fue sólo por la Fortuna por lo que Roma llegó a su actual plenitud de poder, sino por la paciente resistencia y valor de aquellos que afrontaron peligros en su nombre!*

Así les habló Craso en un esfuerzo por animar a sus hombres.

Las legiones avanzaron de nuevo sobre la llanura de Carrhae.

Vanguardia parta

—¿Qué hacemos? —preguntó Sillaces a su líder.

Surena, con la cabeza del hijo de Craso clavada aún en la punta de su lanza, sintiendo la sangre del enemigo abatido resbalando entre sus dedos, sonrió mientras respondía:

—Hacemos lo mismo que hemos hecho antes: *Mig.* Otra nube acabará con ellos.

—*Mig* —repitió Sillaces.

Vanguardia romana en el centro de la llanura

—¡Aggh! —Sexto aulló cuando le cayó una flecha en el escudo con tanta fuerza que lo atravesó hasta clavársele en el ante-

---

28. Todo el texto en cursiva de esta intervención y la siguiente de Craso es literal de *La vida de Craso* de Mestrio Plutarco.

brazo izquierdo. Ni siquiera podía soltar el escudo: el dardo había juntado brazo herido y arma defensiva, y el dolor era insufrible.

—¡Aguanta! —dijo Cayo. Lo ayudó a levantarse y a replegarse junto con el resto de los supervivientes de la centuria—. Sigamos al centurión.

Druso consiguió que la mitad de sus hombres regresasen vivos de un nuevo enfrentamiento desigual contra los *catafractos*. La historia se repetía con terquedad. Los romanos intentaban desbaratar a los arqueros de la caballería ligera parta, que no dejaba de lanzarles flechas, pero en cuanto salían varias cohortes para tal efecto, aparecían los pesados *catafractos* y trituraban a los legionarios.

Aquello simplemente no tenía sentido.

Los gritos de los romanos que sucumbían en combate o eran acribillados por las flechas partas crecían infinitamente hasta transformarse en un largo lamento eterno.

El sol empezó a ponerse en el horizonte.

Sólo la llegada de la noche detuvo la lenta masacre.

Sexto hablaba mientras caminaba penosamente, con una mano intentando tapar la hemorragia de su herida, ayudado siempre por Cayo.

—Esas nubes de flechas y polvo son las nubes negras de la maldición de Ateyo.

39

LA RETIRADA

En las proximidades de Carrhae
Noche del 6 al 7 de mayo de 53 a. C.

Centro de la llanura

El ejército romano languidecía a la luz de las estrellas. El frío del desierto pesaba sobre los legionarios después del horrible calor del día y las flechas inclementes de los partos. Sexto gimoteaba en el suelo. Entre su compañero Cayo y el centurión Druso habían conseguido sacarle la flecha, pero el dolor era horrible y el *medicus* de la legión apenas había tenido tiempo para coserle la herida.

—Dale esto —dijo Druso a Cayo y le entregó un odre en el que aún quedaba algo de líquido—. Es vino. Lo guardaba para mejor momento, pero él lo necesita ahora. Cuídalo. Voy a ver cómo está el resto de los heridos.

Cayo vio a su centurión caminando entre las sombras: Druso había combatido todo el día con valor y ahora atendía a sus hombres durante la noche sin desfallecer. ¿Y si en lugar del cónsul Craso hubieran tenido al mando a alguien como el centurión Druso?

En el praetorium *de campaña*

—¿Qué vamos a hacer? —preguntó uno de los tribunos.

—Nos retiraremos aprovechando la noche —respondió Marco Licinio Craso.

—¿Y los heridos? —planteó Casio.

—Ralentizarán el repliegue —dijo otro de los tribunos, pero en voz baja, como hablan los cobardes que parecen nunca decir nada pero siempre lo dicen todo.

—Pero no podemos abandonarlos en medio de la llanura —opuso el *quaestor*—. Los partos los matarán al amanecer. —Como no veía demasiada compasión, sino sólo miedo, entre aquellos oficiales y hasta en el propio cónsul, Casio buscó argumentos adicionales para salvaguardar a los heridos—. Además, si nos marchamos, sus gritos implorando que no los abandonemos pondrán sobre aviso al enemigo sobre nuestros movimientos.

—¡Por Júpiter! —estalló Craso—, ¿crees acaso que a mí me gusta la idea? ¿Se te ocurre acaso algo mejor? —Pero no dejó ni siquiera un mínimo espacio de tiempo para que su oponente en aquel debate militar pudiera decir nada y siguió hablando—: ¡Esto es una guerra, no un paseo por el foro de Roma! ¡Yo he perdido a mi hijo! ¡Todos sufrimos! —El cónsul se volvió hacia los dos tribunos más proclives a la huida—. ¡Salimos de inmediato!

Centro de la llanura

—Vamos, amigo, aguanta —dijo Cayo, y además del vino del centurión le dio unas *buccellata* que había conseguido de otros compañeros—. Come las galletas. Te darán fuerza.

Sexto comía y bebía en silencio. El dolor era muy fuerte, pero el apoyo insospechado de Cayo lo animó. Nunca pensó que Cayo fuera a reaccionar así si él caía herido. Y menos aún el centurión.

—Nos vamos. —Era la voz de Druso, como siempre potente, pero se acercó al herido y le habló en tono normal—. La orden es dejar a los heridos atrás. ¿Puedes andar, Sexto?

El legionario no estaba seguro. Había perdido mucha sangre. Nunca había estado tan débil. Pero Cayo no dejó que Sexto respondiera sino que habló en su lugar.

—Podrá, mi centurión.

—Bien —aceptó Druso—. Pues vamos allá.

Sexto se puso en marcha apoyándose en Cayo y junto a ellos los legionarios de su centuria aún supervivientes, en total unos cincuenta hombres.

Atravesaron la llanura repleta de heridos, quienes, al observar que el ejército se ponía en movimiento sin tenerlos en cuenta, empezaron a aullar pidiendo ayuda para que los transportaran, pero nadie se detenía. La orden del cónsul era que todos los hombres útiles se pusieran en marcha hacia la pequeña fortaleza fronteriza de Carrhae, donde pensaba encontrar algo más de protección para sus tropas frente a las malditas flechas de los partos. Algunos legionarios intentaban, como Cayo con Sexto, ayudar a algún compañero herido a avanzar, pero no había suficientes soldados fuertes y compasivos para asistir a tantos heridos como había tumbados bajo el cielo estrellado del desierto.

Campamento parto

—¿Qué es ese ruido? —preguntó Sillaces en voz alta.

Surena estaba a su lado bebiendo vino y comiendo un cabrito recién sacrificado. Las victorias siempre le daban hambre.

—Es como si los romanos se movieran —comentó uno de los oficiales partos—, pero no entiendo esos lamentos.

Surena se chupó los dedos. La salsa era excelente.

—Es una *lāb*, una súplica. Están huyendo —dijo el jefe del ejército parto—, pero abandonan a sus heridos y éstos lloriquean como mujeres asustadas.

—¿Y qué vamos a hacer? —preguntó Sillaces con algo de preocupación. No le gustaba nada que el ejército enemigo se moviera al abrigo de la noche.

Surena se reclinó entre sus cómodos cojines y puso las dos manos encima de su repleta barriga. Estaba saciado.

—Nosotros nos vamos a dormir. —Sin embargo, Sillaces y algún otro oficial parecían algo inquietos, así que añadió—: Disponed patrullas nocturnas de jinetes que nos aseguren que los romanos no se atreven a venir contra nosotros y atacarnos en la noche, algo que considero improbable, pero no está de más ser precavido. Más allá de eso no se me ocurre nada mejor que dormir. Nos conviene descansar, porque mañana vamos a matar a muchos más romanos y matar es un esfuerzo agotador.

Vanguardia romana en retirada

Llegaron a las puertas de la fortaleza de Carrhae, que estaba en manos romanas. Éstas se abrieron y el penoso ejército de Craso entró en la pequeña ciudad para encontrar un techo donde refugiarse. El cónsul no tenía grandes planes más allá de hallar un sitio donde poder estar a salvo de nuevos ataques de los arqueros enemigos.

Amanecer del 7 de mayo de 53 a. C.

Ejército parto

Al alba el ejército parto entró de nuevo en la llanura de Carrhae. Ante ellos había un mar de heridos romanos abandonados. Se les oía gemir, lamentarse, gritar.

—¿Qué dicen? —preguntó Sillaces.

—Imagino que imploran clemencia —respondió Surena.

—¿Y cuáles son tus órdenes? —indagó su lugarteniente.

Surena se tomó unos instantes para valorar cuánto tiempo necesitarían. Quizá una hora, o dos. Eso los retrasaría, pero también enardecería los ánimos de sus hombres para futuros encuentros con el enemigo. Por otro lado, mirando con detenimiento a aquellos heridos que estaban más próximos a él, concluyó que lo que habían dejado los romanos en su huida nocturna tras de sí eran los hombres en peor estado. Estaba claro que aquellos que podían andar habían hecho el esfuerzo para no quedarse descolgados del grueso de su ejército. Esto implicaba que los que yacían en aquella llanura desértica no valdrían para esclavos, pues estaban condenados, por los cortes y golpes recibidos, a quedar tullidos de por vida. Y si no valían como esclavos, como prisioneros tampoco parecían tener utilidad, pues si su cónsul los había abandonado no era probable que fueran a pagar un rescate por recuperarlos.

—¡Matadlos a todos! —ordenó Surena. Para dar ejemplo, desmontó de su caballo, se acercó a dos legionarios que tenían aún clavadas flechas en las piernas y les hundió una lanza en el pecho, primero a uno y luego a otro. Y continuó matando más heridos, seguido de cerca por Sillaces y el resto de los oficiales.

Pasó una hora entera.

Surena se detuvo y pidió agua.

En efecto, matar era agotador.

—Hay alguien que quiere ver a nuestro líder —dijo Sillaces y ante un gesto afirmativo de Surena, su lugarteniente se hizo a un lado y dejó a la vista la figura encogida del árabe Ariemnes.

—Veo que el espíritu de Zoroastro ha guiado sabiamente al gran Surena hacia la victoria absoluta —dijo el viejo mercader haciendo una larga reverencia y sonriendo tanto que dejó a la vista sus dientes podridos.

—No es aún una victoria absoluta, pero con algo más de tu ayuda podría serlo —respondió Surena.

—Nada me daría más placer que colaborar con el jefe de este gran ejército parto —dijo Ariemnes.

—A cambio de que luego te deje circular con tu *kārwān* [caravana] por nuestro territorio cobrándote muy poco dinero, ¿no es así?

Ariemnes giró las manos boca arriba, hacia el sol, dejando que éste bañara sus palmas abiertas llenas de arrugas entre dedo y dedo.

—Un módico precio por unos servicios que creo que están siendo beneficiosos para el valeroso jefe de los partos.

Surena sonrió cínicamente. Detestaba a aquel árabe. Estaba seguro de que si la situación fuera al revés, si los romanos fueran los que estuvieran venciendo en aquella contienda, Ariemnes ya estaría pactando con ellos. Pero en cualquier caso, los servicios prestados por el árabe se habían probado útiles al conseguir persuadir al cónsul romano de que se alejara del río y se adentrara en el desierto. Quizá aún podría hacer algo más aquel viejo.

Cohortes romanas perdidas

—No llegaremos nunca —dijo Sexto exhausto.

Varias cohortes se habían perdido durante la noche: en lugar de seguir a las legiones de vanguardia hacia Carrhae, se habían extraviado en el desierto. Eran las tropas que llevaban a algunos heridos a los que, contraviniendo las órdenes del cónsul, no habían querido abandonar, pero éstos, en efecto, habían ralentizado la marcha.

—¡Preparaos para el combate! —ordenó Druso sin dar más explicaciones.

No era necesario: la caballería parta, después de haber aniquilado a todos los heridos de la llanura, había salido en su persecución y les había dado alcance con facilidad.

—¡Hacia aquellas rocas, rápido, por Hércules! —exclamó Druso, que ya hacía rato que había decidido no volver a aceptar demasiadas órdenes de unos superiores que lo único que habían hecho era conducirlos a la derrota total para luego, además, prácticamente abandonarlos en el desierto.

Los hombres del centurión corrieron hacia aquellos peñascos y se protegieron entre ellos. Había cavidades estrechas entre las piedras que los resguardaban de la nueva lluvia de flechas enemigas. A su alrededor podían ver cómo iban cayendo decenas, centenares de legionarios que, con sus mandos confundidos, vagaban de un lugar a otro buscando una salida de aquella nueva masacre.

Los mataron a todos.

Cuatro mil legionarios más muertos.

Al cabo de unas horas, con la caída de la tarde, sólo quedaban los cincuenta hombres de Druso luchando entre las piedras. Las flechas, para sorpresa de los partos, no conseguían el efecto acostumbrado, porque los legionarios iban ocultándose entre los recovecos más angostos para evitar la mayoría de ellas, así que los partos se vieron obligados primero a conducir sus *catafractos* contra aquellos últimos supervivientes y luego, como ni siquiera los jinetes acorazados podían pasar por según qué lugares por la estrechez, Sillaces ordenó que doscientos de sus hombres desmontaran y dieran muerte a aquellos malditos romanos en combate cuerpo a cuerpo.

—¡Por fin! —gritó Druso—. ¡Ahora acabaremos con ellos uno a uno!

Empezó a distribuir a sus hombres por cada una de las entradas al complejo laberinto de pasadizos de aquellas rocas que, tras varias horas de recorrerlo para protegerse de las flechas, habían aprendido a conocer como si llevaran en ellos toda la vida.

Los partos enviados por Sillaces avanzaban entre los peñascos y eran atacados por los romanos, que combatían con tanta saña como desesperación. Caían hombres muertos de ambos bandos. Como los partos eran mucho más numerosos era sólo cuestión de tiempo que consiguieran acabar con todos los hombres de Druso, aunque por cada romano abatido eran tres o cuatro los partos atravesados por los *gladios* de aquel pequeño grupo de irreductibles.

—¿Qué ocurre aquí? —preguntó Surena al personarse en aquel punto donde parecía que no era posible reducir a unos pocos supervivientes romanos.

Sillaces lo puso al tanto de todo lo acontecido en aquel sector de la nueva batalla.

—¿Y cuántos hombres llevamos perdidos aquí? —preguntó entonces Surena.

Sillaces, de pronto, tuvo miedo de decir la cifra, pues nada más serle reclamada comprendió que todo aquello estaba siendo un empeño muy doloroso para ellos.

—Más de setenta.

Surena suspiró y luego negó con la cabeza varias veces.

—Traed al árabe que sabe latín —dijo el líder parto.

En cuanto Ariemnes estuvo frente a él, Surena le instruyó sobre lo que debía decir.

—Parece que quieren parlamentar —dijo Druso, y el aguerrido centurión de Cartago Nova se echó a reír. Eran carcajadas de pura ansia, de pura histeria, después de tanto luchar y herir y matar. Pero eran carcajadas limpias que se contagiaron a todos sus hombres. Sin embargo, igual de rápida que llegó la risa ésta desapareció en un instante.

Sexto miró a Cayo.

—No creo que tenga fuerzas para matarme —le dijo a su compañero—. ¿Cuento contigo?

Cayo asintió.

—Serás el último hombre al que mate antes de suicidarme.

Aquello pareció tranquilar a Sexto. Ni el uno ni el otro tenían mucha esperanza en las negociaciones que pudieran entablarse con los partos.

—¡Romanos! —se oyó desde fuera de las rocas.

—¿Qué? —preguntó Druso en nombre de todos. Sin muchas palabras. No estaba para discursos.

—¡Vais a morir si seguís resistiendo! ¡El gran Surena os ofrece el perdón por vuestro valor! ¡Salid de las rocas y os permitiremos cruzar nuestras líneas para que os unáis con vuestro ejército en Carrhae!

Druso miró hacia el exterior: el que hablaba parecía ser aquel maldito mercader árabe del que se había fiado Craso unas semanas atrás; visto lo que había pasado en los últimos días no era como para confiar de nuevo en él, pero el centurión miró a sus hombres. Estaban agotados, exhaustos.

—No podemos vencer —comentó Druso mirando a sus legionarios.

Nadie supo bien qué decir, hasta que Cayo se atrevió a tomar la palabra.

—Mejor morir luchando. —Todos asintieron. Quedaban sólo veinte legionarios.

A Druso le conmovió tanto valor. Si aquellos hombres hubieran estado guiados por un buen *imperator* la conquista de Partia sí habría sido posible. Difícil, pero posible.

—Es mejor sobrevivir —respondió Druso, sorprendiendo

a todos—. Haremos lo siguiente: yo saldré primero. Si respetan mi vida, salid el resto. Si me matan... haced lo que penséis mejor. Luchad contra el enemigo o suicidaos. Ambas cosas son honrosas.

—Pero pueden esperar a que salgamos todos para matarnos como perros luego fuera de las rocas —opuso Cayo con rapidez en cuanto vio que el centurión se ponía en marcha.

—Sin duda. Pero yo voy a intentarlo. —Y no esperó a más parlamentos con sus hombres. Intuía que quizá el líder parto quería dejarlos vivos para que llegaran a Carrhae y desanimaran al grueso del ejército contando lo que había pasado. Pero era sólo una intuición.

Ejército parto

—Salen —dijo Sillaces, pero enseguida se corrigió—. No, sólo es uno de ellos. ¿Lo matamos ya o esperamos a que salgan los demás? —preguntó en voz baja a su líder, como si temiera que el oficial romano que salía de entre las rocas pudiera entender lo que decían.

—Esperaremos a que salgan todos —respondió Surena y miró a Ariemnes, que comprendió de inmediato que debía decir algo al oficial romano que se acercaba hacia ellos.

—¡Han de salir todos! —dijo el mercader árabe.

—Antes quiero la palabra del líder de los partos de que no nos matarán y de que cumplirá lo prometido —replicó Druso con la serenidad que otorga saber que todo está perdido—. Sólo entonces les pediré que salgan. Si nos vais a matar, prefiero elegir dónde han de morir mis hombres.

Ariemnes tradujo las palabras de Druso con cierto miedo. No tenía claro que aquel discurso fuera a ser del agrado del líder parto.

Surena escuchó con atención primero y luego se echó a reír y con él Sillaces y el resto de los oficiales partos.

—Dile que tiene mi *padistud*, mi palabra —respondió al fin.

En cuanto Druso escuchó al mercader se volvió hacia las rocas.

—¡Salid!

Sillaces aproximó su caballo al de su líder y volvió a hablarle al oído.

—Pero seguimos matándolos cuando salgan todos, ¿no es cierto?

Surena guardó silencio mientras veía cómo Sexto y Cayo y el resto de los legionarios salían, todos cubiertos de sangre, de entre los peñascos en los que se habían refugiado. Los miró a la cara y observó que ninguno tenía problemas en sostenerle la mirada. Hombres valientes como pocos y mandados por un oficial inteligente que había sabido escoger dónde combatir mucho mejor que su estúpido cónsul.

—No, no los mataremos —respondió Surena en voz alta para que lo oyeran bien todos—. En esta ocasión, cumpliremos la palabra dada.

Tiró de las riendas de su caballo para dejar paso a la triste comitiva de Druso y sus veinte legionarios ensangrentados. Triste pero recia, orgullosa, digna. Los veinte caminaron entre un estrecho pasillo de caballos acorazados mientras las bestias piafaban y relinchaban como si estuvieran ansiosas por pisotearlos a todos y acabar con ellos de una vez. Pero nadie los atacó.

Druso avanzaba mirando al frente, sin prestar atención a los enemigos. Daba igual. Si querían matarlos lo harían en cualquier momento y si, en efecto, querían dejarlos marchar, daba igual dónde mirar.

Más lejos ya, junto a las rocas, Sillaces se encaró con Surena.

—No me parece buena idea dejarlos irse así.

—No te parece buena idea porque no valoras la bravura en los hombres —le respondió Surena con desdén—. Por eso yo mando este ejército y tú obedeces mis órdenes. Los dejamos marchar, entre otras cosas, porque, ¿quién mejor que esos mensajeros derrotados y ensangrentados para llevar a Carrhae las noticias de que hemos acabado con otros cuatro mil de sus malditos legionarios? Y por encima de todo, estúpido Sillaces, hoy necesito que los romanos crean en mi palabra.

Surena tiró nuevamente de las riendas de su caballo y empezó a trotar para ordenar el reagrupamiento de sus fuerzas. Junto a las rocas quedó un Sillaces incómodo y rencoroso. No le gustó nada que Surena lo hubiera llamado *estúpido* delante de todos los demás. Y Sillaces no era hombre de olvidar afrentas.

Fortaleza de Carrhae

Druso y sus hombres fueron recibidos como unos héroes en Carrhae y Craso citó enseguida al bravo centurión en el *praetorium*. El cónsul quería reunir el máximo de información sobre el enemigo, su posición y su ánimo. Y es que las circunstancias, pese a estar cobijados en aquella fortaleza, no eran buenas: no había víveres suficientes para unas tropas tan amplias como las que el cónsul había conducido allí, la moral de los legionarios estaba por los suelos y faltaba agua.

—Hay que emprender la marcha lo antes posible —había pedido Casio, quien intuía que un cerco a la plaza podría ser un nuevo desastre. No obstante, una vez más Craso dudaba y mientras meditaba sobre qué opción seguir el tiempo pasaba y los partos se aproximaban.

—¿Sólo habéis quedado vosotros de las cohortes que se perdieron en la noche? —preguntó el cónsul sentado desde su *sella curulis* a un Druso que permanecía en pie y ensangrentado frente él. Craso quería confirmación sobre todos los puntos clave de la historia que acababa de referirle el centurión.

—Sólo nosotros —confirmó el oficial.

—¿Y es cierto que Surena cumplió su palabra de dejaros marchar? —inquirió el cónsul con vivo interés. Le sorprendía que el líder parto hubiera respetado un pacto. ¿Se podría parlamentar con Surena?

—Así es —afirmó Druso.

—Es extraño que los haya dejado marchar libres —comentó entonces Casio.

—¿Es tan peculiar que un enemigo se admire del valor de un grupo de valientes legionarios? —le espetó Craso, como acusando a Casio de valorar menos la bravura de Druso y sus hombres que los propios partos.

—Surena no se mostró clemente ni con los heridos de la

299

primera batalla ni con el resto de las cohortes extraviadas —se defendió el *quaestor*—; por eso digo que me parece peculiar que ahora el líder de los partos exhiba clemencia.

Un tribuno irrumpió en el *praetorium*. Craso lo miró girando las manos con la palma hacia arriba, como preguntando qué pasaba ahora.

—¡Por Marte! ¡Es ese árabe miserable! — exclamó el tribuno.

—¿De quién hablas? —preguntó el cónsul irritado—. No estoy para acertijos.

—El mercader Ariemnes, mi cónsul. Ha regresado y está a las puertas de la fortaleza.

Craso se levantó apretando los puños.

—De buen grado estrangularía ahora a ese miserable. Por su culpa nos encontramos en este trance.

Pero el tribuno tenía la faz pálida. Parecía que la presencia del mercader no era lo peor.

—¿Pasa algo más? —inquirió Craso.

—Es lo que ha gritado desde el exterior, hacia las murallas, mi cónsul.

—¡Te he dicho que no estoy para adivinanzas! —gritó el cónsul—. ¡Di todo lo que tengas que decir de una vez, por Júpiter!

El tribuno miró al *quaestor*, luego a Druso y, finalmente, al cónsul. Al fin habló.

—El mercader árabe dice que Surena promete respetar la vida y dejar marchar a todas las legiones supervivientes en paz a cambio de una condición. —Calló un instante, pero como vio el rostro rojo de ira de Craso continuó hablando antes de que el cónsul se arrojara sobre él para estrangularlo por seguir jugando con su paciencia y no transmitir el mensaje del maldito mercader completo—: Surena respetará a todos los legionarios si entregan al cónsul y a sus oficiales. Eso ha dicho Ariemnes; eso jura el mercader árabe que ha prometido Surena.

Craso miró ahora a su alrededor confuso. Retrocedió y se sentó de nuevo en su *sella curulis*.

—¿Has hablado, centurión, de lo que os ha pasado con Surena, de cómo os perdonó la vida? —planteó ahora el cónsul con rapidez; estaba atando en su cabeza todos los hilos de aquella telaraña que el líder parto estaba tejiendo a su alrededor—. ¿Has contado a alguien más antes que a nosotros lo que os ha pasado?

Druso comprendía la gravedad de la situación y por eso, al contrario que el tribuno, fue directo al asunto clave.

—Yo sólo he hablado aquí, pero mis hombres se han quedado entre el resto de los legionarios y a buen seguro lo habrán contado todo. No pensé en ordenarles que callaran, mi cónsul.

Craso asintió varias veces, lentamente.

Ningún tribuno ni ningún otro oficial tenía ganas ni valor para hablar. Sólo Casio se atrevió a poner en palabras lo que todos pensaban, mirando al centurión Druso.

—Ya sabemos por qué Surena respetó vuestras vidas: ahora los legionarios creen en su palabra y están desesperados. Estamos al borde de un amotinamiento general. El líder parto juega a dividirnos y, por todos los dioses, sabe hacerlo.

40

LA FIESTA DEL REY DE ARMENIA

Artaxata, capital de Armenia
Mayo de 53 a. C.

En el palacio imperial del rey de Armenia se celebraba una gran fiesta. Ni Artavasdes, el rey del país, ni Orodes, el gran rey de reyes, el *Šāhān Šāh* de Partia, querían, en realidad, enfrentarse. Al menos Artavasdes no estaba dispuesto a hacerlo sin haber conseguido refuerzos, como las legiones romanas de Craso, pero como el cónsul no se había avenido a un pacto no disponía de esos refuerzos. Por su parte, Orodes tampoco quería tener dos frentes a un tiempo: uno al norte en Armenia y otro al oeste, en el Éufrates, contra los romanos. Por eso los dos gobernantes hicieron algo inteligente para ambas partes y muy malo para los romanos: llegaron a un pacto entre ellos.

—Sí, es hermosa —confirmó Orodes al ver a la hermana del rey de Armenia.

—Satisfará a vuestro hijo Pacoro y así sellaremos la paz y la reconciliación entre nuestros reinos —dijo Artavasdes de Armenia.

Hubo una gran celebración, música y bailarinas; mucha comida, salsas sabrosas, vino, licores exóticos y entretenimientos de todo tipo.

Fraates, otro de los hijos del rey de reyes, también presente en el banquete, estaba incómodo con todo aquello: primero su padre le negaba liderar las fuerzas partas contra los romanos que habían cruzado el Éufrates, pues había puesto a Surena al mando, y luego casaba a su hermano Pacoro con la hermana del rey de Armenia. Fraates veía que constantemente era relegado de cualquier maniobra que pudiera acercarlo al poder, por eso se dirigió a su padre en un momento de la fiesta. Aprovechó la música, que hacía imposible que alguien los oyera. Quería demostrar al rey de reyes que era inteligente e intuitivo, por lo tanto apto para empresas de envergadura, así que volvió a plantear una preocupación que ya mencionara en el pasado y que con la información que llegaba del frente romano parecía cobrar fuerza.

—Hemos conseguido la paz en el norte, padre, con este matrimonio, pero ¿no teme acaso el gran *Šāhān Šāh* que si Surena triunfa contra los romanos pueda tener ideas de llegar a cotas más altas de poder que las que el propio rey de reyes le concede? Las noticias que llegan desde Carrhae son precisamente que los romanos están retrocediendo.

—¿Por qué siempre insistes en esta cuestión? —preguntó Orodes mientras estiraba el brazo para que un esclavo le sirviera más vino.

—Porque Surena ya salió victorioso del enfrentamiento contra Mitrídates,[29] tu hermano rebelde, y un nuevo éxito podría... darle ideas.

Orodes se quedó reflexionando sobre las palabras de su hijo mientras bebía: Él, con ayuda de su hermano Mitrídates, había asesinado a su propio padre Fraates III para conseguir el poder absoluto en Partia. En un principio cedió Media a su hermano, pero al final Orodes decidió deponerlo y quedarse con todos los reinos de Partia. Su hermano huyó a Siria pero regresó con un ejército y puso en peligro su gobierno. Surena se enfrentó a Mitrídates con las tropas que el propio Orodes le proporcionó y lo derrotó en Seleucia, junto al Tigris. Quizá, después de todo, no era descabellado lo que decía ahora su hijo: una segunda gran victoria, en este caso sobre los romanos, podría envalentonar a Surena y animarlo a codiciar el cetro absoluto de Partia, pero él ya había pensado en todo eso y tomado medidas.

Orodes respondió a su hijo sin mirarlo, con sus ojos clava-

29. Se trata de otro Mitrídates diferente al Mitrídates de la época de Trajano. El de la época de Craso era hermano de Orodes y el de la época de Trajano era hermano de Osroes.

dos en una de las hermosas danzarinas armenias y sin perder la sonrisa mientras hablaba.

—Yo también he recibido informes sobre los avances de Surena contra los romanos, pero no te preocupes, hijo mío. Vigilo atentamente a todos los ambiciosos como Surena.

No dijo más.

Fraates no tenía claro si aquellas palabras iban sólo contra Surena o contra él mismo. ¿Habría averiguado su padre algo sobre lo que había estado tramando los últimos meses?

41

LA SEGUNDA RETIRADA

Mesopotamia
53 a. C.

Ejército romano

Avanzaban otra vez en medio de la noche.

Marco Licinio Craso había optado por dar la orden de salir de inmediato. En esta ocasión Casio lo apoyó. Por una vez, coincidía con el cónsul en que lo mejor era no dejar tiempo para pensar sobre la promesa de Surena a unos legionarios con la moral por los suelos. Muchos podían verse tentados a aceptar la macabra propuesta del líder parto de entregar a los tribunos, al *quaestor* y al cónsul a cambio de una prometida libertad.

—Lo que no entiendo es por qué Surena no nos persigue más de cerca —dijo Casio, pero ni Craso ni nadie quiso dar respuesta a sus dudas, hasta que al cabo de varias horas de atravesar valles pedregosos y zonas desérticas en medio de un gran frío nocturno tuvieron la sensación de estar pasando por un lugar que les resultaba demasiado familiar.

—¿Es posible que los guías de la región nos estén llevando en círculo? —preguntó entonces Craso en voz baja a sus tribunos.

Como siempre, fue Casio el único que tuvo agallas para definir con palabras lo que estaba ocurriendo.

—Me temo que sí.

Ejército parto

Seguían el rastro de las legiones romanas que habían huido de Carrhae. Los jinetes de reconocimiento que se habían adelantado por orden de Surena regresaron al grueso de la formación.

—Están muy próximos, mi señor —dijo el oficial al mando de la patrulla.

—Bien —respondió Surena—. Que liberen a un puñado de prisioneros. Eso bastará para conseguir nuestro objetivo.

Ejército romano en retirada

—¡Han llegado prisioneros liberados! —gritaba Cayo a todo el mundo.

Al instante se creó un tumulto de legionarios que se arracimaban alrededor de los recién llegados a la retaguardia de las legiones. Druso acudió de inmediato para mantener la disciplina.

—¡Volved a la formación! ¡Por Hércules! ¡Aún seré yo el que os mate a todos! ¡Volved a la formación!

Pese a los esfuerzos del centurión de Cartago Nova, tal fue el revuelo que muy pronto la liberación de los prisioneros era el único tema de conversación entre los legionarios de todas las cohortes del ejército; en concreto hablaban, sobre todo, de lo que los prisioneros repetían una y otra vez: Ariemnes y otros mercaderes árabes les habían insistido en que Surena, admirado por la lealtad de los legionarios romanos que no se habían rebelado contra sus mandos, estaba decidido a pactar una retirada de todos ellos, a saber: legionarios, tribunos, cónsul y *quaestor*. Y es que, relataban los recién liberados, lo que más interesaba a los partos y a los árabes era el restablecimiento de una paz que permitiera de nuevo la circulación de las caravanas de productos transportados desde los reinos de Bactria, Sogdiana, Fergana y la lejana Xeres en dirección a Occidente; pero para acordar esa paz final, Surena reclamaba parlamentar de tú a tú, personalmente, con Craso y sus oficiales. El mensaje que habían llevado consigo aquellos prisioneros liberados era claro: con una entrevista entre Craso y Surena terminarían todos los sufrimientos por los que estaban pasando desde que empezó aquella maldita campaña.

Los legionarios no podían hablar de otra cosa que no fuera eso.

Llegó la rebelión.

El *praetorium* de campaña, levantado de forma rápida e improvisada por orden del cónsul cuando hubo comprobado que los guías locales no los estaban alejando del enemigo, fue rodeado por una multitud de soldados encrespados y nerviosos que exigían, con puños en alto y a voz en grito, que Craso fuera a negociar con Surena.

La tensión era palpable en los serios rostros de todos los presentes en aquella tienda de mando. ¿De mando?

—En cuanto resolvamos esto quiero que ejecuten a la mitad de los guías locales —dijo el cónsul con las manos sobre una mesa en la que estaba desplegado lo que creía que era un buen mapa de la zona—. Eso quizá ayude a que los otros recuperen la memoria para conducirnos con rapidez de regreso al Éufrates.

—Eso me parece bien —coincidió Casio—, pero ahora hemos de dar respuesta primero a las exigencias de nuestras tropas.

—¡Los están engañando, por Júpiter! —exclamó Craso con violencia—. ¿No lo veis? ¿Acaso alguien cree aquí en las palabras de esos miserables, de Surena o de ese traidor mercader, Ariemnes?

—¡La cuestión no es ya lo que nosotros pensemos o dejemos de pensar! —le replicó Casio también airado por el cúmulo de despropósitos de aquella campaña que los había conducido del desastre absoluto a, finalmente, un motín del ejército—. ¡Lo que importa ahora es lo que creen los legionarios, y esos miserables partos se las han ingeniado para que crean que se puede pactar con ellos! ¡Por Júpiter, nuestras tropas confían más en el enemigo que en nosotros!

—¿Y qué propones? —le preguntó Craso acercándose al *quaestor* hasta quedar apenas a un palmo de él—. ¿Que nos rindamos? ¿Quieres acaso que rinda a cuarenta mil hombres?

—¡No, por todos los dioses! ¡Pero tendremos que ir a parlamentar! ¡Alguien tendrá que ir y me parece que tendrá que ser el que nos ha traído aquí a todos!

Y Casio miró a dos de los tribunos más veteranos, Octavio y Petronio, en busca de apoyo, pero ni siquiera ellos se atrevieron a decir nada.

—Enviaremos emisarios a Surena para decirle que queremos parlamentar —aceptó al fin Craso—. Eso tranquilizará a los legionarios y, por otro lado, podrán preguntar a Surena con quién desea hablar de todos nosotros. Eso haremos. A fin de cuentas, ¿no estamos haciendo ya todo lo que el líder parto quiere?

Y se sentó en la *sella curulis*.

En efecto, en cuanto los legionarios fueron informados de que se enviaban emisarios para iniciar las negociaciones para acordar una retirada pactada, los ánimos se sosegaron y la calma regresó a las tropas, que volvieron a formar mientras aguardaban resultados.

Los emisarios no tardaron mucho tiempo en retornar al *praetorium* de campaña.

—Surena dice que sólo hablará con el cónsul de Roma.

Craso asintió. Era lo que esperaba. Se levantó despacio y miró a Casio.

—Sé que he cometido errores —le dijo mirándolo a los ojos—, y sé que me culpas por ello. He pagado un precio muy alto por mi ambición, Casio, la vida de mi propio hijo y, seguramente, ahora lo pagaré con mi propia vida, pues acudo a este parlamento con los partos persuadido de que camino hacia mi muerte. Te dejo el mando de las tropas. Si la negociación es sólo una farsa más de los partos para acabar con mi vida, conduce a tantos como puedas a través de las montañas de regreso al Éufrates. Sólo una cosa te pido, os pido a todos. —Y miró a las caras de todos los oficiales allí presentes—: *Romanos y oficiales aquí reunidos, veis que acudo a este encuentro obligado, y sois testigos de la violencia que se ha ejercido sobre mí, pero contad al mundo, si regresáis vivos a casa, que Craso pereció porque fue engañado por sus enemigos y no porque fue entregado a ellos por sus compatriotas.*[30] Que eso no se diga de estas tropas. Me consta que hay hombres valerosos entre ellos.

—Así se hará —confirmó Casio.

Craso no añadió más y salió del *praetorium* seguido por los *lictores* de su guardia.

En el interior de la tienda, Octavio miró a Casio y le habló con decisión.

—Me gustaría acompañar al cónsul.

—También es mi deseo acompañarlo. No es justo dejarlo solo con el enemigo —añadió Petronio.

Octavio y Petronio eran los tribunos que más años llevaban al servicio de Craso. Su lealtad en aquellos momentos era propia de hombres honorables.

—Acompañadlo, si ése es vuestro deseo —dijo Casio y luego miró al resto de los tribunos—. ¿Alguien más quiere acudir con el cónsul al encuentro con Surena?

Pero nadie más dijo nada.

Octavio y Petronio salieron de la tienda.

Casio habló en cuanto éstos abandonaron el *praetorium.*

—Disponedlo todo para partir al amanecer. Yo tampoco espero nada bueno de este encuentro, pero sólo así entenderán las tropas que lo único que podemos hacer es permanecer unidos y marchar hacia las montañas a toda velocidad. Allí los malditos *catafractos* no pueden maniobrar y hay multitud de lugares donde protegerse de las flechas de sus arqueros. Nunca debimos abandonar el Éufrates y luego las montañas. —Y concluyó en voz más baja, mirando al mapa de Mesopotamia—: Es más, nunca debimos ni tan siquiera iniciar esta campaña.

Avanzadilla del ejército parto

Un pequeño grupo de jinetes *catafractos* se habían adelantado al grueso de las tropas. Entre ellos estaba Surena. Se habían detenido en el lugar designado para el encuentro con el cónsul.

---

30. El fragmento en cursiva es literal de *La vida de Craso* de Plutarco.

—Vienen a pie —dijo Sillaces.

—Curioso —comentó Surena.

—Quizá sea su costumbre.

—Seguramente.

Craso llegó junto con Octavio y Petronio y los *lictores* al lugar acordado y se detuvo a unos diez pasos de Surena.

—Aquí estamos —dijo el cónsul en griego.

—Y por Zoroastro, yo me alegro de que por fin podamos hablar, en vez de luchar —respondió Surena, también en griego.

—¿Qué propones? —preguntó Craso.

Surena habría preferido algo más de preámbulo, pues estaba disfrutando con ver a aquel cónsul accediendo a una entrevista contra su voluntad, pero si el romano deseaba ir directamente al grano, tampoco tenía problema en seguirle la corriente. En cualquier caso, todo aquello eran palabras y lo que importaba era seguir con la progresiva destrucción del ejército enemigo.

—Lo que quiero, cónsul, es que las legiones se retiren de nuevo al oeste del Éufrates.

—Eso era lo que estábamos haciendo —replicó Craso con hastío, rabia, asco. Estaba hablando con quien había dado muerte a su hijo y exhibido su cabeza como un trofeo bárbaro. El recuerdo de aquel fatal suceso, aún demasiado reciente en su memoria, hacía que le hirviera la sangre.

—Lo sé —respondió Surena—. Lo que quiero es, además, un pacto por el cual el cónsul romano se comprometa a que ningún otro ejército romano cruce el Éufrates nunca más.

Craso sabía que no tenía la potestad para hacer eso sin un debate en el Senado, pero no tenía ganas de entrar en una explicación de derecho romano con aquel parto desafiante.

—Sea, de acuerdo —respondió.

Se hizo entonces un silencio extraño para todos.

—Me gustaría que esto se pusiera por escrito —dijo entonces Surena—. Propongo que nos veamos en un mes en Zeugma, a orillas del Éufrates, y que se firme este acuerdo que asegurará la paz entre Roma y Partia para siempre.

A Craso le sorprendió la arrogancia de aquel general. Hablaba como si se considerara él rey de reyes de todos los partos. Quizá ése era su plan. Haber expulsado a las legiones romanas atacantes tal vez le daría fuerza para rebelarse contra el propio Orodes y suplantarlo en el poder. Eso era interesante: una guerra civil debilitaría a Partia. A Craso se le iluminaron los ojos con un brillo especial. Ése sería el momento de volver a atacar a los partos y tomarse justa venganza por la muerte de su hijo. No todo estaba perdido. Todo podía conseguirse. Quizá el sacrificio de su hijo no terminara siendo completamente en vano. Lo esencial era ahora seguir la corriente a Surena.

—De acuerdo —dijo Craso—. En un mes nos veremos en Zeugma.

Y el cónsul hizo ademán de retirarse, pero Surena volvió a hablar.

—Pero no parece adecuado que todo un cónsul de Roma regrese andando a su campamento cuando yo he venido hasta aquí a caballo.

—Es nuestra costumbre acudir así a un parlamento con… —no le pareció oportuno decir «el enemigo» y se corrigió mientras hablaba—. A un parlamento con otro líder de un ejército. En todo caso, no tengo caballos aquí.

—Pero yo sí —dijo Surena y miró a uno de los jinetes de caballería ligera que los acompañaban en la retaguardia. Al momento varios desmontaron y uno de ellos le acercó un hermoso caballo blanco al cónsul.

Craso no sabía bien qué hacer, pero aceptó coger el animal por las riendas.

—Permíteme que mis hombres te ayuden a montar —añadió Surena.

Cuatro partos más se aproximaron al cónsul.

En ese momento, Octavio y Petronio se interpusieron en el avance de los guerreros enemigos.

—No se toca al cónsul.

Pero uno de los partos, rápidamente, los rodeó y se situó junto al cónsul, no estaba claro con qué fines, si para ayudarlo a montar en el caballo o si con otra idea. En cualquier caso, Octavio se revolvió con rapidez y decidió no correr riesgos, o correrlos todos, pues desenvainó su *spatha* e hirió mortalmente al caballero parto.

Los otros partos desenfundaron entonces y empezó la lucha entre ellos y los dos tribunos. Los *lictores* se aprestaron a unirse al combate, pero se vieron rodeados por los *catafractos* de Surena, liderados por Sillaces. Los jinetes acorazados partos comenzaron a atravesar los pechos de los *lictores* consulares con las lanzas. La sangre empezaba a correr por todas partes. Craso estaba en lo alto de su caballo y a punto de escapar cuando un parto consiguió herirlo en una pierna y tiró del cónsul hasta descabalgarlo. Uno de los jinetes partos que había desmontado se abalanzó en ese momento sobre Craso, que estaba desasistido, pues tanto los dos tribunos como los *lictores* luchaban ya no por defenderlo sino por sus propias vidas. El guerrero parto atravesó entonces el cuerpo de Craso sin tan siquiera darle la oportunidad de desenvainar su arma.

El grito del cónsul distrajo a Octavio y a Petronio y sus enemigos aprovecharon el momento para herirlos mortalmente. Al poco, cónsul, tribunos y media docena de *lictores* yacían muertos en el suelo mientras que la otra media docena de la guardia de Craso corría despavorida hacia el ejército romano.

—Dejadlos —dijo Surena con tranquilidad—. Ya los capturaremos luego. —Miró al guerrero que había abatido al cónsul—. ¿Cómo te llamas?

—Pomaxatres —respondió el caballero parto.

—Bien, Pomaxatres —continuó Surena—. Termina lo que has empezado.

—Sí, mi señor.

Y Pomaxatres hincó una rodilla junto al cuerpo inerte del cónsul de Roma, le cortó la cabeza con la espada y luego repitió la operación con el brazo derecho. Envainó el arma, cogió la cabeza de Craso del pelo con una mano y con la otra levantó el brazo arrancado, exhibiendo ambos pedazos del cuerpo del cónsul muerto ante su líder.

—Bien. Parece ser que ya hemos acabado de parlamentar —añadió Surena, siempre con voz serena—. Ahora vamos a perseguir a esas legiones hasta el mismísimo Éufrates.

—Lo que no entiendo es —dijo Sillaces a Surena—: ¿por

qué tanta charla cuando habíamos decidido matarlos desde un principio?

—Y lo que nos hemos divertido, ¿qué? —le replicó Surena—. Tu problema, Sillaces, es que no sabes disfrutar de la vida.

Ejército romano

Las noticias de la muerte de Craso y los dos tribunos convulsionaron a los legionarios, que comprobaron cómo habían forzado a su jefe supremo a un encuentro absurdo con un enemigo traidor y vil en grado sumo. Ya nadie pensaba en otra cosa que en atender las órdenes recibidas por el nuevo oficial al mando, en este caso el *quaestor* del ejército.

Casio organizó una veloz retirada en dirección a las montañas más próximas. No se paró a dar instrucciones sobre cuántos víveres llevar o qué hacer con los heridos que aún quedaban entre las filas de las legiones supervivientes a toda aquella desastrosa campaña. Simplemente se puso en vanguardia y echó a andar seguido de cerca por varios tribunos y el *primus pilus* de la primera legión del ejército. Los demás que los siguieran y los que no pudieran que se las entendieran con el enemigo.

La retirada se convirtió en una auténtica cacería, donde los partos abatían constantemente a legionarios que quedaban rezagados mientras que las tropas de la vanguardia romana, a cada nuevo ataque del enemigo, no hacían más que acelerar el paso.

Ejército parto

—Nos convendría ir haciendo prisioneros en lugar de matar a todos los que encontramos —dijo Surena a sus oficiales.

El líder parto ya estaba pensando más en términos económicos que militares. La campaña estaba del todo ganada. Ahora se trataba de sacar el mayor rédito posible y, teniendo en cuenta que los romanos no llevaban apenas provisiones y nada de oro u otros objetos de valor, sólo quedaba una cosa con la que conseguir un botín notable con el que enriquecerse personalmente y con el que dar satisfacción a su jefe supremo, el rey de reyes: esclavos.

Retaguardia del ejército romano

Druso estaba en forma y era fuerte, pero varios de sus hombres se encontraban completamente exhaustos; en particular los veinte supervivientes de la centuria inicial. El cónsul no les había dado tiempo para recuperarse cuando llegaron a Carrhae después de una jornada en la que habían combatido sin descanso. Ninguno de ellos podía dar apenas un paso. Se limitaban a medio arrastrarse por la arena del desierto junto con otros centenares de hombres que se encontraban en circunstancias parecidas.

Y de cientos de rezagados pasaron a varios miles.

Druso trepó a unas grandes dunas en un intento por ver la situación del ejército romano. Lo que detectó era terrible: la larga columna en retirada se había partido en dos mitades: unos veinte mil legionarios, quizá más, avanzaban *magnis itineribus*, a marchas forzadas, hacia las montañas; luego había un gran espacio de un par de millas donde los hombres estaban esparcidos aquí y allá y, al final, unos diez mil legionarios más rezagados, exhaustos o heridos o ambas cosas al tiempo, que, sin duda, no tardarían en ser alcanzados por los partos.

Druso, en lo alto de aquella gran duna, meditó unos instantes. Si aceleraba podría alcanzar al primer gran grupo de cohortes y seguramente ponerse a salvo en las montañas. La otra opción era quedarse con sus hombres y guiarlos en una lucha suicida.

El oficial de Cartago Nova descendió de la colina de arena y se unió de nuevo a su centuria. Cayo, que continuaba ayudando al muy débil Sexto a seguir andando sin retrasarse más, lo miró sorprendido.

—No pensaba que fuera a volver, mi centurión —dijo el legionario.

Druso se encogió de hombros mientras respondía:

—Soy un imbécil.

Sin embargo, nadie de los que seguían a Druso pensaba que aquel centurión fuera un imbécil. De hecho, todos y cada uno de aquellos hombres, admirados por la lealtad de su superior, estaban dispuestos a seguirlo hasta el fin del mundo. Ninguno podía intuir entonces que, precisamente, eso era lo que iban a hacer: seguir a Druso hasta más allá de donde nunca había llegado ningún romano en búsqueda de un destino incierto.

Vanguardia del ejército romano

El terreno empezaba a resultar rocoso, irregular o, lo que era lo mismo, incómodo para los *catafractos* y para el resto de los jinetes partos. La salvación estaba cerca. Casio se detuvo y miró hacia atrás. Como llevaban ya un tiempo ascendiendo podía contemplar el valle desértico que habían dejado a sus espaldas. El espectáculo era deprimente. ¿Dieciséis, veinte, quizá más cohortes? Todas esas tropas se habían quedado rezagadas en la llanura de aquel valle maldito y los partos estaban repitiendo la operación de rodearlos. Pronto empezaría la carnicería. Casio se volvió rápidamente y empezó a vomitar. ¿Era por el esfuerzo de ascender por aquel terreno abrupto a toda velocidad o por la sensación de ignominia al haber abandonado a todas aquellas tropas a su suerte frente al mortal enemigo parto?

Casio se limpió las babas de la boca con el antebrazo derecho.

Ningún tribuno dijo nada. Nadie culpaba al *quaestor*. Si se trataba de buscar cobardes o lo eran todos o nadie. La decisión era difícil: perecer todos o salvar parte del ejército.

Casio no lo tenía tan claro: quizá si hubieran formado todos juntos podrían haber detenido el avance parto. O quizá no y todo habría sido como en la primera batalla. ¡Dioses, qué desastre! ¡A qué fracaso tan deshonroso los había conducido la ambición desmedida y egoísta de un solo hombre, del vanidoso Marco Licinio Craso! El *quaestor* estaba intentando extraer alguna enseñanza de todo aquello. Lo único bueno, concluyó en su rápido repaso por lo acontecido en las últimas semanas, era que el inútil de Craso estaba muerto. Quedaban en Roma, no obstante, dos ambiciones encontradas: la de Pompeyo y la de Julio César. El último, en particular, parecía tener un ansia de poder tan grande o incluso superior a la de Craso. ¿No tendría sentido acabar antes con un hombre así que dejar que un loco como ése condujese a legiones enteras a un desastre como el vivido en Carrhae? Existía la posibilidad de que alguien como César, más hábil a todas luces que Craso a la hora de comandar legiones, pudiera conseguir victorias en lugar de derrotas como la que había cosechado recientemente en la Galia, pero ¿en qué lugar quedaría entonces el Senado? ¿En qué se transformaría Roma entonces? Los partos, en Carrhae, les habían hecho, pese al desastre, un favor. Mejor sería, no obstante, que en el futuro los trapos sucios los arreglaran en Roma antes de involucrar a tantos legionarios valerosos que habían dado su vida inútilmente. Sí, tenía que pensar en eso de acabar con Julio César de alguna forma. De cualquier forma.

—Deberíamos seguir con la marcha —le dijo uno de los tribunos.

Casio asintió mientras seguía mirando hacia el valle y veía cómo los partos concluían la maniobra envolvente con la que, una vez más, habían rodeado a numerosas cohortes romanas en medio de una llanura desértica.

—Sí, vámonos —aceptó Casio—. No quiero ver esto.

En el centro del valle

Druso veía la nube de polvo que empezaban a levantar los cascos de los caballos partos que los habían vuelto a rodear. Un poco más y habrían conseguido llegar a las montañas, pero lamentarse no servía de nada. Todos los legionarios de las centurias próximas miraban a Druso en espera de sus órdenes. Allí ya no había tribunos y muy pocos centuriones, y los que había o eran muy jóvenes o estaban heridos. A todos les parecía bien seguir las órdenes de aquel oficial de Cartago Nova.

—¡Formación en *testudo*! —aulló él con energía. Y siguió gritando para enardecer los ánimos de los que le escuchaban, para hacerse oír por encima de los tambores partos que anunciaban la nueva lluvia de flechas—. ¡Cargaremos contra esos malditos! ¡Moriremos matando! ¡Muerte o victoria!

Y todos los legionarios de las centurias que seguían a Druso se acogieron a aquellas palabras y las repitieron como un himno de lucha con el que se lanzaron contra las sorprendidas filas de los *catafractos* partos, que no esperaban resistencia alguna de unas tropas abandonadas por sus líderes y exhaustas.

—¡Muerte o victoria! ¡Muerte o victoria!

Ejército parto

—Ese tipo de resistencia me es familiar —dijo Surena contemplando el arrebato de las tropas romanas que atacaban a los *catafractos*.

—Acabaremos con ellos de cualquier forma —dijo Sillaces.

—Eso desde luego —confirmó Surena—, pero vamos a ofrecerles un pacto. Engañarlos nos ahorrará esfuerzos y perder hombres de nuestro ejército. Da orden de que los *catafractos* se retiren y detén también la lluvia de flechas.

Sillaces no era hombre de pactos y negociaciones, pero Surena era el que mandaba... por el momento.

Ejército romano del valle

—Se retiran —dijo un jadeante Cayo en voz baja, como si no se lo creyera al principio.

—¡Se retiran! —repitieron los legionarios a su alrededor.

En la retaguardia, donde habían quedado los hombres heridos, Sexto también observaba el repliegue de los jinetes acorazados partos.

—Ahora vendrán las flechas —dijo Druso en la vanguardia romana.

Se hizo un silencio lleno de miedo.

—*Testudo!* —aulló el centurión y todos sus hombres y los de las cohortes que los seguían formaron con los escudos en alto protegiéndose de las flechas.

Pero los temidos dardos no llegaban.

Nadie decía nada.

Druso asomó la cabeza por encima de los escudos: los partos enviaban a un jinete a parlamentar.

Era raro que se propusiera otro pacto, y después de lo que había pasado con el cónsul y la fallida última negociación, las palabras de Surena ya no ofrecían tanta seguridad, pero ya estaba todo perdido. Por escuchar no empeoraría su situación.

—Esperad aquí —dijo Druso y se adelantó; al llegar a la altura de Cayo lo miró un instante—. Ven conmigo y también esos dos de allí. No quiero morir solo.

Cayo y los otros legionarios obedecieron convencidos de que caminaban hacia la muerte, pero ya les daba igual un poco antes o un poco después y caer al lado del centurión les parecía bien, noble, honroso.

El jinete parto se detuvo y Druso y sus hombres caminaron hasta quedar frente al caballero acorazado.

—Surena os ofrece la vida si os rendís —dijo el *catafracto* en griego.

—Una vida como esclavos, quieres decir —respondió Druso también en un griego algo más tosco que el del parto; lo suyo no eran las lenguas, pero sus padres lo educaron en Hispania pensando que llegaría a algo grande. Druso prefirió no pensar en eso ahora.

—No estáis en posición de obtener nada más —replicó el jinete acorazado.

El centurión se pasó el dorso de la mano derecha por los labios resecos. Daría cualquier cosa por tener agua.

—Que nos traigan agua y comida mientras lo pensamos

—dijo Druso. El jinete parto lo miró perplejo, pero el oficial romano ya había dado media vuelta y lo dejaba atrás.

Ejército parto

—¿Agua y víveres? —repitió Sillaces indignado—. Están locos esos imbéciles.
—Dadles lo que piden —contrapuso Surena con serenidad—. Un centenar de odres de agua y otro centenar de cestas de pan.
Sillaces lo miró con odio inyectado en los ojos.
—¿Por qué?
Pero Surena no respondió.

Ejército romano del valle

—Están dejando agua y pan justo donde se detuvo el jinete a negociar —dijo Cayo—. ¿Por qué todo esto?
—Los muertos no valen como esclavos —dijo Druso y miró a los oficiales que estaban junto a él—. Esto es lo que hay: Surena ofrece no matarnos a cambio de nuestra rendición. Sin duda está pensando que ha obtenido poco botín pese a la gran victoria que ha conseguido y quiere compensar sus esfuerzos con un buen número de esclavos. Somos unos... diez mil legionarios. Hay muchos heridos, pero otros no lo están y algunos heridos pueden curarse. Somos un buen botín. Por eso nos ofrece algo de agua y alimento. La rendición es indigna, pero la forma en la que el cónsul Craso ha conducido esta campaña tampoco ha sido muy digna. El más noble ha sido su hijo y está muerto. Personalmente, yo prefiero ser esclavo. Los esclavos pueden ser reclamados por Roma; el Senado puede ofrecer un rescate en algún momento por nosotros, aunque lo dudo. Los esclavos también pueden intentar huir. Los muertos no tienen nada. He luchado en muchas regiones del mundo al mando de muchos cónsules y tribunos, pero esto no ha sido una guerra, sino un desastre. Somos víctimas del error de

Craso. Ésta no es mi guerra. Yo me rindo, pero nadie tiene por qué seguirme.

Y no dijo más sobre el asunto, sino que dio instrucciones para que se recogiera el agua y el pan que habían llevado los partos para que se distribuyeran primero entre los heridos y luego entre todos los legionarios del ejército. No tocaba a mucho, pero sí resultó reconfortante. Era comida del enemigo y el camino hacia la esclavitud, pero los ánimos ya no estaban para acciones valerosas y menos si Druso, al que todos miraban como su líder natural, decía que lo mejor era rendirse. El desánimo se había apoderado de todos.

Era el fin.

Había llegado así. De golpe.

Ejército parto

—Están entregando las armas —dijo Sillaces sorprendido por la facilidad con la que los romanos habían pasado de una acción de ataque desesperada a la rendición absoluta—. Es curioso que aún crean que vamos a respetar sus vidas después de lo que hicimos con su cónsul.

Y Sillaces estalló en una sonora carcajada.

—Esta vez honraremos el acuerdo —dijo Surena con tranquilidad—. Necesitamos esclavos que ofrecer a Orodes. Nuestro *Šāhān Šāh* necesita botín de guerra, no sólo victorias. Es el oro el que hace poderoso, no la gloria. Se puede sacar mucho dinero con diez mil esclavos, u obligarlos a construir edificios o fortificaciones que nos harán aún más fuertes.

42

LA FIESTA DEL REY DE PARTIA

Artaxata, Armenia, 53 a. C.

—La victoria, padre, ha sido completa —explicaba Fraates al *Šāhān Šāh* Orodes; éste, aunque ya sabía todo lo acontecido, escuchaba con atención porque le interesaba ver de qué forma narraba los sucesos de la derrota de Craso su hijo Fraates. Y es que el joven hablaba con una preocupación enorme, como si Surena ya estuviera a punto de rebelarse y reclamar para sí el trono de rey de reyes de Partia. Fraates parecía sufrir con aquella posibilidad no como si fuera uno de los treinta hijos del *Šāhān Šāh*, sino como si fuera el heredero designado, cuando Orodes aún no se había pronunciado sobre el asunto y, de hecho, si nombraba sucesor, antes elegiría a Pacoro, al que acababa de casar con la hermana del rey de Armenia, pues era más dócil y aparentemente más leal que el intrigante Fraates.

—Surena también ha conseguido muchos prisioneros —respondió al fin el rey de reyes a su inquieto hijo.

—Eso enriquece notablemente a Partia —comentó Artavasdes, el rey de Armenia, también presente en aquella conversación que tenía lugar en medio de un segundo banquete para festejar la boda de su hermana con Pacoro, el matrimonio que sellaba la paz entre Partia y Armenia, al menos por un tiempo.

El primer banquete había corrido por cuenta de Artavasdes como hermano de la novia, pero este segundo banquete, según la costumbre, corría a cargo de Orodes, el *basileús basiléon* o rey de reyes y padre del novio.

—Sin duda, los prisioneros que ha conseguido Surena suponen un gran botín —comentó Orodes con satisfacción, como si la inquietud que manifestaba Fraates sobre la posible rebelión de Surena no estuviera en su mente—. Muchos esclavos, sí. Creo que hemos apresado a más de diez mil legionarios. Nunca habrá otro líder romano que se atreva a adentrarse en nuestro territorio. Ningún romano volverá a cruzar el Éufrates para atacar Partia.

—O para atacar Armenia —apostilló Artavasdes subrayando el pacto de protegerse mutuamente de cualquier agresión, algo acordado junto con aquella boda que estaban celebrando.

—Correcto, por Ahura Mazda y por Zoroastro —confirmó Orodes corrigiendo sus palabras—. Ningún romano se atreverá a atacar Partia o Armenia jamás. Y más después de lo que van a ver algunos de esos prisioneros que Surena me ha enviado como muestra de su victoria.

—¿Han llegado algunos romanos presos? —preguntó Fraates. De eso no sabía nada.

—Sí, así es, hijo —confirmó Orodes—. Han venido junto con Sillaces, el lugarteniente de Surena, que nos ha traído esas noticias. Y con ese tal Pomaxatres, el hombre de Surena que dio muerte al cónsul Craso.

El rey de reyes señaló en dirección al lugar donde, en efecto, Sillaces y el aludido ejecutor del cónsul romano se sentaban cómodamente, entre grandes cojines, rodeados de esclavas que los abanicaban mientras bebían y comían en abundancia. Orodes los estaba agasajando con generosidad como muestra de su reconocimiento a la tarea realizada.

—Y esos prisioneros ¿dónde están? —preguntó Pacoro, el novio, muy callado siempre aunque en aquella ocasión sentía gran curiosidad por ver a legionarios romanos por primera vez en su vida.

La música se detuvo de golpe y se hizo un gran silencio.

—Ahí están los prisioneros —dijo Orodes con satisfacción.

Una docena de romanos, con los uniformes destrozados por la guerra y las penurias sufridas en aquella calamitosa campaña de Oriente, entró en la gran sala central del palacio real de Artaxata. Todos caminaban penosamente, pues llevaban grilletes en tobillos, cuello y muñecas; algunos, demasiado prietos, les causaban heridas y sangraban. Entre ellos estaban Druso, Cayo y Sexto. Y para mayor humillación de Roma, varios soldados partos exhibían los estandartes con las águilas de las unidades legionarias capturadas.

—¿Cuál es la idea de traerlos al banquete? —preguntó Fraates, que no entendía a qué venía permitir el acceso al gran banquete de bodas de uno de los hijos del rey de reyes a aquellos prisioneros de guerra.

Aquí Orodes se permitió una gran sonrisa. Le encantaba ver las limitaciones de su hijo Fraates. Quizá, pese a su gran ambición, no era tan de temer como había pensado: le costaba mucho entender las sutilezas del gobierno de un imperio.

—Quiero que asistan a la representación —respondió el *Šāhān Šāh*.

Y acto seguido, mientras situaban al grupo de prisioneros en un extremo de la sala pero en un punto con visibilidad suficiente, se despejó el centro de la gran estancia para dar cabida a los actores que iban a representar una obra de teatro griego, tan del gusto de armenios y partos.

—*Las Bacantes* de Eurípides —dijo Orodes ante la mirada inquisitiva de Artavasdes.

—Ah, magnífica elección —contestó el rey de Armenia. Todos los nobles partos conocían el interés que las grandes tragedias griegas despertaban en Artavasdes y comprendieron que el rey de reyes hacía lo posible por agradar a su consuegro. Era evidente que entre la boda y aquellos banquetes, Orodes quería garantizarse la tranquilidad en su frontera norte durante mucho tiempo.

La representación comenzó: el dios Dioniso llega a la ciudad de Tebas enfurecido porque sus habitantes no le rinden culto, pues no lo reconocen como un auténtico dios ya que es hijo de Zeus, el dios supremo, sí, pero engendrado con una mortal. El viejo Tiresias aparece en escena para defender que hay que adorar a Dioniso como a cualquier otro dios, pero Penteo, rey de Tebas, orgulloso, plantea que Dioniso trajo el vino que vuelve locas y lujuriosas a las mujeres. Tiresias contraargumenta que el vino, no obstante, nos trae el placer del sueño y el olvido de los males y que las mujeres son o no lujuriosas en función de su carácter, no del vino. Entretanto hay un extranjero, que no es otro que el propio dios Dioniso disfrazado, quien, acompañado por unas adoradoras, las bacantes, va por la ciudad de Tebas promoviendo el culto, precisamente, de sí mismo. El joven rey Penteo ordena que lo apresen. Dioniso, que no desvela su auténtica identidad, se deja capturar y es llevado a prisión. Las bacantes escapan, pero lloran el apresamiento de su dios.

Como era de esperar, Dioniso, haciendo gala de su poder, se libera del encierro y provoca un terremoto que derrumba el palacio de Penteo. Para colmo de males, las bacantes armadas han atacado varios pueblos, descuartizado animales y herido a muchas personas sin que nadie pueda detenerlas. Y lo peor de todo, Ágave, la madre de Penteo, parece haber sucumbido al embrujo de Dioniso y se ha unido a las adoradoras como una bacante más. Un mensajero del dios le pide a Penteo que adore a Dioniso y así pondrá fin a los males que asolan su reino, pero el rey no da su brazo a torcer y se niega. En su lugar está pensando en alzar al ejército contra las bacantes, pero como teme que éstas hagan huir sus tropas con algún hechizo decide ir primero a espiarlas disfrazado él mismo como una mujer.

Mientras la obra de teatro continuaba, algunos asistentes tenían preocupaciones más allá de lo que se estaba representando ante ellos.

De hecho, Fraates no era el único que estaba confundido respecto a por qué el *Šāhān Šāh* había decidido llevar a aquel pequeño grupo de prisioneros romanos al banquete. El propio Druso estaba extrañado en grado sumo y temía lo peor. La diosa Fortuna y su propio valor le habían salvado la vida ya en dos ocasiones: primero cuando Surena le perdonó junto a sus veinte hombres supervivientes de su maltrecha centuria en aquellas rocas y, en segundo lugar, en la última batalla, cuando luchaban entre las cohortes rezagadas que se habían separado de las fuerzas de Casio y, una vez más, los partos decidieron dejar de masacrarlos y ofrecer una rendición. Llegaron entonces las cadenas y el penoso traslado hacia el interior de Partia. Hasta ahí todo normal. Lo peculiar había sido que Surena, por voluntad propia o por orden recibida del rey de reyes, decidió conducir a unos pocos prisioneros a aquel banquete en Armenia. Druso había concluido que quizá fueran a ser entregados como regalo al rey de Armenia, o que simplemente el rey parto quería exhibirlos a modo de muestra de su poder ante su hasta hace poco enemigo del norte, como una forma de avisarlo de lo que les podía esperar a los armenios si se rebelaban de nuevo contra Partia. Pero lo que de ningún modo entendía Druso era por qué dejarlos allí mientras se representaba aquella obra. ¿Acaso iban a formar ellos parte de alguna macabra exhibición final? Prefería no seguir pensando en ello y centró la atención en la obra de teatro para así intentar olvidar.

El griego del centurión de Cartago Nova no era el mejor del mundo, pero sí suficiente para seguir el desarrollo de la obra. Los padres de Druso ciertamente habían recurrido al mejor *paedagogus* de la ciudad hispana. En su momento albergaron aquellas grandes esperanzas para el futuro de su hijo. Druso no pudo evitar que se le encogiera el corazón cuando pensó en la reacción de su familia en Hispania cuando oyeran que había caído muerto o, peor aún, prisionero de los partos en la maldita campaña de Craso en Oriente. No había llegado a tener hijos. Al menos por ahí no había que añadir más sufrimiento, pero lamentaba saber que ya nunca tendría la posibilidad de tenerlos. Ni de estar con mujer alguna. Ni nietos, ni descendencia. A todos nos gusta pensar que algo vivo nuestro va a quedar en el mundo una vez que desaparecemos, pero él tenía claro que su futuro sería una lenta tortura hasta llegar a la muerte. Ante tales pensamientos oscuros, la tragedia de Eurípides le pareció catártica: Penteo seguía negándose a adorar al dios Dioniso y éste había destruido ya su palacio, parte de su reino y transformado en bacante a Ágave, su madre.

Por su parte, en el otro extremo de la gran sala de banquetes, Fraates volvió a plantear a su padre su incomprensión ante la presencia de los prisioneros romanos en aquella fiesta.

—Sigo sin considerar apropiada su presencia, padre: son esclavos —insistió Fraates.

—Quiero que vean la obra hasta el final, hijo —respondió

el rey de reyes—, y luego enviaré a seis de esos prisioneros de regreso a Roma para que cuenten lo que han visto y otros seis de regreso junto al resto de los prisioneros, ya esclavos como tú bien dices, para que sepan en Roma y entre los apresados lo que el *Šāhān Šāh* hace con sus cónsules: eso les hará pensar a los senadores, por un lado, que no es buena idea volver a cruzar el Éufrates y, por otro, a los legionarios esclavos les hará reflexionar sobre lo que puedo llegar a hacer con ellos si se rebelan.

—¿Y todo eso lo vas a conseguir con una obra de Eurípides? —insistió Fraates con incredulidad.

—Ah, ésta es una representación diferente —respondió Orodes sonriente—. No hay que subestimar el poder del teatro.

Entretanto, en la esquina de los prisioneros, Druso, junto a sus hombres, seguía viendo la obra, que estaba llegando al momento climático: Ágave, madre del rey Penteo, confundida por el dios Dioniso, enloquecida y transformada en bacante, no reconoce a su hijo cuando éste cae preso de las adoradoras del dios y, pese a que Penteo ruega que ella lo reconozca, lo mata y le corta la cabeza sin ser consciente de que está matando a su propio hijo con la fuerza brutal que le ha proporcionado el dios. Ágave regresa entonces a Tebas con la cabeza de su hijo Penteo, al que acaba de decapitar, embriagada por el vino de Dioniso, pensando que lo que ha matado es un león.

En ese momento uno de los actores, de nombre Jasón, interpretando el trágico papel de la madre que asesina a su hijo Penteo sin saberlo, dio varios pasos al frente hasta salirse de la improvisada escena de la gran sala real de Artaxata y cogió, no sin esfuerzo, algo pesado que le proporcionaron unos soldados partos. Tomó aquel presente con fuerza, pero ocultándolo con su cuerpo mientras retornaba al centro del escenario. Una vez allí dio media vuelta y encaró de nuevo al público de nobles armenios y partos, exhibiendo lo que había cogido y mostrándolo como si fuera la cabeza del malogrado Penteo, hijo de Ágave, al tiempo que pronunciaba las famosas palabras de la madre aún bajo los efectos del vino de Dioniso:

—Ἀσιάδες βάχχαι [¡Bacantes de Asia!] —dijo Jasón encarnando a Ágave.

Y los actores que hacían de coro miraron a Jasón/Ágave y preguntaron todos al unísono:

—τί μ' ὀϱοθύνεις, ὤ; [¿Por qué nos llamáis?]

Y Ágave respondió los siguientes versos:

—φέϱομεν ἐξ ὀϱέων
ἕλικα νεότομον ἐπὶ μέλαθϱα,
μακάϱιον θήϱαν.

[traemos desde las montañas
Una pieza de caza fresca y tierna,
Una maravillosa presa.]

Pero la cabeza que exhibía ensangrentada, que representaba ser la del malogrado Penteo, no era de cerámica pintada de rojo con una peluca, sino que se trataba de una cabeza de verdad, dorada, bañada en oro para preservarla como trofeo brutal, y no era otra que la del cónsul Marco Licinio Craso. Aquella exhibición del enemigo abatido, expuesto en forma de despojo descarnado a la par que resplandeciente, llevó al delirio a todos los partos presentes. Orodes estalló en grandes y sonoras carcajadas, a las que se unieron, por puro placer o por pura conveniencia, las risas del rey de Armenia y sus súbditos. Y aquellas malditas carcajadas penetraron en la cabeza de Druso, Cayo, Sexto y el resto de los prisioneros romanos como cuchillos afilados que les removieran en las entrañas. Uno de los romanos se volvió hacia un lado y vomitó. Aquello, lejos de incomodar a los soldados partos, sólo provocó más risas. El actor Jasón no sabía muy bien qué hacer, pero Orodes, el *Šāhān Šāh*, se lo aclaró desde su cómoda posición, reclinado entre un montón de suaves cojines.

—¡Que la obra siga! —exclamó—. ¡Es la mejor representación de Eurípides nunca vista! ¡Nadie la olvidará, por los siglos de los siglos!

Y volvió a reír. Se le saltaban las lágrimas de los ojos.

Jasón asintió y prosiguió actuando en medio de la algarabía general, hasta que los soldados partos vieron que la obra continuaba y controlaron sus risas para seguir prestando atención a ver qué nuevas sorpresas les deparaba el final de aquella representación que les regalaba su rey de reyes.

Llegó el instante en que los actores del coro volvieron a

hablar al unísono y, en esta ocasión, plantearon una nueva pregunta a Ágave.

—τίς ἁ βαλοῦσα; [¿Quién lo ha matado?]

El actor Jasón, que hacía de Ágave, iba a responder, pero en ese momento se levantó de entre el público uno de los guerreros partos, justo en el lugar donde estaban sentados los caballeros y soldados encabezados por Sillaces y enviados por Surena. Quien se alzó no fue otro que Pomaxatres, quien, sin dudarlo un momento, se situó en el centro de la escena, cogió la cabeza que sostenía el actor y la exhibió en su lugar. El comediante, por cierto, se quedó aliviado al poder alejarse de aquel despojo de Craso.

Pomaxatres miró entonces a todo el público asistente, sin importarle para nada la mueca de muerte de aquella cabeza del cónsul romano decapitado, más bien enorgulleciéndose de ese grito ahogado de Craso, y exclamó henchido de vanidad y júbilo:

—πρῶτον ἐμὸν τὸ γέρας. [¡Mío es el honor!]

Si ya antes había habido carcajadas, ahora todos los partos y armenios presentes estallaron de felicidad y volvieron a reír durante un rato largo que se hizo eterno en los oídos de Druso, Cayo, Sexto y el resto del pequeño grupo de prisioneros romanos. Al centurión de Cartago Nova no le importaba ya tanto la cabeza del cónsul Craso, que, a fin de cuentas, se había labrado su destino. A Druso le deprimía ver las águilas de la legión exhibidas como botín de guerra del enemigo victorioso.

Aún entre risas, sollozando por tanta carcajada, Orodes se inclinó hacia donde estaba sentado Fraates.

—¿Entiendes ahora por qué quería que estuvieran esos romanos presentes en la representación de esta tragedia griega? —y continuó riendo sin esperar respuesta alguna de su hijo.

Artavasdes, en un afán de congraciarse con su temible vecino del sur, apuntó un comentario en tono jocoso.

—Más que una tragedia griega, esta representación es una tragedia romana.

La broma del rey de Armenia por inesperada e ingeniosa hizo reír aún más a todos los allí reunidos, menos, por supuesto, a los legionarios y oficiales romanos presos.

Los actores permanecían detenidos, a la espera de que su público se sosegara antes de proseguir con la representación y dar término a la obra de Eurípides retomando su hilo argumental original sobre el fallecido Penteo, la trastornada Ágave y el dios Dioniso.

Las carcajadas desaparecieron por fin. El público volvió a comer y beber. Tanta risa daba sed y hambre y los actores aprovecharon el silencio de los que callaban por satisfacer su apetito y saciar su sed para continuar con el desenlace de la obra, que culminaba con el destierro de Ágave por Dioniso, ahora ya atormentada de por vida porque al recuperar la razón es consciente de la atrocidad que ha cometido al matar, aunque fuera sin saberlo, a su propio hijo.

El rey de Armenia, por su parte, ponderaba qué bien había hecho en abandonar a Craso a su suerte frente a los partos y, en su lugar, pactar con Orodes. Más le habría valido al cónsul romano no ser tan orgulloso y haber aceptado su ayuda en su momento para acabar con el loco de Orodes. Ahora le tocaba a él convivir con el maldito rey de reyes, pero al menos seguía vivo, mientras que el cónsul romano estaba decapitado y su cabeza exhibida humillantemente en aquella macabra representación. Artavasdes, además, viendo que su comentario irónico al calificar la obra de «tragedia romana» había caído bien en el entorno del *Šāhān Šāh*, se atrevió a formular una pregunta que hervía en su interior.

—¿Y qué piensa hacer el gran rey de reyes de Partia con todos los prisioneros romanos que tiene en su poder?

—Ya lo he comentado antes: seis de esos presos serán enviados a Roma para que informen a su Senado sobre cómo tratamos aquí a los *imperatores* que cruzan el Éufrates con legiones —repitió Orodes sin dejar de masticar la carne de caza que tenía en su boca—; y otros seis de regreso a Partia para que se unan al resto de los prisioneros.

Artavasdes asintió, pero no era aquélla su pregunta.

—No, gran *Šāhān Šāh*. Me refiero a qué va a hacer el rey de reyes con esos diez mil prisioneros de guerra, no con estos pocos que han traído hasta aquí.

Orodes movió la cabeza afirmativamente dando muestra

de que había entendido la pregunta al tiempo que tragaba el jugoso bocado de comida. El rey de reyes se acercó muy lentamente al rey de Armenia y le habló al oído:

—A esos diez mil les tengo preparado algo especial.

HISTORIA DE TRAJANO

Principios del siglo ii d.C.

Libro III
ARMENIA

43

UN ENCUENTRO EN ATENAS

Atenas
Otoño de 113 d. C.

Marco Ulpio Trajano se levantó de su *triclinium* en cuanto lo vio entrar en el atrio.

—Mestrio Plutarco en mi casa —dijo al tiempo que le ponía la mano en el hombro e invitaba al anciano a acomodarse en un lecho que había dejado vacante a su lado izquierdo—. Es un gran honor. ¿Has tenido un buen viaje?

—El César me abruma con su generosidad —respondió Plutarco mientras se tumbaba en el *triclinium* lentamente. Sus más de sesenta años aconsejaban movimientos sosegados.

—¿Están bien los caminos desde Queronea? —se interesó Trajano.

—Razonablemente, César. Y la distancia entre mi ciudad y Atenas no es grande, pero mi cuerpo viejo ya no está para viajes, ni siquiera para pequeños desplazamientos, al contrario que acontece con el emperador, quien en pocas semanas ha sido capaz de ir desde Roma hasta Atenas. Es mi mayor deseo que el viaje haya sido sereno y sin sobresaltos.

Trajano, en efecto, había salido de la capital del Imperio por la *Via Appia*, luego había tomado la *Via Traiana* hasta Brundisium y a continuación había embarcado en un *trirreme* hasta llegar al golfo de Corinto. Luego, por tierra, se había desplazado hasta Atenas.

—Se te ha echado de menos en Roma —dijo entonces Trajano haciendo señas a los esclavos para que llevaran agua, vino y comida al recién llegado.

Plotina, a la derecha del emperador, miraba con recelo al

invitado de su esposo. Igual que no le gustaba demasiado el filósofo Dión Coceyo, también la incomodaba Plutarco: aquel viejo magistrado griego, escritor y hasta sacerdote del templo de Apolo en Delfos con capacidad de augur tenía una mirada demasiado inquisitiva. La emperatriz escuchaba atentamente. ¿Por qué habría invitado Trajano a aquel hombre? Su esposo no hacía nada sin motivo. Podía llevarse mejor o peor con él, no ser amantes, pero Plotina siempre reconocía que su marido era, cuando menos, astuto.

También asistían a aquel encuentro Lucio Quieto y Nigrino, que acompañaban a Trajano en su viaje hacia Oriente. Ambos estaban destinados a hacerse cargo de algunas de las legiones que se estaban concentrando en Antioquía, donde esperaba Adriano. Completaban el grupo de elegidos algunos magistrados y otras autoridades locales de renombre que habían sido recibidas en la residencia ateniense del César, cerca de la Acrópolis, en aquella escala del viaje imperial hacia Oriente. El banquete que celebraban era un gesto de Trajano por mostrarse próximo a las autoridades locales de cada uno de los lugares donde se detenía en su ruta hacia el Éufrates. Todos habían sido recibidos amablemente, pero Trajano sólo se había levantado de su lecho con la llegada de Plutarco.

El viejo magistrado, además de haber viajado por diferentes lugares del Imperio como embajador, había hecho amistad con distintos senadores de Roma, algunos de los cuales intercedieron para que se le concediera la ciudadanía romana recientemente. Los escritos de Plutarco sobre diferentes gobernantes del pasado, que todos conocían con el nombre de *Vidas*,[31] lo habían hecho famoso.

—El viaje, mi buen Mestrio —respondió el emperador—, ha sido bueno. Tuve que retrasar mi partida por la muerte de mi querida hermana Marciana. Ya sabes cuánto la quería y quise darle el funeral que merecía. Despúes salimos de Roma hasta Brundisium, un barco hasta Corinto y finalmente un breve trayecto hasta aquí. Como te decía, te he echado de menos.

---

31. El título *Vidas paralelas* es un sobrenombre dado a la obra de Plutarco a partir del Renacimiento. Hasta entonces se la conocía sólo como *Vidas*.

—Siento que el emperador me haya echado en falta y lamenté mucho en su momento el fallecimiento de la augusta hermana del César —se disculpó Plutarco—, pero en la vejez parece que uno busca el amparo de su tierra natal. Envié una carta al César al saber lo de la augusta Marciana.

—Y llegó, sí. Te lo agradezco —confirmó Trajano.

—He traído ahora un pequeño presente para el César con el que espero ganarme algo de su perdón por no viajar ya a la capital del Imperio como hacía antaño. —El anciano extrajo entonces de debajo de su capa un rollo de papiro y se lo entregó al César—. Sé que hoy día parecen empezar a valorarse más los códices de pergamino, especialmente en los viajes, pero a mí me sigue gustando usar un buen papiro.

Trajano tomó el rollo con ambas manos, como quien coge un objeto sumamente delicado, pero entonces se dio cuenta de que tenía los dedos pegajosos por la fruta que había estado comiendo. Dejó el papiro en el *triclinium* y se limpió los dedos con rapidez en su propia toga. Luego lo cogió de nuevo y lo desplegó un poco, lo suficiente para poder leer el título.

—*La vida de Escipión el Africano*[32] —leyó Trajano visiblemente emocionado.

—Alguien que me consta despierta la admiración del César; alguien de quien se puede aprender mucho. Sé que el César ya la ha leído, pero ésta es una copia escrita por mí, aunque con mi viejo pulso, no sé si hago un buen o un mal regalo.

—Un gran regalo. No lo dudes —le agradeció Trajano. Volvió a enrollar el papiro y miró a su espalda.

Allí estaban Liviano y Aulo, siempre pendientes de la seguridad del César, pero un poco más atrás, en una esquina, estaba el joven Fédimo. Aulo comprendió a quién buscaba Trajano con la mirada y se hizo a un lado. El joven secretario se acercó al emperador, cogió el papiro al tiempo que hacía una leve reverencia y regresó a su discreto lugar.

—¿Y no sería más útil leer la vida de Craso? —preguntó Plotina como quien dice algo a la ligera, sin pensar, mientras

32. Libro actualmente desaparecido.

estiraba la mano para que le escanciaran algo más de vino. Afrontaba la forzosa separación de Adriano aumentando la ingesta de alcohol, aunque el emperador bebía tanto que, a su lado, las copas de más de la emperatriz pasaban desapercibidas.

Trajano la miró de reojo.

—Ya he leído la vida de Craso de Plutarco, esposa mía —respondió con serenidad—. Y he procurado aprender las lecciones más importantes que de ese gran libro se pueden extraer, en particular con relación a los errores de Craso en aquella nefasta campaña.

Plutarco percibió cierta tensión y decidió intervenir.

—Recogí en aquel relato no sólo el desastre de Craso, sino también el pésimo final de los partos que lo atacaron.

—¿Ah, sí? —continuó Plotina—. Yo creía que los partos vencieron. Recuerdo haber leído muchas de tus «vidas», Mestrio Plutarco, y ahora mismo no recuerdo bien el final de la de Craso, más allá de que el cónsul muere y de que los partos usan su cabeza en una obra de teatro o algo así. Además de que el enemigo se quedó con diez mil de nuestros legionarios como prisioneros.

Plutarco miró al emperador y éste asintió mientras le servían más vino.

—La emperatriz lo ha expresado perfectamente —dijo el escritor griego y resumió los acontecimientos finales de la derrota de Craso y cómo éste terminaba con su cabeza en medio de la representación de las *Bacantes* de Eurípides ante el rey Orodes de Partia, al tiempo que confirmó lo de los diez mil prisioneros de guerra; pero, en lugar de detenerse aquí, Plutarco prosiguió relatando los sucesos que él mismo narraba en la parte final de aquel libro que la emperatriz parecía no recordar—. Surena, el líder parto que había derrotado a Craso en Carrhae, estaba rabioso por haberse visto privado de la posibilidad de exhibir los despojos del cónsul romano, en este caso su cabeza y su brazo, ante sus familiares y amigos, pues éstos se llevaron ante el mismísimo Orodes, que los reclamó. Pero como Surena era hombre más de acción que de lamentarse, ideó un plan para no quedarse sin disfrutar de las mieles de su victoria: Surena ordenó que *se enviaran mensajeros a Seleu-*

cia con la información de que él llevaba hasta allí a Craso vivo y que preparaba una procesión burlesca a la que denominó, para humillar aún más a Roma, triunfo. Hizo que uno de los prisioneros que más se parecían a Craso, un tal Cayo Pacciano, se pusiera una túnica real de mujer y que respondiera siempre al nombre de Craso o de Imperator cuando alguien se dirigiera a él, y se le paseó a caballo. Por delante de éste iban trompeteros y unos pocos lictores sobre camellos; se colgaron bolsas de las fasces de los lictores y se ataron a sus hachas cabezas romanas recién cortadas; tras ellos iban cortesanos de Seleucia, músicos, que cantaban muchos cánticos ignominiosos y ridículos sobre lo afeminado y lo cobarde que fue Craso. Y todos allí pudieron ver este desfile.[33] Todos se mofaron así del supuesto Craso y Surena vio engrandecida su imagen en toda la región. Demasiado engrandecida. Las noticias de aquel falso triunfo llegaron pronto a oídos de Orodes y el rey de reyes vio claro que la incontenible ambición de Surena lo conduciría a reclamar pronto para sí el trono de Partia entera. La respuesta del *Šāhān Šāh* ante la exhibición de Surena fue contundente: tras los banquetes en Artaxata, envió a Sillaces de regreso al territorio bajo control de Surena con la misión aparente de felicitarlo, pero en realidad, las órdenes de Orodes eran diferentes: Sillaces se aseguró de que Surena terminara sus días súbitamente envenenado. Orodes disfrutó así de unas semanas de victoria absoluta: derrotados Craso y Roma, envenenado el ambicioso Surena y pactada la paz con Armenia. Todo parecía estar ocurriendo de forma que el rey de reyes pudiera tener un largo y próspero reinado, pero la ambición por el poder también corría fuerte a sus espaldas o, para ser exactos, dentro del palacio imperial.

—Fraates —dijo Trajano apurando su copa de vino.

A Plotina no se le escapó que su esposo parecía estar muy al tanto de traiciones pasadas en la historia en otras dinastías imperiales.

—Así es, César —confirmó Plutarco, y continuó explicándose—: Fraates, el hijo envidioso de Orodes, consiguió que su padre también fuera envenenado, pero como Orodes parecie-

---

33. El texto en cursiva se corresponde con una sección final de *La vida de Craso* de Plutarco, con alguna pequeña modificación por parte del autor.

ra negarse a morir pese a haber ingerido el veneno que debería haber resultado letal, el mismísimo Fraates, ignorando ya cualquier discreción, estranguló al *Šāhān Šāh* hasta darle muerte. Al mismo tiempo, confabulado con varios altos oficiales de Partia, quizá descontentos por haber sido gobernados por un rey que pactaba con enemigos como Artavasdes de Armenia o que envenenaba a generales partos como Surena que derrotaban a los romanos, apoyaron a Fraates en su camino hacia el trono imperial de Partia. De este modo, en apenas unos días murieron violentamente no sólo Pacoro, el hijo de Orodes, quien con su boda con la hermana del rey de Armenia simbolizaba un pacto con el enemigo del norte que muchos despreciaban, sino también se dio muerte casi al tiempo a los otros treinta hermanos de Fraates. En cuestión de días no quedó ni un solo hijo de Orodes, ya de una esposa o de una concubina, con vida. Sólo Fraates. Nadie podía disputarle ya el trono de Partia y fue él quien se quedó con el poder durante muchos años. Cuando Marco Antonio atacó Oriente, Fraates aprovechó para acabar también con Artavasdes, el rey de Armenia, en su contraofensiva. La campaña de Marco Antonio fue otro desastre militar, pero desde el punto de vista de Roma, no obstante, Fraates impartió cierta justicia al eliminar a todos aquellos que habían sido los artífices del desastre de Craso: Orodes, Surena y Artavasdes.

Trajano asintió ante el preciso relato de Plutarco. Todo el mundo se quedó en silencio un rato. Plotina no quiso hacer más preguntas para no indisponerse con su esposo y, al igual que el emperador, bebió algo más de vino. Lucio Quieto, sin embargo, planteó una cuestión que parecía haber quedado olvidada por todos los presentes.

—¿Y qué fue finalmente de aquellos diez mil prisioneros? He oído, bueno, creo que todos hemos oído muchas versiones sobre lo que pudo pasar con ellos, pero ¿qué es lo que piensa nuestro insigne invitado?

Quieto no sólo se dirigía con respeto a Plutarco por el aprecio que le había mostrado el emperador, sino porque Plutarco, entre otros diferentes cargos, era el sacerdote supremo del Templo de Apolo en Delfos y además era augur. Es decir, podía predecir el futuro y, a la luz de lo que había escrito, también sabía mucho del pasado.

—Por Hércules, es verdad que hay muchas teorías sobre aquellos diez mil legionarios —confirmó Plutarco—. Es difícil saberlo con seguridad. Horacio cita en sus odas, concretamente en la número V de su libro III, lo siguiente:

Caelo tonantem credidimus Iouem
regnare: praesens diuus habebitur
Augustus adiectis Britannis
imperio grauibusque Persis.

Milesne Crassi coniuge barbara
turpis maritus uixit et hostium,
pro curia inuersique mores!
consenuit socerorum in armis

sub rege Medo Marsus et Apulus
anciliorum et nominis et togae
oblitus aeternaeque Vestae,
incolumi Ioue et urbe Roma?

[Creemos que el atronador Júpiter gobierna el cielo.
Augusto es considerado un dios en la tierra,
Por sumar a los britanos, y además
El peso de los persas a nuestro Imperio.

¿No vivieron los soldados de Craso en viles matrimonios
Con esposas bárbaras, y (¡a causa de nuestro
Senado y sus perversas costumbres!), envejecieron,
Al servicio de sus hostiles padres?

¿Gente de Marsia y Apulia gobernados por un meda,
Olvidando sus escudos, sus nombres romanos y togas,
Y a la eterna Vesta, aunque los altares de Júpiter
Y la ciudad de Roma permanecieron sin daño?]

»Con lo que se nos da a entender que los diez mil terminaron integrándose vilmente entre los partos. Algo que a mí me cuesta creer. Yo pienso que hay otros finales más posibles para su triste historia.

—En todo caso, Horacio no es quién para hacer tanto escarnio de quien se rindió —intervino Trajano—. A fin de cuentas, él mismo huyó de la batalla de Filipos cuando luchaba en el bando de Bruto contra Augusto.

—Quizá tuvo el don de la adivinación y anticipó el desenlace de la batalla —opuso Plutarco con el sosiego de saberse amigo del emperador y, en consecuencia, poder permitirse contradecirlo en algún punto—. Personalmente, me alegro de que huyera y nos dejara sus poemas. Quintiliano muchas veces decía que eran de los pocos poemas que merecían la pena en latín.

—Sobre poesía no discuto —respondió Trajano entre sorbo y sorbo de vino—. Ahí el experto es mi sobrino segundo Adriano, que no está aquí, sino en Siria.

—Trabajando para el emperador —apostilló Plotina.

—Trabajando para Roma —corrigió Trajano.

Plutarco pudo sentir, de nuevo, la tensión entre el emperador y su esposa y decidió volver a introducir el tema que tanta curiosidad despertaba entre Quieto, primero, y ahora parecía que también entre todos los presentes, como forma de evitar un aumento en las réplicas y contrarréplicas que se lanzaban el César y su mujer.

—Pero no quiero dejar sin respuesta la pregunta del noble Lucio Quieto —continuó Plutarco—. La otra posibilidad, según nos narra el propio Plinio el Viejo,[34] es que los diez mil legionarios prisioneros fueran conducidos en lo que debió de ser una muy penosa marcha, por unas larguísimas mil quinientas millas desde Carrhae hasta el otro extremo del Imperio parto, hasta la ciudad fortificada de Merv. Esta población supone la frontera oriental de Partia y es allí donde termina prácticamente el mundo que conocemos. Dicen que sólo Alejandro Magno avanzó más, llegando a Bactria. En fin, en ese remoto lugar, en Merv, los países se nos confunden: en aquel tiempo estaban los reinos de Sogdiana, Margiana y Fergana, hoy día casi todos ellos integrados en el Imperio kushan, y en algún punto aún más lejano estaba entonces y

---

34. Plinio el Viejo, *Naturalis historia*, libro VI.

sigue estando la siempre enigmática Xeres, donde se produce la carísima seda.

La carísima seda. Plotina sintió un destello de inspiración en su interior. Hasta ese instante no había terminado de intuir por qué su esposo estaba organizando una campaña contra Partia de dimensiones colosales. ¿Sólo por el control de Armenia? Su marido no era hombre de movilizar decenas de miles de legionarios sólo por orgullo. Tenía que haber algo más en todo aquello. La emperatriz fingió una dulce sonrisa frívola y señaló su vestido.

—¿Xeres es de donde viene seda como ésta?

—Precisamente, augusta —confirmó Plutarco.

Pero la respuesta del sacerdote no era lo que le interesaba a Plotina, que seguía acariciando su hermoso vestido a la espera de...

—También dice Plinio el Viejo —interpuso Trajano de nuevo mirando a su esposa—, que *ex illo namque margaritas mittit. minimaque computatione miliens centena milia sestertium annis omnibus India et Seres et paeninsula illa imperio nostro adimunt: tanti nobis deliciae et feminae constant.* [Seguramente nuestros placeres y nuestras mujeres juntos son tan costosos para nosotros que no pasa un año sin que nos gastemos dinero en perlas, perfumes y sedas; India y China y la península de Arabia se llevan al menos cien millones de sestercios de nuestro dinero procedente de todos los confines de nuestro Imperio.][35]

Eso era exactamente lo que quería la emperatriz: saber qué pensaba su esposo de Xeres y el costoso comercio con aquel remoto imperio. Plotina hizo ademán de decir algo, pero Trajano volvió a hablar y ella... a escuchar.

—Hasta creo recordar que el propio emperador Tiberio se quejaba de algo parecido cuando decía *illa feminarum propria, quis lapidum causa pecuniae nostrae ad externas aut hostilis gentes transferuntur.* [Nuestro dinero se exporta al extranjero o a países enemigos por las piedras preciosas que tanto gustan a las mujeres.][36]

35. Plinio el Viejo, *Naturalis historia*, libro XII.
36. En Tácito, *Annales*, 3, 53.

Plotina calló y se limitó a dejar la copa de vino despacio sobre la mesa tapándose la mano derecha con la izquierda, para ocultar así de la vista todos sus anillos más lujosos. Sonrió como si estuviera incómoda, pero en su interior latía no sólo la llama de la inspiración: acababa de entender, por fin, qué movía a su esposo a lanzarse contra Partia. No tenía nada que ver con el rey de Armenia depuesto por Osroes; eso era tan sólo una excusa que había estado buscando su marido para atacar Oriente con el beneplácito del Senado. Lo que su esposo realmente quería era terminar con la actividad de los partos como intermediarios en todo aquel creciente comercio con Oriente, con India, con los kushan y, sobre todo, con Xeres. Lo de Arabia lo había resuelto ya anexionándose los territorios nabateos de Petra y otras ciudades. Ahora le tocaba el turno a Armenia, Mesopotamia y Partia entera. Una cuestión económica y no otra cosa era lo que movía a su esposo. Plotina estaba convencida de que lanzarse contra Partia era una locura, pero en sus ojos brillaba el destello de la admiración. Incluso si no se sentía cómoda con su esposo, no podía evitar apreciar el valor de la audacia cuando la tenía ante sí: su marido estaba organizando no ya la mayor campaña militar de Roma en toda su historia, sino, probablemente, también el diseño de un nuevo mundo comercial donde, sin Partia, Roma tendría mucho dinero a ganar. Cantidades inimaginables. Todo ello, por supuesto, si se conseguía la victoria absoluta contra Partia, algo en lo que, hasta la fecha, Roma siempre había fracasado.

—Así es, augusta —confirmó Plutarco a la emperatriz, dejando de lado las alusiones económicas de Trajano para retomar el asunto de los diez mil e intentar alejarse, de nuevo, de las tensiones entre emperador y emperatriz—, seda como ésa; pero nuevamente divago. Decía que los prisioneros de Carrhae, posiblemente, fueron obligados a trabajar en penosas condiciones reforzando las fortificaciones de aquella ciudad.

—¿Y por qué ese afán en fortificar tanto el enclave llamado Merv? —inquirió entonces Lucio Quieto.

—Veamos, esto es interesante —continuó el sacerdote y escritor griego—. Parece ser que entre Partia y Xeres, si bien hoy tenemos el Imperio kushan, como he dicho antes, en aquella época, sin embargo, sólo estaban los reinos que he mencionado antes y algunas tribus guerreras tremendamente hostiles. Imagino que sería contra esas tribus, cuyos nombres desconozco, contra las que los partos levantaban sus fortificaciones de Merv para...

—Sin embargo... —lo interrumpió el emperador—, yo tenía entendido que Augusto recuperó los estandartes de las legiones perdidas en Carrhae, esos mismos que exhibía Orodes en sus fiestas, además de algunos prisioneros supervivientes.

—El César, como siempre, está muy bien informado —aceptó Plutarco—, pero como también saben todos los aquí presentes, tras el desastre de Craso, el propio Marco Antonio intentó atacar Partia, como he apuntado, para vengar el orgullo romano mancillado o para incrementar su poder frente a Octavio Augusto, pero su campaña contra los partos también terminó en otro desastre. No tanto por perder una batalla, como le ocurrió a Craso, sino porque Marco Antonio quiso abarcar demasiado territorio en poco tiempo, como si se hubiera planteado la conquista de Partia en una única campaña. Los partos se replegaron y dejaron avanzar a Marco Antonio; luego llegó el invierno y la retirada de éste y sus hombres por las montañas de Oriente, entre el frío y la nieve, generó aún más muertos que la batalla de Carrhae. Y también prisioneros. No sabemos si los prisioneros romanos que los partos devolvieron a Augusto cuando se firmó un tratado de paz entre los dos imperios provenían de Carrhae o de la campaña de Marco Antonio. Mi parecer es que eran más bien de esta última campaña y que los diez mil legionarios de Craso se perdieron en los confines más orientales del Imperio parto. Y no creo que nunca sepamos qué fue de ellos.

Mientras el escritor griego culminaba su relato, un pretoriano había asomado la cabeza por el extremo de la sala en la que se encontraban los invitados del emperador. Liviano dirigió una mirada a Aulo y el tribuno fue a hablar con el soldado de la guardia imperial para averiguar qué ocurría. Aulo escuchó al pretoriano, que le habló al oído; asintió y luego se encaminó de regreso a su posición, donde, hablándole también al oído, le explicó a Liviano algo en pocas palabras. El jefe del pretorio afirmó un par de veces con la cabeza y se acercó al César.

—La embajada parta ha llegado antes de tiempo —le dijo Liviano a Trajano en voz baja agachándose para que no lo oyera el resto—. ¿Les hacemos esperar, augusto?

—¿Han pedido ser recibidos? —indagó Trajano dejando la copa en la mesa que tenía frente a su *triclinium*. De pronto todo el efecto del vino parecía haberse desvanecido.

—Sí, César.

Trajano lo meditó unos instantes con la rapidez propia del hombre de acción. Habían llegado mensajeros a Roma, en los días en los que enterraba a su hermana, indicando que Osroes quería parlamentar sobre la situación de Armenia. Trajano, entonces, invitó a que se le enviara una embajada oficial parta a la ciudad de Atenas, pero no se esperaba la llegada de los nuevos emisarios de Osroes hasta pasadas unas semanas. Parecía que el rey parto tenía prisa en comunicarse con él. Quizá quería detenerlo antes de que pusiera pie en Asia y ya no hubiera marcha atrás a su decisión de atacar.

—Pues que pasen —dijo al fin. Si terminaba de hablar con aquellos partos pronto, aún podría disfrutar del postre y de un poco más de vino y olvidar su inoportuna llegada. Además, tenía curiosidad por saber con qué actitud iban hasta él los enviados del emperador Osroes, ese que se autoproclamaba, en lo que Trajano consideraba una muestra de innecesaria ostentación, *basileús basiléon*, rey de reyes.

Aulo acudió raudo a la puerta de la sala de invitados y salió en busca de los embajadores extranjeros. Trajano se dirigió entonces a Plutarco con una sonrisa.

—Tanto hablar de los partos, aquí han venido. Hemos debido de atraer su presencia.

El escritor griego sonrió, pero brevemente. Todos estaban poniéndose serios: Plotina, Quieto, Nigrino, Liviano, Aulo... Todos con la misma pregunta en su mente: ¿cómo trataría Trajano a estos mensajeros del emperador de Partia?

344

44

EL VIAJE DEL ANTICRISTO

Mar Mediterráneo, sur de Italia
113 d. C.

Navegaban entre Sicilia y el sur de Italia. Marción, en proa, escudriñaba vigilante el horizonte del amanecer. Aunque no había piratas en el *Mare Nostrum* desde que Pompeyo el Grande acabara con ellos en época de Julio César, al rico comerciante cristiano le gustaba observar los barcos con los que se cruzaban para intentar averiguar el objetivo de su viaje, intuir qué mercancías llevaban o adivinar su destino. Desde que salieran de Bitinia se habían cruzado con barcos fenicios cargados de colorantes, buques griegos con especias y varios *trirremes* militares romanos repletos de grano proveniente, seguramente, de Egipto.

A Marción no le había costado rehacerse tras su detención por el gobernador de Bitinia. Tenía muchos negocios en el Ponto y toda vez que negó ser cristiano, los romanos no lo molestaron más. Es cierto que eso lo había distanciado de su padre, obispo de Sinope, y de muchas autoridades cristianas. Lo consideraban débil, blasfemo, un apóstata. Pero él sabía que el tiempo corría a su favor. Y el dinero. A medida que sus negocios crecían, en especial desde que se había dedicado al comercio de la seda, cada vez más preciada en Roma, disponía de más sestercios, dracmas y talentos para repartir entre las diferentes comunidades de cristianos de Asia Menor. Y con el dinero, las críticas de sus hermanos cristianos, poco a poco, se iban diluyendo.

Había enviado también una carta a Ignacio, muy débil y enfermo, pero aún vivo y siempre con enorme carisma en todas las comunidades cristianas de Oriente y hasta de Occidente. En la carta, Marción se disculpaba por su inmensa cobardía al negar a Cristo ante el gobernador de Bitinia y explicaba que estaba dedicando todo el dinero de sus negocios a respaldar a las comunidades cristianas de Asia.

Ignacio, hombre práctico a la par que cauto, le había respondido con pocas palabras: aceptaba el dinero, pero le conminaba a perseverar en su penitencia, pues su pecado había sido enorme, en especial al dar un pésimo ejemplo ya que, tras él, muchos cristianos se habían desvinculado de la vida en Cristo. Marción aceptó la crítica y siguió inyectando sestercios a las comunidades cristianas. En realidad, estaba persuadido de que las dudas de Ignacio sobre su fe no eran tanto por el episodio de haber negado a Cristo ante el gobernador de Bitinia, como porque no veía con malos ojos algunas ideas de los docetas y los gnósticos. Por eso Ignacio pensaba que él podía ser otro anticristo. ¿Lo era en realidad? Se encogió de hombros. Ni siquiera él tenía decidida su opinión final sobre los gnósticos, sobre si Dios nació en verdad como hombre o no. Pero más allá de aquellas disquisiciones teóricas, en cualquier caso había conseguido una reconciliación con su padre y con algunos otros obispos y volvió a profesar los ritos de Cristo en su comunidad de Nicomedia. A esto ayudó la repentina muerte del gobernador Plinio. Marción difundió el rumor de que él mismo había rezado a Dios para que castigara a aquel gobernador que tanto le había hecho pecar y que tanto daño había causado a los cristianos de Nicomedia y Bitinia. Al menos, hasta que recibió una carta del emperador Trajano que parecía sugerir una actitud más tolerante no aceptando ya acusaciones anónimas. Aquella misiva de Marco Ulpio Trajano había relajado la presión sobre los cristianos en todo el Imperio, pero Marción sabía que quedaba mucho por hacer. Faltaba lo más importante. Por eso viajaba ahora hacia Roma. Ya le había dicho a Ignacio años atrás que lo haría y éste avisó de que acudiría y le explicaría al obispo de Roma y a sus asistentes un plan perfecto para preservar y hacer crecer el cristianismo en todo el Imperio, e incluso más allá de sus fronteras. El emperador Trajano no parecía ver límites a Roma. Ya había hecho conquistas más allá del Danubio y en todos los puertos se hablaba de que el César estaba considerando lanzarse a conquistar territorios más allá del Éufrates. Si Trajano no ponía límites a su imperio, ¿por qué debían recortarse ellos, los cristianos, posibilidades de crecer más allá de cualquier río, frontera o mar? Estaba convencido de que en ese aspecto tenían que aprender de Trajano.

Se cruzaron con una *liburna birreme* que confundió a Marción: ya se alejaba pero estaba seguro de haber visto en la proa de aquel barco militar romano a una niña de unos doce años. ¿Qué tripulación romana de guerra llevaría consigo a una niña? ¿Qué misión podía tener aquella nave? ¿Cuál sería su destino final?

Marción no tenía respuesta para ninguna de aquellas preguntas.

La *liburna birreme* desapareció en la distancia y el comerciante de Bitinia se olvidó de aquel extraño suceso y volvió a pensar en cómo explicar a Alejandro, el obispo de Roma, su plan secreto para salvar al cristianismo y convertirlo en la religión más fuerte del Imperio.

45

EL RÍO DE TRAJANO

Mar Mediterráneo, próximos a las costas de Egipto
113 d. C.

Navegaban con viento a favor. Aun así, Arrio ordenó que los remeros siguieran bogando a buen ritmo.

—¿Por qué tanta prisa? —preguntó Marcio al capitán.

Arrio respondió sin mirar atrás, mientras oteaba el horizonte en busca de tierra.

—Las tormentas nos han retrasado ya varias semanas. Hemos tenido que atracar en varios puertos que no tenía pensado y el buen tiempo puede abandonarnos en cualquier momento. Si ahora está con nosotros, hay que aprovecharlo al máximo.

Marcio levantó las cejas y dio por buena la respuesta. Estaban en proa. Se volvió y encaró la cubierta del barco. Desde allí podía ver a todos los tripulantes de la nave: una decena de marinos seleccionados por el propio Arrio, que ejercía al tiempo de capitán, piloto y oficial militar al mando; tres pretorianos enviados en el último momento a embarcar en Ostia por el tribuno Aulo, o eso decían ellos; el mercader Titianus, el joven gladiador Áyax, Alana, Tamura y cincuenta remeros para bogar en las entrañas de aquella *liburna*. No era aquél un barco grande. Marcio se preguntaba por qué el emperador no les había dado un barco mayor y más fuerte.

—¿Por qué no nos habrá dado el César una embarcación más grande si tan importante es esta misión para él? —preguntó el veterano gladiador y *lanista* volviéndose de nuevo hacia Arrio.

El capitán se volvió hacia el antiguo gladiador y se echó a reír. Cuando terminaron sus carcajadas habló:

—Si es cierto lo que me han contado los marinos de las *tabernae* de Ostia, el emperador nos ha dado el barco que necesitamos.

Pero aquella respuesta enigmática no aclaró nada a Marcio. Sin embargo, su orgullo de viejo gladiador no le permitió insistir y darle la satisfacción a Arrio de sentirse en posesión de información que le resultara relevante. Marcio se alejó de la proa y, en efecto, el capitán se quedó allí algo decepcionado, pues había esperado más preguntas por parte de aquel *lanista* que tantos aires de importancia parecía darse ante todos.

Marcio pasó junto a Tamura que, en medio de la cubierta, se ejercitaba con una espada. Áyax estaba allí mismo, pero en lugar de mirar a la niña, oteaba también, como Arrio, el horizonte. Estaba anocheciendo.

El veterano gladiador llegó junto a Alana, sentada al otro lado de la cubierta. Se sentó a su lado, le puso la mano derecha suavemente en la espalda y le habló en voz baja.

—No me gusta ese Arrio. No me fío de él.

Ella no dijo nada. Pero permanecía quieta, junto a él, sintiendo sus caricias. Le encantaba que alguien tan fuerte como Marcio mostrara esa dulzura con ella. El barco seguía surcando un mar en calma, algo que Alana agradecía después de las últimas tormentas que tanto los habían retrasado.

—Huelo una traición —añadió Marcio.

—¿Por qué? —preguntó Alana.

—El emperador tiene enemigos en Roma. Nos citó de noche, de forma no oficial, con pocos testigos. Eso es que quería ocultar esta misión de respuesta al embajador kushan. Quizá alguien quiera evitar que lleguemos a nuestro destino.

—¿Y sospechas de ese Arrio?

—Sí —confirmó Marcio.

—Puede ser, pero a mí me incomodan más esos tres pretorianos que llegaron el día que embarcamos en Ostia —dijo la mujer sármata mirando hacia donde los tres guardias imperiales, sentados en cubierta, se entretenían con algún juego para el que habían pintado unas rayas en el suelo de la cubierta.

—Sólo lo digo para que estemos atentos —completó Marcio.

Alana asintió.

—¿Qué es eso? —Era Tamura, que se había acercado a ellos al comprobar que sus intentos por llamar la atención de Áyax exhibiéndose con la espada no surtían el más mínimo efecto sobre el joven gladiador griego.

—No lo sé —dijo Alana mirando hacia el agua, hacia donde señalaba su hija—. Es una luz en medio del mar.

Titianus, el mercader, se había aproximado también a ese lado de la cubierta y fue quien los sacó de dudas.

—Es el viejo faro de Alejandría. La torre que ordenó levantar el faraón Tolomeo II para guiar a los barcos que se acercaban a Egipto, como hace ahora con nosotros.

—Ésa será nuestra entrada en Egipto —dijo Marcio dando aquello por hecho cierto, pero el mercader negó con la cabeza.

—No, espero que no.

—¿Y eso por qué? —preguntó entonces el veterano gladiador. Por algún motivo, quizá porque el viejo mercader no se daba aires altaneros, a Marcio no le hería su orgullo preguntarle a aquel hombre, a diferencia del agrio Arrio.

—Tenemos el barco bien cargado de ánforas con aceite y vinos, mercancías de gran valor, muy apreciadas en todas partes, pero en especial en Oriente. Productos que espero cambiar por seda y lacados, entre otras cosas, lo que hará relativamente rentable este viaje, más allá de servir al César, claro. El caso es que lo habitual era descargar todas estas mercancías en Alejandría en pequeñas falúas, unas embarcaciones de vela mucho más pequeñas, para transportarlas Nilo arriba y luego pasarlas a camellos y seguir por tierra hasta Arsinoe. Todo eso alargaba el viaje, pero el emperador Trajano ha ordenado recuperar el viejo canal de los faraones.

—¿El canal de los faraones? —repitió Tamura muy intrigada y poniendo palabras a la curiosidad que también sentían sus padres por todo aquello.

Mientras el mercader seguía explicándose, dejaron la luz del faro de Alejandría atrás y continuaron navegando hacia el este.

—La idea es continuar hasta Peluse, un puerto antiguo donde el emperador ha ordenado construir una nueva gran bahía. Esto es porque desde Peluse se puede ascender por el delta oriental del Nilo con barcos más grandes que las pequeñas falúas. De ahí deberemos seguir hasta Daphne y luego a Zagazig. Allí es donde realmente empieza el canal. La ruta desde Peluse hasta Zagazig es hacia el suroeste, o sea como si fuéramos hacia atrás, pero es por donde se puede navegar con barcos como éste. En Zagazig deben de estar dragando el viejo canal de los faraones. Dicen que ahora va a llamarse *Amnis Traianus*, el río de Trajano, en honor al emperador, quien ha ordenado a Apolodoro, su gran arquitecto, que se ocupe de todos los trabajos de recuperación del canal. Dicen que sólo un arquitecto como él podrá recuperar esta vía fluvial, la más importante del mundo. Una ruta de agua que une el Mediterráneo, el *Mare Nostrum*, como les gusta denominarlo a los romanos, con el mar de Eritrea. Esto evita tener que trasladar mercancías de un barco a otros barcos, luego a camellos y así, tal y como os contaba antes. Todo ello entorpecía el comercio enormemente. Ahora llegarán más mercancías que nunca de Oriente y también podremos enviar más productos hasta aquellos remotos lugares. Trajano es un César con más visión comercial que sus antecesores.

El viejo mercader siguió narrando algunas historias más relacionadas con aquel canal desconocido para Marcio, Alana y Tamura.

—Se cuenta que algún faraón de los tiempos más remotos ya pensó en unir los dos mares, pero que desestimó la idea porque temió que el Nilo se inundara de agua salada. Lo mismo parece que pensó Darío I, en los tiempos en que dominaba Egipto. El caso es que los faraones tolemaicos sí lo llevaron a término.

Tamura, pese a lo intrigada que estaba por todo aquello, no pudo evitar dar un bostezo.

—Es tarde —dijo el mercader—. Lo mejor será dormir. Al amanecer llegaremos a Peluse.

Aquello pareció sensato y Marcio y Alana se echaron en un lado de cubierta, donde dormían habitualmente a causa del calor excesivo de la bodega, y, junto a Tamura, cerraron los ojos.

Pasó un rato.

Alana notó el ansia de Marcio creciendo bajo la ropa del gladiador.

—Está Tamura —dijo ella.

—Duerme —respondió él . Todos duermen, menos el piloto, y no nos puede ver desde el timón.

Alana comprendió que su esposo no estaba por recibir negativas. Ella sonrió. Le encantaba seguir despertando en él aquella pasión.

Lo hicieron en silencio. Despacio. Bien.

Luego se quedaron abrazados.

El veterano gladiador intentaba mantener los oídos atentos a cualquier movimiento extraño. En su cabeza bullía aún el miedo a una traición. Estuvo pensando en todo lo que Titianus les había contado para mantenerse despierto, pero el sueño, después de hacer el amor, lo venció con rapidez.

Nada sucedió por la noche.

Los rayos del alba despertaron a Marcio.

Alana ya estaba en pie mirando hacia la línea de costa.

—Eso debe de ser Peluse —dijo la mujer.

Tal y como el viejo Titianus les había explicado entraron con la *liburna* en una gran bahía de piedra, levantada una vez más por orden de Trajano, para dar acceso al cada vez más numeroso tránsito de embarcaciones comerciales que se adentraban en el interior de Egipto siguiendo aquella ruta: primero llegaron al puerto de Daphne, en el que no se detuvieron, y continuaron hasta Zagazig, donde tuvieron que esperar para poder entrar en el canal propiamente dicho. Dejaron entonces el Nilo y se introdujeron en un canal excavado desde tiempos inmemoriales. Marcio, Alana, Tamura, Áyax, los pretorianos, los marineros, todos, hasta Titianus y Arrio, miraban admirados cómo la *liburna* cabía en aquel estrecho camino de agua. Podían ver a numerosos legionarios y a muchos operarios llegados desde todas partes de Egipto trabajando intensamente con grandes tornillos hidráulicos con los que se extraían enormes cantidades de agua en un espacio excavado que discurría contiguo al canal ya abierto para la navegación.

—Están ampliándolo —dijo Titianus.

Vieron entonces a un hombre mayor, algo encogido ya por los años, dando órdenes a legionarios y operarios sin parar un instante. Todos parecían obedecerlo de inmediato.

—Nunca pensé que lo vería —dijo entonces Titianus.

—¿Quién es? —preguntó Tamura.

—Apolodoro, Apolodoro de Damasco —precisó el mercader sirio y añadió algo con una sonrisa en la boca—: Ha construido el mayor puente del mundo sobre el Danubio, el puerto de Ostia en Roma, el foro del emperador Trajano, con sus bibliotecas, su Basílica Ulpia y la columna que rememora la victoria sobre los dacios. Y ahora ha reabierto el viejo canal de los faraones. Sólo un sirio es capaz de tanto.

Nadie criticó aquel arranque de orgullo patrio de Titianus. Las obras de dragado del viejo canal y los trabajos de ampliación eran tan sorprendentes que nadie dijo nada durante un buen rato, hasta que llegaron a Babilonia del Nilo,[37] en medio del canal, donde se alzaba una gran fortaleza romana.

Arrio se alejó del grupo y fue a proa.

—¿Por qué nos detenemos? —preguntó Marcio.

—Aquí se paga el impuesto a Roma por cruzar del Mediterráneo a la mar Eritrea. El emperador ordena grandes obras pero luego sabe sacarles rendimiento —se explicó Titianus—. Si Trajano se hubiera dedicado directamente al comercio habría sido un gran mercader.

—Quizá un emperador, a fin de cuentas, no sea otra cosa que un gran mercader, el mercader más grande —dijo Tamura mirando las obras del canal y todos la miraron con los ojos muy abiertos.

Arrio resolvió el pago con los legionarios apostados en la fortaleza y la *liburna* siguió su curso hasta alcanzar la población de Herópolis, el lago Timsah, el lago Amers, la ciudad de Kabret y, por fin, un último tramo de canal hasta desembocar en la mar Eritrea. Todo eso sin tener que descargar nada del barco.

—Esta noche llegaremos a Arsinoe —añadió Titianus—. Ése será realmente el principio de nuestro viaje.

37. Población diferente a la famosa Babilonia situada en Mesopotamia.

Marcio volvió a mirar desde cubierta hacia abajo y pudo comprobar una vez más que en algunos segmentos del canal la *liburna* pasaba con apenas unos pies de margen por cada lado. El veterano gladiador ya tenía claro por qué Trajano les había entregado aquella embarcación y no una más grande para aquel viaje.

46

EL ORÁCULO DE DELFOS

Atenas
113 d. C.

En el exterior de la residencia de Trajano en Atenas

Partamaspates reflexionaba con el ceño fruncido recordando las palabras de su padre.

«Acudirás como embajador ante el emperador romano, pero no te identificarás nunca como mi hijo. No quiero que puedan usarte como rehén. Por otro lado, te envío a ti, hijo mío, porque tengo plena confianza en tu lealtad y en que sabrás representar a Partia y sus intereses con dignidad y firmeza ante el emperador romano.» Luego le explicó lo que quería que dijera al César Trajano.

—Viene un oficial de la guardia romana —dijo uno de los nobles partos que lo acompañaban en aquella delicada embajada. El joven Partamaspates parpadeó varias veces abandonando sus pensamientos y retornando a su realidad más próxima: Atenas.

Aulo se detuvo frente a Partamaspates. Era al que todos los demás partos miraban, así que el tribuno pretoriano lo tuvo fácil para intuir a quién debía dirigirse.

—El emperador recibirá la embajada —dijo Aulo en su limitado griego, suficiente para hacerse entender.

Interior de la residencia imperial

En la gran sala, el banquete se había interrumpido. Nadie se sintió molesto porque la curiosidad por saber qué querían plantear los partos al emperador de Roma era enorme. Y era llamativo que Trajano fuera a recibir a los embajadores de forma tan abierta, rodeado por todo tipo de personas. En aquel momento ya cualquier hombre de reputación o fortuna sabía que Roma estaba concentrando numerosas legiones en Siria para intervenir en Armenia, cuando no en toda Partia. Atacar Oriente era algo siempre anhelado por los romanos, pero desde los desastres de Craso y luego de Marco Antonio, era también la campaña más temida de todas. ¿Sería capaz Trajano de sobrevivir a semejante empresa? ¿No sería mejor pactar una paz duradera con los partos ahora que aún se estaba a tiempo?

—Ave, César —dijo Partamaspates y alzó el brazo con la palma extendida hacia abajo como le había instruido su padre que hiciera. Saludar a la usanza romana no tenía por qué suponer prejuicio ni humillación; además, la embajada era muy difícil y había que intentar encontrar algo que aplacara la aparente cólera del emperador romano: era eso o la guerra total.

—Ave, embajador de Partia —respondió Trajano levantando levemente la mano derecha.

Partamaspates esperaba que Trajano le pidiera que se identificara y ya había previsto hacerlo con otro nombre para no desvelar su parentesco con el rey de reyes, pero su sorpresa fue grande cuando Trajano no le preguntó por su identidad. Que el emperador romano no se molestara ni en averiguar con quién hablaba no presagiaba nada bueno o, al menos, nada pacífico.

—¿Qué es lo que los emisarios de Partia desean? —inquirió Trajano en griego, sereno pero distante, no con tono despreciativo, pero sin ofrecer nada de comer o beber a los recién llegados: media docena de nobles partos vestidos con hermosas túnicas de colores muy vivos, con los cabellos y las barbas acicaladas en abundantes rizos.

—El *Šāhān Šāh*, el *basileús basiléon*, no entiende, mi señor, por qué el emperador de Roma está concentrando tantas legiones en Siria. El rey de reyes quiere transmitir al emperador de Roma que en ningún caso los cambios acontecidos en Armenia suponen amenaza alguna para las fronteras entre Roma y Partia.

—El rey de Partia —replicó Trajano, siempre sereno y reduciendo los títulos del monarca parto a simplemente «rey» y no «rey de reyes», ya fuera en latín, parto o griego— no me consultó cuando depuso a Exedares y coronó a Partamasiris, su hermano, en el trono de Artaxata por su cuenta y... riesgo. Así que no veo por qué ha de consultarme ahora por los movimientos de mis legiones dentro de las fronteras del Imperio romano.

—Estimado emperador —continuó Partamaspates al tiempo que hacía una leve reverencia ante el César—, el rey de reyes Osroes admite que quizá deponer a Exedares sin consultar al emperador romano haya sido un error, pero este malentendido puede subsanarse según los convenios firmados entre Partia y Roma. Exedares no era de fiar.

En este punto, Trajano cogió de nuevo su copa de vino y echó un largo trago. Quería ahogar su irritación en el vino. Luego miró fijamente a los ojos del embajador.

—Quién es de fiar o no para Roma es algo que decidimos en Roma, pero dejando esa precisión de lado, me alegra ver que el malentendido se resolverá con rapidez: entiendo que Exedares será entronizado de nuevo y Partamasiris retornará a Partia. Si es eso lo que has venido a anunciarme, me interesa.

Los nobles partos se miraron entre ellos. Partamaspates volvió a hablar.

—Eso no va a ser posible, César.

—¿Por qué no, embajador? —inquirió Trajano.

Hubo un breve silencio.

—Exedares ha... muerto —anunció, al fin, Partamaspates.

Esta vez el silencio en la sala era denso, pesado.

—Hemos traído regalos para el emperador de Roma —añadió Partamaspates en un intento por quebrar aquella sensación de rabia e indignación que parecía dibujarse en la faz del emperador.

En un instante los nobles que acompañaban a Partamaspates exhibieron pequeños cofres que abrieron rápidamente. Contenían abundantes monedas de oro y plata, esmeraldas y rubíes. Un sustantivo tesoro.

—Hay más oro en un gran cofre que hemos traído desde

Cesifonte hasta Atenas para el César, pues el rey de reyes piensa...

Pero en ese momento, Marco Ulpio Trajano se levantó del *triclinium.*

—¿Creéis de verdad, por Cástor y Pólux, que la voluntad de Roma, de su Senado y de su emperador se compran con regalos? ¿Acaso creéis que tratáis con un simple mercader? Decid a Partamasiris —y aquí Trajano tuvo mucho cuidado en no mencionar a Osroes, sino de centrarse en el trono de Armenia, como si no pensara para nada en Partia— que más le vale que cuando llegue a Artaxata con mis legiones, por su propio bien, encuentre el trono de Armenia vacío; de lo contrario, yo me ocuparé de que quede vacío. No sé si he acertado a explicarme con claridad.

Partamaspates dio un par de pequeños pasos hacia atrás. El emperador romano, puesto en pie, era mucho más alto de lo que había imaginado al verlo por primera vez reclinado en aquel lecho en el que les gustaba recostarse a los romanos cuando comían. Pero él era hijo del rey de reyes. No era hombre que fuera a amilanarse por una amenaza como la que el emperador romano acababa de pronunciar.

—Partamasiris es rey de Armenia y amigo de Partia, y Partia nunca se ha mostrado débil ante Roma —replicó Partamaspates con decisión mientras los nobles partos que lo acompañaban asentían, aunque muy tímidamente—. Roma ya ha sufrido penosas derrotas cuando ha cruzado el Éufrates. Como amigo quiero aconsejar al emperador Marco Ulpio Trajano que no repita los errores de sus antepasados.

—Pero Partia ha roto nuestros acuerdos sobre Armenia al coronar a Partamasiris sin consultarme —repuso Trajano con firmeza.

—Eso es cierto —aceptó Partamaspates—, por eso estos regalos, a modo de disculpa, no de compra de voluntades, sino como muestra de amistad; y por eso, además, exponemos que estamos dispuestos a negociar un nuevo acuerdo sobre Armenia que pueda ser satisfactorio para Roma y para Partia. Quizá el César necesite un tiempo para pensar en ello. Sólo pedimos eso: que piense en algún acuerdo que evite... una confrontación.

Trajano guardó silencio mientras paseaba, muy lentamente, entre los cofres abiertos con oro y plata y piedras preciosas que habían distribuido los emisarios partos por la sala. Al fin, el César se detuvo frente a Partamaspates.

—Meditaré sobre lo que hemos hablado, pero llevaos los regalos de regreso a Cesifonte. Si queréis mi respuesta a vuestra idea de un nuevo acuerdo, podéis enviar otra embajada a Antioquía donde espero reunirme con mis legiones en tres meses.

—En Antioquía en tres meses —repitió Partamaspates—. Así se hará.

Luego se volvió hacia sus compañeros de embajada y les dijo unas palabras en parto. Los nobles empezaron a cerrar los cofres y a recogerlos para seguir a Partamaspates en su salida de aquella gran sala de banquetes de la residencia del emperador romano a su paso por Atenas.

Trajano miró a los músicos.

—Tocad de nuevo. —Se dirigió a los esclavos—: Y traed el postre y más vino para todos.

El emperador, contrariamente a su costumbre, repitió varias veces en los postres y probó muchos más confitados de lo que era usual en él. Plotina sabía que quería dar una sensación de completa seguridad, que después de haber despachado a los partos sin aceptar sus obsequios se sentía tranquilo y confiado. Y, desde luego, Trajano consiguió transmitir esa impresión a todos.

Uno a uno, los invitados fueron despidiéndose del César con la llegada de la hora duodécima. Sobre todo las autoridades romanas en Atenas no querían parecer impertinentes quedándose hasta más tarde. La propia Plotina se retiró nada más llegar la noche y lo mismo hicieron Nigrino y otros hombres de confianza del emperador. Al final sólo quedaron dos hombres, además de Liviano, Aulo y el resto de los pretorianos: Lucio Quieto, por propia iniciativa, y Mestrio Plutarco, a petición del César. El escritor griego observó que el jefe de la caballería de Roma lo miraba incómodo y comprendió que Quieto quería hablar a solas con el emperador.

—Con el permiso del César —dijo Plutarco—, voy a tomar

algo el aire en el atrio contiguo. Parece que a mi edad necesitamos el fresco con más frecuencia.

—De acuerdo —concedió Trajano—, pero no te vayas.

—No, César —aceptó Plutarco y se inclinó primero ante el César y luego ante Quieto que, inclinando levemente la cabeza, agradeció la discreción del griego.

El emperador miró a Liviano y el jefe del pretorio hizo indicaciones para que Aulo y el resto de los pretorianos abandonaran la sala. Algo excepcional. De hecho, el único hombre con el que Liviano y el resto de la guardia pretoriana se atrevían a dejar solo al emperador era, precisamente, con Quieto. La lealtad del norteafricano era total y, cada vez más, Trajano parecía apreciar al *legatus* y jefe de la caballería romana como un hijo o un muy querido hermano menor.

—Ya estamos solos —dijo Trajano—. Tú dirás.

Quieto fue al grano.

—Si la decisión de atacar Armenia y luego Partia está tomada, ¿por qué les has dado esperanzas? Puedo entenderlo en parte, para que piensen que aún hay posibilidad de paz y no se preparen del todo, pero citarlos en Antioquía... ¡por todos los dioses! ¡Eso les permitirá ver el ejército que estamos reuniendo y cuántos somos!

—En efecto, amigo mío —respondió Trajano inclinándose hacia adelante y sirviéndose algo más de vino de una jarra que había quedado en la mesa frente a su *triclinium*—. Quiero que vean que estoy reuniendo el mayor ejército que Roma ha concentrado en su historia. Y con un solo objetivo: lanzarnos contra ellos. Quiero, Lucio, que sientan... miedo.

Y bebió la copa de un trago.

Quieto asintió. Se levantó, se llevó el puño al pecho, se inclinó ante el César y salió de la estancia.

Trajano se sentó en el *triclinium*. Le costó levantarse. Había bebido demasiado, pero su fortaleza era aún poderosa y se sobrepuso al mareo del licor y se levantó al fin.

Salió al atrio y allí encontró a Plutarco. En las esquinas había varios pretorianos de guardia.

—Gracias por esperar, Mestrio —empezó Trajano. Plutarco hizo una reverencia.

—Siempre al servicio del emperador.

—Lo sé. Hombre leal, hombre estudioso, culto. Sabes mucho del pasado y por ello leo tus *Vidas*, pero ya imaginarás por qué te he citado ahora a solas.

—Por el futuro —dijo el escritor griego y sacerdote del Templo de Delfos.

—Así es. ¿Qué puedes decirme a partir de los sacrificios que has hecho en Delfos con relación a mi futuro?

Mestrio Plutarco inspiró profundamente. El emperador le había hablado en susurros y él le había imitado en las respuestas. Parecía que Trajano no quería que los pretorianos escucharan lo que tenía que decirle.

—Lo que he leído en las entrañas de los animales y en el vuelo de los pájaros, y los sacrificios que he hecho en nombre de César en el Templo de Delfos no son... concluyentes.

—¿Qué has visto, sacerdote?

—He visto grandes victorias. Pueblos enteros que se rinden al César, un Imperio romano como nunca antes se haya conocido, como quizá ya nunca vuelva a conocerse, pero...

—¿Pero...? Dímelo todo, Mestrio. No he llegado a emperador de Roma sin haber tenido que enfrentarme con grandes infortunios y desafíos. Si tengo más pruebas delante de mí quiero saberlo. Sólo quiero estar preparado.

Plutarco suspiró lentamente y miró al suelo.

—He visto, César, mucho sufrimiento para el emperador. Y he visto su muerte.

Fue ahora Trajano el que inspiró profundamente. Si hubiera tenido vino cerca habría tomado otra copa, pero quizá mejor digerir aquello con un mínimo de sobriedad. Se aclaró la garganta antes de volver a hablar.

—Todos morimos, Mestrio. En mi caso, prefiero que sea en campaña. —El César se quedó en silencio mirando las estrellas del cielo; al poco volvió a hablar—. Ayer recibí una carta desde Bitinia. Un tribuno militar me informaba de la muerte de Plinio.

—¿El sobrino del autor de la *Naturalis historia*? —preguntó Plutarco.

—El mismo —confirmó Trajano sin dejar de mirar las estrellas—. ¿Lo ves, Mestrio? Todos morimos. En su caso es una pérdida grave para Roma: era un hombre culto, gran abogado y un senador honesto. Y, en lo que sé, buen gobernador. Tenía ilusión de reunirme con él cuando llegara a Asia, pero los dioses lo han dispuesto de otra forma. Sí, todos morimos.

Trajano calló. El sacerdote de Delfos intuyó que el César deseaba estar a solas con su silencio y sus recuerdos sobre Plinio.

Plutarco se inclinó una vez más ante el emperador y lo dejó allí en medio del atrio. El escritor griego se volvió un instante antes de salir y vio que Trajano seguía en el punto donde lo había dejado, solo, en el centro de aquel patio porticado, mirando las estrellas.

47

LUZ EN LA NOCHE

Mar Eritrea
113 d. C.

Los tres pretorianos se llamaban Vibio, Numerio y Servio. Eso era todo lo que Marcio había podido averiguar. Eso y que se habían incorporado a la expedición a Oriente por orden del tribuno Aulo. Pero Marcio desconfiaba. Aulo era, sin duda, uno de los hombres más próximos al emperador, pero él no lo había visto con aquellos pretorianos y desde que Alana le dijera que sospechaba que de haber una traición tendría que provenir de aquellos hombres, el veterano gladiador no dejaba de vigilarlos. Por otro lado, su preocupación sobre el capitán Arrio había disminuido. El marino se mostraba hábil en la navegación. Lo había sido frente a las tormentas en el Mediterráneo y en los estrechos canales del río de Trajano para llegar hasta la mar Eritrea. Y una vez allí, guiado por el mercader Titianus, había ido pasando de un puerto a otro sin problema: de Arsinoe fueron a Myos Hornos. Fue un trayecto corto porque Titianus se entretuvo en adquirir tejidos y ropas que, según él, además del aceite y el vino, serían de interés para otros comerciantes en otras ciudades por las que pasarían. La idea de Titianus parecía ser tener siempre abundante carga con la que poder comerciar en todo momento y circunstancia.

—Si tienes algo que vender, puedes llegar a cualquier lugar del mundo —solía decir el viejo mercader—. Si no tienes nada que vender, no eres nadie en estos puertos.

Por eso se desviaron a una población que llamaban la Villa Blanca, en las costas de Arabia de la mar Eritrea. Allí encontraron otra fortaleza romana con un centurión al mando encargado de cobrar hasta un 25 por ciento de impuestos por todas las mercancías que se compraban y vendían en la ciudad. Marcio no entendía de comercio pero aquellos impuestos le parecieron excesivos.

—¿No es mucho dinero? —preguntó el veterano gladiador.

—Lo es, desde luego —confirmó Titianus—, pero hasta la Villa Blanca llega una calzada que conecta esta población hacia el interior directamente con Petra y en Petra hay de todo. Nos interesa comprar y pagar.

Marcio se encogió de hombros. Su misión era preservar la vida de aquel hombre y asegurarse de que se llegaba hasta el final del viaje, hasta el Imperio kushan, donde se entregaría el mensaje a su emperador para luego regresar a Roma.

De la Villa Blanca cruzaron la mar Eritrea en diagonal, o eso aseguró Arrio, para llegar hasta la lejana Berenice, a más de 1.800 estadios de distancia.[38] Era la tierra de los bereberes, los comedores de carne de vaca, como los llamaban los marinos. Luego llegaron más días de navegación para alcanzar la aún más remota Ptolemais, a más de 4.000 estadios[39] de Berenice, ahora siempre en la costa del lado egipcio. El marfil era el producto más preciado que se podía adquirir en este territorio. Titianus no dudó en adquirir una importante cantidad de cuernos de rinocerontes y elefantes a cambio de trigo, vino, aceite de oliva, ropas y cristal que llevaban en las bodegas de la *liburna*.

Navegaron otros 3.000 estadios más hacia el sureste, siempre costeando las tierras al sur de Egipto, y llegaron a Adulis, pero no fondearon en la bahía de aquella población, sino en la Isla Montaña, un promontorio marino que se erigía a 200 estadios de aquel puerto.

Marcio no entendía por qué echaban el ancla tan lejos de la costa, cuando tanto remeros como el resto de la tripulación

38. Unos 288 kilómetros. 1 kilómetro equivale aproximadamente a 6,25 estadios griegos. El estadio griego (que trataba como patrón de longitud el estadio de Olimpia) era la unidad de medida de distancia para muchos marinos.
39. Más de 640 kilómetros.

parecían necesitados de estirar las piernas en tierra firme. Su relación con el capitán Arrio no era ya de sospecha, pero tampoco cordial. El viejo Titianus, sin embargo, se mostraba mucho más proclive a explicar todo lo relacionado con el viaje y hacia él dirigió el veterano gladiador sus dudas.

—¿Por qué no atracamos en el puerto, como hemos hecho en otras ciudades? A la tripulación le vendría bien caminar un poco.

—*Los barcos que vienen a esta ciudad echan anclas aquí porque temen ser atacados desde tierra* —empezó a explicarse Titianus—. *Antes fondeaban en la bahía misma, en una isla llamada Diodorus, muy cerca de la costa y a la que se podía llegar incluso a pie desde tierra, que era por donde los nativos bárbaros atacaban la isla. (...) A tres días de viaje está Coloe, una población del interior y el primer mercado de marfil. Desde esa ciudad hasta la población habitada por los llamados auxumites hay cinco días de viaje más. Hasta allí se lleva todo el marfil venido de las regiones más allá del Nilo cruzando el territorio llamado Cyeneum, y de ahí hasta Adulis. Prácticamente todos los elefantes y rinocerontes que se cazan viven en el interior aunque ocasionalmente se les ha capturado en la línea de costa, incluso cerca de la propia Adulis.*[40] Todo ese comercio del marfil hace que toda la región en general y la ciudad de Adulis en particular sean lugares peligrosos. No parece prudente que arriesguemos nuestra embarcación y con ella toda la misión de mensajeros imperiales en un puerto tan inestable.

Partieron al día siguiente sin aventurarse a establecer contacto alguno con la gente de Adulis. Aún tenían provisiones suficientes y siguieron navegando varios miles de estadios más hacia el sur, hasta alcanzar la zona del golfo de Arabia, el punto donde la mar Eritrea se estrechaba más. Anclaron cerca de Avalites, pero de nuevo, temiendo ataques de los bereberes de la región, aún más salvajes que los del norte, no se aproximaron demasiado a la costa.

---

40. La sección en cursiva está transcrita literalmente de Περίπλους τῆς Ἐρυθρᾶς Θαλάσσης (*El periplo por la mar Eritrea*), texto sobre navegación en el mar Rojo y el océano Índico escrito en griego probablemente por algún comerciante, quizá egipcio, entre los siglos I a III d. C.

Marcio se dio cuenta de cómo, poco a poco, el poder de Roma se iba diluyendo a medida que navegaban por la mar Eritrea hasta convertirse apenas en un sueño que se desvanecía en el horizonte a sus espaldas.

Ochocientos estadios más y vislumbraron la pequeña población de Malao, donde Titianus aseguró a Arrio que los habitantes eran más pacíficos. Enviaron entonces a algunos remeros y marinos a la costa para reabastecerse de agua y otros víveres. Pero no fue hasta que se arribó a Mundus, una ciudad-mercado importante de la región, que Arrio se decidió a dar permiso a toda la tripulación para que bajaran a tierra, como habían hecho en la ya lejana y casi olvidada Arsinoe. De este modo, todos podrían caminar y relajarse un poco después de varias semanas de navegación.

El barco quedó fondeado en una pequeña isla junto a Mundus y la tripulación se tuvo que trasladar a la costa en un pequeño bote que usaban donde no hizo un puerto con calado suficiente para la *liburna*. Esto hizo que, al disponer de sólo un bote donde apenas cabía una docena de personas, la operación de desembarcar a los remeros y el resto de la tripulación se alargara más de dos horas.

En esta ocasión Marcio sí se decidió a hablar de nuevo con el capitán y centurión naval Arrio.

—No me parece prudente dejar la nave sin protección —dijo el veterano gladiador.

—Los tres pretorianos harán un primer turno de guardia junto con un par de mis hombres. Y la nave se ve desde el puerto. Si pasa algo yo mismo vendré con el resto de los marinos a poner orden.

Marcio asintió, pero seguía sintiéndose inquieto. Que los pretorianos fueran a hacer guardia juntos no le satisfacía en absoluto. El joven Áyax estaba al lado, escuchando la conversación.

—Si quieres yo puedo quedarme también en este turno, hasta la caída de la noche —dijo el joven gladiador—. Luego puedes venir tú a relevarme.

Marcio se volvió hacia el luchador griego. Tampoco era hombre que despertara una enorme simpatía en él porque sabía que Tamura se quedaba medio atontada mirándolo de vez en cuando, pero lo había seleccionado para aquella misión porque confiaba plenamente en él como combatiente. Si Áyax se quedaba junto con los otros dos marinos, los tres pretorianos lo tendrían ya francamente difícil en caso de que fueran a intentar alguna cosa; además, eso le permitiría desembarcar con Tamura y Alana. Él también tenía ganas de estirar las piernas.

—De acuerdo —dijo Marcio—. A medianoche vendré a relevarte con más gente.

Era por la tarde cuando desembarcaron, pero, aprovechando la última luz del día, el mercado aún seguía muy activo. Se veían puestos de frutas y otros víveres, también había artesanos que ofrecían una gran variedad de vasijas, frascos, vasos y otros utensilios, y unas curiosas lucernas decoradas con dibujos rojos que daban luz con aceite que llamaron la atención de Marcio, pero lo que concitaba el interés de Titianus, al que seguían el veterano gladiador, Alana y Tamura, eran los comerciantes de incienso, mirra y unas resinas extrañas. También se vendían algunos esclavos.

—Para encontrar esclavos fuertes hay que ir más al sur, lejos de aquí, pero ahora no es lo que tenemos en mente —dijo Titianus mientras observaba con atención algunos puestos con aquella resina extraña—. Esto es copal de la India, muy apreciado por los árabes al otro lado del golfo —continuó detallando Titianus en latín, pero enseguida cambió al griego y se puso a hablar en voz alta con el comerciante de aquellas resinas, inciensos y mirra, en lo que a Marcio y a Alana les pareció más una discusión que una negociación.

Al final todo quedó en un intercambio de algunas monedas que Titianus entregó al comerciante a cambio de unos pequeños sacos con copal.

—A los mercaderes de aquí los llaman *skleros*, que quiere decir «duros» en griego, pero los productos son buenos. Ah... —Titianus calló un instante, se acercó a otro puesto y repitió de nuevo aquella discusión acalorada que terminó en un nuevo intercambio de monedas, ahora por sacos de lo que parecía un incicnso algo diferente—. Es *mocrotu,* el mejor incienso de la región. El secreto no es tener a veces mucha cantidad, sino tener muy buenos productos. Así me he hecho respetar en toda la mar Eritrea hasta la India —concluyó el viejo mercader al tiempo que le entregaba algunos sacos a Marcio, ya que él no podía con todo lo que había adquirido.

La noche estaba cayendo y regresaron al puerto. Fue entonces cuando vieron aquella gran luz en medio del ocaso resplandeciendo sobre el agua del mar.

—¿Qué es eso? —preguntó Alana.

—¡Es nuestro barco! —exclamó Tamura—. ¡Está ardiendo!

Arrio, que parecía haber detectado el problema al mismo tiempo, apareció corriendo en el puerto y fue a toda velocidad a por el bote. Marcio, Alana y Tamura lo siguieron. Arrio disponía de media docena de sus hombres; el resto seguía repartido por el puerto, ajeno a las tribulaciones que los acuciaban. Los seis marinos, Arrio, Marcio, Alana y Tamura, raudos, subieron al bote. Los hombres de Arrio empezaron a remar.

—¡Rápido, por Júpiter! ¡Más rápido! —exclamaba el capitán. Su frente estaba llena de un sudor frío.

Marcio y Alana apretaban los dientes con rabia.

Tamura oteaba el horizonte negro sobre el que se dibujaba el perfil de la nave en llamas.

En tierra, Titianus, rodeado de los pequeños sacos de incienso y copal que había adquirido en Mundus, se pasaba el dorso de la mano derecha por los labios y tragaba saliva. Si no salvaban el barco todo estaría perdido.

El bote se acercaba ya a la nave.

Además del fragor de las llamas que se extendían ya por más de media cubierta, se oían gritos. De pronto aparecieron las siluetas de los tres pretorianos combatiendo contra Áyax y uno de los marinos de Arrio. Del otro hombre que el capitán dejara a bordo no se sabía nada hasta que súbitamente oyeron un impacto seco en el bote y miraron al agua que los rodeaba. Allí, junto a todos ellos, flotaba un cadáver degollado.

Ahora era Arrio quien apretaba los puños con cólera mal contenida.

—¡Agggh! —aulló el otro marino al ser atravesado por uno de los *gladios* de los pretorianos. Áyax mantenía a raya a su oponente, pero ahora los otros dos pretorianos se le aproximaban por la espalda. No tenía ni una oportunidad y aún estaban demasiado lejos para poder asistirlo.

—¡Remad más rápido, por todos los dioses! —insistió Arrio a los marinos del bote.

Áyax consiguió herir al pretoriano con el que luchaba, pero no mortalmente.

—¡A tu espalda! —le gritó entonces Marcio para avisarlo.

Ayax se volvió veloz y pudo esquivar el ataque de sus dos nuevos enemigos, pero el tercer pretoriano herido se recuperó y blandió su espada para clavársela a traición. Y nadie podía ayudar a Áyax.

¿Nadie?

Tamura se levantó en medio del bote. Cogió una flecha de las que siempre llevaba a la espalda, junto con su saco de pertenencias personales, y la dispuso en su arco. Apuntó con rapidez. El bote se movía, el blanco se veía confuso entre el humo y la oscuridad, sólo iluminado de forma intermitente y temblorosa por las llamas del incendio del barco. La muchacha soltó la cuerda del arco y la flecha surcó perfecta el aire nocturno de la mar Eritrea.

—¡Agggh! —exclamó el pretoriano que iba a atacar a Áyax por la espalda. No pudo gritar mucho más porque la flecha le acababa de atravesar la garganta. Cayó de espaldas, sobre la barandilla de cubierta y por el peso de su pecho dio una vuelta de campana y se desplomó sobre el agua.

Áyax seguía combatiendo contra los otros dos pretorianos, pero al oír aquel grito ahogado a su espalda se volvió un instante y eso permitió que los otros dos se le acercaran aún más. Áyax, no obstante, dio un paso atrás y reanudó el combate contra aquellos guardias imperiales, pero éstos no eran principiantes y se separaron. Numerio buscaba la espalda del gladiador. Nadie puede defenderse solo por mucho tiempo por delante y por detrás. Áyax comprendió la estrategia de sus enemigos y se puso a combatir con la barandilla de cubierta a su espalda. Aun así era difícil batirse con aquellos hombres recios y experimentados en mil combates de frontera, desde el Rin hasta la Dacia.

Tamura seguía en pie en medio del bote. Marcio pensó en advertirla de que tuviera cuidado de no herir a Áyax, pero le pareció una tontería decir algo tan evidente y calló. En su lugar pensó en otra cosa.

—Si dejan de remar —dijo el veterano gladiador—, mi hija podrá apuntar mejor. Están luchando demasiado cerca y un fallo puede ser fatal.

Arrio asintió.

—¡Ya habéis oído! ¡Dejad de remar!

Y pararon. El bote dejó de moverse tanto como antes.

Tamura ya tenía una segunda flecha en el arco.

Era difícil apuntar porque había más humo que antes y Áyax, al haber buscado tener a su espalda la barandilla del barco, se interponía entre la flecha de Tamura y los pretorianos que tenía frente a él.

—Lo saben —dijo Alana—. Saben que hemos disparado con flechas y usan a Áyax de escudo.

Tamura no soltaba la cuerda del arco.

La muchacha empezó, por primera vez en su vida, a sudar antes de disparar una flecha. No le había pasado nunca. Hasta tenía gotas en las manos. Estaba aterrada. Sentía pánico ante la posibilidad de herir a Áyax. Tanto que no se atrevía a disparar. Justo en ese momento, el joven gladiador hizo algo muy inteligente: se agachó de golpe.

Tamura soltó la cuerda del arco. Una segunda flecha salió impulsada con la fuerza de toda la rabia de una joven guerrera sármata indómita y, aunque no lo entendiera aún, enamorada.

—¡Agggh! —gritó Numerio mientras la punta de la flecha le atravesaba el pecho.

Áyax aprovechó el desconcierto del tercer pretoriano y hundió su espada en las costillas. Luego se acercó a Vibio, el último pretoriano, que aún agonizaba.

—¿Quieres pedirme algo antes de morir? ¿Vas a rogar que te perdone la vida? —le preguntó el joven gladiador.

Vibio negó con la cabeza.

—La guardia pretoriana ni se rinde... ni ruega clemencia...

—dijo Vibio echando sangre por la boca—. Mis últimas palabras serán para... rogar... a los dioses... porque la venganza te alcance... —continuó el pretoriano moribundo y empezó a ahogarse en su propia sangre.

Comenzaban a ascender a cubierta desde el bote. Áyax podía oír las voces de Arrio y Marcio. El joven gladiador sonrió mientras dedicaba una última mirada a Vibio y luego lo degolló.

Se levantó.

Arrio, Marcio, Alana y Tamura estaban en cubierta, junto a él, mientras los marinos intentaban apagar el fuego con algunos cubos de agua que llenaban lanzándolos con una cuerda al mar.

—¿Que ha pasado? —preguntó Arrio viendo cómo su nave se consumía por las llamas—. ¡Por todos los dioses! ¿Qué ha ocurrido?

—¡Han sido los pretorianos! —respondió Áyax con rapidez y miró a Marcio—. Teníais razón desde el principio, tú y Alana. No eran de fiar. Ellos prendieron fuego a la nave, en la bodega. Aprovecharon las túnicas y otras telas que Titianus había comprado en Arsinoe. Los marinos y yo intentamos apagar el fuego, pero entonces los pretorianos nos atacaron. El resto ya lo sabéis.

—¡No hay nada que hacer, mi centurión! —dijo uno de los marinos con un cubo vacío en la mano—. ¡El fuego está por todas partes y el viento que se ha levantado aviva las llamas!

—Son las telas, el aceite, todas las mercancías que llevamos en la bodega —confirmó Arrio con una serenidad gélida—. El barco está perdido y con él toda su carga. Vámonos antes de que las llamas alcancen el bote también.

Descendieron rápidamente y se alejaron en la pequeña barca, todos cariacontecidos, mientras veían cómo el fuego se apoderaba ya de los mástiles y las velas.

Cuando llegaron al puerto un gran gentío se había congregado para ver el espectáculo.

—Todo está perdido —dijo Arrio al viejo Titianus.

En un cónclave improvisado, viendo cómo la *liburna* que los había llevado hasta allí desde Roma empezaba a hundirse en el mar, Arrio, Titianus, Marcio, Alana, Áyax y Tamura, junto con algunos de los marinos supervivientes al desastre y los remeros del barco, hablaban sobre qué hacer.

—Todo está perdido —repitió Arrio.

—Podemos hacernos con otro barco y seguir adelante —propuso Marcio, nunca habituado a darse por vencido con facilidad.

—Sin la mercancía que iba en el *liburna* no tengo nada con lo que comerciar, y sin nada que vender no podemos adquirir un nuevo barco —comentó Titianus—. Además, una nueva embarcación necesitará más tripulación y los remeros cobran. Sin mercancías no puedo conseguir el oro necesario para pagar todos esos gastos. Siento decirlo, pero el capitán Arrio tiene razón: éste es el fin de la misión.

Tamura se había alejado un poco del grupo y miraba hacia el barco que seguía hundiéndose lentamente en el mar, consumido por las últimas llamas. Áyax la vio y se le acercó despacio.

—Gracias —le dijo.

Ella no miró hacia el joven gladiador. Estaba sonrojada y no quería que la viera así.

—No ha sido nada —respondió ella sin dejar de mirar hacia la nave incendiada. Sentía un fuego igual de caliente en su interior y, aunque quizá estuviera mal, en medio del desastre se sentía plenamente feliz, pues al volverse al fin y posar sus ojos en los de Áyax vio que el gladiador ya no la miraba como si fuera una niña.

48
—

UN CÉSAR EN ASIA

Seleucia de Pieria
113 d. C.

Adriano se pasaba los dedos de la mano por la boca. El calor era bochornoso y el sudor impregnaba todo su cuerpo. Vio cómo su tío descendía del barco escoltado por Liviano y el resto de la guardia pretoriana. Trajano apenas lo saludó un instante.

—Las tropas están reunidas según lo que tú ordenaste... —empezó Adriano, pero su tío se limitó a dar una breve respuesta sin detenerse.

—Eso más tarde. —Y el emperador prosiguió su marcha acompañado por Quieto y Nigrino.

La guardia pretoriana pasó y luego llegó Plotina.

—¿Ves como todo sigue igual? —le dijo Adriano a la emperatriz.

Ella sonrió amablemente. Estaban rodeados por esclavos y algunos pretorianos más. Plotina se salió de la ruta de la comitiva imperial para departir con más intimidad con su sobrino político.

—Hemos de ver cómo se desarrolla todo —respondió intentando aplacar a Adriano por el desaire de su tío—, y ahora es mejor no hablar. Nos observa.

—Si ni siquiera nos mira —dijo Adriano señalando hacia el emperador, que se alejaba dándoles la espalda.

—El emperador tiene mil ojos, Adriano.

Y el sobrino segundo del César se encogió de hombros y se calló.

Plotina y él se separaron.

Adriano se quedó solo en el puerto de Seleucia de Pieria.

Su conversación con el emperador tendría que esperar, pero, en ese momento, llegó alguien por detrás. Uno de los legionarios de confianza de Adriano.

—Hay alguien que quiere ver al gobernador.

Ese anuncio misterioso sólo podía significar una cosa. Adriano asintió, caminó hacia los *horrea* de almacenamiento de grano del puerto y allí, entre las sombras de las grandes estructuras de ladrillo se encontró, como esperaba, con su antiguo tutor.

—Ave, Atiano —dijo Adriano—; ¿tú también has venido a recibir al César?

—No, mi señor. Eso ha sido sólo una coincidencia en el tiempo. Yo he venido a informar.

—Espero que sea algo bueno, porque no estoy para más desaires.

—Es algo bueno, mi señor —confirmó Atiano—: La misión que el César había puesto en marcha con ese Titianus ha quedado... abortada.

Adriano no pudo evitar esbozar una media sonrisa. Aquélla era una dulce venganza ante la frialdad con la que su tío lo había saludado.

—¿Cómo pueden estar tus hombres tan seguros de ello?

—Titianus ha perdido el barco. Hubo un enfrentamiento entre... bueno, entre unos y otros, una lucha descarnada, muertos y un incendio. No tienen ni barco, ni dinero ni medios con los que proseguir el viaje. Tendrán que regresar y asumir su fracaso ante el César.

Adriano fruncía el ceño. Le parecía demasiado sencillo. Le cayera mejor o peor su tío, no le gustaba infravalorarlo. Era peculiar que el César hubiera seleccionado gente de tan pocos recursos para una misión secreta que parecía relevante, al menos, para el propio César.

—¿Y si se rehacen? —inquirió el sobrino segundo del emperador.

—Aún tengo un infiltrado en la misión. Si encontraran la forma de continuar con el viaje, esta persona acabaría con todos si hace falta. Es implacable.

—De acuerdo. En todo caso, sería interesante que esa per-

374

sona pudiera averiguar el auténtico objetivo de esa misión. No me creo que mi tío se ande con tanto secreto sólo para enviar una respuesta a una embajada pública del emperador kushan. Debe de haber algo más en esa misión. Quizá tu hombre pueda aprovechar el viaje de vuelta para averiguar esto.

—Le transmitiré instrucciones para que arroje luz sobre este asunto.

—Bien —aceptó Adriano y suspiró antes de cambiar de tema—. ¿Mantenemos aún contacto con Liberal en Chipre y con Pompeyo Colega en Cirene?

—Sí, mi señor.

—Bien, ve primero a Chipre. Puedes embarcar aquí mismo y está a pocos días. Luego ve a Cirene. Asegúrate de que siguen siendo nuestros amigos.

—Sí, mi señor. Necesitaré dinero.

—Usa todo el que haga falta —respondió Adriano. Sin dudarlo, sacó una bolsa repleta de monedas de oro de debajo de su toga y se la entregó a Atiano como quien entrega un puñado de sestercios.

Atiano cogió la bolsa, se inclinó y para cuando volvió a levantar la mirada, Adriano ya había doblado la esquina del almacén y había desaparecido seguido de su guardia personal. Atiano no entendía bien el interés de Adriano por mantener aquellas relaciones abiertas con aquellos dos senadores caídos en desgracia e «invitados» por Trajano a hacerse cargo de ciudades remotas del Imperio, pero no se cuestionó las órdenes recibidas y fue en busca de un barco.

Antioquía, 113 d. C.

Trajano, ya fuera porque había sido demasiado rudo en su saludo a su sobrino, o porque éste había realizado bien la labor de concentrar tropas en Seleucia, Antioquía y en diversos puntos de la ribera del Éufrates bajo control romano, empezó a mostrarse más cordial con Adriano. Así, cuando llegaron diversas embajadas de reyes y gobernantes de multitud de pueblos y regiones limítrofes, Trajano invitó a Adriano al *consilium augusti*, junto con Quieto y Nigrino, que había establecido en su nueva residencia de Antioquía.

El primero en llegar al edificio que hacía de palacio imperial en Antioquía, en la provincia romana de Siria, fue Mannus, un líder árabe que se puso al servicio del emperador de Roma de inmediato y sin dudarlo. Trajano aceptó su ofrecimiento, pero, una vez que se quedaron solos, se dirigió a sus hombres.

—Está bien que se nos ofrezcan, pero esta campaña la hemos de organizar con nuestros recursos y, sobre todo, nuestras ideas.

—Negarse a recibir ayuda, por ejemplo de Armenia, fue uno de los errores más graves de Craso —contrapuso Adriano.

—Yo no he dicho que no aceptemos ayuda, sólo que desconfiemos de toda la que se nos pueda ofrecer —opuso Trajano—. Especialmente de quien se ofrece demasiado rápido y sin condiciones, pues alguien así es quien primero traiciona, en cuanto siente que el viento sopla en otra dirección. Y, desde luego, no haremos caso de consejos que pudieran suministrarnos los árabes. Eso sí sería repetir el error de Craso de confiar en Ariemnes. Eso, y no otra cosa, es lo que he querido decir, sobrino.

Quieto y Nigrino, y Liviano, que como jefe de la guardia siempre estaba presente en el *consilium*, detectaron la creciente tensión entre Trajano y Adriano, pero no fue necesario intervenir porque Fédimo, el secretario del César, también admitido en aquel selecto cónclave, anunció la llegada de otro embajador: en este caso un enviado de Sporaces, gobernante de Anthemusia, que también decidió inclinarse ante el emperador de Roma, aunque sus palabras fueron incómodas.

—He venido hasta aquí para saludar y mostrar la admiración de mi señor Sporaces, rey de Anthemusia, señor de Batnae, ante el gran César de Roma —dijo, pero lo que añadió hizo que Trajano torciera el gesto—: También mi señor respeta a Osroes, rey de reyes, y quiere manifestar al emperador romano que el reino de Anthemusia se mantiene neutral en el conflicto que pueda tener lugar entre Roma y Partia.

Y ofreció algunos regalos.

Trajano asintió y no dijo nada. El embajador, confuso pero desconocedor de las costumbres de los emperadores de Roma, decidió, quizá con buen criterio, salir de allí sin reclamar una respuesta más precisa por parte del César.

Adriano no tardó en aprovechar la salida del embajador de Anthemusia para lanzarse a degüello contra el proyecto de su tío.

—Ni siquiera habiendo concentrado tantas tropas nos temen —dijo—. Sólo hemos conseguido el apoyo de un árabe en el que ni tan sólo el César confía.

—Falta la embajada de Osroene —interpuso Quieto con rapidez—. Osroene es un reino importante. Abgaro, su rey, controla toda Mesopotamia norte. Si se decantara por estar a nuestro lado, la campaña de Armenia, al menos, sería muy fácil, pues no tendríamos que vigilar nuestro flanco sur.

—¿A quién ha enviado Abgaro? —preguntó Trajano a Fédimo, que estaba en la puerta de la sala de audiencias de la residencia imperial del César en Antioquía.

—A Arbandes, su hijo —respondió el secretario.

—Ah —dijo el César.

Abgaro había rehuido acudir en persona, pero enviar a su hijo, que podría ser usado como rehén en caso de que la embajada terminara mal, era una señal de cierta confianza ante el emperador de Roma. Y como decía Quieto, tener a Osroene como aliado podía facilitar toda la campaña de Armenia y luego los planes futuros de extensión de fronteras romanas hacia Oriente.

—Que pase —dijo Trajano.

Frente a la sala de audiencias

Arbandes esperaba sentado en un *solium* que habían dispuesto para él por orden de Fédimo. El secretario había seguido las instrucciones de Trajano de que se proporcionara asiento a los embajadores de linaje real que fueran enviados a Antioquía y Arbandes, pese a ser joven y fuerte, decidió hacer uso de esa prerrogativa que le concedía el César, aunque sólo fuera por marcar diferencias con los emisarios de distintos puntos de Asia que estaban llegando a aquella sala de audiencias del César de Roma y que no tenían un linaje real equiparable al suyo.

El joven repasaba las palabras de su padre Abgaro antes de partir en aquella misión.

—Nuestra posición es la de neutralidad, hijo —le había dicho su padre antes de que saliera de Edesa, la capital de Osroene—, pero haz todo lo que esté en tu mano para que el emperador de Roma entienda que ésta puede ser una neutralidad más amistosa hacia Roma que hacia Partia.

—¿Y cómo puedo persuadir a alguien como el César, padre? —había preguntado Arbandes confuso—. Todo el mundo dice que ese Trajano es muy desconfiado.

—Y en eso hace bien. Sólo así habrá podido llegar a ser quien es y gobernar sobre tantos pueblos del mundo; pero tú, hijo mío, tienes algo que ningún otro embajador tendrá.

—¿Y qué es eso, padre?

Abgaro, rey de Osroene, sonrió.

—Eres de linaje real y, sobre todo, eres joven y hermoso. Y me consta que el emperador de Roma siente debilidad por los jóvenes bellos como tú. Quizá Trajano quiera emular al gran Alejandro no sólo en el campo de batalla. ¿Me entiendes, hijo?

—¿Quieres que sea el Hefestión de Trajano?

—Eso es mucho querer, hijo mío, pero cuanto más te aproximes a ser uno de sus amigos favoritos, íntimos, más seguridad para el reino de Osroene. Yo, entretanto, intentaré mantener las negociaciones abiertas con Osroes. El tiempo dirá qué debemos hacer en cada momento: si apoyar a Roma o si pasarnos al bando de Partia.

—Cuando dices el tiempo, padre, te refieres a la fuerza militar de Trajano y Osroes en cada momento, ¿verdad?

Abgaro sonrió.

—Me alegra ver, hijo mío, que no sólo eres hermoso, sino también inteligente.

—El emperador Trajano recibirá ahora al emisario de Osroene.

La voz de Fédimo hizo que los recuerdos y pensamientos de Arbandes se desvanecieran. El hijo de Abgaro se levantó y, con decisión, entró en la sala donde esperaba el emperador de Roma.

Sala de audiencias

Arbandes se acercó hasta quedar a unos pasos de distancia del César y allí hincó la rodilla derecha en tierra.

—Levántate —dijo Trajano.

El joven embajador obedeció. El César lo miró de arriba abajo y a Adriano no se le escapó lo que había en la mirada del emperador. Hacía tiempo que no veía ese brillo en los ojos de su tío; exactamente desde la muerte de Longino en la Dacia. Pero en aquel tiempo el destello en la mirada del César era por un romano y ahora era por un posible enemigo. Para Adriano su tío se mostraba cada vez más imprevisible y eso resultaba cada vez más peligroso para Roma.

—Te escucho, enviado de Osroene —dijo Trajano invitando al recién llegado a que hablara.

—Mi padre, el rey Abgaro, señor de Edesa y de todo el norte de Mesopotamia, presenta sus respetos al emperador de Roma, al hombre más poderoso del mundo —explicó Arbandes—. Es un honor para nuestro reino que el César esté tan cerca de nosotros y sólo queremos que el emperador de Roma sepa que Osroene nunca atacará los ejércitos del emperador.

—Eso es muy interesante, pero ¿y si mis ejércitos entran en conflicto con los de Osroes de Partia?

Aquí Arbandes inspiró profundamente. No se andaba con remilgos ni rodeos el emperador de Roma.

—Mi padre me ha autorizado para que garantice al César que nuestra embajada es una muestra no de indiferencia ante cualquier conflicto entre Roma y Partia, sino una muestra de auténtica y sincera amistad de Osroene con el César.

—¿Amistad a cambio de qué?

—Osroene, César, es un lugar hermoso y Edesa una de las ciudades más bellas de Asia. No queremos que la guerra arrase nuestro territorio.

Trajano apretó los labios antes de responder.

—Le puedes decir a tu padre que el César de Roma nunca atacará Osroene si su reino se mantiene como mi amigo. Si nada malo me viene desde Osroene, nada malo llegará a esas tierras desde el César.

Arbandes asintió lentamente. Eso implicaba no dejar pasar las tropas de Osroes hacia el norte si el rey de reyes se decidía a atacar al César romano. De momento, el rey de reyes se estaba replegando al oeste del Tigris, pero si Osroes cambiaba de estrategia, negarles el paso a los partos sería lo mismo que declararse aliados de Roma... Suspiró levemente: todo eso aún estaba lejos y muchas cosas podían ocurrir antes de que evitaran tomar una decisión en un sentido o el otro.

—Nada malo saldrá desde Osroene contra Trajano —confirmó Arbandes con aplomo forzado, pero que sonó a decisión.

Fédimo asomaba por la puerta del fondo de la sala de audiencias y miraba hacia Trajano con cierto nerviosismo. Alguien importante acababa de llegar, pero el César, en ese momento, no entendía bien quién pudiera ser más importante que los enviados del poderoso reino de Osroene.

—Parece que ahora no dispongo de más tiempo para departir con el valeroso Arbandes —dijo Trajano—. Quizá podamos hablar con más sosiego en otro momento si el hijo de Abgaro se queda unos días en Antioquía.

—Por supuesto, César —respondió Arbandes. Hizo una leve reverencia, dio media vuelta y emprendió la marcha hacia la salida. En la puerta se cruzó con quien menos quería cruzarse en aquel momento: Partamaspates, hijo de Osroes, entraba en la sala de audiencias como embajador del mismísimo rey de reyes de los partos. Partamaspates lanzó una mirada asesina a Arbandes, como había hecho con el resto de los embajadores que esperaban aún fuera. Era como si les advirtiera con los ojos de que Partia tomaba nota de todos los que se habían congregado como ratas cobardes en torno al emperador de Roma en lugar de quedarse en sus respectivos reinos a la espera de recibir órdenes desde Cesifonte, la capital de Partia.

—No ha querido esperar, mi señor —dijo Fédimo en la sala de audiencias—, y no entiendo por qué los pretorianos lo han dejado pasar...

—Lo han dejado pasar porque di orden, Fédimo, de que no se interpusieran en el camino del enviado de Osroes si éste regresaba a por la respuesta que le prometí dar en Atenas hace unas semanas. Quizá debería haberte hecho partícipe de esta orden, joven secretario.

No era habitual que el emperador se disculpara de nada ante nadie y aquello llamó la atención de Adriano. Era evidente que su tío tenía muy buena relación con ese secretario. Tomó nota mental de ello.

Entretanto, Partamaspates se había situado justo donde hacía unos instantes había estado Arbandes.

—Nos volvemos a ver —dijo Trajano saltándose el ceremonial de los saludos, siempre usando el griego, como toda aquella mañana, como lengua de comunicación con las embajadas de Oriente.

El hijo de Osroes tampoco estaba para mucha parafernalia.

—El enviado del rey de reyes vuelve a verse, en efecto, con el César de Roma. Se me citó aquí la última vez que hablamos en Atenas y aquí he venido en busca de la respuesta a la propuesta de acuerdo y paz del Šāhān Šāh.

—¿Y has traído los regalos que ofreciste en Atenas? —preguntó Trajano para sorpresa de Quieto, Nigrino y hasta del propio Adriano.

Partamaspates se relajó levemente, aunque, hombre prudente, no bajó la guardia del todo. Quizá el emperador romano hubiera reflexionado y aún hubiera una posibilidad de acuerdo.

—Los he traído, pero si el César se aviene a negociar una solución para Armenia, aún enviaremos más regalos que complacerán mucho a Roma.

—No lo dudo —continuó Trajano aparentemente conciliador, pero pronto borró la media sonrisa tenue de su boca para volver a ponerse serio y firme—, pero mucho me temo que tendrás que llevarte tus regalos de nuevo. A no ser que...

—¿A no ser qué? —inquirió Partamaspates nuevamente tenso—. ¿Qué condición busca el César para poder llegar a una paz duradera?

—A no ser que Partamasiris sea depuesto y sea ahora Roma

la que decida quién va a ser soberano de Armenia —sentenció Trajano de forma tajante.

—¿El César quiere decir que busquemos a un sustituto de Partamasiris de forma negociada?

—No, quiero decir que será Roma la que decida quién es rey de Armenia.

—Pero eso no es lo que dicen nuestros tratados —contrapuso Partamaspates.

—Cierto. —Trajano tuvo que pensar un momento; el griego del enviado parto era más fluido que el suyo y al César le costó encontrar las palabras exactas: quería ser muy preciso—. No veo yo qué problema hay en que Roma decida quién es rey de Armenia sin consultar. ¿Acaso no es eso lo que habéis hecho al asesinar a Exedares y poner a Partamasiris en el trono en su lugar? Si yo no he de sentirme molesto por eso, ¿por qué habría de sentirse molesto Osroes porque yo haga lo mismo que él ha hecho antes sin consultarme?

Partamaspates abrió la boca pero no dijo nada. No tenía argumentos. Miró a algunos nobles partos que lo acompañaban. Se miraban entre ellos, pero nadie apuntó consejo alguno. El hijo de Osroes se volvió de nuevo hacia el César.

—Lo que pide el emperador de Roma no es aceptable para Partia.

Durante unos instantes nadie habló.

—Entonces esta conversación ha terminado —dijo Trajano reclinándose hacia atrás en la *cathedra* en la que recibía a los embajadores—. Creo que a partir de ahora Roma y Partia se hablarán de otra forma.

Nadie había mencionado la palabra guerra aún. Partamaspates tenía la misión de salir de allí dejando alguna posibilidad de negociación abierta y no quería defraudar a su padre. «Las negociaciones, al menos, hijo —le había dicho Osroes—, nos dan tiempo para reunir nuestros ejércitos o traer tropas desde el frente oriental, donde luchamos contra Vologases. Si no consigues hacer entrar en razón al César romano, al menos consígueme tiempo.» Además, Partamaspates había visto un incontable número de legionarios romanos concentrados en Antioquía y sus hombres le habían comentado que en otras poblaciones del alto Éufrates, en la ribera romana, había aún más legiones. Tenía que ofrecer algo al César para rebajar su impulso guerrero y dar ese tiempo a su padre que tanto necesitaba para organizar la defensa.

—Prometo que Osroes hablará con Partamasiris para que éste ponga a los pies del César de Roma su corona. ¿Aplacaría ese gesto algo la cólera de Trajano?

El emperador giró levemente la cabeza hacia un lado y luego la levantó y asintió un par de veces.

—Sería un principio de algo diferente. Eso lo admito —dijo.

Partamaspates asintió también. Pero había prometido demasiado en su afán por evitar una declaración de guerra total entre los dos imperios.

—Si Partamasiris entrega su diadema al César —continuó Partamaspates—, quedará en manos del César decidir si lo acepta como legítimo gobernante de Armenia.

—Sí —confirmó Trajano—. Si Partamasiris tiene ese gesto quedará en manos de Roma el destino de Armenia. Acepto que eso es así.

—Sea, entonces el *Šāhān Šāh* hablará con Partamasiris. El emperador de Roma tendrá noticias desde Armenia por carta en pocas semanas.

—Bien —dijo Trajano.

Partamaspates comprendió que la negociación, o más bien la cesión de Partia ante Trajano, había llegado a su término. No había conseguido mucho, pero la palabra *guerra* no se había mencionado. Quizá si su padre convencía a Partamasiris para que tuviera el gesto de arrodillarse ante Trajano, toda la exhibición de fuerza de Roma quedara en nada, sólo en eso, en una muestra de su poder, y todo volvería a su cauce. Pero ¿qué podía usar su padre para convencer a su tío Partamasiris de que entregara la diadema de Armenia a Trajano? Partamaspates salió con pensamientos oscuros de aquella sala de audiencias, pero se consoló pensando que si en algo era bueno su padre, era en intrigas. Algo se le ocurriría al *Šāhān Šāh* para que Partamasiris intentara aplacar a Trajano.

49

MARFIL

Mar Eritrea, 113 d. C.

—Debe de haber algo que podamos hacer —dijo Marcio, que se resistía a abandonar el encargo imperial de llegar hasta el reino de los kushan y entregar el mensaje que llevaba Titianus en un papiro enrollado que le había dado el César en aquella lejana y secreta reunión en la *Domus Flavia*.

La oscuridad se había vuelto a apoderar por completo de la bahía, pues el barco había sido ya completamente engullido por el mar y las llamas se habían apagado.

—Sin barco no podemos cruzar el océano que nos separa de la India y sin mercancías no tengo con qué negociar para conseguir otro barco —insistió Titianus exponiendo, una vez más, la cruda realidad.

Marcio paseaba por el muelle con los brazos en jarras, mirando al suelo. Titianus se había sentado sobre unas grandes piedras que algunos canteros habían abandonado allí, seguramente porque quien las encargó en el norte de Egipto o se había quedado sin dinero o había muerto y no envió a nadie a por aquel material. Arrio, Alana, Tamura, Áyax y los marinos supervivientes lo imitaron. De los remeros ya no se sabía nada. Era como si hubieran desaparecido engullidos por el mar igual que la nave. Estaba claro que ya intuían que no había más dinero para pagarles y se habían perdido por las tabernas del puerto en busca de algún otro barco de otro comerciante, más afortunado que Titianus, que sí pudiera pagar por sus servicios.

Marcio dejó de caminar arriba y abajo y se encaró con Titianus señalando los pequeños sacos de incienso, mirra y copal que acababan de adquirir en el mercado de Mundus.

—Tienes eso y algo más de oro —dijo el veterano *lanista*—. Yo te he visto un pequeño saco con monedas con el que has estado comprando esos productos.

Titianus asintió y sonrió como quien lo hace a un niño ingenuo que no entiende la magnitud de los problemas a los que se enfrenta.

—Sí, gladiador, tengo algo más de oro y estos sacos, pero no es suficiente para comprar un barco de dimensiones apropiadas para cruzar la gran mar Eritrea que nos separa de la India, ni siquiera aprovechando los vientos favorables de estas fechas.

—¿Y qué barco se puede comprar con lo que tenemos? —preguntó Marcio que, obstinado, no abandonaba tan fácilmente la idea de seguir con el viaje.

Titianus ladeó la cabeza e hizo un gesto de apretar los labios mientras pensaba.

—Una, quizá dos falúas —respondió el mercader—, pero poco más. Y eso con suerte. Ya has visto que los comerciantes aquí son duros de roer y en Mundus ya todos saben que estamos desesperados. Intentarán aprovecharse; aunque tengo algún comerciante conocido que quizá pudiera ofrecerme un precio justo. Pero ésa no es la cuestión: las falúas son barcos demasiado pequeños, de muy poco calado, incapaces de afrontar con seguridad una travesía como la que tendríamos que hacer si siguiéramos con el viaje hasta la India. Sería un suicidio. Pregúntale a nuestro capitán.

Titianus miró hacia donde estaba sentado Arrio.

—Es cierto, con una falúa es imposible cruzar la gran mar Eritrea de aquí a la India —confirmó el centurión naval—. Sería una muerte segura. Conmigo y mis hombres no contéis para esa locura.

—Pero tú, como yo, como todos —insistió Marcio—, tienes, tenemos la orden imperial de llegar hasta el Imperio kushan.

Arrio se levantó y se encaró con el veterano gladiador. Áyax se puso en pie también y se situó por detrás de Marcio, y con él fueron Alana y Tamura, mientras que los marinos del centurión también se situaban detrás de su jefe.

—Tengo esa orden, gladiador —dijo Arrio—, y estoy dispuesto a cumplirla, pero no con algo que sea un suicidio. Muertos no servimos al César. Dame otra opción. ¡Por todos los dioses, dame otro barco como el que teníamos y yo os llevaré hasta la India!

—¿Y volver hacia atrás para contactar con el emperador y que nos proporcione otro barco? —preguntó Alana.

—Ésta es una misión secreta —respondió Titianus—. Tendríamos que ir hasta Egipto y desde allí convencer al gobernador de que contacte con el emperador, que seguramente ya no estará en Roma, sino por Asia. Se tardaría meses en recibir la nueva orden del César. Es una posibilidad pero perderemos los vientos favorables para navegar hacia la India. Y se corre el riesgo de que en Egipto se pregunte sobre el objeto de nuestro viaje. No creo que al César le gustara que actuáramos de esa forma.

Marcio y Arrio permanecían apenas a un palmo de distancia el uno del otro, ambos con las manos en las empuñaduras de sus espadas, al igual que los que estaban detrás de uno y otro. Ambos contenían la respiración, hasta que Marcio cedió, exhaló mucho aire de golpe y se volvió separándose de Arrio y todos fueron relajándose hasta que quedaron, de nuevo, sentados sobre aquellas piedras abandonadas en el muelle del puerto de Mundus.

Marcio estaba sentado junto a Titianus.

—De acuerdo: lo de volver atrás y pedir ayuda al César puede revelar el objetivo de nuestro viaje y eso no podemos hacerlo, pero ¿no hay forma de conseguir otro barco sin retornar hasta Egipto? —preguntó el *lanista*.

Hubo un instante de silencio. El hecho de que Titianus tardara en responder le hizo ver a Marcio que algo podía hacerse pero que, por algún motivo, el mercader no era proclive a proponer esa alternativa.

—¿Hay alguna forma? —repitió Marcio, levantando el tono de voz.

—En Muza venden barcos adecuados para el viaje —respondió el mercader, al fin.

—¿A cuánto de distancia está eso? —inquirió Marcio mirando a Arrio.

—Unos días —respondió el capitán—. Hay que retroceder algo, pero se puede llegar en poco tiempo. Está al otro lado del golfo de Arabia.

—Pero ahí se podría llegar con una falúa, ¿no? —continuó Marcio.

—Sí, hasta ahí sí —admitió Arrio con algo de rabia por el tono de cierto desprecio con el que le había hablado el *lanista*.

—Pero no tenemos dinero con que comprar el barco —intervino entonces Titianus.

—Sí, pero te has callado unos instantes cuando te he preguntado si no hay forma de conseguir otro barco y eso es porque crees que sí hay una forma. Así que, por Némesis, ya nos estás diciendo cuál es esa forma —expuso Marcio a toda velocidad, como si no quisiera dejar a Titianus más tiempo para pensar.

—Es peligroso —replicó el mercader.

—Todo este viaje es peligroso. Vivir es peligroso —apostilló el *lanista*.

—Marfil —respondió entonces el mercader.

—¿Marfil? —repitió Marcio—. ¿Y cómo vamos a conseguir marfil si no tenemos casi dinero ni mercancías?

—Bueno —empezó el mercader después de carraspear un par de veces—. El mismo dinero puede comprar más o menos productos dependiendo del precio de lo que compras y las mismas cosas no valen lo mismo en todos los sitios. Con el incienso y la mirra podemos conseguir una falúa y con el copal y el oro que tengo se puede conseguir bastante marfil como para comprar otro barco más grande en Muza si entregamos también la falúa.

—Entonces todo está resuelto —dijo Marcio levantándose de golpe, dispuesto ya a ponerse manos a la obra.

—No es tan fácil —prosiguió Titianus—. El marfil es normalmente muy caro. Por eso en Muza con una falúa de marfil seremos ricos y podremos comprar un barco más grande y hasta mercancías para llevar a la India, pero para que podamos comprar ese marfil a un precio barato hay que ir a buscarlo lejos.

—En Avalites he visto algo de marfil y eso no está muy lejos

—replicó Marcio, que seguía sin ver problema alguno en la operación propuesta.

—Y en Adulis también —añadió Titianus algo exasperado porque no le dejaban explicarse hasta el final—, pero os recuerdo a todos que cuando pasamos por allí ya no nos acercamos a Adulis. Donde hay mucho marfil hay mucha violencia. Y además en Adulis el precio sigue siendo alto, fuera de nuestro alcance, porque está muy cerca de Muza. No, el marfil barato está muy lejos de aquí, a semanas de navegación hacia el sur. Hay que llegar allí donde terminan los mapas. En Raphta tenemos mucho marfil a un precio muy barato, porque está lejos y porque es muy difícil volver... vivo. Yo fui una vez y me juré que nunca más lo intentaría.

Se hizo un breve silencio.

—Entonces... ¿es mejor volver a Roma y enviarle al emperador Trajano un mensaje diciéndole que hemos fracasado? —preguntó Marcio.

—No —respondió Arrio y suspiró antes de continuar—. Tendremos que ir hasta Raphta, comprar el marfil y regresar hasta Muza para cambiarlo por un barco en condiciones.

Pero no parecía satisfecho con el plan.

Fue Tamura la que planteó la pregunta clave.

—¿Por qué es peligroso ir hasta Raphta?

Titianus iba a responder, pero Arrio se le adelantó mientras se levantaba despacio.

—Piratas.

50
—

UN SUEÑO IMPOSIBLE

**Antioquía
113 d. C.**

Tras la entrevista con Partamaspates, Trajano decidió no recibir a nadie más hasta la tarde. Quería comer algo primero y reunir fuerzas para los embajadores que aún quedaban por presentar sus respetos. Adriano aprovechó el intermedio y ni siquiera esperó a que los esclavos distribuyeran toda la comida por las mesas, entre los *triclinia* que se habían dispuesto para el resto de los miembros del *consilium augusti.*

—Esta campaña es un error, César —dijo el sobrino del emperador sin tomar nada de la abundante fruta que se le ofrecía ni coger una copa de vino como ya habían hecho Quieto, Nigrino y hasta el propio Trajano.

—¿Por qué? —preguntó el emperador.

—Esta campaña de Oriente es un error, César, porque terminaremos todos como la legión perdida —insistió Adriano.

—En quince años al mando del Imperio no he perdido ni una legión —contraargumentó Trajano—. Ni siquiera he sufrido una derrota.

—Pero Partia no es el Rin o la Dacia —opuso Adriano—. Si cruzamos el Éufrates terminaremos como Craso. ¡Por todos los dioses! ¡Lo que propones no puede hacerse! Todos lo piensan pero nadie se atreve a decirlo.

Quieto y Nigrino dejaron de beber.

—Lo que puede hacerse o no puede hacerse depende, sobrino, de cómo se piensa. Si algo no puede hacerse no hay que dejar de hacerlo sino cambiar de forma de pensar. Yo no pienso como Craso, y mis legiones no serán como la legión perdida. Yo no he salido a perderme sino a encontrar: voy a crear un imperio más grande del que nadie en Roma soñó nunca antes.

—Exactamente de eso hablas, tío: de sueños imposibles.

—No, de sueños inmortales. Si conquistamos Partia, Roma durará otros mil años tal y como la conocemos. Por el contrario, si no tenemos la riqueza de Oriente bajo nuestro control, Roma no podrá resistir. Necesitamos más recursos para proteger nuestras fronteras del norte. O para cambiarlas. Quedarnos quietos será nuestra muerte.

Adriano suspiró profundamente y negó con la cabeza. Estaba claro que no había forma de hacer cambiar de opinión a su tío. Trajano parecía tenerlo todo ya muy decidido. Lo que dijeran todos los embajadores de Osroes o de los reinos vecinos no tenía realmente peso en la determinación del emperador.

Adriano se levantó.

—Preferiría no tomar parte directa en esta locura.

Trajano asintió.

—No pensaba que formaras parte activa en ningún momento. Si alguien no cree en lo que hace no lo hace bien. Te quedarás en retaguardia, aquí en Siria, controlando el flujo de aprovisionamiento de las legiones. Supongo que eso podrás hacerlo.

Adriano se contuvo ante el tono de desprecio de su tío.

—Eso sabré hacerlo, sí... César.

Adriano dio entonces media vuelta y se marchó del improvisado almuerzo del *consilium augusti.*

—Estaremos mejor sin él —dijo Trajano y apuró su copa.

Hubo un rato de silencio hasta que Quieto se atrevió a decir algo práctico.

—Con Osroene a nuestro lado el avance sobre Armenia será más sencillo.

Trajano y Nigrino asintieron.

Se habló poco más sobre el resto de los embajadores, más allá de que el emperador subrayara el hecho de que Sporaces tendría que ser castigado en el futuro por su deslealtad con Roma al proclamarse neutral. El César dejaba claro con aquella afirmación que ya no toleraba neutralidades de nadie.

Lucio Quieto y Nigrino se fueron a descansar.

Trajano imaginó adónde habría ido su sobrino a buscar consuelo: Plotina recibiría a Adriano con los brazos abiertos. ¿Había hecho bien llevándola allí, donde Adriano y Plotina podrían estar de nuevo juntos? ¿O habría sido mejor haber dejado a la emperatriz en Roma? Pero eso último habría hecho que Adriano hubiera tenido un contacto directo en la capital del Imperio con el Senado, donde había muchos que, como su sobrino, dudaban de la posibilidad de éxito de la campaña de Oriente. Llevar a Plotina era una forma de reunir a sus «opositores» en la familia, pero también de tener a ambos alejados del Senado. Hiciera lo que hiciese, cada opción tenía unas ventajas y unas desventajas.

Suspiró. Se llevó las manos a las sienes. A veces tenía unos grandes dolores de cabeza, pero al final se pasaban en poco tiempo.

Él también necesitaba algo de consuelo.

Pensó en alguno de los jóvenes esclavos, pero no.

Llamó a Fédimo.

El secretario acudió de inmediato.

—¿Qué puedo hacer por el César?

—El embajador de Osroene.

—Sí, César. El joven Arbandes, el hijo del rey Abgaro.

—El mismo. Tráelo a mi cámara privada. Quiero...

Pero Trajano no terminaba de hablar.

—El César... quiere... —repitió Fédimo en busca de completar la frase.

El emperador, al fin, concluyó sus instrucciones.

—Quiero... hablar con él.

Fédimo tuvo cuidado en no mostrar aprobación ni desaprobación en el rostro al recibir aquella orden y se inclinó ante el emperador. La vida íntima del César no era asunto suyo. No era asunto de nadie.

51

LA HERMOSA YAN JI

Loyang, 114 d. C.

Cámara del emperador
Palacio imperial de Loyang

Yan Ji estaba desnuda. Y hermosa.

Era la más guapa de todas las concubinas del joven emperador An-ti, que, a sus dieciocho años, estaba más concentrado en descubrir los lunares repartidos por la piel de sus esposas que en aprender cómo gobernar uno de los dos mayores imperios del mundo. Sus sesenta y cinco millones de súbditos no eran de su especial interés. Los documentos administrativos que el *t'ai-tzu t'ai-fu*, su tutor jefe, había llevado para que se familiarizara con diferentes asuntos de Estado estaban sin tocar sobre una repisa al otro lado de la habitación. Él se centraba en las jóvenes, cada vez más bellas, que los funcionarios imperiales le ofrecían como concubinas. Yan Ji era una de las más recientes adquisiciones y, sin duda, la que lo había trastornado por completo.

La muchacha, de pronto, se rio. Se sentó en la cama y se cubrió los pechos con los brazos.

—Me haces cosquillas.

—Ven aquí, Yan Ji —dijo el joven emperador invitándola a que volviera a acostarse.

—No —respondió ella con voz de niña enfadada.

Todo parecía un juego, pero Yan Ji se levantó y se fue a la otra punta de la habitación.

A An-ti le encantaba verla moverse desnuda, pero como heredero del trono imperial era caprichoso por poder tenerlo todo cuando quería, de modo que le incomodaba aquella rabieta de su anhelada favorita.

—¡Ven aquí he dicho! —le ordenó de forma tajante, pero ella se sentó en el suelo en una esquina y se acurrucó.

El emperador se levantó, fue a donde estaba ella y estiró de uno de sus brazos hasta ponerla primero en pie y luego arrastrarla de regreso a la cama. La arrojó con fuerza contra el colchón y luego se puso encima. Ella no opuso resistencia y él empezó a hacer lo que quería hacer, pero la muchacha no ponía nada de su parte y a él le gustaba tanto que ella se implicara en el asunto que, ya fuera por eso o por el licor consumido, se hizo a un lado y la dejó estar.

—¿Qué ocurre esta vez? —preguntó el emperador An-ti mirando al techo de su cámara privada.

Ella dio media vuelta y se acurrucó de lado en posición fetal. Yan Ji había conseguido con aquellas rabietas los mejores vestidos de palacio, las mejores habitaciones y las más eficaces sirvientas. Ahora quería más.

—Es Li —dijo ella, al fin.

Li era una de las esposas del emperador.

—¿Qué pasa con Li? Apenas la veo. No puede ser que estés celosa de ella.

—Pues lo estoy —insistió Yan Ji siempre dándole la espalda. Él seguía mirando al techo.

—No lo entiendo —dijo el emperador.

Ella se volvió y se acercó cariñosamente hacia él acariciando su pecho desnudo con su pequeña mano izquierda. De forma muy suave y tierna. Estuvo masajeando al emperador un rato. Él se dejó hacer. Las caricias empezaron a reavivar el ansia sexual de An-ti, lo que la joven pudo comprobar al crecer algo debajo de la sábana que tapaba al emperador de cintura para abajo. Ésa era la señal que esperaba para empezar a hablar de nuevo.

—No son celos de ella —se explicó la muchacha, siempre sin dejar de acariciar el pecho del emperador—. Es por su hijo.

—¿El pequeño Liu Bao? —preguntó An-ti al tiempo que cerraba los ojos y se dejaba masajear. Al momento empezó a sentir besos, los labios de Yan Ji por todo su cuerpo.

—No me parece justo que siendo yo tu favorita, sea el hijo de Li quien esté designado como futuro emperador —se explicó Yan Ji entre beso y beso.

—¿Y qué es lo que quieres que haga?

—Quiero que el emperador me haga un hijo y que ese hijo sea luego el sucesor en el trono de los han.

—No se puede... ah... tener todo en la vida, Ji —dijo el emperador entre pequeños gemidos de placer pues las manos de Yan Ji estaban ocupadas ya en otras partes de su cuerpo mientras seguía besándolo—. Mi madre... además... está contenta con el nombramiento de Liu Bao como heredero... piensa que eso da continuidad... a la dinastía... y sin su consentimiento... no puedo hacer nada...

Ella detuvo en seco sus caricias y sus besos. Deng. Siempre la emperatriz madre y viuda Deng se interponía en todo. Pero Yan Ji se contuvo y reactivó sus diferentes masajes al cuerpo extasiado del emperador An-ti.

—Yo creo que sí se puede tener todo. Yo lo quiero todo... y no tengo nada... —susurró ella al oído imperial mientras mordisqueaba dulcemente la oreja de su joven majestad.

—Me gustaría complacerte... —continuó él—, pero... no puedo contradecir a mi madre... en ese punto la apoyan sus excelencias... los ministros... Y sí que tienes muchas cosas...

—No tengo nada... —Hablaba un poco y proseguía con sus caricias de todo tipo; luego volvía hablar—. Li ha sido elegida emperatriz consorte... y su hijo Liu Bao es el único hijo del emperador, su heredero. Yo... no tengo nada...

Y calló unos momentos para continuar dando placer al emperador hasta conducirlo al éxtasis máximo.

—Ahhh —gimió él.

Ella se separó y se limpió las manos y el cuerpo en la sábana.

No dijeron nada durante unos instantes.

Él se sentó en la cama y cogió un vaso con más licor.

—¿Has pensado en algo? —preguntó An-ti en cuanto terminó de beber. Él también estaba cansado de la emperatriz viuda, pero no veía cómo imponerse.

Yan Ji sonrió malévolamente y habló mirando al emperador.

—Tengo un plan.

Las tres excelencias y los nueve ministros habían abandonado la estancia. Fan Chun, sin embargo, permaneció en la sala con la emperatriz.

—¿De qué quiere hablarme mi fiel *yu-shih chung-ch'eng*, mi leal asistente del ministro de Obras Públicas? —preguntó la emperatriz desde el trono imperial.

—Dos son las cuestiones sobre las que deseaba departir con su majestad.

—Te escucho.

Fan Chun miró a uno de los funcionarios que lo acompañaban. El hombre se acercó con una pequeña caja y la entregó al consejero imperial, quien, a su vez, la ofreció a la emperatriz después de abrirla. Fan Chun la sostenía en alto mientras mantenía la cabeza agachada mirando al suelo.

—¿Qué es esto? —preguntó la emperatriz cogiendo con las manos lo que parecía una pequeña tela donde se podía leer un poema—. ¿Quieres que hablemos de literatura?

—El texto no es importante aquí, majestad —se explicó el consejero—. Se trata del material en el que está escrito.

La emperatriz examinó con detalle aquel tejido. Lo levantó hacia arriba y lo miro por debajo. Lo dobló.

—Es una tela extraña —dijo ella—. Y de poca calidad. Una vez doblada no parece volver a su textura inicial. No creo que tenga mucho valor. Estoy segura de poder rasgarla en dos sin el más mínimo esfuerzo.

—Con permiso. —Fan Chun, con cuidado de no tocar la mano de la emperatriz, cogió la muestra con el poema—. Su majestad, no obstante, habrá observado que el material es muy fino y que se lee bien el texto escrito sobre él.

—Sí, eso es cierto —concedió la emperatriz.

—Y su majestad recordará el enorme problema de espacio que tenemos en los archivos imperiales con los informes funcionariales que se redactan siempre sobre bambú.

—Sí.

—En este material podríamos tener todos los archivos del Imperio han en mucho menos espacio que lo que ocupa el bambú. Y es más fácil de trasladar y de almacenar. El funcionario Cai Lun ha estado trabajando sobre este material desde hace unos años y tenemos textos que se conservan perfectamente desde entonces.

—Pero es más frágil que el bambú —contrapuso la emperatriz Deng.

—Sin duda, su majestad tiene razón en ese punto. Eso es indiscutible, pero también lo son sus otras ventajas.

La emperatriz Deng juntó las manos mientras pensaba.

—¿Cómo se llama este material nuevo? —preguntó su majestad.

—Papel.

—Papel —repitió la emperatriz Deng—. Bien, ¿y qué propones?

—Solicito el apoyo de su majestad ante los ministros y sus excelencias para que se permita el uso del papel en palacio, sin dejar de emplear el bambú en los documentos más importantes, pero como forma de recoger los archivos de las cuestiones más triviales de modo que se ahorre espacio. Y también me gustaría que se empezaran a copiar algunos de nuestros textos clásicos en este material, de forma que podamos enviar copias a diferentes ciudades. Creo que el papel puede ayudar a divulgar más el conocimiento en el Imperio han y me consta que la emperatriz siempre ha estado interesada en que esta extensión del saber sea una realidad.

Su majestad volvió a pensar un momento.

—De acuerdo —dijo, e hizo un gesto para que Fan Chun le acercara de nuevo la muestra. Su consejero le llevó la caja y la emperatriz tomó otra vez en las manos la pequeña hoja de papel—. Curioso. Y sí, es muy ligero. Quizá pase el tiempo y todos recuerden a Cai Lun por su descubrimiento.

Su majestad dejó la muestra de nuevo en la caja y Fan Chun la cerró, la entregó al funcionario y se quedó mirándolo un instante. El ayudante del consejero se inclinó, dio media vuelta y salió de la estancia dejando al asistente del ministro de Obras Públicas a solas con la emperatriz.

—Ahora me hablarás del segundo asunto que te interesa —comentó la emperatriz.

—En efecto, majestad. Como habrá oído por las explicaciones de los ministros, hay rebeliones en las regiones más occidentales del Imperio han y ataques de los *hsiung-nu* allí donde la Gran Muralla termina, y esto, unido al hecho de que puede estar a punto de estallar una guerra entre el imperio de Anshi y el imperio de Da Qin, según informan los mercaderes que llegan de Occidente, puede afectar enormemente a nuestro comercio en la ruta de la seda.

—Sí, he escuchado con preocupación las explicaciones sobre esos dos temas —confirmó la emperatriz.

—Y su majestad, con gran sabiduría, ha aceptado el consejo de sus excelencias y ministros de enviar tropas de refuerzo a esas regiones fronterizas de nuestro Imperio. Yo sugiero además que entre esas tropas incorporemos a algún oficial de la nueva guardia; un hombre de confirmada lealtad a la emperatriz Deng para que nos mantenga bien informados de todo lo que ocurre allí.

—Si tu intuición te hace creer que eso es importante, seguiré aquí tus consejos, tal y como hacía mi querido esposo, el emperador He. Selecciona pues a quien tú creas mejor y que viaje con capacidad de decisión a esas regiones junto con el resto de los coroneles.

El asistente del ministro de Obras Públicas hizo una larga reverencia.

—Gracias, majestad.

Despacho del asistente Fan Chun

Li Kan estaba de pie y en silencio frente al asistente del ministro de Obras Públicas, que permanecía ocupado leyendo informes en un tejido extraño que no era bambú ni otra tela que él hubiera visto antes. Se preguntaba por qué aquel consejero que tenía tanta influencia sobre la emperatriz no había sido ascendido a ministro o excelencia.

Aún tardaría tiempo en averiguarlo.

Podría haberlo preguntado. El consejero parecía tenerlo en mucha estima y había ya una gran confianza entre ambos, pero aquello era muy personal y Li Kan no tenía claro que fuera correcto plantearlo.

—Bien —dijo Fan Chun dejando los papeles que tenía en las manos sobre la mesa y, mirando a Li Kan, añadió—: Vas a partir hacia las regiones occidentales.

—¿Con el ejército?

—Sí. Quiero un oficial de confianza en esta campaña contra los *hsiung-nu*. Tú eres leal, lo has demostrado estos años y tienes una experiencia en combate que será de gran ayuda a nuestras tropas en Occidente, pero escúchame bien.

—Sí, asistente. —Li Kan se puso muy firme.

—Hemos perdido el control sobre algunos de esos territorios y la región nos es esencial para mantener nuestra ruta comercial con los Yuegzhi y con el Imperio an-shi. Si perdemos esos dominios será mucho más difícil exportar la seda, lacas y otros productos y perderemos unos ingresos que necesitamos para mantener el ejército han en pie, que es lo mismo que mantener el imperio en sí. ¿Me entiendes?

—Sí, asistente.

—Bien. Veamos, ¿qué más? Ah sí, esto también es importante: los mercaderes informan de que una guerra puede estallar, si es que no ha empezado ya, entre An-shi y el remoto Da Qin. Quiero que estés muy atento a cualquier información sobre esto. Cualquier mensajero, cualquier comerciante que nos aporte luz sobre este asunto es relevante. Si esos dos imperios entran en guerra puede que eso afecte también a nuestra ruta de venta de la seda y otras mercancías. Quiero..., esto es, la emperatriz Deng desea estar bien informada. La mayoría de los oficiales carecen de tu intuición para discernir lo que es importante de lo que no. Cuento con tu discreción para que me hagas llegar cualquier noticia sobre esa lejana guerra. Una guerra de tan gigantescas proporciones, por muy distante que esté de nosotros, no es un asunto menor.

Li Kan asintió.

—Dejas, por el momento, la guardia imperial y te reincorporas al ejército de nuevo, pero con grado de *Hsiao-wi*.

—¿Yo? ¿Coronel?

—No te sorprendas. Espero que llegues alguna vez a *chiang-chün.*

Li Kan abrió la boca. La cerró. Se inclinó ante el *yu-shih chung-ch'eng.* Se volvió. Se detuvo. Volvió a encarar al consejero. Fan Chun estaba leyendo de nuevo aquellos documentos escritos en aquel material extraño. El asistente lo miró.

—¿Alguna duda?

—No, asistente. Es decir, sí.

—No me gustan los circunloquios. No son apropiados para un oficial del Imperio han.

Li Kan asintió y formuló su interrogante con rapidez.

—Me pregunto: ¿cómo es posible que el asistente del ministro de Obras Públicas, estando en el círculo más próximo a la emperatriz Deng, y teniendo tanta influencia en el gobierno del Imperio han no haya sido nombrado ya ministro o excelencia?

Fan Chun tardó en responder, pero cuando lo hizo fue con precisión milimétrica.

—Tu pregunta es relevante, y el hecho de que te atrevas a formularla indica que asumes un grado de confianza conmigo propio de una gran lealtad y eso me conmueve, pero el hecho de que no des aún con la respuesta me hace ver que aún tienes camino que recorrer para llegar a general. Si tan intrigado estás te sugiero que releas un libro que imagino que ya habrás leído.

—¿Qué libro, asistente?

—El 孫子兵法, el *sūnzǐ bīngfǎ.* Supongo que como todo buen militar lo habrás leído.

—Sí, asistente, por supuesto, he leído *El arte de la guerra* de Sūn Tzu.

—Pues reléelo y en él encontrarás la respuesta a tu pregunta. De hecho el día que me des la respuesta correcta propondré tu ascenso a general.

Li Kan se inclinó, dio media vuelta y salió de la oficina del asistente. Tenía una copia de *El arte de la guerra* en sus dependencias personales de palacio y quería empezar su relectura de inmediato.

Fan Chun se quedó pensativo. ¿Cuánto tardaría el joven Li Kan en comprender? Estaba claro que el nuevo coronel del ejército han se había ido concentrado en encontrar la respuesta a su pregunta, hasta el extremo de que había dejado la puerta del despacho abierta. Fan Chun suspiró lentamente, pero con sosiego. Podía dar una voz y que alguno de los sirvientes cerrara la puerta, pero le molestaban tanto los gritos... Se levantó y caminó hacia allí. Estaba satisfecho. Con Li Kan en las regiones occidentales tendría información fresca sobre la posible guerra entre Da Qin y An-Shi, además de disponer de un gran oficial frente a los irritantes e incansables *hsiung-nu*, y, por último, los asuntos de palacio parecían controlados. Al llegar a la puerta vio a la hermosa Yan Ji, la nueva favorita del emperador An-ti, cruzar el patio inferior de palacio con una sonrisa en los labios. ¿Realmente estaba todo controlado?

52

LA RUTA DE TRAJANO

A lo largo del alto Éufrates
Primavera de 114 d. C.

Trajano salió de Antioquía en primavera. Su objetivo era apoderarse de Armenia aquel año. El tiempo y las circunstancias dirían si eso sería posible o no, pero su determinación era firme. También su intención de tener presentes los errores de Craso para no repetirlos.

De la gran ciudad de Siria, el emperador, junto con Quieto, Nigrino y otros *legati* al mando de varias legiones, partió hacia el este hasta llegar a Beroea,[41] y de allí hacia el norte hasta Zeugma, donde les esperaba la legión IV Scythica para unirse al gran ejército imperial. Allí fue donde Craso cruzó el Éufrates, pero Trajano decidió continuar hacia el norte siguiendo el curso del río por la ribera derecha, es decir, por el lado del Éufrates controlado por Roma. Así, sin oposición ni problemas de abastecimiento de agua y víveres, Trajano llegó hasta Samosata. Allí esperaba la legión VI Ferrata, que también se unió al ejército imperial.

—Ha llegado una carta —dijo Fédimo mientras el emperador comía algo del rancho de las legiones frente a una tienda de uno de los *quaestores* del ejército.

El emperador entregó el cazo de arcilla con gachas a Aulo, que lo cogió sin saber bien qué hacer con él y se lo quedó en la mano, pero siempre con gesto marcial en el rostro.

—¿Carta de quién? —preguntó el César mientras alargaba el brazo para coger el papiro que le entregaba su secretario.

---

41. Actual Alepo, en Siria.

—Es de Partamasiris. —Fédimo estuvo atento a no decir del *rey* Partamasiris, pues precisamente ésa era la cuestión de toda aquella campaña.

Trajano la leyó con rapidez y luego se la devolvió desplegada a Fédimo. Lucio Quieto y Nigrino miraban al César en espera de algún comentario, pero Trajano se limitó a retomar el cazo con comida de Aulo y a volver a llevarse la cuchara la boca con auténtica ansia. Había pasado varias noches con Arbandes en Antioquía y era como si hubiera rejuvenecido varios años. Comía más y se sentía más fuerte. Marchaba a pie como sus legionarios y necesitaba reponer energías.

—¿Qué dice Partamasiris? —preguntó Lucio Quieto, que no pudo resistir más.

—Dice que... saldrá a mi encuentro... —Trajano hablaba sin dejar de comer— y que me presentará la diadema de Armenia para que... sea yo el que... se la ciña... de nuevo en la cabeza... y firma como rey de Armenia. Esta comida está buena, pero es poco abundante —añadió mirando a los *quaestores*—. Los legionarios aún tienen una larga marcha hasta el corazón de Armenia. Dad más comida a mis hombres.

Trajano devolvió el cazo esta vez directamente a uno de los *quaestores*, que se quedó mirando el tazón de arcilla con la frente arrugada.

—Harán falta entonces más víveres, augusto, si hemos de incrementar las raciones —dijo el *quaestor* sosteniendo el cuenco vacío del emperador—. Siento tener que comentarlo, pero es así, César.

Trajano lo miró apreciativamente. Le gustaba cuando un oficial decía lo que tenía que decir en cada momento. Es más, le gustaba ver que sus oficiales se atrevían a informar de lo que era necesario en cada circunstancia.

—Lo que dices es correcto, *quaestor* —respondió Trajano poniendo la mano sobre el hombro del oficial—. Tú, junto con el resto de los *quaestores*, seguid mis instrucciones de incrementar las raciones y yo, como *imperator* al mando, me ocuparé de que tengáis los víveres que precisáis.

Trajano no dijo más y echó a andar para seguir revisando el estado de las tropas y los pertrechos. Quieto, Nigrino, Liviano, Aulo y ahora también Fédimo, con la carta de Partamasiris en una mano, lo seguían de cerca.

—Avanzaremos ahora hacia Metilene —se explicó Trajano—. Es una ciudad rica y fértil. Allí podremos aprovisionarnos con todo lo necesario.

Quieto y el resto asintieron. Aquello era sensato y seguro.

Fédimo, cuando vio que el asunto de la ruta y de los víveres parecía resuelto, volvió al tema de la carta.

—¿Hay respuesta para Partamasiris, augusto?

Trajano se detuvo en seco y miró a su joven secretario.

—No —dijo tajante—. Ha firmado la carta como rey de Armenia. —Miró entonces a Lucio Quieto—. Seguiremos avanzando y reuniendo más legiones. Ya se le irán bajando los humos.

El ejército romano llegó a la rica Metilene en pocos días.

En efecto, tal y como había comentado el emperador, aquella población poseía el mayor *canabae legionis* de la región: una especie de ciudad paralela junto a la población original, en donde se habían reunido todos los comerciantes, artesanos y agricultores que proveían de víveres y todo tipo de pertrechos a las legiones de Roma. Allí, además, se unió al ejército imperial la legión XII Fulminata.

Llegó a Metilene una segunda carta de Partamasiris.

Trajano sonreía mientras la leía una noche en la tienda del *praetorium* de campaña.

—Parece que Partamasiris quiere negociar —dijo el César.

—El cordero ve al lobo cerca y le ha entrado miedo —comentó Quieto.

—Eso parece —aceptó el César—, pero seguiremos su juego y enviaremos a un tribuno a hablar con Partamasiris. Selecciona a alguien de confianza, Lucio. Me encanta que crea que puede hacerme cambiar de planes. Si no fuera tan patético, sería hasta divertido.

Se envió al tribuno Junio, hijo de uno de los *legati*, con la respuesta de que el César se avenía a negociar siempre que Partamasiris entregara la diadema real que luego Trajano volvería a colocar sobre la cabeza del rey de Armenia.

—¿Y entretanto? —inquirió Nigrino, que preveía que el

César no iba a quedarse quieto esperando la respuesta de Partamasiris.

—Entretanto cruzaremos el Éufrates.

Se hizo el silencio.

Hasta aquel momento todo había ido bien. Se habían ido reuniendo tropas y aprovisionándose de todo lo necesario para una larga campaña a la espera de adentrarse en Armenia en busca del enemigo, pero, de algún modo, todos seguían temiendo cruzar el río.

—Va a ser sólo una prueba —se explicó Trajano—. Yo también soy consciente del temor de las tropas a cruzar el Éufrates, pero nos vamos a plantear ahora sólo un objetivo pequeño y luego nos retiraremos. Podéis transmitir esta información a las tropas: tener la certeza de que mi plan incluye un rápido repliegue; eso les dará firmeza y seguridad en este primer ataque.

Y así fue.

Las legiones de Trajano cruzaron el Éufrates y tras varios días de marcha llegaron frente a la primera gran ciudad Armenia: Arsamosata.

Las puertas de las murallas se abrieron para el César. Los habitantes de la ciudad, que no habían recibido tropas de Armenia central por parte de su rey, decidieron no enfrentarse al magno ejército invasor de Roma. La primera ciudad conquistada fue muy fácil. Pese a ello, Trajano se mantuvo fiel a su plan y a su promesa hecha a sus oficiales y legionarios y se replegó con la mayor parte de sus tropas, cruzando de nuevo el Éufrates y acampando en la fortaleza romana de Satala, de vuelta en la ribera derecha y romana del gran río mesopotámico. De alguna forma, quería ir mostrando tanto a oficiales como a soldados que, bajo su mando, se podía cruzar el Éufrates, conquistar ciudades y regresar indemnes. El ánimo de las tropas estaba alto. Trajano ordenó repartir vino adicional entre los legionarios para festejar esa primera pequeña victoria, pero que sabía a muy grande después del miedo acumulado por los romanos a cruzar el Éufrates durante decenios y decenios. Por si eso fuera poco, a Satala fueron llegando aún más y más tropas: además de las legiones IV Scythica, VI Ferrata o

XII Fulminata, que se les habían unido por el camino hacia el norte, y de la XVI Flavia Firma de Capadocia apostada en aquella ciudad, y de las III Cirenaica y la III Gallica y la X Fretensis de Judea, con las que había partido inicialmente desde Antioquía, acamparon alrededor de Satala dos legiones más completas: la I Adiutrix y la XV Apollinaris, que habían alcanzado aquella posición haciendo un largo viaje desde sus campamentos de las regiones del Danubio, cruzando Asia Menor central para, vía Ancyra,[42] llegar hasta Satala. Esa ruta para los legionarios, pues la mayoría de los pertrechos, armamento y otros materiales para la guerra habían sido remitidos por mar desde Tomis[43] hasta Trapezus[44] a través del mar Negro, según instrucciones de Trajano, ahorrando así gran parte del esfuerzo a sus hombres. Pero, por si eso fuera poco, el emperador había hecho llegar, también por tierra y por mar, numerosas *vexillationes*, o unidades complementarias, de la legión VII Claudia, de la XIII Gemina, la II Traiana Fortis, la XII Primigenia, la XXX Ulpia Victrix, la XI Claudia, la I Itálica y la V Macedónica. Trajano había reunido en Satala para su campaña de Oriente tropas provenientes de diecisiete legiones diferentes, en lo que terminaba siendo un equivalente a bastante más de ocho legiones completas. Se trataba de casi un tercio del poder militar de Roma, casi cien mil hombres, la mayor concentración de legiones romanas nunca conocida.

---

42. Actual Ankara.
43. Actual Constanza en Rumanía.
44. Actual Trabzon en la costa norte de Turquía.

53

EN EL FIN DE LOS MAPAS

Costa de Azania[45]
114 d. C.

Marcio estaba inquieto. Aquélla era una misión que estaba diseñada para llegar al final del mundo conocido, y ahora, antes de llegar al Imperio kushan, tenían que viajar primero bordeando la costa de los reinos al sur de Egipto hasta llegar a lugares remotos que no aparecían en los mapas.

Tardaron unos días en conseguir que Titianus hiciera las transacciones necesarias con varios comerciantes para tener una falúa en condiciones que a Arrio le pareciera lo suficientemente sólida como para navegar hacia aquellos lejanos parajes en los que debían adentrarse siempre en dirección sur. Marcio aprovechó e hizo también algunas adquisiciones por su cuenta con el poco oro que tenía.

—¿Dos lucernas y grasa? —preguntó Alana cuando vio lo que había comprado.

—Titianus y Arrio se encargan de las provisiones, yo de la seguridad del viaje —respondió Marcio sin aclarar nada más sobre los productos que había comprado.

Alana iba a preguntarle, pero sabía que, en el fondo, a Marcio le gustaba tener sus pequeños secretos y dejó la cuestión de lado. Quizá Marcio había simplemente pensado en tener luz por la noche en la embarcación. Llevaban un trozo de acero y pedernal para prender fuego cuando hiciera falta, pero era cierto que no tenían lucernas. En fin, seguramente, en algún momento, se resolvería el enigma.

45. Costas de África oriental.

Empezó la navegación, pero apenas iniciado el que debía ser un largo trayecto, Titianus, que no dejaba de mirar el agua del mar, se dirigió a Arrio nervioso.

—Busca una bahía segura donde fondear.

—Acabamos de empezar —replicó el centurión naval algo molesto, pues el navío no era veloz y los estadios a surcar hasta alcanzar los confines desconocidos del sur de la gran mar Eritrea eran miles, decenas de miles quizá. Así no llegarían nunca.

—Estamos a la altura del cabo Elefante, justo antes de llegar al cabo de las Especias, ¿verdad? —preguntó el mercader.

—Sí, hace dos días que dejamos Mosyllum.

—Eres hombre de mar, Arrio, eso me consta. Tu cruce del canal de Trajano fue impecable, pero no has estado nunca en estas aguas. Míralas —le invitó Titianus extendiendo la mano por encima de la barandilla del barco.

—Están muy oscuras.

—Busca una bahía y rápido. Ese color aquí es el preludio de una gran tormenta.

Arrio tuvo el sentido común de hacer caso a Titianus y dirigió el barco a una cala donde pudieron fondear a resguardo de un viento que, de pronto, empezó a agitar el agua que veían en el mar abierto.

La tormenta fue muy fuerte, pero anclados en la bahía, consiguieron que sólo quedara en anécdota, pues los arrecifes de ambos lados de la playa actuaban de muros de contención contra los vientos y las grandes olas. Todos sabían que Titianus era el que más sabía de los parajes que iban surcando en aquella larga navegación, pero aquel día desde Marcio hasta Áyax, desde Arrio hasta su media docena de marinos, todos aprendieron a respetar aún más al viejo mercader de ojos pequeños que miraba, una vez más, hacia el horizonte desde proa.

La navegación continuó tranquila durante varios días.

Desde que viraron hacia el sur en el cabo de las Especias, cada día de viaje los alejaba de la India, al otro lado del gran océano. En su lugar, seguían navegando lentamente junto a la costa de los reinos al sur de Egipto. Pasaron cerca de la desembocadura de un río al que llamaban allí el pequeño Nilo y siguieron más hacia el sur: cuatrocientos estadios más y alcanzaron la población de Pano, y tras cuatrocientos más, la ciudad de Opone. Habían llegado a la región de Azania. Desde la falúa podían ver a muchos nativos en pequeñas embarcaciones hechas con un solo tronco largo, surcando la costa en busca de pescado entre la desembocadura de pequeños ríos donde Tamura, por primera vez en su vida, vio cocodrilos en libertad. Los únicos que había visto hasta entonces era en algunas de las *venationes* o cacerías salvajes del Anfiteatro Flavio. Los cocodrilos de Azania, sin embargo, eran mucho más grandes.

—No suelen atacar a los hombres —dijo el viejo Titianus para tranquilidad de todos, aunque luego añadió algo menos relajante—. Aquí los peligrosos, como en casi todas partes, son los hombres.

Áyax se acercó a Tamura y se apoyó en la barandilla de babor junto a ella. Ambos miraban a los nativos que pescaban en el horizonte de palmeras.

Tamura sostenía uno de los libros que Dión Coceyo le había regalado en el puerto de Ostia, concretamente el de Plutarco sobre la vida de Craso, en griego. La costumbre de Tamura de llevar siempre consigo aquellos libros en una bolsa, junto con su arco y sus flechas, había permitido que Áyax se salvara del incendio de la nave en Mundus.

—¿Qué son exactamente? —preguntó Áyax a la joven señalando los pequeños códices de pergamino cosido.

—Son libros —respondió Tamura ilusionada de poseer algo que llamara la atención de Áyax y que él no conociera. Así, la muchacha siguió hablando emocionada—: están en diferentes lenguas. Tengo éste en griego sobre la vida de un cónsul romano que murió luchando contra los partos y luego está éste, escrito por el propio Julio César, donde narra la guerra civil entre él y Pompeyo el Grande; también tengo éste otro, más corto, con textos en sánscrito de un profeta...

—Lo importante en este mundo es luchar bien —la interrumpió el gladiador con cierto desdén hacia las explicaciones de la muchacha—. Los libros de los que hablas no valen para nada. Mejor sería que siguieras entrenándote con la espada. Eres muy buena con el arco, pero alguna vez puede que te haga falta luchar con una espada. No pierdas el tiempo con esos… libros.

Y se alejó de aquel lado de la embarcación dejando a Tamura de nuevo sola y enrabietada. El desprecio de Áyax hacia sus libros le dolió tanto… Y ella que pensaba que tenía algo con lo que atraer su atención de nuevo. Sin poder evitarlo soltó una lágrima que brilló iluminada por el sol de la costa de Azania. Miró al mar y cogió la pequeña bolsa con sus tres libros. Echó la vista atrás: Áyax la observaba de reojo, sentado en la barandilla de estribor. Él disimulaba pero ella sabía que la miraba. Tamura cogió la bolsa con fuerza con la mano derecha y extendió el brazo por encima de la barandilla de la pequeña falúa. La bolsa estaba apenas a un par de pies del agua. Sólo tenía que abrir la mano y los libros que Dión Coceyo le había regalado caerían al mar y se perderían para siempre. Quizá eso hiciera que Áyax viera que ella apreciaba sus ideas.

—¡Por Júpiter, mirad! —dijo uno de los marinos de Arrio.

El grito hizo que Tamura, instintivamente, en lugar de soltar, asiera con fuerza la bolsa y la llevara de nuevo de regreso a su costado, donde la ajustó con rapidez mientras dirigía sus ojos, como el resto, hacia la costa: se veía un barco grande, no sabía bien de qué tipo, acercándose a los nativos de las pequeñas embarcaciones, atacándolos. Algunos guerreros habían descendido del barco y mataban a varios nativos mientras que a otros les lanzaban redes o los golpeaban dejándolos sin sentido para luego subirlos al barco.

—¿Piratas o mercaderes de esclavos? —preguntó Marcio.

—Aquí no hay diferencia entre unos y otros —respondió Titianus—. En un par de meses la mayoría de los miserables que sobrevivan al ataque serán vendidos en el sur de Egipto. Son hombres sanos y fuertes. Buenos esclavos.

—¿Nos atacarán luego a nosotros? —indagó entonces Arrio.

Titianus miró hacia el interior de la falúa.

—No lo creo probable. Vamos hacia el sur. Saben que vamos vacíos. Somos pocos, de modo que suponemos poco botín como esclavos cuando pueden escoger entre centenares desperdigados por la costa. No, ahora nos dejarán seguir. Pero nos esperarán o nos seguirán. Cuando estemos cargados con algo de valor, entonces sí que vendrán a por nosotros. Quizá los esquivemos, pero son astutos. Por eso el marfil en esta región es barato.

Todos miraron de nuevo hacia el barco pirata: tenía dos grandes mástiles y varias hileras de remos. Al menos cien piratas iban en su interior. Si se decidían a atacarlos no tendrían ni una sola posibilidad.

Nadie dijo nada.

La navegación continuó.

Seis días de pequeñas bahías y luego varios días más de una larga e infinita playa que parecía no terminar nunca. Era como si hubieran llegado al final del mundo. Marcio, como el resto, pese al respeto que tenían por el viejo Titianus, empezaba a preguntarse si aquel mercader sabía realmente hacía dónde iban. ¿Habría en verdad marfil, allí tan lejos de todo y de todos?

Apareció entonces una pequeña ciudad.

—Sarapion —precisó Titianus y con calma añadió—: Aún nos faltan varios días de navegación.

Todos empezaron a comprender por qué pocos se aventuraban a buscar el marfil en aquel territorio. Llevaban más de un mes surcando el océano siempre hacia el sur y aún faltaban más días; por no mencionar que habían dejado atrás a piratas esperándolos por si conseguían regresar con algo que mereciera la pena.

Pasaron por delante de Nicon.

Y siguieron más hacia el sur.

Todo era ahora pájaros de vivos colores, por todas partes, y más cocodrilos aún mayores si cabía que los que habían visto más al norte. Y tortugas enormes, como ninguno de ellos había encontrado en su vida. Por fin, varias jornadas después, Titianus señaló hacia la costa con seguridad.

—Rhapta.[46] El último puerto del mundo conocido. La última población de Azania. Aquí encontraremos el marfil al mejor precio.

46. En la costa oriental de África, a la altura de Madagascar.

—¿Y qué hay más al sur? —preguntó Tamura, pues el mar seguía y seguía sin fin.

—*Más allá de este lugar el océano se dobla hacia el oeste, y extendiéndose por las regiones al sur de Etiopía, Libia y África, se mezcla con el mar de Occidente.*[47] Eso dicen algunos navegantes, pero no conozco a ninguno que haya vuelto para contármelo a mí en persona. No sé pues realmente qué hay más allá. Hemos llegado al final de los mapas.

47. Literal del *Periplo por la mar Eritrea.*

54

REESCRIBIENDO LA HISTORIA

Elegeia,[48] **114 d. C.**

Anchialos, rey de los heníocos y los maquelones de la Cólquida,[49] la región costera más oriental del mar Negro, se humilló ante Trajano en Satala. Nadie había visto nunca un ejército como el que el emperador romano acababa de reunir en la frontera de Armenia y muy pocos se atreverían a plantar cara a semejante poder.

—¿Lo volvemos a hacer? —preguntó Lucio Quieto al emperador.

—Sí, por Júpiter —respondió Trajano.

El ejército romano volvió a ir más allá del Éufrates adentrándose ahora directamente en Armenia más de cien millas, hasta alcanzar la ciudad de Elegeia, a menos de doscientas millas de la capital del reino de Partamasiris.

Hacía un calor abrasador. El sol de junio caía a plomo sobre una llanura elevada donde los veranos eran calurosísimos y los inviernos helados. Aquel territorio debía conquistarse antes de que llegaran las nieves o todo se complicaría. Al menos había que tener controlado el centro del reino.

Una vez más tampoco salió ejército alguno desde Elegeia para combatir contra los romanos, pues la ciudad era el lugar acordado por Trajano y Partamasiris para entrevistarse y resolver de una vez por todas el asunto de la coronación del rey de Armenia.

—Se retrasa —dijo Nigrino a un Trajano pensativo, que

---

48. En las proximidades de la actual Erzurum, Turquía oriental.
49. Actuales Abjasia y Georgia.

paseaba por la interminable ciudad de tiendas de campaña que constituía el campamento de su gigantesco ejército de conquista.

—Partamasiris quiere que pensemos que no nos tiene miedo —dijo Trajano mientras se detenía un momento para beber algo de agua—. Esperaremos —añadió devolviendo el cuenco vacío a un pretoriano.

Partamasiris llegó a la reunión con el emperador de Roma una semana después de la fecha acordada. Eso sí, en cuanto estuvo en Elegeia no se detuvo ni para entrar en la ciudad y, aparentando viajar sin apenas descanso desde Artaxata, se presentó ante Trajano en el *praetorium* militar del César y le habló en griego.

—Llevo todo el polvo de los caminos sobre mi piel, augusto. Han sido los bandidos que apoyan aún al depuesto Exedares los que me han retenido —se excusó Partamasiris exhibiendo su habitual sonrisa de pocos dientes, desagradable para cualquiera que la contemplase, e inclinándose levemente ante Trajano—. Pero estoy seguro de que una vez que el emperador de Roma me confirme como rey de Armenia, esos rebeldes comprenderán que no tiene sentido su lucha.

Trajano no dijo nada durante unos momentos en los que se pasó el índice de la mano izquierda por la nariz, como si se rascara.

—Veo que llevas la diadema del rey de Armenia sobre la cabeza —comentó el César.

Tanto el emperador de Roma como el líder de Armenia habían pasado por alto los saludos protocolarios. Partamasiris intuía en la mirada fría de Trajano que el César no estaba por dar rodeos en aquella negociación. Al rey de Armenia, en realidad, no le convencía nada haber tenido que presentarse al fin ante Trajano en persona, pero su hermano Osroes no le había dejado margen. El *Šāhān Šāh* le había negado tropas de apoyo para enfrentarse con Trajano y le había conminado a presentarse ante el emperador de Roma, humillarse ante él y hacer todo lo posible para que ofreciendo la diadema al César, este último consintiera en ponérsela de nuevo en la cabeza, de modo que se cumpliera el protocolo de que el rey de

Armenia era aceptado tanto por Partia como por Roma. Partamasiris no estaba seguro de que Trajano fuera a admitir simplemente una humillación del rey de Armenia como disculpa por el agravio cometido al haber depuesto a Exedares sin consultarle, pero ¿qué otras opciones tenía? No disponía de tropas suficientes para oponerse al ejército de las casi diez legiones, según le habían informado sus hombres de la frontera, que había introducido Trajano en Armenia. Sin apoyo de Partia, Partamasiris sólo podía rendirse, huir o negociar. La primera opción era inaceptable, la segunda no llevaría más que a ser exterminado si permanecía en Armenia o a ser apartado de la corte en Cesifonte si optaba por regresar a Partia. Negociar parecía la mejor elección. Osroes, además, le había incentivado confirmando que casaría a Aryazate con él si conseguía, de la forma que fuera, hacer entrar en razón a Trajano para que se retirara sin invadir más territorios. Siempre la hermosa Aryazate en el horizonte de su deseo, del deseo de tantos...

Partamasiris levantó los brazos, se llevó las manos a la cabeza y, con cuidado, se quitó la preciada diadema de rey de Armenia, dio dos pasos al frente y la puso a los pies del emperador de Roma.

Era el momento clave.

Más no se podía humillar ningún rey.

Quieto, Nigrino, Liviano, Aulo, Fédimo, todos los romanos presentes en el *praetorium* no dejaban de admirarse. Lucio veía que desde la conquista de la Dacia los reinos limítrofes con Roma simplemente se rendían: Arabia había pactado ser absorbida por Roma y reconvertida en provincia sin apenas oponer resistencia; el reino de Osroene se declaraba amigo de Trajano, según el rey Abgaro; y multitud de reyezuelos de las costas del mar Negro y de otras regiones próximas a donde se encontraban se humillaban. Ahora estaban ante el gobernante del poderoso y rico reino de Armenia y éste ponía la corona a los pies de Trajano.

—Este gesto tuyo me parece correcto —dijo el César y se levantó lentamente de su *sella curulis*, dio tres pasos al frente y, por primera vez en mucho tiempo, se agachó delante de alguien, pero fue sólo para coger la diadema del suelo. La acercó a sus ojos para apreciarla bien; su vista ya no era la de antaño. Era de oro con piedras preciosas en la parte frontal y los laterales. Era muy hermosa. Sin duda, una joya digna de un rey.

Trajano miró a Partamasiris, que permanecía arrodillado ante él en espera de que el emperador depositara la corona sobre su cabeza. El César hizo ademán de acercarse hacia el rey humillado, pero, en el último momento, se volvió, dio unos pasos y se detuvo ante su joven secretario.

—Fédimo, coge esto y custódialo —le dijo Trajano al tiempo que le entregaba la diadema real—. Custódiala bien: es un despojo de guerra que representa una gran victoria para Roma.

La orden del César dada a Fédimo había sido en griego, de forma que Partamasiris pudo entenderlo, pese a que no daba crédito a lo que estaba pasando. Era evidente que Trajano quería que él comprendiera todo lo que estaba diciendo.

—Pero César... —empezó Partamasiris, ya en pie—. No ha habido guerra alguna. Mi diadema no puede tomarse como despojo de guerra. No he sacado mis ejércitos para luchar. He venido a resolver nuestras diferencias... a buscar una paz con el emperador de Roma...

—Oh, sí que ha habido una guerra —dijo Trajano volviéndose para encarar a su interlocutor ya sin corona—. Yo he traído hasta aquí a mis legiones. Que tú hayas decidido no luchar y rendirte es asunto tuyo. Es cierto que me has ahorrado algunos esfuerzos y en recompensa por facilitarme la anexión de Armenia al Imperio de Roma estoy dispuesto a respetar tu vida y la de tu familia. Teniendo en cuenta tu cobardía, creo que puedes considerarte un hombre afortunado.

Partamasiris miró hacia el pequeño grupo de nobles armenios y partos que lo habían acompañado para ver al César. Estaban mudos. Ninguno quería irritar al todopoderoso emperador de Roma que, a lo que veían, había viajado a Asia a poner y quitar reyes, a reorganizar todo el mundo conocido; en definitiva: a quedarse.

Trajano señaló a uno de los *legati* presentes.

—Tú, Catilio Severo. Tengo buenos informes sobre tu valía. Serás el primer gobernador de la provincia de Armenia.

Severo miró a Quieto y a Nigrino. Éstos levantaron las cejas tan sorprendidos como él.

—Sí, César —dijo el recién nombrado gobernador de la nueva provincia de Armenia y se llevó el puño al pecho.

—Esto ha llegado demasiado lejos, augusto —dijo Partamasiris de forma triste, porque pedir cuando no se tiene fuerza para hacerlo entre poderosos siempre resulta patético, a no ser que se trate de alguien de virtud intachable; pero Partamasiris precisamente virtuoso nunca había sido.

Trajano, ignorando las quejas del depuesto rey, se dirigió ahora a Quieto.

—Puedes informar a las legiones de que hemos conseguido una gran victoria.

—Sí, César —respondió Lucio con rapidez; estaba aprendiendo a no sorprenderse ya por nada que propusiera o hiciera Trajano. Nunca había visto una anexión tan veloz de un territorio, pero estaba claro que con el César hispano ya nada era como había sido hasta entonces: ahora todo era posible. Trajano pensaba en otra dimensión diferente. Quieto tenía claro que sólo debía observar, obedecer y aprender. Salió de la tienda para informar a los tribunos de las legiones. Una gran victoria requería una celebración a la altura de las circunstancias.

—Esto no acabará así —dijo Partamasiris respirando muy rápidamente, como un perro acorralado.

Trajano le dedicó entonces una breve mirada.

—No, seguramente esto es sólo el principio de algo más grande, pero creo que demasiado grande para que un ser despreciable como tú tome parte en ello. —Y se dirigió a Liviano—: Escoltadlo fuera del campamento. A él solo. —Miró entonces a los nobles armenios y partos—. A vosotros os sugiero que los que sois armenios paséis el resto de la noche en Elegeia. Por vuestra seguridad. A los que sois de Partia, coged vuestros caballos y marchad de regreso a Cesifonte.

Todos los nobles asintieron, se inclinaron ante el César y salieron de allí lo más rápido que pudieron, decididos unos a atrincherarse en sus mansiones de Elegeia y no asomar las narices fuera de sus muros hasta nueva orden directa del emperador de Roma, y los demás decididos a cabalgar sin descanso hasta Cesifonte. Eran supervivientes naturales y solían tener claro cuándo el viento cambiaba de dirección. De Partia no llegaba ni una tenue brisa, mientras que de Roma soplaba un viento irrefrenable de nombre Trajano.

Aulo cogió a Partamasiris por el brazo, pues éste se resistía a abandonar el *praetorium*. En cuanto el rey depuesto sintió que lo cogían se sacudió la mano del pretoriano.

—¡No me toques!

Aulo iba a repetir el gesto, pero Partamasiris echó a andar hacia la salida de la gran tienda de campaña y no hizo falta tocarlo más.

Liviano miró al César con un interrogante en el rostro.

Trajano asintió una sola vez.

Liviano se llevó el puño al pecho y salió detrás de Partamasiris junto con el resto de los pretorianos.

Todos los armenios y partos habían abandonado el *praetorium*.

Trajano se sentó en la *sella curulis*.

Lucio Quieto entró de nuevo en la tienda.

De pronto se empezó a oír un clamor por todas partes. Decenas de miles de legionarios gritaban una sola palabra al unísono. Hasta los muros de Elegeia parecieron estremecerse.

—*Imperator, imperator, imperator!*

Marco Ulpio Trajano era, una vez más, aclamado como emperador por sus tropas.

—Es momento de que aprovechemos toda esta euforia para hacer efectiva la conquista de Armenia —dijo el César—. Veamos, hablo de memoria, pero si me dejo algo, me corregís: Brutio Praesens, con una legión, acudirá a las montañas del Ponto; la IV Scythica, que será la que dejaremos en Armenia hasta que la región sea segura, avanzará hasta el océano Hircanio[50] para comprobar que no hay oposición ni peligro desde esa zona. Otra legión quiero que vaya hasta los pasos de las grandes montañas del norte, mientras Lucio Quieto irá con la caballería y tantas cohortes como necesite al lago Van, donde

50. El océano Hircanio era el actual mar Caspio.

sabemos que están la mayor parte de los que se nos pueden resistir. El resto de las legiones permanecerán aquí dispuestas a acudir en ayuda del que más lo necesite. Quiero Armenia asegurada y sometida de forma efectiva antes del invierno.

Todos saludaron al emperador y salieron de la tienda.

—Lucio, espera —dijo Trajano cuando Quieto iba a abandonar el *praetorium*—. Me consta que los guerreros más rebeldes están en la zona que te he asignado. Te he dejado lo más difícil.

—Cualquier otro encargo me habría defraudado, César.

Trajano sonrió.

—No te pongas en peligro de forma innecesaria.

—No, César.

Quieto dio media vuelta y salió.

En la tienda sólo estaban Fédimo y el emperador. Aulo y otros pretorianos vigilaban rodeando el *praetorium* por el exterior.

—Deja esa diadema, Fédimo y prepárate para que te dicte una carta.

El secretario obedeció y al instante estuvo dispuesto.

—A Osroes, señor de Partia —empezó Trajano evitando utilizar los títulos de rey de reyes, *Šāhān Šāh* o *basileús basiléon*—. La muerte de Partamasiris, hermano tuyo, ha sido un lamentable incidente que yo he intentado evitar a toda costa.

Aquí el joven secretario dejó de escribir y miró al emperador.

—Continúa, Fédimo, continúa tomando nota.

—Sí, César. Perdón.

—Parece ser que Partamasiris intentó huir de la escolta que lo conducía de regreso a Partia y alguno de mis pretorianos se excedió en su celo hiriéndolo mortalmente. Siento lo sucedido y espero que esto no sea inconveniente para que podamos consolidar la situación actual, en la que Armenia pasa a formar parte de los dominios de Roma. —Trajano se detuvo un momento antes de seguir hablando—. Firmado por Marco Ulpio Trajano, *Imperator Caesar Augustus et cetera*. Que salga hoy mismo un mensajero con la carta hasta el Éufrates y que la lleve por barco hasta Zeugma. Allí que se entregue la carta a alguno de los barcos de mercaderes que van hacia el sur. No quiero que ningún legionario o pretoriano pague la posible ira de Osroes por ser mensajero de estas noticias.

Justo en ese instante, el jefe del pretorio, con la espada envainada pero goteando sangre, entró en el *praetorium*.

—Está hecho, César. Ha implorado por su vida como un niño, llorando.

—Cobarde hasta el final —comentó Trajano. Se levantó y, personalmente, se sirvió un vaso de vino y sirvió otro que ofreció a Liviano.

—Gracias, augusto.

—Bueno, la... digamos, confusa muerte de Partamasiris tras una negociación se parece mucho a la también confusa muerte de Craso tras su parlamento con Surena hace ciento setenta y siete años. Roma es, en ocasiones, algo lenta, pero al final siempre reescribe la historia. Da gran placer tener la última palabra en algo que pasó hace tanto tiempo. Imagino que ahora —añadió Trajano mirando el vino de su copa—, Osroes empezará a entender que esto va en serio, que yo no soy Craso y que mis legiones no son la legión perdida.

55

EL CÓNCLAVE SECRETO

Roma, 114 d. C.

Se reunieron en una pequeña *domus* de una de las regiones periféricas de la ciudad de Roma. Estaban sentados en el atrio y corría el aire. Marción estaba a un lado y el obispo Alejandro, muy mayor y quizá enfermo, en el otro extremo, flanqueado por Sixto, también mayor pero más fuerte y a quien todos consideraban el sucesor de Alejandro, y por Telesforo, de origen griego, más joven y menos ortodoxo en sus ideas. Marción confiaba en este último para que alguien de aquella tríada recibiera con más apertura de miras su plan para preservar y extender la fuerza del cristianismo. No había nadie más con ellos. Era un cónclave secreto donde se iba a debatir sobre ideas que quizá nunca deberían desarrollarse. Fuera había un pequeño grupo de fieles cristianos apostados en la calle, frente a la puerta de entrada de la *domus*, charlando de mercaderes y viajes, como si fueran vecinos del barrio departiendo con sosiego en medio del día. Realmente vigilaban.

—Lo mejor será que nos digas lo que tengas que decirnos con rapidez —empezó el obispo Alejandro en el interior de la casa—. La política ambigua de Trajano, si bien ha detenido la brutalidad sin control contra los cristianos, ha dejado que todo dependa mucho de la interpretación que hace cada gobernador o cada mandatario romano. Y Trajano y su tolerancia se encuentran ahora lejos de Roma, en Oriente, precisamente de donde tú vienes. He pedido a Sixto, mi brazo derecho, y a Telesforo, hombre de fina intuición y que sigue el camino marcado por Cristo con ejemplaridad para todos, que me acompañen para escucharte.

Marción se aclaró la garganta.

—Se trata de preservar a Cristo —dijo el mercader llegado de Asia.

—Eso ya me lo ha explicado por carta Ignacio —respondió Alejandro con dificultad; le costaba hablar y miró a su derecha.

—Ignacio ya nos explicó por carta —continuó Sixto con más decisión y fuerza en su voz— que te preocupa sobre todo el hecho de que todos los discípulos de Jesús han muerto y que por tanto temes que se pierda su mensaje. Nosotros compartimos esa preocupación, pero para eso precisamente estamos nosotros, los que seguimos a Jesús y luego a Pedro. Ignacio nos advertía de que, más allá de la Iglesia, tú propones un plan adicional para preservar ese mensaje. Te escuchamos, pero ve al grano.

Marción asintió y se lanzó a explicar su plan con precisión pero sin extenderse en detalles. Sabía que entre obispos de Cristo era fácil perderse en minucias absurdas y no llegar nunca a nada concreto.

—Mi teoría es sencilla: los judíos llevan años, siglos, preservando sus creencias pese a haber estado esclavizados o subyugados por diferentes imperios, desde el Egipto de los faraones hasta el Imperio romano. Yo creo que parte de la clave de la supervivencia de su credo es que además de la fe y la tradición oral, poseen textos escritos sagrados y eso les da una fuerza más allá de cualquier profeta, de cualquier apóstol o de cualquier obispo, porque siempre tienen algo escrito, algo que pueden leerse unos a otros de un siglo a otro y así preservar su mensaje.

—Nosotros también aceptamos algunos de los textos judíos —apuntó Telesforo—, como la Biblia de los setenta...

—Pero ése es otro error —lo interrumpió Marción con vehemencia—. Perdón, pero esto es importante. —Los tres lo miraban atentos, con incredulidad Alejandro, con desprecio Sixto y con curiosidad Telesforo—. Ése es el segundo problema que tenemos: ¿somos judíos o somos cristianos? —Marción levantó la mano para que no le respondieran aún—. Evidentemente que no somos lo mismo que los judíos, pero el hecho de que compartamos esa Biblia y otros escritos con ellos nos debilita, confunde a los propios seguidores de Cristo. De hecho, la mayoría de los romanos no distingue demasiado entre ser judío o cristiano. Y yo digo que en eso quizá tengan algo de razón los romanos. Hemos de diferenciarnos de los judíos, pero aprender de ellos: necesitamos nuestro propio libro sagrado, nuestro propio texto que nos una a Dios a través del mensaje de Cristo.

—¿Otra Biblia? —preguntó Alejandro en un esfuerzo genuino por entender pese a sus dudas al personaje que tenía enfrente.

—Algo parecido, pero un libro centrado sólo en Jesús, en su vida.

—Tenemos la palabra de Jesús de Juan, de Marcos, de Lucas y de muchos más de sus discípulos —apuntó Telesforo de forma conciliadora. Había mucha tensión en aquel encuentro.

—Son demasiados textos. Nadie ha dicho cuál es la versión más fiel al mensaje de Cristo y quizá debiéramos decidirlo —argumentó Marción.

—A veces, la verdad sobre una persona, o sobre Dios, o sobre Jesús en este caso —expuso Telesforo con serenidad—, es poliédrica, sujeta a más de una perspectiva, y tener los relatos de más de un discípulo ayuda a comprender mejor lo que Jesús nos quiso decir cuando estuvo entre nosotros.

Alejandro y Sixto asintieron.

Marción suspiró. Se pasó la mano por la cara, luego por el cogote mientras agachaba la cabeza.

—Aun así —continuó el mercader de Asia—, la complejidad de un mensaje, sus múltiples caras, dificulta que llegue al mayor número de gente. Si queremos que el cristianismo sea la creencia de todos, del mayor número posible, el mensaje ha de ser recogido en palabras simples y de una sola forma. Necesitamos que se decida qué versión es la válida, recopilar los textos que creemos más acertados y divulgar entonces la palabra de Jesús sólo con ellos.

—Sabemos que prefieres la versión de Lucas sobre la vida de Cristo —apuntó entonces Sixto, que había investigado mucho sobre Marción antes de aquella reunión—, pero incluso usando sólo esa versión, omites los capítulos que hacen referencia a la natividad de Jesús. ¿Sigues a los gnósticos y dudas del nacimiento de Cristo? Eso nos perturba, como nos incomoda tu proximidad a esos supuestos filósofos o a los anticristos de los docetas. Y, además, no hace mucho negaste ser cristiano ante el gobernador de Bitinia para salvar tu vida.

—Otros antes que yo pecaron, desde Pedro hasta Pablo, y luego retomaron el camino de Cristo —dijo Marción para preparar su defensa; había esperado ese ataque en algún momento y había llegado—. Yo he pecado, y mi alejamiento de Jesús no ha sido menor y hago penitencia por ello. He estado distribuyendo la mayor parte de las riquezas de mis negocios por todas las comunidades de Asia, siempre atendiendo a los cristianos que más dificultades pasaban. He obrado mal pero me he esforzado en hacer mucho bien desde entonces. Ya lo hice antes y lo vuelvo a hacer ahora, pero no soy perfecto.

—No has respondido al asunto de si aceptas o no la natividad de Cristo como humano —interpuso Alejandro con su fino hilo de voz, pero no por ello dejaron de resonar sus palabras en aquel pequeño atrio.

—Si empezamos a debatir sobre puntos concretos del mensaje de Cristo y sobre su vida no damos respuesta a la cuestión que yo veo más urgente ahora: crear nuestro propio libro —opuso Marción sin responder al asunto planteado sobre el nacimiento de Jesús.

—Las evasivas no te ayudarán en este cónclave —le dijo Sixto.

—El tiempo y la indecisión corre contra nosotros —insistió Marción.

Se hizo un silencio.

—Quizá sea relevante decidir sobre el asunto de un libro sagrado —dijo, al fin, Telesforo, como mediando entre sus colegas y el mercader llegado desde el otro extremo del Imperio—, pero no es menos cierto que tu pasado, Marción, nos incomoda y que lo que propones, si bien a todas luces es interesante, me atrevería a decir que incluso estimulante, es un paso muy grande para la Iglesia que no debemos dar sin meditarlo bien y sin recurrir al consejo de quien sintió las manos de Cristo sobre sus sienes.

—¿Sugieres consultar a Ignacio? —preguntó Alejandro.

—Así es.

—¡Pero si Ignacio me envió a vosotros para que decidieseis! —exclamó Marción, levantándose de su asiento y casi volcando la silla al alzarse con cierta violencia. Sus tres oponentes, eso sentía que eran aquellos hombres, lo miraron con gesto de desaprobación—. Lo siento —dijo—, pero yo entendí que todo se decidiría aquí y ahora.

—Ignacio te envió a nosotros para que te escucháramos en persona —añadió el obispo de Roma con su débil voz—, pero una decisión tan audaz como la creación de un libro sagrado de los cristianos, un libro único, por lo que he entendido, requiere el consejo de los que más saben y, si es posible, de los que más cerca han estado de Cristo. La propuesta de Telesforo me parece buena: transmitiremos... continúa tú... me cuestan... tantas palabras... —Y volvió a mirar a su derecha.

—Enviaremos una carta —dijo Sixto retomando el discurso de Alejandro e intentando interpretar el sentir del obispo de Roma—. En ella explicaremos a Ignacio la magnitud del plan que propones y nuestras propias impresiones, la de cada uno de nosotros con relación al mismo. He de decirte que yo, personalmente, no lo veo con buenos ojos en absoluto, pero estoy dispuesto a escuchar a Ignacio e incluso a cambiar de parecer si éste nos habla apoyando tu propuesta. Ahora mismo, como el propio Ignacio nos dijo en su momento, no sé si eres un enviado de Dios o de Satanás. Quizá él haya tenido más tiempo y más clarividencia para discernir la respuesta que debe darse a tu idea de un libro sagrado de los cristianos.

El cónclave se terminó.

Alejandro primero, y luego Sixto y Telesforo abandonaron aquel atrio.

Marción se quedó solo mirando al suelo.

No entendían nada.

En medio de aquellas columnas, negó varias veces con la cabeza.

Él no pensaba esperar.

56

LA CONQUISTA DE ARMENIA

Invierno de 114-115 d. C.

Senado de Roma

—Bien, entonces leeré lo que se ha votado y decidido enviar al César en Oriente. —El senador Palma se aclaró la garganta antes de leer el papiro que sostenía en las manos con la declaración del Senado que se acababa de aprobar—: A Marco Ulpio Trajano, *Imperator Caesar Augustus*: el Senado y el pueblo de Roma aclaman al César como vencedor en su campaña de castigo contra los partos en Armenia, se congratulan enormemente por la anexión de Armenia como nueva provincia del Imperio romano y nombran, por segunda vez, al emperador como *Optimus*, el mejor de los gobernantes posibles.

Hubo aplausos por todas las bancadas, aunque ni a Palma ni a Celso se les escaparon algunos rostros sombríos, como los de Julio Urso Serviano, cuñado de Adriano, o Cayo Fusco Salinator, hijo político del anterior.

—Los que disienten y temen el desenlace final del conjunto de la campaña de Oriente del César no se atreven a hablar —comentó Celso—, pero al más mínimo error abrirán la boca y lanzarán sus críticas. No lo dudes.

—Seguramente, amigo, pero para eso estamos tú y yo aquí: para que eso no pase y con las noticias que van llegando de Oriente, el emperador nos ha impuesto una tarea muy sencilla —concluyó Palma con optimismo.

Celso asintió, pero sin sonreír. Intuía maquinaciones en las sombras del poder, pero no podía identificar a nadie en concreto. Le incomodaba en particular el silencio de Serviano.

Éste y Adriano habían tenido diferencias en el pasado, por el aparente apoyo de Trajano a su sobrino segundo. Quizá esas diferencias persistieran entre ambos. Eso sería lo mejor porque Serviano era un senador de Barcino veterano y muy respetado en Roma. También muy hábil. Sí, los enemigos del César estaban muy callados en Roma. Quizá hubiera otros, también en silencio, fuera de Roma, en otro lugar del Imperio.

Cirene, norte de África

El veterano senador Pompeyo Colega leía una carta enviada por Atiano, el antiguo tutor del sobrino segundo del César. Parecía que Adriano seguía interesado en saber si se podía contar con él, igual que con Salvio Liberal en Chipre y con otros amigos senadores en Roma, que veían con cierta aprensión el alejamiento de un tercio de la fuerza militar romana que Trajano se había llevado más allá del Éufrates.

Pompeyo Colega no consideró que la respuesta a esa carta debiera ser dictada a los oídos de ningún secretario y él mismo se sentó frente a su escritorio en el *tablinum* de su residencia como gobernador de Cirene, y se aprestó a escribir una respuesta que pudiera ser del agrado de Atiano y de su señor Adriano. Pompeyo Colega redactó la carta con un rictus serio en el rostro. Hacía tiempo que no sonreía, pero quien ríe el último ríe mejor y él era un hombre paciente.

Montañas del lago Van, Armenia

Cubierto por pieles, con barba de varios días, el casco bien ajustado y la espada desenvainada y aún con sangre del enemigo corriendo por el filo, Lucio Quieto parecía más un oso de las montañas que un alto oficial romano. Había descabalgado y lo mismo habían hecho sus hombres de confianza. Tras dos meses de lucha encarnizada con los últimos armenios que se resistían al poder de Roma en su reino, por fin habían alcanzado el lago Van.

Lucio Quieto pasó por encima de varios cadáveres de guerreros enemigos abatidos por flechas de los arqueros romanos o ensartados por los *pila* de su caballería y caminó hasta la orilla misma del lago. Hacía mucho frío y le sorprendía que, pese a lo gélido de aquel invierno y las montañas nevadas, el lago, sin embargo, no estaba congelado como habría sido de esperar en aquellas circunstancias.

Se arrodilló, hundió la mano en el agua fría y se la llevó a la boca.

—¡Agh! —exclamó y la escupió—. Está salada —dijo y se levantó. Él no lo entendía, pero por eso no se congelaba—. Alejad los caballos del lago y que los lleven a beber al río que hemos cruzado antes. Si las bestias o los hombres beben del lago enfermarán.

Las órdenes de Quieto se transmitieron con rapidez.

—Ya no quedan enemigos que abatir —dijo uno de los oficiales.

—No, aquí no —confirmó Lucio Quieto—. Envía un jinete a Artaxata con este mensaje para el emperador: Armenia está completamente conquistada.

—Sí, mi *legatus* —respondió el oficial mientras veía cómo Lucio Quieto retornaba sobre sus pasos, pasando de nuevo por encima de los cadáveres del enemigo destruido para volver a montar en su caballo. Todos contemplaban a Quieto no ya como el jefe de la caballería de Roma, sino como el oficial más valiente y eficaz del emperador. Todos en la campaña de Oriente hablaban de Quieto como el hombre llamado a suceder a Trajano.

Palacio real de Artaxata, Armenia

Trajano leyó la carta de Lucio Quieto personalmente. Ni siquiera Fédimo las abría. Todo lo que el brazo derecho del emperador enviaba llegaba a las manos del César directamente. El emperador miró a su joven secretario.

—Lucio ha sometido los últimos centros de resistencia, Fédimo: Armenia es nuestra de forma absoluta.

—El *legatus* Quieto siempre cumple con eficacia las órdenes del César —respondió el secretario.

—Así es —confirmó el emperador y se levantó para asomarse por una de las ventanas desde las que veía las murallas y hasta parte del foso de la ciudad de Artaxata, que también se había rendido sin luchar y eso que las fortificaciones eran extraordinarias. Eran increíbles los muros que el temor podía levantar sin ni siquiera desenvainar una espada. Murallas enormes construidas por el gran Aníbal.

—Sigue leyendo el pasaje de la *Vida de Lúculo* que escribió Plutarco, Fédimo —dijo el emperador.

—¿Donde explica la fundación de esta ciudad?

—Exacto —respondió Trajano sin dejar de mirar por la ventana.

El secretario se aprestó a leer.

—*Se dice que el cartaginés Aníbal, después de que Antíoco fuera derrotado por los romanos, lo dejó y fue ante el rey Artaxias de Armenia, a quien hizo sugerencias excelentes. Por ejemplo, como observó que una sección del país que disponía de una magnífica situación natural estaba sin uso y abandonada, planeó construir allí una ciudad, y llevó entonces a Artaxias a aquel lugar y le mostró sus posibilidades, y le conminó a ordenar aquella construcción. El rey estaba encantado y rogó a Aníbal que fuera él mismo quien supervisara los trabajos, de todo lo cual emergió una hermosa ciudad llamada a partir del propio rey Artaxias como Artaxata, que sería proclamada capital de Armenia.*[51]

Y Fédimo calló.

Trajano hizo un gesto con la mano y el secretario comprendió que el emperador quería estar a solas y meditar. El joven se levantó y dejó al César solo en su cámara.

Trajano escudriñaba el horizonte de Armenia desde el alféizar de aquella ventana en lo alto de la colina en la que se levantaba el palacio donde tantos reyes antes que él habían vivido. Aníbal diseño la ciudad. ¿Sería él, Marco Ulpio Trajano, capaz de hazañas similares a las del cartaginés? Conquistar Artaxata y Armenia entera era algo meritorio, pero el propio

51. De la *Vida de Lúculo* (31, 3-4) de Plutarco.

428

Lúculo había conseguido rendirla en tiempos de Julio César y Pompeyo y Craso... siempre Craso. Luego el *legatus* Corbulón, de quien tanto había aprendido el padre de Trajano, también la atacó y la destruyó en gran parte. Nerón envió luego mucho dinero para reconstruir Artaxata. El César inspiró profundamente: no, entrar en Armenia era importante, pero no cambiaría el mundo. Lo que revolucionaría todo sería mantener los territorios de forma permanente. Transformarlos en provincias romanas, como había hecho con la Dacia primero y luego con Arabia. Ése era el plan, el objetivo, el sueño.

Trajano bebió algo del vino que tenía en la copa. Casi siempre llevaba una en la mano. Quieto había rendido a los guerreros del lago Van, y el resto de los *legati* habían asegurado los límites de Armenia en el norte y el este. ¿Qué hacer ahora?

Empezó a nevar.

Trajano negó en silencio con la cabeza: moverse con aquel clima helado no era buena idea. Ése fue uno de los graves errores de Marco Antonio en su campaña de Oriente: trasladar sus tropas en pleno invierno armenio. No. Él no haría eso. El ejército se quedaría allí mismo, unido, seguro y bien abastecido de víveres y agua. La primavera próxima se lanzaría hacia el sur, hacia Mesopotamia, pero sin alejarse del río Éufrates para mantener bien sus líneas de aprovisionamiento y para disponer de agua y no repetir el error de Craso de adentrarse en el desierto. Trajano asintió para sí mismo: aprender del pasado para construir un nuevo futuro. Echó un trago de su copa de vino. Y con Lucio Quieto como su brazo armado implacable. No podrían detenerlos.

En lo que no quiso pensar Trajano fue en lo que le había dicho Plutarco en Atenas sobre su muerte en aquella campaña. No tenía sentido pensar en lo inexorable. Dejó de mirar por la ventana y cerró los ojos concentrado en sus planes de conquista.

57

EL ATAQUE PIRATA

Costas de Azania, 114-115 d. C.

En el puerto de Raphta, tal y como había anunciado en repetidas ocasiones Titianus, encontraron, en efecto, mucho marfil y a un precio tan barato que con el poco dinero que tenían junto con el incienso y el copal, consiguieron llenar la falúa de alargados cuernos de elefante y rinoceronte hasta que la embarcación no podía aguantar más sin hundirse.

—Tapadlo —dijo el mercader a Arrio.

Todos entendieron que era un intento por ocultar el preciado oro blanco que transportaban de miradas indiscretas, ahora que iniciaban el regreso hacia el norte a lo largo de aquella infinita costa.

No habían pasado ni dos días de navegación cuando incluso antes de llegar de vuelta al puerto de Nicon, un gran barco pirata apareció desde detrás de una de las pequeñas islas que había en aquella remota esquina del mundo.

—Son ellos, ¿verdad? —preguntó Arrio.

—Sí —confirmó Tamura, que era, de largo, la que mejor vista tenía de todos.

—Nos han seguido —añadió Alana.

—Cuanto más al sur atacan, menos testigos hay de lo que hacen —explicó Titianus—. Luego llevarán el marfil ellos mismos más al norte y lo revenderán.

El barco pirata había aparecido a su espalda, por el sur, pero parecía ganarles terreno rápidamente.

—La falúa es demasiado lenta y vamos demasiado cargados —dijo Arrio con cierta desesperación—. Hay que prepararse para luchar.

Titianus miraba con inquietud hacia el barco que se aproximaba.

—Podemos amenazarlos con arrojar la carga al mar —dijo el mercader—. Eso quizá los detenga, al menos un día, mientras piensan qué hacer.

—¿Sabes acaso su lengua? —indagó Alana.

—No son negros como los nativos que vimos pescando —dijo Tamura, que ahora que el barco estaba más próximo, podía distinguir a los piratas mejor aún que cuando los vieron atacando a los pescadores nativos de las playas del norte.

—Son árabes —concretó Titianus—. Y trabajan para los mercaderes de Muza, en el interior de la mar Eritrea, a miles de estadios de aquí.

—¿De Muza? —Arrio no daba crédito a lo que oía.

—Claro —confirmó Titianus—, ¿por qué van a pagarnos este marfil a precio de oro en Muza si pueden conseguir que sus piratas nos lo arrebaten aquí, lejos de todos? ¿Crees acaso que van a dejar a alguno de nosotros con vida para contarlo?

—Aquí vendría bien un Pompeyo —dijo Tamura para sorpresa de todos, en particular de Titianus. Ése fue el momento en el que el mercader se percató de que la que consideraba hasta aquel momento una jovencísima guerrera, muy brava pero inculta, tenía secretos extraños en su educación.

—Sí, sin duda, pequeña —aceptó Titianus—. Un Pompeyo el Grande con su gran flota de *trirremes* romanos, que acabó con los piratas de Cilicia y de todo el Mediterráneo en tiempos de César y Craso, sería algo muy bueno en estas costas, pero la larga mano de Roma nunca ha llegado hasta aquí. Estamos solos.

—Y esta charla no nos ayuda nada —añadió Arrio que, impotente, observaba cómo el barco pirata estaba cada vez más y más cerca.

—Hemos de luchar —dijo Áyax, contundente, desenvainando su espada. La media docena de marinos romanos lo imitaron. Titianus negaba con la cabeza.

—Es mejor intentar negociar —insistió el mercader, pero Áyax y los marinos romanos no estaban por la labor. Arrio se concentraba en el pilotaje de la pequeña nave en un fútil intento por optimizar al máximo las capacidades de la misma, pero iban demasiado cargados y la galera pirata se aproximaba hacia ellos inexorablemente. Tamura no sabía qué hacer, pero había cogido su arco y tomado una flecha y se aprestaba a apuntar hacia el barco enemigo. Alana fue la única que reparó en que Marcio no estaba con ellos, sino que había ido a la parte de proa. En ese momento, la guerrera sármata lo vio reaparecer portando un cubo con grasa en una mano y una lucerna encendida en la otra.

—Hay un hueco entre el marfil en proa donde hace menos viento —le dijo Marcio dando una explicación que Alana aún no entendía—. Así he podido encender más rápidamente la lucerna con el pedernal y la punta de acero.

El veterano *lanista* le dio un beso al pasar a su lado, pero de inmediato la dejó y fue junto a la joven Tamura.

—Dame la flecha —le dijo su padre.

La muchacha se mostró confusa y tardó en reaccionar.

—¡Por Némesis, niña, dame esa maldita flecha! —le espetó Marcio algo airado.

—Dásela —dijo Alana con voz más dulce, situándose detrás de su esposo y poniendo la mano sobre su hombro para intentar tranquilizarlo.

Tamura le entregó el dardo. Su padre lo cogió y hundió su punta en la grasa negra, de forma que cuando la extrajo llevaba un montón adherida a la punta. Luego acercó ese extremo de la flecha a la llama de la lucerna y el dardo prendió con rapidez.

—Toma —le dijo Marcio ahora a la joven.

Tamura no necesitó que se le explicara lo que debía hacer. Cogió la flecha que ardía en su punta y la situó en el arco. Apuntó hacia el barco y la lanzó con su destreza habitual. Sin embargo, para sorpresa de todos menos de Alana, por primera vez en aquel viaje, por primera vez en mucho tiempo, la joven Tamura erró en su objetivo, y eso que el blanco, un gran *trirreme*, era bien grande y estaba próximo. La flecha cayó al agua antes de llegar al barco pirata, se hundió velozmente y su furia en llamas se apagó al tiempo que desaparecía la última esperanza de los viajeros de la falúa.

Tamura miró a sus padres aún más confundida, impotente.

—Con la grasa y la llama, la punta pesa más —le explicó Alana—. Has de disparar más alto para alcanzar un objetivo que está más bajo.

—Sí, madre —aceptó la niña. Entretanto, Marcio ya tenía otra flecha en llamas preparada.

Tamura repitió la operación: situó la flecha en el arco y apuntó, esta vez algo más alto.

—Más arriba aún —dijo Marcio—. Has de darle a las velas.

—Sí, padre —dijo ella.

Arrio, Titianus, Áyax y los marinos romanos asistían a aquel cónclave familiar de guerreras sármatas y padre gladiador entre atónitos y esperanzados. Era increíble ver con qué frialdad aquella familia se aprestaba no ya a defenderse sino a atacar a la enorme embarcación pirata que se les echaba encima. No tenían como acompañantes en aquel viaje a gente normal.

—¿Qué es eso? —preguntó Áyax.

Se oía un murmullo extraño que llevaba el viento del mar desde donde estaba el barco pirata.

—Son carcajadas —aclaró Arrio—. Se ríen de nosotros.

Tamura disparó.

La flecha voló en una larga parábola surcando el espacio que había entre la pequeña falúa cargada de marfil y el *trirreme* enemigo. La vela principal era un blanco grande y estaban ya a menos de doscientos pasos. El dardo cayó del cielo con rapidez y acertó en un lateral del velamen mayor.

—Más —insistió Marcio y le dio otra flecha prendida a su hija.

Tamura disparó de nuevo.

Ahora dio en la segunda vela. La primera flecha había prendido ya y el fuego empezaba a consumir la gran tela blanca.

—Otra —dijo Marcio.

Arrio, Áyax, Titianus, Alana y el resto contenían la respiración mientras padre e hija seguían con la operación de prender flechas y de lanzarlas sobre el bajel enemigo.

Las velas del barco pirata estaban ya completamente en llamas.

Se hizo el silencio en el mar.

—Ya no se ríen —dijo Titianus a la vez que presenciaba los lanzamientos de Tamura, asistida por su padre, impresionado por el ingenio de Marcio y la pericia de su hija. Hasta aquel momento no había entendido muy bien por qué Trajano había seleccionado a aquel hombre y a su curiosa familia para aquel viaje, pero estaba claro que eran gente de recursos.

—Sin velas pierden velocidad —dijo Arrio.

—Sí, incluso ya ni reman —añadió Áyax—.Todos parecen ocupados en apagar el fuego.

Los piratas se esforzaban en subir cubos de agua del mar con cuerdas y los echaban sobre los mástiles para evitar que las llamas de las velas pudieran incendiar el resto de la embarcación. Estaban ahora luchando por su propia supervivencia.

En la falúa todos esperaban que el fuego de las velas fuera el fin del *trirreme* enemigo, pero los árabes mercenarios de Muza que lo comandaban tampoco eran gente falta de arrestos y consiguieron controlar el incendio. Sólo habían perdido las velas.

—¡A los remos! —gritaron los jefes piratas al resto de sus hombres.

Y remaron.

En la falúa las sonrisas y la sensación de victoria duraron poco tiempo.

—¡Vuelven a ganar velocidad! —exclamó Arrio, una vez más contrariado—. ¡Aun sin velas son muchos remos contra nuestra poca velocidad!

Nadie dijo nada. Todos miraron a Marcio con la esperanza de que el veterano *lanista* tuviera quizá alguna otra estratagema con la que afrontar el peligro que, de nuevo, se cernía sobre ellos.

—Creo que esta vez sí tendremos que luchar —dijo al fin Marcio para desesperación de todos.

Miraron entonces a Titianus.

—Ya no se puede negociar —dijo el viejo mercader—. Les hemos destrozado las velas y les hemos herido en su orgullo. Ya no sólo quieren el marfil: anhelan venganza.

Áyax volvió a desenfundar su espada y ahora lo imitaron todos, incluidos Alana y Marcio.

El barco pirata volvía a estrechar la distancia que los separaba de él y se les aproximaba cada vez más.

—Aún nos queda una posibilidad —dijo entonces Arrio y señaló hacia la costa.

—¿Vas a fondear? —preguntó Marcio inquieto, que no veía de qué forma podía eso serles de utilidad: los piratas harían lo mismo y los cazarían en tierra firme como habían visto unas semanas atrás que lo hacían con los nativos pescadores de Azania.

—Nadie va a fondear —aclaró Arrio mientras cambiaba el curso de la navegación de la pequeña falúa—. Al menos, no nosotros.

Titianus frunció el ceño. El mercader empezaba a intuir lo que tramaba el capitán.

—Arrio quiere navegar lo más próximo a la costa que pueda nuestra falúa, ¿no es así? —indagó Titianus.

Arrio asintió.

—El *trirreme* tiene un calado superior al nuestro —añadió el capitán—. Veremos si pueden seguirnos.

—Si fueran inteligentes, en lugar de acercarse a la playa tras nosotros deberían navegar en paralelo, rebasarnos e interponerse en nuestra ruta por delante —dijo Titianus.

Arrio pilotaba la falúa. El resto miraba hacia el barco pirata.

El *trirreme* enemigo viró siguiendo la estela que dejaba la pequeña embarcación llena de marfil. Los corsarios de Muza parecían estar demasiado obcecados en llegar a la pequeña nave lo antes posible. Estaban cegados por la rabia y el orgullo herido. Quizá pensaron que podrían hacerlo antes de que las aguas fueran demasiado poco profundas.

—¡Se ve el fondo! —exclamó uno de los marinos romanos que observaba aquellas aguas transparentes como el cristal—. ¡No más de cuatro o cinco pies!

Arrio sabía que no podía acercarse más, pues estaban cargados al máximo, pero tenía que arriesgarse para que el *trirreme* se confiara.

Se oyó un crujido en la parte inferior de la falúa.

Arrio viró ligeramente, un poco, para alejarse de la costa.

—¿Hay vías de agua? —preguntó el capitán.

Todos miraban por todas partes. Nadie vio nada. Todos sudaban profusamente y no era por el sol.

De pronto oyeron un crujido mucho mayor, enorme, brutal, pero provenía de atrás, de muy atrás; llegó hasta ellos desde la embarcación pirata. Luego oyeron los gritos de rabia: el *trirreme* había embarrancado por acercarse demasiado a la costa.

—Su odio los ha cegado —sentenció Titianus.

Arrio se alejó entonces un poco más de la costa y siguió navegando hacia el norte sin detenerse en lugar alguno durante cientos y cientos de estadios.

El viejo mercader, sentado en popa, vio cómo el navío pirata quedaba atrás, como una terrible pesadilla que nunca hubiera existido. Miró entonces hacia los tripulantes de la falúa: Áyax y los marinos romanos habían acabado con los traidores pretorianos; Marcio, Alana y Tamura habían contribuido de forma esencial, junto con la habilidad de Arrio, para escapar de los piratas. Y él, bueno, había ideado el plan del marfil de Raphta. Ahora obtendrían el dinero suficiente para reemprender la marcha hacia Oriente. Trajano había seleccionado bien a los integrantes de aquella locura. Le había sorprendido, en particular, la jovencísima guerrera sármata. La vio en una esquina de la falúa, leyendo uno de sus libros, casi en secreto, como si no quisiera que nadie supiera lo que hacía.

El barco seguía navegando suavemente hacia el norte.

Cayó la noche.

Tamura se levantó y se sentó junto a una de las lucernas que su padre mantenía encendidas. Por si acaso.

Tamura, en efecto, leía ahora a escondidas.

No quería que Áyax la viera con esos códices que él despreciaba, pero había decidido no arrojarlos. En un mundo tan extraño, lejos de todo y de todos, siempre a punto de morir, aquellos libros que le regaló su viejo tutor la acompañaban.

La lucerna proyectaba una luz temblorosa pero suficiente.

En el otro extremo de la embarcación, Alana se acercó a Marcio y lo abrazó por la espalda.

—Hoy has estado bien —dijo ella.

—¿Hoy? —preguntó él con un tono de fingida molestia—. Yo siempre estoy bien.

Ella sonrió sin dejar de abrazarlo.

—¿Quieres seguir estando bien ahora conmigo?

Marcio, lentamente, se volvió sin deshacer el abrazo de Alana y la besó en la boca.

En el otro lado de la falúa, oculta por la montaña de marfil, Tamura releía el final de la *Vida de Craso*. Pero el relato no aclaraba qué fue de los diez mil prisioneros romanos de aquella legión perdida. Dión Coceyo le dijo que Plinio el Viejo y otros sabios romanos decían que quizá fueron llevados a la lejana Merv, una fortaleza al oriente del Imperio parto.

Tamura miró hacia el este.

Sólo se veía un gran manto oscuro: el océano y el misterio del pasado, del presente, del futuro.

¿Estaba todo conectado?

La joven cerró el códice y lo guardó en su pequeño saco.

Se apoyó en la barandilla de la falúa.

¿Sería cierto que los diez mil fueron llevados a esa lejana ciudad de Merv? ¿Averiguaría ella alguna vez el final de la historia de la legión perdida?

HISTORIA DE LA LEGIÓN PERDIDA

Tiempos de Julio César, Pompeyo y Craso,
mediados del siglo I a. C.

Libro IV

58

MERV

Extremo oriental del Imperio parto, Asia central
44 a. C.

—Pásame el agua —dijo Druso.

—Sí, centurión —respondió el legionario y le entregó el odre medio vacío.

El oficial de Cartago Nova bebió poco. Los partos escatimaban en los suministros que les daban para aquellas misiones de reconocimiento en el fin del mundo, que era como se referían a las regiones limítrofes de su imperio. Más allá de Merv estaban los reinos de Margiana, Fergana y Sogdiana, razonablemente autosuficientes, algunos decían que hasta ricos, por la ruta de la seda que provenía de la remota Xeres.

—Esta vez ha habido suerte, centurión —dijo el veterano Sexto. Allí todos eran ya muy veteranos. Llevaban casi nueve años combatiendo en aquella frontera. Sexto seguía esgrimiendo con torpeza el escudo en combate, pues nunca se había recuperado del todo de la flecha recibida en la campaña de Carrhae, pero era tan valiente como el que más y junto con Cayo eran los dos hombres de confianza del centurión Druso en aquella región perdida en el centro de Asia, obligada a vigilar la frontera oriental de los partos.

—Regresemos, por Júpiter —dijo Druso y echó a andar.

—¡Vamos allá! —aullaron al unísono Sexto y Cayo, y varios miles de legionarios se pusieron en marcha.

Druso tenía callos en los pies, como casi todos en sus tropas. Los partos sabían lo que se hacían: les daban alimento y bebida, pero siempre muy justa, en especial cuando salían de patrulla. Con los pocos suministros que les proporcionaban no podían alejarse mucho de Merv sin quedar a merced de la naturaleza o de los enemigos.

Druso repasaba en su mente todo lo vivido en los últimos años, desde la derrota de Carrhae hasta su actual situación como tropas semiesclavas al servicio de los partos. No era una revisión nostálgica, sino un intento por ponderarlo todo, por valorar hasta qué punto sus hombres serían capaces de seguirlo en el plan que había ideado las últimas semanas. Para empezar Cayo, Sexto y él fueron obligados a ver cómo Craso terminaba con la cabeza cortada y usada en una representación teatral para deleite de armenios y partos. Luego los llevaron de regreso junto al grueso de los prisioneros y se les obligó a cruzar a pie todo el Imperio parto en pocas semanas, en la marcha más larga y más penosa que Druso había hecho en su vida. Los legionarios caían muertos, ya fuera por enfermedad o por agotamiento, a decenas primero, luego a centenares, a miles. De los diez mil que habían iniciado aquella marcha obligada por sus captores, sólo llegaron seis mil a Merv. A los partos les daba igual lo que les pasara. Cuando llegaron a la ciudad del extremo oriental de su imperio, Druso lo comprendió: primero se les obligó a trabajar en las canteras y allí lo único que interesaba eran hombres fuertes, resistentes, capaces de picar piedra durante horas bajo un sol inclemente, así que la gran marcha sirvió para seleccionar a los mejores de la legión perdida.

De las canteras fueron conducidos a la mismísima Merv para que realizaran los trabajos más duros de la construcción de los muros de aquella ciudad. Unas murallas imponentes. A Druso le quedó claro que los partos temían mucho a alguien en aquella región para levantar semejante fortificación.

—Es por los hunos —le explicó un prisionero griego a Druso una mañana en la que coincidieron en la construcción de la muralla norte de la ciudad.

Ésa fue la primera vez que Druso oyó hablar de los hunos.

—Son los guerreros más terribles del mundo —le explicó aquel esclavo griego—. Asolan los reinos de Fergana, Sogdiana y Margiana; atacan a los wusun, que son vasallos de los han de Xeres. Incluso atacan el gran Imperio han. Llevan siglos en guerra con ellos y no se rinden nunca. Por eso estas murallas, romano, y por eso os han traído aquí. Os van a obligar a luchar contra ellos. Entiendo algo de parto y he oído cómo hablaban sobre el asunto varios oficiales de Merv.

Y así fue: terminadas las fortificaciones, los partos, para sorpresa de los legionarios, les dieron instrucciones sorprendentes:

—Avanzaréis diez millas hacia Oriente y acamparéis allí. Desde la ciudad os veremos, desde lo alto de las murallas. Se os entregarán regularmente agua y víveres y os daremos armas: lanzas y escudos. Nada de flechas. Si viene el enemigo defenderéis la ciudad. Si lo hacéis de forma eficaz se os premiará con más comida y agua. Si huis, cuando terminemos nosotros con los hunos os buscaremos y os daremos a todos la peor de las muertes.

Druso organizó el campamento. No quedaban tribunos entre la legión perdida y Druso era el centurión de mayor rango. No se les permitía levantar una empalizada, pues los partos temían que se hicieran fuertes en algún altozano próximo, de modo que el centurión ordenó que varias patrullas se adentraran más aún hacia Margiana para poder detectar el avance de cualquier guerrero enemigo y así evitar ataques por sorpresa.

Pasaron varios meses de aquella forma y no había actividad de combate relevante, así que Druso obligó a las tropas a hacer marchas rápidas por la zona para mantenerse en forma y a practicar el combate cuerpo a cuerpo y las formaciones de ataque y defensa, como la *testudo*. Tampoco podía forzar a sus hombres a una actividad física demoledora porque los suministros de víveres y agua siempre eran escasos y no podía agotarlos si no tenía alimento y líquido suficiente para que recuperaran sus fuerzas.

Un amanecer llegaron varios jinetes de una *turma* al galope.

—¡Son millares, centurión! —dijo el decurión al mando de aquella unidad.

No pudo decir mucho más porque la tierra empezó a temblar bajo sus pies.

Druso echó al suelo la poca comida que le quedaba en el cuenco que tenía en la mano y cogió su espada y su *pilum*. Se alegró de haber insistido y de haber conseguido espadas para la mayoría de sus hombres. Los partos habían entendido que sin ellas los legionarios, una vez arrojados los *pila*, estarían desarmados ante el enemigo y, por tanto, no valdrían de nada como soldados.

—¡Todos en *testudo*! —gritó Druso mientras se ajustaba su casco.

Seis mil legionarios formaron un largo muro de escudos impenetrable a diez millas de las murallas de Merv.

Los partos lo observaban todo desde lo alto de los muros. Veían la gran polvareda de la caballería de los hunos aproximándose hacia la ciudad y la formación compacta de los romanos.

—No resistirán ni la primera acometida —decía un oficial parto a otro.

—No, por Zoroastro. Son hombres muertos. Tendremos que luchar nosotros —respondió otro.

En la llanura frente a Merv, Druso sentía el movimiento de la tierra bajo la palma de su mano derecha, que tenía apoyada en el suelo. Sudaba, como todos sus hombres. Ahora comprobarían si lo que habían ensayado serviría de algo.

Druso miraba por un resquicio entre su escudo y el del legionario que estaba a su derecha. La caballería enemiga estaba a quinientos pasos, a cuatrocientos, a trescientos cincuenta. Se oyó un zumbido inmenso.

—¡Aguantad! ¡Aguantad, por Hércules! —gritó Druso—. ¡Escudos en alto!

Las flechas enemigas cayeron brutalmente sobre los legionarios. Muchos fueron heridos, pero no tantos como cuando los partos habían lanzado sus mortales dardos en Carrhae. Los arcos hunos no eran tan fuertes y sus flechas, si bien causaron bajas, no terminaron de descomponer la formación romana.

Estaban ya a trescientos pasos y avanzando al galope. Doscientos cincuenta. Doscientos.

—¡Preparad *pila*! —aulló Druso.

—¡Preparad *pila*! ¡Preparad *pila*! —repitieron Sexto y Cayo y todos los oficiales de la larga formación romana.

Ciento cincuenta pasos.

Todos los legionarios contenían la respiración. El suelo vibraba. Se oía a los caballos del enemigo relinchando.

A cien pasos.

—¡Ahora! ¡Ahora! —exclamó Druso.

Y cinco mil *pila* volaron por el cielo.

Centenares de jinetes de la caballería huna cayeron abatidos, pero el resto aún seguía avanzando.

—¡Pasillos! ¡Ahora! —ordenó el centurión de Cartago Nova en medio de las llanura de Asia central.

La estrategia era tan sencilla como genial, la misma que Escipión había usado en Zama. Al abrir pasillos, los caballos, que de natural no desean pisar a nadie, se dirigieron hacia los espacios que los romanos dejaban libres. En cuanto los hunos penetraron esos pasillos, Druso dio la nueva orden.

—¡Atacad! ¡Contra los hunos, contra los caballos! ¡Por Marte!

Los legionarios herían a los guerreros de las estepas del norte de Asia en las piernas, en el costado si alcanzaban, y cuando llegar a los jinetes resultaba muy penoso simplemente hundían sus espadas en los vientres de los animales. Los caballos malheridos se ponían a dos patas o coceaban bestialmente y descabalgaban con su furia a muchos hunos que, una vez que daban con sus huesos en el suelo, eran aniquilados por los romanos, quienes luchaban a la desesperada.

Al cabo de un breve pero feroz combate, los jefes hunos dieron la orden de retirada. La carga de la caballería enemiga había sido rechazada. Los legionarios aclamaron a Druso como si de un auténtico *imperator* se tratara, pero la felicidad del centurión de Cartago Nova y de sus oficiales apenas duró unos instantes. En cuanto empezaron a contar cadáveres pudieron comprobar que habían perdido varios centenares de legionarios, mientras que apenas habían conseguido dar muerte a unos doscientos hunos.

—Volverán —dijo Druso entonces—. Y ahora ya no podremos sorprenderlos.

Y la escena se repitió en numerosas ocasiones. Los hunos parecían disponer de tropas sin fin, sin embargo los legionarios de Druso no tenían reemplazos que sustituyeran a los caídos. Tras largo tiempo vigilando la frontera de Merv, ya sólo quedaban tres mil romanos listos para el combate. Había otros mil heridos o tullidos. El resto había muerto en combate.

Druso repasaba los años pasados en Merv y había concluido que su existencia, la suya y la de todos sus hombres, era sólo una lenta y prolongada agonía encaminada a la aniquilación, defendiendo una frontera que no era la suya y luchando por unos amos, los partos, que los despreciaban y apenas les daban lo mínimo para subsistir penosamente.

—Esta vez ha habido suerte —repitió Sexto, ya que en la última incursión realizada hacia Margiana los hunos habían rehuido el combate. De hecho llevaban dos meses en los que apenas atacaban. Y era extraño.

—Están en guerra civil —dijo Druso a Sexto y Cayo.

—¿Guerra civil? —preguntaron los dos a la vez.

—He hablado con un prisionero de Sogdiana —se explicó el centurión sin dejar de caminar hacia el campamento de las afueras de Merv—. Lo interrogué como hago siempre y tuve la fortuna de que sabía griego; un artesano apresado por los hunos que había salvado la vida al forjarles armas de acero; parecía buen herrero. Me contó lo que está pasando más allá de la frontera: los hunos se han dividido en dos bandos. Por un lado está Huhanye y por otro Zhizhi. Los dos se han declarado como *chanyu* o jefe de todo su pueblo. *Chanyu* es como ellos mismos o los de Xeres llaman a sus líderes. Lo esencial es que parece que son dos hermanos enfrentados mortalmente: Huhanye ha conseguido la ayuda del Imperio han, pues les ha prometido vasallaje o algo parecido. Zhizhi, su contrincante, es el más violento y terrible, según decía el herrero de Sogdiana apresado. Todos lo temen: los han de Xeres, los partos, los habitantes de Margiana, Sogdiana y Fergana y hasta muchos hunos que se han pasado al bando de Huhanye. Pero pese a estar solo, Zhizhi se ha quedado con los guerreros más brutales y se ha apropiado de gran parte de Sogdiana y Margiana. No nos ataca ahora porque está ocupado luchando contra su hermano, pero si gana lo único que podemos esperar es que se acuerde de nosotros y venga con todo lo que tiene. El sogdiano, que ha estado entre los hunos de Zhizhi, dice que su líder está preparando un ataque a gran escala contra Partia para apoderarse de Merv. Y ya os podéis imaginar quiénes seremos los primeros en morir.

Druso dejó de hablar. Cayo y Sexto no dijeron nada en un rato largo.

Llegaron al campamento y los legionarios se distribuyeron entre sus tiendas para descansar y comer el rancho del atardecer. No había vino. Los partos sólo les daban algo después de un combate victorioso, pero sin lucha no había recompensa alguna.

Cayo se acercó a Druso, que oteaba el horizonte de Oriente en la puesta del sol.

—No eres hombre de hablar mucho ni de dar largas explicaciones —dijo Cayo—, así que si nos has contado todo esto es por algo.

Druso asintió y volvió a hablarles sin dejar de mirar hacia el este, con el sol moribundo a sus espaldas.

—No pienso quedarme en Merv y morir defendiendo esta maldita ciudad de los partos.

Cayo y Sexto se miraron.

—Incluso si conseguimos huir, no podremos cruzar Partia —se atrevió a decir al fin Sexto—. Los partos nos matarían si nos revolviésemos contra ellos e intentáramos cruzar su territorio. Son centenares de millas...

—Unas mil quinientas, quizá más —lo interrumpió Druso mirando hacia la noche de Oriente—. Todo eso ya lo he pensado. Ya perdimos cuatro mil hombres cuando cruzamos Partia como prisioneros. Si lo intentamos como enemigos, como dices, no llegaremos ni uno vivo más allá del Tigris. El Éufrates ni lo avistaremos. No, ésa es una empresa tan suicida como permanecer aquí. Pero yo no he dicho nada de cruzar Partia.

Silencio.

Las estrellas iluminaron el cielo negro sobre sus cabezas.

—¿Entonces? —preguntó Sexto.

Druso no dijo nada, sino que señaló hacia el este.

—Ése es el único camino que los partos no tienen controlado —apostilló el centurión. Ante la mirada de sorpresa de sus oficiales, se explicó con más detalle: tenía que convencer-los; con el apoyo de Cayo y Sexto podría conseguir que muchos más legionarios lo siguieran en aquella locura—: Mi plan es abandonar una noche este maldito campamento y no volver a ver las murallas de Merv. Nos adentraremos en Margiana y buscaremos a los hunos. Zhizhi, el más violento, es el que nos interesa. Dicen que está loco, pero el sogdiano me aseguró que este líder de los hunos está buscando mercenarios para combatir contra su hermano entre los habitantes de los reinos vecinos. Si nos presentamos ante él es muy posible que nos acepte en su ejército. Hay guerra en Oriente y nosotros somos guerreros. Hemos luchado contra los partos, contra los propios hunos y, antes de esta pesadilla, muchos de nosotros combatimos contra germanos, britanos, galos y no sé cuántos bárbaros más. Si hay algo que llevamos en la sangre es luchar. Hemos sobrevivido a derrotas brutales y nos hemos sobrepuesto a todo. Zhizhi nos ha visto combatir y detener varias cargas de su caballería en campo abierto. No dudará en alistarnos en su ejército. Nuestros servicios serán bienvenidos por un líder huno que está en guerra y necesita hombres. Nos ofreceremos a luchar a su lado a cambio de ser tratados como mercenarios a sueldo, libres y no como esclavos. Quizá nunca regresemos a Roma, eso es algo que veo imposible, pero no estoy dispuesto a vivir como esclavo de los partos. Éste es mi plan.

Druso calló y exhaló un largo suspiro. Ya lo había contado todo. Ahora sólo quedaba ver cómo respondían sus hombres de mayor confianza a aquella propuesta de locos.

—A mí me parece bien —susurró Sexto, confundiendo su voz con el silbido del viento de la noche.

—A mí también —dijo Cayo con voz algo más decidida—. Estoy harto de luchar para esos miserables partos. Aunque lo más probable es que nos maten los hunos de ese Zhizhi o sus enemigos si éste nos acepta como mercenarios. Pero, como dice el centurión, prefiero morir luchando como un legionario libre.

Druso no pudo evitar sonreír en las sombras de la noche ante el arrojo de sus oficiales.

—Seguramente, Cayo —confirmó el centurión—, nos matarán unos u otros, pero nos llevaremos por delante a tantos como podamos.

Y se quedó mirando hacia el este. Lo que no dijo Druso era que para llegar hasta el líder de los hunos había que salvar un gran obstáculo natural: el río Oxo. Pero un líder sabe hasta dónde puede desvelar de la cruda realidad a sus hombres. Cada cosa en su momento.

HISTORIA DE TRAJANO

Principios del siglo II d.C.

LIBRO IV

MESOPOTAMIA

59

LA DOBLE COLUMNA

Artaxata, Armenia
Abril de 115 d. C.

«Ríos, ríos, ríos —pensaba Trajano—. La clave son siempre los ríos.» En la Dacia lo fue el Danubio, allí la clave estaba en el control del Éufrates y el Tigris.

El emperador había reunido a sus mejores hombres. No lo había hecho en su residencia de la capital de Armenia, sino en el *praetorium* de campaña de las legiones apostadas frente a sus murallas. Todos los allí presentes tenían claro que el emperador no estaba de paseo por Oriente, sino en guerra.

—¡Cierra! —dijo Trajano a Aulo. El tribuno corrió las cortinas de la tienda. En el interior estaban el César, Lucio Quieto, Nigrino y Liviano. También Fédimo, como siempre en una esquina.

—Trae esos planos —le dijo Trajano a su secretario— y ponlos en la mesa.

Fédimo desplegó un par de papiros que, unidos adecuadamente, conformaban un plano de toda Mesopotamia.

—Veamos —empezó Trajano con brillo en los ojos—. Os voy a explicar cómo vamos a hacer esto y cuáles son los objetivos para la campaña de este año. Acercaos. Trae otra lucerna, Fédimo. Bien. Así mejor. Mirad, estamos aquí, al norte de Armenia. Hemos asegurado este reino, gracias en gran medida al duro invierno que ha pasado Lucio en las montañas, donde ha acabado con la resistencia —y miró a Quieto con agradecimiento; el norteafricano se limitó a llevarse el puño al pecho—. Bien. Pero esto es sólo el principio de algo mucho más grande. Una posibilidad para invadir Mesopotamia es aden-

453

trarse por uno de sus dos grandes ríos, el Éufrates o el Tigris. De hecho, lo más lógico sería que descendiéramos por el Éufrates, pues dominamos su ribera occidental y es una fuente segura de abastecimiento de agua y de suministros para las legiones, pero este plan tiene un grave riesgo. —Aquí se detuvo y miró a sus hombres; ninguno parecía intuir el peligro—. Si descendemos por el Éufrates, los partos, con mucha probabilidad, no opondrán resistencia sino que nos dejarán avanzar. ¿Por qué? —Volvió a mirar a sus hombres pero ninguno parecía tener respuesta a la pregunta—. Ya veo que calláis. El caso es que no sé si yo habría tenido en cuenta el peligro del que os voy a hablar si no hubiera tenido a mi disposición esta información. —Miró a Fédimo, que rápidamente puso sobre la mesa, junto a los mapas, un papiro con anotaciones—. Son de Julio César —aclaró Trajano ante los boquiabiertos Nigrino y Liviano; Quieto, que ya sabía de la existencia de aquel documento, pues Trajano le había descubierto casi todos sus secretos, no se asombró tanto, pero estaba igual de interesado que el resto en saber cuál era el peligro de descender sólo por el Éufrates. Trajano continuó hablando—. Es un papiro encontrado por Suetonio hace años, cuando le pedí que reorganizara las bibliotecas de Roma. Augusto ordenó esconder algunos escritos de Julio César junto con diferentes poemas que no vienen al caso, porque en ellos había planes de conquista más allá del Danubio o del Éufrates. Augusto nunca pensó que se debieran cruzar esos ríos, pero como veis yo soy de otro parecer. Ya lo hicimos todos juntos en la Dacia y ya tuve allí en consideración ideas de Julio César; de la misma forma pienso tener muy presentes sus planes para operar más allá del Éufrates, especialmente en Mesopotamia. Esta vez Roma no avanza hacia Oriente de la mano de un inútil como Craso, sino siguiendo ideas de Julio César que estoy dispuesto a ejecutar hasta las últimas consecuencias. La Vestal Máxima ha custodiado este papiro durante años, hasta que he decidido recuperarlo para poner en marcha lo que aquí se propone.[52] Los partos

52. Para saber más sobre cómo encuentra Trajano ese documento, ver la novela *Circo Máximo*.

no saben con quién se enfrentan esta vez. —Y sonrió, pero rápidamente desdibujó su sonrisa y se puso, de nuevo, muy serio—. Pero al asunto: el avance hacia Mesopotamia. El caso es que es evidente, pero el afán de conquista nos puede cegar a todos: si descendemos sólo por un río, el Éufrates, los partos pueden ascender con su ejército por el Tigris y luego atacarnos por la retaguardia. ¿Cuál es la solución que propone Julio César y que habría ejecutado si no lo hubieran apuñalado en las *idus*[53] de marzo?

—¿Avanzar por los dos ríos a la vez? —apuntó Quieto con dudas.

—Exacto, muy bien, Lucio —confirmó Trajano ilusionado al ver que su mejor hombre estaba bien centrado en la estrategia—. Eso es lo que propone Julio César aquí, en estas notas. Ya hemos cruzado el Danubio con éxito y ahora le toca al Éufrates.

—¿Y el Rin? —preguntó Nigrino, encendido por las conquistas en ciernes.

Trajano sonrió.

—Todo a su debido tiempo —respondió el César—. Esto del Éufrates aún nos va a llevar un tiempo, concentrémonos en lo que tenemos entre manos. Pero me gusta tu espíritu, Nigrino. Veamos: sí, la cuestión es dividir nuestras fuerzas en dos mitades. Una parte del ejército comandada por mí descenderá por el Éufrates con el objetivo de subyugar a ese impertinente de Sporaces, el rey de Anthemusia.

—¿El que se declaró neutral? —preguntó Liviano.

—El mismo —ratificó Trajano—. Hemos de hacerle ver con nitidez que no hay neutralidad posible. Pero Anthemusia es un bocado pequeño. Este ejército ha de ocuparse de Anthemusia y Osroene. Anthemusia no debe de ser muy difícil, pero Osroene es un reino importante. Esta primavera comprobaremos si la supuesta alianza con Roma del rey Abgaro y de su hijo Arbandes es real o ficticia.

—Eso es lo que hará la mitad de nuestras tropas, ¿y el resto de las legiones? —inquirió Quieto, que ya intuía su misión.

53. *Idus* es femenino en latín.

—La otra parte del ejército, bajo tu mando, Lucio, avanzará hacia el sur desde Artaxata, pasará por las montañas que has asegurado este invierno y someterá a los Mardi para de inmediato ir al objetivo principal.

—Adiabene —dijo el norteafricano, señalando el reino más importante de Mesopotamia nororiental.

—Eso es, por Júpiter. Lo más importante —y aquí Trajano hizo una pausa en la que inspiró mucho aire—, lo más difícil será cruzar el Tigris, pero has de hacerlo. Necesitamos hombres a ambos lados del Éufrates, pero también a ambos lados del Tigris. Sólo así podremos lanzarnos con seguridad hacia el sur de Mesopotamia, hacia el corazón del Imperio parto, hacia Cesifonte. Sólo atacaré su capital si tengo la retaguardia y esos dos ríos controlados. Entonces sí, entonces Partia entera será nuestra. —Miró a Quieto fijamente—. ¿Podrás cruzar el Tigris, amigo mío?

—Lo cruzaré, augusto, o moriré en el empeño.

Palacio real de Cesifonte, Partia
Abril de 115 d. C.

—¿Y bien? —preguntó Mitrídates a su hermano, el *Šāhān Šāh*.

—¿Y bien qué? —respondió Osroes devolviendo la interrogante con otra.

—¡Por Ahura Mazda y Zoroastro! ¡Eres el rey de reyes! —gritó Mitrídates poniéndose en pie y haciendo aspavientos—. ¡El emperador romano ha matado a Partamasiris, que, aunque no lo tuviéramos en gran estima personal, era nuestro hermano! ¡Y no hemos hecho nada! ¡Ese maldito Trajano ha declarado la anexión de toda Armenia, toda, al Imperio romano! ¡Y no hemos hecho nada! ¿Hasta cuándo vas a permanecer en esa actitud? Vologases sigue proponiéndose como rey de reyes en el este y cada vez más consejeros y *magi* empiezan a considerar que un cambio de *Šāhān Šāh* puede ser lo que Partia necesite para detener al emperador romano en su voracidad sin límites! ¿Y me preguntas «y bien qué»?

Osroes sabía que todo lo que su hermano decía era cierto.

—Ni tú ni yo ni nadie esperábamos que el César romano se atreviera a matar a Partamasiris y mucho menos a anexionarse Armenia.

—Eso es verdad, pero lo ha hecho. Hemos de actuar.

—Hemos de actuar —confirmó Osroes—. Tengo un plan para detenerlo. Trajano no va a conseguir lo que se propone.

—¿Y cuál es tu plan? —inquirió Mitrídates sentándose junto a su hermano.

El *basileús basiléon* se inclinó hacia adelante para explicarse.

—Trajano ha dividido su ejército en dos columnas. Una desciende por el Éufrates y la otra avanza hacia el Tigris.

—Lo quiere todo —sentenció Mitrídates.

—Vamos a demostrarle que ha abierto demasiado la boca: la loba romana va a atragantarse este verano, pero primero dejaremos que antes engulla algunos pedazos de carne para que se confíe.

Osroes explicó a su hermano su estrategia.

Y Mitrídates, después de escucharlo atentamente, sonrió.

En las proximidades de Batnae
Reino de Anthemusia, Mesopotamia noroccidental
Junio de 115 d. C.

Dos meses después de haber explicado el plan de ataque a sus más altos oficiales, Trajano se sacudía el polvo de más de doscientas millas. Habían ido de Artaxata a Elegeia y luego a Satala y de ahí de regreso al Éufrates para abastecerse de agua. Los víveres y suministros de guerra llegaron a las tropas en Metilene, primero, y a continuación en Samosata, en un continuo avance sin oposición hacia el sur. Llegaron por el río hasta Zeugma y abandonaron entonces el cauce de agua en el mismo punto y siguiendo la misma ruta de Craso 168 años antes, sólo que con una pequeña gran diferencia: toda Armenia al norte estaba ahora conquistada y anexionada al Imperio romano, con lo que no había que preocuparse por esa región que ya no existía como reino independiente. Eso les daba seguridad a todos, al propio Trajano y a sus miles de legionarios, para superar, o al menos adormecer, el síndrome de la legión perdida. ¿Lo conseguiría? El emperador estaba convencido de que sí.

Llegaron a Batnae, capital del pequeño reino de Anthemusia, sede del trono de Sporaces, uno de los reyes que se había declarado neutral en el conflicto entre Partia y Roma y que había enviado una embajada a Trajano a Antioquía el año anterior para expresar su neutralidad.

—Apenas hay murallas —dijo Nigrino.

—Batnae es una ciudad comercial —comentó Trajano oteando el horizonte, donde se vislumbraba la población—. Una parada en la ruta de la seda hacia Xeres. Comerciantes y artesanos: eso es lo que tiene Batnae. No es una ciudad guerrera, nunca lo ha sido. Por eso Craso no pudo refugiarse en ella cuando huía de Carrhae. Por eso ahora tampoco podrán defenderla bien contra nosotros.

—A no ser que Osroes haya enviado refuerzos a Sporaces —apuntó Nigrino.

—Sí —aceptó Trajano—, pero eso sólo lo averiguaremos de una manera.

Y ordenó el avance de dos legiones contra las murallas.

El César se quedó pensativo mientras sus legionarios atacaban la ciudad con furia. ¿Dónde pensaba Osroes plantarle cara? Armenia había sido casi un paseo militar excepto por la campaña que Lucio tuvo que luchar bravamente en las montañas del lago Van. Los armenios podrían haber resistido más si el que se consideraba rey de reyes les hubiera enviado tropas, pero Osroes había decidido no luchar el año pasado. ¿Pensaba hacerlo ahora? ¿En dónde? ¿Allí en Batnae, en Anthemusia? ¿En Osroene? Si fuera en Osroene, el pacto de su rey Abgaro y los abrazos de su hijo Arbandes se probarían falsos. ¿O sería en Adiabene adonde Osroes enviaría sus tropas, allí adonde había enviado a Lucio Quieto a cruzar el Tigris?

—Están entrando ya en la ciudad —dijo Nigrino.

Y así era.

—No parece que Sporaces haya recibido refuerzos de Partia —comentó Trajano.

En pocas horas la ciudad de Batnae estaba rendida, rodeada por las legiones de Trajano y aseguradas todas sus calles por miles de legionarios armados hasta los dientes. Los comerciantes y los artesanos estaban aterrados, pero cuando vieron que no había pillaje empezaron a tranquilizarse e incluso a aclamar al emperador romano en su entrada triunfal en la ciudad. Los combates se habían reducido a los enfrentamientos de las murallas próximas a las puertas de la ciudad. Las legiones apenas habían sufrido bajas y Trajano había ordenado que no hubiera saqueos. Pensaba concentrar toda su rabia en una sola persona.

Sporaces estaba arrodillado al pie de su trono cuando Trajano entró en su palacio. A ambos lados del rey de Anthemusia había pretorianos con espadas desenvainadas.

Trajano se sentó en el trono. Para no tener el título de rey de reyes, se estaba sentando en muchos tronos últimamente. No era una silla muy grande. Tampoco se trataba de un reino muy poderoso, pero sí rico.

—Apenas ha habido resistencia, mi señor —dijo Sporaces en griego.

—Es tarde para las palabras —le respondió Trajano—. Tuviste la oportunidad de aliarte a Roma el año pasado; otros así lo hicieron enviando mensajeros a tal efecto cuando yo estaba en Antioquía. Ahora, Sporaces, no estás en condiciones de decir nada. Te equivocaste.

—Yo no sabía que el César venía a quedarse —se atrevió a decir el rey de Anthemusia arrodillado ante Trajano; la desesperación era la que le hacía hablar—. Otras veces han venido los romanos y luego se han marchado, y éramos nosotros, los reyes de Anthemusia, de Osroene o de Adiabene, los que nos quedábamos para recibir la ira del rey parto si colaborábamos con vuestro imperio. Si yo hubiera sabido que la intención del César era la de quedarse en Oriente no me habría declarado neutral. El emperador de Roma puede estar seguro de que Anthemusia será un reino leal a Roma.

—¿Un reino? —se preguntó Trajano apoyando su espalda cómodamente en el trono—. No. Hay demasiados reinos, demasiados tronos en esta parte del mundo. Anthemusia es incluso pequeño para una provincia romana. Si acaso un distrito de una provincia romana. Te lo repito, Sporaces: es tarde para palabras. —Se agachó para dirigirse al monarca humillado—. Un rey de verdad debe intuir cuándo está cambiando la historia, cuándo van a ocurrir cosas que no han pasado nunca antes. Los que no saben ver esos cambios no son reyes: son esclavos de su miedo y el miedo, Sporaces, cuando no se sabe dominar, siempre conduce a la muerte.

Trajano volvió a reclinarse en el trono y miró a Liviano. El jefe del pretorio, acostumbrado ya a terminar con su espada lo que las legiones empezaban con los *pila*, hizo un gesto a Aulo y entre el tribuno y otro pretoriano sacaron a rastras al rey Sporaces de su palacio mientras no dejaba de gritar y patalear como un cerdo conducido al sacrificio.

—Esto ha sido fácil —dijo Nigrino.

—Demasiado fácil —confirmó Trajano meditabundo y arrugando el ceño. ¿Dónde estaban los partos? ¿Dónde pensaba Osroes intentar detener su avance? ¿Cómo le iría a Lucio en el Tigris?

60

UN NUEVO BARCO

Costeando la mar Eritrea
Abril de 115 d. C.

Llegar a Muza en la pequeña falúa cargada hasta los topes de marfil costó más de lo que habían imaginado. Tenían que detenerse en prácticamente cualquier población que veían para abastecerse de agua y comida, pues el marfil ocupaba todo el espacio dedicado a la carga y eso no les permitía almacenar suficientes víveres y agua para una navegación más continuada sin tocar tierra. Además cualquier nube que amenazara lluvia, según Arrio, aconsejaba acercarse a la costa aún más y refugiarse al abrigo de la primera bahía que encontraran.

A Titianus todo este retraso parecía ponerlo muy nervioso, algo que llamó poderosamente la atención de Marcio, pues no era habitual que el viejo mercader se sintiera incómodo. El veterano exgladiador sólo había visto al mercader tan preocupado tras la pérdida del barco en el incendio de Mundus.

—¿Qué te preocupa? —le preguntó Marcio un atardecer en el que el resto había desembarcado para aprovisionarse y él se había quedado con el mercader para vigilar la preciosa mercancía, siempre tapada con mantas para evitar las miradas de los curiosos que pudieran acercarse a la playa. O las de otros barcos con los que se cruzaban que muy bien podían ser más piratas viajando de incógnito hacia el sur, hacia Azania, camuflando sus auténticos objetivos con una aparente actividad de barcos mercantes.

Al principio Titianus no dijo nada, pero luego miró al que fuera *lanista* y le habló con sinceridad.

—Sospecho.

—¿De qué o de quién? —continuó preguntando Marcio.

—Verás: voy a ser plenamente sincero contigo, pues el emperador parecía tenerte en mucha estima y se supone que tú eres el principal encargado de la seguridad en este viaje de locos —empezó a explicarse el viejo—. Estoy preocupado porque vamos muy lentos. Ya tendríamos que estar en Muza y aún nos faltan semanas.

—Según Arrio hemos de extremar el cuidado en la navegación hacia Muza o podemos perder la mercancía en cualquier tormenta.

—Sí, eso dice —aceptó Titianus—, y también es cierto que el marfil no deja sitio para muchos víveres, pero aun así estoy incómodo: cada semana que pasa, es una semana del viento de Hippalus[54] que perdemos.

—¿Qué es el viento de Hippalus? —preguntó Marcio.

—Durante los meses de estío, en las costas en las que navegamos el viento sopla con fuerza hacia Oriente y eso hace posible que con un barco de buenas velas se pueda cruzar el gran océano que nos separa de la India, pero a partir de octubre, el viento de Hippalus cambia y sopla durante todo el invierno en dirección contraria, hacia el oeste, de forma que es imposible navegar contra él. Si no conseguimos llegar pronto a Muza y adquirir con rapidez un nuevo barco con grandes velas, no podremos salir en dirección a la India hasta de aquí un año, hasta el próximo verano. Eso es lo que me preocupa.

Marcio asintió.

—Ya —dijo entonces el antiguo preparador de gladiadores—, pero además sospechas. —De pronto, tuvo una intuición muy fuerte—. ¿Crees acaso que Arrio está ralentizando la navegación para provocar ese nuevo retraso?

—Eso me temo —admitió el mercader—. No puedo evitar la sensación de que alguien de los que estamos en esta misión sigue intentando obstaculizarla, pero no tengo pruebas de nada contra nadie.

54. No está confirmado, pero parece ser que el navegante griego Hippalus fue uno de los primeros en descubrir el funcionamiento del viento monzón y su importancia para la navegación.

—Yo también tengo esa sensación —dijo Marcio—. Vayamos eliminando sospechosos y aceptemos que ni tú ni yo estamos interesados en detener el viaje —Marcio miró al mercader y éste cabeceó afirmativamente como si aceptara aquel punto de partida—; bien, entonces te puedo asegurar que ni mi mujer Alana ni mi hija Tamura están contra nosotros. Supongo que eso lo puedes aceptar tú también. Ya viste cómo luchamos contra los piratas, en especial Tamura.

—Sí, eso ya lo he pensado.

—Nos quedan Áyax, Arrio y sus marineros —continuó Marcio—. Áyax es callado, pero fue quien descubrió la traición de los pretorianos.

—Eso también lo he pensado —apostilló Titianus, que veía cómo el antiguo gladiador estaba llegando a su misma conclusión.

—Eso sólo nos deja a Arrio y sus marineros —dijo Marcio poniendo palabras a lo que Titianus pensaba—. Por eso crees que retrasa nuestra llegada a Muza.

—Sí, eso pienso, pero, por otro lado, no podemos prescindir de él sin disponer de otro piloto. Como navegante, más allá de su exceso de celo con la falúa y el marfil, ha sido un buen capitán hasta la fecha, pero... Ya llegan. —Señaló a la comitiva con Áyax al frente, Tamura y Alana detrás, y Arrio y sus hombres cerrando el grupo, que regresaban a la embarcación con comida y agua.

Marcio se acercó al mercader y le habló al oído.

—Lo estaré observando. —Y miró hacia Arrio.

Muza, mayo de 115 d. C.

Llegaron al puerto de Muza, el gran mercado de la mar Eritrea, el punto de confluencia de las riquezas de Petra por tierra y de las extravagancias y lujos del más lejano Oriente transportados por mar desde la India o desde Xeres: telas púrpura refinadas y otras más burdas, túnicas cosidas al estilo árabe, diferentes vinos, trigo, azafrán, muselinas, mantas exuberantes, otras muy sencillas, vasos de cobre, de plata, de oro, mirra, alabastro, caballos, mulas. Todo se podía encontrar en Muza. Incluso barcos para cruzar el mundo conocido y adentrarse en el desconocido.

Hasta allí llegaron, al fin, Titianus, Marcio, Alana, Tamura, Áyax, Arrio y su media docena de marineros con el marfil. Tal y como había anticipado el viejo mercader, la visión del oro blanco que habían llevado impactó en el mercado de Muza y eso que allí estaban acostumbrados a la llegada de grandes barcos con preciados cargamentos, pero de inmediato corrió la voz de que Titianus estaba dispuesto a ofrecer aquel marfil a muy buen precio, pues lo había adquirido en las lejanas, baratas pero muy peligrosas, costas de Azania.

Todo parecía marchar a pedir de boca hasta que Arrio empezó a poner problemas a la hora de encontrar un barco adecuado para la gran travesía hacia la India: los que no eran demasiado pequeños para ofrecer suficiente seguridad en la gran travesía del océano eran desechados por el capitán romano por demasiado grandes.

—No tenemos bastantes hombres para gobernar este *trirreme* —decía Arrio ante un barco que a todos los demás les parecía impecable.

Titianus y Marcio se miraron, pero no dijeron nada. Titianus optó, en un principio, por no enfrentarse, pero ante la constante negativa de Arrio a aceptar un barco u otro el mercader se encaró, por fin, con el piloto.

—Elígelo tú, pero elígelo pronto —le dijo—, pues las semanas han pasado y el verano se nos termina.

—De acuerdo —aceptó Arrio, pero puso condiciones—. Lo ideal es un barco similar al que teníamos, una *liburna*, pero en cualquier caso tendremos que contratar algunos marineros más. Los barcos pequeños no ofrecen seguridad en el océano y uno como el que necesitamos precisa de más marineros; en todo caso evitaremos un *trirreme* que es demasiado grande y requiere mucha tripulación, como os decía antes.

Titianus se desesperaba. Buscar hombres retrasaría más aún la partida.

—Yo buscaré los marineros —dijo Marcio, que estaba es-

464

cuchando aquella conversación con la misma incomodidad que el viejo mercader.

—¿Y cómo vas a saber tú quién de entre los desharrapados que hay por el puerto de Muza es en verdad buen marino y quién sólo un muerto de hambre que no se mareará nada más nos hagamos a la mar? —le preguntó Arrio con cierto desprecio.

Marcio y Arrio no se habían gustado nunca, pero el antiguo gladiador no quiso añadir más problemas.

—Los buscaremos entre los dos —propuso Marcio.

—Bien —aceptó Arrio.

Titianus suspiró.

El capitán se adentró en el muelle para mirar los nuevos barcos que habían llegado aquel día a Muza en busca de uno que lo satisficiera para la travesía proyectada. Marcio iba a seguirlo, pero Titianus lo cogió del brazo.

—¿A qué viene eso de que quieres seleccionar a los marineros? —le preguntó el mercader en voz baja.

—Cada vez me fío menos de Arrio y temo que contrate miserables que luego se nos rebelen y hagan imposible la travesía —respondió el antiguo *lanista*.

Titianus asintió y soltó el brazo de Marcio.

Los únicos que no parecían inquietos por todo aquel retraso eran Tamura y Áyax. La estancia en Muza les había dado tiempo para estar juntos. En la pequeña falúa no había sitio para hablar sin ser observados por los demás. Tamura percibía que Áyax buscaba con ella mayor intimidad que la de una conversación privada paseando por el puerto o por el mercado de la ciudad, pero, pese a haber matado a sus tres primeros enemigos hacía ya mucho tiempo, tal y como una guerrera sármata debía hacer para poder tener contacto carnal con un hombre, aún tenía miedo a dar ese paso. Áyax, por el momento, parecía esperar, aunque Tamura sabía que el gladiador había acudido en alguna ocasión, desde que llegaron a Muza, a ciertas casas donde las mujeres yacían con hombres por unas monedas. Eso no la preocupaba más allá de que él pudiera perder interés en ella. Lo cierto era que la muchacha estaba hecha un lío. Algún día habían pasado junto a un puesto donde un anciano vendía pergaminos y papiros con textos en griego y otras lenguas que ella no conocía. Le habría encantado detenerse y hojear todo aquello pero iba con Áyax, a quien le seguía ocultando que leía a escondidas los tres libros que le regaló Dión Coceyo, así que pasó de largo sin mirar ningún papiro. Sí, estaba confundida entre querer gustar a aquel gladiador, entre lo que a ella le gustaba de verdad, con lo que sentía por dentro y por unas ansias que parecían arder en su interior, en su cuerpo.

Todos daban la impresión de estar muy ocupados buscando barcos, marinos o provisiones para la gran travesía y no los observaban. Todos menos Alana. La madre de Tamura también sospechaba de Arrio, pero no todo en la vida era aquella misión, y para ella había otros asuntos tanto o más importantes que aquel viaje, así que si Marcio se ocupaba de Arrio, ella vigilaba cada paso que daba su hija con la discreción de una guerrera oculta entre los árboles. No los seguía. No le hacía falta. Bastaba con estar atenta a cómo, día a día, la mirada de su hija cambiaba y cómo crecía ese brillo especial en sus ojos.

Alana se lo comentó un día a Marcio.

—Con alguno tendrá que ser —le respondió él—. Áyax, al menos, ha demostrado ser leal.

Alana no insistió. Los hombres son tan ciegos. Marcio hablaba de lealtad con relación a la misión, pero a ella le preocupaba la lealtad de Áyax con respecto a Tamura. No le preocupaba que el joven gladiador se acostara con otras mujeres. Lo que incomodaba a Alana era que percibía que para Áyax la pasión creciente de Tamura era sólo un desafío, un juego, un pasatiempo. Los hombres, a excepción de algunos como Marcio, vienen y se van. Pero te dejan como te dejan.

Una mañana temprano Alana fue la primera en ir al mercado. No quería compañía. Examinó los puestos con atención. Estaba segura de que en el mercado de Muza, igual que se encontraban productos de Xeres o India, tendría que haber mercancías de algunas regiones de la africana Cirene. Y así fue: vio la planta que buscaba en una esquina del mercado, expuesta junto con otras muchas raíces y hierbas, en un puesto que regentaba una mujer. Era lógico que fuera una mujer. Alana se detuvo y le preguntó en latín.

—¿Tienes *silphium*?

—*Silphion*, sí —respondió la mujer en griego, pero muy claro. Se entendieron—. ¿*Silphion* de Persia?

—No —dijo Alana—. Quiero *silphium* de Cirene.

—Ah. —La mujer sonrió—. Es el mejor, sin duda. Pero muy caro, tanto como comprar plata.

—No importa —respondió Alana. Tras vender el marfil, Titianus había repartido algún dinero entre todos los miembros de la expedición. La mayor parte, por supuesto, se la quedó para financiar la compra del nuevo barco y de víveres, pero dar algo de dinero a todo el mundo, en medio de una ciudad comercial como Muza, levantó los ánimos. Alana nunca pensó que fuera a tener que usar casi todos sus denarios de plata, y los de Marcio, que se los había entregado para que los custodiara, en hacerse con un poco de *silphium*.

Dudó.

En una mano tenía el *silphium* y en la otra la bolsa con las monedas.

Pensó en Áyax.

Pensó en Tamura.

Se decidió y entregó los denarios a la anciana.

—Es muy fuerte —le dijo la vieja—. Si se atreve a usarlo, que tome siempre muy poco. Demasiado puede ser mortal.

61

LA MARCHA DE QUIETO

**Río Tigris en la frontera de Adiabene Mesopotamia nororiental
Mayo de 115 d. C.**

Lucio Quieto ordenó el avance de sus tropas cruzando las montañas del lago Van. La primavera había abierto todos los pasos y la nieve sólo se veía en las cumbres más altas. Los belicosos mardi eran los primeros contra los que tendrían que luchar en la misión que le había asignado Trajano para ese año. Sea porque se vieron solos o porque tenían noticias de la capacidad destructiva de los legionarios y la caballería de Quieto, fueron derrotados con facilidad.

—Luchan sin convicción —dijo uno de los tribunos a Quieto.

El norteafricano bajó de su caballo junto a uno de los pequeños riachuelos que cruzaban en su avance hacia Adiabene y el Tigris y entregó las riendas a un oficial.

—Que beban bien todos los animales y los hombres —dijo el *legatus.*

Se pasó la mano por el cuello sudoroso. Todo marchaba bien. Apenas habían tenido bajas en su enfrentamiento contra los mardi. Si todo continuaba así podría reunirse con Trajano antes incluso de lo previsto.

Pasaron los días y llegaron al gran río: el Tigris, con el deshielo de la nieve de las montañas y las lluvias de primavera, fluía con enorme fuerza. Era ancho, era caudaloso, era veloz. Tumultuoso.

—El río rápido —dijo Quieto entre dientes y como uno de sus tribunos lo miró como si no hubiera entendido bien, el *legatus* se explicó—: eso es lo que dicen que significa su nombre, «el río rápido», al contrario que el tranquilo Éufrates. Viéndolo parece que el nombre tiene sentido. Por aquí es imposible cruzar. Seguiremos hacia el sur.

Tuvieron que avanzar en paralelo al Tigris, por su ribera derecha, durante bastantes millas en busca de un lugar donde poder atravesarlo. El líder norteafricano ordenó que varias *turmae* fueran por delante para prevenir ataques y también para localizar el punto donde el río fuera, por fin, vadeable. Durante el avance se rindieron las ciudades de Thebeta, Singara y hasta la inexpugnable Hatra. Esta última, situada sobre una meseta y con enormes fortificaciones, con un pozo de agua en su centro y bien aprovisionada, podría haber resistido durante meses, pero el *mry*, el gobernador Elkud, decidió rendirla en busca de la magnanimidad de Quieto, algo que consiguió.

Luego cayó Libana.

Todo marchaba bien.

Una tarde, una de las patrullas regresó al galope. El decurión fue directo a ver a Lucio Quieto.

—¿Qué ocurre? —preguntó el *legatus*.

—Hemos encontrado un lugar donde cruzar el río —dijo el oficial de caballería, pero con la voz temblorosa.

—Eso son magníficas noticias —replicó Quieto con entusiasmo, pero ante la extraña actitud del decurión añadió—: ¿hay algún imprevisto?

—Mi *legatus*, todos los partos del mundo están esperándonos en ese punto. Es imposible cruzar.

Lucio Quieto sorbió por la nariz. Los cambios de temperatura de las montañas a los valles lo habían constipado un poco. Se aclaró la garganta y escupió desde lo alto del caballo.

—Lo que es posible o imposible en este ejército, decurión, lo decido yo.

—Sí, *legatus*. Lo siento —respondió el oficial y bajó la cabeza. Cuando la volvió a levantar el jefe de la caballería romana ya no estaba allí, sino galopando hacia el sur en busca de todos los partos del mundo.

Quieto llegó, junto con la vanguardia de su ejército, hasta el lugar avistado por la patrulla de reconocimiento. En efecto, miles de soldados enemigos esperaban al otro lado del Tigris. Estaban armados y formando un campamento de enormes dimensiones.

—¿Hay árabes entre ellos o me lo parece? —preguntó Quieto estirando el cuello en lo alto de su caballo.

—Los hay —confirmó uno de los tribunos.

—Es el ejército completo del rey Mebarsapes de Adiabane —dijo otro.

—Ha venido con todo lo que tiene —aceptó Quieto—. Eso está claro, y además están llegando refuerzos partos.

—Muchos, *legatus* —dijo otro tribuno y se corrigió enseguida—. Bueno, parecen bastantes.

—Tenemos cuatro legiones —dijo Quieto ignorando el último comentario; lo único importante era evaluar correctamente la situación—. ¿Diríais que nos igualan en número?

Se hizo un silencio. No estaba claro. De pronto uno de los decuriones llamó la atención de Quieto señalando hacia el este.

—Con esos que llegan quizá sí, mi *legatus*.

Lucio Quieto miró hacia donde señalaba el oficial y comprobó que una columna de caballería parta se aproximaba para unirse al resto del ejército ya congregado en la ribera izquierda del Tigris. El líder norteafricano se debatía en una tormenta de sentimientos: había prometido a Trajano que cruzaría el Tigris, pero ni él ni el emperador, estaba seguro de ello, habían previsto una concentración de tropas tan potente del enemigo en un único punto. Era como si Osroes hubiera dado la orden de situar todas sus tropas y las de sus aliados para hacer frente sólo a uno de los dos ejércitos romanos. Ante esa estrategia, ¿debía seguir con el mandato de Trajano de cruzar el Tigris como fuera? Quieto dudaba entre cumplir la promesa dada o seguir su intuición militar y contenerse.

—¿Qué vamos a hacer? —preguntó uno de los tribunos.

Quieto volvió a sorber por la nariz. Luego miró a sus oficiales.

—Le prometí al César que cruzaríamos este maldito río. Si los partos han decidido oponer resistencia, peor para ellos.

Pero ante la enorme concentración de tropas enemigas, la

bravura del *legatus* norteafricano no pareció persuadir a todos los oficiales allí reunidos. Y Quieto se dio cuenta. Si atacaba, sería contra el criterio de muchos de los tribunos. Pero una promesa a Trajano no era un compromiso del que uno pudiera desprenderse con facilidad. Ni siquiera cuando el sentido común dicta retractarse.

—Aunque muera en el empeño —susurró Quieto para sí mismo contemplando al enemigo.

62

LA DESCENDENCIA DE SERVIANO

Residencia imperial, Antioquía
Mayo de 115 d. C.

La cabeza del rey Sporaces, expuesta en una mesa en el centro del atrio, parecía mirarlos desde sus cuencas casi vacías con restos de ojos podridos.

Adriano y Plotina se habían quedado solos.

—La ha enviado con Nigrino —dijo el sobrino del César apurando su copa—. Quería asegurarse de que fuera exhibida por las calles de toda Antioquía.

—Es un despojo de guerra, un trofeo de una victoria —dijo Plotina mirando la cabeza desgajada y fétida con curiosidad—. Sporaces no aceptó humillarse ante Trajano y éste ha querido mostrar a todos lo que les ocurre a los que no se le rinden.

—Mostrar a todos... no —contrapuso Adriano—. A mí. Mi tío ha querido hacerme llegar el mensaje claro y nítido sobre cómo es capaz de conseguir los objetivos que se propone. Si hubiera querido persuadir a los enemigos de Roma de que o se humillan o mueren, no habría enviado la cabeza de este imbécil de Anthemusia aquí, sino al frente de guerra, a Adiabene o a Osroene. —Adriano hablaba levantando la voz.

—¿Por qué te irritan tanto las victorias de Trajano? —preguntó Plotina con serenidad. Le hacía cierta gracia verlo desencajado, aunque ella, en gran medida, compartiera su nerviosismo por lo que estaba ocurriendo.

—Me desespero —dijo Adriano levantándose y caminando por el atrio en torno a la cabeza de Sporaces—, porque al final mi tío es como esos Artavasdes u Orodes de antaño: se ríe con las cabezas del enemigo abatido cuando está cometiendo un enorme error, un error que puede arrastrarnos a todos al fin del Imperio. Craso se equivocó al cruzar el Éufrates, murió y bien se rieron de él Artavasdes y Orodes; y a Marco Antonio atravesar el mismo río le costó una derrota humillante y miles de hombres.

—Trajano ha cruzado con éxito el Éufrates —dijo Plotina a modo de sentencia—. Eso no admite discusión, te guste o no.

—Pero el Éufrates no es en sí mismo el problema —replicó Adriano colérico—. Ese éxito envalentona a mi tío: ahora querrá cruzar el Tigris y luego el río siguiente y así sin fin. ¿Crees acaso que los partos no decidirán atacar a las legiones con todo lo que tienen en algún momento? Partia, simple y llanamente, no se puede conquistar. Acometer una campaña de castigo, deponer a un rey en Armenia y luego retirarse, eso es posible y puede que hasta sea necesario para salvaguardar nuestro poder en las provincias de Asia, el Ponto Euxino y Siria, pero pretender, como está haciendo mi tío, anexionarse Armenia y los territorios de Mesopotamia y sólo los dioses saben cuántos más es una locura. Roma no tiene recursos suficientes para extender tanto sus fronteras. Se lo he dicho al César una y otra vez y se ha negado a escucharme. Me considera un cobarde. Sin agallas. Pero él sabe que he combatido bien; en la Dacia lo hice.

Plotina asintió levemente mientras humedecía sus labios en el vino. Luego habló, siempre con sosiego, con tiento, pero con palabras precisas.

—Sabes que no eres el único que piensa así. Yo misma me siento inquieta con tantas legiones de Roma más allá del Éufrates. Un fracaso bélico allí dejaría a todo el Imperio sin un tercio de su capacidad militar, y eso podría ser un desastre para defender el Rin y el Danubio. Esa preocupación nos une, sobrino... y otras cosas... —Sonrió levemente; él, en pie, desde el centro del atrio, afirmó una vez con la cabeza pero sin sonrisa; desde luego Adriano no era un romántico. Plotina prosiguió su discurso—. En todo caso, el nerviosismo por esta campaña, pese a las victorias de Armenia y ahora de Anthemusia, es compartido por otros muchos. Si ni tú ni yo somos capaces de hacer ver a Trajano el riesgo en el que está poniendo a Roma, quizá debiéramos buscar aliados en el Senado.

—Ya he pensado en ello muchas veces —respondió Adriano cogiendo una copa medio llena que había dejado alguno de los invitados; no quería llamar a ningún esclavo que pudiera escuchar lo que decían—. Mi tío ya ha tomado medidas y tiene el Senado controlado: ha dejado a Celso y a Palma en Roma para vigilar a todos los *patres et conscripti* y ha exiliado a los pocos amigos que tenía como Pompeyo Colega o Salvio Liberal. Están en Chipre y Cirene. Mantengo contacto con ellos, pero poco pueden hacer desde allí. Y el viejo Cacio Frontón murió ya. El Senado está de rodillas ante Trajano y su locura.

Plotina dejó su vaso de vino en la mesa e hizo como que se arreglaba las arrugas de su túnica de seda.

—Tienes a tu cuñado Serviano —dijo la emperatriz.

—Sabes que Serviano y yo estamos enemistados —replicó Adriano sentándose de nuevo en su *triclinium*—. Nunca le gustó que Trajano pareciera favorecerme durante los primeros años de mandato. Se creía con derecho a todo y yo me interpongo en su camino.

—Pero Serviano es de los pocos senadores muy respetados por el resto de los *patres et conscripti*, si te gusta usar su nombre más antiguo. Tú lo sabes. Lo necesitas. Ahora todo va bien en la campaña de Oriente, pero cuando empiecen los problemas, si los hay, el Senado será un hervidero de víboras y has de tener allí la más fuerte, la más venenosa. Serviano, tu cuñado, el famoso senador de Barcino, es tu hombre.

—Pero ¿qué puedo ofrecerle? Aunque pactara con él que si me ayuda a detener esta locura de la invasión de Partia lo nombraré mi sucesor, es algo irreal. Serviano es muy mayor. Es imposible que pudiera suceder a alguien de mi edad, mucho más joven.

—Eso es cierto —concedió Plotina—. Pero Serviano y tu hermana Paulina tienen a Julia, tu sobrina. Y la niña ya no es niña, sino una joven mujer que se avaba de casar con Salinator. Me lo ha comunicado Paulina misma por carta. Es lo que tiene mantener los lazos familiares, algo de lo que tú nunca te

474

preocupas, pero no quiero desviarme del tema. Tu sobrina es joven y sana y es hija de Serviano. Pronto tendrá, seguramente, algún hijo; Salinator no es como Trajano: a Salinator le gustan las mujeres. Serviano sueña con un heredero de todo su clan de Barcino, alguien en quien concentrar toda su fuerza en el Senado. Tú le puedes ofrecer que si te ayuda a detener a Trajano, si se presenta la ocasión para tal maniobra, ese nieto suyo puede heredar algún día algo más que unas cuantas villas y un puesto en la Curia. Dile que ese posible nieto puede ser algún día emperador de Roma. Si le prometes eso, Serviano te apoyará hasta el fin de sus días. Y ha sido dos veces cónsul con Trajano, gobernador de Germania y Panonia y no sé cuántas cosas más. Muchos lo seguirán y podrás maniobrar cuando tengamos... cuando tengas que hacerlo.

Adriano la miraba con los ojos muy abiertos.

—Eres algo más que una mujer bella —dijo el sobrino de Trajano.

Ella negó con la cabeza, aunque se sonrojó levemente con la aparente inocencia de una virgen.

—No finjas una pasión que no sientes, pero gracias por el cumplido. Me basta con que me hagas el amor esta noche y con que nunca me tomes por idiota.

Adriano se acercó y la cogió de la mano.

Juntos salieron del atrio y juntos fueron a la cámara de la emperatriz.

Adriano se levantó en medio de la noche, salió de forma sigilosa del lecho de Plotina y fue a su cámara personal. Iba a acostarse. Hacer el amor cuando no se siente pasión es agotador y estaba exhausto. Pero en ese instante vio que los esclavos habían dejado un mensaje en papiro sellado encima de la mesa.

Adriano rasgó la cera y desplegó el papiro que acercó a la llama de la lucerna de la mesa. Leyó en silencio, sin ni siquiera mover los labios.

La misión secreta se ha rehecho. Han conseguido hacerse con un nuevo barco y navegan hacia India. Como dije, tengo un hombre infiltrado aún entre ellos. Él se encargará de averiguar el objetivo de ese viaje y abortará que se consiga.

No había firma y Atiano se había preocupado de dictarla para que nadie reconociera su letra. Adriano, muy serio, acercó el papiro a la llama de la lucerna hasta que prendió. Lo sostuvo en la mano mientras se quemaba tanto tiempo como le fue posible. Cuando sólo quedaba una esquina por arder, lo soltó y el resto del papiro se consumió en su lento trayecto hacia el suelo. Sólo quedaron cenizas de aquel mensaje que serían barridas por los esclavos al amanecer.

63

LA CARTA DE LI KAN

Kasgar, regiones occidentales del Imperio han
115 d. C.

Li Kan estaba cubierto de sangre.
Se palpó bien el cuerpo.
Nada.
Como en otras ocasiones, era sangre *hsiung-nu*. Se despidió de los otros oficiales y entró en su tienda. El general al mando lo había felicitado, lo había señalado como el *Hsiaowei*, como el coronel más valiente del ejército, pero eso no era lo que ahora tenía en mente. Lo que ansiaba era escribir su carta mensual a Fan Chun. El general en jefe ya comunicaba todo lo referente a la guerra en las regiones occidentales a las tres excelencias y a los nueve ministros; éstos, a su vez, a la emperatriz Deng y, si lo preguntaba, al emperador An-ti, quien seguía sin tener mucho interés por los asuntos de Estado y menos aún por las guerras. Pero Fan Chun le había encomendado informar cada mes dando su parecer sobre la guerra y sobre cualquier otra circunstancia o pensamiento que tuviera. Y ahora tenía ideas que compartir con aquel viejo funcionario.

Li Kan cogió el pequeño pincel de mango de bambú y pelo de conejo en la punta y empezó a escribir con cuidado. No quería que sus trazos resultaran vulgares. Esta vez iba a escribir una carta inusual. Iba a empezar copiando algunos fragmentos de *El arte de la guerra* y debían quedar plasmados con la elegancia adecuada para un texto tan valioso. Del capítulo primero transcribió una sección amplia:

兵者，詭道也。故能而示之不能，用而示之不用，近而示之遠，遠而示之近。利而誘之，亂而取之，實而備之，強而避之，怒而撓之，卑而驕之，佚而勞之，親而離之。攻其無備，出其不意，此兵家之勝，不可先傳也。

Todo el arte de la guerra está basado en el engaño. Por lo tanto, cuando se puede atacar, tenemos que parecer incapaces; cuando usamos nuestras fuerzas, tenemos que parecer inactivos; cuando estamos cerca, debemos hacer creer que estamos lejos al enemigo. Finge confusión y aplástalo.

Si está asegurado en todos los frentes, dispone para él. Si sus fuerzas son superiores, evítalo.

Tenemos que hacer creer al enemigo que estamos en la lejanía; cuando alejados, tenemos que hacerle creer que estamos al lado. Lanza señuelos para atraer. Si el temperamento de tu oponente es colérico, persigue irritarle. Simula ser débil, que pueda crecer su arrogancia.

Si se está tomando un respiro, no le des descanso. Si sus fuerzas están unidas, sepáralas.

Atácale donde no está preparado, aparece donde no se te espera.

Estas estratagemas militares, para que conduzcan a la victoria, no deben revelarse de antemano.

Y del capítulo séptimo, el que versaba sobre las maniobras en combate, copió una frase breve:

故兵以詐立，(以利動)

En la guerra practica el engaño y tendrás éxito.

Luego empezó con sus propias palabras:

Al asistente del ministro de Obras Públicas

Ya imagino que el yu-shih chung-ch'eng tendrá todos los informes sobre la campaña. Sólo puedo confirmar que los hsiung-nu han sido derrotados en Kasgar y han retrocedido, de forma que la ruta comercial con Occidente vuelve a estar abierta para las caravanas que transportan la seda, lacas y otros productos de nuestro imperio hacia los Yuegzhi, el Imperio an-shi o incluso el lejano Da Qin. En cualquier caso será, a mi parecer, necesario mantener aún un número de tropas extraordinario en esta región del Imperio han si queremos consolidar esta victoria y seguir asegurando la ruta hacia Occidente.

Hay otro asunto sobre el que quería comunicar con el asistente: como se verá he transcrito algunas secciones de El arte de la guerra *de Sūn Zǐ. Después de repasar con mucha atención este libro, de acuerdo con la recomendación que me hizo el asistente en nuestro último encuentro, creo haber encontrado la respuesta a mi pregunta sobre por qué el funcionario Fan Chun, a quien dirijo esta carta, sólo ostenta ese cargo y no uno de más alto nivel, como entiendo yo que sería lógico teniendo en cuenta la gran confianza que el antiguo emperador He tenía en su persona y la tremenda estima que la emperatriz Deng tiene en la actualidad por el* yu-shih chung-ch'eng.*

Si nos centramos en los textos que he transcrito podemos ver que su autor insistió una y otra vez en que el engaño y el disimulo son esenciales en la guerra. En general, hacer creer al enemigo lo que no es termina siendo siempre el camino hacia la victoria. Y he concluido que si Fan Chun fuera o bien ministro o bien una de las tres excelencias, su nombre estaría en boca de todos y todos los funcionarios lo envidiarían. Sus movimientos serían mucho más observados que ahora, pues ¿quién va a fijarse en un asistente de un ministro allí en Loyang, donde tantos asistentes hay? Por otro lado, es un cargo desde el que se puede tener acceso directo a todos los archivos del Imperio y, si la emperatriz lo permite, acceso directo también a su majestad. Es pues un mero engaño la posición que Fan Chun ocupa en la corte han. Una estratagema hábil del difunto emperador He, mediante la cual ha ocultado a su mejor consejero entre el ejército de asistentes y funcionarios de la corte. Una estrategia que la emperatriz Deng ha imitado.*

Ésta es, pues, a mi parecer, la respuesta a lo que para mí había sido un misterio durante años. Espero haber acertado y espero seguir creciendo en sabiduría sin que por ello reduzca mis esfuerzos en las artes de combate cuerpo a cuerpo.

Li Kan
Coronel del ejército del Imperio han

Palacio imperial de Loyang

Fan Chun dejó la carta de Li Kan en la mesa y esbozó una muy tenue sonrisa.

—Prepara los documentos para el nombramiento de un general —dijo mirando a uno de los secretarios que lo acompañaban en su oficina del Ministerio de Obras Públicas.

479

El secretario en cuestión se levantó, hizo una reverencia y salió a por lo que se le había solicitado. Fan Chun tenía que consultar las fórmulas precisas del nombramiento. No se elegía a un general todos los días y casi nadie recordaba de un nombramiento a otro las palabras exactas.

Se oyeron entonces algunos gritos y llantos.

—Ve y averigua qué pasa —le dijo Fan Chun al secretario que aún estaba con él.

El hombre salió de inmediato.

El asistente aguardó con paciencia que se le llevara la información solicitada. Muchos se habrían asomado, pero cuando un suceso ha provocado el llanto no suele tener solución y no importa tener pleno conocimiento del mismo un poco antes o un poco después. Salir corriendo a ver qué pasaba era cosa de los eunucos intrigantes o de los funcionarios que siempre estaban al acecho de cualquier acontecimiento que pudiera poner en peligro su puesto o proporcionarles un ascenso.

El secretario regresó.

—La emperatriz consorte Li ha muerto —dijo el joven funcionario.

—¿Ha muerto alguien más? —preguntó Fan Chun.

—No que yo sepa, *yu-shih chung-ch'eng.*

—¿Está bien la emperatriz Deng? —inquirió Fan Chun de forma concreta.

—Sí, eso lo he preguntado.

—¿Y el pequeño príncipe Bao, hijo de la emperatriz consorte Li y el emperador An-ti? ¿Está bien?

—Sí, *yu-shih chung-ch'eng.*

—Bien, y el emperador An-ti imagino que también, ¿no es así?

—Así es —confirmó el secretario.

Fan Chun suspiró.

—¿Se sabe por qué ha muerto la emperatriz consorte Li?

El secretario se lo pensó un poco antes de responder. Aquel pequeño retraso fue suficiente para que Fan Chun intuyera el motivo y por ello habló antes que el joven funcionario.

—La han envenenado, ¿verdad?

—Sí —respondió el secretario sorprendido por la clarividencia de su superior.

Fan Chun hizo una señal para que lo dejara solo y el secretario se retiró. El asistente necesitaba pensar. Los asesinatos en palacio habían empezado antes de lo que él había imaginado. La hermosa Yan Ji parecía tener mucha prisa por llegar al poder, mucha más que el débil emperador An-ti, su esposo.

—Lo siento —dijo el primer secretario que regresaba con los documentos para el nombramiento de general—. No sé si el *yu-shih chung-ch'eng* desea hacer esto ahora o mejor en otro momento.

—Ahora, sin duda —respondió Fan Chun con rapidez—. Mi intuición me dice que en este momento el nombramiento de este general es más necesario que nunca.

64

EL BOSQUE DE NÍSIBIS

Mesopotamia
Julio de 115 d. C.

Trajano dirigió sus tropas desde Batnae, bordeando el sur de Osroene hasta la temida Carrhae. Decidió no detenerse en aquel lugar de infausto recuerdo, aunque no pudo evitar, mientras cruzaba aquel valle maldito para los romanos, pensar en cómo los partos rodearon a Craso hijo y lo mataron allí mismo. Pero las legiones del César hispano siguieron avanzando. Era curioso, no obstante, ver cómo, sin que el emperador lo hubiera pedido, los miles de legionarios que lo seguían pisaban aquella arena del desierto en silencio. El ejército de Trajano se convirtió en una misteriosa procesión armada y muda que serpeaba por entre las colinas donde se había derramado la sangre de sus antepasados. Muchos creían que los lémures, los espíritus de los legionarios muertos en aquella batalla, aún seguían vagando por aquella tierra marchita y temían despertarlos. Allí se había perdido mucho, pero Trajano estaba dispuesto a recuperarlo todo y a conseguir mucho más de lo que ningún romano hubiera imaginado nunca, con la excepción, claro está, de Julio César.

Dejaron atrás el terrible valle y siguieron bordeando el reino de Osroene. El rey Abgaro había enviado de nuevo a su hijo Arbandes como mensajero y Trajano lo había recibido.

—Mi padre me envía a confirmar y reiterar los lazos de amistad que le unen a Roma y a su César —dijo Arbandes—, e invita al *imperator* a venir a Edesa, nuestra capital, cuando lo desee, donde será recibido como un gran conquistador y auténtico rey de reyes.

La mención del título de «rey de reyes» era particularmente indicativa del reconocimiento que hacía Abgaro a Trajano.

—Puedes decir a tu padre que me será grato acudir a Edesa cuando termine esta campaña y que si él es fiel a su palabra de no cooperar en modo alguno con Osroes, yo seré generoso y magnánimo con Osroene.

Arbandes se inclinó ante el César. Iba a marcharse, pero, aunque estaban presentes Nigrino, Liviano y otros *legati* y tribunos, el joven y hermoso hijo de Abgaro se atrevió a añadir unas palabras.

—Y si se me permite decir algo más... —Trajano hizo un gesto en ese sentido y el joven continuó hablando—, para mí será un placer personal recibir al César de Roma en mi ciudad.

No se dijeron más.

No era el lugar.

Trajano sonrió.

—Nos veremos, joven Arbandes, nos veremos pronto —apostilló Trajano.

El hijo del rey de Osroene hizo una reverencia y entonces se marchó.

—Continuemos —dijo el César levantándose. Le dolía todo el cuerpo. Se empeñaba en seguir dando ejemplo y hacer las largas caminatas a pie, igual que sus legionarios, pese a que no era ya un joven oficial, sino que tenía más de sesenta años, muchísimos más que la media de edad de las tropas. Trajano se quedó pensativo. Hasta su médico, Critón, le había sugerido que combinara marchas a pie con jornadas en las que se desplazara a caballo, pero Trajano siempre se negaba.

—El ejercicio me hace bien —respondía él a Critón—. Me mantiene con energía.

Y el médico callaba.

—Nísibis está cerca —dijo Fédimo interrumpiendo los pensamientos del César y recogiendo los documentos del *praetorium*. El secretario se había percatado de la incomodidad física del emperador. Parecía ser el único. Nísibis era el objetivo que Trajano había marcado en sus planes de conquista para aquel año. Esto es, Nísibis él y el Tigris para Quieto.

El César carraspeó.

Sí, Fédimo se había percatado de que le dolían los pies y las piernas y los brazos... Miró a su alrededor. Todos habían salido menos el secretario.

—Me hago mayor —admitió entonces Trajano.

—Sólo de cuerpo, augusto, no de ánimo —respondió Fédimo.

Trajano sonrió por segunda vez aquella mañana.

—Pero necesito un cuerpo que me acompañe en estas campañas. Ningún espíritu conquista nada.

—Augusto, mi anterior amo, Suetonio, el *procurator bibliothecae*, solía decir que el espíritu de nuestras acciones es lo que nos sobrevive. Nuestro cuerpo es secundario.

Trajano lo miró y apretó los labios mientras meditaba. ¿Qué quedaría de todo cuanto estaba haciendo? Difícil saberlo, y lo del cuerpo...

—Eso del cuerpo como algo secundario es una creencia cristiana, ¿no es así? —indagó el emperador.

La conversación sobre si Fédimo era o no cristiano nunca había llegado a su término. El secretario, una vez más, evitó el tema.

—Es una creencia también de los egipcios, augusto.

Y el secretario salió de la tienda.

Trajano suspiró. Inspiró. Dio un paso al frente, dos, tres. Cruzó la cortina del *praetorium*, salió al exterior y se puso al frente de sus legiones.

Avanzaron por un terreno abrupto en ocasiones y llano en otras.

Los días se sucedieron sin enfrentamientos hasta que, como había anunciado Fédimo, Nísibis apareció en el horizonte antes de que el agotamiento hiciera mella en el emperador.

—Las murallas son más altas y mejor protegidas que las de Batnae —comentó Nigrino.

—Sí, pero están solos —dijo Trajano señalando hacia lo alto de los muros—. Tienen pocos hombres en las defensas y no se ven armaduras como las de los partos. Me parece que Osroes también ha dejado esta ciudad a nuestra merced.

—O están escondidos —apuntó Aulo en voz baja.

—Es posible —admitió Trajano sin mostrarse molesto

por el comentario del pretoriano—. Sólo hay una forma de saberlo.

Durante dos semanas los defensores de Nísibis lucharon como jabatos, pero como había apuntado el emperador, parecían no tener suficientes hombres si se atacaba por diferentes lugares a la vez. Aun así los dos intentos que habían hecho para conquistar las murallas habían sido, por el momento, infructuosos.

Trajano llamó entonces a Nigrino.

—¿Has visto esa montaña? —preguntó el César.

El *legatus* miró donde indicaba el emperador.

—¿El monte Massius? —preguntó Nigrino.

—Tiene un gran bosque —dijo Trajano—. Quiero dos torres de asedio. Eso terminará con la resistencia.

—Sí, César.

Las construyeron en pocos días.

Las murallas no eran excesivamente altas y las torres no tenían por qué ser infinitas. El emperador ordenó que se siguiera con los ataques, sin intentar acometer la conquista de los muros, para que los defensores estuvieran exhaustos. Así, sin tiempo para que los soldados de Nísibis pudieran recuperarse, un amanecer de julio, las dos torres fueron empujadas por los legionarios por dos extremos opuestos de la muralla, al tiempo que por otros enclaves se atacaban las defensas con escalas y todo tipo de armas arrojadizas. Los escorpiones se activaron todos a la vez.

Nísibis sucumbió al mes y medio de asedio.

Una gran victoria para el César y una nueva inyección de moral y ánimo para las legiones. Cruzar el Éufrates cada vez parecía más fácil y resultaba ser a cada momento una mayor fuente de alegrías.

—*Imperator, imperator, imperator!* —gritaban las legiones de Roma.

Nigrino miraba al emperador admirado: era la undécima aclamación imperial de Trajano, ¿o la duodécima? El *legatus* había perdido la cuenta. Combatían bajo el mando de un César sin límites.

Trajano desfiló orgulloso ante sus tropas mientras se saqueaba Nísibis. No hubo misericordia. La ira del emperador de Roma iba en consonancia con la resistencia que presentaba el enemigo. Era una lección para futuras campañas, pues aquello sólo estaba empezando. Los objetivos se habían conseguido: Anthemusia reducida, Sporaces muerto, Nísibis conquistada y Osroene había aceptado el vasallaje. Llegó entonces un mensajero desde Adiabene con noticias de las legiones de Quieto.

—¿Ha cruzado ya el Tigris? —preguntó Trajano al decurión enviado desde el este sin darle tiempo ni a presentarse.

—No, augusto.

El tono del mensajero era de preocupación. Aquel decurión estaba muy nervioso.

Marco Ulpio Trajano pidió un asiento y de inmediato llevaron su *sella curulis*. Nigrino, Liviano y el resto de los *legati*, junto con algunos tribunos, se habían congregado frente al *praetorium* para saber de primera mano cómo le iban las cosas al segundo cuerpo de ejército desplazado a Mesopotamia. Todos estaban exultantes con la conquista de Nísibis y sólo esperaban recibir más buenas noticias de Lucio Quieto, un *legatus* que nunca había fallado a Trajano, aunque a nadie se le escapaba que el mensajero permanecía en pie, tragando saliva y mirando al suelo.

—Explícate entonces, decurión —dijo Trajano llevándose la palma de la mano izquierda a la boca.

—El avance inicial fue más o menos fácil —empezó a narrar el mensajero de Quieto—. Redujimos a los mardi y seguimos hasta el Tigris para detenernos a la altura de Cizre, que es el punto mejor para cruzar el río.

—Por allí cruzó Alejandro Magno —apuntó Trajano a modo de confirmación de que la idea de vadear el Tigris en ese lugar era correcta.

—Pero, augusto, el rey Mebarsapes de Adiabene había concentrado allí todas sus tropas y había recibido fuerzas árabes de apoyo y una innumerable cantidad de jinetes partos llegados del sur. Había en total un ejército enemigo de cuarenta mil hombres, entre infantería y caballería. Pese a ello, el *legatus* Quieto intentó atravesar el río con la caballería por de-

486

lante, pero los arqueros partos nos masacraron y tuvimos que retirarnos.

—¿Quieto está bien?

—Sí, César. Una flecha le rozó un hombro, pero está bien. Lo ha preparado todo para un nuevo intento combinando caballería e infantería y aprovechando que no ha llovido en las últimas semanas y que el nivel del agua ha descendido un poco, pero...

—¿Pero...? —repitió Trajano.

—El *legatus* Lucio Quieto, augusto, no cree que se pueda conseguir cruzar el río sin perder, al menos, diez o veinte mil hombres. Incluso cree que puede no conseguirse el objetivo y pide confirmación de la orden recibida de cruzar el Tigris a toda costa. Me ha dicho el *legatus* que si el César confirma la orden, lanzará sus cuatro legiones y toda la caballería contra el enemigo. Y que siente no poder enviar noticias mejores.

Todos callaron.

—¿Qué piensas, Nigrino? —preguntó Trajano.

—Yo creo, César, que Quieto es, sin duda, el mejor de tus *legati*. Si él cree que cruzar el río con todas esas tropas enemigas, con sus jinetes y sus arqueros esperando en la otra ribera, es una locura, es que lo es. Pero el César que nos ha dirigido a todos tiene más clarividencia y más ánimo que todos nosotros juntos para valorar lo que puede o no puede hacerse.

Trajano se levantó y caminó entre sus oficiales con los brazos en jarras.

Se detuvo y miró a Nigrino y a Liviano.

—Perder una o dos legiones por cruzar el Tigris es un precio demasiado elevado que no podemos permitirnos. Estoy seguro de que en el Senado hay algunos que sólo esperan una noticia de ese tipo para empezar a criticar esta campaña olvidando en un instante todas las grandes victorias conseguidas, las ciudades rendidas y los territorios anexionados al Imperio. No. Lucio Quieto ha sido prudente al pedirme confirmación de la orden que le di. Por otro lado, tenemos que cruzar ese maldito río. —Trajano se puso las manos en el cogote y miró hacia el suelo mientras seguía hablando—. Parecía que Osroes no quería participar en esta guerra, pero ya lo ha hecho.

Y lo ha hecho bien, a lo grande: ha adivinado nuestra estrategia de descender por los dos ríos a la vez y ha decidido que eso no lo vamos a hacer. Quiere evitarlo le cueste lo que le cueste.

—Entonces ¿cambiamos de estrategia? —preguntó Nigrino.

Trajano bajó los brazos.

—Ah, no, por Júpiter, Nigrino, eso nunca. ¿No lo ves? El hecho de que Osroes, que hasta ahora había dejado que nos apoderáramos de Armenia, de Anthemusia, de Nísibis y ha dado por perdido el reino de Osroene sin intervenir, haya enviado todas las tropas que ha podido reunir a Cizre es porque ahí está el punto de inflexión de toda esta campaña. Alejandro Magno cruzó por allí y consiguió todo lo que se propuso. Osroes ha aprendido del pasado. —Trajano miró fijamente a Nigrino—. Hemos de cruzar el Tigris en ese lugar, pero Lucio Quieto no puede hacerlo solo. Y ha sido inteligente. Lo ha intentado y ha comprobado que con las legiones que tiene y los medios de los que dispone le es imposible cumplir con el objetivo asignado. Hemos de buscar la forma de hacer posible lo imposible... —Y miró de nuevo hacia el bosque del monte Massius—. Dile al *legatus* Lucio Quieto que no lo vuelva a intentar, decurión. Que mantenga allí tres legiones bien pertrechadas y bien guarnecidas en un campamento a prueba de ataques del enemigo. Igual que nosotros no podemos cruzar, ellos tampoco podrán si mantenemos allí un buen número de tropas. Veamos. Sí, dile eso y que luego se reúna conmigo en Edesa al final del verano con una de sus legiones. No quiero que se desplace por territorio enemigo sin buena protección.

Todo eso lo dijo Trajano sin dejar de mirar al bosque que habían usado para conseguir la madera precisa para las torres de asedio con las que habían conquistado Nísibis.

Aún quedaban muchos árboles.

¿Suficientes?

65

EL GRAN OCÉANO

El mar infinito rumbo a la India
Finales de septiembre de 115 d. C.

La gran mar Eritrea, el gran océano que separa los últimos puertos de Arabia de la lejana India, estaba agitada como si se tratara de un gigante dormido que estuviera despertándose. Los vientos parecían estar confundidos, como si chocaran unas brisas con otras. Las olas crecían. Las nubes del cielo eran negras y el barco parecía una cáscara de nuez en una ciclópea piscina de aguas turbulentas. La *cladivata* de dos mástiles que habían comprado en Muza se hundía en las aguas como si fuera a ser engullida por el oscuro océano en cualquier momento para, de repente, ascender vertiginosamente hacia el cielo. Tamura, Alana, Áyax y hasta Marcio estaban completamente mareados en el interior de la bodega. Todos habían vomitado y nadie decía nada. Titianus también estaba entre ellos. El viejo mercader no parecía sufrir tanto con el brutal oleaje, pero sus escasas fuerzas no le permitían ya salir a cubierta.

—¿Es esto normal? —le preguntó Marcio en cuanto pudo rehacerse un poco.

—Es una tormenta —respondió Titianus.

—¡Por Némesis, viejo! ¡Ya sé que es una tormenta! ¿Pero es normal tan fuerte en estas fechas?

—Nosotros nos hemos retrasado y hemos salido a finales de septiembre. La tormenta se ha adelantado. Es más propia de noviembre en adelante, pero ha pasado lo que me temía. Ahora dependemos de Arrio y su pericia.

Marcio suspiró.

—Incluso si es un traidor imagino que no querrá morir en medio del océano —concluyó el antiguo *lanista.*

—Imagino que no —aceptó Titianus.

En cubierta

—¡Bogad, bogad! ¡Tenemos que seguir remando! —aullaba Arrio a sus marinos. Sólo si embestían las olas en vez de dejarse llevar a la deriva podrían salir de allí con vida.

La nave crujía como si se fuera a partir en dos mitades en cualquier momento, el agua volaba por los aires como si el mar entero los envolviera. Aquello parecía el fin.

Arrio cedió en su lucha y viró hacia el sur. Aquello los alejaría de la ruta, pero la tormenta era demasiado fuerte y seguir enfrentándose a ella suponía un combate excesivamente desigual. A medida que se alejaban del rumbo planeado, la mar empezó a sosegarse, los vientos aflojaron y las olas disminuyeron.

Todo, poco a poco, fue calmándose.

Finales de octubre de 115 d. C.

Habían salido de Eudaemon Arabia, la «próspera» según lo que su significaba nombre, y la idea habría sido arribar a Barbaricum, en las costas ya dominadas por el Imperio kushan, lejos del control de Partia. Sin embargo, la tormenta los había desviado más al sur y ahora oteaban el horizonte en busca de un puerto que Titianus pudiera identificar como seguro para poder acercarse a la costa y desembarcar.

—No deberías haberte alejado tan pronto de Arabia —le dijo Marcio a Arrio.

—Tuve que hacerlo para acortar el viaje —le replicó el piloto romano con el desdén habitual—. Si no lo hubiera hecho, en vez de una tormenta habríamos sufrido dos en el mismo viaje y esta nave no resiste dos tormentas. Tuve que ir hacia el sur para salvar el barco, para salvarnos a todos. De nada.

Y se alejó del antiguo gladiador.

Marcio seguía sospechando, pero también pensaba que si realmente hubiera querido impedir todo avance de la misión podría haber dado la vuelta durante la tormenta. Claro que Titianus sí se habría dado cuenta al leer las estrellas. Tanto Arrio como el viejo mercader se orientaban mirando el cielo por la noche. En cualquier caso, el capitán había vuelto a retrasarlos. No era de fiar.

—Es Barigaza —dijo entonces Titianus señalando un puerto en la costa—. Mal sitio —comentó entre dientes, pero todos pudieron oírlo y vieron cómo miraba al cielo del anochecer: la luna llena estaba en lo alto—. ¡Y en el peor momento posible! —exclamó el viejo—. ¡Hay que alejarse de la costa, Arrio! ¡Aléjate de la costa!

El capitán no entendía bien a qué venían aquellos nervios y aquella prisa repentina de Titianus, pero había aprendido a respetar los conocimientos que el mercader tenía de todas aquellas remotas costas por las que iban navegando desde hacía meses e intentó que el barco virara girando el timón. Al principio la *cladivata* obedeció a la perfección y cambió su curso 180 grados. Todo parecía ir bien hasta que Arrio empezó a sudar.

—¡No navegamos hacia adelante, sino hacia atrás! —Y gritó a los marineros, pues ya no había viento que empujara las velas—: ¡Remad, remad!

Los marineros se esforzaron. Lo dieron todo como habían hecho durante la tormenta. Marcio y Áyax se pusieron a remar también, y hasta Alana y Tamura, pues el mar seguía arrastrándolos hacia la costa, hacia la desembocadura de un río.

—¿Qué está ocurriendo? —preguntó Arrio ya muy angustiado mirando a Titianus.

—¡Vuelve a girar el barco y encara la costa! —le ordenó el mercader—. ¡La corriente en noches de luna llena es imbatible en Barigaza cuando empuja hacia la costa! ¡Lo único que puedes intentar es buscar un arenal donde encallar el barco!

Arrio obedeció de nuevo. Explicar cómo conocía aquel viejo tantos rincones del mundo era algo que requeriría sin duda miles de historias junto a un buen fuego, pero ahora no había ni un instante para relatos de ancianos viajeros. La *cladivata* volvió a encarar la costa y ésta, con sus arrecifes y bancos de arena, los miraba amenazadora. Hacía tan sólo una semana, en medio de la horrible tormenta que habían sufrido, habrían dado cualquier cosa por avistar la costa y ahora que la tenían delante de ellos les parecía a todos el más peligroso de los monstruos: las rocas eran dientes afilados y las palmeras proyectaban largas sombras fantasmagóricas sobre las playas a la luz de la luna.

De pronto las aguas se quedaron tranquilas.

—¡Por todos los dioses! —gritó Titianus—. ¡Agarraos a la nave con todas vuestras fuerzas! ¡Agarraos todos!

Y cuando las aguas estaban quietas, en el momento justo de llegar a la desembocadura del río de Barigaza, se oyó un ruido como los gritos de un ejército que viniera desde lejos; y de pronto el mar mismo se lanzaba contra los bancos de arena de la costa con un desgarrador rugido.[55]

El barco se estrelló contra la playa. Arrio tuvo la habilidad de hacer que la *cladivata* enfilara contra la arena de la misma forma que lo había hecho contra las olas gigantes en medio de la tormenta. Aquello redujo el efecto del choque, aunque todos salieron disparados hacia adelante. El que no dio con su cabeza con un remo, chocó con su cuerpo contra las barandillas de cubierta. Y hubo quien salió volando del barco y cayó en la playa donde, gracias a los dioses, la arena amortiguó el golpe.

—¿Qué locura es ésta? —preguntó Arrio en cuanto se rehízo, mirando desde lo alto de cubierta hacia el mar que entraba con enorme fuerza en dirección a la costa.

Pero Titianus parecía más relajado.

—Lo peor ya ha pasado, amigos —les dijo—. Arrio es un buen piloto, eso hay que reconocerlo —añadió—. La mayoría no consigue evitar que los barcos vuelquen. Bienvenidos a la India.

Marcio puso pie a tierra un momento y comprobó que

---

55. La sección en cursiva es una descripción de esa costa transcrita literalmente del *Periplo por la mar Eritrea*.

492

aunque el agua sólo le llegaba por los tobillos, ésta lo arrastraba ahora mar adentro como si un gigante lo estuviera agarrando por los pies. El antiguo gladiador volvió a subir al barco.

—Esperaremos —dijo.

Tuvieron que permanecer en la *cladivata* hasta el amanecer para que la marea cambiara y poder desembarcar con sosiego. El tiempo lo dedicaron unos a curarse las heridas de los golpes que se habían dado al encallar el barco, y a comer y beber algo, los otros.

Tamura y Áyax comieron uno al lado del otro. Últimamente pasaban cada vez más tiempo juntos.

—Ya estamos muy cerca del Imperio kushan —dijo él entre bocado y bocado de las galletas que estaba masticando—. Pronto terminará nuestra misión y podremos volver a Roma.

Tamura comía sin decir nada. Lo pensó varias veces. Había prometido no contárselo nunca a nadie, pero allí, en las lejanas costas de la India, una promesa como aquélla, aunque la hubiera hecho al mismísimo emperador Trajano, no parecía tan absoluta, tan inquebrantable. Además, Áyax, como el resto, tendría que enterarse pronto de lo que el César le había dicho. Quizá debería decírselo primero al viejo Titianus, tal y como la había instruido el César, o, puestos a romper la palabra dada, decírselo primero a su padre y su madre, pero ella anhelaba tanto resultarle cada vez más interesante a Áyax que siempre buscaba algo con que sorprenderlo. En el mar había podido disfrutar de su compañía con frecuencia, pero ahora que estaban llegando a una nueva costa, estaba segura de que el joven gladiador, en cuanto pudiera, buscaría algún lugar donde estar con una mujer. Siempre lo hacía. Al principio eso no le importaba, pero de un tiempo a esta parte, sin entender muy bien por qué, aquello cada vez la molestaba más. ¿Y si le dijera un gran secreto a Áyax? Quizá eso la haría más misteriosa, más atractiva ante sus ojos hermosos y sus brazos y piernas fuertes, musculadas, su piel tersa y firme...

—Llegar al Imperio kushan no es la misión —dijo ella.

Áyax dejó de masticar y la miró con asombro en los ojos. Ella siguió hablando. Era curioso. Lo que más le había costado era quebrar el voto de silencio sobre aquel secreto, pero una vez roto, Tamura lo contó todo. Le explicó a Áyax cómo el propio emperador Trajano la había hecho capturar en las calles de Roma y cómo la habían conducido a su presencia y cómo el mismísimo César le había explicado cuál era el auténtico objetivo de la misión. Y, al final de todo, cuando la boca dulce de Áyax estaba apenas a un palmo de su propia boca, ella, bajando la voz, porque el secreto era el de un emperador o porque quería inconscientemente que Áyax se fuera acercando aún más y más, le contó también qué era lo que Trajano le había revelado aquella noche en Roma, a solas.

Áyax parpadeó dos veces.

No dijo nada.

Ella estaba tan entregada que pensó en desvelarle también el secreto de la pequeña estatuilla de Júpiter que el emperador le había entregado aquella extraña noche, en la lejana Roma, en lo que ya parecía otra vida, en otro mundo... y estaba a punto de hacerlo pero, justo en ese instante, el gladiador recorrió el mínimo espacio que lo separaba de Tamura.

Se besaron.

66

ARMENIA ET MESOPOTAMIA IN POTESTATEM P.R. REDACTAE[56]

Osroene y norte de Mesopotamia
Octubre de 115 d. C.

Abgaro recibió a Trajano como a un héroe mítico. Ordenó que la gente saliera a las calles de Edesa y vitoreara al emperador romano no ya como un amigo, sino como un liberador que había fulminado con su poder el yugo con el que los partos tenían sometido al reino de Osroene.

El emperador hispano caminó por las calles de una ciudad engalanada con guirnaldas en medio de gran júbilo flanqueado por Aulo y Liviano y rodeado por el resto de su guardia pretoriana. Liviano, en particular, no se fiaba de aquellas enormes muestras de simpatía. Trajano las estaba disfrutando aunque en su fuero interno, al igual que su jefe del pretorio, el emperador albergaba siempre una pequeña duda sobre la sinceridad de Abgaro. En la versión sobre el desastre de Craso narrada por Plutarco, el traidor que confundió a los romanos fue el árabe Ariemnes, pero en otras versiones se atribuía a otro Abgaro, anterior al rey de Osroene pero de la misma dinastía, la autoría de la traición que condujo a las legiones de Craso a combatir en Carrhae. Y Trajano no podía evitar que le vinieran a la mente, ahora que iba a encontrarse con aquel rey, aquellas otras historias del pasado.

Pero los esfuerzos de la campaña habían sido enormes, en especial los requeridos para rendir Nísibis, y verse rodeado de

---

56. Armenia y Mesopotamia han sido sometidas a la autoridad del pueblo romano.

felicidad, saludado como amigo y agasajado en un gran banquete era, cuando menos, muy agradable.

Trajano se acomodó sobre unos cojines de seda especialmente llevados para él, según decía el rey Abgaro, en el lugar de honor del palacio del rey de Osroene. Allí mismo, junto con sus hombres de confianza, recibió nuevas embajadas de reyes de otros estados y ciudades próximas que, a cada momento, temían más y más la cercanía del emperador romano y acudían a humillarse con la esperanza de ver salvados sus pequeños reinos de la ira del César, como Abgaro había conseguido con Edesa y todo Osroene. Entre otros muchos destacaba un enviado del *mry* Elkud, gobernador parto de la ciudad fortificada de Hatra, quien intentaba evitar que la ira de Trajano llegara hasta sus murallas. De hecho, Elkud había rendido la ciudad a Lucio Quieto, pero lo que el emperador no sabía entonces era que ese mismo Elkud, al tiempo que hacía que un embajador suyo se humillase ante el César y dejaba pasar a Quieto hacia el sur sin enfrentarse con él, había enviado un contingente de guerreros a la ribera del Tigris para luchar junto con el rey Mebarsapes de Adiabene y Mitrídates de Partia contra las legiones que el propio Trajano tenía allí apostadas.

Mas en aquel momento, con aquellos gobernantes a sus pies y una copa en la mano, el emperador sintió cómo la vanidad se apoderaba de él. Edesa se llama así en honor a la Edesa macedónica, nombre puesto por Seleúco, uno de los generales de Alejandro Magno. La sombra de Alejandro estaba por todas partes en Oriente y Trajano se sentía como si fuera un nuevo Alejandro que estuviera reconstruyendo el legendario imperio del más grande de los conquistadores.

En medio de aquel festival de lisonjas y festejos, Arbandes, el hijo de Abgaro, vestido con apenas algo que ocultara sus partes más íntimas, cubierta su piel tostada con aceites brillantes, inició una misteriosa y sensual danza guerrera que a todos llenó de asombro. Muy particularmente Trajano, que ya tenía debilidad por el joven príncipe, se sintió conmovido y, una vez más, aquella noche el emperador de Roma no la pasó solo.

—¿Todo va bien entre tú y el César, hijo? —preguntó el rey Abgaro a su vástago al día siguiente cuando se encontraron a solas, mientras la mayoría de los oficiales romanos descansaban, excepto un amplio número de pretorianos que se turnaban, por orden de Liviano, para hacer guardia y vigilar que ni el emperador ni sus hombres de confianza fueran molestados por nadie.

—Todo marcha perfectamente, padre —respondió Arbandes—. Yo creo que el emperador me tiene afecto sincero.

—Eso es bueno, hijo. No queremos terminar ni como Partamasiris ni como Sporaces.

—No, padre.

Entretanto, el emperador se levantaba en su cámara y llamaba a Fédimo.

—Escribe a Quieto. Dile que he cambiado de opinión. Escríbele indicando que yo iré a reunirme con él en Cizre.

—Sí, César.

Trajano comunicó entonces a Abgaro que dejaba las comodidades de Edesa, pero que regresaría en poco tiempo.

—Siempre al servicio del emperador de Roma —respondió Abgaro, que deseaba preguntar, más que otra cosa en el mundo, adónde pensaba ir el emperador, pero tuvo el buen criterio de no hacerlo.

Trajano dejó a Nigrino al mando de las legiones en Osroene para asegurar que el territorio permanecía leal a Roma, y cabalgando con la guardia pretoriana llegó a Cizre en pocas jornadas.

Lucio Quieto salió a recibirlo.

—Lo siento, augusto, lo siento una y mil veces. —El norteafricano se arrodilló ante Trajano.

—¿Qué sientes, amigo mío?

—No haber podido cumplir mi promesa de conseguir cruzar el Tigris.

—¡Por Júpiter! —exclamó Trajano—. ¡Mil veces mejor que te tengas que excusar por eso que por perder dos o tres legiones! Pero no nos lamentemos inútilmente y enséñame cómo están las cosas.

Lucio condujo a Trajano junto al Tigris: en la ribera romana estaban las cuatro legiones apostadas construyendo un imponente campamento para pasar el invierno.

—Iba a mandar una de regreso según las órdenes del César —dijo Quieto.

—Sí, nos llevaremos una de regreso, pero dejaremos tres. Eso será suficiente para mantener la posición. —Luego miró al otro lado—. Veo que efectivamente son muchos los enemigos. ¿Cuarenta mil?

—Seguramente algo más, César —respondió Quieto—. Mis espías aseguran que cuarenta y cinco mil. Quizá una cifra superior.

—Está claro que Osroes no quiere que juguemos a descender por los dos ríos a la vez según lo que tenemos planeado.

—¿Y qué hacemos? —preguntó Quieto—. Aquí no hay madera ni para construir botes. Hay bosques más al norte, en las montañas del lago Van, pero eso está a mucha distancia.

—Hay un bosque en Nísibis y eso está más cerca —dijo Trajano—. Convoca a los zapadores y a los ingenieros de las legiones. Tengo trabajo para todos ellos. Van a tener un invierno muy activo.

—¿Y nosotros? —inquirió Quieto.

—Nosotros nos retiraremos a Antioquía a pasar el invierno, pero volveremos, Lucio. Con la primavera volveremos. Y cruzaremos ese maldito río.

Roma

—*ARMENIA ET MESOPOTAMIA IN POTESTATEM P.R. REDACTAE* —dijo Celso en medio del Senado—. Ése es el texto que se imprimirá en las nuevas monedas que se acuñarán para celebrar que nuestro *Imperator Caesar Augustus* ha incorporado al Imperio las nuevas provincias de Armenia y de Mesopotamia. Pero eso no me parece suficiente para conmemorar semejante hazaña: propongo que se declare *Parthicus* a nuestro César, por sus inmensas victorias contra los ejércitos y los aliados de aquel imperio que tanto daño nos causó en el pasado y sobre el que Trajano está imponiendo la fuerza incontestable de las legiones bajo su hábil mando.

Ningún senador se opuso.

Serviano salió del Senado en silencio.

—Te veo meditabundo —le dijo su yerno Salinator. Se acababa de casar con Paulina, la hija de Serviano, apenas hacía unos meses—. ¿Te preocupa, como a tantos otros, lo mucho que se alarga la guerra de Oriente?

—Sí, en parte es eso.

—¿Hay algo más?

Los dos hombres se detuvieron en el foro, cerca de los *rostra*. Serviano miró a su alrededor. Nadie parecía reparar en ellos ni escuchar su conversación. Aun así respondió en voz baja.

—He recibido una carta de mi cuñado.

—¿De Adriano, el sobrino del emperador? —dijo Salinator con asombro. Adriano estaba enemistado con Serviano, o eso pensaba Salinator.

—Sí, carta de Adriano.

—¿Y?

—Y propone cosas interesantes para mí y también para ti. Sabe que Paulina, mi hija, tu esposa, está embarazada.

Su yerno afirmó con la cabeza.

—Se lo diría Paulina a la emperatriz Plotina. Se escriben con frecuencia, pero no entiendo qué tiene eso de relevante para Adriano —dijo Salinator con el ceño fruncido.

—El sobrino del César, aunque cueste imaginarlo, nos propone aquí cosas muy interesantes relacionadas con el embarazo de Paulina.

Fue ahora Salinator quien miró a su alrededor. Tampoco vio nada ni a nadie que lo inquietara.

—¿Qué cosas?

Serviano negó con la cabeza.

—No es el momento ni el lugar para hablar de ello, pero digamos que hemos de estar preparados.

—¿Preparados para qué? —inquirió Salinator, a quien todo aquello le parecía cada vez un galimatías misterioso y confuso. Nunca había sido hombre de muchas luces y no podía intuir qué podía tener que ver una carta del sobrino del emperador con el nacimiento de un hijo suyo y de Paulina. No era capaz de trazar conexiones.

—Hemos de estar preparados para cuando el César sufra su primer revés en la campaña de Oriente —le precisó Serviano—. Y Adriano dice que pese a las victorias conseguidas hasta la fecha, las legiones de Quieto han quedado atascadas en el Tigris sin poder cruzarlo. Seguramente el emperador intentará vadear el río la próxima primavera, pero nadie puede cruzar un río como el Tigris con cuarenta mil enemigos o más enfrente. Ni siquiera Trajano podrá. Es muy posible que no tengamos que esperar mucho para empezar a decir en el Senado lo que pensamos de toda esta locura. Y tú me apoyarás.

Salinator asintió. Seguía sin ver la relación de todo aquello con Paulina y su embarazo, pero compartía el temor a que las legiones terminaran aquellas campañas con una terrible derrota en Oriente.

Serviano continuó hablando, pero en voz baja. Se trataba más bien de sus pensamientos, a los que el veterano senador ponía palabras. A veces decir en frases completas lo que meditaba lo ayudaba a extraer conclusiones.

—Roma no puede ir tan lejos, cruzando un río tras otro, sin detenerse nunca, como si no hubiera límite a lo que puede ser conquistado. Más tarde o más temprano los partos asestarán un golpe mortal a Trajano, y entonces ¿qué? Tenemos que defender las fronteras del Rin y el Danubio, y Britania, África y Egipto. Con un tercio de las legiones en Oriente todo queda debilitado... en eso estarás de acuerdo conmigo, ¿verdad, muchacho?

—Verdad —repitió Salinator con los ojos muy abiertos.

Serviano lo cogió del brazo.

—Podemos acabar todos como la legión perdida —le dijo el veterano senador a su yerno al oído, como un susurro henchido de miedo, un miedo que seguía aún muy dentro de los corazones de todos los senadores aunque ya hubieran pasado más de ciento cincuenta años desde el desastre de Craso. E insistió, siempre en voz baja, confundiendo sus palabras con el viento de otoño que se arrastraba por el foro—: Trajano acabará como la legión perdida: en medio de algún remoto lugar de Asia, prisioneros, esclavos o errantes en un mundo desconocido quién sabe con qué absurdo destino final.

HISTORIA DE LA LEGIÓN PERDIDA

Tiempos de Julio César, Pompeyo y Craso,
mediados del siglo I a. C.

LIBRO V

67

LA HUIDA

Merv, extremo oriental del Imperio parto
43 a. C., diez años después del desastre de Carrhae

Druso convenció a Sillaces, el líder parto que estaba ahora a cargo de la defensa de la frontera oriental del Imperio como *mry* de Merv, de que la legión necesitaba construir una empalizada para protegerse de los ataques de los hunos. Los partos se habían mostrado siempre en contra de esta posibilidad, pero al final, tras un ataque del enemigo que causó centenares de bajas entre los romanos, Druso les hizo ver que muertos no valdrían para defender aquella frontera. Quizá fuera por eso, o quizá porque los propios partos estaban más ocupados en sus guerras internas: Surena había sido envenenado por orden del rey de reyes Orodes y el propio Orodes había sido, a su vez, asesinado por Fraates, uno de sus hijos, que se estaba haciendo con el poder absoluto en el Imperio parto. Seguramente, en medio de ese caos, la petición de Druso fue considerada sin mucha atención ni ganas de discutir por parte de un Sillaces más pendiente del desarrollo de los acontecimientos en el interior de Partia que en la frontera que él debía vigilar.

—De acuerdo —le respondió al fin Sillaces a Druso tras aquella última batalla que resultó tan desastrosa para los romanos de Merv—; pero una empalizada de poca altura.

—Sólo necesitamos unos parapetos que impidan que los hunos puedan atacar con toda su caballería sin encontrar otro obstáculo que nosotros con nuestros escudos —replicó a su vez el centurión de Cartago Nova—. De hecho, para que veáis que no queremos construir una fortaleza, iré preparando la empalizada por partes, sin montarla. Cuando tenga todas las partes os la mostraremos y sólo entonces, si os parece bien lo que hemos hecho, levantaremos los parapetos.

Sillaces, que tenía prisa y quería leer las cartas llegadas desde Ctesifonte para saber si realmente era Fraates quien se había hecho con el control de la capital, pareció satisfecho con aquel plan y Druso puso de inmediato a todos sus hombres a trabajar.

Se talaron árboles y se fueron preparando pequeños segmentos de empalizada donde se ataban hasta un máximo de diez o quince troncos, dependiendo del grosor, y luego se empezaba con otro segmento. Los trozos de parapeto se amontonaban unos sobre otros, a la espera de que, una vez revisados por los partos y conseguido el visto bueno según lo pactado entre Druso y Sillaces, pudieran luego los romanos proceder al montaje completo de la empalizada defensiva en la llanura frente a la ciudad de Merv.

—No entiendo, centurión —se atrevió a decirle un día Sexto a Druso—, por qué hemos aceptado esperar a tenerlo todo antes de montarlo. Si los hunos atacaran ahora, todo el trabajo no valdría de nada.

—Si clavamos en el suelo cada segmento de la empalizada, nos costará luego más llevárnoslo todo —le respondió Druso, y bajando la voz añadió—: ¿Acaso has olvidado que vamos a irnos?

Sexto y Cayo, que estaba a su lado en aquella conversación, se miraron un momento frunciendo el ceño. Ninguno de los dos había olvidado que el plan era irse de allí, pero no habían relacionado la empalizada con el plan de huida. Pensaban que la idea era construir aquellos parapetos de troncos para poder defenderse mejor de un ataque sorpresa de los hunos que tuviera lugar antes de que hubieran tomado la decisión final de alejarse de Merv.

—Además —apostilló Druso enigmáticamente—, no estamos construyendo una empalizada. Lo esencial es que no haya rendijas entre los troncos. Supervisad que no haya rendija alguna.

Cayo iba a preguntar por qué era tan importante pero el

centurión se alejó de ellos sin aclarar qué era lo que estaban haciendo con todos aquellos troncos apilados, así que dirigió su duda hacia Sexto.

—¿Y eso de que no haya rendijas?

—Yo qué sé —respondió Sexto encogiéndose de hombros—. Imagino que no querrá que ninguna flecha enemiga pueda atravesar los parapetos. Yo tampoco entiendo mucho, pero el centurión nos ha mantenido vivos todo este tiempo y lo que diga se hará.

Cayo asintió varias veces.

Llegó la primera noche sin luna desde que habían planeado fugarse de Merv en dirección al este para intentar unirse a Zhizhi, el salvaje líder de los hunos.

Druso miró al cielo negro de la noche de Asia.

—Los partos que vigilan las murallas no podrán ver cómo nos vamos —dijo y dio la orden de partida.

Los legionarios se pusieron en marcha. Para sorpresa de todos ellos, Druso dio instrucciones precisas de que se transportaran también los diferentes segmentos de empalizada en los grandes carros de los que disponían para el aprovisionamiento de víveres. El centurión se había preocupado de que, al tiempo que se hacían los parapetos, se prepararan, además, aún más carros a escondidas. Había habido tanto trabajo de carpinteros al mismo tiempo aquellas semanas que los partos que acudían regularmente a comprobar lo que hacían los romanos no repararon en ello.

—Pero este transporte nos ralentizará el viaje —dijo Cayo al centurión hispano.

—Sí, eso es cierto, pero necesitamos el material —respondió Druso—. Contamos con una noche entera de ventaja sobre los partos. Y luego espero que tarden en tomar la decisión de salir en nuestra búsqueda algún día más. Eso suponiendo que lo hagan. Seguramente, Sillaces pedirá permiso al rey de reyes. Eso son mensajeros que han de viajar a Cesifonte. Es tiempo que vamos ganando. Podemos permitirnos el lujo de ir despacio transportando todo lo que hemos construido.

—Aun así, mi centurión —insistió Cayo—, Sillaces podría decidir salir en nuestra búsqueda y darnos caza por su cuenta.

Todavía no se sabe bien quién gobierna Partia en estos meses, tras el asesinato de Orodes.

—Es una posibilidad. Por eso, por Cástor y Pólux, adelante, rápido.

Murallas de Merv, al amanecer

—¿Lo ve, mi señor? —dijo uno de los guardias partos de las murallas—. No están. Se han marchado.

—Ya veo que se han ido. Por Ahura Mazda, pero ¿adónde y por qué?

Nadie supo qué responder.

Sillaces se pasaba los dedos de la mano izquierda por la barba. Debería informar al rey de reyes, pero tampoco tenía claro qué contarle a Fraates.

—Enviaremos patrullas en su busca. Quiero saber hacia dónde han ido. Luego decidiremos.

La legión de Druso, cincuenta millas al este de Merv

—Allí, mi centurión —dijo Sexto señalando hacia el oeste.

En lo alto de unas colinas se veía a un pequeño grupo de jinetes partos.

—Sillaces ha enviado patrullas —dijo Druso—. Yo habría hecho lo mismo. Son pocos y no nos atacarán. No tienen nada que hacer si no vienen con el grueso de su caballería. Hemos de seguir avanzando. Cada hora de marcha es esencial.

Merv, residencia del gobernador

Sillaces volvía a acariciarse la barba.

—¿Van hacia el este?

—Sí, mi señor —respondió el jinete de la patrulla que había divisado a la legión romana adentrándose en territorio enemigo.

—No tiene sentido —continuó Sillaces—. En esa dirección sólo encontrarán a hunos que acabarán con ellos. Si hubieran ido hacia el norte, o mejor aún, hacia el sur, lo entendería. Eso indicaría que buscaban el mar, que intentaban regresar hacia Roma, aunque saben que tendrían, en algún momento, que volver a entrar en territorios controlados por nosotros y que se las tendrían que ver con alguno de nuestros ejércitos. Hacia el sur lo tendrían muy muy difícil, pero aún tendrían alguna posibilidad. Eso pienso yo. Pero hacia el este... es cosa de locos.

—¿Informamos al rey de reyes? —preguntó uno de los oficiales partos.

—¿Informar a Fraates de que se nos han escapado varios miles de prisioneros armados? No —respondió Sillaces tajantemente—. ¿Cuánta distancia nos llevan de ventaja?

—Calculo, mi señor —dijo de nuevo el jinete de la patrulla—, que en estos momentos, teniendo en cuenta dónde los vimos y que he tenido que venir cabalgando desde allí, unas cien o ciento cincuenta millas.

—Pero con los caballos podemos darles alcance si vamos a buena marcha —comentó Sillaces en busca de confirmación por parte de sus oficiales.

—Sin duda, mi señor —respondió otra vez el jinete de la patrulla—. Y, si se me permite, no hará falta ni ir al trote: se han llevado consigo los parapetos que estuvieron construyendo y eso ralentiza su marcha aún más. Llevan carros de los que ellos mismos tiran, pero su avance es penoso. A caballo, al paso, en tres días, cuatro a los sumo, los alcanzaremos.

Sillaces lo meditó unos instantes.

Se decidió.

—Vamos a por ellos: no podemos permitir que se escapen, incluso si caminan hacia su muerte contra los enemigos. Unos prisioneros del Imperio parto no tienen derecho a elegir cómo morir. Ni eso. ¡Mi caballo, rápido!

Ejército romano aproximándose a la frontera de Sogdiana.[57]
Tres días después

—Es raro que no hayamos encontrado hunos en todo este tiempo —dijo Sexto.

—He enviado a los prisioneros sogdianos por delante para que hablen con los hombres de Zhizhi —respondió Druso—. Nos esperan al otro lado del gran río.

—¿Gran río; qué río es ése, centurión? —preguntó Cayo.

—El Oxo.

Sexto y Cayo no dijeron nada, pero todos allí habían oído hablar del río que hacía de frontera entre los últimos territorios de Partia y el reino de Sogdiana. Era muy ancho, muy caudaloso y profundo. Ambos iban a preguntar cómo iban a cruzar un río de esa envergadura cuando varios legionarios dieron la señal de alarma.

—¡Más jinetes partos, mi centurión! —exclamó Sexto.

Druso miró hacia atrás.

—¿Más patrullas o una avanzadilla del ejército de Sillaces? —preguntó el centurión hispano en voz alta, pero no esperó respuesta y dio la única orden que llevaba repitiendo toda aquella semana agotadora—: ¡Adelante, adelante! ¡Mas rápido, más rápido! ¡Por Júpiter, corred por vuestra vida!

En el horizonte de la retaguardia romana se fueron dibujando las siluetas de más y más jinetes partos. No era todavía una fuerza importante, pero Cayo y Sexto tenían cada vez más claro que la respuesta a la pregunta que había hecho su centurión era que se trataba de la avanzadilla del ejército entero de Sillaces, que había salido de Merv en su busca sin tan siquiera esperar órdenes de Fraates desde Cesifonte.

—*Magnis itineribus!* ¡Marchas forzadas! —aulló Druso, casi a la carrera.

Los legionarios trotaban por aquel terreno desértico. No

57. Sogdiana, junto con Fergana y Margiana, era un reino fronterizo en esta época entre el Imperio parto y el Imperio chino. Abarcaba desde el río Oxo hasta el Yaxartes. En el siglo I d. C. sería anexionado por el emergente Imperio kushan.

había vegetación ni un lugar donde protegerse en caso de que los partos los rodearan. Seguir arrastrando los carros con los parapetos era un esfuerzo brutal, pero muchos legionarios empezaban a pensar que el centurión había planeado usar los parapetos no ya contra los hunos sino contra los propios partos que los perseguían ahora.

—¡Por eso habrá querido el centurión... que llevemos los malditos... parapetos! —dijo Sexto a Cayo casi sin aliento mientras seguían avanzando hacia el este.

Su compañero no respondió. No quería perder fuerzas hablando.

De pronto, al descender de unas colinas lo vieron.

Era enorme, caudaloso, imponente, en medio de la nada.

—El Oxo —dijo Druso deteniéndose un momento, con los brazos en jarras, algo inclinado hacia adelante, intentando recuperar el aliento después de la carrera que acababan de hacer.

Sexto y Cayo miraron a su alrededor: no había puente a la vista y no había con qué hacer barcas ni seguramente tiempo para construirlas con el ejército parto de Sillaces pisándoles los talones. La legión entera fue avanzando hasta llegar a la ribera misma del río. Allí se detenían todos los hombres y miraban a su centurión mientras veían cómo los jinetes partos, todavía a una distancia prudencial, los seguían de cerca, amenazadoramente con sus carcaj repletos de flechas, esperando tranquilos a que llegara Sillaces con el grueso de la caballería parta, para masacrarlos junto al río infranqueable.

—¿Y ahora qué, mi centurión? —preguntó Cayo muy tenso, sudando por el esfuerzo y por el miedo—. Los partos no habrán venido hasta aquí para pedirnos amablemente que regresemos a Merv. Nos van a acribillar con sus flechas como castigo. Nos van a matar a to...

—¡Silencio, imbécil! —gritó Druso—. ¡No os he traído aquí para morir! ¡Eso ya llegará, pero no aquí, no hoy contra los partos! ¡Un día imagino que no muy lejano, moriremos, pero hoy no es ese día! ¿Para qué creéis que os he hecho cargar con todos los parapetos que hemos construido con los árboles de Merv? ¿Es que no lo veis? —Pero sus hombres, quizá por el miedo o por el cansancio o porque no daban para más no respondían—. ¡No son parapetos! ¡Son balsas!

Ejército parto

Sillaces miraba hacia el Oxo desde lo alto de las colinas. Había llegado demasiado tarde. Para cuando el grueso de sus tropas se unieron a los jinetes de la avanzadilla, los romanos, haciendo uso de más de un centenar de balsas, habían cruzado el río y se reagrupaban al otro lado, en territorio de Sogdiana, controlado en aquel momento por los hunos del temible Zhizhi.

—¿Qué hacemos, mi señor? —preguntó uno de los oficiales.

—Nada. No tenemos con qué cruzar el río y, aunque pudiéramos, no me aventuraría con la caballería más allá del Oxo sin el permiso o sin las órdenes del rey de reyes.

—Entonces... ¿los dejamos marchar?

—Patrullaremos a lo largo del río para asegurarnos de que no intentan ir ahora hacia el sur. Eso es todo. Si el curso del Oxo hubiera ido en esa dirección quizá lo podrían haber aprovechado con las balsas, pero el río va hacia el norte, hacia su desembocadura en el mar Khuarazm[58] y no quieren ir al norte helado. Por el motivo que sea están decididos a marchar hacia el este, hacia el territorio conquistado por ese loco de Zhizhi. Caminan hacia su muerte y no lo saben. —Y como si de un oráculo se tratara, Sillaces pronunció su dictamen final sobre aquellas cohortes romanas que veía alejándose hacia el Asia más remota, hacia regiones en las que nunca antes había estado un legionario romano—: Morirán todos. Se convertirán en una legión perdida, en un fantasma que atormentará a los romanos durante siglos. El Senado de Roma nunca se sobrepondrá al miedo de que algo así les vuelva a ocurrir a otros ejércitos suyos que ataquen Partia. Vámonos de aquí.

Y escupió en el suelo.

58. Mar de Aral.

68

MERCENARIOS

Asia central, 43 a. C.

Druso y sus hombres avanzaban ahora hacia la ciudad sogdiana de Samarkanda, que según lo que sabían también había caído en manos del huno Zhizhi.

—¿Cuál es tu nombre? —le preguntó el centurión al herrero sogdiano que les hacía de guía desde hacía varios días. Druso pensaba que era importante desarrollar más la relación que tenían con aquel hombre, quien hablaba el suficiente griego para comunicarse con ellos a la vez que dominaba el sogdiano y quizá otras lenguas.

—Nanaifarn —respondió el hombre que caminaba junto a Druso.

—¿Cómo es que conoces tantas lenguas, Nanaifarn? —continuó preguntando en griego el centurión, esforzándose en pronunciar bien aquel nombre.

—Muchos en Sogdiana vivimos del comercio. Algunos somos artesanos, como yo, que trabajo el hierro, pero lo esencial es vender lo que producimos. A Sogdiana, hasta hace muy poco, llegaban mercancías del gigantesco Imperio han, más al este, o del sur, desde la India y desde Partia. Creo que incluso nos llegaban cosas de tu imperio, ese que vosotros llamáis Roma. Y para vender, lo mejor es hablar muchas lenguas, aunque sea sólo un poco de cada una.

—Sí, está claro —dijo Druso—, pero hablas en pasado, como si ya no llegaran mercancías hoy día.

—La guerra no es buena para el comercio y Zhizhi ha conquistado Margiana, Sogdiana y Fergana; casi todos los territorios desde el río Oxo hasta muy al norte, hasta el gran

Pu-Ku,[59] como lo llaman los han, están bajo su control, de modo que los han tienen miedo de enviar caravanas. Mira a tu alrededor.

Estaban pasando por lo que debía de haber sido no hacía muchos meses una población floreciente, con mercado, artesanos y mucha gente intercambiando productos, pero todo lo que veían eran casas semiderruidas, ruinas de lo que debió de ser una incipiente muralla defensiva y algún animal doméstico suelto. No se veía a nadie. Era un pueblo fantasma.

Cuanto más se adentraban en los dominios de Zhizhi la desolación era creciente.

—Dicen que el jefe huno quiere cambiar esto, que quiere afianzarse en el poder y volver a abrir la Ruta de la Seda, entre el Imperio han y Partia, pero no sé qué pasará. Para eso Zhizhi ha de negociar con el emperador han: de momento el Imperio han mantiene a su hijo como rehén para que deje de atacar las regiones occidentales de los han.

—Y sin embargo —interpuso Druso—, crees que nos podemos unir a él.

Nanaifarn se detuvo y miró al centurión.

—¿Cuántos hombres tienes ahora bajo tu mando, centurión?

—Unos tres mil.

—Sois suficientes hombres para resultar interesantes a Zhizhi, como mercenarios para que lo ayudéis allí donde tenga más problemas, para atacar o para defenderse de los han, pero sois demasiado pocos para enfrentaros a él vosotros solos y cambiar las cosas. Unirse a Zhizhi es la única solución para vosotros, para mí y mis compañeros sogdianos. Espero que cuando nos encontremos con ellos digas que soy de los vuestros. Zhizhi no valora a los artesanos, ni siquiera a los herreros como yo. A él sólo le interesan los guerreros. Vosotros le interesaréis.

—Puedes estar seguro de que diremos que tú y tus hombres sois de los nuestros —le respondió Druso—. Además de estar agradecido porque nos has ayudado a escapar de Partia

---

59. Lago Balkash.

por esta ruta, por si mi agradecimiento no te ofrece suficiente seguridad, sabes que te necesitamos como intérprete con los hunos. Mi vida y las de los míos también están en tus manos. Nos necesitamos el uno al otro.

—Eso es cierto —admitió Nanaifarn, y pareció que lo dijo con más sosiego.

Llegaron entonces unos legionarios que Druso había enviado por delante como patrulla de reconocimiento, a pie a falta de caballos. Pero mejor era eso que avanzar en un territorio hostil completamente a ciegas.

—Los hunos, mi centurión, miles de ellos —dijo uno de los legionarios casi sin aliento.

Druso inspiró profundamente.

—¡Formad en cohortes a lo largo de todo el valle y que los dioses nos asistan! —Luego se dirigió a Nanaifarn—. Te adelantarás con Sexto y un puñado de mis hombres. Eres herrero, pero me has dicho que también comerciante, ¿no es así?

—Así es —respondió el sogdiano tragando saliva.

—Y los sogdianos sois capaces de venderlo todo, ¿no es cierto?

—Es cierto.

—Entonces, Nanaifarn, ve adelante y véndenos a todos como mercenarios. Dile a Zhizhi que por poco dinero no encontrará mejores guerreros en toda la región.

Nanaifarn no tenía nada claro que todo aquello fuera a salir bien, pero ése era el plan desde un principio y el momento clave había llegado. Y, cosa extraña, aquel oficial extranjero, romano, como se denominaba él mismo, transmitía una seguridad, una fuerza, una decisión embriagadora. ¿Sería eso suficiente para pactar con alguien tan terrible como el líder de los hunos?

Por el extremo del valle se dibujaba la silueta del imponente ejército de caballería de Zhizhi: más de siete mil jinetes que se repartían por toda la anchura del valle. Estaba claro que el líder huno no se tomaba a la ligera la proximidad de aquellas tropas desconocidas en su territorio.

Druso vio cómo Nanaifarn se adelantaba junto con Sexto para negociar. El centurión esperaba que el líder de los hunos enviara a algún oficial de alto rango, pero no: en su lugar vio cómo el jinete al que todos los demás miraban, el que sin duda debía de ser el mismísimo Zhizhi, se adelantaba junto con una treintena de sus jinetes.

Se hizo un gran silencio en aquel valle en la ruta hacia Samarkanda. Ningún romano había llegado hasta allí antes. Druso empezó a pensar que seguramente ya no irían más lejos. Miró las montañas. Pasado el Oxo el terreno había cambiado y se veían profundos bosques. Era un lugar hermoso para morir. De pronto, se oyó una gigantesca carcajada. El valle, hondo, parecía tener la acústica de un gigantesco teatro griego y la risa del líder de los hunos retumbó por cada esquina de las montañas.

Nanaifarn regresó junto con Sexto.

—¿Qué ha dicho? ¿Por qué se ha reído? —pregunto Druso con sudor en la frente y asiendo su *gladio* con fuerza.

—Ha dicho que estamos locos, pero que locos es precisamente lo que necesita. Ha ordenado que lo sigamos hasta la ciudad de Talas,[60] donde está en este momento. Allí lucharemos contra los wu-sun y, si hace falta, contra los guerreros del Imperio han. Ha dicho que si combatimos bien os premiará.

—¿Y si no?

—Zhizhi ha dicho que si huimos del campo de batalla nos buscará hasta los confines del mundo y nos dará muerte uno a uno de mil formas diferentes y horribles. Ha dicho que si lo traicionamos caerá sobre todos nosotros como la invencible fuerza de un terremoto. Es entonces cuando se ha echado a reír.

La devastadora desolación que habían visto de camino hasta aquel valle parecía confirmar que el líder de aquellos hunos no fanfarroneaba con su capacidad de destrucción. Druso pensó que la comparación que había hecho Zhizhi de su propia brutalidad era muy certera y el centurión repitió aquellas últimas palabras en voz baja, como si intentara asimilar por completo la importancia de aquella advertencia:

—Como un terremoto.

60. Hoy llamada Taraz, al sur de Kazajistán.

HISTORIA DE TRAJANO

Principios del siglo II d.C.

LIBRO V
LA CÓLERA DE LOS DIOSES

69

UN RUGIDO DEL INFRAMUNDO

Antioquía, Siria. Invierno de 115 d. C.

Trajano, con una amplia sonrisa en su rostro, reclinado en su *triclinium*, contemplaba la llegada de todos los invitados a la cena en el gran atrio porticado de su palacio de Antioquía. Había habido varios días seguidos de extrañas y poderosas tormentas, pero aquella tarde el tiempo había mejorado y el emperador había ordenado que todo lo necesario para la velada se dispusiera en los jardines de aquel inmenso atrio. Para Trajano, examinar a la luz de las antorchas incandescentes que estaban dispuestas por todas partes el rostro de cada uno de los que entraban y se iban acomodando a su alrededor era la mejor forma de intuir el grado de lealtad de *legati*, consejeros y, por qué no decirlo, familiares: la anexión de Armenia era un hecho consolidado y la de Mesopotamia, quizá algo aventurada, ya había sido propuesta al Senado. Todo eran grandes victorias. ¿Les gustaba eso a sus invitados? El viejo Dión Cocceyo, que acababa de llegar desde Roma, parecía relajado, comiendo fruta, bebiendo vino y admirando la belleza de alguna de las esclavas egipcias que servían la comida. A Trajano le gustaba que el sabio aún tuviera aquellos apetitos: eran muestra de vitalidad y quería a aquel hombre de inteligentes consejos cerca de él en medio de aquella campaña tan ambiciosa como compleja. Y más cuando no todos estaban a favor de sus conquistas: Trajano podía ver a su sobrino Adriano bebiendo serio, en silencio, sin apenas mirar a nadie.

Fédimo entró en el gran atrio y le entregó una carta del Senado. El emperador la abrió y la leyó atentamente.

—¿Algún problema en Roma? —preguntó Plotina intrigada.

—Eso depende de cómo se mire —respondió Trajano enigmáticamente, pero con una sonrisa en el rostro—. Me han nombrado *Parthicus*. A mí me parece una buena noticia, pero no sé si todos aquí lo ven igual —añadió mirando hacia Adriano.

—¡Yo brindo por ese nombramiento! —exclamó Quieto levantándose con una copa en la mano.

—¡Yo me uno a ese brindis! —dijo Nigrino, alzándose también.

—¡Y yo!

—¡Y yo!

Así hicieron todos los *legati* presentes, tribunos, autoridades de Antioquía; el propio Dión Coceyo, con algo de esfuerzo, se levantó también. Plotina los imitó con una sonrisa en el rostro, sincera o fingida, pero sonrisa al fin y al cabo, al tiempo que miraba a Adriano. El sobrino segundo del César fue el último, pero se levantó también con la copa en la mano.

—Veo ese reconocimiento un poco prematuro aún —dijo Adriano ante el estupor de Quieto y el resto de los *legati*—, pero brindo por él y por la salud del César.

Todos miraron al emperador, a la espera de su reacción ante el evidente desafío de su sobrino segundo.

Trajano bebió de su copa y todos los imitaron, incluido Adriano. A continuación el César volvió a reclinarse en su *triclinium*. Todo se hacía en medio de un silencio incómodo. Nadie se atrevía aún a decir nada.

—Es prematuro decir que Partia está conquistada —aceptó Trajano mientras cogía algo más de fruta a la espera de las suculentas carnes que estaban siendo cocinadas en las cocinas del palacio de Antioquía—, pero todo marcha bien. En un año, dos a lo sumo, el curso entero del Éufrates y del Tigris estarán bajo el control de Roma. Cesifonte, Babilonia, hasta el puerto de Carax estarán bajo nuestro poder y nos abrirán las rutas comerciales a la India, al Imperio kushan... —Y calló, para beber algo más de vino.

—¿Hasta dónde se propone llegar mi esposo? —preguntó Plotina, más que nada para evitar que Adriano volviera a indisponerse con su tío—. ¿Cuál es el límite de esta serie de campañas?

—Ésa es la pregunta clave —admitió Trajano sin mirarla, con los ojos clavados en el fondo de su copa vacía—. ¿Tenemos realmente límites?

Plotina miró entonces a Dión Coceyo, como buscando que alguien inteligente y de confianza del César pusiera freno a su marido. Trajano observó el gesto de su esposa y también se volvió hacia el anciano consejero y filósofo, quien, no obstante, dudaba si intervenir o no.

—La emperatriz se interesa por tu opinión sobre este punto de la expansión del Imperio, Dión, y yo también estimo tus pensamientos —le dijo el César—. Habla, te escuchamos todos.

El filósofo carraspeó un par de veces y bebió de su copa como intentando aclararse la garganta, aunque lo que realmente buscaba eran unos instantes para encontrar las palabras adecuadas.

—Ciertamente, César, todo debe tener algún límite —dijo Dión Coceyo—, aunque nadie como el emperador para vislumbrar mejor que ningún otro cuál debe ser esa frontera. El emperador ha conducido hasta ahora a las legiones de Roma de victoria en victoria. Hemos de pensar que el César sabe lo que se lleva entre manos y hemos de rogar a Júpiter para que vele por su salud y su clarividencia.

—¿Crees que mi clarividencia puede estar menguando? —indagó Trajano con rapidez.

—Creo, augusto, que todos somos susceptibles de caer, ocasionalmente, en un exceso de confianza —apostilló el filósofo con tiento.

Se hizo un nuevo silencio.

—Lo que dices es muy cierto —respondió Trajano al fin—. La prudencia debe ser siempre compañera de quien decide el destino de diez legiones, pero la audacia debe ir también de la mano de quien rige una Roma que vive presa de sus fantasmas.

—Un fantasma como el de la legión perdida —apuntó Plotina.

—Precisamente —aceptó Trajano—, la clave es qué o quién es más fuerte: ¿el miedo de todo un pueblo o la audacia de un César? —Y se volvió hacia a Dión Coceyo como si le trasladara aquella pregunta.

—No lo sé, César —respondió el filósofo.

Trajano no insistió, sino que miró en ese momento a Arbandes, el joven y hermoso heredero del trono de Osroene, su invitado personal en aquella fiesta, y Arbandes comprendió que el emperador, más allá de conquistas, guerras o miedos, no quería pasar solo aquella noche.

A Quieto no se le escapó aquel intercambio de miradas entre Trajano y Arbandes. Al *legatus* norteafricano le preocupaba aquella relación íntima entre el César y el heredero de Osroene, pero quién era él, quién era nadie para inmiscuirse en la vida privada del emperador. Además el propio Trajano, al percibir sus temores, le había asegurado que, más allá de sus placeres íntimos, tener a Arbandes en Antioquía era una forma de garantizarse la lealtad de su padre, Abgaro, pues si este último decidía pasarse al bando de Osroes, Arbandes sería usado como rehén por ellos. Aquello le pareció inteligente a Quieto, pero el norteafricano seguía temiendo que el César se cegara y que su pasión por el hermoso Arbandes le impidiera ver que realmente aquel joven príncipe sólo era leal a sí mismo. Nadie de fiar.

Los músicos empezaron a tocar y los pensamientos de todos se relajaron.

Trajano bebió un nuevo trago de su copa. Pronto iniciaría Arbandes una de sus majestuosas danzas y el emperador no quería perderse el espectáculo. Desde Pylades no había encontrado nada igual, pero Trajano temía tener que ausentarse a mitad del baile para acudir a la letrina. De un tiempo a esa parte tenía la sensación, cada vez más evidente, de que necesitaba orinar con más frecuencia que antaño. Había consultado a su médico, pero todo lo que Critón supo sugerir fue que bebiera algo menos de vino y eso era algo a lo que Trajano, sencillamente, no pensaba renunciar. ¿Qué sabían los médicos?

Marco Ulpio Trajano se levantó de su *triclinium* y miró a su esposa.

—Ahora vuelvo. —Sin esperar respuesta, seguido de cerca

por Aulo y una docena de pretorianos, cruzó por en medio del banquete en dirección a la puerta que daba acceso a las habitaciones privadas de la familia imperial. Se detuvo, no obstante, un instante ante el *triclinium* del príncipe de Osroene—. No empieces la danza hasta que regrese —dijo el César.

Arbandes se levantó al tiempo que respondía:

—Esperaré al emperador, por supuesto. No podría bailar si aquel que más valora mi danza no está presente. —Y sonrió.

Trajano le devolvió la sonrisa mientras se volvía ya hacia la puerta al fondo del atrio. El César caminaba rápido. Un poco porque realmente tenía necesidad de aliviarse y un mucho porque cuanto antes regresara antes podría disfrutar del encanto del baile de Arbandes.

Mientras andaba podía oír las pisadas fuertes de las sandalias de Aulo y el resto de los pretorianos a su espalda. Trajano sonrió otra vez, ahora levemente, para sí mismo. Aulo le había sido y le era leal desde incluso antes de ser César. Sí, pese a Adriano y algunos otros intrigantes en Roma, podía considerarse afortunado por disponer de al menos un puñado de hombres leales a su alrededor.

Llegó a su cámara. Dos pretorianos se adelantaron y abrieron las puertas de bronce para facilitar la entrada del César. Trajano cruzó el umbral seguido sólo por Aulo, quien se adelantó para abrir personalmente la puerta de madera que daba acceso a una habitación donde el César había dado orden de que se instalara una letrina cómoda y limpia para su uso personal. Se trataba de una pequeña sala de uso privado que antecedía a otra mucho mayor, de su uso personal también, donde había una piscina de agua templada que aprovechaba las aguas termales de los baños públicos que se erigían justo enfrente del palacio. Trajano acudía con frecuencia a los baños públicos, en su política de dejarse ver por aquellos a los que gobernaba, como alguien próximo a ellos, pero aquella letrina y la piscina contigua le permitían un aseo personal cómodo en medio de unas campañas militares que estaban siendo particularmente exigentes con su cuerpo. Ya no era un joven de veinte años, ni siquiera un hombre maduro y recio de treinta, sino casi un viejo de sesenta años, ¿o eran sesenta y uno? Hacía tiempo que prefería dejar de llevar la cuenta.

Se sentó en la letrina para aliviarse.

Miraba al suelo.

Había sido injusto con su pensamiento sobre Critón. Su médico, otro hombre leal, sólo le aconsejaba lo que estimaba mejor para su bienestar. Trajano sacudió levemente la cabeza. Se había convertido en un viejo, además, bastante cascarrabias.

Se iba a levantar cuando, de pronto, como surgido desde el mismísimo inframundo, se oyó el rugido descomunal de una gigantesca bestia. Marco Ulpio Trajano se quedó petrificado.

Nunca había oído nada igual en su vida. Y nunca volvería a oírlo.

Sabía que Aulo lo esperaba junto a la puerta, en la cámara imperial.

—¿Qué ha sido eso? —preguntó el César.

—No lo sé —respondió Aulo, sin siquiera añadir el oportuno «augusto», algo muy extraño en alguien tan respetuoso como él; pero ni el tribuno pretoriano ni el emperador estaban para títulos honoríficos.

Trajano se levantó de la letrina y se ajustó la ropa con rapidez, con la sensación de urgencia de quien intuye el desastre absoluto. El emperador salió del baño y junto con Aulo, sin saber ninguno de los dos muy bien por qué, se situaron en el centro de la cámara imperial mirando al suelo. De pronto todo empezó a temblar: las baldosas de mármol se resquebrajaban una tras otra reventando como si algún ser gigantesco estuviera comprimiendo la habitación o el palacio entero con sus ciclópeas extremidades en un abrazo mortal e incontenible.

Aulo y Trajano retrocedían en dirección al baño intentando librarse de aquel suelo que estallaba bajo sus pies cuando, de pronto, lo de menos era lo que estaba ocurriendo con las baldosas: las paredes empezaron a resquebrajarse y enormes trozos del techo pintado caían ante ellos como piedras arrojadas desde catapultas.

—¡Hay que salir de aquí! —gritó Trajano, pues había que gritar a pleno pulmón para hacerse oír por encima del estruendo ensordecedor que se había apoderado de todo el palacio, que parecía estar derrumbándose sobre ellos.

En los jardines del atrio

—¿Qué ha sido eso? —preguntó Lucio Quieto levantándose *ipso facto* al oír aquel rugido que parecía ascender desde el Hades.

Nadie supo qué responder, pero los músicos dejaron de tocar, todos dejaron de beber y de comer y no quedó ni una sonrisa en el grupo de invitados al banquete del César.

En ese momento, dos de las columnas del extremo opuesto a donde se encontraban la emperatriz y Adriano y Quieto parecieron reventar desde dentro y se desplomaron hacia el interior del jardín, cayendo en mil pedazos sobre el sector donde estaban Arbandes y otros invitados extranjeros. Los gritos de los heridos estremecieron al resto, pero no hubo tiempo de ocuparse de nadie, porque acto seguido otras muchas columnas del atrio se agitaron como si fueran ramas de árbol estremecidas por un fuerte viento invisible capaz de tumbarlas sin apenas esfuerzo.

Todos se levantaron.

Quieto fue el primero en reaccionar.

—¡Al centro! ¡Al centro del jardín! —Y miró a Adriano—. ¡Hay que alejarse de las columnas, de los muros...!

Adriano asintió y repitió la orden de Quieto con fuerza.

—¡Al centro! ¡Alejaos de las columnas!

El viejo Dión Coceyo no estaba ya para carreras y tropezó. Quieto lo levantó con energía y lo ayudó a alejarse de las columnas, que seguían cayendo a su alrededor.

—¡El emperador...! —dijo entonces el anciano filósofo. Quieto lo miró y se quedó inmóvil.

—El emperador... —repitió el veterano *legatus* mirando hacia las columnas derruidas donde hasta hacía un momento estaba la puerta que daba acceso al interior del palacio. El norteafricano fue entonces directo hacia Adriano y volvió a hablar a gritos—: ¡Hay que ir a por el emperador!

Adriano miró hacia los muros, que seguían cayendo. Una enorme nube de polvo emergía de la tierra envolviéndolos a todos, casi cegándolos.

—¡No podemos hacer nada! —respondió Adriano.

Quieto negó con la cabeza, dio unos pasos y empezó a gritar.

—¡Nigrino, Nigrino!

Al momento, escupiendo polvo por la boca y con un brazo sangrando, apareció el otro *legatus*.

—¡Estoy aquí! ¡Aquí! —aulló mientras se cogía el brazo herido con la mano que aún parecía sana.

Quieto comprendió que Nigrino no estaba en condiciones de ayudarlo.

—¡Quédate aquí! —dijo y echó a andar hacia la nube de polvo.

—¿Adónde vas? ¿Estás loco?

—¡Voy a por el emperador!

—¡Espera! ¡Voy contigo! —dijo Nigrino, pero en ese instante una gran zanja surgió entre los dos. La tierra se abría por diferentes puntos. Se oyeron los gritos de los que caían en algunas de esas zanjas, que también de golpe se cerraban, estrujando sin clemencia a quien pudieran haber aprisionado en su interior. Era como si la tierra fuera un gran dragón que engullera seres humanos como el león que se divierte cazando moscas.

—¡No hay tiempo! —vociferó Quieto y volvió a encaminarse hacia donde había estado la puerta del palacio.

La nube de polvo lo envolvía todo y costaba respirar. El norteafricano se agachó. La tierra se agitaba bajo sus pies y, como si se inflara el mundo, Quieto sintió que el suelo se hinchaba de súbito y lo levantaba por el aire para luego desaparecer y dejarlo caer de golpe. Era tierra y yerba y el golpe no fue particularmente doloroso, pero la sensación de terror y de impotencia absoluta atenazó a Lucio Quieto unos instantes.

Se arrodilló como pudo.

La tierra seguía temblando. Apenas habían transcurrido unos segundos desde el principio de aquella locura, pero parecía que hubieran pasado horas.

El norteafricano gateaba luchando contra la nube.

—¡Hay que ayudar... al emperador! —exclamó mientras lloraba de rabia y miedo, con el polvo cegándole los ojos. Pero todo eran gritos, y arena en el aire, y trozos de paredes y columnas que rodaban por el suelo y aquel temblor que no parecía detenerse nunca.

En el interior del palacio

Trajano y Aulo consiguieron llegar a la sala de la piscina. Se quedaron atónitos al comprobar que el gran tanque de agua estaba completamente vacío porque se había abierto una gran grieta en su interior. Todo seguía derrumbándose a izquierda y derecha, por delante de ellos y a sus espaldas. Estaban perdidos. El palacio entero se desplomaba sobre sus cabezas sin que pudieran hacer nada por evitarlo. Podían oír los aullidos de dolor de algunos de los pretorianos, atrapados bajo algunos de los escombros que seguían cayendo de los techos del palacio.

—¡Allí! —gritó Aulo señalando un gran ventanal abierto en la pared occidental de la sala. Estaba elevado por encima de la altura de un hombre, pero no era momento de dudas.

Trajano fue corriendo al ventanal e intentó alcanzarlo, pero no lo consiguió ni dando un salto. El muro de aquella pared parecía ser más grueso que el resto y resistía, mientras las otras paredes se agrietaban y el techo se partía arrojando más trozos de ruinas sobre sus cabezas. Aulo ya estaba ensangrentado en varios sitios y el emperador mismo sentía dolor en brazos y piernas, pero no había tiempo ni para palparse el cuerpo. Aulo llegó junto a él y puso las manos juntas para que Trajano pudiera encaramarse a ellas y, acto seguido, con el impulso que le dio el tribuno, alcanzar el gran alféizar de aquel gigantesco ventanal. Desde allí pudo observar que no era sólo el palacio el que se estaba derrumbando, sino que todos los edificios de la ciudad estaban siendo agitados por aquella extraña fuerza incontenible e irrefrenable en su furia.

—¡Vamos, Aulo! —exclamó Trajano tumbándose a lo largo del gran alféizar y extendió el brazo en busca de la mano del tribuno.

Aulo se estiró y asió el brazo que le tendía el César. Trajano tiró de él con fuerza, a la que se añadió el impulso que el propio Aulo se dio desde el suelo, mayor de lo imaginado porque en medio de aquella furia desatada sobre ellos, la adrenalina le proporciona al ser humano energías suplementarias que nadie piensa tener en su interior. Aulo consiguió que sus manos se asieran al borde del alféizar del gran ventanal. Trajano tiró entonces de su ropa hacia arriba y, al final, con gran esfuerzo pero con rapidez, Aulo estaba encaramado junto al emperador. Justo en ese momento la pared del otro extremo de la sala se desplomaba escupiendo polvo y ladrillos y grava. Instintivamente, los dos hombres se cubrieron el rostro con los brazos.

La inmensa nube de polvo impulsaba todo lo que encontraba frente a ella: capturó al César y al tribuno, acurrucados en aquella gran ventana, y los elevó por el aire, arrojándolos al exterior de la sala, que colapsaba por completo, hasta depositarlos sobre la hierba de uno de los jardines imperiales del palacio como si se tratara de la gigantesca mano de un cíclope que lanzara una piedra, sólo que la piedra eran ellos dos. El golpe no fue rotundo y seco, pues la sala de la piscina estaba medio excavada para aprovechar las aguas termales y la altura desde la que fueron arrojados contra el suelo no era grande. Rodaron varios pasos por la hierba, hasta que sus maltrechos cuerpos se detuvieron.

El primero en incorporarse fue Aulo, que escupió tierra por la boca con sangre y babas.

—¡Agh! —dijo mientras, ahora sí, se palpaba el rostro, los brazos y las piernas en busca de heridas. Le dolía todo el cuerpo pero no parecía tener nada roto. De pronto notó algo diferente.

La tierra había dejado de temblar.

Se levantó y miró a su alrededor: allí ya no estaba el palacio imperial de Antioquía, sino sólo ruinas, columnas partidas, paredes derruidas, polvo y un silencio tan extraño como tenebroso. ¿Y el emperador? Tan preocupado como había estado por sí mismo y aturdido por el constante rugido y el temblor de la tierra bajo sus pies, el tribuno se había olvidado de que había salido despedido de la gran ventana de la sala de la piscina junto con el César. Miró a su derecha, a su izquierda: sí, allí, tumbado, estaba el emperador.

Aulo se arrodilló junto a él.

—¡César, César! —gritó el tribuno a la vez que asía a Trajano por los hombros e intentaba incorporarlo. El emperador no respondía. Aulo depositó de nuevo la espalda del César en el suelo con cuidado y le giró entonces la cabeza. Trajano tenía los ojos cerrados y una brecha en la frente por la que no paraba de manar sangre.

—¡César, César! —repetía Aulo una y otra vez entre lágrimas.

70

EL INGENIO DE ZHANG HENG

**Loyang, capital del Imperio han
115 d. C.**

El *Taixue* o Academia Imperial estaba a pleno rendimiento, pero la emperatriz Deng no estaba satisfecha con el nivel de conocimientos de los funcionarios del Estado. Su majestad preguntó entonces a Fan Chun por alguien capacitado para evaluar a los miles de candidatos que deseaban acceder a la Secretaría Imperial y al Censorado, las oficinas administrativas de máximo rango en todo el imperio. El asistente del ministro de Obras Públicas no lo dudó ni un instante.

—Zhang Heng es la persona indicada, majestad, para dirigir esos exámenes.

—¿Y por qué estás tan seguro de ello, Fan Chun? —preguntó la emperatriz Deng—. Sinceramente, pensaba que me pedirías unos días para pensarlo.

—Ah, pero en este caso está claro. Es cierto que tenemos a Wang Fu, pero es persona tan poco práctica como lúcida; su falta de pragmatismo lo hace inadecuado para la tarea. Y hay otros que son buenos matemáticos o calígrafos, pero Zhang Heng domina todos los campos con maestría pese a su juventud: sus dotes en matemáticas lo han llevado a ser Astrónomo Jefe, como la emperatriz muy bien sabe, encargado del calendario oficial entre otras obligaciones relevantes. Además, Zhang es un genio como calígrafo, domina el arte de la escritura como pocos y compone poemas, muchos de ellos de mérito, a mi modesto entender. Y finalmente, Zhang Heng es hombre que entiende el funcionariado y sus engranajes. Si él se encarga de seleccionar a los candidatos al Secretariado Imperial y el Censorado, estoy convencido de que elevará el nivel de estas oficinas hasta la excelencia, majestad.

Y así fue. Heng instauró un examen que los candidatos a los más altos puestos del funcionariado chino debían superar mostrando, entre otras aptitudes, su dominio en caligrafía, de más de nueve mil caracteres. Eso para empezar. Los suspensos se contaban por miles, pero el nivel de la administración han se elevó de forma sobresaliente. Gracias a aquel éxito, cuando Zhang Heng, a través de Fan Chun, pidió una audiencia con la emperatriz ésta se la concedió.

—Sabes que estamos satisfechos con tu trabajo como Astrónomo Jefe y como examinador oficial del Secretariado Imperial —dijo la emperatriz al recibirlo ante los nueve ministros, sus tres excelencias y una docena de asistentes de alto rango, entre los que, por supuesto, se encontraba también Fan Chun—. Me dice ahora el asistente del ministro de Obras Públicas que querías hablar conmigo.

—Sí, majestad —dijo Zhang Heng e hizo una pronunciada reverencia—. Se trata de algo en lo que llevo pensando hace tiempo, pero para lo que necesito materiales... algo costosos... Me explicaré... —Pero calló; miró al suelo, levantó la cabeza y volvió a hablar mirando un instante a la emperatriz—. Creo que sería más fácil si le enseño algo a su majestad.

—Adelante —respondió la emperatriz intrigada.

Zhang Heng miró a Fan Chun y éste hizo una señal a unos guardias. Éstos salieron y, al instante, entraron de nuevo en la sala de audiencias del palacio imperial de Loyang portando una especie de gigantesca vasija de metal que tenía una docena de dragones de hierro con la boca cerrada a su alrededor.

Los ministros y sus excelencias murmuraban.

—Esto es un prototipo de hierro —se explicaba Heng—. Lo ideal sería hacerlo de bronce de la mejor calidad y he de trabajar más en las conexiones entre el péndulo central y los dragones, pero en esencia en esto es en lo que desearía trabajar en los próximos años, con el permiso de su majestad y, por supuesto, sin desatender mis otras obligaciones como Astrónomo Jefe y examinador oficial del Secretariado Imperial.

La emperatriz no pudo evitar sonreír.

Fan Chun se acercó por detrás a Zhang Heng y le habló al oído.

—No has dicho de qué se trata.

—Ah, sí, claro, perdón, majestad —dijo Heng en voz alta, mirando al suelo, azorado por su torpeza y hablando muy rápido—. Esto pretende ser lo que yo he dado en llamar 候風地動儀, *houfeng didongyi*, la veleta de los temblores de tierra, majestad. La idea es que pueda detectar terremotos que hayan ocurrido a miles, a decenas de miles de *li* de distancia de aquí.

—¿Dices que esa máquina podría detectar terremotos? —preguntó la emperatriz asombrada. Era un hombre docto, culto y leal el que hablaba y, en consecuencia, no se tomaba a la ligera sus aseveraciones; no obstante, aquello parecía increíble.

—Pero incluso si esa máquina funcionara —intervino entonces su Excelencia de la Guerra, celoso de la relevancia que Heng estaba adquiriendo en la corte—, ¿qué utilidad puede tener saberlo? Lo interesante sería poder impedir un terremoto, o al menos predecirlo. No veo qué interés tiene que la máquina lo diga. Si hay algún terremoto en algún lugar del imperio, o fuera de él, ya nos llegará esa información de cualquier forma. Además, los terremotos son cosa de los dioses.

La emperatriz asintió y su Excelencia de la Guerra se mostró orgulloso de su intervención mirando al resto de arriba abajo.

—¿Qué tienes que decir a esto? —preguntó Deng en tono más conciliador al astrónomo.

—Bueno, majestad; para empezar, no tengo claro que los temblores de tierra sean algo de los dioses... pero más allá de ese asunto delicado, si bien es cierto que a Loyang siempre llega información sobre los terremotos que ocurren en el imperio, ésta llega tarde: me consta que hemos sufrido varias de estas desgracias en los últimos años y que su majestad siempre se ha esforzado en que se envíe ayuda de todo tipo a las regiones afectadas. Pero una forma de ayudar sería poder enviar todo cuanto es necesario lo más rápidamente posible. Desde que ocurre un terremoto hasta que nos llega un correo imperial pasa un tiempo precioso que podría haberse dedicado a preparar los víveres y otros suministros que se desean enviar al lugar en cuestión. La máquina haría que la ayuda del emperador, de la emperatriz, llegara mucho antes a los que más la necesitan, pues advertidos por la máquina del suceso, para cuando llegaran los mensajeros, en Loyang ya estaría todo dispuesto.

Se hizo un profundo silencio.

—Pero la máquina es un prototipo —comentó entonces Fan Chun—. Heng necesitaría financiación para una máquina más grande, de bronce y más sensible a estos temblores.

—¿Y cómo sabemos que esta máquina funciona? —interpuso entonces su Excelencia de la Guerra paseándose por un lado del prototipo. Justo en ese instante la cabeza de dragón más próxima a su Excelencia se abrió y dejó caer una bola de hierro pequeña que se paseó por la sala hasta parar en los pies de Fan Chun.

—Cuando la máquina detecta un movimiento en alguna dirección el péndulo debe hacer que la cabeza más próxima a ese punto suelte una bola, pero lo cierto es que este prototipo es muy inestable y la boca del dragón puede haberse abierto simplemente por la proximidad de los pasos de su Excelencia. O... —Heng calló.

—¿O? —preguntó la emperatriz.

—O quizá haya tenido lugar un terremoto a muchas decenas de miles de *li* de distancia, en algún remoto lugar de Occidente.

Su Excelencia negaba con la cabeza.

—No creo que dedicar recursos a estos artilugios mecánicos valga para nada que no sea malgastar el dinero recaudado entre los súbditos del Imperio han —concluyó.

La emperatriz levantó la mano y todo el mundo calló.

Deng miró aquel ingenio con interés: saber de inmediato que había tenido lugar un terremoto y hasta tener noción sobre más o menos en qué región no parecía para nada algo baladí.

—Zhang Heng, puedes pedir al ministro de Finanzas que financie tus trabajos para crear una nueva máquina, que probaremos en el futuro y con la que averiguaremos si el dinero ha sido bien o mal empleado. No tengo ganas de escuchar hoy a nadie más —sentenció la emperatriz rápidamente levantando aún más la voz y alzando las dos manos, para dejar claro que nadie se dirigiera a ella con el fin de contravenir su mandato. Su Excelencia de la Guerra, que iba a intentar contraargumentar, captó el mensaje, se inclinó ante su majestad y calló, y lo mismo hicieron el resto de excelencias, ministros y asistentes.

Todos fueron saliendo, incluido Heng, pero cuando Fan Chun estaba en la puerta uno de los guardias lo cogió por un brazo y lo hizo volver.

—La emperatriz desea hablar con el *yu-shih chung-ch'eng* a solas.

—Por supuesto —dijo Fan Chun y se acercó de nuevo al trono imperial.

—No tengo ganas de más debates hoy, pero estoy intrigada por si hay noticias de Occidente —comentó la emperatriz.

—¿De la guerra entre Da Qin y An-shi?

—Exacto —confirmó la emperatriz.

Hacía unos meses que varios mercaderes de la Ruta de la Seda habían comunicado que el camino terrestre hacia los remotos imperios de Occidente estaba cortado porque ambos reinos lejanos estaban en guerra. Esto estaba suponiendo una pérdida importante de ventas de seda, lacas y otros productos y, como era lógico, tenía a la emperatriz preocupada.

—Sí, majestad. Ayer mismo, Li Kan me escribió que había hablado con más mercaderes que acababan de llegar del territorio de los Yuegzhi. Estos comerciantes dicen que es difícil que las caravanas con la seda puedan llegar muy lejos, pues la guerra sigue. Parece ser que el emperador de Da Qin ha cruzado uno de los dos grandes ríos de An-shi, pero que el emperador de An-shi, por su parte, resiste con su ejército en el segundo río. Yo creo que todo dependerá de si el emperador de Da Qin consigue cruzar ese segundo río. Si lo hace, An-shi será suyo.

La emperatriz asintió.

—¿Y crees que ese emperador de Da Qin seguirá avanzando hasta cruzar el río Ili?[61]

—No lo veo probable, majestad. Mucha es la distancia que separa los ríos centrales de An-shi del Ili, pero estaremos atentos al desarrollo de los combates.

—Bien —confirmó la emperatriz. Y suspiró—. Ahora sí que me retiraré.

Fan Chun se inclinó, dio media vuelta y esta vez ningún guardia lo detuvo cuando salía de la gran estancia central del palacio imperial de Loyang. Justo al lado de la puerta estaba Zhang Heng, aún arrodillado junto a su ingenio mecánico, como si examinara con detalle alguno de sus mecanismos inferiores invisibles desde arriba.

—¿Algún problema? —preguntó Fan Chun, agachándose junto a él.

—Ah, no, no —dijo Heng incorporándose. Lo mismo hizo el asistente del ministro de Obras Públicas. El astrónomo siguió hablando—. Es que no entiendo por qué se ha abierto la boca del dragón y ha caído la bola.

—Bueno, por lo que has dicho antes, ¿no? —comentó Fan Chun repitiendo la explicación que el propio Heng acababa de dar en la sala de audiencias—. Quizá porque su Excelencia de la Guerra se había acercado demasiado.

—No. Eso lo he dicho para no quedar como un idiota delante de todos.

Fan Chun guardó silencio un instante.

—Entonces, después de todo, quizá haya habido algún terremoto en algún lugar de Occidente.

—Eso creo —dijo Heng—, pero no puedo estar seguro. Si llegara algún correo con noticias de un terremoto en las regiones occidentales, dímelo, por favor.

—Por supuesto, claro que si el terremoto ha sido fuera del Imperio han será difícil tener información sobre el mis-

---

61. Río Oxo para los romanos y griegos, río Amu Daria en la actualidad que desemboca en el mar Aral y que marcaba la frontera entre Partia y el Imperio kushan.

mo. Pero ¿podría tu maquina detectar algo que ocurriera tan lejos?

Heng, Astrónomo Jefe de la corte han en Loyang, se encogió de hombros.

—No tengo ni idea.

71

LOS SUPERVIVIENTES

Atrio en ruinas del palacio imperial de Antioquía, Siria
Invierno de 115 d. C.

Los supervivientes se levantaban del suelo quebrado en mil pedazos y se abrazaban entre sí. La tierra se había detenido al fin, pero el silencio que siguió los espantaba casi tanto como el temblor constante que los había aterrorizado durante lo que ellos creían que había sido una hora eterna, aunque en realidad apenas habían transcurrido unos instantes.

Nigrino se levantó también y miró hacia donde había estado la puerta de entrada al palacio. Llamarlo así ya no tenía mucho sentido. Varios árboles yacían tumbados, desencajados de la tierra, con sus raíces al descubierto. El *legatus* vio entonces a Lucio Quieto avanzando por encima de las ruinas, gritando, llamando al emperador.

—¡César, César! —aullaba el líder norteafricano mientras se encaramaba a columnas derrumbadas y escalaba por las paredes abiertas como si las hubieran fulminado los rayos del mismísimo Júpiter.

Nigrino se dirigió entonces a Adriano.

—¿Está bien la emperatriz? —preguntó al sobrino del César, pues Plotina estaba en el suelo, junto a él.

—Sí —respondió Adriano—. Parece algo aturdida pero bien.

—Voy a ayudar a Quieto. Hemos de encontrar al emperador y sacarlo de allí, de esas ruinas, como sea.

Adriano miró hacia la montaña de piedra desencajada de lo que había sido hasta hacía tan sólo unos instantes un imponente palacio. No tenía claro que su tío hubiera sobrevivido a aquello. Lo que, por cierto, abría posibilidades muy interesantes a su futuro. Adriano miró hacia Quieto. El norteafricano había desaparecido entre el mar de ruinas. Aún se oía el ruido que algunos muros hacían al seguir desplomándose. ¿Sería aquél el día en el que vería no sólo el fin de Trajano sino también el de Quieto? ¿Sería posible tanto en tan poco tiempo?

—Sí, ve con Quieto. Yo me ocupo de ver cómo está todo el mundo aquí —respondió Adriano con una serenidad controlada.

Nigrino partió raudo tras Quieto.

Avanzó con tiento sobre piedras que se movían, entre una nube espesa de polvo volátil y, tras superar una gran montaña de ruinas, vio a su compañero en medio de lo que debía de haber sido la cámara personal del emperador, ahora transformada en un montón de grava y ladrillos partidos. Nigrino caminó como pudo, esquivando los agujeros que dejaban las ruinas a su alrededor como trampas mortales, y llegó junto al norteafricano.

Se veían varios brazos de cadáveres emergiendo de entre las piedras.

—No son del César —dijo Quieto en cuanto sintió la presencia de Nigrino.

—¿Aulo y los pretorianos? —preguntó Nigrino.

—He tirado de varios de ellos y llevaban el uniforme de los pretorianos, sí —dijo Quieto mientras miraba a un lado y a otro. Empezaron entonces los gemidos. Ya no había silencio, sino alaridos horribles de los que estaban atrapados bajo las ruinas, allí mismo y en otras partes del palacio. Los aullidos de dolor extremo se convirtieron en un inmenso coro de lamentos que emergía de todas las esquinas de la ciudad de Antioquía.

—Debe de haber cientos de personas bajos los escombros —dijo Nigrino.

—Miles... —precisó Quieto— y uno de ellos es el César...

Pero en ese momento oyeron otro grito diferente.

—¡Aquí, aquí!

—¡Es Aulo! —exclamó Quieto con sorpresa, con esperanza, al reconocer la voz del tribuno. Los dos *legati* escalaron otro montón de ruinas y vislumbraron al tribuno pretoriano junto al cuerpo de otro hombre.

—¡Está con el emperador! —dijo Nigrino.

—¡Vamos allá! —exclamó Quieto.

Tuvieron que descender por una ladera de escombros que se movían si pisabas donde las piedras no estaban asentadas y el camino fue peligroso, pero la posibilidad de encontrar al emperador con vida los animaba y les daba el valor para lanzarse por aquella vertiente de ruinas con el arrojo de quien lucha por la vida de un amigo al que hasta hace sólo un momento han dado por muerto.

—¿Cómo está? —preguntó Quieto nada más ver la herida del emperador.

—No lo sé, pero respira —respondió Aulo.

Quieto se dirigió entonces a Nigrino.

—Has de volver a donde estaban los invitados y traer a Critón... si es que aún vive. El César necesita al médico de inmediato.

—De acuerdo.

Pero cuando Nigrino estaba a punto de marcharse una voz los detuvo a todos.

—¿Qué ha pasado? —preguntó Trajano, que acababa de abrir los ojos y se llevaba una mano a la frente—. ¿Un terremoto?

—Sin duda, César —dijo Aulo.

—Ayudadme a levantarme —dijo Trajano mientras apoyaba la mano llena de sangre en el suelo para intentar alzarse.

—Quizá sería mejor que el César descansase —dijo Lucio Quieto.

Trajano lo miró con severidad.

—¿Te parece, Lucio, éste un momento adecuado para descansar? ¿Me dirías eso en medio de una batalla?

—No, César —admitió Quieto.

Trajano se levantó ayudado por Aulo y Nigrino.

—Pues esto es lo más parecido a una batalla que he visto nunca, ¿no crees, Lucio?

El norteafricano miró a su alrededor. Todo eran ruinas y cadáveres y heridos y llamadas de auxilio de los que estaban atrapados por todas partes.

—Sí, sí que lo es.

—Pues sea quien sea el enemigo, porque no sé quién o qué crea un terremoto, no parece que estemos ganando, Lucio, así que tendremos que organizarnos —continuó Trajano a la vez que asía por el brazo al norteafricano en señal de amistad y agradecimiento por preocuparse por él, pero rápidamente indagó sobre la situación—. ¿Dónde está el resto?

—Hacia allí, César —respondió Nigrino, señalando el lugar donde debían de encontrarse los invitados supervivientes, más allá de varias montañas de escombros.

—Bien, vamos allí y dadme algo con lo que taparme esta herida... —dijo llevándose la mano a la frente ensangrentada.

Quieto se arrancó parte de su túnica y se la entregó al César.

—Parece que sangra menos, César —dijo Aulo.

Y echaron a andar por encima de las ruinas del palacio.

72

LA DECISIÓN DE ARRIO

Costa occidental de la India
Invierno de 115 d. C.

La *cladivata*, pese a haber encallado en Barigaza a causa de las poderosas mareas de la región, no estaba muy dañada y eran pocos los desperfectos. Aun así no pudieron ponerse con las reparaciones durante unas semanas porque la temporada de lluvias se alargó y fue imposible trabajar hasta que las nubes despejaron. Una vez recuperado el barco, se echaron a la mar de nuevo, esta vez costeando la India hacia el norte. La línea de costa era sinuosa, con fuertes corrientes y vientos, y Arrio fue progresando muy lentamente hacia el objetivo: alcanzar territorio bajo el control de los kushan.

—Allí —dijo una mañana Titianus señalando hacia tierra.

Todos miraron hacia donde apuntaba el índice del mercader: se veía un enorme delta donde varios brazos de un mismo río vertían una enorme cantidad de agua a la mar Eritrea.

—¿Es el Sinthus?[62] —preguntó Arrio, que había oído hablar de un río gigantesco que desembocaba en la mar Eritrea desde las tierras más profundas de la India.

—Así es —confirmo Titianus—. *Es el más grande de todos los ríos que fluyen hacia la mar Eritrea, vertiendo una enorme cantidad de agua, de forma que durante un largo trecho de mar, antes de llegar aquí, el agua del océano es fresca.*[63]

—¿Y ahora qué hacemos? —preguntó de nuevo Arrio,

---

62. Río Indo.
63. Literal de *Periplo por la mar Eritrea*, al igual que las siguientes frases en cursiva que dice Titianus.

pues no sabía por cuál de todos aquellos brazos del gran río ascender en busca de la ciudad de Barbaricum. El delta se le antojaba como un complejo laberinto imposible de descifrar.

—*Este río tiene siete brazos, muy poco profundos y pantanosos, así que no son navegables, excepto el del centro* —dijo Titianus y lo señaló para que Arrio pudiera conducir la *cladivata* en esa dirección—. *En la ribera de ese brazo del río encontraremos la ciudad de Barbaricum.* Tradicionalmente ha estado bajo el control de los partos durante muchos años, pero los kushan han luchado por conseguir una salida directa al mar y arrebataron el control de este puerto a los gobernantes de Cesifonte hace un tiempo. En cuanto atraquemos en Barbaricum estaremos rodeados de guerreros kushan. Nos acercamos al final de nuestro viaje.

Cuando Tamura escuchó aquellas palabras del mercader, comprendió que era momento de desvelar a Titianus, y a sus padres también, lo que ya había contado a Áyax.

Y lo hizo.

El mercader se quedó mirando a la muchacha perplejo.

—Así que el emperador quiere que sigamos más allá del Imperio kushan. Desea que lleguemos hasta la mismísima Xeres. Me parece increíble.

—Si mi hija lo dice es que es así —dijo entonces Marcio, convencido de que si Tamura había dicho lo que había dicho, tenía que ser cierto.

—Es sorprendente —apuntó Arrio con cierta desconfianza— que el emperador informe del auténtico objetivo de esta misión a una niña y no al viejo Titianus o a cualquier otro de nosotros. No digo que no sea cierto, pero me parece extraño.

—Quizá Trajano no confía en nadie y pensó que una niña preservaría mejor el secreto de la misión que ninguno de nosotros —contrapuso Marcio empezando a respirar con fuerza. Arrio lo incomodaba cada vez más: primero había estado retrasando la navegación por las costas de Azania, luego puso todo tipo de impedimentos a la hora de comprar un nuevo barco en Muza; seguidamente retrasó el viaje por el océano, las reparaciones en Barigaza y hasta la navegación por las costas de la India. Y ahora dudaba de la palabra de Tamura.

La muchacha, entretanto, estaba muy enrabietada por la insistencia tanto de su padre como de Arrio en referirse a ella como una «niña». Sentía que cada vez que decían aquella palabra, Áyax, casi inconscientemente, se separaba un poco de ella. La confusión de sus sentimientos le hizo olvidar que ella también había desvelado a Áyax no sólo el objetivo final del viaje, sino también lo que Trajano le había dicho que debía transmitir al emperador de Xeres si llegaban alguna vez hasta él. Pero no, en aquel momento, Tamura sólo pensaba en que no era una niña y en que iba a demostrárselo muy pronto a Áyax. No ya luchando ni lanzando flechas, sino de la única forma en que una mujer puede dejar bien claro ante un hombre que ya no es una niña.

—No pasa nada —intervino Titianus intentando sosegar los ánimos encrespados entre Arrio y Marcio—. Siempre he querido tener una buena excusa que me empujara a ir más allá de Kasgar.

—¿Kasgar? —preguntó Marcio.

—Está en la frontera entre el Imperio kushan y los territorios controlados por Xeres. Las órdenes del Trajano nos obligan a seguir más allá de ese punto y a mí, personalmente, me ilusiona.

—Pues yo no pienso seguir —dijo Arrio.

Marcio se llevó la mano a la empuñadura de su espada.

Titianus se interpuso entre ambos y eso dio tiempo a que Arrio se explicara con más detalle.

—Yo estoy en esta misión como piloto, como capitán de barco del Imperio romano. Os he llevado en barco por el Mediterráneo, a través del Canal de Trajano; luego he navegado por todas las costas de Egipto y Azania y hasta he cruzado la gran mar Eritrea y os he conducido por las costas de la India, pero en Barbaricum el mar termina. Yo no seguiré. Me quedaré en este puerto y esperaré vuestro regreso.

Pero no dijo nada de impedir al resto que prosiguiera con el viaje. Eso relajó a Marcio. De hecho dio por bienvenida aquella decisión de Arrio: así se desharían de aquel marino sospechoso de estar retrasándolos siempre.

—Por mí de acuerdo —dijo el antiguo gladiador.

—De acuerdo todos entonces —aceptó Titianus y volvió a señalar, ahora hacia la ribera del río por el que ascendían—: Barbaricum.

Desembarcaron y el mercader dirigió la venta de parte de los productos que llevaban: diferentes telas, algo de topacio, coral, incienso, vasijas de vidrio, una vajilla de plata y un poco de vino. Titianus ordenó que el resto se cargara en mulas para ser conducido hacia el interior del imperio. Los caminos hacia el norte eran razonablemente seguros para los mercaderes, pues los kushan favorecían el comercio que cruzaba su territorio. Para eso habían luchado por tener un puerto en la mar Eritrea. Y el comercio además en aquel momento era muy intenso en la ruta kushan, pues la guerra entre Partia y Roma había desviado a la mayoría de las caravanas que iban desde Xeres hacia el puerto de Barbaricum. La ciudad bullía con una actividad febril. El trasiego de barcos de todo tipo era constante, de modo que lo más difícil fue encontrar un muelle libre para desembarcar la mercancía.

Con las mulas cargadas, algunos productos vendidos y otros nuevos recién adquiridos, todo estaba dispuesto para proseguir el viaje hacia el norte, hacia Bagram, hacia la capital del Imperio kushan.

—Hasta luego —dijo Arrio a Titianus en el muelle de Barbaricum donde permanecía anclada la *cladivata*—. Esperaré aquí vuestro regreso. ¿Cuánto tiempo crees que necesitaréis?

Titianus meditó un momento. Llegar hasta Bagram aún les llevaría un mes. Luego allí tendría que esperar hasta conseguir ver al emperador y, aunque se identificaran como embajadores de Trajano, eso podía llevar un tiempo. Después estaba el viaje hasta Samarkanda y luego Kasgar. Y a partir de ahí, lo desconocido: cruzar Xeres entera en busca de su capital, conseguir hablar con el emperador de aquellas tierras y regresar. El mercader no pudo evitar sonreír cuando dio su respuesta.

—Si estamos aquí en Barbaricum en año y medio me consideraría afortunado.

Arrio asintió. Le pareció razonable.

—Esperaré dos años —dijo el capitán romano—. Si en dos

años no habéis regresado volveré a Roma y diré que no hay... respuesta de la embajada. ¿Lo ves bien, mercader?

Titianus miró a Marcio. El antiguo *lanista* movió la cabeza afirmativamente.

—De acuerdo —dijo entonces el mercader.

—Que los dioses os protejan —añadió Arrio al despedirse.

Titianus lo miró en silencio. «Lo necesitaremos», pensó, pero no dijo nada y se puso en marcha junto con Marcio, Alana, Tamura y Áyax. Atrás quedaban Arrio y sus marinos.

73

EN GUERRA CONTRA LOS DIOSES

Circo Máximo de Antioquía
115 d. C., dos horas después del terremoto

Trajano, pese a sus heridas en la cabeza y los brazos, tomó el mando de la situación. Su primera orden fue la de trasladar a todo el mundo del palacio imperial a la gran explanada central del Circo Máximo de Antioquía. Todos los familiares del emperador, sus altos oficiales, consejeros, libertos y esclavos supervivientes al desastre cruzaron por encima de las ruinas del palacio imperial y se adentraron en el Circo Máximo de la ciudad. Sólo había que atravesar una gran avenida que separaba el palacio del gigantesco estadio pues, a semejanza de Roma, el gran Circo estaba justo al lado de la residencia imperial.

—Será mejor evitar los accesos habituales, César —sugirió Nigrino, quien, por mandato del emperador, se había adelantado para ver en qué estado se encontraba el Circo—. Parte de las gradas se ha derrumbado y temo que puedan seguir cayendo más secciones, pero hay una apertura, pasando por encima de la zona destruida, que sería el camino más rápido y seguro para acceder al centro de la explanada.

—Cruzaremos por allí —confirmó Trajano.

Y así se hizo.

A partir de ahí, el emperador reunió a sus consejeros y *legati*. Todos cubiertos de polvo y algunos con heridas leves, pero todos dispuestos a las órdenes de un Trajano cuya templanza en aquel momento de desastre los tenía admirados. Allí estaban, en un gran círculo, sobre la arena del Circo, Adriano, Lucio Quieto, Nigrino, Aulo y el viejo Dión Coceyo que, pese a su edad, ayudado por unos y por otros, había conseguido salvarse del desastre. Plotina y el resto de las mujeres de la familia imperial estaban un poco más separadas, todas bien, con alguna herida y, desde luego, mucho terror, atendidas por Critón, el médico imperial. También se había salvado Arbandes, quien, por orden imperial, fue conducido a una tienda confortable donde poder descansar y recuperarse del miedo pasado y de alguna leve herida en un brazo.

Trajano aún se sostenía con una mano el vendaje que el propio Critón le había hecho en la cabeza después de limpiarle la herida, pero hablaba con una energía que transmitía seguridad a todos los presentes en medio de aquella oscuridad lúgubre que se cernía sobre una ciudad destrozada. Habían encendido antorchas, pues el atardecer alargaba las sombras de los edificios en ruina. De vez en cuando aún se oía el bramido de alguna pared desplomándose y nuevos gritos, que se unían a los lamentos constantes que llegaban de todos lados y que partían los sentimientos hasta del hombre más recio y endurecido por la guerra.

—Veamos —empezó el emperador—. Por partes: primero, ¿cuál es la situación? Segundo, ¿qué ha ocurrido? Y tercero, ¿qué vamos a hacer? Sobre lo primero, veo que la familia imperial está bien y vosotros también. Todos tenemos alguna herida, pero viendo lo ocurrido podemos darnos por satisfechos. Por cierto, cuando pase todo podéis agradecerme que decidiera celebrar el banquete en el atrio y no en el interior de palacio; quizá todavía no nos han abandonado los dioses del todo. Pero volviendo al asunto de los supervivientes: no sé dónde están Liviano o, por ejemplo, Fédimo. ¿Sabemos algo de ellos?

Lucio Quieto fue el primero en hablar.

—Liviano ha enviado un mensajero desde el campamento pretoriano en las afueras de la ciudad y dice que el regimiento y la caballería a su cargo están bien en su mayoría, así como las legiones acantonadas en diferentes puntos alrededor de la ciudad. El hecho de que los campamentos sean provisionales, con tiendas en su mayor parte en lugar de con construcciones, parece que ha mitigado los efectos de este... —el norteafricano aún no sabía muy bien cómo definir lo que había ocurrido, aunque todo apuntaba a un gran terremoto—, de este... desastre, César.

—Bien, esto es importante —dijo Trajano asintiendo sin retirar la mano derecha del vendaje; la cabeza le dolía, pero no era momento de quejarse, sino de actuar—. Y de Fédimo, mi secretario, ¿sabemos algo...?

Pero antes de que nadie pudiera decir nada, se oyó la voz del aludido.

—Fédimo está aquí, al servicio del emperador, como siempre, César.

Trajano se levantó de la *sella* en la que se encontraba y saludó afectuosamente a su joven secretario asiéndolo de ambos brazos sin importarle ensuciarse con el polvo que cubría su piel sudada y sucia.

—Estás bien, estás bien... —repetía Trajano.

—Había dejado el banquete para ir a la biblioteca de la ciudad, César: quería consultar algunos documentos y encontrar algún mapa de Mesopotamia, tal y como deseaba el emperador, pero tuve la fortuna de que la tierra empezara a temblar cuando ya estaba fuera, de regreso al palacio. El temblor me sorprendió por las calles y pude evitar que el edificio se desplomara sobre mí. La biblioteca está... arrasada, César.

—Bien, bien... —dijo Trajano volviendo a sentarse—, pero mis hombres de confianza están bien. —Paseó los ojos por todos y cada uno de los que lo rodeaban, incluyendo una rápida mirada a un Adriano que permanecía en silencio, cabizbajo. Trajano se preguntó qué estaría pensando su sobrino, pero no tenía tiempo para divagar y retomó su discurso—. Los edificios, Fédimo, no son tan importantes como las personas. Un edificio como la biblioteca, como el palacio imperial o como este circo que nos rodea puede ser levantado de nuevo, aunque sustituir la lealtad de un buen secretario, de un buen *legatus* o de un buen consejero es infinitamente más difícil. Pero sigamos: he de entender que la ruina que veo a mi alrededor es en esencia un reflejo de lo que hay por toda la ciudad.

—Eso es lo que me ha dicho el mensajero de Liviano, augusto —confirmó Lucio Quieto.

—Eso también es lo que yo he visto viniendo aquí desde la biblioteca, César —apostilló Fédimo.

—Bien, bien... —Trajano apretó los labios y bajó la mirada

mientras seguía hablando, o, más bien, dando voz a sus pensamientos—. Así es como están las cosas: Antioquía está prácticamente arrasada. Pasemos entonces a la segunda cuestión. —Levantó los ojos de nuevo y los fijó en Dión Coceyo—. Esto que ha ocurrido es un terremoto, ¿no es así, Dión?

El anciano Dión se levantó de su *sella*, no sin esfuerzo, y dio un paso al frente. Era el único, además del emperador, que estaba sentado, por razón de su edad, cuando se reunía el *consilium augusti* de Trajano. Una vez en pie, el filósofo dio respuesta a la pregunta del César.

—Sí, augusto: no hay duda alguna de que lo que acabamos de experimentar todos ha sido un terremoto, pero ciertamente uno de los de mayor magnitud de los últimos años, quizá decenios.

—¿Por qué aquí y en este preciso día y qué podemos esperar en las próximas horas? —preguntó Trajano con los ojos brillantes y un tono vibrante. Antes de decidir necesitaba saber.

El filósofo carraspeó, lo que anunciaba una respuesta extensa, pero en aquel momento todos daban por bienvenido a alguien que pudiera arrojar algo de luz sobre aquella noche oscura.

—Por qué ocurre un terremoto, César, es algo que realmente no sabemos bien. Anaxágoras, creo recordar, pensaba que los terremotos se producen cuando hay demasiada agua en la corteza terrestre y el agua, de algún modo, se filtra por las cavidades de la tierra y las zarandea a su paso. Demócrito pensaba algo parecido, pero Anaxímenes creía que era casi lo contrario: que por falta de agua algunas partes de la tierra caían en cavidades vacías y creaban estos temblores al desplazarse. Y Aristóteles también pensaba que el calor del sol evaporaba grandes cantidades de agua y la desaparición de ésta junto con los movimientos del propio vapor podrían crear una inestabilidad que facilitara estos desplazamientos de tierras. En fin, realmente no sabemos bien por qué ocurre esto. Otra cosa es lo que la gente piense y... —Pero aquí se detuvo el filósofo.

—No, habla, sea lo que sea —dijo Trajano—. No es momento para remilgos. ¿Qué pensará la gente?

—Muchos atribuyen estos terremotos a los dioses, ya sean

547

a los nuestros o las suyos propios. Habrá cristianos que atribuyan este terremoto al control al que están sometidos por las autoridades del Imperio y pensarán que su dios castiga al César. También habrá judíos que piensen que su dios se venga ahora de los romanos que destruyeron su templo hace unos años, no importa que fuera en tiempos de Vespasiano y Tito: la demolición de su templo es algo que ni olvidan ni perdonan. Y muchos ciudadanos romanos, y seguramente muchos legionarios del ejército tendrán simplemente... miedo, César, a que sus dioses los hayan abandonado. Algunos volverán a hablar de la legión perdida y quizá concluyan que se trata de un aviso para que no se vuelva a cruzar el Éufrates, como hizo Craso, o una advertencia de que lo que no debe intentarse de ningún modo es cruzar también el Tigris. Siento ser tan incómodo en mis comentarios, pero el César me ha pedido que exprese todos mis pensamientos.

Trajano inspiró profundamente. Los llantos que seguían oyéndose por las ruinas que los rodeaban, los estallidos de las piedras que continuaban cayendo en medio de la noche que ya los envolvía por completo y los gritos de pena o terror que se oían intermitentemente por el exterior del Circo, subrayaban el impacto de las palabras del filósofo.

Trajano asintió una vez más y volvió a preguntarle:

—No me has respondido aún a una parte de lo que te he planteado.

—Es cierto —aceptó el anciano—. ¿Qué podemos esperar a partir de ahora? No soy experto en el asunto de los terremotos, pero sí que he leído en varios textos que es frecuente que tras un gran temblor se sucedan otros en los días sucesivos, quizá no de tanta importancia, pero sí grandes. Esto aumentaría los destrozos, el número de víctimas y el terror de todos. Yo sugeriría al César abandonar la ciudad y trasladarse a otro punto de la provincia, y quizá tratar de enviar ayuda desde allí, alimentos y algunas tropas que mantengan el orden mientras se intenta recomponer algo en esta ciudad herida mortalmente para siempre. Ése, César, es mi consejo.

Dión Coceyo dio un paso atrás y se quedó en pie, frente a su silla, pero sin tomar asiento.

—Siento que hayas tenido que sufrir este desastre con nosotros —dijo Trajano mirándolo fijamente—, pero es una suerte disponer de tus conocimientos en un momento tan grave como el que vivimos. Gracias, Dión, puedes sentarte. —El emperador volvió a mirar a su alrededor—. Bien, por Júpiter, tenemos una idea aproximada de lo que ha ocurrido y a lo que nos enfrentamos. Queda decidir qué vamos a hacer a partir de este momento.

Varios jinetes entraron en el Circo Máximo al galope por la sección de los *carceres* que, a lo que se veía, también estaba resquebrajada y permitía el acceso de aquellos *singulares*, pues se trataba de caballería pretoriana, a la explanada del estadio.

El *consilium augusti* estaba custodiado por un nutrido grupo de pretorianos de infantería supervivientes al desastre del palacio imperial que impidieron el acceso de estos recién llegados al consejo del César. Trajano miró a Quieto y éste no necesitó palabras. El norteafricano fue rápidamente a donde estaban los jinetes y departió con ellos unos momentos. Nadie hablaba en el consejo. El crepitar de las antorchas se mezclaba con más gemidos llegados de todas las direcciones posibles. Era como si la ciudad entera de Antioquía llorara sin parar.

Quieto regresó al cónclave imperial.

—Los envía Liviano —empezó el norteafricano—. El prefecto de la ciudad ha muerto. No hay autoridad ni control en las calles, La gente anda perdida, sin rumbo, buscando a sus familiares. Hay casas que siguen cayendo. Liviano pide instrucciones para él y para el resto de los *legati* al mando de las legiones. Quiere saber adónde hay que trasladar al ejército y si hay que marcharse esta misma noche o esperar al amanecer, César.

Se hizo un incómodo silencio.

—Lo mejor es irse cuanto antes —propuso Adriano.

Trajano se levantó, dio un par de pasos y se situó en el centro del *consilium augusti*. Inspiró, una vez más, muy profundamente, apretó los labios y, por fin, exhaló lentamente el aire de los pulmones. Miró entonces a Quieto sin tener en cuenta, al menos por el momento, el comentario de su sobrino.

—Dile al mensajero de Liviano que la guardia pretoriana

se queda aquí, en Antioquía, y que lo mismo pasa con el resto del ejército. Que informe a todas las legiones. No nos moveremos ni esta noche ni en mucho tiempo de esta ciudad. Hemos venido a pasar el invierno a Antioquía y lo pasaremos aquí...

—Pero la ciudad está destruida —intervino de nuevo Adriano entrando en el discurso del emperador como un tropel de disconformidad irrefrenable—: pronto empezarán los saqueos. Y con tantos heridos y muertos vendrán las enfermedades. Estoy seguro de que el sistema de abastecimiento de agua de la ciudad estará destrozado. La mayor parte si no todos los acueductos estarán derruidos. En unos días empezará la sed y los tumultos por falta de comida. No podemos poner en peligro a las legiones en medio de este caos. Lo prudente es trasladar el ejército y, desde un lugar seguro, si el emperador lo desea, asistir a Antioquía. —Pero como veía que su tío se mantenía inmóvil, con los brazos en jarra, sin apariencia de que ninguno de esos argumentos fueran a hacerlo cambiar de opinión, Adriano intentó añadir miedo, si no para asustar al César, quizá sí para introducir el temor en las venas de sus oficiales más fieles—. Además, augusto, mañana o en unas horas sólo, la tierra volverá a temblar y quizá esta segunda vez no tengamos tanta suerte ninguno de nosotros. Lo sensato es, si mi consejo no es del agrado del emperador, aceptar el consejo de Dión Coceyo, a quien el César siempre ha tenido en gran estima. Y él mismo ha sugerido que lo prudente es marcharse...

—¡No nos iremos! —lo interrumpió Trajano levantando la voz y con una determinación casi hostil. Y se volvió hacia Quieto—. ¡Y he dado una orden para Liviano que espero que sea transmitida literalmente!

Quieto se llevo el puño al pecho, dio media vuelta y fue a hablar con el mensajero del prefecto del pretorio. Todos vieron el asombro, la sorpresa y aun el miedo, ese terror que Adriano quería sembrar, en la faz de aquel jinete, que asintió y partió al galope para llevar las órdenes del César a sus pretorianos y *legati*. Las miradas del círculo del consejo imperial volvieron sobre el emperador, que seguía en el centro.

—No, no nos iremos de aquí. No seré yo un emperador de quien pueda decirse que ante un terremoto abandoné a los ciudadanos de una ciudad del Imperio a su suerte, a un destino que con nuestra partida no puede ser otro que el que ha descrito Adriano: muerte, pánico y caos. Pero si nos quedamos y luchamos contra el desastre que nos rodea, si lo hacemos juntos, unidos, entonces podemos revertir esa terrible serie de acontecimientos que ha expuesto mi sobrino. —Y dijo «sobrino» a conciencia, intentando que sonara a pequeño, a infantil, a miedoso; no añadió más connotaciones porque no sabía cómo; pero siguió hablando—. Yo no les tengo miedo a los ejércitos enemigos como tampoco temo a los terremotos o las inundaciones o lo que sea que nos sobrevenga. Si hay alguien que tiene que dar ejemplo en circunstancias totalmente adversas es el emperador. Además, si esto no os convence... —se detuvo un instante y miró directamente a los ojos de Adriano, que lo miraba a su vez con rabia contenida— os diré algo más en lo que quizá no hayáis pensado. —El crepitar de las antorchas, las sombras temblorosas de los presentes en aquel cónclave, el cielo raso cubierto de estrellas, los aullidos de dolor de heridos y gentes desesperadas que transitaban por las calles de una ciudad mordida por los infiernos... todo parecía dar vueltas en torno a aquel grupo de oficiales y consejeros que escuchaba a un solo hombre, a uno al que hacía años el Senado había elegido para ser *imperator*, hablar con una decisión y una fortaleza que los dejaba mudos—. ¿No os habéis planteado lo que van a pensar de nosotros, de mí, del ejército de Roma, de todos si nos vamos en medio de la noche, como niños que corren porque tienen miedo a la oscuridad? ¿Qué van a concluir los ciudadanos de Antioquía? ¿Y los de otras ciudades y colonias del Imperio cuando lleguen noticias de nuestra marcha? ¿Creéis acaso que todos van a pensar que el emperador fue «prudente»? ¿De verdad sois tan ingenuos? No, yo os diré lo que van a decir en las termas de Roma, en las tabernas de los puertos de todo el Mediterráneo, yo os diré lo que dirán los oficiales de Osroes, en Partia, os diré lo que pensarán en la Dacia y en todas las fronteras del Imperio: «Trajano tuvo miedo». Eso dirán de mí, y de vosotros y de las legiones. «Salieron corriendo abandonando a todos.» Antioquía nos ha recibido y nos ha dado apoyo como base de operaciones en la conquista de Armenia y Mesopotamia, y ahora que Antioquía nos necesita, ¿vamos a abandonarla? ¿Es eso realmente justo? Incluso llego a preguntarme si marcharnos de aquí ahora, desde un punto de vista puramente de gobierno, es realmente sensato —y detuvo su discurso atronador mirando, de nuevo, a Dión Coceyo.

El filósofo griego se levantó por segunda vez de su asiento.

—No sabría decir, tras escuchar al César, si quedarse es o no lo más sensato, pero me parece indiscutible que permanecer en Antioquía es, sin duda, lo más compasivo y lo más audaz. Un César, un emperador, ha de obrar normalmente con sensatez antes que nada, pero en ocasiones dramáticas como ésta la audacia es admirable. ¿Dónde está la frontera entre la prudencia y la insensatez cuando un desastre se ha cernido sobre todos? Aquí me rindo a la clarividencia del emperador. Y sus reflexiones sobre la forma en que tanto Roma como los reyes extranjeros evaluarán las acciones del César en un día tan nefasto como el de hoy tienen mucho fundamento y son aspectos que no había tenido presentes en mi primer consejo. Por eso yo sólo soy eso, consejero, y el César es César. Una solución intermedia es alejarse unas millas, pero no tengo claro que eso sea muy diferente a quedarse, pues los temblores que puedan sobrevenir asolarán un territorio amplio y si el emperador no está considerando alejarse hacia el sur o hacia el norte más de cien o ciento cincuenta millas, quizá quedarse pueda ser tan bueno como alejarse un poco. Sólo puedo añadir que si el César se queda en Antioquía mis viejos brazos y mi humilde ingenio estarán, como siempre, a su servicio aquí y ahora. A fin de cuentas, lo que veo a mi alrededor se parece más que a otra cosa al escenario de una batalla terrible, y quien sabe más de batallas y de guerras es el César.

Se inclinó levemente ante el emperador. No lo hizo más porque su espalda no se lo permitía. Trajano lo sabía. Se acercó al anciano y lo acompañó personalmente a su asiento para que el filósofo, que como el resto también tenía alguna herida y magulladuras varias, pudiera sentarse de nuevo y descansar.

Pero de inmediato, Trajano se volvió hacia el resto de los presentes.

—En efecto, nuestro viejo Dión tiene razón en que lo que ha ocurrido bien se asemeja a una guerra y que yo sepa a ninguno de los presentes nos ha gustado tener que retirarnos en una batalla, así que tampoco lo haremos ahora. Éste es un buen momento para recordar el espíritu de Plinio el Viejo, que fue personalmente con la flota imperial de Miseno a asistir a todos los heridos por la erupción de Vesubio que arrasó Pompeya y Herculano. —En cuanto lo dijo supo que no había elegido el mejor ejemplo, pues precisamente Plinio el Viejo falleció asfixiado intentando ayudar con los barcos imperiales a los que huían de la erupción; en todo caso, nadie pensó en recordar ese funesto final, o quizá no tuvo oportunidad de hacerlo, porque Trajano se lanzó a dar múltiples órdenes a toda velocidad—. Veamos: Quieto, quiero que vayas a por los hombres de las legiones IV Scythica y VI Ferrata y que se dediquen, en diferentes unidades, barrio por barrio, a intentar sacar a cuantos heridos puedan de debajo de los escombros. Un mapa, necesitamos un plano de la ciudad... —y miró a Fédimo, quien para sorpresa de muchos pero no para Trajano extrajo de inmediato un plano de la ciudad, pues el joven secretario había accedido a la biblioteca, tal y como había explicado, para conseguir planos de Mesopotamia, pero también de Antioquía, ya que el César le había comentado que quería hacer algunas modificaciones en el trazado de varias calles para mejorar la ciudad en su conjunto; ahora eran otras las circunstancias, totalmente diferentes, pero quizá esos mismos planos fueran seguramente aún más útiles—. Bien, bien, bien... —dijo Trajano señalando el suelo—. Ponlo aquí, muchacho. —Fédimo extendió el mapa en el suelo. El emperador hincó una rodilla junto al plano, un pretoriano acercó una antorcha y Quieto, Nigrino y el resto se aproximaron para seguir bien las indicaciones—. Quieto, con esas legiones, ha de peinar el distrito III, el del palacio imperial, o lo que queda de él, las gradas del circo que nos rodea y las termas; la legión XII Fulminata, con Nigrino al mando, que se ocupe de los sectores I y II, aquí y aquí. El sector IV es muy grande... veamos, del teatro y el foro hacia el norte se ocupará la legión XVI Flavia Firma con Adriano al frente y la legión III Cirenaica, bajo mi mando personal, se centrará en la parte sur de ese mismo sector. Las legiones III Gallica, X Fretensis, I Adiutrix y XV Apollinaris permanecerán en reserva. Luego se incorporarán a los trabajos por turnos, pues aquí va a haber tareas para todo el mundo. Liviano patrullará con la guardia pretoriana toda la ciudad y se encargará de evitar cualquier tipo de saqueo. Quiero que los heridos se lleven a los *valetudinaria,* a los hospitales de las legiones y que nuestros *medici* se ocupen de atender a todos, sin importar su origen o condición, sean civiles o militares, ciudadanos romanos, sirios, cristianos o judíos. Y en una cosa tiene razón Adriano. —Lo miró un instante, como en un intento de un mínimo de reconciliación; los necesitaba a todos unidos, incluso a su sobrino, en torno a aquel hercúleo empeño por retomar el control de una ciudad en ruinas—. Él ha mencionado el problema del abastecimiento de agua y debe de estar en lo cierto: que los zapadores del ejército examinen el estado de todos los acueductos y que calculen los daños. La reconstrucción de los acueductos tiene prioridad absoluta sobre cualquier otro edificio. La reconstrucción de Antioquía empezará por los acueductos, porque no dudéis de que vamos a levantar esta ciudad de nuevo. Fédimo, quiero que escribas una carta a Apolodoro. Está en Egipto, drenando los canales que dan acceso a la mar Eritrea. Dile que lo necesito aquí lo antes posible. No, dile que lo necesito ya mismo.

—Sí, César —confirmó el secretario.

—Bien, bien —continuó Trajano mientras analizaba el plano con detenimiento y repasaba mentalmente las instrucciones que había dado—, la familia imperial y yo mismo permaneceremos aquí, en esta explanada. Parece un sitio razonablemente seguro. ¿Alguna pregunta?

Nadie dijo nada.

El emperador se levantó y los demás lo imitaron.

—Sólo una cosa más —dijo Trajano—. Dión ha dicho que puede haber nuevos temblores. Advertid a los oficiales y a los legionarios a vuestro mando de esta posibilidad. Decidles que ésta es una guerra como las demás y que la vamos a ganar, pero que no hay victoria sin bajas. Decidles que Trajano está con ellos. —Se quedó un momento pensativo, asintió y volvió a hablar—. Decidles que los dioses me protegen, necesitamos que piensen que nuestros dioses no nos han abandonado. Mañana mismo haremos sacrificios y después, al amanecer, organizaremos la distribución de alimentos. Las legiones estaban bien pertrechadas con grano, aceite y todo lo necesario. Nadie ha de pasar hambre o sed en una ciudad en la que Trajano esté viviendo, incluso si la cólera de un dios desconocido se ha desatado sobre nosotros. Mañana los alimentos. Ahora empezaremos a rescatar heridos. Quieto, Nigrino, Adriano y yo haremos un primer turno hasta la tercera vigilia. Luego que los oficiales de cada legión continúen hasta el amanecer. Así tendremos unas horas de descanso. Espero veros aquí con la primera luz del alba.

—Ave, César —dijo Lucio Quieto y, al instante, incluido Adriano, aunque quizá sin tanto entusiasmo, el resto de los altos oficiales del emperador repitieron el saludo al unísono.

—¡Ave, César!

Y todos dieron media vuelta para empezar a trabajar. Fédimo se arrodilló para recoger el plano y enrollarlo con cuidado mientras el viejo Dión se acercó al emperador.

—El César se ha olvidado de asignarme alguna tarea; soy viejo pero quizá aún pueda ser útil al emperador de Roma —dijo el filósofo.

Trajano lo miró arrugando la frente.

—¿A qué te refieres?

El filósofo sonrió.

—El emperador hace bien en intentar que los legionarios y los ciudadanos de Antioquía piensen que los dioses no han abandonado al César —se explicó—, pero me temo que ante una tragedia como la que acaba de acontecer, muchos serán los que duden del afecto de los dioses por Trajano, o, al menos, serán numerosos los que piensen, en efecto, que otros dioses como el judío o el cristiano nos están castigando. O quizá Ahura Mazda, el dios supremo de los partos. El César necesita un arma más fuerte que sus legiones para vencer en una guerra contra dioses enemigos.

—Sigo sin entenderte. ¿Qué arma es ésa, más poderosa que los sacrificios oportunos, que pueda persuadir a mis enemigos de que los dioses romanos velan por mí y por aquellos que me siguen?

—Bueno... no creo que lleguemos nunca a persuadir a los enemigos de la religión romana, pero sería ya una gran victoria asegurarse de que los legionarios y los ciudadanos fieles al Imperio sientan que Trajano está, en verdad, bendecido por los dioses de Roma.

—Te escucho —dijo Trajano, sentándose un momento al tiempo que el filósofo se le acercaba lentamente, hablando en voz baja, buscando que sólo el César oyera sus palabras.

—Para combatir las creencias de judíos y cristianos y de los legionarios que dudan de esta campaña contra Partia, el César necesitará el arma más fuerte que existe.

—¿Cuál es esa arma? —insistió Trajano con algo de irritación en su voz. Apreciaba a Dión Coceyo en grado sumo pero no estaba para acertijos.

—Un rumor.

Trajano tragó saliva.

—No te entiendo —dijo el emperador y suspiró—, y hoy no estoy para enigmas...

—¿Cómo se ha salvado el emperador de una muerte segura en medio de este terremoto? —lo interrumpió el filósofo con una pregunta veloz—. Porque si bien nosotros estábamos al aire libre, en el jardín del gran atrio del palacio, y eso sin duda nos ha salvado, el César estaba en el interior del propio edificio. Pero Trajano, en lugar de yacer como tantos otros bajo los escombros, sigue aquí vivo y dando órdenes a sus *legati*.

El emperador volvió a arrugar la frente mientras repasaba en voz alta lo que había ocurrido desde el rugido inicial que dio paso al gran temblor.

—Se oyó aquel aullido infernal, luego un silencio... estaba con Aulo. —El pretoriano, que se había acercado al César y al filósofo, igual que había hecho Fédimo, asintió—. Juntos vimos que el suelo se deshacía bajo nuestros pies y luego las paredes; fuimos entonces a la sala de la piscina, vimos la ventana y nos encaramamos a ella, y no sabíamos bien qué hacer cuando una enorme nube de polvo nos empujó al exterior e imagino que tuvimos la fortuna de no matarnos al ser expelidos de aquella parte del palacio que se nos venía encima. Eso es lo que recuerdo —y calló mirando a Aulo.

—Eso mismo recuerdo yo, augusto —confirmó el tribuno.

Dión volvió a sonreír.

—Así que el César fue salvado por una misteriosa nube. ¿Y si esa nube hubiera sido en realidad un ser gigantesco enviado por los dioses para salvar al César?

Trajano guardó silencio.

—No creo que fuera el caso —dijo al fin el emperador.

—Yo tampoco —admitió Dión Coceyo—, pero lo importante en un rumor no es lo que crean quienes lo inventan, sino lo que crean los que lo escuchan.

El emperador meditó nuevamente unos instantes.

—Sea —dijo al fin—. Si crees que promover ese relato puede ayudar a que los legionarios y los ciudadanos de Antioquía se sientan más seguros, adelante con ello, pero no sé cómo vas a conseguir crear un rumor como ése y que se difunda con rapidez.

—Oh, César —respondió el filósofo inclinándose—, que el emperador permita que ésa sea mi tarea esta noche.

—De acuerdo.

—Necesitaré la ayuda del secretario imperial, si esto es posible —requirió Dión.

—Sea —aceptó Trajano y se dirigió a Aulo—. Vámonos. Tenemos que acudir con una legión al sector IV de la ciudad y ver a cuánta gente podemos rescatar de las ruinas antes de la tercera vigilia.

Marco Ulpio Trajano se alejó seguido por Aulo y la guardia pretoriana.

El joven secretario y el viejo filósofo se quedaron a solas junto a dos antorchas que continuaban ardiendo allí donde acababa de tener lugar aquel *consilium augusti* de emergencia.

—¿Cómo se crea un rumor? —preguntó Fédimo en voz baja.

—Ah, pero eso es muy fácil, muchacho —se explicó el filósofo—. Sólo tenemos que contar a diez personas cada uno de nosotros esta noche la historia del ser gigante que rescató al emperador en medio del terremoto, levantándolo por el aire y poniéndolo a salvo por una ventana.

—¿Y eso bastará? —preguntó con incredulidad el secretario imperial.

—No. A cada una de esas personas, joven Fédimo, les haremos jurar que no lo cuenten a nadie, pues no estamos seguros de que sea cierto. Pidiéndoles eso, nos aseguraremos de que mañana, pese al terremoto, nadie hablará de otra cosa que no sea el misterioso rescate del César por un ser enviado por los dioses de Roma.

«[3] γενήσεσθαι. πρῶτον μὲν γὰρ μύκημα ἐξαπίνης μέγα ἐ βρυχήσατο, ἔπειτα βρασμὸς ἐπ᾽ αὐτῷ βιαιότατος ἐπεγένετο, καὶ ἄνω μὲν ἡ γῆ πᾶσα ἀνεβάλλετο, ἄνω δὲ καὶ τὰ οἰκοδομήματα ἀνεπήδα, καὶ τὰ μὲν ἀνέκαθεν ἐπαιρόμενα συνέπιπτε καὶ κατερρήγνυτο, τὰ δὲ καὶ δεῦρο καὶ ἐκεῖσε κλονούμενα ὥσπερ ἐν σάλῳ περιετρέπετο, καὶ ἐπὶ πολὺ καὶ τοῦ ὑπαίθρου προσκατελάμβανεν.

»[5] τοσαῦτα μὲν τότε πάθη τὴν Ἀντιόχειαν κατειλήφει· Τραϊανὸς δὲ διέφυγε μὲν διὰ θυρίδος ἐκ τοῦ οἰκήματος ἐν ᾧ ἦν, προσελθόντος αὐτῷ μείζονός τινος ἢ κατὰ ἄνθρωπον καὶ ἐ ξαγαγόντος αὐτόν, ὥστε μικρὰ ἄττα πληγέντα περιγενέσθαι, ὡς δ᾽ ἐπὶ πλείους ἡμέρας ὁ σεισμὸς ἐπεῖχεν»

«Primero vino, de súbito, un gran rugido, y éste fue seguido por una tremenda sacudida. Toda la tierra se levantó, y los edificios saltaban por los aires; algunos ascendían para luego desplomarse y quedar hechos añicos, mientras que otros eran sacudidos hacia un lado y hacia otro como si fueran mecidos por el mar, y se derrumbaban, y el desastre se extendió por un amplio territorio (...).

»Así de grandes fueron las calamidades que se cernieron sobre Antioquía en aquel tiempo. Trajano [no obstante,] escapó por una ventana de la habitación en la que se encontraba. Algún ser, de estatura mayor que la de cualquier hombre, llegó hasta él y lo guio al exterior de modo que escapó con apenas unas leves heridas; y como fuera que los temblores prosiguieron durante días, vivió al aire libre en el hipódromo.

DIÓN CASIO, Libro 68, 24, 3 y 25, 5.

74

EL IMPERIO KUSHAN

Bagram
Finales de 115 d. C.

El consejero Shaka recibió a Titianus, a Marcio y a Áyax en su residencia a las pocas semanas de haber llegado a Bagram.

—Ha sido más rápido de lo que esperaba —dijo Titianus a Marcio en voz baja mientras aguardaban la llegada del consejero del emperador. El mercader había pasado los primeros días comerciando en la capital, hasta que identificó a guardias del palacio imperial y se dirigió a ellos en griego. Tuvo la fortuna de que el oficial comprendía lo suficiente para entender la petición de Titianus de entrevistarse con algún consejero del emperador kushan con el fin de transmitirle un mensaje de un poderoso señor de Occidente. El guardia se mostró receloso, pero tuvo el buen criterio de transmitir la petición a sus superiores y éstos llegaron a Shaka, que ahora iba a recibirlos.

Alana y Tamura, como no eran hombres, estaban fuera de la sala, en una estancia contigua, donde otras mujeres escribían en grandes papiros.

Sala de embajadores del palacio de Bagram

—Os escucho, pero sed breves —dijo Shaka en griego, en pie, muy serio, frente al extraño y exótico grupo de, según le habían dicho, enviados de un poderoso señor de Occidente. Y el caso era que la faz de uno de ellos le resultaba familiar, la del guerrero más veterano, pero el consejero Shaka no podía recordar por qué o de dónde.

559

—Somos mensajeros del emperador romano Trajano —empezó Titianus en griego, lo que de inmediato captó la atención del consejero.

—Ah, sí —lo interrumpió entonces Shaka y señaló con su índice a Marcio—. Yo te he visto a ti en el gran Circo Máximo, en Roma.

El griego de Marcio no era en absoluto fluido y miró a Titianus, que le tradujo.

—Es posible, sí, consejero, que nos hayamos visto allí —dijo Marcio en latín.

Titianus volvió a traducir.

—Bien, bien —continuó el consejero—. Esto es prueba de que seguramente sois quienes decís ser, pues a uno de vosotros lo he visto próximo al César romano. Perfecto. Ahora sí os escucharé con atención. Espero, Titi...

—Titianus —completó el mercader.

—Espero que comprendas que son muchos los que quieren ver a su majestad Kanishka, y muy pocos los que pueden tener el privilegio de acceder a él. Pero hablad, hablad.

—Mucho me temo, consejero, que el César desearía que habláramos personalmente con el emperador... Kadphises.

—Kadphises ha muerto hace poco y ahora es su hijo Kanishka quien rige los designios del Imperio kushan, pero no se le puede molestar. El emperador está muy ocupado atendiendo los asuntos relacionados con el cuarto concilio.

Titianus se rascó la cabeza. Había un nuevo emperador y se hablaba de un concilio. Se pasó la palma de la mano derecha por la boca.

—¿Cuarto concilio? —preguntó al fin el mercader, un poco por aclarar aquel asunto y otro poco por tener tiempo para pensar.

—El emperador Kanishka se ha decantado por favorecer el desarrollo del conocimiento de las enseñanzas de Buda y ha reunido en Bagram a los más doctos conocedores de su mensaje para hacer un compendio de sus enseñanzas recopilando los textos más relevantes sobre los pensamientos del gran profeta. Es la cuarta vez que algo así se hace, y a estas reuniones las hemos llamado concilios. Pero este cuarto concilio de las creencias budistas va a marcar un antes y un después. Es un asunto de la máxima importancia. Por eso el emperador no puede atender ahora a ningún embajador, sea quien sea ni venga de donde venga. Pero hablar conmigo es como hablar con el emperador. No hablar conmigo es dudar del emperador kushan. Yo transmitiré vuestro mensaje si es relevante y, si en efecto lo es, el propio emperador quizá quiera recibiros y daros respuesta personalmente para vuestro César.

Titianus vio que no había mucho margen. Era mejor hablar.

—El César Trajano se ha lanzado a la conquista de Partia siguiendo los consejos de los enviados del anterior emperador kushan, entre los que creo que se encontraba el propio consejero Shaka.

—Lo sabemos —confirmó el propio Shaka que, como todos en Oriente, a través de la Ruta de la Seda, tenía noticias de la guerra entre Partia y Roma y de los avances de Trajano, además de recordar la conversación que había mantenido hacía unos años con el mismísimo César para sugerirle que pusiera en marcha semejante guerra.

—Bien. El emperador Trajano espera que los kushan ataquen Partia por su lado oriental para de esa forma debilitar aún más los ejércitos partos y poder derrotarlos con mayor facilidad. Luego el Imperio parto se repartirá entre Roma y el emperador kushan.

Shaka asintió una vez, muy lentamente. El mensaje era correcto. Trajano había tardado mucho en poner en marcha aquel ataque, pero al final lo había hecho. Ahora les tocaba a ellos.

—Hablaré con su majestad el emperador Kanishka —dijo Shaka. Iba a marcharse, pero Titianus volvió a hablar.

—Una cosa más, consejero: necesitamos permiso del emperador kushan para seguir nuestro viaje comercial hacia Xeres.

—¿Hacia Xeres? —preguntó Shaka confundido. Eso no era nada habitual y desde luego nada relacionado con lo hablado con Trajano. Las caravanas de Xeres dejaban sus productos en el Imperio kushan, que actuaban de intermediarios, como hacían los partos. Luego se llevaba todo a Barbaricum y allí se embarcaba en barcos de mercaderes griegos, indios, árabes o hasta romanos, pero nunca se había permitido que un romano cruzara todo el Imperio kushan para adentrarse en Xeres y contactar con el emperador han.

—No estoy seguro de poder garantizaros que se os vaya a conceder ese permiso. Además —añadió Shaka en un intento por justificar esa negativa—, el César Trajano esperará la respuesta de su majestad Kanishka. Seguir hacia el este os retrasará a la hora de llevar las respuesta del Imperio kushan.

—Bueno, el ataque de los kushan sobre Partia será la mejor respuesta para el emperador de Roma —replicó Titianus, que ya había pensado en un razonamiento de aquel tipo por parte de la corte de Bagram—. Cuando eso ocurra, el augusto Trajano sabrá que hemos cumplido la primera parte de la misión.

—¿Y la segunda parte en Xeres cuál es? —inquirió Shaka frunciendo el ceño y con tono de gran desconfianza.

—Oh, mi señor, en Xeres el emperador Trajano sólo busca invitar a las autoridades de ese imperio a incrementar su comercio con Roma, comercio que pasa por el Imperio kushan y que, si se incrementa, aumentará la riqueza de vuestro pueblo. Que se nos permita seguir hacia Xeres sólo puede redundar en beneficio de su majestad Kanishka.

El consejero Shaka inspiró profundamente. La respuesta era satisfactoria. Podría ser cierto o no lo que acababan de decirle, pero era una posibilidad aceptable.

—Transmitiré vuestro mensaje y vuestra petición a su majestad Kanishka.

Estancia de los copistas kushan, junto a la sala de embajadores

Alana y Tamura no eran mujeres de quedarse quietas en una esquina. En particular Tamura quien, movida por la curiosidad innata de su juventud, se aventuró a acercarse a las otras mujeres que había en aquella estancia, que parecían escribir largos textos bajo la atenta vigilancia de una mujer más mayor y veterana en aquella tarea.

La muchacha sármata y romana se detuvo junto a una de las copistas y, mirando por encima de su hombro, empezó a leer algunas palabras escritas en símbolos que para Alana eran aún difíciles. El alfabeto kushana[64] le seguía resultando complejo de recordar. Otro asunto distinto era recordar de memoria cómo se pronunciaban las palabras. La mujer kushan mayor se aproximó a Tamura por detrás. Alana temió que fuera a recriminarle algo, pero antes de que pudiera interponerse, ya estaba hablando en una lengua desconocida.

—¿Entiendes sánscrito?

Tamura se volvió dando un respingo, pero la sonrisa de la mujer que le acababa de hacer la pregunta la tranquilizó a ella y a Alana, aunque esta última no entendiera nada de lo que se decía.

—Muy poco. Palabras. Números sobre todo cuando está escrito con las letras del latín; con vuestras letras me cuesta mucho —dijo Tamura. Se llevó las manos al pequeño saco que siempre llevaba consigo y extrajo el libro con textos en sánscrito transcritos en el silabario kushana y en el alfabeto latino que le regalara Dión Coceyo de eso hacía ya tres años. Ella había seguido leyendo aquel libro, junto con el de griego y el de latín.

La mujer miró con un brillo dulce en los ojos el pequeño volumen que sostenía Tamura en la mano.

—¿Puedo? —preguntó.

La muchacha le entregó el libro y la mujer lo examinó con atención. En particular el título del volumen. En la primera página se podía ver la siguiente palabra:

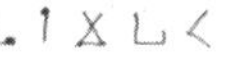

—Se trata del *Dharmapada* —dijo la mujer aún más sorprendida—. ¿Puedes leerlo? —Se lo devolvió a Tamura.

La muchacha lo cogió con más cuidado del habitual, pues la persona con la que estaba hablando no parecía tratar aquel

64. Cuando se hace relación al alfabeto o silabario de los kushan, el adjetivo es kushana.

libro como algo con lo que simplemente aprender una lengua extraña. Tamura pasó unas hojas y buscó uno de los pasajes que tenía mejor aprendidos y que, además, tenía escrito en los dos alfabetos, el latino y el kushana. Lo leyó despacio en voz alta.

Yathā saṅkāradhānasmiṃ
ujjhitasmiṃ mahāpathe
Padumaṃ tattha jāyetha
sucigandhaṃ manoramaṃ.

Evam saṅkārabhūtesu
andhabhūte puthujjane
Atirocati paññāya
sammāsambuddhasāvako.

[Así como un deleitable
y perfumado loto crece allí,
en una pila de basura
que ha sido desechada en el camino,
de la misma forma,
entre la basura de los seres,
el discípulo del Buda brilla con su sabiduría
sobrepasando a la ciega humanidad.][65]

—Lo has leído muy bien, pero ¿lo entiendes? —le preguntó la mujer, siempre con una gran sonrisa en los labios que tranquilizaba a Tamura.

—Entiendo cada palabra, pero cuando pienso en todo a la vez ya no lo entiendo.

—Lo que acabas de leer quiere decir que hay flores muy bellas que son capaces de crecer en lugares horribles y del mismo modo podemos encontrar a personas muy buenas pese a que entre los hombres abunden las personas malvadas. ¿Así lo entiendes mejor?

—Algo más.

65. *Dharmapada.* Enseñanzas del Buda, versos 58 y 59. Traducción de Bhikku Nandisena.

—Pero no del todo.

—Del todo no.

—Eres sincera. —La mujer volvió a sonreír—. Yo creo que tú y yo tenemos mucho de que hablar, pero te advierto que a veces entender es sufrir. Eso al principio. Luego, comprender es paz. Mi nombre es Buddahamitra y soy monja seguidora de las enseñanzas del gran Buda. Tu libro es una pequeña parte de sus enseñanzas. Aquí —y señaló a las otras mujeres con sus grandes papiros— estamos recogiendo todos los escritos que hablan de las enseñanzas de Buda. —Y mientras Tamura miraba a las otras mujeres que seguían con su trabajo, Buddahamitra miró a Alana—. ¿Quiénes sois vosotros?

—Mi nombre es Tamura y ella es mi Matṛ.

—Tu madre —repitió Buddahamitra—. Ella no nos entiende, ¿verdad?

—No.

—¿Y quién te ha enseñado sánscrito?

—Mi maestro Dión Coceyo.

—Nunca he oído hablar de él, pero debe de ser sabio para que alguien de tan lejos como venís vosotros se haya preocupado o interesado en Buda. Dile a tu madre que pienso que tiene una hija muy inteligente.

Tamura se sonrojó pero tradujo.

Alana asintió despacio y miró a aquella mujer con el sosiego de saber que habían encontrado una amiga. Ella no era de libros, pero su instinto guerrero le decía que siempre era bueno tener amigos, especialmente en lugares desconocidos donde cualquier cosa, buena o mala, podía ocurrir.

Por las calles oscuras de Bagram

Era de noche.

Áyax salió de la casa que se les había asignado por el consejero Shaka para su estancia en Bagram. Marcio no sospechó porque intuía que iba a por lo que iba siempre que estaban en una ciudad. Tamura también pensaba lo mismo, pero a ella que Áyax saliera en busca de mujeres ya no le hacía ninguna gracia. Se habían estado besando a escondidas desde Barigaza y Barbaricum hasta Bagram, pero la muchacha comprendió aquella noche, para su dolor, que los besos no bastaban a un gladiador como Áyax. La decisión que había tomado Tamura de hacerle ver que era toda una mujer le parecía, a cada momento, más urgente. Ella deseaba estar con él y, al tiempo, no quería que él estuviera con ninguna otra. Pensó en seguirlo, pero sabía que confirmar lo que creía sólo le haría más daño, de modo que se agarró con fuerza a la almohada de su lecho e intentó dormir, entre lágrimas de rabia e impotencia.

Áyax, entretanto, no fue en busca de mujeres, sino que llegó a la residencia del consejero Shaka y pidió ser recibido.

—Espero que tengas un buen motivo para importunarme en medio de la noche —le espetó el consejero cuando lo recibió en un patio al aire libre, en el interior de su casa—. El viejo mercader de tu grupo o ese guerrero más veterano parecían tener más criterio que tú sobre las horas oportunas para trasladar mensajes.

Shaka hablaba en griego, pero Áyax, como era de Grecia, se sentía muy cómodo en su lengua nativa.

—Siento molestar al consejero, pero el emperador Kanishka haría mal en permitir que mis compañeros sigan hacia Xeres.

Shaka abrió bien los ojos.

—¿Y por qué no debemos dejarlos pasar? —preguntó el consejero.

—Porque Titianus ha mentido: no vamos hacia Xeres con una misión comercial, sino en una misión de guerra.

Shaka guardó unos instantes de silencio. Se sentó en un taburete con almohadón que había en una esquina del patio. Dos guardias vigilaban. Les hizo una señal y desaparecieron del patio. Estaban a solas.

—¿Por qué me cuentas esto? —inquirió Shaka—. ¿Por qué traicionas a tus compañeros de viaje?

—Porque no todos servimos al emperador Trajano en este grupo —dijo Áyax.

—Ah, no. Esto es interesante de verdad —admitió Shaka contento de estar obteniendo mucha información. Quizá con todo lo que aprendiera aquella noche podría proporcionar a su majestad Kanishka datos suficientes para volver a ser considerado un gran consejero. Desde el desastre del intento fallido de envenenamiento de Aryazate, la hija de Osroes, el emperador Kanishka ya no confiaba tanto en él. Y su posición en la corte imperial de Bagram era muy endeble. Siempre había consejeros más jóvenes con ansias de arrebatarle su puesto.

—Mis órdenes son impedir que esta misión llegue a su destino final —precisó Áyax.

—Órdenes... ¿de quién?

—De quien será el próximo emperador de Roma, un nuevo César.

—Ah. —Shaka asintió. Le habría gustado más precisión en esa última respuesta, pero lo esencial, por el momento, era que había que impedir que aquellos mensajeros siguieran hacia Xeres, hacia el Imperio han, algo que, por cierto, coincidía con sus intuiciones, que no solían errar. Volvió a mirar a aquel joven guerrero—. Una misión de guerra, eso has dicho.

—Sí, consejero.

—¿Y sabes el mensaje que el emperador Trajano quiere enviar a Xeres?

—Sí.

—Te escucho.

Áyax le contó lo que Tamura le había confesado el día en que se besaron por primera vez en Barigaza.

Cuando el gladiador terminó, Shaka se levantó despacio.

—Hablaré con el emperador, pero no dudo de cuáles serán sus instrucciones.

—¿Matarlos? —preguntó Áyax.

—A todos —confirmó Shaka—, menos, por supuesto, a quien se ha mostrado tan leal a nuestra causa. Aunque sólo sea porque obedece a alguien que quiere ser emperador romano en lugar del César Trajano.

—Matar al viejo mercader es cosa fácil, pero el guerrero veterano, Marcio, y su esposa son buenos luchando. Si no lo hacemos bien, si sospechan, pueden escapar. La niña, aunque parezca muy joven, es muy buena con el arco y hay que andarse con cuidado con ella, pero la tengo engañada.

—¿Engañada cómo?

—De la forma en la que los hombres solemos engañar a las mujeres.

Shaka levantó las cejas y sonrió.

—No pareces alguien de muchos escrúpulos —dijo Shaka—. Me gustas. Cuando resolvamos todo esto puedes volver a Roma y retornar con aquel a quien sirves, pero si quieres quedarte aquí, yo siempre tengo trabajo y oro para alguien como tú.

—Lo pensaré.

—Perfecto —dijo el consejero—. Hablaré con el emperador y tú y yo estaremos en contacto. El asunto del concilio no era una excusa y es posible que me cueste tener acceso al emperador Kanishka en un tiempo. Entretanto te sugiero que te diviertas con esa niña estas semanas, ahora que aún está viva.

75

EL PODER DE IGNACIO

Antioquía
Finales del 115 d. C.

El rumor de Dión Coceyo sobre cómo el emperador Trajano había sido salvado por alguna gigantesca y divina criatura enviada por los dioses romanos surtió efecto y muchos hablaban de aquello en medio de las obras de reconstrucción de la ciudad. Seguramente, aquel relato fantástico habría persuadido hasta a los cristianos de Antioquía de no ser por la presencia allí también del anciano Ignacio. Éste, aunque ya muy mayor, no aflojaba en la constante defensa del dios cristiano y pronto empezó a difundir entre todos los que lo escuchaban que el terremoto que había asolado la ciudad no era sino un castigo del Señor a los romanos por sus crímenes contra el mundo, en general, y contra los cristianos, en particular. Si el castigo había recaído también sobre los habitantes de Antioquía esto se debía a que la ciudad había dado acogida cómoda y feliz a las legiones de Trajano, que partían de allí cada primavera para extender más un imperio basado en dioses falsos y diabólicos.

Ignacio, como siempre, no dejaba espacio para matices.

Todo esto, por supuesto, llegó a oídos del César.

—¡Que lo traigan a mi presencia de inmediato! —exclamó Trajano en cuanto le informaron de lo que el líder cristiano de la ciudad estaba diciendo por todas partes—. ¡Por Júpiter, que me lo traigan ya mismo!

Aulo no tuvo que buscar demasiado. Ignacio no se escondía y fue arrestado y conducido ante el *praetorium* de campaña del emperador, que seguía instalado en el centro del hipódromo de la ciudad.

Trajano lo miró en silencio un rato: ante él tenía a un hombre anciano, adusto, enjuto, pero con aire de dominio, de control, de poder. ¿Cómo alguien tan débil podía sentirse así? El César se temía lo peor: fanatismo.

—Me dicen que cuentas a todo el que te quiere escuchar que el terremoto que hemos sufrido ha sido enviado por tu dios.

—Lo que digo es que el único dios y señor que existe ha querido castigar la vanidad de los romanos que adoran a dioses diabólicos y falsos.

Dión Coceyo, que estaba presente, levantó las cejas y lanzó un suspiro. Sabía de los intentos de magnanimidad que el emperador había tenido para con los cristianos y otras religiones, pero un desafío de aquel calibre y en un momento de tanta tensión después del devastador terremoto no iba ser recibido de forma amable por el César.

—No te he llamado para hablar de religión —le espetó Trajano con cierto desprecio, despertado, entre otras cosas, por la ausencia de términos de respeto en la respuesta anterior de Ignacio. El emperador habría agradecido que aquel cristiano se hubiera dirigido a él empleando los acostumbrados «augusto» o «César», al principio o al final de sus palabras—. En cualquier caso, ya que tú mismo mencionas el tema, entiendo que niegas a nuestros dioses y que te reconoces seguidor y adorador de ese al que vosotros llamáis Cristo. Piensa bien tu respuesta, pues, tal y como le dije un día al gobernador de Bitinia, el senador Plinio, si niegas seguir a ese Cristo y aceptas a los dioses romanos, te dejaré en libertad, pero de lo contrario, si te reafirmas en manifestarte públicamente —y el emperador enfatizó aquella palabra cuando la pronunció, como si quisiera dar a entender que le daba igual lo que cada uno hiciera en privado, que sólo le importaba la actitud pública de los ciudadanos del Imperio—, si públicamente, insisto, te reconoces como seguidor de Cristo, no me dejarás otra opción que condenarte a muerte.

Ignacio no dudó como otros. Eso lo diferenciaba de Marción, ese maldito hijo de Satanás que sí había negado a Cristo ante aquel gobernador que el César acababa de mencionar.

Él, Ignacio, también podría negar a Cristo y así salvarse para seguir luchando contra el creciente poder de los gnósticos, los docetas y hasta de ese miserable mismo de Marción, que acababa de sacar a la luz un libro que presentaba como el compendio de los textos sagrados de los cristianos. Y lo había hecho sin la aquiescencia ni de Alejandro ni de Sixto ni de Telesforo. Lo había hecho solo; peor, lo había hecho contra todos ellos. Y lo terrible era que aquel maldito libro estaba haciéndose tremendamente popular. Sí, era tentador salvarse para seguir luchando por Cristo y ayudar a eliminar el libro hereje del mismísimo Marción, pero eso sería rebajarse a su nivel: negar a Cristo lo convertiría en otro terrible ejemplo para todos y eso no podía ser.

—Sólo hay un Dios, César, y no es ninguno de vuestros entes diabólicos.

—Entonces no me dejas otra opción que condenarte a muerte. —Y miró a Aulo—. Que lo encadenen y que lo envíen a Roma para ser ejecutado en el Anfiteatro Flavio.

Ignacio ni se manifestó contra aquella sentencia ni opuso resistencia alguna a los pretorianos que lo condujeron fuera del *praetorium.*

—¿Algún problema? —preguntó Trajano mirando a todos los miembros de su *consilium augusti*—. Sé que no es bueno soliviantar los ánimos religiosos de los ciudadanos de Antioquía que puedan seguir a ese profeta, pero no podemos permitir que desafíos como el suyo queden impunes. Y menos después de lo que ha pasado, menos después de lo mucho que estamos trabajando reconstruyendo esta ciudad mientras la tierra sigue temblando, como Dión nos anticipó. He de demostrar a todos este invierno que el emperador no teme a otros dioses, a ningún dios. Sigo aquí, reconstruyo Antioquía y no me tiembla el pulso ante ningún profeta o charlatán, me da igual lo que sea, que no reconoce mi autoridad y la autoridad de Roma. Y en primavera saldremos de aquí e iremos al maldito Tigris y lo cruzaremos, igual que hicimos con el Éufrates, y ninguna de mis legiones terminará jamás como la legión perdida.

Y miró a todos.

—Creo que el César no tenía ningún margen con ese profeta —dijo Dión Coceyo.

Sus palabras sosegaron el ánimo del emperador, que observó entonces que Adriano miraba al suelo ensimismado. Como siempre, a Trajano le incomodaba no poder intuir qué estaba pensando o, peor, tramando su sobrino segundo.

Todos salieron del *praetorium* en silencio.

Adriano fue el último en hacerlo. Caminaba, pero seguía mirando el suelo. Estaba tan feliz... por fin había dado con la clave de todo: la religión podía ser el elemento desequilibrador. El fanatismo de ese Ignacio se lo había mostrado bien a las claras. El radicalismo judío o cristiano —él no tenía claro que hubiera diferencia entre unos y otros— era una herramienta demoledora con la que su tío, que siempre parecía tenerlo todo pensado, no había contado. Ése y no otro podría ser su gran error.

La sonrisa de Adriano, en medio de las ruinas de Antioquía, a solas en su ruta hacia el distrito IV de la ciudad, era tan amplia como intrigante.

76

LA CARTA DE FAN CHUN

Yutian,[66] reino de Yutian
Una de las regiones occidentales del Imperio han

Li Kan miraba por la ventana de la torre. Estaba a más de 11.700 li[67] de distancia de Loyang. Técnicamente había salido del Imperio han, pues el reino de Yutian era más bien un estado independiente, vasallo de los han, eso sí. Pero era un punto clave en la Ruta de la Seda y hasta allí había ido Li Kan para asegurar las fronteras del reino y evitar los ataques de los *hsiung-nu* y, peor aún, de la creciente influencia de los Yuegzhi, que con su nuevo emperador Kanishka amenazaban con controlar aquel reino por completo. De hecho la religión budista era ya la más importante en Yutian. Se empezaba por la religión y luego llegaba el control por las armas. Pero, por el momento, hasta allí llegaba el correo imperial de Loyang. Li Kan bajó la mirada y, aprovechando la luz de la ventana, leyó con atención la última carta de Fan Chun:

Al *chiang-chün* Li Kan, al mando del ejército han
en las regiones occidentales

Espero que tu delicada misión de mantener el afecto del reino de Yutian para con nuestro Imperio vaya por buen camino. Si los defiendes de los ataques hsiung-nu, *estoy seguro de que su rey comprenderá que no necesita la ayuda de los Yuegzhi para tal empresa. Confío ciegamente en tu destreza militar para tal empeño y tu capacidad negociadora, creciente con tus años de experiencia.*

66. En el oeste de China.
67. Aproximadamente 4.400 kilómetros.

En otro orden de cosas, la emperatriz Deng ha sido informada de todo cuanto se me explicó en la última misiva que enviaste hace unas semanas. Su majestad se ha mostrado particularmente interesada por la guerra que se está desarrollando entre Da Qin y An-shi, interés regio que muestra su buen criterio y lucidez. Sin duda, dicha guerra es de gran relevancia para nuestros intereses comerciales. Aunque las caravanas sigan su curso por territorio Yuegzhi hasta sus puertos y de ahí a Occidente evitando la guerra en An-shi y Da Qin, eso sólo hace más fuertes a nuestros incómodos vecinos. Conviene que reúnas tanta información como te sea posible mediante mercaderes o de cualquier otra persona que, a tu criterio, pueda aportar información relevante sobre estos acontecimientos bélicos en el remoto occidente del mundo. Como general has mostrado gran capacidad y como persona me has hecho ver que has madurado y reflexionado, pero creo que por edad y experiencia aún estoy en situación de permitirme darte algunos consejos. Concretamente me gustaría que tuvieras en consideración dos muy precisos: primero, sobre la cuestión de reunir información de aquella lejana guerra, piensa que a veces lo que nos interesa puede llegarnos de la forma más inusual y sorprendente; así que no debes menospreciar lo inesperado, por muy extraño que pueda parecer. Mantenme informado de cualquier suceso de la frontera que te resulte inusual. Y mi segundo consejo: ya eres general, pero no por ello eres inmune al error. Te sugiero que no hagas nunca lo que hizo el chanyu *Zhizhi con embajadas o mensajeros y, por supuesto que no tomes decisiones precipitadas como la inicial del general Chen Tang. Que Tang solucionara al final su error de base no quiere decir que no partiera de un error. Todo esto, como sabes, lo tienes en las memorias del general Tang en el* 前漢書,[68] *libro del que, por si acaso, te envío copia. Como siempre espero que el espíritu de Confucio te guíe en tus actos y decisiones con la sabiduría e inteligencia que has demostrado hasta la fecha.*

Fan Chun
yu-shih chung-ch'eng

Li Kan se alejó de la ventana y dejó la carta sobre la mesa. Se sentó en una silla. Como siempre quería ponderar con tiento las palabras de Fan Chun y, en aquel momento, muy en particular, sus consejos. Sólo que él no necesitaba releer el *Han Shu* para saber qué ocurrió con Zhizhi y aquella embaja-

---

68. El *Han Shu* o *Historia de la antigua dinastía Han.*

574

da han, o qué decisión precipitada tomó el general Chen Tang. No, él sólo tenía que cerrar los ojos y recordar la vieja historia que su padre le contó poco antes de morir. Para entender aquellos consejos, Li Kan sólo tenía que rememorar el pasado de su familia.

Había cerrado los ojos, pero, de golpe, los abrió.

¿Hasta qué punto Fan Chun intuía su origen secreto? Li Kan nunca lo había desvelado a nadie. El viejo asistente del ministro de Obras Públicas no podía conocerlo. Era imposible. Sacudió la cabeza.

¿O sí?

El viejo consejero se escudaba en textos antiguos pero siempre daba consejos como si supiera todo el pasado de su familia, el secreto de su padre...

En cualquier caso, hasta la fecha, Fan Chun había actuado con él como un auténtico protector. ¿Por qué? ¿Les unía algo?

Li Kan volvió a cerrar los ojos y se concentró en recordar la historia de Druso, la legión perdida de Da Qin, el temible *chanyu* Zhizhi y, sobre todo, la decisión del general Chen Tang.

Porque esa decisión fue la que lo cambió todo. Una decisión precipitada, algo que él, tal y como decía Fan Chun, no debía hacer nunca.

¿Nunca?

Li Kan se concentró. Era como si pudiera escuchar aún a su padre contándole aquel episodio de la legión perdida...

77

LOS RECUERDOS DE LI KAN

Ciudad de Yu-yang
Frontera norte del Imperio han (China),
próxima a la Gran Muralla
Primer año del reinado del emperador An-ti (106 d. C.)

—Escúchame, Li Kan, hijo mío. Antes de que me reúna con nuestros antepasados he de terminar mi relato. Estoy débil y me fallan ya las fuerzas, pero has de conocer la historia hasta el final...

»Druso unió a los hombres de la legión perdida a las fuerzas de caballería de los hunos liderados por Zhizhi. Oh, muchacho, fue una combinación demoledora. Y eso que a Druso apenas le quedaban unos miles de hombres bajo su mando. Pero aquella infantería perfectamente adiestrada en combinación con una de las mejores caballerías del mundo asoló Asia central. En pocos años Huhanye, el hermano de Zhizhi, tuvo que refugiarse más al este, en territorio han, porque era incapaz de hacer frente al ejército de su mortal enemigo. Zhizhi consiguió además sumar sogdianos, hombres de Kangchú, a sus tropas, como el herrero Nanaifarn, pues el líder de los hunos aceptó desposarse con la hija del rey de Kangchú.[69]

»Con su ejército reforzado, Zhizhi fue asentando su poder no sólo en aquel reino, sino también en Dayuán,[70] un territorio tradicionalmente tributario de los han pero que terminó teniendo que pagar a Zhizhi para evitar verse arrasado por el

---

69. Kangchú es la forma en la que los chinos se referían a Sogdiana, reino limítrofe entre Partia y el Imperio han.
70. Reino de Fergana según la terminología china.

pillaje de las tropas de aquel huno a quien nadie podía controlar. Zhizhi, junto con la legión perdida, derrotó también a los Wusun del norte y éstos tuvieron que retirarse a los lugares más inhóspitos de las estepas. Zhizhi se autoproclamó *chanyu* de todos los hunos, repudió a la hija del rey de Kangchú y se erigió en soberano de los reinos de Kangchú y Dayuán. Todos los valles desde la frontera con An-shi hasta los ríos que desembocan en el gran Pu-Ku estaban bajo su control. Y eso, muchacho, implicaba que el comercio de la seda tenía que contar con él o ninguna caravana podría llegar hasta An-shi, el imperio de los Yuegzhi, Shendu o reinos más occidentales, lejanos y desconocidos como el remoto Da Qin.[71]

»A los únicos a los que no atacaba directamente Zhizhi era a los han. Pero no por temor a su ejército. Estaba convencido de que su caballería, junto con las tropas reclutadas en Kangchú y la infantería de la legión perdida, serían capaces, combinadas sus fuerzas, de derrotar a cualquier ejército que los han se atrevieran a enviar contra él. No, Zhizhi no atacaba al Imperio han simplemente porque el emperador Yuan retenía a su hijo como rehén desde hacía años. ¿Que cómo podía ser esto? Te lo explicaré: tiempo atrás, cuando Zhizhi y Huhanye luchaban por el dominio sobre los *hsiung-nu*, el propio Zhizhi negoció con la corte han para conseguir su apoyo contra su hermano, pero el emperador Yuan, intuyendo lo violento e imprevisible del carácter de Zhizhi, optó por apoyar a Huhanye. Zhizhi había enviado a su propio hijo en una embajada a la corte han, y cuando el emperador Yuan tomó la decisión de apoyar a su hermano en lugar de a Zhizhi, ordenó retener al hijo de este último para evitar que el *hsiung-nu* más violento de cuantos habían conocido los han se atreviera a atacarlos directamente. La estratagema funcionó durante varios años, hasta que, al final, derrotado Huhanye, los ministros aconsejaron al emperador Yuan volver a negociar con Zhizhi. Y es que el autoproclamado único *chanyu* de todos los *hsiung-nu* con-

71. El padre de Li Kan, lógicamente, sigue usando nombres chinos: Pu-Ku es el lago Balkash, An-shi es el Imperio parto, los Yuegzhi son los kushan y Shendu se refiere a la India.

trolaba ya un vasto territorio clave para la Ruta de la Seda y había cortado el comercio. Se quisiera o no, había que volver a hablar con él y negociar una fórmula para que las caravanas pudieran viajar de nuevo hacia Occidente. Se acordó, Li Kan, enviar una gran embajada del Imperio han a la ciudad fortaleza de Talas en Kangchú, al suroeste del Pu-ku, y que con esa embajada fuera el hijo de Zhizhi, que el Imperio han devolvía a su padre como muestra de confianza y prueba de amistad para conseguir reabrir la Ruta de la Seda.

»Pero nada salió como se esperaba. Con Zhizhi nunca ocurría nada según se planeaba. El día en que llegó la embajada de los han, muchacho, Druso comprendió que tenían un problema grave, tan enorme como haber sido prisioneros de los partos, sólo que ahora estaban en mitad de Asia central, sentados sobre un avispero a punto de estallar...

HISTORIA DE LA LEGIÓN PERDIDA

Tiempos de Julio César, Pompeyo y Craso,
mediados del siglo I a.C.

LIBRO VI

78

LA EMBAJADA HAN

Fortaleza Talas en Kangchú, capital del reino huno de Zhizhi.
Suroeste del lago Balkash, Asia central
42 a.C.

—Ya están aquí —anunció Nanaifarn.

Druso se levantó con rapidez, dejando a un lado a la joven esclava sogdiana que estaba acostada junto a él, y empezó a vestirse.

—¿Has avisado a Cayo y a Sexto? —preguntó el centurión.

—Sí. Ya vienen.

Nanaifarn seguía actuando como intérprete con Zhizhi y se había ganado la confianza plena de los romanos. El herrero sogdiano estaba agradecido por estar bajo la protección de aquellos guerreros llegados del fin del mundo, porque con Zhizhi como amo y señor de todos los territorios en miles y miles de *li* a la redonda, en cualquier momento un sogdiano podía ser ejecutado. Si el líder huno había ordenado la muerte de la hija del mismísimo rey, con quien se había desposado, ningún sogdiano estaba a salvo de sus arrebatos de ira, cada vez más frecuentes. Pero Zhizhi respetaba la eficacia de los romanos en combate y permitía que vivieran con autonomía dentro de aquel ejército que regía los destinos del corazón de Asia. Nanaifarn se sentía entonces seguro integrado en aquellas tropas, que se autodenominaban «legión» en su lengua extraña.

—¿Cuántos son? —preguntó Druso andando ya de camino a la sala central del palacio de Zhizhi, acompañado por Cayo y Sexto.

—Por lo menos una veintena de hombres —explicó Nanaifarn—. Al frente de la embajada está un tal Ku Chi, un renombrado oficial del Imperio han. El emperador de Xeres está demostrando que considera a Zhizhi como un auténtico soberano y ha enviado una embajada de gran envergadura. Además, han traído a su hijo de vuelta con su padre.

—Entonces Zhizhi estará satisfecho —dijo Druso.

—Eso nunca se sabe con Zhizhi —apostilló Nanaifarn apretando los labios y levantando las cejas.

Los tres romanos y el sogdiano entraron en la gran sala. El *chanyu* les permitía acudir a las reuniones relevantes que tuvieran lugar allí como hacía con otros líderes de sus tropas sogdianas.

Druso suspiró. Lo que vio lo relajó enormemente: Zhizhi estaba sonriente, incluso riendo a carcajadas en ocasiones de pura felicidad, con su hijo sentado ya a su lado, viendo cómo los embajadores han abrían, uno tras otro, diferentes cofres con maravillosos presentes enviados por el emperador de Xeres desde la remota Loyang. Y los sirvientes de los hunos se afanaban en preparar un montón de mesas con todo tipo de sabrosos manjares, carnes de caza con salsas, pescados del río Talas y aves de todo tipo sazonadas con especias de mil lugares diferentes. Se preparaba un gran festín.

—Hoy comeremos bien —confirmó Sexto.

—Eso parece —dijo Druso. Más tranquilo de lo que había estado en semanas, se sentó a una de las mesas junto con sus oficiales y con Nanaifarn.

Al poco, el propio Zhizhi hizo indicaciones a los miembros de la embajada del Imperio han para que se sentaran también y disfrutaran de la comida.

Todo iba de maravilla.

Druso, mientras masticaba un delicioso venado, empezó a pensar que quizá podrían disfrutar de un período de paz, y la verdad era que no iría mal algo de reposo para todos ellos: llevaban años de luchas descarnadas contra sogdianos, contra los hunos que aún apoyaban a Huhanye y contra los brutales wusun. Era cierto que los habían derrotado a todos, pero una paz con los han, que controlaban a los hunos de Huhanye y que podían influir sobre el resto de los opositores a Zhizhi, podría ser el principio de un tiempo de gran prosperidad para la zona. Y por las dimensiones del banquete y las continuadas carcajadas de Zhizhi, parecía que hasta el gran *chanyu* de Asia central pensaba lo mismo.

Druso había bebido y comido demasiado y estaba cayendo en las manos de Morfeo, que parecía acariciarle las sienes, por lo que no reparó en que una cincuentena de los más fieles guerreros de Zhizhi entraba, poco a poco, en el palacio y se situaba detrás de los miembros de la embajada. De hecho, los han también habían bajado la guardia y, como Druso, comían y bebían confiadamente, satisfechos de ver que sus objetivos de pactar una alianza con Zhizhi para reabrir la Ruta de la Seda iban por muy buen camino

De pronto, el último pedazo de venado que Druso sostenía en la mano se salpicó de un líquido espeso de color rojo oscuro. El centurión, incluso en medio de aquella somnolencia que lo invadía, identificó con rapidez el olor de la sangre humana fresca o, mejor dicho, aún caliente. Se volvió y vio cómo las espadas de los hunos atravesaban a todos y cada uno de los embajadores han. A varios los habían decapitado y de una de esas ejecuciones había brotado la sangre que acababa de salpicar a Druso y a sus oficiales. A otros les hundieron los sables por la espalda, retorciéndolos al sacarlos. El primero en ser ejecutado, porque aquello fue una ejecución en toda regla, fue el mismísimo Ku Chi. Hubo algunos gritos, pero pocos. A la mayoría de los han los habían cogido por sorpresa. Hubo uno que estuvo más atento y consiguió levantarse y desenvainar su propia espada, pero tres hunos lo acribillaron con flechas.

Todo fue muy rápido.

Se hizo un silencio breve, pero rápidamente las carcajadas de Zhizhi retornaron. Se calló y dijo unas palabras. Luego volvió a reír e hizo gestos para que todos sus hombres siguieran con el festín como si allí no hubiera pasado nada en absoluto.

—¿Qué ha dicho? —preguntó Druso a Nanaifarn.

—No estoy seguro. Ha hablado en su lengua, pero creo adivinar que ha comentado algo así como que «ahora aprenderán los han lo que pasa por retener a un hijo mío durante varios años».

—Esto traerá consecuencias —dijo Cayo a Druso acercándosele al oído.

—Sin duda, y muy graves —confirmó Druso.

—¿Qué hacemos? —preguntó Sexto.

—Comer —respondió el centurión con voz seria; de pronto, se le había pasado todo el sueño—. Y si es posible, reír también, tanto como podáis. Como hacen ellos, como si aquí no hubiera ocurrido nada.

Pero había pasado todo.

79

EL GENERAL CHEN TANG

Ch'ang-an, capital del Imperio han del oeste
Residencia del emperador, sala de audiencias
36 a.C.

El emperador Yuan-ti escuchaba con aire cansado a las excelencias, a los ministros y a los consejeros que se arracimaban en torno al trono.

—Su majestad no debe dejarse llevar por la ira. Zhizhi ha cometido una gran afrenta, pero...

—¿Una afrenta? —lo interrumpió otro—. ¿Así hemos de considerar el asesinato a sangre fría de todos los miembros de nuestra embajada justo cuando entregábamos a ese salvaje a su hijo libre como muestra de buena voluntad?

—Pero lo esencial es el comercio —terciaba un tercero.

—Eso es cierto —intervino un cuarto ministro—. Y Zhizhi está dejando que éste se reinicie con los territorios de An-shi y Shendú. Que la ruta de las caravanas vuelva a abrirse para nosotros en dirección a Occidente es clave. Estoy de acuerdo en que no debemos atacar a Zhizhi cegados por el ansia de venganza.

La discusión continuó durante horas.

No hubo acuerdo entre los consejeros aunque eran más numerosos los que aconsejaban a su majestad imperial no llevar a cabo ninguna campaña de castigo. El hecho de que pasara el tiempo y que Zhizhi no atacara directamente al Imperio han parecía darles la razón a los ministros y a las excelencias que sugerían contención: daba la impresión de que si se dejaba en paz al maldito autoproclamado *chanyu* supremo de los hunos, éste se conformaría con los territorios que tenía bajo su dominio. Además, era cierto que la presión sobre las caravanas se había relajado y la Ruta de la Seda, aunque de forma débil, empezaba a recuperarse.

Hubo varias reuniones más sobre el asunto. El emperador Yuan-ti terminaba siempre bostezando. Su política había sido siempre la misma. no hacer nada y dejar que todo se resolviera o se pudriera por sí solo. Y así se había mantenido en el poder. No veía por qué tenía que cambiar su forma de actuar ahora. ¿Por un montón de embajadores muertos? ¿Por orgullo? ¿Por temor a que ese maldito Zhizhi se atreviera a más?

Volvió a bostezar.

Provincia del Imperio han limítrofe con Kangchú (Sogdiana)
Residencia del gobernador de Gansu
36 a.C.

El general Chen Tang, sin embargo, no bostezaba. Él no estaba dispuesto a que el asesinato de los embajadores quedara sin castigo. Tang era uno de esos eslabones de la larga cadena de la historia que deciden no permanecer quietos y hacen que entonces, de repente, todo cambie. Pero para transformar la historia de un imperio hacen falta muchos hombres. Tang calculaba mientras hablaba: ¿Diez, veinte, treinta mil?

—No podemos permitir que Zhizhi siga controlando Kangchú y Dayuán[72] —se quejaba reiteradamente el general Chen Tang a Kan Yen, el *shou*, el gobernador de la región de Gansu, limítrofe con los territorios dominados por el *chanyu* rebelde—. Ese maldito está construyendo un imperio entre nosotros y An-shi: tiene subyugados a los habitantes no sólo de esos reinos, sino también a los de Kangchú, donde ha fijado su capital. Hasta los wusun lo temen y se revuelven contra nosotros. Está alterando toda Asia central.

—Lo sé —le respondió lacónicamente el viejo gobernador—; sabes que comparto tu visión sobre todo el asunto y que así lo he transmitido al emperador, pero sus excelencias no lo ven así.

72. Sogdiana y Fergana para los han.

—Insisto de nuevo, mi *shou*. —Tang reiteró su razonamiento.

El gobernador suspiró. Cualquier otro habría escrito a la capital del imperio acusando a Tang de insubordinación, pero el gobernador sabía que entre los asesinados por Zhizhi en aquella malograda embajada había varios familiares del airado general.

—Sé que además hay motivos personales que te impulsan a reclamar esta campaña de castigo contra Zhizhi —le volvió a responder el *shou* de Gansu—, y por eso he tenido paciencia contigo, pero esta conversación ha terminado. Para siempre.

Tang era un hombre paciente.

Esperó seis largos y lentos años, hasta que un día el gobernador Kan Yen cayó enfermo.

El general reunió en cuestión de semanas un imponente ejército de cuarenta mil hombres. Eran sorprendentes las ganas de reunirse que los soldados han y los de otras regiones y territorios aliados tenían para atacar a Zhizhi. Eran ya muchos años de terror y brutalidad.

Chen Tang lo tenía todo dispuesto.

Justo entonces Kan Yen se recuperó, con la suficiente fortaleza para llamarlo a su presencia en cuanto se enteró del ejército que su subordinado, sin permiso de nadie, había reclutado en poco tiempo.

—¿Qué crees que estás haciendo, general? —preguntó el gobernador a Tang en cuanto éste entró en el despacho personal de la residencia del *shou* de Gansu.

—Lo que tendríamos que haber hecho hace mucho tiempo —respondió Tang desafiante.

El gobernador negó con la cabeza al tiempo que hablaba.

—Crees que lo tienes todo pensado pero no llegarás muy lejos. ¿Te has olvidado de 玉門關; de *Yumen Guan*?

Yumen Guan, el paso fronterizo de la gran Puerta de Jade, en el sector oeste de la Gran Muralla, el límite occidental de la frontera de Gansu. Era la puerta por la que pasaban todas las grandes caravanas de la Ruta de la Seda, muchas de ellas también cargadas con jade, de donde la puerta había tomado su legendario nombre. Era la entrada al 河西走廊 —el Hexi

587

Zoulang—, el corredor de Hexi, la red de oasis entre el desierto del norte[73] y la gran meseta del sur.[74] El *Yumen Guan* era el único camino posible para entrar en las regiones dominadas por Zhizhi.

—No se atreverán a detenerme —dijo Chen Tang con cierto aplomo, pero su voz dejó entrever algo de la incertidumbre que aquel paso despertaba en su ánimo.

El gobernador, con sosiego y una pequeña sonrisa de victoria, le habló despacio.

—La Puerta de Jade de la Gran Muralla está custodiada por tropas imperiales que sólo reciben órdenes del emperador en persona. ¿Crees, de verdad, que esos hombres van a dejarte salir del imperio con cuarenta mil guerreros? ¿O acaso, a la insubordinación de reclutar un ejército sin mi permiso, vas a añadir el enfrentamiento directo con un regimiento de soldados del emperador? ¿Es eso lo que vas a hacer? Porque si lo haces, resultes vencedor o no contra Zhizhi, olvídate de regresar al Imperio han. Y piensa en lo que el emperador ordenará que hagan con todos los miembros de tu familia.

Tang dudó unos momentos, pero volvió a hablar.

—Zhizhi ha atacado la mismísima Kasgar. Cada vez se atreve a más. Es sólo cuestión de tiempo que el *chanyu* de los *hsiung-nu* se plante ante la propia Puerta de Jade. Entonces los guerreros del emperador ya no serán suficientes para defenderla. Entonces los ministros y sus excelencias nos ordenarán que reclutemos un ejército, pero ya será tarde. Zhizhi resultará demasiado poderoso y ni la Gran Muralla será suficiente para contenerlo, y eso el gobernador de Gansu lo sabe.

—Lo sé —respondió con serenidad gélida el *shou* de la provincia—. Claro que lo sé. ¿Crees acaso que no veo cómo Zhizhi crece en poder cada mes, cada semana, cada día, y crees que no siento rabia extrema por la inacción de los ministros del emperador, incapaces de ver lo que ocurrirá si no hacemos algo ya? ¿Crees acaso que he llegado a gobernador por influencias y no por mérito propio?

73. El Gobi.
74. El Tíbet.

Todo el mundo era conocedor de la valía del gobernador de Gansu y de su noble carrera militar y política. El general Tang también lo sabía. Por eso calló y no dijo nada.

El gobernador abrió un cajón de la mesa frente a la que estaba sentado y sacó un documento.

—Toma —dijo y lo puso en el borde de la mesa más próximo a su subordinado.

El general Tang se acercó, cogió el documento y lo leyó en silencio.

—Es un permiso del emperador Yuan-ti para cruzar la Puerta de Jade con mi ejército, firmado por él mismo y por el *shou* de Gansu —dijo Tang asombrado.

—Mi firma es real; la del emperador, como imaginarás, está falsificada. Asumo la responsabilidad. Eres tan animal que te veo capaz de perder guerreros inútilmente luchando contra los soldados imperiales de la puerta de la Gran Muralla. Y no estamos en condiciones de desperdiciar ni uno solo de los hombres que has reunido. No te confíes. Pese a la gran cantidad de soldados que has reclutado, muchos son de regiones aliadas, muy rabiosas contra Zhizhi, eso es cierto, pero sin gran preparación militar. Los *hsiung-nu* de Zhizhi son brutales, inmisericordes y muy experimentados. Y me consta que cuentan entre sus filas con mercenarios de lugares del mundo que ni tú ni yo conocemos. Seguramente son menos que tu ejército, pero conocen bien el territorio que pisan y han demostrado ser capaces de poder con todo y con todos. No te confíes. Y ahora márchate. No, no digas nada. No me agradezcas nada. Ve y venga a tus familiares, pero acaba con ese maldito Zhizhi. Sólo si traes su cabeza en una estaca es posible que el emperador decida no cortarnos las nuestras. Yo saldré al atardecer y me uniré con tu ejército. Necesitarás en algún momento, quizá, algún asesor político en esta campaña, pero el mando militar es tuyo.

Chen Tang abrió la boca varias veces. La cerró cada vez. Saludó marcialmente. Enrolló la orden imperial falsificada y se la introdujo en un bolsillo debajo de la cota de malla. Dio media vuelta y salió de la residencia del gobernador.

Kan Yen se levantó despacio. Acababa de tirar toda una

vida sin tacha al servicio del imperio por la ventana. Había falsificado una orden imperial. La pena para semejante delito no era otra que la muerte y la deshonra para él y toda su familia para la eternidad. Pero el impertinente Tang tenía razón: ante la ceguera del emperador y sus consejeros debían actuar ya e intentar detener a Zhizhi antes de que fuera un monstruo tan poderoso que ya nadie pudiera derrotarlo.

Kan Yen inspiró profundamente.

¿Cuánto tiempo pasaría antes de que el emperador se enterara de la salida de aquel ejército han? ¿Tendría Chen Tang tiempo suficiente para conseguir la victoria y regresar? ¿Conseguiría, en efecto, una victoria o Zhizhi con sus *hsiung-nu* y sus misteriosos mercenarios derrotarían a los cuarenta mil soldados de Tang?

Kan Yen, de forma instintiva, sin darse cuenta, se pasó por el cuello los dedos de la mano derecha. Le costaba tragar.

80

LA PUERTA DE JADE

Frontera occidental del Imperio han
36 a.C.

Los guerreros de la torre de vigilancia de la Puerta de Jade se quedaron muy quietos durante unos instantes, hasta que uno de ellos, tras parpadear varias veces, se rehízo de la sorpresa y bajó corriendo por la escalera. Si los que se acercaban a la puerta hubieran llegado desde fuera del imperio, los otros guerreros han que aún quedaban en lo alto de la torre ya habrían puesto en marcha la catapulta que hiciera volar un proyectil incendiado para avisar al resto de las torres de vigilancia de la proximidad de un ataque enemigo.

—Mi *hsiao-wei*, viene un ejército hacia la muralla.

El coronel imperial se levantó de la mesa en la que estaba desayunando aún.

—¿Cuántos son?

—Miles, mi *hsiao-wei*. Son miles.

—¿Habéis dado la señal?

—No, *hsiao-wei*.

El coronel se quedó petrificado. No daba crédito a lo que acababa de decirle su subordinado.

—¡Lo primero es dar la señal, imbécil!

—Es que no vienen de fuera, *hsiao-wei*. Vienen de dentro del imperio.

El coronel ya no entendía nada. No tenían ninguna notificación oficial sobre ningún desplazamiento de tropas imperiales en la provincia de Gansu. Ni por parte del emperador ni del gobernador. Subió velozmente por la escalera y una vez en lo alto miró hacia donde señalaban sus hombres, hacia el camino de Gansu que llevaba hasta la Puerta de Jade que custodiaban. No se veía caravana alguna, como era lo habitual, sino una infinita columna de soldados de infantería y de caballería que se aproximaba a buen paso.

El coronel se sorbió los mocos. Aquella noche seguramente se había destapado y se había resfriado, pero eso ahora no era lo que lo preocupaba.

—Llamad a todos los hombres y distribuidlos por la muralla —ordenó a uno de sus guerreros.

—¿Con las ballestas, *hsiao-wei?*

—¡Con las ballestas preparadas, claro que sí, estúpido! —le espetó el coronel imperial.

—Es el general Tang —dijo entonces otro de los guerreros han de la muralla.

El coronel se volvió de nuevo hacia el camino de Gansu. Y sí, al frente de aquel ejército, porque aquello era un ejército en toda regla, y muy grande, cabalgaba el *chiang-chün* Chen Tang. El coronel asintió: era de esperar. Entre los militares de toda la provincia no se hablaba de otra cosa desde hacía varios años: ¿cuánto tardaría Tang en reclutar un ejército y lanzarse contra el temible Zhizhi para vengar a sus familiares asesinados por el cruel líder de los *hsiung-nu?*

El coronel bajó de la torre acompañado por una decena de sus hombres y se situó en medio de la Gran Puerta de Jade, que permanecía completamente cerrada.

El general Tang se detuvo junto a la torre, desmontó de su caballo y, seguido por un grupo de sus guerreros, caminó para encontrarse con el guardián imperial de la puerta.

—Te saludo, *hsiao-wei* —dijo el general.

—Y yo saludo al general Tang —respondió el coronel.

—Solicito que nos abras la puerta para que mis tropas y yo podamos pasar.

El coronel no respondía. Llevaba sólo unos meses en la provincia, pero conocía la fama de Tang: un militar tan eficaz como reacio a seguir los métodos burocráticos correctos.

El silencio del guardián de la puerta empezó a resultar incómodo tanto para los guerreros que acompañaban al general como para los que estaban tras el propio coronel.

—No he recibido notificación alguna de que un ejército han tenga que salir del imperio —dijo al fin el *hsiao-wei*.

El general Tang asintió. Se llevó la mano debajo de la coraza y extrajo un documento que acercó al coronel. Este último lo cogió y lo leyó. Una vez. Dos. Tres. Inspiró profundamente.

—Lleva las firmas del gobernador y del propio emperador —dijo Tang.

—Las lleva, sí —admitió el coronel—. Aun así es muy peculiar que no me haya llegado aviso a través del correo imperial de un movimiento de tropas tan importante.

—A mí el emperador tampoco me notifica cuándo reemplaza al coronel de la Puerta de Jade o cuándo sustituye a cualquier otro mando del imperio. ¿Acaso crees que el emperador debe consultártelo todo? —Se echó a reír y con él los guerreros que acompañaban al general.

El coronel, no obstante, no se hizo a un lado de inmediato, sino que, muy lentamente, fue desplazándose hacia un extremo del camino.

—Pienso solicitar confirmación oficial a la capital, a Loyang —dijo.

—Solicítala, pero hazte a un lado, di a tus hombres que dejen de apuntarnos con las ballestas y abre las puertas de una maldita vez. Dudas del documento que te acabo de enseñar, pero piensa que estás dificultando un plan diseñado por el emperador en persona.

Aquí el coronel empezó a sudar. Se volvió hacia lo alto de la muralla e hizo una indicación con las manos para que los arqueros bajaran las ballestas y otra a los que controlaban las puertas, para que las abrieran.

Cuando el coronel se volvió de nuevo el general Tang ya estaba montando en su caballo y aprestándose a cruzar la Puerta de Jade con todo su ejército.

El *hsiao-wei* subió de nuevo a la torre para observar toda la operación. El ejército de Tang era inmenso y las puertas tuvieron que estar abiertas durante largo tiempo.

En el exterior, el general Chen Tang tiró de las riendas de su caballo para que el animal se saliera del camino. El gran *chiang-chün* dedicó una mirada larga a la Gran Muralla de arcilla y troncos entremezclados que defendía el Imperio han: se extendía hasta más allá de donde se podía abarcar con la vista. Una obra imponente. El general se sintió orgulloso de pertenecer a un imperio que había sido capaz de hacer una obra semejante, pero sintió también aún más rabia al pensar que ese mismo imperio había dejado pasar seis años sin castigar la brutal afrenta de Zhizhi al ejecutar a todos los miembros de una embajada han. Miró entonces al suelo. Tendría que controlar sus sentimientos o éstos entorpecerían sus cálculos, y en la guerra, como decía Sūn Tzu, todo era cuestión de cálculo. Le vendría bien que se les uniera el propio Kan Yen. Tang preveía una campaña difícil en lo militar y compleja políticamente. La derrota sería el desastre para él, para todos, para el Imperio han en su conjunto. La victoria... la pena de muerte para él, pero quizá salvar la honra de su familia.

El general Chen Tang escupió en el suelo. Quizá eso era lo que hacía falta para derrotar a Zhizhi: alguien que ya estuviera muerto. Sólo el que ha sentido la muerte muy de cerca o el que siente cómo se aproxima se atreve a todo.

HISTORIA DE TRAJANO

Principios del siglo II d.C.

Libro VI
EL INVENCIBLE TIGRIS

81

EL FANTASMA DE LA LEGIÓN PERDIDA

Antioquía
Marzo de 116 d.C.

Los trabajos de reconstrucción de Antioquía aún estaban en marcha, pero la primavera se aproximaba.

—No podemos retrasarnos —dijo Trajano a Quieto, que lo acompañaba en el *praetorium* de campaña instalado todavía en el centro del hipódromo de Antioquía—. Los cielos están despejados. Sale el sol. Es el momento de ponernos en camino.

—¿Y la ciudad? —preguntó Lucio.

—Dejaremos a una legión entera aquí para los trabajos de reconstrucción y cuando regresemos tras la nueva campaña, el resto de las tropas seguirán ayudando hasta que Antioquía resurja de sus escombros, pero ni siquiera un terremoto puede detener la conquista de Partia, Lucio. Tenemos ya las nuevas provincias de Armenia y Mesopotamia. Este año es el turno de Asiria. Este invierno vi la muerte muy de cerca, cuando se desplomaba el palacio sobre mi cabeza, pero sobreviví, Lucio, y siento que ahora ya nada ni nadie podrá detenernos. El sacerdote de Delfos, Plutarco, me dijo en Atenas que había visto mi muerte. Quizá fue este terremoto lo que vio, pero los dioses han querido salvarme. Estoy convencido de que ya nada podrá impedirnos la conquista total de Partia.

Lucio no quería contradecir al César, pero seguía habiendo un problema pendiente de la campaña anterior y se sintió en la penosa obligación de recordárselo al emperador.

—El Tigris continúa allí —dijo el norteafricano—, y Mebarsapes y su ejército y todos los partos del mundo también.

—Lo sé —aceptó Trajano—; pero yo también te dije que incluso pese a todos ellos cruzaremos el Tigris en Cizre.

No hubo oportunidad para razonar más. El emperador no dio margen para continuar con aquella conversación.

—¡Qué preparen las legiones! —exclamó el César hispano.

Lucio Quieto vio cómo Trajano echaba a andar en busca del caballo que le preparaba Aulo. Un animal que sólo montaría para salir de la ciudad, pues luego, fiel a su afán de ejemplaridad, el emperador desmontaría para emprender el largo camino hacia Cizre a pie, como todos sus soldados. Quieto sacudió la cabeza. Pese a los años que llevaba con Trajano nunca pensó que estaba bajo el mando de alguien a quien ni los terremotos más devastadores podían parar. ¿Sería suficiente esa fortaleza de ánimo para cruzar un río tan caudaloso como el Tigris, con miles de arqueros partos preparados en la ribera opuesta dispuestos a acribillarlos a todos en cuanto intentaran acceder a la otra orilla?

De camino a Cizre
Marzo-abril de 116 d.C.

La ruta fue la ya acostumbrada: de Antioquía a Zeugma, donde el gran ejército imperial romano cruzó, una vez más, el Éufrates, algo que ya había dejado de impresionar a los legionarios, pues se estaba convirtiendo en costumbre con Trajano. De Zeugma fueron directamente a Edesa. El rey Abgaro, junto con su hijo Arbandes, volvió a recibir al César con agasajos.

—Sólo podemos quedarnos una noche —dijo el emperador a Abgaro.

—Procuraremos que sea una velada de grato recuerdo —respondió Abgaro y miró hacia su hijo.

Arbandes sonrió y se inclinó levemente ante la mirada de Trajano.

El emperador no pasó a solas esa noche.

Cámara privada del rey Abgaro
Abril de 116 d.C.

Estaba a punto de amanecer. Su hijo entró con sigilo.

—Padre —dijo en voz baja.

—¿Sí? ¿Ha pasado algo? No me digas que el emperador te ha echado de su lecho.

—No, no es eso, padre —dijo el muchacho.

—Ah, dioses —suspiró el rey—. Entonces todo está bien.

—No, todo no está bien, padre —replicó Arbandes irritado.

Había una concubina en la cama del rey. Abgaro le dio una palmada en la espalda y la muchacha salió a toda velocidad sin hacer preguntas.

—¿Qué ocurre, entonces? —dijo el rey a su hijo.

Algunos guardias asomaron por la puerta, pero el rey hizo un gesto para que los dejaran solos.

—¿Hasta cuándo tendré que acostarme con el emperador de Roma? —preguntó Arbandes.

No era habitual que su hijo fuera tan directo. Sin duda estaba cansado de hacer lo que fuera que el emperador romano le pedía en aquellas veladas íntimas los dos solos.

—Creía que te gustaba —respondió Abgaro con tiento. No quería que su hijo reaccionara de forma imprevisible.

—Al principio era... —empezó el muchacho, pero tardó en encontrar una palabra adecuada para sus sensaciones—. Era... divertido. Sí, eso. Me entretenía ser el hombre que se acostaba con el emperador de Roma al que todos temen tanto. Desnudo no parece gran cosa, padre. Se hace viejo por momentos. Yo diría que, aunque sólo lleva tres años en Asia, es como si llevara veinte. Y se cansa cada vez antes.

—¿Se cansa? —indagó Abgaro, que buscaba confirmar un punto de aquella conversación que le parecía especialmente relevante.

—Cuando estamos juntos... en la cama...

—Ya veo. Eso es interesante.

Los dos guardaron silencio un rato mientras Abgaro se echaba por la cara un poco de agua de una bacinilla de oro que tenía en una mesa de su cámara privada.

—No creo que tengas que acostarte con el emperador de Roma muchas más veces, hijo mío —dijo al fin Abgaro en un susurro.

—¿Ah, no? ¿Por qué, padre?

—Tengo información de lo que Trajano se va a encontrar en Cizre: Osroes ha apostado fuerte por evitar el avance romano en ese lugar, pero por lo que tú mismo me has dicho que Trajano te ha contado, el César está empeñado en cruzar el Tigris en ese punto exacto, este año, a toda costa. Osroes ha concentrado tantos arqueros que aquello será una lluvia tan mortal como la que acabó con Craso en Carrhae. Pronto no habrá una sola legión perdida romana, sino varias más, y la cabeza de Trajano será usada en una nueva representación de las *Bacantes* de Eurípides a la que tú yo asistiremos invitados por el mismísimo Osroes, victorioso y triunfante.

—Pero, padre, si nosotros hemos arriesgado todo a que Trajano ganará esta guerra. Si es cierto lo que dices, cuando Osroes derrote a Trajano en el Tigris, vendrá con todo su ejército y arrasará Edesa, y seremos tú y yo los que perdamos la cabeza.

Abgaro sonrió. Su hijo era hermoso, capaz de encandilar con bailes y caricias a un emperador que se hacía viejo, pero, desde luego, no era particularmente sagaz. Aún tenía mucho que aprender para ser un digno sucesor suyo.

—Siéntate, muchacho —le dijo Abgaro—, y escúchame bien y aprende cómo se gobierna un reino pequeño como Osroene, que está en medio de dos gigantes como Roma y Partia: cuando el viento ha soplado desde Roma nos hemos rendido sin combatir al César, pero cuando el emperador romano sea derrotado en el Tigris, éste, igual que ha hecho ahora, regresará por la misma ruta en busca de refugio y nosotros se lo daremos y tú, con tus caricias y besos, lo consolarás... por última vez: en medio de la noche, cuando el César duerma, le cortarás la cabeza al tiempo que mis guardias y mis soldados se enfrentarán a lo que quede de las tropas medio aniquiladas con las que Trajano regrese del Tigris. Regalaremos entonces la cabeza de Trajano a Osroes en una bandeja y eso, no lo dudes, aplacará por completo su cólera hacia nosotros. Y con eso habremos conseguido salvar de la destrucción a Edesa y todo Osroene en medio de la más brutal de las guerras. Así, hijo, se gobierna y se salvan nuestras posesiones y nuestro poder.

—Entonces ¿siempre hemos estado engañando a Trajano?

—Desde tu primer beso —le confirmó su padre—. Mi único temor era que te encariñaras del César, pero ya veo que eso no ha pasado.

—Ni pasará, padre —reafirmó Arbandes sonriente.

—Es sólo cuestión de semanas que uses este cuchillo para matar al César.

Abgaro le mostró una preciosa daga con esmeraldas y rubíes ensartados en la empuñadura.

—Es un arma preciosa, padre.

—Sólo lo mejor para el emperador Trajano.

Se echó a reír mientras guardaba la daga en el cofre del que la había extraído; su hijo lo acompañaba en aquellas carcajadas hermanas de la traición y la muerte.

Nísibis
Abril de 116 d.C.

Lucio Quieto se quedó boquiabierto cuando llegaron a Nísibis, la última parada de importancia antes de retornar a Cizre: una legión entera había estado trabajando durante todo el invierno, construyendo toda clase de ingenios de madera extraños para los que el *legatus* norteafricano no encontraba nombres adecuados.

—¿Son barcos? —pregunto a Nigrino, que estaba a su lado.

—Ni idea —respondió el otro *legatus*, tan confuso como él.

—Venid —dijo Trajano, sorprendiéndolos por la espalda.

Los dos lo siguieron junto con otros *legati*, Liviano, Aulo y un nutrido grupo de pretorianos que siempre acompañaban al César a todas partes. El jefe del pretorio, desde lo ocurrido con el terremoto, había ordenado que el emperador nunca estuviera solo ni para ir al baño. Sólo podía estar a solas con

Lucio Quieto, con Aulo o cuando tenía alguna aventura licenciosa como la de Arbandes. A Liviano no le gustaban los devaneos privados del César, pero todo Osroene parecía tan sometido y Abgaro tan servicial que el jefe del pretorio había dado por buena también aquella excepción.

Trajano y sus hombres llegaron al lugar donde un hombre pequeño, rodeado de artesanos y zapadores, daba algunas indicaciones sobre cómo proseguir con los trabajos de construcción de diversos ingenios de madera.

—Apolodoro —dijo Trajano.

El arquitecto de Damasco se volvió y se inclinó ante el César.

—Aquí estoy, augusto. Siempre al servicio del emperador.

—¡Por Cástor y Pólux! No te dejo tiempo para que permanezcas ocioso, ¿verdad? —le dijo Trajano acercándose y poniéndole la mano encima del hombro—. Has reabierto el canal que conecta el mar Mediterráneo con la mar Eritrea y ya te he traído aquí para que nos ayudes a cruzar el Tigris.

—El trabajo me gusta, César, y los retos son siempre estimulantes —respondió Apolodoro.

—¿Y bien? ¿Lo tienes todo preparado? —preguntó el emperador.

—Necesitaría una semana más. Lo tengo todo pero faltan algunas carretas, grandes, especiales, para llevar todo lo que hemos hecho. Hay algunos pontones que ya hemos transportado, pero me faltan las balsas más grandes. Están desmontadas, en piezas, para facilitar el transporte. Luego necesitaremos dos o tres días más allí, en Cizre, para montarlo todo. No sé si esto es excesivo tiempo...

—No, está bien. Una semana aquí y luego dos, tres días junto al Tigris. Bien. Dedicaré ese tiempo a preparar las tropas.

Trajano se despidió del arquitecto y se alejó del lugar para dejar a Apolodoro trabajar tranquilo. Una vez a doscientos pasos de donde se terminaban los ingenios de madera, el emperador se detuvo y anunció los planes para acometer la empresa, aparentemente imposible, de atravesar el Tigris con un inmenso ejército en la orilla opuesta esperándolos para acribillarlos con flechas.

—En quince días iniciaremos los ataques para cruzar el río.

Todos permanecían en silencio.

—César, los informes que nos llegan de Cizre indican que los partos han concentrado un número jamás conocido de arqueros —dijo Lucio Quieto—. Sé que yo no fui capaz de cruzar el río y es por mi culpa que estamos aquí, pero temo que todo esto termine...

—¿Ibas a decir como en Carrhae? —preguntó Trajano.

Quieto inspiró profundamente, pero al fin respondió:

—Sí, César.

Trajano suspiró algo exasperado. Si Lucio, su mejor y más leal hombre, estaba inquieto, ¿qué sería de los demás? Le habían llevado su *sella curulis*. Se sentó.

—Después de tantas victorias como se han conseguido bajo mi mando, ¿aún dudáis todos de mí? —Por primera vez en mucho tiempo el emperador parecía realmente molesto con lo que había dicho Lucio y eso sorprendió aún más a todos los presentes—. Decidme. —Se levantó y paseó entre los miembros de su *consilium augusti* de campaña, levantando la voz—. ¡Decidme, por Júpiter! ¿cuándo he sido yo derrotado? ¡Vamos, decidme, mencionad tan sólo una derrota sufrida por mí! ¡Ya sea aquí o en el Danubio o en el Rin! ¡Dadme el nombre de alguna batalla en la que estando yo al mando hayamos sufrido una derrota!

Nadie dijo nada.

No había batalla alguna que mencionar.

—¿Creéis acaso que me he vuelto loco o viejo o las dos cosas a la vez? ¿No he venido a pie, andando, como el resto de los legionarios del ejército? ¿No como acaso su rancho, no bebo el agua de la tropa, no duermo en las tiendas de campaña cuando estamos en marcha? ¡Habladme, por Hércules! —Trajano casi gritaba, rojo, encolerizado como no lo habían visto casi desde la muerte de Longino. Se puso en pie—. Decidme, de una vez por todas y para siempre, ¿cuántas victorias he de conseguir para que comprendáis que yo nunca nunca entro en combate si no sé que voy a conseguir la victoria? ¡Lo calculo todo una y mil veces, lo pienso todo una y mil veces, por Cástor y Pólux! ¡No hago caso a consejeros extranjeros en los que no se puede confiar! ¡Escucho vuestras dudas cuando las tenéis y cambio de criterio cuando vuestras apreciaciones son justas! —Suspiró, puso los brazos en jarras; volvió a hablar con voz algo más serena, pero con la misma indignación—. Lucio Quieto vino a mí el año pasado a Edesa y me dijo que no había podido cruzar el Tigris y me explicó las circunstancias. ¿Le recriminé yo algo su acción? Ni lo más mínimo. ¿Por qué? Porque había sido prudente e inteligente. Yo di una orden, pero las circunstancias hacían imposible su cumplimiento sin perder una enorme cantidad de hombres, y aun así quizá ni siquiera se habría conseguido el objetivo de cruzar el río. Pero ahora hemos vuelto aquí porque tengo todo preparado y dispuesto, como lo tuve cuando cruzamos el Danubio y atacamos a Decébalo, o como cuando nos lanzamos sobre Armenia tras atravesar el Éufrates y la conquistamos, o como cuando el año pasado nos hicimos con Batnae y Nísibis. Y todo va a salir igual de bien aunque al otro lado del Tigris estén todos los arqueros, o más, que los que acabaron con Craso hijo y con las legiones de Craso padre. Aunque los dioses hayan lanzado terremotos contra mí, pese a eso, pese a todo, vamos a cruzar ese maldito río y vamos a descender luego por el Éufrates y el Tigris en paralelo y vamos a conquistar Cesifonte. Y si me veis perturbado, nervioso al hablaros, es sólo por agotamiento, porque yo puedo derrotar a tantos enemigos como se pongan delante de mí. Tengo con vosotros la fuerza y la lealtad y la valentía para conseguir tantas victorias como hagan falta para doblegar a Partia entera, pero ¿sabéis una cosa? Hay un enemigo al que no puedo vencer y eso me exaspera, porque está aquí, siempre, entre vosotros, y nos acompaña siempre desde que cruzamos el Éufrates por primera vez hace ya dos años.

Trajano no desveló el nombre del enemigo en cuestión. En su lugar, calló y volvió a sentarse, cabizbajo, como agotado, vencido.

—¿Qué enemigo es ése, augusto, al que no podemos vencer? —preguntó Lucio Quieto.

Trajano levantó la cabeza y lo miró con una sonrisa de impotencia.

—La legión perdida. Contra la legión perdida no puedo. Nadie puede derrotar a un fantasma, a un espíritu del pasado.

Puedo doblegar a los dacios, a los armenios, a los partos y a todos los pueblos del mundo, pero no soy capaz de derrotar a esa maldita legión perdida y el miedo que causa su recuerdo entre mis legionarios. Veo el eterno terror a la legión perdida reflejado en vuestros rostros. Así no puedo luchar más. Pensaba que con Armenia y Mesopotamia sometidas, habiendo cruzado el Éufrates en varias ocasiones y habiendo obtenido sólo victorias, ese miedo se habría disipado de una vez por todas, pero no. Contra esa legión todo es poco, todo es inútil. Quizá si Plutarco escribe mi vida lo pondrá en uno de sus papiros: «Y Trajano fue vencido al fin por la legión perdida, por el recuerdo a una derrota que ni sus mejores oficiales podían olvidar nunca». —Suspiró de nuevo; más profunda e intensamente que las veces anteriores—. Nos retiramos. Hemos sido vencidos antes de ni siquiera intentarlo.

El silencio más sepulcral se apoderó del cónclave de militares romanos.

—Seguramente el emperador Trajano no merece oficiales tan torpes como nosotros —dijo Lucio Quieto agachándose de cuclillas para hablar cara a cara al emperador, que se había sentado—, pero sí hay algo que puedo garantizarle al César: yo no temo ni a fantasmas ni a legiones perdidas. Sólo me inquietan veinte mil arqueros enemigos dispuestos a masacrarnos, diez mil infantes y diez mil jinetes que los apoyan, pero sé que tenemos el mejor César que ha habido nunca, un emperador que es simple y llanamente invencible. Nunca ha sido derrotado y nunca lo será y yo lo seguiré hasta la muerte, hasta el fin del mundo o hasta el Hades, si es eso lo que Trajano quiere conquistar un día.

Trajano sonrió algo más relajado.

—¿Cuál es el plan de ataque, augusto? —preguntó entonces Quieto.

Trajano asintió al ver que Nigrino, Liviano, Aulo y el resto de los allí reunidos cabeceaban afirmativamente, como si Quieto hablara por todos ellos.

—Traed un plano del valle de Cizre y del Tigris —respondió el emperador.

Se lo llevaron de inmediato.

82

LA BATALLA DEL TIGRIS

Cizre
Mayo de 116 d.C.

Ribera oriental del Tigris

Mebarsapes, rey de Adiabene, estaba junto a Mitrídates, hermano de Osroes, rey de reyes de Partia. Éste había enviado a su hermano junto con un importante contingente de arqueros de la caballería ligera parta y *catafractos* para evitar, como fuera, que los romanos cruzaran el Tigris. Era algo arriesgado, pues esas tropas las habían tenido que retirar del territorio más oriental, donde se seguía luchando contra el irreductible Vologases, quien continuaba reclamando para sí el título de auténtico *Šāhān Šāh*. Mitrídates era consciente de que ya que disponía de aquellos soldados y jinetes debía hacer el mejor uso posible de ellos. En Oriente se había quedado su hijo Sanatruces con menos efectivos de los necesarios para contener a Vologases.

—Hemos de acabar con esto pronto —dijo Mitrídates—. He de retornar al este con gran parte de este ejército o Vologases nos pondrá allí en un aprieto.

El rey de Adiabene era consciente de las preocupaciones de su aliado parto.

—Los romanos desistirán en cuanto vean que es imposible lo que se proponen —comentó Mebarsapes y, de súbito, señaló hacia la otra orilla—. Mira. ¿No es ése el emperador Trajano?

Los dos vieron a un hombre mayor, a caballo, rodeado de jinetes pretorianos, paseando por la ribera enemiga. Aquel hombre era el único de todo el ejército romano que tenía el pelo completamente gris.

—Sí, sin duda, ha de ser él —confirmó Mitrídates—. Me han comunicado desde Osroene que esta vez venía el propio emperador romano para intentar cruzar el Tigris y es el hombre de más edad y a quien todos parecen obedecer. Observa cómo se hacen a un lado cuando se acerca con sus pretorianos. Y... se ha detenido. Por Zoroastro y Ahura Mazda, juraría que nos está mirando.

Ribera occidental del Tigris

Trajano miraba fijamente hacia la orilla opuesta.

—Parece que aquéllos de allá fueran sus jefes —dijo.

—Si es así, uno debe de ser el rey de Adiabene, Mebarsapes —contestó Lucio Quieto—. El otro no lo sé. Parece un alto oficial parto.

—¿Sabemos a quién ha enviado Osroes para liderar sus arqueros y *catafractos*? —preguntó Trajano—. Tiene que ser alguien de su familia y muy leal, pues lo ha enviado con muchas tropas. No parece su hijo. Se mueve con menos soltura que Partamaspates, a quien vimos al frente de las últimas embajadas partas en Atenas y Antioquía.

—Quizá un hermano de Osroes —sugirió Nigrino.

—Pues el único hermano vivo que le queda a Osroes es Mitrídates —concluyó Trajano—. Pero eso ahora no importa. Empezad con el plan.

Y Quieto y Nigrino, junto con otros tres *legati*, Julio Máximo, Julio Alejandro y Erucio Claro, azuzaron sus caballos para ir cada uno a los puntos designados por Trajano y en su plan de ataque.

Sector norte, ribera occidental

Lucio Quieto se dirigió a sus legionarios con ansia de batalla.

—¡Vamos, por Hércules! ¡A las balsas, todos! ¡Rápido!

Varias cohortes romanas subieron a grandes balsas construidas bajo la supervisión de Apolodoro en Nísibis el invierno anterior. Estaban en el flanco izquierdo de la posición romana.

Flanco derecho del ejército parto y de Adiabene, frente a la posición de Quieto

Mitrídates había acudido hasta el lugar más estrecho del río. Estaba seguro de que Trajano intentaría cruzar por ese punto y, en efecto, por allí estaban iniciando el embarque de tropas enemigas en grandes balsas.

—Bien —dijo entre dientes y con una amplia sonrisa en el rostro—: los esperaremos aquí y los acribillaremos. —Luego elevó el tono de voz y gritó sus órdenes—: ¡Por delante la caballería ligera con los arcos preparados! ¡Por detrás los *catafractos*! ¡Por Ahura Mazda, por Partia, por el *Šāhān Šāh*!

Centro del ejército parto y de Adiabene

Mebarsapes se había quedado en el centro de la formación con el grueso de sus tropas. Le habría gustado ser el primero en la línea de combate, pero era evidente que Mitrídates se quería llevar el honor y la gloria de aquella fácil victoria. Justo en ese momento llegaron jinetes que tenía patrullando en el sector más al sur, a lo largo del Tigris.

—Majestad, los romanos están embarcando tropas no sólo al norte, sino también al sur.

El rey asintió y pensó con rapidez: era razonable. El emperador romano intentaba atacar por los dos puntos más estrechos del río. El Tigris hacía un gran meandro en aquel lugar y ese maldito Trajano iba a intentar cruzarlo por el norte y por el sur, justo allí donde el río, aunque de aguas algo más rápidas, era un poco más estrecho. Y lo intentaba por los dos puntos a la vez.

—Sea, pues acudiremos nosotros al sur —dijo Mebarsapes mirando a uno de sus oficiales—. Tú ve al norte y comunica a

Mitrídates que los romanos también están intentando cruzar el río en el sur y que nosotros nos ocuparemos de que no lo hagan. No va a quedar ni uno de esos malditos con vida. Ni uno de los que se mojen los pies en el Tigris.

Centro de la formación romana

Trajano observaba cómo Lucio Quieto por el norte y Julio Máximo por el sur iniciaban el despliegue de balsas repletas de legionarios. Él, entretanto, se encontraba en una gran plataforma de madera desde la que podía ver todo lo que ocurría a su alrededor: el grueso de las legiones estaba en una especie de península natural, creada por el meandro del Tigris, con agua al norte, al este y al sur. Los legionarios, en grandes balsas con parapetos para protegerse de las flechas enemigas, navegaban ya tanto al norte como al sur del meandro. Trajano tenía ante él la parte más tranquila del Tigris, pero también la más ancha. Había enviado una legión con Lucio Quieto al norte y otra con Julio Máximo al sur. En el centro del meandro cuatro legiones más permanecían inmóviles. Entre cohorte y cohorte había grandes bultos, cuyo contenido estaba oculto por enormes telas color arena que se confundían con el terreno.

Nigrino había regresado de revisarlo todo.

—Estamos listos, augusto —dijo el *legatus*.

—Esperaremos —respondió Trajano—. Quiero que los partos y el rey de Adiabene se convenzan de que nuestros objetivos son el norte y el sur del meandro, los pasos estrechos del río. Sí, esperaremos. —Miró al cielo—. No hay nubes y el sol aún está ascendiendo. Tenemos tiempo. Hemos de confundirlos y gastar sus recursos.

Sector norte del meandro

Navegando por el río, los legionarios se apretaban contra los parapetos. Sabían lo que se les venía encima y no les hacía ninguna gracia. Pero sus oficiales, desde los centuriones hasta los tribunos, incluido el *legatus* Lucio Quieto, les habían hablado con una seguridad tan embriagadora que se agarraban a las palabras que les habían repetido todos sus superiores una y otra vez como si fueran su gran esperanza.

—¡Trajano nunca ha sido derrotado! ¡Nunca!

Eso les habían dicho y era cierto.

La lluvia de flechas parta empezó.

Los pensamientos se quebraron.

Llegó el sudor frío.

—¡Desdoblad los parapetos! —aulló Lucio Quieto.

De inmediato los legionarios levantaron los parapetos que estaban plegados sobre sí mismos, de modo que al desplegarlos del todo ya no eran de un metro de altura, sino de más de dos, con lo que tenían protección contra las flechas enemigas tanto frontalmente como por arriba. Además, Apolodoro había dispuesto que hubiera parapetos en un extremo de la balsa y en diferentes puntos en su interior, de forma que el peso de todos los legionarios se distribuyera proporcionalmente para impedir que las gigantescas balsas se desestabilizaran y se hundieran por un lado.

¡Clac, clac, clac...!

Los dardos enemigos, una lluvia de flechas tan brutal como la que los partos habían lanzado contra las tropas de Craso años atrás, se les vinieron encima a las tropas de Lucio Quieto, pero los parapetos los protegían y apenas hubo bajas o heridos. Los remeros de las balsas, resguardados también en cada extremo de las extrañas pero eficaces embarcaciones, remaron para seguir avanzando hacia la otra orilla.

Estaban en el centro del río.

¡Clac, clac, clac...!

Otra andanada de flechas enemigas.

Y otra más y otra...

Pero la casi totalidad de las flechas enemigas se estrellaba contra los parapetos.

Orilla oriental del Tigris, ejército parto en el sector norte

Mitrídates estaba siendo testigo de cómo la mayor parte de las flechas arrojadas por sus jinetes no conseguían causar apenas bajas entre los romanos.

—¡Disparad más alto, imbéciles! ¡Más alto! —gritó el hermano de Osroes—. ¡Las flechas han de caer casi en picado para superar esos parapetos!

Y como no parecía estar seguro de que sus hombres fueran a entenderlo, él mismo se acercó a uno de sus jinetes.

—¡Dame! —le espetó.

El caballero parto le entregó el arco y Mitrídates se acercó a la orilla cabalgando y, al más puro estilo parto, sin detener a su montura, apuntó hacia el cielo y lanzó la flecha. Ésta surcó el aire trazando una gran parábola hasta que perdió fuerza, el peso de la punta se impuso y empezó entonces un descenso brutal silbando de un modo mortífero hasta caer sobre la cabeza de un legionario romano que no estaba completamente protegido por arriba, reventándole el cráneo y el cerebro y haciendo que su cabeza estallara por dentro.

Mitrídates detuvo su caballo.

—¡Así!

Centenares, miles de jinetes empezaron a imitar a Mitrídates.

Sector norte del río, en el centro de las aguas

Lucio Quieto había visto las nuevas órdenes y la exhibición que había hecho el líder parto.

—¡Inclinad parapetos!

Y los legionarios tiraron de los parapetos hacia ellos de forma que éstos quedaban en diagonal con la superficie de las balsas, actuando casi como un techo protector.

¡Clac, clac, clac...!

La nueva andanada de flechas enemiga se estrelló una vez más, pese a la gran parábola trazada por los dardos enemigos, en aquellos parapetos, que parecían ya auténticos puercoespines por la innumerable cantidad de dardos clavados en ellos.

—¡Anclad! ¡Anclad las balsas, por Júpiter! —aulló ahora Lucio Quieto, quien hasta el momento seguía milimétricamente las instrucciones recibidas por el propio emperador en el último *consilium augusti* anterior a la batalla.

Los legionarios arrojaron anclas desde las balsas y todas las embarcaciones quedaron detenidas tras haber recorrido dos tercios de la anchura del Tigris en aquel punto norte del meandro.

Lucio Quieto caminaba por su balsa sudando y haciendo grandes gestos para comunicarse con los tribunos y centuriones de las embarcaciones que tenía a su alrededor. Y, mientras tanto, empezó a mascullar entre dientes, con rabia:

—Ahora nos toca a nosotros. Ahora es nuestro turno, por Marte y por Cástor y Pólux y por todos los dioses. Se van a enterar ahora esos malditos partos de una vez para siempre. El año pasado me detuvisteis, pero esta vez vais a ser vosotros los que os vais a ahogar en sangre.

»¡Descorred ventanas! —ordenó a pleno pulmón.

Y los legionarios levantaron tablas estrechas que había a intervalos regulares en todos los parapetos, dejando al descubierto un montón de pequeñas ventanas por las que se podía ver y, sobre todo, disparar.

Los legionarios que llevaba Quieto no eran legionarios cualesquiera, sino los mejores de las mejores *cohortes sagitarii* del ejército del emperador: los más diestros arqueros del Imperio.

—¡Disparad! ¡Disparad! —gritó Quieto y poco faltó para que él mismo cogiera un arco y se pusiera a lanzar flechas como loco. Pero se contuvo. Su misión era dar órdenes, supervisarlo todo, mantener la formación de las balsas, animar a los arqueros y estar atento al momento en que Trajano diera la auténtica orden de ataque. Porque de momento aún no estaban en la ofensiva.

Aún no.

Se asomó por una de las ventanas: decenas de jinetes partos caían abatidos por las flechas romanas. En aquella orilla nadie tenía parapetos. Y se retiraban. Lucio Quieto sonrió. Para ser aquello sólo una maniobra de distracción estaba causando auténtico daño en el enemigo.

Centro del ejército romano

Nigrino, acompañado por otros *legati,* miraba al emperador.

—¿Empezamos?

Trajano había estado mirando al norte y estaba satisfecho con los progresos de Lucio Quieto en aquella parte del río. Levantó la mano para que Nigrino no le hablara por unos instantes. Se volvió entonces hacia el sur.

—Parece que Julio Máximo está emulando los logros de Quieto, si bien él lo hace frente al rey de Adiabene. —Luego miró a Nigrino—. No hay prisa. Más aún, vamos a hacer una nueva maniobra de engaño. Ordenad que de las cuatro legiones, dos se posicionen justo en la ribera del Tigris como apoyo posible para Quieto en el norte y Julio Máximo en el sur, como si vaciáramos nuestro centro. Pero que nadie embarque. El plan original sigue en pie.

—Sí, César —dijo Nigrino y dio media vuelta para transmitir las órdenes necesarias.

Sur del río, ejército de Adiabene

Los arqueros del rey Mebarsapes se mostraban impotentes para causar bajas entre los romanos parapetados detrás de las protecciones de sus balsas.

—Tú —dijo el monarca señalando a uno de sus oficiales—. Ve al norte y dile a Mitrídates que necesito más arqueros y refuerzo de *catafractos* por si los romanos llegan a desembarcar.

—Sí, majestad.

El oficial partió al galope. Mebarsapes se pasó el dorso de la mano derecha por la boca. La tenía reseca. Aquello no le estaba gustando nada. Los parapetos y las balsas eran algo tan sencillo como eficaz. Aquel Trajano no era un enemigo al uso.

Ribera oriental, sector norte

A Mitrídates le temblaba la boca y al final tuvo que desahogarse.

—¡Mebarsapes es un imbécil, por Zoroastro! —exclamó el

hermano de Osroes ante el perplejo mensajero enviado por el rey de Adiabene. Mitrídates siguió diciendo más cosas, pero mascullando, para sí mismo—. Y un débil y un flojo... pero es lo que tenemos... —Miró de nuevo al enviado de Mebarsapes—. De acuerdo, dile que le enviaré más tropas de refuerzo, pero por lo que más quiera, tu rey ha de evitar que los romanos lleguen a la orilla en su sector; ¿está claro, muchacho? Si los romanos llegan a cruzar esto se puede poner muy mal para todos. Díselo. ¡Sal ya! ¡Corre!

Mitrídates acompañó sus gritos de aspavientos exagerados con los brazos, de forma que el mensajero salió a toda velocidad de regreso a las posiciones que defendía su rey. El hermano de Osroes se volvió entonces hacia sus oficiales, pero antes de que pudiera decir nada uno de ellos señaló hacia los romanos. Mitrídates se volvió y vio las maniobras que Trajano había ordenado.

—Están vaciando su centro —comentó mientras sus hombres asentían—. El emperador romano se lo va a jugar todo a intentar cruzar por el norte y por el sur a la vez.

—El centro del meandro es muy ancho —se atrevió a decir uno de los oficiales partos.

—Es cierto —aceptó Mitrídates—. Por eso se concentra en el norte y el sur, los puntos más estrechos del río. Pues nosotros vaciaremos también nuestro centro: que la mitad de las tropas que tenemos allí venga aquí para seguir impidiendo que los romanos crucen al norte y que la otra mitad vaya de apoyo a Mebarsapes. Cuantos más partos haya con ese inútil, mejor.

Nadie se atrevió a comentar que pese a las maniobras que estaba realizado el enemigo, los romanos aún disponían de dos legiones situadas en el centro.

Ejército romano en tierra

Trajano observó cómo los partos distribuían sus reservas para detener el avance de las balsas de Lucio Quieto al norte y de Julio Máximo al sur.

—Ahora —dijo Trajano sin levantar la voz, pero con la seguridad firme de quien ha esperado el momento justo para el golpe clave.

Nigrino y Julio Alejandro salieron al galope en dirección a la orilla. Sus legiones estaban apostadas en la parte central que dibujaba el trazado del largo meandro del Tigris.

—¡Ahora, por Júpiter, ahora! —aullaron ambos *legati* a sus tribunos y éstos a los centuriones y legionarios.

Las grandes telas que cubrían los otros artefactos que había construido Apolodoro durante el invierno en Nísibis se descubrieron a toda velocidad. Centenares de legionarios empezaron a llevar con grandes carretas pequeñas barcazas que alineaban una tras otra desde la orilla occidental, de forma que, al unirlas y atarlas bien con sogas gruesas, iban construyendo un improvisado puente sobre el Tigris. La obra, no obstante, requeriría una hora o dos de tiempo, pese a la celeridad con la que miles de legionarios se aprestaban a aquella faena agotadora. Como en ese punto el Tigris era más ancho tenían la ventaja de que las flechas no podían alcanzarlos desde la orilla opuesta, además de que, por las maniobras de engaño realizadas por Trajano, todas las fuerzas enemigas estaban al norte y al sur de aquella posición central. Por otro lado, intentar construir el puente de barcazas en aquel lugar tenía la enorme desventaja de que aquél, en efecto, era el punto más ancho y, por tanto, se necesitaban más barcazas, más tiempo y más esfuerzo para conseguir terminar aquella sorprendente obra de ingeniería.

—Los trabajos van rápido —dijo Liviano a Trajano.

—Sí, pero los partos se darán cuenta y revertirán las órdenes dadas —contrapuso el tribuno Aulo—. Pronto habrá arqueros enemigos en la otra orilla y cuando el puente llegue a la mitad del río, nuestros zapadores estarán ya al alcance de sus flechas.

—Cierto —confirmó Trajano—. Y eso no podemos permitirlo. Que salgan ya las nuevas balsas.

—Sí, César —dijo Aulo, que recibió aquella orden con alivio.

Las instrucciones de Trajano se transmitieron velozmente y a ambos lados del puente en construcción empezaron a embarcar tropas de las dos legiones de reserva del centro del ejército imperial. Lo hicieron en grandes balsas con parapetos similares a las de los extremos norte y sur, sólo que éstas tenían, además de los parapetos, torres de madera en su centro desde donde los arqueros romanos podían disparar en altura contra el enemigo.

Entretanto, los que trabajaban en el puente seguían anclando bien cada barcaza al lecho del río y atando una a la otra para mantener la estabilidad de toda aquella obra. El propio Apolodoro, siempre protegido por un grupo de pretorianos, dirigía los esfuerzos de los legionarios desde una barca que iba acercándose, peligrosamente, según avanzaban la construcción, hacia el centro del río.

Orilla oriental, sector norte

Mitrídates vio lo que estaba pasando y comprendió que Trajano había jugado a engañarlos.

—Hemos de llevar tropas al centro de nuevo ya mismo, o los romanos terminarán ese puente en poco tiempo y no encontrarán oposición en ese enclave.

—Pero no podemos dejar ahora el norte sin defensa o los legionarios de esas malditas balsas desembarcarán, mi señor —dijo un oficial nervioso.

Mitrídates asintió.

—Nos hemos de volver a repartir entre el norte y el centro, y en el sur que se apañe Mebarsapes con sus hombres. Envía un mensajero para que los *catafractos* y la caballería ligera que le habíamos enviado como apoyo regresen, y me da igual lo que diga el rey de Adiabene. ¡Necesitamos a nuestra caballería acorazada en el centro!

En el medio del río, sector central

Nigrino vio que los partos emplazaban tropas frente a ellos para intentar detener la construcción del puente.

—¡Parapetos arriba!

Y la escena que se había visto al norte y al sur se repitió. Las andanadas de flechas partas eran detenidas por las protecciones de madera de las balsas. Pero eso no era suficiente ahora: una cohorte de legionarios entró por la parte del puente que estaba construida. La mitad eran arqueros, que de inmediato tomaron posiciones para disparar contra los partos, mientras que el resto de los soldados defendían con sus escudos a los zapadores, los que maniobraban con las barcazas, para protegerlos de las flechas durante sus trabajos de atar con las gruesas maromas las nuevas barcas, además de anclarlas al lecho del río. Empezaron a darse bastantes bajas romanas entre los ingenieros, los arqueros y los legionarios que protegían, o lo intentaban, a los zapadores.

Parecía que la construcción del puente iba a desbaratarse.

Todo el plan original de Trajano, centrado en aquel puente, empezaba a resquebrajarse. ¿O no?

Centro del ejército romano en tierra

Trajano miró a Aulo y a Liviano:

—Que Nigrino y Julio Alejandro comiencen a disparar con sus arqueros, de lo contrario perderemos el puente —dijo con seriedad—, y que Lucio haga lo planeado en este momento. Si esperamos más todo el trabajo habrá sido en vano.

Varios mensajeros partieron raudos a transmitir las órdenes hacia las posiciones de los *legati* que había mencionado Trajano.

El emperador miró hacia el sur: los partos se retiraban y dejaban a Mebarsapes sólo con sus hombres frente a Julio Máximo. Si en ese lugar pudieran desembarcar, eso desequilibraría la batalla, pero pese al repliegue parto, los hombres de Adiabene luchaban con furia y el intercambio de andanadas de flechas de un lado y otro era brutal y continuo.

—Luchan por su tierra —dijo Liviano, que parecía haber interpretado bien los pensamientos del César.

—Que pronto dejará de ser suya —apostilló el emperador

con una seguridad y una determinación que sorprendieron al jefe del pretorio, pues el desarrollo de la batalla hacía difícil aún predecir su resultado final.

El aplomo del César en aquellos momentos de incertidumbre tenía una virtud: era contagioso; lástima que los legionarios no pudieran oír a su emperador. De pronto, Trajano, como si fuera él ahora quien interpretaba bien las ideas de su mejor pretoriano, habló de nuevo:

—Creo que ha llegado el momento, Liviano, de que nos acerquemos al río personalmente Todos los legionarios han de ver que su César cree en la victoria. Eso les dará ánimos para redoblar esfuerzos.

A Liviano nunca le gustaba que el emperador se expusiera en una batalla de forma inútil, pero en aquel momento, en aquella guerra, en medio de aquel pulso entre los dos imperios, entre Partia y Roma pugnando por el control del Tigris, quizá no fuera mala idea que se dejara ver más próximo a la línea de combate.

En el río, sector central

Los zapadores de las legiones, protegidos por los arqueros de las *cohortes sagitarii,* progresaban en la construcción del puente. Tanto Nigrino como Julio Alejandro gritaban sin parar para enardecer los ánimos de todos sus hombres y que la lluvia de flechas sobre el enemigo no decayera en ningún momento.

—¡*Legatus,* se nos están acabando las flechas! —exclamó uno de los tribunos a Nigrino, pero el líder hispano se volvió y señaló una larga hilera de barcas que se les acercaban por detrás.

—El emperador lo ha previsto todo, tribuno —le respondió Nigrino—: ahí llegan más dardos. Todas esas embarcaciones están llenas. Organiza la distribución de forma que no quede ninguna balsa sin flechas.

—Sí, *legatus* —dijo el tribuno con determinación.

En el río, sector norte

Un centurión tocó a Lucio Quieto por la espalda.

—¿Qué pasa? —preguntó el norteafricano irritado y volviéndose bruscamente.

—Están haciendo la señal, mi *legatus*, en la ribera del río —se explicó el centurión.

Quieto miró hacia donde se le indicaba y observó a uno de los tribunos con el brazo derecho en alto. Ése, en efecto, era el gesto pactado para la siguiente fase: la ofensiva.

—¡Bien, centurión, por Júpiter! ¡Has hecho bien en avisarme!

Quieto hinchó los pulmones para proferir la orden con fuerza suficiente para que se oyera en medio del fragor de la batalla, al menos, por los centuriones de las balsas más próximas, quienes, a su vez, irían repitiéndola, apoyados también por las trompetas de los *buccinatores*, de modo que en poco tiempo todos estuvieron haciendo lo mismo:

—¡Levad anclas! ¡Dejad que las balsas sean arrastradas por la corriente!

De inmediato los remeros, que no estaban ocupados hasta ese momento, empezaron a tirar de las cadenas de las anclas y en cuestión de unos instantes todas las balsas de la legión de Quieto empezaron a ser arrastradas por el flujo constante de las aguas del Tigris.

Ribera oriental, sector norte

—¿Qué hacen ahora? —preguntó Mitrídates a sus oficiales.

—Se dejan arrastrar por la corriente, mi señor —respondió uno de ellos.

—¡Eso ya lo veo, imbécil! —le espetó el hermano del rey de reyes—, pero ¿por qué lo hacen? —No esperó a que le respondiera ninguno de sus hombres: él mismo dio todas las explicaciones en voz alta para que los oficiales más torpes comprendieran la sorprendente estrategia del enemigo—: Van hacia el puente que están construyendo en el centro del meandro. El emperador romano está concentrando cada vez más balsas allí. Trajano va a cruzar por el centro. Sus ataques por el norte y el sur eran... engaños. ¡Malditos engaños! ¡Por Ahura Mazda, todos hacia el centro! ¡Seguidme!

Mitrídates se lanzó al galope hacia el lugar donde se estaba construyendo el puente romano y donde la batalla parecía más encarnizada. La caballería ligera, con sus arqueros pero sin protecciones, lo siguió con rapidez, y galopando pudieron mantener el ritmo de las balsas de Quieto. Desde allí, no obstante, se les empezó a impedir el avance por la ribera del río, porque no dejaban de dispararles flechas desde detrás de sus protecciones. Mitrídates veía cómo muchos de sus mejores jinetes caían derribados por la continua lluvia de dardos enemigos. Miró también hacia atrás y comprobó que, como imaginaba, los pesados *catafractos*, bien guarnecidos con sus armaduras y más a salvo de las flechas, sin embargo, se quedaban rezagados. A ese ritmo era muy posible que la caballería acorazada no llegara al lugar donde los romanos estaban ya acabando el gigantesco pontón de barcazas a tiempo de detener a las tropas enemigas, que por lo que veía empezaban a entrar en el puente desde la orilla romana.

En el río Tigris, del norte hacia el centro

—¡Acribilladlos! ¡Acribillad a esos malditos! —aullaba Quieto casi enloquecido de ansia de victoria.

Aquéllos eran los mismos partos que le habían impedido cruzar el Tigris el año anterior. Ver cómo navegaban ahora seguros en aquellas balsas fortificadas y cómo podían abatir a aquellos jinetes partos era uno de los mayores placeres de los que Quieto había disfrutado desde las victorias en la Dacia.

Orilla occidental del Tigris, junto al puente

El emperador Trajano ya no se conformaba con dejarse ver por sus tropas y por los enemigos. Quería mandar un mensaje aún más osado a los legionarios que estaban terminando el puente y a los que defendían a los zapadores desde las incontables balsas que llenaban el Tigris.

—Voy a cruzar, Liviano —dijo el César desde su caballo.

La guardia pretoriana observó a su emperador con una mezcla de admiración y temor; pero enardecidos ante aquella exhibición de pundonor militar, se aprestaron a situarse en columna de a cuatro por detrás del César.

—¡Augusto, por favor, una cosa es acercarse a primera línea y otra querer cruzar el puente el primero en medio de la lluvia de flechas que lanzarán los partos!

—¡Y una cosa es ser un simple rey y otra un César! —respondió Trajano.

—Ruego, augusto —imploro Liviano—, que, al menos, pasen primero dos *turmae* pretorianas con Aulo al frente y luego el César.

Trajano miró a su jefe del pretorio y, sin pensarlo mucho, aceptó. La propuesta de Liviano parecía una combinación razonable de prudencia con arrojo. Sólo quedaba una duda que disipar. El arquitecto Apolodoro había regresado a la orilla occidental, toda vez que el puente de barcazas estaba prácticamente terminado y que tenía orden de no ponerse en peligro dirigiendo los trabajos en un lugar donde pudieran alcanzarlo las flechas enemigas. El emperador lo quería vivo para futuras empresas.

Trajano lo vio desembarcar y se acercó a él.

—¡Dijiste que el puente aguantaría el paso de mi caballería! —le dijo Trajano a voz en grito—. ¿Estás seguro?

Apolodoro miró hacia el puente: las barcazas estaban todas ancladas al lecho del Tigris, la curva que trazaba el meandro ralentizaba el flujo del agua en aquel punto, no había olas y todas las piezas de la construcción estaban bien ligadas con maromas muy gruesas. La madera era muy resistente. Los carpinteros habían trabajado bien en invierno y los legionarios y zapadores con valentía en el montaje durante aquella batalla brutal.

—El puente aguantará la caballería imperial, César —sentenció el arquitecto—. Va mi vida en ello.

El emperador se echó a reír.

—No, amigo mío, va a ir la mía —dijo el César cuando detuvo su risa y clavó los ojos de nuevo en el arquitecto—. ¿Y resistirá el peso de los carros con los escorpiones, también?

Apolodoro miró a aquellos carros cuyo montaje había supervisado él mismo: estaban tirados por dos mulas cada uno con un pequeño escorpión preparado para lanzar grandes *pila* con una potencia como no se había visto nunca en Oriente, una versión mejorada de los carroballistas usados en Adamklissi. Pero eran vehículos pequeños, nada que ver con las grandes carrozas y acémilas con material para torres de asedio que habían puesto en peligro su puente sobre el Danubio la primera vez que lo cruzaron las legiones de Roma.

—Los carros de los escorpiones pasarán también, César.

—¡Sea; entonces adelante, por Júpiter! —exclamó Trajano y azuzó su caballo para volverse hacia el puente—. ¡Aulo, pasa con tus *turmae*!

—Sí, César.

Y Aulo entró el primero en el puente de barcazas sobre el Tigris, seguido por sesenta jinetes y, tras ellos, con su pelo gris al viento, despeinado, sudoroso, pero con su espada en alto, bien visible para todos los legionarios de la orilla y de las balsas, entró Marco Ulpio Trajano cabalgando al trote por encima de las maderas, que crujían asombradas al haberse convertido en la alfombra firme sobre la que un emperador de Roma, por primera vez en la historia, intentaba cruzar el río Tigris.

83

LA PRUDENCIA DE KANISHKA

Bagram, capital del Imperio kushan
Primavera de 116 d.C.

Tal y como había anticipado Shaka, conseguir una audiencia con el emperador Kanishka le había costado meses. Para empezar, él, Shaka, desde su fracaso en el asunto de intentar dar muerte a Aryazate, la hija de Osroes, ya no estaba entre los consejeros predilectos del emperador kushan. Para continuar, el emperador Kanishka estaba realmente absorbido por las reuniones del cuarto concilio y parecía tener tiempo sólo para los monjes budistas y para los largos debates sobre qué textos eran más apropiados para recordar siempre las enseñanzas del gran maestro.

Shaka, no obstante, había tenido la fortuna de que la embajada de Trajano lo buscara a él como referencia en la corte kushan. Eso, más toda la información que le había proporcionado el gladiador Áyax, y que Shaka acababa de presentar al emperador, lo podían devolver a la primera línea de consejeros imperiales.

—Veamos si lo he entendido bien —dijo Kanishka en un intento por recapitular y repetir de forma ordenada los sorprendentes datos que Shaka le acababa de exponer en aquella audiencia privada—: Estos hombres son una embajada enviada por el emperador romano Trajano en respuesta a nuestro plan de que Roma atacara Partia por un lado mientras nosotros hacíamos lo propio por el otro extremo. Es decir, son la respuesta a una embajada enviada en tiempos de mi padre Kadphises.

—Así es, mi señor —confirmó Shaka.

—Y piden que ahora nosotros cumplamos con nuestra parte del plan diseñado por mi padre: que ataquemos a los partos desde nuestra frontera con su territorio para obligarlos a luchar dos guerras a un tiempo y así poder acabar con su imperio.

—Sí, mi senor.

—Adicionalmente, esta embajada solicita permiso para poder seguir camino hacia el Imperio han con fines comerciales, para ampliar el intercambio de mercancías entre Roma y los han, algo que, sin duda, nos beneficiaría al ser intermediarios de dicho comercio, los únicos una vez eliminada Partia; no obstante, a esto se añade la sorprendente confesión de uno de estos embajadores, una especie de luchador de nombre Áyax, que dice que no debemos dejar que la embajada romana prosiga con su camino pues no se trata de una misión comercial sino militar.

—Así es, majestad —repitió Shaka.

—Una misión que lleva al Imperio han una propuesta de guerra que me acabas de explicar. Áyax, que ha desvelado esta cuestión secreta de la misión, lo ha hecho porque trabaja para alguien que, parece ser, está llamado a suceder a Trajano y que no tiene interés en continuar con sus planes de expansión más allá de los ríos de Partia.

—El emperador ha resumido a la perfección todo lo que he dicho —dijo Shaka y se inclinó ante su señor.

Kanishka guardó silencio un rato.

Unos guardias abrieron las puertas de la sala y anunciaron que la monja Buddhamitra esperaba ser recibida.

—Decidle que espere un poco —respondió el emperador.

Shaka miró hacia atrás. Las puertas volvieron a cerrarse. El consejero se volvió de nuevo hacia el emperador.

—Creo que habría que matarlos a todos —dijo Shaka, que, nada más pronunciar aquella sentencia mortal miró a su alrededor, pero sólo vio a los guardias del emperador en las esquinas de la gran sala.

—Desde luego la embajada no puede seguir su camino hacia el Imperio han —aceptó Kanishka—, pero impedir su camino nos enemistaría con Trajano y matarlos aún mucho más. No, esa última opción es inadmisible. A estas alturas, después de varios meses en Bagram todo el mundo sabe que hay unos embajadores romanos en la corte. ¿Crees que es un buen mensaje para el resto de las embajadas de reinos e imperios fronterizos que se difunda la idea de que damos muerte a quien viene a negociar con nosotros? No, eso, sencillamente, no podemos hacerlo.

—Pero no podemos tampoco, mi señor, dejarlos continuar camino ni dejar que regresen para que cuenten que les impedimos hacerlo —comentó Shaka algo confuso.

—No. Por lo tanto, hemos de buscar otra solución —dijo el emperador aunque luego guardó silencio. Tenía curiosidad por ver si Shaka era capaz de intuir lo que debía hacerse, pero el consejero no decía nada. A Kanishka le quedó claro que Shaka se había hecho viejo y lento con los años. Ya no era aquel hombre hábil, astuto y rápido a la hora de extraer conclusiones de la época de su padre.

—Ha de parecer un accidente, o varios si es necesario —dijo al fin el emperador Kanishka—. Si estos hombres y mujeres, pues me has dicho que los acompaña una mujer adulta y una muchacha, mueren por accidente o por enfermedad, lo tendremos todo resuelto: nadie de Roma llegará al Imperio han con el mensaje de Trajano ni nadie regresará a Roma para decir que se les impidió seguir camino. En su lugar enviaremos mensajeros a la corte romana explicando las desdichas acaecidas sobre sus mensajeros. Eso evita que nos enemistemos con Trajano, caso de que éste consiga triunfar sobre los partos, y también conseguimos que esté satisfecho aquel líder romano para el que trabaja ese Áyax, pues la misión de llegar al Imperio han habrá quedado abortada. Ésa, y no otra, es la solución perfecta.

—¿Y el asunto de atacar Partia desde nuestro lado? —peguntó Shaka.

Aquí Kanishka no lo dudó ni un instante.

—Esperaremos. Los partos han detenido a Trajano en el Tigris. No creo que el emperador romano consiga cruzar ese río.

—Pero ¿y si lo hace?

—Si lo hace, seguiremos esperando a ver cómo se desarrolla la campaña. Siempre podemos decir que no atacamos porque hacerlo sería atacar a Vologases, que es quien tiene sus tropas partas más próximas a nuestra frontera. Y si atacamos a Vologases haremos que éste no pueda luchar contra Osroes, algo que ahora le favorece a Trajano. No, Shaka, esta guerra entre Roma y Partia es muy compleja. Por el momento nos mantendremos al margen, da igual lo que hubiera propuesto mi padre. Además, Trajano tardó años en ponerse en marcha contra Partia. También podemos tomarnos nosotros un tiempo antes de responder a su petición actual. Entretanto, hay que ocuparse de los accidentes de los enviados de Trajano. Veamos, Shaka: toda la información que has reunido sobre este asunto te hace, a mis ojos, merecedor de que vuelva a confiar en ti, aunque estés un poco más lento en tus reacciones. Te pondré a prueba: ¿crees que podrás ocuparte de hacer desaparecer a esos mensajeros romanos de forma discreta, sin que sospeche nadie de la corte kushan ni los embajadores extranjeros que tenemos ahora en Bagram? Recuerda que con el concilio budista, los ojos de media Asia están puestos en nosotros. No quiero asesinatos en la corte en estos meses.

—Por supuesto que sabré ocuparme de esto con discreción, majestad —respondió Shaka con aplomo.

Kanishka hizo una señal a los guardias para que abrieran las puertas de nuevo. La monja Buddhamitra entró en la sala sin esperar a ser invitada. El emperador miró a Shaka mientras éste se inclinaba ante él.

—Espero que no falles como te ocurrió anteriormente con Aryazate —dijo Kanishka en voz baja—. No soy un emperador que acepte ser decepcionado por un consejero dos veces seguidas.

Shaka, que ya se había incorporado, asintió sin decir nada. Dio media vuelta y su mirada se encontró con la de la monja. Buddhamitra lo miró como si fuera capaz de leer en su cabeza. Al consejero siempre lo incomodaba aquella monja, pero la eliminó con rapidez de sus pensamientos. Tenía un asunto urgente del que ocuparse. Y, como había dejado bien claro el emperador, no podía fallar.

Sonrió.

No pensaba hacerlo.

84

EL INFRANQUEABLE TIGRIS

Cizre
Mayo de 116 d.C.

Sector sur del río, orilla oriental

—¡Resistid, hombres de Adiabene! ¡Resistid! —aullaba el rey desesperado al ver cómo los aliados partos los abandonaban para, según decían, impedir el avance romano por el puente que habían estado construyendo—. ¡Resistid! ¡Lucháis por vuestra tierra, por vuestras mujeres y casas! ¡Por vuestra vida!

Las balsas romanas se habían acercado aún más y estaban muy próximas a la orilla. Los arqueros de Adiabene seguían intentando hacer blanco en los legionarios de aquellas barcas, pero estaban demasiado bien protegidos y lo único que veía Mebarsapes era cómo, uno tras otro, sus hombres caían acribillados. Quizá fuera mejor dejarlos desembarcar y, una vez que los legionarios enemigos abandonaran las barcas, podrían luchar cuerpo a cuerpo contra ellos. Quizá ahí tuvieran una oportunidad mejor para defender su reino. Era una locura, era drástico, era ceder terreno con la idea de poder detener el avance romano, pero no había nada más que hacer.

—¡Replegaos! ¡Replegaos! ¡Alejaos de la orilla! —aulló el rey.

En el río, sector sur

Julio Máximo vio la retirada de los guerreros de Mebarsapes. Estaba seguro de que era algo táctico y no definitivo. Estaban más protegidos en las barcazas, tras los parapetos, pero si podía desembarcar y romper las filas de los guerreros de Adiabene, la llegada de su legión por la retaguardia enemiga desequilibraría la batalla de forma decisiva. Y la orden del César era clara:

—Si te dejan desembarcar, desembarca y avanza. —Así le había hablado Trajano antes del combate.

—¡Remad, remad, remad! —gritó Julio Máximo, enardecido aún más al ver que el emperador se lanzaba con la caballería pretoriana a cruzar el puente de barcazas—. ¡Hacia la orilla!

Sobre el puente

Trajano galopaba con su espada en alto, como un espíritu, andando sobre las aguas del Tigris.

—¡Adelante! ¡Por Roma, por nuestros antepasados muertos, por la legión perdida!

Y el emperador avanzaba como si con el ruido de los cascos de la caballería pretoriana triturara los recuerdos de una de las peores pesadillas de toda la historia de Roma: la derrota de Craso sería ahora su victoria, la lluvia incesante de flechas partas era ahora la tormenta irrefrenable de los dardos romanos que seguían siendo arrojados sin descanso desde centenares de balsas, y el recuerdo de la legión perdida ya parecía, por fin, sólo una pesadilla ajena a todos los legionarios que luchaban bajo el mando de un emperador invencible.

Balsas al norte del puente

Lucio vio a Trajano sobre el puente y observó que los partos se aprestaban a esperar al César y recibirlo con todas las flechas y lanzas que les quedaban en la orilla oriental. Los partos no daban por perdida la batalla en absoluto y tenían razón en pensar que nada había aún decidido.

—¡No podemos dejar al emperador solo, por Hércules y todos los dioses! ¡Remad hacia la orilla!

Ejército parto en el centro, frente al puente

—¡Mataremos a su emperador en cuanto éste pise tierra! —vociferó Mitrídates al tiempo que todos sus arqueros y jinetes apuntaban con los arcos hacia el final del puente.

El emperador cabalgaba hacia la conquista, hacia la victoria o hacia el infierno...

Balsas de Quieto, al norte del puente

—¡Disparad, disparad! ¡Por Roma, por el emperador! —ordenó Quieto.

Balsas de Nigrino, al norte del puente

—¡Ahora, ahora, lanzadlo todo, por Júpiter!

En el aire

Las flechas partas volaban a toda velocidad en busca del corazón de Trajano, pero se encontraban con miles de dardos romanos surcando la ruta contraria y las armas arrojadizas de los unos y los otros chocaban con virulencia infinita por encima de las cabezas de la caballería pretoriana, que seguía cabalgando, escudos en alto, para protegerse de los dardos que pudieran caerles encima. Hubo algún herido, pero la mayoría, incluido Trajano, llegaron al final del puente mientras que la mayor parte de las flechas enemigas fue bloqueada por las continuas andanadas de dardos romanos.

Al final del puente

Trajano se detuvo un instante. Tenía que evaluar la situación. Las balsas de Nigrino estaban ya muy próximas a la ribera oriental y desde sus torres los legionarios de las *cohortes sagitarii*, aprovechando la altura en la que se encontraban, acribillaban sin descanso alguno a los partos, quienes, sin esperar ya órdenes de sus líderes, empezaban a dispersarse y a replegarse para huir de aquella lucha desigual, pues la mayor parte de los romanos seguía disparándoles desde parapetos que los protegían mientras que ellos no disponían de una salvaguarda similar.

Los hombres de Quieto aprovecharon la desbandada enemiga para empezar a desembarcar y el propio Trajano los recibió dando personalmente las órdenes de cómo distribuirse a lo largo de la ribera en formación de *testudo,* centuria a centuria, como si decenas de gigantescas tortugas empezaran a emerger de las aguas del Tigris.

Ejército parto

Mitrídates no lo había dado aún todo por perdido. No había podido impedir el desembarco romano pero ahora, con retraso pero aún con tiempo de hacer daño, llegaron sus *catafractos*. Les ordenó que se arrojaran contra las centurias romanas en *testudo* que avanzaban alejándose cada vez más del río, adentrándose ya en el reino de Adiabene.

—Veremos si pueden con los *catafractos*. Aún los devolveremos a todos al río; sus cadáveres flotarán hasta llegar podridos a Cesifonte —masculló entre dientes con rabia eterna.

Ejército romano en la orilla oriental

—¡Los carros, los carros! —aulló Trajano.

Los escorpiones romanos, tirados por las mulas, empezaron a desembarcar desde el puente y sus conductores y artilleros recibieron la orden, del propio Trajano, de disparar sus misiles mortíferos contra la caballería acorazada del enemigo. Ésta trotaba ya contra los legionarios, que poco podían hacer para detenerlos sólo con sus escudos y sus *pila.*

—¡Largad, largad! —gritó Trajano desde lo alto de su caballo.

Una flecha enemiga pasó rozando la cara del emperador y Aulo ordenó que varios pretorianos rodearan aún más de cerca al César.

Los artilleros soltaron las cuerdas de los escorpiones y un sinfín de lanzas mortales, impulsadas con una potencia arrolladora, impactaron en las armaduras de los temibles *catafractos*. Las corazas fueron perforadas por aquellas lanzas brutales arrojadas con el equivalente a la fuerza de veinte brazos humanos y decenas de *catafractos* primero y luego más de un centenar cayeron abatidos.

Retaguardia del ejército parto

Mitrídates sabía que si ordenaba a los *catafractos* atacar, pese a las bajas sufridas, aún podría infligir mucho daño entre los romanos; lo que no tenía nada claro ya es que pudiera conseguir una victoria. La determinación de aquel maldito emperador romano en cruzar el Tigris era tan obstinada como incontestable.

Dudaba.

Llegó un mensajero del sur de la batalla.

—¡Mebarsapes no ha resistido y se repliega hacia aquí! ¡Los romanos del sur nos van a rodear!

Mitrídates inspiró profundamente. Se debatía entre sus ansias por vengar a los *catafractos* muertos y su intuición militar. Aún estaba a tiempo de retirarse en orden con una parte importante de sus tropas intactas para luego plantear batalla de nuevo a Trajano más adelante, en otro momento más propicio y en un lugar más apropiado.

Le dolió en las entrañas cuando lo dijo, pero lo dijo:

—¡Nos retiramos!

Y Mitrídates, seguido por su caballería ligera, esto es, por lo que quedaba de ella y por la mayor parte aún de sus *catafractos*, dio media vuelta y se alejó en medio de una gran nube de arena y polvo, una nube muy distinta a las terribles polvaredas que antaño envolvieran a los hombres de Craso. Aquella jornada la nube levantada por los partos sólo anunciaba su derrota.

Vanguardia romana en la orilla oriental del Tigris

Trajano lo contemplaba todo desde lo alto de su caballo. Estaba en tensión, los músculos que asían la espada marcando sus curvas con precisión. El César aún no se fiaba.

Mitrídates se retiraba. Eso era evidente, pero había otra nube de polvo a la derecha.

—Es Mebarsapes, augusto —dijo Nigrino—. Julio Máximo ha conseguido doblegar su resistencia cuando el rey se ha quedado sin el apoyo de los partos.

—¡Está solo! ¡Rodeadlo! —ordenó Trajano.

La infantería romana se extendió en perpendicular desde el río, impidiendo la retirada de Mebarsapes, cuyo ejército, en desbandada y sin el apoyo de la caballería parta, ya lejos del lugar de la batalla, quedó envuelto por una maraña espesa de cohortes romanas.

Mebarsapes, herido en piernas y brazos, fue llevado ante el emperador.

No hubo conversación. Sólo una palabra pronunciada de forma lapidaria por el César:

—¡Ejecutadlo!

Aulo, junto con dos pretorianos, iba a llevarse al rey vencido cuando éste empezó a chillar en griego.

—¡No podéis ejecutarme! ¡Soy el rey de Adiabene!

Trajano ya se había dado la vuelta, pero ante los gritos de Mebarsapes se detuvo, se volvió y lo encaró, acercándose hasta quedar a apenas a tres pasos del mismo.

—Si fueras rey no te mataría, pero para ser rey tendrías que tener un reino y Adiabene ya no lo es. Adiabene acaba de transformarse en la provincia romana de Asiria. ¡Lleváoslo! —Trajano vio entonces a Quieto, Nigrino y otros *legati*, que se aproximaban para recibir instrucciones—. Mebarsapes servirá de ejemplo, como en su momento nos valió la ejecución de Partamasiris. Todo Oriente ha de saber que quien se una a nosotros, como Abgaro y su hijo Arbandes de Osroene, será respetado por mí, pero quien se atreva a oponerse a nuestro avance terminará flotando en uno de esos ríos que aquí se empeñan en llamar infranqueables.

Todos los *legati* asintieron.

—¿Y cuáles son las órdenes ahora? —preguntó Quieto.

Trajano miró hacia el río y luego hacia el este, en dirección a donde se había replegado la caballería parta de Mitrídates.

—Calculo que han perdido un tercio de sus hombres, les quedan dos tercios —empezó Trajano pensando al tiempo que hablaba—. ¿Os parece una estimación razonable?

—Sí, César —admitió Nigrino mirando hacia la ribera del río.

—Dos tercios es aún un ejército poderoso —continuó Trajano—. Sería peligroso alejarnos del río y perseguirlos. No, la aniquilación del enemigo tendrá que esperar. Hemos de asentar antes nuestras posiciones aquí y nuestro control sobre Cizre. El dominio del río en este punto es clave para nuestro futuro avance hacia el sur.

Nuevamente todos afirmaron en silencio. Las consideraciones del emperador parecían llenas de prudencia: no era aquél un César que se cegara por una victoria, no importa lo grande que ésta hubiera sido.

—Hay muchos cadáveres —dijo entonces Quieto—. ¿Los quemamos?

Trajano desmontó de su caballo, pidió agua y se la dieron de inmediato. El resto de los *legati* lo imitó: bajaron de sus monturas y también bebieron agua. El emperador se quedó entonces mirando hacia el río con los brazos en jarras.

—No, Lucio. Enterraremos a nuestros legionarios caídos en la batalla, pero quiero todos los cadáveres de los partos y de los hombres de Mebarsapes flotando en el río. El Tigris se encargará de llevarlos hasta las murallas de Cesifonte. Será una bonita forma de saludar a Osroes.

Y empezó a reír, una risa a la que todos los presentes se unieron. Pero Trajano, de pronto, se llevó la mano derecha a la cabeza y calló de golpe, aunque nadie se percató de ello.

Quieto se le aproximó ebrio de victoria, tanta que no se daba cuenta del sufrimiento del emperador.

—Hemos cruzado el Tigris, augusto —dijo el norteafricano—. Está claro que Trajano es un César que puede conseguir cualquier cosa que se proponga. No importan los fantasmas del pasado. El emperador ha derrotado a la legión perdida.

Trajano suspiró. El dolor se iba.

—Lo he conseguido contigo, Lucio. Lo hemos conseguido juntos, y quién sabe: quizá tengas tú que terminar lo que yo estoy empezando.

—¿Acaso esto tiene fin, César? Creía que no había límites para el emperador Trajano.

El César sonrió, pero no dijo nada. El dolor volvía.

Marco Ulpio Trajano se alejó de Quieto con una mano en la sien. Aquellas punzadas en el interior de su cabeza eran intensas, pero se esforzó por no mostrar sufrimiento en sus facciones. Retiró la mano de la cabeza y la llevó a la empuñadura de la espada. Así, Trajano, caminando con paso firme por encima de miles de partos muertos, en la ribera oriental del Tigris, allí adonde ningún otro emperador romano había llegado nunca, se paseaba como un dios bajado a la tierra ante los ojos de decenas de miles de legionarios que, al unísono, lo aclamaban una y otra vez:

—*Imperator, imperator, imperator!*

El infranqueable Tigris había dejado de serlo.

85
—

LAS CADENAS DEL PROFETA

Mar Mediterráneo, costas del sur de Grecia
Primavera de 116 d.C.

Todos los legionarios de la galera estaban nerviosos. Habían soportado ya dos tormentas durísimas. Una nada más partir desde las costas de Siria y otra antes de alcanzar la costa griega. Estaban atemorizados.

—Es por el profeta bárbaro que llevamos en la bodega —dijo uno de los soldados en un susurro.

Sus compañeros no dijeron nada pero asintieron en silencio. Todos en el barco pensaban lo mismo. No eran normales dos tormentas tan duras como las que habían sufrido cuando ya estaba bien entrada la primavera.

—Eso es su maldito dios que lo protege —señaló otro legionario.

—No quiere que lleguemos a Roma —respondió otro—. Allí le espera la muerte a su profeta con los leones en el Anfiteatro Flavio. Por eso su dios nos manda estas tormentas.

—¡Basta ya de cháchara! —los interrumpió el centurión naval al mando de la tropa de la galera—. ¡Dispersaos y dejad de cuchichear como los viejos!

Pero el centurión también se sentía inquieto. En su momento, el encargo de llevar unos cuantos prisioneros a Roma para ser juzgados y casi con toda seguridad ejecutados no le pareció una mala misión. No había piratas en el Mediterráneo desde hacía decenios y no era época de tormentas. Por eso, él, como el resto de sus hombres, no entendía bien por qué Neptuno agitaba tanto las olas. ¿Sería cierto lo de que el dios del prisionero profeta intentaba evitar que llegaran a Roma?

El centurión descendió a la bodega. Los legionarios apostados como centinelas se hicieron a un lado para dejarlo pasar. El oficial entró en un pasillo angosto al que daban las celdas de aquella prisión flotante.

—¡Agua, por todos los dioses, agua! —decían varios de los prisioneros, pero sin atreverse ninguno a sacar la mano entre los barrotes. Ya lo había hecho uno de ellos y los legionarios habían respondido cortándole el brazo entero. Ahora el desgraciado se desangraba en una esquina de su celda, pues el *medicus* de a bordo apenas había mal cosido la terrible herida.

El centurión se detuvo en la última celda al fondo de aquel pasillo del terror.

—¿Y tú no pides nada? —dijo el oficial mirando hacia el interior de la celda.

—Nada necesito —respondió Ignacio sentado, entre las sombras.

Al centurión le sorprendió la voz por su fuerza. Aquel hombre era un anciano pero hablaba como si tuviera treinta años, recio y fuerte.

—He pensado que podríamos eliminar las cadenas —dijo el oficial—. Los demás van sin ellas. Aunque tus crímenes sean peores, si me prometes no intentar nada, daré orden de que te quiten las cadenas.

Silencio.

Nadie se movió en el interior de la celda. El oficial frunció el ceño. Había pensado que si trataban algo mejor a aquel profeta quizá su dios dejara de martirizarlos a todos con más tormentas.

—¿Qué me dices, profeta? —insistió el centurión levantando la voz.

—Estas cadenas son un orgullo para mí —respondió Ignacio sin moverse del fondo de la celda—. Son una prueba del amor perfecto de Dios, que ha permitido que vaya encadenado como lo fue Pablo en el pasado.

El centurión resopló de pura rabia. No entendía nada de lo que decía aquel lunático. Estuvo tentado de ordenar que lo azotaran, pero tuvo miedo y calló.

86

LA SOMBRA DE TRAJANO

Palacio real de Cesifonte
Primavera de 116 d.C.

—¡Eres un inútil! —exclamó Osroes enfurecido—. ¿Has visto el río? En Cesifonte no se habla de otra cosa que no sean los cadáveres de nuestros soldados partos flotando en el Tigris.

—Puede que sea un inútil —le replicó su hermano Mitrídates acercándose hasta hablarle apenas a un palmo de distancia—, pero soy el único de los dos que se ha puesto al frente de un ejército y ha defendido Partia de ese maldito Trajano. Es más, hermano, he sido el único de los dos que ha luchado durante años, junto con mi hijo Sanatruces, contra el rebelde Vologases en el este. Puedes llamarme lo que quieras, pero eso no va a evitar que las siluetas de las águilas de los estandartes romanos estén pronto a las puertas de Cesifonte. La sombra de Trajano se acerca, queramos o no, pero es así.

Osroes dio media vuelta, anduvo unos pasos para alejarse de Mitrídates y se sentó en su preciado trono de oro macizo. Le irritaba tener que admitir que todo lo que decía su hermano era cierto. Pero él no podía arriesgarse en primera línea de combate.

—Soy el *Šāhān Šāh* —replicó Osroes intentando hablar con más sosiego. Su hermano había fallado en el frente, pero era leal, al menos por el momento—. Que yo sepa, un rey de reyes no acude a primera línea de combate, sino que gobierna y envía a sus generales a la guerra.

—Ésa es, en efecto, nuestra costumbre —aceptó Mitrídates.

—Y la costumbre de los romanos durante mucho tiempo.

—Ha habido excepciones —contrapuso Mitrídates algo

más sereno también—. Hablo de memoria, pero creo que Vespasiano o Tito sí lucharon en primera línea.

—Antes de ser emperadores. Después nunca —contestó Osroes.

—Es verdad —dijo Mitrídates—, pero por el motivo que sea, Trajano es diferente a todos ellos: lleva años siendo emperador, luchó en el Rin cuando aún no lo era y conquistó la Dacia siéndolo. Y no satisfecho con ello se ha anexionado Arabia Nabatea, o Félix, como la llaman en *Hrōm*, luego Armenia y todo el norte de Mesopotamia. Apenas han pasado unos días desde la batalla de Cizre en el Tigris y algunos de nuestros soldados que han escapado de las garras romanas dicen que el César se va a anexionar Adiabene como la provincia de Asiria.

—Seguramente los habrán dejado escapar para que nos llegue ese mensaje —dijo entre dientes Osroes—; ese miserable Trajano quiere que sepamos que no se va a detener. No quiere castigarnos por manipular Armenia. Quiere aniquilarnos.

—Es posible, sí, como es probable que haya dejado marchar a esos soldados con la idea de que nos llegue el mensaje de que va a ir engulléndonos, poco a poco, pedazo a pedazo, sin parar nunca. Pero eso no cambia lo sustancial: Marco Ulpio Trajano marcha al frente de sus legiones y combate en primera línea de forma ejemplar. De hecho creo que si no se hubiera lanzado a galopar sobre el puente junto con su caballería quizá sus legionarios no habrían combatido con tanta pasión y seguridad en la victoria y podríamos haberlos detenido. Pero ¿qué guerrero va a dejar de dar lo mejor de sí mismo con un líder que muestra tanto arrojo como ingenio? Nunca ha sido derrotado.

—Tendrías que haberlo conseguido en el Tigris, hermano —replicó Osroes suspirando—. Ya habíamos cedido Armenia sin combatir. No pudimos defendernos en Mesopotamia por la traición de Abgaro; sin Osroene de nuestra parte aquella región estaba perdida. Nos hemos centrado en defender Adiabene al lado de Mebarsapes y sólo tenemos un rey aliado muerto, diez mil cadáveres de partos flotando en el río y un puente romano hecho con barcazas. Ya me dirás qué queda por hacer.

Mitrídates anduvo un par de veces de un extremo a otro de la sala del trono con los brazos en jarras. Se detuvo y miró al rey de reyes.

—Me consta que Trajano avanzará hacia el sur ahora que tiene las espaldas bien guardadas, y seguramente lo hará tanto por el Tigris como por el Éufrates. Tengo una idea.

—Te escucho, hermano —respondió Osroes. La situación era tan crítica que, pese a la rabia que sentía hacia él por haber sido derrotado en el Tigris, estaba dispuesto a oír cualquier plan que pudiera ayudar a contener a los romanos.

—Cesifonte es fuerte y tiene la protección natural del río Tigris —empezó Mitrídates—. Voy a coger la mitad de las tropas y me iré al este para unirme a las fuerzas de mi hijo Sanatruces e intentar acabar con Vologases de una vez por todas. El pacto con él es imposible. Ya lo probamos en el pasado y no hubo forma. Pero mi hijo me ha informado de que Vologases ha sido derrotado por primera vez en una gran batalla. No está acabado, pero si llego con refuerzos quizá terminemos con él para siempre. Con la otra mitad de la caballería y la infantería de la que disponemos aún se puede defender bien Cesifonte. Como te decía, el río es un foso natural muy difícil de franquear. Sólo si los romanos tuvieran una flota importante podrían asediar por tierra y agua a la vez, haciendo que la defensa de la ciudad fuera mucho más complicada. Pero la flota romana, y ésta es la clave de todo mi plan, no está en el Tigris, sino en Zeugma, en el Éufrates. Trajano la hará navegar hacia el sur por el Éufrates y podrá transportar incluso hasta armas de asedio; pero sin barcos que la ataquen, Cesifonte resistirá meses. Y eso me dará tiempo para retornar y atacar a los romanos por la retaguardia. Contigo en la ciudad, con miles de arqueros partos protegidos en las murallas arrojando flechas contra los romanos y con mi caballería acosándolos, Trajano tendrá que retirarse o arriesgarse a ser aniquilado al tener que combatir en dos frentes a la vez.

—Todo tu plan depende de que los romanos no tengan flota en el Tigris y de que dobleguéis, tú y tu hijo, a Vologases de una vez por todas.

—Lo primero es seguro, y lo segundo, después de la derrota que ha sufrido Vologases, puede serlo. En cualquier caso —añadió Mitrídates—, estaremos en contacto, y si Cesifonte es asediada me replegaré con la mayor parte del ejército que pueda reunir en el este para asistirte en la defensa de nuestra capital y rodear a Trajano.

—De acuerdo —aceptó al fin Osroes para, frunciendo el ceño, sumar una idea adicional al plan de su hermano—. Sí, vamos a maniobrar como has propuesto, pero te voy a demostrar que un *Šāhān Šāh* también puede hacer cosas muy valiosas sentado en su trono de oro, aunque tú no lo creas.

Mitrídates lo observó intrigado. Conocía muy bien esa mirada torcida de su hermano. No quería que Osroes pusiera esa mirada pensando en él o en su hijo.

—Abgaro —dijo Osroes por toda respuesta.

—Es un traidor —dijo Mitrídates—. Recurrir a él es inútil.

—Yo no lo creo, hermano —respondió Osroes con seguridad—. Abgaro es un traidor, una serpiente, pero falta por ver traidor a quién. El rey de Osroene ha visto cómo los romanos han venido otras veces a Oriente y luego se han ido, y sabe qué hemos hecho los partos con los traidores en cuanto los romanos se han replegado. Él lo sabe y estoy seguro de que teme que, en cualquier momento, el viento sople desde Cesifonte y no desde *Hrōm*. Pero como ahora la tormenta romana ha sido más fuerte que nunca se ha pasado al otro bando. Hasta ha hecho, me consta, que su hijo Arbandes se haga amigo íntimo, muy íntimo, del emperador romano.

—Más a favor de lo que te digo: es imposible que vuelvan a nuestro lado.

—Abgaro es voluble, como la brisa. Imposible es una palabra demasiado definitiva hablando de un rey de Osroene. Además está el asunto que tú mismo has comentado de la importancia del líder romano ante sus hombres. Quizá si consiguiéramos descabezar a *Hrōm*, si pudiéramos matar a Trajano, toda esta pesadilla terminaría. Sin Trajano, el Imperio romano se contraerá. No hay nadie con su ambición y su fuerza para sustituirlo.

Mitrídates recibió la propuesta del *Šāhān Šāh* con sorpresa. Osroes era ciertamente osado cuando se lo proponía.

—¿Estás tratando de decirme que Abgaro y su hijo Arbandes se van a arriesgar a intentar asesinar al César?

—Bueno, habrá que motivarlos un poco: les ofreceremos mucho oro, el perdón cuando todo esto acabe y la mano de Aryazate Arbandes para sellar nuestra alianza.

—A Trajano, me consta, lo asesinar cuando invadió la Dacia, y salió mal. Todos los conspiradores están ahora muertos.

—Sin duda, infravaloraron a Trajano, pero conozco a Abgaro personalmente, hermano: es el ser más vil y traicionero que he conocido en mi vida y ya sabes que he tratado a unos cuantos. No me extrañaría que hasta él mismo haya pensado en esto. El águila romana es demasiado inocente. No tiene ni idea de con quién se está acostando.

87

LA CACERÍA DEL TIGRE

Un bosque al norte de Bagram
Primavera de 116 d.C.

Marcio caminaba feliz en medio de aquel bosque de las colinas al norte de Bagram.

Todo estaba bien. Como hacía tiempo. Tanto que ya casi ni lo recordaba. El consejero Shaka les había asegurado que el emperador Kanishka les facilitaría todo lo necesario para proseguir su viaje hacia Xeres. La espera, no obstante, había sido larga. El consejero había estado en lo cierto con relación a que el emperador kushan tenía en aquel momento su atención puesta en la religión más que en otros asuntos. Por eso habían tenido que aguardar tantas semanas para obtener una respuesta, pero la espera había merecido la pena. Entretanto, habían sido alojados confortablemente en unas habitaciones cómodas. Y no era fácil, pues la ciudad de Bagram estaba repleta por un gentío inmenso. La gran reunión religiosa sobre aquel profeta antiguo del que todo el mundo hablaba allí parecía ser un acontecimiento muy importante para ellos. A Marcio aquello le interesaba más bien poco. Y menos ahora que no interfería con la misión. No se le escapaba, no obstante, que a Tamura, con su conocimiento de sánscrito, sí parecía resultarle más interesante todo lo relacionado con aquel encuentro de monjes. Y monjas. Había una en particular, Buddhamitra, que recibía a menudo a Tamura y la instruía en textos antiguos, como había hecho Dión Coceyo en el pasado. Marcio no pensó que hubiera ningún mal en ello. Si hasta Trajano quiso que la niña fuera educada en lenguas diferentes —por motivos que a él siempre se le escaparon—, las enseñanzas de la monja budista no eran, a sus ojos, otra cosa que una especie de continuación de lo que había hecho el pedagogo griego en Roma y, por tanto, no le parecían algo negativo.

Alana tampoco veía con malos ojos a aquella mujer religiosa, así que las visitas de Tamura a Buddahamitra se convirtieron en algo habitual. Como habitual fue ver que la muchacha también había incrementado su interés por Áyax. Ya no ocultaban su relación. A Marcio tampoco le parecía mal. Áyax era un gladiador, un guerrero, era fuerte y, todo tenía que pensarse, podría proteger a Tamura cuando él o Alana ya no estuvieran. Porque ellos, alguna vez, no estarían.

Era duro pensarlo, pero era ley de vida.

De muerte.

Marcio suspiró mientras seguía caminando por el bosque.

No se lo había dicho a nadie, ni a Alana, pero se sentía cada día más débil, con menos fuerzas. No sabía exactamente qué le pasaba. Hubo un momento en que pensó que quizá fuera la comida o el agua, pero comía y bebía lo mismo que Áyax y éste estaba bien. No. Era la edad. Tenía más de cincuenta años. Unos cuantos más. Bastantes más. Nunca supo exactamente su edad. La mayoría de los gladiadores morían antes de los treinta. Teniendo en cuenta su vida, había llegado más allá de lo que nadie hubiera pensado posible.

El bosque del norte de Bagram emitió un poderoso rugido.

—Es el tigre —dijo Áyax, que lo acompañaba.

Alana y Tamura eran mujeres y los kushan no iban a entender que eran guerreras, así que acordaron con las dos que sería mejor que ellas permanecieran en Bagram. Y el anciano Titianus no estaba para cacerías. Por eso sólo Marcio y Áyax acudieron a aquella batida como invitados.

—Sin duda. Es el tigre —repitió Marcio. Un rugido tan brutal sólo podía ser de una bestia felina de dimensiones gigantescas, y ya les habían dicho allí que los tigres eran de los más grandes que nunca se hubieran visto.

Marcio se sintió algo aturdido.

Quizá no debería haber aceptado ir a aquella cacería con Áyax y un grupo de soldados imperiales, pero era una especie de regalo que les hacía el mismísimo emperador para distraerlos, para agasajarlos. No quiso oponerse. Y Titianus dijo que sería conveniente que al menos Áyax y él aceptaran la invitación para no indisponerse con un emperador que se había mostrado proclive a dejarlos seguir su ruta hacia Xeres.

De pronto, Marcio se acordó de otra cacería, en otro tiempo, en el otro extremo del mundo, y los recuerdos enturbiaron su mente con pensamientos oscuros. ¿Sería esta nueva cacería algo más de lo que parecía? No, no tenía sentido. Los malos pensamientos lo asaltaban, estaba seguro, porque se encontraba algo débil, enfermo, y eso le hacía ver fantasmas donde no los había.

¿O sí?

El rugido resonó con mucha más fuerza que antes.

—Está muy cerca —dijo Marcio—. Deberíamos detenernos y esperar a los soldados del emperador.

—De acuerdo —dijo Áyax.

Se habían adelantado a los guardias imperiales por sugerencia de Áyax, que había dicho que muchos hombres de avanzadilla asustarían al tigre.

Marcio se llevó la mano a la frente. Estaba sudando y no lo entendía. No había comido más que la misma carne que había llevado Áyax aquella mañana.

—De parte del mismísimo Kanishka —había dicho Áyax cuando llevó el venado asado, según él, de las cocinas del emperador kushan.

Marcio se detuvo y se apoyó en un árbol con un brazo, con la cabeza baja, mirando al suelo. Lo cierto era que le costaba respirar.

Áyax había estado consiguiendo comida especial para ellos, o si no el consejero Shaka. Marcio lo había dado todo por bueno porque encajaba: eran muestras, debían de serlo, de que Kanishka quería tenerlos satisfechos mientras esperaban para partir hacia Xeres. Y el único que se encontraba mal era él. Ni el joven gladiador ni Alana ni Tamura, ni siquiera el viejo Titianus, se habían quejado de nada relacionado con la comida.

¿Qué le estaba pasando?

El rugido del tigre se volvió a oír, pero ahora parecía que estaba más lejos.

—Los soldados del emperador serán los que se encarguen de él —dijo Áyax.

Marcio asintió, pero siguió apoyado en el árbol, mirando al suelo. Y pensando. Áyax los había separado de la guardia del emperador. Los pensamientos volvió sombríos retornaron a la cabeza del viejo exgladiador. Se volvió para hablar con el joven luchador griego para, de pronto, encontrarse la espada de Áyax apuntando a su pecho.

Y Áyax, sin dudarlo un instante, con firmeza, la empujó contra su cuerpo resquebrajando piel y costillas.

Marcio no tuvo ni tiempo ni fuerzas para defenderse.

Se derrumbaba, agarrado al árbol, intentando comprender. ¿No era Arrio el traidor? Sí, primero los pretorianos, luego Arrio... ¿y ahora Áyax?

—No lo entiendes, ¿verdad? —le dijo el joven agachándose con la espada en la mano derecha que goteaba sangre de su víctima por todo el filo.

A Marcio le costaba hablar. Y no entendía por qué no tenía energías para luchar. Aun gravemente herido, su ánimo, su voluntad, le gritaban que se levantara como fuera y que, al menos, lanzara algún golpe contra aquel miserable que, de cuclillas frente a él, parecía reírse de todo. Pero, simplemente, Marcio no podía.

—Pero si tú... nos defendiste de los pretorianos... cuando éstos incendiaron el barco... —dijo al fin el veterano *lanista* agonizante.

—Lo que visteis fue a los pretorianos luchando contra mí —se explicó Áyax—. Yo fui quien prendió fuego al barco en Mundus pero los pretorianos me sorprendieron, aunque tú y tu hija, tu preciosa Tamura, fuisteis tan amables de socorrerme y de ayudarme a eliminar a los que me habían rodeado. Sin vuestra intervención los pretorianos me habrían matado y nada de esto habría ocurrido. Quizá fuiste un buen gladiador en tiempos pasados, y un buen preparador, pero como estratega te queda bastante que aprender. Y ya no tendrás tiempo.

Marcio se llevó, lenta y pesadamente, la mano a la empuñadura de su espada.

—No creo que consigas desenfundarla siquiera —le dijo Áyax con sosiego, sin hacer ademán de levantarse para alejarse y ponerse en guardia—. Verás: te hemos estado envenenando estos últimos días. Poco a poco. Aquí en Bagram parece que quieren que todo sea con... ¿cómo dice el consejero Shaka? Ah, sí: con discreción. Hoy acabamos contigo. Mañana con el resto. Diremos que ha sido un accidente. Que el tigre te sorprendió. Ya nos encargaremos de que el animal te dé un par de arañazos cariñosos, pero no te preocupes: tú ya estarás muerto para cuando te desgarre con las zarpas. Con eso bastará para disimular la herida de mi espada.

Marcio tragaba y lo que tragaba era sangre, su propia sangre.

Áyax seguía hablando. Parecía que contarle todo a su víctima le hacía sentirse bien, más fuerte, poderoso, inmenso.

—Titianus es un viejo y tu mujer Alana no es la de antaño, según ella misma ha dicho más de una vez. No nos preocupan. Pero tú eras algo especial. Yo querría haberlo hecho sin veneno, pero el consejero Shaka parece temer cualquier error y se encargó de esa parte. Al menos te he herido de frente y caes muerto por un gladiador. Uno que te ha traicionado, pero eso tampoco es tan ajeno al mundo del anfiteatro.

—No... me preocupa mi... muerte... —consiguió decir Marcio entre espumarajos de sangre que le salpicaban de babas espesas y rojas la barbilla y el cuello. Las manos las tenía sobre la herida, haciendo la poca presión que podía hacer, pues, en efecto, el veneno lo había dejado sin energía alguna.

—No, claro —le dijo Áyax—. Te preocupan los que faltan por morir: tu esposa y la joven y hermosa Tamura. Lo tendré fácil. Tamura hace todo lo que yo quiero. Y todo lo incluye todo. Es muy dulce la joven fierecilla cuando quiere serlo.

—Tus palabras no me causan dolor —le respondió Marcio con un aplomo que sorprendió a Áyax. El joven gladiador había esperado vislumbrar horror ante el futuro de muerte o tortura que podía esperar a Alana y a Tamura, su mujer y su hija, y, sin embargo, Marcio lo miraba desafiante, como si el que fuera a morir fuera otro.

—Pienso disfrutar de Tamura un tiempo —continuó Áyax en busca de algo que consiguiera hacer sufrir aún más al *lanista* agonizante—. No he decidido aún si matar primero a la madre o primero a la hija. ¿Quién crees que sufriría más de ver morir a la otra?

—Has conseguido... matarme a traición... pero no vas a lograr que tema por el... futuro de Alana y Tamura... porque sé cuál ha sido mi... error y... mientras tú hablas... yo estoy enmendando aquello en lo que me equivoqué...

Áyax frunció el ceño.

—Hablas en enigmas —dijo—. Quizá la proximidad de la muerte te haya hecho perder la razón.

Pero Marcio negó con la cabeza levemente. La sangre brotaba entre los dedos de sus manos. La vida se le escapaba, pero la suya no había sido una existencia cualquiera: conjurado para asesinar a dos emperadores de Roma, guerrero indómito al norte del Danubio junto con los sármatas y el gladiador más victorioso de los últimos años en Roma. La muerte, en efecto, estaba allí, ya muy cerca, pero usó las últimas energías para enmendar su error.

—Hace semanas... desde que llegamos a Bagram... —decía mientras seguía escupiendo más y más sangre por la boca—, que dejé de rezar a Némesis... me confié... pensé que con Arrio lejos... que acogidos por Kanishka... todo estaba bien... Ése fue mi error... pero desde que estás ahí... agachado... frente a mí... sólo he hecho que... —Estaba sentado, apoyado en el árbol, pero se iba cayendo de lado al tiempo que seguía hablando—. Sólo he hecho que rezar a Némesis y... rogar venganza.

—Curioso —replicó Áyax con tranquilidad y una gran sonrisa en su boca—. Uno de los pretorianos del barco también pidió venganza cuando moría. Y ya ves que los dioses no lo han escuchado.

—Pero hay una diferencia... entre ese pretoriano... y yo —masculló Marcio.

—¿Una diferencia? ¿Qué diferencia?

Marcio ya estaba completamente tumbado en el suelo, desangrándose por completo, con los ojos abiertos, pero sin ver otra cosa que una inmensa luz que lo cegaba. No era consciente de que estaba mirando, por un claro entreabierto entre las ramas del árbol, directamente al sol y sus retinas se estaban quemando.

—A mí... Némesis... no me ha fallado nunca...

Y dejó de respirar.

Y Marcio se quedó inmóvil mirando al cielo.

Una brisa suave se levantó.

Un rugido bestial sorprendió a Áyax por la espalda.

88

UN NUEVO PRETENDIENTE

Palacio de las mujeres de la corte, Cesifonte
116 d.C.

La hermosa Rixnu, la *Šhar Bāmbišn*, la reina consorte favorita de Osroes, sonrió a la joven Aryazate. Esta última, con sus dieciséis años, sabía que la siempre controvertida cuestión de su matrimonio debería ser resuelta ya muy pronto. Y de eso estaba hablando con la bella Rixnu. Aryazate la idolatraba como si la *Šhar Bāmbišn* fuera una diosa. No era para menos: en el muy convulso mundo del *bānūg*, la corte de jóvenes nobles partas, concubinas y esposas del rey de reyes, las envidias y las rencillas eran algo muy común, pero Rixnu, que se reconocía en una Aryazate diez años más joven que ella, la había adoptado como si de su propia hija se tratara, en especial desde que muriera la verdadera madre de la muchacha.

—¿Por qué sonríes? —preguntó Aryazate intrigada, arrodillada a los pies de Rixnu. La *Šhar Bāmbišn* estaba reclinada en una butaca cómoda contemplando el estanque y el jardín del palacio de las mujeres. Aryazate estaba sentada en el suelo, al borde mismo del agua, jugando con una de sus manos a ver si capturaba alguno de los escurridizos peces. Algo que no conseguía nunca.

—Sonrío porque tu suerte parece estar cambiando al fin —respondió Rixnu.

—¿Lo dices porque ya sabes con quién me casarán?

—Así es —le confirmó la *Šhar Bāmbišn*.

Aryazate, por pura inercia, siguió con la mano en el agua, pero ya no tenía su atención en el juego con los peces. Hacía años se había hablado de casarla con el salvaje Vologases, el miserable, brutal y violento primo que se había rebelado contra su padre reclamando el trono de oro de Partia para sí. Ella iba a ser usada como moneda de cambio para conseguir la paz. Aquellos meses en los que no se hablaba de otra cosa que su programada boda con Vologases fueron terribles para la pequeña Aryazate. Y justo cuando se dejó de hablar de ello llegó una idea aún peor: casarla con el viejo Partamasiris, su asqueroso tío de dientes sucios y podridos cuyo mal aliento se dejaba notar a distancia y era comentado y maldecido por cualquier mujer que hubiera estado con él. El emperador romano, al que llamaban Trajano, le había hecho un favor, al menos Aryazate lo sentía así, al matar a su tío tras arrebatarle Armenia. La joven lamentaba la pérdida de un reino tan grande e importante como Armenia, pero respiró muy tranquila cuando llegó hasta sus oídos la noticia de la muerte de su tío a manos de aquel emperador extranjero. Sin duda, ese Trajano debía de ser otro salvaje, como Vologases —quizá aún peor que él, porque ni siquiera era parto—, pero en su fuero interno, la muchacha le estaba agradecida. Luego, con relación a su matrimonio, llegó un tiempo de sosiego en el que ella siguió creciendo y poniéndose, según decía Rixnu, aún más hermosa, pero Aryazate no estaba segura de ello, pues sabía que la Šhar Bāmbišn era parcial con respecto a ella.

La joven aún no sabía que una mujer no suele hacer un cumplido sobre belleza a otra mujer si no es cierto. Las mentiras a ese respecto suelen ser más bien propiedad de los hombres. Aún le quedaba mucho por aprender. Sea como fuere, al final Aryazate reunió la valentía suficiente como para preguntar, una vez más, sobre su futuro próximo.

—¿Y con quién ha pensado casarme ahora mi padre?

—Con un príncipe guapo, mi pequeña, y como tú muy bien sabes, no hay muchos.

—¿Quién es? ¿Puedes decírmelo, por favor? —insistió Aryazate con la más dulce de sus voces.

Rixnu le acarició sus largos cabellos negros y lacios y brillantes.

—Con el príncipe Arbandes, el hijo del rey Abgaro de Osroene. Pero esto, pequeña, es un gran secreto.

—Arbandes —masculló Aryazate entre labios. Aquel príncipe era alto y joven y guapo. Eso decían todos. De pronto, la muchacha sacó la mano del agua y la puso sobre las rodillas de Rixnu—. Y si es un secreto ¿cómo puedes estar tan segura de ello? Mi padre, el *Šāhān Šāh* Osroes no comenta nada del gobierno de Partia ni de sus planes sobre nosotras con ninguna mujer, nunca. Ni siquiera contigo. Tú misma me lo dijiste. Y no creo que mi padre haya cambiado ahora de forma de ser. Si algo he aprendido es que los hombres son como son y no cambian nunca. Eso también me lo dijiste tú.

Rixnu se echó a reír. Era increíble cómo la muchacha lo absorbía todo. Pero ella se sentía feliz y orgullosa. Sólo le había proporcionado buenos consejos a la joven, de forma que sólo había aprendido cosas buenas y útiles que quizá le sirvieran en el futuro. De pronto, no obstante, la *Šhar Bāmbišn* sintió un ataque de profunda pena. Y Aryazate lo detectó.

—¿Qué ocurre? —preguntó la muchacha visiblemente preocupada—. ¿He dicho algo que te ha molestado? Si es así, lo siento de veras. Cuando se habla de mi boda me pongo muy nerviosa, mucho y...

—No pasa nada, mi pequeña —la tranquilizó Rixnu acariciando una vez más su cabeza mientras pasaba sus finos dedos entre sus cabellos negros—. No pasa nada más que me he apenado al recordar que algún día esa famosa boda tuya que tanto se ha hecho esperar tendrá lugar y eso nos separará para siempre. Pensar en ello me ha llenado de tristeza, pero no tiene sentido alguno lamentarse por lo que no se puede evitar. Y, en cuanto a tus preguntas, es muy cierto que Osroes no ha cambiado y no comenta nada sobre sus planes con ninguna de sus esposas, ni siquiera conmigo ni con Asiabatum, la reina de reinas. No, el rey de reyes sólo nos informa de sus decisiones cuando ya están tomadas y nos afectan directamente. Un día vendrá aquí y te dirá que te casas con Arbandes. Lo sé porque...

Pero calló.

—¿Qué...? —empezó Aryazate hasta que se dio cuenta de que un *šabestān*, uno de los eunucos guardianes de las mujeres del *Šāhān Šāh*, se acercaba y entonces ella también guardó silencio. El hombre, o medio hombre, como ellas los llamaban, pasó a su lado sin decir nada.

—Siempre están vigilando —dijo Rixnu en un susurro—. Nunca confíes en ningún *šabestān*.

—Pero ellos nos guardan, nos protegen —respondió Aryazate.

—Nos guardan sólo para Osroes, pero como quien guarda un mueble o este estanque —continuó explicándose Rixnu, siempre en voz baja—. No te fíes de ellos. Si un día el rey de reyes se cansa de cualquiera de nosotras, un *šabestān* como el que acaba de pasar te arrojará fuera de aquí. Y eso no es lo peor que pueden hacernos.

Rixnu lamentó haber hablado de más.

—¿Qué es lo peor que puede hacernos un *šabestān?* —preguntó Aryazate y la *Šhar Bāmbišn* no la culpó por ello; la que estaba en falta era ella por hablar de más, pero tenía la solución perfecta para que Aryazate se olvidara de aquel asunto de los eunucos y las órdenes que podían llegar a recibir del rey de reyes.

—Aún no te he dicho por qué sé lo que sé sobre tu futura boda con Arbandes.

—Es verdad —dijo Aryazate olvidando por completo, tal y como quería Rixnu, todo lo relacionado con los eunucos, pues en su mente ya nada era importante si no estaba relacionado con su futura boda, el matrimonio que habría de cambiar su vida para siempre—. ¿Cómo lo sabes?

—Como bien decías, Osroes no ha cambiado y no comenta nada de sus ideas con nosotras, ni conmigo ni con Asiabatum, la mismísima *Bāmbišnān Bāmbišn*, la reina de reinas. Pero como soy la favorita, Osroes pasa sus noches conmigo y el rey de reyes, pequeña, habla en sueños. Por eso lo sé. Pero no se lo digas a nadie o podrían castigarnos a las dos.

Aryazate asintió. No pensaba desvelar aquello jamás. Suspiró. Arbandes. De todos los pretendientes a su mano que se habían considerado en los últimos años, por fin el *Šāhān Šāh* había pensado en alguien joven y guapo. Era un gran alivio, casi un sueño... De pronto, una idea cruzó por la mente de Aryazate.

—¿Siempre ha hablado mi padre en sueños?

—No, pequeña, siempre no. Lo hace desde hace unos meses.

Pero Rixnu no quiso concretar más y Aryazate no preguntó. La muchacha volvió a inclinar la cabeza sobre el regazo de la *Šhar Bāmbišn* y a meter la mano en el agua del estanque para jugar con los peces.

Por su parte, Rixnu guardó un largo silencio. No quería explicarle a Aryazate por qué motivo pensaba ella que Osroes hablaba durante los últimos meses en sueños y por qué sufría constantemente terribles pesadillas. A la *Šhar Bāmbišn*, con buen criterio, no le pareció adecuado compartir con Aryazate que ella estaba segura de que Osroes no dormía bien y mascullaba frases enteras en sueños porque tenía miedo, porque desde que el emperador romano Trajano había cruzado el Tigris estaba completa y totalmente aterrorizado. Y cuando un hombre tiene pesadillas constantemente y es incapaz de tener una erección es que tiene tanto terror en el cuerpo que no puede ni tan siquiera hacer el amor, no importa cuán bella sea la mujer que esté a su lado. A Rixnu no se le olvidaba la cara de rabia y desesperación del rey de reyes la primera vez que no pudo consumar el acto. Ella lo intentó tranquilizar con besos y caricias, pero aquello no pareció consolarlo. Y todo fue peor las veces siguientes. Por un momento, Rixnu temió perder su puesto como favorita del rey de reyes, pero Osroes debió de pensar, con acierto, que el problema no era ella y por eso no hizo desfilar a una concubina tras otra para comprobarlo. Por eso, porque pensaba que era cuestión suya, o porque, imaginó Rixnu, Osroes no quería que todo el *bānūg*, todas las mujeres de su corte, supieran que desde que Trajano había cruzado el Tigris él estaba impotente. Impotente no sólo para defender su imperio, sino incapaz también en la cama. Por eso pasaba las noches sólo con Rixnu. A fin de cuentas era su favorita desde hacía tiempo y nadie sospechaba nada extraño. Pero a la hermosa *Šhar Bāmbišn* no se le olvidaría nunca el tono frío con el que Osroes le habló la segunda noche que no pudo conseguir una erección.

—No se lo digas nunca a nadie.

—No, mi señor —había respondido ella. Y nunca más hablaron de ello.

Desde entonces, aunque lo ocultaba, Rixnu estaba muy preocupada: cuando un emperador no era capaz ni de yacer con una mujer, o con un hombre, con alguien, es que los problemas del imperio eran mucho más grandes de lo que nadie podía sospechar. Quizá si la boda de Aryazate con Arbandes se celebraba pronto, al menos la pequeña muchacha podría escapar de Cesifonte. Por primera vez en su vida, Rixnu contemplaba en silencio los muros de la capital de Partia y ya no sabía si estaba en el más hermoso de los palacios del mundo entero o en la más mortífera cárcel de un imperio que se desmoronaba.

89

EL DESCANSO DEL ÁGUILA

Edesa, capital de Osroene
Verano de 116 d.C.

Los estandartes de las legiones del ejército imperial romano se clavaron en los alrededores de Edesa. Trajano, junto con su guardia y su caballería de *singulares*, entró en la ciudad y en el palacio real donde Abgaro, como siempre, lo recibió, lo felicitó por la gran victoria conseguida en el Tigris y lo agasajó.

Llegó la hora de acostarse y el emperador miró a Arbandes con ansia. El joven príncipe sonrió y asintió.

—Todo ha estado delicioso, un banquete digno del mismísimo Alejandro —dijo Trajano al rey de Osroene recordando al gran conquistador macedonio, a quien, cada vez de forma más evidente, estaba emulando—, pero he de descansar. La victoria del Tigris me ha abierto el camino hacia el sur de Mesopotamia y he de reponer fuerzas para las empresas que aún he de acometer antes del próximo invierno.

—Por supuesto, César —respondió Abgaro y se levantó para acompañar a su huésped especial, pero Trajano le hizo un gesto para que se detuviera.

—Ya conozco el camino... aunque si tu hijo quiere recordármelo... Es mejor que el rey se quede con el resto de sus invitados —añadió Trajano señalando a los nobles de Osroene que se habían dado cita en el palacio de Edesa para rendir pleitesía al victorioso César.

Arbandes se levantó de inmediato.

—He de... hablar un momento con mi padre, César —dijo el joven príncipe—; tenemos asuntos pendientes sobre cómo Osroene puede proveer mejor de víveres y otros pertrechos a las legiones del emperador, pero si el César desea verme me reuniré con él en poco tiempo.

—No me hagas esperar, joven príncipe —dijo Trajano, pero sin tono de irritación, más bien con la dulce ansia del amante.

En cuanto Trajano salió de la sala, Abgaro cogió a su hijo por el brazo y lo condujo también fuera del recinto donde celebraban el banquete con los nobles de Osroene. Antes de salir, el monarca hizo una señal a uno de sus sirvientes y las flautas volvieron a sonar y las bailarinas a danzar. El rey llevó a su hijo a su cámara personal, alejada del bullicio de la fiesta. A medida que se adentraban en el palacio de Edesa, se cruzaban con guardias de Osroene, pero también con pretorianos que patrullaban para asegurar la vida del César.

—Cierra la puerta —le dijo Abgaro a su hijo una vez que entraron en su dormitorio.

—¿Lo vamos a hacer esta noche, padre? —preguntó el príncipe inquieto—. Esto no era lo acordado, pues el plan era terminar con la vida del emperador cuando éste regresara de una terrible derrota, casi sin tropas y abatido. No es ése el César que tenemos esta noche en nuestra casa, padre.

—No, en efecto, no lo es —aceptó Abgaro—, y tenemos varias legiones romanas rodeando Edesa. El plan que convinimos, hijo mío, era el que era en su momento; sin embargo las cosas han cambiado.

—A eso me refiero, padre: Trajano sigue consiguiendo victorias...

—Yo no me refiero a la batalla del Tigris, muchacho, sino a esta carta. —El monarca abrió un pequeño cofre que había en la mesa y mostró una carta a su hijo al tiempo que hablaba—. Es de Osroes, muchacho, y nos propone una firme alianza si acabamos con la vida del emperador romano.

Arbandes no dijo nada, sino que dio media vuelta y empezó a caminar en círculos con ambas manos en la nuca.

—Pero, padre, todo está infestado de pretorianos —dijo el príncipe sin dejar de caminar.

—Se les puede matar. Difícil, pero puede hacerse.

Arbandes se detuvo entonces y miró a su padre.

—¿Y las legiones que rodean Edesa? ¿También podemos acabar con ellas?

—No, muchacho, pero podemos cerrar las puertas de la ciudad y resistir un asedio durante meses. Tenemos todos los víveres y el agua que hemos reunido para las malditas legiones de Trajano. Pueden valernos para resistir mientras llega ayuda de Osroes, a quien enviaré un mensajero esta misma noche, de forma que sepa lo que hemos hecho.

—¿Y por qué iba a asistirnos?

—Porque está tan deseoso de venganza que no dudará, y más si sabe que el ejército romano ha sido descabezado.

—¿Y no sería mejor, padre, seguir como ahora?

—Fuiste tú, hijo, el que me dijo que no le gustaba ya acostarse con el César.

El príncipe suspiró.

—Eso es verdad.

—Y te está esperando —insistió Abgaro—; ¿qué me dices?

Hubo un silencio por el que se filtraron algunas risas que llegaban desde la fiesta. El banquete seguía en marcha.

—He dado mucho vino a los pretorianos y también a las legiones. Sé que los que están de guardia no deben beber, pero son un ejército victorioso y se sienten invencibles. Ya han estado aquí otras veces y siempre les ha ido todo bien. Están confiados. Si te atreves a hacerlo, hijo mío, adelante. No tendremos una oportunidad mejor.

Arbandes miró al suelo. Los brazos le colgaban como muertos. Parecía una estatua. Habló sin moverse.

—Después de acostarnos, padre; cuando el emperador ha satisfecho sus ansias conmigo, se queda dormido. Entonces lo haré.

—Muy bien —dijo Abgaro.

Fue a la mesa y del mismo cofre de donde había extraído la carta de Osroes, sacó la daga con la empuñadura repleta de esmeraldas y rubíes que ya enseñó a su hijo hacía unos meses, sólo que ahora no se limitó a mostrársela, sino que se la puso en las manos al tiempo que le hablaba:

—Úsala bien, hijo mío: pulso firme. No dudes en el momento culminante. La determinación es clave cuando se elimina a un enemigo mortal. Y Trajano lo es.

El muchacho cogió el puñal con la mano derecha y aprisionó fuertemente su empuñadura repleta de piedras preciosas.

—No dudaré, padre.

—Muy bien, muchacho. No sé si eres consciente, pero el futuro de Osroene, de Partia y hasta de Roma está en tus manos. Ahora ve, hijo, ese maldito Trajano te espera con ansia. Sírvele por última vez y luego mátalo sin piedad.

En la cámara del emperador Trajano
Palacio real de Edesa

Marco Ulpio Trajano está desnudo y sudoroso.

Arbandes también está desnudo, pero apenas corren gotas transparentes por su piel tersa. El emperador cierra los ojos. El príncipe de Osroene espera unos instantes. La respiración del emperador de Roma es rítmica, sosegada, tranquila. Aún se oye la música del banquete. Su padre sigue agasajando a los nobles del reino congregados en Edesa. A Arbandes le parece oír risas más próximas y a hombres hablando en latín. El vino distribuido por su padre quizá está empezando a tener el efecto esperado.

Arbandes gira levemente la cabeza, aún acostado junto al emperador. Encima de la mesa está su túnica y en ella la daga. Los pretorianos ya no se molestan en comprobar si lleva armas o no. Su padre tiene razón: las victorias han hecho a los romanos cada vez más confiados.

El emperador está dormido.

El príncipe se incorpora muy despacio y se sienta en la cama.

Espera un momento.

La respiración del César sigue como antes.

Arbandes se levanta entonces y va hasta la mesa.

Introduce las manos en la túnica y con la derecha coge fuertemente la empuñadura de la daga.

90

LOS BESOS DE TAMURA

Bagram
Verano de 116 d.C.

Desde la muerte de su padre, Tamura se había volcado aún más en su relación con Áyax.

Echada de costado en la cama suspiró.

Áyax.

Su joven gladiador había sobrevivido al tigre. De hecho apenas había sufrido algún pequeño rasguño. Los soldados kushan llegaron a tiempo de abatir al salvaje animal con sus flechas, pero no fue suficiente para salvar a su padre también. Ahora ella estaba con su madre y con Áyax.

Marcio, el gran gladiador de Roma, había muerto.

Su padre había estado allí todo aquel viaje, para protegerla, para cuidarla, a ella y a su madre. Ahora, ante su repentina e inesperada ausencia, se había refugiado en los abrazos de su joven y fuerte gladiador, como si buscara un sustituto ante la enorme pérdida que acababa de sufrir.

Tamura, en ocasiones, lloraba en silencio por las noches.

Hacía el amor con Áyax, pero se sentía sola.

Al principio no lo notó, pero luego empezó a tener la sensación de que él no sentía la misma pasión por ella. Más tarde concluyó que todo aquello eran conjeturas suyas absurdas, por la rabia, la pena y el dolor que tenía por la muerte de su padre. Marcio había salvado a su madre de las locuras de Roma y luego, cuando fue atrapado de nuevo por los romanos, había conseguido regresar, con el apoyo incluso del propio Trajano, para rescatarlas a ellas de una Dacia destrozada por la guerra. Les había proporcionado una existencia segura en la gran Roma.

Una ciudad que a ella nunca le gustó, pues Tamura siempre echaba de menos los verdes e inmensos hayedos del norte del Danubio, aquellos frondosos bosques donde creció de niña y que ella continuaba considerando su auténtico hogar. ¿Regresaría alguna vez a ese hogar? ¿Sentiría de nuevo, en alguna ocasión, la plácida sensación de estar en casa?

Durante el viaje había empezado a considerar que el auténtico hogar era allí donde estaban sus padres, pero ahora, de pronto, sin el aviso lento de una enfermedad, sin el vaticinio de ningún oráculo, sin la incertidumbre de una guerra, Marcio, su padre, había muerto despedazado por un tigre.

Por eso se volvió hacia Áyax en busca de abrazos y caricias y besos. Los sentimientos que la sacudían por dentro sólo encontraban refugio junto al joven gladiador griego. Incluso si éste se mostraba algo más distante en la relación que ella. Quizá los hombres eran siempre así: más fríos, más lejanos. Ella no tenía experiencia. Había pensado en hablar de ello con su madre, pero Alana estaba demasiado entristecida aquellas semanas como para que pareciera buena idea hablar de relaciones con hombres.

Tamura, aquella noche, echada de lado en la cama, con Áyax tumbado junto a ella, durmiendo, mantenía los ojos muy abiertos.

Cuando terminaban de hacer el amor, él se quedaba con frecuencia dormido, pero a veces sólo estaba en duermevela mientras se recuperaba para yacer de nuevo con ella con la misma intensidad que al principio de la noche. Tamura no sabía si Áyax estaba en ese momento dormido del todo o sólo rehaciéndose. De pronto sintió que la cama se movía y supo que el gladiador, su gladiador, retornaba hacia ella. Suspiró lentamente.

—Ven a mí —dijo él.

Y ella se volvió y lo miró con dulzura.

—Eres hermosa —dijo Áyax con la satisfacción de quien poseía un objeto bonito.

Ella sonrió y se sonrojó un poco. Estaba completamente desnuda. Él, en cambio, había llegado de una reunión con el consejero Shaka, la última, había dicho él, antes de que partieran hacia Xeres, y se había acostado con ella sin despojarse de la ropa. Ni siquiera se había quitado el cinturón del que colgaba su espada. La había poseído con gran ansia. Y ella, como tantas otras veces, se había dejado hacer.

—Voy a ti... siempre... —dijo ella acercándose despacio, como una gata en celo—, pero desnúdate. Yo también quiero verte.

A Áyax le divertía tanto ver hasta qué punto la tenía en sus manos que se tomó aquella petición como un puro halago: ella quería ver su hermoso cuerpo de gladiador desnudo, con sus poderosos músculos, su tersa piel.

Áyax se levantó, se quitó el cinturón de la espada y lo lanzó contra la esquina de la habitación. Ella se puso también en pie y anduvo hacia él hasta abrazarlo y quedar los dos desnudos, piel con piel. Luego hubo besos y caricias, hasta que ella se separó ligeramente y lo cogió de la mano y lo condujo de vuelta a la cama.

—Esta vez yo arriba —dijo ella.

A él le daba igual. De hecho mejor. Estaba cansado. La joven hija de Marcio era incansable en el lecho.

Tomaron posiciones.

Él debajo, ella encima.

Áyax había pensado en que lo prudente sería envenenar primero a Tamura y luego al resto, pero la muchacha le proporcionaba un gran placer físico en la cama, y mental fuera de ella: era un auténtico disfrute para su intelecto retorcido ver, día a día, cómo la podía tener tan engañada sobre todo: sobre lo que iba a ocurrir con la misión, sobre su fingida pasión por ella y sobre la muerte de su padre.

Tamura le estaba besando el cuello. Con la dulzura de siempre, con la ternura ingenua de aquella inocencia tan enorme. Era el engaño lo que más excitaba al gladiador. Habían empezado a envenenar ya a Titianus. El viejo no aguantaría mucho y por su edad nadie sospecharía. Luego vendría la muerte de Alana y, sí, seguramente también el envenenamiento de la propia Tamura y el regreso a Roma donde sus servicios serían recompensados con una enorme cantidad de oro y una vida cómoda para siempre. Áyax lo tenía todo perfectamente planeado y tenía a todas las personas de su entorno próximo controladas. Nada podía fallar.

Tamura le besaba ahora el otro lado del cuello, con la misma pasión que había exhibido en el de antes. Él dio una profunda inspiración. Ya estaba preparado, con la misma ansia y la misma potencia que cuando había entrado en aquella habitación al principio de la noche.

Ella se levantó para facilitarlo todo. Luego se dejó caer. Él se sintió encantado, tanto que no reparó en cómo la muchacha, de besarle el cuello, pasó a estirarse. Él creyó que iba a cambiar la posición de la almohada del lecho. A veces lo hacían, o en ocasiones la usaban mientras estaban juntos. Que Tamura se estirara un poco más de lo habitual no resultó nada extraño para él. La muchacha era muy flexible.

De súbito, Áyax sintió una especie de mordedura en el cuello que no supo bien a qué atribuir, porque no era como si le hubiera mordido, algo que había hecho alguna vez, sino más bien como si algo frío lo hubiera rasgado.

«¿Qué es esto?», creyó decir Áyax, pero ni una palabra salió de su boca, porque la garganta estaba seccionada y sólo le brotaba sangre por la boca.

Le costaba respirar.

Tamura se levantó, separando su pequeño cuerpo de la piel del gladiador. La sangre empezaba a inundar la cama entera, porque las manos de Áyax apenas podían contener la hemorragia por la que se le escapaba la vida y sus planes y sus sueños forjados sobre el engaño, la traición y el horror.

No, no podía hablar, pero su mirada lo decía todo, lo preguntaba todo.

Ella, desnuda, con el puñal que había cogido de debajo de la cama, clavaba los ojos en él con una rabia y un odio como nunca había visto jamás en nadie. Era como si Tamura supiera a la perfección que todo había sido una inmensa mentira durante meses, que nunca había sentido amor por ella y que además era él quien había matado a su padre. Pero ¿cómo podía saberlo todo?

—Buddahamitra —dijo ella, en pie, con los ojos inyectados en una ira bestial que no parecía verse saciada por aquel corte certero y limpio en el cuello de quien tanto mal le había causado—. Buddahamitra —repitió Tamura, con el placer de darse cuenta de que las palabras podían causar aún más daño en el maldito y miserable Áyax, quien, sin dar crédito aún a lo que pasaba, parecía, por la expresión de pavor de su rostro, que empezaba a cobrar conciencia de que era ya hombre muerto. Así que Tamura, rápidamente, se lo reveló todo con palabras exactas, precisas. Su moribundo interlocutor no tenía tiempo para circunloquios—: Uno de los libros que despreciaste, el que tenía escrito en sánscrito, me unió a Buddahamitra. Despertó el interés de ella por mí. Un día ella me llevó a una habitación y me contó la más terrible de las historias: resulta que el emperador Kanishka quiere usar la religión budista para unir su imperio con algo más fuerte que las armas, pero hay monjes que desconfían de hasta dónde quiere llegar el emperador con su control de la religión y lo vigilan de cerca. Tienen espías en la corte, y Buddahamitra es uno de esos espías. La monja lo sabe todo: tiene guardianes que le cuentan todo lo que los consejeros hablan con el emperador. Ella no interviene en nada si no tiene que ver con Buda y el cuarto concilio, pero igual que averigua otras cosas, se enteró de tu miserable traición, de cómo planeaste matarnos a todos nosotros, uno a uno, ayudado por el consejero Shaka, y me informó de que la muerte de mi padre había sido un asesinato perpetrado por esas manos tuyas con las que intentas detener la sangre que mana sin control de tu cuello.

Tamura andaba desnuda por la habitación, con la daga ensangrentada en la mano, de un lado a otro, hablando rápido y mirando de forma intermitente a Áyax, que seguía intentando, infructuosamente, detener la hemorragia.

—Al principio —continuó ella—, me negué a creerla, pero ella hizo que un guardia me contara todo el plan de la cacería. Pero yo seguía sin creerla, así de cegada estaba por mis sentimientos hacia ti. Entonces me dijo que ahora estabais envenenando a Titianus y te vigilé. Sin creerla todavía, porque no era posible que tú, el hombre al que me he entregado, el hombre al que he amado como no he amado a nadie en mi vida, pudiera ser el asesino de mi padre y el traidor que nos ha estado acompañando todos estos años durante este viaje sin fin. Pero te vigilé, te observé con mis propios ojos y vi cómo vertías líquido en una copa de vino que tú mismo entregaste a Titianus. Y aun así seguí pensando que todo era una locura, una insidia creada por la corte kushan para dividirnos, para que no siguiéramos nuestro viaje, para volvernos a todos locos. Pero seguí vigilándote y descubrí dónde escondías el líquido que llevas días mezclando con el vino que sirves a Titianus, y cogí el pequeño frasco y lo vertí, entero, en un poco de carne que di a unos gatos de la calle. Y los tres gatos, los tres, Áyax, murieron en el acto. Y entonces pensé en cómo tus abrazos eran fríos y distantes, cómo tus besos eran gélidos y cómo sólo te interesaba poseer mi cuerpo pero no a mí, no a mí. Tú sólo te quieres a ti mismo y nos has ido usando y engañando todo el viaje y, lo peor de todo, he estado ciega mientras matabas a mi padre, a mi propio padre... Podría haberlo evitado y no supe verlo... no quise verlo... —Tamura se detuvo al fin sollozando; dejó de moverse por la habitación y lo miró fijamente—. Pero tú ya estás muerto. Cuando comprendí que todo lo que Buddhamitra me había contado era cierto, me arrodillé en el suelo e imploré a Némesis, la diosa a la que tanto veneró mi padre, que me guiara.

Tamura calló. Áyax apenas respiraba, pero la seguía observando con aquellos ojos henchidos de miedo. La muchacha clavó los ojos en su mano. Soltó el puñal. Un clang anunció su impacto con el suelo.

—Y Némesis me ha guiado y me ha dado fuerzas para acostarme una noche más contigo. Tenía planeado matarte nada más entrar. Pero venías con tu espada en la cintura y eres mucho más fuerte que yo. Supongo que menos rápido, pero muy fuerte y muy bien entrenado, porque te ha adiestrado el mejor de los preparadores de lucha que nunca jamás ha tenido Roma: mi propio padre. Tuve miedo de fallar, de sólo herirte y de que tuvieras oportunidad de contraatacar. Morir me da igual, pero no vengar a mi padre... eso no podía permitirlo. Así que me desnudé para ti y te besé como tantas otras veces te he besado y estoy seguro de que no has notado absolutamente nada, porque, Áyax, las mujeres también podemos engañar como los hombres, incluso infinitamente mejor que los hombres cuando nos lo proponemos. Y yo me lo propuse. Te he dejado volver a estar conmigo. He hecho todo lo que a ti te gusta, aunque se me revolvían las entrañas al sentirte dentro de mí y notar que te daba placer con ello, pero Némesis me ha dado las fuerzas necesarias para sobreponerme al asco que me embargaba y aguantar cada instante, cada abrazo tuyo, cada vez que empujabas dentro de mí como un animal. No, peor que un animal. No hay animal en el mundo que sea tan vil, tan cruel y tan traidor como tú. Muere para siempre, Áyax, muérete, con lentitud.

Y se arrodilló junto a él, que seguía intentando decir alguna palabra, pero sangre, sólo sangre emergía de su boca.

—En tu propio nombre llevabas la condena —le susurró ella al oído—. Pero tú que nunca has leído nada, no podías saber que el auténtico Áyax murió por despreciar a los dioses. Creo que hoy Némesis ha sabido darme la suficiente fuerza para que veas lo que ocurre a los que reniegan de todos los dioses del mundo. —Calló un momento—. Parece que ya no me oyes.

El gladiador ya no respiraba. Tenía los ojos abiertos, sin parpadear, con esa mirada de terror absoluto de quien no sabe enfrentarse a la muerte.

Tamura se pasó el dorso de una mano por la boca y por los ojos medio cerrados por donde brotaban lágrimas, pero no por su amor perdido, no por esa pasión que nunca fue real, sino por la muerte de su padre.

Se quedó quieta.

Junto al cadáver.

Durante horas.

Se empezaron a oír los primeros pájaros del amanecer.

Ella despertó como por sorpresa.

De pronto sintió unas arcadas terribles, irrefrenables, y se puso a vomitar al lado de la cama.

—¡Dioses! —exclamó en voz alta llevándose las manos al vientre. Estaba embarazada del asesino de su padre.

91

LA MUERTE DE TRAJANO

Cesifonte, capital de Partia
Verano de 116 d.C.

Partamaspates entró en el salón del trono de oro del *Šāhān Šāh* de Partia acompañado por un hombre.

—Padre, Abgaro ha enviado un mensajero.

Había gran número de nobles partos reunidos con el rey de reyes. Osroes miró a su hijo frunciendo el ceño y Partamaspates comprendió lo que preocupaba a su padre.

—El *Šāhān Šāh* hará bien en escuchar a este mensajero de Osroene delante de todos sus nobles y consejeros. De hecho, creo que éste es el lugar y la compañía adecuados para recibir, no; mejor aún, padre: para disfrutar de esta noticia. Todas nuestras preocupaciones han terminado.

Osroes suspiró y se pasó los dedos de la mano izquierda por los labios. Tenía la boca reseca. Desde que Mitrídates se había ido al este con más de la mitad del ejército, los días se le hacían lentos y eternos.

—¿Qué es lo que tiene que decir este mensajero que va a resultar tan estimulante para todos? —preguntó al fin el *Šāhān Šāh*.

El enviado de Osroene dio varios pasos al frente hasta situarse justo ante el trono de oro del *basileús basiléon* y habló alto y claro.

Sólo tres palabras.

No hacía falta más para explicar que el mundo entero había cambiado en una noche.

—Trajano ha muerto.

Silencio.

Murmullos.

—¿Qué has dicho? —preguntó Osroes inclinándose tanto hacia adelante en su trono que a punto estuvo de caerse de él.

—Trajano ha muerto —repitió con el mismo aplomo de la primera vez el mensajero de Osroene.

—¿Muerto? —insistió en sus dudas el rey de reyes—. ¿Estás seguro de ello? ¡Quiero pruebas!

—Mi señor, yo he tenido que partir de Edesa en medio de la noche y he cabalgado durante días sin apenas descanso para poder traer la noticia lo antes posible a Cesifonte. Ésas eran mis instrucciones, pero mi señor el rey Abgaro me ha dicho que puedo explicar al *Šāhān Šāh* cómo ha sido la muerte del emperador romano.

—Por favor —dijo Osroes apoyando la espalda de nuevo en el trono en el que, por primera vez desde hacía meses, volvía a sentirse cómodo.

—El príncipe Arbandes, arriesgando su vida, lo asesinó por la noche, cuando el emperador estaba en su cámara privada del palacio real de Edesa.

—El príncipe Arbandes... —repitió Osroes—. Y Trajano muerto. —Tenía que decírselo a sí mismo varias veces. Y lo hizo. Y, al fin, estalló en una gran carcajada a la que enseguida se unieron todos los nobles allí presentes.

—Y el rey de reyes —dijo el mensajero en cuanto las risas se relajaron y ya pudo hacerse oír de nuevo— se alegrará de saber que la cabeza del emperador romano está esperándole en Edesa. Sólo que...

Osroes dejó de llorar. La risa le había hecho saltar las lágrimas, pero ya intuía que todo no podía ser tan simple.

—¿Sólo que qué? —preguntó desde el trono.

—*Šāhān Šāh*, mi rey y el príncipe han arriesgado todo su reino con esta acción y ahora las legiones rodean Edesa. Mi rey y todo Osroene necesitan la ayuda del rey de reyes.

Osroes asintió varias veces. No le gustaba tener que enviar tropas al norte, pues sabía que los romanos, además de las legiones apostadas en Edesa, disponían de otro ejército más allá del Tigris y él no tenía hombres para formar una fuerza militar con la que ayudar a Edesa a no ser que dejara Cesifonte sin suficientes guerreros en sus murallas. Por otro, lado, si Abgaro había tenido las agallas de acabar con Trajano, no podía dejarlo sin ayuda. Osroes, como todos en Oriente, estaba convencido de que sin el emperador romano era sólo cuestión de tiempo que todos los ejércitos de *Hrōm* terminaran por retirarse de Partia, Adiabene, Mesopotamia y quién sabía si también de Armenia.

—Es justo lo que pide tu rey, mensajero —respondió Osroes—. Partirás en cuanto hayas comido y descansado un poco. Se te entregará un caballo nuevo, el mejor que tengamos en mis cuadras, y acudirás de regreso a Edesa, donde espero que encuentres la forma de cruzar entre las tropas romanas que la asedian en busca de venganza para informar a tu monarca de que pronto llegarán refuerzos desde Cesifonte para asistirlo en su lucha contra las legiones.

El mensajero se inclinó y, acompañado por dos guardias, salió de la sala del trono. Osroes se levantó y se dirigió a todos los nobles de Partia allí congregados:

—Amigos y consejeros: quiero que sepáis que lo que acabáis de oír ha sido fruto de un plan urdido por mí. Ahora comeremos y beberemos para disfrutar de esta gran noticia con un banquete como pocas veces se ha celebrado en este palacio y, además, engalanaremos toda la ciudad y habrá festejos en todas las calles de Cesifonte. Empezad sin mí. Voy a ocuparme con mi hijo de ponerlo todo en marcha. Hoy es un gran día, un grandísimo día para Partia y para todos los reinos sobre los que gobernamos: el invasor extranjero ha muerto.

Osroes salió de la sala acompañado por su hijo en medio de grandes gritos de júbilo.

Una vez en el exterior, el rey de reyes cogió a su hijo por el brazo y lo llevó a una esquina de uno de los grandes patios del palacio, alejándose de los guardianes partos que los escoltaban.

Osroes miró a Partamaspates a los ojos y le habló en voz baja.

—Deja partir al mensajero de Osroene y al instante sal tú mismo con un regimiento de caballería ligera. Toma unos quinientos hombres. Ve hacia el norte y consígueme confirmación de lo que nos ha contado ese hombre. No dudo de que Abgaro odiara a Trajano y quizá su hijo también, pero antes de enviar las tropas que tengo en Cesifonte hacia Edesa o antes de reclamar refuerzos a mi hermano, tu tío Mitrídates, hemos de estar bien seguros de que Trajano está muerto: una y mil veces muerto.

92

LA FLOR DE LOTO

Asia central
Verano de 116 d.C.

Alana encontró a su hija Tamura junto al cadáver frío de Áyax.
Era madre.
Podía digerir cualquier cosa que hubiera hecho su hija.
La joven abrió los ojos.
Lloró un rato largo en los brazos de su madre antes de
poder hablar.

Su hija le contó todo lo ocurrido, desde los reiterados engaños del joven gladiador y el asesinato de su padre hasta la
forma en la que ella le había dado muerte.

Alana suspiró y abrazó a la que siempre sería su pequeña.
Estuvieron así unos instantes, pero Alana rápidamente se puso
en acción: era de prever que el consejero Shaka echara pronto
de menos a Áyax, pero quizá aún disponían de algunas horas.
Tamura fue en busca de Buddhamitra para pedirle ayuda
mientras Alana hablaba con Titianus. La monja budista, como
esperaban, no les falló y con sus múltiples contactos en Bagram les consiguió caballos y un guía que los sacó de la capital
del Imperio kushan con discreción.

Cabalgaron hacia el norte, en busca de Samarcanda. Se trataba de llegar a la Ruta de la Seda lo antes posible para, enmas-
carados como comerciantes, seguir su camino hacia Xeres.

El guía, un budista completamente leal a Buddhamitra,
los condujo hasta aquella ciudad en pocos días. Todo parecía
ir bien, pero el poder del Imperio kushan era cada vez mayor
y se expandía. La ciudad de Yarkand estaba ya totalmente bajo
su poder y la influencia del emperador Kanishka se dejaba

notar en el reino limítrofe de Yutian, tradicionalmente vasallo del Imperio han, pero ahora un territorio en disputa entre ambos: Xeres y los kushan.

Aun así, todo marchó bien hasta que llegaron al puesto fronterizo. Un soldado kushan los detuvo y habló con Titianus. Utilizaron palabras en sogdiano habituales entre los comerciantes de la Ruta de la Seda.

—Espera un momento —dijo el guerrero.

Alana miraba, sin desmontar del caballo, a un lado y a otro del camino de piedra en el que se encontraban. Había una veintena de tiendas de los soldados que vigilaban aquel extremo del Imperio kushan.

—Esto no me gusta —le comentó Alana a Tamura.

—¿Crees que les habrá llegado algún mensaje desde Bagram sobre nosotras? —preguntó la muchacha.

—Buddhamitra nos ha ayudado a escapar de allí —respondió Alana—, pero no creo que pueda controlar al consejero Shaka y es muy probable que éste haya enviado mensajeros a los diferentes puestos fronterizos, especialmente los del este, pues sabe que queremos ir hacia Xeres.

El soldado regresó acompañado de una docena de hombres armados con espadas y arcos. El que parecía ser el líder del puesto de guardia volvió a hablar con Titianus. El mercader levantó algo la voz, lo mismo hizo el soldado kushan y se disponía a desenfundar su espada, pero el viejo comerciante agachó entonces la cabeza y la calma pareció regresar.

Titianus se acercó entonces a Alana y a Tamura.

—No nos dejan pasar —explicó—, y eso no es lo peor. Dicen que una docena de sus hombres nos van a escoltar de regreso a Bagram.

—Esto es cosa del consejero Shaka —dijo Alana enfurecida.

—Seguramente, pero no podemos hacer nada —señaló el mercader.

Alana respiraba rápidamente.

Miró a su hija.

Tamura asintió una vez, con claridad y asió las riendas del caballo con fuerza.

—Sube a tu caballo, mercader —le pidió Alana a Titianus.

El viejo sintió el tono vibrante con el que la mujer le había hablado y también comprendió.

—No saldrá bien —dijo en voz baja—. Son demasiados.

—¿Se te ocurre algo mejor? —preguntó Alana mientras veía cómo los guerreros kushan montaban en sus propios caballos y empezaban a rodearlos.

Titianus suspiró.

—No, no se me ocurre nada mejor —admitió. Fue hasta su caballo y, con cierta dificultad, consiguió subirse de nuevo a él.

Alana sacudió las riendas del suyo, lo mismo hizo Tamura y Titianus las imitó. El guía budista se quedó quieto, sin entender bien qué pasaba o qué pretendían. En su cabeza no cabía la posibilidad de intentar cruzar un puesto fronterizo de la guardia imperial kushan a la fuerza.

—¡Aaaahh! —aulló Alana. Su hija hizo lo mismo y Titianus espoleó con los talones también a su caballo lo mejor que pudo.

Ninguno de los guerreros kushan se esperaba aquella reacción de un viejo y dos mujeres. La sorpresa ayudó inicialmente a Alana, Tamura y Titianus y les permitió alejarse más de cien pasos antes de que los soldados reaccionaran e iniciaran una persecución.

—¡Vamos, vamos! —gritó Alana mientras se hacía a un lado para que Tamura y Titianus la adelantaran. Ella quería cerrar el grupo para asegurarse de que ninguno de sus dos compañeros de huida quedaba rezagado, en particular su hija.

Un silbido pasó junto a Tamura y otro rozando la oreja de Titianus.

—¡Vamos, más rápido! ¡Dioses! —insistió Alana azuzando también su caballo para alejarse todo lo posible de aquella lluvia de flechas.

Les estaban arrojando dardos mortales, pero al hacerlo ni sabían apuntar bien ni podían mantener la velocidad en la persecución. Los kushan no eran jinetes partos capaces de disparar con perfecta puntería mientras galopaban. Eran lo uno o lo otro. Dejaron entonces de disparar y se centraron en la persecución. Pero los caballos que la monja Buddhamitra había elegido para su apreciada Tamura, su madre y su amigo mercader, no eran caballos cualesquiera, sino animales seleccionados entre los mejores caballos de Fergana, la región legendaria por sus animales veloces como el viento.

La distancia entre los jinetes que huían y sus perseguidores se ampliaba. Pronto, el líder de la patrulla kushan comprendió que no les darían alcance. No sólo era una cuestión de que los caballos de los escapados eran mejores, sino que además el peso de Alana, Tamura o del viejo y enjuto Titianus era mucho menor que el de sus grandes guerreros. Era imposible dar caza a los huidos.

—¡Deteneos y disparad! ¡Disparad todas vuestras flechas!

Y los jinetes frenaron los caballos, cogieron las flechas, tensaron los arcos y lanzaron tantos dardos como tenían. La mayoría se perdió sin dar en los objetivos que se iban alejando en el horizonte, pero el oficial al mando del puesto fronterizo juraría que, al menos, un par de flechas habían alcanzado a los escapados.

—¡Al galope! —ordenó de nuevo.

Quería comprobar si había algún herido, pero los huidos no aflojaban el ritmo. No, no podrían cogerlos.

—Ahí —indicó uno de los jinetes kushan señalando el suelo, a un lado del camino. El oficial miró y vio que había sangre.

Sonrió.

Los habían alcanzado.

—Los perseguiremos sin descanso hasta el anochecer —dijo y azuzó a su caballo seguido por el resto de la patrulla de guerreros kushan.

A un par de millas de distancia

Por delante seguían galopando Tamura y Titianus, y tras ellos, Alana, cerrando el grupo. Ninguno se había quejado y los tres mantuvieron la velocidad hasta que Alana calculó que ya tenían una distancia importante ganada sobre sus perseguidores.

—¡Ahora al trote! ¡Si no los caballos no aguantarán!

Los tres ajustaron el ritmo de la marcha y así continuaron

durante una hora larga, hasta que el sol empezó a caer en el horizonte. Alana miraba a intervalos regulares hacia atrás para asegurarse de que los kushan no les daban alcance. El camino daba muchas vueltas y curvas, de forma que era difícil tener una visión muy extensa hacia el sol poniente, por donde llegaban los perseguidores, pero era de pura lógica que los soldados habrían tenido también que ralentizar el ritmo de sus caballos o éstos habrían caído exhaustos.

—Seguiremos mientras haya luz —dijo Alana.

—Sí, madre —contestó Tamura.

El viejo mercader asintió, pero se le veía pálido y agotado. Alana sabía que quizá todo aquello era demasiado esfuerzo para un hombre de tanta edad como Titianus, pero no habían tenido opción y por eso el propio mercader no planteaba alternativa alguna a la idea de seguir cabalgando. Haber regresado a Bagram habría supuesto una condena a muerte para todos.

Anocheció.

El camino entraba en un gran valle.

—Nos saldremos de la ruta y nos alejaremos un par de millas, hacia el sur —propuso Alana—. De esa forma, si siguen cabalgando por la noche nos rebasarán y perderán nuestro rastro.

Y así hicieron.

Se apartaron tanto como les fue posible, hasta que, ya sin luz y con un terreno desconocido e impracticable, lo prudente fue desmontar, atar los caballos a un árbol y sacar las mantas para pasar la noche.

—No podremos encender fuego —indicó Alana.

Aquella región era muy calurosa durante el día, pero fría por la noche pese a que estaban en mitad del verano. Sin embargo, era evidente que no podían encender una lumbre para calentarse, pues delataría su posición a los kushan.

Titianus bajó del caballo, dio dos pasos y se derrumbó.

Tamura acudió en su ayuda.

—Le han alcanzado, madre —dijo la joven, pero Alana no respondía y la muchacha levantó la mirada y vio que su madre permanecía en pie, pero abrazada al cuello de su caballo. Tenía una flecha clavada en la espalda, igual que Titianus. Como Alana se había quedado siempre por detrás de ella, Tamura no había visto que un dardo enemigo la había herido. Y en Titianus, la verdad, no se había fijado. Ahora resultaba que ambos habían sido alcanzados por los arqueros kushan.

—Qué lástima —dijo Titianus mirando hacia la oscura noche sin luna en dirección al este—. Casi llego hasta la Torre de Piedra. Marca el principio de los estados bajo el control de Xeres... pero yo ya no lo conseguiré.

El anciano estaba muy débil. Tamura lo ayudó a tumbarse mientras no dejaba de mirar a su madre. En cuanto depositó al viejo mercader en el suelo fue con Alana y la ayudó también, en su caso, a sentarse.

—Hay que arrancar la flecha —dijo Tamura en cuanto estuvo a su lado.

—¡No! —dijo Alana casi en un grito—. No —repitió con voz más serena. No quería dar explicaciones, pero se sentía muy débil. La herida era mortal.

—Te recuperarás, madre, como lo has hecho siempre. Como hiciste en la Dacia, ¿recuerdas? Cuando yo sólo era una niña y huíamos de los romanos. Esto será igual.

Alana miró a Tamura con dulzura. Luego se volvió hacia Titianus.

—¿Cómo está? —preguntó Alana.

Tamura fue hasta el viejo mercader. No se movía, tenía los ojos abiertos y no parecía respirar. La muchacha volvió junto a su madre.

—Ha muerto —dijo la joven.

Ninguna de las dos dijo nada en un rato.

Tamura cogió una de las mantas y se las ingenió para romperla en pequeñas tiras para, al menos, contener la sangre que manaba por la espalda de su madre.

—Deberíamos quitar la flecha —insistió la muchacha.

Pero su madre volvió a negar con la cabeza.

—Por todos los dioses —dijo Alana—, te vas a quedar sola.

—No, madre, no. No digas eso. No puede ser. Tú eres fuerte, siempre lo has sido. No vas a morir, madre, no.

Alana se tumbó de lado.

—Lo siento, mi pequeña. Es mi culpa. No fue buena idea intentar huir de los kushan. Deberíamos haber vuelto. Quizá Buddahamitra podría habernos ayudado de nuevo...

—No es culpa tuya, madre. Es culpa de ese miserable de Áyax, y mía por haberle contado el secreto que el emperador Trajano dijo que no revelara a nadie. —Tamura empezó a sentir un miedo férreo, pétreo, completo, que se apoderaba de ella, y comenzó a llorar. Se abrazó a Alana—. No, madre, no puedes morir. Tú no. Por favor, madre, no me dejes sola.

—Escucha, hija —le replicó Alana con gravedad en la voz—. Mi herida es mortal... Moriré está noche, pero moriré en tus brazos. Es una buena muerte para una guerrera sármata. Caída en combate y abrazada hasta el último minuto por su hija. Pero ahora no digas nada... no tengo ya muchas energías para muchas palabras. Has de pensar como guerrera. ¿Me escuchas? Llora si quieres, pero ¿me escuchas?

—Sí, madre —dijo Tamura reprimiendo un poco el mar de lágrimas que la invadía por dentro.

—Bien. Esta noche no darán contigo. Has de partir al alba. Coge los tres caballos. Retoma al camino si los kushan aún no están en él. No lo creo... ellos tampoco habrán podido seguir en esta noche sin luna... Galopa con el primero, todo lo que puedas. Luego abandónalo y cambia de caballo... y lo mismo con el segundo... hasta que te quedes con uno solo... eso te dará aún más ventaja...

—¿Pero adónde voy a ir, madre?

—Hacia Xeres. Si regresas, los kushan te ejecutarán, pero si vas hacia Xeres serás embajadora del emperador Trajano... allí tu vida tiene sentido... has de seguir hacia el este... y no tengas tanta pena... los padres mueren... hemos vivido juntos, en tiempos terribles y en los buenos... no hay que llorar tanto...

Pero Tamura estaba desconsolada hasta límites inimaginables para su madre. La muchacha se acercó más aún a Alana y le habló al oído, porque hay cosas que sólo se pueden confesar en voz muy baja, en un susurro ahogado, como si uno intentara que no fueran reales.

—Madre, estoy embarazada de Áyax. Voy a tener un hijo del asesino de mi padre.

Alana dejó de respirar.

—¡Madre, madre! —gritó la muchacha.

—Sssshh; silencio, muchacha —le dijo Alana—. No sabemos cuánta distancia nos... separa... de los kushan.

—Lo siento.

Alana acarició la mejilla de su hija.

—Una guerrera sármata tiene los hijos que elige tener y con quien ella quiere. Tú no quieres un hijo del asesino de tu padre, así que... no lo tendrás.

Tamura no entendía bien cómo podía hacerse eso, pero su madre señaló al caballo que había estado montando.

—Tráeme la bolsa azul que cuelga de la grupa del animal —dijo la mujer. Tamura fue rauda a por aquel pequeño saco y se lo entregó a su madre.

—Aquí está.

—Ábrelo y busca un frasco que hay envuelto en un paño verde.

Tamura encontró el trapo, lo sacó y lo desenrolló con cuidado. En el frasco había un líquido oscuro.

—Es *silphium* —dio Alana—. Toma un pedazo pequeño de una de las mantas de lana e imprégnalo con un poco de ese líquido. Luego métetelo dentro. Dentro. ¿Entiendes? Y ese niño no nacerá de tu vientre... Y ahora tengo que dormir... —Se recostó de lado—. No pierdas tiempo en enterrarnos... no es un deshonor alimentar a los lobos... todos tenemos que vivir en este mundo...

—Madre —dijo Tamura en voz baja, con tono de súplica, pero Alana parecía haberse dormido de golpe.

La muchacha le puso la mano en la espalda, con cuidado de no tocar la flecha que seguía clavada en la piel morena, y percibió que continuaba respirando. Quizá no fuera todo tan terrible. A lo mejor su madre había exagerado el alcance de la herida. Puede que quitarla no fuera una buena idea, pero igual, al alba, su madre estaría algo más fuerte y podría montar y juntas alcanzarían una ciudad adonde los kushan no pudieran llegar y allí habría médicos. Seguro que habría médicos en Xeres. Quizá mejores que en Roma. Y curarían a su madre.

Sí, eso es lo que iba a pasar.

Se lo repitió una y mil veces, pero el miedo le mordía las entrañas. Se dio cuenta entonces de que tenía el frasco con las hierbas en su mano izquierda. *Silphium.* Lo había oído mencionar alguna vez a su madre: una hierba que hervida con agua y otras sustancias hacía que de tu cuerpo se desprendiera de un niño si no deseabas tenerlo, pero siempre pensó que era una leyenda.

Miró el frasco.

Pensó en Áyax y en sus besos de mentira, en su mente retorcida y vil y cruel. Recordó a su padre muerto. Pensó que tenía algo del asesino de su padre creciendo en sus entrañas y no lo dudó. Fue a por una de las mantas y seccionó un pedazo pequeño de una esquina con su cuchillo de caza. Quitó también el tapón del frasco y echó un poco en el trozo de manta.

¿Cuánto es un poco?

Pensó en Áyax y la rabia la cegó por un instante y vertió más líquido sobre aquel trozo de lana. Vació medio frasco. ¿Era eso un poco o mucho? Luego se sentó y se arremangó la túnica que la cubría hasta dejar descubiertas sus partes íntimas. Separó las piernas. Hizo una pequeña bola con aquel pedazo de manta empapado en el *silphium* de su madre y se lo introdujo dentro.

No sintió ni daño ni gusto.

No sintió nada.

¿Haría efecto así? No pasaba nada. Le preguntaría a su madre al amanecer. Quedaba aún medio frasco más. Debería haber suficiente para acabar con aquello que Áyax había dejado en su ser. Y si no se mataría. Pero ese niño nunca nacería. Eso lo tenía claro. Si su madre moría y se quedaba sola allí, en el fin del mundo, suicidarse no parecía una mala opción.

Tenía que dormir.

«Piensa como guerrera.» Eso le había dicho su madre y, como siempre, llevaba razón. Y una guerrera debe dormir o de lo contrario no valdrá al día siguiente. Dormir un poco.

Cerró los ojos, pero todos sus pensamientos eran negros: su padre muerto, Titianus muerto, Áyax un traidor, ella embarazada del asesino de su padre, su madre... su madre tenía que ponerse bien... tenía que pensar en algo bueno, en algo dulce y bonito que le hubiera pasado recientemente para poder conciliar el sueño.

No le venía nada a la cabeza hasta que recordó su último encuentro con Buddahamitra. Y se acordó de la conversación que tuvieron. Eso empezó a sosegarla un poco.

«¿Por qué me has ayudado tanto? —le había preguntado ella a la monja budista cuando ésta le informaba de dónde recoger los caballos y reunirse con el guía que debía sacarlos de Bagram—. Y ¿por qué me revelaste todo lo de Áyax?»

«¿Recuerdas el poema de Buda, el que me leíste de tu libro la primera vez que nos vimos? ¿Lo recuerdas?»

Y Tamura lo recitó de nuevo:

> —Yathā saṅkāradhānasmiṃ
> ujjhitasmiṃ mahāpathe
> Padumaṃ tattha jāyetha
> sucigandhaṃ manoramaṃ.
>
> Evam saṅkārabhūtesu
> andhabhūte puthujjane
> Atirocati paññāya
> sammāsambuddhasāvako.
>
> [Así como un deleitable
> y perfumado loto crece allí,
> en una pila de basura
> que ha sido desechada en el camino,
> de la misma forma,
> entre la basura de los seres,
> el discípulo del Buda brilla con su sabiduría
> sobrepasando a la ciega humanidad.]

«¿Lo entiendes ahora?», preguntó la monja.

«No del todo, lo siento.»

Buddahamitra sonrió.

«Tú, mi pequeña, eres esa flor de loto que es capaz de crecer entre la basura de los hombres que engañan, que mienten y que matan. Y a la flor de loto hay que salvarla siempre. Cuando pienses que todo está perdido, recuerda que el espíritu de Buda está en ti. Y con él todo es posible.»

Tamura se abrazó a esas palabras y concilió un sueño débil y quebradizo, es cierto, pero al fin y al cabo pudo dormirse.

93

NAHARMALCHA

Río Éufrates
Verano de 116 d.C.

Trajano estaba vivo, muy vivo.
A la cintura llevaba una maravillosa daga engalanada con piedras preciosas en su empuñadura. Un regalo de su amante Arbandes. El hijo del rey de Osroene lo había sorprendido en medio de la noche con aquel presente en la mano. Él había sentido que el joven se levantaba y cuando se volvió en la cama lo vio con aquel hermoso puñal.
—¿Qué es eso, Arbandes? —había preguntado él muy serio.
El hijo del rey de Osroene había dado un pequeño respingo, sobresaltado.
—Creía... que el César dormía y... —empezó a decir de forma balbuceante.
—¿Y? —había insistido Trajano con el ceño fruncido.
—Y quería preparar este presente para que el César lo encontrara junto a él al amanecer —había continuado Arbandes de forma más decidida.
A Trajano le enterneció que el muchacho se pusiera nervioso al ser sorprendido mientras preparaba el regalo.
—Ven aquí —le había dicho.
Y Arbandes dejó el puñal y fue.
Trajano sonreía al recordar todo aquello y al palpar con su mano derecha la empuñadura de aquella daga, regalo de su amante de Edesa.
Suspiró de forma relajada.
Más allá de su vida íntima, también estaba satisfecho en lo militar.

Todo había salido perfectamente en la nueva campaña desde que habían salido de Osroene: Quieto había descendido por la ribera oriental del Tigris, toda vez que ya habían conseguido su control capturando Nínive, Arbela y Gaugamela sin encontrar gran oposición. Del mismo modo, Nigrino, por la ribera occidental del mismo Tigris, había podido descender casi hasta Babilonia sin encontrar resistencia. Eso sí, al llegar cerca de Cesifonte, Nigrino se había alejado para evitar las fuerzas que Osroes tenía concentradas en torno a la capital. El *legatus* había cumplido así las órdenes que había recibido de no atacar la capital parta con sólo un tercio del ejército imperial.

Trajano asintió para sí mismo. La idea era reunir todas las tropas para ese golpe final. La cuestión clave era cómo reagrupar ahora sus tres ejércitos, pues además de las legiones de Quieto y Nigrino estaba la flota imperial, que Trajano comandaba personalmente: el César había descendido por el Éufrates con cincuenta buques militares desde Zeugma, cincuenta barcos atestados hasta los topes de legionarios y pertrechos para el asedio de Cesifonte. Otras muchas cohortes habían hecho el viaje a pie, siempre al lado del río, y en paralelo con la flota imperial, bajo el mando de Julio Máximo y Julio Alejandro. La flota y las legiones habían seguido el curso del Éufrates hasta llegar a la altura donde se encontraba Cesifonte, sólo que la capital parta estaba situada a unas cincuenta millas de donde se habían detenido. Nigrino, por su parte, había ascendido ahora desde las proximidades de Babilonia, con lo que ya estaban a punto de unirse dos de los tres ejércitos. Pero Lucio Quieto seguía al oeste del Tigris, a la espera de que Trajano se lanzara a por Cesifonte desde el este. De esa forma convergerían legiones romanas sobre la capital enemiga desde ambos flancos.

Pero Trajano quería más.

Sabía que necesitaba más.

—Osroes ha concentrado todas las fuerzas de las que dispone en Cesifonte —se explicó Nigrino confirmando lo que Trajano sospechaba—. No hemos encontrado apenas oposición lejos de la ciudad y no hay caballería parta de aquí a Babilonia, pero si uno se intenta acercar a la capital, empieza a encontrarse caballería ligera parta e incluso hemos visto unidades de *catafractos* patrullando en las proximidades.

—Es posible que se replieguen al interior de la ciudad si nos acercamos —apuntó Julio Máximo en aquella nueva reunión del *consilium augusti* de campaña.

—Sí, pero eso no evita el hecho de que Osroes dispone de tropas más que suficientes para defender Cesifonte durante meses —opinó Nigrino—. Cesifonte es inconquistable si no atacamos por varios puntos a la vez. Lo ideal sería combinar un ataque de Lucio Quieto por el este y nosotros desde el oeste, pero, sin la flota, la mayor parte de las murallas son inaccesibles. Ante esos muros no nos bastarán las barcazas que se usaron en Cizre para cruzar el Tigris.

Atardecía en el campamento imperial a orillas del Éufrates. Trajano estaba sentado en su *sella curulis* y los *legati* en pie a su alrededor. Liviano y Aulo guardaban, como de costumbre, la espalda del César.

—Nigrino tiene razón —confirmó Trajano—. Tenemos a Quieto a un lado de la ciudad, ya en la otra ribera del Tigris, y eso nos da una ventaja importante, pero Lucio también está a merced de un ataque enemigo si llegaran refuerzos desde el frente de guerra que Osroes tiene abierto en Oriente contra Vologases. Necesitamos un puente o una flota que permita, en cualquier momento, transportar tropas de un lado a otro del Tigris. No se puede asediar una ciudad rodeada por un gran río sin puentes o sin flota. Y lo mejor para atacar las murallas es tener flota. He estado pensando mucho en esto y la única solución para rendir Cesifonte pasa por tener un gran número de barcos, algo similar a la flota que tenemos aquí anclada junto a nosotros en el Éufrates, pero en el otro río.

—He visto algunos pequeños grupos de árboles en la zona —apuntó Julio Alejandro.

—Insuficientes para construir una flota como la del Éufrates —dijo una voz nueva que se incorporaba al *consilium augusti*.

Los *legati* se volvieron y vieron al arquitecto imperial. Abrieron el círculo para facilitar que se uniera a la reunión. Todos lo habían respetado siempre por la construcción del gran puente sobre el Danubio, pero a partir del exitoso cruce del Tigris, ayudados por las barcazas y balsas con parapetos y torres diseñadas por aquel pequeño individuo de Damasco, éste se había ganado la admiración de todos los militares allí presentes.

Trajano se había llevado al arquitecto con él desde Cizre de regreso a Osroene y luego lo había embarcado en su buque insignia en Zeugma. El emperador estaba seguro de que sus servicios podrían ser útiles en aquella audaz campaña, en cualquier ocasión complicada, y el momento había llegado.

—¿Y si te trajéramos madera desde más al norte? —preguntó Nigrino.

—¿Cuánto tiempo dispondría para construir esa flota? —inquirió entonces el arquitecto mirando a Trajano.

—Necesitamos una flota en el Tigris en menos de un mes —respondió el emperador—. El verano terminará pronto y, además, cada semana que pasa posibilita que Osroes reúna refuerzos de entre los que luchan contra Vologases. No, no hay tiempo para construir una flota nueva para la que, además, no hay madera próxima. La solución es el Naharmalcha.

Ninguno de los *legati* tenía idea de a qué se refería Trajano. Apolodoro, no obstante, respondió con naturalidad.

—Era una muy buena idea, César, pero ayer mismo fui a revisarlo y está inutilizado. El rey de los partos ha debido de pensar que lo usaríamos, lo ha rellenado de tierra en múltiples puntos y ha abierto vías en los diques de contención. Los trabajos de reparación pueden hacerse, sin duda, pero llevarán meses.

—Parece que Osroes —dijo Trajano en voz baja—, aunque rehúye el combate en primera línea, no para de urdir estrategias de defensa. Puede que no sea un valiente, pero no es un estúpido. No me sorprende que haya inutilizado el Naharmalcha. Cuando envió todas sus tropas a Cizre para defender el Tigris ya demostró que sabe leer los planes de su contrincante y ha previsto que pudiéramos usar el viejo canal.

Durante un rato nadie dijo nada hasta que Nigrino se dirigió al emperador de nuevo.

—¿Qué es el Naharmalcha, augusto?

El César miró a Apolodoro y fue el arquitecto el que respondió.

—Es un antiguo canal que conectaba el Éufrates con el Tigris desde hace siglos. No estaba recientemente en todo su esplendor, pero quizá con algún pequeño trabajo adicional de ampliación en alguna sección nos habría servido para pasar la flota del Éufrates al Tigris. Pero, como he dicho antes, los partos lo han desecado en diferentes puntos y lo han rellenado de tierra. En cualquier caso, he observado que el Naharmalcha desemboca al sur de Cesifonte y eso obligaría a la flota a tener que remontar el río en un lugar donde la corriente del Tigris es muy fuerte, lo que dificultaría enormemente las maniobras de la flota en su ataque a la ciudad.

Trajano suspiró. Luego preguntó:

—¿Y hacer nosotros un canal nuevo?

—Lo he considerado y he encontrado un punto donde los dos ríos, el Éufrates y el Tigris, apenas están separados por veinte millas. Pero hay varios inconvenientes. El primero y el más evidente es el asunto del tiempo: una obra así también precisaría bastante esfuerzo y meses sin descanso. Pero además hay un problema insoslayable que hace imposible hacer cualquier canal en ese lugar.

—¿Qué problema? —preguntó Trajano.

—El Éufrates, augusto, discurre a más altura en ese punto que el Tigris. La diferencia de niveles podría provocar que se desecara un río y se inundara el otro y todo su valle. Sería un desastre que además escaparía a nuestro control. Por eso los arquitectos de antaño hicieron el canal de los reyes, que es lo que significa Naharmalcha, más al sur, donde los niveles de los ríos son casi iguales.

—¡Por todos los dioses! —exclamó el emperador—. ¡No tengo recursos ni tiempo para construir una nueva flota en el Tigris! ¡No se puede usar el Naharmalcha y no se puede hacer un canal que una los dos ríos! Resumiendo: aunque tengo una magnífica flota aquí, apenas a doscientos pasos de donde estamos hablando, una flota con la que la capital parta caería rendida, no hay forma alguna de conseguir que estos barcos lleguen al Tigris.

Trajano solía mostrarse animoso ante cualquier contratiempo, de forma que su desesperación impactó en sus oficiales y el abatimiento se contagió con rapidez a los *legati*, quienes, cabizbajos, miraban al suelo sin saber qué decir.

—Yo no he dicho eso, César —añadió entonces Apolodoro de Damasco para sorpresa de todos.

—¿Qué es lo que no has dicho? —preguntó el emperador.

—Yo no he dicho que la flota del Éufrates no pueda llevarse hasta el Tigris en relativamente poco tiempo. Sólo he explicado que no puede hacerse por un canal.

—¿Y cómo piensas transportar cincuenta barcos, arquitecto, a lo largo de veinte millas de tierra? —preguntó Trajano exasperado—. ¿Volando?

Apolodoro, muy serio, negó con la cabeza. Luego sonrió e hizo una pregunta sencilla.

—¿Son los legionarios del César fuertes?

—Lo son —respondió el emperador enarcando las cejas, confuso.

—¿Muy muy fuertes? —insistió Apolodoro.

—Mis hombres son todo lo fuertes que haga falta —sentenció Trajano categórico.

—Entonces, augusto, no tenemos tiempo que perder.

Trajano había planeado conectar el Éufrates mediante un canal con el Tigris, de forma que pudiera llevar sus barcos río abajo por esta ruta (...). Pero al averiguar que el Éufrates discurría en este punto a una altura más elevada que el Tigris, no lo hizo, por temor a que el agua se escapara toda del Éufrates creando una inundación y dejando el río innavegable. Así que empleó máquinas para arrastrar los barcos a través del estrecho espacio que separaba los dos ríos.

DIÓN CASIO, libro LXVIII

94

LA DECISIÓN DE OSROES

Cesifonte
Verano de 116 d.C.

—¡Por tierra! ¿Cómo que por tierra? —preguntaba Osroes una y otra vez—. ¡Eso no es posible!

—Lo está haciendo, padre —le insistía Partamaspates—. Lo he visto con mis propios ojos: los barcos van sobre una gran base, como una balsa gigante con innumerables ruedas, de la que tiran caballos y legionarios. Han hecho cincuenta de esas gigantescas carretas. ¡Por Shamash! ¡Padre, es como si la flota enemiga navegara por la tierra que separa el Éufrates del Tigris! Van muy despacio, pero es cuestión de uno o dos días como mucho que consigan llegar con todos los barcos enemigos al Tigris. Han sabido elegir un punto donde los dos ríos navegan muy próximos el uno del otro.

Osroes lo había escuchado todo con los ojos muy abiertos. Se aferraba con la mano izquierda a su trono de oro con ansia, como si al asirse a él con mucha fuerza fuera más difícil derrotarlo. El índice y el anular de la mano derecha estaban en sus labios, una vez más resecos, ásperos. Apenas bebía agua desde que se había enterado de que Trajano no había muerto.

—Ahura Mazda nos ha abandonado —dijo al fin el rey de reyes en voz baja, aunque allí sólo estaba su hijo y la guardia personal del *Šāhān Šāh*—. Ahura Mazda, Shamash, Angra Mainyu, Anahita, Mitra... todos los dioses y las diosas nos han abandonado. Hasta el espíritu de Zoroastro parece lejos de nosotros. Trajano no sólo es invencible sino inmortal, o eso dicen todos en Cesifonte, y quizá lleven razón: derrotó a mis mejores arqueros en el Tigris, lo que nunca antes había conseguido ningún romano, y ahora sus barcos navegan por tierra. —Se llevó las yemas de los dedos índice y anular de ambas manos ahora a las sienes—. Primero Abgaro nos dice que está muerto, luego que no, que el imbécil de su hijo no pudo hacerlo al final, que el César lo sorprendió en el momento clave y todo el plan se fue abajo. Menudo plan estúpido y qué poca diligencia en su ejecución. Pero ya arreglaré yo cuentas con Abgaro y con su hijo Arbandes. Ya nos ocuparemos de la traición de Osroene en su momento. Ahora he de pensar bien. Y rápido. Hemos de encontrar una solución. Pero no la hay, no la hay aquí, hijo mío. No ahora. Hemos de retirarnos, sí, hemos de abandonar Cesifonte. Resistiremos en las montañas. Incluso a Trajano se le terminará por atragantar tanto territorio. En algún momento la larga cadena que aprovisiona a su ejército se quebrará y entonces regresaremos con todas nuestras tropas, pero ahora no. Ahora es imposible enfrentarse a ese maldito Trajano.

—Pues si mi padre cree que debemos huir —dijo Partamaspates— tendríamos que apresurarnos: las legiones avanzan junto a los barcos del emperador romano por el oeste, mientras que por el norte, a este lado del Tigris, las patrullas han avistado dos o tres legiones más, las que cruzaron el Tigris en Cizre, que avanzan también hacia Cesifonte.

Osroes dejó caer las manos sobre los reposabrazos de oro macizo del trono.

—Llevas razón: hay que salir ya mismo. Hay que salir a toda velocidad. —Acariciaba el trono de oro como sopesando si llevárselo o no: fue su decisión más difícil—. Lo dejaremos todo detrás. Que preparen la caballería. Nos marchamos de inmediato.

Partamaspates asintió, pero había algo pendiente.

—Voy a avisar a las mujeres —dijo el hijo del rey de reyes—. Hablaré con la *Bāmbišnān Bāmbišn* para que ponga en marcha los preparativos para desplazar a todo el séquito de mujeres y niños del *Šāhān Šāh*.

—¡He dicho que hemos de salir ya! —le gritó Osroes bajando del trono; le costaba dejarlo, pero no había otra solución. Ya lo recuperaría o ya forjaría otro nuevo con el oro que acumulara en años posteriores si es que los romanos se lo llevaban de allí. Miró con furia a su hijo—. ¡Voy a perder mi trono y tú me hablas de las mujeres! ¿Eres acaso un imbécil? ¡Por Ahura Mazda, por Zoroastro mismo! ¡No entiendes que las mujeres nos retrasarían!

—Pero, padre, no podemos dejarlas aquí, no podemos permitir que tus esposas, la reina consorte y la reina de reinas y todas tus otras esposas y tus hijas caigan en manos de los romanos: no podemos permitir que atrapen a tus hijas, a princesas de la dinastía arsácida.

—¡Claro que no podemos permitirlo, muchacho! ¡Eso nunca! ¡Matadlas a todas! —aulló Osroes sin un ápice de duda. Aquélla era una orden que no necesitó pensar ni un solo instante. Su rostro, no obstante, mostraba cierta pena al ver su trono de oro... pero no: llevarlo implicaría una carreta... tenían que salir a caballo, al galope...

Partamaspates se quedó mirando a su padre con la boca abierta. No era ajena a la dinastía arsácida aquella decisión final: entre los partos, en situaciones límite, en medio de brutales guerras civiles, quien perdía una gran batalla ordenaba en ocasiones la ejecución de todas las mujeres de su séquito, pues ralentizaban la huida hacia las montañas. Por supuesto, ningún contendiente quería dejar que el contrario se apropiara de sus esposas e hijas ya fuera para torturarlas o para incorporarlas como esclavas a su propio séquito de esposas e hijas, y crear nuevos enemigos al dejarlas embarazadas.

Partamaspates había oído hablar de esa costumbre, pero él era muy joven y no recordaba las guerras entre Vologases II —su primo y padre del Vologases que ahora estaba en rebeldía en el este— contra Pacoro II, su tío. En aquellos años también se ejecutaron brutalidades como la que acababa de ordenar su padre en aquel mismo instante.

Osroes veía que Partamaspates estaba paralizado, pero él ya había tomado todas sus decisiones y no pensaba permitir que ni siquiera su hijo, con su posible aversión a llevar a término aquella instrucción, fuera a ralentizar su huida. Se le acercó y le habló a la cara, muy muy cerca del oído. Sin elevar la voz, pero con la rabia perfectamente encauzada fluyendo salvajemente en la retahíla cruel de cada una de sus palabras:

—Vas a ir al palacio de las mujeres y personalmente dirigirás la matanza de todas y cada una de mis esposas e hijas. Se salvarán sólo los niños mayores, los que ya no están en el palacio de las mujeres. Hablarás con los eunucos y éstos te ayudarán porque les explicarás que ellos sí vienen con nosotros. Siempre es fácil encontrar nuevas esposas y engendrar con ellas más hijas hermosas y sumisas, hijo mío, pero no es sencillo encontrar un buen *šabestān* capaz de custodiarlas cuando nos son útiles y de ejecutarlas en momentos de extrema necesidad como el que nos ocupa. Verás como a ellos no les tiembla el pulso y como no dudarán ni un instante en ejecutar la orden que te acabo de dar. Cumplirás este mandato y antes de que el sol esté en lo alto te reunirás conmigo en la puerta principal de la muralla para partir hacia el este. Si no lo haces, te abandonaré junto con ellas en Cesifonte, pero que sepas que para cuando regrese, y te juro por el profeta Zoroastro, por Ahura Mazda y todos los dioses que pienso regresar, te daré a ti muerte el primero. Luego vendrán todos y cada uno de los romanos del mundo. No ha nacido aún el César, invencible o inmortal, que no vea yo replegarse hacia *Hrōm* por haber cometido el error de intentar lo que no se puede hacer: Partia nunca jamás pertenecerá a esa maldita y miserable loba romana. Ahora, hijo, ¿serás capaz de cumplir mis órdenes sin vacilar? El sol está ascendiendo rápido esta mañana. Las legiones avanzan contra Cesifonte y los barcos del enemigo, tú lo has dicho, navegan por la tierra de nuestros antepasados.

Partamaspates tragaba saliva, miraba al suelo y asentía lentamente.

—Quiero una respuesta, hijo.

—¿A todas? —preguntó sin levantar la mirada del suelo el joven príncipe, con un tono de ruego, de súplica—. ¿A Rixnu también, a tu favorita?

—A la *Šhar Bāmbišn* la primera —replicó su padre, feliz de acabar con la mujer que había presenciado su creciente impotencia en la cama. Le causaba alivio eliminarla.

—¿Y a Aryazate también? ¿A tu hija preferida?

—A ella también. ¿Te han quedado claras mis instrucciones? Los guardias, ante un gesto del rey de reyes, ya avanzaban hacia la puerta. Habían escuchado lo esencial y sabían que era momento de apresurarse para salir con vida de Cesifonte.

—Sí, padre: he entendido las órdenes —dijo Partamaspates como quien pronuncia la más horrible de las sentencias.

—Muy bien. Nos reuniremos en la puerta principal de la ciudad. Sé veloz. Las mujeres mueren con facilidad. Son débiles y, como aprenderás hoy, totalmente prescindibles.

En el palacio de las mujeres

Partamaspates entró, por primera vez desde que era adulto, en el palacio de las mujeres. El *šabestān* jefe, un eunuco ya entrado en años pero gigantesco, una enorme masa de músculos entremezclados con una protuberante barriga que no parecía tener fin, salió a su encuentro.

—Traigo una orden del *Šāhān Šāh* y hay que ejecutarla sin dilación —dijo el joven Partamaspates, quien, pese a los comentarios de su padre, no tenía para nada claro de qué forma iba a reaccionar aquel ciclópeo guardián.

—Las órdenes del rey de reyes deben cumplirse siempre —respondió el eunuco.

El príncipe parto se pasó la lengua por los labios antes de hablar de nuevo.

—El *Šāhān Šāh* ha dado instrucciones de partir de Cesifonte a toda velocidad. Los romanos se acercan desde el este y el norte y también traen una flota por el Tigris. Me ha dicho que os preparéis, pues desea que los eunucos, todos, nos acompañéis en el viaje a las montañas, pero antes se ha de dar muerte a las mujeres.

El *šabestān* no cambió la expresión seria del rostro. Ni siquiera parpadeó.

—¿A todas? —preguntó en busca de más precisión.

—A todas —confirmó Partamaspates.

—Bien —aceptó el *šabestān* jefe—. Contaremos con la reina de reinas.

—¿Asiabatum ayudará? —Partamaspates estaba perplejo.

—Oh sí. La *Bāmbišnān Bāmbišn* cooperará. Estoy seguro de ello. Siempre ha sido una firme defensora de las costumbres partas hasta las últimas consecuencias.

Y el eunuco dio media vuelta al tiempo que desenvainaba su espada. Dio una voz y varios eunucos más salieron a su encuentro.

—Nos vamos de Cesifonte con el rey de reyes —les explicó con rapidez—, pero antes hemos de eliminar a todas las esposas y las hijas del *Šāhān Šāh*. Es su orden. La instrucción viene por boca del príncipe Partamaspates.

Todos asintieron y desenvainaron las espadas.

Había dos muchachas junto al estanque, hablando con sosiego, ajenas a todo lo que ocurría en la ciudad. En el palacio de las mujeres no había ventanas al exterior y no se veía a los jinetes del *Šāhān Šāh* reuniéndose con celeridad frente al palacio del rey de reyes para partir hacia el este. Las muchachas, simplemente, no sabían nada.

—¿Empezamos ya? —preguntó uno de los eunucos más jóvenes.

El *šabestān* jefe vio a las dos muchachas.

—Sí.

Sin dudarlo, el eunuco más joven se acercó a las incautas princesas, cogió a una por el pelo, por la espalda, tirando de la cabeza de la chica hacia arriba y pasó el filo de su espada por el cuello. No hubo gritos. Todavía no. Su compañera estaba petrificada. De tanto terror no le salía la voz. Otro eunuco la sorprendió por la espalda también e hizo lo mismo con ella. Sus asesinos soltaron los cabellos de sus víctimas y los cuerpos de las muchachas cayeron a plomo sobre el estanque. Su sangre empezó a teñir de rojo el agua.

Partamaspates lo contemplaba todo boquiabierto. Él había guerreado y matado enemigos en combate, pero aquello era diferente. Sentía que el estómago se le estaba revolviendo.

Asiabatum apareció por un extremo del patio del estanque y se dirigió a los eunucos con un puño en alto, como si fuera a luchar.

—Es orden del *Šāhān Šāh* —dijo el *šabestān* jefe—. El rey de reyes parte ahora mismo de Cesifonte. Las mujeres no van.

Asiabatum bajó el puño.

Se quedó quieta un momento. No miraba a las jóvenes recién ejecutadas. Necesitaba unos instantes para pensar. El eunuco gigante esperó. Si la *Bāmbišnān Bāmbišn* cooperaba todo sería mucho más fácil y, sobre todo, mucho más rápido.

Asiabatum se dirigió a Partamaspates, que, aunque pálido, permanecía en pie.

—¿Osroes ha dado la orden? —preguntó la mujer.

—Sí —respondió Partamaspates lacónicamente.

—Entonces debe hacerse —aceptó Asiabatum y se dirigió al *šabestān* jefe—. Yo os acompañaré habitación por habitación, pero todo se hará sin ultrajar a ni una de las mujeres, sean jóvenes, mayores, niñas o niños pequeños.

El gran eunuco asintió. Y estaba encantado. Con Asiabatum al frente de toda la operación acabarían muy pronto y eso les permitiría llegar a tiempo de unirse con Osroes, pues temía que el rey de reyes no los esperara si se retrasaban. El *šabestān* conocía al *Šāhān Šāh* y no las tenía toda consigo de que éste fuera a esperarlos a ellos, ni siquiera de que fuera a esperar a su propio hijo, si no eran eficaces en acabar con todas las mujeres con rapidez.

Asiabatum dirigió al que ya era un nutrido grupo de eunucos, más de veinte, a la primera de las grandes salas donde estaban las jóvenes que esperaban ser casadas muy próximamente. Partamaspates sabía que su hermana Aryazate estaría allí y temía encontrársela. Había llegado a pensar en que si hubiera dispuesto de algo de tiempo podría haberla avisado de alguna forma para facilitar que huyera. Por otro lado, pensaba que aquélla era una idea impropia de un príncipe parto y que rayaba la traición. Eran sus costumbres. Peor sería que las mujeres cayeran en manos de los romanos y fueran ultrajadas por ellos o torturadas...

Empezaron los gritos. Las primeras no tuvieron ocasión de decir nada, pero en cuanto las otras vieron cómo los eunucos cortaban el cuello a sus compañeras empezaron a gritar... Partamaspates seguía repasando en su cabeza la orden recibida y sus motivaciones en busca de una justificación lógica... ¿Por qué no llevárselas? Pero no, claro que no.

Cuando entraron en otra sala, donde había niños, el príncipe parto vio cómo las que acababan de dar a luz se aferraban a sus niños recién nacidos y el resto a sus pequeños vástagos, fueran niños o niñas. No reparó en que las mujeres no hacían distinción a la hora de defender a su descendencia entre ni ños o niñas. No, no reparó en ello. Estaba centrado en justificar lo que estaba viendo, lo que él mismo había ordenado... no, no... esto lo había mandado su padre... pero él había hecho de mano ejecutora... los niños berreaban como cerdos antes del sacrificio. Algunos salían corriendo. A una niña la encontraron escondida por su madre en una gran tinaja. El *šabestān* jefe tumbó de una patada la gran tinaja, sacó de la misma a la criatura tirándole de los pelos. La pequeña le mordió con saña, pero él le cortó el cuello como al resto; mientras tanto, otro de los eunucos asesinaba a la madre. Pero Partamaspates había encontrado algo a lo que agarrarse y que daba sentido a lo que hacían: estaba claro que las mujeres no se desprenderían nunca de sus niños, y éstos sí que ralentizarían cualquier marcha hacia las montañas y eso no podía permitirse. Estaba claro que un *Šāhān Šāh* no podía depender de unos niños. Sí, la orden era lógica. Brutal quizá, descarnada, pero necesaria desde un punto de vista militar.

—Falta Rixnu —dijo Asiabatum con firmeza. La *Bāmbišnān Bāmbišn* tenía sangre en las manos. Partamaspates la había visto coger a varias niñas y abrazarlas fuerte para que les cortaran el cuello, facilitando así la labor de los verdugos eunucos—. Falta Rixnu —repitió.

Al príncipe parto le pareció percibir cierto arrebato de felicidad en la reina de reinas. Seguramente, a Asiabatum no le gustó nunca ver cómo crecía la influencia de la *Šhar Bāmbišn*, más joven e infinitamente más hermosa, sobre las decisiones de Osroes. Era probable que verla morir fuera algo que la hiciera feliz, algo bonito con lo que irse de este mundo pese a hacerlo en medio de aquella locura. «Falta Rixnu», pensó Partamaspates y eso le hizo ver que también faltaba Aryazate. Su hermana de dieciséis años no se encontraba en la primera sala, que era donde debería haber estado, pero el príncipe recordó que Aryazate había trabado una enorme amistad precisamente con Rixnu. Quizá estarían juntas. En ese momento, Partamaspates tomó una decisión, la única decisión propia que tomaba en mucho tiempo: si encontraban a Aryazate ésta moriría por su espada, no por la de ningún eunuco, y no sujetada por Asiabatum. Lo haría él.

Salón personal de la Šhar Bāmbišn

Rixnu estaba contando a Aryazate más historias sobre Babilonia, su ciudad natal, pero la *Šhar Bāmbišn* sólo necesitó oír los primeros gritos de una de las víctimas de la primera sala, para entender qué estaba ocurriendo. Aryazate la miró sorprendida y asustada.

—Vamos a ver qué pasa —dijo la muchacha.

—No, no salgas —le replicó Rixnu con un tono tan firme como gélido. No era una sugerencia, sino una orden como las que daba siempre Asiabatum y Aryazate se sintió dolida. Rixnu nunca se había dirigido a ella de esa forma y, de pronto, intuyó que algo terrible debía de estar pasando y que por eso la *Šhar Bāmbišn* le había hablado de ese modo... Más gritos. Un torrente de ellos que llegaba a la cámara de Rixnu por todos los rincones. Aullidos desgarradores.

—¿Qué ocurre, Rixnu? —preguntó Aryazate con voz temblorosa—. ¡Por Ahura Mazda! ¿Qué está pasando?

La reina consorte miraba hacia la puerta. Ya apenas tardarían nada en llegar a donde estaban. ¿Podían intentar huir las dos juntas? No. Ella no sabía nadar. Nunca pensó que fuera a serle necesario. Pero Aryazate sí sabía. Siempre diferente a todas, la pequeña había aprendido allí mismo, en aquel muelle, de niña, jugando con su propio hermano Partamaspates. En el pasado. En otro tiempo. Cuando todo iba bien...

—¡Ven! —gritó Rixnu a la muchacha y abrió una puerta trasera, medio oculta por la pintura de las paredes—. Por aquí se va al embarcadero. Era mi camino cuando el rey de reyes me requería y no deseaba que nadie, ni siquiera Asiabatum, supiera que estábamos juntos. También era la ruta que Osroes usaba para entrar en nuestro palacio en medio de la noche, para estar conmigo o con cualquiera de sus otras esposas. Huye por ahí. —Pero Aryazate no se movía pese a que ya se oían las pisadas de los eunucos acercándose, al igual que los gritos de las que morían se percibían cada vez más próximos— ¡Corre, corre y que Anahita te proteja!

El grito de Rixnu pareció despertar a Aryazate de su estado de estupefacción total y empezó a caminar hacia la puerta trasera. En ese momento entraron los eunucos con su hermano al frente, seguido por la terrible Asiabatum.

—¡Corre! —repitió Rixnu, cerrando la puerta trasera en cuanto ella la cruzó.

—¡Matadla! —exclamó entonces Asiabatum señalando a Rixnu—. ¡Tendré el placer de verte morir antes de que sea mi turno! —aulló la reina de reinas como si escupiera cada palabra.

Rixnu se arrodilló, como para facilitar la labor de quien fuera a ser su verdugo, pero lo hizo frente a la puerta por la que acababa de huir Aryazate.

—¡Apartadla de ahí! —gritó el *šabestān* jefe, que de ningún modo quería que se le pudiera escapar ni una sola de las esposas o hijas, niños y niñas del rey de reyes.

Dos eunucos arrastraron a Rixnu a un lado, Partamaspates empujó la puerta con el hombro y está cedió de golpe. El príncipe cayó al suelo, pero se rehízo con rapidez. Aún pudo ver a su hermana corriendo hacia el muelle privado que usaba el *Šāhān Šāh* en sus noches de lujuria. Se volvió hacia los eunucos.

—¡Acabad con las dos! —les espetó con firmeza—. ¡Yo me encargo de ella!

Dio media vuelta y salió corriendo tras Aryazate.

El *šabestān* jefe frunció el ceño, pero una orden de un príncipe era innegociable. Miró a Asiabatum. La reina de reinas asintió y se arrodilló despacio, pero siempre sin dejar de mirar a Rixnu.

—De acuerdo —se reafirmó Asiabatum—, pero después de ella.

El *šabestān* jefe hizo una señal a los otros eunucos y uno de ellos puso el filo de su espada en el cuello de Rixnu. Ella levantó la cabeza y fijó los ojos en sus verdugos.

—Sois muy valientes contra mujeres y niños, pero pronto llegarán los romanos y serán sus espadas las que corten vuestros cuellos —dijo la reina consorte con odio inyectado en la mirada—. Con esa idea muero feliz.

La espada, inexorable, inclemente, se deslizó por su garganta.

La sangre de Rixnu fluía a borbotones. Ella cerró los ojos y cayó de lado. Para desazón de Asiabatum, la joven reina de reinas ni siquiera hizo una mueca de dolor en su muerte y seguía con la faz tan hermosa como en vida, pero Asiabatum no tuvo tiempo de más reflexiones, porque el *šabestān* jefe le estaba cortando ya su propio cuello. La mujer sintió que no podía hablar, que no podía respirar, que no veía nada...

Junto al muelle del palacio de las mujeres

Aryazate corría a toda velocidad hacia el muelle. El camino empedrado estaba repleto de escalones y también de varios cadáveres de otras princesas asesinadas que habían llegado hasta allí arrastrándose, medio moribundas, quizá con la misma idea de arrojarse al Tigris en busca de una escapatoria. Pero los eunucos cortaban los cuellos con precisión y las muchachas que yacían muertas en su camino hacia el muelle del palacio se habían desangrado todas antes de alcanzar su objetivo. Sin embargo, Aryazate estaba viva, intacta, sin heridas y corría como si fuera el viento del río, como un pájaro, como un águila que volara a ras de suelo.

Se volvió un instante para ver si la seguían.

Vio a su hermano que gritaba su nombre.

Tenía en su memoria todos y cada uno de los escalones del recorrido. Pero, distraída por la voz de su hermano, no se percató de uno de los cadáveres cruzados en su trayecto: tropezó con él y, aunque se estaba rehaciendo y recuperando la estabilidad, resbaló con el otro pie en la sangre roja que seguía manando del cuello de la muchacha muerta.

Su caída la detuvo.

Cuando se empezó a levantar, la espada de su hermano estaba ya en su cuello.

—Soy tu hermana, Partamaspates. Soy tu hermana... —dijo Aryazate entre sollozos. ¿Qué más podía decir? Si aquello no era suficiente para detenerlo, nada lo sería... pero siguió hablando porque notó que la espada, aunque en su garganta, estaba detenida, como si el arma dudara—. Jugábamos de niños, aquí mismo, en este palacio. Nos bañábamos juntos en ese mismo muelle. Nos atábamos con cuerdas para que el agua del Tigris no nos arrastrara sin control. Por Anahita, hermano, tú me enseñaste a nadar.

Partamaspates estaba petrificado. Había transmitido la brutal orden de su padre, pero miró el filo de su espada: brillaba al sol. Ella también se dio cuenta y volvió a hablar.

—Tu espada está limpia, hermano. No has matado a ninguna de las otras mujeres, ¿y me vas a matar a mí?

—Si no lo harán los romanos —dijo él, rehaciéndose, rebuscando en su cabeza las razones que lo forzaban a hacer lo que iba a hacer—. Te ultrajarán y luego te matarán. Créeme, esta muerte es mejor.

—Pero yo no quiero morir, no por ti. No por mi hermano.

—Volvió a llorar, aunque, de súbito, dejó de hacerlo y lo miró a los ojos, fijamente, con la fuerza que tiene una bestia acorralada—. Los dioses maldecirán este sacrilegio. Zoroastro no aprobaría nunca esto. Es una costumbre vieja de la que la nueva religión abomina. Seguro que mi padre dio la orden sin que estuvieran presentes ni los *magi* ni los sacerdotes de Zoroastro.

En eso su hermana tenía razón.

—Pero no puedo dejar que caigas en manos de los romanos —insistió él sin bajar la espada, que ya había hecho un pequeño corte en el cuello de Aryazate por el que manaba un poco de sangre. No era ni mucho menos una herida mortal. Todavía no. Era sólo el preludio del gran festín que iba a darse el arma del príncipe en poco tiempo. ¿O no?

—Los romanos no me cogerán viva, hermano. Aunque sepa nadar la corriente del Tigris es muy fuerte. Me ahogaré, pero no seas tú el que me mate. No seas tú... por favor...

Partamaspates retiró muy lentamente la espada. Ella se llevó la mano al cuello. Le dolía, pero podía respirar bien y se sentía fuerte. Aryazate no dudó ni un instante. Se levantó, salió corriendo, alcanzó el muelle y se tiró al agua.

Partamaspates se quedó allí quieto un momento. Vio que su espada tenía un poco de sangre. Poca. Con rapidez se agachó y la hundió en el cuello de la muchacha muerta con la que había tropezado su hermana hacía sólo unos momentos. La extrajo completamente manchada de sangre roja. Se incorporó y miró hacia el río. No pudo ver el cuerpo de su hermana. Era como si el río se lo hubiera tragado. La distancia con la costa era demasiado grande. Nadie, ni el más fuerte de los guerreros partos, podría cruzarlo con aquella corriente. El Tigris, el río veloz, era muy traicionero. Por eso se ataban con cuerdas de niños cuando se arrojaban a él. Aryazate estaría ya ahogándose.

Dio media vuelta.

En el fondo se alegraba de no haber sido él.

No sabía si estaba feliz o triste o aturdido.

Se cruzó con el *šabestān* jefe, que acudía a comprobar que todo se hubiera ejecutado hasta el final.

—Ya está hecho —dijo Partamaspates y exhibió su espada goteando sangre—. Su cuerpo ha caído al río.

Algo había en el tono de voz del príncipe parto que hizo que el eunuco frunciera el ceño. El *šabestān* pasó a su lado y siguió andando hasta llegar al muelle. Paseo por encima de las maderas mirando hacia el río. No veía el cuerpo de la joven princesa Aryazate.

—Se hace tarde —dijo Partamaspates a su espalda.

—Es verdad —admitió el eunuco olvidándose de la princesa desaparecida y preocupándose más por sí mismo—. Hemos de ir a la plaza frente al palacio del rey de reyes o nos quedaremos solos en Cesifonte sin guerreros que nos defiendan de los romanos.

Partamaspates y los eunucos salieron corriendo de aquel palacio sin mirar atrás.

Aryazate respiraba aceleradamente. Estaba asida a uno de los postes del muelle. Oculta para quien mirara desde el camino del palacio, pero no si alguien se asomaba desde arriba. Podía oír las pisadas de su hermano y del eunuco jefe y escuchaba sus palabras. Sabía que no podía intentar cruzar el río a nado. Era un suicidio y ella quería vivir. Vivir.

Su hermano y el *šabestān* se alejaban.

Aryazate se quedó allí, inmóvil, abrazada a aquel poste con todas sus fuerzas, sintiendo el Tigris deslizarse a su alrededor con la fuerza del agua de las montañas del norte.

Ella seguía allí.

Agarrada, quieta.

95

ENCUENTRO ENTRE DOS MUNDOS

Marinus nos dice que un macedonio[75] llamado Maes, también conocido como Titianus, mercader, hijo de mercader, anotó la distancia de este viaje [hasta la Torre de Piedra], aunque él mismo no llegó a Xeres, sino que envió a otra persona [para continuar el viaje].

CLAUDIO PTOLOMEO, I, XI.

En algún lugar de Asia central. Frontera entre el Imperio kushan y los protectorados más occidentales del Imperio han.
Verano de 116 d.C.

Tamura abrió los ojos cuando el sol ya estaba en lo alto. El agotamiento había podido con ella y el resplandor del alba no fue suficiente para despertarla.

Se levantó de un respingo y se pasó ambas palmas de las manos por la nuca. Sudaba. El sol calentaba mucho en aquella remota región del mundo. El cuerpo de Titianus seguía allí, tendido, boca arriba, con los ojos abiertos, mirando a ningún sitio. ¿Y su madre?

Fue junto a ella.

Parecía dormida, con los ojos cerrados, pero el corazón de Tamura se quedó helado. Ya había visto mucha gente muerta en su vida y podía reconocer un cadáver con rapidez.

Se arrodilló junto al cuerpo.

—Madre... —dijo.

---

75. «Macedonio» de cultura, pero según diversos autores (ver bibliografía) probablemente nacido en Siria, y por eso me he referido a él como sirio en la novela.

Cogió la mano de Alana despacio. Estaba fría pese al sol del mediodía.

—Madre —repitió y se echó a llorar.

Todos sus músculos vibraban mientras se derretía en lágrimas.

—Madre... —repetía intermitentemente, siempre sin soltar la mano de quien la había traído a este mundo, de quien la había amado, cuidado, protegido...

Su llanto duró un rato largo.

Hasta que se le secaron los ojos.

Se levantó despacio y oteó el paisaje.

Se concentró en pensar, mejor dicho: en intentar pensar algo. A sus padres les hubiera gustado que ella no se quedara allí, quieta, perdida, pero antes de que hubiera podido concluir nada sobre qué hacer, más allá de que deseaba enterrar a Titianus y a su madre, sobre todo a su madre, se dibujó en el horizonte un grupo de jinetes. Tamura habría llorado más de pura rabia si aquello le hubiera servido de algo y si aún le quedaran lágrimas, pero las dimensiones del desastre eran ya tan grandes como irresolubles. Su padre muerto, asesinado por Áyax; su madre muerta también y, para colmo, ella, su supuesta intrépida hija, embarazada de Áyax, había sido además tan torpe de no alzarse al amanecer para continuar la huida por la que Alana lo había arriesgado todo.

Miraba hacia Occidente protegiéndose los ojos del sol: eran los jinetes kushan. Una docena. Quizá más. Pensó en montar en los caballos e intentar huir de nuevo al galope, pero ya fuera por cansancio físico o por falta de ánimo, sola como estaba en medio de Asia, o porque los kushan ya la estaban rodeando, Tamura se quedó quieta, como una estatua, junto al cadáver de su madre.

—¡Ja, ja, ja! —empezaron a reír todos los soldados del imperio de Kanishka, en particular el oficial del puesto fronterizo, por satisfacción y de puro nervio, pues de no haber encontrado a los escapados muy posiblemente el castigo para él podría haber sido terrible. Pero el oficial ya estaba tranquilo y seguro de sí mismo: dos de los escapados estaban muertos y sólo quedaba en pie la muchacha.

La rodearon por completo.

El oficial empezó a preguntarse si no sería justo entretenerse, él primero y sus hombres luego, con la muchacha antes de enviarla de regreso, convenientemente encadenada, a Bagram. Su intento de huida bien merecía un escarmiento de ese tipo. No era cuestión de que se corriera la voz de que los puestos fronterizos vigilados por los kushan eran fáciles de sortear hasta para las muchachas.

El guerrero kushan al mando se dirigió a los otros y las risas volvieron a sonar en aquella estepa de pocos árboles, mucho calor bajo el sol y frío por las noches.

Tamura vio cómo desmontaban varios de los hombres y cómo se situaban delante y detrás de ella, a su izquierda y a su derecha. Si cargaba el arco ellos harían lo mismo. Optó por desenfundar su espada.

Las risotadas de los kushan fueron aún mayores. Dos de ellos apuntaron hacia Tamura con los arcos en tensión y sendas flechas astifinas orientadas hacia el pecho de la joven sármata.

—¡No! ¡La quiero viva! —dijo el oficial al mando. Y desenfundó también su arma. Se lanzó contra Tamura sin apenas darle tiempo a defenderse, pero la muchacha era veloz como una gacela y paró los golpes de la espada con tal brío que la resistencia inesperada de la joven fugitiva sorprendió al oficial y a todos sus hombres.

Tamura resoplaba de puro miedo.

El miedo.

Ella no tenía miedo a nada. Eso le había dicho al emperador Trajano hacía tanto tiempo, en otro mundo, en otro tiempo, y el emperador romano le había dado una respuesta enigmática que la muchacha recordaba ahora mientras mantenía la espada en alto en previsión de un nuevo ataque de los kushan.

«No tener miedo no hace a alguien valiente —así le había hablado el emperador de Roma—. Uno es valiente de verdad cuando conoce el miedo y es capaz de enfrentarse a él y superarlo. Eso es valor. Lo demás es imprudencia, locura. Pero no te preocupes. Un día conocerás el miedo, cuando menos lo esperes y de la forma más brutal e inesperada éste te encontrará. Nos encuentra a todos. Ése será el día en el que averiguarás si realmente eres valiente.»

Y ella ahora tenía mucho miedo: sin sus padres, perdidos en pocos días uno y otra, embarazada del asesino de uno de ellos, sola, rodeada por un grupo de guerreros kushan que lo más dulce que podían hacerle era matarla. Sí, estaba aterrada. Pero Tamura, quizá porque todo estaba ya perdido, quizá porque, simplemente, sí era valiente, se sobrepuso y empezó a dominar su pánico: si atacaba, al fin tendrían que matarla, y eso ahora le parecía lo mejor y también lo más digno para con el sacrificio de su madre. Por lo menos morir luchando y no siendo violada por uno tras otro de aquellos salvajes crueles.

Y se lanzó con su espada contra el oficial. Muy rápido.

Un ataque era lo último que aquel guardián de fronteras esperaba y la espada de Tamura encontró el pecho sin coraza de aquel oficial con increíble facilidad, penetró en él y los huesos crujieron. La sangre salió a borbotones cuando la muchacha tiró de su arma. El oficial kushan soltó la espada, que cayó al suelo, y se llevó las dos manos a la herida. Se desplomó de golpe. El resto de los hombres tardaron en reaccionar. Ella sabía que no debía darles cuartel y se lanzó contra otro, sorprendiéndolo también e hiriéndolo en un brazo, pero eran demasiados. No doce, sino hasta veinte kushan eran ya los que se habían reunido a su alrededor. Había matado a uno y herido a otro. El resto dio un par de pasos hacia atrás. Los arqueros apuntaban hacia ella. Tamura asintió para sí misma. Las flechas serían bienvenidas. Eso acabaría con ella y con la descendencia de Áyax a la vez.

—¡Vamos, dispara! —gritó Tamura en sármata, en latín, en griego—. ¡Disparad!

Y varias flechas mortales volaron clavándose con perfecta puntería.

Dardos brutales tan poderosos como los de los partos, sólo que los kushan no poseían arcos que pudieran disparar con potencia tan irrefrenable y los partos estaban a miles de kilómetros de allí luchando entre ellos o contra las legiones de Trajano. Los jinetes kushan cayeron uno tras otro abatidos por disparos certeros que llegaban desde la espalda de Tamura. La muchacha se volvió para mirar y observó que se aproximaba un regimiento de caballería con arqueros de un ejército desconocido para ella. Para cuando encaró de nuevo a sus enemigos, Tamura vio cómo los kushan que aún estaba vivos, no más de media docena, galopaban hacia el oeste como llevados por el viento.

La muchacha quedó de nuevo sola, en pie, rodeada ahora por más de una docena de cadáveres kushan además de los cuerpos sin vida de Titianus y de su madre. Los nuevos jinetes la rodearon de inmediato y la apuntaron con unos arcos extraños que ella no había visto nunca, como pequeñas catapultas que se sostenían en la mano, como arcos tumbados con una barra en el centro en la que los soldados recién llegados apoyaban las flechas que ahora la apuntaban.

Luego miró a los hombres en sí, a las caras, y observó que tenían los ojos más rasgados que hubiera visto nunca. Eran diferentes a las gentes de Bagram o incluso a los que vivían en el puesto fronterizo de Yarkand. ¿Quiénes eran? ¿Iban a matarla?

«El valor consiste en sobreponerse al miedo. Es entonces cuando se demuestra si uno es realmente valiente.»

Tamura, de pronto, comprendió muchas cosas que le habían enseñado Dión Coceyo y hasta el propio Trajano y, de inmediato, bajó la espada en señal de paz, de entrega, al tiempo que pronunciaba aquellas palabras en sánscrito que su viejo maestro griego le enseñara años atrás. Las mismas cuyo significado tanto tardó en revelarle y que ahora parecían ser la única posibilidad de supervivencia.

—*Adhīśvaras āhvāyaka.*

Y las repitió una y otra vez, sin descanso, como una letanía eterna. Y a esas palabras añadió el nombre que Buddhamitra le había dicho que significaba «Roma» para los hombres de Xeres.

—*Adhīśvaras āhvāyaka Da Qin.*

Los guerreros de aquel extraño regimiento la miraban confusos. Uno de ellos dijo algo y el resto bajó los arcos. Ya no la apuntaban, pero tampoco se movían. Otro dio media vuelta, dejó el círculo de jinetes y marchó al galope, como si fuera a buscar a alguien. Tamura tragó saliva. ¿Habría alguna persona que entendiera sánscrito? Miró entre los caballos y la muchacha no daba crédito. No estaba con un pequeño grupo de guerreros como los kushan que la habían perseguido: ahora había centenares, miles de hombres armados iguales a los jinetes que la rodeaban. Todo un ejército de Xeres avanzaba hacia ella. Estaba claro que quien gobernara aquel imperio no quería que los kushan entraran en él o en sus reinos vasallos. Tamura pensó que cuanto mayor fuese el ejército que se cruzaba en su camino, más posibilidades tendría de que hubiera alguien que la entendiera. Ella seguía repitiendo a intervalos regulares de tiempo sus palabras.

—*Adhīśvaras āhvāyaka Da Qin.*

Los jinetes la miraban pero no decían nada.

Esperaban.

Tamura bajó la espada. Nadie parecía que fuera ni a acercarse ni a alejarse. Empezó entonces a cavar con la espada en el suelo un hoyo ante la mirada de aquellos hombres, más intrigados por sus movimientos que nerviosos. Tamura había decidido aprovechar el tiempo de espera, hasta que llevaran a alguien que decidiera qué hacer con ella, para preparar con rapidez una tumba para su madre. No tenía nada claro lo que iba a pasar con ella y si podía, al menos, enterrarla, evitaría que los lobos o los buitres se la comieran. No importaba lo que hubiera dicho su madre; le había pedido que no la enterrase sólo para que pudiera huir con rapidez. Ahora todo aquello parecían ya palabras de otro mundo.

Había llovido en los últimos días y la tierra húmeda se extraía fácilmente, de forma que en poco tiempo tuvo terminado el agujero. Tamura sudaba por la frente, por los brazos, por los cuatro costados. Estaba sucia, cubierta de polvo y barro y sangre de los kushan con los que había luchado. Ante la atenta mirada de los jinetes han, arrastró el cuerpo de su madre hasta el agujero y, una vez depositado en su interior, con sus propias manos, con lágrimas en los ojos y un fuerte dolor en el vientre que no entendía, empezó a enterrar el cadáver de Alana. Apenas había terminado cuando se oyeron voces. Tamura se levantó. Los jinetes han se hicieron a un lado para dejar pasar un caballo montado por quien debía de ser un oficial muy respetado, pues se hizo un silencio sepulcral.

Tamura repitió las palabras que le enseñara Dión Coceyo y las que había aprendido de Buddhamitra.

—*Adhīśvaras āhvāyaka Da Qin.*

El oficial era alto, más que la mayoría del resto de los hombres han y tenía los ojos rasgados también, de una forma diferente. ¿Menos alargados que el resto? Desmontó y dio unos pasos hacia adelante, acercándose a ella. Tamura pensó que cubierta de tierra y sudor y sangre debía de resultar alguien bastante desagradable a quien mirar y, sin saber bien por qué, le supo mal que aquel hombre al que todos parecían respetar tanto la viera así.

Li Kan permanecía en pie y en silencio mirando a la muchacha. No entendía el significado de lo que la joven mujer repetía una y otra vez. Paseó los ojos por lo que había ante él: un grupo de guerreros kushan muertos, la mayoría por flechas de sus hombres, aunque dos tenían heridas de lucha. La muchacha era pequeña, pero se la veía ágil, en forma. Muy sucia. Sostenía una espada extraña, extranjera, pero que a Li Kan le trajo recuerdos que el general se guardó para sí mismo. Había también un viejo muerto y una tumba recién excavada. La espada de la joven tenía restos de tierra y barro. También se veía más barro en sus manos. Acababa de enterrar a alguien. Todo aquello era muy peculiar. ¿Quiénes eran aquella muchacha cubierta de tierra y sangre y aquel viejo muerto? ¿De quién era la tumba? Huían de los kushan. Eso podía ser bueno a los ojos del Imperio han, pero no necesariamente.

Un intérprete mayor, con el pelo gris, ya estaba junto al general.

—Pregúntale quién es —ordenó Li Kan.

Tamura escuchó, por fin, a alguien hablando en una lengua que ella entendía, al menos en parte.

—¿Entiendes lo que digo? —preguntó el intérprete han en sánscrito.

Tamura suspiró largamente. Era el primer alivio, mínimo, pero alivio, en días.

—Sí —respondió ella—. Mi nombre es Tamura —y repitió

el mensaje que había estado recitando desde hacía una hora a la espera de que alguien entendiera las palabras que Dión Coceyo le enseñara hacía años.

El hombre del pelo gris tradujo.

—Dice, mi *chiang-chün*, que su nombre es Tamura, o algo parecido, y...

—¿Y...? —inquirió el general con firmeza.

—Y que es mensajera del emperador de Da Qin.

Li Kan se quedó en silencio. Nadie se atrevía decir nada. Tamura tampoco. La muchacha se quedó muy quieta. Intuía que todo dependía de lo que aquel hombre al que todos obedecían decidiera hacer con ella. El oficial alto volvió a hablar con el hombre que traducía, y este último se dirigió a ella de nuevo.

—El *chiang-chün* desea confirmar que hemos entendido bien: ¿vienes realmente de Da Qin?

—Sí —insistió Tamura con aplomo—. Y traigo un mensaje del emperador de Da Qin para vuestro emperador.

El intérprete volvió a traducir con ojos de incredulidad y asombro. Pero sus palabras fueron fieles a las que había dicho Tamura.

Li Kan volvió a meditar en silencio. Estaba recordando las palabras que el asistente del ministro de Obras Públicas le dijo cuando lo enviaron a las regiones occidentales: «Una guerra puede estallar, si es que no ha empezado ya, entre An-shi y el remoto Da Qin... Cualquier mensajero, cualquier comerciante que nos aporte luz sobre este asunto es esencial... La emperatriz Deng desea estar bien informada sobre esto... La mayoría de los oficiales carecen de tu intuición para discernir lo que es importante de lo que no. Cuento con tu discreción para que me hagas llegar cualquier noticia sobre esta guerra».

A Li Kan le costaba convencerse de que aquella muchacha sucia y evidentemente asustada que se decía mensajera del remoto Da Qin pudiera ser, en efecto, importante para Fan Chun, pero tampoco quería pasar por alto algo que pudiera ser de interés para la emperatriz Deng. ¿Una muchacha? ¿Podía ser importante en el mundo una muchacha, por muy guerrera que aparentara ser? ¿No se reirían de él en Loyang? La joven, por puro miedo, podría estar, simple y llanamente, mintiendo, inventándose una historia fantástica para que la protegieran... Recordó entonces un pasaje de una de las cartas del asistente del ministro de Obras Públicas:

> *Sobre la cuestión de reunir información de aquella lejana guerra, piensa que a veces lo que nos interesa puede llegarnos de la forma más inusual y sorprendente; así que no debes menospreciar lo inesperado, por muy extraño que pueda parecer. Mantenme informado de cualquier suceso de la frontera que te resulte inusual.*

A Tamura aquel silencio se le hacía eterno. Estaba segura de que aquel oficial estaba examinándola y de que no le gustaba ni le convencía lo que veía. Y no sabía ya si era por los nervios, por el agotamiento o por qué, pero las piernas empezaban a temblarle. Comenzaba a sentirse muy débil, pero Tamura reunió fuerzas de donde ya no le quedaban para mantenerse firme, en pie, y esperar el veredicto de aquel oficial de aquel ejército desconocido...

Pero, decididamente, algo le estaba pasando por dentro. Y le dolía.

—Pregúntale a quién está enterrando en la tumba —dijo Li Kan al intérprete.

El hombre del pelo gris tradujo.

—A mi madre —respondió Tamura.

Cuando el intérprete le transmitió la respuesta de la muchacha, Li Kan se quedó aún más sorprendido, pero, pese a aquel nuevo dato extraordinario, él ya había tomado la decisión de enviar a aquella extraña joven a Loyang. Era mejor que Fan Chun se riera de su exceso de celo en cumplir sus mandatos que dejar pasar por alto algo o, en este caso, a alguien que, aunque sólo remotamente, pudiera ser relevante para el Imperio han.

Ante la revelación de que la tumba que la muchacha parecía haber excavado hacía sólo unos instantes era de su madre, Li Kan se volvió hacia un oficial que estaba tras él.

—*Pao chu* —dijo el general.

En cuestión de instantes, unos soldados llevaron todo lo

necesario a Li Kan: le entregaron unos trozos de bambú fresco y una pequeña antorcha encendida. El general dio varios pasos hacia Tamura. La muchacha, por pura inercia, dio los mismos pasos hacia atrás, aunque eso la alejaba de la tumba de su madre. También por puro instinto levantó la espada que tenía desenvainada. Los arqueros volvieron a apuntarle directamente al corazón. Li Kan levantó la antorcha y dio una voz. Los soldados bajaron las ballestas y Tamura también bajó su espada. Li Kan dobló una pierna hasta hincar su rodilla derecha junto a la tumba de Alana, depositó el bambú sobre la tierra aún húmeda y suelta que la cubría, lo prendió y dio un par de pasos hacia atrás. El *pao chu* de bambú fresco empezó a crepitar con fuerza haciendo un sonido que Tamura percibió como un ultraje al reposo eterno de su madre. La muchacha dio dos pasos rápidos y con una patada certera alejó el maldito bambú, aún ardiendo y crepitando, lejos de la tumba.

—¡Ooooh! —dijeron todos los soldados al unísono.

El intérprete tragó saliva. Tamura vio cómo su faz se tornaba totalmente blanca y dirigió entonces la vista al oficial jefe que había puesto el bambú ardiendo sobre la tumba de su madre: éste la miraba con furia en los ojos, pero contenida por una fuerza de voluntad muy bien adiestrada. Tamura no tardó en comprender que había hecho algo muy mal, pero no podía entender qué. Desde luego, pasara lo que pasase, no iba a permitir que ultrajaran la tumba de su madre de modo alguno. El dolor del interior de su vientre volvía a morderla por dentro.

—Has humillado al *chiang-chün* Li Kan —le dijo el intérprete en voz baja.

La muchacha sólo sentía dolor y no entendía nada.

—¿Quién es Li Kan? ¿Qué es un *chiang-chün*? —preguntó arrastrando las palabras. Le costaba hablar.

—*Chiang-chün* significa general y Li Kan es el general más importante del Imperio han. Nosotros quemamos bambú fresco sobre nuestros muertos más queridos porque el crepitar que hace al arder ahuyenta los malos espíritus. El general Li Kan se había arrodillado ante la tumba de tu madre en señal de respeto y te había honrado con su acto, pero tú, al darle una patada al bambú, al *pao chu*, lo has humillado como nunca nadie lo había hecho y, además, lo has hecho delante de sus hombres.

Tamura luchaba por mantenerse en pie, pero ya no podía más, no entendía más. Sintió la sangre, su sangre resbalando por sus muslos. Miró al general, pero éste estaba dando media vuelta y se alejaba.

—No lo sabía... —empezó la joven pero cada palabra era una tortura—; estoy muy débil...

Cerró los ojos.

Perdió el conocimiento.

Se derrumbó.

Sangre, mucha, brotando de entre sus piernas.

Laser e silphio profluens quo diximus modo inter eximia naturae dona numeratum plurimis compositionibus inseritur, per se autem algores excalfacit, potum nervorum vitia extenuat. feminis datur in vino et lanis mollibus admovetur vulvae ad menses ciendos. Pedum clavos circumscariphatos ferro mixtum cerae extrahit. urinam ciet ciceris magnitudine dilutum.

[El láser, un jugo que se extrae del *silphium*, tal y como ya hemos comentado, considerado uno de los mayores regalos de la naturaleza, se utiliza en muchos preparados medicinales. Por sí solo calienta y revive a personas entumecidas por el frío y, tomado bebido, alivia afecciones de los nervios. Se da también a las mujeres con vino y se usa con lana suave como un pesario (supositorio vaginal) para provocar hemorragias menstruales (de forma artificial).]

PLINIO, EL VIEJO, *Historia Natural,*
Libro XXII, capítulo XLIX

96

LA VICTORIA ABSOLUTA

Cesifonte
Principios de septiembre de 116 d.C.

La imponente flota de Trajano surcaba las aguas del Tigris: el majestuoso barco insignia, que navegaba en primer lugar desplegando enormes velas con el nombre del César trenzado con hilo de oro, impresionaba y aterrorizaba a partes iguales a los ciudadanos partos, que contemplaban cómo el emperador romano se acercaba a una ciudad, Cesifonte, que ya no tenía soldados para defenderse. Tras la gigantesca embarcación del César llegaban cincuenta naves más repletas de legionarios armados y dispuestos a todo. Y no sólo eso: si los habitantes de Cesifonte, abandonados por el *Šāhān Šāh*, por un rey de reyes que había huido con su ejército dejándolos desasistidos en el momento de mayor necesidad, miraban hacia el este, descubrían entonces que las legiones de Lucio Quieto, el lugarteniente del César romano, se aproximaban también hacia las murallas de la ciudad desde el otro extremo.

Cesifonte estaba rodeada, por tierra y por el agua.

Los ciudadanos se rindieron a la evidencia y decidieron ahorrarse el penoso sufrimiento de un asedio. En su lugar, optaron por confiar en la magnanimidad de un emperador extranjero invencible. No tenía sentido intentar resistir.

Las puertas de la capital de Partia se abrieron.

Trajano desembarcó y, a caballo, escoltado por los mejores *singulares* de su guardia pretoriana, con Aulo y Liviano a ambos lados, siempre atentos, siempre protegiéndolo, entró en Cesifonte.

Palacio de las mujeres

Aryazate había visto los barcos romanos aproximarse a la ciudad. Para todos sus compatriotas aquello era terrible, pues los eternos enemigos estaban a punto de entrar en la capital, pero para ella significaba que sus verdugos, los crueles eunucos del *Šāhān Šāh,* habían desaparecido. Y su maldito padre con ellos. Sí, la presencia de la flota romana implicaba que el rey de reyes y hasta su propio hermano Partamaspates estarían ya a mucha distancia de allí.

Aun así le costó reunir las fuerzas para trepar por aquel tronco del muelle del palacio de las mujeres. Lo hizo muy lentamente. Viendo la flota romana junto a los muros de Cesifonte, Aryazate, de pronto, se detuvo en seco. ¿Y si su padre hubiera ordenado que quedara algún *šabestān* en el palacio para matar a cualquier mujer superviviente? Parecía una locura, pero después de ver a Asiabatum colaborando en aquella sinrazón no le parecía imposible que hubiera algún eunuco suicida esperándola con una espada ensangrentada en la mano.

La muchacha llegó a lo alto del muelle y asomó la cabeza un momento para, de inmediato, volver a esconderse. Sus ojos parecían haber confirmado que el camino hasta el palacio desde el muelle estaba desierto. Sólo le había parecido ver el cuerpo tendido de alguna de sus compañeras asesinadas.

Volvió a asomarse.

No se veía nada.

Trepó del todo y empezó a andar por el camino hacia el palacio. Siempre encogida, temerosa, casi temblando. No sabía si era por el frío del agua del río en contacto con el viento de Cesifonte o por puro miedo, pero sentía espasmos por todo su cuerpo que no podía controlar.

Pasó por encima de los primeros cadáveres tendidos, inertes.

Procuró no mirar hacia abajo, pero patinó con la sangre, aún no seca del todo, y a punto estuvo de caerse. Se reequilibró con la habilidad de la juventud, pero decidió que tendría que mirar al suelo para evitar los charcos de sangre. No pudo entonces evitar ver las muecas de horror de sus compañeras sorprendidas por sus verdugos, tumbadas aún allí, en el camino, o en las primeras estancias del palacio por las que ya avanzaba. Sin casi darse cuenta, como en un sueño, llegó hasta la estancia donde había estado con Rixnu por última vez: la Šhar Bāmbišn yacía tendida, como todas las demás, pero con el rostro hacia abajo. Aryazate se descompuso. No podía resistirlo más. No era un desastre, como un terremoto o una inundación: se trataba de un exterminio ejecutado por aquellos que se suponía que debían protegerlas. Rompió a llorar y su cuerpo se convulsionó. Todo el silencio en el que había estado mientras había permanecido asida al poste del muelle, por temor a ser descubierta, se quebró de golpe y su dolor emergió por todos los poros de su piel.

—¡Asesinos! —gritó ya sin temor a ser vista por alguien; incluso si algún eunuco quedaba allí le daba igual: de pronto la muerte sería bienvenida por ella. ¿No era casi peor ser la única superviviente? Habría sido mejor no esconderse y morir con las demás. Rixnu muerta y todas sus hermanas y amigas. Hasta sintió lástima de la implacable Asiabatum, cuyo cuerpo estaba allí a unos pasos, también degollada. Cruel como los verdugos, pero víctima al mismo tiempo. La mente de Aryazate empezó a ver claro en medio del terror y el sufrimiento total. Era la clarividencia de quien lo ha perdido todo y que rápidamente instaura en su mente una nueva jerarquía de prioridades, un nuevo orden que dé sentido a la supervivencia.

»Asesino —dijo ahora en singular en un susurro que se deslizó por las paredes de aquella sala como una serpiente en busca de una presa. Sí, había pasado del plural al singular pero no por un descuido, sino por la necesidad que tenemos todos en medio de las mayores injusticias de buscar un culpable concreto en quien concentrar nuestra rabia y nuestra ansia de venganza completa. En este caso la búsqueda del culpable absoluto no fue difícil.

»Asesino —repitió Aryazate de nuevo en voz baja, posando la mano dulcemente sobre el pelo de su querida Rixnu primero y luego sobre la mejilla, girando un poco su cabeza para dejar de nuevo a la vista el más bello de los rostros. Pero era una faz helada. Separó la mano del cuerpo de la *Šhar Bāmbišn*. La más hermosa de las esposas del *Šāhān Šāh* llevaba horas muerta.

»Asesino —dijo por última vez pensando únicamente en aquél a quien hacía responsable de aquella matanza: su padre, el *basileús basiléon*, un rey de reyes incapaz no ya de defender a sus mujeres, sino tan siquiera de llevárselas en su huida. Esposas, concubinas, niños y niñas, todos muertos por orden de su maldito padre. Y Rixnu también. La dulce amiga, la que siempre la había consolado, había dado la vida por ella, para protegerla en el último momento.

Aryazate dejó de llorar.

¿Acaso las lágrimas eran la moneda justa con la que pagar a Rixnu por su inmenso sacrificio?

La joven princesa parta negó en silencio con la cabeza. Luego se quedó perfectamente inmóvil. Volvió a hablar en un susurro.

—Muerto, he de verte muerto y con la cabeza a mis pies —dijo mientras se levantaba lentamente y se ponía a caminar de nuevo, pisando la sangre de sus hermanas, sorteando los cadáveres de mujeres y pequeños, andando sin rumbo hacia no sabía dónde. Pero ¿cómo una princesa de dieciséis años, desarmada y sin ejército, podría con un rey de reyes armado, escondido en las montañas, mortífero, cruel, inmisericorde...? Oyó entonces ruido y quiso esconderse, pues ahora que anhelaba venganza, la muerte ya no era tan bienvenida por su corazón, pero no hubo tiempo de nada. Sus pensamientos oscuros la habían distraído y sus sentidos no se habían percatado de la llegada de los legionarios hasta que fue demasiado tarde. Una docena de veteranos de la legión V, que pasaban por encima de los cadáveres de las mujeres y los niños, a los que miraban con ojos grandes de asombro, la encontraron allí, sola, en pie, junto al cadáver de otra mujer, la más hermosa de cuantas habían visto. Tanta era la belleza de Rixnu que ni la muerte pudo turbarla en su macabra visita. Tanta hermosura que los legionarios tardaron en darse cuenta de que la joven que estaba en pie también era muy bella.

Muy joven.

Muy deseable.

Nadie dijo nada durante unos momentos que se hicieron

interminables para todos, romanos y princesa parta, hasta que Aryazate habló en griego.

—Quiero ver a vuestro César —y lo dijo con el aplomo no de una niña, ni siquiera de una joven mujer que se sabe muy hermosa, sino con la fuerza de una princesa, hija de reyes de una dinastía centenaria.

Los legionarios, con el ansia insatisfecha de hacía meses, se miraban entre sí inquietos. No entendían griego. Las palabras no podían detenerlos. ¿Podían poseerla y luego degollarla como a las demás? Por un cadáver más nadie diría nada.

Se acercaron lentamente a la muchacha. Aryazate supo leer sus miradas y comprendió que antes de la muerte habría más horror en aquella sala, junto al cadáver de Rixnu.

Aryazate volvió a hablar elevando la voz. Tenía que haber alguien que la entendiera. No tenía más defensa que su voz.

—¡Soy Aryazate, hija del rey de reyes, princesa de Partia! ¡Nadie puede tocarme o la maldición de Ahura Mazda caerá sobre todos vosotros, perros malditos!

Pero los legionarios no la entendían y aunque la hubieran comprendido nada temían de dioses extranjeros de reyes derrotados. Se acercaron aún más. Podían oler la mujer que había dentro de aquella túnica aún empapada por el agua del Tigris. Y les gustó aquel aroma joven, intenso, fuerte...

—¿Qué pasa aquí?

Todos se detuvieron en seco y dieron varios pasos atrás.

La voz del *legatus* Lucio Quieto congeló a los legionarios, que se tragaron sus ansias como quien engulle un mal trago con rapidez para que pase lo antes posible.

—¿Qué pasa aquí? —repitió Quieto al ver a la joven muchacha en pie, firme, con los ojos muy abiertos, mirándolo fijamente.

Palacio imperial de Cesifonte

En el centro de la ciudad, Trajano cruzó las lujosas estancias del palacio del rey de reyes, ahora un fugitivo escondido con su ejército en algún lugar del Oriente más lejano.

—Se ha escapado antes de que pudiéramos bloquear su huida —dijo Liviano al César.

—No te preocupes —le respondió Trajano con tranquilidad—. Ya le daremos caza. Al final caerá, como caen todos los cobardes. Ahora acompáñame.

Y Trajano entró, siempre escoltado por el jefe del pretorio y por el tribuno Aulo en el salón del trono del *Šāhān Šāh* de Partia. Al fondo se veía el inmenso asiento de oro macizo. Marco Ulpio Trajano anduvo el espacio que lo separaba de aquella gigantesca *cathedra* dorada y, sin dudarlo, se sentó, y con él toda Roma, en el trono imperial de Partia. Y a sus hombres aquel gesto, después de tres años de campaña en Oriente, les supo a gloria.

Trajano señaló entonces hacia una de las esquinas de la gran sala.

Liviano y Aulo se volvieron para ver qué había llamado la atención del César.

Y lo vieron: allí, en pie, había un estandarte de una legión romana olvidada en el tiempo.

Aulo se acercó, lo cogió y lo acercó al emperador.

—¿Será de la legión de Craso? —preguntó el tribuno.

—Seguramente —confirmó Trajano.

—Entonces la historia de la legión perdida es toda cierta —añadió Liviano.

—Toda cierta —repitió Trajano sin dejar de mirar aquel viejo estandarte con el águila repleto de polvo, historia y derrota—. Y éste es su final —sentenció el César—: Enviaremos el estandarte de la legión de Craso de vuelta a Roma. Eso impresionará a mis amigos y acallará a mis enemigos en el Senado.

De pronto entró Lucio Quieto en la sala.

—¿Qué te parece, mi buen Lucio? —le preguntó Trajano antes de que el norteafricano pudiera decir nada—. Estoy sentado en el trono de oro de Partia y hemos recuperado el estandarte de la legión perdida.

—Por Júpiter, todo me parece perfecto, César —respondió Quieto y no dijo más durante unos instantes. Todos, incluido el que acababa de llegar, querían saborear aquella visión del emperador Trajano sentado en el trono de Osrocs y ver el estandarte de la legión de Craso en manos, de nuevo, de Roma.

—Hay alguien que quiere ver al emperador —dijo al fin el *legatus* norteafricano.

—¿Alguien? ¿Quién? —preguntó Trajano genuinamente intrigado, pues ya había hablado con una especie de delegación de los ciudadanos de Cesifonte que no habían podido o no habían tenido tiempo de emprender la huida y le habían implorado que se respetaran sus propiedades, sus hijos y sus mujeres (la petición había venido formulada en ese orden), en compensación por no haber opuesto resistencia alguna y haber abierto las puertas de la ciudad. Algo a lo que él se había comprometido. ¿Quién podía quedar aún en la ciudad con autoridad suficiente como para atreverse a solicitar una audiencia con el César?

—Es la hija de Osroes —se explicó Quieto.

Todos se miraron entre sí.

—¿Y por qué no la has traído contigo? —inquirió Trajano.

—La princesa prefería permanecer junto al cuerpo muerto de una amiga, o eso he entendido. El emperador sabe que mi griego no es muy bueno. En cualquier caso, creo que es conveniente que el César vea lo que ha ocurrido en el palacio de las mujeres.

Trajano se levantó del trono, pero se volvió para admirarlo una vez más. Costaba despegarse de él.

—Nos lo llevaremos a Roma —dijo, pensando en lo que estaba llamado a ser el mayor triunfo que hubieran visto nunca los ciudadanos de la capital del Imperio; luego miró a Quieto—. Los senadores, todos y cada uno de ellos, especialmente los que más han dudado de esta campaña, han de ver, Lucio, que nos hemos traído hasta el trono mismo de Partia. —Y sonrió.

—Así debe ser, César —respondió el norteafricano sonriendo también.

Trajano cruzó la sala de audiencias y, siempre escoltado por Aulo, Liviano y el propio Quieto, se adentró en las calles semidesiertas del que hasta entonces había sido el gran bastión del Imperio parto. Los habitantes que aún quedaban en la ciudad se habían atrincherado en sus casas rogando a Ahura Mazda y al profeta Zoroastro que el emperador romano cumpliera con su palabra de respetar sus vidas y sus propiedades. Nadie los había atacado, pero les costaba creer que el invasor pudiera ser con ellos clemente y más magnánimo que su propio rey de reyes, Osroes, que los había abandonado.

Trajano cruzó la ciudad y la parte del río que separaba Cesifonte de la pequeña isla donde estaba el palacio de las mujeres del séquito imperial parto. Mientras navegaban por el río, Lucio Quieto informó al emperador sobre todo cuanto había visto en el lugar hacia el que se aproximaban.

El emperador de Roma desembarcó en el muelle donde hasta hacía muy poco atracaban los barcos de la familia real arsácida.

Echó a andar.

Había legionarios romanos apostados a ambos lados del camino, firmes ante su César.

Trajano reparó de inmediato en que había un cadáver a un lado de aquel sendero. Y no era de un hombre, lo que encajaba con el sorprendente relato de Quieto, que lo seguía de cerca. El César no dijo nada y siguió avanzando. Entró en el palacio y encontró más cuerpos de mujeres degolladas. Los había por todas partes. Luego empezó a ver los cadáveres de los niños. Todos habían visto mujeres y pequeños muertos antes, pero nunca tantos juntos, en medio de un palacio tan ricamente adornado, y todos degollados, como si se hubiera llevado a cabo una larga y lenta ejecución sin cuartel, sin piedad ni misericordia.

Trajano miró a su alrededor. Veía a niños abrazados a sus madres, todos degollados. Todos muertos. El suelo estaba empapado de sangre por todas partes y era fácil resbalar sobre el mármol allí donde el líquido rojo permanecía aún fresco.

—¿Contra quién luchamos? —preguntó entonces Trajano—. ¿Quién puede ser capaz de algo así contra su propia gente, contra su propio séquito, su familia?

Nadie respondió.

En ese momento llegó un grupo de legionarios custodiando a una mujer muy joven.

—¿Es ésta? —preguntó Trajano en voz baja a Quieto.

—Sí, augusto —respondió el *legatus* norteafricano—. Según lo que me dicen todos es la única que hemos encontrado con vida.

—Supongo que estoy ante el emperador de Roma —dijo Aryazate en griego, con decisión, sin muestra alguna de miedo ni de sumisión.

A todos les sorprendió que la muchacha se atreviera a hablar sin que el César se hubiera dirigido a ella. Hasta el propio Trajano la miró con asombro.

—Ante él estás —confirmo el César también en griego—. ¿Eres, de verdad, hija de Osroes?

—Así es, César —respondió la joven, siempre con una extraña serenidad.

Hubo un breve silencio. Trajano la miró de arriba abajo. A él no le interesaban las mujeres desde un punto de vista sexual, pero aquello no era impedimento para que pudiera apreciar la belleza de una princesa parta, así como su fortaleza en tiempos de destrucción y sangre.

—¿Qué ha pasado aquí? —preguntó el emperador—. Mis hombres no son responsables de estas muertes. Yo no tengo por costumbre ejecutar a mujeres y niños y mis oficiales lo saben y no permiten semejantes actos a mis legionarios. No es mi forma de hacer la guerra, a no ser que se me traicione.

—Esto ha ocurrido por orden de mi padre —explicó la muchacha. La voz empezó a fallarle por momentos, por lo que se vio obligada a hablar muy despacio. No quería llorar más, y menos ante el emperador de Roma—. Los partos, César, no tienen por costumbre llevarse a sus mujeres y niños cuando se retiran. Creen que ralentizan su marcha. Pero tampoco quieren que éstas caigan en manos de sus enemigos. Por eso... esto.

—Pero tú estás viva.

—Me escondí. Tenía miedo a la muerte.

—¿Y por qué has salido ahora de tu escondite? —inquirió Trajano.

La muchacha se permitió una sonrisa que más pareció una mueca cínica, sorprendente en alguien tan joven.

—No era mi escondite un lugar en el que pudiera ocultarme por mucho tiempo más, César, y además... —Pero no terminó la frase.

—¿Además...? —insistió Trajano.

—Además... ya no temo a la muerte. Todas mis hermanas y mis amigas están muertas, ejecutadas por orden de mi padre. He visto a mi propio hermano entre los verdugos. Sea de la forma que sea, la muerte que desee darme el César de Roma será bienvenida por mí. Sólo quiero reunirme con los espíritus de mis hermanas, pues lo único que pensé que podría dar sentido a mi vida es algo que ahora está ya fuera de mi alcance.

Trajano negó con la cabeza lentamente.

—No seré yo quien ordene la ejecución de una princesa parta, pero me gustaría que esta decisión no aumentara tu infortunio ni tu tristeza. Me gustaría poder hacer algo para mitigar un poco el enorme sufrimiento que padeces.

—Sólo hay dos cosas que podrían proporcionarme consuelo, pero no creo que el César sea capaz o tenga la disposición para hacerlas.

—¿Cuáles?

—Que el emperador abandone Partia y sus reinos vasallos sería una —afirmó la joven con seriedad.

Trajano no se molestó. Era una reclamación lógica en boca de una princesa que había sido educada como tal.

—No puedo hacer lo que me pides, pero puedo intentar ser un gobernante menos temible de lo que suponéis tú y tu pueblo. Pero has dicho dos cosas. ¿Cuál es la otra que piensas que tampoco puedo cumplir?

—Que el emperador romano capture un día a mi padre y lo mate ante mis ojos. Amo Partia, pero odio a quien por no saber defenderla ha condenado a muerte a niños y mujeres indefensas.

Quieto, Liviano y el resto de oficiales que entendían algo de griego asistían asombrados ante aquel intercambio de frases henchidas de sentimiento y furia contenida que cruzaban la princesa parta y el emperador.

—Lo de capturar a tu padre es algo que sí está en mis manos, y si lo ejecuto, te garantizo que será ante ti —aseguró

Trajano—. Entretanto, quedarás bajo mi protección. Sólo es cuestión de tiempo que consigas tu venganza.

La muchacha, para sorpresa de todos, incluido una vez más el mismísimo Trajano, negó con la cabeza y volvió a hablar cuando el emperador parecía haber dado por terminada ya aquella conversación.

—El César no debería infravalorar a mi... padre. —A Aryazate le costó pronunciar aquella palabra otra vez; antes la había usado por pura inercia; pero añadió aún algo más—: Que Osroes se haya retirado no quiere decir que hayáis terminado con él. Alguien que ha ordenado estas ejecuciones para facilitar su huida es capaz de regresar de entre los mismísimos muertos y morder de nuevo a quien cree que lo ha derrotado. El César piensa que ha vencido y no es así. Aún no.

Trajano asintió lentamente, como si asimilara aquel aviso, pero no dijo nada y se mantuvo en silencio mientras sus hombres, a una señal suya, escoltaban a aquella joven en dirección a la salida.

Lucio Quieto se acercó al emperador y le habló en voz baja.

—¿Crees en esa advertencia?

—Es una mujer muy joven, casi una niña —respondió Trajano con serenidad—. Y está aterrorizada, trastornada por el horror que ha vivido. No está en condiciones de evaluar nada. No es una guerrera o una gladiadora acostumbrada a la lucha y los cadáveres. Debe de ser la primera vez que la guerra llega tan cerca de ella y no piensa con frialdad. Y, la verdad, por Cástor y Pólux, mi querido Lucio, no veo yo que podamos temer mucho ya de Osroes. La sangre de sus mujeres y niños sólo me hace ver cuán desesperada ha sido su huida.

Lucio Quieto asintió. Todo cuanto decía Trajano tenía perfecto sentido y, sin embargo, el norteafricano, en el cénit de sus facultades, unos años más joven que el César, militar hasta la médula, intuitivo y despierto, presentía que quizá las palabras de aquella princesa podían contener más verdad que locura.

Roma
Principios de otoño de 116 d.C.

Serviano se sentó frente a la mesa del *tablinum* de su vieja *domus* familiar en el centro de Roma. Acababa de regresar de la última sesión del Senado. Los *patres conscripti* habían designado a Trajano, por segunda vez, *Parthicus*, le habían reconocido el derecho a una nueva aclamación como *imperator* por las legiones de Asia, la decimotercera de su principado y, más aún, le habían reconocido el derecho a celebrar no ya uno sino tantos triunfos como desease para conmemorar la reciente caída de Cesifonte y las sucesivas anexiones de Armenia, Mesopotamia, Asiria y, ahora, la provincia de Babilonia.

Serviano suspiró. Luego, cogió un *papiro* nuevo y empezó a escribir.

A Publio Elio Adriano, gobernador de Siria:

La nuestra es una causa perdida. La entrega en el Senado del estandarte de la legión perdida de Craso, recuperado por el ejército de Trajano, es el fin de nuestros planes. Nadie nos apoyará ahora.

Julio Urso Serviano

Breve. Por escrito no quería ser más preciso. Tampoco era necesario. Las noticias de todo lo decidido aquella mañana en el Senado llegarían pronto al sobrino segundo del César por correo imperial. Eso sería suficiente para que entendiera. Serviano dobló el *papiro* lentamente. Era como si con aquella carta se pusiera fin a un gigantesco sueño que había incluido, en los momentos de mayor optimismo, conseguir que alguien de su familia, en un futuro no muy lejano, hubiera llegado a ser César. Delirios absurdos de grandeza. No entendía cómo Adriano podía ni tan siquiera haber llegado a sugerir tales cosas. Trajano era invencible y no importaba lo lejos que se encontrara de Roma con sus legiones: era el emperador indiscutible, con amigos en el Senado, con el Imperio controlado y con las legiones rendidas a sus pies. Era cierto que había algunos problemas en las fronteras de Britania y el Danubio, pero ante la enormidad de las victorias del César, aquellos escarceos de britanos o sármatas iaziges resultaban insignificancias.

Vertió cera de una vela y presionó con su anillo sobre ella para sellar la misiva.

Se levantó. Suspiró de nuevo.

Así terminan los sueños.

Carax
Otoño de 116 d.C.

La flota imperial atracó en Carax, en las costas mismas del golfo Pérsico. El emperador fue el primero en pisar tierra. Liviano y Aulo lo escoltaron mientras descendía del gran buque insignia.

Trajano se detuvo un instante y miró a su alrededor: pescadores, marineros de mil lugares diferentes, mercaderes, mujeres de toda condición, desde esclavas hasta esposas ricamente enjoyadas, niños, niñas. Miles de personas estaban inmóviles y en silencio en aquel inmenso puerto. Ninguno de ellos había opuesto resistencia ni pensaba oponerla al gran César de Roma. Allí todos eran marinos o comerciantes, cuando no ambas cosas, y lo único que les interesaba era que el comercio siguiera fluyendo entre su ciudad y los confines de la India o de la aún más remota Xeres.

Bajo la mirada atenta del jefe del pretorio, varias centurias de legionarios desembarcaron y velozmente fueron apostándose a lo largo de todo el muelle para interponerse entre aquel gentío de curiosos y el emperador. Trajano caminó con lentitud. No lo vitoreaban, pero tampoco lo miraban con gesto amenazador o de disgusto. Los únicos que podrían haber supuesto un problema, los soldados imperiales de Partia, fieles a Osroes, habían desaparecido hacía semanas, casi al mismo tiempo de la caída de Cesifonte. Desde entonces todos allí esperaban la llegada de aquel César romano, de quien se decía, entre otras muchas cosas, que era inmortal y todopoderoso. Ciertamente nunca se había visto una flota tan imponente como la romana en aquella bahía desde... nadie podía recordar desde cuándo.

El emperador, por su parte, repasaba en su mente la última carta del Senado: le ofrecían una aclamación como *imperator*, una más, la decimotercera y, nuevamente, el título de *Parthicus* que él rechazara el año anterior. Esta vez había aceptado ambas, la aclamación y el título. Ahora ya no había duda de que Partia estaba completamente subyugada. Apresar a Osroes era algo secundario. Trajano sonreía satisfecho mientras seguía caminando por aquel gran muelle. Era bueno que lo vieran seguro de sí mismo. Y no, no debían temer nada de él. Trajano se consideraba el más interesado en que el comercio con India y Xeres siguiera fluyendo desde allí. De hecho, por ese comercio había dado comienzo toda aquella guerra. ¿Armenia? Una bonita excusa y un territorio rico, pero no lo primordial: lo relevante era que habían eliminado a uno de los grandes intermediarios entre Roma y Xeres. Todos los aranceles que cobraban antes los partos ya no saldrían de las arcas de Roma. Más bien al revés: ahora sería Roma la que controlaría todo aquel inmenso y creciente comercio entre Oriente y Occidente. Se preguntaba quién de entre su familia o de entre sus más fieles colaboradores era capaz de entender lo que estaba haciendo. Adriano, desde luego, no. Quieto quizá intuyera algo, pero debía hacérselo ver con claridad. ¿Plotina? Pudiera ser. Su esposa más sabía cuanto más callaba, y últimamente callaba mucho. Pocas cartas de ella.

Trajano se detuvo ante un gran altar en cuyo relieve se veía lo que parecía ser un emperador parto siendo investido como tal por alguien poderoso. Pero ¿quién podría ser más poderoso que un emperador? ¿Un dios? Sí, quizá aquella deidad del altar fuera Ahura Mazda, de la que tanto hablaban los sacerdotes partos.

Como era habitual en aquel muelle, junto a aquella imagen y su gran altar de piedra, aunque a una distancia prudencial por respeto, había fardos de todo tipo de productos: especias, cereales, frutos secos... y Trajano, algo sudoroso por aquel lento paseo bajo el sol del golfo Pérsico, inclemente incluso en otoño, se sentó sobre uno de aquellos sacos, copiando así, sin él saberlo, el gesto que diecinueve años antes un viajero chino llamado Kan Ying había hecho en su truncado periplo rumbo a Roma desde la remota y, para el propio César, desconocida Loyang.

Trajano nada sabía del viaje de aquel enviado de la corte han a quien los kushan y los partos impidieron llegar a Roma. El César, allí sentado, empezó a considerar el futuro y sus enormes posibilidades tras aquellas tres campañas victoriosas en Oriente: había eliminado a los partos como intermediarios en el comercio con Xeres sin la colaboración de los kushan, que, pese a la embajada enviada a Roma hacía años, no parecían haber atacado con saña a los partos desde su extremo del mundo. ¿Tendría sentido seguir avanzando hacia Oriente, hasta llegar a la mismísima India, igual que había hecho Alejandro siglos atrás?

Aquí Trajano miró un momento al suelo, carraspeó y escupió. Se sentía viejo. Le dolían los huesos y había días en los que se levantaba con aquel terrible dolor de cabeza que parecía no abandonarlo nunca...

—Si tuviera diez años menos... —dijo en voz baja.

Ni Aulo ni Liviano lo oyeron. Estaban pendientes de la guardia pretoriana, del gentío, de los legionarios. Trajano volvió a fijar los ojos en el suelo: tenía a Quieto. Él supondría esos diez años que le faltaban. Su brazo derecho, su más leal hombre, podría conseguir aún más.

El emperador miró entonces hacia el mar: una nave, la última de aquella temporada, se dibujaba aún en el horizonte, navegando rumbo, precisamente, hacia la India. ¿Qué habría sido de sus mensajeros enviados a Xeres? ¿Qué sería del mercader Titianus, del centurión naval Arrio, del gladiador Marcio, su esposa sármata y, sobre todo, qué sería de aquella niña, casi mujer, Tamura, a la que confió su mensaje secreto para el emperador de Xeres? Trajano negó con la cabeza. Aquella misión había sido una locura. Ahora lamentaba haber enviado a aquellos hombres y mujeres a un empeño imposible, pero en su momento consideró que podía tener sentido contactar con Xeres sin nadie interfiriendo, ni partos ni kushan. Pero ahora, viendo que él mismo había necesitado tres años de guerra, apoyado por diez legiones, para doblegar Partia, ¿cómo imaginar que alguien de aquella misión de locos pudiera llegar hasta Xeres, evitando las costas controladas por Osroes y engañando al emperador de los kushan?

No, nunca llegarían noticias de ellos. Ojalá alguno o alguna sobreviviera para contarlo.

El emperador dejó entonces de pensar en Titianus, Marcio, Alana o Tamura para fruncir el ceño muy profundamente. ¿Podrían las legiones acabar también con el Imperio kushan y que Roma y Xeres comerciaran sin intermediarios? Y, ya puestos... ¿podría una legión romana salir victoriosa en combate contra un ejército desconocido del emperador de Xeres, allá en los confines del mundo?

Trajano lanzó entonces una sonora carcajada echando la cabeza hacia atrás. Casi le lloraban los ojos y se los limpió con el dorso de la mano mientras se levantaba bajo la curiosa mirada de Liviano y Aulo, quienes pensaron que el César reía de pura felicidad por haber conseguido llegar hasta donde ningún otro emperador romano había llegado nunca antes. No entendían que Trajano se había reído por pensar en imposibles.

Aún sacudía la cabeza pensando en aquella locura mientras caminaba de regreso al barco: para Trajano, una legión romana contra un ejército de Xeres era algo que sencillamente nunca jamás había ocurrido y que nunca jamás ocurriría.

Trajano se encogió de hombros mientras seguía negando con la cabeza. Sueños absurdos de la imaginación.

Claro que el emperador hispano nunca pudo leer las memorias del general Tang.

HISTORIA DE LA LEGIÓN PERDIDA

Tiempos de Julio César, Pompeyo y Craso,
mediados del siglo I a.C.

Libro VII

97

EL PLAN DEL GENERAL TANG

Asia central
Final del otoño de 36 a.C.

Hacía frío en el campamento del ejército del Imperio han, al sur del desierto de Taklamakán.

—El invierno parece querer adelantarse, *shang chiang-chün* —dijo el gobernador Kan Yen abrazándose, en un intento por mantener algo del calor de su cuerpo—. Si eso ocurre tendremos muchos problemas.

El general Tang no dijo nada. Miraba hacia el mar de tiendas de su ejército mientras tomaba una infusión caliente.

—Te he hablado, *chiang-chün*, y un gobernador tiene por costumbre recibir respuesta de sus generales. ¿O es que una vez que te he acompañado en esta locura, rebelándonos contra la autoridad del emperador del pueblo han, ya no atiendes a ninguna jerarquía?

Tang se volvió y miró al viejo gobernador.

—No, no es eso. Respeto la autoridad del *shou* de Gansu y las regiones occidentales del imperio. Estaba pensando.

—¿En qué?

—En que voy a dividir las tropas en dos columnas de ejército similares, para avanzar con dos fuerzas en paralelo en nuestra aproximación al territorio controlado por Zhizhi.

El anciano gobernador asintió despacio. Dejó caer los brazos. El frío no se le iba del cuerpo de ninguna forma. Dividir el ejército en dos mitades era algo frecuente en las campañas han. Y podía tener sentido en las actuales circunstancias.

—Te escucho, *chiang-chün* —dijo el gobernador Yen.

Tang hablaba señalando hacia las tiendas del campamento.

—Verás que el ejército ya lo he dividido en dos grandes mitades. Allí, a la izquierda, hay tres *tu-wei-fu*, tres regimientos. Al frente de cada uno he puesto un *hsiao-wei* de mi confianza. Los tres son coroneles experimentados ya en la guerra contra los *hsiung-nu*. A la derecha, en aquel sector, están acampados otros tres regimientos, con tres coroneles más al mando de cada unidad. Mi plan es rodear la cuenca del río Tarim. Una columna del ejército lo hará por el sur del desierto, para luego cruzar Dayuán y llegar a Kangchú[76] desde ese extremo. Nosotros, con los otros tres regimientos, seguiremos la ruta al norte del desierto, la de las montañas. Es más difícil y nos acercaremos al territorio en disputa entre los guerreros de Kangchú gobernados por Zhizhi y sus enemigos los wusun, pero es la mejor forma de garantizarnos que peinamos todas las regiones al sur de la capital de Zhizhi. No quiero alcanzar su fortaleza y cuando la asediemos encontrarme con que un ejército de Kangchú o de los *hsiung-nu* del maldito Zhizhi nos ataca por la espalda. Eso no debe ocurrir. Este doble avance ralentizará algo la campaña, pero lo veo necesario.

—Pasaremos más frío en las montañas —dijo el gobernador.

—Lo pasaremos, sí —aceptó el general Tang.

—No obstante, parece sensato lo que planteas, y en todo caso, tú eres el *chiang-chün*, el general, el militar —respondió Kan Yen.

—Gracias, gobernador. Es importante que nos mantengamos unidos, en especial cuando dé las órdenes a cada *hsiao-wei*. Nuestra unión dará confianza a los coroneles y ellos la transmitirán a los soldados. Voy a convocarlos...

El general Tang empezó a andar en dirección a la tienda de los oficiales, cuando el anciano gobernador le dirigió la palabra una vez más.

—Hay algo que deberías saber antes de dar las órdenes.

Tang se detuvo y se volvió hacia el gobernador.

—He enviado una carta al emperador —dijo Kan Yen.

76. Dayuán es el reino de Fergana y Kangchú el de Sogdiana, según la llamaban los han.

—¿Una carta? ¿Qué carta?

—Una carta en la que explico a su majestad imperial que hemos falsificado su firma para crear una orden falsa suya con la que poder cruzar la Puerta de Jade con un ejército de cuarenta mil hombres —dijo el viejo gobernador.

—Pero ¿por qué has hecho tal cosa? —preguntó Tang, que no daba crédito a lo que estaba escuchando.

—Oh, no hay que alterarse demasiado, general: sin duda, el propio coronel de la Puerta de Jade habrá informado ya al emperador de lo ocurrido y nuestros nombres ya estarán proscritos y condenados por las tres excelencias y los nueve ministros imperiales, pero he creído pertinente que el emperador tenga la oportunidad de tener nuestra versión: es esencial que su majestad sepa que no hemos renegado de estar bajo sus órdenes. Algún ministro innoble, y te aseguro que hay muchos en la capital del imperio, podrían convencerlo de que nuestra intención podría ser la de unirnos a Zhizhi para crear ese gran imperio central que tanto tememos y que tanto daño haría al pueblo han. No, eso no puede ser. He informado al emperador de que hemos salido del imperio para enfrentarnos con Zhizhi, exterminar su ejército, aniquilar su poder y, a ser posible, poner la cabeza del temible *chanyu* en una lanza han.

—¡Pero acabas de condenarnos a nosotros y a nuestras familias a muerte! —exclamó Tang, que siempre había pensado en una campaña relativamente rápida que les permitiera regresar con la cabeza de Zhizhi y así aplacar la cólera del emperador antes de que ésta fuera ya del todo irreversible.

—Tú eres militar; yo *shou*, gobernador, político. Te voy a explicar cómo funciona esto: estamos condenados a muerte desde que cruzamos la Puerta de Jade y dudo de que nada de lo que consigamos pueda revertir eso, pero los dos tenemos familias, en efecto, y la pena de muerte podría extenderse con facilidad a nuestras mujeres e hijos. Con la carta he intentado hacer ver al emperador que estamos locos, pero que no somos traidores. Las familias de un gobernador y un general trastornados aún pueden conseguir el perdón. Las de unos traidores, nunca. Y me he asegurado de que esa carta sea entregada por hombres de mi confianza en mano sólo al emperador, sin ministros o excelencias de por medio. Esa carta, mi querido general, es la que puede salvar a nuestros seres queridos. En lugar de enrabietado, deberías estarme agradecido.

Cheng Tang asimiló todo lo que el viejo *shou* había dicho. El *chiang-chün* no se movía.

—Ahora voy a descansar —continuó el gobernador—. Este frío acabará conmigo. Pero tú ibas a convocar a los coroneles. No dejes de hacerlo. Una victoria absoluta es lo único que puede salvarnos a ti y a mí y, sin duda, lo único que puede ayudar a nuestras familias más allá de esa carta mía. No lo olvides. Una victoria total o será el desastre para todos.

Fortaleza del líder huno Zhizhi en Talas, Kangchú (Sogdiana)
Suroeste del lago Balkash, Asia central

Druso estaba en pie con ambas manos en el cogote mirando hacia el este, en lo alto de una de las torres de vigilancia de la empalizada que estaban construyendo alrededor de la fortaleza de Zhizhi. A su lado, Sexto y Cayo, con aire de derrota miraban al suelo de madera y negaban con la cabeza. Nanaifarn estaba junto a ellos, en silencio.

—Repite lo que nos acabas de decir —dijo Druso sin mover las manos del cogote y sin dejar de mirar hacia el este.

—He oído que el pueblo han ha enviado un ejército de decenas de miles de soldados contra Zhizhi —reiteró el sogdiano, que seguía siendo el cordón umbilical de comunicación entre los romanos de la legión perdida y los hunos de aquella ciudad de guerreros salvajes bajo el mando del implacable Zhizhi.

—Tenía que pasar y ya ha pasado —dijo Sexto al cabo de unos minutos de silencio—. Era de esperar que más tarde o más temprano los han enviaran a un ejército para vengarse de sus compatriotas asesinados en aquella embajada. Pero no pensé nunca que enviaran a tantos.

—Los han siempre han sido lentos en actuar —dijo Nanaifarn—, pero cuando lo han hecho ha sido a lo grande.

Druso bajó las manos y las apoyó en la barandilla de la torre.

—¿Qué vamos a hacer? —preguntó Cayo.

Pero el centurión seguía oteando el horizonte y no decía nada.

—Una idea sería huir, como ya hicimos en Merv —sugirió Sexto.

—En eso he estado pensando —admitió Druso rompiendo su silencio—, pero huir... ¿hacia dónde? El norte es aún más gélido e inhóspito. No sobreviviríamos al primer invierno. Hacia el este están los han y ese ejército que se acerca y hacia el oeste los partos nos esperan para aniquilarnos si osamos desandar el territorio que nos alejó de ser esclavos suyos.

—Queda el sur —se atrevió a apuntar Cayo.

Druso sacudió la cabeza.

—No. —Y se volvió un instante hacia Nanaifarn—. Cuéntales a ellos lo que me explicaste a mí antes.

—El general que comanda el ejército han lo ha dividido en dos columnas que rodean el desierto de Taklamakán —se explicó el sogdiano—. Una columna se acerca hacia nosotros por el este y la otra por el sur.

—O sea que no tenemos más que el norte helado o los partos al oeste —concluyó Sexto.

—O quedarnos aquí —dijo Druso, siempre con las manos apoyadas en la barandilla de aquella torre.

—Pero es una batalla perdida —opuso Cayo—. Zhizhi apenas cuenta con un par de millares de su caballería de hunos, otros tantos sogdianos, que falta por ver que sean leales cuando las cosas se pongan mal, y nosotros, que apenas sobrepasamos el millar.

—Por eso vamos a construir más torres —replicó Druso—; reforzaremos la empalizada, revisaremos la muralla interior de arcilla y construiremos un foso alrededor de toda la empalizada exterior. El trabajo nos mantendrá ocupados. Es mejor no pensar. En cualquier caso, siempre será preferible luchar protegidos que en campo abierto. Hemos sobrevivido a la inutilidad del maldito Craso, a las flechas de los partos, a su crueldad sin límites, a la marcha desde el Éufrates hasta Merv; hemos escapado de la esclavitud, combatido contra los wusun y conquistado territorios para el lunático de Zhizhi. Hemos conseguido victorias inimaginables y soportado sufrimientos que habrían terminado con cualquier otra unidad militar. Si ahora hemos de enfrentarnos contra los ejércitos de ese imperio que todos llaman han, lo haremos. Y sobreviviremos como hemos hecho siempre, o les haremos tanto daño mientras nos matan que pasaremos a los anales de sus historiadores si es que tienen alguien que se ocupe de recoger las gestas de sus generales.

Druso habló con tanta fuerza y sentimiento que insufló a Sexto y Cayo la valentía que parecía habérseles agotado. Ambos parecieron sentir vergüenza de haber dudado sobre qué debía hacerse, hasta que Sexto se atrevió a hablar de nuevo.

—Muerte o victoria, mi centurión.

—Muerte o victoria —confirmó Druso—. Una legión de Roma no conoce otro camino. Nuestro destino, nos guste o no, está unido al de ese loco de Zhizhi.

Ejército han en ruta hacia Talas
Valle del río Ili, Asia central

El avance del *ying*, la división del ejército al mando directo del general Chen Tang, fue más lento de lo esperado: montañas, arroyos y con frecuencia noches frías generaban toda clase de inconvenientes en su progreso hacia el norte rodeando el desierto de Taklamakán. Pero, por encima de todo, la escasez de víveres empezó a preocupar al *chiang-chün*, que veía cómo sus soldados iban consumiendo las provisiones sin tener posibilidad de conseguir ningún alimento nuevo. Las aldeas que encontraban estaban o abandonadas o desabastecidas, con graneros vacíos y granjas sin animal alguno.

—Los guerreros de Kangchú[77] y los *hsiung-nu* de Zhizhi se lo han llevado todo —decían los pocos habitantes de aquellos pueblos miserables.

Pero una mañana ocurrió algo inesperado:

77. Es decir, sogdianos pero según la denominación de los han.

—Hemos detectado una columna de jinetes de Kangchú a cincuenta *li* de distancia, *chiang-chün* —le dijeron al general Tang los soldados de una de las patrullas que siempre iban por delante del ejército han para evitar que una emboscada enemiga los sorprendiera—. Y llevan mucho ganado con ellos —añadieron los guerreros con claras muestra de ansia.

La faz casi siempre atribulada del general Tang se permitió esta vez una sonrisa.

—En esta ocasión el hambre nos ayudará en esta guerra —comentó el general en cuanto se quedó de nuevo a solas con el gobernador Kan Yen.

—¿Crees que por conseguir el ganado del enemigo nuestros guerreros van a luchar con más bravura? —preguntó el viejo *shou*.

—Tú sabes de política y de administración, yo de guerras y soldados. No dudes ni por un instante que los soldados de nuestro ejército se batirán como tigres hambrientos por una presa. Hoy haremos bueno a Sun Tzu cuando nos dice en el *Arte de la guerra* que «conseguir las provisiones arrebatándoselas al enemigo es una doble victoria».

Cheng Tang no se equivocaba.

Sus tropas rodearon a la caballería sogdiana y *hsiung-nu* en un amplio valle y se lanzaron contra ellos con auténtica voracidad de victoria y carne. Los *hsiung-nu* se defendieron, pero cometieron el error de seguir a varias unidades han que se replegaban. Eso hizo que quedaran al alcance de los arqueros han más experimentados y éstos, con sus grandes ballestas, acribillaron a la mayor parte de los *hsiung-nu*. Los sogdianos fueron más prudentes y se mantuvieron en el centro del valle, próximos al gran rebaño de reses que habían acumulado durante las últimas semanas por orden del mismísimo Zhizhi, con la doble intención de dejar sin provisiones al ejército han en su avance y de proveerse de carne para el largo invierno que se aproximaba a la fortaleza de Talas, al suroeste del Pu-Ku.[78]

—¿Y ahora qué vas a hacer? —le preguntó Kan Yen a Tang.

El general lo contemplaba todo muy atento desde lo alto

78. Lago Balkash.

de la ladera sur del valle. Estaba satisfecho con haber destruido la caballería *hsiung-nu*, pero el alimento aún seguía fuera de su alcance.

—Somos muchos más que ellos —dijo con seguridad, cubriéndose los ojos del sol mientras inspeccionaba toda la longitud del amplio valle—. Hasta ahora hemos jugado a escondernos para sorprenderlos, pero ahora ya no necesitamos dar más sorpresas. Ahora vamos a exhibirnos. Quiero que sepan cuántos somos. Veremos entonces qué pasa.

Y dio orden de que todas las *hou-kuan*, todas y cada una de las compañías de su ejército, se mostraran por ambas laderas de aquella depresión.

—¿Esperas que se rindan? —preguntó el viejo gobernador.

—Espero que, al menos, acepten negociar.

—Después de falsificar una orden imperial, de cruzar la Puerta de Jade con cuarenta mil guerreros y de bordear todo el desierto de Taklamakán, yo creía que habíamos venido hasta aquí para vengarnos de aquellos que habían matado a nuestros familiares de la embajada; creía que habíamos venido a exterminar a Zhizhi y a todos sus hombres y aliados.

—Los hombres de Kangchú[79] siempre han sido razonables —contraargumentó Tang— y no sólo hemos de conseguir una victoria absoluta, gobernador, sino también reabrir la Ruta de la Seda. Cuando acabemos con Zhizhi, y juro que lo haré aunque sea lo último que haga en esta vida, necesitaremos a alguien que gobierne este territorio como se hacía antes de que irrumpiera ese lunático. No pensar en lo que va a ocurrir después de una guerra en un territorio es no entender que cualquier guerra, si no se es un loco, debe tener un plan para la paz posterior.

El viejo Kan Yen asintió en silencio. El general parecía saber no sólo de guerra. Eso le dio esperanza en la victoria final, si bien temía por todos los guerreros de mil lugares diferentes que Zhizhi había reunido en Talas. En particular le preocupaba aquella guardia de guerreros mercenarios extranjeros que Zhizhi había conseguido llevar al reino de Kangchú y que na-

79. Sogdianos.

die sabía bien de dónde provenían. El gobernador había departido con Tang sobre aquellos soldados desconocidos, pero el general han no se había mostrado particularmente preocupado por ellos. A Kan Yen, no obstante, los años le habían enseñado que nunca había que infravalorar aquello que no se ha visto antes. Lo desconocido puede ser débil, pero también muy poderoso.

El gobernador no dijo nada. Ahora era momento de hablar con los guerreros de Kangchú del valle. En eso Tang tenía razón: un pacto con ellos podría ayudar en la guerra y luego en la paz.

Fortaleza de Talas, en Kangchú (Sogdiana)
Suroeste del lago Balkash

Druso, seguido de cerca por Sexto, Cayo y el sogdiano Nanaifarn, irrumpió en el palacio de Zhizhi. Los guardias *hsiung-nu* se abalanzaron sobre ellos para detener su avance. El centurión romano no estaba dispuesto a que nadie se interpusiera en su camino y, sin dudarlo, desenvainó su *gladio*. Sexto y Cayo lo imitaron. Nanaifarn contuvo la respiración. Los guerreros *hsiung-nu* dieron dos pasos hacia atrás, pero también sacaron sus espadas.

—¡Zhizhi! ¡Maldito seas! —aulló Druso exhibiendo su espada amenazadoramente.

Nanaifarn no tuvo que traducir.

El líder de los hunos enarcó las cejas, separó de su trono a dos mujeres que estaban arrodilladas a sus pies, acariciándole las piernas, y se levantó para ver quién osaba interrumpirlo en su descanso placentero con sus esposas y oficiales más próximos. En cuanto vio al jefe de los mercenarios extranjeros sonrió y se volvió a sentar, pero dio una orden a sus hombres.

—¡Dejadlo acercarse!

Los *hsiung-nu*, de mala gana, se hicieron a un lado, pero sin envainar sus armas. Druso, Sexto, Cayo y Nanaifarn caminaron de nuevo con paso firme hasta situarse justo enfrente del trono. El centurión guardó entonces su *gladio* y sus hombres lo imitaron.

—¡Los han avanzan y se han hecho con ganado suficiente para poder alimentar a sus tropas todo el invierno! —exclamó Druso sin más preámbulos, y miró a Nanaifarn para que éste tradujera de inmediato sus palabras. El sogdiano lo hizo añadiendo algunas formas adicionales de respeto a la persona de Zhizhi.

El líder de los *hsiung-nu* no pareció inquietarse. Él ya sabía de la derrota de sus hombres en aquel valle al sur del río Ili y de la pérdida del ganado, pues los sogdianos de aquel regimiento, al fin, habían pactado su libertad a cambio de entregar el ganado a los han.

Druso seguía encendido. La inacción de Zhizhi mientras los han iban aproximándose a la fortaleza de Talas, haciéndose cada vez más fuertes sin que el jefe de los hunos hubiese hecho nada por evitarlo, había provocado que ya no pudiera contenerse y decidiera ir a hablar directamente con Zhizhi. La última vez que había departido directamente con el jefe *hsiung-nu* había sido durante la campaña contra los wusun, pero entonces todo marchaba bien y se consiguió una victoria tras otra. Ahora, desde que Zhizhi había construido aquella fortaleza, era como si el veterano y brutal guerrero huno de antaño hubiera perdido su furor por el combate justo en el peor momento posible para semejante relajación.

—Que los han hayan conseguido un poco de ganado no cambia nada —respondió Zhizhi hablando en sogdiano. Nanaifarn actuaba de intérprete entre el huno y el centurión romano—. En vez de morir de hambre, los han morirán ahora de frío. El invierno está ya cerca y nosotros tenemos el abrigo de nuestra ciudad fortificada, mientras que ellos tendrán que soportar el gélido hielo y la nieve húmeda en sus miserables tiendas de campaña. El invierno luchará por nosotros.

—Yo no estoy seguro de que sean tan imbéciles como para esperar al invierno —interpuso Druso con furia—. Atacarán antes.

—Tenemos la empalizada y la muralla —respondió Zhizhi siempre sin alterarse, acariciando el pelo lacio y oscuro de una de sus esposas, que seguía arrodillada a sus pies.

—Los han nos atacarán de inmediato, están acampando ya muy cerca —insistió Druso—. Muchos sogdianos, muchos guerreros de Kangchú, han desertado de nuestras tropas desde la derrota del valle del Ili, donde los han se hicieron con el ganado. No confío en la lealtad de los sogdianos, de los guerreros de Kangchú que nos quedan aquí, y no estoy seguro de que la caballería *hsiung-nu* y mi infantería romana puedan ser suficientes para defender las fortificaciones. No contra cuarenta mil guerreros enemigos.

Zhizhi dejó de acariciar a la hermosa mujer, borró su sonrisa del rostro y, por primera vez en aquella conversación, mostró incomodidad en su faz.

—En la próxima primavera castigaré sin piedad a todos los hombres de Kangchú, de Sogdiana, como la llamas tú, que nos hayan traicionado. Los que siguen con nosotros lo saben y por eso permanecerán a nuestro lado. Saben que mi ira no tiene límites con los traidores. Tendremos hombres suficientes para defender la empalizada que han construido tus soldados y la muralla que han levantado mis guerreros y los propios sogdianos.

Druso suspiró. Se pasó el dorso de la mano por la frente mientras Nanaifarn le traducía las palabras del líder de los *hsiung-nu*.

—Aun así —insistió el centurión romano—, deberíamos atacar a los han ahora que aún no han reunido todas su tropas.

Zhizhi escuchaba muy serio al jefe de sus mercenarios extranjeros. Le resultaba muy desagradable su aire de independencia, sus ademanes desenvueltos y la falta de respeto que mostraba hacia él. La forma en que el traductor sogdiano suavizaba cada comentario del mercenario no le engañaba. Los gestos y la mirada de Druso eran demasiado desafiantes para estar en consonancia con las palabras que emitía el sogdiano, que trataba de transmitir las opiniones de aquel guerrero extraño llegado, junto con sus tropas, de algún recóndito y desconocido reino del mundo, más allá de las fronteras conocidas. Pero detrás de ese evidente aire desafiante, Zhizhi había aprendido a valorar las opiniones militares de aquel jefe de sus mercenarios, y era cierto que la situación era bastante comprometida, quizá más de lo que había sido nunca desde que se hiciera con el poder absoluto en los reinos de Sogdiana y Fergana.

—¿Qué propones? —preguntó, al fin, Zhizhi.

Aquella interrogante llegó a los oídos de Druso como una bendición del dios Marte de la guerra. Quizá aún se acordara de ellos pese a encontrarse más allá de los confines de Roma, de Partia y de cualquier lugar conocido por los hijos de la loba que alimentara en el pasado legendario a Rómulo y Remo.

—Los han están acampando, pero sólo ha llegado hasta aquí la primera parte de su ejército. No atacarán hasta que llegue el segundo cuerpo de sus tropas. Los sogdianos, los guerreros de Kangchú, tienen espías que me han confirmado esto varias veces. Yo cargaría con la caballería contra ellos ya mismo, para demostrarles a los han que la lucha será descarnada y cruel por nuestra parte y para hacer ver a los sogdianos que están en la ciudad que no habrá pacto posible con los han, como pasó en el valle del Ili. Ese ataque nos dará fuerza ante nuestros enemigos han y ante los que duden de nuestra resolución aquí dentro.

Zhizhi asintió varias veces sin decir nada. Bajó la mirada e hizo un gesto a una de sus esposas, que de inmediato volvió a arrodillarse junto a él. El guerrero huno acarició ahora la mejilla de la mujer. Era hermosa. La deseaba. Volvió a afirmar con la cabeza. La poseería aquella misma mañana, antes de salir a combatir.

—De acuerdo —aceptó Zhizhi en voz alta—. Saldré con mi caballería este mismo día y acosaremos a los han mientras intentan montar su campamento. Eso, como dices, parece una buena idea. Ahora regresa a la empalizada y a las torres y cumple con tus obligaciones de vigilar al enemigo.

Druso parpadeó varias veces cuando escuchó la última traducción de Nanaifarn. No había esperado una respuesta tan activa por parte del líder de los hunos.

—Sea —dijo el centurión y dio media vuelta. Cruzó el salón del trono de Zhizhi a toda velocidad, seguido por Sexto y Cayo. La guerra contra los han estaba a punto de empezar. Seguramente sería la última batalla de la legión perdida.

98

LA CARGA DE LA CABALLERÍA *HSIUNG-NU*

**Talas, en Kangchú (Sogdiana), suroeste del lago Balkash
36 a.C.**

Torre de la empalizada
Posiciones de la infantería romana

—¿Habéis reforzado los escudos? —preguntó Druso.

—Sí, bueno, en ello están todos los hombres —respondió Sexto—, pero al final pesarán mucho.

Druso no respondió, pues en ese instante estaba concentrado en observar desde lo alto de la torre en la que se encontraban cómo sus legionarios abrían las puertas de la empalizada para dar paso a Zhizhi, quien, imponente a lomos de su gran caballo de Fergana, salía para liderar la carga de su temible caballería contra los guerreros han, apostados frente a las fortificaciones de la muralla.

—¿Pesados? —preguntó al fin el centurión.

—Los escudos, sí —insistió Sexto—. Con todos esos refuerzos que has pedido será difícil maniobrar con ellos y casi imposible hacer una larga marcha.

—No creo que vayamos a tener oportunidad de hacer grandes marchas ya, amigo mío —le dijo Druso y se volvió de nuevo para mirar a los jinetes *hsiung-nu*, quienes sin pensárselo mucho ya empezaban a galopar para encontrarse con el enemigo han—. O Zhizhi destroza a los guerreros de Xeres en esta salida o empezará un asedio del que dudo que salgamos vivos.

743

El *chiang-chün* Cheng Tang estaba montado sobre su caballo. No se sorprendió cuando vio salir a los *hsiung-nu* lanzándose contra ellos mortalmente, con una brutal carga destinada a barrerlos de la tierra. No, no le resultó inesperada aquella estrategia, pero habría preferido que el ataque del enemigo hubiera tenido lugar en unos días, cuando ya hubiera llegado la segunda columna de su ejército y la superioridad numérica le hubiera dado muchas más garantías de resistir aquella embestida. En cualquier caso, ya no había marcha atrás.

—¡Allí está el asesino *hsiung-nu* que a tantos han ha matado! ¡Hoy es el día de la venganza! —empezó a gritar Cheng Tang a sus hombres paseando con su caballo por delante de las líneas de su infantería y arqueros—. ¡Hoy es el día en que empieza el fin de su terror y sangre! ¡Hoy es el día en el que el pueblo han va a conseguir la victoria sobre su enemigo más cruel! ¡Recordad que habrá recompensas para todos los que seáis capaces de abatir a un maldito guerrero *hsiung-nu*! ¡Pero recordad que, por encima de todo, hoy luchamos por detener a este asesino que amenaza nuestras fronteras, nuestras ciudades y mujeres y niños! ¡Recordad que ellos no entienden nada más que la fuerza de nuestras armas! ¡Apuntad bien y no desperdiciéis ninguna flecha! ¡Esperad a mi señal! ¡Por el emperador de los han!

El general Tang azuzó entonces a su caballo y se posicionó justo por detrás de sus tropas de infantería y arqueros. Todo estaba en marcha. Había dispuesto a sus hombres en tres líneas: en primer lugar los soldados de cabeza afeitada, argolla de hierro en el cuello y túnicas rojas. Todos ellos eran convictos, criminales de la peor calaña a los que se había reclutado con la promesa de una redención de la totalidad o de gran parte de su pena si combatían con valor. La argolla de hierro al cuello era símbolo de que eran presos, al igual que sus cabezas afeitadas eran símbolo de la decapitación que les esperaba si se mostraban cobardes en la lucha. No disponían de armadura ni de protecciones especiales de ningún tipo. Eran lo peor de lo peor y como tales se los trataba. Y, pese a ello, muchos se sentían agradecidos de disponer de una oportunidad para recuperar la libertad, aunque cuando el suelo empezó a temblar bajo sus pies por la proximidad de la caballería *hsiung-nu*, y se oyeron los gritos salvajes de aquellos guerreros del norte que cargaban al galope contra ellos, todos los túnicas rojas del ejército han empezaron a dudar de si no habrían estado mejor en la peor de las prisiones del imperio que encontrarse aquella mañana en aquel lugar maldito del mundo.

A una señal de los oficiales levantaron las lanzas que les habían entregado como única arma frente al enemigo, que se aproximaba como un torrente desbordado en medio de la mayor de las tormentas.

En segunda línea, Tang había dispuesto la infantería regular han, hombres adiestrados militarmente, con casco de metal, escudos de mimbre y lanzas en sus manos, protegidos por cotas de malla unos y por gruesas corazas de cuero otros. Al igual que los túnicas rojas, tampoco estaban muy convencidos de salir vivos de allí, aunque la victoria sobre los guerreros de Kangchú semanas atrás en el valle del Ili, la abundancia de alimento desde aquel día y el prestigio del general Tang, que nunca había sido derrotado en una lucha contra los *hsiung-nu*, les daba el ánimo que necesitaban para asir con fuerza sus lanzas, a la espera de encontrarse cara a cara con los temidos jinetes *hsiung-nu*.

Luego estaba la tercera línea del ejército han: arqueros, miles de ellos, de todo tipo y condición, también subdivididos en diferentes líneas: en primer lugar los mercenarios vietnamitas que Tang había incorporado de campañas anteriores en el norte; luego los arqueros regulares con arcos convencionales y, repartidos entre ellos, numerosos grupos de arqueros con ballestas. Todos estaban preparados para arrojar sus dardos mortíferos contra el enemigo que se acercaba. Tenían miedo, como todos, pero se sentían más seguros por detrás de las líneas de los túnicas rojas y de la infantería regular. Finalmente estaban los *chueh chang*, auténticos gigantes, los hombres más fuertes del ejército han que, contrariamente a lo que se podría haber supuesto, no estaban incluidos en la infantería de combate, sino armados con unas ballestas de grandes dimensiones, portentosas máquinas cuyo alcance superaba a la de cualquier arco aliado o enemigo, pero que requerían de una enorme fuerza para ser cargadas y, en consecuencia, sólo podían ser operadas por los hombres más fuertes y corpulentos. Todos habían tensado ya sus gigantescas ballestas y las tenían preparadas apuntando hacia los jinetes *hsiung-nu*.

Finalmente quedaba la caballería han, reducida en aquella *ying*, pues la otra división que tenía una ruta más larga de aproximación a Talas era la que se había quedado con la mayoría de los jinetes. Por eso Tang habría preferido haber reunido sus dos divisiones antes de la carga de Zhizhi. El general han sabía que no podía usar sus pocos cientos de jinetes para detenerlos, de modo que los había dispuesto en retaguardia.

Tang se situó entre la segunda y la tercera línea, justo por delante de los arqueros. Montado sobre su caballo, resultaba bien visible para los oficiales de infantería y para todos los arqueros. El fragor de la caballería *hsiung-nu* se apoderó de la pradera. No era sólo el ruido de sus miles de caballos, sino también los gritos salvajes de los hunos. Tang, no obstante, se mostraba imperturbable sobre su caballo negro y aquella fría serenidad transmitía un poderoso magnetismo a sus oficiales y soldados. Hasta los túnicas rojas de primera línea, que no paraban de tragar saliva, lo miraban con admiración y esperanza. Todo dependía de la pericia de aquel hombre: o Tang sabía lo que se hacía o morirían todos aquella mañana.

Los *hsiung-nu* estaban ya muy cerca de los convictos han de primera línea. Éstos esgrimían sus lanzas, asiéndolas con manos temblorosas y con un sudor frío resbalando por sus cabezas rapadas. El general levantó el brazo y miró al oficial jefe de los *chueh chang*, que asintió a la espera de la orden definitiva.

La caballería de Zhizhi estaba apenas a unos centenares de *bu*,[80] pero aún demasiado lejos para los arqueros vietnamitas, los regulares del ejército han o los portadores de ballestas convencionales. Dar la orden de que dispararan sería desperdiciar una enorme cantidad de flechas que luego echarían de menos. Demasiado lejos para todos aún, excepto para los *chueh chang*.

80. Un *bu* equivalía aproximadamente a 1,2 metros.

El general Tang bajó la mano.

El oficial de los arqueros especiales también.

Los gigantes portadores de las grandes ballestas han soltaron las cuerdas de sus máquinas y las flechas más brutales del ejército que había cruzado la Puerta de Jade hacía sólo unos meses salieron disparadas con una velocidad tan fulgurante como destructiva. Volaron por encima de la infantería y de los túnicas rojas. Volaron sobre la hierba de la pradera que aún separaba al ejército han de la caballería enemiga. Y llegaron a las primeras líneas de jinetes *hsiung-nu* con tanta fuerza que allí donde encontraban a un hombre —estuviera o no protegido con cotas de malla, cuero o escudo—, sólo de la potencia del impacto bestial era impulsado hacia atrás, de modo que la mayoría caían derribados e impactaban con el suelo, en muchos casos heridos de muerte.

Caballería hsiung-nu

Zhizhi veía cómo decenas de sus hombres caían bajo las flechas de los han pese a encontrarse aún a una gran distancia. Lo peor no eran los guerreros muertos o heridos, sino que al caer de los caballos, arrastrados por la fuerza de aquellas portentosas flechas gigantes, los abatidos entorpecían el avance del resto de la caballería. Los caballos no querían pisar a los *hsiung-nu* caídos y se hacían a un lado para esquivarlos, chocando entonces unos con otros.

A punto estuvo aquella primera andanada de amilanar la furia de los hunos, pero su líder aulló con fuerza y dio ejemplo avivando aún más su galope.

Sus hombres lo siguieron.

Ejército han

El general Tang había vuelto a levantar el brazo. Las flechas de los *chueh chang* habían sido certeras y habían causado bastantes bajas en el enemigo, pero no habían sido suficientes para detenerlos. El *chiang-chün* contaba con ello. Ahora, no obstante, tardaría un rato en disponer de una nueva andanada de las grandes ballestas, pues incluso los experimentados y corpulentos *chueh chang* necesitaban de un tiempo para volver a tensar las cuerdas de sus enormes armas. No, ahora era el momento de los otros arqueros.

Tang bajó el brazo mirando a los oficiales vietnamitas y a los arqueros regulares y a los de las ballestas convencionales. El avance imparable de los *hsiung-nu* sólo tenía una ventaja: ya estaban a tiro de todos.

La lluvia de flechas fue como una gran nube que oscureció el cielo por momentos.

Caballería hsiung-nu

—¡Disparad, disparad! —ordenó Zhizhi a sus hombres.

Veía la nube de flechas que se aproximaba contra ellos y quería que sus guerreros lanzaran también las suyas antes de perder a muchos bajo los dardos han.

Los *hsiung-nu* apuntaron al cielo y depararon sus arcos sin dejar de galopar.

Miles de flechas de unos y de otros chocaron en el aire, pero otros miles cayeron sobre los hunos hiriéndolos en brazos, piernas, cabeza, pecho...

—¡Agggh!

Los aullidos de dolor se extendieron por toda la caballería *hsiung-nu*, que no había recibido un castigo semejante en todo el tiempo que había estado bajo las órdenes de Zhizhi.

Ejército han

Los túnicas rojas sufrieron más que nadie la lluvia de flechas hunas. Desprovistos de protecciones de defensa adecuadas, muchos de los dardos enemigos los hirieron. Los oficiales han tuvieron que emplearse a fondo gritando una y otra vez.

—¡Mantened la posición! ¡Mantened la posición!

—¡El que retroceda será ejecutado!

La amenaza del castigo capital retuvo a la mayoría, aunque algunos huyeron hacia las montañas.

El general Tang observó aquello con preocupación. No le inquietaba que se fugaran unos pocos prisioneros —ya los buscarían y los matarían al final de la batalla—, pero sí le preocupaba sobremanera que su ejemplo pudiera ser copiado por la infantería regular. Eso le hizo cambiar de opinión y se volvió hacia uno de los oficiales de su caballería, que estaba junto a él.

—Rodead nuestras líneas y dad muerte a esos túnicas rojas cobardes, a ser posible antes de que se alejen y queden fuera de la visión de los soldados.

El oficial asintió y partió raudo a cumplir las instrucciones. Comprendía y compartía la importancia y la urgencia de ejecutar con rapidez aquella orden.

Primera línea de combate

Zhizhi había sobrevivido a las flechas. En el fondo creía que el sol, la luna, el cielo y la tierra y sus antepasados lo protegían siempre. Ésa era su religión y su fuerza. Quizá estaba loco, pero nadie podría llamarlo nunca cobarde.

El impacto de la vanguardia de la caballería *hsiung-nu* contra los túnicas rojas de los han se saldó con sangre y muerte por todas partes. El espeso líquido rojo lo salpicaba todo, pues los hunos pugnaban por abrirse paso como si estuvieran segando trigo con sus espadas cuando lo que cortaban eran brazos o cabezas del enemigo.

Los convictos que intentaban alejarse del combate fueron interceptados por los pequeños contingentes de la caballería han, insuficientes para hacer frente al grueso de los *hsiung-nu* pero muy capaces de hacer cambiar de opinión a los túnicas rojas que intentaban huir de la batalla. Éstos daban media vuelta y se aprestaban a reincorporarse al combate, pues contra los hunos, si sobrevivían, aún tenían la esperanza del perdón.

Toda la primera línea de lucha se había transformado en una maraña confusa de caballos, lanzas, espadas, convictos y hunos.

Centro del ejército han

El general Tang estuvo tentado de dar la orden a sus arqueros de que dispararan contra aquella masa confusa de hombres y bestias, pues, al fin y al cabo, sólo se trataba de *hsiung-nu* y de prisioneros han, pero estos últimos, sobre todo los que se habían quedado desde el principio haciendo frente a los hunos, estaban luchando con bravura, ya fuera por conseguir sobrevivir o por obtener el perdón; aquella lucha de los convictos no merecía ser castigada con una lluvia de flechas que matara a unos y otros.

—La infantería —dijo Tang a sus oficiales, que se aprestaron a transmitir la nueva orden a los guerreros del ejército regular.

Primera línea de combate

—¡Avanzad, ahora! ¡Avanzad por el emperador de los han! —gritaban unos.

—¡Dejad paso, retiraos por los pasillos! —aullaban otros oficiales a los convictos para que permitieran la incorporación a la primera línea de lucha a las tropas de refresco.

Los túnicas rojas no necesitaron que se les repitiera la orden y, rápidamente, se retiraron por los pasillos que la infantería había dejado en retaguardia.

En cuestión de pocos minutos, los *hsiung-nu* se encontraron combatiendo cuerpo a cuerpo contra toda una nueva primera línea de guerreros que llegaban frescos al combate; mientras que muchos de ellos estaban con heridas, algunos habían perdido los caballos y todos estaban agotados, sin que hubieran conseguido poner en fuga a los han.

Torres de la empalizada de la fortaleza de Talas

Druso, junto con Cayo y Sexto, contemplaba el desarrollo de la batalla.

—¿Habéis visto la potencia de las flechas han? —preguntó el centurión.

—Sí —dijeron Cayo y Sexto al unísono.

—Ahora ya sabéis por qué quería nuestros escudos muy reforzados. Nanaifarn me había hablado de los arqueros han y acabo de ver que no exageraba.

Los dos asintieron.

—Zhizhi no va a poder romper las filas del ejército han —dijo Sexto al cabo de unos minutos.

—No, no lo va a conseguir —coincidió Druso—. Es más, si no se retira pronto, mucho me temo que la lucha se puede transformar en una derrota absoluta para los hunos. Y eso nos dejaría solos frente a los han.

Nadie dijo nada más durante un rato.

El fragor de la batalla, los gritos de los oficiales y los alaridos de dolor de los que eran heridos o muertos llegaban hasta ellos reptando por las praderas del centro de Asia, como serpientes que anunciaran con silbidos de muerte un próximo desenlace funesto para todos los que miraban en silencio la batalla de Kangchú.

Vanguardia de los hsiung-nu

Zhizhi acababa de cortarles el cuello a dos convictos han que le habían dado la espalda para escapar de la lucha y ser reemplazados por la infantería regular. Estaba encendido y presto a acabar con tantos han como se interpusieran en su camino y, aparentemente, pese a las numerosas bajas sufridas, sus hombres parecían compartir con él el ansia de vengar a los compañeros caídos en la carga de la caballería. Sentía un incendio que le quemaba por dentro, pero Zhizhi no habría llegado a hacerse con el reino entero de Kangchú, y a controlar una vasta región de Asia central si no fuera por su fino instinto guerrero. Sabía que los nuevos soldados han entraban frescos en el combate y él no había organizado bien la lucha. Había contado con una rápida retirada de los enemigos ante una carga directa y brutal, pero los han habían resistido. Tenía que plantear la batalla de nuevo, pero de otra forma. Desde la fortaleza. Aún tenía el grueso de sus tropas con él, al menos dos tercios de las mismas. Seguía siendo poderoso y con las fortificaciones, la empalizada exterior, el muro interior, los guerreros de Kangchú y aquellos mercenarios llegados del fin del mundo podía atrincherarse en la ciudad y esperar a que el invierno, tal y como había pensado desde un principio, acabara con los han.

—¡Retirada! ¡Retiraos conmigo todos! —vociferó el gran Zhizhi a sus hombres, y la caballería de los *hsiung-nu*, disciplinada, dio media vuelta de inmediato y empezó a galopar de regreso a la empalizada. Podían parecer una jauría de lobos que atacaran sin orden, pero eran rápidos en responder a su líder. Hasta los lobos tienen estrategia cuando cazan.

Centro del ejército han

—¡Disparad otra vez! —ordenó el general Tang mirando una vez más a los oficiales de los *chueh chang*, y las gigantescas ballestas volvieron a escupir flechas mortíferas que, pese a la veloz huida de los hunos, aún alcanzaron a varios jinetes en su repliegue.

—No han caído muchos ahora. —Era la voz del viejo gobernador Kan Yen, que parecía algo repuesto de sus dolencias en pies y manos y se había acercado hasta Tang para ver cómo iba la batalla—. ¿Por qué no ordenas a nuestros propios jinetes que los persigan? Podrían acabar con algunos más en la confusión de su huida.

—No —respondió Tang contundente—. Si nuestros jinetes se acercan demasiado a sus fortificaciones estarán al alcance de sus arqueros, y no tengo suficiente caballería como para permitirme el lujo de perder a un centenar por intentar herir a otros tantos hunos en su retirada. Y que no te engañen, viejo *shou*, Zhizhi se ha replegado y hemos ganado este primer pulso, pero esto no ha hecho más que empezar.

—Sí, pero has resistido bien su primer ataque. Ahora se lo pensarán dos veces antes de volver a salir y en pocos días recibiremos los refuerzos de la segunda división de nuestro ejército, que está ya a pocas jornadas de marcha de aquí.

—No, no saldrán más —aceptó Tang—, pero ésa no es la cuestión, gobernador. La cuestión es que hemos de conseguir entrar nosotros en su ciudad antes de que llegue el crudo invierno. Y no será tan sencillo.

Empalizada de la fortaleza

Las puertas se abrieron con rapidez empujadas por soldados hunos y sogdianos que las custodiaban. Druso y sus hombres estaban en lo alto de las torres. Zhizhi cruzó la puerta principal al galope, seguido por el resto de la gran caballería *hsiung-nu*. Se habían batido con furia y con valor, pero no habían podido contra los arqueros y la infantería han. Zhizhi desmontó de su caballo de un salto. Druso había descendido de lo alto de los puestos de vigilancia de la empalizada. Quería saber qué órdenes daba el jefe de los hunos. Nanaifarn iba junto con el centurión y sus dos hombres de confianza, Cayo y Sexto.

Casi sin darse cuenta Zhizhi se encontró de cara con el jefe romano.

—Ya hemos hecho la salida —dijo el líder de los *hsiung-nu*, sudoroso, con sangre enemiga salpicada por rostro y brazos y protecciones de cuero en su cuerpo fornido de guerrero indómito.

Druso no necesitó traducción para entenderlo. Después de años con los hunos comprendía algunas frases, y el tono y los gestos de Zhizhi mandaban un mensaje claro de rabia y tensión. Pero luego, el jefe de los hunos añadió algo más mirando fijamente a los ojos al propio Druso y también a varios oficiales sogdianos, para acto seguido desaparecer con sus hombres de confianza adentrándose en la muralla que protegía el interior de la fortaleza.

Druso miró a Nanaifarn.

—Ha dicho que ahora es nuestro turno de luchar. Quiere que defendamos la empalizada. Y que ya llegará el invierno.

El centurión romano asintió. La salida de la caballería huna no había surtido el efecto deseado, pero había que intentarlo.

—La verdad es que lo del ataque de los *hsiung-nu* no ha valido de mucho —dijo Cayo—. Además han tenido muchas bajas y no sé hasta qué punto nos valen los sogdianos.

—Bueno, de algo ha valido este combate —contrapuso Druso dando ya media vuelta y dirigiéndose hacia las torres de la empalizada.

—¿De qué ha servido? —inquirió Sexto, que como Nanaifarn y Cayo se aprestaba a seguir al centurión.

—Sabemos dos cosas —respondió Druso—: para empezar que el general de los han es un militar capaz y valiente.

Pero no dijo más.

Siguieron avanzando entre los jinetes heridos, que estaban siendo atendidos por los curanderos de los hunos y por varias mujeres.

—Has dicho dos cosas, pero solamente has mencionado una —comentó Sexto intrigado—. ¿Qué más sabemos después de este combate?

Ascendieron con rapidez por la escala que los conducía hasta lo alto de una de las torres. Druso miraba hacia el campamento han. Los soldados del enemigo estaban recogiendo flechas de entre los muertos *hsiung-nu.* Su general debía de haber ordenado que recuperaran tantos dardos como fuera posible. El oponente al que se enfrentaban era un optimizador magistral de recursos.

—Sabemos... —empezó Druso lentamente—; sabemos... que el general del los han no esperará al invierno. Atacará en cuanto lleguen sus refuerzos.

99
—

LA BATALLA DE KANGCHÚ

Fortaleza de Talas, Kangchú
Suroeste del lago Balkash, Asia central
Finales de otoño de 36 a.C.

Ejército han

La segunda división de los han llegó a la semana siguiente. El general Tang había observado cómo los defensores de la fortaleza habían excavado un foso alrededor de la empalizada y lo habían llenado con agua del río Talas, que fluía próximo a la ciudad, para impedir que nadie pudiera acercarse a la empalizada.

—Ésos son los mercenarios de Zhizhi —dijo el gobernador Kan Yen una mañana, cuando miraban hacia las posiciones del enemigo y veían cómo progresaban aquellos trabajos defensivos—. Ése foso no nos facilitará las cosas —continuó el viejo gobernador—; ¿por qué no los atacas mientras lo construyen?

—Lo hemos hecho —respondió el general Tang—, pero la infantería no puede acercarse sin quedar al alcance de los arqueros de la empalizada, y cuando nuestros propios arqueros han disparado *más de un centenar de sus soldados de infantería se han puesto en formación a ambos lados de aquella puerta, protegiéndose con los escudos como si formaran así las escamas de un pez, como si practicaran un ejercicio de maniobras.*[81] Las flechas chocan contra los escudos y luego siguen con el trabajo del foso. No

81. Literal de «Las memorias del general Cheng Tang» incluidas en el 後漢書, es decir el *Hou Han Shu* o *Libro de la Dinastía Han Posterior*.

había visto nunca nada igual. Esos hombres son los únicos que me preocupan. Los guerreros de Kangchú están desmotivados y los *hsiung-nu* son buenos en campo abierto, donde los hemos vencido ya, pero no sabrán defenderse bien en una fortaleza, pero esos mercenarios extraños van a ser un problema.

—¿Por qué no has usado a los *chueh chang* contra ellos? —inquirió el gobernador—. Sus ballestas grandes podrían hacerles mucho daño.

—Tengo a los *chueh chang* ocupados construyendo ballestas aún más especiales y, además, tengo una solución para lo del foso.

Dio media vuelta. Tenía muchos asuntos de los que ocuparse y una reunión con cada *hsiao-wei*. Tenía que explicar bien a los seis coroneles de su ejército cuál era el plan de ataque.

En lo alto de la empalizada

—Ahí vienen —dijo Sexto.

—No han tardado ni un día desde que llegaron sus refuerzos —añadió Cayo mirando al centurión de Cartago Nova, quien, como en tantas otras ocasiones, había deducido certeramente el desarrollo de los acontecimientos.

Pero no habían estado ociosos: en previsión de un ejército enemigo aún más poderoso, Druso había pedido a sus hombres que excavaran un gran foso alrededor de toda la empalizada que habían llenado con agua del río Talas. ¿Sería eso suficiente para detener a aquel general han?

Oyeron un tumulto a sus espaldas y se volvieron: Zhizhi y sus oficiales también salían del recinto amurallado y se dirigían hacia una de las torres. El huno parecía hacerse acompañar no sólo de guerreros, sino también de algunas de sus mujeres. Ante la mirada inquisitiva de sus hombres, Druso les aclaró las ideas.

—Zhizhi querrá comprobar cómo se desarrolla la defensa de la ciudad sin dejar de divertirse con sus esposas.

—No parece muy propio de un guerrero —sugirió Sexto.

—No lo es —confirmó Druso, pero se oyeron tambores.

El ejército han de cuarenta mil hombres avanzaba hacia la empalizada: la infantería iba por delante: primero los guerreros vestidos con túnicas rojas, luego otros con corazas de cuero y cotas de malla y, por detrás, incontables arqueros con armas de todo tipo.

—Lo que no veo son esos guerreros altos que manejaban aquellos arcos especiales de largo alcance —dijo Sexto.

—Yo tampoco —añadió Druso con aire inquieto. Entonces observó que una unidad de infantería enemiga se desgajaba del grueso del ejército han e iba en dirección a un lateral de la empalizada y tras ellos caminaban aquellos guerreros altos con sus pesados arcos—. Allí están.

—¿Por qué allí? —preguntó Nanaifarn.

—No lo sé... —añadió Druso con el ceño fruncido. Tenían el foso lleno de agua y una empalizada con torres, y todo construido sobre un altozano, no pronunciado pero sí algo elevado, lo que les otorgaba una posición de ventaja. El centurión no dejaba de mirar hacia aquella unidad de infantería enemiga escindida del resto—. Hemos de detenerlos como sea —dijo Druso con rapidez—. ¡Rápido, Sexto, Cayo, coged a todos los hombres y vamos hacia aquel extremo de la empalizada!

—Pero... ¿por qué? —inquirió Cayo.

—¡Por Hércules y todos los dioses, Cayo! —exclamó Sexto— ¡Hagamos lo que dice!

Druso ya caminaba en aquella dirección y no miraba atrás.

Infantería han, flanco izquierdo

El general Tang en persona comandaba la unidad de infantería que se había separado del resto de las tropas. Había dejado al viejo gobernador Kan Yen al mando supremo, y confiaba en que cada *hsiao-wei* supiera mantener el orden y la disciplina durante el ataque.

—¡Aquí! —ordenó Tang, y la unidad de infantería se detuvo. Estaban a unos trescientos *bu* de distancia de la empalizada y el foso—. ¡Empezad a cavar! —exclamó con energía y luego se dirigió a los *chueh chang*—. ¡Y vosotros preparad las ballestas!

Torre del sector oeste de la empalizada

—Eso es... —dijo Druso entre dientes.

—Están cavando una zanja —comento Sexto enarcando las cejas y restregándose los ojos.

Nanaifarn y Cayo no decían nada, pero compartían la confusión de Sexto. Druso asintió varias veces en silencio hasta que se decidió a hablar. Y rápido. No había tiempo o los han se saldrían con la suya.

—Quieren vaciar el foso —dijo el centurión, pero como sus hombres no parecían entenderlo, se explicó—. ¡Por Júpiter! ¿No lo veis? Estamos en un leve altozano, toda la fortaleza lo está y hemos llenado el foso sacando agua del río Talas, pero están cavando en una zona donde el terreno es inferior. Si esa zanja conecta con el foso, toda el agua que rodea la empalizada se escapará por allí e inundará aquella zona, hacia el oeste.

—Y sin el foso será mucho más fácil para los han atacar la empalizada —concluyó Sexto—. Todo el trabajo de estos días no habrá valido para nada.

—¿Y qué hacemos? —preguntó Cayo.

Druso inspiró profundamente. Luego exhaló todo el aire de golpe.

—Están fuera del alcance de nuestros arqueros. Hemos de salir y atacarlos...

—Zhizhi se negará —dijo Nanaifarn.

Nadie dijo nada. Todos sabían que el sogdiano llevaba razón.

—¿Entonces? —preguntó Cayo.

Druso se pasaba el dorso de la mano derecha por los labios.

—Entonces nos tocará a nosotros defender el foso. Esperaremos a que se aproximen con su zanja y estén a tiro de nuestros arqueros. En ese momento los masacraremos con todo lo que tengamos. Preparad arcos y flechas, todas las que tengáis y... —miró a Nanaifarn—, mira tú a ver si puedes convencer al resto de los sogdianos para que se concentren en ayudarnos.

—De acuerdo —respondió Nanaifarn y partió en busca de refuerzos.

Unidad militar han al suroeste de la empalizada

—¡Cavad, cavad, cavad! ¡Por el emperador! ¡Cavad! —gritaba Cheng Tang desde lo alto de su caballo.

Los túnicas rojas se afanaban con tesón en aquella obra. Los han estaban acostumbrados a excavar y a levantar muros. Eran disciplinados y silenciosos. Sudaban con profusión, pero nadie se detenía para secarse las gotas que resbalaban por la frente.

Cavar, cavar, cavar...

Torre del extremo suroccidental de la empalizada

—¡Trabajan a una velocidad sorprendente! —exclamó Sexto.

—Como si la vida les fuera en ello —añadió Cayo.

—Seguramente les va —sentenció Druso. Nanaifarn ya les había explicado que los túnicas rojas eran prisioneros, condenados, convictos. Aquella tenacidad en el trabajo sólo podía deberse a que su propia vida estaba en juego.

—Pronto estarán a tiro —añadió Sexto—. ¿Preparamos a los arqueros?

—Sí —ordenó Druso.

Había una docena en la propia torre y luego en varios puntos de la empalizada próximos a donde los túnicas rojas trabajaban. También había un importante grupo de arqueros romanos por detrás de la empalizada apuntando hacia el cielo. Estos últimos dispararían a ciegas, pero Druso había insistido en que lo esencial era disponer del máximo número de arqueros a un mismo tiempo.

—Preparaos... a mi voz... —dijo el centurión mirando a Sexto—; cuando baje el brazo...

Unidad militar han al suroeste de la empalizada

El general Tang miraba hacia la fortificación. Podía ver perfectamente a los arqueros enemigos dispuestos para arrojar una lluvia de flechas sobre los túnicas rojas. No sentía lástima por los convictos que iban a morir, pero era importante que pudieran seguir trabajando en la zanja hasta alcanzar el agua del foso. La clave de aquella batalla era drenar el río artificial de agua que protegía la empalizada de la ciudad de Talas. Si lo vaciaban todo era posible, si no estaban bloqueados.

Tang miró a su espalda. Un centenar de *chueh chang* habían cargado las ballestas más grandes nunca antes empleadas por un ejército han.

—¡Largad! —ordenó Tang.

En lo alto de la torre suroeste

Druso estaba a punto de dar la misma orden cuando las gigantescas flechas de las ballestas enemigas empezaron a impactar por todas partes. Una de ellas destrozó uno de los pilares de madera del techo de la torre y parte de la estructura se vino abajo. Otra atravesó el cuerpo de uno de los arqueros por completo, salpicando de sangre a todos los que allí estaban y clavándose al fin en la pared posterior de la garita de vigilancia. Otras muchas se clavaban en la empalizada causando graves desperfectos, cuando no matando directamente a los arqueros romanos, que caían a plomo sobre los arqueros de detrás de la estructura defensiva. La andanada de flechas han, enormes, poderosas y lanzadas desde una cómoda lejanía para estar a salvo de cualquier contraataque, había causado una escabechina entre las tropas romanas.

—¡Por todos los dioses! —gritó Druso gateando por el suelo de la torre y mirando a Sexto—. ¡Que disparen nuestros arqueros, los que hayan sobrevivido! ¡Que disparen ya!

Cayo y Sexto dieron la orden vociferando, tumbados en el suelo de la torre, mientras una segunda andanada de flechas han volaba por encima de ellos.

Los arqueros romanos supervivientes apuntaban contra los túnicas rojas desde lo alto de la empalizada y consiguieron abatir a algunos, pero la segunda andanada de flechas han acabó con ellos. Sólo quedaban los que estaban protegidos detrás de la empalizada, quienes disparando al cielo, sobrevolando la estructura defensiva de madera, conseguían alcanzar a algunos túnicas rojas, muy pocos, que seguían, sin descanso, trabajando en la zanja. Las flechas romanas no eran tan certeras, pues disparaban a ciegas. Pero aun así causaban algunas bajas y empezaban a generar algo de confusión entre los convictos del enemigo.

Unidad militar han al suroeste de la empalizada

—¡Apuntad a lo alto! —ordenó ahora el general Tang—. ¡Las flechas deben caer justo detrás de la empalizada!

Los *chueh chang* no necesitaban más explicaciones. Su vida había sido, desde siempre, disparar dardos con arcos y ballestas. Entendían perfectamente de qué se trataba y apuntaron de forma certera hacia el cielo calculando bien la parábola de sus flechas mortíferas.

Torre suroccidental

—¡Los han matado a todos! —exclamó Cayo—. ¡A todos!

—¡No nos quedan arqueros! —gritó Sexto gateando por el suelo de la torre. Y luego murmuró unas palabras para sí mismo—: Más nubes oscuras de flechas. La maldición de Ateyo nos perseguirá hasta el fin del mundo.

—¡Abajo, abajo! —ordenó Druso.

Aquél era un desastre tan brutal como el de Carrhae. O peor. La caballería *hsiung-nu* había sido repelida por los arqueros han y su infantería y ahora sólo con las ballestas gigantes acababan de aniquilar a los arqueros de los que disponían. Más de un centenar de hombres muertos.

Druso, Sexto, Cayo y Nanaifarn estaban ya al pie de la empalizada, muy pegados a la estructura con el fin de evitar ser alcanzados por una nueva lluvia de flechas. Además se protegían con los escudos.

—¿Qué hacemos? —preguntó Sexto.

—¡Salimos! —aulló Druso encolerizado, pero con la mente fría—. ¡Es lo único que no esperan! ¡Salimos y matamos a todos los túnicas rojas que podamos y nos retiramos! Contra sus arqueros no podemos, pero vamos a detener esa maldita zanja. —Se dirigió a los legionarios que estaban junto a la puerta de aquel sector—. ¡Abrid, por Hércules, abrid y seguidme! ¡Formación en *testudo*! —Y continuó para sí mismo mientras se ajustaba el casco—: Se van a enterar esos malditos guerreros han de Xeres. Se van a enterar de cómo se las gastan los legionarios de Roma.

Unidad militar han al noroeste de la empalizada

La zanja progresaba.

Aniquilados los arqueros enemigos, no parecía haber ya nada que pudiera importunar los trabajos. El general Tang estaba satisfecho y seguro de conseguir el objetivo marcado en poco tiempo cuando, de pronto, se abrió la puerta de la empalizada más próxima al lugar donde estaban cavando la gran zanja y, por un puente improvisado preparado por los enemigos y dispuesto sobre el foso a toda velocidad, salieron aquellos mercenarios extranjeros llegados de no se sabía dónde.

—¡Salen, mi *chiang-chün*! ¿Qué hacemos? —preguntó uno de los coroneles.

Tang no daba crédito a lo que veía: como en ocasiones anteriores, un regimiento de aquellos mercenarios salía de la fortificación cubriéndose con los escudos, como si fueran un gigantesco pez de escamas enormes en las que confiaban para protegerse de las flechas.

—¡Disparad! —ordenó Tang a los arqueros convencionales de los han.

Y lanzaron una andanada de flechas.

Tropas romanas en el sector suroccidental

—¡Aguantad! ¡Resistid! —aullaba Druso con toda la potencia de sus pulmones.

Clac, clac, clac... la lluvia de flechas cayó sobre ellos como si de granizo se tratara. Los escudos fuertemente reforzados de los romanos resistieron la andanada de dardos convencionales. Muchos de ellos quedaron clavados en los escudos, pero pese al peso extra, los romanos siguieron avanzando hacia los túnicas rojas que continuaban cavando la zanja.

Al poco, Druso y sus hombres llegaron a la zanja.

—¡Matad, matad! ¡Por todos los dioses, matadlos a todos! —ordenó el centurión al tiempo que separaba levemente su escudo del de su compañero para sacar el gladio y pinchar y pinchar y pinchar, hasta que la sangre roja de aquellos han de cabeza rapada se vertía por todas partes, por sus propios escudos, por sus caras, hasta por los ojos.

Sangre, sangre, sangre.

—¡Matad, matad, matad!

Posición de retaguardia de la unidad militar han en el sector suroccidental

El general Tang se volvió hacia los *chueh chang.*

—¡Disparad sobre ellos, que no quede uno vivo!

Y las ballestas gigantes soltaron su muerte perfecta.

Tropas romanas en el sector suroccidental

—¡Aggh! —gritó Cayo al tiempo que una enorme flecha atravesaba su escudo y se le clavaba en el hombro.

Y se oyeron un centenar de gritos más a su alrededor. Los dardos de las grandes ballestas atravesaban incluso los escudos reforzados de los romanos. Muchos caían heridos o muertos. El *testudo* se deshacía.

—¡Replegaos! ¡Ahora, todos! —ordenó Druso con frialdad.

Y los legionarios se retiraron superados por la última andanada de flechas, pero sólo después de haber dejado un montón de muertos entre los túnicas rojas, hasta el punto de haber conseguido detener el avance de la zanja.

El repliegue fue ordenado y veloz. En apenas unos instantes estaban todos los supervivientes de regreso en la empalizada, e iban ya a retirar el puente del foso y a cerrar la puerta, cuando Sexto empezó a gritar.

—¡Cayo, Cayo!

El oficial herido se arrastraba ya sin escudo ni gladio, con una enorme flecha que lo atravesaba por el hombro, de parte a parte, dejando un largo reguero de sangre en su retirada.

Sexto no se lo pensó y fue a por el amigo herido.

Los legionarios no sabían exactamente qué hacer y miraron a Druso.

—¡Esperad! —ordenó el centurión.

Sexto ya estaba con Cayo.

—¡Vamos, vamos, amigo mío! ¡Yo te ayudaré! —dijo el recién llegado, pero Cayo se desplomó sobre el suelo de aquella ladera de la fortaleza de Talas.

—Estoy... muerto... —dijo Cayo mirando al cielo azul—. Hasta aquí ha llegado mi viaje.

—¡No, tú regresarás conmigo! —dijo Sexto, abandonando su propio escudo, que lo protegía de las flechas enemigas, y levantando a Cayo al tiempo que gritaba con intensidad propia de un salvaje—: ¡Aaahhh! ¡Vamos, amigo mío!

Tropas han en el sector suroccidental

Los *chueh chang* aún estaban intentando recargar sus grandes ballestas, pero los arqueros convencionales ya estaban todos preparados y apuntando hacia aquel oficial mercenario que intentaba retirar a uno de los heridos.

—¡Esperamos la orden! —dijo el coronel al general, pero Tang guardaba silencio.

El *chiang-chün* Cheng Tang, jefe militar de la provincia de Gansu y las regiones occidentales del Imperio han, miraba cómo aquel mercenario llevaba en brazos, lentamente pero sin detenerse, como podía, a su compañero herido y cómo hasta había abandonado su escudo protector para ayudarlo. Aquellos malditos mercenarios habían acabado con más de un centenar de túnicas rojas y habían detenido, al menos por el momento, el avance de la zanja que tenían que cavar para drenar el foso. Sus hombres anhelaban matar a tantos de aquellos malditos mercenarios como pudieran, de cualquier forma, en cualquier modo. Pero Tang se volvió hacia su coronel y negó con la cabeza.

—No —dijo el general—. Nosotros no hacemos la guerra matando a los que arriesgan su vida para retirar a un compañero herido. Yo no hago la guerra de ese modo. Bajad los arcos. Todo el esfuerzo de esos guerreros es en vano. Nos reharemos y terminaremos la zanja que hemos empezado, pero hay que reconocerles pundonor a esos soldados del fin del mundo aun cuando sólo es cuestión de tiempo que los aniquilemos a todos.

Puerta suroccidental de la empalizada

Druso vio cómo los arqueros han dejaban de apuntar a Sexto y a Cayo en su lenta retirada hacia la puerta.

—Podría haberlos matado y no lo ha hecho —dijo entre dientes el centurión, pero no tuvo tiempo de pensar mucho más en aquella acción del líder de los han, pues Sexto ya estaba sobre las maderas que permitían superar el foso—. ¡Vamos, ayudadlo a entrar, retirad el puente y cerrad la puerta!

Sexto dejó a Cayo en el suelo.

—Estoy muy mal... —insistió Cayo.

—Te pondrás bien, por Cástor y Pólux, y acabaremos con todos esos malditos guerreros de Xeres, y yaceremos con muchas mujeres aún, de las de Zhizhi, de los sogdianos y hasta de los han —le respondió Sexto mientras le limpiaba el pecho para ver la herida, pero la sangre manaba a borbotones y supo, aunque se lo negaba una y otra vez, que todo era ya inútil.

Cayo ya no volvió a hablar, y al poco dejó de respirar. Sexto se abrazó al cadáver de su amigo y los legionarios hicieron un corro de silencio y respeto a su alrededor.

Entretanto Druso había subido a lo alto de la torre suroccidental, que aunque dañada por las flechas gigantes de los han, aún se tenía en pie. Lo acompañaba Nanaifarn y un par de *optiones* a la espera de órdenes.

—El general enemigo está sustituyendo a los túnicas rojas que hemos matado por soldados de su infantería regular para seguir con la zanja —dijo Nanaifarn—. Todo ha sido en vano y hemos perdido muchos hombres.

—En vano no —respondió Druso, que aún no daba aquella locura por perdida—. Yo he aprendido dos cosas con esta salida: primero, que el general enemigo es alguien con quien se puede negociar si conseguimos llegar a ello en algún momento.

Pero Druso calló. Estaba evaluando la situación mientras miraba hacia el exterior y al interior de la empalizada. A ambos lados.

—¿Y cuál es la otra cosa que dices que has averiguado, romano? —preguntó Nanaifarn.

—Que los han necesitan bastante tiempo para recargar esos arcos gigantes mortíferos. Demasiado tiempo. Aunque es cierto que el precio que hemos pagado para averiguar estas dos cosas ha sido muy caro.

Miró ahora hacia el corro de hombres que rodeaban el cadáver de Cayo. En aquella salida había perdido a uno de sus dos hombres de máxima confianza y a más de un centenar de legionarios. Apenas quedaban trescientos soldados de la legión perdida. Estaban al borde mismo de la aniquilación absoluta.

Unidad militar han en el sector suroccidental de la empalizada.

El general Tang observaba cómo los túnicas rojas supervivientes al ataque de los mercenarios de Zhizhi retiraban a los cadáveres y a los heridos. No era sólo por respeto a los caídos o mutilados, sino porque además, de no hacerlo, no tenían forma material de continuar cavando la zanja. Algunos ya empezaban a recuperar las palas, dejando las lanzas en el suelo, para reiniciar los trabajos, pero el *chiang-chün* podía percibir el desánimo. Los mercenarios habían perdido muchos hombres en aquella salida, pero habían sembrado la desesperanza entre los convictos.

—Que la infantería sustituya a los túnicas rojas en primera línea y que continúen con la zanja —ordenó Tang mirando a sus oficiales.

Y suspiró. Miró hacia el grueso de las tropas, a varios *li* de distancia, y sus ataques hacia la empalizada en otros sectores de la fortaleza: los arqueros de su ejército estaban causando múltiples bajas en el enemigo, y ni los guerreros de Kangchú ni los *hsiung-nu* parecían ofrecer una resistencia que fuera a ser duradera en el tiempo. Todo se podía conseguir. Sólo aquellos malditos mercenarios desconocidos plantaban cara como fieras salvajes acorraladas.

En la torre

—Hemos de volver a salir. Es una locura pero es lo único que no esperan —dijo Druso, aunque aún no era una orden, sino un pensamiento en voz alta—. Su infantería está a punto de concluir la zanja, y si lo hacen, entonces...

Pero no pudo terminar su frase. Unos sogdianos llegaron al pie de la torre y gritaron a Nanaifarn.

Sexto, que acababa de subir a la torre, miró al sogdiano.

—¿Qué ocurre? —preguntó el de Corduba, ya que Druso ni siquiera se había vuelto, pues mantenía la mirada fija en la zanja que seguían excavando los guerreros han.

—Los arqueros enemigos han herido a Zhizhi y éste se ha retirado junto con sus esposas y sus oficiales al interior del sector amurallado. Todos los *hsiung-nu* han abandonado la empalizada. Sólo quedan los míos, los guerreros de Sogdiana, defendiendo la fortificación de madera...

Ahora fue Nanaifarn el que no pudo continuar hablando, porque un extraño estruendo, como si un gran río de aguas bravas se les echara encima, se oyó a los pies de la torre. Todos se acercaron al borde las protecciones, justo allí donde el centurión de Cartago Nova seguía clavado, observando los trabajos de los han.

—Ya lo han conseguido —dijo Druso en voz baja.

Y es que los hombres del general enemigo habían logrado que la zanja llegara hasta el mismísimo foso. Los romanos no disponían ya de arqueros con los que desalentar a los infantes han y éstos habían logrado su objetivo. La zanja había abierto una gran brecha en el foso y como la zanja estaba en la pendiente y el foso en una zona más alta, toda el agua de aquel canal artificial se iba en un gigantesco reguero de barro, agua y piedras, arrastrándolo todo a su paso. Tal era la fuerza del agua del foso liberada que los guerreros han tuvieron que correr hacia los lados de la zanja a toda velocidad para ponerse a salvo y no verse arrastrados por aquella corriente descontrolada. No todos lo consiguieron.

—Algunos caen en su propia trampa —comentó Sexto algo ilusionado.

—No te engañes —le replicó Druso—. Es mayor nuestra pérdida.

Pero el centurión no dio más detalles sobre sus oscuros pensamientos.

Miró al cielo: estaba nublado y la tarde caía sobre Asia. Pronto sería de noche. Una noche muy larga. Druso escupió en el suelo. El general enemigo no era hombre de tomarse ni siquiera una noche de descanso.

Ejército han

Centenares de guerreros bajo el mando del general Tang reunían grandes montones de madera en primera línea. Varias docenas de hombres la untaban con grasa y añadían estiércol seco del ganado que, semanas atrás, arrebataran a los guerreros de Kangchú en el valle del río Ili. El *chiang-chün* había ordenado almacenar madera y estiércol desde que se habían instalado frente a la ciudad fortificada. Todos, hasta el gobernador Kan Yen, habían concluido que el general, con buen criterio, estaba acumulando leña para el gélido invierno que se aproximaba.

—Pensaba que la madera era para el frío que se nos vendrá encima en unas semanas —dijo Kan Yen al general Tang. El viejo *shou* era el único con autoridad suficiente para cuestionar o indagar sobre una orden del jefe militar supremo de aquel ejército.

—No tengo intención de pasar el invierno aquí, gobernador —respondió el general y se alejó junto con sus oficiales hasta que su figura se desvaneció en medio de las sombras de aquella noche sin luna.

Kan Yen no preguntó más. Observó que la noche había caído sobre el campamento pero que nadie había encendido antorchas. Estaban totalmente a oscuras.

—¿No vais a encender hogueras? —preguntó el viejo *shou* a uno de los coroneles.

—Son instrucciones del general, mi señor —respondió el *hsiao wei*—: nada de fuego hasta nueva orden... —El alto oficial dudó—, pero si el gobernador cree que debemos...

—No —respondió Kan Yen con rapidez—. Si el general Tang ha dado esas órdenes debemos seguirlas.

El oficial se inclinó ante el gobernador y Kan Yen, con el paso lento de la edad, se separó un poco del coronel escrutando con los ojos la negrura que lo envolvía todo.

En el interior de la fortaleza

Druso miraba al cielo repleto de estrellas. Luego se quedó inmóvil, escuchando.

—¿Pasa algo? —preguntó Sexto en voz baja.

—¿No lo oyes? —respondió Druso con otra interrogante y una mano en alto para que nadie hablara.

El de Corduba se quedó quieto, intentando captar algún ruido.

—No se oye nada —dijo Sexto en voz baja.

—Precisamente —confirmó el centurión de Cartago

Nova—: Nada. Sólo silencio. No es normal. Primero forzaron a la caballería de los *hsiung-nu* a retirarse cuando éstos los atacaban. Luego hirieron al mismísimo Zhizhi, consiguieron vaciar el foso y nos causaron innumerables bajas... ¿Y no lo celebran?

—Es raro, sí —admitió Nanaifarn, que, como siempre, hacía la ronda nocturna con ellos. A Druso le gustaba tenerlo siempre próximo para poder comunicarse con los oficiales sogdianos.

De pronto se oyeron gritos.

—¿Qué ocurre? ¿Qué dicen? —preguntó Druso.

—¡Fuego! —respondió Nanaifarn—. Dicen que hay un fuego...

—No —le corrigió Druso—: hay varios.

Y el centurión señaló a diferentes puntos de la empalizada donde las llamas lamían los postes de madera consumiéndolos.

—¡Por Hércules, por eso era tan sumamente importante el foso! —exclamó Sexto, que ahora entendía la insistencia de su centurión en intentar mantener aquella barrera de agua. Sin ella, los han habían podido acumular madera en diferentes sectores de la empalizada y, aprovechando la noche, incendiarla para quemar toda la barrera fortificada exterior de la ciudad.

Ejército han

Fue cuestión de poco tiempo. Una vez iniciadas las llamas, alimentadas por la grasa y el estiércol, éstas quemaron con rapidez la empalizada, quebrándola en varios puntos.

—¡No os confiéis! —aullaba el general Tang galopando con su caballo entre sus hombres. Los guerreros ya habían encendido antorchas para iluminarse y poder maniobrar sin tropezar los unos con los otros, además de que contaban con la inestimable ayuda de los incendios aún en progreso de la empalizada—. Apuntad hacia las llamas. Todos preparados, a mi señal.

Interior de la fortificación

—¿Qué hacen? —preguntó ahora Sexto señalando a decenas de jinetes *hsiung-nu* que se lanzaban en desorden hacia las aberturas de la empalizada—. Es una locura intentar defender la fortificación en medio de las llamas.

—No van a defenderla —precisó Druso.

—¿A qué van entonces? —inquirió Nanaifarn.

—Intentan huir.

Ejército han

—¡Ahora, ahora, por el emperador! —gritó el general Tang.

La lluvia de flechas de todo tipo y dimensión se adentró en el mar de llamas justo cuando los primeros jinetes *hsiung-nu* galopaban en su avance desesperado entre el fuego, en busca de una escapatoria a aquella batalla del infierno. Los dardos se clavaron tanto en hombres como en bestias. Los animales relinchaban aterrorizados por las heridas y el fuego que los rodeaba.

Fue una masacre completa.

Ni uno solo de aquellos jinetes consiguió escapar de la fortaleza de Talas.

En el interior del sector amurallado

Druso, Sexto y el resto de los romanos supervivientes, junto con Nanaifarn y los guerreros sogdianos, se replegaron al interior de la parte amurallada de la fortaleza.

Las puertas se cerraron.

La empalizada ardía a su alrededor y el humo hacía que muchos guerreros y habitantes de la capital del imperio de Zhizhi tosieran y les costara respirar. El viento del norte se despertó en medio de aquella noche de fuego y aunque avivaba el incendio de la fortificación exterior, facilitó que el humo se alejara de la parte amurallada del centro. Aunque pequeño, aquello supuso un alivio para los guerreros romanos, sogdianos y hunos que aún quedaban en aquella ciudad asediada.

Druso, junto con Sexto y Nanaifarn, fue admitido en la torre donde Zhizhi, herido en la cara, con un ojo vendado, y aún sangrando por la sien, daba todavía órdenes a los oficiales que habían permanecido fieles a su causa y que no habían intentado huir.

—No lo da todo por perdido —tradujo Nanaifarn en voz baja para que Druso y Sexto pudieran saber lo que decía—. Se han recibido mensajeros anunciando la inminente llegada de refuerzos sogdianos que atacarán a los han esta misma noche. No cree que el general Tang vaya a retirarse, pero basta con que se alargue el asedio y llegue el invierno.

—En eso puede tener razón —comentó Sexto.

—Es posible —admitió Druso, pero sin convicción. Olía la derrota a millas de distancia y sentía que el imperio de Zhizhi se desmoronaba por momentos. Pero no podían salir de allí sin ser masacrados por los han, tal y como les había pasado a los jinetes hunos que habían intentado huir. Su destino, para bien o para mal, estaba ligado al desenlace de aquella batalla en el centro de Asia, luchando en el bando de un loco contra un general hábil y astuto. El invierno, ciertamente, era lo único que podía salvarlos.

Ejército han

Las llamas remitían y la infantería han había cruzado los rescoldos que atestiguaban que hacía unos momentos allí había habido una gran empalizada. Las tropas tomaban ahora posiciones alrededor de toda la gran muralla interior de arcilla que protegía el centro de Talas.

—No es de piedra —dijo el gobernador Kan Yen—. ¿Podrás con este nuevo obstáculo como lo hiciste con el foso y la barrera de madera?

—No se trata de poder, sino de querer —sentenció Cheng Tang.

—Las estrellas están desapareciendo —continuó el ancia-

772

no *shou*, para quien los motivos de preocupación no parecían tener fin—. Eso significa nubes y con el frío que hace no será lluvia, sino nieve. Y ésta animará a los defensores e inquietará a nuestros soldados.

—Más motivo para persistir en el ataque.

—¡*Chiang-chün!* —exclamó uno de los coroneles.

Tang se volvió.

—¿Qué ocurre?

—Vienen refuerzos para ayudar a Zhizhi. Centenares de jinetes. Algunos hablan de miles.

—¿Guerreros de Kangchú o *hsiung-nu*? —preguntó el general Tang.

—No lo sé, mi señor —respondió el *hsiao wei* con expresión confusa en el rostro. No entendía qué importancia podía tener aquella precisión. Tang, que comprendió la incapacidad de su interlocutor para valorar lo que era relevante de lo que no, lo empujó a un lado y fue a por su caballo.

—Si son de Kangchú pactaré con ellos —dijo Tang mirando al gobernador, como si buscara su aprobación en un asunto que era ya no sólo militar, sino también político.

—Hemos venido aquí para terminar con Zhizhi y su imperio de locura, no con el reino de Kangchú —confirmó el anciano *shou*—. Actúa según creas oportuno, con la fuerza o con la negociación.

—Con ambas —replicó el general Tang mientras azuzaba su caballo—. Sólo desde la fuerza aceptarán un pacto.

En lo alto de la muralla

Druso observaba, junto con un pequeño grupo de sus hombres, la llegada de los jinetes sogdianos en medio de la noche. Era difícil calcular su número, pues había que orientarse por las antorchas que éstos portaban, pero todos convinieron en que eran al menos dos o tres mil.

—No son suficientes para forzar a los han a levantar el asedio —comentó Sexto.

—No, pero sí suficientes para incomodar sus operaciones,

alargar la lucha y... —Druso extendió la mano y sintió el gélido frío de los primeros copos—. Está empezando a nevar. Ese miserable de Zhizhi siempre ayudado por sus dioses del sol, la tierra, el fuego y el aire. Es sorprendente cuánta suerte puede tener un ser tan loco y cruel.

—Quizá sean nuestros dioses los que nos ayudan —sugirió Sexto.

—Desengáñate, amigo —contrapuso el centurión de Cartago Nova—: desde que cruzamos el Oxo, los dioses de Roma son sólo una sombra lejana que ni gobierna ni influye en las guerras de este lugar perdido del mundo. O esos jinetes alargan el asedio y el invierno fuerza a los han a retirarse o estaremos solos, con nuestros trescientos *gladios* y escudos, frente a un ejército imperial han.

—Trescientos, como en las Termópilas —dijo Sexto entonces, con una sonrisa.

—Esto no es las Termópilas, Sexto. Algo me dice que de esta batalla se hablará poco en el futuro y de nosotros aún menos.

—¿Por qué se hablará poco de nosotros? —inquirió Sexto.

—Nadie quiere recordar las derrotas.

Ejército han

La caballería de Kangchú recién llegada había decidido no intentar rodear al ejército han que asediaba la fortaleza de Talas. Eso les habría obligado a diseminarse demasiado y preferían permanecer juntos, al menos durante la noche.

El general Tang estaba cansado. Llevaba toda la noche sin dormir, y lo mismo gran parte de sus tropas. Acababa de establecer los primeros turnos para que soldados, arqueros y jinetes han pudieran descansar unas horas mientras otras unidades equivalentes permanecían en guardia.

Había escaramuzas constantes, pero los arqueros han y las ballestas gigantes de los *chueh chang* eran suficientes para obligar a los jinetes enemigos a retirarse.

—Combaten sin creer en la victoria —dijo el gobernador Kan Yen—. ¿Por qué no negociar con ellos ya?

—Aún no —replicó el general Tang. Y ordenó que la infantería se posicionara en formación de ataque allí donde la caballería enemiga parecía estar reagrupándose. Además dio instrucciones de que los soldados han dejaran de lado sus lanzas y, en su lugar, se equiparan con tambores, cacerolas, sartenes y todo tipo de utensilios de cocina.

El gobernador veía cómo tenían lugar aquellas extrañas operaciones con el ceño fruncido, pero la seguridad del general hizo que se mantuviera en silencio.

La luz del alba rasgó el cielo por el este.

La caballería de Kangchú, más de tres mil jinetes, cargó contra la infantería han, tan inapropiadamente equipada para repeler su ataque. Los soldados de Tang echaban de menos sus lanzas y tenían puestas sus esperanzas en los arqueros que estaban posicionados tras ellos. El general Cheng Tang se situó junto a los *chueh chang*. La caballería de Kangchú se lanzaba ya al galope contra ellos. Puede que hubieran combatido con titubeos durante la noche, pero aquella carga era un ataque en toda regla.

—¡Ahora! —gritó Tang.

—¡Ahora, ahora! —repetían los coroneles y el resto de los oficiales del ejército han.

Pero nadie disparó una sola flecha. La caballería estaba a tiro de los *chueh chang* y seguía avanzando. En lugar de dardos silbando en el aire, se oyó el enorme estruendo de miles de tambores y utensilios de metal de toda condición siendo golpeados los unos contra los otros. Además, todos los soldados han gritaron con todas sus fuerzas, por un lado porque el general así lo había ordenado y por otro de puro miedo. Muchos habrían gritado de igual forma aunque no se les hubiera dado instrucciones en ese sentido. Tambores, miles de utensilios de metal golpeados unos contra otros y alaridos de terror. Fue un estruendo gigantesco que sacudió las entrañas mismas del valle y llegó hasta las murallas de la fortificación de Zhizhi, pero, sobre todo, alcanzó la primera línea de la caballería de Kangchú. Los animales se vieron aturdidos por aquel inesperado estruendo y, confundidos unos, asustados otros y todos muy nerviosos intentaron detenerse o dar media vuelta, creando un caos completo. Unos jinetes caían de los aterrados caballos y se partían el cuello al impactar a toda velocidad con el suelo. Otros conseguían mantenerse sobre las monturas, pero sus compañeros que llegaban detrás chocaban con ellos y bestias y guerreros terminaban cayendo al fin heridos, contusionados. Fueron unos instantes de confusión absoluta donde los jinetes de Kangchú perdieron a muchos hombres antes de que sus oficiales consiguieran reorganizar las primeras líneas de la caballería y reiniciar la carga contra un enemigo cuyo ruido metálico y cuyos tambores ya no sorprendían ni a caballos ni a guerreros. El ataque se retomaba de nuevo, pero el ímpetu de la gran carga inicial se había perdido.

—¡Largad! —ordenó entonces el general Tang.

Y ahora sí, miles de arqueros han junto con las ballestas de los *chueh chang* escupieron infinidad de flechas sobre el enemigo.

Los sogdianos se batieron en retirada de inmediato.

Tras ellos dejaban un largo reguero de muertos y heridos.

—Ahora negociaremos —dijo el general Tang al gobernador—. Les hemos causado muchas bajas, pero aún son suficientes para incomodarnos en nuestro asedio a la fortaleza. Sin embargo, ahora se avendrán negociar. —Miró al gobernador directamente a los ojos—. ¿Puedo dejar esto en tus manos mientras yo me ocupo de Zhizhi, los *hsiung-nu* y sus malditos mercenarios?

—Puedes —dijo Kan Yen.

En lo alto de la muralla

Druso vio cómo la caballería sogdiana se retiraba y cómo salían mensajeros han tras ellos, al tiempo que todo el ejército de aquel general enemigo daba media vuelta y encaraba de nuevo la muralla de la fortaleza. Los túnicas rojas marchaban una vez más en primera línea; al menos lo que quedaba de ellos, pues muchos habían muerto en la salida que hiciera Zhizhi hacía unos días y luego en los trabajos de la zanja. Tras aquéllos iba la infantería enemiga al completo. Llevaban más antorchas y escalas de todo tipo. Era el ataque final.

—Nos retiramos de la muralla —dijo Druso en voz baja a Sexto—. Pasa la orden al resto de los hombres. Que los sogdianos que quedan o los hunos defiendan esta posición. Es sólo cuestión de tiempo y sangre que el enemigo escale la muralla, y no será nuestra sangre la que se vierta en esta nueva lucha.

—¿Y Nanaifarn?

Druso se detuvo un momento.

—Siempre nos ha sido leal —respondió el centurión—. Dile que si quiere venir con nosotros, puede hacerlo. En todo caso se trata sólo de morir antes o después. Que elija él cuándo y con quién.

Ejército han

El general Tang comprobó que la lucha por acceder a lo alto de la muralla fue mucho menos cruenta de lo que había imaginado. Sólo había costado unos centenares de túnicas rojas y unos pocos infantes. Era un precio aceptable por aquel nuevo avance.

Tomada la muralla, sus hombres abrieron las puertas con rapidez y el grueso de las tropas han, incluida la caballería, con Tang al frente, entraron en la fortaleza de Zhizhi. El *chiang-chün* paseó la mirada por el interior del recinto amurallado y evaluó la situación con rapidez mientras un *hsiao wei* lo informaba.

—La mayoría de los guerreros de Kangchú que quedaban han muerto en la muralla y los *hsiung-nu* se han refugiado en el palacio.

—Ya veo —dijo el general Tang—. ¿Y los mercenarios?

—No lo sabemos, *chiang-chün*.

—Pues hay que averiguarlo: son pocos pero peligrosos —ordenó Tang y azuzó su caballo para adentrarse en la ciudad rodeado por su caballería.

Había muchas viviendas arracimadas unas con las otras por todas partes. Se veían tiendas cerradas y lo que quizá en su momento fueron tabernas, pero ahora mucho de todo lo que se podía observar estaba o en llamas o abandonado. La gente salía de sus casas y se arrodillaba implorando clemencia. La mayoría eran artesanos y comerciantes que vivían bajo el gobierno de Zhizhi. En algunos casos habían acudido allí por avaricia, para enriquecerse gracias al pillaje con el que el *chanyu* de los temibles *hsiung-nu* tenía sometida a toda la región, pero otros habían sido llevados allí a la fuerza por los hombres del implacable líder de los hunos de Asia central. Tang podía leer en las caras el terror y el sufrimiento de muchos de aquellos hombres, mujeres y niños. Pero también había guerreros de Kangchú y *hsiung-nu* ocultos entre la gran masa de la población que se rendía en busca también de clemencia, intentando pasar desapercibidos entre el resto.

El palacio fue rodeado.

—¡Quemadlo! —ordenó el general Tang sin un ápice de duda.

Las llamas pronto lamieron la gran construcción de madera del centro de la ciudad de Talas, donde Zhizhi se había refugiado con sus esposas, cien guerreros leales y su heredero al trono.

Al poco tiempo, los primeros guerreros empezaron a salir de entre las llamas gritando, tosiendo, unos a gatas, otros armados con espadas encarando a los soldados han. Los que buscaban lucha eran acribillados por los arqueros; los otros eran apresados y conducidos a una gran explanada en el centro de la ciudad. Al fin, el propio Zhizhi salió andando del palacio en llamas, herido en la cara y el costado, asistido por su hijo, el heredero al trono de aquel imperio de Asia central que estaba desapareciendo, aquel que había estado retenido por los han años atrás y que retornó con la embajada que fue masacrada por el propio Zhizhi. Ahora el círculo de aquella historia llegaba a su fin. También fueron apresadas varias de las esposas. Todos fueron conducidos, junto con el resto de los guerreros *hsiung-nu* y de Kangchú que se rendían, a la plaza de la ciudad en ruinas.

Una vez allí, los coroneles, siguiendo las instrucciones del general Tang, hicieron dos grandes grupos.

—A la derecha, mi *chiang-chün* —dijo uno de los oficiales mirando a Tang montado a lomos de su caballo—, están los que nos han parecido comerciantes, artesanos u otras gentes, junto con la mayoría de las mujeres y los niños. Hay algo más de mil. A éstos no los hemos contado aún del todo. A la izquierda están los guerreros *hsiung-nu* y de Kangchú, el heredero al trono, las esposas de Zhizhi, algunos niños de su familia y el propio Zhizhi. Éstos suman un total de mil quinientos dieciocho. También hemos encontrado las credenciales de Ku Chi y el resto de los embajadores han asesinados por orden de Zhizhi hace unos años. Ahora... ¿qué hacemos?

El general Tang no dijo nada. Desmontó de su caballo lentamente y paseó por delante de todos los prisioneros hasta detenerse ante Zhizhi. Éste, aunque con heridas múltiples, aún orgulloso y desafiante, permanecía en pie.

—Arrodíllate —ordenó Tang en chino.

Zhizhi no se movió.

El general volvió a hablar.

—Arrodíllate... si quieres vivir.

Zhizhi tragó saliva y sangre. Como tantos otros hunos, entendía suficiente chino, la lengua del enemigo permanente, como para comprender la oferta que se le estaba haciendo. No había pensado ni por un solo instante que el general enemigo fuera a concederle la posibilidad de permanecer con vida, pero ante aquella oferta se tragó todo su orgullo y se arrodilló con rapidez.

Cheng Tang asintió varias veces.

—Sólo quería saber si eras realmente valiente o sólo un miserable cobarde —dijo Tang mientras desenvainaba su espada *jian* de doble filo. Sin decir más dio un paso atrás, asió con ambas manos fuertemente la afilada arma y la dirigió a toda velocidad contra el cuello de Zhizhi.

La cabeza del líder de los *hsiung-nu* de Asia central voló por los aires con una estúpida mueca de sorpresa.

El general Tang envainó entonces el arma y se dirigió al *hsiao wei* que tenía a su lado.

—Cortad vosotros las otras mil quinientas diecisiete cabezas de este grupo —dijo y echó a andar para acercarse a su caballo—. Al resto perdonadles la vida.

Ya tenía al animal cogido por las riendas cuando llegó

un oficial corriendo desde las proximidades del palacio incendiado.

—Ya hemos encontrado a los mercenarios, mi *chiang-chün* y...

—¿Y? —preguntó el general Tang mientras subía a lo alto de su caballo como si aquello no fuera ya una gran noticia.

Pero el oficial tardaba en responder, hasta que la mirada del general, inquisitiva y exigente, lo forzó a explicarse con más precisión.

—No se rinden.

Tang apretó los puños al tiempo que hablaba. Estaba exhausto. Llevaba casi dos días sin dormir. No fueron palabras. Era casi como un rugido de rabia.

—¿Cuántos son?

—No más de trescientos, mi señor.

—Y nosotros treinta y nueve mil. ¿Y aun así no se rinden?

—No, mi señor.

Tang se llevó las yemas de los dedos de su mano derecha a los ojos. El sueño lo vencía por momentos. Suspiró al tiempo que dictaba sentencia.

—Pues tendremos que acabar con todos.

HISTORIA DE TRAJANO

Principios del siglo II d.C.

LIBRO VII
LA REBELIÓN

100

LA MALDICIÓN DE BABILONIA

Puerta de Istar, Babilonia
Noviembre de 116 d.C.

El emperador de Roma entró en Babilonia.
¿Hacía mal?
Los antiguos sacerdotes caldeos ya avisaron a Alejandro Magno de que no entrara en la ciudad, pero el gran conquistador macedonio desafió aquella advertencia. No quería someterse a unos sacerdotes extranjeros de un pueblo derrotado.
Trajano lo estuvo considerando todo el tiempo desde que ascendiera por el curso del Éufrates desde Carax y el golfo Pérsico con su flota imperial. Decidió desoír los avisos de aquellos sacerdotes del enemigo, pero estaría atento a prodigios o señales funestas. El César recordaba las palabras de Plutarco sobre Alejandro Magno y también sobre sí mismo, sobre Trajano, de quien el augur griego había dicho que había visto su muerte en aquellas campañas de Oriente, pero el emperador seguía persuadido de que lo que había percibido el sacerdote de Queronea era su muerte en el terremoto de Antioquía; sin embargo él había sobrevivido. Por eso se sentía más seguro. Estaba convencido de que los dioses romanos habían decidido protegerlo contra todo y contra todos. Otro asunto era lo que Plutarco había escrito sobre el legendario conquistador macedonio: según el sacerdote griego, cuando Alejandro llegó a las puertas de Babilonia vio a unos cuervos luchando entre ellos e hiriéndose unos a otros con brutalidad y algunos de aquellos pájaros negros terminaron cayendo muertos a los pies del gran macedonio. Plutarco también recordaba que se había hecho un sacrificio en honor al propio Alejandro

y que faltaba parte del hígado del animal sacrificado, lo que los augures de su época interpretaron como un terrible designio. Y Alejandro Magno, conquistador de la mayor parte del mundo conocido, a las puertas de Babilonia, tuvo, por fin, miedo.

Y no entró, sino que acampó a las afueras de la ciudad durante días en los que se acumularon aún más señales y prodigios terribles. Pese a todo, al final, Alejandro Magno optó por quebrantar el consejo de todos sus augures y, para mostrar al mundo que él no tenía miedo ni a ejércitos ni a designios, entró al fin, por la gran Puerta de Istar, en la ciudad de Babilonia. Pero a los pocos meses, Alejandro murió de unas fiebres. No se supo nunca si por causa natural o por envenenamiento.

Los remeros del barco insignia de la flota imperial romana dejaron de bogar Éufrates arriba cuando llegaron a la altura de la entrada norte a la ciudad de Babilonia, la mítica Puerta de Istar. Trajano, seguido de cerca por Liviano, el prefecto de la guardia pretoriana, descendió de la embarcación. Con él desembarcaron Lucio Quieto, Nigrino y otros *legati* de la expedición romana a Oriente: Julio Máximo, Erucio Claro o Julio Alejandro, entre otros. Algunas autoridades locales se habían reunido junto a la gran puerta de azulejos azules y ocres para recibir al victorioso César, pero Trajano los ignoró. No por afán de humillarlos, sino porque había aprendido que allí sólo se valoraba al soberano que se comportaba con desdén aparente hacia sus súbditos. En Partia imponía más el oro de las letras tejidas en las velas de los barcos de la flota romana, o la pose altanera y distante con la que Trajano avanzaba, subido a lomos de un hermoso caballo blanco hacia la gran Puerta de Istar, que cualquier acto magnánimo. No por ello se conducía como un tirano ni tomaba decisiones crueles contra los conquistados, pero sabía que no debía mostrarse particularmente proclive a la condescendencia en actos públicos. Y la entrada en Babilonia del emperador de Roma era uno de los actos públicos más importantes que nunca un conquistador podía hacer en su vida. Por otro lado, Trajano no tuvo que esforzarse para no prestar atención a aquella comitiva de ciudadanos de Babilonia, pues sus ojos estaban clavados en la gigantesca entrada norte a la ciudad: la Puerta de Istar. Desde lo más alto hasta la base misma, toda aquella parte de la muralla, el arco de entrada de la puerta y las paredes de la calle que se adentraba hacia el interior de la legendaria ciudad estaban recubiertos de unos azulejos azules y ocres que refulgían bajo la poderosa luz del sol. Estaban próximos al invierno, pero allí el calor aún era notable. Babilonia, rodeada por las aguas del Éufrates y numerosos canales, podía resultar inhabitable en los meses de verano, por eso Trajano, siguiendo en este punto los consejos de su médico, el griego Critón, había esperado hasta el final del otoño para acercarse a la ciudad donde murió Alejandro Magno.

—César —dijo Quieto. Trajano se volvió hacia él.

El norteafricano señalaba hacia un grupo de legionarios que custodiaban a una joven.

El emperador asintió e hizo una señal a los legionarios para que acercaran a la muchacha. Cuando estuvo apenas a unos pasos de su montura, Trajano se dirigió a ella en griego.

—He pedido a mis hombres que encontraran a alguien que supiera de Babilonia y su pasado y mis oficiales me han dicho que tú, Aryazate, hija de Osroes, les comentaste que sabías mucho de esta ciudad. ¿Es esto cierto?

—Así es, César —respondió la joven con templanza.

—¿Y cómo puede ser eso si siempre has vivido en Cesifonte?

—Porque Rixnu, la antigua reina consorte del *Šāhān Šāh* Osroes, era gran amiga mía y ella provenía de Babilonia y siempre me contó historias sobre su ciudad, César.

El César asintió.

—Que le den un caballo —ordenó Trajano.

Los caballos de la comitiva imperial, con el emperador siempre al frente, avanzaron hacia la Puerta de Istar. Al poco estaban al pie mismo del gran arco de entrada. Las autoridades de la Babilonia sometida, reunidas a un lado de la entrada abierta, se inclinaron en señal de sumisión. Trajano frenó su caballo y todo el séquito quedó detenido.

El César miró hacia los azulejos brillantes.

Entrar o no entrar en Babilonia. ¿Le pasaría a él lo que a

Alejandro? Critón le había aconsejado esperar a las temperaturas más tibias de noviembre, pues estaba convencido de que en las ciudades rodeadas de pantanos o canales había siempre más fiebres con el calor que en épocas más frescas. El médico griego siempre se había mostrado certero en sus consideraciones y Trajano había aceptado aquel consejo. Pero más allá de aquella prudente prevención, detenerse ahora y no entrar sería una muestra de debilidad enorme que un conquistador no podía permitirse. Los babilonios se reirían de él y en poco tiempo la noticia de que Marco Ulpio Trajano, *Imperator Caesar Augustus*, había dado media vuelta frente a la Puerta de Istar y había decidido no entrar en Babilonia por miedo a fantasmas del pasado llegaría a todos los puntos de las nuevas provincias de Mesopotamia, Armenia y Asiria, además de, por supuesto, Babilonia. Y el eco de aquel acto de miedo —o prudencia quizá, pero que siempre sería interpretado como miedo, en particular por sus enemigos—, se extendería por todos los confines de Oriente: su decisión sería motivo de conversación y burla en la corte kushan de Bagram y quién sabía si más lejos, en la desconocida Xeres, hacia donde había mandado a emisarios con un mensaje secreto; de saberse allí que no se había atrevido a entrar en Babilonia dicho mensaje perdería toda fuerza y sentido. También se extendería la noticia de su miedo por Occidente: llegaría primero a Antioquía, a los oídos de su ambicioso sobrino Adriano, que vería en aquel gesto una prueba, por primera vez, de miedo en su tío, y eso lo animaría aún más en sus planes, fueran los que fuesen, para acercarse al poder absoluto que tanto anhelaba. Trajano sabía que tenía que resolver, y pronto, el asunto de la sucesión... Pero la noticia de su miedo a entrar en Babilonia llegaría también hasta la mismísima Roma, donde los senadores enemigos, que los tenía, se frotarían las manos viendo, por primera vez, una grieta en la fortaleza de la autoridad imperial. Él no se había detenido ante el fantasma de la legión perdida ni en el Éufrates ni en el Tigris. Tampoco lo haría ahora.

Trajano miró entonces al cielo.

No se veían ni cuervos ni ningún otro pájaro.

Durante los sacrificios, nadie había observado nada extraño en las vísceras de los animales. Los dioses romanos seguían con él.

El emperador sacudió las riendas de su caballo y éste echó a andar de nuevo.

Marco Ulpio Trajano cruzó el arco de la gran Puerta de Istar y entró en la ciudad de Babilonia.

—¿Ha progresado el emperador en el objetivo de atrapar a mi padre, el *Šāhān Šāh* Osroes? —preguntó Aryazate sin pensar en que el César no se había dirigido a ella. La joven era una princesa parta prisionera, pero de sangre real, y no veía por qué no podía interpelar directamente al César con algo que la inquietaba.

Trajano, sin dejar de mirar hacia los refulgentes azulejos, respondió con serenidad.

—Osroes está escondido en algún lugar remoto del oriente de su antiguo imperio, sus ejércitos están derrotados y Armenia, Mesopotamia, Asiria y hasta Babilonia misma, en la que nos encontramos, sometidas como provincias romanas. Su capital, Cesifonte, es ahora un cuartel para mis legiones y los reinos que rendían vasallaje antes a Osroes, como Osroene, no reconocen ahora otro señor que no sea Roma.

—Pero mi padre sigue libre —replicó la joven, que cabalgaba al paso junto al César—. No debería el emperador de Roma infravalorar a mi padre. Es como una serpiente que parece muerta cuando sólo está dormida.

Trajano sabía del odio que había acumulado la joven hacia su padre después de que éste diera la orden de que se ejecutara a todas las mujeres de su séquito, incluida ella misma. Era normal esa rabia y más en alguien de sangre joven, pero la muchacha era incapaz de entender cuándo un imperio había sido completamente derrotado por otro. Trajano decidió dejar de lado aquel asunto y preguntó sobre los motivos ornamentales de aquellos magníficos azulejos azules y ocres.

—Veo muchos animales que conozco, como esos leones o aquellos otros de allí, pintados en ambas paredes, pero desconozco ese animal cuya imagen se repite una y otra vez.

—*Mušḫuššu* es su nombre —respondió Aryazate— en la lengua antigua de Babilonia. Se trata de un animal diferente, entre serpiente y dragón. Su cuerpo está cubierto de escamas, su lengua es como la de la serpiente pero tiene garras de águila en las patas traseras y de león en las delanteras, larga cola y cuello y una cresta.

—¿Un animal imaginado o quizá la imagen de un dios?

—Oh, no, César —respondió la joven princesa—. Es un animal que existía en tiempos de Nabucodonosor, sólo que ahora parece haber desaparecido.

—Ya veo —aceptó Trajano, siempre mirando desde lo alto de su caballo hacia aquellas paredes de ladrillos azules esmaltados que los envolvían con su ejército de animales silentes pero vigilantes.

—El César hace bien en admirarse de la belleza de la Puerta de Babilonia dedicada a la diosa Istar —continuó la muchacha con cierta felicidad al poder contar ahora algo de lo mucho que Rixnu había compartido con ella en el pasado; era como si su amiga aún estuviera allí—. Esta entrada de Babilonia estaba diseñada para llegar hasta el centro mismo de la ciudad, donde se levantaba la derruida gran torre de Babel que alcanzaba hasta el cielo. Ésta ha desaparecido, pero esta gran Puerta de Istar permanece como una de las grandes maravillas del mundo, según algunos. Me consta que depende de quién refiera el listado de maravillas del mundo, unos la incluyen y otros no. Si no recuerdo mal, augusto, según Filón de Bizancio, para ver las maravillas del mundo *hay que trasladarse a Persia, atravesar el Éufrates, viajar al Egipto, irse a vivir con los eleos de la Hélade, llegar a Halicarnaso de Caria, navegar a Rodas y contemplar Éfeso en Jonia.*[82] Sin embargo, para Antípatro de Sidón, las maravillas son las pirámides de Egipto, el Templo de Artemisa en Éfeso, el gran Mausoleo de Halicarnaso, el Coloso del Sol de Rodas y las enormes murallas y los grandes jardines colgantes de esta misma ciudad, de Babilonia, incluida esta gran Puerta de Istar. El coloso de Rodas creo que ya ha desaparecido, o eso me contó Rixnu, pero hoy el César puede contemplar dos de estas maravillas. Espero algún día poder

82. Literal de Filón de Bizancio según la traducción de Fernando Báez (2012). Ver bibliografía.

ver el resto de las mismas, pues esto es cuanto han podido ver mis ojos por el momento.

Y la princesa calló.

Trajano se quedó en silencio. La joven de dieciséis años sólo había visto una de esas maravillas —o dos si se aceptaba que en Babilonia había dos—, pero es que él, el magno emperador de Roma, preocupado constantemente por gobernar el mayor de los imperios, pese a todo su poder acumulado, no había visitado ni Egipto, ni Éfeso, ni Halicarnaso. Él no había visto de esas maravillas más que lo que habían contemplado los ojos de aquella joven princesa parta y Grecia. Trajano se juró a sí mismo que, cuando regresara a Roma, durante su trayecto de retorno a la capital de su Imperio, haría todo lo posible por detenerse en la mayor parte de aquellas ciudades y contemplar aquellas maravillas de las que tantos sabios hablaban y que la propia Aryazate acababa de recordarle. Aunque eso sí, él había cruzado el Éufrates varias veces y siempre con éxito. Eso no se lo podía quitar ya nadie. Y en ello encontró bastante consuelo y satisfacción, pero su pensamiento volvió veloz hacia el presente inmediato.

—El Coloso de Rodas, en efecto, se derrumbó en un terremoto hace ya tiempo —dijo el emperador como toda respuesta—. Ahora, no obstante, me interesa detenerme en aquella gran casa, donde veo a los legionarios de mi guardia personal.

—¿Por qué está el César interesado justo en ese lugar? —preguntó la princesa.

—Porque ése debería ser —y se volvió hacia Lucio Quieto— el lugar donde murió Alejandro Magno.

—Debe de serlo, augusto —confirmó el norteafricano—. Pedí a Aulo y a su guardia pretoriana que se concentraran frente al emplazamiento que los babilonios identificaran como el lugar de la muerte de Alejandro, César. Y allí está Aulo.

—Cerca del Gran Templo de Marduk, el dios de Babilonia —dijo Aryazate señalando hacia un gran edificio en el centro de la ciudad—, y de los templos de las diosas Istar y Nanal.

Trajano asintió sin decir nada al tiempo que desmontaba de su caballo. Lucio Quieto, Nigrino y Liviano lo imitaron y siguieron al César. El resto de los miembros de la comitiva imperial, a falta de una señal explícita del emperador, esperaron en medio de la gran travesía central de Babilonia, entretenidos y admirados ante los brillantes ladrillos esmaltados y sus detallados ornamentos.

Aulo se puso firme y saludó militarmente al emperador en la puerta de la antigua casa de descanso de Alejandro Magno.

—¡Ave, César!

Trajano movió de forma afirmativa la cabeza y puso su mano derecha sobre el hombro de Aulo.

—Vayamos adentro —dijo el César, pero se volvió un momento hacia los que lo seguían—, y que venga la princesa parta. Sin duda, aun sin haber estado aquí antes, sabe más que todos nosotros de este sitio.

El pequeño grupo cruzó varias estancias iluminadas con antorchas nuevas preparadas por los pretorianos. Había guardias dispuestos por Aulo en cada una de las habitaciones, todas lujosamente pintadas o con más ladrillos esmaltados en donde esta vez se combinaban más motivos animales, mitológicos y vegetales de color azul, ocre y rojo intenso.

Llegaron a una gran terraza desde la que se divisaban grandes piscinas de agua procedente de los canales del Éufrates y, más lejos, se veían parte de los inmensos jardines colgantes que aún quedaban en aquella ciudad eterna, que había visto el nacimiento y la desaparición de varios imperios y que, sin embargo, allí seguía, entre majestuosa y triste, entre gloriosa y decadente.

—El emperador me ha llamado —dijo Aryazate con su voz dulce de jovencísima mujer.

Trajano rebuscó entre su uniforme militar y extrajo un papiro mal enrollado y desgastado por el uso frecuente.

—Hablas griego —le dijo el César a la princesa parta—, pero ¿puedes leerlo?

Aryazate, estirando el brazo para coger el papiro, respondió con su resolución habitual.

—Sí puedo, César.

—Pues lee esto, el capítulo LXXVI —añadió Trajano.

Su vista ya no era la de antes y le costaba mucho leer, pero se negaba a admitirlo ante otros. Por otro lado, aunque sus hombres más leales pudieran entender algo de griego, el emperador no tenía mucha confianza en que ni Quieto ni Nigrino ni Liviano ni Aulo, allí presentes, supieran leerlo con fluidez.

Aryazate fue desenrollando el papiro en busca del capítulo indicado.

—Aquí está —dijo, y empezó a leer despacio, pero en voz alta y clara, no muy rápido; el contenido del texto parecía invitar a esa lectura pausada que hacía la muchacha parta—. «Capítulo *LXXVI*. *En el diario se hallan así descritos los trámites de la enfermedad* [de Alejandro Magno]: *En el día decimoctavo del mes Desio se acostó en el cuarto del baño por estar con calentura*»...[83] aquí me cuesta leer —dijo Aryazate interrumpiendo unos momentos la lectura.

Trajano no dijo nada. Sabía que había leído tantas veces aquel papiro que en algunos lugares las líneas estaban medio borradas. Tenía que hacerse con una copia nueva.

—¿Qué mes es «Desio»? —preguntó Quieto situándose junto a Trajano al final de la terraza, encarando las impresionantes vistas que desde allí se divisaban de la gran Babilonia.

—Δαίσιος —precisó Trajano—. Es el octavo mes del calendario macedónico. Entre nuestro mayo y junio, Lucio.

—«*Al día siguiente*... —dijo Aryazate, que ya tenía claro lo que ponía el texto, pero se detuvo y miró al César. Trajano hizo un gesto afirmativo y la princesa siguió leyendo—, *después de haberse bañado,* [Alejandro Magno] *se trasladó a su cámara y lo pasó jugando a las tablas con Medio. Bañóse a la tarde otra vez, sacrificó a los dioses, y habiendo cenado tuvo de nuevo calentura aquella noche. El vigésimo día del mes se bañó e hizo también el acostumbrado sacrificio, y habiéndose acostado en la habitación del baño, se dedicó a oír a Nearco la relación que le hizo de su navegación del gran Océano. El día vigésimo primero ejecutó lo mismo que el anterior, y, habiéndose enardecido más, pasó mala noche, y al día siguiente fue violenta la calentura. Se lo trasladó entonces a la gran pieza del nadadero,*

83. Esta sección y el resto que sigue en cursiva, literal de la *Vida de Alejandro*, que Plutarco escribió, al parecer, según los *Diarios reales de Alejandro* o las *Efemérides* de Eumenes de Cardia.

donde se puso en cama, y trató con los generales acerca del mando de los regimientos vacantes, para que los proveyeran, haciendo cuidadosa elección. El día vigésimo cuarto, habiéndose arreciado más la fiebre, hizo sacrificio, llevado al efecto al altar, y de los generales y otros líderes mandó que los principales se quedaran en su cámara, y que los comandantes y capitanes durmieran en la parte de afuera. Se lo llevó ahora al traspalacio, donde el día vigésimo quinto durmió algún rato, pero la fiebre no remitió. Entraron los generales, y estuvo aquel día sin habla, y también el día vigésimo sexto; de cuyas resultas les pareció a los macedonios que había muerto, y dirigiéndose al palacio gritaban y hacían amenazas a los más favorecidos de Alejandro, hasta que al fin les obligaron a abrirles las puertas, y, abiertas que les fueron, llegaron de uno en uno hasta la cama. En aquel mismo día, Pitón y Seleúco, enviados a consultar a Serapis, le preguntaron si llevarían allí a Alejandro; el dios les respondió que lo dejaran donde estaba, y el día vigésimo octavo por la tarde... —Aryazate levantó la mirada del texto y fijó los ojos en el emperador de Roma antes de pronunciar las últimas palabras del capítulo— *y el día vigésimo octavo, Alejandro Magno murió.*»

Trajano suspiró profundamente.

—Fue aquí, en esta casa —dijo el César señalando hacia las piscinas que se veían abajo—. Y en alguna de esas balsas de agua es donde se bañaba.

Nadie dijo nada durante un rato.

—Murió coincidiendo con el final del año —comentó Aryazate quebrando el silencio.

El emperador la miró con el ceño fruncido.

—El año no termina en mayo —dijo Trajano, sin enfado, simplemente subrayando algo evidente.

—En Roma no —aceptó la princesa—, pero en Partia *Spandarmatī*, que se corresponde con vuestro mayo, es el último mes del año.

Trajano asintió y no dijo nada. Al cabo de un rato, dejó la terraza y volvió a entrar en aquella mansión del pasado que una vez había albergado al más grande de los conquistadores. El emperador fruncía el ceño, de nuevo pensativo. ¿O era él, Trajano, el más grande? ¿No se extendía su Imperio desde las remotas costas de Caledonia, el frío Rin o los bosques de la

Dacia, hasta más allá del Éufrates y el Tigris? Era cierto que Alejandro había avanzado aún más hacia Oriente, hasta llegar al río Indo, pero no poseía dominios en Occidente, ni la península Itálica, ni en Hispania o la Galia ni en todo el norte de África o la lluviosa Dacia, ni Iliria, Panonia o Moesia estuvieron bajo control del gran macedonio. Era difícil ponderar quién era más grande. Trajano se detuvo un instante. Quieto lo seguía de cerca y el César intuía su poderosa presencia tras de sí. Con Lucio a su lado se sentía siempre capaz de todo. Sí. Asintió sin decir nada. Si se lanzara más hacia Oriente y atacara a los kushan ya no habría dudas de quién era más grande, pero... eso, nuevamente, entraría en colisión con el mensaje que Titianus y sus hombres llevaban a la lejana y desconocida Xeres. Trajano inclinó un poco la cabeza hacia la derecha al tiempo que se pasaba la palma de la mano por el cuello. Sentía otra vez ese dolor extraño en ese punto, pero no le dio importancia. Ni siquiera se lo había comentado a Critón. Como en otras ocasiones, volvió a preguntarse por aquella misión de locos que había puesto en marcha años atrás en Roma.

¿Habría llegado Titianus más allá del Imperio kushan? ¿Y aquel veterano gladiador y su esposa sármata y, sobre todo, la joven Tamura, hija de ambos? Tamura era la clave de todo aquel viaje. ¿Seguiría viva? ¿Tenía sentido mantenerse fiel a aquel mensaje secreto o, conquistada Partia, era más audaz ir más allá de su sueño, más allá de lo que Craso deseó, más allá de lo que nadie había imaginado nunca e intentar dominar desde Caledonia hasta la India?

Pasaron varios días en los que el César se relajó en Babilonia, mientras recibía informes de diferentes puntos de las nuevas provincias, de la retaguardia en Antioquía o del más lejano Senado de Roma.

Todo iba bien.

—Han traído los bueyes —dijo Liviano una mañana.

—Perfecto —respondió Trajano y se dirigió a Quieto y al resto de los *legati*—. Hagamos los sacrificios programados.

Todos se dirigieron al gran altar del templo de Semíramis.

Hacía unos días habían hecho un sacrificio en la mismísima casa donde murió Alejandro, pero el lugar no era adecuado para un ritual de grandes dimensiones públicas y por eso el emperador había ordenado que se hicieran nuevos sacrificios a la luz del día y ante los ojos de todos los habitantes de Babilonia en el gran altar del templo de Semíramis en el centro de la antigua ciudad.

Los grandes bueyes empezaron a ser sacrificados según los ritos romanos ante Trajano, *pontifex maximus.*

—Parece que hemos superado la maldición de Babilonia, Lucio —le dijo en un receso del ritual a su mano derecha en aquella campaña de conquista y fuerza.

—Eso parece —respondió el líder norteafricano.

Aryazate, presente en los actos religiosos, miraba hacia el altar de sus antepasados y pensaba en Ahura Mazda, el espíritu supremo del zoroastrismo. Los *legati* pensaban en Júpiter. Trajano en sí mismo.

En ese momento se oyó el galope de un caballo que llegaba a toda velocidad por la Puerta de Istar. El ruido de los cascos del animal ascendía por los refulgentes ladrillos esmaltados azules y ocres.

Trajano miraba hacia el altar sin prestar atención a la llegada de aquel jinete inesperado, pero Lucio Quieto se volvió lentamente con la sensación del guerrero que, en plenas facultades de combate, intuye una emergencia militar.

El mensajero se detuvo al pie del templo de Semíramis. Quieto descendió por la escalera y se situó junto al recién llegado.

—¿Qué ocurre? —preguntó el norteafricano sin preámbulo alguno.

—Hay un levantamiento —dijo el jinete, pero dudó en decir más y miró hacia el emperador, que seguía de espaldas a ambos.

—¿Un levantamiento? —dijo al fin Trajano volviéndose muy despacio y empezando a descender también por la escalera del templo.

—¿Dónde? —preguntó Lucio Quieto.

El mensajero romano, como viera que el emperador ya se aproximaba y que escuchaba atentamente, respondió.

—En Seleucia...

—Bueno... —dijo Trajano—. Enviaremos algunas cohortes para resolverlo...

Pero el mensajero añadió algo más.

—Y en Hatra... En general toda Mesopotamia está en armas contra nosotros.

—De acuerdo —admitió el emperador—. Necesitaremos movilizar una o dos legiones. Era raro que no se hubieran rebelado en ningún sitio en todo este tiempo. Ya nos pasó en la Dacia, ¿recuerdas, Lucio?

—Sí, César. —Pero el tono de Quieto no sonaba completamente convencido y eso fue lo que alertó a Trajano. Lucio tenía clavados los ojos en el mensajero. El emperador lo miró entonces con más atención y observó que el jinete tenía el rostro muy pálido.

—¿Es eso todo o hay más, decurión? No me gusta recibir los mensajes por partes.

Ante la advertencia del César, el mensajero tragó saliva y luego habló muy deprisa.

—Seleucia, Hatra, toda Mesopotamia. Es un levantamiento general, augusto. Armenia ha expulsado a nuestras tropas y también se han rebelado Nísibis y Edesa, todo el reino de Osroene. Además, nuestras patrullas al este de Cesifonte han detectado una enorme concentración de tropas partas. Es como si nos quisieran atacar desde dos frentes a un tiempo, César, desde oriente y desde nuestra retaguardia.

—¿Osroene también? ¿Estás seguro de lo que dices? —insistió Trajano con el gesto ya agrio.

Todos callaban. Osroene en armas contra Roma significaba que Abgaro y su hijo Arbandes, el último amor del César, habían traicionado la confianza del emperador.

—Osroene también, augusto —confirmó el mensajero—. Hemos perdido media cohorte en el levantamiento de Edesa. Allí han sido particularmente crueles con nuestros hombres.

—La traición siempre lo es —dijo Trajano con los brazos en jarras y mirando al suelo. Luego continuó en voz más baja—: La maldición de Babilonia parece seguir siendo poderosa. —Miró entonces a Quieto—. Pero nosotros seremos más fuertes, Lucio. Hemos de serlo. Alejandro estaba solo, pero yo te tengo a ti.

En ese momento, Aryazate se acercó y pronunció unas palabras.

—No es Babilonia. Es mi padre, el *Šāhān Šāh* Osroes: una serpiente que se arrastra sigilosamente, César. El emperador de Roma nunca conseguirá Partia mientras él siga vivo. No importa que parezca acorralado. Su picadura sigue siendo mortal.

Trajano miró hacia Aryazate y luego hacia la estatua del dios Marduk.

—Sea la maldición de una deidad o el último coletazo de Osroes —dijo el César—, no me echará nadie de Oriente. Aunque me vaya la vida en el empeño. No retrocederé. Nunca.

101

LA POLÍTICA DE KANISHKA

Palacio imperial de Bagram
Finales de otoño de 116 d.C.

—La joven escapó —dijo el emperador Kanishka, señor del Imperio kushan—. Eso me dicen mis soldados de la frontera. ¿Es eso cierto?

—El gladiador veterano está muerto, mi señor —respondió el consejero Shaka con rapidez—. Y también el joven luchador. Y el líder, el anciano que los dirigía, el mercader Titianus, también. Hasta la mujer que los acompañaba ha muerto.

—Pero la joven ha escapado, ¿o acaso mis soldados me engañan?

—Es apenas una niña, mi señor. Una niña. La matarán. Eso con suerte para ella. Seguramente le harán cosas peores antes.

—Es probable que ése sea su destino. No, con toda seguridad ése y no otro será su fin, pero más allá de eso, me preocupa que se te haya escapado una niña. Eso me hace plantearme, viejo consejero, ¿qué se te escapará la próxima vez?

El silencio era intenso.

—La próxima vez no se me escapará nadie, majestad.

—Sin duda, de eso estoy seguro. ¿Sabes por qué? —inquirió Kanishka.

El viejo consejero temía preguntar, pero sentía que el emperador deseaba oír la interrogante, así que la planteó.

—¿Por qué, mi señor? ¿Por qué ya no se me escapará nadie?

—Porque ya no habrá próxima vez. —Y Kanishka miró a los guardias que había apostado en el interior de la sala de audiencias—. Lleváoslo —dijo. No se molestó ni en levantar la voz.

—El emperador se equivoca al prescindir de mí —dijo Shaka en un intento desesperado por revertir el curso de los acontecimientos, pero Kanishka ni siquiera lo miró.

Shaka sintió las manos de los soldados kushan en sus hombros. No luchó. Dio media vuelta y los siguió hacia su muerte segura. Al salir de la sala de audiencias se cruzó con Buddhamitra. Ella representaba el poder ascendente y él, el final de una época antigua.

—Todos están muertos —dijo él rebosante de rabia con una sonrisa malévola en los labios.

—La muchacha sobrevivió —respondió ella deteniéndose un momento y sin alterarse lo más mínimo, con la serenidad de las personas religiosas coherentes con sus creencias.

Los soldados se pararon también para permitir que el consejero sentenciado y la monja budista hablaran. No se detuvieron por respeto a Shaka, sino por Buddhamitra. Sabían que era confidente y consejera del emperador.

—Es apenas una niña —replicó Shaka aún con más odio—. La apresarán los han primero, o los hunos o cualquier otro pueblo salvaje de las estepas de Oriente, la violarán y finalmente la esclavizarán. Mejor le habría sido morir.

Para sorpresa de Shaka, ahora fue Buddhamitra la que sonrió.

—Siempre me has menospreciado y no por budista, sino por mujer. Has infravalorado a todas las mujeres y, sin embargo, te ejecutan por causa de una, la que tú consideras una niña. ¿No crees que es una curiosa paradoja?

Shaka enrojeció de ira, pero Buddhamitra no se quedó para escuchar su respuesta. Dio media vuelta y entró en la sala de audiencias para hablar con el emperador. Eso sí, mientras caminaba podía oír las maldiciones que aquel viejo consejero condenado profería imprecando a dioses antiguos y olvidados. La monja reflexionó en silencio al tiempo que se acercaba al trono del emperador kushan: ¿Sobreviviría la joven Tamura? Era una flor de loto. Y era valiente. La muchacha lo llevaba escrito en su mirada. Pero necesitaría encontrar a alguien que supiera leer en aquellos ojos bravos de mujer indómita. Shaka, en eso, llevaba razón: la muchacha lo tenía muy difícil.

102

PARTIA ORIENTAL

Campamento de Osroes en algún lugar remoto
del extremo oriente del Imperio parto
Otoño de 116 d.C.

—Tenemos a Trajano entre dos fuegos —dijo Osroes cómodamente sentado en una gran butaca cubierta de pieles en el centro de aquella tienda—. Eso no lo esperaba el César de Roma. —Miró hacia los sirvientes que estaban en la entrada de la tienda—. ¡Vino, traed más vino!

Partamaspates estaba en pie, frente al *Šāhān Šāh* de Partia. Pero el hijo de Osroes miraba al suelo. ¿Realmente estaba ante el rey de reyes? Su padre, en menos de tres años, había perdido el control de Armenia, de Osroene, de todas las tierras entre el Éufrates y el Tigris, de las ciudades de Hatra, Babilonia y hasta Cesifonte... pero seguía hablando mientras estiraba el brazo para que un esclavo escanciara más vino en su copa de oro. Algo del poco oro que se habían podido llevar de la capital, ahora en manos del enemigo.

—Sé que estás deprimido, hijo mío, pero hemos hecho una retirada táctica. Hemos alejado al emperador romano de sus fuentes de abastecimiento en la retaguardia y he conseguido que se alcen contra él Osroene y Hatra, lo que dificultará aún más que puedan llegar víveres y suministros a las legiones de Trajano. Y hemos reunido un importante ejército aquí en el oriente de nuestro imperio. Es el momento de lanzarse para recuperarlo todo, muchacho.

—Sí, padre —respondió Partamaspates sin mucho convencimiento.

Osroes percibía aquella desazón en su hijo pero decidió

no insistir en animarlo. Cuando todo cambiara, ya comprendería su hijo inexperto que lo que habían hecho tenía sentido. Estaba seguro de que no se podía derrotar a Trajano en un enfrentamiento cara a cara, no después de lo ocurrido en la batalla del Tigris. Había que debilitar sus líneas de abastecimiento primero, alzando en armas diferentes territorios en la retaguardia del César. Eso minaría la moral de las tropas romanas. Y todo ello se había conseguido al fin gracias a su diplomacia secreta con el siempre cambiante Abgaro de Osroene.

—Escúchame bien, hijo: Ahura Mazda va a estar de nuevo con nosotros en cada paso que demos, pero no me fío de mi hermano Mitrídates. Tu tío ha insistido en encabezar el nuevo ejército junto con su propio hijo Sanatruces. En el consejo de las familias nobles y entre los *magi*, muchos son los que lo ven como el nuevo *Šāhān Šāh*; él y Sanatruces quieren arrebatarnos Partia, pero eso está por ver. Yo me voy a quedar aquí, para controlar el consejo y evitar que el miserable de Vologases nos ataque ahora a nosotros mientras estamos recuperando el terreno perdido contra Trajano. Pero he de enviar a alguien de mi plena confianza con este ejército que avanza hacia Cesifonte, alguien que pueda vigilar a Mitrídates y a Sanatruces, y ese alguien, como siempre que he tenido una misión realmente importante, has de ser tú. ¿Puedo confiar en ti?

—Sí, padre. Pero si se consigue la victoria contra Trajano, Mitrídates se verá reforzado en sus pretensiones para ser proclamado como único rey de reyes.

—No adelantemos acontecimientos. Preveo una victoria, pero ésta puede llegar de muchas formas, y en el consejo de familias nobles saben que Osroene y Hatra se han alzado a petición mía. Saben que aún tengo influencia. En una gran batalla pueden pasar muchas cosas, pero es cierto que la ambición de tu tío Mitrídates y de tu primo Sanatruces es creciente, por eso has de vigilarlos de cerca. ¿Lo entiendes?

Partamaspates asintió.

—Bebe algo de vino, muchacho. Y descansa. Saldrás al amanecer con el resto de las tropas.

Su hijo bebió algo. Poco. Osroes lo vio salir de la tienda

aún cabizbajo. Estaba así desde la salida de Cesifonte. El *Šāhān Šāh* no tenía claro que pudiera fiarse ni siquiera de Partamaspates. Ya no tenía la mirada orgullosa de los días en los que lo envió a negociar con Trajano a Atenas o Antioquía. Su hijo había perdido la fe en sí mismo y, estaba convencido, en él, en su padre.

El rey de reyes suspiró largamente. No podía fiarse de nadie. Al final tendría que arreglarlo él todo, de eso estaba seguro. Nadie entendía que las guerras, como las partidas, se ganan al final y que lo esencial era ver cuántos jugadores llegaban al desenlace con opciones. De momento estaban en aquella partida de tronos y poder él mismo y su hijo Partamaspates, su hermano Mitrídates y su hijo Sanatruces. Y siempre, Trajano.

Cinco.

Echó un trago más de vino.

Demasiados para un solo trono.

Quizá fue por el licor, pero se olvidó de que eran seis en la partida. No había contado a Vologases, que seguía agazapado en las montañas sin reconocer la autoridad de ninguno de los otros cinco contendientes.

Osroes echó un trago más de vino.

Cerró los ojos.

Se durmió.

103

EL DESPERTAR

**Frontera entre el Imperio kushan y las regiones
occidentales del Imperio han, Asia central
Final de otoño de 116 d.C.**

El aborto la había tenido en cama durante varios días, pero el apetito había vuelto y Tamura empezó a comer un cereal hervido del que parecían disponer en abundancia los han. No le era desconocido: lo había visto en algunas guarniciones romanas en la Dacia y, según decían, lo importaban de Egipto; luego lo había vuelto a ver en gran cantidad en los puertos de la mar Eritrea por los que habían pasado, pero nunca lo había probado hasta esa semana. Estaba bueno. Recordó que Dión Coceyo le había hablado de aquello y que le había explicado que era un cereal de Oriente que las tropas de Alejandro Magno llevaron a Grecia y otras regiones cuando regresaron de Asia. Lo llamaban arroz.

Se levantó y salió fuera de la tienda. El aire frío de las estepas la sorprendió. No había reparado en un brasero que calentaba el interior de la tienda y no había sido consciente hasta entonces de que el invierno se estaba acercando a aquella región remota del mundo.

Llevaba dos días sin hablar con nadie. Se sentía inmensamente sola. El intérprete que sabía sánscrito sólo la había visitado en un par de ocasiones para ver cómo se encontraba. De aquellas breves conversaciones, Tamura había entendido que había perdido el niño que llevaba en sus entrañas. El *silphium* que le había proporcionado su madre había resultado muy eficaz. Quizá en exceso. Ella debía de haber empleado más de lo apropiado, pues la hemorragia que había sufrido, según los médicos, había sido muy abundante. Por eso había tenido que permanecer en reposo durante un tiempo. Tamura también había entendido que aquello, su inesperada enfermedad, había indispuesto aún más al general Li Kan contra ella, pues había tenido que retrasar el repliegue de sus tropas. Estaban en un territorio fronterizo en disputa entre los kushan y los han, pero como los médicos habían sugerido que moverla a ella en aquellas condiciones podría terminar con su vida, el general Li Kan había decidido esperar a que se recuperase. Parecía ser que el interés del general radicaba en si era cierto que ella era la embajadora del emperador de Da Qin. Su persona, según Li Kan, tenía que ser protegida por el ejército han, había dicho el intérprete.

Dos breves conversaciones pero intensas, cargadas de información que Tamura seguía sopesando mientras miraba a su alrededor: había un sinfín de tiendas militares por todas partes, pero se veía a poca gente. El ejército habría salido en busca de enemigos para protegerse de algún ataque o en una misión de reconocimiento. O quizá a cazar y a por otros suministros. Los guerreros que quedaban la miraban desde lejos, pero ni se acercaban ni la interpelaban en modo alguno.

Tamura inspiró profundamente y enseguida su nariz se arrugó casi de forma instintiva. Olía mal. El campamento no: ella. No se había lavado desde que saliera de Bagram, de eso hacía muchos días. Había combatido, visto morir a su madre, la había enterrado con sus propias manos y había sufrido un aborto. Los médicos han quizá la habían cuidado, pero nadie se había molestado en proporcionarle nada para lavarse. Volvió a mirar a su alrededor. Los guerreros han seguían mirándola, pero no veía deseo en sus ojos, sino una mezcla de curiosidad y fastidio. Quizá también la culpaban, como su general, por el retraso en partir de aquel territorio hostil para ellos.

Se pasó la mano por el pelo largo. Estaba pegajoso. No se sentía cómoda consigo misma.

Iba a entrar de nuevo en la tienda cuando se oyeron gritos. Estaban en un campamento militar en una posición fronteriza de un gran imperio, de modo Tamura no necesitó mucho tiempo para intuir que alguien daba la alarma. La muchacha corrió hacia el interior de la tienda y buscó con rapidez. Sus armas estaban allí, junto a la cama: una espada y su arco especial con un carcaj repleto de flechas. Era embajadora, no prisionera, y no le habían retirado sus armas. Tomó la espada y se la enfundó en la cintura primero y luego cogió las flechas y el arco y volvió a salir de la tienda.

Un grupo de jinetes se acercaba al galope. Eran al menos una cincuentena, quizá algunos más. Era difícil saberlo.

Los pocos guerreros han que quedaban de guardia en el campamento habían cogido también sus armas, pero no parecía haber arqueros entre ellos, sino soldados con lanzas. Aunque, de pronto, aparecieron media docena de han con ballestas.

Le gritaron algo, pero ella no los entendió. Señalaban a la tienda. Seguramente querían que entrara y que se quedara dentro. Para que no estorbara en la lucha o para que no la viera el enemigo o para protegerla mejor. Fuera como fuese, Tamura no obedeció sino que cogió una flecha y cargó su arco.

Los jinetes kushan se acercaban al galope. Sería una patrulla enemiga que habría burlado el grueso del ejército de Li Kan y aprovechando la ausencia de las tropas principales quería saquear y destruir el campamento de sus oponentes.

Tamura observó que a los guerreros con ballestas les temblaba el pulso de puro miedo. El general se habría llevado a sus mejores hombres y había dejado en retaguardia a los más inexpertos, sólo que ahora la retaguardia estaba en primera línea de combate. Los jóvenes arqueros han no resistieron la tensión y dispararon demasiado pronto. Las flechas no alcanzaron a ninguno de los jinetes kushan. Tamura apuntó hacia ellos, tensó la cuerda del arco, pero esperó a que se acercaran más. Un poco más. Un poco más.

Disparó la primera flecha y ésta voló a toda velocidad hasta hundirse en la garganta de uno de los atacantes. Cogió otra flecha. Apuntó. Disparó de nuevo. Un segundo kushan cayó abatido. Para entonces los arqueros han ya habían conseguido recargar las ballestas y disparar. Esta vez, con el enemigo ya mucho más cerca, hirieron a tres kushan más. Tamura, entretanto, había herido a otros dos, pero los jinetes ya galopaban entre las tiendas del campamento. Los guerreros han se interpusieron en su galope con las lanzas por delante. Eran valientes. Aunque inexpertos, el general Kan debía de haberles insuflado algo de pundonor. Varios caballos fueron alcanzados y algunos jinetes cayeron y se vieron forzados a luchar cuerpo a cuerpo contra los han que los rodeaban. Empezó a haber muertos de un bando y otro. Tamura siguió disparando flechas y abatió a dos kushan más, pero la lucha entre unos y otros era ya confusa, no sabía identificarlos bien y dejó de disparar. De pronto, tras un rato de lucha cerrada, sólo veía en pie guerreros kushan y más jinetes de su ejército a caballo. Si había soldados han, ya estaban escondidos. Los kushan la vieron. Iban a acercarse. Tamura volvió a apuntarlos con el arco. En ese momento se oyó una voz de uno de los kushan. El oficial al mando hizo una señal con el brazo y todo el destacamento emprendió la huida, dejando a una veintena de guerreros han muertos, junto con otros tantos de sus hombres.

Tamura vio la nube de polvo que dejaban al galopar hacia el oeste y, de entre la niebla de arena, emergió el ejército de Li Kan, que regresaba al campamento.

Bajó el arco.

Se fijó en cómo el general Li Kan hablaba con uno de los pocos han supervivientes al ataque y cómo éste se explicaba con grandes aspavientos, señalando de vez en cuando hacia ella.

La joven guerrera sármata, hija también de uno de los mejores gladiadores de Roma, se sintió orgullosa. Ahora aquel general sabría al menos que ella era valiente y una gran luchadora, pero, para sorpresa de la muchacha, Li Kan la miró desde lejos con gesto de desprecio, dio media vuelta y se alejó al tiempo que daba órdenes a gritos. Los soldados empezaron a desmontar de inmediato las tiendas, mientras algunos retiraban a los muertos y comenzaban a cavar agujeros en el suelo.

El viejo intérprete apareció de nuevo y se acercó a Tamura con gesto contrariado.

—El general está colérico —dijo el hombre en sánscrito.

—¿Y ahora qué he hecho mal? —preguntó Tamura.

—El general te considera culpable del retraso en replegar

su ejército, responsable por tanto de la muerte de esos guerreros que custodiaban el campamento. Además, tu destreza con el arco ha generado cierta admiración entre sus hombres.

—¿Y eso último también es malo?

—Bueno, al general le incomoda que la joven mujer que lo humilló hace unos días, cuando apagaste el bambú que él había encendido sobre la tumba de tu madre, sea admirada por sus hombres.

Tamura se quedó pensativa. Estaba claro que el general Li Kan y ella nunca se entenderían.

—¿Y ahora adónde vamos? —preguntó al ver que desmontaban las tiendas del ejército con rapidez.

—A Loyang.

—¿Qué es Loyang? ¿Dónde está?

El intérprete la miró y sonrió ante tanto desconocimiento por parte de aquella supuesta embajadora llegada desde Da Qin. Pero respondió con precisión, para aclararle las ideas a aquella guerrera desconocida.

—Loyang es la capital del Imperio han. Loyang es el centro del mundo. Allí se decidirá sobre ti.

Y volvió a sonreír, pero con desdén. A Tamura le resultó evidente que aquel hombre no consideraba muy posible que las autoridades imperiales fueran a conceder mucho crédito a que ella fuera embajadora de Da Qin y que eso, probablemente, la conduciría a un pésimo final. Pero no se arredró. Tenía el mensaje secreto de Trajano para el emperador del Imperio han. Y una estatuilla de Júpiter como regalo. Era todo lo que tenía, pero no era poco. Volvió a arrugar la nariz. Tenía eso y un montón de suciedad por todo el cuerpo. ¿Cuándo podría lavarse?

104

EL BRAZO DERECHO DEL CÉSAR

Edesa, Osroene, Mesopotamia norte
Noviembre de 116 d.C.

Lucio Quieto entró en Edesa a sangre y fuego. Había recibido la noticia de la muerte del *legatus* Julio Máximo de Mesopotamia y estaba aún más enfurecido que cuando inició la campaña de castigo contra Osroene. No todas las noticias eran malas: Erucio Claro y Julio Alejandro habían arrasado Seleucia y, en general, con la excepción de Hatra, el resto de las ciudades de las nuevas provincias de Mesopotamia y Asiria, incluida la gran Babilonia, volvían a aceptar, aunque fuera por la fuerza, la autoridad de Trajano. Ya en Osroene, Nísibis había rendido las puertas de sus fortificaciones sin prestar demasiada resistencia. La sola promesa de Lucio Quieto de ser clemente si la ciudad se entregaba sin lucha había sido suficiente para que los habitantes cedieran ante el avance de las cohortes bajo su mando. Y tenía perfecto sentido aquella reacción de los habitantes de estas ciudades de Osroene, pues el rey Abgaro y su hijo Arbandes habían concentrado el grueso de sus tropas sólo en Edesa, la capital, abandonando a otras ciudades a su suerte.

Pero hasta Edesa misma llegó el hombre fuerte de Trajano. Los combates en las murallas de la capital fueron encarnizados: Quieto lanzó una y otra vez sus hombres contra las fortificaciones enemigas sin descanso y construyó más catapultas, que añadió a las que ya había llevado por barco desde Babilonia en previsión de un duro asedio como el que estaba teniendo que afrontar.

—Llévate todo cuanto necesites, Lucio —le había dicho

Trajano antes de su partida—. Iría contigo, pero aquí soy necesario para prepararlo todo para una nueva batalla contra los partos frente a Cesifonte. Será la batalla final, la que lo decidirá todo en esta guerra contra Partia. Además... —Y aquí el emperador se tomó unos instantes antes de continuar—. Además, a mí me podría faltar decisión contra Edesa. Has de ir tú.

Lucio Quieto había comprendido a qué se refería Trajano: en Edesa estaba Arbandes, el príncipe de Osroene, hijo de Abgaro. El hermoso Arbandes, el amante del César. Ahora era sólo un traidor más, pero Lucio comprendió que Trajano dudaba de sí mismo. El emperador no estaba seguro de actuar de la forma implacable que correspondía ante un traidor si tenía ante sí la hermosa y musculada figura de Arbandes.

—Tienes que ir tú, Lucio. Tráemelos vivos. A los dos, a Abgaro y... a Arbandes. Nos mantendremos comunicados por correo —dijo el César alejándose del barco en aquel muelle del puerto de Babilonia.

Quieto había tenido que combatir con sus hombres durante un mes en Edesa, pero al fin habían conquistado con una torre de asedio el acceso a un sector de la muralla. Fue como recolectar fruta madura. Desde esa posición, los legionarios se lanzaron con furia contra el resto de la ciudad. Los numerosos compañeros caídos en aquellos treinta días de asedio los empujaban en pos de venganza sin que Quieto tuviera que dar apenas orden alguna. Por fin pudo empezar a enviar buenas noticias por carta al emperador. Los correos imperiales llegaban casi a diario y la comunicación entre el César y él era constante.

Empezaron los incendios y las ejecuciones en masa.

Los muertos entre los habitantes de Edesa se contaban por miles.

Por decenas de miles.

Las llamas lo consumían todo.

Una ciudad enemiga requería crueldad en su sometimiento, pero una ciudad traidora, como Edesa, requería la destrucción total.

Lucio Quieto entró en el palacio real y, mirando a ambos lados, distribuyó a sus legionarios de más confianza.

—¡Por Hércules! ¡Vosotros por la derecha y vosotros por la izquierda! ¡Nosotros iremos por el centro! —ordenó—. ¡Al rey y al príncipe los quiero vivos! ¡Es orden del César!

Lucio avanzaba por entre los grandes patios del palacio real de Abgaro buscando al rey y a su hijo. El norteafricano iba seguido por un nutrido grupo de los jinetes de su caballería. En una ciudad conquistada no había mucho trabajo para las *turmae* romanas, pero aquéllos eran los hombres con los que Quieto venía combatiendo desde la Dacia y, en algunos casos, desde antes. Eran hombres fieles a Quieto hasta las últimas consecuencias y los combates en Armenia, Mesopotamia, Asiria y Cesifonte no habían hecho sino afianzar esos lazos de lealtad. Muchos eran, como el propio *legatus*, norteafricanos. Por eso, en medio del palacio de un rey y un príncipe traidores, Lucio quiso rodearse de los más leales. Eran casi como sus propios *singulares*, una especie de escolta similar a la del César, tanto en capacidad de combate como en nivel de lealtad total. Además, no era mal mensaje mostrar incluso a los más fieles cómo pagaba Roma a los traidores.

De súbito apareció un grupo de guerreros de Osroene. Lucio Quieto no tuvo tiempo ni de desenfundar su espada: sus hombres se interpusieron entre él y los soldados de Abgaro. La lucha fue encarnizada, pero sólo al principio. El empuje de los caballeros de Quieto fue tal que al instante varios guerreros enemigos cayeron abatidos mientras el resto escapaba por pasadizos y puertas. Pronto el *legatus* norteafricano volvía a tener el camino libre.

La misma circunstancia se repitió en dos ocasiones más, pero cada vez con menos enemigos y cada vez con menos y menos resistencia.

—¡Por Júpiter, los tenemos! —dijo uno de los oficiales romanos y señaló hacia la entrada de uno de los patios del palacio.

Quieto dirigió sus pasos hacia el lugar y allí, en medio, junto a una fuente de aguas ensangrentadas —pues varios heridos habían acudido hasta la misma para beber o limpiarse—, estaban Abgaro y su hijo Arbandes. Ninguno portaba espada. Abgaro miraba a su alrededor buscando. Arbandes, acurrucado junto a la fuente, escondía la cabeza entre las manos.

En cuanto el rey vio a Quieto ya supo a quién dirigirse.

—¡No nos puedes matar! —gritó Abgaro en una mezcla de griego y latín en un intento desesperado por hacerse entender *in extremis*. No estaba seguro de que Quieto supiera mucho griego. Pero entre lo que entendía el norteafricano y algunas expresiones latinas, el rey de Osroene pudo comunicarse con el *legatus*.

—¿Por qué no puedo mataros a los dos, traidores? —preguntó Quieto desenfundando lentamente su espada.

—He oído a tus oficiales —insistió Abgaro—. El César nos quiere vivos. Y has dado orden de que no se nos matara.

Lucio Quieto dejó de andar y se detuvo a unos cinco pasos de Abgaro.

—¡Por Júpiter, eso es cierto! —aceptó el *legatus* y volvió a enfundar su espada para decepción general de sus hombres, que, como el resto de los legionarios que saqueaban e incendiaban Edesa, sólo deseaban dar muerte al rey y el príncipe de Osroene que habían traicionado la confianza del emperador y de Roma.

Muchos soldados romanos, compañeros de los legionarios que estaban ahora en el palacio real, habían muerto en aquel levantamiento y la sangre reclamaba sangre. Pero el *legatus* mandaba, y por encima de todo estaban las órdenes del emperador. No sabían bien por qué, pero pese a la instrucción de atrapar con vida a Abgaro y a Arbandes los legionarios habían albergado la esperanza de que el *legatus* no pudiera contener su cólera y los atravesara con su espada en el instante mismo en que se cruzara con ellos. Pero no. Su líder enfundó el arma y con ese gesto dejaba insatisfecha la sed de venganza de miles de legionarios.

—Eso es cierto —repitió Lucio Quieto, parado, sin moverse.

Ver al *legatus* inmóvil pareció animar algo a Arbandes, que se levantó poco a poco y se situó junto a su padre.

—Todo ha sido un malentendido —continuó Abgaro sin mirar a su hijo—. Osroes nos mintió. Dijo que había barrido a las legiones de Trajano en Cesifonte. Nosotros siempre hemos querido ser fieles a Roma...

Quieto suspiró y negó con la cabeza. ¿Cuánto puede llegar a mentir un rey traidor? Lo de que hubiera un contacto entre Abgaro y Osroes podía ser más que cierto, pero que les hubiera mentido con lo de haber derrotado a Trajano resultaba más difícil de creer. Abgaro tenía sus propios medios para haber confirmado aquella noticia. No. Quieto estaba persuadido de que Abgaro sabía del levantamiento de las otras provincias y del avance de un nuevo ejército parto y que todo era parte de un mismo plan al que había decidido sumarse por propia voluntad. Pero no tenía pruebas.

En ese momento ocurrió algo inesperado para Quieto y, sobre todo, para el propio Abgaro.

—Lo que dice mi padre no es cierto —dijo Arbandes alejándose un par de pasos del rey, pero no más porque los soldados de Quieto los rodearon con sus *gladios* y *spathae* desenfundadas de forma amenazadora.

—¡Calla, insensato! —le espetó Abgaro, pero Quieto levantó la mano para silenciar al rey.

—No, que hable el príncipe de Osroene: veamos qué es lo que tiene que decirnos el heredero del trono —dijo el *legatus* norteafricano, enfatizando las palabras «heredero» y «trono», como dando a entender que eso precisamente era lo que estaba en juego y que Arbandes podría aún verse beneficiado de todo lo que había pasado. Quieto escupió en el suelo. Un traidor de traidores, con eso parecía que estaba tratando. Sentía asco, pero quería escuchar lo que el príncipe tenía que decir.

Arbandes miró al *legatus*. El joven heredero del trono de Edesa, que veía cómo toda la ciudad ardía, había concluido que el viento aún soplaba con fuerza desde Occidente, desde Roma, y no desde Partia, y decidió, sencillamente, abandonar a su propio padre.

—Nosotros sabíamos que hay un ejército parto que avanza contra Cesifonte y que varias regiones recién conquistadas por Trajano se han levantado en armas. Mi padre quiso unirse a la rebelión de acuerdo con Osroes —se explicó Arbandes con rapidez mientras Abgaro se tornaba rojo de ira, pero permanecía en silencio con la espada de un legionario en su cuello—. Yo no quería rebelarme. Deseaba avisar al emperador de Roma, pero mi padre me impidió enviar a mensajero alguno. Ésa es la verdad de lo que ha ocurrido.

Quieto miraba a uno y a otro. Los dos mentían. No necesitaba a nadie para llegar a esa conclusión.

El *legatus* norteafricano volvió a desenfundar su espada. Sus hombres se hicieron a un lado mientras su superior caminaba hacia el rey de Osroene.

—No puedes matarnos —insistió Abgaro pese a que podía sentir el *gladio* de un legionario en su garganta. Quería desvelar también cómo Arbandes había estado a punto de asesinar a Trajano, pero ahora lo urgente era detener la espada del norteafricano—. ¡No puedes contravenir la orden de Trajano! ¡Piensa lo que haces! ¡Eres un *legatus augusti*! ¡Te debes a tu emperador, a tu César!

Lucio Quieto sonrió.

—La orden exacta es que mis hombres os atrapen vivos, sí, pero ¿sabes para qué?

Abgaro no dijo nada, sino que se limitó a negar con la cabeza. El sudor le inundaba la frente.

—Para que os mate yo.

Y Lucio Quieto hundió su espada en el pecho del rey de Osroene. Lo hizo una vez. Dos. De puro pánico y sorpresa, Abgaro no gritó. Se desplomó en el suelo y empezó a arrastrarse hacia su hijo, que daba pasos hacia atrás.

Quieto contempló la agonía del rey traidor. Una tercera herida sería la definitiva y terminaría con el sufrimiento de Abgaro, pero Lucio optó por no volver a clavar la espada en aquel enemigo abatido. Era justo que sufriera una muerte lenta, desangrándose despacio. Miró entonces a Arbandes. El príncipe se arrodilló, se postró por completo e, ignorando a su agonizante padre, empezó a implorar.

—No, Trajano no puede desear lo mismo para mí. No. Todo ha sido culpa de mi padre. Él es el traidor. Siempre lo ha sido.

Y Arbandes empezó a lloriquear como un niño pequeño.

—Agggh —dijo el moribundo Abgaro en un intento final por hablar y desvelar que su hijo estuvo de acuerdo en intentar asesinar a Trajano. Pero las palabras ya no brotaban de la boca del rey moribundo, sólo espumarajos rojos de sangre y bilis.

Su hijo seguía postrado ante Quieto, llorando, hablando, implorando...

—El emperador sabe que yo lo estimo, que lo quiero, que lo amo. Trajano lo sabe. El César no puede desear mi muerte.

Lucio Quieto tenía unas ganas infinitas de acabar con la vida de aquel hombre cobarde y rastrero, pero recordó en ese instante las palabras de Trajano, enviadas por carta desde Cesifonte hacía apenas una semana. La última carta que Trajano, por el momento, le había enviado. En cuanto Quieto recibió aquella misiva, días atrás, de inmediato intuyó su contenido: «No deseo dar muerte al príncipe de Osroene». Eso había escrito el César.

—Levanta, príncipe —dijo al fin Lucio, pero como el joven no se atrevía a despegar el rostro del suelo, el *legatus* tuvo que añadir más información para alimentar la esperanza del príncipe humillado a sus pies—. Llevas razón: el emperador me ha dicho por carta que no desea darte muerte. —Miró a Abgaro, que aunque incapaz de hablar, aún parecía poder oír—. Sí, el emperador no desea su muerte —repitió el norteafricano mirando fijamente al agonizante Abgaro.

Ésas fueron las últimas palabras que escuchó el rey de Osroene y con ellas murió, sabiéndose traicionado por su propio hijo, que se las había ingeniado para sobrevivirlo y no acompañarlo en su funesto final. Una cosa es morir y otra dejar este mundo henchido de rabia y odio e impotencia.

Entretanto, Arbandes, algo más confiado, se levantó muy despacio, aún con cara de miedo y lágrimas en las mejillas, pero con un fulgor especial en los ojos: el brillo de la felicidad que sobreviene después de haberlo visto todo perdido; cuando, de repente, el cielo vuelve a ser azul y el sol resplandece una vez más. De pronto, el príncipe de Osroene sonrió, y al instante inició una risa convulsa y nerviosa. Trajano no podía ordenar su muerte.

—Trajano... me quiere... vivo...

Arbandes seguía con aquella carcajada histérica. El emperador romano no había podido olvidar todas sus caricias y sus besos. ¡Qué importaba que todos aquellos besos y caricias fueran entregados por su parte desde la mentira, sin sentimientos reales de amor sino sólo para conseguir el afecto del emperador de Roma, del hombre más poderoso del mundo! Lo esencial era que en el pecho del César había prendido la llama de la pasión por él, por Arbandes, y esa pasión le impedía a Trajano ordenar su muerte.

El príncipe de Osroene siguió con aquella risa altisonante y desencajada, odiosa para todos los legionarios que lo rodeaban. Con cuánta ansia lo ensartarían con sus *gladios*, pero las órdenes eran las órdenes. Pocas veces les había costado tanto obedecer.

Quieto miraba al sonriente Arbandes con seriedad, con la boca cerrada y apretando los dientes. «No puedo ordenar su muerte, no puedo hacerlo», había dicho Trajano en su carta y el César continuaba justificándose:

Sé que un traidor merece la muerte, pero en el caso de Arbandes me siento atrapado por su hermosura y me es imposible decretar que sea ejecutado; pensé que desde la distancia podría en algún momento escribirte esta orden mortal que no pude darte de viva voz en Babilonia, pero los días y las semanas han pasado y sigo sintiéndome incapaz de dar esa maldita orden.

Lucio Quieto desenfundó su espada con parsimonia infinita ante los ojos sorprendidos de Arbandes, que empezó a andar hacia atrás y a negar una y otra vez con la cabeza. Quizá no debería haberse reído. Quizá esa carcajada había ofuscado al *legatus* romano.

—No puedes contravenir una orden de Trajano —empezó a decir el príncipe una vez más cuando no pudo seguir retrocediendo porque los jinetes de Quieto se lo impidieron—. Eres el hombre de más confianza de Trajano. ¿Cómo crees que reaccionará si le desobedeces? —Pero como Lucio Quieto no se detenía, Arbandes rebuscó en lo más profundo de los secretos para intentar frenar el avance de aquel *legatus* que lo miraba con ojos de furia incontenible—. Yo sé... yo sé... muchas cosas de Trajano, más de lo que ni tú ni nadie sabe... El emperador habla en sueños cuando duerme... y Trajano piensa en ti como sucesor al frente del Imperio... Trajano quiere nombrarte augusto antes de que acabe la campaña y casarte con alguna de sus sobrinas, para que así, emparentado con su familia, estés al mismo nivel que Adriano...

Quieto se detuvo. Parpadeó. Mantenía su espada en alto. Los legionarios callaban. Todos querían gritar a pleno pulmón: «¡Mátalo, mátalo!». Pero nadie osaba hablar, ni siquiera los caballeros norteafricanos de la escolta del *legatus*. Aquella batalla había empezado para destronar a un rey traidor, pero ahora parecía, al final de la contienda, que lo que había en juego era la designación del César de Roma.

Arbandes, que veía cómo sus palabras habían penetrado en Quieto y cómo con ellas podía manipularlo, volvió a sonreír levemente.

—Entre lo que me ha confesado y lo que ha dicho en sueños, sé todo eso, *legatus* —continuó el príncipe limpiándose las lágrimas con una mano mientras que la otra la cerraba y la movía arriba y abajo para dar más fuerza a lo que decía—. Lucio Quieto, *legatus*, dejará de ser sólo un general más de las legiones para ser el emperador de Roma. Pero si me matas ahora, estoy seguro de que Trajano se retractará y cambiará de idea. Y tú perderás toda Roma por un instante de locura. Quieto es cualquier cosa menos un loco.

Todos guardaban silencio en el patio.

Los legionarios miraban a su superior entre admirados y... ¿sorprendidos? No tanto. Todos sabían que Quieto era la mano derecha de Trajano desde hacía tiempo y a ninguno de los romanos allí presentes les parecía mal la idea de que fuera nombrado sucesor de Trajano. El *legatus* norteafricano era el más fuerte, el más hábil y el más apreciado de todos los *legati* de las legiones. Aquel nombramiento tenía sentido, pero, y en esto tenía razón el miserable Arbandes, si Quieto incumplía una orden de Trajano, el líder norteafricano podría perder no ya sólo la confianza del César, sino también el nombramiento como sucesor; perder en definitiva un imperio: el Imperio de Roma, y no cualquiera, sino el Imperio romano más grande nunca conocido.

Lucio Quieto permanecía inmóvil esgrimiendo su espada frente a Arbandes. El príncipe volvió a sonreír. Para los legionarios era increíble cómo aquel hombre podía pasar de implorar postrado a sonreír satisfecho y seguro de sí mismo.

Pero a Arbandes nada le importaba la opinión de aquellos soldados. Se sabía victorioso. Ahora sí. Estaba seguro de ello. Nadie, simplemente nadie quiere perder un imperio. No importaba lo mucho que aquel *legatus* anhelara su muerte. Nadie puede estar tan trastornado como para ceder un poder tan grande y que está a punto de pasar a sus manos.

—Sólo tienes que enfundar tu espada, *legatus* —dijo Arbandes con la voz suave de una meretriz mentirosa—. Guarda ahora tu *gladio*, Lucio Quieto, y yo me acostaré de nuevo con el César y me aseguraré de que Trajano, en cada noche de placer, recuerde que tiene ese placer por ti, por su mejor hombre, por el *legatus* que merece heredar su Imperio.

Lucio Quieto, sin embargo, ante la incredulidad de Arbandes, dio un paso al frente y, como si no pensara en nada, casi con la mirada vacía, hundió su espada hasta el fondo en el pecho hermoso del príncipe de Osroene.

—¡Agghhh! —aulló Arbandes como un cerdo que estuviera siendo sacrificado—. ¿Qué haces, maldito...? ¡El César te odiará... eternamente...!

Quieto retorció entonces la espada aún con más saña brutal, levantando y bajando la empuñadura para causar el máximo destrozo posible en el interior del pecho de aquel príncipe traidor, hijo de rey traidor y capaz de mentir acerca de todo, por todo y, al fin del camino, para nada. O peor aún: capaz de decir la verdad sólo cuando ésta puede doler.

Arbandes cayó de bruces con las manos en el corazón intentando inútilmente contener el río de sangre que manaba de su pecho.

—¡Loco maldito...! ¡Loco maldito...! —aullaba Arbandes retorciéndose de dolor en el suelo y dando patadas sobre las losas de mármol como un niño enfurruñado que cree que con una rabieta podrá, una vez más, salirse con la suya.

Quieto contemplaba la escena con seriedad. Enfundó, ahora sí, su espada, se agachó junto al príncipe herido y empezó a decir en voz alta las últimas palabras de aquella carta enviada por Trajano desde Cesifonte.

—Te diré, príncipe Arbandes, lo que me escribió el César al final de su última carta: «No, yo, Marco Ulpio Trajano, no puedo ordenar la muerte de Arbandes». Eso, en efecto, dijo el emperador, pero añadió algo más, príncipe de Osroene: «Por eso te envío a ti, Lucio Quieto, *legatus* y jefe de la caballería de Roma, para que hagas con Arbandes lo que tú consideres que sea justo. Soy consciente de que como César debo ordenar su muerte, pero como hombre sabes que me tiembla el pulso. Que sea el discernimiento de Lucio Quieto, el brazo derecho del César, el que decida lo que debe hacerse con el príncipe de Osroene. Y lo que decidas, aunque resulte doloroso para mí como hombre, será lo correcto para mí como César». Ésa fue la orden completa de Trajano, joven príncipe —añadió Quieto poniéndose ya de cuclillas para que el agonizante Arbandes pudiera oírle bien—. Y ni tus besos ni tu hermosura, ni tus caricias ni tus mentiras han podido persuadirme de que no merecieras otra cosa que la muerte propia de un traidor. Ni siquiera por heredar Roma entera puedo traicionar al César Trajano.

—Te maldigo... te maldigo... —escupió Arbandes quedándose por fin inmóvil y con los ojos muy abiertos.

Quieto se incorporó de nuevo, indiferente a la maldición de aquel traidor.

—Cogedlo por los pies, a él y a su padre, y atad sus cuerpos a sendos caballos. Que los arrastren por toda la ciudad en llamas. Y dejad ya de matar. Necesito que haya supervivientes para que cuenten cómo trata Roma a los traidores. ¡Por Cástor y Pólux, a ver si hay nuevos levantamientos en las provincias conquistadas después de esto! Sólo los fanáticos serían capaces de no entender el mensaje.

105

LOS IMPUESTOS DE ROMA

Antioquía, Siria
Invierno de 116 d.C.

Atiano entró en la sala de audiencias del palacio del gobernador de Siria. Adriano lo recibió a solas. Ni siquiera había guardias en las esquinas de la estancia.

—Aquí estoy, mi señor.

El sobrino segundo del César no respondió de inmediato. Aquel silencio y la ausencia de testigos eran circunstancias que Atiano conocía bien. Adriano estaba, sin duda, a punto de darle alguna orden importante y... secreta.

—Mi tío, el emperador de Roma, reclama más tropas que he de enviar hacia Oriente. Esta vez he de remitir estos nuevos contingentes a Cesifonte. Y más tropas, amigo mío, significa más dinero. Pero Roma ya no tiene más dinero.

Atiano frunció el ceño. En ningún momento había oído en el Senado, en el foro de la capital o en ningún lugar que hubiera visitado recientemente, que un gobernador, tribuno o prefecto se quejara de que el Estado romano estuviera desabastecido. Las campañas de Oriente eran costosas, eso era cierto, pero Trajano se había preocupado de enviar también importantes cantidades de oro y plata fruto de los saqueos de las ciudades conquistadas. En particular, el gran trono de oro del rey de Partia, arrebatado a los enemigos eternos precisamente en Cesifonte, había sido y seguía siendo objeto de todo tipo de comentarios elogiosos hacia Trajano.

—Puedo ver por tu frente arrugada que disientes de mi afirmación —continuó Adriano. El interpelado fue a hablar, pero el gobernador se lo impidió haciendo uso de la palabra—. Nos

818

conocemos hace mucho tiempo, Atiano, y puedo leer tus pensamientos en las muecas de tu faz como si fueras un papiro desplegado y escrito en tinta roja. ¡Por Hércules, ya sé que hay fondos, bastantes, para suministrar a mi tío lo que me pide, en particular mas *vexillationes* de sármatas mercenarios de la conquistada Dacia, pero eso no es lo relevante! ¡Por Júpiter Óptimo Máximo! También se supone que estando a cargo de la administración de las legiones, en retaguardia, he de prever y proveer no sólo para el presente, sino también para el futuro. Y pregunto yo: ¿tendrá mi tío suficiente con estas nuevas unidades de caballería y unas cuantas cohortes más o necesitará en breve muchas más tropas? —Una vez más Atiano abrió la boca para decir algo, pero de nuevo Adriano se lo impidió prosiguiendo con su discurso desde la silla de gobernador de Siria—. Y no sólo eso, amigo mío: ahora mi tío afronta un contraataque total de los partos. Es posible que el César venza, o no, pero incluso si lo hace, ¿acaso Marco Ulpio Trajano se detendrá en Cesifonte? ¿Se conformará mi tío con haber anexionado las nuevas provincias de Armenia, Mesopotamia, Asiria y Babilonia al Imperio romano o querrá continuar avanzando hacia el este, siguiendo la ruta de Alejandro Magno y llegar hasta el Indo y quizá incluso luchar contra los reinos indios del sur o contra el mismísimo Imperio kushan del norte? Todo he de preverlo y para todo se me exigirá que provea. Y si pensamos así, a lo grande, como le gusta decir a mi tío, ¿no crees que entonces sí que hará falta más dinero del que Roma tiene ahora?

Aquí Adriano guardó silencio un rato.

—Sí, imagino que así será, mi señor —aceptó Atiano—. Si el César se planteara esas nuevas conquistas, es posible que hubiera que buscar una estrategia complementaria para refinanciar al Estado romano.

—¡Exacto, por Júpiter! Eso mismo he concluido yo —respondió Adriano satisfecho de haber llevado a su servicial interlocutor, por fin, a su terreno.

Un nuevo silencio. Atiano intuyó que Adriano esperaba una pregunta, es decir, la pregunta.

—¿Y cómo se va a refinanciar Roma para esas posibles nuevas conquistas?

—Subiendo los impuestos, por supuesto —respondió Adriano.

Era ahora Atiano quien callaba, pero, al cabo de unos instantes, se atrevió a decir algo que pesaba en su ánimo.

—Trajano, el emperador, nunca ha subido los impuestos. Es una medida impopular.

—Impopular, sí —admitió Adriano—, pero reconocerás que a la luz de las previsiones de las más que posibles futuras acciones de mi tío es mi obligación tener en cuenta esta medida excepcional.

Atiano, que veía que Adriano no iba a echarse atrás en su decisión, asentía lentamente mientras seguía pensando, mirando al suelo.

—¿Cuánto? —preguntó.

—Un cinco por ciento para los ciudadanos romanos, y un diez por ciento para los que no lo son —respondió Adriano.

Atiano se pasó la palma de la mano derecha por la frente. Eran cifras desorbitadas.

—Sólo el emperador en persona puede ordenar una subida generalizada de esa magnitud.

—Por supuesto. El edicto lo firmaré en su nombre —explicó Adriano mirándose las uñas de la mano derecha.

—Puede haber disturbios en algunas provincias, gobernador. Creo que el gobernador de Siria debería...

—¿Reconsiderar mi decisión? Es eso lo que ibas a decir, ¿no es así?

—Sí, mi señor.

—Pues no, no voy a cambiar de parecer en modo alguno.

Atiano negaba con la cabeza. Estaba sudando. Suspiró un par de veces.

—Las provincias donde hay judíos, no sólo Judea sino también Cirene o Chipre u otros muchos lugares, es casi seguro que se rebelarán. Son comerciantes en su mayoría y, en consecuencia, los que más tendrán que pagar.

—Muy cierto —convino Adriano—, muy ajustado tu comentario, Atiano. Hemos de asegurarnos de que esas rebeliones tendrán lugar: asegúrate de que se dé orden de que a los judíos en concreto se les incrementen los impuestos hasta un 15 por ciento. —Atiano abrió la boca, pero una nueva pregunta del gobernador de Siria le impidió oponer razonamiento alguno a la última orden recibida—. ¿Seguimos en contacto con Salvio Liberal, Pompeyo Colega y los demás?

—Sí, gobernador —respondió Atiano suspirando y negando más veces con la cabeza, pero sin atreverse ya a decir nada, pues era evidente que Adriano no buscaba dinero, sino revueltas, disturbios; en definitiva, todo tipo de problemas.

—Y siguen como gobernadores en... ¿qué provincias?

—Cirene y Chipre —dijo Atiano.

—Por Júpiter, justo donde viven más judíos. Todo encaja perfectamente. Por fin van a sernos útiles después de estar comiendo del Estado durante todos estos años. Has de notificarles a Liberal y a Colega en concreto que sean implacables con las revueltas. Quien no pague debe ser ejecutado y quien reclame, encarcelado.

—Todo esto puede terminar en un gran incendio dentro del Imperio, mi señor... Entiendo que el gobernador desea que haya problemas para que Trajano detenga sus conquistas, pero esto es muy peligroso. La situación puede volverse en contra de los propio Liberal y Colega, en nuestra propia contra, en contra de todos. Iniciaríamos un incendio que quizá no podremos apagar nunca...

Adriano levantó la mano para que Atiano callara y, a la vez, se levantó y empezó a caminar alrededor de su interlocutor.

—Colega y Liberal tendrán que saber moverse en medio de las llamas. Un incendio es lo que necesitamos, pero no padezcas demasiado: serán los propios hombres de Trajano los que tengan que apagarlo, y después, de las brasas de este desastre surgirá una nueva Roma: surgiré yo.

Se hizo un silencio espeso. El sudor corría en enormes gotas por la faz de Atiano. Había hecho muchas cosas terribles en su vida y dado muerte a más de un inocente, pero lo que Adriano pretendía podía adquirir unas dimensiones muy peligrosas, imprevisibles.

—Los judíos se volverán locos con todo esto —comentó Atiano—. Son fanáticos.

—Fanáticos es precisamente lo que necesitamos —respondió Adriano frío, inalterable.

—Va a morir mucha gente —insistió Atiano.

—Todos los días muere mucha gente y no pasa nada. La vida es así.

—¿Y no teme el gobernador de Siria la reacción del César cuando se entere de quién ha dado la orden de subir los impuestos?

—Para cuando eso ocurra, amigo mío, creo que el emperador tendrá asuntos más urgentes de los que ocuparse.

Atiano se quedó perplejo ante tanta osadía; asintió una vez más, suspiró y se llevó el puño al pecho. Ya iba a dar media vuelta cuando Adriano habló de nuevo.

—Hay un asunto más.

—Sí, mi señor.

—Quiero que avises a Julio Urso Serviano de todo esto. Mi viejo cuñado está demasiado desalentado con las victorias de Trajano. Quiero que esté advertido de la subida de impuestos, de modo que pueda preparar un buen discurso para despertar al Senado de su letargo. Sí, amigo mío, viene un gran incendio. Un incendio purificador. Insisto: ¿no dice acaso mi tío, el César, que hemos de pensar a lo grande? Pues bien, si Nerón incendió Roma, nosotros, Atiano, vamos a incendiar el Imperio entero.

106

LA CAPITAL DE LOS HAN

Imperio han
Invierno de 116 d.C.

Llegaron a una enorme muralla que se extendía hasta más allá de donde podía abarcar la vista, ya mirara uno hacia el norte o hacia el sur. Tamura no podía creer lo que veía. Nadie le explicaba nada. El intérprete parecía haber quedado en las remotas regiones fronterizas y ella estaba incomunicada. Ningún guerrero del ejército de Li Kan se dirigía a ella y la sirvienta que le había asignado el general para asistirla durante el largo viaje hacia la capital del Imperio han parecía de humilde condición y temerosa de dirigirse a ella.

Así, la joven guerrera sármata, embajadora del emperador Trajano, no sabría hasta mucho más tarde que acababa de cruzar la Puerta de Jade de la Gran Muralla: la entrada al imperio de Xeres.

Avanzaron luego durante días por una calzada despejada y en buen estado por la que le sorprendió que sólo se cruzaban con otros soldados, como si nadie más pudiera usar aquel camino. De hecho, cuando Tamura, desde lo alto de su caballo, miraba a izquierda y derecha, veía a comerciantes y campesinos, con carros o a pie, por pequeños senderos que discurrían paralelos a la gran carretera de grava por la que avanzaba el ejército de Li Kan.

Llegaron a una enorme ciudad, tan grande como Roma. Tamura estaba convencida de que aquél era el destino final, la gran capital de los han, pero se sorprendió al ver que apenas estuvieron en ella una jornada, en la que el general aprovechó para hacer acopio de provisiones, dejar muchos soldados e incorporar a otros, para, al día siguiente, continuar por aquella calzada que parecía no tener fin.

La mayor parte de las tropas se quedó en esa gran ciudad que la sirviente, ante las insistentes preguntas de Tamura, pareció llamar Ch'ang-an o algo parecido. Li Kan había reducido notablemente el contingente y ahora eran apenas un centenar de hombres a caballo los que proseguían en aquel largo viaje al corazón de aquel gigantesco imperio. Tamura concluyó que las tropas, como en Roma, eran necesarias sobre todo en las zonas fronterizas y no tanto en el interior de los dominios del emperador de los han.

El emperador de los han.

Tamura meditaba.

Tenía mucho tiempo para hacerlo durante aquel largo desplazamiento. Observar y pensar, eso era todo cuanto podía hacer. Se había percatado de que la disciplina era muy importante y muy tenida en cuenta entre aquellos guerreros que miraban a su general con auténtica devoción, casi como si se tratara de un dios.

El emperador de los han.

Aquella idea iba y venía constantemente a su cabeza. ¿Cómo sería el hombre a quien tenía que entregar aquel mensaje secreto? ¿Sería receptivo a las palabras de Trajano? ¿Creería en ellas o la despreciaría por ser una mujer la mensajera de Roma? ¿La ejecutarían? ¿Algo peor? ¿La respetarían? Imposible saberlo. Seguir pensando en ello era torturarse sin sentido.

Un día, cuando el sol estaba en lo alto del cielo y se divisaba otra ciudad tan grande o quizá mayor aún que Ch'ang-an, el propio Li Kan se acercó a ella y le dijo una palabra. La primera desde que se saludaran cuando ella estaba aún junto a la tumba de su madre y rodeada de kushan muertos.

—Loyang —dijo Li Kan, y se alejó.

La muchacha recordó que el viejo intérprete le había mencionado aquel nombre como la capital del Imperio han, adonde debían conducirla. El general había querido informarla de que habían llegado al final del viaje, pero ni siquiera la miró cuando dijo aquella palabra.

Murallas, puertas enormes, templos, carros, palacios, guardias, mercados y, sobre todo, gente, Tamura veía muchísima gente por todas partes: un tumulto infinito de personas que iban y venían que de inmediato le trajeron a la memoria las atestadas calles de Roma próximas al *Macellum* y al foro.

Se detuvieron frente a la entrada del palacio más grande.

Las puertas se abrieron y Li Kan al frente, junto con sus jinetes, y ella al final cruzaron el umbral.

Una vez en el interior de lo que parecía ser el gran palacio imperial, contrariamente a lo que imaginaba Tamura, no la condujeron ante el emperador, sino a una cámara confortable, rodeada de paneles de madera, donde había algo similar a una bañera de bronce, muy grande, con patas también de bronce y con un gran dragón esculpido en uno de los extremos a modo de decoración, agua templada y caliente en diferentes recipientes y dos sirvientas que se inclinaron ante ella.

Una de las sirvientas señaló la bañera. Tamura no necesitó que insistieran. En las casas de postas militares donde habían pasado las noches durante el largo trayecto por la calzada militar desde la frontera hasta Loyang había podido observar que en algunas de estas posadas había, a veces, un edificio donde los soldados entraban sucios y salían más limpios, pero sólo entraban hombres allí y nadie le propuso hacer uso de aquellos baños. Ni ella se habría atrevido. Lo máximo que le habían ofrecido para su aseo personal durante el viaje desde la frontera kushan había sido alguna toalla húmeda con la que procuraba limpiarse algo del polvo de los caminos del mundo que llevaba pegado a su piel. Desde Bagram la muchacha no había disfrutado de un baño en condiciones. La bañera que se le ofrecía ahora le parecía a la joven guerrera una bendición de los dioses, un regalo después de tanto sufrimiento.

La ayudaron a desnudarse e hicieron todo lo posible por no mostrar que olía mal.

Tamura entró en la bañera y disfrutó de sentir el contacto del agua tibia primero y luego caliente resbalando por su piel.

La lavaron bien. El mal olor, por fin, se desvaneció.

Luego le ofrecieron ropa.

Eso fue divertido: las sirvientas o quien las hubiera enviado no tenían claro qué desearía ponerse y le habían llevado ropas de hombre y de mujer. Pues, ¿qué era ella? ¿Una mujer o un guerrero? ¿Y cómo vestirían allí de dónde provenía? Tamura estaba convencida de que alguien se habría hecho esas preguntas y ante la ausencia de respuesta clara habría optado por enviarle ropa limpia de ambos sexos para que decidiera qué ponerse.

Aunque era invierno y la ropa acostumbrada para la estación sería la de color negro —a diferencia de la de color verde o amarillo más propias de otras estaciones—, todo lo que se le ofrecía era de color rojo. Tamura no podía saber aún que aquél era el color más respetado por simbolizar el fuego sagrado. La muchacha optó por una especie de pantalón y luego se ciñó una gran capa o túnica, alrededor de la cual las sirvientas ajustaron un cinturón.

Llamaron a la puerta. Las mujeres la abrieron y salieron con rapidez de la estancia. Li Kan entró despacio. De pronto se quedó inmóvil contemplando a Tamura. La muchacha se dio cuenta de que algo cambiaba en la mirada del general. ¿Sería por su pelo largo, lacio y negro, ahora limpio y cepillado con cuidado que brillaba a la luz del sol que entraba por las ventanas de la estancia? ¿O el hecho de que la túnica que había seleccionado Tamura dejaba al descubierto sus brazos y su piel tersa y sin polvo parecía ahora suave como la más fina de las sedas? ¿O sería porque la muchacha lo miraba directamente a los ojos y le sonrió? ¿O sería por todo a la vez? El caso es que Tamura comprendió que el general que tanto la había despreciado durante todo aquel tiempo la miraba ahora con ojos diferentes. Con ojos de ansia. La muchacha mantuvo su sonrisa, pues conocía bien, pese a su juventud, esa mirada y no sentía precisamente temor, hasta que Li Kan hizo un gesto para que ella lo siguiera. Tamura salió tras el general de quien acababa de averiguar que, además de un gran líder militar, era también un hombre a quien su joven cuerpo de mujer sármata, exótica y desconocida en aquella región del mundo, resultaba, sin duda alguna, atractivo. A Tamura le gustó saber que además de su espada y su arco disponía ahora de otra arma.

Cruzaron varios patios con árboles gigantes y estanques con flores de loto flotando. Tamura se acordó de la monja Buddhamitra. Dejaron grandes edificios a un lado y a otro de su camino por aquel complejo de palacios diversos donde se veía a multitud de hombres yendo y viniendo, la mayoría con pequeñas maderas llenas de dibujos y enrolladas, que llevaban de un lado a otro de aquel laberinto de casas de madera. Los dibujos eran la forma en que los han escribían. Había visto al intérprete de la frontera haciendo trazos similares en lo que el hombre dijo que era una carta para un funcionario.

Tamura observó que todos se apartaban ante Li Kan y se hacían a un lado. Era un hombre respetado no ya sólo por los soldados de la frontera, sino por los funcionarios de la capital del imperio. Un hombre muy importante al que ella, en varias ocasiones, aún sin quererlo, había ofendido. Pero un hombre que acababa de descubrir que ella le resultaba atractiva. Un hombre, en suma, con muchas caras. ¿Con secretos?

Se detuvieron ante una puerta abierta y él señaló hacia el interior.

Tamura entró.

Era una sala pequeña, con una mesa baja tras la que había un anciano de rodillas que le hizo un gesto para que ella se pusiera en la misma postura frente a él. La muchacha ya había advertido que aquélla era la forma habitual en la que los hombres de aquel imperio se disponían ante una mesa para descansar, comer o hablar.

—El general Li Kan dice que entiendes sánscrito, la lengua de los monjes budistas de las remotas regiones de Occidente —dijo el anciano en ese idioma.

—Así es. Algo, señor —respondió Tamura. Le costaba hablar después de tantas semanas de silencio, pero se sintió feliz de poder comunicarse de nuevo con alguien. Tanto que casi ni le importaba cuál fuera su destino. Por fin podía hablar y alguien la entendía—. Gracias por el baño —añadió Tamura. Fue lo primero que le vino a la mente.

El anciano sonrió.

—Es algo que se te debería haber ofrecido hace mucho tiempo —respondió el anciano—. Li Kan es un gran general y gran militar, pero creo que en las pequeñas grandes cosas de la vida se pierde. Además parece muy confuso contigo.

—¿Por qué confuso? —preguntó Tamura.

El anciano levantó la mano.

—No. Empecemos bien. Presentémonos. Mi nombre es Fan Chun y soy el *yu-shih chung-ch'eng*, algo así como el asistente del ministro de Obras Públicas, que es, a su vez, uno de los principales consejeros del emperador. Y estoy aquí para evaluar si debemos o no llevarte ante su majestad.

Tamura asintió y a continuación hizo lo propio:

—Mi nombre es Tamura. Soy hija de una guerrera sármata y un guerrero de Roma, que es ese imperio lejano que creo que aquí llamáis Da Qin. Eso entendí con el intérprete que conocí en la frontera. Traigo un mensaje del emperador Trajano de Roma, de Da Qin, para el emperador de Xeres, es decir, del Imperio han.

Fan Chun suspiró.

—¿Cómo es que entiendes y hablas sánscrito?

—Primero me enseño mi maestro en Roma, en Da Qin. Dión Coceyo era su nombre. Alguien muy... sabio. —Tamura calló unos instantes, que dedicó a pensar en su viejo pedagogo. ¿Qué sería de él? Pero rápidamente volvió al presente y siguió hablando—. Luego la monja Buddahamitra de Bagram me ayudó a entenderlo y hablarlo mejor.

—De acuerdo. Puede ser, pero comprenderás que el conjunto de tu historia es muy improbable. Poco creíble.

—¿Porque soy una mujer?

—Entre otras cosas, sí —admitió Fan Chun—. Pero aunque fueras un hombre me resultaría difícil creer que hayas cruzado el mundo entero y... sobrevivido.

—Éramos más en la embajada: había un capitán de barco romano, guardias imperiales, soldados, mi padre y mi madre, que eran grandes guerreros, un comerciante que conocía la ruta del viaje y otro... —Tamura no sabía muy bien cómo hablar de Áyax—, y otro... guerrero. Éramos un grupo grande cuando partimos de Roma.

—¿Y dónde está ahora toda esa gente de la embajada?

—Murieron.

—Es un viaje peligroso. Sí, es cierto. Y según me informa Li Kan, no parece que los *Yuegzhi*, los kushan para ti, estuvieran deseosos de dejaros pasar hacia nuestro imperio. ¿Por qué?

—Porque uno de los nuestros nos traicionó. Llegamos a Bagram, la capital del imperio de los kushan, de los *Yuegzhi*, como embajadores del emperador Trajano, pero en realidad queríamos, debíamos, llegar hasta el Imperio han. Cuando el traidor de nuestro grupo desveló al emperador Kanishka nuestra auténtica misión, tuvimos que salir huyendo de allí y... fue difícil. Sólo yo he sobrevivido.

Tamura decidió omitir el asunto del incendio del primer barco, el marfil, los piratas, las tormentas y otras peripecias de aquel viaje para centrarse sólo en lo más próximo.

—¿Y tú tienes el mensaje para nuestro emperador? —preguntó Fan Chun.

Tamura asintió.

—Enséñamelo —dijo el consejero.

Pero Tamura negó con la cabeza.

—No está escrito, pero conozco el mensaje. El emperador Trajano en persona me lo dijo hace de eso ya... tres años. Lo memoricé.

—Bien. Dime entonces el mensaje.

Pero Tamura volvió a negar con la cabeza.

—El emperador Trajano me insistió en que sólo debía entregar mi mensaje en presencia del emperador de Xeres, del Imperio han.

Fan Chun guardó silencio un rato.

—Podría forzarte a que me dijeras el mensaje. Hay formas —dijo el asistente del ministro.

—He perdido a mi madre y a mi padre en este viaje. He perdido a un hijo que llevaba en mi vientre. Estoy sola en un mundo que no conozco y donde apenas puedo hablar con nadie que me entienda. Estoy sola y siento tanto dolor por dentro que recibir dolor físico se me antoja una liberación. Haz conmigo lo que quieras, pero lo único que me queda, lo único que da sentido a mi vida es este maldito mensaje, y lo entregaré al emperador han en persona o moriré con él.

Tamura había hablado con una serenidad tan fría que hasta el viejo Fan Chun se sorprendió. Y él no se admiraba de nada ni de nadie desde hacía mucho tiempo.

—¿Qué edad tienes? —preguntó el consejero a la muchacha dejando el asunto del mensaje por el momento.

—Dieciséis, creo —dijo ella.

Fan Chun asintió. El corazón mismo de la juventud. Una edad donde en lo poco que se cree se cree hasta el final. Podrían torturarla, pero ¿merecía la tortura aquella joven enviada desde el otro extremo del mundo o merecía más bien el reconocimiento de la corte imperial por haber conseguido hacer lo que nunca nadie había logrado antes? Si era cierto lo que decía, la joven había llegado hasta Loyang con un mensaje del emperador de Da Qin. Cuando el emperador He envió a Kan Ying hacia Occidente, éste no pudo ir más allá de la frontera de An-shi.

—Li Kan ya me había advertido de que eras... ¿cuáles fueron sus palabras exactas? Ah sí: asombrosa, luchadora y valiente, y que habías sufrido mucho para cruzar las tierras de los *Yuegzhi*, de los kushan. Pareces haberle causado una impresión importante a nuestro mejor *chiang-chün*, aunque intuyo que se siente herido, ofendido por ti de alguna forma; lo conozco y sé interpretar tan bien sus palabras como sus silencios.

Tamura bajó la mirada mientras intentaba explicar los diferentes desencuentros vividos entre ella y el general: el malentendido del bambú sobre la tumba de su madre, su aborto, cómo su debilidad obligó a retrasar el repliegue de las tropas y el hecho de que ella luego se descubriera como una hábil arquera después de haberlo ofendido anteriormente.

—Es difícil hacer cambiar una primera impresión —replicó Fan Chun—, pero cambiar tres malas primeras impresiones es imposible. Ahora entiendo la contrariedad en el rostro de mi general. Le gustas pero te desprecia, todo a la vez.

El consejero calló y cogió algo que parecía un papiro. Dibujó algunos trazos con los signos de los han. Luego lo dejó sobre la mesa. Suspiró y, al fin, volvió a hablar.

—Te llevaré ante su majestad —dijo Fan Chun y se levantó con rapidez inesperada en alguien de su edad.

Antes de que pudiera darse cuenta, la muchacha caminaba de nuevo tras la poderosa figura de Li Kan, esta vez acompañada por aquel anciano consejero, rodeados los dos por una nutrida escolta de soldados han.

—En la sala de audiencias guardarás silencio total hasta que su majestad se dirija a ti, ¿entiendes? —preguntó Fan Chun a Tamura mientras avanzaban a paso rápido por el complejo entramado de edificios oficiales del palacio imperial de Loyang.

—De acuerdo —aceptó Tamura.

—En la sala de audiencias habrá varios consejeros muy importantes —continuó explicando Fan Chun—. Están los nueve ministros y sus tres excelencias. Ellos hablarán primero y departirán con su majestad. Puede que pase mucho tiempo antes de que su majestad decida dedicarnos su atención. Incluso puede decidir no dedicarnos nada de su precioso tiempo hoy. Y quizá tampoco mañana. Lo importante es que estés en perfecto silencio y que sólo hables cuando se te pregunte. Si el momento oportuno llega, yo mismo actuaré como intérprete entre su majestad y tú. ¿Lo has entendido?

—Sí, señor.

—Bien, bien.

Llegaron a la gran sala de audiencias. Apenas se podían ver las decoraciones de los paneles de madera, pues tal y como había anticipado Fan Chun, estaba atestada de consejeros y funcionarios imperiales, pero Tamura pudo identificar al fondo, próximo al trono imperial de su majestad, a un grupo de nueve personas, que rápidamente concluyó que serían los nueve ministros y, al otro lado del trono, otros tres consejeros más, más veteranos que el resto, que debían de ser las tres excelencias. Todos vestían túnicas de fina seda roja. Uno de ellos estaba hablando con la persona que estaba sentada en el trono. Hasta ahí todo le encajaba perfectamente a Tamura. Todo menos un pequeño gran detalle. Nadie le había avisado a Tamura de que la persona que estaría sentada en el trono del Imperio han no sería un hombre. En el trono había una mujer. Tamura se quedó boquiabierta, con los ojos clavados en la emperatriz Deng.

107

EL DISCURSO DE QUIETO

Cesifonte
Invierno de 116 d.C.

Campamento romano frente a la ciudad

Lucio Quieto, sin darse ni un día de descanso, cabalgó desde la sometida Edesa hasta entrar, casi sin aliento, en el *praetorium* de campaña del emperador de Roma levantado junto a Cesifonte. Allí encontró al César reunido con el resto de los *legati* del *consilium augusti* preparando la estrategia para la batalla final. Trajano, nada más verlo entrar, no se anduvo con rodeos.

—¿Lo has matado?

El *legatus* norteafricano no necesitó que el emperador fuera más preciso. Tanto él como el resto de los allí presentes sabían que el César preguntaba por Arbandes, el príncipe de Osroene.

Lucio Quieto tragó saliva y luego respondió.

—Sí. He dado muerte a los dos, al príncipe y a su padre.

Trajano se pasó la lengua por los labios. Luego miró al suelo. Levantó entonces los ojos, rodeó la mesa de los mapas y se acercó a Quieto, que permanecía inmóvil esperando, como todos, la reacción del emperador.

El César alzó el brazo derecho con lentitud y, al fin, posó la mano sobre el hombro del líder norteafricano.

—Eres más fuerte que yo, Lucio —dijo Trajano mirándolo fijamente y, acto seguido, paseando los ojos por los rostros de los que los rodeaban, añadió unas palabras—: Si en algún momento me pasa algo en la batalla, Lucio Quieto asumirá el mando absoluto en la contienda y en la campaña si es necesario.

A todos les pareció bien aquella orden.

Lucio, en silencio, mientras el César volvía a tomar su posición junto a la mesa para explicar cómo afrontar la lucha del día siguiente, se quedó pensativo. Quizá la única verdad que Arbandes había dicho en su vida era que Trajano realmente pensaba en él como sucesor.

Ejército parto frente a Cesifonte

Mitrídates miró a Sanatruces y a Partamaspates.

—Hoy es el día en el que barreremos a esos romanos de Partia para siempre.

Sanatruces asintió en apoyo de las palabras de su padre. Partamaspates, el hijo de Osroes, que había podido departir con Trajano en persona varias veces y que había visto el lento pero inexorable avance del César por Armenia, Osroene, Mesopotamia y Asiria hasta llegar a Cesifonte, no hizo gesto alguno. Eso sí, tras ellos, más de sesenta mil partos, caballería ligera, *catafractos* y aliados de todo Oriente, bien equipados y con ansias de venganza, parecían dar mucha fuerza a la seguridad de Mitrídates. Los romanos eran expertos en el combate, veteranos, pero muchos de los partos allí reunidos llevaban también años curtidos en la lucha diaria contra el rebelde Vologases. La batalla, cuando menos, iba a ser muy reñida.

Ejército romano a las afueras de Cesifonte

Marco Ulpio Trajano paseaba con su caballo por delante de las legiones. Con él iban Liviano y Aulo y, tras ellos, Lucio Quieto.

Trajano ya no pensaba en príncipes sino en el enemigo, en cómo acabar con él de una vez por todas. Los partos habían reunido una hueste ingente, un ejército temible, pero él estaba seguro, como siempre, de la victoria: había diseñado una estrategia para acabar con el nuevo ejército parto de una forma lenta pero metódica: carroballistas contra los *catafractos*, como habían empleado en Adamklissi, en el pasado en la Dacia; luego una maniobra envolvente... Sería una batalla que duraría desde el alba hasta el atardecer y correría mucha sangre, pero Trajano estaba convencido de que sería, por encima de todo, sangre parta. Y ésta constituiría la batalla definitiva. Estaban ante el último intento desesperado de Osroes y su hermano Mitrídates de recuperar el trono de Partia, su imperio perdido.

Todo iba bien, según lo previsto, hasta que, de pronto, Marco Ulpio Trajano se encogió en lo alto del caballo. Soltó las manos de las riendas y se las llevó a las sienes.

—Aaahh —exclamó en un grito ahogado.

El caballo se detuvo.

El emperador intentó incorporarse de nuevo, pero el dolor lo atormentaba de tal manera que se hubiera dejado caer desde lo alto de la montura de no ser porque Aulo, rápido, se situó a su lado y lo ayudó a mantenerse sobre el animal.

El tribuno miró al jefe del pretorio, quien, ante la cara de preocupación de Aulo y el gesto inconfundible de dolor en la faz del César, comprendió que alguna dolencia grave había hecho mella en la fortaleza casi indestructible del emperador.

Liviano y Aulo bajaron a Trajano con rapidez del caballo y lo ayudaron a caminar de regreso a la tienda del *praetorium*, pero aun así resultó evidente para muchos que el César se encontraba mal, muy débil.

Quieto, que había permanecido junto a las legiones a la espera de noticias de Aulo sobre el estado del César, sabía que aquella imagen del emperador teniendo que ser ayudado para desmontar de su caballo y luego asistido por el jefe del pretorio y por un tribuno para poder caminar en dirección a su tienda, era, sin duda, la peor de las imágenes que un legionario podía tener en su mente antes de entrar en combate contra un poderoso ejército que había llegado hasta ellos repleto de veteranos, henchido de sed de venganza y muy bien pertrechado. El *legatus* norteafricano recordaba cómo en la gran batalla del Tigris el arrojo personal del emperador lanzándose a cruzar el primero el río sobre aquel puente de barcazas fue lo que, en gran medida, determinó el curso de aquel enfrentamiento clave. Y ahora todo ese valor, toda esa fuerza, estaba fuera de la batalla que iba a comenzar en unos instantes. Quieto vio a Aulo salir de la tienda, coger su caballo y galopar raudo hasta su posición.

—El César no puede combatir —dijo el tribuno en voz baja al líder norteafricano—. Critón dice que ha de reposar. De hecho, he visto que el emperador apenas puede moverse.

—Bien. Vuelve con él —respondió el *legatus.*

Aulo volvió a galopar de regreso al *praetorium* en la retaguardia del ejército imperial.

Lucio Quieto miraba desde lo alto de su caballo ahora hacia las primeras líneas de las cohortes romanas. Sólo leía debilidad, como la que había mostrado el César, sin desearlo, por causa de aquella dolencia inesperada. Debilidad y miedo. Y con miedo no se puede luchar. Con miedo no se puede vencer.

El *legatus* empezó a trotar para alejarse rápidamente del lugar central del ejército romano donde los legionarios habían presenciado cómo el César tenía que ser retirado por los pretorianos. Quieto albergaba la esperanza de que el miedo sólo hubiera llegado a las cohortes centrales de las legiones, pero, para su desesperación, no importaba lo mucho que se distanciara del centro de la inmensa formación romana, pues en todas partes veía lo mismo reflejado en las caras de los legionarios: temor, pánico, duda. Eso era lo que mostraban las miradas de todos. El miedo es como una mancha de aceite que se extiende sin que nada ni nadie pueda detenerlo.

Quieto tiró de las riendas de su caballo para regresar al centro de las legiones. Ahora cabalgaba mirando la crin de su montura, apretando los labios, muy concentrado.

—Los partos, *legatus,* avanzan —dijo uno de los tribunos que seguían al jefe de la caballería romana y ahora líder absoluto de las legiones por designación de Trajano.

Quieto miró hacia el este. En efecto, así era. El ejército enemigo avanzaba hacia ellos. Lentamente, pero se aproximaba. El norteafricano no dijo nada, no detuvo su caballo y siguió mirando hacia la crin del mismo. Ahora no le importaban los partos. La derrota no la llevaban ellos, sino el miedo que había invadido a los legionarios por la debilidad del César, de su César. Y de pronto, Lucio Quieto simplemente tornó su rostro rojo por pura ira, por la rabia más absoluta que hubiera sentido en mucho tiempo. Frenó su caballo, lo hizo girar y encaró a las legiones del centro del inmenso ejército y empezó a hablar.

—¡Por Júpiter! ¡Leo el miedo en vuestros ojos y me avergüenzo! ¡Leo la duda en vuestra mirada y me dais asco! ¡Leo la debilidad en vuestros rostros y siento cólera!

Nadie esperaba un arrebato tan descarnado por parte del *legatus* norteafricano. Ni los tribunos ni los centuriones ni mucho menos los legionarios habían visto nunca antes al jefe de la caballería de Roma tan iracundo y rudo en sus palabras. Pero el *legatus*, tras un muy breve pero intensísimo instante de pausa, continuó hablándoles:

—¿No sois acaso los mismos que derrotasteis a los bárbaros en Germania? ¿No sois acaso los mismos que vencisteis a los enemigos en la Dacia? ¿Y a los sármatas y a los roxolanos y a tantos aliados de los dacios como se unieron a ellos? ¿No sois acaso vosotros los mismos que conmigo, por orden de Trajano, sometisteis Armenia?

El ejército parto avanzaba. Era una inmensidad de soldados y jinetes y *catafractos* que se aproximaban lenta pero inexorablemente. Las fuerzas estaban igualadas en número. ¿Igualadas en ánimo?

Quieto sabía que sus oficiales estaban nerviosos por la proximidad del enemigo, que esperaban que diera una orden, pero Quieto no les prestaba atención ni a ellos ni a los malditos partos. A él sólo le interesaba el corazón de sus legionarios.

—¿Acaso no sois vosotros los mismos que cruzasteis el Éufrates y conquistasteis Mesopotamia? ¿Acaso no sois vosotros los mismos que atravesasteis el Tigris pese a que todos los partos del mundo y todos los soldados de Mebarsapes os esperaban en la otra orilla armados hasta los dientes? ¿No sois los conquistadores de Asiria, los que rendisteis Cesifonte, la capital del enemigo que se acerca, la capital que ahora mismo ocupamos? ¿No sois los mismos que entrasteis en Babilonia, los que llegasteis al golfo Pérsico? ¿No sois vosotros acaso los mismos que extendisteis las fronteras de Roma hasta unos límites jamás conocidos, jamás pensados, jamás soñados? —Y alzó aún más la voz—. ¡Habladme, malditos! ¡Responded a mis preguntas! ¿No sois acaso vosotros los mismos que habéis conquistado medio mundo para Roma?

Silencio. Sólo silencio entre las legiones. Y tambores. Los tambores del enemigo acercándose.

—¡Sí, lo somos! —gritó uno de los centuriones de primera línea.

De pronto, como una ola de respuestas, miles, decenas de miles de gargantas, empezaron a responder al unísono.

—¡Sí, somos nosotros! ¡Somos nosotros!

Quieto soltó las riendas de su caballo y levantó las manos extendiendo los brazos.

Sesenta mil legionarios callaron.

—¡Y ahora todos vosotros tenéis miedo! ¡No hace falta que me digáis nada sobre esto! ¡Está grabado con fuego en vuestras miradas de duda! Y todo ¿por qué? ¡Porque el César está indispuesto! ¡Claro, me diréis, todas las victorias que he referido han sido porque estábamos todos, vosotros y yo, todos juntos, guiados en Germania, en la Dacia, en Armenia, en el Éufrates, en Asiria, en el Tigris, en Cesifonte, en Babilonia, en todas partes hemos estado siempre guiados por el mejor de los *imperatores* posibles, por el *Optimus Princeps*, por Marco Ulpio Trajano, *Dacicus* y *Parthicus*! ¡Me diréis: sí, él nos guiaba y por eso ganamos, por eso vencimos, por eso derrotamos uno tras otro a tantos enemigos de Roma como nos salieron al paso en el pasado! ¡Y ahora os sentís huérfanos porque el emperador está enfermo y ha tenido que ser conducido a su tienda! ¡Eso es lo que pasa! ¡Porque ahora tenéis miedo de que sin el César ese ejército que se aproxima pueda derrotarnos, porque os falta, porque nos falta el guía, el líder, el mejor de los generales!

Y Quieto calló.

A sus espaldas los tambores de los partos resonaban cada vez con más fuerza.

Lucio no se molestó en volverse.

Seguía sin importarle lo más mínimo quiénes eran o cuántos o dónde estuviera el enemigo. A él seguía interesándole tan sólo el ánimo de los legionarios de Roma.

—Pues... ¿sabéis lo que os digo?

Nadie respondió.

Sólo tambores acercándose.

—¡Os digo lo que os he dicho al principio: que me dais asco y pena y rabia! ¡Os digo que me dais vergüenza! ¡Incontables victorias os ha regalado Trajano con su mando sobre vosotros, con su hábil dirección! ¡Innumerables victorias, una tras otra, os ha entregado el César! ¡El mismo emperador que ha comido siempre vuestro rancho, bebido vuestra misma agua y caminado las mismas millas que vuestras sandalias! ¡El mismo que se ha preocupado de los heridos cuando los ha habido, el mismo que ha enterrado con honor a los caídos cuando ha habido víctimas y el mismo que os ha premiado una y otra vez cuando conseguíamos la victoria con tierras para los veteranos, con dinero para los que seguían luchando y, constantemente, con aprecio hacia vuestros esfuerzos! ¡Eso ha sido simple y llanamente siempre! ¡Porque siempre os ha conducido a la victoria! ¡Desde Germania hasta Oriente, pasando por medio mundo: ni una sola derrota!

Aquí volvió a callar.

Los tambores sonaban ya potentes. Los oficiales querían interrumpir al jefe de la caballería romana, pedirle una orden, la que fuera, para detener aquel avance del enemigo, pero nadie, absolutamente nadie se atrevía a decir nada. Era cuestión de tiempo que los partos lanzaran a la caballería ligera o, peor aún, a los temidos *catafractos* contra ellos y que la interminable lluvia de flechas hasta oscurecer el cielo empezara una vez más, como siempre que se combatía contra aquel portentoso enemigo al que habían dado por destruido y que, como si resucitara, parecía retornar de entre los muertos cargado de aún más odio y fuerza y ansia.

—¡Ni una sola derrota! —repitió Lucio Quieto—. ¡Trajano sólo os ha dado victorias! ¡Pero hoy, es cierto, Marco Ulpio Trajano está enfermo! ¡Hoy no podemos disponer de su guía! ¡Sólo hoy nos ha fallado su fuerza, su resolución, su vigor! ¡Sólo hoy no tenemos su arrojo! ¡Sólo una vez! ¡Y yo, por Cástor y

Pólux y todos los dioses de Roma, os pregunto alto y claro!: ¿No sois capaces vosotros de regalarle, por una vez, por una sola vez, por una sola y maldita vez, no sois capaces de regalarle una victoria al César? ¿No sois capaces de entregarle al emperador que está intentando aún, estoy seguro de ello, levantarse de la cama en la que está postrado contra su voluntad y, aun enfermo, volver a subir al caballo para luchar cuando lo que necesita, por una vez, por una única vez, es descansar? ¿Y vosotros no podéis llevar por esta vez la cabeza de nuestro enemigo en una bandeja y decirle al César: «Aquí están los partos, rendidos a los pies de nuestro *imperator*, muerto su líder a los pies de nuestro *Optimus Princeps*»? ¿No sois capaces de ganar, una sola vez, solos? ¿Ninguno de vosotros es capaz? ¿Nadie? Yo insisto: *quis potest?* ¿Quién puede?

Hubo otro silencio de Quieto.

—Los *catafractos* del enemigo se adelantan, *legatus* —dijo uno de los tribunos en voz baja, al fin, al líder norteafricano—. Van a cargar contra las cohortes de primera línea. Deberíamos poner en marcha las instrucciones del César.

Pero el oficial calló y se retiró luego hacia atrás.

Quieto pareció no haberlo oído. No se movió ni un ápice. Él sólo tenía ojos para las legiones de Roma.

—*Ego possum!* ¡Yo puedo! ¡Yo soy capaz! —dijo de nuevo otro de los centuriones de primera línea.

—¡Y yo!

—¡Y yo!

Y un mar de yoes empezó a resonar entre las legiones. Hasta que todos, desde los tribunos hasta el último legionario de la última cohorte pronunciaron aquellas palabras, aquel compromiso, aquella promesa.

Tal fue el clamor de aquellas decenas de miles de voces romanas que los tambores del enemigo dejaron de oírse, ahogados por los pulmones de las legiones de Roma.

—Ahora sí —dijo Quieto en voz baja y se volvió hacia el tribuno que tenía a su derecha—. Lanzad a los carroballistas ya contra los *catafractos*.

Luego miró de nuevo hacia las legiones levantando su escudo y golpeando su espada con el mismo. Sesenta mil romanos lo imitaron y el estruendo llegó hasta oídos de los *catafractos* que avanzaban y que, de pronto, por primera vez en su vida sintieron algo muy parecido a la duda, algo muy semejante a la inquietud, algo igual al miedo.

Lucio Quieto cogió las riendas de su caballo, tiró de ellas y lo situó de lado entre un pasillo de las cohortes. Levantó la mano y clavó los ojos en los centuriones de primera línea. Las miradas ya no eran de terror, sino de anhelo puro por entrar en combate. Quieto podía ver que a todos aquellos legionarios les faltaba tiempo para empezar a matar y matar enemigos no por ellos, no por sobrevivir, no por Roma, sino por la lealtad infinita que todos sentían en su pecho por alguien llamado Marco Ulpio Trajano.

—¡Por el emperador! ¡Por Trajano! —aulló Quieto.

Bajó el brazo y sesenta mil hombres se lanzaron tras los carroballistas, enormes carros con ballestas de gran tamaño que ya embestían a los *catafractos* de los partos arrojándoles durísimas e irrefrenables lanzas que destrozaban sus protecciones, los herían o mataban y detenían por completo su marcha.

Y hacia ellos avanzaban los legionarios, a por los que quedaran de los *catafractos* y a por las flechas de la caballería ligera enemiga, a combatir bajo nubes de hierro protegidos por parapetos como los que usaron en el Tigris; todos unidos para luchar sin desfallecer un instante hasta poder entregar a su César, tal y como había pedido Quieto, la cabeza del líder de sus enemigos. Todos los legionarios tenían sólo una idea en la cabeza: que por una vez, por una maldita vez, conseguirían ellos la victoria para Trajano.

108

EL MENSAJE SECRETO

Loyang, capital del Imperio han
Invierno de 116 d.C.

Tamura acariciaba su pequeña bolsa, que llevaba, como siempre, atada a su cuerpo, colgando del hombro derecho y que ahora quedaba oculta por la túnica roja de seda que llevaba puesta. Los libros que le regalara Dión Coceyo los había dejado en la habitación que le habían asignado en palacio. Sólo había cogido la estatuilla de Júpiter que le regaló Trajano. Ojalá le trajera suerte. La joven vio cómo cada uno de los nueve ministros y cada una de las tres excelencias departía largo y tendido con aquella mujer sentada en el trono. La emperatriz miraba en ocasiones a un lado o a otro, como si buscara el asentimiento o la negativa del resto de los consejeros a aquello que parecían proponer sus servidores del gobierno imperial. Tamura se dio cuenta de que la emperatriz miraba con frecuencia hacia Fan Chun y, en un par de ocasiones, hacia ella misma. Tamura bajó en ambas ocasiones la mirada.

Al cabo de un largo rato de debates que a Tamura se le hicieron eternos, los altos funcionarios del Estado han empezaron a abandonar la gran sala hasta que sólo quedaron los guardias, la emperatriz, Fan Chun, el general Li Kan y ella. Tamura vio que el anciano consejero hablaba ahora con la emperatriz. No los entendía pero intuía que hablaban de ella.

—¿Ésta es la joven portentosa que viene desde Da Qin? —preguntó Deng.

—Así es —confirmó Fan Chun—. Al menos, eso dice ella.

—¿Cómo podemos estar seguros de que no miente? —indagó la emperatriz—. ¿Cómo podemos saber si lo que dice es verdad y no extrañas mentiras?

—Es difícil de dilucidar si lo que dice es cierto o no, pero la experiencia me demuestra que cuanto más improbable es lo que alguien cuenta suele ser más próximo a la verdad, pues la realidad es, a menudo, muy sorprendente.

—Y decías que traía un mensaje —continuó la emperatriz—. Dile que nos cuente ese mensaje que, según explicabas, tiene orden de entregar sólo a mi persona.

Fan Chun tradujo la petición de la emperatriz al sánscrito mirando a la joven sármata y Tamura asintió, dio un paso pequeño adelante, se arrodilló y fue al grano directamente. Comprendía que ante una mujer que mandaba sobre un imperio tan gigantesco como el de los han no tenía sentido ni era prudente andarse con rodeos.

—Mi señor, el emperador Marco Ulpio Trajano de Roma, del imperio que aquí se conoce como Da Qin, desea hacer saber a quien gobierne en Xeres, esto es, en el Imperio han, que él, mi señor, va a atacar y conquistar el imperio de An-shi. Mi emperador desea informar al emperador han de que su interés sólo es eliminar a un vecino traidor y, a la vez, suprimir también así un intermediario incómodo para el comercio entre los grandes imperios de Da Qin y el de la emperatriz Deng. Quedará después de esta conquista sólo el Imperio kushan entre ambos, y mi emperador sugiere que, si los han lo desean, pueden anexionárselo, de forma que así en el mundo habrá sólo dos grandes imperios y no cuatro, que podrán tratar y comerciar entre ellos de igual a igual, en paz y sin intermediarios que encarezcan los productos o que tergiversen y mientan sobre los unos y los otros, impidiendo, como hasta ahora, que los romanos y los han puedan establecer contacto directo y entenderse en beneficio mutuo. Ése, augusta, emperatriz... —Tamura no sabía bien qué título emplear para referirse a Deng— es, en suma, el mensaje de mi emperador, el César de Roma, el señor de Da Qin.

Fan Chun, por primera vez en muchos años, se quedó boquiabierto y en silencio.

—¿Y bien? —preguntó la emperatriz más intrigada que

nunca, en particular ante el gesto de asombro de Fan Chun, un consejero al que no había visto asombrarse nunca antes.

El asistente del ministro de Obras Públicas parpadeó un par de veces, se volvió hacia la emperatriz y tradujo.

Ahora era Deng la que parpadeaba y guardaba silencio.

Fan Chun, Li Kan, también con gesto de asombro, y la propia emperatriz no quitaban los ojos de una Tamura que permanecía inmóvil, arrodillada, respirando deprisa, intentando controlar sus nervios.

—¿Qué piensas de esto? —preguntó la emperatriz al *yu-shih chung-ch'eng*.

—No sé qué pensar, majestad —admitió el consejero—. Esperaba un mensaje de toma de contacto, no una explicación detallada sobre movimientos militares tan enormes.

—¿Das crédito a esta joven? —insistió Deng.

—Su historia, una vez más, es tan improbable que sólo una lunática podría inventarse algo así.

La emperatriz miró entonces a Li Kan.

—Con nosotros está mi mejor general. Como militar, ¿qué piensas de proyectos de tal envergadura?

Li Kan dio un paso al frente.

—No sabría bien qué decir. An-shi, por las referencias que tenemos de textos antiguos y por lo que dicen los mercaderes de la Ruta de la Seda, es un imperio muy poderoso, tanto o más que el de los kushan. De Da Qin sabemos muy poco. No sabría quién podría vencer en una confrontación de esa envergadura. Sólo sé que... —Se detuvo.

—Di todo lo que pienses, general. No estoy acostumbrada a que se me responda a medias.

Li Kan asintió y continuó con rapidez.

—Sólo sé que una guerra entre esos dos imperios debe de ser un conflicto de dimensiones colosales, majestad, y quien decida iniciarlo debe de ser alguien poderoso y audaz.

—La verdad —intervino de pronto Fan Chun— es que la eliminación de intermediarios entre nosotros y el imperio de Da Qin podría ser beneficiosa para el comercio. Ya en el pasado los *hsiung-nu* de Zhizhi supusieron un problema para la Ruta de la Seda y el general Tang tuvo que eliminarlos. Hoy día los kushan y An-shi encarecen las mercancías que nos llegan de Occidente de forma exagerada. Ciertamente, que el emperador de Da Qin eliminara An-shi de la Ruta de la Seda sería beneficioso. No hemos de olvidar que no dejaron que nuestro mensajero Kan Ying entrara en contacto con Da Qin.

—¿Y tendríamos nosotros capacidad militar para derrotar a los kushan y extender el control a más regiones al oeste de nuestros protectorados occidentales, más allá de Dayuán o Kangchú?[84] —preguntó Deng mirando al *chiang-chün.*

—Sería una empresa arriesgada y muy costosa —respondió el general.

—Pero ¿posible? —insistió la emperatriz.

—Si ése fuera el deseo de su majestad me encargaría de que fuera posible —respondió Li Kan con una decisión que impactó a su interlocutora de sangre imperial.

—¿Recomendarías tú una empresa semejante? —preguntó entonces Deng a Fan Chun.

—No lo sé. Es todo muy precipitado. Tendría que pensarlo. Además, no sé si ante un emperador tan audaz como parece ser el de Da Qin no nos interesaría más tener a los kushan de por medio. Pues de hecho, si An-shi fuera absorbido por Da Qin...

—Nadie nos asegura que si desaparecen los kushan este mismo emperador de Da Qin no nos ataque directamente también a nosotros —dijo la emperatriz interrumpiendo a su consejero.

—Yo no podría haberlo expresado mejor, majestad —aceptó Fan Chun.

Un silencio.

Tamura tragaba saliva. No entendía nada de lo que se decía a su alrededor, pero resultaba evidente que su mensaje había causado cierto impacto en la emperatriz y sus consejeros. Decidió permanecer callada y de rodillas.

—Todo esto parece una locura —dijo al fin la emperatriz—, a la que no pienso dar crédito sin una prueba de que esta joven es algo más que una lunática con gran imaginación

---

84. Fergana y Sogdiana.

y, según decís, una gran guerrera. No me basta para tomarme todo esto en serio. Dile que aporte una prueba de que algo de lo que dice es cierto, de que realmente es enviada por alguien poderoso o, de lo contrario, que se vaya de aquí. Ya decidiré luego si la condeno a prisión, al exilio o qué hacemos con ella.

Fan Chun bajó la cabeza y suspiró. Comprendió que se había dejado llevar por su ilusión de poder contactar con un imperio tan lejano, por su pasión por conocer y saber más de otros mundos. Lo que ahora pedía la emperatriz lo debería haber exigido él mismo antes a aquella extranjera, pero se había cegado por su ansia de creer en viajes del todo imposibles. El asistente se volvió hacia Tamura y le demandó alguna prueba que apoyara su fantástico relato.

Tamura, siempre sin levantarse, hundió la mano en el interior de su túnica y extrajo de su pequeña bolsa la estatuilla de arcilla del dios Júpiter que Trajano le entregara años atrás.

—Éste es un presente de mi emperador para la emperatriz Deng de los han —explicó ella en sánscrito mientras exhibía la pequeña figura.

Fan Chun se acercó y tomó la estatuilla del dios supremo de Roma. Le pareció una curiosidad, pero nada más. La acercó a la emperatriz, que la cogió y la examinó con atención para luego devolverla a su viejo consejero.

—Es sin duda una estatuilla diferente a las nuestras y a cualquier cosa que haya visto antes, pero eso sólo prueba que la muchacha puede venir de muy lejos, no que sea la enviada de un emperador todopoderoso que decide anexionarse imperios vecinos como quien decide si desayuna fruta o arroz.

La emperatriz suspiró ahora.

Estaba cansada.

Fan Chun percibía el agotamiento de su majestad y lamentaba de nuevo, en su fuero interno, haber dado tanto crédito a las palabras de aquella joven extranjera. Su intuición de viejo consejero, no obstante, se obstinaba en decirle aún una y otra vez que nadie, de hecho nadie, ni un loco, podría inventarse algo tan sorprendente e increíble. Era todo tan irreal que precisamente por eso tenía que ser todo cierto. Pero una estatuilla peculiar era poca prueba...

—¿Puedo disponer de un poco de agua en una bacinilla y que se me devuelva la estatuilla un instante? —rogó Tamura mirando al consejero e interrumpiendo sus pensamientos con aquella extraña petición.

Fan Chun enarcó las cejas, inspiró profundamente, exhaló el aire despacio, se volvió hacia la emperatriz y tradujo. Deng levantó las manos como quien diera su visto bueno pero sin fe alguna en que dar curso a aquella petición tuviera sentido. Estaba perdiendo la paciencia. Había sido una mañana de deliberaciones larga.

El agua fue llevada de inmediato.

Tamura tomó la estatuilla que le devolvía el consejero. La muchacha se levantó y, antes de que nadie pudiera decir nada, la joven arrojó al suelo con todas sus fuerzas la figura de arcilla del dios Júpiter. La pieza, lógicamente, se hizo añicos, excepto en su parte central. Los pequeños brazos y las piernas divinos estaban repartidos por las cuatro esquinas de la sala, pero el centro seguía en apariencia intacto. La muchacha cogió el torso desnudo de la figura de arcilla, lo hundió en la bacinilla de agua y lo restregó con los dedos con fuerza hasta que, cuando lo extrajo del líquido enrojecido por el barro, ya no había torso alguno de ningún dios, sino una gigantesca piedra preciosa de color rojo que brillaba a la luz del sol de aquella parte del mundo. Era un rubí, el rubí más grande que nadie hubiera visto antes en el Imperio han.

La muchacha lo entregó de nuevo a Fan Chun y éste, rápidamente, casi como si la joya le quemara en la mano, a su majestad imperial.

—Es un presente del César de Roma, de Da Qin, para la emperatriz Deng como muestra de sus buenas intenciones —dijo Tamura y volvió a arrodillarse y a mirar al suelo mientras seguía hablando—. A mi emperador le habría gustado enviar un tesoro mayor, pero estaba seguro de que algo más llamativo o más grande nunca habría llegado hasta el final del viaje.

La emperatriz Deng examinaba ahora aquella hermosa joya tallada, tan grande como inesperada, que había viajado miles y miles de *li* para terminar ahora en sus manos.

—Quizá la muchacha, después de todo —aceptó la emperatriz— sí que es la enviada de alguien muy poderoso. Lo que no entiendo... —La emperatriz calló mientras arrugaba la frente.

—¿Puedo ayudar a su majestad? —inquirió Fan Chun inclinándose a la vez que formulaba la pregunta, pero más tranquilo al ver que quizá, después de todo, su intuición seguía sirviéndole bien.

—No entiendo por qué un emperador de un lugar tan poderoso como seguramente sea Da Qin decide enviar a una empresa tan compleja como la de cruzar el mundo con un mensaje imperial secreto a la que, sin duda, cuando dio comienzo su misión, era tan sólo una niña. ¿Harías tú algo así, asistente?

—No, no lo haría, majestad.

—Y tú, me lo has probado en muchas ocasiones, eres alguien sabio y prudente. Entonces, o todo esto es una mentira de esta joven, aunque su historia encaja con que ella posea una joya de estas dimensiones, o el emperador de Da Qin es un insensato que confía una empresa casi imposible a una niña.

—Lo que su majestad dice es muy razonable —respondió Fan Chun con serenidad, ponderando bien cada una de sus palabras—. Sólo podemos hacer una cosa para intentar desentrañar el misterio.

—¿Qué? —inquirió la emperatriz Deng.

—Preguntar a la que se dice mensajera y ver si su respuesta es lógica o absurda.

La emperatriz levantó las cejas como quien no cree mucho en aquella idea, pero levantó las manos una vez más invitando a que su viejo consejero procediera.

Fan Chun miró a Tamura y le habló, como siempre, en sánscrito.

—No entendemos por qué el emperador de Da Qin confió un mensaje tan importante a una niña. Comprenderás que es algo muy absurdo.

La joven guerrera sármata cabeceó lentamente al tiempo que comenzaba a responder despacio, como si, a la vez, pusiera en orden sus propios pensamientos.

—Yo misma me he hecho esa pregunta muchas veces: ¿por qué confiar un mensaje como ése a mí y no al comerciante Titianus, que conocía la ruta, o a mi padre, un gran guerrero, o a cualquiera de los pretorianos, o al otro gladiador, o incluso a mi madre? Los acontecimientos me hicieron ver que el emperador no confiaba en los guerreros adultos de su palacio ni tampoco en el capitán del barco, ni siquiera en Titianus. Después de pensarlo mucho tiempo, y he tenido muchos días de silencio desde que llegué al Imperio han para meditarlo bien, he concluido, majestad... —y aquí Tamura se permitió una breve pausa y, por primera vez, mirar a los ojos de la emperatriz Deng—; he concluido que el César Trajano, el emperador de Da Qin, sólo confiaba en mi padre y en mi madre y, además, estaba seguro de que ambos darían la vida no ya por proteger el mensaje, sino por salvarme a mí si fuera necesario en algún momento. Por eso el César Trajano me confió el mensaje a mí, porque estaba convencido de que de llegar alguien hasta aquí, esa persona sería yo. Alguno de los guerreros adultos, ciertamente, fueron desleales al emperador de Da Qin y, por otro lado, mi padre primero y mi madre después, en efecto, dieron la vida por mí. Este mensaje quizá no sea muy importante para la emperatriz Deng, para su majestad, pero este mensaje es para mí lo más importante de mi vida, pues entregándolo honro la memoria de mis padres y haciéndolo me siento más cerca de ellos, de su recuerdo, que es todo lo que poseo.

Fan Chun asintió lentamente. Luego tradujo.

La emperatriz Deng escuchó con atención.

Al principio no dijo nada. Luego se quedó mirando un largo rato el hermoso rubí gigantesco que exhibía en la palma de su mano. Al fin habló:

—Honrar la memoria de los padres es muy importante para nosotros. Tienes todo mi respeto por ello. Consideraré con atención el contenido del mensaje que has traído y por el que tanto ha sufrido tu familia. No puedo reparar tu pérdida, pero te garantizo que, hasta que decida, junto con mis consejeros, qué respuesta dar a tu emperador, serás atendida y tratada en Loyang como embajadora de Da Qin.

109

LA CABEZA DE SANATRUCES

Cesifonte
Invierno de 116 d.C.

—¡Tengo que levantarme! ¡Dejadme! —gritaba Trajano mientras intentaba zafarse de los brazos del viejo médico Critón y del enjuto secretario Fédimo—. ¡Dejadme salir! ¡Por Júpiter! ¡No puedo dejar a mis legionarios solos…!

Hizo falta que Aulo asiera fuertemente al César para que éste, por fin, cediera.

—¡Dejadme! —dijo una vez más, pero su ímpetu perdió vigor y se dejó caer en la cama.

—Está sudando —comentó Fédimo.

—Está fuerte —apostilló el tribuno pretoriano—. Parece haber recuperado el movimiento y la energía, al menos en parte.

—Es posible, pero ha de descansar. En estos casos, tras un ataque como el que ha sufrido, lo esencial es el descanso o nunca se recuperará. Recuerda que cuando lo trajisteis a la tienda apenas podía mover los brazos y las piernas.

El pretoriano asintió.

—Decidme, al menos, cómo va la batalla —dijo el César en un débil susurro.

En el exterior se oía el fragor de la contienda.

—Iré a ver —dijo Aulo.

—¡No! —exclamó el médico—. Mejor que vaya Fédimo. Si el emperador vuelve a tener un arrebato sólo tú puedes contenerlo.

—De acuerdo —aceptó Aulo y miró al joven secretario, que cabeceó afirmativamente y se dirigió raudo a la entrada de la tienda imperial.

En el exterior del praetorium *de campaña*

Fédimo miró hacia la batalla. Él no era militar. Aulo habría sabido interpretar con más rapidez lo que observaba: las legiones estaban en formación, haciendo una gigantesca uve, como si estuvieran envolviendo al enemigo. ¿Y los temidos *catafractos*? No se los veía por ninguna parte. No, Fédimo no era militar, pero aquello no daba para nada la sensación de una derrota, sino todo lo contrario. Pero eso sí, los partos cedían terreno sólo muy lentamente. Había una lucha encarnizada en las primeras líneas. Aquella inmensa uve intentaba engullir a un enemigo tan poderoso como indigesto. ¿Lo conseguirían?

Fédimo parpadeó. El sol lo deslumbraba.

¿Y Lucio Quieto?

No veía al *legatus* norteafricano por ningún lado.

En el interior de la tienda

Pasaron horas. El fragor de la lucha parecía debilitarse poco a poco, como una fiera gigantesca que se fuera durmiendo poco a poco y cuyos rugidos fueran perdiendo fuerza poco a poco. Ya había pasado un buen rato desde que el joven secretario regresara al interior de la tienda y anunciara que, a su entender, la batalla iba bien, aunque no estaba concluida. Explicó lo que había presenciado.

—Una maniobra envolvente —dijo Trajano—. Bien por Quieto, aunque habrá tenido que abrir la formación de las legiones enormemente para poder realizar esa estrategia contra un enemigo tan numeroso.

—El *legatus* Lucio Quieto puede conseguirlo —comentó Aulo convencido.

—Y habrá lanzado los carroballistas contra los *catafractos* —añadió Trajano, pero con voz débil—. Estoy cansado...

El emperador cerró los ojos y cayó en un extraño duermevela entre el mundo de los despiertos y el mundo de los sueños. De pronto, vio una infinita serpiente que se acercaba hacia su cama y reptaba hasta rodear su cuerpo maltrecho con las escamas gélidas de aquella piel de animal traidor. La serpiente lo abrazaba con tal fuerza que apenas podía respirar. Trajano quiso liberarse de aquella bestia que lo atacaba, pero no podía, no podía... y pensó en pedir ayuda a Quieto:

—¡Lucio, Lucio! —gritó.

El César abrió los ojos y vio al líder norteafricano allí, en pie, junto a la cama, pero éste permanecía inmóvil, todo cubierto de sangre, y era él quien lo llamaba como si, herido mortalmente, le pidiera ayuda...

—¡César, César, César! —decía aquella voz quebrantada de Quieto, mientras la serpiente no dejaba de aprisionarlo y él, Trajano, no podía hacer nada ni por liberarse ni por asistir a su brazo derecho, a su amigo. De pronto, se dio cuenta de Quieto no era Quieto, sino Longino, que parecía llamarlo desde el Hades.

—¡César, César!

Trajano se llevó las manos a la cara y se frotó los ojos y vio entonces a Quieto de nuevo: seguía cubierto de sangre, pero no se le veía ni triste ni preocupado ni débil, sino exultante. Y sí, el líder norteafricano lo llamaba, pero con la alegría de quien trae buenas noticias.

—¡César, ha sido una gran victoria!

Trajano se incorporó lentamente en la cama. Critón lo ayudó poniendo algunos almohadones en su espalda para que pudiera estar sentado con más comodidad.

—¿Qué ha pasado? —preguntó Trajano mirando aún confuso a su alrededor.

—El César se ha quedado dormido un par de horas —explicó Fédimo.

—Y ha tenido pesadillas —precisó Critón—. La fiebre ha hecho que el emperador viera cosas extrañas, monstruos, fantasmas.

—Sí, recuerdo una serpiente... —dijo Trajano, pero al mirar a su alrededor allí no había reptil alguno que lo intimidara. Sólo estaban Critón, Fédimo, Aulo, Lucio Quieto y él mismo.

—El emperador habrá tenido pesadillas, pero aun así el César ha conseguido una nueva victoria total para Roma —dijo Lucio Quieto mientras se limpiaba con el dorso de la mano derecha algo de la mucha sangre parta que tenía por el rostro.

—¡Los carroballistas! —exclamó el César—. Los carros con ballestas, ¿los has usado?

—Igual que en Adamklissi contra los *catafractos* sármatas de la Dacia —precisó Quieto—. Y con el mismo buen resultado. El resto ha sido cuestión de voluntad y las legiones de Trajano tienen sólo voluntad de victoria.

Aulo, que ya tenía noticia, por cuenta de otros pretorianos, del emocionante discurso de Quieto a las tropas antes de entrar en combate, no dijo nada. Pero apreció la humildad de un líder como el *legatus* norteafricano, que no se apuntaba la victoria como algo personal cuando era evidente para todos allí, en la tienda del *praetorium*, como fuera, como en todo el campamento del ejército imperial, que esta vez el gran Lucio Quieto había sabido comandar las legiones con la misma destreza del emperador. Como si fuera otro César.

—¿Una victoria absoluta? —preguntó Trajano, siempre cauteloso—. ¿Estás seguro de lo que dices?

Lucio Quieto esperaba una reacción similar por parte del emperador, así que no se sintió incómodo por la pregunta, sino que, tranquilamente se volvió e hizo una señal a unos legionarios que estaban a la puerta del *praetorium*. Éstos entraron entonces con rapidez portando una cesta tapada con un paño de tela blanca manchada de la misma sangre roja que se iba vertiendo por la parte inferior del cesto.

—Dejadlo ahí, a los pies del emperador, que es donde debe estar —ordenó Quieto.

Los legionarios obedecieron sin dudarlo, con orgullo y alegría, depositaron su extraño cargamento junto a la cama donde reposaba el César y se retiraron unos pasos. Lucio Quieto se acercó entonces al cesto, se agachó, cogió con la mano derecha el paño que cubría el contenido de la cesta y lo retiró de golpe: una cabeza con mirada vacía, boca torcida, barba rizada, todo ello repleto de sangre, apareció ante el emperador de Roma.

—Sanatruces —aclaró Quieto—. La cabeza del hijo de Mitrídates, el líder del último ejército que los partos han osado enviarnos. Sus tropas han sido totalmente doblegadas. En su desesperación habían reclutado incluso hasta un regimiento compuesto sólo por eunucos de los que vigilan a las esposas de los nobles. Los hemos masacrado, incluido su líder, un gigantón a quien Liviano atravesó con su espada. Apenas han sobrevivido algunas unidades del enemigo. Un pequeño grupo ha huido hacia el norte, dirigidos por Mitrídates, que se nos ha escapado, y otra pequeña parte de los supervivientes se ha rendido bajo el mando de Partamaspates, el hijo de Osroes.

Trajano suspiró aliviado y dejó que todo el peso de su cuerpo cayera sobre los almohadones de su espalda.

—En efecto, una gran victoria —aceptó al fin con satisfacción—. Una victoria tuya, Quieto. Tu primera gran victoria.

—Una victoria del César y de Roma —replicó el norteafricano negándose a recibir los honores por haber derrotado al inmenso ejército parto.

Trajano sonrió.

—Como quieras. Una victoria de todos, porque todos han participado en ella. ¿O me equivoco?

—Hasta el último legionario de la última cohorte de la última legión ha luchado con furia, augusto —confirmó Quieto—, eso es cierto. Sí, una victoria de todos.

Se hizo un breve silencio.

—Llevaos ese despojo —dijo entonces Trajano señalando la cabeza de Sanatruces—. Dádselo a los perros más hambrientos que encontréis. Ahora nos queda recuperar Hatra. Pero no podemos lanzarnos contra ella dejando nuestra espalda descubierta. Osroes aún está allí y cada vez pienso más que la princesa Aryazate tiene razón: es una serpiente como la que se me aparece en mis peores sueños, un reptil que nos morderá siempre que le demos ocasión hasta que consigamos darle muerte de una vez por todas.

—¿Dividimos el ejército? —sugirió Quieto, pensativo, pero feliz de ver al emperador lo suficientemente recuperado como para debatir sobre estrategia a gran escala—. ¿Dejamos unas legiones en Cesifonte y avanzamos con otras hacia el norte, hacia Hatra?

—No —respondió Trajano muy tajante—. Hatra es una

ciudad casi inexpugnable y esta campaña muy compleja. No, no dividiremos las tropas. Iremos todos a Hatra.

—¿Y Cesifonte y Babilonia? —preguntó Aulo.

Trajano miraba al suelo. Se había jurado una y mil veces que nunca se replegaría. Era difícil tragarse el orgullo. A cualquiera le cuesta; a un emperador acostumbrado a las victorias una tras otra, aún más. Levantó la mirada y se dirigió una vez más a sus hombres.

—Traed a Partamaspates. Y, por todos los dioses, traed vino. Esta victoria hay que celebrarla.

Aulo fue en busca del hijo de Osroes.

Quieto, por su parte, estaba feliz, pero Critón, el médico, se le acercó por la espalda y lo cogió por el brazo para conducirlo a la puerta del *praetorium*.

—Voy a examinar a nuestro *legatus* —dijo el médico a modo de explicación—. Veo alguna herida que me incomoda.

—Si no tengo nada... —interpuso el norteafricano intentando zafarse del médico, pero Trajano se lo recriminó.

—Ve con Critón y que te cure las heridas. Roma te necesita vivo. Yo te necesito vivo —dijo el César con una sonrisa en la cara.

Quieto cedió y acompañó a Critón fuera de la tienda. En cuanto estuvieron en el exterior, el médico soltó el brazo del *legatus*, se detuvo y lo miró fijamente a la cara.

—El emperador me preocupa —dijo—. No debería beber tanto. No creo que el vino sea la mejor de las soluciones para su dolencia. Un nuevo ataque puede ser definitivo. Mortal. Puede quedarse paralizado por completo. Para siempre.

—Ya —admitió Quieto—. Lo imagino. Pero no podemos cambiar la naturaleza del César, no podemos hacer que deje de ser quien ha sido siempre.

Critón exhaló todo el aire de sus pulmones.

—No, supongo que no podemos.

110

LA SANGRE DE LOS CRISTIANOS

Roma
Febrero de 117 d.C.

En el centro de la arena del Anfiteatro Flavio

Ignacio caminaba hacia las fieras con los ojos cerrados y las manos en alto mientras oraba.

—A ti me entrego, mi Señor y Dios, hacia ti voy con las manos desnudas sin nada que llevarme de este mundo que no sea la bondad de haber tenido la dicha de conocer tu mensaje a través de Cristo. Afortunado fui por haber sido bendecido por las manos mismas de Jesús, hijo de ti, mi Señor. Y hacia ti voy, oh Dios eterno todopoderoso, hacia ti camino con los pies descalzos sobre esta arena como Cristo caminaba sobre las aguas del mar...

Se detuvo.

Las fieras rugían a su alrededor, pero él permanecía inmóvil sin decir palabra alguna. Rezaba en silencio, moviendo apenas los labios. Ya no se sentía en la tierra, sino en la gloria de Dios.

El público se admiraba de cómo los leones no se aproximaban al prisionero cristiano, como si temieran algo de aquel viejo.

En las puertas de la salida de las fieras

—Es porque no se mueve —dijo uno de los *bestiarii* desde una de las puertas a pie de la arena del Anfiteatro Flavio—. Los cristianos creerán que se trata de uno de esos milagros de sus hombres sagrados de los que tanto hablan, pero los leones no atacan porque no se mueve.

—Pero al final se lo comerán —respondió otro de los pretorianos que vigilaba aquella puerta—. Siempre lo hacen.

—Sí —aceptó el que había hablado primero.

En la arena

Ignacio seguía en pie, casi en el centro del Anfiteatro Flavio.

—Que la gloria de Dios me alcance pronto y viva en ella alejado de las turbulencias terrenales, de nuestros pecados y debilidades, de nuestros egoísmos y miserias, de nuestras traiciones constantes a tu palabra y a tu mensaje...

En las últimas gradas

Entre el público un hombre contemplaba la escena desde los asientos más lejanos con pena en el corazón y lágrimas contenidas en los ojos.

—Dios, en efecto, lo protege —dijo Alejandro, el obispo de Roma en secreto, entre la multitud del público inmerso.

—Sin duda —confirmó Telesforo, que acababa de regresar a las gradas desde las celdas del hipogeo, donde se le había permitido entrevistarse con Ignacio unos instantes antes de que fuera arrojado a los leones.

—¿Qué te ha dicho? —le preguntó Alejandro entre la pena y el ansia y el horror—. Necesitamos su último consejo más que nunca. ¿Lo has visto con temple?

—Temple infinito. Dios está no ya con él, sino en él, y le ha dado fuerzas para enfrentarse a su final terrible con la serenidad que vemos —le confirmó Telesforo.

—¡Aaaahhh! —gritó una mujer y luego un clamor enorme lo invadió todo. La gente se puso en pie. Algunos intercambiaban monedas sobre las apuestas cruzadas con respecto a qué león sería el primero en atacar.

Alejandro y Telesforo no se alzaron como el resto. Ya sabían lo que estaba ocurriendo y no querían presenciar aquella locura de sangre y terror con más detalle. Ignacio, simplemente, ya no estaba con ellos sino en los cielos, con Dios. Un lugar mucho mejor.

—Paz a su alma y que el Señor la acoja en su seno como merece —dijo Telesforo en un susurro.

La gente volvía a sentarse. Ambos pudieron ser testigos de cómo un grupo de leones despedazaba restos del cuerpo de quien para la multitud era un hombre viejo y traidor al Imperio. Eso era lo que veían los romanos.

—Entonces ¿te ha dicho algo sobre Marción y su maldito libro? —preguntó Alejandro con rabia en los labios. Era difícil contenerse ante tanta barbarie y tanta injusticia juntas.

—Me ha dicho que al diablo hay que combatirlo con las armas del diablo —respondió Telesforo con el ceño fruncido.

—¿Y qué ha querido decir con eso? —indagó Alejandro decepcionado porque el último mensaje de Ignacio fuera un acertijo.

Telesforo negó con la cabeza en señal de desamparo.

—No lo sé, pero era como si fuera Dios quien hablara por su boca.

—Con las armas del diablo... —repitió Alejandro en voz baja sin entender nada.

Telesforo, a su lado, miraba hacia el suelo, pensativo, sin decir nada.

111

UN NUEVO PLAN

Hatra
Marzo de 117 d.C.

Trajano contemplaba las murallas de Hatra con el semblante serio. Se había conseguido una gran victoria contra los partos en Cesifonte, pero aun así la extensión de los territorios conquistados era tal y la complejidad de mantenerlos controlados tan enorme, que había tenido que tomar una de las decisiones más dolorosas de su vida: dejar la provincia de Babilonia de nuevo en manos del enemigo, en este caso bajo el control de un títere, Partamaspates, el hijo de Osroes, bajo la promesa de éste de estar sometido al Imperio del pueblo de Roma, como si el nuevo rey de reyes fuera sólo un muñeco.

Aun así, aunque Partamaspates hubiera aceptado, al menos nominalmente, la sumisión al César, aquella concesión era un repliegue. Armenia al norte también estaba siendo amenazada con nuevas revueltas, impulsadas parecía ser por Mitrídates, el único líder parto relevante de la familia de Osroes que había salido con vida de la batalla de Cesifonte. Con ese repliegue estratégico, que Trajano quería considerar sólo como algo temporal, las provincias de Mesopotamia y Asiria eran las únicas que estaban controladas directamente por las legiones.

Ahora lo esencial era terminar con la rebelión de Hatra, pues su ejemplo podía suponer un estímulo para que otras poblaciones se unieran a una prolongada resistencia contra Roma que Trajano sabía que no podía permitirse. La idea era aceptar aquella retirada de Babilonia y Cesifonte, para, rindiendo Hatra, hacerse de nuevo fuerte en Asiria, Armenia y Mesopotamia, de modo que las legiones pudieran, una vez más, descender sobre la capital de Partia, apartar a Partamaspates y recuperar todo aquel territorio como provincia del Imperio. El hijo de Osroes, al entregarse, ya había dado clara muestra de no ser un enemigo temible.

Era un buen plan.

Había enviado a la princesa Aryazate a Antioquía. Un rehén en retaguardia siempre podía ser útil. Curiosamente, la joven no había pedido reencontrarse con su hermano Partamaspates en Cesifonte y quedarse allí. Era un comportamiento peculiar, pero Trajano no tenía tiempo para pensar en lo que pasaba por la cabeza de una princesa parta con respecto a su destino. Sólo tenía tiempo y energías para su plan de contraataque.

Trajano, muy restablecido de la extraña dolencia que había padecido en Cesifonte y que había paralizado sus extremidades durante horas, miraba ahora en pie, con los brazos en jarras, hacia los muros de Hatra.

Su buen plan pasaba, no obstante, por rendir aquella fortaleza.

Quieto llegó a caballo, desmontó y se situó junto al César.

—Ya tengo toda la información que me pediste —dijo el norteafricano.

—Te escucho —respondió Trajano sin dejar de mirar hacia las murallas.

—Hatra está construida sobre el promontorio que vemos —empezó el jefe de la caballería con tono serio, marcial, sin mostrar miedo, pero tampoco dando a entender que lo que describía fuera un objetivo fácil de conquistar—. Toda Hatra está rodeada por una doble muralla de más de cuatro millas de perímetro. La muralla exterior es de tierra apelmazada; luego tenemos una especie de zanja o foso y viene la segunda muralla de piedra. En ésta hay cuatro grandes puertas fortificadas, una hacia el norte, otra hacia el sur, una más hacia el este y una última hacia el oeste. Incluso si conseguimos superar la primera muralla de tierra será difícil conquistar la segunda. Hay más de ciento sesenta torres desde las que los arqueros pueden hacer que cualquier aproximación a la ciudad resulte muy peligrosa, casi imposible.

—Podríamos rendir a sus defensores por hambre —sugirió Trajano—, aunque eso lleva tiempo y no me gustaría tener que pasar aquí meses. Imagino que se habrán pertrechado bien de víveres antes de rebelarse contra nosotros.

—Varios comerciantes árabes —comentó entonces Quieto— nos aseguran que Elkud, el *mry* o gobernador de Hatra, hizo acopio de provisiones para resistir todo un año si fuera necesario.

—No nos podemos permitir un año —dijo Trajano suspirando—. Y pensar que los gobernadores de Hatra enviaron una embajada a Edesa humillándose ante Roma cuando habíamos cruzado el Éufrates, al mismo tiempo que ya entonces enviaban a guerreros de Hatra a luchar contra nosotros en el Tigris; ¿recuerdas, Lucio?

—Sí, augusto. Parece que aquí en Oriente todos juegan a estar en los dos bandos a la vez, con nosotros y con los partos.

—No, Lucio —lo corrigió Trajano—. Aquí todos juegan a estar en un único bando: el suyo propio, y para vencer, para mantenerse como gobernadores o sátrapas o reyes de sus ciudades o reinos están dispuestos a prometerlo todo a todos, pero luego, al final, no hay lealtades ni entre ellos mismos. Ahí tienes a los partos divididos ahora entre Mitrídates en Armenia, Partamaspates en Cesifonte, Osroes oculto en las montañas del este y ese desconocido Vologases que se disputa con todos el trono desde la frontera del Imperio kushan. Por eso han sido y son débiles y pudimos derrotarlos en un principio, pero por eso mismo cuesta tanto controlar luego los territorios conquistados. No cumplen ninguna promesa, ningún pacto. Pero los derrotaremos definitivamente, Lucio, lo haremos aunque sea lo último que haga en esta vida.

Trajano hablaba rojo de rabia.

—El emperador no debería alterarse tanto —añadió Quieto preocupado por que el César sufriera otro ataque paralizante que lo apartara de la dirección de las legiones. El jefe de la caballería romana no temía hacerse de nuevo con el mando, pero sabía que aquello sería otra vez muy desmoralizador para las tropas y perder el ánimo era lo último que podían permitirse en aquellos momentos de pulso permanente con un enemigo, dividido, sí, pero resistente como pocos.

—Estoy bien —respondió Trajano serenándose un poco y volviéndose hacia las murallas para contemplarlas de nuevo con la frente arrugada—. Podríamos rendirlos por sed, como hicimos con los dacios de Sarmizegetusa, cortándoles el suministro de agua.

—Lo hemos mirado, César, pero Hatra se abastece de un gran pozo que tienen en el centro de la ciudad, tan profundo que es inalcanzable para nuestros zapadores. Por el contrario, el agua que tenemos a nuestra disposición es escasa y de no muy buena calidad. Aquí no llueve en meses, el sol es abrasador, los hombres tienen que beber y tendremos que transportar agua desde muy lejos. Va a ser algo complicado.

El César asintió, pero sin dar muestras de desánimo en su rostro.

—Envía una legión en ofensiva contra las murallas, pero sin arriesgar hombres innecesariamente —dijo Trajano—. Que sientan nuestro aliento y nuestra determinación. Lo haremos poco a poco, como se hacen las grandes cosas, Lucio. Pero lo haremos

—Sí, César.

Pero no fue fácil.

Los combates se alargaron durante días y los legionarios apenas conseguían causar algunas bajas entre los defensores. Para lograr acceder a la primera muralla habrían sido necesarias torres de asedio, pero alrededor de Hatra tampoco había bosques que proporcionaran la madera necesaria para semejantes obras. Y no tenían a Apolodoro, a quien Trajano, en un exceso de confianza, había devuelto a Egipto para que culminara las obras del canal que unía el Mediterráneo con la mar Eritrea. El César ordenó entonces que los zapadores excavaran minas, con las que se pudo debilitar la tierra apelmazada en un sector del muro exterior al crear un corrimiento de la superficie que abrió una brecha en la gran estructura. No era mucho, pero después de tanto esfuerzo, los legionarios lo celebraron como una gran victoria. Estuvo bien porque las tropas necesitaban animarse, pues los días pasaban bajo un sol abrasador que derretía sus frentes y los debilitaba hasta dejarlos extenuados. Y el agua, tal y como había previsto Lucio, era escasa y se tenía que racionar.

—Hemos de aprovechar la ilusión que esa brecha en la muralla externa ha encendido en nuestros hombres —dijo Trajano subiendo a su caballo.

—¿Qué va a hacer el César? —preguntó Quieto con cierto nerviosismo.

—¡Voy a lanzarme con mis *singulares* hacia la brecha! ¡Será como cuando crucé el puente sobre el Tigris en medio de la batalla! —respondió el emperador enfervorecido—. ¡Hay que arremeter contra el único punto débil del enemigo! ¡Que los arqueros nos cubran! Sé que no vamos a conseguir entrar con este primer ataque, pero mis legionarios han de ver que estoy con ellos.

Lucio Quieto asentía desde lo alto de su propio caballo mientras veía cómo Liviano, detrás del César, le hacía señales negando con la cabeza. Lucio sabía que quizá el emperador aún no estaba completamente recuperado del ataque paralizante que sufrió en Cesifonte apenas hacía tres meses, pero, por otro lado, las penalidades que estaban pasando los legionarios en aquel asedio eran tales que la presencia del emperador en primera línea sería un revulsivo. Eso era indudable. Los soldados se veían obligados a compartir su comida con millones de moscas que rodeaban cualquier lugar donde hubiera alimento. El agua seguía faltando y el sol suponía siempre una tortura creciente. Quieto vio cómo Liviano, ante su silencio, se le acercaba.

—Al menos que el César se quite el *paludamentum* púrpura —le dijo el jefe del pretorio en voz baja al norteafricano—. No hace falta que lo exhiba para que lo identifiquen nuestros hombres, pero llevarlo, sin embargo, lo hace demasiado visible para los arqueros enemigos.

Quieto sopesó el consejo de Liviano. Miró hacia los pretorianos y vio cómo Aulo, con el que Liviano ya debía de haber hablado del asunto, afirmaba varias veces, rápidamente, con la cabeza, pero sin decir nada. Trajano, ocupado en ajustarse la coraza con ayuda de dos *calones*, no parecía reparar ni en las

miradas ni en los gestos de los hombres de su guardia pretoriana. Los esclavos llevaron entonces el gran manto púrpura
para ceñirlo al cuello del César.

—Quizá el emperador se sentirá más ágil sin el *paludamentum* púrpura —apuntó Quieto.

Trajano, que había doblado su cuerpo para que los *calones*
pudieran ceñirle el manto resplandeciente y brillante del poder absoluto de Roma, se incorporó de nuevo sin dar tiempo
a que los esclavos se lo pusieran.

—Lo que pasa es que tenéis miedo de que los arqueros
enemigos se centren en mí —dijo Trajano, pero sin rabia ni
despecho.

—Eso también —aceptó Quieto—. Nuestros legionarios
ya conocen la figura del César sin necesidad de que lleve la
púrpura.

Trajano miró a un lado y a otro.

—Parece que lo tenéis todo hablado entre vosotros —dijo
observando a Liviano.

El jefe del pretorio callaba. Fue Aulo quien habló por
todos.

—La misión de toda la guardia pretoriana y de toda la caballería de *singulares*, augusto, es proteger al César en todo momento —dijo el tribuno bajando la mirada.

Trajano los contempló a todos muy serio.

En el campo de batalla, varias cohortes se acercaban hacia
la brecha. En las murallas se podía ver a los arqueros enemigos preparándose.

Trajano sonrió.

—En efecto, Aulo, ésa es vuestra misión. Si os sentís mejor,
dirigiré esta carga sin el *paludamentum* púrpura.

Liviano, Aulo, muchos pretorianos y hasta el propio Quieto exhalaron un largo suspiro de alivio.

—¡Vamos allá, por Júpiter! —exclamó entonces el emperador sin dejarles tiempo para disfrutar de aquel instante de
serenidad.

Elkud, *mry* de Hatra, miraba hacia las cohortes que se aproximaban a la brecha abierta por los romanos en la primera muralla. Él era el gobernador de la ciudad en nombre del rey de reyes de Partia. En aquel momento no estaba claro quién era realmente el *Šāhān Šāh*, si Partamaspates que se sentaba de forma efectiva en el *parwāngāh*, en el trono de Cesifonte, Mitrídates en Armenia, Osroes refugiado en las montañas o el eterno rebelde Vologases. Pero eso en ese momento a Elkud no le importaba demasiado. Se había levantado en armas contra las legiones del César y ahora tenía que resistir como fuera. Hasta el final. Intuía que el emperador romano querría darles un escarmiento ejemplar si entraba en la ciudad, así que eso, sencillamente, no debía ocurrir nunca.

—Sin torres de asedio lo que han conseguido no les valdrá de nada —dijo Elkud a sus oficiales.

—Pero les da esperanza, padre, donde antes no tenían nada —apuntó Nash Rihab, hijo del gobernador.

—Por Shamash, muchacho, en eso llevas razón. Necesitaríamos algo con lo que compensar esta pequeña victoria moral de los romanos, algo con lo que hundirlos y acelerar que abandonen el asedio. Nunca conseguirán rendirnos, pero salvaríamos hombres y ahorraríamos sufrimiento a nuestro pueblo si logramos que se den cuenta de tal imposibilidad pronto y no dentro de varios meses. No tenemos problemas de agua, pero los víveres podrían empezar a sernos insuficientes si el asedio se alargara hasta un año.

—Pero eso ellos no lo saben, padre.

—Siempre hay traidores, muchacho —añadió Elkud mirando hacia el ejército romano que avanzaba contra ellos—. No dudes, hijo mío, que en el momento que tengamos el más mínimo problema de abastecimiento, algún traidor informará al enemigo. La guerra, muchacho, es hija de muchas deslealtades.

Guardaron silencio un rato hasta que Nash Rihab vio la caballería de élite romana aproximándose hacia la brecha.

—¿Qué utilidad puede tener la caballería allí, padre, para los romanos?

—Apoyar a su infantería si abriéramos la puerta y lanzáramos a nuestros jinetes para intentar impedir los trabajos de sus zapadores. Deben de estar excavando ya un nuevo túnel para tratar de quebrar los cimientos de la segunda muralla.

—No podrán romper la roca sobre la que se asienta la segunda muralla —apostilló Nash Rihab.

—Me gustaría ver la cara de sus zapadores cuando sus picos choquen con la roca... —comentó entonces Elkud, pero calló por un instante mientras observaba con atención a un grupo de jinetes que cabalgaba próximo a la brecha—. ¿Hasta qué edad combaten en la caballería romana?

Nash Rihab se quedó confundido ante la inesperada pregunta de su padre, cuando al mirar hacia la dirección que Elkud señalaba con el índice, vio un jinete romano con todo el pelo completamente gris. Era extraño.

—Es él —dijo Elkud.

—¿Quién?

—Trajano. —El gobernador se dirigió hacia sus oficiales sin dudarlo un instante—: ¡No lleva su capa púrpura, pero es él! ¡Deberían haberle puesto casco! ¡Que todas las flechas vayan contra el jinete del pelo gris! —Y luego añadió algo entre dientes pero que su hijo oyó perfectamente—: Si abatimos al César, la brecha que habremos abierto en la confianza de los romanos será mucho más grande que la que ellos han abierto en nuestra muralla. El valor de Trajano es la única arma realmente peligrosa que nuestros enemigos tienen en este asedio. Ese emperador es nuestro enemigo, pero he de reconocerle una bravura que no había visto nunca antes. Si en el *parwāngāh* de Cesifonte se hubiera sentado alguien como él, todo esto habría sido distinto.

Caballería pretoriana, frente a la brecha de la muralla exterior de Hatra

El César llegó hasta donde los zapadores dirigían el trabajo de las minas nuevas. Desmontó de su caballo. Liviano, Aulo y un puñado de pretorianos a los que el jefe del pretorio miró lo rodearon para evitar que ninguna flecha pudiera llegar al César. De hecho todos, desde el propio Liviano, pasando por Aulo hasta el último de los pretorianos que envolvían al emperador, llevaban grandes escudos que desataron con rapidez de sus caballos para usarlos como protección. Por el momento todo parecía exagerado, porque ningún arquero enemigo disparaba.

—¡Hay que seguir con las minas! —exclamó Trajano para animar a los zapadores que se habían aproximado al César para recibir instrucciones.

—Hemos chocado con una gran base de roca, augusto —dijo uno de los oficiales al mando de la excavación.

—¡Pues hay que quebrar esa roca como sea! —insistió Trajano.

—Se tardará tiempo, augusto, y no sé...

Pero Trajano no quiso escuchar lamentos. No había ido hasta allí para eso, sino para insuflar nuevas energías a sus hombres.

—¡Por Júpiter, habéis conseguido una gran victoria al abrir la brecha en la primera muralla! ¡No desfallezcáis! ¡Si hay roca, cavad más bajo! ¡Y emplead todo el tiempo que os haga falta! ¡Yo estoy aquí con vosotros y esperaré a que lo consigáis! ¡Sabed que los dioses nos ayudarán, sabed que el César comparte vuestra lucha y sabed que lo conseguiréis! ¡Recordad que Trajano, vuestro César, nunca ha sido derrotado! ¡Jamás!

Alrededor del emperador se había reunido un gran número de ingenieros, zapadores, legionarios y jinetes. Todos lo escuchaban absortos. Todos menos Liviano, que miraba hacia las torres de la segunda muralla de Hatra cubriéndose con la palma de la mano para protegerse del sol cegador.

—¿Llegan hasta aquí las flechas enemigas? —preguntó el jefe del pretorio en voz baja a uno de los ingenieros de la mina.

—Sí —respondió éste también en voz baja—, pero hemos levantado un parapeto que nos protege y parece que los arqueros de Hatra no quieren desperdiciar flechas que quizá luego puedan necesitar.

Liviano asintió mientras examinaba la pared de madera

que protegía las excavaciones. Eso tenía sentido. Por muchas penalidades que las legiones estuvieran pasando, poca agua, moscas en la comida, sol abrasador y frío gélido nocturno, tenían la gran ventaja de poder reabastecerse de armamento, todo tipo de materiales y de nuevos víveres siempre que hiciera falta. Incluso, aunque fuera penoso y difícil, se podía llevar agua en cántaros desde millas al oeste. Los sitiados, sin embargo, tenían que economizar víveres y armamento. Agua era lo único que les sobraba. Nada estaba decidido.

Segunda muralla de Hatra, torre junto a la puerta sur

—El jinete del pelo gris ha desmontado y se ha refugiado detrás de los parapetos que los romanos han levantado para proteger sus trabajos en la mina —dijo Nash Rihab—. Disparar por encima del parapeto es como disparar a ciegas. Perderemos muchas flechas y abatiremos a muy pocos enemigos.

—Pero ¿cuándo tendremos a su emperador más cerca, muchacho? —opuso Elkud y miró hacia sus oficiales—. ¡A discreción!

Parapeto de la mina romana frente a la brecha
de la muralla exterior de Hatra

—¡Nunca han conseguido vencerme! ¡Recordadlo siempre! ¡Por todos los dioses: nunca, nadie! —continuaba Trajano que, por fin, parecía haber hinchado tanto los pechos de los ingenieros, zapadores y legionarios que estaban dispuestos ya a comerse la roca subterránea a mordiscos si fuera necesario—. ¡Derrotamos a los dacios en Sarmizegetusa y a los roxolanos en Adamklissi! ¡Hicimos huir a los partos de Armenia, cruzamos el Éufrates, conquistamos Osroene! ¡Atravesamos el Tigris contra miles de enemigos armados hasta los dientes! ¡Nada ni nadie nos ha detenido nunca ni nadie lo conseguirá...!

Iba a seguir, pero en ese instante empezaron a caer flechas por todas partes al tiempo que se oían centenares de golpes secos de otros dardos que se estrellaban contra la madera del parapeto. La mayoría de las flechas enemigas eran detenidas por la pequeña fortificación que los romanos habían levantado para proteger los trabajos de la mina, pero nunca antes habían lanzado los defensores de Hatra una lluvia tan densa y constante de flechas. Era como si les estuvieran arrojando de una sola vez absolutamente todo lo que tenían y ni los parapetos parecían ser suficiente defensa para contener una lluvia tan incesante de dardos.

—¡El emperador, el emperador! —gritó Liviano, que, con rabia e impotencia, se percató de que se había alejado demasiado de los parapetos al hablar a los zapadores. Varias flechas estaban cayendo justo al lado del César. Zapadores, ingenieros y legionarios corrían a por sus escudos o hacia el interior de la mina para protegerse de aquel inesperado ataque, sorprendente sobre todo por lo inusitado de la intensidad. Era una lluvia tan inclemente e inmisericorde que en muchos pechos legionarios se despertó, una vez más, el miedo al desastre de Craso.

Aulo era el que estaba más cerca de Trajano y fue junto al César raudo como una centella. El emperador no llevaba escudo alguno. Lo había dejado para hablar a sus legionarios y así tener ambas manos libres para gesticular y subrayar sus palabras, sus frases, su mensaje de victoria eterna con los brazos extendidos.

Aulo cubrió al César con su propio escudo y evitó que una flecha se clavara en el cuerpo del emperador, pero al hacerlo, el tribuno dejó su propio cuerpo descubierto y un dardo certero, diseñado para acabar mortalmente con un enemigo de los dioses de Hatra, se hundió en su espalda y la punta de la flecha se abrió camino, punzante y desgarradora, hasta el mismísimo corazón del tribuno.

Aulo sintió cómo, de súbito, le abandonaban las fuerzas, pero aun así no bajaba el brazo con el escudo que protegía al César.

—¡Aulo, Aulo! —gritó Trajano abrazando el cuerpo del tribuno y sintiendo la sangre caliente de su mejor guardián brotando de su espalda.

El emperador apretó con las palmas de las manos la zona

alrededor de la flecha clavada en el cuerpo del tribuno en un intento por detener la hemorragia, pero la sangre de su guardián eterno, de su vigilante de siempre, desde que años atrás le anunciara en Germania que Nerva lo había adoptado, esa sangre del más leal de los pretorianos, el mismo que había estado siempre junto a él en Roma, en la Dacia, en aquellos bosques donde lo rodearon los traidores renegados enviados por Decébalo, la sangre del más fiel de la guardia imperial, se escapaba entre los dedos del emperador, que seguía abrazándolo y aullando con rabia y dolor y odio...

—¡Aulo, Aulo!

Las flechas seguían cayendo.

Trajano soltó el cuerpo de su guardián, de su pretoriano, de su amigo, pero lo acompañó en su lenta caída hasta dejarlo de costado sobre la tierra de Mesopotamia. Los dardos continuaban rodeando al emperador.

Trajano tenía sangre en el pecho.

—¡Han alcanzado al César! —gritó Liviano.

Lucio Quieto fue hasta el lugar al galope para socorrer a Trajano, pero para cuando llegó ya parecía que todo estaba perdido. Vio al emperador cubierto de sangre por el pecho, en las manos, gritando y siendo arrastrado por el resto de la guardia hacia uno de los caballos para intentar sacarlo de allí a toda velocidad.

—¡Han matado a Aulo! —le dijo Liviano al pasar a su lado—. ¡Y han herido al César!

—¿No será la sangre de Aulo la que lleva el emperador en su cuerpo? —preguntó Quieto con algo de esperanza dentro del desastre.

Nadie respondió.

No era necesario: el César llevaba una flecha clavada en el hombro, por la espalda.

En el praetorium *de campaña*

Trajano, con una venda en el hombro, cubierto con una túnica de lana blanca y con sus sandalias militares puestas, estaba sentado en su *sella curulis* en la tienda del *praetorium*. Le habían dibujado un plano aproximado de las fortificaciones de Hatra y estaba examinándolo con detalle cuando entró Lucio Quieto con el semblante sombrío.

—No es grave —dijo el emperador al ver la faz de su segundo en el mando—. Es sólo un rasguño de una flecha. Estaba clavada en la coraza, pero la punta apenas me rozó la piel. La mayor parte de la sangre que me cubría era de Aulo. Lo irreparable es su muerte. He perdido a un hombre leal hasta el fin. Quedan pocos como él. La conquista de Partia me está consumiendo, por dentro y a mi alrededor, arrebatándome a hombres como Aulo. He ordenado a Fédimo que envíe cartas a su familia. No les faltará de nada a ninguno de los suyos. Es lo menos que puedo hacer.

El César dobló el mapa de Hatra con cierto desdén, con rabia.

—Sí, la muerte de Aulo ha sido un duro golpe para todos —admitió Quieto, sin añadir nada más.

—Esta rebelión de Osroene y Hatra nos ha sorprendido a todos —continuó Trajano—. Quizá no evalué bien los riesgos de unas conquistas demasiado rápidas, pero aún pienso que todo puede rehacerse. Primero hemos de centrarnos en la caída de Hatra. ¡Por Júpiter! ¡Cómo lamento haber enviado a Apolodoro a Egipto! He pensado en reclamarlo, pero para cuando llegue mi carta a Alejandría él ya habrá partido hacia Roma. Quería completar algunas cosas del foro y le di permiso. Fui un estúpido. Si estuviera aquí ese arquitecto ingeniaría algo con lo que ayudarnos a quebrar esas fortificaciones. La pared de roca del subsuelo de la ciudad parece impenetrable. Los zapadores han vuelto a informarme de que los trabajos de la mina están atascados. Y sé que falta agua. Y este sol abrasador que cada día va a más. Y ahora la muerte de Aulo. No sé, quizá estoy equivocándome. A lo mejor todos los demás tienen razón y yo no... —Pero Trajano calló al ver que Lucio paseaba por la tienda sin decir nada; aquél era un comportamiento extraño—. ¿Qué ocurre, Lucio? Apenas he estado unas horas alejado de primera línea. No puede haber pasado nada tan grave para explicar que ya ni siquiera tengas interés en escucharme.

—El problema no está en vanguardia —dijo Quieto deteniéndose frente al César.

Trajano parpadeó un par de veces. ¿Qué podía haber pasado en Roma o en cualquier otro punto del Imperio que pudiera causar ese peculiar tono de preocupación en Lucio? Su jefe de caballería, su segundo en el mando, no era hombre de incomodarse ni por batallas ni por guerras ni por muertes. Algo grande estaba pasando en el Imperio. Algo grave.

—¿En retaguardia? —preguntó Trajano—. No puede ser que Osroene se haya alzado en armas de nuevo, no desde que tú estuviste allí y resolviste el asunto en Edesa.

—No es Osroene: es todo el Imperio —respondió Quieto—. Llegó una carta de Adriano mientras Critón atendía al César. Llegó en medio de la confusión, no sabía siquiera si el emperador estaba gravemente herido o no, y decidí leerla. Podría habérsela dado a Fédimo, pero la leí yo. No sé si hice lo correcto.

—No vengas ahora con remilgos, Lucio. No me importa si tú o Fédimo sois los primeros en leer una carta. Por Júpiter, ve al asunto.

Quieto extrajo un papiro doblado de entre los dobleces de su uniforme y lo puso sobre la mesa del *praetorium*, junto al mapa doblado de Hatra. Trajano reconoció la letra de su sobrino Adriano en el mensaje.

—No voy a perder el tiempo en leer un mensaje de mi sobrino. Me basta con que me expliques qué está pasando.

—Hay algunos problemas en las fronteras, en Mauritania, en Britania y en la Dacia también, allí con algunas tribus de los roxolanos.

—Nada de eso es nuevo —replicó Trajano poniendo las manos sobre la mesa, al lado mismo de la carta de Adriano—; mi sobrino no puede haberte preocupado tanto por los viejos problemas de esas fronteras. Son asuntos menores. Ya los resolveremos cuando consolidemos nuestras posiciones aquí... Debe de haber algo más serio.

Quieto asintió.

—Los judíos se han rebelado.

—¿Eso es todo? ¡Por Cástor y Pólux! ¡No puede ser que el invencible Lucio Quieto se haya puesto nervioso por eso!

—No es como otras veces. Si lo que cuenta Adriano es cierto, tenemos un problema muy grave.

—¿Qué dice mi sobrino?

—Es un levantamiento global. Se han alzado los judíos en las ciudades en las que hemos estado hace poco, como Babilonia, pero también en Alejandría, Chipre o Cirene y por supuesto en toda Judea. Los judíos están como poseídos, trastornados: «*En Cirene han puesto a un tal Andreas como líder y atacan tanto a ciudadanos romanos como a los griegos. Comen la carne de sus víctimas, se hacen cinturones con sus entrañas, se bañan en su sangre y usan la piel de los cadáveres para hacerse ropa; a muchos los han serrado en dos, de cabeza abajo; a otros los lanzan a las fieras y al resto los obligan a luchar como gladiadores. En total han muerto más de doscientas veinte mil personas. En Egipto también han perpetrado locuras similares, y en Chipre, dirigidos por un tal Artemion, lo mismo. Allí han muerto doscientas cuarenta mil más*».[85] Es una sangría sin límite conocido y Adriano dice que el Senado reclama el regreso de las legiones para poner orden dentro del Imperio y proteger las fronteras del norte.

Trajano no dijo nada. Abrió despacio el mapa de las fortificaciones de la ciudad de Hatra de nuevo, de modo que cubrió la carta de Adriano. Lucio se mantuvo también en silencio.

—Supongo que Hatra tendrá que esperar —dijo el emperador—. Nunca me había retirado antes de un asedio.

---

85. Literal de Dión Casio, libro LXVIII, 32.

112

EMPUJAR

Loyang
Marzo de 117 d.C.

Yan Ji se sentó al borde de la cama y se cubrió el cuerpo con su túnica de seda roja. El emperador An-ti, como siempre, dormía plácidamente después de haberla poseído por enésima vez. Ella torció el gesto.

Se levantó y se sentó en el suelo de madera, acurrucándose, cogiéndose las rodillas con sus brazos pequeños: sí, llevaba casi tres años como favorita del emperador, pero qué había conseguido. Ni siquiera estaba embarazada. Cierto que tampoco había habido más embarazos y eso que el emperador yacía ocasionalmente con otras esposas. An-ti no paraba de beber y de comer. Había engordado. Pero la verdad era que todo eso no importaba demasiado. No por el momento. Lo del hijo tendría que resolverse al final; aún tenía esperanza. Lo que la reconcomía por dentro era esa falta de ambición de su esposo, que a sus veintidós años seguía siendo un títere en manos de su madre. La emperatriz Deng lo controlaba todo, lo gobernaba todo, lo poseía todo. Ellos no tenían nada. Bueno, sí, el emperador tenía a sus mujeres, a ella misma para empezar, y bebida y dinero, pero nadie les prestaba atención. ¿De qué servía ser la esposa y favorita de un emperador que en realidad no ejercía como tal?

Sin embargo, ya nadie podía deshacer aquel enlace que la unía a él. Sería eternamente la esposa de alguien que no era nadie. Pero ella se rebelaba contra esa idea. No había sido educada en palacio para ser la sirvienta de una emperatriz mayor que hacía y deshacía a su antojo. Además, una preocupación adicional era que, en cualquier momento, An-ti podría caprichosamente buscarse otra favorita y Yan Ji sabía que entonces el consejero Fan Chun, algunos ministros y la propia Deng se lanzarían contra ella por la muerte de la consorte Li, la madre del príncipe Liu Bao, el único hijo del emperador. Deshacerse de Li fue arriesgado. Sonrió. Pero necesario. Aunque después de aquello se vio obligada a adoptar una actitud sumisa y discreta durante largo tiempo. Demasiado tiempo. Había pensado que sería ya el emperador el que empezaría a actuar... pero no. Ése había sido su único error de cálculo.

Yan Ji había pensado mucho en los últimos meses.

Había considerado incluso deshacerse también del pequeño Bao, pero el maldito asistente del ministro de Obras Públicas lo había alejado de la corte, llevándolo a Ch'ang-an, dejándolo así fuera de su alcance.

No.

Tenía que pensar en otra cosa si quería cambiar aquella situación.

De pronto se quedó muy muy quieta.

Sus ojos miraban a la pared, pero no veían el panel de madera. La joven esposa no estaba mirando a ningún sitio. Miraba hacia el futuro.

¿Cómo no lo había pensado antes? ¿Cómo no se le había ocurrido? Todo era tan sumamente sencillo. Todo tenía una solución perfecta. Sólo hacía falta audacia, valor y cierta destreza.

Sonrió por segunda vez aquella mañana.

Ya lo había hecho antes. Podría hacerlo de nuevo. Era aún más arriesgado, sí, pero nada osado de verdad carece de peligro. El objetivo de su ataque ahora sería mucho mayor, mucho más importante que una simple esposa consorte, pero, en consecuencia, el premio a conseguir sería mucho más grande: sería todo.

Todo.

Y ella lo quería todo.

Y podría hacerlo porque ninguno esperaba que apuntara tan alto. A veces es mejor una certera flecha en el líder del enemigo que centenares de dardos en los pechos de sus soldados. Esta vez Fan Chun no podría detenerla ni tampoco ese general del norte, Li Kan, que actuaba ahora casi como jefe de la guardia imperial de la emperatriz Deng. Ambos, además, estaban distraídos con aquella extranjera llegada de no se sabía dónde. El viejo Fan Chun parecía tan interesado en lo que aquella mujer pudiera contar y, por su parte, el general Li Kan estaba... enamorándose, eso es, de la joven extranjera como sólo se enamoran los hombres: sin saberlo. Estaban ambos con la mente en otras cosas. Era su oportunidad.

—¿Yan Ji? —preguntó el emperador, que se despertaba en la cama.

La joven esposa parpadeó.

—Sí, mi señor, aquí estoy.

Y se levantó despacio. Su marido la deseaba.

Todos deseamos cosas. Muy pocos las consiguen. Los cobardes nunca. Yan Ji se sabía audaz, quizá imprudente, pero nunca diría nadie de ella que era cobarde. ¿Ambiciosa? Sí, pero ¿para qué se casa una con un emperador si no es para gobernar el mundo? Y en ocasiones hay que dar algún empujoncito para que, por fin, gobierne ese emperador con el que te casaste.

—Aquí estoy —repitió ella dulcemente.

Él la tumbó con rapidez, separó sus piernas y se puso encima de ella y, sin más, empezó a empujar con ansia.

Yan Ji cerró los ojos. Eso mismo... pensaba hacer ella... empujar...

113

LA EXTENSIÓN DEL IMPERIO

Antioquía
Abril de 117 d.C.

—¿Sabes quiénes son Nergal, Atamatis o Shamash, sobrino? —preguntó Trajano.

Adriano había pensado muchos principios para la conversación del reencuentro con su tío, pero aquél no lo había imaginado.

—No, no lo sé, augusto.

—Son dioses de la ciudad de Hatra a quienes Elkud, su *mry*, su gobernador, estará haciendo sacrificios de agradecimiento desde hace semanas por tu incompetencia, sobrino. Eso son.

—Yo no tengo la culpa si... —se defendió Adriano, pero Trajano lo cortó de inmediato.

—Tu misión era ocuparte de la retaguardia y asegurarte de que no surgieran problemas en el resto del Imperio y has fallado. —Trajano hablaba de pie, dando vueltas en torno a una gran mesa donde estaba desplegado un gran mapa del Imperio con varios círculos rojos en diferentes lugares; Adriano escuchaba también de pie, en silencio, apretando los labios. El emperador se detuvo y fue señalando cada uno de esos círculos a la vez que enumeraba a qué hacían referencia—. Cirene, Chipre y Egipto. Judíos en rebelión, y lo mismo en Judea. Y ataques en las fronteras de Britania y el Danubio.

—También Mauritania —añadió Adriano.

Trajano levantó la mirada del mapa y encaró los ojos desafiantes de su sobrino. El emperador sabía que aquélla no era una frase pronunciada por Adriano al azar. Mauritania era la tierra de Lucio Quieto. Su sobrino no estaba dispuesto a dejar pasar un levantamiento como ése sin acusar a Quieto.

—Lucio se ocupará de resolver ese problema en su momento —replicó el emperador—, pero primero tendrá que terminar con el alzamiento de Judea, que es mucho más grave y da alas al resto de los judíos del Imperio. Si no hubieras dejado, sobrino, que se abrieran tantos frentes, no nos veríamos faltos de *legati* capaces para atender los ataques allí donde han surgido, ¿no crees?

—El emperador se ha llevado un tercio del ejército de Roma a los confines de Asia. ¿Cómo se supone que he de mantener un territorio de fronteras tan extensas con cien mil legionarios menos..., César?

Como siempre, a su sobrino parecía atragantársele la palabra «César» para referirse a él. Trajano enrojeció.

—¡Usando mi nombre, sobrino! —gritó. No era habitual que el emperador elevara la voz y eso sorprendió a Adriano, que esta vez sí guardó silencio sin atreverse a tentar más su suerte irritando a su tío, que seguía hablando a gritos—. ¡Mi nombre, sobrino, bastó a Palma para que los árabes se rindieran! ¡Mi nombre, sobrino, hizo que se conquistara Armenia, Mesopotamia y hasta gran parte de Partia con todos los ejércitos huyendo de mí! ¡Mi nombre, sobrino, debería haberte bastado para, al menos, evitar alguna de estas rebeliones! ¡Yo me llevé cien mil hombres a Partia, pero dejé doscientos mil en la retaguardia!

—¡Las fronteras del Imperio son demasiado extensas ya, tío! ¡No podemos defender tanto territorio! ¡No podemos anexionarnos más reinos! ¡Es... una locura... *Imperator Caesar Augustus*! —Adriano intentó compensar con la enumeración de títulos honoríficos haberse referido al emperador como «tío» en su arranque de rabia.

Trajano suspiró y, aún rojo de cólera, se sentó en la *cathedra* que Fédimo había dispuesto para él junto a la mesa antes de salir y dejar al emperador a solas con su sobrino.

—Sí se puede. Si se quiere se puede defender todo el Imperio y las nuevas provincias —insistió el César conteniéndose para no seguir gritando. Su sobrino lo exasperaba, pero se

877

sentía agotado y enfermo y no se veía con fuerzas para discutir más tiempo. En medio de tantos levantamientos necesitaba de todos los hombres posibles, legionarios y altos oficiales, y eso incluía al mismísimo Adriano, aunque lo que más deseaba en aquel momento era abofetearlo y arrojarlo del *praetorium* a patadas, como a un perro... Se contuvo. Volvió a hablar—. Lo que está a nuestro alcance o no, Adriano, no depende de las circunstancias, sino de nuestra voluntad de llevarlo a cabo. Y tú, sencillamente, no has querido ni quieres tan siquiera intentarlo. Por eso, sobrino, tú no serás quien me suceda como emperador.

Se hizo un silencio espeso.

Trajano permanecía sentado, inmóvil, apenas respirando.

Adriano, en pie, miraba al suelo y apretaba los puños.

—Nombrar a Lucio Quieto como sucesor es un error —respondió Adriano con una serenidad fría que en cualquier otro momento habría sorprendido a Trajano. Pero el emperador, inmóvil, parecía estar demasiado cansado como para escuchar a su sobrino con atención. No le importaba lo que dijera o lo que pensara.

—Casarte con Vibia... eso sí fue un error del que nunca me he lamentado lo suficiente, pero no cometeré un segundo error nombrándote sucesor.

—Quieto conducirá al Imperio a su autodestrucción —argumentó Adriano intentando, en vano, defenderse de la ira de su tío—. Nos invadirán por todas partes y será el fin de Roma.

—Sal de aquí —espetó Trajano en voz baja, casi como un susurro, pero Adriano se resistía a retirarse sin terminar aquella conversación—. ¡Sal de aquí! —repitió el César como en un grito ahogado, apenas un hilo de voz pero repleto de cólera pura.

Adriano tragó saliva, dio media vuelta y encaró la puerta del *praetorium*.

—¡Abrid! —aulló Adriano y las puertas de metal de la gran sala militar de Antioquía se abrieron. El sobrino del César salió. Las puertas se cerraron de inmediato.

Trajano se encontró solo en medio del *praetorium* del palacio del gobernador de Siria, sentado frente a la mesa del gran mapa del Imperio. Seguía completamente inmóvil.

El tiempo pasaba con una lentitud escalofriante.

Marco Ulpio Trajano empezó a llorar. Lo sabía porque notaba las lágrimas deslizándose con lentitud por las mejillas aún enrojecidas por su arrebato de cólera o quizá por la propia enfermedad.

No se movía.

No había llorado desde la muerte de Longino. En la Dacia, en otro tiempo, en otro mundo.

Intentó tragar saliva pero tampoco lo consiguió. Tenía la garganta del todo seca. Quizá por eso no había podido elevar más la voz cuando ordenó a Adriano que se marchara. ¿O era el miedo? Se acordó en ese instante de la conversación que tuvo con aquella joven muchacha hija del gladiador Marcio y de una guerrera sármata, Tamura, a la que había enviado al fin del mundo con un mensaje secreto, aquella que le confesó no tener miedo de nada y él se rio por su enorme ingenuidad. «El miedo viene cuando lo hemos perdido todo y estamos solos; es en ese momento cuando uno se enfrenta consigo mismo y descubre si realmente tiene el valor de doblegar el miedo.» Eso le había dicho a la muchacha y se creyó muy sabio cuando lo hizo. Buscó saliva en el fondo de la garganta y, al fin, encontró algo.

Seguía completamente inmóvil.

Pensaba, recordaba.

«El emperador sólo podrá ser derribado desde dentro.» Algo así le había dicho la vestal Menenia antes de partir de Roma. Él siempre pensó en una traición que había identificado en la persona de Adriano, pero ahora ese «desde dentro» cobraba una nueva dimensión: una dimensión aterradora como nada que hubiera sentido o visto o temido nunca antes.

Él siempre pensó que era valiente: había perdido a Longino y luego se había sentido solo en innumerables ocasiones y ahora estaba perdiendo, una tras otra, todas las nuevas provincias conquistadas. Sentía que lo estaba perdiendo todo, pero cuán ingenuo había sido, él que tan sabio se había sentido ante aquella joven Tamura, él que creía que podía dar lecciones de valentía, nunca pensó que se pudiera sentir tanto terror como el que se había apoderado ahora de él.

Y lloraba. Sentía más lágrimas por las mejillas.

Apenas habían pasado unos instantes desde que Adriano lo dejara solo, pero al emperador se le antojaba que habían pasado horas enteras. El llanto continuaba brotando sin parar. Si hubiera podido se las había secado con el dorso de una mano, aunque sólo fuera por pudor, por vergüenza, pero permanecía sentado exactamente en la misma posición en la que estaba cuando Adriano abandonó la sala.

Inspiró aire.

Intentó serenarse.

Sonrió con amargura. Al menos quería pensar que sonreía. No estaba seguro de si lo hacía.

Ahora se vería si era valiente o sólo un cobarde más sobre la faz del mundo.

Tenía que llamar a Fédimo, pero sentía pánico a intentarlo y no poder.

Consiguió reunir algo más de saliva en la boca y entonces tragó. Humedecer la garganta lo hizo sentirse mejor. Era increíble cómo, de pronto, podemos valorar algo tan básico como tener saliva. Hacía rato que había dejado de intentar mover las manos y mucho menos levantarse.

—Fédimo —dijo al aire que lo rodeaba, pero fue un suspiro casi inaudible. Trajano tragó más saliva. Tenía que conseguir que acudiera Fédimo. No podía permitir que ninguna otra persona lo viera en esa condición. Ni Plotina y, por supuesto, nunca Adriano. No debían saber lo que le ocurría. Quizá fuera pasajero, como sucedió en Cesifonte, sólo que ahora había llegado con mucha más fuerza. Tenía que agarrarse a esa esperanza. Eso le dio el valor para volver a intentarlo.

—¡Fédimo!

Esta vez había elevado bastante el tono de voz, pero las puertas de bronce eran gruesas. Su asistente estaría fuera esperando, pero quizá no lo oía.

—¡Fédimo! —repitió el emperador y rompió a llorar aún más, esta vez de forma desconsolada, como un niño que se derrumba, frágil, completamente derrotado—. ¡Fédimo...!

—volvió a pronunciar en medio de un sollozo que ya no era capaz de controlar.

Las puertas del *praetorium* de Siria se abrieron de par en par y Fédimo apareció en el interior de la sala. En cuanto vio al emperador, se volvió y ordenó que las puertas se cerraran con rapidez antes de que nadie pudiera ver al César. Fédimo era de la confianza absoluta del emperador y los pretorianos no dudaron en obedecer. Las puertas volvieron a cerrarse. Fédimo se volvió de nuevo y se aproximó al César lentamente. Trajano, que parecía haber recuperado el control sobre su llanto, había dejado de llorar y miró fijamente a Fédimo.

—Has de llamar a... Critón. Fédimo... haz que Critón venga a verme ahora mismo... ¿me entiendes? —Y como si lo pensara mejor, cambió de idea—. No, no vayas tú. Manda a alguno de los pretorianos a por Critón y tú quédate conmigo. No me dejes... solo, Fédimo.

—Pero ¿qué ocurre, augusto? —Fédimo no sabía bien como decirle al César las siguientes palabras—. ¿El emperador no se encuentra bien? El médico vendrá enseguida. Ahora daré orden de que lo llamen...

Trajano lo interrumpió.

—Fédimo, no puedo moverme. Ni brazos ni piernas, nada. Estoy paralizado. Por completo. Es como si ya estuviera... muerto.

—Voy a por el médico, augusto.

Dio media vuelta para dejarlo solo. Trajano ardía por dentro. No podía entender cómo el leal Fédimo era capaz de desobedecerlo en algo tan concreto en un momento tan grave.

—¡Fédimo, Fédimo, no me dejes solo! —gritó Trajano con todas sus fuerzas.

El secretario se volvió hacia el emperador.

—No se entiende nada de lo que dice el César —dijo el secretario despacio, pues ya no sabía siquiera si el emperador podía oírlo o comprenderlo—. No se entienden las palabras del César. Es como si Trajano quisiera hablar, pero no le salen bien las palabras. El emperador sólo... balbucea sonidos sinsentido. Voy a llamar al médico.

Marco Ulpio Trajano comprendió entonces la dimensión

del ataque que acababa de tener. El más indómito de los espíritus estaba atrapado en un cuerpo roto. La maldición de Babilonia, la misma que había derrumbado al omnipotente Alejandro, terminaba ahora con él. La advertencia de Menenia y los augurios de Plutarco se acababan de cumplir: el emperador de Roma moría lentamente en aquella campaña de Oriente, derrotado desde dentro, desde dentro de sí mismo.

HISTORIA DE LA LEGIÓN PERDIDA

Tiempos de Julio César, Pompeyo y Craso,
mediados del siglo I a.C.

LIBRO VIII

114

EL FINAL DE LA LEGIÓN PERDIDA

Fortaleza de Talas, Kangchú (Sogdiana)
Suroeste del lago Balkash, Asia central
Finales de otoño de 36 a.C.

Ejército han en la fortaleza de Talas

Los túnicas rojas supervivientes al último enfrentamiento con los extraños mercenarios enemigos regresaban cubiertos de sangre, casi todos heridos. Y contentos. Porque volvían. Sus compañeros muertos no habían sido tan afortunados.

El general Tang, sentado sobre un taburete para descansar algo su exhausto cuerpo, seguía dando las órdenes a sus hombres. Aún no se había tomado tiempo para dormir desde que empezara aquel largo asalto final a la fortaleza. Llevaban dos horas acosando a aquellos malditos mercenarios y no habían conseguido mucho más que muertos entre sus soldados y, quizá, algunas bajas en los contrarios.

—¡La infantería! ¡Ahora la infantería! —exclamó con voz potente, pero sin levantarse—. ¡Y mientras relevan a los túnicas rojas, que los arqueros masacren a esos miserables!

Supervivientes de la legión perdida en Talas

Se habían refugiado entre las pocas casas de piedra que había en aquel Talas en ruinas. Los hombres de Druso hacían salidas en pequeñas formaciones en *testudo* por las estrechas calles, y cuando llovían las flechas se protegían primero con los escudos y luego replegándose en las casas que habían ocupado.

Eran almacenes de grano. Tenían acceso a un pozo con agua y a un almacén con víveres. Podrían resistir allí días, semanas.

Clac, clac, clac.

Los dardos enemigos golpeaban los tejados.

—Pronto nos lanzarán algo mas que flechas —dijo Sexto.

—Es posible —admitió Druso muy pegado a una de las paredes de piedra para protegerse de las flechas—. Pero resistiremos.

Clac, clac, clac.

Luego silencio.

—¡Nos han rodeado! —exclamó un legionario.

—Saldremos en cuatro formaciones pequeñas, una en cada dirección —ordenó Druso.

Sexto lo cogió del brazo.

—Lo siento, centurión, pero ¿no será el momento de una *devotio*?

Druso miró la mano de Sexto y éste le soltó el brazo de inmediato.

—Haz lo que quieras —respondió el centurión—. Pero yo soy de los que prefieren morir matando. —Y echó a andar con su escudo en el brazo izquierdo y el *gladio* en la mano derecha. Se detuvo y se volvió un instante—. Yo creo que a Cayo le habría gustado que nos lleváramos a tantos han de ésos como pudiéramos. Y eso voy a hacer.

Sexto asintió varias veces.

—Eso es cierto. —Y desenfundó su *gladio* con rapidez y rabia—. ¡A por ellos! ¡Por Marte, por Roma, por Cayo!

Ejército han en el interior de la fortaleza

El viejo gobernador Kan Yen vio a los guerreros han de infantería regresar heridos, aturdidos y ensangrentados, igual que había pasado con los túnicas rojas. Apenas quedaban ya convictos que usar como carnaza contra aquellos mercenarios extranjeros que se resistían. Por su parte, Tang no parecía tampoco dispuesto a cejar en su empeño de seguir hostigándolos con todo lo que tenía hasta aniquilarlos por completo.

—Creo que quizá el general Tang podría considerar otras posibilidades.

El *chiang-chün*, que oyó al gobernador a su espalda, se volvió y le respondió aún sentado en su banqueta.

—Yo no he interferido en cuestiones políticas. No creo que sea el momento ni el lugar para que el gobernador de Gansu me dé lecciones militares.

El viejo *shou* no pareció ofenderse por el tono hostil con el que acababa de ser recibida su sugerencia y sonrió. Guardó luego un tiempo razonable de silencio hasta que se decidió a volver a hablar.

—Pero lo que ocurre ahora es ya una cuestión política. —Y como Tang iba a replicarle, el gobernador levantó la mano con autoridad, de modo que el general, ya fuera por cansancio o por obediencia, calló—. Sí, mi querido *chiang-chün*. La batalla de Kangchú ha terminado y ahora es el tiempo de la política: mi tiempo y mi autoridad. Sí, ya sé que tenemos a un puñado de mercenarios extranjeros atrincherados en una esquina de la fortaleza, pero ésa no es, de momento, la cuestión clave. Aunque puede llegar a serlo y por eso me veo obligado a intervenir. Hace unas horas me pediste que negociara con los jinetes de Kangchú, venidos para apoyar a sus compatriotas que estaban en Talas luchando junto a Zhizhi. Y he negociado con ellos una paz duradera. Les he hecho ver que nosotros no tenemos interés en quedarnos en Kangchú, sino que sólo nos movía el deseo, la necesidad, de eliminar al lunático de Zhizhi y vengar la afrenta de nuestra embajada asesinada por los *hsiung-nu*. Ambos objetivos los hemos conseguido, todo ello gracias a una muy eficaz dirección militar por tu parte, general Tang, pero ahora, a mi entender, el gran *chiang-chün* que nos ha llevado a la victoria sobre los *hsiung-nu* y todos sus aliados está cansado, y su razón nublada por el agotamiento. Los guerreros de Kangchú con los que he pactado están tan contentos o incluso más que nosotros por la desaparición de Zhizhi. Si nos retiramos ellos gobernarán este territorio, desde el Balkash hasta Fergana, en paz con el Imperio han. La Ruta de la Seda hacia Occidente volverá a abrirse en beneficio de todos. La paz y la prosperidad retornarán a estas tierras y las regiones occidentales de nuestro imperio. Y todo esto se habrá conseguido sin apenas bajas militares. Hemos perdido a casi todos los convictos, eso es cierto, pero los túnicas rojas no cuentan a los ojos de nadie, incluido nuestro emperador Yuan-ti. Pero si ahora, empecinado en masacrar a esos pocos mercenarios que se resisten a rendirse, empezamos a acumular bajas en la infantería imperial, nuestra gran victoria puede tornarse en una victoria costosa a los ojos del emperador y he de recordarte que estamos aquí sin el permiso de su majestad. Nuestras cabezas aún están en juego. Y las de nuestras familias también. Los mercenarios tienen agua y víveres. Las casas de piedra los protegen de las flechas y combaten como tigres heridos. Pueden alargar este combate durante semanas. ¿Es eso lo que nos interesa? Creía que el invierno era algo que debíamos evitar.

Tang suspiró. Era cierto que estaba agotado. Quizá la última decisión de arremeter contra aquellos irreductibles mercenarios con la infantería podía haber sido algo precipitada. Y lo que decía Kan Yen sobre que los objetivos principales estaban conseguidos era cierto.

—Todo lo que dices tiene sentido. Podríamos asfixiarlos con humo.

—El viento no va en dirección a esas casas. Nos asfixiaremos nosotros antes que ellos —respondió el gobernador.

—Puede ser. Sí, es cierto —aceptó Tang y volvió a suspirar—. Y no es menos cierto que necesito descansar. ¿Qué propones?

—Que duermas —respondió el viejo *shou*.

Legionarios romanos atrincherados en Talas

—Viene un anciano escoltado por un grupo de guerreros —dijo Sexto.

Druso se asomó desde una barricada de piedras y tejas rotas que habían acumulado en una de las calles para incomodar el avance de los han.

—Llama a Nanaifarn —dijo el centurión—. Nos van a volver a hacer falta sus servicios.

888

115

EL PRINCIPIO

Frontera entre Kangchú (Sogdiana) y el Imperio han
Invierno de 36 a.C.

Druso miraba a sus hombres, un puñado de supervivientes. Ciento cincuenta y cuatro legionarios que habían sobrevivido al desastre de Carrhae, la esclavitud en Merv, la guerra contra los hunos, las luchas como mercenarios bajo el lunático de Zhizhi y, finalmente, la brutal batalla de Kangchú.[86] Un puñado de hombres. Eso era todo. Druso sonrió. Un puñado de héroes. Pero héroes sin patria. Ciento cincuenta y cuatro y Nanaifarn. El sogdiano, al final, había decidido acompañarlos. Había perdido a toda su familia en la contienda; se había convertido en otro hombre sin pasado. Su desgracia había servido para que ellos dispusieran de un intérprete en aquella nueva etapa de aquel periplo sin fin aparente. Los han, o al menos el anciano con el que negociaron y algunos guerreros, comprendían el suficiente sogdiano como para entenderse con Nanaifarn.

Druso repasaba los últimos acontecimientos mientras marchaban integrados como una unidad militar independiente en un inmenso ejército de Xeres. El acuerdo fue simple: se les ofreció ser soldados al servicio del emperador... ¿Yuan-ti? El centurión de Cartago Nova no estaba seguro de recordar bien el nombre de su nuevo señor. Pero el pacto era bueno y eso era lo esencial.

---

86. Esta batalla también es conocida como batalla de Talas. Pero no hay que confundirla con otra posterior batalla de Talas en 751 entre árabes y turcos contra chinos. Véase la nota histórica.

La larga columna del ejército han se detuvo en medio de una gran llanura.

Druso vio a Nanaifarn, que regresaba de recibir instrucciones de uno de los oficiales de Xeres que sabía sogdiano.

—Dicen que acamparemos aquí y que el general Tang quiere verte.

Tienda del chiang-chün *del ejército expedicionario han en Asia central*

El general Tang repasaba una carta que le había entregado hacía un rato el gobernador Kan Yen. El emperador Yuan-ti no les concedía recompensa alguna por su victoria sobre Zhizhi, ni tan siquiera mostraba agradecimiento por haber reestablecido el orden en aquella región y permitir así la reapertura de la Ruta de la Seda hacia Occidente; pero su majestad imperial tampoco hablaba de castigos ni de represalias contra él o contra el gobernador ni contra sus familias. Teniendo en cuenta que habían reclutado un ejército de cuarenta mil guerreros sin permiso imperial y que lo habían sacado de los límites del imperio en una campaña militar no autorizada para combatir en una guerra no reconocida, aquella carta sabía a victoria. En ese momento entraron un par de guerreros escoltando al líder de los mercenarios extranjeros y el sogdiano que hacía de intérprete.

Tang, para sorpresa de Nanaifarn, se dirigió a él en sogdiano, pero sin dejar de mirar de reojo al recio líder de la unidad militar extranjera.

—Dile a tu jefe que los han son un pueblo de palabra. Dile que he buscado un enclave próximo a la frontera pero dentro de nuestro territorio, donde podrán establecerse como una unidad mercenaria al servicio del imperio. Se les proporcionarán víveres y madera para que construyan allí un campamento estable. Hay bosques alrededor por si precisan de más madera, y un río, de modo que el abastecimiento de agua lo tienen garantizado.

Tang hizo una breve pausa para que Nanaifarn tradujera.

Mientras el sogdiano hablaba en voz baja en griego, el general han examinaba el rostro ajado por cicatrices de guerra de Druso. Tang tenía claro que estaba ante alguien que había visto mucho, luchado constantemente y, pese a todo, mantenido la dignidad. Algo difícil cuando uno lleva años lejos de su tierra natal.

Nanaifarn calló.

—También os enviaré mujeres —continuó Tang—. Vuestros hijos serán buenos guerreros y el imperio necesita de combatientes fuertes en sus fronteras. A cambio de todo esto, tanto vosotros como todos vuestros descendientes durante diez generaciones tendréis la obligación de defender las fronteras del Imperio han siempre que se os reclame en las líneas defensivas.

Se detuvo una vez más. Nanaifarn tradujo. Druso miró al general, se llevó el puño al pecho y asintió.

Tang interpretó aquel gesto como una muestra de aceptación.

—¿Cómo se llama vuestra unidad militar? —preguntó entonces el general.

Druso parpadeó varias veces cuando escuchó la traducción de Nanaifarn.

—*Legio* —respondió el centurión, sin entender bien a qué venía aquella pregunta.

—De acuerdo —aceptó el general Tang—: *Li-chien* —repitió modificando la pronunciación de Druso—. *Li-chien* será el nombre de vuestro campamento.

No hubo más palabras.

Druso miró a los ojos del general un instante. Tang le mantuvo la mirada. El centurión volvió a saludar con el puño en el pecho y, al ver que los guerreros han abrían las telas de la entrada a la tienda, dio media vuelta y salió de allí junto al intérprete.

Tang se inclinó sobre la mesa donde había un mapa de la provincia de Gansu y otras regiones occidentales del imperio y, despacio, con tinta oscura, escribió en un extremo el nombre de aquel nuevo campamento. Le gustaba tener bien ubicados todos los puestos militares de la frontera. Nunca se sabía dónde podía atacar el enemigo.

Druso hizo que todos sus hombres, empezando por Sexto, madrugaran al día siguiente para que estuvieran dispuestos para la marcha los primeros. El general Tang estaba siendo fiel al pacto, y el centurión pensó que era buena idea dar una imagen de tropas disciplinadas. Eran pocos, pero debían verse bien organizados pese a los años de viaje, penurias y exilio.

—Parece que ellos también madrugan bastante —comentó Sexto.

—Tendrán ganas de regresar a su imperio —respondió Druso ajustándose bien la coraza dispuesto para un nuevo día de marcha.

—Ganas de volver. Sí, eso puedo entenderlo —dijo Sexto.

Druso detectó la melancolía en su respuesta pero no hizo comentarios. No había nada que decir.

Avanzaron durante horas por un camino largo y serpenteante que parecía no tener fin hasta que, con la caída del sol, los hombres de la legión perdida vieron algo que no esperaban. Estaban perplejos, boquiabiertos: ante ellos emergía una muralla de más de veinte pies de altura, con torres fortificadas enormes a intervalos regulares y cuyo principio o final era... ninguno. Aquella muralla no tenía fin. Mirara uno hacia el norte o hacia el sur, sólo se veía una muralla interminable, inabarcable.

—¿Qué es esto? —preguntó Sexto y se respondió a sí mismo—: Estamos en el fin del mundo.

Druso, superada la sorpresa inicial, negó con la cabeza, puso la mano derecha en el hombro de su mejor oficial y sonrió al responderle.

—No, amigo mío. No es el fin del mundo, sino el principio de otro.

Los legionarios, abrumados ante aquella muralla, se habían hecho a un lado, para no entorpecer el avance de las unidades de infantería y caballería han que los seguían. Los guerreros de Xeres no parecían en absoluto sorprendidos por la muralla. De pronto, la silueta inconfundible del general Tang se hizo visible para Druso.

El *chiang-chün* pasó junto a los nuevos mercenarios del Imperio han y, al ver cómo todos tenían clavados los ojos en la Gran Muralla, echó la cabeza atrás al tiempo que lanzaba una sonora carcajada.

Druso no se lo tomó a mal. Al contrario, quizá por los nervios o por el cansancio, se echó también a reír. Un buen rato. Hasta que le saltaron las lágrimas.

—Ahora sí que hemos llegado al final de nuestro viaje, Sexto —dijo el centurión secándose las lágrimas de los ojos con el dorso de la mano. Luego miró a Nanaifarn y le habló en griego—. Averigua si hemos de cruzar nosotros la muralla con el resto de su ejército.

El sogdiano preguntó al general.

—También —respondió Tang—. Li-chien está justo al otro lado. Allí os quedaréis. Yo seguiré hasta Loyang, hasta la capital del mundo.

Para cuando Druso escuchaba la traducción que hacía Nanaifarn, el general Tang cabalgaba ya hacia aquel muro sin fin.

—Pues tendrán alguna puerta —comentó entonces Sexto a su espalda.

—Imagino que sí —aceptó Druso.

En cuanto pasó la última unidad militar del ejército han, los romanos se reincorporaron al camino y siguieron a los soldados de un imperio que había sido capaz de construir el mayor muro que nunca hubieran visto en su vida. Y habían visto muchas cosas.

Al descender una colina, una gigantesca puerta fortificada, guarnecida con torres de vigilancia, apareció ante sus ojos.

—Ahí tienes tu puerta, Sexto —dijo Druso.

—Pues... vamos allá, supongo —dijo el de Corduba.

—Sí, por Júpiter. Crucemos esa muralla —apostilló Druso.

En poco tiempo, el centurión de Cartago Nova, al mando de ciento cincuenta y cuatro supervivientes de la legión perdida, cruzó la Puerta de Jade del Imperio han, la puerta a un nuevo mundo, la puerta que los convertía en leyenda.

HISTORIA DE TRAJANO

Principios del siglo II d.C.

LIBRO VIII

EL FINAL DE UN SUEÑO

116

LA SUCESIÓN

Selinus,[87] costa de Cilicia
Julio de 117 d.C.

La humedad y el calor hacían que todos sudaran profusamente. Trajano había pedido que lo subieran a cubierta porque en el interior del barco el aire le resultaba ya del todo irrespirable. Estaba mareado y, una vez más, no sentía ni las piernas ni las manos ni los brazos. Y aunque había recuperado parcialmente la facultad del habla, le costaba enormemente pronunciar cada palabra. Después de una lenta recuperación le había dado otro ataque y volvía a estar postrado, sin casi poder moverse. La sugerencia de Plotina de detenerse en el primer puerto seguro y quedarse allí hasta que se encontrara mejor parecía razonable a ojos de todos: de Fédimo, el joven secretario del César, de Liviano, el jefe del pretorio, de Critón, el médico del emperador, y de Matidia, la sobrina segunda de Trajano, que también acompañaba al César en su lento periplo de regreso hacia Roma.

Trajano los vio a todos tan de acuerdo que no se opuso, aunque él era de la opinión de proseguir el viaje por muy agotador que éste fuera. Tenía la sensación de que cuanto más cerca estuviera de Roma, del Senado, próximo a Celso, Palma y Nigrino, más seguro estaría de poder hacerlo todo como debía hacerse. El asunto de la sucesión era ahora lo primordial. Quieto estaba en campaña de castigo contra los judíos. Tenía que llegar hasta Celso, Palma y Nigrino lo antes posible.

---

87. Selinus se corresponde con la ciudad actual de Gazipasa, al sur de Turquía.

Suspiró.

El barco se aproximaba a la bahía.

Debería haber resuelto el asunto en Antioquía. Debería haber nombrado un regente, quizá alguien veterano, respetado por todos, y luego proponer un listado de nombres, no muchos, unos diez, de entre los que el Senado podría escoger al mejor para la tarea de gobernar Roma. Adriano no estaría en ese listado. No después de su incapacidad para mantener el Imperio en paz cuando él estaba en el frente de Oriente. Siempre había tenido sus dudas con respecto a su sobrino pero ahora ya estaba decidido a dejarlo de lado en todo lo relacionado con la sucesión. No importaba la insistencia de Plotina en que era familia por haberse casado con su sobrina Vibia Sabina. Ése había sido otro error. Pero un error no se soluciona ahondando en él, sino corrigiendo en todo lo posible lo hecho. No era fácil deshacer el matrimonio, pero sí podía dejar a Adriano fuera de la sucesión.

Entraron por la desembocadura de un río y ascendieron por él apenas media milla, hasta el embarcadero donde amarraron el barco.

Trajano asintió para sí mismo, en silencio. Le llevaron algo de agua. Bebió. Con dificultad. Le costaba tragar. Le costaba todo. Su cuerpo lo estaba abandonando.

Lucio Quieto estaría el primero en la lista y Celso, Palma y Nigrino maniobrarían en el Senado para que fuera el preferido por Roma. Su capacidad militar era incuestionable, era inmensamente popular en las legiones de Oriente, en Mauritania y África, y también en las del Danubio. Nadie podría disputarle el puesto, con lo que se evitaría el riesgo de una guerra civil que el Imperio no podía permitirse en modo alguno.

Trajano agrió el gesto.

Sólo Adriano podría cuestionar aquella decisión. Pero ¿qué podía argüir su sobrino segundo? ¿Diría que Quieto era norteafricano, un provincial? No. Ellos también lo eran: de Hispania. Aquella norma no escrita de que todo emperador debía ser nacido en Roma, o al menos en Italia, había terminado cuando Nerva lo eligió a él como sucesor. No, ésa no podía ser la línea de defensa de Adriano. Su sobrino agitaría el miedo a un Imperio demasiado grande y se apoyaría en todos aquellos que veían el cruce del Éufrates como una locura. Adriano avivaría el recuerdo de la legión perdida de Craso y el miedo que aquel fracaso había dejado en Roma. No importarían todas las victorias conseguidas ni las nuevas anexiones de las cuatro provincias orientales. El miedo y la debilidad podrían hacer que muchos senadores se dejaran llevar por los fantasmas que exhibiría Adriano ante todos ellos: fronteras desguarnecidas, un Imperio penetrado por hordas enemigas cruzando el Rin, el Danubio y el temido Éufrates. Les intentaría persuadir de que ni siquiera alguien como Quieto podría mantener la seguridad de Roma. Muchos de esos senadores podrían no ver, o no querrían ver, que Roma era más fuerte si se aseguraban las nuevas provincias orientales, con sus riquezas y con todo el oro que podría entrar en las arcas del Estado controlando la ruta del comercio con Xeres, eliminados los traidores partos como intermediarios. Sus cuatro provincias de Oriente. Ahora sólo quedaban dos de forma efectiva: Mesopotamia y Asiria. Armenia estaba en rebelión y Babilonia con Cesifonte en manos de un rey títere como Partamaspates. Pero todo podía revertirse. Quieto podría hacerlo.

Empezaron a bajarlo del barco entre varios esclavos que levantaban el *solium* en el que estaba sentado. Tuvieron que poner dos pasarelas juntas para poder realizar bien la operación. En su pésima condición física todo costaba el doble, el triple. Y él, impotente, no podía hacer nada más que pensar y pensar...

Pero con él en Roma, rodeado por Palma y Celso y Nigrino, conseguiría hacer valer su opinión, y con Quieto elegido César todo podría conseguirse, afianzarse... Sólo así podría vencer al maldito *lemur* de la legión perdida de una vez por todas, de una vez para siempre...

Pasaron unos días.

El descanso le hizo bien.

Pidió entonces que lo subieran a la ladera de la montaña de aquella pequeña población marítima. Quería contemplar el atardecer reflejado sobre el Mediterráneo, ese mar cuyas costas controlaban por completo, esas aguas que eran el centro de todo pero pronto pasaría a ser un mar más de los muchos que debían controlar: había que someter las poblaciones del norte del Ponto Euxino,[88] adentrarse en el océano Hircanio[89] y asegurar también toda la ruta marítima de la gran mar Eritrea,[90] desde Egipto hasta Carax y las costas de la India. ¡Por Júpiter, había tanto por hacer! Dejaba una gran tarea a Quieto. Ni siquiera el norteafricano podría acometerla en su totalidad. Harían falta varias generaciones para completar su gran sueño. Un sueño inmortal.

La subida fue por un camino tortuoso y empinado. Los esclavos sudaban enormemente. Pese a que el sol ya estaba muy bajo en el horizonte, su poder extenuante se sentía aún con fuerza, su calor los asfixiaba aún a todos y la humedad lo hacía todo pegajoso, espeso, agotador. El mar parecía muy sereno, como si estuviera recubierto por una fina capa de aceite por la que se deslizaban algunos barcos pequeños de pescadores que retornaban después de una dura jornada de trabajo. Allí estaba: el Mediterráneo del Imperio. Inmóvil, detenido.

Llegaron a lo alto de la montaña.

—El sueño de Trajano —dijo el emperador entre dientes.

Fédimo se acercó.

—¿El César desea algo? —preguntó el joven secretario.

Trajano negó con la cabeza. No quería hablar. Sólo pensar.

Estaban en Selinus, un antiguo puerto de piratas cilicios sometido por Pompeyo el Grande. ¿Y él, Trajano, había sido grande? Desde allí arriba todo se veía muy pequeño: las casas de Selinus, el Odeón donde se reunían las autoridades de la ciudad portuaria, el acueducto, los baños públicos. Quizá desde más alto, desde el Olimpo, desde donde miraban los dioses, hasta los imperios parecerían pequeños, ya fueran Roma, la destruida Partia, el distante Imperio kushan o la desconocida Xeres. Recordó, como hacía ocasionalmente, a sus mensajeros enviados más allá de todos los límites conocidos. ¿Habría conseguido alguno, o alguna, llegar hasta Xeres? ¿Qué sería

88. Mar Negro.
89. Mar Caspio.
90. Mar Rojo y océano Índico.

de ellos, del gladiador Marcio, su esposa Alana, su hija Tamura, a la que le encomendó aquel mensaje secreto? ¿Lo habría entregado? Si así era, resultaba entonces aún más necesario que Quieto fuera quien lo sustituyera y no Adriano.

Adriano.

Todo volvía a Adriano.

—Bajemos —ordenó Trajano.

El emperador no pudo evitar descender aún más triste que cuando había subido a contemplar, sin él saberlo, la última puesta de sol que había de ver en su vida.

Residencia del emperador en Selinus

Terminó julio.

Llegó el 9 de agosto de 117 d.C., esto es, del año 870 *ab urbe condita*, desde la fundación de Roma.

El emperador ya no salía al exterior. Apenas podía moverse. Plotina había asumido los cuidados del César como algo personal, de modo que ya nadie que no fuera ella podía acercarse a Trajano. A Liviano le dijo que el emperador se aturdía si veía a más gente en la habitación y lo conminó a hacer guardia alrededor de la villa que el séquito imperial ocupaba. El jefe del pretorio accedió sin comprender que los enemigos de Trajano en Selinus podían estar más bien dentro que fuera de la residencia del César.

Al médico Critón, Plotina le tomó la palabra de que el César estaba ya más allá de toda posible recuperación y por eso le indicó que sus servicios no eran ya necesarios, que si surgía alguna crisis grave nueva que hiciera relevante su asistencia lo llamaría.

A Matidia, la única sobrina de Trajano que estaba en Selinus, la entretuvo responsabilizándola de supervisar la intendencia doméstica de la residencia mientras permanecieran en Selinus.

Y por fin, al joven Fédimo, Plotina le explicó que la vista del César no era la de antes, ni su entendimiento el mismo, de forma que sería ella, durante unos días al menos, hasta que el emperador se recuperara, la que leería el correo enviado al emperador desde todas las esquinas del Imperio romano.

Nadie sospechó.

No entonces.

Todos sabían que Trajano estaba muy enfermo y que lo probable sería que muriera. Incluso si alguien lo envenenara quizá le estuviera haciendo un favor, pues su cuerpo había dejado de responderle hasta para las acciones más elementales. Por eso ni Liviano ni Critón ni Fédimo ni Matidia vieron peligro alguno en que sólo fuera Plotina quien entrara en la habitación donde convalecía Trajano.

Sólo ella.

Algún día hubo en ese *interim* en el que Trajano tuvo alguna leve mejoría, pero no lo suficiente como para ni tan siquiera pedir salir de nuevo para contemplar el sol en la bahía de Selinus, desde lo alto de aquella ladera tan escarpada.

—¿Y el correo? —preguntó Trajano.

—Fédimo se ocupa y me selecciona las cartas relevantes —respondió Plotina—. La rebelión judía se ha controlado en casi todos los puntos del Imperio, en Cirene, en Chipre, en Alejandría, hasta en Judea parece que las cosas van mejor.

—Eso está bien. Podremos así volver a concentrar los esfuerzos de las legiones en... asegurar las conquistas de Oriente... —dijo Trajano, pero le costaba hablar. Tenía la sensación de farfullar, de balbucear, más que hablar.

Hubo un largo silencio. El César se volvió hacia su esposa, que estaba sentada en un *solium* a su lado. Tenía que intentar hacerle ver a su mujer... tenía que hacerle entender...

—Adriano te traicionará. Has de alejarte de él. Busca protección en Liviano y sus pretorianos, son de toda confianza. Y cuenta con Fédimo para que te ayude en asuntos administrativos y con las cartas que hay que enviar. Hay que escribir a Lucio Quieto y reclamar que venga aquí, Plotina. Hemos de hacer todo esto con rapidez. Ahora lo veo todo claro. La enfermedad nubló mis sentidos durante días, pero ahora he podido pensar y sé lo que hay que hacer. —De pronto las palabras parecían brotarle con una facilidad inusual. Trajano podía ver los ojos abiertos como platos de su esposa. Sabía que estaba dándole mucha información a mucha velocidad, pero no había tiempo que perder, sentía que no le quedaban ya muchas energías y era muy importante poder tenerlo todo bien organizado—. Debería haber hecho todo esto mucho antes, pero ahora no tiene sentido lamentarse, sino poner solución a los errores del pasado —continuaba Trajano sin dejar de mover los labios a gran velocidad. Plotina seguía allí, junto a él, escuchándolo muy atenta, y eso le dio fuerzas para continuar—. Nombraremos a Quieto mi sucesor oficial. Lo adoptaré y lo nombraré César. Y enviaremos cartas informando de esta adopción al Senado y luego a todos los *legati* de las treinta legiones de Roma. He pensado en hacer un listado con varios nombres y que luego eligiera el Senado, pero no podemos permitirnos ni eso: no hay tiempo y ahora veo claro que un listado podría generar la guerra civil. No, ha de ser todo mucho más preciso. Sin margen para el debate. Quieto es muy popular en Oriente, en el Danubio y en África. Nadie osará oponerse a él y contamos con Celso y Palma y Nigrino en el Senado. Ellos conseguirán que éste reconozca su adopción por mí. Sí, si hacemos todo esto, Quieto terminará con la rebelión judía y luego afianzará nuestras conquistas en Oriente. Esas nuevas provincias son la clave para una Roma mucho más poderosa. Adriano es el único problema y él se opondrá, pero si hacemos todo esto que te he dicho, no podrá tener ni el apoyo del Senado ni de las legiones. Es importante que Adriano no venga, Plotina. Sé... —Esto le costaba decirlo, pero era importante; no era momento ni de remilgos ni de dudas, sino de grandes verdades, dichas en voz alta y clara. Marco Ulpio Trajano cogió la mano de su esposa por primera vez en mucho tiempo, en uno de los pocos movimientos que aún podía hacer, y siguió con su discurso de palabras al que Plotina continuaba atendiendo con los ojos bien abiertos y el ceño fruncido, como si estuviera confusa; Trajano comprendía que tanta sinceridad de golpe costaba de digerir, pero tenía que continuar—. Plotina, no importa la relación que hayas tenido o que tengas o que creas que tienes con Adriano ahora. Te traicionará. En el momento en el que yo muera, sólo le interesarás para que le des tu apoyo, pero si estás con Liviano y con

Quieto no podrá reclamarte nada, ni tan siquiera acercarse a ti. Adriano no te quiere, Plotina. Adriano sólo se quiere a sí mismo. Si no actuamos juntos, Plotina, primero moriré yo, luego Adriano te usará para conseguir el poder y matará a Fédimo y a Liviano y a tantos como se interpongan en su camino. Quieto no lo aceptará y habrá una gran guerra civil, que es lo último que necesita el Imperio en estos momentos, cuando aún estamos apagando la gran revuelta de los judíos. No es justo que la lealtad de Fédimo o Liviano y de tantos otros sea pagada con la muerte. No lo es. Por eso hemos de evitarlo. No hemos sido el mejor de los matrimonios, pero, Plotina, estamos hablando no ya de nosotros sino de Roma. Adriano debilitará Roma. Si nos retiramos de Oriente ahora, la frontera del Éufrates será una constante guerra que nos debilitará y que contribuirá a una lenta caída del poder romano. Hay que acabar con los partos ahora que somos fuertes y ellos siguen divididos; ¿me entiendes, Plotina? Lo más importante ahora es que Adriano no venga a Selinus.

En ese momento ocurrió lo que Trajano más temía y sin embargo era, al tiempo, lo que Plotina llevaba esperando días: la puerta de la habitación se abrió y una de las esclavas anunció que Adriano, el sobrino segundo del César, gobernador de Siria, acababa de llegar a Selinus y estaba allí mismo, al otro lado de la puerta, esperando para entrar.

Trajano negó con la cabeza, pero la esclava miraba a su señora.

—Que pase —ordenó Plotina.

Publio Elio Adriano entró en el dormitorio de su tío.

Se acercó despacio, siempre mirando hacia la cama. Trajano soltó la mano de su esposa, cerró la boca y miró hacia el techo de la habitación. No tenía ni deseos ni fuerzas para una nueva discusión con su sobrino.

—¿Cómo está? —preguntó Adriano.

Trajano escuchaba atento, pero sin dirigir la vista ni a su esposa ni a su sobrino.

—Mal —respondió Plotina y se explicó mirando hacia su marido—. A veces dice alguna palabra que puedo entender, como esta mañana que ha preguntado por el correo. Yo le he respondido por si es capaz de entender algo, pero luego se pone a farfullar un sinfín de palabras que nadie puede comprender. Es como si creyera que habla y que lo entendemos, pero realmente no se le entiende nada. Y él sigue balbuceando sin parar, a toda velocidad.

Marco Ulpio Trajano cerró los ojos y empezó a llorar en silencio.

—¿Lo tienes todo preparado, según hemos hablado? —preguntó Adriano acercándose a la ventana de la habitación para mirar desde allí hacia la bahía y el mar que bañaba las costas de todo el Imperio. Sonrió. Su Imperio.

—Sí —respondió Plotina dejando de mirar a su marido y, por tanto, sin ver las lágrimas que empezaban a brotar de sus ojos—. Todo.

—Perfecto —dijo Adriano volviéndose hacia Plotina y borrando la sonrisa de su rostro para, de nuevo, poner una faz que mostrara preocupación. Pensó en besar a Plotina, pero se limitó a ponerle la mano con suavidad en el hombro y hablarle al oído—. Que no pase de esta noche.

Plotina asintió. Adriano se fue.

Y el sol desapareció en el horizonte.

Y se hizo la noche.

Pasó la primera vigilia y la segunda.

Las sombras se arrastraban ya por todo el Imperio romano, desde Selinus hasta Caledonia, desde Hispania hasta Siria.

Una esclava llevó el caldo caliente que el emperador tomaba en medio de la noche.

—Déjalo ahí —dijo Plotina—. Yo se lo daré.

La esclava obedeció y salió de la habitación con rapidez.

La emperatriz se levantó, fue a la mesa donde estaba el caldo humeante y puso junto a él un pequeño frasco con un polvo blanco que había tenido en la mano durante las últimas horas del día, desde que Adriano la dejara a solas con el César. Plotina abrió el frasco y vertió todo su contenido en el caldo. Luego, con la cuchara, le dio vueltas hasta que los polvos se diluyeron por completo. Cogió entonces el caldo y lo llevó en las manos, con cuidado de que no se derramara nada, hasta el *solium*, y volvió a sentarse.

Trajano, como le solía ocurrir varias veces a lo largo de la noche, se despertó.

Ella se levantó, fue hacia la cama y le acercó el caldo a los labios.

Él la miró.

—¿Dolerá? —preguntó el César con sorprendente claridad en la pronunciación.

A Plotina le tembló entonces el pulso y derramó un poco del caldo sobre las sábanas. Se separó con el cuenco del emperador y volvió a sentarse en el *solium*. Ella lo miraba con cierta perplejidad. ¿Hasta dónde entendía su esposo lo que estaba pasando? ¿La había visto verter el veneno? ¿Tenía sentido decirle que ella iba a anunciar en poco tiempo que había fallecido y que en su lecho de muerte había adoptado a Adriano como hijo y como sucesor? Plotina sabía que su esposo no veía esa opción con buenos ojos; incluso aunque no había entendido todos los discursos farfullados por el César en los últimos días, sabía que Adriano no sería el elegido por su esposo si estuviera bien. Pero, por otro lado, ¿qué sentido tenía alargar la agonía de un hombre que no iba a recuperarse nunca? Entretanto, los partos se rehacían en Oriente, los judíos aún pugnaban en Judea, el Imperio estaba en un momento delicado y requería de un líder fuerte e inteligente. Ella estaba convencida de que Adriano era ese líder. Además, por su intimidad con él también creía que podría influir para que, de un modo u otro, se respetara la memoria de Trajano y parte, al menos parte, de sus grandes logros, más allá de las diferencias que Adriano y su tío pudieran haber tenido en los últimos años. Pero Trajano tenía que morir ya para poder poner todo este plan en marcha.

—No, no dolerá —dijo ella mirándolo fijamente a la cara—. Es para terminar con esta... lenta... muer...

No acabó la última palabra.

Trajano suspiró primero, luego asintió levemente y cerró los ojos. Ella volvió a levantarse y a aproximarse a la cama. El César sintió el calor del cuenco en sus labios y entreabrió la boca para empezar a sorber. Sabía que caminaba hacia la muerte, hacia una tumba bajo la gran Columna que Apolodoro había levantado en Roma que conmemoraba su gran victoria sobre los dacios.

Los dacios.

Recordó otra tumba, muy lejos de Selinus, en medio de la lluvia, en la necrópolis de Sarmizegetusa Ulpia Traiana, más allá del Danubio y el gran puente que ordenara construir para anexionar aquella región al Imperio. Era la tumba de Longino. Siguió sorbiendo lenta, pero constantemente. El caldo sabía bueno, como siempre y no, no sentía dolor alguno. ¿Sería ésta la primera vez que lo envenenaban o llevaban haciéndolo poco a poco durante las últimas semanas? ¿Meses? ¿Desde que llegó a Antioquía? ¿Desde que embarcaron? ¿Desde que llegaron a Selinus? ¿O quizá su muerte era por aquella enfermedad extraña que lo paralizaba y el veneno sólo ayudaría a terminar antes con el dolor y la impotencia, como decía Plotina? ¿Quizá sentía algo más de sueño que habitualmente? Casi lo agradeció. No podía decir bien más que alguna palabra de cuando en cuando. Insuficiente, ya lo había comprobado, para hacerle entender a Plotina lo que estaba haciendo Adriano, cómo la estaba usando... Pero no, no quería tener esos pensamientos ahora. Estaba impotente para influir ya en modo alguno en los destinos de Roma. Roma misma buscaría su propio camino. Quizá Lucio Quieto y Celso y Palma y Nigrino juntos serían aún capaces de consolidar el rumbo que él, Marco Ulpio Trajano, había iniciado para el Imperio, pero él ya no estaría allí para verlo. Puede que los cuatro pudieran contra Adriano...

Esa lucha ya no estaba en sus manos.

Quizá el Senado lo deificara, lo harían un dios y desde arriba podría contemplar qué dirección tomaba el gran barco de Roma en el océano de la historia.

¿Un dios? No le importaba tanto eso como llegar, por fin, al Hades y reunirse de nuevo con Longino.

El caldo se acabó.

Plotina apartó el cuenco de los labios del César, que parecía dormido, se separó del lecho y llevó el tazón vacío a la mesa. Desde allí oyó que Trajano volvía a balbucear de nuevo esa serie de sílabas ininteligibles, incomprensibles por com pleto. Ella se acercó a la cama y lo miró, por primera vez en mucho tiempo, con lástima, mientras Trajano movía los labios aún húmedos por el caldo recién ingerido y seguía emitiendo aquellos sonidos inconexos y sin sentido. Haciendo un gran esfuerzo, que debía de dolerle según reflejaba el rictus agrio de su rostro, Trajano levantó el brazo derecho todo cuanto pudo como si quisiera coger algo o a alguien invisible hasta que, por fin, el brazo cayó a plomo sobre la cama y el César guardó silencio. El rostro del emperador se quedó entonces completamente inmóvil, igual que sus manos, sus brazos, sus piernas, su corazón y su alma. Trajano apenas respiraba, creía que hablaba, pero sólo pensaba...

—Hacia ti voy, viejo amigo. Longino, me estoy acercando. Más allá de tu tumba en la Dacia, más allá de las batallas y las guerras y los imperios y las traiciones y los odios y las envidias. Más allá de las miradas de romanos y bárbaros, más allá de los pensamientos de sacerdotes y sicarios, más allá de las deslealtades de todos, esposa y sobrino incluidos, más allá de las carreras del Circo Máximo o las luchas del Anfiteatro Flavio, más allá de la lujuria y la sabiduría, más allá de batallas y conquistas, asedios y fortalezas inexpugnables, más allá de vestales, oráculos y mensajes secretos, más allá del Rin y del Danubio y del Éufrates y el Tigris; más allá de la Dacia y Arabia y Armenia y Osroene y Mesopotamia y Asiria y Babilonia y Carax y la mar Eritrea, más allá de los kushan o la desconocida Xeres, más allá de mi padre, de mi esposa, de mi familia. Camino, por fin, hacia lo que más he deseado siempre desde que me dejaste. Camino hacia ti, Longino, y nos encontraremos ya mismo y pronto volveremos a las montañas de Hispania y saldremos, como cuando éramos muchachos, jóvenes y fuertes y valientes, a cazar el más grande de los linces, que sigue, amigo mío, estoy seguro de ello, esperándonos allí para retarnos una vez más a la más épica de las cacerías. ¡Tira ahora de mi brazo, Longino, y no me dejes caer en el abismo! ¡Tira de él, por Júpiter, como hiciste aquella vez en Hispania! ¡Tira de mí hacia ti y llévame contigo al Hades! ¡No me dejes morir solo! ¡Longino! ¡No me dejes solo!

El propio Trajano sospechó que su enfermedad se debía a un veneno que se le había administrado, pero otros afirman que se debía a que la sangre, que desciende todos los años a las partes más bajas del cuerpo, vio su flujo habitual bloqueado. Había sufrido también un ictus, de forma que una parte de su cuerpo estaba paralizada, y estaba siempre somnoliento. Al llegar a Selinus, en Cilicia, que también llamamos Traianópolis, de pronto expiró después de haber gobernado diecinueve años, seis meses y quince días.

DIÓN CASIO, Libro LXVIII, 33.

117

EL REGRESO DEL REY DE REYES

Cesifonte
Agosto de 117 d.C.

Osroes entró de nuevo en el salón del trono, ahora sin trono, de Cesifonte. Trajano le había arrebatado la gran butaca de sólido oro sobre la que el rey de reyes de Partia se sentaba y decidía acerca de los designios de millones de personas desde Armenia hasta el Imperio kushan y la India. Es decir, cuando Armenia estaba sometida a su control y el rebelde Vologases arrinconado en las montañas. Ahora Armenia estaba bajo el poder de su traidor hermano Mitrídates y el maldito Vologases dominaba amplias regiones del oriente de Partia. A esto había que sumar que Trajano también le había robado su honor al despojarlo del poder, al haberlo obligado a huir teniendo que dar muerte a su séquito de mujeres y niños. Todo ello después de haberle infligido tremendas derrotas militares. Particularmente dolorosa en su memoria era la batalla del Tigris, donde había estado convencido de que podría haber detenido el avance de aquel loco emperador romano.

Entraron varios soldados portando un enorme nuevo trono, de piedra maciza pero con joyas incrustadas.

—Ponedlo ahí —indicó el *Šāhān Šāh* señalando el lugar que hasta hacía sólo unos meses había ocupado el trono dorado de oro—. De momento valdrá —apostilló.

Luego Osroes salió de la sala y, siempre escoltado por sus hombres, llegó a las murallas de Cesifonte, y desde lo alto de una de las torres contempló cómo los barcos de Partamaspates se alejaban hacia el norte, río arriba. Su hijo ni siquiera se había atrevido a luchar contra él. A Osroes le bastó descender de las montañas con su ejército de leales para que Partamaspates saliera huyendo. El plan inicial había sido que su hijo aceptara ser rey vasallo de Trajano sin realmente serlo, pero Partamaspates se había hecho fuerte en Cesifonte ignorando las cartas de su padre, como si hubiera decidido ser leal al César romano. Por eso ahora había tenido el buen criterio de escapar. Temía la reacción violenta de su padre. Osroes sonreía malévolamente. Partamaspates hacía bien. No había visto Osroes con buenos ojos esa independencia de su hijo y pensaba castigarlo. No había habido oportunidad. Tiempo al tiempo. Hijos rebeldes. Venganza lenta. Todo llegaría. Roma lo daba por derrotado, como Mitrídates en el norte o Vologases en el este, pero ya se vería. Quien ríe el último ríe mejor.

Por otro lado, nadie en Cesifonte quiso apoyar a Partamaspates, un gobernante puesto a dedo por Roma que se había atrevido a pactar con aquellos que habían destrozado el poder parto en el mundo. Osroes mantenía su sonrisa. Los extranjeros no entendían Partia y su hijo tampoco. Sabía que en Cesifonte y en otras ciudades de Mesopotamia lo preferirían a él antes que a nadie que pactara con los romanos. Y el estúpido de su hijo le había obedecido y había llegado a un acuerdo con Trajano sin darse cuenta de que así se descartaba como candidato apreciado por el pueblo para el trono. Si hubiera respondido a sus cartas de forma sumisa podría haberlo mantenido junto a él, quizá no en Cesifonte, pero sí en alguna otra ciudad. Pero ya nada. En todo caso, su lento plan de retorno al poder absoluto marchaba bien. Y es que ésa era su estrategia: ir eliminando competidores poco a poco: su hermano Partamasiris y su sobrino Sanatruces muertos por Trajano mismo, Partamaspates en franca huida, el propio Trajano en retirada. Partia se le había indigestado. Quedaban Mitrídates en Armenia y Vologases en el este.

Regresó a la gran sala de audiencias y se sentó en su nuevo trono.

Resultaba incómodo, así que pidió que le llevaran cojines.

Éstos le fueron proveídos de inmediato. Volvió a acomodarse en aquel nuevo asiento.

Mejor.

Osroes I Euergetes Dikaios Epiphanes Philhellene miró hacia la enorme sala vacía. Pronto acudirían de nuevo embajadores y emisarios de todas las esquinas de Partia y Mesopotamia y hasta de la mismísima Armenia y otras regiones y reinos. Al fin de todo, tal y como él había intuido, la tormenta de Trajano, la invasión de aquel emperador romano, había terminado siendo eso: sólo una tormenta. Pronto volvería todo a su sitio mientras las aguas del Éufrates y el Tigris seguían navegando, como siempre, hacia el mar del sur, lamiendo las murallas de Babilonia y Cesifonte, como si acariciaran el amanecer del resurgir de Partia.

Mitrídates en Armenia y Vologases en el este.

Frunció el ceño.

Vologases seguía siendo el problema primordial.

Pero tenía solución.

A veces, después de tantas vueltas, lo mejor es volver al principio.

Aryazate.

Osroes había descubierto ya que su hija había sobrevivido. Al principio lo consideró un problema. Pero de las crisis había que hacer virtud. Y él era un genio en eso. Por eso sobrevivía. Siempre.

118

EL ASALTO AL PODER: IMPERIO ROMANO

Selinus
Agosto de 117 d.C.

En el praetorium

El *praetorium* estaba lleno de papiros y documentos. Fédimo había estado usando la sala como despacho a la espera de la recuperación del César. Ahora eso ya no iba a pasar nunca. El secretario cogió cuatro papiros enrollados y lacrados con el sello imperial de Trajano y los entregó a los cuatro pretorianos que tenía con él. Estaba a punto de hablar cuando se empezaron a oír gritos y golpes. Los cuatro pretorianos se volvieron hacia la puerta. La lucha había empezado. Los cuatro pretorianos se llevaron las manos a sus espadas y las desenvainaron con rapidez al tiempo que se volvían hacia la puerta.

—¡No! —les espetó Fédimo con tanta autoridad que, sorprendidos, se volvieron de nuevo—. ¡No! —repitió el secretario del emperador—. ¡Vuestra misión ha de ser otra! Dejad que Liviano proteja esa entrada. Coged estos papiros. —Y se acercó a cada uno de ellos para entregarles, uno a uno, cada rollo lacrado mientras les daba instrucciones—. Tenéis que entregar estos mensajes a sus destinatarios. Tres viajaréis en un barco que he dispuesto en el puerto con dirección a Atenas para seguir luego rumbo a Roma. Allí os dividiréis y entregaréis vuestros papiros en los lugares indicados: Faventia, Baiae y Tarracina. Tú —y se dirigió al cuarto pretoriano elevando algo la voz para hacerse oír por encima del ruido de la lucha encarnizada que se estaba librando en el exterior— tienes otra embarcación que te conducirá a Antioquía y de ahí has de llegar a Jerusalén a toda velocidad. Como viajáis la mayor parte de los trayectos en barco podréis entregar los mensajes en cuestión de una semana en Asia y de dos semanas en Italia. Quizá algún día más, pero sed veloces. El factor tiempo es clave. ¡Ahora marchad!

Fédimo les abrió una pequeña puerta trasera.

—¡Por aquí! ¡Y no os detengáis por nada del mundo!

Los cuatro hombres envainaron las armas, asieron con fuerza sus papiros y salieron por la puerta que el secretario les había abierto.

En cuanto el último cruzó el umbral, Fédimo la cerró. Suspiró algo más sereno. Aquellos pretorianos entregarían los mensajes. Eran hombres totalmente leales seleccionados por el propio Liviano a petición suya para enviar aquellas misivas.

Fédimo fue junto a la mesa donde cogió varios documentos. Los golpes de lucha seguían en el exterior. Oyó un grito ahogado.

En el exterior del praetorium

Liviano cogió con las manos la lanza que acababa de atravesarlo. Aún permanecía en pie, pero la sangre brotaba como un torrente por la herida abierta. Se sentía no ya traicionado, sino estúpido por no haberlo visto llegar.

Cayó de rodillas.

Tendría que haberlo previsto cuando Adriano llegó a Selinus con varios barcos y un pequeño ejército de tres cohortes. Con esos legionarios, los ciento cincuenta pretorianos que acompañaban al César no tenían ninguna posibilidad. Liviano sospechó que Adriano tramaba algo, pero no que fuera a actuar ni tan pronto ni con aquella saña propia de un desesperado. Liviano, aún de rodillas, sangrando, las manos en la lanza, pensó en Lucio Quieto. Si él hubiera estado allí... todo habría sido distinto. Para empezar Quieto viajaba siempre con trescientos jinetes de su caballería... pero igual que con Marco Antonio y Julio César... la historia se repetía: separaron a Marco Antonio de Julio César y asesinaron a este último; Trajano mandó a Quieto a luchar contra los judíos y Adriano... aprovechó...

Los pensamientos se enturbiaban.

El jefe del pretorio cayó de costado sobre el suelo. Su cabeza se golpeó con el mármol y perdió el conocimiento. Eso le ahorró la deshonra de ver cómo los legionarios lo decapitaban igual que lo hacían con otros pretorianos.

Dentro de la sala del praetorium

Fédimo fue sorprendido mientras fingía repasar el correo imperial que iba a presentar a la emperatriz. La puerta por la que habían salido los correos estaba cerrada y ninguno de los legionarios reparó en ella. Estaban demasiado ocupados en matar como para pensar en otras puertas o en mensajes.

Al contrario que Liviano, cuando el joven secretario vio entrar a aquellos soldados armados y con las espadas aún vertiendo sangre pretoriana, no opuso resistencia alguna. Los legionarios no se ensañaron. Así como sentían envidia por los elevados salarios de la guardia pretoriana, no tenían nada personal contra aquel escribano. Se limitaron a cumplir las órdenes recibidas. La recompensa era grande. Ahora ellos serían los nuevos pretorianos.

Fédimo se arrodillo.

Pensó en Cristo.

Cerró los ojos.

Lo degollaron desde atrás.

En el Odeón

Critón, el médico del César, fue directamente convocado por Adriano al Odeón de Selinus, donde el sobrino del ya fallecido emperador estaba tomando decisiones y organizando el mundo después de Trajano.

—¿Has visto a mi tío? —preguntó Adriano siendo cuidadoso de no denominarlo ya emperador, pues el César tenía que ser ya otro, es decir, él.

—Sí... gobernador —respondió Critón sin estar muy seguro de con que título referirse a su ilustre interlocutor—. Está muerto.

—¿Alguna opinión sobre por qué ha muerto? —preguntó Adriano mientras hacía como si leyera unos papiros.

—Estaba muy enfermo, gobernador. Había tenido varios ataques. La sangre no fluía bien por su cuerpo.

—Bien —dijo Adriano y miró entonces al griego—. Y eso será también lo que escribirás y lo que contarás al Senado, ¿no es cierto?

Critón lo pensó unos instantes.

—Así es, gobernador.

—Entonces puedes marcharte.

Critón se inclinó ante Adriano dos veces. Tres. Cuatro. Se fue andando hacia atrás, sudando profusamente y haciendo más y más reverencias. Había visto a los legionarios atacando a los pretorianos por las calles de Selinus y no había que ser muy inteligente para comprender que Adriano se estaba haciendo con el poder no precisamente de una forma muy consensuada. Había estado convencido de que después de los pretorianos y Fédimo el siguiente en la lista sería él, pero se acababa de dar cuenta de que si redactaba en su escrito al Senado la versión del gobernador de Siria sobre la muerte del César, Adriano respetaría su vida, porque era más convincente que el relato de la muerte del emperador viniera confirmado por su médico de confianza que por otro desconocido que pudiera haber en Selinus o que pudiera seleccionar el propio Adriano.

Critón no era un héroe y, además, se decía a sí mismo una y otra vez que Trajano habría muerto en pocas semanas en cualquier caso. ¿Qué importaba si alguien lo había envenenado o no un poco antes del inevitable final?

El médico se adentraba en la ciudad portuaria ensimismado, mirando al suelo.

Adriano permanecía en el Odeón.

Tras el médico griego llegó el turno de las autoridades de la ciudad.

A las gradas del recinto llegaban aún ecos de algunos gritos y golpes de espadas. Los últimos pretorianos fieles a Liviano y al emperador fallecido estaban siendo abatidos por las tropas del gobernador de Siria.

—¿Sabéis quién soy? —preguntó Adriano sentado en el centro de las gradas del Odeón.

Los miembros del pequeño grupo del concejo local de Selinus se miraron entre sí. Nadie parecía reunir el valor suficiente para aventurar una respuesta que todos intuían que o era la correcta o conduciría al que la pronunciara hacia un destino similar al de los pretorianos.

Adriano suspiró. Olía el miedo. Eso estaba bien. No obstante, no se permitió ninguna sonrisa. No cuando quedaba tanto para asegurarse el poder.

—Os explicaré lo que está pasando —dijo al fin el sobrino segundo de Trajano.

Y lo hizo.

Le llevó un tiempo. Tenía muchas instrucciones que dar a aquellos hombres. Luego lo haría con otros muchos a lo largo y ancho del Imperio, pero en aquel momento se concentró en Selinus. Todo lo grande empieza con algo muy pequeño. Estaba ya a punto de terminar de enumerar sus instrucciones a las autoridades locales cuando Plotina apareció en el Odeón seguida por un grupo de soldados que la escoltaban, que la vigilaban.

—¿Era necesaria toda esta sangre? —preguntó la emperatriz delante de todo el mundo.

Adriano se llevó la palma de la mano izquierda a la boca y la barba. Miró a los hombres de Selinus a los ojos.

—Ya he terminado con vosotros. Haced lo que os he dicho.

Todos partieron del Odeón a toda velocidad, contentos de salir vivos de allí. Nadie miró hacia atrás.

Plotina y Adriano quedaron frente a frente en el recinto, con las gradas vacías, sin público. Sólo había soldados en las entradas al pequeño Odeón y dos más detrás del gobernador.

Adriano ignoró la pregunta de la emperatriz.

—Ah, mi querida Plotina: te alegrará saber que he dado orden a las autoridades de la ciudad para que se construya un gran cenotafio, un monumento funerario permanente a la memoria de mi tío. Aunque se lleven luego las cenizas a Roma para su gran funeral, Selinus recordará siempre que aquí fue donde expiró un emperador de Roma. El primero de una nueva dinastía. Y también les he notificado que a partir de hoy mismo Selinus ya no sólo llevará ese nombre sino que será conocida en todo el Imperio con el apelativo de Traianópolis. Imagino que todo esto te satisfará.

—¿Hacía falta tanta sangre? —insistió ella—. Ése no era el plan. La idea era que yo anunciaría que mi esposo te adoptaba en su lecho de muerte y que el Senado decidiría. Con mi apoyo y ese documento y la ayuda de Serviano y otros senadores se habría podido conseguir que una mayoría aceptara tu nombramiento. Ésa era la idea. Matar a Liviano, a Fédimo y a todos esos pretorianos no era necesario ni estaba en el plan del que hablamos. Los senadores tienen suficiente miedo a un Imperio demasiado grande con unas legiones demasiado alejadas de Roma. Hay muchos que no quieren una nueva guerra en Oriente. Con eso tenías suficiente para ser elegido el nuevo *Imperator Caesar Augustus*. Ahora, después de esta sangría va a haber senadores que se opondrán a tu elección con todas sus fuerzas.

—Entonces haré lo que tenga que hacer.

—Has ordenado dar muerte a un jefe del pretorio leal y a un secretario. ¿Vas a dar instrucciones para matar a senadores también? Nadie se ha atrevido a tanto desde tiempos de Domiciano. Ni Nerva ni Trajano ordenaron nunca la ejecución de un senador. Hasta los más miserables y corruptos vieron que su pena en tiempos de Trajano era devolver el dinero y luego el exilio, pero nunca la muerte. No puedes matar a senadores o el Senado te verá como un nuevo Domiciano. ¿Es eso acaso lo que quieres?

—Esta conversación, querida tía, ha terminado. —Y se levantó dispuesto a marcharse de allí.

—No, esta conversación acaba de empezar —replicó ella y se interpuso en su camino.

Adriano se detuvo, se acercó lentamente a ella, la asió con suavidad pero con fuerza también por la cintura, la apretó contra sí, le dio un beso en la mejilla y le habló al oído.

—Es posible que esta conversación sólo haya empezado, pero ahora no tengo tiempo para continuarla, mi querida tía.

El abrazo, el tono suave de otro tiempo y el beso la cogieron por sorpresa y para cuando ella quiso reaccionar, Adriano ya abandonaba el recinto seguido por sus hombres. Plotina se quedó sola en un Odeón de gradas vacías. El cuerpo de su esposo aún no estaba frío y Adriano ya estaba fuera de su control. Plotina intuía que se había equivocado, pero ya era tarde para detener el curso de la historia.

Un barco atracado en el puerto de Selinus

Desde la cubierta, Publio Acilio Atiano vio cómo el gobernador de Siria llegaba al barco, ascendía por la pequeña pasarela y bajaba al interior del buque. Un soldado se le acercó y le indicó que debía seguirlo. Atiano fue tras el legionario y éste lo condujo a la estancia del capitán en la bodega del barco. No era una habitación grande, pero sí confortable, con pieles de fieras por el suelo y las paredes y una mesa amplia repleta de viandas diversas: carne seca de jabalí, fruta y queso. También había jarras con agua y vino. Y hacía menos calor allí dentro que en el exterior. Adriano sostenía una copa de oro en la que un esclavo estaba escanciando lo que, sin duda, sería un excelente licor de Baco de la región. El esclavo salió y cerró la puerta.

—Si tienes hambre o sed, sírvete tú mismo —le dijo Adriano y luego echó un trago largo de su copa de oro.

—Quizá luego... augusto.

Adriano sonrió al ver que Atiano se dirigía a él ya como emperador.

—Veo que no has tardado mucho en reconocer mi actual condición. Eso está bien. Eres el primero que lo hace. Lástima que no todos serán tan raudos en aceptar mi adopción por parte de mi recién fallecido tío.

—Pero... ¿tenemos el documento? —indagó Atiano algo inquieto.

—Lo tenemos —confirmó Adriano sirviéndose algo más de vino.

—¿Y la emperatriz respaldará con su testimonio el contenido de ese documento?

Adriano apretó los labios y alzó las cejas. Se quedó inmóvil un instante, pero al fin asintió.

—Sí. La emperatriz está incómoda con las ejecuciones de Liviano y los pretorianos y con la muerte de ese secretario de mi tío, pero ¿qué otra cosa puede hacer sino seguirnos ya el juego hasta el final?

—Podría... —Pero Atiano no se atrevió a seguir.

—Di, di lo que sea que estás pensando. Me interesa.

—Podría contactar con algunos de los senadores más leales a Trajano o con el mismísimo Lucio Quieto y ofrecerles su apoyo. Podría... revolverse contra nosotros.

Adriano inspiró profundamente.

—Es posible —admitió—. Pero no lo creo. A Plotina le gusta maquinar, es cierto, pero sólo cuando ve clara la victoria. Sabe que contamos con Serviano en Roma. —Se permitió una pequeña risa—. Y fue por sugerencia suya que reactivé ese contacto, pero bueno... —Volvió a adoptar un tono serio—. Todo eso ahora ya no importa. La vigilaremos, pero no actuaremos en modo alguno contra ella. Estoy seguro de que si mi tía ve que la respeto a ella y a Matidia y al resto de las mujeres de la familia, incluida mi querida esposa Vibia... —Volvió a detenerse y echó otro trago de vino—. Estoy convencido de que si no voy contra ellas directamente, Plotina se mantendrá en la línea de lo que hemos pactado. Otra cosa es si se organiza una revuelta poderosa contra mí, pero para que eso no ocurra, cuento contigo; ¿no es así, Atiano?

—Sí... César.

—César, sí. Por fin César. Pero hemos de asegurarnos de que ese título es el que al final recogerán los anales que se escriban siglos después de que tú y yo hayamos muerto, y para eso hemos de terminar con los pequeños cabos sueltos de nuestro plan.

—¿Que son...? —preguntó Atiano que, aunque intuía la respuesta, pensaba que en asuntos de tanta importancia era conveniente tener una noción precisa de cada detalle.

—Celso, Palma, Nigrino y Quieto.

Atiano miró al suelo con el ceño fruncido.

—Nigrino y Quieto lo entiendo, pero ¿realmente hay que

incluir en la lista a Celso y a Palma? Son más políticos que hombres de acción. La conquista de Arabia por parte de Palma fue sin batallas de relevancia. No los veo capaces...

—Hemos iniciado un camino que no permite dejar ni la sombra de una posibilidad de enemigo en la retaguardia, amigo mío. Ya ves que a mi tío nunca lo derrotaron en una batalla, sólo hubo revueltas y traiciones a sus espaldas. No seré yo quien, por un absurdo exceso de magnanimidad, caiga en el mismo error. Los tres primeros están en Italia y allí puedes contar con la colaboración de Serviano y sus aliados. Que se haga lo que se tenga que hacer. Que se compre a quien haga falta y que se les prometa a los hombres que nos sean necesarios lo que pidan. Haz que salga un barco con un mensaje para Roma hoy mismo.

—Me han informado de que han salido del puerto esta misma mañana un par de embarcaciones con pretorianos. Deben de llevar mensajes —comentó Atiano.

—Ni los mensajes ni los mensajeros importan —replicó Adriano—. Lo esencial es eliminar a los destinarios de esos mensajes. Que las misivas les lleguen o no me da igual. Que Serviano se centre en los receptores de esas cartas.

—¿Y Quieto?

—¡Por Júpiter, Quieto, siempre Quieto! —exclamó Adriano arrojando su copa de oro contra una piel de león del suelo. Acto seguido puso los brazos en jarras y miró a su interlocutor con los ojos inyectados—. Quieto, con toda seguridad, será uno de los que reciban a esos mensajeros. Quiero que te ocupes tú personalmente de él. Está acabando con la rebelión en Judea, gran labor que está haciendo para el Imperio, pero ése, Atiano, ha de ser el último servicio que Quieto preste nunca más a Roma.

Hubo un largo silencio durante el cual Adriano se volvió hacia la mesa, cogió otra copa de oro —había tres más— y escanció vino, que esta vez rebajó con un poco de agua. Tenía todavía varios asuntos más de los que ocuparse y no podía permitirse estar ebrio a media tarde. La gran celebración tendría que esperar al momento en que Atiano le enviara la confirmación de que el asunto del maldito Lucio Quieto había quedado solucionado para siempre, de forma drástica y definitiva.

—Cuando el César dice que hay que terminar con los cabos sueltos y que me ocupe de Quieto, el César está dando a entender lo que yo creo que está dando a entender.

Adriano se volvió lentamente.

—Te tenía por un hombre inteligente, Atiano.

El aludido tragó saliva, pero aun así quería confirmación.

—Son senadores. Nadie ha... obrado mortalmente contra un senador desde Domiciano.

Adriano sonrió. Era la segunda vez que recibía la misma advertencia en menos de una hora.

—Yo creía que tú, Publio Acilio Atiano, querías ser senador.

—Así es, César.

—Pues habrá que ir haciendo sitio. En el edificio de la Curia no cabe todo el mundo a la vez. Tú mismo.

119
—

EL ASALTO AL PODER: IMPERIO HAN

Loyang
Verano de 117 d.C.

Palacio imperial, en la puerta de la sala del té

Quizá fue porque la joven Tamura estaba en lugares inespera-
dos o porque los dioses lo quisieron así.

Sea como fuere, el caso es que la mensajera de Trajano en
la corte imperial han se encontraba justo en ese momento en
la pequeña sala donde se preparaba el té para la emperatriz
Deng. Las sirvientas de su majestad lo habían dejado ya todo
dispuesto. Tamura sentía curiosidad por ver más de cerca
aquellas piezas tan hermosas de cerámica en las que la emperatriz bebía sus infusiones. Los soldados de la puerta, por supuesto, se interpusieron en su camino y cruzaron sus lanzas
impidiéndole el acceso al pequeño cuarto. Ella tenía permitido desplazarse con libertad por el recinto del palacio imperial, pero con frecuencia se le negaba el acceso a distintas dependencias. Tamura dio un paso atrás para no crear una
situación incómoda para nadie. Era lógico que allí donde se
preparaba el té de su majestad imperial sólo pudieran acceder
las sirvientas que se ocupaban de atender personalmente a la
emperatriz o, quizá, algún miembro de la familia. Esto último
lo pensó Tamura porque vio que dentro estaba Yan Ji, la favorita del emperador An-ti, aparentemente verificando que todo
estuviera bien dispuesto: tazas policromadas, tetera humeante
y pequeñas cucharillas de jade blanco.

Yan Ji se sintió observada y le extrañó tener esa sensación porque había contado con que los guardias estarían de espaldas, como en efecto estaban. Eran otros los ojos que la miraban con atención. Demasiada atención. Una mirada felina e inteligente la vigilaba. Yan Ji sonrió siniestramente cuando comprobó que aquellos ojos no eran otros que los de la mensajera enviada desde el lejano Da Qin: esa joven extraña por la que tanto interés parecían tener en las últimas semanas la emperatriz Deng, su consejero Fan Chun o hasta el general Li Kan. Los guardias continuaban de espaldas con las lanzas cruzadas para no permitir que aquella extranjera entrara allí donde se había preparado el té de la emperatriz. Pese a ello, la extraña llegada desde el otro extremo del mundo la observaba con el ceño fruncido. Las lanzas la impedían pasar, pero sí podía ver. Los guardias no se volvieron. Yan Ji amplió su sonrisa malévola. ¿Qué podía importar que aquella extranjera fuera testigo de cómo ella ejecutaba su plan, ese plan que con tanto tiempo había diseñado en silencio, entre la rabia y la envidia y las ansias de acceder al poder sin tener que esperar más a que la vieja y maldita Deng muriera? ¿Qué podría hacer aquella extranjera aunque la viera verter el contenido de su diminuto frasco en la tetera imperial? Nada podría comunicar a nadie una extranjera que no conocía la lengua de los han. La mente de Yan Ji bullía con millones de pensamientos veloces mientras extraía el frasco de debajo de sus ropas de seda brillante. Era cierto que la extranjera había empezado a ser instruida en la cultura han por la tutora que reemplazaba a la fallecida Ban Zao, antigua institutriz de la emperatriz, pero ¿cuánto podía haber aprendido la joven en unas pocas semanas de su lengua? Apenas la había oído pronunciar saludos concisos y breves expresiones de agradecimiento cuando se le servía algo de comida o bebida; pobre vocabulario era ése para intentar explicar a los guardias imperiales lo que estaba a punto de ocurrir. ¿Y si gritaba? Eso detuvo la mano de Yan Ji, pero sólo un instante. Pensarían que estaba loca. A fin de cuentas a menudo se comportaba de forma inusual. Yan Ji ya sabía cómo la extranjera había humillado en varias ocasiones al mismísimo *chiang-chün* Li Kan con sus reacciones inesperadas y absurdas. En la corte aquellos cotilleos se extendían con velocidad. Siempre en voz baja, pero siempre con rapidez.

La favorita del joven emperador An-ti volvió a sonreír, pese a la mirada atenta de Tamura, que seguía allí, al otro lado de los guardias, vigilándola. El hecho de que la extranjera no contara con la confianza de Li Kan fue lo que inclinó al fin la balanza donde Yan Ji estaba sopesando mentalmente si seguir adelante con el plan o si detenerse.

Yan Ji vertió, al fin, el contenido del pequeño frasco en la tetera caliente.

Tenía que hacerlo ya. Algunos consejeros imperiales, en especial aquel maldito Fan Chun, desconfiaban cada vez más de ella, y cada día que pasaba se incrementaba la seguridad en torno a la emperatriz Deng. En ese momento aún tenía la oportunidad de hacer lo que iba a hacer, pero ¿quién podía garantizarle que al día siguiente seguiría permitiéndosele, por ejemplo, el acceso a la sala donde se preparaba el té de la emperatriz? Hasta ahora Fan Chun no se había atrevido a sugerir que se le restringieran los movimientos por el palacio, pues era la favorita del emperador y una prohibición semejante podría encender la cólera de su joven e impetuoso esposo. Sin embargo, la sospecha, de eso estaba segura, aumentaba en la cabeza siempre demasiado pensante de aquel consejero imperial. No, no podía perder la oportunidad que el destino le brindaba aquel día porque simplemente estuviera siendo observada por aquella extranjera llegada desde el fin del mundo. Una testigo, sí, pero una testigo muda a efectos reales, una testigo que no podría comunicarse con nadie del palacio. ¿Sería la maldita extranjera capaz de hacerse entender si llamaba a alguno de los sabios que traducían textos budistas del sánscrito? Era una posibilidad, pues la muchacha sí parecía conocer esa lengua, pero para cuando los llamara el poder ya estaría en manos de su esposo, el emperador An-ti, esto es, en sus propias manos. Había que tener en cuenta, claro, a aquel miserable e insidioso Fan Chun, que parecía saber también aquella lengua de los budistas, pero el consejero no estaba ese día en la ciudad. Por eso había elegido aquella jornada para actuar. La joven extranjera no tendría pues nadie con quien entenderse aquel día. El plan debía, en consecuencia, seguir hasta su inexorable desenlace.

A la puerta de la sala del té

Tamura parpadeó varias veces, como si no creyera lo que estaba viendo: Yan Ji acababa de verter el contenido de un frasco en la tetera de la emperatriz. Si la joven favorita del emperador An-ti la hubiera mirado con ingenuidad o con simple indiferencia cuando sus miradas se encontraron, Tamura no habría pensado en nada especial —quizá sólo era una especia que se añadía al té de la emperatriz—, pero los ojos inyectados de rabia y odio y ansia y desprecio y risa de victoria y muerte de Yan Ji se lo dijeron todo sin pronunciar palabra alguna. Tamura estaba segura de que ese frasco que acababa de ser vertido en el té de la emperatriz Deng era veneno.

Dentro de la sala de té

Yan Ji se guardó el frasco ya vacío, cogió la bandeja con el té y dio una voz. Los guardias se volvieron y separaron sus lanzas para dejarla salir sin sospechar nada. Tamura quería advertirlos pero no sabía cómo. Yan Ji la volvió a mirar sonriente, triunfante. En el fondo estaba doblemente feliz de ver que alguien que no podía desvelar nada ni intervenir en forma alguna para impedir su plan compartía su secreto. Era como tener público el día de su gran asalto al poder; todo se disfrutaba más. Habría sido una pena hacer algo tan osado y no poder contarlo a nadie, que nadie valorara su audacia. La cara de terror de Tamura la hacía deleitarse aún más en su victoria.

Tamura vio entonces cómo regresaban dos sirvientas de la emperatriz y cómo los guardias se hacían a un lado. Una de las sirvientas cogió la bandeja con la tetera humeante directamente de las manos de Yan Ji, mientras la otra entraba en la sala de té y cogía una segunda bandeja con las tazas y las cucharillas de jade. Siempre varias tazas y varias cucharillas para que la emperatriz, si tomaba más de un taza de té, tuviera a mano una limpia para repetir.

Las bandejas, las sirvientas y, tras ellas, los guardias, custodiando ahora lo que deberían haber custodiado mucho mejor apenas hacía unos instantes, desfilaron ante sus ojos. Nadie podía sospechar que Yan Ji o cualquier otro miembro de la familia imperial estuviera dispuesto a hacer algo tan atrevido, tan brutal. Tamura lo veía todo impotente. Quizá el viejo consejero Fan Chun, con el que había hablado alguna vez en sánscrito, estuviera en la puerta de la sala de audiencias hacia donde se dirigía el té envenenado, y a él sí podría advertirlo de lo que estaba a punto de ocurrir. Ésa era su gran esperanza, así que Tamura se unió rápidamente al cortejo de guardias que iban tras las sirvientas con el té de su majestad Deng.

La joven sármata los siguió hasta la sala de audiencias y buscó desesperadamente al consejero Fan Chun con la mirada, pero no lo vio por ninguna parte. No importaba: empezaría a dar su mensaje en sánscrito en voz alta por si Fan Chun estuviera entre alguno de los funcionarios que se arracimaban ya frente a la puerta de la sala de audiencias pasando entre los numerosos guardias imperiales.

—*Bhaṭṭārikā, víṣa, ánta!* [Reina madre, veneno, muerte] —advirtió una y otra vez en la lengua que antaño le empezara a enseñar su viejo maestro Dión Coceyo por orden de Trajano.

Nunca pensó que aquella lengua le fuera a servir para algo tan importante. Un idioma que ya le salvara la vida a ella misma en la frontera entre el Imperio kushan y el Imperio han tenía que valer ahora para salvar también a su majestad Deng, la emperatriz que la protegía en aquel mundo extraño en el

que estaba completamente sola. Una lengua que luego Buddahamitra se ocupó de que aprendiera aún mejor...

Pero nadie reaccionaba a sus palabras.

No tenía nadie con quien entenderse.

Fan Chun no estaba, no estaba por ninguna parte y ninguno de los otros viejos consejeros que la miraban confusos ante
sus voces parecía poder comprenderla.

¿Y en la lengua de los han? Lo intentaría con algunas palabras de chino pero no sabía cómo se decía ni veneno ni peligro, ni reina madre ni emperatriz ni nada parecido.

La bandeja pasaba ya entre los soldados sin que nadie hiciera nada por impedirlo. Tamura giraba buscando un rostro
amigo. Su mirada se encontró, una vez más, con la de la triunfante Yan Ji. Su sonrisa era un puro desafío.

Tamura volvió a dar voces en sánscrito con las palabras
clave, pero sus gritos sólo generaban estupor entre soldados y
funcionarios. Sabían que era una extranjera peculiar, pero
aquello era excesivo, más allá de una excentricidad.

—Será mejor que se la lleven —dijo uno de los ministros a
Li Kan, que, ante aquella algarabía, se había acercado a la
puerta de la sala de audiencias.

El general, como todos, estaba sorprendido por el extraño
comportamiento de la mensajera de Da Qin. Una vez más la
joven obraba de modo impropio e inoportuno. El recio *chiang-
chün* sabía que la emperatriz Deng le había tomado cierto
aprecio a la extranjera y no quería que alguna de sus peculiares ocurrencias la indispusiera con la guardia imperial o con
consejeros y funcionarios: tenerla allí gritando palabras en
idiomas extraños sin que quedara claro a qué o a quién se refería era ciertamente perturbador.

Li Kan asintió mirando al ministro.

—Yo me ocuparé —dijo el general, con ese tono de quien
está acostumbrado a comportamientos absurdos por parte de
la persona de la que ahora, una vez más, tenía que hacerse
cargo. Lo único que había cambiado en la mente de Li Kan
era que consideraba a la extranjera muy hermosa, pero ésa no
era la cuestión.

Tamura se dio cuenta de que todos la miraban contraria-dos y de que en lugar de advertir sobre lo que estaba a punto de pasar lo único que había conseguido era ponerse en ridículo o, peor aún, que pensaran que estaba completamente loca. Su idea de dar voces en sánscrito había sido un total desastre. Y aquel general con el que nunca se entendía se acercaba con cara de pocos amigos.

Tamura, aun así, volvió a repetir en sánscrito las palabras «veneno» y «reina madre». Era un último intento.

—*Bhaṭṭārikā, víṣa!*

Aún tenía la esperanza de que quizá alguno de los consejeros más ancianos que estaban entrando en la sala de audiencias de Loyang pudiera entenderla, pero todos sus esfuerzos eran en vano. Sin Fan Chun toda comunicación parecía imposible. Su comportamiento era tan inusual e incomodaba tanto a todos, que los consejeros y funcionarios pasaban a su lado con rapidez, sin mirarla, sin escucharla. Tamura pensó que en aquel momento, incluso si fuera capaz de explicar lo que había visto en la lengua de los han, éstos ya ni la escucharían. Todo estaba perdido. La emperatriz Deng estaría muerta en poco tiempo. Seguramente Fan Chun y algún otro sospecharían de Yan Ji, pero con el emperador An-ti ya como único gobernante del imperio nadie podría actuar contra la esposa favorita y Tamura intuía muchas más muertes y sangre y horror en aquella corte donde su propia supervivencia estaba también en juego. ¿Cuánto tardaría Yan Ji en sugerir al emperador que se la alejara de allí o, directamente, que se la ejecutara? Yan Ji podría decir que ella, la extranjera, había llevado mala suerte o algún tipo de maldición y culparla a ella por la muerte de la emperatriz. O, ¿por qué no?, involucrarla en el envenenamiento. Todo apuntaba al desastre. Había sido una tonta. Ahora entendía por qué Yan Ji había sonreído: para transmitirle lo que iba a hacer, para provocar que hiciera lo que había hecho, ponerse en ridículo; incluso quizá para usarla como posible chivo expiatorio en una eventual caza de culpables por la muerte de la emperatriz.

Tamura apretó los puños con rabia. Li Kan ya estaba frente a ella. Tamura sabía que no debería haber dicho nada y haber dejado que Yan Ji se saliera con la suya sin intervenir. La emperatriz Deng estaría muerta, pero quizá ella aún tendría una oportunidad de sobrevivir y, sin embargo, algo la había incitado a intentar denunciar la acción de Yan Ji. Sí, algo tan sencillo como la amistad que sentía que la unía a la emperatriz Deng. Su majestad se había mostrado como una persona generosa hacia ella, la había acogido en la corte y le había proporcionado una tutora para intentar que pudiera, de alguna forma, adaptarse a aquel nuevo mundo que sólo bajo la hospitalidad de la emperatriz había dejado de resultar hostil y temible. Por eso había actuado y quería seguir intentándolo. Le debía a la emperatriz lealtad, pero ¿cómo advertir a aquel general que la volvía a mirar, como tantas otras veces, con ese gesto entre confusión y menosprecio, entre intriga y rechazo?

Li Kan se dirigió a dos de los guardias.

—Cogedla y llevadla a sus aposentos y que no salga de allí hasta que se calme y deje de gritar palabras extrañas —ordenó.

Los soldados se volvieron hacia la muchacha pero ésta dio un paso atrás, dos, tres y no se dejó detener con facilidad.

Tamura decidió concentrarse en aquel maldito general. Era cierto que nunca se habían entendido ni comprendido ni caído bien, pero, al menos, tenía su atención puesta en ella y eso era más de lo que estaba haciendo ningún otro de aquellos estúpidos hombres de la corte imperial.

—*Bhaṭṭārikā, víṣa, ánta!* —repitió una vez más en sánscrito, como si repetir palabras desconocidas pudiera servir para algo.

Li Kan la miró muy serio hasta que empezó a negar con la cabeza y volvió a dirigirse a los soldados.

—Lleváosla —insistió el general.

Tamura siguió retrocediendo. Los ojos de Li Kan aún estaban clavados en ella. ¿Qué más podía hacer? ¿Y si usara gestos? Hizo entonces ademán con una mano como si bebiera algo y entonces puso cara como de asco, como si le pasara algo doloroso, pero ni Li Kan ni los soldados parecían entender nada y eran los únicos que la miraban ya.

Estaban solos en la entrada de la sala de audiencias. Todos los consejeros y funcionarios habían desaparecido en el interior. Estaban, no obstante, las puertas abiertas. ¿Y si volviera a gritar? ¿La oiría quizá la emperatriz? ¿Serviría eso de algo? Pero en ese mismo instante las puertas empezaron a cerrarse. Decidió no gritar. No se la entendería, eso había quedado claro. Y la emperatriz, aunque sentía simpatía por ella, tampoco era persona a quien le agradaran los comportamientos peculiares. Aún tenía allí a Li Kan mirándola. Entre pensamiento y pensamiento los soldados la habían cogido por los brazos y empezaban a arrastrarla alejándola de la sala de audiencias. Pero Li Kan seguía mirándola.

120

LOS MENSAJES DE FÉDIMO

Faventia, norte de Italia
Verano de 117 d.C.

—Que le den comida y bebida —dijo Nigrino a Calvencio Víctor, el jefe de su guardia personal, señalando al pretoriano que, sudoroso y exhausto, acababa de entregarle el mensaje de Fédimo.

Nigrino se retiró a su *tablinum* y allí leyó con atención la carta del secretario de Trajano. El senador se llevó un momento el dorso de la mano a la boca, justo en el punto donde Fédimo describía la muerte de Trajano.

Siguió leyendo.

Terminó la carta. Dejó el papiro sobre la mesa. Sabía que el tiempo corría en su contra; en la suya y en la de sus amigos en el Senado. Fédimo explicaba que había enviado mensajeros a Celso, Palma y Quieto. Nigrino cogió una hoja de papiro en blanco y la puso delante de él, sobre la mesa. Se quedó inmóvil unos instantes. Tenía que escribir a Celso y a Palma y convocarlos a una reunión en Roma. Quieto tendría que ingeniárselas para llegar a África por su cuenta, con sus hombres. Era muy posible que lo consiguiera si su caballería no lo abandonaba en el último momento. Todo tendría que verse. De momento había que convocar la reunión con Celso y Palma.

Se puso a escribir.

Las manos le temblaban.

Trajano había muerto. Tenía que pasar. Estaba muy enfermo. Pero le costaba creerlo... asumir que había ocurrido...

Nigrino inspiró profundamente. Debía mantener la serenidad.

Cogió otra hoja, y esta vez con pulso más firme reinició la escritura.

Lida, provincia romana de Judea
Verano de 117 d.C.

Quieto miraba hacia la ciudad de Lida. Llevaban varias semanas de asedio. Sabía que los habían cogido por sorpresa. Los judíos no contaron con la rapidez de la caballería africana y los jinetes sorprendieron a los habitantes en el proceso de reunir víveres suficientes para soportar un largo asedio. Lucio Quieto examinaba las murallas, no muy altas, mientas trazaba en su mente un plan de ataque. Había rendido a los judíos de Mesopotamia y a casi a todos los de Judea, pero en Lida, los líderes Julián y Papo se habían hecho fuertes. Terminar con ellos era poner fin a la revuelta.

Inspiró profundamente.

Tiberio, su segundo en el mando de la caballería, le habló por la espalda.

—Ha llegado un mensajero.

Quieto no se movió un ápice. No le importaban los mensajeros, sino terminar con aquella rebelión.

—Viene de Selinus, de parte del secretario del emperador Trajano —insistió Tiberio.

—¿De parte de Fédimo? —preguntó el *legatus* volviéndose con rapidez para encarar al mensajero.

El pretoriano que estaba junto a Tiberio extendió el brazo con un papiro enrollado en la mano. Quieto cogió el mensaje. Desplegó el papiro con rapidez y lo leyó en silencio.

Tiberio, el pretoriano y varios tribunos y oficiales esperaron con paciencia. Todos aguardaban recibir instrucciones del *legatus* norteafricano, pero Lucio Quieto volvió a enrollar el papiro despacio y, sin decir nada a nadie, cabizbajo, pasó entre todos los tribunos, centuriones y demás oficiales sin ni siquiera levantar la mirada. Abrió las telas de la puerta de la tienda del *praetorium* de campaña y se desvaneció en su interior. Afuera todos permanecieron en silencio, esperando.

Pasó un rato.

El *legatus* no salía de la tienda.

—¿Qué hacemos con el asedio? —preguntó uno de los tribunos sin mirar a nadie en particular, pero todos sabían que se dirigía a Tiberio, el segundo al mando.

Tiberio Claudio Máximo no supo muy bien qué decir. En su lugar miró al pretoriano recién llegado desde Selinus y lo interrogó.

—¿Está todo bien en Selinus con el César Trajano?

El pretoriano negó con la cabeza al tiempo que daba respuesta.

—No. El emperador Trajano ha muerto.

El silencio retornó al cónclave de oficiales.

—Voy a hablar con el *legatus* —dijo al fin Tiberio y fue al *praetorium* de campaña.

Los legionarios que custodiaban la tienda donde se encontraba Lucio Quieto se hicieron a un lado al ver a Tiberio Claudio Máximo aproximándose. Éste llegó a la entrada cubierta por varias telas y oyó algo extraño. Como el sollozo de un niño.

Tiberio se volvió hacia los centinelas.

—¿Ha entrado alguien además del *legatus*? —preguntó. Al líder norteafricano le gustaba relajarse con alguna esclava de cuando en cuando, pero lo de los niños no era común en él.

—No —respondió uno de los legionarios—. El *legatus* está solo.

Tiberio asintió.

Se volvió de nuevo y encaró la entrada al *praetorium*. Se lo pensó unos instantes, pero, al fin, descorrió lentamente las telas y cruzó el umbral. Una vez en el interior vio al comandante en jefe de las tropas romanas desplazadas a Judea sentado en el borde de un *triclinium*, encogido, con la cabeza casi a la altura de las rodillas y las manos sobre el cogote, temblando. Y el llanto estaba ahí, pero no había niño alguno. Sólo Lucio Quieto, *legatus augusti*, jefe de la caballería romana, gobernador de Judea y senador de Roma, llorando.

Tiberio no dijo nada.

Dio media vuelta y salió de la tienda del *praetorium*.

934

—Podéis marcharos —les dijo a los centinelas—. Yo haré guardia durante una hora, hasta el relevo. Estoy esperando instrucciones del *legatus.*

Los legionarios asintieron y se fueron.

Tiberio no quería que nadie oyera al jefe de la caballería de Roma llorando.

Se acercaron varios tribunos, pero Tiberio les habló antes de que pudieran formular pregunta alguna.

—Mantened las posiciones. El *legatus* me ha dicho que atacaremos mañana.

Los tribunos aceptaron las palabras del segundo en el mando y fueron hacia donde estaban acampadas sus tropas.

Tiberio se quedó plantado delante de la tienda del *praetorium.* El sollozo ahogado seguía en el interior, cada vez más tenue, desvaneciéndose muy lentamente.

121

EL MUNDO ESTÁ LLENO DE SORPRESAS

Loyang
Verano de 117 d.C.

—Lleváosla —repitió el general Li Kan.

Tamura estaba desesperada. Lo había intentado todo y nada había servido. La emperatriz Deng estaría muerta en unos instantes y ella no podía hacer nada por evitarlo. Lo único que tenía eran los ojos de Li Kan clavados en ella, con una mirada llena de confusión y ansia y duda. Nada más. Pero Tamura recordó entonces las palabras de su anciano tutor: «Cuando tengas problemas graves, usa todo lo que creas que pueda ser útil para encontrar la solución, pero cuando nada haya hecho efecto, entonces usa también todo lo que creas inútil, pues el mundo está lleno de sorpresas». Algo así le había dicho Dión Coceyo. En otro tiempo, en otra vida. ¿Valían los consejos de una esquina del mundo en la esquina opuesta, en otro mundo distinto?

Su limitado chino no valía para nada. Sus palabras en sánscrito eran incomprensibles para aquel general que seguía con sus ojos vigilantes detenidos en ella. ¿Qué sentido tenía usar otras lenguas? Pero Dión Coceyo lo había dicho... Usó el griego.

—Ἡ Βασίλισσα καταφαρμαχθήσεται! [La emperatriz va a ser envenenada.]

Pero como Tamura imaginaba, Li Kan no pareció entender nada, hasta el punto de que el general se volvió y le dio la espalda para encaminarse a las puertas de la sala de audiencias que, lentamente, se estaban cerrando.

¿Qué le quedaba a ella?

No tenía nada más que usar. El griego había sido su último

recurso. Algo absurdo, pero recordó que el griego le había servido en numerosos lugares distantes de Roma y por eso lo había empleado. Dión Coceyo dijo cualquier cosa aunque parezca inútil. ¿Qué podía haber más inútil que usar el griego? El latín.

¿La lengua de Roma para dirigirse a un general del Imperio han?

No había nada más absurdo ni más inútil.

Pero Tamura lo empleó.

—*Imperatrix venenabitur!* [La emperatriz va a ser envenenada.]

Las puertas de la sala de audiencias, una vez que Li Kan había entrado, se seguían cerrando lenta pero inexorablemente.

Tamura volvió a gritar una vez más aquella frase en latín más como una forma de sacar fuera de su cuerpo toda la rabia de su impotencia que porque pensara que aquello tenía ya algún sentido.

—*Imperatrix venenabitur!*

Los guardias la arrastraron y las lágrimas le impidieron ver que las puertas de la sala de audiencias volvían a abrirse y que el general Li Kan salía y caminaba veloz hacia donde ella estaba.

La voz del *chiang-chün*, que ella reconoció enseguida, hizo que Tamura parpadeara varias veces para poder limpiarse los ojos y ver al general dando voces a los soldados, que forcejeaban para alejarla de aquel lugar.

—Deteneos y soltadla —ordenó Li Kan en la lengua de los han. De pronto, mirándola con una intensidad que nunca había visto en los ojos del general, se dirigió a ella con palabras que, aunque pronunciadas de una forma distinta a la que estaba acostumbrada, Tamura pudo entender perfectamente—: *Quid dicisti?* [¿Qué has dicho?]

Para Tamura fue como si el mundo y el tiempo y la vida se hubieran detenido.

¿Cómo podía saber latín aquel *chiang-chün* del Imperio han?

Pero la muchacha recobró su acostumbrada capacidad de reacción rápida y comprendió que no era ni el momento ni la circunstancia para preguntas superfluas, de modo que se centró en lo único sustancial en aquel instante:

—*Potio imperatricis a Yan Ji venenata est.* [La bebida de la emperatriz ha sido envenenada por Yan Ji.] —dijo Tamura con concisión, en un latín sencillo y claro que, sin que ella pudiera entender cómo, Li Kan pareció comprender perfectamente.

La faz del general se tornó pálida de inmediato y los ojos se le abrieron como platos, como si de súbito pudiera ver más allá de todo y de todos. Se volvió y dio varias voces más. Los guardias lo miraron perplejos. Tamura no tenía ni idea de qué podía estar diciendo Li Kan, pero vio cómo los guardias abrían las puertas de la sala de audiencias de par en par a toda velocidad, de modo que cuando Li Kan llegó a ellas ya estaban completamente separadas. Los soldados que habían estado asiendo y arrastrando a Tamura la habían soltado y ella pudo acercarse un poco hacia la puerta, con cuidado, pues no quería que los guardias volvieran a cogerla, pero éstos parecían estatuas. ¿Qué habría dicho Li Kan? La muchacha se aproximó un poco más a la entrada de la sala de audiencias. Desde allí pudo ver cómo el general se abría paso a gritos entre los atónitos funcionarios, consejeros y ministros de la corte del Imperio han. Todos se volvieron hacia él y lo miraron sorprendidos. Para Tamura era evidente que Li Kan estaba actuando contraviniendo todos los usos y las costumbres de la corte, pero fuera lo que fuese que decía, todos se hacían a un lado.

Al apartarse los funcionarios se abrió un largo pasillo por el que Tamura pudo ver cómo Li Kan avanzaba raudo hasta detenerse justo frente a la emperatriz, donde cayó de rodillas y, mirando al suelo, sin atreverse a levantar el rostro hacia su majestad, volvió a decir la frase que llevaba repitiendo desde que ella lo había advertido. Tamura vio que la emperatriz inclinaba un poco la cabeza hacia un lado. En la mano derecha sostenía ya una taza de té. Su majestad imperial miró entonces hacia la taza, luego hacia Li Kan y, de súbito, a lo largo de aquel estrecho pasillo de funcionarios, los ojos de la emperatriz Deng se clavaron en sus propios ojos, sármatas y romanos. Tamura se quedó boquiabierta un instante y luego, como Li Kan, bajó la mirada, pero sólo un momento. Para cuando volvió a alzar los ojos, la muchacha vio que la emperatriz ponía con cuidado la taza en el suelo, al pie de su trono imperial. Nadie decía nada en toda la sala. Li Kan permanecía arrodillado, mirando la taza.

Uno de los gatos de la emperatriz Deng se acercó, ajeno al silencio y a las disputas, traiciones y ansias de los seres humanos y, como tantas otras veces había hecho, se acercó a lamer los restos de comida o bebida que la emperatriz solía ofrecerle. No era un gato ni particularmente querido ni especial, pero la emperatriz favorecía que se les diera de comer y que no se los molestara, pues mantenían el palacio limpio de otros animales mucho más perniciosos.

El pequeño felino pardo llegó junto a la taza de té y bebió de ella.

El silencio de la sala de audiencias del palacio imperial de Loyang era absoluto.

No pasaba nada.

Al gato no pareció agradarle que sólo hubiera té en la taza. Había esperado algo más sustancioso: quizá una galleta, como en otras ocasiones, así que empezó a dar media vuelta y alejarse del trono indiferente al numeroso público que lo observaba con mucha atención.

Tamura perdió de vista al gato entre el tumulto de funcionarios.

La muchacha empezó a sudar profusamente. Quizá todo había sido su imaginación y ahora tendría que afrontar la ira no sólo de los consejeros y del propio general Li Kan, al que, una vez más, habría puesto en ridículo, sino que ahora habría perdido también el favor de la emperatriz por interrumpir una de sus audiencias imperiales y además habría acusado a la favorita del emperador An-ti de intentar asesinar a la emperatriz. De pronto, todos los presentes en la sala parecieron exhalar un «ah» de asombro.

Tamura no podía verlo, pero el gato pardo había caído muerto apenas a cinco pasos del trono de la emperatriz Deng.

122

UN NUEVO EMPERADOR

Faventia, norte de Italia
20 de septiembre de 117 d.C.
Hora sexta

Nigrino acababa de hacer sacrificios a los dioses. Tenía la intuición de que Roma caminaba hacia una nueva guerra civil con batallas tan duras como la que se librara en aquella misma ciudad del noroeste de Italia años atrás, en los tiempos finales de la república, cuando los *optimates* y los populares combatieron por el control del Estado. Metelo derrotó a Cayo Mario, el tío de Julio César, en aquella misma ciudad. ¿Se iban a repetir luchas semejantes?

Nigrino miró al cielo. Estaba nublado. Y sin pájaros. Ningún mensaje que leer por los augures en el aire. Las entrañas de las bestias sacrificadas parecían estar bien y, sin embargo, se sentía inquieto. ¿Cuántas Faventias harían falta para que el nombre de Quieto no fuera cuestionado por nadie? En el Senado tendrían la oposición de Serviano, reconciliado con su cuñado Adriano, pero con Celso y Palma y otros se podría conseguir una votación favorable a Quieto.

—Es la hora —dijo Calvencio Víctor a su espalda.

Nigrino bajó la mirada y cogió las riendas del caballo que le ofrecía el jefe de su guardia personal. Eran tiempos donde moverse por Italia sin un grupo de leales resultaba peligroso. ¿Hasta dónde sería capaz Adriano de llegar para que el Senado reconociera aquel documento del que todos hablaban pero que nadie había visto, en el que supuestamente Trajano lo había adoptado ya en su lecho de muerte nombrándolo sucesor? Nigrino no estaba dispuesto a admitir la legitimidad de aquel documento nunca, y muchos otros tampoco. No importaba que la augusta Plotina dijera que era veraz. Todos sabían que la antigua emperatriz estaba bajo el halo de poder de Adriano. O algo más que eso.

Suspiró.

Había que hacerse fuerte en Italia, controlando el Senado para dar tiempo a que Lucio Quieto llegara a África desde Judea. En Mauritania y África, Quieto podría hacerse con un poderoso ejército con el que retar la autoridad de Adriano.

Nigrino, siempre con el ceño fruncido, montó en su caballo. Lo ideal sería disponer del apoyo de Tercio Juliano, Cincinato y otros oficiales del norte del Imperio para hacerse con el control de las legiones del Danubio o del Rin, pero Nigrino había recibido noticias de que Adriano pensaba dirigirse precisamente hacia el Danubio antes de ir a Roma. Era listo, Adriano.

Nada iba a ser fácil.

Cabalgaban al paso por las calles de Faventia, entre los talleres de alfarería y tejidos que daban fama a la ciudad. Nigrino montaba muy erguido en el caballo y los que lo miraban lo hacían con admiración y silencio. Todos sabían que era uno de los más próximos al gran emperador Trajano, recientemente fallecido, y muchos intuían también un enfrentamiento entre hombres como él y el sobrino del César. El pueblo sabía que Adriano se había autoproclamado emperador pese a que el Senado aún no había dado a conocer su parecer sobre un asunto de tanta importancia. Cualquier cosa podía ocurrir.

Calvencio Víctor y los veinte hombres de la guardia de Nigrino siguieron a su líder hacia la calzada romana que los conduciría de regreso a Roma. Calvencio sabía que su jefe iba al encuentro de Celso y Palma. También era conocedor de lo que su líder planeaba con relación a Adriano. Calvencio había estado con Nigrino desde las campañas de Partia, donde había reemplazado a otro oficial de confianza de Nigrino que había fallecido por enfermedad en su viaje del Danubio a Antioquía. Calvencio había luchado, desde entonces, junto a Nigrino, y éste siempre lo había considerado hombre leal.

Calvencio desenfundó la *spatha* sin hacer ruido. Ninguno de los otros diecinueve jinetes hizo nada por alertar a su líder. Calvencio Víctor le clavó la *spatha* por la espalda. Nigrino se revolvió herido ya de muerte y dio con sus huesos en el suelo desde lo alto del caballo, lo que automáticamente provocó que Calvencio le extrajera la espada del cuerpo, ampliando la herida y partiendo en dos el corazón de Nigrino.

Nigrino apenas tuvo tiempo de volver los ojos hacia Faventia, como si quisiera buscar ayuda. Faventia significaba «brillo entre los dioses». No pudo gritar. Todo su cuerpo se paró de golpe.

Calvencio Víctor desmontó y se acercó al cuerpo del senador abatido para asegurarse de que estaba muerto. No se sentía especialmente orgulloso de aquel acto, pero Serviano y Atiano le habían prometido que el nuevo emperador Adriano sería muy generoso y Calvencio, pese a las tramas de algunos senadores de Roma, tenía la convicción de que el viento soplaba a favor del nuevo autoproclamado emperador que regresaría de Oriente pronto. Siempre le había gustado luchar a favor del viento.

Cesifonte, 20 de septiembre, al atardecer

Osroes miraba hacia el Tigris desde lo alto de las murallas de la ciudad. No era una inspección rutinaria, sino de necesidad: Vologases volvía a atacar desde las posiciones más orientales del debilitado Imperio parto y con su sobrino Sanatruces muerto y su hermano Mitrídates en rebelión en Armenia, nada ni nadie parecía oponérsele en su avance sobre Cesifonte. Osroes sabía que contaba con su propio ejército, el mismo que le había valido para expulsar a su hijo Partamaspates de la ciudad y rehacerse con el poder de nuevo y en solitario en la capital del Imperio parto, pero estaba intranquilo. Igual que nadie había querido ayudar a Partamaspates contra él, ¿cuántos aliados iba a encontrar ahora para luchar contra el eterno enemigo Vologases? Osroes percibía el resentimiento de los ciudadanos de Cesifonte por haber sido abandonados a su suerte cuando el emperador Trajano marchaba sobre la ciudad. ¿No le pagarían con la misma moneda y se mostrarían renuentes a combatir contra Vologases por él? En un asedio necesitaría no sólo a su ejército, sino también el apoyo de la población.

Osroes oteaba el horizonte. El *Šāhān Šāh* había hecho correr aún más rumores sobre las supuestas crueldades de Vologases en Oriente, historias en las que el usurpador mataba niños, violaba mujeres y torturaba hombres lentamente hasta su muerte delante de sus familias. La idea era que el pueblo le prefiriera a él, a Osroes I, pese a sus faltas pasadas, en lugar de a aquel salvaje inmisericorde que se aproximaba, pero aun así el rey de reyes ya no estaba seguro de hasta qué punto todos creían aquellas historias. Tenía que encontrar algo adicional con lo que detener el avance de Vologases antes de que sus tropas aparecieran dibujadas en el perfil del horizonte y fueran visibles desde las murallas de Cesifonte.

Por eso se le había ocurrido la idea de escribir al que todos consideraban ya el nuevo emperador de Roma y reclamarle algo que los romanos tenían y que era suyo, muy suyo. Adriano no era Trajano: quizá se lo devolviera. A cambio de algo. Todo tenía un precio, pero satisfacer a un nuevo César en aquel momento, por una vez, podía tener sentido.

Pero no había respuesta alguna de Occidente. Adriano, por el momento, guardaba silencio. Osroes estaba intranquilo. Su plan se podía resquebrajar. El rey de reyes, desde lo alto de las murallas de Cesifonte, oteaba el horizonte en busca de un mensajero de Roma que no parecía llegar nunca.

Baiae, Campania, sur de Italia
20 de septiembre
Hora octava

Celso había recibido una carta de Nigrino convocándolo a una reunión en Roma en los próximos días. Allí se verían con Palma y otros senadores incómodos con la supuesta adopción de Adriano por parte del moribundo Trajano y por las confusas noticias que llegaban de Oriente, donde se hablaba de que la muerte del César había tenido lugar en extrañas circunstancias, y de una posterior retirada de las legiones de muchas posiciones tanto en la Dacia como en Mesopotamia. Además, nada se sabía de Liviano, el jefe del pretorio, ni de Fédimo, el secretario de Trajano.

Esos silencios eran los que más perturbaban a Celso mientras entraba, ya desnudo, en el gran estanque central de las Termas de Mercurio en Baiae.

Se hundió en el agua cálida y miró hacia lo alto, hacia la bóveda con un gran orificio central en lo alto por el que pasaba aún la última luz del atardecer. Palma preveía unos próximos días, quizá semanas o meses, muy intensos, y había decidido relajarse una última vez en las tibias aguas de aquel complejo termal famoso en todo el Imperio desde tiempos inmemoriales.

Absorbido como estaba por sus pensamientos, no se percató de que los soldados con los que se hacía acompañar últimamente no estaban en ningún punto visible de aquella gran estancia. Tampoco pensó que fuera extraño que hubiera tan poca gente en las termas; lo atribuyó a que en Baiae la mayoría prefería la mañana a la tarde para bañarse.

Celso cerró los ojos y se hundió por completo en las aguas de las Termas de Mercurio.

Al cabo de unos instantes de inmersión para sentirse envuelto por la calidez del abrazo de aquel maravilloso líquido tibio fue a emerger para recuperar el aliento y poder inflar sus pulmones de nuevo de aire, pero, de pronto, alguien lo retuvo bajo el agua. Celso, que aún no acertaba a entender qué estaba pasando, se concentró en oponerse a la fuerza que lo retenía debajo de la superficie, pero no podía liberarse. Alguien lo tenía cogido por los hombros y lo mantenía sin posibilidad de emerger. Abrió los ojos. Sólo vio dos, tres cuerpos quizá, desnudos como el suyo. Lo habían rodeado los otros bañistas. Sacudió las manos en la superficie y salpicó de agua impotente a unos y otros, pero no le permitieron en ningún momento volver a emerger. El aire se le agotaba. Dio un puntapié, dos, pero no se retiraban, sino que otros se sumaban al grupo que lo mantenía sumergido. Abrió la boca a sabiendas de que no debía hacerlo, tragó agua y quiso toser, pero sólo sentía más y más agua por dentro y por fuera, por todas partes...

—Es suficiente —dijo una voz desde fuera del estanque—. Hace rato que ya no mueve las manos.

Los hombres se separaron y el cuerpo del senador Celso se hundió por completo en el agua de las Termas de Mercurio de Baiae. Aún tardaría un rato en flotar.

Tarracina, sur de Italia
20 de septiembre
Hora décima

Palma también había recibido carta de Nigrino convocándolo a una reunión de un grupo de senadores en Roma. En principio había pensado esperar a que Celso llegara desde Baiae y juntos seguir por la Via Appia hasta la capital del Imperio, pero el senador Palma se había sentido incómodo en Tarracina y, al caer la tarde, ordenó a su escolta que lo dispusieran todo para partir.

Viajar de noche no era una buena idea, pero presentía que quedarse quieto en Tarracina podía ser peor.

Salieron de la ciudad y enfilaron por el nuevo camino que Trajano había financiado para que la Via Appia acortara su ruta al aproximarse a Tarracina. ¿Cuándo tendría Roma a otro igual, a otro capaz de mover las legiones por todo el mundo conocido, conseguir una victoria tras otra y, a la vez, preocuparse por las calzadas, la administración, los acueductos, los puentes...? Adriano, en su opinión, igual que para muchos de sus colegas en el Senado, era un enorme paso atrás. Quizá Trajano se había aventurado demasiado en las campañas de Oriente, pero con Quieto al mando, las conquistas se podían afianzar y con esos territorios se conseguiría un enorme caudal de riqueza que repercutiría positivamente en todo el Imperio en poco tiempo. Era una apuesta audaz, pero *fortuna audaces iuvat.*

—Hay alguien allí delante, senador —dijo uno de los hombres dc la escolta.

Palma observó que a unos cien pasos un grupo de jinetes avanzaba hacia ellos. Era peculiar que alguien más quisiera viajar con la noche ya casi sobre ellos, pero en la luz débil del atardecer no se distinguía bien si eran soldados o civiles. No llevaban carro alguno, luego no era probable que fueran comerciantes.

—¿Bandidos? —preguntó Palma a sus hombres, pero cuando se volvió para escuchar su respuesta descubrió que lo habían abandonado. No se habían ido por la calzada —en ese caso habría oído los cascos de los caballos sobre las piedras—: se habían adentrado en el bosque.

Palma miró de nuevo al frente. Los jinetes desconocidos se acercaban al trote.

Ya estaba seguro de que no eran bandidos. Al salir de Tarracina, lo único que había conseguido era adelantar su muerte un par de horas. Desenfundó su espada. Un *legatus* de Trajano muere luchando. Él había conseguido la anexión de Arabia. No podía rendirse como un cobarde.

No le dieron ni esa posibilidad.

Primero fueron los silbidos. De inmediato, las flechas.

Cayó del caballo.

Aún con tres dardos en el cuerpo intentó levantarse.

No pudo.

Para cuando llegaron los jinetes estaba bocarriba con los ojos abiertos.

—Trai... do... res... —dijo.

Le clavaron un *pilum* en el centro del pecho.

Ya no dijo más.

123
—

EL DESTINO DE ARYAZATE

Selinus, Cilicia
Octubre de 117 d.C.

Adriano dejó la carta de Osroes I sobre la mesa del *tablinum*
que usaba a modo de despacho en la residencia que las autoridades de Selinus le habían proporcionado durante su estancia en la ciudad. Después de las ejecuciones del jefe del pretorio, el secretario de Trajano y los pretorianos, nadie en toda la
región osaba poner la más mínima dificultad a Adriano, al
menos mientras estuviera en Asia. Luego ya dictarían los acontecimientos. El nuevo César, no obstante, tenía decidido que
sería él quien dirigiera esos acontecimientos. Dirigir te permite conducir a todos hacia donde tú deseas. Y él tenía claros sus
anhelos.

Adriano percibía la tensión en el ambiente. Había tenido
que derramar sangre y tendría que verter aún más para con-
solidarse como nuevo *Imperator Caesar Augustus*, pero sabía
también que debía emprender acciones en sentido contrario,
actos no virulentos, decisiones que lo reconciliaran con el pasado cercano y también con los enemigos de la frontera. Ambas cosas.

Salió de la estancia, cruzó el atrio y, escoltado por soldados
de su más estricta confianza, una nueva guardia pretoriana,
abandonó la residencia para, dejando atrás el Odeón, los baños y hasta el acueducto de la ciudad, llegar al emplazamiento
donde se estaba levantando ya el monumento funerario a su
tío. Trajano ya había sido incinerado, no allí, sino en Seleucia
de Pieria, y sus cenizas iban ya camino de Roma, custodiadas
por Plotina y Matidia, para la celebración de un gran triunfo y

funeral a la vez. Pero eso no era óbice para que él hiciera levantar un gran templo funerario en memoria de su tío Trajano justo en la ciudad donde éste había fallecido. A fin de cuentas, Selinus, ahora Traianópolis, tendría que ser reconocida y recordada por el Senado y por todo el Imperio eternamente como el lugar donde Trajano había muerto y... había adoptado a Adriano, llamado a ser el nuevo emperador.

Con Plotina lejos, se sentía más libre aún para actuar sin las ataduras de la antigua emperatriz. ¿Querría Plotina aliarse con los senadores amigos de Trajano? Adriano sonrió. Quizá sí, quizá no, pero incluso si así fuera, para cuando ella llegara a Roma, éstos ya no deberían suponer una amenaza a sus planes. Esto es, si Serviano y Salinator hacían lo pactado.

Quien golpea primero, ya se sabe, golpea dos veces.

Luego estaba la misión de Atiano en el sur de Judea. Sin duda lo más complicado y la clave de todo.

Adriano visitó, como hacía cada día, los trabajos del gran cenotafio a su tío sin prestar mucha atención a las explicaciones del arquitecto. Su mente estaba en otros asuntos; ni siquiera recordaba el nombre de quien le hablaba, pero sí constató que se habían allanado los terrenos y que se habían marcado ya los lugares donde se levantarían hasta ciento diez columnas que rodearían el monumento funerario en memoria a Trajano. También habían empezado la excavación en el centro de la llanura de lo que estaba llamado a ser un gran nicho a modo de supuesta tumba del emperador. Tampoco iba a ser un monumento faraónico, pero sí un recuerdo razonable en presupuesto y tamaño para que nadie en Roma pudiera criticarlo por no marcar el lugar donde había muerto el último César. Adriano, además, había ordenado que se acuñaran ya allí mismo algunas monedas con la imagen del monumento en una cara y la de Trajano en la otra. Aunque tenía que destruir la oposición de los más cercanos a Trajano, al mismo tiempo debía consolidar la conexión con su tío. Era una compleja estrategia de búsqueda de equilibrios, entre la sangre y la memoria, entre la traición y la apariencia de lealtad.

En medio de la llanura, rodeado por sus hombres primero y luego por decenas de artesanos que se afanaban en levantar las primeras columnas del monumento, Adriano recordó la carta que le había llegado desde Cesifonte. Osroes y Partia. Adriano había ordenado la retirada de las tropas de Asiria y de todas las ciudades de Mesopotamia en las que aún había fuertes romanos. También había dejado todo el reino de Osroene en manos del defenestrado Partamaspates, el cobarde hijo de Osroes que, huyendo de Cesifonte, incapaz de enfrentarse contra su padre, había buscado ayuda en él. Adriano lo había nombrado rey de Osroene, con capital en la destruida Edesa. Siempre era mejor tener a un cobarde como vecino que a un intrigante como el propio Osroes. Todo volvía al final al eterno rey de reyes de Partia. El nuevo emperador se dirigió a uno de sus oficiales.

—Llamad a la princesa Aryazate. —Y como vio que el nuevo pretoriano no parecía entender, añadió un comentario—: La joven que hemos traído hasta aquí en el barco desde Antioquía.

La muchacha había sido llevada desde Cesifonte hasta Antioquía por Trajano primero y luego, por orden del propio Adriano, había sido conducida desde la capital de Siria hasta Selinus. La joven era un rehén de lujo que Adriano había pensado que podía serle útil en algún momento, y ese momento había llegado.

Selinus
Hora duodécima

Estaba anocheciendo cuando Aryazate entró en el atrio de la residencia de quien todos consideraban ya nuevo emperador de Roma. La joven albergaba la esperanza de que el César planeara retomar las acciones bélicas contra el Šāhān Šāh. Ver sufrir a su padre, rodeada Cesifonte una vez más por legiones romanas, era su más preciada fantasía, incluso si eso conllevaba de nuevo la derrota de los guerreros partos de su dinastía. A veces se sentía confusa sobre sus propios sentimientos. Una de las cosas que más había temido en un principio, tras la muerte de Trajano, era ser conducida a Roma con las cenizas del viejo emperador. La muchacha, a falta de nadie más con quien hablar, se entretenía conversando cuanto podía con las esclavas griegas que se habían puesto a su disposición en reconocimiento de que, aunque prisionera, era una princesa. Éstas le habían explicado que se preparaba un gran desfile que los romanos llamaban *triunfo* para conmemorar las victorias de Trajano sobre Osroes y que allí se exhibirían todo tipo de despojos de guerra, incluidos rehenes y esclavos. Ser paseada por las calles de Roma como una vulgar prisionera de guerra encadenada la había atemorizado durante semanas, y, hasta cierto punto, Aryazate pensaba que las esclavas habían disfrutado un poco, o mucho, insuflando ese miedo en sus venas.

Pero las cenizas de Trajano partieron hacia la lejana Roma y ella seguía allí. ¿Por qué la habría llamado el nuevo emperador? Seguramente para hablar sobre su futuro. El nuevo César partiría pronto hacia Occidente. ¿Iba ir con él? ¿Como prisionera, como esclava, como princesa?

—Tu padre, Osroes, te reclama —le anunció Adriano sin más preámbulos desde un *triclinium* en que estaba recostado.

La muchacha, en pie frente a él, lo miraba con los ojos muy abiertos y en silencio. Él había hablado en griego y ella lo entendió perfectamente, pero su silencio pareció confundir a Adriano.

—¿Me entiendes cuando te hablo? —inquirió Adriano.

—Sí, César —respondió ella.

—Bien —dijo él con un suspiro—. Entonces te diré lo que vamos a hacer. Mi interés ahora es mantener la paz con Partia, de forma que te voy a devolver a tu padre, a quien espero que le dirás que has sido tratada correctamente, tanto por parte de mi tío ya fallecido como por mí. Partirás hacia Cesifonte...

Pero Aryazate se arrodilló ante el César, acercándose tanto al *triclinium* que puso sus pequeñas manos de dedos finos y suaves sobre el mueble, de modo que los guardias se sintieron alarmados y desenfundaron las espadas de inmediato. Adriano levantó la mano para que se detuvieran. La muchacha hablaba en griego, pero tan rápido que a Adriano le costaba seguirla bien y agachaba la cabeza para oírla mejor.

—Por lo que más quiera el nuevo emperador de Roma,

por todos sus sagrados dioses y sus familiares: que no se me envíe de regreso a Cesifonte. A mi padre no, por Ahura Mazda, por las enseñanzas de Zoroastro y por todos sus dioses, por ese Júpiter al que tanto adoran en Roma, que no se me devuelva a mi padre. Eso nunca. ¡Nunca!

Adriano conocía la historia de las ejecuciones masivas de mujeres y niños del séquito real parto cuando su tío entró en Cesifonte y que sólo aquella princesa se las había ingeniado para sobrevivir. Podía comprender que la muchacha no quisiera retornar hacia un padre que había sido capaz, en un momento de crisis, de ordenar su muerte, pero ¿a quién le interesaba satisfacer? ¿A aquella muchacha aterrada que, por muy princesa que fuera, ningún poder tenía contra él? ¿O a aquel maldito emperador parto que después de tantas batallas, ciudades conquistadas y luego perdidas, después de tantos legionarios muertos, volvía a estar sentado en el trono de Cesifonte? Adriano olvidó que al menos el trono ya no era de oro macizo, pues ése le había sido arrebatado por Trajano y estaba ya en Roma esperando desfilar ante todo el pueblo. La memoria, la de todos, es selectiva. La de Adriano, mucho.

—Lo siento, princesa, pero satisfaré el deseo de tu padre —respondió el César con cierto tono de aburrimiento. Aquellos ruegos le parecían infantiles, impropios de una mujer de dinastía real y, desde luego, inoportunos.

—¡No, no, no! —empezó entonces ella a gritar y esta vez se acercó aún más, como si fuera a abrazar al César.

Aquí los nuevos pretorianos del emperador se aproximaron con rapidez, cogieron a la princesa por los hombros y tiraron de ella para alejarla del César. Esta vez Adriano no hizo nada para detenerlos. Cuando Aryazate vio que todos sus ruegos eran inútiles para ablandar al nuevo emperador, transformó y concentró toda su rabia en amenazas:

—¡Imploraré a Ahura Mazda eternamente que un día alguien te arrebate lo que más quieras, augusto! ¡Lo rogaré a mi dios cada mañana y cada noche y un día Ahura Mazda, todopoderoso, arrancará al nuevo César lo que el emperador romano más adore!

Adriano no le dio importancia a aquella maldición.

—¡Lleváosla! —exclamó Adriano con desdén mientras se llevaba la copa de vino a la boca.

Bebió un buen trago. A sus oídos llegaban aún los gritos desesperados de aquella estúpida princesa que parecía proferir ahora maldiciones no sólo en griego, sino también en parto. Más tonterías pueriles.

Aún habrían de pasar años antes de que en medio de las lágrimas, junto al cuerpo de su amado Antinoo, Adriano recordara a Aryazate y comprendiera que la fuerza del odio de una princesa parta era capaz de atravesar el tiempo y la distancia para retornar y morder con la furia de la venganza.

Pero en aquel momento, Adriano estaba feliz. Todo marchaba según sus planes.

124
—

LA DETENCIÓN DE QUIETO

Sur de Judea
Noviembre de 117 d.C.

Lucio Quieto vio a aquel jinete acercándose al galope. No le ponía nervioso. Lo que le reconcomía por dentro era que sus patrullas habían detectado dos legiones enteras desplazadas desde Egipto hasta la frontera entre Judea y Arabia y él no había sido informado de ese importante movimiento de tropas por nadie.

Se cubrió la frente con la mano para protegerse del sol.

El jinete seguía acercándose.

Dos legiones enteras en la frontera sur de Judea.

¿Por qué?

La guerra contra la rebelión judía en la región había llegado prácticamente a su término. Apenas quedaban algunas revueltas en lugares remotos y aislados de la provincia. Jerusalén estaba sometida. A sangre y fuego. Los judíos no le habían dejado otra opción. Y sus líderes Julián y Papo habían sido detenidos y ejecutados. Con la rebelión descabezada todo había sido más fácil. Quieto aún recordaba su última conversación con aquellos líderes fanáticos en Lida:

—*Si vuestro dios es tan poderoso como decís, que os rescate de mis manos* —les había dicho él cansado de sus quejas e insultos hacia Trajano.

—*Tú ni siquiera eres merecedor de que Dios haga un milagro por tu causa.* —Eso le habían respondido y aún se habían atrevido a añadir más—: *Pues ni tan siquiera eres un gobernante independiente, sino el siervo de otro superior.*[91]

91. La sección en cursiva es transcripción literal del diálogo según vie-

953

Eso le dijeron.

Estaban muertos.

Sin embargo, aquel mensajero romano que se acercaba y, sobre todo, aquellas dos legiones llegadas desde Egipto, justo ahora que él pensaba dirigirse de regreso a su tierra, a Mauritania, no presagiaban nada bueno. Su idea era confirmar que el levantamiento judío también se hubiera controlado en Egipto y luego seguir hacia África. Pero ahora dos legiones enteras, enviadas no sabía por quién, se interponían en su ruta. Y en la de su caballería. Trescientos jinetes, los mejores del ejército imperial de Roma. Quieto no hacía ya ni un solo desplazamiento sin aquellos jinetes que le eran completamente leales. Con ellos había combatido en la Dacia, en Armenia, en Mesopotamia, en Osroene, en Asiria, en el Tigris y en Partia entera. Le seguirían hasta el fin del mundo.

Frunció aún más el ceño.

¿Por eso habían enviado dos legiones enteras? ¿Quién estaba al mando?

—¿De que se tratará? —preguntó Tiberio Claudio Máximo, el decurión que actuaba como segundo en el mando en aquella caballería de élite. Tiberio había sido licenciado con grandes honores apenas hacía unos meses, pero, de camino a Grecia, ante la rebelión judía, se había reincorporado a la caballería de Quieto por petición de éste, quien, según le había dicho, necesitaba de los mejores hombres para acabar con aquella revuelta.

En aquel momento, la rebelión judía ya estaba, *de facto*, resuelta, pero todo se había complicado con la enfermedad del César y el acceso al grado de *imperator* de Adriano. Sin buscarlo, Tiberio se veía envuelto en una confrontación entre Adriano y los senadores y *legati* amigos de Trajano, entre los que destacaba, por encima de todos, el propio Lucio Quieto. A Tiberio también le extrañaba la aparición de aquellas dos legiones llegadas desde Egipto sin aviso alguno.

---

ne reflejado en *History of the Jews* de Heinrich Graetz (1891). En otras versiones Julián y Papo se salvan de la sentencia a muerte.

—¿Serán refuerzos que llegan tarde para asistirnos en la lucha contra los judíos? —añadió Tiberio.

—No lo sé, pero saldremos de dudas de inmediato —respondió Quieto sin dejar de mirar hacia el mensajero, que ya estaba llegando a su posición.

Tiberio era un hombre de su máxima confianza y jinete de gran valor: fue el que dio muerte ni más ni menos que al mismísimo Decébalo en la Dacia. Era uno de esos hombres con los que cualquiera se sentía más seguro al lado si entrabas en combate cuerpo a cuerpo. Sabías que nunca iba ni a retroceder ni a dejarte solo. Por eso Quieto lo llamó de nuevo a filas. Lo necesitaba.

—¡Ave, Lucio Quieto! —dijo el mensajero sin bajar del caballo, sin añadir la palabra *legatus* al final y presentando un papiro doblado que acercó alargando el brazo.

Quieto cogió el mensaje, rompió el sello de cera con un dedo y leyó con rapidez, también montado en su caballo.

—Es de Atiano —dijo Quieto sin dejar de mirar el papiro, como si necesitara leerlo varias veces para confirmar lo que allí se decía—. Me informa de que el nuevo emperador Adriano me reclama en Selinus, donde ha fallecido Trajano. Quiere que deje de dirigir las operaciones militares en Judea y Egipto y que retorne a Roma, al Senado, pero antes el nuevo augusto quiere verme en su residencia de Selinus.

Tiberio Máximo asintió, pero no parecía que las noticias le gustaran.

—Espera aquí —dijo Quieto al mensajero y tiró de las riendas para alejar su caballo unos pasos de aquel enviado. Tiberio lo siguió. Un poco más allá estaban los trescientos jinetes en perfecta formación, aguardando órdenes.

Una vez que estuvieron a una distancia prudente del mensajero, Lucio Quieto volvió a hablar.

—¡Por Cástor y Pólux, esas dos legiones están bajo el control de Atiano!

—Y Atiano es el perro de presa del nuevo César —apostilló Tiberio Máximo con rabia.

—Así es. Y desean que vaya a Selinus —añadió Quieto con ira mal contenida.

—Eso está al norte.

—Sí, y nos aleja de nuestro objetivo, de Mauritania —confirmó Quieto.

Tras haber recibido información confusa sobre las posibles muertes de Celso, Palma y Nigrino en Italia, Lucio Quieto tenía muy claro que debía refugiarse —y si era posible hacerse fuerte—, en Mauritania y África, provincias en donde tenía familiares, amigos y muchos ciudadanos proclives a apoyarlo en una rebelión contra Adriano. Las ejecuciones de los tres senadores amigos de Trajano, si realmente habían tenido lugar, habrían indispuesto a gran parte del Senado contra Adriano...

—El nuevo emperador quiere evitar a toda costa que el *legatus* Quieto llegue a Mauritania —dijo Tiberio como si le leyera el pensamiento.

—En efecto —admitió el aludido, pero acto seguido suspiró profundamente antes de seguir hablando—. Pero son dos legiones, Tiberio. No tenemos ni una sola oportunidad. Adriano es un miserable y un traidor. Estoy seguro de que no va a luchar por recuperar las conquistas de Trajano. No tiene ni las agallas ni la inteligencia para saber cómo retener esas nuevas provincias que tanto dinero pueden suponer en un futuro próximo. Trajano se metió en esta guerra con fines muy concretos y ahora que hemos superado primero la rebelión de Osroene y Mesopotamia y luego también la de los judíos, va a ser el propio Adriano el que se retire sin más.

—Un cobarde —sentenció Tiberio.

—Pero un cobarde listo: está usando a Atiano para todo el trabajo sucio aquí en Oriente e imagino que a Serviano, su cuñado, en Roma.

—A ambos les habrá prometido grandes cosas.

—De eso puedes estar bien seguro, pero todo vuelve a lo mismo —insistió Lucio Quieto arrugando el papiro con el maldito mensaje entre los dedos de su mano derecha—. Dos legiones. No tenemos ninguna posibilidad. ¡Por Hércules! ¡He sido un imbécil! Debería haber previsto esto antes. Debería haber salido de Jerusalén incluso antes de haber terminado con la rebelión y dejar esos problemas para Adriano mientras nosotros nos preparábamos en Mauritania para levantarnos contra él, pero ahora es tarde para todo. Es tarde hasta para lamentarse.

—Podemos luchar —sugirió Tiberio.

—Es un suicidio que esta fuerza de caballería no merece.

—Podemos hacerles mucho daño —añadió Tiberio.

—Pero sin posibilidad de victoria, decurión. Amigo mío, te tengo en demasiada estima a ti y al resto de los hombres. No os puedo ordenar eso. No sería noble que te pidiera que te reincorporaras a mi caballería para que luego tengas que morir por mí. Para luchar por Roma sí, para suicidarte en mi defensa, no. Estoy seguro de que puedo negociar una entrega pactada. Es a mí a quien quiere Atiano, a quien persigue Adriano. A vosotros os dejará en paz si no intervenís. En el fondo sabe que sois una unidad de caballería muy útil. Os enviará a alguna frontera lejana. Quizá a Britania o Germania, pero con eso podéis vivir. En unos años bajo Adriano, vuestros servicios bajo mi mando, bajo el mando de Trajano, quedarán olvidados y seréis hombres bien vistos en la nueva Roma que está naciendo sobre la sangre de Celso, Palma y Nigrino.

—Pero Adriano ejecutará al *legatus* Quieto en cuanto llegue a Selinus, quizá antes...

Pero Quieto ya se alejaba en busca del mensajero sin tan siquiera dar opción a Tiberio Máximo para que contraargumentara. El decurión azuzó su caballo. Cuando llegó junto a su superior, el enviado ya daba media vuelta y galopaba en dirección sur.

Campamento militar romano entre la frontera de Arabia y Judea junto a la costa del mar Mediterráneo

—Quiere hablar —dijo Clemenciano, nuevo gobernador de Judea por designación de Adriano y *legatus* al mando de aquellas legiones de Egipto junto con Atiano, el enviado del nuevo César para detener a Lucio Quieto antes de que abandonara la provincia en dirección a Mauritania.

Publio Atiano cabeceó afirmativamente antes de hablar:

—Sea, pues, negociaremos. Tú espérame aquí.

—Vienen tropas —dijo Tiberio.

—Ya imaginaba que no vendría solo, pero no pensaba que fuera a tener tanto miedo: trae al menos una cohorte —respondió Quieto.

—La primera cohorte —precisó Tiberio—, pues cuento más ochocientos que quinientos legionarios aproximándose.

—Permaneceremos en nuestra posición —dijo Quieto.

Pasó un rato hasta que las tropas de infantería se detuvieron en seco a no más de mil pasos.

—Se adelanta alguien a caballo y va solo —dijo Tiberio.

—Es Atiano. Esperadme aquí.

De nuevo no hubo tiempo para réplica alguna.

Publio Atiano y Lucio Quieto se encontraron a una distancia equidistante de la primera cohorte de la primera legión del ejército enviado por Adriano y de la caballería de élite del líder norteafricano.

—Te escucho —dijo Atiano en cuanto ambos estuvieron apenas a cinco pasos de distancia.

Quieto asintió. Otro miserable, como Adriano, pero iba al grano. Eso le pareció bien.

—Me alegro de que no te andes con rodeos —empezó Quieto sin usar ningún título de respeto ante su interlocutor, que también se había saltado todas las formalidades—. No hay nada que odie más en este mundo que los que se andan por las ramas. Bueno, sí. Hay algo que desprecio más: a los traidores.

Atiano no dijo nada. Ni sonrió ni hizo tampoco mueca alguna de enfado. Permaneció impasible. Quieto comprendió que estaba ante un perro de presa eficaz que se concentraba en sus objetivos. Nada lo distraería hasta cumplir las órdenes recibidas.

—Me entregaré a ti si se respeta la vida de mis hombres —dijo entonces Quieto.

—Nadie te está arrestando —opuso Atiano—. El César simplemente te reclama en Selinus.

—Por Hércules, sé que estás acostumbrado a mentir a los estúpidos, pero no insultes mi inteligencia —replicó Quieto con desdén y escupió en el suelo—. Otra cosa es que no tengas autoridad suficiente para negociar esto que te pido. No sé si trato con un perro de presa o sólo con un perro faldero de Adriano.

—Se te ha olvidado decir *augusto* delante del nombre del nuevo emperador —le recriminó Atiano, por primera vez, algo exasperado.

Ahora fue Lucio Quieto el que no quiso responder.

El silencio empezó a hacerse incómodo para los dos. El sol estaba en lo alto. Hacía un calor insoportable pese a que ya estuviera bien entrado el otoño. Parecía que allí nunca llegaba el frío. Sólo por las noches.

—Sí que tengo autoridad para aceptar lo que propones —dijo, al fin, Atiano.

—Entonces... ¿aceptas?

—De acuerdo —respondió sin pestañear Atiano—. Despídete de tus hombres y entrégate solo. Si haces eso, te juro por Júpiter que tu caballería será respetada. Nada tiene el César contra ellos. Son buenos jinetes.

—Son los mejores de la caballería de Roma —apuntó Quieto—, pero no te considero capacitado para debatir sobre la habilidad de mis hombres ni tengo deseo alguno de alargar esta conversación llena de traición al gran Trajano, un César de verdad, como no lo habrá nunca más. Me despediré de mis jinetes y regresaré solo.

En ese momento Lucio Quieto se dio cuenta de que el horizonte, por detrás de la cohorte que había acompañado a Atiano, empezaba a llenarse de más y más legionarios. Miró hacia atrás y también vio más legionarios, y lo mismo si se volvía hacia Oriente. Sólo el oeste, donde se vislumbraba el mar, permanecía sin soldados. Estaban rodeados, con el Mediterráneo como única salida. Una ruta imposible sin barcos.

—¿Te has traído las dos legiones enteras contigo hasta aquí? —preguntó Quieto.

—Subestimar a alguien nunca ha sido mi costumbre —se explicó Atiano.

Lucio Quieto asintió. Si había albergado alguna mínima esperanza, como la de huir al galope, ésta acababa de ser aniquilada. Carraspeó, volvió a escupir en el suelo y sin decir nada más, sin tan siquiera saludar formalmente al enviado del emperador Adriano, tiró de las riendas de su caballo y dio media vuelta para, al trote, regresar, por última vez, junto a sus hombres.

125

TRES OPCIONES PARA TAMURA

Loyang
Octubre de 117 d.C.

La emperatriz Deng hablaba a intervalos regulares, haciendo pausas en las que Fan Chun podía ir traduciendo al sánscrito la esencia de lo que su majestad estaba explicando a Tamura. Por su parte la emperatriz aprovechaba los momentos en los que el consejero traducía para beber un poco de té muy caliente en pequeños sorbos. Té sin veneno, gracias a que se habían adoptado mayores medidas de seguridad desde que la joven sármata salvara la vida de su majestad. Entre otras enviar a Yan Ji lejos de la corte.

—Su majestad te ha hecho llamar, joven mensajera de Da Qin —dijo Fan Chun a una Tamura que escuchaba con enorme interés—, porque te tiene mucho aprecio. Este respeto te lo has ganado de dos formas fundamentales, joven mensajera: primero por conseguir cruzar el mundo conocido y desconocido para traer un regalo y entregar un mensaje de tu poderoso emperador. Has tenido éxito en un viaje donde hasta los más osados hombres han fracasado, y la emperatriz se congratula en que sea una mujer la que haya conseguido esta hazaña. En segundo lugar, te has ganado el afecto de su majestad al intervenir en un momento clave, cuando intentaban envenenarla con su té. Por todo ello, la emperatriz Deng ha pensado mucho en el futuro de la mensajera de Da Qin y quiere presentarte tres opciones para que elijas tu camino con libertad.

Tamura miraba a Fan Chun, pero en cuanto éste terminó de hablar, él volvió los ojos hacia la faz maquillada de blanco de la emperatriz. La muchacha asintió entonces mirando un instante a la emperatriz.

Deng volvió a hablar un rato. Calló. Cogió de nuevo su taza de té. Fan Chun reinició la traducción.

—Su majestad ha reunido información suficiente gracias a nuestros guerreros en la frontera e informes de diferentes caravanas de la Ruta de la Seda como para saber que el emperador de Da Qin, esto es, tu señor, se está retirando del Imperio an-shi, abandonando sus conquistas. Hay incluso quien dice que el gran emperador está muy enfermo o ha muerto. Sea como sea, tendrá un sucesor. La cuestión es que la primera posibilidad sobre tu futuro es que retornes a Da Qin con una respuesta para su emperador: un mensaje de parte de la propia emperatriz del Imperio han.

Tamura miraba al suelo mientras escuchaba atenta. Tres opciones. Tenía que elegir una. Podía oír la voz de su majestad hablando de nuevo. La joven mantuvo la mirada baja, hasta que el viejo *yu-shih chung-ch'eng* volvió a hablar.

—La segunda opción es que permanezcas aquí, en la corte, a mi lado, donde serás siempre respetada y donde podrás seguir tu instrucción con preceptores adecuados de nuestra lengua y nuestra cultura. A su majestad le encantará poder compartir contigo algunas tardes y, cuando hables bien nuestro idioma, departir sobre los misterios de Da Qin y sobre todos los lugares que has visitado en tu largo viaje: An-shi, Shendú, el Imperio *Yuegzhi* y tantos otros reinos y ciudades que has conocido en tu periplo.[92]

Tamura volvió a asentir. Esperaba que su majestad Deng hablara de nuevo, pero la emperatriz callaba.

—¿Cuál es la tercera... cosa... posible... que tengo, majestad? —se atrevió a preguntar Tamura en un mal chino, pues desconocía la palabra «opción». Ni siquiera estaba segura de haber entonado bien para no resultar ofensiva, pero vio que la emperatriz sonreía antes de volver a hablar. En esta ocasión su parlamento fue muy breve.

92. An-shi es Partia, Shendu la India y el Imperio *yuegzi*, los kushan de Asia central.

Fan Chun tradujo de inmediato.

—Su majestad se pregunta si no te satisface alguna de esas dos posibilidades. Porque si así fuera, ya no haría falta tener en cuenta la tercera y última opción.

Tamura parpadeaba.

Marchar de regreso a Roma o quedarse en Loyang. No tenía ni idea de qué hacer. Estaba confusa, perdida. Se pasó una mano por el rostro suave de piel tersa y joven. No sabía qué hacer. ¿A quién preguntar?

126

LA CABALLERÍA DE QUIETO

Sur de Judea
Otoño de 117 d.C.

—¡Voy a entregarme y, por Cástor y Pólux y todos los dioses, no quiero que intentéis nada! —ordenó Lucio Quieto a sus hombres, que lo miraban muy serios, asiendo las riendas de sus caballos con fuerza, inmóviles, casi como estatuas marmóreas de un ejército fantasma que de pronto, sin líder, quedara condenado a vagar por el mundo sin señor ni dueño.

—*Legatus...* —empezó a decir Tiberio Claudio Máximo, pero Quieto lo interrumpió.

—Decurión, ya lo hemos hablado antes. No tenemos ni una sola posibilidad: estamos rodeados. Sólo me quieren a mí. He pactado con Atiano, ese miserable, que nada se haga contra vosotros. Seréis reasignados a alguna misión en una provincia lejana de Oriente y de África. Las brumas de Britania o Germania os esperan. —Guardó unos instantes de silencio antes de continuar—. Ha sido un honor dirigir la mejor caballería del mundo. En los bosques de la Dacia, en las montañas de Armenia o luchando contra los mismísimos *catafractos* de Partia, siempre habéis salido victoriosos. Las conquistas de Trajano han encontrado en vosotros un poderoso brazo ejecutor de sus órdenes. Aunque sean otros los que os manden ahora, continuáis pensando en el gran Trajano. Imaginad que seguís bajo sus órdenes pues, estoy seguro, el espíritu del emperador os acompañará hasta los confines del Imperio.

No dijo más. Dio media vuelta y empezó a cabalgar al paso hacia el lugar donde se encontraba Atiano con la primera cohorte de su ejército.

Publio Acilio Atiano sonrió mientras veía cómo el gran líder de la caballería romana se separaba, poco a poco, de sus hombres. No tenía claro que Adriano fuera a respetar su acuerdo de no atentar contra la vida de aquellos jinetes que ahora abandonaban a su jefe de caballería, bajo cuyo mando habían combatido durante tantos años, pero si el nuevo emperador cumplía o no lo pactado, no era asunto suyo. Su misión era conducir a Selinus a Lucio Quieto solo y desarmado y, si no se entregaba, acabar con él y con todos aquellos que se opusieran a su arresto. Parecía que iba a ser la primera de las dos opciones. En la vida todo es elegir. Quieto podía rendirse o luchar, y entregarse era lo sensato.

Atiano estaba satisfecho. Ufano. Todo había sido mucho más fácil de lo que había anticipado. No había contado con el amor de un *legatus* noble hacia sus hombres. No había pensado que Lucio Quieto fuera a ser capaz de negociar su entrega a cambio de que no se actuara contra sus soldados. Atiano había estado persuadido de que Quieto habría reaccionado como él mismo habría hecho: pidiendo a sus hombres que lucharan hasta el final. En fin. Quieto era hombre noble, era innegable, pero poco práctico. Cierto que no tenían ni él ni sus jinetes ni una sola posibilidad contra dos legiones, pero... Publio Acilio Atiano borró la sonrisa de su rostro.

—¿Qué hacen? —preguntó de forma retórica. No esperaba respuesta de nadie. Se volvió rápidamente hacia sus oficiales y empezó a gritar—: ¡Formación de ataque, maldita sea, formación de ataque!

Y es que tras Lucio Quieto, pese a las órdenes dadas por éste, los trescientos jinetes de su caballería habían empezado a avanzar siguiendo a su *legatus*. Quieto vio los movimientos de las tropas de Atiano y, con el ceño fruncido, miró hacia atrás, por encima del hombro. Vio entonces que sus hombres, rebelándose contra sus órdenes, lo seguían en un bloque compacto.

Lucio Quieto se detuvo y lo mismo hicieron los trescientos jinetes.

—¡¿Estáis locos?! —les gritó—. ¡Acabarán conmigo y luego con todos vosotros! ¡Por Hércules! ¡No deis ni un solo paso más!

Y azuzó otra vez a su caballo, pero mirando hacia atrás para comprobar si sus hombres lo obedecían.

No lo hacían.

Avanzaban todos de nuevo, como una gran falange de caballería, tras la estela de su líder.

Lucio Quieto volvió a detenerse.

—¡Os he dado una orden! ¡Que nadie vuelva a avanzar! —les espetó de nuevo, con rabia, con furia entremezclada, no obstante, con cierta conmoción de sentimientos. Sus hombres se negaban a abandonarlo. Estaban dispuestos a seguirlo a donde fuera. Pero ¿eran conscientes de que cabalgaban hacia un suicidio colectivo?—. ¿Acaso ya no obedecéis mis órdenes? —les preguntó entre iracundo y emocionado.

Tiberio Claudio Máximo agitó las riendas de su caballo y se adelantó al resto hasta llegar a la altura donde se encontraba el *legatus*. Y habló en voz bien alta, para que todos los demás jinetes pudieran oírlo.

—¡Con el debido respeto, *legatus*! ¡Esa orden, la de permanecer impasibles mientras nuestro jefe es detenido por Atiano, es la única orden que nunca cumpliremos! ¡Cualquier otra instrucción de nuestro jefe de caballería será seguida hasta el final...! ¡Hasta la última gota de nuestra sangre!

Lucio Quieto soltó una de las riendas y se pasó la mano derecha por el cogote, acariciándolo varias veces al tiempo que miraba al suelo.

—Sabes que no tenemos ninguna opción —insistió Quieto mirando al decurión fijamente a los ojos.

—Ésa, mi *legatus*, no es la cuestión —respondió Tiberio.

—¿Ah no? ¿Y cuál es la cuestión?

—La cuestión es que nunca combatiremos bajo el mando de Adriano.

—Pues, por todos los dioses, moriréis aquí, hoy, todos.

—Yo ya he encargado mi tumba —respondió Tiberio Claudio Máximo. No era una figura retórica, sino que ya había enviado el texto que quería que figurara en la misma por carta a un artesano de Filipos, en Grecia, donde había pensado retirarse, pues allí tenía familiares y acceso a tierras de cultivo propias, cuando sobrevino la rebelión judía y todos sus planes se truncaron.

Lucio Quieto negaba con la cabeza.

—¿Y el resto? —preguntó el *legatus*—. ¿También han comprado tumbas?

—Cada uno a su manera, pero todos están de acuerdo en seguir a nuestro *legatus* hasta el fin.

Retaguardia de las legiones

Mientras tenía lugar aquel debate, Atiano había aprovechado para situarse en la retaguardia de sus tropas, junto con Clemenciano, y disponer que varias cohortes se fueran aproximando hacia la caballería de Quieto, cerrando el cuadrado alrededor del enemigo, con tres lados repletos de legionarios y un cuarto limitado por la playa. Los soldados de los extremos norte y sur se extendían hasta que una parte de ellos se hundía en el agua del mar. Atiano quería asegurarse de que ningún jinete podría escapar de aquel cerco galopando por la playa.

—Va a ser como pescar —dijo Clemenciano.

—Sólo que los peces no tienen armas —respondió Atiano muy serio—. Que se preparen los arqueros por detrás de las cohortes de vanguardia.

Centro del cuadrado

—Esto se parece a Carrhae —dijo al fin Lucio Quieto—. Al final, después de todo, parece que vamos a acabar como la maldita legión perdida. Primero vendrá una lluvia de flechas, luego los *pila* de las cohortes de primera línea. Lo único razonable es lanzarnos contra un punto concreto e intentar romper la línea del enemigo para poder escapar al galope, lo ideal en dirección sur.

—Me parece un buen plan... César —respondió el decurión de forma categórica. Como vio que el *legatus* se sorprendía añadió unas palabras—: Todos nosotros sabemos que el emperador Trajano pensaba en el *legatus* como futuro César. Adriano ha manipulado todo para que parezca que él es el elegido, pero para nosotros, Lucio Quieto es el único *Imperator Caesar Augustus*. Además, si nos quieren matar a todos es porque Adriano ve en el *legatus* Lucio Quieto al auténtico César.

Quieto inspiró profundamente. Era un día de verdades. Luego miró a su alrededor y, por fin, detuvo sus ojos en el decurión.

—No parece que el mío vaya a ser un largo principado, Tiberio. Pero los enemigos se acercan. Se me ocurre...

Quieto calló.

—¿Qué, augusto? —preguntó Tiberio con interés. Había detectado un tono especial en la última frase de su superior: el mismo timbre de voz que ponía cuando tenía una buena idea de estrategia.

—Se me ocurre que nos concentremos en el flanco sur junto al mar. Los caballos pueden moverse con más destreza que un hombre si están sólo un poco sumergidos en el agua, mientras que los legionarios, con todo el equipo, serán muy torpes en la playa. Quizá en ese punto podamos abrir una brecha. Es muy difícil, seguramente imposible, pero es lo único que nos queda.

Tiberio Claudio Máximo asintió una vez.

Lucio Quieto desenfundó su larga *spatha*.

—Por Roma —dijo Quieto en voz baja mirando a Tiberio—. Y por el César Trajano.

—Y por el emperador Lucio Quieto —añadió Tiberio.

—Vamos allá —aceptó el norteafricano sacudiendo la cabeza—. Estamos locos. Todos.

El *legatus* alzó el arma al cielo. El decurión lo imitó y ambos se lanzaron al galope en dirección al mar, en diagonal, buscando el punto donde los legionarios que se les oponían hundían sus sandalias en la arena húmeda de la playa.

Retaguardia de las legiones

—¡Que disparen los arqueros! —ordenó Atiano.

—No tienen ninguna oportunidad —dijo a su espalda Clemenciano.

Publio Acilio Atiano no dijo nada, ni siquiera se volvió para mirar a su interlocutor.

Caballería de Quieto

Primero fueron las flechas y luego los *pila* de las cohortes, tal y como el propio Lucio Quieto había anticipado. Muchos jinetes fueron abatidos y otros heridos en piernas y brazos. Los caballos atravesados por dardos o lanzas se derrumbaban y relinchaban como bestias malheridas, pero, pese a los caídos y los alcanzados por las armas arrojadizas de las legiones, la mayoría de los jinetes llegó hasta la primera línea de las cohortes, ya en la playa. El combate que se trabó allí fue encarnizado e inmisericorde, en especial por parte de los hombres de Quieto, enfurecidos por la traición, por los amigos heridos, por los compañeros muertos, por la rabia de verse rodeados no ya por bárbaros sino por tropas legionarias.

Las espadas de los norteafricanos volaban estrellándose contra las cabezas de los soldados enviados por Adriano desde la tranquilidad de su residencia provisional en Selinus. Las armas chocaban contra los cascos de los legionarios y los yelmos de metal reventaban o se mostraban insuficientes ante la brutalidad de los golpes de aquella caballería herida mortalmente, pero que se negaba a ser aniquilada por completo. La primera línea de legionarios de la playa fue barrida, y la segunda y la tercera y la cuarta y la quinta. Todo un manípulo destrozado, casi una cohorte completa... Los jinetes se abrían paso dirigidos por Quieto, matando, pisando con sus caballos a los legionarios abatidos o heridos.

El agua del mar se tiñó de rojo oscuro.

Retaguardia de las legiones

—¡Enviad nuestra caballería! —aulló entonces Atiano.

Clemenciano, que seguía a su espalda, ya no decía nada. Estaba perplejo. Los jinetes de Quieto estaban abriendo una brecha y se encontraban a punto de superar la posición de las cohortes más próximas a la playa.

Caballería norteafricana

—¡Aghhh! —gritó Quieto.

Un legionario había conseguido herirlo en una pierna. El *legatus* le hundió su *spatha* en el hombro y Tiberio, que estaba a su lado, lo remató por la espalda. El decurión no tuvo ningún remilgo por acometer aquella acción: a los traidores se los mata hasta por la espalda, de lado, a mordiscos si es necesario.

—¡Hércules! —aulló ahora el propio Tiberio. Otro legionario lo había herido en la pierna. La operación de contrataque se repitió, pero a la inversa: Tiberio hirió en el cuello, mientras que Quieto ejecutó al legionario por la espalda.

Siguieron avanzando.

Por lo menos ciento cincuenta jinetes, la mitad de la fuerza original, había logrado desbordar las líneas de las cohortes.

—Podemos conseguirlo —dijo Quieto entre dientes. Azuzó aún más a su caballo para empezar a abandonar la playa roja de sangre y cabalgar ya sobre arena más firme en dirección al sur.

Quieto estaba emocionado. Si escapaban aún podrían llegar a Alejandría. Allí conocía gente. Un barco. Navegarían hasta África y Mauritania. Se harían fuertes de nuevo. Reuniría un ejército poderoso. Contactaría con senadores amigos. Habría mucho odio en el Senado hacia Adriano, especialmente si la información sobre las ejecuciones de Celso, Palma y Nigrino era cierta. Enviaría mensajeros a la Dacia, donde estaban Tercio Juliano, Cincinato y otros. Atacaría a Adriano desde el norte y el sur... Todo podía hacerse...

De pronto, ante él, apareció la caballería de las legiones de Atiano y Clemenciano. Los esperaban a quinientos pasos. Quieto aminoró la velocidad de su galope.

En cualquier otra circunstancia habría estado seguro de la victoria, pese a que los jinetes que se les oponían los doblaran en número, pero vio que Atiano estaba haciendo maniobrar al resto de las cohortes para que los rodeasen de nuevo. Aquellas *turmae* que Atiano les había enviado no tenían la misión de derrotarlos, por eso se habían detenido a quinientos pasos. Su función era la de retenerlos, la de ganar tiempo para que las legiones maniobraran.

—¿Qué hacemos? —preguntó Tiberio, resoplando. Le faltaba el aire por el esfuerzo de la lucha, por la sangre que perdía por la herida abierta.

—No tenemos tiempo. Hemos de arremeter contra su caballería y abrir una nueva brecha antes de que Atiano tenga tiempo de situar otras cohortes detrás de sus *turmae*.

Tiberio asintió. Era una locura, pero todo lo era desde que decidieron no abandonar a su líder.

—¡Vamos allá! ¡Por Júpiter! —gritó Tiberio mirando a los jinetes norteafricanos que se iban incorporando al grupo que había conseguido rebasar la línea de legionarios de la playa.

Retaguardia de las legiones

—Los arqueros ya vuelven a estar en posición, *legatus* —dijo uno de los oficiales a Atiano. Éste se limitó a asentir.

Clemenciano se acercó.

—¿Crees que podrán romper otra vez el cerco?

—Es difícil, pero no imposible —respondió Atiano—. Estamos aniquilando la mejor unidad de caballería del Imperio. Es normal que resulte difícil.

—Cuando me dijiste en Alejandría que necesitaríamos dos legiones para detener a Quieto me pareció una exageración —reflexionó Clemenciano en voz alta—, pero ahora veo que tenías razón.

Las flechas legionarias volvieron a causar una segunda masacre entre los jinetes de Quieto, pero, como en el caso anterior, se mostraron insuficientes para detener la carga de aquella caballería de héroes. Quieto fue atravesado por una flecha en un brazo y su caballo herido en el lomo. El animal relinchó con furia, pero no era una herida mortífera y la decisión en las riendas de su veterano jinete hizo que siguiera galopando contra las tropas que había ante ellos.

El choque de las *turmae* de las legiones y la caballería norteafricana de élite fue como cuando un elefante lucha contra una manada de leones hambrientos. Quieto y sus hombres se quitaban de encima unos jinetes romanos poco acostumbrados a luchar en batallas en primera línea de combate, pero eran muchos y entraban frescos en la batalla. La mayoría de aquellas *turmae* había intervenido en operaciones de reconocimiento o de castigo, cuando el enemigo ya huía y era fácil masacrarlo por la espalda. La caballería de Quieto, por el contrario, ni huía ni daba la espalda. Nada de eso. Los jinetes de las legiones se encontraban con espadas mortíferas, rabia sin control y una fuerza desmedida como no habían visto ni volverían a ver en su vida. Si sobrevivían.

La línea de caballería de las legiones de Egipto fue quebrada con más rapidez de lo que el propio Quieto o Tiberio podrían haber imaginado nunca. Allí no había valor. Además, tanto a los jinetes como a los legionarios contra los que luchaban les faltaba algo: convicción. A ninguno de ellos le gustaba tener que estar combatiendo contra una caballería que siempre había batallado a favor de Roma.

Y sin convicción se combate mal.

Brecha abierta.

Quieto aulló alzando su espada al viento.

—¡Por Roma, por Trajano, por el Imperio!

Y un centenar de jinetes lo siguieron con sus espadas en alto, mientras la desconcertada y confundida caballería de las legiones, es decir, los que habían sobrevivido al enfurecido envite de Quieto y sus hombres, intentaba reorganizar sus destrozadas líneas.

«Puede conseguirse», pensó Quieto aún con fe en escapar vivo de aquella trampa mortal de Adriano, pero las legiones habían tenido tiempo de maniobrar y, una vez más junto a la playa, estaban rodeados por nuevas cohortes.

Todo se repetía.

Quieto, al fin, comprendió que no había esperanza alguna. La estrategia de Atiano no era brillante, pero sí eficaz: los rodearía una y otra vez. Lanzaría andanadas de flechas cada vez que arremetieran contra los nuevos legionarios o jinetes que se interpondrían eternamente en su ruta de huida, y mientras abrían otra brecha, perderían más jinetes. Era una lenta y larga agonía, pero no sólo de un hombre, sino de toda una unidad militar especial. Quieto comprendió que a Atiano no le importaba que se llevaran por delante a doscientos, trescientos, quinientos o mil hombres. Sabía que no podían acabar con los más de quince mil hombres que los rodeaban. Era una cuestión de tiempo. Y sangre.

Mucha sangre.

El Mediterráneo estaba rojo a lo largo de una milla de playa.

Y aquello aún no había terminado.

127

EL CONSEJO DE LA EMPERATRIZ DENG

Loyang
Otoño de 117 d.C.

La emperatriz volvía a sorber té lentamente. Tamura miró a su alrededor: había una docena de guardias apostados por las esquinas de la sala, tres sirvientas a los pies de su majestad por si ésta deseaba cualquier cosa, un escriba que tomaba algunas notas y, por fin, el general Li Kan, como jefe de la guardia de palacio, detrás de la propia Tamura. La muchacha sentía su mirada clavada en ella constantemente. ¿Por qué la miraba con esa intensidad? No estaba gritando ni haciendo nada extraño.

—¿Puedo pedir consejo a la emperatriz sobre estas dos opciones? —preguntó entonces Tamura mirando a Fan Chun.

El consejero trasladó a su vez la cuestión a la emperatriz inclinando la cabeza a modo de reverencia y Tamura lo imitó. Estaban solicitándole algo, y aunque sólo fuera consejo, al pedir debían mostrar sumisión. La joven comprendió que no lo había hecho bien, pero Fan Chun, al hacer la traducción de su pregunta, le dio la oportunidad de corregir el error. La reverencia de Tamura fue muy marcada, evidente, clara.

La emperatriz habló de nuevo, esta vez largo y tendido. Cuando terminó, Fan Chun parpadeó un par de veces. Tenía que ver cómo resumir las ideas de su majestad apropiadamente.

—La emperatriz Deng —empezó, al fin, el asistente del ministro de Obras Públicas— considera que la primera opción no es buena por dos motivos: por un lado, las posibilidades de que vuelvas a conseguir cruzar el Imperio *Yueghzi* y Anshi por segunda vez sin perder la vida son mínimas; tus padres dieron su vida para que lo lograras en el viaje de ida. Has pagado un precio muy caro sólo por ese trayecto. Por otro lado, ¿cómo podemos saber si el nuevo emperador de Da Qin está interesado en retomar los planes de su antecesor, quien te envió hasta aquí? Su majestad manifiesta interés en entablar contacto con Da Qin, pero no quiere arriesgar la vida de una joven a quien tanto debe. Por eso te sugiere desestimar esta primera opción. Si la emperatriz quiere contactar con Da Qin ya encontrará otro modo u otras personas. En cuanto a la segunda opción, ésta es, sin duda, la que más complacería a la emperatriz desde un punto de vista egoísta, pero esta posibilidad, la de que permanezcas en Loyang, tiene el manifiesto peligro de que tu vida y tu tranquilidad sólo estarían aseguradas mientras su majestad viva. Yan Ji no ha sido ejecutada. El joven emperador An-ti la protege y su majestad no quiere abrir un conflicto directo con el heredero del trono han. Su favorita ha sido «exiliada», enviada lejos, como sabes, pero la emperatriz piensa que el joven emperador han puede insistir en que Yan Ji regrese a la corte en cuanto la emperatriz ya no esté aquí para protegerte de su venganza por descubrir e impedir su plan. Lo más probable es que entonces la hermosa pero cruel favorita del emperador decida tomarse venganza en tu persona. Por eso esta opción tampoco satisface a la emperatriz que, en el fondo de su corazón, desea conseguir lo mejor para ti.

—Entonces... —Pero a Tamura le fallaban las palabras en la lengua han y decidió usar el sánscrito de nuevo mirando a Fan Chun—. Entonces sólo me queda la tercera opción. ¿En qué consiste esta última posibilidad?

La emperatriz suspiró y miró por encima de los hombros de Tamura. No por sentirse superior, sino porque sus ojos se estaban fijando en la faz siempre seria y fría del general Li Kan.

128

LA TERCERA OPCIÓN DE QUIETO

Sur de Judea
Otoño de 117 d.C.

Retaguardia de las legiones

—No pensé nunca que Quieto se decidiera por la tercera opción —comentó Atiano con sus ojos vueltos hacia el mar rojo sangre.

—¿La tercera posibilidad? —Clemenciano no parecía entender.

Atiano se explicó con su cara vuelta hacia la playa. No le interesaba explicar nada a Clemenciano. Aquel inútil le daba, no obstante, la excusa para poner voz a sus pensamientos.

—En la vida todo son opciones, eso he creído siempre, y somos hijos de nuestras decisiones. Quieto tenía, en principio, como todos cuando se compite por el poder, dos opciones: rendirse o luchar. Al final pareció elegir la segunda, pero en las legiones de Roma siempre queda una tercera opción. Una por la que muy pocos se deciden. Ya no quedan valientes.

—¿Cuál es esa tercera opción? —preguntó Clemenciano arrugando la frente.

Atiano enarcó las cejas antes de responder. La incapacidad de entender nada del nuevo gobernador lo exasperaba.

—Morir, Clemenciano, morir luchando hasta el final. Ésa es la tercera opción cuando las legiones entran en combate, y es la que ha elegido Quieto. No quedan hombres así.

Clemenciano se encogió de hombros. Luego pidió agua y vino y queso y carne seca de jabalí.

—¡Agh! —dijo el nuevo gobernador de Siria escupiendo

el licor que acababa de ingerir—. El vino de las legiones no se puede beber ni mezclado con agua.

Cogió en su lugar algo del queso que habían puesto un grupo de *calones* en una pequeña mesa portátil junto a los dos poderosos hombres de Adriano.

—Quizá no sea el momento más adecuado para beber o comer —comentó Atiano sin dejar de mirar hacia la playa.

—¿Acaso crees que corremos algún peligro? —preguntó Clemenciano con nerviosismo—. Creía que lo teníamos todo controlado. Cada vez son menos. Es cuestión de tiempo, pero se hace largo. Me ha entrado hambre.

Atiano sacudió la cabeza. Estaban eliminando a los mejores para entregar las provincias de Roma a gente como Clemenciano. No, no tenía ganas de comer o beber. El hecho de que tuviera que hacer el trabajo sucio del nuevo emperador no quería decir que estuviera particularmente orgulloso de ello. Él, como todos, buscaba lo mejor para su entorno próximo, para su familia. Un puesto en el Senado era inaccesible para Atiano por dinero; tenía que ganarlo prestando otros servicios. Primero sería jefe del pretorio, luego el Senado. Miraba hacia la playa. Apenas quedaba un puñado de jinetes de Quieto luchando junto a su líder. Atiano echó a andar sin decir nada a Clemenciano, quien, ocupado como estaba en reclamar otro vino mejor, no se percató de que se marchaba.

En la playa, supervivientes de la caballería de Quieto

Tiberio Claudio Máximo cayó de su caballo abatido por varias flechas y un *pilum* que le atravesó el corazón. No tuvo mucho tiempo para repasar su vida. Al instante se vio con su cuerpo hundiéndose en el agua roja del mar. Su último pensamiento fue para aquella tumba que había encargado. Siempre le había gustado hacer las cosas con tiempo. Incluso había especificado en una misiva el texto de la inscripción: además de su gran gesta de atrapar y dar muerte a Decébalo, la inscripción debía contar que Tiberio Claudio Máximo había combatido bajo las órdenes del divino Trajano. Siempre pensó que el se-

977

nado deificaría al emperador. ¿Lo harían? Él ya no estaría allí para averiguarlo... Sería una bonita tumba... el artesano la haría... había adelantado el dinero para su realización... una tumba sin cadáver...

A cien pasos del cuerpo de Tiberio

Los legionarios se hacían a un lado a medida que Publio Acilio Atiano se acercaba. Por el largo pasillo de soldados, el enviado de Adriano para arrestar a Lucio Quieto avanzaba en silencio.

Llegó a primera línea.

Ya no era una primera línea de combate, sino sólo de muerte: los cadáveres de los jinetes de la caballería del líder norteafricano flotaban en el agua roja junto con decenas, centenares de cuerpos de legionarios también muertos o mutilados o gravemente heridos.

Atiano comprobaba que la lucha había sido brutal, inmisericorde y sin pausa durante más de una hora. Sólo un hombre permanecía en pie en medio de los cadáveres flotantes: Lucio Quieto, con varias flechas en el hombro, los brazos y la pierna, seguía blandiendo su espada contra más de un centenar de soldados de las legiones enviadas desde Egipto para detenerlo. Se había llevado por delante con su caballería a más de mil legionarios y a otros cien o doscientos jinetes de las *turmae*.

Para Atiano aquél era un precio muy caro para detener a un solo hombre, pero la absoluta lealtad de su caballería había hecho imposible evitar aquella carnicería. Sería mejor que no se escribiera acerca de lo que acababa de ocurrir; muchos en Roma lo usarían contra el nuevo emperador. No obstante, echar tierra sobre lo acontecido en aquella playa era asunto del César Adriano, no suyo. Atiano no tenía la más mínima duda de que el nuevo emperador encontraría la forma de que todo aquello se... olvidara. Pero quedaba aún aquel *legatus* en pie, esgrimiendo tozudamente su espada, aun después de tantos muertos y tanta sangre. Ninguno de los legionarios se le aproximaba para darle el golpe de gracia. Atiano arrugó la frente y miró a su alrededor. Los legionarios no se movían. ¿Era por miedo, por vergüenza o por admiración? Atiano comprendió en aquel momento por qué Adriano había insistido tanto en que se debía dar muerte a Lucio Quieto. La propuesta de arresto era toda una pantomima: Atiano tenía la orden de ejecutarlo en cuanto sus jinetes lo abandonaran. Pero la caballería de Quieto había luchado hasta el final, hasta el último hombre.

—¿Cuántos? —preguntó Atiano a un tribuno al que le había ordenado que le informara con precisión de las bajas.

—Mil trescientos legionarios muertos, más de quinientos heridos, ciento ochenta jinetes de nuestras *turmae* abatidos y otros muchos, heridos. Han destrozado prácticamente media legión y sólo eran trescientos.

Atiano asintió y levantó la mano.

Por el momento no quería saber más.

—¡Cobardes! ¡Miserables! ¡Traidores! —aulló el *legatus* norteafricano escupiendo espumarajos de sangre por la boca—. ¿Nadie se atreve a intentar darme muerte?

Quieto era casi un cadáver más que, sin saber cómo, tenía energía aún para insultarlos.

Atiano no había visto nunca tal tenacidad, tanta capacidad de resistencia. Media legión, Quieto había destrozado casi media legión sin tener posición de ventaja, estando rodeado, siendo traicionado, luchando bajo una lluvia de flechas. Flechas. Atiano miró a su espalda. Se había hecho acompañar por un grupo de arqueros. El enviado de Adriano se hizo a un lado y éstos se situaron en primera línea, frente al agonizante *legatus*. Atiano se limitó a cabecear levemente. Los arqueros cargaron sus arcos y los tensaron apuntando hacia el *legatus*.

Lucio Quieto vio que lo iban a acribillar como a un perro rabioso.

—¡Cobardes hasta el final! —gritó—. ¿Ni siquiera se me va a permitir morir como un hombre? —preguntó mirando hacia Atiano.

El enviado de Adriano alzó la mano y los arqueros bajaron sus arcos.

—¿Qué quieres? —preguntó Atiano.

—Un instante... —respondió Quieto escupiendo más sangre—. Sólo necesito un instante... no me hace falta más...

—Lo tienes —concedió Atiano y levantó los brazos en un claro gesto que todos comprendieron. Los legionarios se hicieron hacia atrás creando un gran círculo en torno al *legatus* malherido.

Lucio Quieto los miró a todos con un desdén y un desprecio tan grandes que la mayoría de los legionarios agacharon la cabeza.

—¡Os enseñaré cómo mueren los hombres! —aulló vomitando más sangre—. ¡Al menos que esta traición os valga para que aprendáis... eso...!

Lucio Quieto, *legatus* norteafricano, jefe de la caballería imperial, brazo derecho del emperador Marco Ulpio Trajano y, para muchos, el señalado por el fallecido César como único sucesor, con capacidad de retener las nuevas conquistas y ser respetado por las legiones y el Senado a un tiempo, asió la empuñadura de su espada con ambas manos, la puso en horizontal, con la punta justo debajo del esternón y lanzó un grito desgarrador mientras la hundía con todas sus fuerzas en su cuerpo.

—¡Romaaaaaa!

Cayó hacia atrás.

Su cuerpo se hundió al principio para salir a flote al momento. Aún agitaba los brazos. Nadie se acercaba.

Quieto flotaba boca arriba, mirando al cielo azul de Judea. Se atragantaba con su sangre, con el agua. Mucha agua, por todas partes, y toda roja.

—Así muere un loco —dijo Clemenciano que, al fin, se había atrevido a seguir a Atiano hasta la playa.

Publio Acilio Atiano se volvió muy despacio y encaró al recién llegado con cara de asco.

—No, gobernador, así muere un César. Si ese hombre hubiera tenido mil jinetes a su mando en lugar de trescientos, a lo mejor los que estarían flotando en la playa boca arriba desangrados, pese a nuestras dos legiones, seríamos tú y yo, imbécil.

Publio Acilio Atiano no se quedó para escuchar lo que tenía que decir Clemenciano. El enviado de Adriano se alejó de aquella maldita playa roja y, por primera vez en su vida, después de un combate, cuando llegó a su tienda de campaña y se quedó a solas, se arrodilló en el suelo y empezó a vomitar.

Adriano, entonces gobernador de Siria, sucedió [a Trajano] *en el trono. Aunque era el único heredero posible dentro de la familia imperial, parece ser que Trajano podría haber estado considerando nombrar a otra persona como su sucesor. El rumor* [sobre si realmente Trajano había adoptado a Adriano como hijo en su lecho de muerte o no] *refleja las serias tensiones que había entre diversos generales veteranos y la familia imperial. En cuestión de meses, incluso antes de que Adriano regresase a Roma, se ejecutaron cuatro de los generales de Trajano con más carisma, bajo la sospecha de estar urdiendo un complot contra Adriano.*

DAVID POTTER, catedrático de griego y latín
del departamento de Estudios Clásicos de la Universidad
de Michigan, en su libro *Emperors of Rome*
(Quercus, 2007)

Palma fue asesinado en Tarracina, Celso en Baiae, Nigrino en Faventia y Lucio en el transcurso de un viaje.

Historia Augusta, 7, 2

129

LA TERCERA OPCIÓN DE TAMURA

Loyang
Otoño de 117 d.C.

Tamura había preguntado por su tercera opción.

Descartada la posibilidad del retorno a Roma, por imposible, o la de permanecer en Loyang largo tiempo porque a medio plazo podría suponer un peligro cuando regresara Yan Ji, sólo parecía quedar la misteriosa tercera opción. Pero nada se había dicho aún sobre la misma. Cuando la joven había preguntado, la emperatriz se había limitado a mirar fijamente al general Li Kan. Tamura no entendía por qué.

La muchacha se volvió y vio la figura robusta y muy firme del *chiang-chün*. Éste no dijo nada, sino que se mantenía serio y en silencio. Tamura se acordó entonces de algo que aún la confundía: ¿por qué Li Kan entendía latín? Pero en todas aquellas semanas el general nunca se había acercado a ella, como si ya no quisiera verla; sin embargo, siempre la miraba fijamente desde lejos. Y cuando le preguntó a Fan Chun sobre el latín y Li Kan, el viejo asistente del ministro de Obras Públicas se limitó a sonreír y no dijo nada. Un misterio.

Su majestad dijo entonces algo y Li Kan asintió una vez, con rotundidad y, Tamura estaba convencida de ello, ruborizándose un poco. La faz del general se tornó roja. ¿Una vez más enfadado con ella? ¿Qué había hecho ahora?

La joven se volvió hacia la emperatriz, que volvía a hablar. Fan Chun escuchaba atento y luego tradujo de un tirón.

—Su majestad ha recibido una petición del *chiang-chün* Li Kan, jefe de la guardia imperial de Loyang y general en jefe del ejército del norte, que ha solicitado permiso para casarse. Un hombre como Li Kan no tiene que pedir permiso para desposarse, pero la emperatriz ve en su gesto una muestra de la gran lealtad del general hacia el Imperio han y su gobierno. Además, en esta ocasión, la petición de permiso tiene más sentido, ya que Li Kan desea casarse con una protegida de su majestad.

Tamura no estaba segura de estar entendiendo bien lo que el consejero traducía. ¿Qué le importaba a ella con quién se quisiera casar Li Kan y qué tenía que ver eso con su tercera opción...? De pronto quedó petrificada. Sin habla. Tragó saliva. Le había costado, pero creía, por fin, entender...

Fan Chun se dio cuenta del aturdimiento de la joven, por eso procuró pronunciar las siguientes palabras con cierta dulzura, sin que pareciera una imposición:

—El general Li Kan ha pedido casarse con la mensajera de Da Qin.

Tamura se volvió de nuevo lentamente y miró a Li Kan. Éste permanecía igual de mudo que ella y aún más firme que antes. Parecía que no respirara, como si se tratara de una de esas estatuas de terracota que había visto en algunos de los patios del palacio imperial de Loyang.

—¿He de aceptarlo? —acertó a preguntar al fin Tamura en el poco chino que había podido aprender con su tutora.

La emperatriz volvió a intervenir en un nuevo parlamento relativamente extenso. Su cara y su gesto eran serios, pero no había ni enfado ni mandato en su expresión.

—La emperatriz —volvió a traducir Fan Chun— insiste en que eres totalmente libre de aceptar o no la oferta del general. Su majestad precisa que las otras dos opciones, aunque desaconsejables, siguen ante ti y puedes elegirlas si lo deseas: intentar regresar a Da Qin o permanecer junto a la emperatriz. Como imagina que también deseas saber su opinión sobre esta última opción, su majestad ha sido muy... explícita. Para ella el matrimonio con Li Kan es, con mucho, la mejor solución para tu dilema, que...

En ese momento la emperatriz se levantó e interrumpió al viejo asistente, que calló de inmediato y dio dos pasos hacia atrás mientras veía que su majestad se acercaba a Tamura lentamente y le hablaba como si de una madre se tratara.

—Mensajera de Da Qin —dijo la emperatriz en chino ante los ojos abiertos como platos de Tamura—. Nos guste o no, éste es un mundo de hombres. Yo, como emperatriz del Imperio han, sólo soy un accidente. No sé si alguna vez éste será un mundo de hombres y mujeres por igual, pero hoy por hoy es y seguirá siendo, por tantos años y siglos como puedo imaginar, un mundo de hombres y para hombres. Una mujer joven y hermosa como tú, por muy valiente y feroz que pueda ser, sólo estará realmente segura bajo la protección de un hombre que la cuide de la estupidez, la lujuria y la crueldad de los otros y, por qué no decirlo, de los celos y la envidia y el rencor de otras mujeres como Yan Ji. La decisión más importante es pues, en tu caso, como lo fue en el mío, tener la oportunidad de elegir bien a ese hombre que te proteja. Yo fui inmensamente afortunada con el emperador He, que siempre me trató con amor y respeto. He observado cómo los ojos del general Li Kan han ido cambiando estas semanas en su forma de mirar a la mensajera de Da Qin: primero había indiferencia, luego curiosidad y ahora veo un brillo que sé reconocer por la experiencia de mis años. Mi mejor general está hechizado por la mensajera de Da Qin, aunque ésta, tan joven, no sabe darse cuenta de ello. He consultado a Fan Chun y él me dice que os entenderéis, que hay algo secreto que os une. No he querido preguntar cuál es ese secreto que os conecta porque los que me han servido bien, y los dos lo habéis hecho, tienen derecho a sus secretos.

La emperatriz llevó entonces su mano de finos dedos a la mejilla de Tamura. La muchacha callaba y observaba. Fan Chun traducía rápidamente mientras la joven sentía la caricia de la emperatriz en su rostro. Su majestad se volvió, caminó de regreso al trono y se sentó de nuevo en él.

—Mi consejo, mensajera de Da Qin, es que te cases con el general Li Kan —dijo Deng y miró a Fan Chun—. Traduce esto también.

Fan Chun obedeció.

—¿Por qué es ésta mejor opción que las otras? ¿Acaso mi vida no correrá el mismo peligro cuando la emperatriz muera? —preguntó la muchacha para sorpresa del asistente, quien, no obstante, tradujo a la emperatriz las dudas de Tamura.

Deng sonrió. Luego miró a Li Kan.

—Mucha pasión por ti no parece sentir la mensajera de Da Qin —dijo la emperatriz—. ¿Mantienes pese a ello tu petición?

—Sí, majestad.

Tamura presenciaba aquel intercambio de palabras sin estar muy segura de lo que pasaba, pero su intuición le decía que seguían hablando de ella.

La emperatriz asintió y se dirigió de nuevo a la joven.

—Ésta es la mejor opción porque Li Kan es el mejor militar del Imperio han y ni siquiera el emperador An-ti querrá eliminar al vigilante más capaz de la frontera del imperio, ni indisponerse contra él ordenando la detención de su esposa, algo que, con toda probabilidad, le pedirá Yan Ji. No, no hay otra opción mejor. Tu vida estará más segura en el Imperio han al lado del general Li Kan. Pero... es tu decisión.

Fan Chun traducía al tiempo que Tamura se pasaba el dorso de la mano derecha por la frente llena de sudor: marchar de regreso a Roma —un viaje imposible, la muerte a cada paso—; quedarse —un tiempo de paz y luego la venganza de la favorita del emperador An-ti—; o desposarse con aquel hombre al que humilló en el pasado y que, sin embargo, ahora pedía su mano. Tamura dio media vuelta y, con una pregunta en su mirada, clavó los ojos en los del general Li Kan: ¿Por qué? ¿Por qué yo? Pero no la formuló en palabras.

Nadie decía nada.

La emperatriz hizo un gesto y una sirvienta rellenó su taza con más té humeante.

Fan Chun fruncía el ceño. No entendía por qué la muchacha no aceptaba sin más. Esto le demostraba cuánto le faltaba aún por conocer del sentir de las mujeres. No podía ser por inexperiencia, pues la mensajera de Da Qin había tenido un aborto, luego había yacido ya con, al menos, otro hombre. Esto había dejado perplejo a Fan Chun cuando Li Kan le manifestó su deseo de desposarse con la muchacha, pues no era virgen. Pero vio sentido al matrimonio por razones... diversas. Sin embargo, aquel terco silencio de la muchacha...

—Me temo que la emperatriz y el general esperan una respuesta, mensajera de Da Qin —dijo Fan Chun con el tono más cordial que supo—. Eres libre de elegir, pero has de elegir.

—Sí —dijo Tamura.

El consejero inclinó la cabeza algo confuso.

—¿«Sí» que vas a darnos una respuesta pronto o «sí» es la respuesta? —intentó aclarar. Era importante saber bien antes de traducir.

—Las dos cosas —afirmó Tamura mirando al suelo—: me casaré con el general Li Kan.

El asistente del ministro de Obras Públicas transmitió la decisión de la joven. La emperatriz cabeceó de forma afirmativa. Luego levantó levemente su mano derecha.

—La audiencia ha terminado —dijo Fan Chun.

Tamura, el consejero y el general, después de inclinarse ante Deng, salían ya del salón del trono de Loyang cuando la emperatriz llamó al *chiang-chün* y éste se detuvo.

Su majestad hizo un gesto con la mano y Li Kan se acercó al trono hasta detenerse e hincar una rodilla en el suelo, a la espera de recibir órdenes. Pudo oír que las puertas se cerraban. Fan Chun y la mensajera de Da Qin ya no estaban en la sala.

—No, esta vez no hay mandato alguno, Li Kan, sólo un consejo.

—Un consejo de su sabia majestad es siempre una orden —dijo él en tono marcial.

—Tómalo como desees, general. Mi consejo es que, si quieres dormir tranquilo y no temer por tu vida, nunca fuerces a la que será tu mujer en poco tiempo a hacer nada que ella no desee. Hay muchas mujeres que sufren a manos de sus esposos y callan y padecen con paciencia; es lo habitual, pero algo me dice que la joven mensajera de Da Qin puede no tener esa paciencia.

Li Kan miró a la emperatriz un instante con ojos de sorpresa ante aquella advertencia.

—No, Li Kan, no te muestres ahora perplejo —continuó la

emperatriz—. Quieres acostarte con una tigresa. Me parece bien, pero el Imperio han necesita a su mejor general vivo, así que no olvides nunca que es con una tigresa con quien vas a compartir las noches. Acaríciala. No la obligues nunca a mostrarte sus garras. Éste es mi consejo no ya de emperatriz, sino de mujer. Serás sabio si lo tienes en cuenta.

130

LOS DETALLES

Roma
Finales de otoño de 117 d.C.

Serviano se levantó de su asiento y se situó en el centro del Senado. Miró a su alrededor. Vio miedo en los ojos de sus colegas. Mucho. Eso, sin duda, le facilitaba la tarea. Él nunca se había distinguido por ser un buen orador, pero aquella mañana la oratoria no iba a ser muy necesaria. Aun así se esforzó en construir un discurso mínimamente organizado.

—*Patres et conscripti*, a vosotros me dirijo usando la fórmula antigua que antaño se empleara entre nuestros venerables antepasados, porque a uno de ellos pienso referirme para explicar que lo que se está haciendo en las lejanas fronteras orientales es lo que debe hacerse. Catón el Viejo decía en su memorable *De Macedonia Liberanda* que en aquel tiempo se debía otorgar la libertad a los macedonios porque el Estado romano no disponía ni de los medios ni de las energías suficientes para protegerlos. Bien, pues eso exactamente y no otra cosa es lo que sucede hoy día con Asiria, Babilonia, Mesopotamia, Armenia y Osroene. Roma no dispone en la actualidad ni de las legiones ni del dinero suficiente para financiar el mantenimiento de esas admirables conquistas del óptimo *Imperator Caesar Augustus* Marco Ulpio Trajano. Admirables victorias, sí, pero imposibles de retener. Empecinarse en mantener lo que no se puede preservar sin poner en riesgo el resto del Imperio es conducir a toda Roma hacia el desastre. Por eso propongo que el Senado aquí reunido apruebe respaldar las decisiones que el nuevo César Publio Elio Adriano se ha visto forzado a tomar en beneficio del bien común: que se apoye su decisión de retirarse de todas las provincias y los reinos que he mencionado anteriormente.

Ni siquiera consiguió un final rotundo para su exposición, pero tras los fallecimientos de Nigrino, Celso y Palma en diferentes puntos de la península Itálica y la detención, aún no estaba claro en Roma si con muerte también, de Quieto en Judea, nadie se atrevió a votar en contra. Otra cuestión eran los sentimientos, pero ni a Serviano ni a Adriano les importaban demasiado en aquel momento los sentimientos del resto de los senadores.

Selinus

Adriano dejó la carta de Serviano sobre la mesa.

—¿Buenas noticias? —preguntó Atiano.

—Las oportunas —respondió Adriano—. En Roma todo está en orden. Serviano se ha ocupado de los senadores incómodos y el resto apoya mis decisiones de retirada de las provincias orientales. La cuestión, no obstante, que más me interesa es si tengo buenas noticias tuyas o no, aunque imagino que verte aquí relajado anticipa que lo que vas a comunicarme me satisfará.

Atiano no se anduvo con rodeos innecesarios. Su señor, de un tiempo a esta parte, parecía, cada día que pasaba, más impaciente y más difícil de mantener contento.

—En Asia ya no hay oposición al nuevo emperador —dijo Atiano.

—¿Ninguna?

—Ninguna —insistió Atiano—. He de reconocer que Lucio Quieto se resistió con enorme coraje, luchó con un arrojo que no había visto...

—Partimos para el Danubio mañana mismo —lo interrumpió Adriano levantándose—. Te has ganado el puesto de jefe del pretorio —le dijo al pasar a su lado—. Ahora falta ver si quieres llegar a senador. Sírveme bien y te haré cónsul. Pero, por favor, no me molestes nunca con detalles. No quiero saber nada sobre la resistencia de Quieto, su coraje o su arrojo. Los detalles, Atiano, me aburren. Los detalles son borrados por la historia: no interesan a nadie. Celso, Palma, Nigrino y Quieto son sólo detalles. Ya me ocuparé de que se olviden. Lo único relevante soy yo.

Adriano se levantó, pasó al lado de su antiguo tutor sin mirarlo y salió de la estancia.

Atiano se quedó solo mirando al suelo. Le había faltado informar al César de las muertes de Salvio Liberal y Pompeyo Colega en Cirene y Chipre. Ambos gobernadores habían muerto en los brutales tumultos provocados por la subida de impuestos contra los judíos. El incendio del Imperio se los había llevado por delante. Pero Atiano supo en aquel momento que ya no diría nada sobre aquellos hombres que habían ayudado al nuevo César en su ascenso. Tenía claro que para Adriano sus muertes también serían detalles.

131

LOS DESCENDIENTES

Loyang
Finales de otoño de 117 d.C.

—Hay algo que nunca he entendido bien —dijo Li Kan.

El asistente del ministro de Obras Públicas levantó la mirada del montón de papeles que estaba revisando. De un tiempo a esa parte pedía que se le entregaran los informes en ese material y no en las pesadas tablillas de bambú. Además de ser más práctico, pues ocupaba mucho menos espacio cada escrito, si quería promover el uso de aquel nuevo material entre los funcionarios de la corte imperial tenía que dar ejemplo. Pero ahora los papeles debían esperar. Li Kan partía hacia el norte con su nueva esposa, la joven mensajera de Da Qin, y había acudido a la modesta oficina del asistente del ministro de Obras Públicas para despedirse en un gesto de amistad y lealtad.

—¿Qué es lo que no entiende nuestro mejor *chiang-chün*? —preguntó Fan Chun dejando los documentos a un lado de la mesa.

—Nunca he terminado de entender por qué he tenido tu apoyo constante en la corte imperial desde que llegue a Loyang.

—Ya, bien —empezó Fan Chun, pero a continuación guardó un largo silencio—. Tu *chi tu-wei*, tu comandante de la Gran Muralla, envió muy buenas recomendaciones desde un principio cuando eras un joven guerrero, y tus acciones militares posteriores te han encumbrado a la posición que has conseguido.

Li Kan asintió, pero no parecía convencido.

—Aun así, tengo la sensación de que el apoyo del asistente

del ministro de Obras Públicas ha sido más intenso de lo que esos informes positivos de mi comandante o la brillantez de mi carrera militar merecían.

—¿Eso crees? —preguntó Fan Chun, pero no dejó que su interlocutor respondiera—. Es evidente que cada vez eres más sabio. Eso te vendrá bien en tu nueva condición.

—¿Mi nueva condición? —inquirió Li Kan algo confundido. Acababa de recibir órdenes de retornar a la Gran Muralla, al norte del país, pero eso no le parecía una nueva situación.

—Me refiero a tu nueva condición como hombre casado.

—Ah.

—La sabiduría deberá guiarte. Tu esposa no es alguien convencional.

Li Kan inspiró aire profundamente. Aquélla era la segunda advertencia que recibía sobre el asunto. Primero la emperatriz y ahora el asistente del ministro de Obras Públicas.

—¿Acaso cree el *yu-shih chung-ch'eng* que he hecho mal al desposarme con esa mujer?

—No. Creo que es una forma correcta de cerrar un círculo.

Li Kan volvió a inspirar profundamente.

—Una vez más el asistente del ministro de Obras Públicas vuelve a dirigirse a mí con enigmas que no soy capaz de descifrar.

Fan Chun sonrió.

—El general tiene razón, pero los enigmas han de terminar ya entre nosotros. Voy a retirarme. Por fin. He conseguido el permiso de la emperatriz para ir al interior, a un templo, para meditar. Tengo interés en reflexionar sobre las enseñanzas de Confucio y de leer con sosiego los textos sánscritos de los nuevos monjes budistas. Mis días en este mundo están llegando a su fin. Y estoy cansado. Las intrigas de palacio son demasiado intensas ya para mí... —El anciano se quedó con la mirada vacía unos instantes—. Pero esto no resuelve el enigma que te he planteado hace un momento y, como he dicho, es hora de que entre tú y yo quede todo dicho. Me explicaré, pero... siéntate.

Li Kan se lo pensó un instante. Nunca antes el asistente del ministro de Obras Públicas le había permitido sentarse en su presencia, ni él, siendo ya general, había reclamado ese derecho. Sabía que le debía mucho a aquel consejero imperial y no quería parecer petulante.

—Siéntate, Li Kan. Mi explicación va ser algo más extensa de lo habitual.

El general obedeció.

—Bien. ¿Por dónde empezar? Sí, veamos. —Fan Chun miró al techo como si buscara inspiración, pero enseguida fijó los ojos en los dos funcionarios que estaban también presentes en la pequeña oficina. Estos hombres entendieron el mensaje, se levantaron y salieron cerrando la puerta del panel de madera, dejando solos al viejo *yu-shih chung-ch'eng* con el general Li Kan—. Veamos, hay algo que nos conecta a ti y a mí, igual que sé que hay algo que te conecta a ti con tu joven esposa extranjera. Oh, no te muestres sorprendido. Conozco tu secreto, siempre lo he sabido. El trabajo de un buen consejero imperial es tener información; cuanta más mejor. Los secretos no pueden existir en mi posición o nunca podría haber aconsejado bien al emperador He antes o a la emperatriz Deng estos últimos años. Una emperatriz o un emperador pueden permitirse el lujo de decir que quienes los sirven bien pueden tener secretos, pero ese lujo lo disfrutan sus majestades porque saben que tienen a otros servidores, como yo, que se ocupan de desentrañar esos secretos y revelárselos si suponen un peligro. Tu secreto, no obstante, nunca ha supuesto una amenaza en la corte y por eso ha permanecido conmigo. Pero vayamos al asunto: verás, sé que desciendes de unos extraños guerreros contra los que el general Tang tuvo que enfrentarse en la legendaria y remota batalla de Kangchú hace ya muchos años. Varias generaciones de nuestros antepasados nos separan de aquellos sucesos, pero tú y yo estamos conectados porque tú desciendes de Druso, el líder militar de aquella unidad extranjera que ellos mismos denominaban... ahora no recuerdo el nombre bien. Lo tengo anotado todo en las memorias de...

—Legión... ellos se llamaban a sí mismos «la legión perdida» —completó Li Kan, que empezaba a comprender que era el momento de la sinceridad absoluta entre él y el *yu-shih chung-ch'eng.*

—Eso es, sí. ¿Lo ves? La memoria empieza a fallarme en cuestiones de importancia. Ya no soy válido para ocupar mi puesto. Torpes son los que no saben ver cuándo hay que retirarse a tiempo, esto es esencial en un campo de batalla pero más importante aún en la vida... Pero vuelvo a mis digresiones y no es el momento para ello. Decía que desciendes de ese Druso, líder de aquella legión perdida. Yo, por mi parte, desciendo directamente del general Tang. Sí, no te sorprendas. Todos tienen descendientes, no sólo tus exóticos antepasados. El general Tang escribió sus memorias y las guardo aquí. —Señaló un estante donde había muchas tablillas de bambú y también papeles modernos—. Veo que frunces el ceño. ¿Crees que es mal sitio para esconder un documento importante? Al contrario. Si quieres esconder un escrito, lo mejor es ponerlo con otros muchos. Aislado llama la atención, pero rodeado de otros miles sólo pasa por uno más.

»Pero retornemos a las memorias en sí: en los anales oficiales de la dinastía han del este sólo se han recogido algunos de los comentarios del general Tang sobre aquella unidad militar. El asunto, por extraño y desconocido, siempre se ha llevado con mucha discreción. El caso es que tu antepasado y el mío fueron primero oponentes en el campo de batalla, pero luego se hicieron amigos. El general Tang, que admiraba las dotes de combate de tus antepasados, consiguió que Druso y los pocos hombres de aquella unidad que sobrevivieron se integraran en el ejército han. Hasta les cedió terrenos para que establecieran un campamento permanente cerca de la frontera occidental. Vosotros, es decir, tú, tu padre, antes tu abuelo, y así de generación en generación, mantuvisteis el secreto de vuestro origen con cuidado cuando empezasteis a diseminaros por el Imperio han. Sólo el general Tang y su familia, es decir, mi familia, mantuvieron y transmitieron de generación en generación el asunto de vuestro misterioso origen y los lugares donde estabais emplazados por la frontera. Que yo tenga conocimiento, tú eres el último descendiente de aquella legión perdida y has heredado las grandes dotes de lucha de aquel extranjero llamado Druso. El resto han ido muriendo o mezclándose con nosotros hasta desaparecer su rastro casi por completo. De algún modo podría decirse que eres el último guerrero de Da Qin aquí en el Imperio han, pues esa legión procedía de aquel lejano mundo. Y yo soy el último descendiente del general Tang. Eso nos une. Por eso, tu sensación de que he estado de alguna forma... ¿cómo decirlo?, sí, tutorizando con amistad tus movimientos desde que llegaste a Loyang, es cierta. Lo he hecho por ese viejo vínculo que nos une, pero también porque creo en tus dotes militares y en tu lealtad. Los diferentes acontecimientos en la frontera y en el palacio imperial han demostrado que he estado acertado. No me has defraudado en ningún sentido.

Li Kan escuchaba en silencio, sin decir nada, sin interrumpir al anciano funcionario y sin moverse un ápice. Casi ni parpadeaba.

—Por todo ello, creo que tu matrimonio con esa joven mensajera de Da Qin es lógico. Cuando yazcas con ella en un lecho cerraréis uno de esos extraños círculos de la historia. Tú provienes de la legión perdida de Da Qin, de Roma, como la llamaba Druso, y la mensajera también procede de allí —continuó el viejo asistente del ministro de Obras Públicas—. Por eso pudiste entender a la muchacha cuando te advirtió del veneno de Yan Ji. Porque te habló en esa lengua de Da Qin de la que tú aún entiendes muchas palabras, porque os la habéis transmitido de padres a hijos como parte de vuestro secreto origen. Ahora volverás a tener a alguien con quien hablarla. Por eso cerráis el círculo. A veces la vida tiene sentido. Pero...
—el anciano inspiró profundamente—, es importante que sigas manteniendo tu secreto. Yo me retiro. Otros vendrán a sustituirme. La emperatriz pronto perderá el control del poder, que pasará a manos de su hijo. El emperador An-ti no es hombre de comprender sutilezas ni de apreciar la riqueza de la variedad en su imperio. Es mejor que de ahora en adelante seas han al cien por cien y sólo han y que, lo antes posible, se olviden en Loyang de tu esposa, de su mensaje y hasta de Da Qin. La emperatriz ha decidido, por fin, no enviar mensaje alguno de respuesta a ese emperador Trajano o a quien lo sustituya. No tiene sentido. Sus ejércitos se retiran hacia el oeste. Eso parece confirmado por todas las caravanas de la Ruta

de la Seda. Da Qin y el Imperio han seguirán siendo gigantes separados. Continuaremos enviando nuestra seda, lacas y otros productos hacia allí, pero no creo que volvamos a tener noticias directas de aquel imperio en varias generaciones. Tú y tu esposa, o Druso y el general Tang en la batalla de Kangchú, sois accidentes de la historia, acontecimientos que quizá nunca deberían haber ocurrido.

El anciano consejero suspiró. Luego inspiró profundamente. Cerró los ojos, los abrió y se quedó, una vez más, mirando al techo, con la mirada perdida en recuerdos remotos al tiempo que volvía a hablar.

—No, ya no quedan más guerreros de Da Qin entre nosotros, no que yo tenga localizados. Ni descendientes del general Tang. Yo no he tenido hijos, aunque tú con esa guerrera de Da Qin puedes alargar la estirpe de la legión perdida, al menos, una generación. Pero pronto no seremos nada, ni un recuerdo, sólo un accidente que quizá desaparezca de la memoria de todos, un relato extraño del que nadie se acuerde. Tú y yo, amigo mío, somos uno de esos imposibles de la historia: reales, pero increíbles. Vive feliz en el norte, vigila las fronteras de nuestro imperio y ten hijos con esa hermosa mensajera de Da Qin, otra persona perdida en la historia. Es un regalo que te envía el viejo imperio lejano del que desciendes. Cuídala. Yo me retiro. Como te decía al principio, la emperatriz me ha concedido mi deseo. En la paz de un pequeño pueblo reflexionaré sobre todo esto y sobre nada. Intentaré, simplemente, conseguir la paz de mi espíritu. He visto demasiadas cosas horribles, he dado órdenes justas e injustas. Tengo demasiados conflictos en mi ser que necesitan ser o borrados o asimilados. Demasiados contrarios enfrentados en mi interior. Quiero llegar a la muerte, si es posible, ya que no en paz con el mundo, algo que se me antoja imposible, sí, al menos, en paz conmigo mismo. Y en cuanto a ti y tu secreto, tu misterioso origen, pronto pasarás a ser una leyenda, luego sólo una sombra destinada al olvido. No hagas nada para cambiar eso. Es el transcurso natural del tiempo para con los sucesos increíbles. Pronto ya nadie nos recordará ni a ti, ni a mí, ni a esa extraña legión perdida.

El viejo consejero calló unos instantes mientras cerraba una vez más los ojos. Se lo veía cansado, agotado después de tantos años de secretos, consejos imperiales y misiones que sólo él conocía.

—Tienes mi bendición, general Li Kan —dijo el anciano retomando el uso de la palabra con su tono habitual de serenidad y control, como si hubiera regresado al mundo real después de aquella letanía de palabras que habían sonado a gran confesión retenida durante años y por fin liberada—. Tenéis mi bendición, tú y tu esposa. Ve al norte, vigila la Gran Muralla y defiéndela de los ataques de los *hsiung-nu* y sé eficaz en tu labor, como has sido siempre. Mientras lo seas, y lo serás porque tienes la inteligencia militar para hacerlo, tu familia estará a salvo. El emperador An-ti no se atreverá a cambiarte de tu puesto. Eso es todo.

Li Kan se levantó. Se quedó un momento detenido frente al viejo consejero imperial, que sin mirarlo ya se centraba en coger los documentos con los que estaba ocupado antes de su llegada. El general comprendió que todas las palabras estaban dichas, así que saludó, se puso firme, dio media vuelta y sin decir nada salió de la oficina de aquel funcionario, de aquel anciano, de aquel amigo.

Li Kan caminó lentamente por los pasillos del palacio imperial de Loyang mientras en su mente oía aún las palabras de viejo asistente: «Pronto pasarás a ser una leyenda, luego sólo una sombra destinada al olvido».

132

EL PUENTE SOBRE EL DANUBIO

Drobeta, Dacia
Final del otoño de 117 d.C.

—¡No puede ser, por Hércules! ¡Ésa no puede ser la orden! —repitió por enésima vez el *praefectus castrorum*.

Tercio Juliano, *legatus* al mando de la VII legión *Claudia*, o de lo que quedaba de ella después de que muchas *vexillationes* y parte de su caballería fueran destinadas a Oriente para la conquista de Partia primero y luego para luchar contra el levantamiento de los judíos, suspiró. El *legatus* ya había previsto la falta de predisposición del jefe del campamento de Drobeta a ejecutar aquella orden, pero nada podía hacerse.

—Cincinato, se trata de una carta con el sello del emperador —se explicó el jefe supremo de la VII *Claudia*—. Entiendo tu rabia, pero nada puede hacerse.

—Lo hemos construido con nuestras propias manos —insistía Cincinato con lágrimas en los ojos.

Hacía tiempo que Tercio Juliano no veía llorar a un oficial.

Tampoco le pareció inadecuado aquel gesto desesperado de su subordinado.

—He pedido confirmación a Turbo, el nuevo gobernador de la provincia de Dacia nombrado recientemente por Adriano, al nuevo emperador mismo que sigue en Asia y hasta al Senado en Roma —respondió el *legatus*.

—¿Y...? —preguntó el *praefectus castrorum* con voz vibrante en busca de un hilo de esperanza al tiempo que se secaba las lágrimas de las mejillas con las manos arrugadas, ajadas por el sol y el frío y el trabajo duro de la guerra.

—El nuevo emperador, el *Imperator Caesar Traianus Hadrianus Augustus Pontifex Maximus* reitera la orden desde Selinus y el tono de la carta es bastante hiriente. Adriano me amenaza con degradarme sólo para empezar. Si no obedecemos la orden tu carrera y la mía terminarán en la arena del Anfiteatro Flavio delante de los leones. Dice que piensa venir a la Dacia personalmente en las próximas semanas para entrevistarse con el gobernador Turbo y quiere comprobar el desmantelamiento del puente. No podemos negarnos, Cincinato. ¿Quieres acabar con los leones?

—Imagino que no. Con los senadores Celso, Palma y Nigrino muertos no parece que muchos se vayan a atrever a contradecir al nuevo César. Pero, la verdad, con ellos muertos, las fieras del anfiteatro ya no se me antojan un final tan malo —se atrevió a decir Cincinato mirando de reojo a su superior a la vez que hacía una pregunta y proponía un plan peligroso—: ¿Y Lucio Quieto? Decían que cabalgaba hacia la provincia de África. Allí tiene muchos amigos y puede hacerse con un ejército. Si le ayudamos desde el norte...

Tercio Juliano no se ofendió por aquella sugerencia de rebelión, pero miró hacia la puerta abierta. Se levantó, pasó junto a Cincinato, llegó al umbral y se asomó. Los guardias estaban a unos pasos. Cerró la puerta, regresó a su *solium* y se sentó de nuevo. Frente a él, al otro lado de la mesa, Cincinato seguía en pie. Tercio Juliano se dirigió a su subordinado en voz baja.

—Por nuestra vieja amistad, por los muchos años en campaña juntos, no tendré en cuenta lo que me acabas de sugerir. Por menos de eso el nuevo emperador ha condenado a muerte a otros. Escúchame bien, Cincinato, porque no lo repetiré: Lucio Quieto ha muerto. Fue interceptado por tropas fieles a Adriano, creo que comandadas por esa rata de Atiano, que se está encargando de todo el trabajo sucio del nuevo César en Asia. De todo lo horrible en Italia ya se está ocupando ese miserable de Barcino,[93] el senador Serviano y todo su clan. El caso es que con Lucio Quieto muerto y los otros senadores

93. Barcelona.

asesinados no hay nadie dispuesto ni capaz de hacer frente al nuevo emperador. ¿Lo entiendes?

Cincinato asintió.

El *legatus* siguió hablando, con voz temblorosa, al tiempo que apretaba los puños mientras continuaba explicándose, luchando por contenerse y no gritar para que no lo oyeran los guardias, sus propios hombres.

—Por todos los dioses, Cincinato, yo mismo pensé en lo que has dicho: con Quieto en África reuniendo hombres y nosotros aquí en la Dacia podríamos haber plantado cara a Adriano. ¿Crees que no lo he considerado viendo cómo el nuevo César ha retirado nuestras tropas de las llanuras de Oltenia y Muntenia y de otras zonas del bajo Danubio? Muchos senadores, hartos de ver cómo entregamos tanto territorio a los bárbaros, nos habrían apoyado y más después de las ejecuciones de Celso, Palma y Nigrino, pero Adriano es muy inteligente y ha acabado con Quieto, cortando toda posible rebelión de raíz. El nuevo César sabe que sin él no hay oposición posible. Así que no nos queda otra, por Cástor y Pólux, nos guste o no, que obedecer los mandatos del nuevo emperador. ¿Entiendes o no entiendes ya lo que te estoy explicando? Tenemos esa maldita orden y hemos de cumplirla. Si no lo haces tú lo haré yo personalmente, aunque tenga que ir con una antorcha de un extremo a otro del puente. —Lanzó un grito y lo subrayó pegando un puñetazo en la mesa—: ¡Dioses!

Cincinato guardó unos instantes de silencio, pero luego aún se atrevió a preguntar más.

—¿Y el Senado también ha confirmado la orden?

—También —respondió Tercio Juliano intentando serenarse; hacía años que no perdía el control—. Tengo una carta de Serviano informando de que el Senado ha votado a favor de la orden de Adriano con respecto al puente. Estamos atados de manos y pies. Así que empieza a reunir a tus hombres y ve dando las instrucciones necesarias.

—Hay legionarios que tienen amigos suyos enterrados entre las piedras del puente. No se lo tomarán bien.

—Lo sé —admitió Tercio Juliano—, pero son legionarios de Roma y cumplirán sus órdenes como siempre.

—¿Incluso si Roma se ha vuelto loca?

—Incluso en esas circunstancias —confirmó Tercio Juliano—. Un legionario ha de cumplir las órdenes. Si no Roma no es nada. Y nosotros tampoco.

—De acuerdo —convino al fin el *praefectus castrorum*, pero pasó a plantear ahora los problemas prácticos que había para ejecutar aquella maldita orden—. La madera de aliso que seleccionó el arquitecto es especialmente resistente al fuego. No será fácil conseguir que arda.

—Cierto. He estado pensando en ello —dijo Tercio Juliano. El tiempo de espera que había tenido al aguardar las cartas que confirmaran aquella maldita orden le habían dado, en efecto, muchos días para estudiar todas aquellas complicaciones técnicas—. Usaremos grasa y aceite. Pintaremos todo el puente con sustancias inflamables y pondremos paja por toda su superficie y también en grandes balsas que situaremos bajo las arcadas del puente, junto a las grandes pilastras de piedra. Estas balsas las habremos llenado también de paja untada con más grasa y aceite. Luego lo prenderemos todo a la vez: unos desde arriba del puente, otros desde los extremos del mismo y otros legionarios lo harán desde barcas junto a las balsas.

Cincinato comprobó que su superior lo tenía todo bien calibrado,

—La falta de lluvias de las últimas semanas ayudará —sentenció, al fin, el *praefectus castrorum*.

Drobeta
Tres días después

Lo hicieron al amanecer.

—Prended —dijo el *legatus* en voz baja, casi como si no quisiera decirlo.

La superficie del puente se resistía a arder, pese a que las grandes montañas de paja que había extendidas por todas partes sí ardían en largas llamas que se elevaban hacia el cielo azul de la Dacia. Sin embargo, las barcazas de debajo del puente prendieron bien y sus lenguas de fuego lamían las entrañas de la gigantesca construcción desde sus cimientos, hasta que en varios puntos, justo en medio del río, las grandes vigas de madera empezaron a crujir al verse rodeadas de más y más llamas incandescentes.

—El puente se quema —dijo Cincinato con nuevas lágrimas en los ojos. Y no era el único. Otros legionarios de la VII *Claudia* que habían contribuido en un pasado nada lejano a construir aquella superestructura de ingeniería civil también tenían los ojos húmedos, y en el brillo de sus pupilas se reflejaban las llamas que consumían el fruto de sus años de esfuerzo.

Nadie entendía aquella orden.

—¿Es por envidia? —preguntó Cincinato al *legatus*.

—Quizá —convino Tercio Juliano—. Aunque ante el Senado Serviano argumentó que el puente de Drobeta es un arma de doble filo; el senador de Barcino insistió en que podría ser usado por bárbaros para entrar en el Imperio. Los roxolanos están muy agitados y rebeldes. Les tienen miedo en Roma.

—Ya no confían en nosotros para defender las fronteras.

—Puede que no. El miedo se ha instalado en Roma. El miedo a crecer, el miedo a ser más grandes, el miedo a todo. Es el principio de un largo y lento fin. Largo y lento porque somos muchos aún los que estamos aquí en la frontera, defendiendo el Imperio, pero fin porque Roma ya no cree en sí misma.

—Con Trajano ha muerto Roma —dijo Cincinato.

—Con Trajano hemos muerto todos, amigo mío.

Las llamas consumían la superestructura de madera. El puente en su totalidad estaba envuelto en el mayor incendio que nunca hubieran visto en aquella región del mundo. El humo podía vislumbrarse desde decenas de millas de distancia.

—¿Cómo murió Lucio Quieto? —preguntó el *praefectus castrorum*—. Era un gran jefe de la caballería de Roma.

—Según he podido averiguar —respondió Tercio Juliano en voz muy baja—, Lucio Quieto murió luchando hasta la última gota de su sangre, como mueren los héroes.

[En tiempos de Adriano] *se dio orden de desmantelar inclu-*
so la superestructura del puente del Danubio levantando aguas
abajo de las Puertas de Hierro, construido por Apolodoro, el
principal arquitecto de Trajano

ANTHONY BIRLEY, *Biografía de Adriano*, pág. 116

133

EL CRUEL VOLOGASES

Cesifonte
Final de otoño de 117 d.C.

Aryazate vio cómo su peor pesadilla se hacía realidad. No sólo no había podido impedir que los romanos la devolvieran a su odiado padre, sino que además éste la usaba, otra vez, como herramienta para mantenerse en el poder, ese mismo poder que había empleado para matar a Rixnu y a todas las mujeres de su anterior séquito real cuando salió huyendo de Cesifonte acosado por Trajano y sus ejércitos.

Aryazate regresó a la ciudad de su niñez para comprobar cómo su padre ya se había hecho con otro nuevo séquito de esposas, muchas de las cuales ya estaban embarazadas por el eterno *Šāhān Šāh*, a quien ni romanos por Occidente ni usurpadores como Vologases por Oriente habían conseguido arrebatarle el poder de forma permanente.

Cesifonte había sido saqueada por los invasores de Roma, pero estaba siendo reconstruida en gran parte, aunque Aryazate no tuvo mucho tiempo para comprobar cuáles eran los designios de Osroes sobre los trabajos de renovación de los edificios imperiales partos, pues su padre la convocó a una audiencia privada apenas al día siguiente de haber llegado desde Edesa.

Aryazate suspiró mientras entraba en la sala del trono de Cesifonte. Su mente repasaba su viaje: de Selinus a Antioquía y de la gran ciudad asiática a Edesa, la capital de Osroene. En la corte de Partamaspates, la joven también había implorado, como ya hiciera ante Adriano, ser acogida allí y no ser entregada de nuevo a su padre. Pero su hermano, débil como siempre, no quiso desobedecer ni a Osroes, su padre, ni mucho menos a su nuevo amo real, el emperador romano. Partamaspates, como ya hiciera en Cesifonte el día del asesinato en masa de todas las mujeres, se hizo a un lado y, una vez más, abandonó a su hermana a su suerte.

Perdida esa última oportunidad, la princesa parta había terminado, al fin, siendo conducida justo allí adonde nunca esperaba tener que regresar: ante los pies de su padre.

La joven entró en la antigua sala del trono dorado de Cesifonte, donde ya no estaba el gran trono de oro macizo que Trajano le había arrebatado al *Šāhān Šāh*. En su lugar, la muchacha vio que Osroes había hecho poner otro de mármol con incrustaciones de piedras preciosas y cubierto con cojines y telas para mayor comodidad. No estaba mal, pero en modo alguno llegaba a impresionar como el trono perdido.

—Es provisional —dijo Osroes como si tuviera la capacidad de leer el pensamiento de su hija. Ella no dijo nada. Su padre continuó—. Pronto tendré el suficiente oro para fundirlo y poder disponer de un nuevo trono dorado igual o aún más grandioso que el anterior. ¿Ves? Todo puede arreglarse. Hasta he conseguido recuperar gran parte del territorio que ese lunático de Trajano pretendía tener bajo su control. Nadie puede contra Partia. No han podido antes y no podrán nunca. Pero nos hemos reunido para hablar de ti. —Se detuvo un instante mientras la contemplaba inquisitivamente—. Siempre me he preguntado cómo te las ingeniaste para sobrevivir, aunque eso... —hizo un gesto con la mano derecha, como quien desecha algo sin importancia—, realmente ya no me interesa. El pasado reciente es mejor olvidarlo. A mí se me habrá de recordar por lo que haga a partir de ahora, y pienso hacer cosas grandes, pero no te he hecho traer para explicarte asuntos que van más allá de tu comprensión, pues como mujer eres incapaz de entender de qué estoy hablando. Sólo te he convocado para informarte de que por fin vas a tener un esposo y que éste será Vologases. Al final, volvemos a la primera opción de todas.

Ella fue a abrir la boca, pero Osroes levantó la mano e hizo un gesto de desaprobación y ella guardó silencio.

—Si consigues que te acepte —continuó el *Šāhān Šāh*— y que detenga sus ataques contra mí, si logras que acepte pactar conmigo, podrás disfrutar de un futuro con tu nuevo esposo, al que le concederé el gobierno de una satrapía en la región oriental del Imperio. Si no consigues que te acepte como esposa, entonces ya no me serás útil y tendré que hacer que lo que ordené en su momento termine por cumplirse, es decir, tendré que asegurarme de que eres ejecutada. Hay quien ha visto en el hecho de que escapases de aquella muerte una señal de Ahura Mazda, pero mis sacerdotes están de acuerdo en interpretar que si fuiste salvada fue para, precisamente, servirnos ahora como escudo contra Vologases. Y no digas nada, no hables: sal y cumple como mujer.

Osroes alzó ambas manos y antes de que Aryazate pudiera decir palabra alguna, varios guardias ya la escoltaban hacia la salida.

Merv, extremo oriental de Partia
Dos meses después

El viaje fue largo y penoso. Hubo vientos huracanados en los desiertos de arena, tormentas de lluvia torrencial en las praderas y siempre mucho frío por las noches y mucho calor durante el día. Aryazate, refugiada en su carromato real parto, custodiado por un pequeño regimiento de caballería ligera imperial, apenas se asomaba de vez en cuando para ver cómo los paisajes cambiaban o de dónde provenía el viento.

Un día el carro se detuvo, pero no fue como otras veces. Sonó a definitivo.

Era el final del camino. ¿También el final de su vida? De una forma u otra era el final de su existencia como la había conocido hasta ahora: o terminaba como esposa de aquel salvaje sanguinario de Vologases o la ejecutarían. La muerte no la asustaba, pero la enervaba llegar a ella sin haber conseguido vengarse de su padre, de aquella maldita orden por la que hizo que dieran muerte a Rixnu y al resto de las mujeres. Aryazate anhelaba venganza con una fuerza tal que había rezado a

Ahura Mazda para que le diera una oportunidad. Una sola. No necesitaría más. Estaba dispuesta a arrastrarse ante quien fuera, pero sabía que necesitaba la ayuda de Ahura Mazda y de todos los dioses en el cielo y de un hombre fuerte en la tierra. Aunque fuera el más vil de los usurpadores sanguinarios, ese ser cruel y horrible, ese hombre despiadado, feo y asqueroso de quien le habían hablado desde niña: ese terrible Vologases que, según le habían contado siempre en Cesifonte, escupía espuma y sangre por la boca cuando aullaba sus órdenes en el campo de batalla, violaba a todas las mujeres que se cruzaban en su camino y asesinaba a los niños por pura diversión delante de sus padres. Ése tendría que ser su único aliado. Y tendría que yacer con él y hacer con él todas aquellas cosas que siempre soñó realizar con un príncipe apuesto y valiente. Le entraron arcadas. Bajó del carro. Se arrodilló. Vomitó a escondidas, sin que nadie la viera, detrás del carromato imperial.

Pasaron unos instantes.

Se sintió algo aliviada. Se incorporó y miró a su alrededor.

Estaban en medio de una gran llanura.

El carro seguía detenido. La pequeña guardia de jinetes estaba inmóvil unos pasos por delante. No la miraban. Los guerreros tenían otras preocupaciones. A lo lejos se veía un gran ejército aproximándose. Las tropas de Vologases pronto los rodearon. Detrás de ellos se vislumbraban las fortificaciones de la ciudad de Merv: una enorme fortaleza que, según había oído contar en Cesifonte, había sido levantada en parte con prisioneros romanos capturados en alguna batalla antigua. Aryazate sonrió con amargura. Ella misma se sentía prisionera en ruta hacia su fatal destino, un final que no preveía mejor que el de aquellos romanos apresados en tiempos pasados por sus antepasados. Estaba a punto de ver al monstruo usurpador, al eterno demonio que acechaba en Oriente desde hacía más de diez años reclamando para sí un trono que no era suyo. Eso le habían enseñado a ella en Cesifonte desde niña una y otra vez. En aquel momento, Aryazate recordó cómo había temido en el pasado casarse con el feo y repulsivo y viejo Partamasiris cuando éste gobernaba Armenia. Ahora aquello le habría parecido un mal menor. Al menos Partamasiris, pese a ser asqueroso y viejo, habría sido uno de los suyos y no un criminal que acechaba el trono de Cesifonte con una guerra brutal y sin cuartel, un ser para quien todo valía: saqueos, asesinatos, tortura...

De entre las tropas que los rodeaban surgió un jinete sobre un poderoso caballo negro que se adelantó seguido de cerca por una veintena de sus guerreros. Avanzó hasta quedar a unos cien pasos de donde se encontraba el carro.

—Ve —dijo el oficial parto al mando de la pequeña escolta de la hija de Osroes.

La muchacha se volvió y vio que el oficial sudaba. Miró entonces hacia las tropas que los rodeaban y observó cómo centenares de arqueros tenían sus armas dispuestas y apuntando hacia ellos.

Aryazate obedeció y se adelantó sola, a pie —nadie le ofreció un caballo—, hacia el criminal de Oriente, hacia el usurpador del trono, hacia el mal hecho hombre, hacia la vileza transformada en guerrero irredento, innoble e implacable. La muchacha se había jurado una y otra vez a sí misma que haría lo que fuera para agradar a aquel ser terrible, pero, de pronto, a cada pequeño paso que daba para acercarse a él sus fuerzas, su decisión y su templanza flaqueaban.

Así, con el vestido de la duda y la pesadumbre y la pena de sentirse tan cobarde, Aryazate llegó frente al gran azote de Oriente.

Vologases dijo algo a los hombres de su guardia que ella no pudo oír. Los guerreros del usurpador se echaron a reír. Ella dejó de caminar. Sentía ganas de llorar, pero fue capaz de no entregarse a esa última humillación. Ya era bastante haber perdido parte de su autocontrol y descubrir su miedo en su mirada.

Vologases desmontó del caballo y se acercó a ella. El criminal asesino de Oriente llevaba el rostro cubierto por un pañuelo. A Aryazate le pareció muy apropiado y casi lo agradeció. Cuanto menos viera de aquel hombre, cuanto menos sintiera su cuerpo, cuanto menos tuviera que besarlo, mejor.

Ella, a su vez, también llevaba el rostro tapado por un fino velo de seda amarilla.

—Descúbrete —le dijo él en parto, la lengua que compartían. Eso le hizo recordar a la princesa que pese a que era un usurpador y un salvaje sanguinario también se decía que era descendiente de alguna de las familias reales de la dinastía arsácida. ¿Sería cierto? Aquello le vino a la mente no sólo por el hecho de que usara el parto y no el griego o una lengua extranjera, sino también porque el timbre de su voz resultaba... agradable, como si quien hablara fuera un hombre fuerte y viril y, quizá, algo totalmente absurdo, apuesto. ¡Cuánto puede engañar una voz sin rostro!

Aryazate se descubrió y desveló su belleza, sus ojos oscuros y grandes, su mirada que revivía algo de la decisión y la fuerza que estaba recuperando poco a poco, pese a seguir presa del pánico. Y como ese terror también se dibujó en su mirada, resultaba una mujer hermosa y asustada, lo que la hacía a los ojos de los hombres un ser carnal aún más apetecible.

—Mi tío abuelo me envía un regalo hermoso —dijo Vologases.

¿Su tío abuelo? Aryazate no entendía bien. De acuerdo que aquel hombre pudiera descender de alguna rama de la gran familia arsácida, pero que fuera sobrino nieto de su padre era algo inesperado y desconocido para ella. ¿Tan próximo estaba aquel salvaje del trono por linaje?

—No soy un regalo y no veo justo que uno de los dos pueda ver al otro y el otro no —dijo ella sorprendiéndose de ver recobrada parte de su energía y templanza, aunque quizá la voz aún le fallase y el tono vibrante de sus palabras desvelara parte del gran miedo que tenía.

Vologases echó la cabeza hacia atrás y se puso a reír con ganas. Una carcajada limpia, alegre, divertida a la que se unieron los hombres de su escolta. Los guerreros del regimiento de Osroes que habían llevado a Aryazate no se rieron nada. Centenares de arcos seguían apuntando hacia ellos y la decisión de que dispararan o no pendía de un fino hilo de seda que intuían que muy pronto sería cortado por quien precisamente estaba riendo en aquel momento.

—Por Ahura Mazda, es justo lo que dices —dijo Vologases. Pero de pronto cambió el tono de su voz y con un timbre grave y siniestro añadió una pregunta—: ¿Seguro que te atreves a verme el rostro?

Aryazate engulló la poca saliva que le quedaba en la garganta.

—Sí —dijo en voz baja, sin convicción, pero lo dijo.

—Tú lo has querido.

Vologases se descubrió el rostro quitando el pañuelo que lo protegía de la arena del desierto. Y, al hacerlo, volvió a reírse con más ganas que antes.

A Aryazate la sorprendieron dos cosas: por un lado que Vologases hubiera mencionado al dios supremo y, por otro, que la faz de aquel ser sanguinario y cruel era un rostro... hermoso, de facciones suaves, ojos de mirada profunda, barba bien cuidada y sin apenas canas. Estaba ante un parto, sobrino nieto de su padre, apuesto y que creía en Ahura Mazda. No era aquello lo que esperaba haber encontrado al final de su viaje.

—Ya me has visto. Ahora dime, si no eres un regalo ¿qué eres? —preguntó Vologases cuando dejó de reír—. O mejor aún: ¿quién eres?

—Soy Aryazate, hija de Osroes, enviada por mi padre para que me aceptes por esposa a cambio de un pacto de paz.

Todo eso ya lo sabía Vologases por las cartas enviadas por Osroes, pero el joven príncipe parto disfrutaba viendo cómo la muchacha se explicaba.

—¿Y qué obtengo yo con esa paz? —preguntó él entonces.

—El gobierno de una satrapía en la región más oriental del imperio, siempre y cuando dejes de atacar con tus tropas al ejército imperial de Cesifonte.

Vologases la miró con ojos admirados. No había oído tantas palabras de una mujer ni de tanta enjundia en mucho tiempo. Concretamente desde que su madre muriera.

—¿Y qué es para mí una satrapía oriental cuando lo que es mío por legítimo derecho es el trono dorado de Cesifonte, el dominio completo de todo el Imperio parto, desde Osroene y Armenia hasta las costas del mar cálido y los ríos que nos separan de los kushan? ¿Cree mi tío abuelo que voy a rendirme después de años y años de lucha por tan poco, por una pequeña esquina de todo cuanto es mío por derecho dinástico?

—Obtienes la paz pese a ser un usurpador y consigues mi cuerpo.

—Tu cuerpo lo puedo conseguir ahora mismo sin pactar nada —dijo él amenazadoramente, transformándose en alguien feroz, temible, acercándose tanto a ella que la joven pudo notar su aliento en sus mejillas enrojecidas por la tensión y las sensaciones contradictorias que sentía por dentro. Vologases le daba miedo, pero no asco.

—Para un usurpador el acuerdo que propone mi padre Osroes es bastante generoso —insistió ella.

Aryazate quería asegurarse de que se consiguiera el pacto. Eso le daría tiempo, quizá el suficiente para empujar ella misma de nuevo a Vologases contra su padre y quién sabía si al final conseguir así su anhelada venganza. Pero era prematuro aún pensar en todo eso, pues Vologases se alejaba unos pasos para, de inmediato, revolverse hacia ella como una fiera enfurecida, casi fuera de sí, que le hablaba ahora a gritos, eso sí, sin escupir ni espuma ni sangre por la boca, sólo rabia y desprecio.

—¿Un usurpador yo? ¿Cuántas veces piensas ofenderme insultándome con esa palabra? Es eso lo que te enseñaron desde niña, ¿verdad? ¡Pues escúchame tú ahora, princesa hija de Osroes, y escúchame bien porque no te lo repetiré más! ¡Yo soy Vologases III, hijo de Vologases II, hijo de Vologases I! ¡Mi abuelo era el *Šāhān Šāh*, el rey de reyes de toda Partia, y heredó el título y los territorios completos del imperio de su padre Vonones II, como éste los había recibido antes de su propio padre Gotarces II! —El príncipe parto continuó ahora con un tono más bajo, pero no menos cargado de rabia—. Mi abuelo tenía varios hermanos: a saber, Pacoro, tu padre Osroes, Partamasiris y Mitrídates. Cuando aquél murió dejó el trono a su hijo, Vologases II, mi padre, pero tu propio tío, Pacoro, hermano de Osroes, le arrebató el trono en una guerra traidora.[94]

»Yo soy de la línea auténtica, la que debería haber seguido gobernando Partia y no ese miserable de Pacoro que, cuando estaba a punto de morir, en lugar de retornarme el trono a mí

---

94. Véase el árbol genealógico de la dinastía arsácida parta en los apéndices.

como heredero de mi padre, entregó el Imperio parto a su hermano, tu padre, Osroes, quien lleva años gobernando de forma ignominiosa Cesifonte y sus provincias. Sólo hay que ver la forma cobarde en la que ha dejado que los romanos arrasen todo el Imperio, que entren en Cesifonte y le arrebaten hasta el magnífico trono dorado de mis antepasados. Un miserable así no merece pasar ni un solo día más en Cesifonte y yo, personalmente, me ocuparé de que Osroes sufra por su traición y la traición de todos cuantos le antecedieron y le apoyaron, y esto incluye a todos sus malditos hermanos, sus hijos y... sus hijas.

Aquélla era una lección de historia sobre la familia arsácida nueva para Aryazate. Nunca le habían contado nada parecido en Cesifonte. Quizá aquel príncipe parto que tenía enfrente completamente encolerizado, que no dejaba de acechar al ejército imperial de su padre desde hacía años, tuviera razón. Aryazate presentía que, conociendo de lo que era capaz su padre Osroes, quizá hubiera más nobleza y más realidad en lo que Vologases decía que en lo que siempre le habían enseñado a ella en el Cesifonte de su infancia.

—Pacoro y Partamasiris ya están muertos —dijo ella por decir algo. No sabía bien por dónde continuar aquella conversación extraña e inesperada. Además, ella estaba en la lista de los que Vologases había jurado exterminar. No parecía que hubiera margen para conseguir nada.

—Pero tu padre Osroes en Cesifonte y su hijo, tu hermano Partamaspates, en Osroene, aún siguen vivos, como mi otro tío abuelo Mitrídates en Armenia, aunque todos cederán o se encontrarán con su destino, es decir, conmigo. Y claro, también estás tú, pero como mujer que eres no cuentas —replicó con rapidez y luego la miró una vez más con desdén, se cubrió de nuevo la cara con su pañuelo y se dirigió a ella con aires de despedida—. Ahora que ya sabes la auténtica historia de nuestra dinastía, princesa Aryazate, te devuelvo a tu padre. Márchate de aquí con esos guerreros aterrados que te acompañan y nunca, ¿me oyes bien?, nunca vuelvas a presentarte ante mí porque ya no seré ni tan generoso ni tan clemente.

Y le dio la espalda.

Aryazate se quedó parpadeando. ¿Volver? ¿Volver a qué? ¿A un padre que había ordenado matarla en el pasado y que ahora, habiendo sobrevivido a la matanza de Cesifonte, la usaba como moneda de cambio otra vez para conseguir mantenerse en el poder? Hoy la ofrecía a Vologases, y mañana... ¿a quién? Era cierto que su padre había prometido ejecutarla si no conseguía que Vologases la aceptara como esposa, pero ella estaba segura de que el *Šāhān Šāh*, en lugar de matarla, la volvería a emplear para casarla con algún otro poderoso de los reinos limítrofes con Partia. Era lo que más la encolerizaba. No temía la muerte, sino la idea de poder ser útil a su padre. Eso la trastornaba por completo.

Eso le dio fuerzas.

—Tú crees que odias a Osroes más que nadie en el mundo —dijo Aryazate a Vologases, que cogía ya las riendas de su caballo para montarse en él—, pero tu odio es apenas una suave brisa al lado de la tormenta de venganza y asco y desprecio que yo siento por él.

Las palabras de Aryazate, de quien no esperaba oír ya nada más ni en aquel momento ni en ningún otro momento de su vida, intrigaron a Vologases. Lo suficiente para que devolviera las riendas de su caballo a uno de sus hombres, se descubriera el rostro de nuevo y se acercara una vez más a la muchacha.

—¿Crees acaso que eres el único que sufre por las traiciones y las insidias de mi padre? —continuó Aryazate decidida a contarlo todo, pues todo lo había perdido y ya nada más tenía que perder, sino la vida, una existencia que se le antojaba insufrible si no conseguía venganza—. Tú, Vologases III, no sabes nada, no tienes idea de nada, y, desde luego, no sabes quién soy yo ni lo que soy capaz de hacer.

Vologases la miró de pies a cabeza. Luego habló con serenidad.

—Eres una princesa parta, hija de la rama más miserable de nuestra gran familia, pero la sangre noble de nuestra dinastía corre por tus venas. Ahora no pareces hablar como enviada de Osroes. Eso, lo admito, ha despertado mi curiosidad. Poco más, pero te concedo un instante para que me digas, según tú, quién eres en verdad.

Aryazate le contó todo lo sucedido cuando los romanos llegaron a Cesifonte: cómo su padre ordenó ejecutar a todas las mujeres y los niños para huir con más rapidez.

—Algo había oído de todo eso —dijo Vologases cuando ella terminó con su intenso y dramático relato—. Y no me extraña: los cobardes sólo son valientes contra mujeres y niños desarmados. Cuando se enfrentan a hombres de verdad palidecen, tiemblan, huyen. Tu padre, no obstante, como imaginarás, se habrá ocupado de confundir a todos y de que muchos piensen que la muerte de todo su séquito de mujeres fue promovida por el propio Trajano. Tu padre hizo uso de una vieja costumbre que algunos de nuestros antepasados emplearon hace años. Una costumbre que yo, como tú, detesto y deploro. Yo creo que quien no es capaz de proteger a sus mujeres y a sus niños no merece gobernar nada, ni un pueblo ni una ciudad y mucho menos Partia. La terrible matanza que me has contado, penosa, sin duda, es, sin embargo, tu tragedia personal y nada tiene que ver conmigo. Siento devolverte a quien legítimamente odias tanto, pero no me eres útil para nada. Tendrás que buscar venganza en otra parte. No cuentes conmigo. Mi lucha por recuperar el trono de Cesifonte es una guerra de honor, no una cuestión personal.

—Eso no es cierto: es una guerra personal desde el momento en que desprecias a mi padre casi tanto como yo —se atrevió a decir Aryazate—. Además, dices que no te soy útil, pero puedo causarte muchos más problemas de los que imaginas: si me dejas regresar, mi padre no dudará en usarme de nuevo para conseguir más apoyos, pero esta vez contra ti. Si tú no te desposas conmigo, mi padre me ofrecerá a quien sea que le envíe refuerzos para seguir manteniéndote acorralado en el extremo oriental de Partia. Me entregará a Mitrídates, mi tío, en Armenia, o incluso a mi hermano en Osroene. No sería la primera vez que hay una boda entre hermanos en nuestra familia y con los recursos y los ejércitos de Osroene o de Armenia mi padre será de nuevo fuerte y tu larga guerra de honor, como la llamas, se prolongará eternamente sin que llegue nunca tu victoria. Te harás viejo y morirás lejos de Cesifonte sin haberte sentado nunca en el trono que, como has dicho, mereces por linaje. De modo que no te vayas de aquí devolviéndome a mi padre y pensando que por ser mujer no cuento, porque sí valgo como moneda de cambio para unir a tus enemigos en la lucha por el trono de Partia. Y tampoco digas que la mía y la tuya son guerras diferentes, porque son sólo parte del mismo combate contra el mismo ser miserable. Un enemigo que primero me humillará y me usará a mí, pero sólo para luego derrotarte a ti.

Se hizo un silencio en el que Vologases se puso muy serio, sombrío.

—Lo que dices está bien razonado —aceptó él—, pero no pienso casarme contigo y aceptar una paz con Osroes. —Calló unos instantes. Suspiró y puso los brazos en jarras mientras la miraba—. Lo que siento es que después de lo que has dicho sólo me dejas un camino sensato, que no es otro que ordenar que te ejecuten aquí y ahora.

—La muerte venida del auténtico heredero del trono de Partia será mil veces mejor a que se me devuelva a manos de mi padre sin posibilidad de conseguir venganza.

La bravura de la joven, que no bajó en momento alguno la mirada, impactó a Vologases como no lo había hecho nada ni nadie en años. Pero tenía que hacerse lo que debía hacerse. La joven princesa lo había dejado muy claro y, con toda seguridad, había resumido muy bien las que serían futuras acciones de su padre con respecto a ella si retornaba viva de aquel encuentro. Se sorprendió de no haberlo pensado antes.

Vologases III, despacio, llevó la mano a la empuñadura de su espada.

Sí, cada vez lo veía más claro: Osroes casaría a aquella muchacha de sangre noble parta con Mitrídates o con Partamaspates. Primero la ofrecería a Mitrídates: más valiente, más fuerte, más peligroso y con un reino, Armenia, de más recursos para prolongar la guerra.

Vologases III desenfundó. La espada silbó al deslizarse hacia el exterior.

—Arrodíllate —dijo.

Aryazate obedeció. La muerte, al fin, llegaba como una

bendición. Al menos no sería su padre quien la matara y no la emplearía para fortalecerse. No haber vengado a Rixnu y al resto de mujeres y niños y niñas la entristecía infinitamente. Pero sólo eso: la falta de venganza. La muerte era bienvenida.

Vologases III se acercó a la muchacha arrodillada.

El líder de Partia oriental fruncía el ceno. Llevaba años de guerra. Había matado a mucha gente, pero nunca a una mujer desarmada. Pero aquélla no era una muchacha sin más: ella misma se lo había buscado al hacerle ver que era una herramienta del maldito Osroes, un arma de su enemigo eterno que debía suprimir en aquel mismo instante o luego se volvería contra él y los suyos durante años...

Aryazate cerró los ojos.

Vologases III levantó su espada. Sus soldados no decían nada. Los guerreros de la princesa parta empezaron a llorar. Vologases intuía que ese llanto no era por lástima de lo que iba a sucederle a la hija de Osroes en un instante, sino porque si la princesa era decapitada imaginaban que su destino no sería mucho mejor.

Vologases oyó aquellos sollozos y miró de reojo hacia aquellos guerreros de Osroes. Luego miró de nuevo a Aryazate, ante él, siempre de rodillas pero sin ni una sola lágrima en el rostro. Tanta cobardía en unos y tanto valor en aquella joven, en una mujer, casi una niña.

—¡Por Ahura Mazda! —exclamó Vologases—. ¡Tú no mereces la muerte!

Y bajó la espada.

Aryazate abrió los ojos y los clavó en él.

—Tú mereces ser mi Šhar Bāmbišn, mi reina.

Aryazate se quedó muy quieta. Apenas respiraba. No estaba segura de entender lo que estaba ocurriendo.

—Levántate —añadió Vologases tendiéndole la mano.

La muchacha alargó el brazo con su propia mano temblorosa. No era miedo: sólo nervios. Seguía sin comprender. No se atrevía a pensar que estaba ocurriendo lo que, en efecto, estaba pasando.

—Nos casaremos esta tarde y esta noche serás mía —continuó Vologases sin dejar de mirarla—. Luego, juntos, marcha-remos hacia Occidente y no nos detendrá nadie hasta llegar a las puertas mismas de Cesifonte. Levántate y ven conmigo: la princesa Aryazate, la que va a ser reina de reinas, tendrá, por fin, su venganza. Eso era lo que querías, ¿no es cierto?

—Sí, mi señor —respondió ella y añadió—. Sí, mi *Šāhān Šāh.*

Vologases sonrió al oír de labios de aquella hermosa princesa el título de rey de reyes referido a su persona.

—Si sabes satisfacer a un hombre en el lecho tan bien como sabes hablar, voy a ser un rey de reyes muy afortunado.

La muchacha vio cómo Vologases pedía que llevaran un carro para ella. Otro distinto al que la había conducido allí desde Cesifonte.

—Gracias —dijo esbozando, por primera vez en aquel intenso encuentro, una tenue sonrisa que, a ojos de Vologases, sólo la hizo aún más bella.

Aryazate subió al carro con la mirada encendida.

En su pequeña cabeza bullían grandes ideas: una guerra mortal contra los ejércitos partos de Occidente, llegar a Cesifonte, un largo asedio y, al final de aquel periplo de sangre, matar a su padre.

Rixnu sería vengada.

Pronto.

Era feliz.

Entretanto, Vologases, una vez que su futura esposa estuvo segura en el nuevo carro, se volvió hacia los guerreros de Osroes que la habían llevado allí. Ya no lloriqueaban. El sorprendente giro que habían tomado los acontecimientos de aquel encuentro les había devuelto la esperanza de retornar sanos y salvos a Cesifonte, donde, sin duda, serían bienvenidos al haber aceptado Vologases a Aryazate como esposa.

El líder de Partia oriental los miraba muy fijamente. Aquellos cobardes no entendían nada. Vologases estaba replanteándose muchas cosas: quizá las mujeres sí contaban, al menos algo más de lo que él había pensado antes; quizá no. Tenía que meditar sobre el asunto, pero había algo que tenía muy claro: él no olvidaba con tanta facilidad las lágrimas en los rostros de los cobardes que apenas unos instantes atrás no habían movido ni un solo dedo por defender a la princesa que escoltaban. Una guardia imperial de miserables.

Vologases miró a sus hombres al tiempo que montaba en su caballo y les dio una orden precisa.

—Matadlos y enviad sus cabezas de regreso a Cesifonte.

134

EL FUNERAL Y EL TRIUNFO DE TRAJANO

Roma
Invierno de 117 d.C.

Entre el Campo de Marte y el foro de Trajano

El Campo de Marte bullía con miles de legionarios llegados de todas las unidades que, de un modo u otro, habían participado en las campañas de Oriente de Trajano. El gran desfile triunfal se estaba organizando allí mientras en el centro de la ciudad se abrían todas las puertas de los templos donde se quemaba incienso en cada *ara*, en cualquier rincón sagrado de Roma. La ciudad entera estaba engalanada con guirnaldas.

Los primeros en entrar en la ciudad cruzando la gran puerta triunfal fueron los senadores, todos menos cuatro. Quieto, Celso, Palma y Nigrino ya no estaban entre ellos y su ausencia pesaba sobre muchos de sus colegas, de forma que la faz seria de la mayoría de los *patres conscripti* contrastaba con la alegría del pueblo de Roma. Y es que Adriano, en una hábil estrategia para ganarse el favor de un pueblo al que le costaba aceptar la retirada de las provincias orientales, había repartido grandes cantidades de dinero. El nuevo emperador había concedido a cada ciudadano romano tres *aureus*, el equivalente a trescientos sestercios para cada habitante libre de Roma.

De entre los senadores, no obstante, algunos rostros parecían estar más en consonancia con el entusiasmo mostrado por el pueblo, en particular el caso de Serviano, que veía cómo el sueño de que uno de sus descendientes fuera nombrado sucesor del nuevo César estaba cada vez más próximo a cumplirse.

Tras los *patres conscripti* iban los *buccinatores*, que con sus trompetas anunciaban la entrada en la ciudad de más de un centenar de carros con despojos de guerra obtenidos por las legiones romanas en Oriente, seguidos por otro centenar de hombres que exhibían grandes cuadros pintados donde se mostraban las mayores hazañas conseguidas por Trajano: la anexión de Armenia, la victoria contra los partos en el Tigris, la flota romana entera transportada por tierra del Éufrates al Tigris, la conquista de Cesifonte, imágenes de ciudades añadidas al Imperio —si bien por la política de Adriano sólo temporalmente—, como Artaxata, Edesa, Babilonia, Nínive, Nísibis o Carax, entre otras muchas. Luego desfilaban más cuadros con las derrotas de los ejércitos de Partamasiris en Armenia, de Osroes en Mesopotamia y de Mitrídates y Sanatruces en Partia, carros cargados de joyas, plata y oro, armas de todo tipo confiscadas al enemigo: lanzas, espadas, escudos y miles de los temidos arcos partos que tanto dolor causaron a los hombres de Craso antaño, armas a las que Trajano supo imponerse, corazas de los terribles *catafractos* enemigos, armaduras de los jinetes y también de los propios caballos. Pero de entre todos los tesoros de guerra arrebatados a los partos destacaba por encima de cualquier otro el gran trono dorado de Cesifonte, portado en una gran acémila, donde brillaba resplandeciente e imponente bajo el sol invernal que bañaba las calles de Roma. La visión de aquel gran asiento de oro macizo henchía los corazones del público de un orgullo especial, pues todos sabían que Adriano había ordenado la penosa retirada de todos esos territorios que Trajano había conquistado, pero, al menos, aquel trono arrebatado al enemigo eterno de Partia ya era suyo para siempre. Se hablaba de que lo fundirían en Roma para hacer monedas, como las que había repartido Adriano entre todos los ciudadanos libres, o quizá lo derretirían para hacer una gran estatua de Trajano. Todo eran rumores sobre más y más monumentos y celebraciones que se iban a realizar para conmemorar las grandes heroicidades del *Optimus Princeps*, el mejor de los emperadores jamás conocido.

Tras el trono de oro de Cesifonte desfilaron decenas de toros blancos que iban a ser sacrificados en el Templo de Júpiter en lo alto del Capitolio. Llevaban los cuernos pintados de dorado, adornados con guirnaldas, y los lomos cubiertos con mantos de fina seda procedente de la remota Xeres.

En el palco imperial del Circo Máximo

La gran procesión victoriosa, que servía al mismo tiempo de funeral, había cruzado la puerta triunfal y serpenteaba por el foro Boario, el velabro, el circo Flaminio, el gran nuevo e imponente foro de Trajano, con sus mercados y bibliotecas y la gran columna, hasta que la comitiva empezó, por fin, a entrar en el Circo Máximo, donde más de doscientas cincuenta mil personas bramaban de júbilo ante aquella exhibición del poder de Roma.

En el palco imperial del Circo Máximo estaban las mujeres de la dinastía Ulpio-Aelia: Plotina, la esposa del fallecido Trajano: Matidia, su sobrina; Vibia Sabina, la mujer de Adriano; Rupilia y otras sobrinas nietas del victorioso César. Adriano, el nuevo emperador, estaba ausente, pues según se había dicho en el Senado, había decidido ir a la Dacia a asegurar la frontera del Danubio, donde los roxolanos estaban causando más problemas de los habituales.

Había también algunos otros ilustres invitados en el palco. En particular destacaba un curioso grupo de tres hombres ya entrados en años, alguno realmente anciano, que asistían con el semblante serio a aquel gran desfile imperial, mezcla de triunfo y funeral.

—La seda que cubre esos toros habría costado muchos menos sestercios si las tropas no se hubieran retirado de Partia —dijo Apolodoro de Damasco en voz alta.

—Sssssh —silbó Suetonio y luego habló en voz baja—. Hay nuevos pretorianos por todas partes. Hay que tener cuidado con lo que se dice.

Apolodoro de Damasco asintió una vez, suspiró y volvió a hablar, esta vez con más tiento.

—Ya he visto bastante de esta pantomima. Ha sido, como siempre, un placer veros, pero me voy a retirar.

—Pues despídete de la emperatriz viuda y de la nueva y alega que te encuentras enfermo —añadió Dión Coceyo, el tercero del grupo.

—¿Tan mal están las cosas con el nuevo César en el poder? —preguntó Apolodoro, algo incrédulo de que fuera preciso andarse con tantos miramientos.

—Si cuatro senadores han sido... eliminados —susurró ahora Suetonio—, no hay nadie a salvo.

—¿Vuelven los tiempos de Domiciano? —preguntó Apolodoro.

Ni Suetonio ni Dión Coceyo respondieron. A ambos aquella conversación les parecía profundamente inoportuna y más en el palco imperial del Circo Máximo, en medio de un desfile triunfal organizado por el Senado en honor a Trajano pero controlado por pretorianos nuevos fieles sólo a Adriano.

—Bueno, yo soy bastante menos prescindible que un senador —añadió Apolodoro con cierta soberbia propia de su carácter—. Cuando necesitan puentes, foros, monumentos, puertos, acueductos o anfiteatros, entonces saben que no hay otro mejor. Eso me mantendrá a salvo de las purgas, si las hay. Pero he de admitir que desde un punto de vista estrictamente personal echaré de menos a Trajano. Era un hombre que sabía reconocer el talento de cada uno y un César que me dio la oportunidad, como nunca antes nadie, de hacer... —La voz del arquitecto adquirió un tinte vibrante cargado, para sorpresa de sus interlocutores, de emoción—... De hacer imposibles. Sí, Trajano me permitió soñar. Me propuso retos inalcanzables: puentes infinitos, canales irrealizables, foros grandiosos. ¿Cuándo habrá otro como él?

Se despidió y, sin alegar enfermedad ni molestia alguna, salió del palco tras limitarse a saludar a la antigua emperatriz de Roma y a la nueva con una sencilla reverencia. Plotina lo miró mientras se alejaba, pero su rostro no mostraba ni enfado ni sorpresa; ya conocía de sobra la personalidad imprevisible de aquel viejo arquitecto. Vibia Sabina aún no sabía qué pensar de nada ni de nadie. Vivía en su propia confusión, casada con el nuevo César, un hombre al que detestaba.

—Su rencor hacia Adriano es por lo que éste ha hecho con el puente, con su puente sobre el Danubio —comentó Suetonio en voz baja a Dión Coceyo.

—¿Qué ha pasado con el puente? —preguntó el viejo filósofo—. Últimamente no salgo al foro. Sólo leo y escribo en mi casa.

—Adriano ordenó incendiarlo. Pensaba que era un riesgo para la frontera, un camino que los roxolanos podían usar para atacar las provincias del norte.

Dión Coceyo cabeceó. No dijo nada. Que fácil era destruir y qué difícil construir. ¿Cambiaría el mundo alguna vez?

Apolodoro se alejaba cabizbajo, ensimismado en sus pensamientos: estaba diseñando en su cabeza una cúpula para un nuevo templo de Roma, un edificio que debía levantarse sobre las ruinas del Templo de Agripa. Una cúpula inmensa, perfecta. Había otras cúpulas importantes en algunos templos y termas, pero aquélla sería la mayor que nadie hubiera hecho nunca. Y de piedra. A prueba de fuegos. Una cúpula que permanecería, una obra que sobreviviría a todos los malditos emperadores de Roma. Ésa sería su venganza por lo del puente.[95]

En las gradas, Dión Coceyo y Suetonio se quedaron mirando hacia la antigua emperatriz.

—Ella no es el problema —dijo Suetonio, siempre en voz baja—. Son Calvencio Víctor y otros como él.

Y señaló disimuladamente hacia la entrada al túnel que conectaba el palco imperial del Circo Máximo con el palacio de la *domus Flavia*. Allí, tieso y examinando con rostro severo los movimientos y los gestos de todos los allí congregados, estaba el tribuno pretoriano aludido por el viejo bibliotecario de Roma, Calvencio Víctor, el asesino de Nigrino —aunque nadie se atreviera a pronunciar semejante acusación—, quizá también relacionado con las misteriosas muertes de los senadores Celso y Palma.

95. Apolodoro está pensando en el Panteón de Roma, cuya construcción en época de Adriano está generalmente atribuida a su persona.

—Dicen que Atiano —continuó Suetonio—, que llegará pronto a Roma acompañando a Adriano en su regreso, es peor, y ya ha sido nombrado nuevo jefe del pretorio. Atiano será el encargado de controlar a los lobos como Calvencio.

Dión Coceyo asintió una vez mas en silencio.

—Las transiciones en Roma rara vez son tranquilas —dijo el filósofo—. Y, por lo que me has contado del puente, entiendo el resentimiento de Apolodoro.

—Aun así debe andarse con cuidado —apostilló Suetonio.

—En eso tienes toda la razón —aceptó Dión Coceyo—. Si me lo permites, todos debemos andarnos con cuidado. Por mi parte, en cuanto termine el funeral, o el triunfo, lo que quiera que sea esto, emprenderé viaje de regreso a mi patria, a Prusa, en Bitinia, y allí me quedaré. Esta vez he venido a Roma sólo por respeto a Trajano, para asistir a este desfile. Entre tantos enemigos suyos, traidores y arribistas, pensé que el anterior César merecía que algunos amigos suyos estuvieran en su funeral. Pero luego retorno a Bitinia. Lo más sensato en las transiciones de un emperador a otro es estar lo más alejado de Roma que se pueda. Yo te aconsejaría que siguieras mi ejemplo y vinieras conmigo o que marcharas a cualquier otro lugar, fuera de la capital del Imperio y, sobre todo, lejos del palacio imperial.

—En tu caso te entiendo, tienes familia allí, pero mi vida, desde hace ya mucho tiempo, está en Roma. Además tengo muy buena relación con Vibia Sabina, la nueva emperatriz. Cuento con que el favor de la esposa de Adriano sea suficiente escudo contra sus ataques de ira o envidia.

Dión Coceyo negó levemente con la cabeza pero no dijo nada. Para el filósofo esa amistad con Vibia Sabina y el hecho de que el viejo *procurator bibliothecae augusti* fuera menos soberbio que Apolodoro podían no ser suficientes virtudes para librarse de los caprichos del nuevo César.

—La verdad es que se hace extraño ver todo este triunfo sobre un montón de pueblos y ciudades que ya hemos devuelto —dijo Suetonio cambiando de tema.

—Extraño, sí —admitió Dión Coceyo.

Los gritos del pueblo ahogaban su conversación y eso era

bueno, porque los ojos y los oídos de Calvencio Víctor no dejaban de vigilar en ningún momento.

El bramido del público que atestaba las gradas del Circo Máximo se debía en aquel momento a la entrada en la gigantesca pista de arena de centenares de cautivos armenios, árabes y partos que Adriano no había entregado a Osroes, pues necesitaba prisioneros que exhibir ante la plebe. También había muchos judíos de las últimas revueltas en Cirene, Chipre, Judea o Babilonia. Carne para las fieras o esclavos para las luchas de gladiadores de los juegos que se iniciarían en los próximos días. Algo tenía que regalar Adriano a los romanos, además de oro, para divertimento y distracción y para que dejaran de una vez de plantearse si la retirada de las conquistas de Trajano era buena o mala idea.

Tras los prisioneros entraron en el Circo Máximo numerosos flautistas que acompañaban con su música a los *lictores*, engalanados con sus mejores túnicas púrpura. Y, por fin, irrumpió en la pista de arena una cuadriga majestuosa tirada por cuatro hermosos caballos blancos en donde, a falta del cuerpo del fallecido César, se había situado una estatua de Trajano, desproporcionada de tamaño, mucho más grande que un hombre normal, para que el emperador representado en ella pareciera un auténtico gigante laureado y victorioso. En esta ocasión no había ningún esclavo diciendo al *imperator*:

—*Respice post te! Hominem te ese memento.* [¡Mira tras de ti! Recuerda que eres un hombre.]

De hecho habría sido inapropiado que se pronunciaran semejantes palabras a la estatua de Trajano, que iba a ser divinizado próximamente por el Senado.

Tras esa primera cuadriga iba una segunda donde los caballos blancos no transportaban estatua alguna, sino un pequeño cofre de oro y plata, engalanado con gemas de todo tipo, en el que se encontraban las cenizas del emperador incinerado en Asia y llevadas hasta Roma por su esposa Plotina con el fin de ser depositadas, al final del triunfo, en el interior de la base de la gran columna que Apolodoro de Damasco había erigido en el centro del foro de Trajano, en cuyos relieves se rememoraban las grandes hazañas de las pasadas victorias contra los dacios. En Roma no se enterraba nunca a nadie dentro del *pomerium* sagrado, dentro del perímetro central de la urbe, pero los flavios rompieron aquella costumbre al levantar el *Templum Gentis Flaviae* para enterrar a los emperadores de su dinastía, y aquella excepción facilitó que las cenizas de Trajano pudieran ser ubicadas al pie de aquella hermosa columna sin oposición del Senado.

Frente al Atrium Vestae

Ajeno a todo el bullicio, al griterío y a la multitud congregada a lo largo de todas las calles, foros y circos, un hombre esperaba en un lateral del *Atrium Vestae*. Nadie lo miraba, pues todos los ojos estaban volcados en disfrutar de aquel despliegue de poder y fuerza que el emperador Adriano había mandado organizar a Serviano para que los romanos tuvieran ocasión de honrar al fallecido Trajano.

El hombre solitario, ya algo entrado en años pero aún fuerte y robusto, aguardaba con la paciencia entrenada de los muchos años de espera. Al fin, una puerta de la casa de las vestales se abrió y por ella salió, dubitativa, casi con miedo, una mujer de unos cuarenta años que caminaba despacio, muy recta, siempre delgada y, pese a la edad, con un porte, un semblante y unas facciones en las que perduraban, de forma excepcional, los rasgos de una belleza serena. Era una mujer soltera, sin hijos, sin padre. Una situación extraña para una romana.

El hombre sonrió al verla. Ella también y se acercó hasta quedar apenas a un paso de distancia.

¿Tocarse? ¿Abrazarse? Llevaban treinta años sin poder hacerlo.

—Gracias por venir —dijo ella.

—Sabes que siempre he estado esperándote —respondió él.

Aún no se tocaban. A ella no la había acariciado nadie desde los once años, con la excepción de un día especial. Todo lo demás fueron jornadas sin contacto físico alguno con nadie. Ni un beso, ni un roce.

Fue él quien se decidió primero y dio el paso que faltaba, pero ella, de pronto, tuvo miedo y retrocedió. Él se detuvo.

—No quería asustarte —dijo el hombre.

—Es todo tan diferente de como imaginé —habló ella de nuevo más serena—. Ya no está él, Trajano, y se me hace muy extraño.

—Siempre se portó como un padre contigo.

—Siempre —repitió ella y una lágrima resbaló por su mejilla y lo miró a los ojos—. ¡Abrázame, Celer! ¡Por todos los dioses, abrázame!

Él la rodeó con sus brazos y Menenia lloró sin que nadie los mirara. La veterana vestal, después de treinta años de sacerdocio, después de haber llegado a ser Vestal Máxima, dejaba la orden y volvía a ser, simplemente, una mujer.

No se movieron en un rato.

En cualquier otro día, en cualquier otro momento, una pareja abrazada en las calles de Roma, en el mismísimo foro, a la puerta del *Atrium Vestae*, habría llamado la atención, habría sido motivo de escándalo, pero no el día del triunfo *post mortem* de Trajano, no el día del funeral del mayor de los emperadores. La plebe estaba entretenida.

Ella, pese a que nadie los mirara, consciente de lo inapropiado de su forma de actuar, se separó.

—Es increíble —dijo Menenia al ver que nadie los observaba, que nadie tenía ojos que no fueran para otra cosa que contemplar el gran desfile triunfal—. Incluso después de muerto, Trajano nos protege.

Él se volvió hacia la multitud que les daba la espalda y luego la miró de nuevo y asintió.

—Tu madre nos espera —le dijo entonces Celer al oído—. No ha querido venir a Roma. Ya sabes que ella siempre dice que ya tuvo su dosis de Césares y no necesita ver más triunfos ni funerales.

El comentario devolvió la sonrisa a la faz de Menenia y la mujer subió al carro que Celer tenía preparado para, al contrario que hacía todo el mundo, en lugar de entrar, salir de la Ciudad Eterna.

135

UN LIBRO PARA UNA NUEVA ALIANZA

Roma, bajo tierra, un lugar secreto
117 d.C.

—¿Me querías ver? —preguntó Alejandro, el obispo de Roma—. Tendrás que disculpar que te reciba en un sótano húmedo en este sector de la ciudad, lúgubre y miserable, pero con la rebelión de los judíos, ningún seguidor de otra religión distinta a la romana es bien visto por los *triunviros* ni por cualquier otra autoridad de la ciudad. Ya sabes que los romanos nunca han sabido distinguir entre los judíos y nosotros. Estoy arriesgando mucho al aceptar reunirnos hoy. Espero que sea importante.

—No habría molestado al obispo de Roma si no lo juzgara así —respondió Telesforo con rapidez.

Luego hubo un breve silencio.

—Tú dirás —invitó Alejandro, tenso, incómodo por la espera.

—Creo que ya sé lo que Ignacio quiso decirnos antes de morir.

—¿De qué me hablas?

—De las palabras que dijo antes de morir en la arena del Anfiteatro Flavio: «Al diablo hay que combatirlo con las armas del diablo».

—Ah, eso. —Alejandro parecía defraudado. En el *mare magnum* de las matanzas contra judíos y, por extensión, de cristianos por parte de los romanos, en medio de aquellos tumultos y violencia general, el obispo de Roma no había tenido tiempo para meditar sobre aquel enigma que les había dejado Ignacio—. Lo había olvidado. Como sabrás, me estoy ocupando de otras cuestiones de más urgencia.

—Pero no hay nada más urgente que derrotar al diablo —opuso Telesforo con vehemencia.

—Sobrevivir, que los cristianos sobrevivamos, me parece más urgente —lo corrigió el obispo de Roma con indignación—. La supervivencia de nuestra religión, de la auténtica fe, me parece más urgente que resolver enigmas, incluso si son de alguien tan digno de recuerdo y respeto como Ignacio.

—Todo va unido —insistió Telesforo y siguió hablando rápido para evitar que el obispo lo interrumpiera o diera fin a aquella entrevista antes de que dijera lo que había ido a desvelar—. Ignacio, maestro, se refería a Marción y a su maldito libro, ese compendio de escritos de la vida de Jesús y cartas de algunos apóstoles que presenta a todos como el libro sagrado de los cristianos. Cada día que pasa, Marción gana más adeptos y es porque tiene algo tangible que enseñar, algo palpable que repartir para que sus fieles puedan leerlo juntos cuando se reúnen. Ese maldito libro lo hace cada vez más fuerte.

—Eso ya lo sé —consiguió decir Alejandro cuando Telesforo tuvo que inspirar aire para no ahogarse—, pero ¿qué tiene eso que ver con el enigma de las palabras de Ignacio?

—Todo, mi maestro —se explicó Telesforo contento de que el obispo, al fin, se hubiera centrado en escuchar lo que tenía que decir—. Ignacio estaba diciéndonos que Marción es el diablo y que debemos derrotarlo con sus mismas armas y su mejor arma es ese libro, así que lo que nosotros, los auténticos cristianos, hemos de hacer es crear un libro semejante al de Marción, pero verdadero. Hemos de sentarnos, el obispo de Roma y los que éste designe, para seleccionar los escritos que mejor y más fielmente describan la vida de Jesús, los textos que mejor expresen su mensaje, y reunir también las cartas de Pablo y otros apóstoles para juntarlo todo en un nuevo libro que será el auténtico. Sólo un libro sagrado bendecido por el obispo de Roma podrá derrotar al libro hereje de Marción. Eso es lo que Ignacio quiso decirnos antes de morir y eso, maestro, es lo que debemos hacer.

Alejandro asintió muy lentamente.

—Quizá tengas razón. Tiene sentido lo que dices.

Hubo un nuevo y largo silencio.

Los dos hombres estaban sentados en la penumbra de aquel sótano.

—¿Y cómo llamaremos a ese libro? —preguntó Alejandro.

—No lo sé aún. Pero será un libro que forjará una nueva unión con Dios —respondió Telesforo con brillo en los ojos—. Quizá Η Διαθήκη, *diatheké*, tendría sentido.

—*Alianza*[96] —repitió Alejandro traduciéndolo del griego—. Me gusta. Un libro para una nueva alianza... aunque seleccionar los textos, ponernos de acuerdo, no será fácil.

—No, no lo será.

—Quizá tardemos generaciones en hacerlo.

—Es posible, pero entretanto haremos algo maravilloso. Dos cosas maravillosas.

—¿Dos?

—Sí, mi maestro: por un lado, tendremos algo con lo que luchar contra el libro hereje de Marción y, por otro, nos pasaremos mucho tiempo, quizá toda nuestra vida y la vida de otros que nos sigan, hablando de Jesús. ¿Qué puede haber mejor que eso?

—Pocas cosas —aceptó Alejandro, pero frunció el ceño con una sombra de duda que se anticipaba al futuro—. Esperemos que esos debates no vayan nunca más allá de las palabras...

Se oyeron gritos.

Los dos hombres miraron hacia la bóveda de aquel sótano.

Eran gritos de júbilo. El desfile triunfal de Trajano estaba pasando por encima de donde estaban.

Los dos hombres permanecieron inmóviles, pensando en las entrañas del Roma sobre aquel futuro libro sagrado mientras Roma entera sólo pensaba en el poder de sus Césares.

---

96. Éste sería el término griego inicial para denominar el Nuevo Testamento. El término en latín *testamentum* se emplearía más tarde.

136

UN EMPERADOR DEMASIADO GRANDE

Roma
Invierno de 117 d.C.

En el Circo Máximo

En el ciclópeo estadio de carreras el desfile de los legionarios victoriosos continuaba. Había *vexillationes* de las legiones IIII *Scythica*, VI *Ferrata*, XII *Fulminata*, XVI *Flavia Firma*, III *Cirenaica*, III *Gallica*, X *Fretensis*, VII *Claudia*, XIII *Gemina*, II *Traiana Fortis*, XII *Primigenia*, XXX *Ulpia Victrix*, XI *Claudia*, I *Itálica* y la V *Macedónica*. Nunca antes se habían reunido tantas unidades de tantas legiones diferentes en un triunfo, pero es que nunca antes un emperador había reunido tantas legiones en una campaña tan ambiciosa como la de Trajano en Partia.

Plotina saludaba a cada estandarte con la mano extendida, igual que hacían el resto de los asistentes del palco imperial y gran parte del público, además de acompañar el saludo con vítores continuos que transformaban todo el gigantesco recinto en un épico clamor en memoria de Trajano.

Dión Coceyo saludaba, como todos. Eso sí, el filósofo lo hacía sin ansia marcial ni deseos de quedar bien ante nadie. Él saludaba por respeto a su amigo Trajano. Sonrió de forma casi imperceptible. Recordó cuando el emperador fallecido le había dicho que muchas veces no entendía lo que él decía, pero que lo respetaba enormemente. Pocos hombres eran capaces de respetar a quien no comprenden del todo.

Dión Coceyo suspiró. Tan largo era el desfile que seguramente la cabeza de la majestuosa comitiva estaría ya llegando al Templo de Júpiter en lo alto de la colina Capitolina para iniciar los sacrificios a los dioses tras rendir ante la estatua de Júpiter el gran trono dorado de Cesifonte. Luego llegaría el momento en el que Plotina misma depositaría las cenizas de su esposo al pie de la Columna en el foro de Trajano.

Trajano.

Dión Coceyo frunció el ceño. Marco Ulpio Trajano, un emperador que pensaba siempre a lo grande, tanto que Roma no había podido seguirlo en sus sueños. Pero, realmente, ¿hasta dónde habían llegado los sueños de Trajano? El viejo filósofo recordó a su joven alumna sármata Tamura, hija de gladiador y guerrera indomable, enviada junto con aquel comerciante... ¿cuál era su nombre? Se hacía viejo. Sí: Titianus. Aquel mercader de Oriente con un mensaje y una misión cuya finalidad última el emperador Trajano nunca desveló a nadie en Roma, ni siquiera a él. ¿Para qué querría el emperador que la muchacha sármata aprendiera griego y hasta el sánscrito que él había conseguido desentrañar de los escritos que el embajador Shaka le dejara en su visita a Roma? Hacía tantos años de todo eso...

En medio de la fanfarria, el estruendo de más y más *buccinatores* y los gritos del pueblo congregado en el Circo Máximo, Dión Coceyo tuvo un momento de intimidad especial para recordar a aquella pequeña adolescente y a sus padres. ¿Seguirían vivos? Nada más se había sabido de ellos. Arrio, el capitán del barco, regresó unos meses atrás, y el filósofo pudo hablar con él en el puerto de Ostia, pues cuando Arrio envió mensajes al palacio imperial sobre aquella misión, el único del *consilium augusti* provisional que sabía algo de la misma era él. Vibia Sabina, ante la ausencia de su esposo Adriano, sugirió que hablara él con aquel veterano capitán de barco que tantas ganas tenía de comunicar sobre su periplo. Los nuevos senadores del *consilium*, como Serviano o Salinator o el pretoriano Calvencio Víctor, no mostraron interés alguno por historias de marinos extraños.

Dión fue pues a Ostia.

Arrio le contó una historia increíble de piratas, marfil y vientos de la gran mar Eritrea que los habían llevado hasta la India. Allí esperó el capitán el regreso de Titianus, de Marcio, el gladiador veterano, y su esposa Alana y la joven hija de ambos, Tamura, y de Áyax, el otro gladiador joven, pero nunca supo nada más de ellos y, al cabo de dos años, el tiempo de espera pactado, regresó al Imperio romano. Nadie podía culparlo. Y muerto Trajano ya nadie indagaría sobre qué fue de aquella misión impulsada por un emperador empeñado en ir siempre un poco más allá de cualquier límite. Dión Coceyo sintió lástima, sobre todo por aquella muchacha adolescente que tan buena alumna había sido. Nunca pensó que una joven pudiera tener esa capacidad para aprender. ¿Le habría sido útil lo que le enseñó o los consejos que le dio? ¿Seguiría leyendo los papiros que le entregó? ¿Estaría aún viva?

El viejo filósofo negó con la cabeza. Tenía que emprender su propio largo viaje de regreso a Bitinia en el oriente del Imperio y por eso pensaba en otros largos viajes imposibles.

Una villa fuera de la ciudad

El trayecto llevó unas tres horas en las que los dos disfrutaron primero de hablar largo y tendido sin estar vigilados por nadie, luego de poder sencillamente cogerse las manos y luego de compartir el silencio mientras veían los árboles a ambos lados de la larga *Via Appia*. Llegaron a la villa en la que la madre de Menenia residía desde hacía años, desde que el emperador Trajano le proporcionara una pensión vitalicia y un alojamiento amplio y cómodo lejos del torrente de personas, miradas e intrigas de Roma.

Domicia Longina salió a recibirlos.

—Madre —dijo Menenia—, no tendrías que haberte levantado.

—Hay ocasiones especiales, hija. Días excepcionales y hoy es uno de ellos. No me levanto por un emperador, pero sí por mi hija, la gran Vestal Máxima de Roma.

—Ya no soy vestal, madre —dijo ella acercándose.

Estaban en medio del camino que ascendía hacia la villa. Celer se mantenía a cierta distancia para proporcionar privacidad a las dos mujeres en su anhelado reencuentro. Aunque ambas habían podido verse ocasionalmente en diferentes visitas que había hecho Menenia a su madre a lo largo de aquellos años, no habían podido tocarse, fieles a las costumbres del sacerdocio de Vesta, excepto una vez y con permiso especial del entonces *pontifex maximus* Trajano. Por eso, para Menenia era muy especial este segundo abrazo del día.

—Vamos adentro —dijo Domicia—, pero despacio. Es cierto que a mis años caminar me parece correr. Y correr sólo un vago recuerdo perdido. Como tantos otros recuerdos...

Domicia Longina sentía el peso de los años. Muchos de ellos vividos entre el terror y la violencia de manos de su esposo Domiciano. Años que envejecen a cualquiera con rapidez. Pero pese a todas las vicisitudes terribles de su existencia, Domicia había conseguido sobrevivir a nueve emperadores: Claudio, Nerón, Galba, Vitelio, Vespasiano, Tito, Domiciano, Nerva y Trajano, hasta llegar al actual Adriano. Había sido esposa de uno de ellos y madre de quien, de no ser por la locura de su esposo, seguramente habría sido también un César. Había sido amante de otro emperador y, en definitiva, los había visto llegar y desaparecer de su vida como las estaciones que vienen, nos acompañan un tiempo y luego se diluyen en otra que nos hace olvidar la existencia de la anterior.

Se sentaron en el atrio de la villa.

Celer, nuevamente, se mantuvo algo alejado, bebiendo un poco de vino rebajado con agua que un esclavo le servía, mientras las dos mujeres seguían conversando.

—Imagino que habría una multitud enorme hoy en Roma —dijo Domicia.

—Inmensa, como nunca se ha visto, madre.

Luego hubo un silencio.

—Trajano siempre fue bueno con nosotras, madre —continuó Menenia—. Adriano ha organizado el mayor de los triunfos. Algo nunca visto antes. Mayor incluso que con la conquista de la Dacia.

—Todo organizado con el dinero que el propio Trajano llevó a las arcas de Roma, hija —comentó Domicia cogiendo una copa de vino ella también. A sus años ya no se privaba de los que ella llamaba pequeños placeres de la existencia—.

Pero ya verás cómo Adriano recortará en los juegos circenses. Cuando quede claro que el Imperio es suyo y que la fortuna de Trajano le pertenece, ya no será tan espléndido con el pueblo. Se concentrará entonces en gastar en él. No me extrañaría que en lugar de tantos edificios públicos como hizo Trajano, Adriano se haga construir algún gran palacio en Roma o cualquier otro sitio con el que se encapriche. De hecho, me alegro mucho de que dejes de ser vestal justo ahora. No es éste un buen momento para estar en Roma y menos con alguien tan imprevisible como Adriano en el poder como *pontifex maximus*. En el silencio de esta villa estaremos bien. Lo esencial será pasar desapercibidas —apostilló Domicia mirando a Celer—. Ya nada de carreras en el circo, muchacho.

—Madre —interpuso Menenia con una sonrisa en los labios—, hace muchos años que Celer no corre en el circo. Entrena caballos, eso es todo. Luego los vende.

—Es cierto. Olvido cosas. Pero mejor que sea así —replicó Domicia—. Si no olvidara algunas cosas, no podría vivir. En cuanto a Celer, que continúe de esa forma: en silencio y lejos de Roma. Eso es lo que nos salvará a los tres.

Menenia asintió despacio.

—Es curioso, madre, es la segunda vez que alguien me comenta lo mismo en pocos días. Dión Coceyo, el viejo filósofo, también me dijo que él pensaba irse de Roma pronto, de regreso a Prusa, su ciudad natal en Bitinia.

—Un hombre inteligente, siempre lo fue —sentenció Domicia y se llevó la copa de vino a los labios.

Menenia volvió a asentir levemente. Si de algo sabía su madre era de Césares y si ella pensaba o intuía que con Adriano habría problemas, seguramente así sería. Por otro lado, Menenia sentía como si al dejar ella su sacerdocio, su intuición hacia el futuro se hubiera diluido.

El futuro.

El presente.

El pasado.

De pronto, un pensamiento cruzó la mente de Menenia.

—Me has dicho, madre, lo que intuyes de Adriano, pero ¿qué piensas tú de Trajano?

—Ah, Trajano —dijo la antigua emperatriz de Roma, pero calló. Quería meditar bien su respuesta. Para ella, la mayoría de los Césares eran sólo unos ambiciosos egoístas crueles, cuando no lunáticos también como su marido Domiciano. Sólo Vespasiano o Tito podían salvarse de un suspenso total en su rápido repaso por los últimos Césares de los últimos tiempos. Quizá Nerva también. Pero ¿y Trajano?

Celer se acercó hacia las dos mujeres. Le intrigaba saber qué opinaba la sabia antigua emperatriz de Roma sobre aquél al que el Senado había calificado como *Optimus Princeps*, el mejor de los gobernantes posibles.

Domicia Longina miró su copa llena de vino mientras pronunciaba su evaluación final sobre el primer emperador hispano.

—Trajano fue un César invencible derrotado sólo por un fantasma de tiempos remotos: el fantasma de la legión perdida de Craso. Ni la plebe ni los patricios ni el Senado terminaron nunca de sobreponerse al miedo de la maldición de Ateyo, nunca superaron el pavor de imaginar que otras legiones podían acabar como la legión perdida si se cruzaba otra vez el Éufrates. Sin embargo, el *Optimus Princeps*, hija mía, pensó que podía derrotar incluso a los fantasmas. Ése fue su único error.

Domicia calló y suspiró. Se llevó de nuevo la copa de vino a los labios hasta apurar todo su contenido en una larga, lenta y dilatada serie de tragos.

—Ah —dijo al retirarse la copa vacía de los labios y añadió—: Como decía el viejo Plinio: *In vino veritas* [En el vino está la verdad.] Menenia, Trajano fue un emperador demasiado grande para una Roma demasiado pequeña.

137

LOS BOSQUES DEL NORTE

Norte del Imperio han
Invierno de 117 d.C.

Los árboles se elevaban hacia el cielo azul del mundo. Ella galopaba a lomos de su caballo esquivando las ramas más bajas con la destreza de un águila en vuelo rasante. El aire intenso, puro, fresco, hinchaba sus pulmones con el sabor dulce de la libertad.

Detuvo a su animal junto a un riachuelo y desmontó. La muchacha se agachó y hundió la mano en el agua fría para de inmediato llevársela a la boca y saciar su sed. Desde hacía unas semanas tenía más ganas de beber y más hambre. Ella sabía por qué. Se acercó al costado del caballo y de una pequeña alforja de cuero extrajo un frasco con cuidado.

Tamura se sentó al borde del arroyo con el recipiente de vidrio en sus manos. Era el *silphium* que aún le quedaba. Pensó en su madre.

«Una guerrera sármata sólo tiene los hijos que quiere tener», eso le había dicho.

Tamura destapó el frasco con la mano izquierda y se lo acercó lentamente al rostro. A la nariz. Lo olió. Pese al tiempo transcurrido desde que lo tomara no parecía haber alterado su extraño aroma denso.

Tamura se lo alejó entonces de la cara y estiró el brazo hasta que su mano con el frasco quedó sobre el riachuelo de aguas bravas. Giró entonces la mano y el *silphium* se vertió, se fundió con el agua y se diluyó en la turbulencia helada del líquido transparente.

Tamura se levantó entonces, guardó el frasco vacío y miró

hacia el bosque hermoso, tan frondoso como los bosques de la Dacia. De alguna forma se sentía, por fin, de regreso en la siempre anhelada patria de su infancia, allí donde había aprendido a montar a caballo o a disparar el arco con su madre y su padre. Miraba a los árboles.

—He vuelto, madre —dijo la joven. No importaba que estuviera a miles de millas de distancia de la Dacia. Aquellos bosques eran como un retorno a un tiempo en el que fue feliz.

El caballo relinchó.

Tiró de él y lo acercó al río para que también pudiera beber. En cuanto el animal pareció estar satisfecho volvió a montarlo y galopó de regreso hacia el campamento militar a los pies de la Gran Muralla.

Las puertas de la fortificación se abrieron cuando la vieron acercarse. Nadie le pidió nada ni se interpuso en su camino. Era la extraña esposa del general Li Kan. Entre mujer y guerrero, alguien que casi nadie allí entendía, pero que, de alguna forma, se había hecho con el afecto de todos. Tamura nunca miraba a nadie con desprecio, pese a ser la mujer del general al mando del ejército del norte. Repartía comida entre los niños más hambrientos del campamento y de las poblaciones vecinas y, por encima de todo, mantenía al general Li Kan de buen humor todo el tiempo. Y los soldados apreciaban en su justa medida lo importante que era eso. Allí, cualquier guerrero han habría dado su vida sin dudarlo por protegerla si fuera necesario. Aunque todos sabían que la joven esposa sabía cuidarse sola.

Había murmuraciones, no obstante. Algunas mujeres no veían con buenos ojos la libertad de aquella esposa llegada del otro extremo del mundo, pero nadie se atrevía a decir nada por temor a contrariar al todopoderoso general que, todo hay que decirlo, mantenía la región protegida de los constantes ataques de los *hsiung-nu*, quienes una y otra vez se estrellaban no ya sólo contra la Gran Muralla de protección del Imperio han, sino contra la destreza sin par de aquel general que sabía cómo utilizar a sus soldados para impedir que nunca un solo bárbaro del norte pudiera ni tan siquiera acercarse a la base de la muralla.

Tamura, una vez dentro del campamento, dejó el caballo en los establos y cruzó la gran plaza central de la fortificación en dirección a la residencia donde vivía con su esposo. Estaba atardeciendo. Era la hora de la cena y la muchacha se apresuraba para estar junto a su marido cuando las sirvientas hubieran dispuesto el arroz y la carne de la última comida del día.

Li Kan la vio sentarse a su lado con la felicidad de saber que tenía, en efecto, tal y como le había dicho la emperatriz, a una tigresa como esposa; hermosa pero libre, misteriosa pero alegre, felina pero dulce.

—¿No crees que no deberías cabalgar tanto en tu estado? —le preguntó él mientras les servían la comida.

Hablaban una mezcla de latín y la lengua han. Él casi todo en la lengua del imperio del dragón y ella casi todo en latín, pero se entendían. Cuando realmente se quiere los idiomas no suponen murallas.

—Cuando piense que no puedo, no lo haré —respondió ella. El embarazo estaba aún en sus primeras semanas y ella, más allá de tener hambre, se sentía en perfecta forma.

Li Kan suspiró. Le resultaba prácticamente imposible conseguir que Tamura cambiara de parecer en nada, pero tenía la esperanza de que cuando naciera el niño —estaba convencido de que sería un niño—, su esposa pasaría más tiempo en casa y menos en los bosques.

Terminó la cena.

Bebían té.

—Tengo miedo de que un día tengas un accidente y pierdas al niño.

—Yo tengo miedo de que un día un guerrero *hsiung-nu* te dé muerte con una flecha. Con una espada sé que es imposible.

Nadie dijo nada durante un rato.

—¿Vamos a dormir? —preguntó él.

—Tú no quieres dormir —replicó ella muy seria, pero de pronto sonrió—. Yo tampoco.

Una vez en el dormitorio ella se desnudó con rapidez. Él la miraba con adoración. Era tan joven, tan bella y se movía, exactamente, como una tigresa en celo.

Hicieron el amor como lo hacían siempre: sin prisa, con furia, con dulzura, con pasión.

Ella se quedaba abrazada a él después del éxtasis, muy quieta. A veces lloraba mientras él le acariciaba el pelo lacio negro, suave, que cubría su espalda desnuda. Él nunca entendía por qué lloraba.

—¿Te he hecho daño? —le preguntaba entonces.

Ella siempre negaba con la cabeza y se acurrucaba a su lado.

A veces no decían nada y se dormían sin más.

A veces hablaban durante horas. De infinidad de cosas. De asuntos triviales, del Imperio han, de otros reinos, de los viajes de Tamura o de las campañas de Li Kan.

—Lloro porque tengo miedo de que todo esto termine alguna vez —le confesó ella una noche.

Él no supo qué contestar, porque en el fondo de su ser compartía el mismo temor. Por eso pensó en cambiar de tema.

—Mi padre me contó muchas veces la historia de la legión perdida —dijo él entonces—, como yo te la he contado a ti ya varias veces, ¿verdad?

—Varias veces —repitió ella con una sonrisa. Eso alegró a Li Kan, porque veía que el temor se borraba de los ojos oscuros de su esposa.

—La legión perdida de Craso —continuó él—. Éste murió porque quería rivalizar en gloria con los otros dos grandes generales de Da Qin, de Roma: Julio César y Pompeyo. Sé bien la historia del final de Craso, pero siempre me he preguntado qué pasó con los otros dos generales romanos que se quedaron en Da Qin. Siempre me he preguntado si lucharon entre ellos. Y si fue así, ¿quién ganaría?

Tamura respiraba despacio. Su marido acariciaba su cuerpo desnudo mientras hablaba. Las manos de Li Kan eran grandes y fuertes. A ella siempre le emocionaba que siendo él tan fuerte nunca le hiciera el más mínimo daño.

—Yo sé el final de esa historia —dijo ella.

Li Kan detuvo la palma de la mano sobre el vientre desnudo de Tamura, allí donde se sentía una pequeña elevación justo estaba gestándose un nuevo ser.

—¿De verdad? —preguntó él con cierto tono de incredulidad—. ¿O te lo estás inventando para agradarme?

Ella cogió la mano de Li Kan y la apartó despacio. Salió de la cama y desnuda cruzó la habitación hasta llegar a un pequeño armario donde guardaba sus cosas, sus pequeños tesoros llevados desde el otro extremo del mundo. Buscó hasta encontrar un códice de pergamino. Lo cogió y regresó a la cama con él.

—Luz —dijo ella y él acercó la pequeña lámpara de aceite a la cama, situándola junto a su esposa.

Tamura empezó a leer.

—Esto lo escribió Julio César. Me lo dio mi maestro en Roma, Dión Coceyo. Un hombre muy sabio. Me enseñó muchas cosas. En este libro Julio César cuenta cómo se enfrentó a Pompeyo y cómo...

—No me cuentes el final —la interrumpió Li Kan.

Ella sonrió.

—Es una gran historia pero es larga —dijo la joven.

—Tenemos tiempo —respondió él.

En una casa de madera, en medio de un campamento militar del Imperio han en la frontera norte, junto a la muralla más grande del mundo, empezó Tamura a leer en voz alta *De Bello Civilli* [*Sobre la guerra civil*] de Julio César:

—*Litteris C. Caesaris consulibus redditis aegre...* [Después de que entregara a los cónsules la carta de Cayo César...]

Li Kan se tumbó por completo en la cama con las manos debajo de la nuca. De cuando en cuando le preguntaba a Tamura por aquellas palabras que no entendía, que eran bastantes, y la muchacha se las explicaba para luego retomar la lectura de aquel relato.

Li Kan cerró entonces los ojos y se concentró en escuchar la dulce voz de su joven esposa, que pronunciaba con cuidado, una a una, las palabras de Julio César narrando su enfrentamiento contra el poderoso Pompeyo el Grande.

Nunca pensó Marco Ulpio Trajano que la historia de Roma fuera a ser leída por una joven guerrera sármata y escuchada a la vez por un general de Xeres, a los pies de la Gran Muralla, una fortificación que ni imaginaban ni conocían en el Imperio romano. Una muralla de otro mundo. Un sitio hasta donde Roma nunca pudo llegar, o no quiso, o no supo hacerlo, por temor, por envidia, por desconocimiento, o porque simplemente estaban convencidos de que más allá de la India sólo había *regiones de difícil acceso por sus inviernos rigurosos y su gran frío, países que no se podían encontrar por algún designio divino de los dioses.*[97]

Unos círculos se cierran, otros se abren. Somos sombras de la historia, leyendas, sueños de vida rodeados de muerte, relatos felices o tristes, con frecuencia las dos cosas al tiempo, sonrisas y lágrimas siempre iguales aunque vengamos de mundos distintos.

97. Literal del final de *El periplo por la Mar Eritrea.*

EPÍLOGO

—

Cesifonte

129 d.C. Doce años después de la muerte de Trajano

—¡Ya no podemos hacer nada, mi señor! —exclamó el guerrero parto cubierto de sangre desde la puerta entreabierta del salón del trono del *Šāhān Šāh.*

El oficial hizo ademán de entrar, pero Osroes se levantó y fue directo a él como una fiera furiosa con su propia espada en la mano.

—¡Fuera, fuera, fuera! —gritó el rey de reyes blandiendo el arma amenazadoramente—. ¡Tu misión y la de tus hombres está ahí fuera, por Ahura Mazda, defendiendo el trono sagrado de Partia! ¡Defendiéndome a mí!

El oficial herido retrocedió unos pasos cuando quedó más allá del umbral de la gran puerta de bronce, y Osroes aprovechó para empujar la pesada hoja de metal hasta cerrarla. Soltó entonces la espada que resonó fuertemente al caer, y con ambas manos cogió el largo pestillo de bronce y trabó las puertas desde dentro.

Se quedó quieto, mirando las enormes hojas de bronce cerradas.

Se oyeron golpes y lamentos al otro lado.

¿Eran sus guerreros que buscaban, como él, un lugar donde refugiarse de la ira del enemigo inmisericorde?

Osroes se llevó el dorso de la mano derecha a la boca y su lengua degustó la sal de su propio sudor. Era el sabor del miedo. El rey de reyes empezó a retroceder, andando hacia atrás y sin coger su espada, que quedó en el suelo, junto a la gran puerta de bronce.

Más golpes sobre las gigantescas hojas de metal.

Y gritos.

La lucha había llegado hasta las mismas puertas del salón del trono.

El trono.

Osroes se volvió y corrió a sentarse una vez más en su sagrado trono de *Šūhān Šāh*. Era suyo de siempre, desde hacía años, por linaje, por derecho dinástico y divino, por designio de Ahura Mazda. Ni siquiera Trajano pudo desbancarlo de allí. Le arrebató el trono dorado, pero nunca pudo imponerse por completo y, al final, el líder romano tuvo que huir y él, como siempre, prevaleció sobre todos sus enemigos. Pero ahora...

Se hizo un silencio al otro lado de la puerta cerrada. El combate había terminado. Osroes sabía lo que llegaría: primero fueron golpes sobre el bronce como los de antes, pero, al poco, empezaron unos enormes clangs que reverberaban por toda la gran sala vacía del trono de Partia. Habían llevado un ariete de metal, fuerte y poderoso, y decenas de hombres lo blandían y lo hacían chocar brutalmente contra las puertas de bronce.

¡Clang, clang, clang!

Osroes se llevó las manos a los oídos. Aquellos golpes metálicos que resonaban por todas las esquinas de la estancia eran ensordecedores. Pero eso no era lo terrible. Lo insoportable es que eran el anuncio del fin.

—¡No, no! ¡Esto no puede estar ocurriendo! —aulló con las manos en los oídos y empezando a llorar como un niño.

De pronto un sonido diferente rasgó los tímpanos del rey de reyes. Osroes, aún con las manos en las orejas, miró hacia la entrada: el gran pestillo de bronce se había partido y las puertas de metal se movían.

¡Clang!

Sonó a definitivo.

Las dos hojas de bronce se abrieron de par en par.

—¡No, no, no! —aulló el rey de reyes una vez más desde su trono, agarrado a los reposabrazos con las manos.

Esperaba que irrumpieran en cualquier momento los guerreros de Vologases, del maldito y eterno Vologases, cuyo ejército lo había asediado durante semanas rodeando toda Cesifonte. De nada habían servido las cartas que Osroes había enviado a su hermano Mitrídates para que lo ayudara con tropas desde el norte, desde Armenia: hacía años que Mitrídates había dejado de colaborar con él en la lucha contra Vologases y lo había dejado solo ante el ejército del usurpador. Sin las fuerzas de Armenia y el norte de Mesopotamia, toda defensa había sido insuficiente ante el avance irrefrenable de aquel miserable de Oriente. Mitrídates, en su egoísmo, no se daba cuenta de que al separarse de él, Vologases acabaría primero con el poder de Cesifonte y luego acudiría al norte para derrotar a las fuerzas de Armenia.

Tampoco había conseguido ayuda de los otros gobernantes de reinos vecinos. En Osroene ya no estaba su hijo Partamaspates, fallecido hacía un tiempo, y el nuevo rey nunca respondió a sus cartas. Ni el *mry* de Hatra ni ningún otro gobernador o monarca.

Lo habían dejado solo.

Pero eso ya daba igual.

Osroes miró hacia puerta, donde las hojas de bronce habían cedido por completo. Un intenso haz de luz cegadora le deslumbró y no podía ver quién estaba entrando en la sala del trono. El *Šāhān Šāh* miraba hacia la luz interponiendo entre ella y sus ojos semicerrados las manos, con los dedos separados levemente, intentando así discernir cuántos eran. Fue entonces cuando se dio cuenta de que se había dejado la espada en el umbral. Pero... no irrumpían guerreros... era una sola persona la que entraba... una mujer.

—Hola, padre.

Osroes seguía cegado por la luz. Apenas veía una silueta oscura, la figura inconfundible de una mujer joven. Y esa voz...

—¿Aryazate? —preguntó Osroes dubitativo.

—Aquí estoy, padre —respondió la mujer—. ¿Me echabas de menos?

—No entiendo... —masculló Osroes—. Te creía muerta. Vologases mató a todos los que te escoltaban...

—A mí no me mató, padre. A mí el único que ordenó matarme alguna vez fuiste tú, ¿recuerdas?

Osroes tragó saliva. Miró a un lado y a otro. Por ambos extremos de la sala serpeaban sendas hileras de guerreros de su eterno enemigo Vologases.

—Pero... no comprendo... ¿entonces?

Me casé con él. Eso era lo que querías, ¿no? —dijo Aryazate mientras desenfundaba una espada que llevaba ceñida a la cintura.

—Pero... ¿qué es esto, hija mía? ¿No pensarás...? Esto es una locura: soy tu padre, siempre lo he sido... —Las lágrimas retornaban a las mejillas de Osroes—. Esto no puede ser, no tiene sentido...

—Sí puede ser, padre. Yo también era tu hija cuando ordenaste mi ejecución. Ahora tu hija regresa casada con tu peor enemigo, alguien que, por cierto, ha resultado ser un noble guerrero y un excelente esposo. Eso, padre, debo agradecértelo. Elegiste bien a mi marido. Ahora el será *Šāhān Šāh* y yo su *Bāmbišnān Bāmbišn*. Sólo nos queda por eliminar un pequeño detalle que ensucia con su traición perenne el trono de Partia. Pero eso, padre, lo vamos a resolver ahora mismo, ¿verdad? Ese detalle, ya lo imaginarás, eres tú.

Los guerreros de Vologases se acercaban al trono al que Osroes se aferraba con ambas manos y gritaba sin parar.

—¡No, no, nunca!

—¡Cogedlo! —exclamó Aryazate—. ¡Esto quiero hacerlo personalmente!

—¡No, no, no...!

Los guerreros obedecieron a su reina y cuatro de ellos cogieron a Osroes por los brazos y lo levantaron del trono, donde el viejo rey se dejó una uña clavada en su intento por permanecer en él hasta el final. Lo golpearon en el estómago, lo doblaron hasta conseguir que quedara arrodillado frente a su hija y un soldado le levantó la cabeza tirando del pelo, de modo que el cuello del rey de reyes quedara al descubierto, sin defensa.

—Rixnu tuvo la dignidad de no llorar ni implorar —dijo Aryazate acercándose con la espada en la mano—. Me decepcionas, padre, aunque no me sorprende que tú no estés a su altura.

—¡No, no, no... agggh!

Aryazate soltó la espada ensangrentada y ésta cayó al suelo. En ese momento. Vologases III entró en la gran estancia del palacio real de Cesifonte. Caminó con paso marcial escoltado por una treintena de sus mejores hombres hasta situarse junto a su mujer y el cuerpo degollado de un Osroes que, aunque muy débil, aún podía oír lo que ocurría a su alrededor mientras se desangraba velozmente por el cuello cortado.

Vologases miró a su mujer y sonrió. Luego se agachó y le habló al moribundo rey de reyes.

—Tienes una hija fascinante.

Osroes se quedó inmóvil con los ojos abiertos.

Vologases cogió de la mano a Aryazate y, juntos, pisando la sangre aún caliente del anterior *Šāhān Šāh*, ascendieron los peldaños que conducían al trono de Partia.

APÉNDICES

1

NOTA HISTÓRICA

(Recomendación: no leer esta sección
hasta terminar la novela)

Trajano

Marco Ulpio Trajano murió en Selinus entre el 9 y el 10 de agosto de 117 d.C. Esta ciudad se corresponde con la actual Gazipasa, al sur de Turquía. A las afueras de esta pequeña población se pueden encontrar las ruinas de la antigua ciudad romana. Apenas quedan vestigios de un acueducto, unos baños, un odeón y restos de una necrópolis. El edificio más importante y razonablemente bien conservado es precisamente el monumento funerario que se levantó por orden de Adriano en honor a Trajano para recordar al mundo que allí fue donde murió el primero de los Césares hispanos y, sin duda, el más grande, al menos el que llevó a Roma a su máxima extensión y poder.

Para llegar a Gazipasa lo ideal es ir a Estambul y de allí en avión a Antalya, al sur del país. Desde Antalya se puede ir en coche (por una buena autovía, aunque se olvidaron de hacer carriles de aceleración y deceleración para salir o entrar en ella) hasta Alanya. En esa ruta conviene visitar el circo de Perge, el imponente teatro de Aspendos y la ciudad romana de Side. Desde Alanya, en coche, por la misma autovía, se puede llegar a Gazipasa.

Encontrar las ruinas de Selinus no es sencillo, pues apenas están señalizadas y la visita depende de si han cortado o no la maleza alrededor de los restos, pero es emocionante llegar al lugar donde murió Trajano.

El emperador hispano fue incinerado en Selinus o en otra ciudad de Oriente, quizá Seleucia de Pieria. Sus restos en forma de polvo fueron depositados en la base de la columna de Trajano en Roma. En algún momento de la convulsa historia de la Ciudad Eterna, probablemente en uno de los saqueos que sufrió la urbe con la caída del Imperio, alguien robó las cenizas de Trajano, con toda seguridad interesado en hacerse con el valioso recipiente en el que estarían depositadas. No sería de extrañar que quien se hiciera con la urna o vasija o cofre vertiera las cenizas allí mismo y saliera corriendo con su botín. Posiblemente las cenizas de Trajano quedarían, al fin, diseminadas por el viento por las ruinas de su gran foro en el centro de Roma, que parece un lugar oportuno para los últimos restos de Trajano.

La sucesión

La muerte del emperador Trajano está envuelta en una gran controversia. Parece ser que murió por algún tipo de enfermedad paralizante que muy probablemente estuviera relacionada con un ictus, o varios. El estilo de vida, la dieta y el amor al vino de Trajano encajarían a la perfección con un final de este tipo. El emperador, muy débil, se vio imposibilitado para resolver el tema de su sucesión de forma adecuada. Trajano hizo muchas cosas muy bien, pero le faltó visión o quizá un ataque cerebral inesperado le impidió dejar resuelto este espinoso e importante asunto cuando ya tenía claro cómo resolverlo.

Si bien Trajano consideró a Adriano como posible sucesor en alguna fase inicial de su gobierno, es más probable que, al final, durante las campañas dacias y en especial en Partia cambiara de opinión. Necesitaba a alguien a favor de su política de conquistas y capaz en el campo de batalla. Se ha apuntado que el César pensó intensamente en Lucio Quieto como sucesor, pese a que era norteafricano. El origen de Quieto podía ser un problema, pero el propio Trajano había quebrado la costumbre de que todo emperador debía ser romano de nacimiento o, cuando menos, itálico. En todo caso, hay muchas teorías al respecto. *La legión perdida* ha ilustrado precisamente la versión de que Trajano pensaba en Quieto como sucesor y no en Adriano, una teoría que, como digo, tiene muchos defensores entre el mundo académico (véase, por ejemplo Potter, 2007).

Adriano

La figura de Adriano ha sido reflejada en la literatura, en particular en *Memorias de Adriano*, de Marguerite Yourcenar, como la de un hombre maravilloso, inteligente, culto y de buen trato. Las fuentes clásicas aportan datos que cuestionan este retrato. La novela de Yourcenar es una excelente obra literaria, pero a mí me cuesta considerarla como histórica. Adriano era muy voluble en su carácter, caprichoso, violento con frecuencia (podía sacar los ojos a un esclavo que no le sirviera como él deseaba) y maltrataba a su esposa Vibia Sabina. Estos rasgos están en las fuentes clásicas, como el hecho de que rompiera la ley tácita de Nerva y Trajano de no sentenciar a muerte a ningún senador, y aún menos sin tener en cuenta al conjunto del Senado. Adriano ordenó o permitió que bajo su mandato se ejecutara a Celso, a Palma, a Nigrino y al propio Quieto. Todos ellos eran rivales y hombres que podían oponerse a la dudosa legalidad de su adopción por un Trajano moribundo, quizá incapacitado en su lecho de muerte para firmar ya ningún documento y que muy probablemente ni siquiera entendiera bien lo que estaba pasando a su alrededor.

Adriano, además, ordenó la ejecución del arquitecto Apolodoro de Damasco, expulsó de la corte imperial a Suetonio (para aislar a su esposa en el palacio imperial, pues el bibliotecario parecía apoyar a la emperatriz en todo momento) y, aunque a este respecto hay teorías diferentes, es muy posible que ordenara la destrucción del puente sobre el Danubio por considerarlo una amenaza en la frontera (otra posibilidad es que el puente fuera desmantelado años después por Aureliano, pero los expertos españoles y rumanos que he consultado consideran más posible la teoría de que fuera destruido en época adriana). De igual forma, Adriano retiró las tropas de todas las provincias orientales anexionadas por Trajano y de parte de la Dacia. Esta política defensiva no surtió el efecto deseado de apaciguar al incómodo vecino parto, pues Vologases IV atacaría en tiempos de la propia dinastía Ulpio-Aelia (o Antonina) las fronteras orientales de una Roma que no quiso asegurar las conquistas de Trajano en aquel territorio.

Adriano era un hombre culto y amante de la poesía, esto es cierto, pero no estoy seguro de que me sintiera cómodo en su corte a no ser que estuviera dispuesto a darle siempre la razón en todo momento.

Adriano también rompió con la costumbre de Trajano de gastar el dinero de Roma en edificios de uso público, programas para los más desfavorecidos o en conquistas para crear nuevas provincias. Sería injusto no reconocer que durante el mandato de Adriano también se hicieron grandes obras públicas, pero ninguna conquista, y, además, gastó grandes cantidades de dinero en caprichos muy costosos, como su maravillosa Villa Adriana fuera de Roma. Eso sí, igual que en el caso de otros emperadores megalómanos, su villa es un lugar precioso para visitar, aunque uno no desearía verlo financiado con el dinero de sus impuestos. También derrocharía millones de sestercios en templos y otros monumentos en honor de su amante Antinoo.

Lo más probable es que Adriano diera un golpe de Estado soterrado para hacerse con el poder, manipulando a un Trajano muy enfermo —algunas fuentes hablan de veneno— y eliminando físicamente a cualquier posible opositor de renombre; esto es lo que he recreado en la novela. En los años siguientes a la muerte de Trajano, Adriano promocionó a Atiano como jefe del pretorio y posteriormente senador y también premió a otros colaboradores en su asalto al poder, como Calvencio Víctor. Con Serviano y su familia se mostró amistoso al principio, pero poco a poco fue maniobrando y nunca consideró la descendencia de su cuñado como posibles herederos al trono. En otras palabras: a Serviano lo engañó vilmente. A Plotina la aisló y lo mismo hizo con su esposa Vibia Sabina.

Por supuesto, de un personaje tan complejo como Adriano se pueden hacer retratos novelescos muy diversos.

El viaje de Titianus

El viaje de Titianus está mencionado en fuentes clásicas. La datación del mismo, no obstante, es controvertida, yendo las fechas que se apuntan para su periplo desde Roma hasta Asia entre la época de Augusto y la del propio Trajano (Cary, 1956). En *La legión perdida* he optado por que el viaje tuviera lugar en la parte final del gobierno de Trajano y he dotado a la audaz misión de motivaciones comerciales y militares. El motivo exacto por el que un César ordenó dicha travesía a un comerciante macedonio o sirio (esto también es objeto de debate) y algún pequeño grupo de colaboradores se desconoce. Lo que sí se sabe con bastante detalle es cómo era el mar Rojo, el océano Índico, la costa arábiga, la costa occidental de India y sus ciudades y puertos, así como la costa de África oriental, y hasta parte de la Ruta de la Seda terrestre que atravesaba el Imperio kushan. Todo esto lo conocemos a partir del texto escrito en griego en el siglo II por algún comerciante anónimo titulado *El periplo por la Mar Eritrea*. El lector verá que ocasionalmente he introducido citas de este texto en la novela, de modo que percibirá hasta qué punto el viaje de Titianus, Tamura, Marcio, Alana, Áyax y Arrio sigue fielmente esta ruta: las mercancías de cada puerto, los días de navegación, la presencia o no de piratas, la caza de esclavos, la compra de marfil, los vientos monzones; todo esto es fiel a los datos que conocemos de aquella época.

La guerra entre Partia y Roma

La mayoría de los personajes del Imperio parto son históricos, igual que casi todos los sucesos relacionados con dicha cultura que se mencionan en la novela: la muerte de Partamasiris, la política de retirada de tropas de Osroes evitando durante mucho tiempo el enfrentamiento directo con Trajano, la batalla del Tigris, cómo Trajano hizo pasar los barcos de la flota de un río a otro por tierra, la conquista de Cesifonte y el asedio de Hatra. Éstos y otros sucesos están descritos según la información que disponemos, que no es tanta. De hecho, ha sido muy complejo reunir datos sobre estos acontecimientos, pues las fuentes sobre la vida de Trajano y sus campañas de Partia, sorprendentemente, están desaparecidas en su casi totalidad. Apenas tenemos los resúmenes del relato de Dión Casio y poco más. Es como si alguien hubiera decidido borrar de los anales la conquista de Partia por parte de Trajano. ¿Tiene Adriano algo que ver en esto?

Está registrado, no obstante, el hecho de que una hija de Osroes fue capturada por Trajano y luego devuelta por Adriano. Lo que se desconoce es el nombre concreto de esa princesa. Ningún historiador lo recogió. Lo que he hecho es recurrir a un listado de princesas partas de la dinastía arsácida incluido en un artículo (Brosius, 2009) de la *Enciclopedia Iránica* para seleccionar un posible nombre de un personaje histórico cuyos datos concretos no han quedado plasmados en ningún texto: así surge Aryazate en la novela. El final de la princesa parta una vez regresa con su padre Osroes nos es desconocido y lo he novelado. Lo que sí es histórico es que Vologases, el eterno enemigo de Osroes (casado o no con esa princesa parta), atacó una vez más al poco tiempo de que los romanos se retiraran y, por fin, consiguió derrocar a Osroes del trono. Partia quedaría entonces bajo el control de Mitrídates y Vologases III, que siguieron batallando hasta que o bien el propio Vologases III o quizá su hijo Vologases IV se hicieron con el poder total y, como he dicho anteriormente, luego se atrevieron a atacar al Imperio romano, demostrando que la idea de retirarse de Adriano no solucionaba los problemas fronterizos con Partia.

La sanguinaria costumbre de dar muerte a todas las mujeres y a los niños cuando un rey parto huía para poder hacerlo más rápido y no dejar atrás posibles rehenes es cierta (recogida por Tácito, Isidoro de Carax o Flavio Josefo). Que Osroes recurriera a esta rutina al huir de Cesifonte cuando se vio acosado por Trajano es algo que no sabemos, pero no sería nada extraño.

Finalmente, con relación a Partia, y como explico de nuevo en el árbol genealógico de la dinastía arsácida, las constantes disputas por el trono entre los miembros de la familia real parta hacen imposible explicar todos los que realmente se disputaron el gobierno de este imperio entre el año 106 y el 117, de modo que he decidido simplificar estas guerras fratricidas eliminando de la novela a aquellos nobles partos que apenas estuvieron unos meses en el trono. Así, por la novela desfilan sólo los partos más destacados de la época: Exedares, Partamasiris, Osroes, Mitrídates, Sanatruces, Partamaspates y Vologases. Con ellos creo que es suficiente para mostrar a los lectores la constante lucha intestina en el seno de Partia.

La India, el Imperio kushan y el budismo

El Imperio kushan emerge como potencia territorial dominante del norte de la India y Afganistán durante el siglo I de nuestra era y se erige como pieza clave en la Ruta de la Seda. Es muy difícil disponer de datos concretos sobre la dinastía kushan, pues los yacimientos arqueológicos donde se estaban encontrando más restos con información están precisamente en Afganistán, y hoy día la exploración arqueológica en la zona es prácticamente nula. En la época de Trajano gobernaba el Imperio kushan Kadphises o quizá su hijo Kanishka. En *La legión perdida* he optado por describir el momento de transición de un emperador a otro.

Las relaciones entre los kushan y el Imperio han de China están documentadas. Los *Yuegzhi*, como los denominan los chinos, y el Imperio han siempre mantuvieron una relación tumultuosa en su frontera, algo que se muestra también en la novela. De todas formas, gobernantes como Kanishka, aunque siempre intentaron expandir su poder, comprendieron que mantener la Ruta de la Seda abierta era interesante para ellos, incluso si eso los forzaba a mejorar puntualmente las relaciones con sus vecinos de Occidente y de Oriente (algo que el huno Zhizhi de finales del siglo I a.C. no supo entender y que a la postre condujo a su aniquilación por los han).

Los emperadores kushan, en particular Kanishka, optaron por promover la religión budista como la fe del Estado, seguramente como un elemento adicional unificador de los territorios bajo su mando. Facilitaron que el cuarto concilio budista pudiera realizarse en su capital. Durante este concilio, los monjes más destacados de esta religión seleccionaron los escritos que mejor reflejaban la vida y las enseñanzas de Buda. Había también algunas monjas influyentes, como es el caso de Buddhamitra, que es, aunque pueda sorprender, un personaje histórico.

El consejero Shaka es un personaje de ficción, pero sí es cierto que llegó una embajada a Trajano desde alguna región de la India cuando el emperador hispano celebraba su triunfo sobre los dacios en Roma. Muchas fuentes consideran que sólo los kushan del norte de la India tenían la capacidad de enviar una embajada de este tipo a un lugar tan lejano, y sin duda Kadphises y Kanishka tendrían consejeros de su confianza, aunque sus nombres no nos hayan llegado. El consejero Shaka rellena este hueco de la historia.

China

China era y sigue siendo ese gigante eternamente desconocido o incomprendido para Occidente. En la época de *La legión perdida*, China era un remoto imperio exótico del que venían productos asombrosos como la seda o las lacas. Aunque el Imperio han desempeña un papel secundario en la novela he procurado realizar una recreación lo más fidedigna posible de su organización, estructura social y militar, así como de los conocimientos que los chinos tenían a principios del siglo II, que no eran pocos. Me parecía particularmente interesante mostrar que mientras en Occidente escribíamos en papiro o pergamino, en China estaban inventando el papel, o que mientras nuestros mejores intelectuales elaboraban extrañas teorías sobre lo que era un terremoto, allí sus matemáticos se esforzaban en construir sismógrafos. La invención del papel tuvo lugar en las fechas que se refieren en la novela, y el sismógrafo unos años después, por eso en *La legión perdida* se presenta a la emperatriz un prototipo y no el aparato definitivo cuya reproducción podemos ver en el Museo de Historia de Pequín. Estos dos ejemplos, la invención del papel y del sismógrafo, intentan ilustrar que la civilización china estaba tan avanzada como la grecorromana de la que procedemos, en algunos casos incluso más. Personajes como el consejero Fan Chun, la emperatriz Deng, el matemático Zang Heng, el joven emperador An-ti y su siempre intrigante favorita Yan Ji existieron en realidad. Igual que la estructura de tres excelencias y nueve ministros, los generales y gobernadores de las provincias o las grandes ciudades de Ch'ang-an y Loyang, tal y como aparecen descritas en *La legión perdida*. De todos estos aspectos me gustaría subrayar uno que, lo reconozco, me sorprendió durante el proceso de documentación: el hecho de que China, un imperio de dimensiones territoriales y demográficas equiparable al Imperio romano, estuviera gobernado de facto por una mujer. Y además bien gobernado. Con cada novela que hago y leyendo cada vez más sobre el pasado voy confirmando que las mujeres han desempeñado un papel mucho más importante en la historia del que habitualmente se nos ha transmitido.

El personaje de Li Kan en China es de ficción, pero si es cierto que hubo supervivientes de la legión perdida no es imposible que alguien así existiera (ahora me referiré más en detalle a este punto). En todo caso, había generales del ejército han de frontera con la misión de mantener a los hunos, a los *hsiung-nu*, en el norte, o a los kushan, los *Yuegzhi*, en Occidente, siempre fuera del imperio. Li Kan ilustra bien cómo sería la vida de uno de esos militares.

Roma y China

Las relaciones comerciales entre Roma y China pueden retrotraerse hasta el principio mismo de la Roma imperial. Ya el historiador Floro refiere una embajada China enviada a saludar al César Augusto, aunque los investigadores desde Yule (1915) en adelante consideran que si realmente existió tal embajada sería de comerciantes privados y no oficial, pues nunca aparece referenciada en el *Hou Han Shu* o libro de *La dinastía Han del Este*, que compendia los datos históricos más relevantes del imperio chino de los primeros siglos de nuestra era. Ocasionalmente hay alguna cita de este valioso texto en diferentes secciones de *La legión perdida*.

La embajada oficial o comercial de Titianus, citada arriba, si parece ser el primer intento serio de Roma por contactar con China, aunque, como he explicado, hay gran controversia sobre la fecha de dicho viaje, que en *La legión perdida* hemos decidido situar en la época de Trajano.

Por su parte, el Imperio han hizo su particular intento de contactar con Roma con la embajada de Kan Ying en tiempos del emperador He. Fue una misión que no pudo culminar su objetivo, entorpecido tanto por los kushan como, sobre todo, por los partos, que no deseaban de ningún modo que Roma y China pudieran interaccionar sin estar ellos como intermediarios. Todo esto viene recreado en la novela.

Más allá del relato de *La legión perdida*, los emperadores Marco Aurelio, Alejandro Severo y Marco Aurelio Caro enviaron nuevas embajadas a China durante los siglos II y III de nuestra era. Posteriormente el Imperio bizantino, desde tiempos del emperador Constancio II (641-668), mantuvo contactos intermitentes con China y Asia central.

Fuera como fuese, Plinio el Viejo, coetáneo de Trajano, ya refería que Roma se gastaba, por lo menos, cien millones de sestercios al año en sus importaciones de China. No quiero pensar en lo que diría el viejo Plinio si levantara cabeza en 2015 y viera cuánto se gasta Occidente hoy día importando productos de China. Como se ve, la historia del comercio con Extremo Oriente empezó hace mucho más tiempo de lo que muchos imaginan.

La legión perdida y la batalla de Kangchú

La batalla que tuvo lugar en torno a 36 a.C. en la fortaleza de Talas enfrentó a fuerzas del líder huno Zhizhi, aliado con tropas sogdianas y una unidad de mercenarios extranjeros, contra el ejército del general han Tang. No hay que confundir esta batalla librada en Talas en 36 a.c. con otra denominada específicamente «batalla de Talas» que tuvo lugar en el mismo emplazamiento siglos después, en 751, entre tropas árabes y turcas contra tropas chinas de la dinastía Tang (la coincidencia en el nombre Tang del general de 36 a.C. y de la dinastía china de 751 es casual). Se trata, pues, de enfrentamientos totalmente diferentes. La batalla de 36 a.c. suele ser denominada en fuentes chinas como batalla de Kangchú, entendiendo que, como se ha explicado en la novela, Kangchú es el nombre que los han daban a Sogdiana.

Hasta aquí todo claro. La controversia (o la magia) surge cuando se intenta determinar quiénes eran los guerreros de aquella unidad de mercenarios que luchaban junto a los hunos del brutal Zhizhi. Se han apuntado teorías de todo tipo (incluso que fueran descendientes de las tropas de Alejandro Magno), pero una de las que más ha impactado es la del británico Dubs, experto en estudios sobre el Extremo Oriente, quien afirma (Dubs, 1957 y 1962) que esos mercenarios eran, precisamente, los supervivientes de la legión perdida de Craso. Las fuentes occidentales (esto es, romanas, representadas por Plinio el Viejo y Plutarco) pierden la pista a esta legión en Merv, el extremo oriental de Partia. No sabemos si la idea de Dubs de que esa legión siguió hacia China es cierta o no, pero el general Tang, tal y como se ha recogido en la novela, describía las técnicas militares de estos guerreros mercenarios (combate en formación de *testudo*, campamentos con empalizadas, etc.) de forma que se puede interpretar que estaba frente a los restos de una legión romana.

La teoría de Dubs ha sido criticada, cuestionada y atacada en multitud de ocasiones. En especial, Ethan Gruber (2007) publicó un demoledor artículo donde muestra todos los puntos débiles de la idea de Dubs. Pero, y esto es lo interesante, incluso Gruber, en honor a la rigurosidad académica y científica, se ve obligado a admitir al final de su artículo que la teoría de Dubs, pese a que él la pueda considerar improbable, «no debe ser considerada una completa imposibilidad». Esto me llevó a pensar que si el mayor detractor de la teoría de

Dubs es incapaz de negarla al cien por cien implica que hay un margen para pensar, para imaginar que quizá los mercenarios de Zhizhi eran, tal y como afirma Dubs, los restos de la legión perdida.

Sólo imaginarlo me resultó fascinante. No sabemos si es cierto o no, pero nadie puede afirmar que no fuera así, de modo que me decidí a pasar de la mera fantasía a novelar con precisión los lugares, ciudades, reinos, lenguas, etnias, religiones, culturas y diferentes técnicas militares de los unos y los otros, dando así, en cierta forma, vida (literaria, al menos) a la teoría de Dubs. Esto es lo que los lectores encuentran en *La legión perdida*: lo que tanto se ha discutido llevado a una novela atendiendo al detalle en las localizaciones, en los combates y en el choque de esos dos mundos, Roma y China. No puedo saber aún, nadie puede a fecha de hoy, si los mercenarios de Zhizhi eran de la legión perdida, pero de lo que sí estoy bastante seguro es de que si realmente lo fueron, tuvieron que seguir la ruta que he descrito y combatieron de forma muy similar a la presentada en la novela. Son ficción la forma de huir de Merv (no hay constancia de cómo sería esta huida), pero son muy reales las luchas entre las diferentes facciones de hunos, el conflicto militar entre los hunos y los han, y la guerra que asoló Sogdiana en esta época por la lucha entre estos dos bandos que pugnaban por controlar la Ruta de la Seda que atravesaba Asia central. Y también es fidedigno, en este caso a las fuentes chinas (no hay otras), el desarrollo de la batalla de Kangchú. Los personajes de Druso, Cayo y Sexto son imaginados, pero si la legión perdida llegó hasta Kangchú y luchó contra un ejército han, algún centurión valeroso habría y estaría acompañado, sin duda, por buenos oficiales romanos, sobre todo si eran hombres que habían sobrevivido a tantas guerras, batallas y penurias.

El asunto de las descendencia de los supervivientes romanos (si aceptamos que hubo romanos en Kangchú luchando contra el general Tang) es también controvertido, pero nuevamente las fuentes chinas indican que a parte de estos mercenarios se les perdonó la vida y se los integró en el ejército regular han. A partir de ahí la imaginación me ha permitido unir este evento de la legión perdida con el viaje de Titianus, en particular con la llegada de Tamura y su encuentro con Li Kan. A este respecto sabemos que Titianus nunca llegó más allá de Asia central, pero el mercader envió a algún miembro superviviente de su misión más hacia el este. ¿Llegó a China?

Es posible que haya quien piense que en esta ocasión he dejado volar mi imaginación muy alto, pero estoy muy acostumbrado, y de antemano pido excusas por el cliché, a comprobar que la realidad siempre supera a la más fantástica de las ficciones. Igual todo ocurrió como he contado, tal vez de forma muy diferente, quizá de forma aún mucho más increíble. Pero sí quiero subrayar que tanto los reinos de Asia central y la China de ambas épocas, el siglo I a.C. y principios del siglo II d.C. han sido descritas de forma fidedigna a los datos que tenemos. Otro asunto es si la legión perdida llegó o no hasta allí y si luego hubo descendientes romanos integrados en el ejército han. En este punto, por el momento, sigue sin haber acuerdo entre los académicos.

Los cristianos y el Nuevo Testamento

Los cristianos aparecen en *La legión perdida* de forma muy secundaria, pero me parecía, como en las novelas anteriores de la trilogía de Trajano, inaceptable escribir sobre esta época sin tener presente lo que estaba pasando en una comunidad religiosa que hoy día es la más relevante en nuestra cultura (más allá del hecho puramente religioso, que, por supuesto, es en sí mismo muy importante también).

Y es que es entre el final del gobierno de Trajano y la época de Adriano cuando los cristianos se ven abocados a un enorme conflicto: ¿qué hacer si el mundo, tal y como creían los primeros cristianos, no acaba y se mueren todos los discípulos de Cristo? ¿Cómo preservar el mensaje de Jesús? A partir de aquí hay varias teorías sobre cómo se llega a la conclusión de que hay que crear un nuevo libro sagrado que compendie los principales relatos sobre la vida y las enseñanzas de Jesús. Una de esas teorías es la de que Marción se anticipó a la comunidad ortodoxa y esto fue lo que motivó, por reacción, que desde dentro de la Iglesia cristiana se decidiera crear un canon de textos sagrados que terminarían siendo lo que hoy conocemos como Nuevo Testamento (Piñero, 2008) Y todo esto mientras Trajano y Adriano se enfrentaban por su forma diferente de concebir el Imperio romano y su expansión.

Me parecía también interesante mostrar cómo en paralelo a la generación del Nuevo Testamento, el budismo, otra de las grandes religiones del mundo, intentaba hacer algo parecido (recopilar textos sobre la vida y las enseñanzas de su gran profeta) en su cuarto concilio bajo el auspicio de los emperadores kushan. Lugares diferentes, religiones distintas, pero siempre el ser humano actuando de formas similares.

El síndrome del Capitán Trueno

Finalmente, la redacción de *La legión perdida* requería soslayar un problema de comunicación entre personajes de muy diferentes culturas evitando caer en lo que, cariñosamente, denomino el «síndrome del Capitán Trueno». Y es que nuestro gran héroe hispano del cómic recorría el mundo entero en tiempos medievales pudiendo hablar con escandinavos, ingleses, árabes, mongoles, chinos o samuráis japoneses sin demasiados problemas de comunicación. Esto no lo digo como crítica a un maravilloso cómic, el de Víctor Mora (guionista) y Miguel Ambrosio (dibujante), cuya función esencial era la de entretener, objetivo que cumplió a plena satisfacción con centenares de miles de lectores, entre los que me incluyo. Pero a la hora de elaborar una novela histórica, aunque también en ella busco entretener al máximo, se ha de tener presente una base de rigor documental y de verosimilitud que requiere resolver el tema de la comunicación entre personajes de diferentes culturas del modo más creíble posible.

Gore Vidal, en su novela *Creación*, donde un personaje viaja también en el mundo antiguo del siglo v antes de Cristo desde Grecia hasta China pasando por toda Asia, resuelve el asunto haciendo que su protagonista sea un muy culto embajador persa que dominaba varios idiomas, lo que le permitirá hablar con Sócrates, Buda o Confucio.

Esto me llevó a investigar sobre las lenguas de comunicación internacional del siglo I a.C. y del siglo II d.C. En ambos casos el griego era fundamental y, de forma complementaria, el sogdiano en el siglo I a.C. y el sánscrito en el siglo II d.C. Esto implicaba que debía de haber personajes que conocieran estas lenguas para poder facilitar la comunicación entre unos y otros. En estos períodos tenemos lenguas *intraimperiales*, por así decirlo, usadas sólo dentro de un imperio, y lenguas *transimperiales*, usadas o comprendidas, al menos, por una élite en más de un imperio. El griego era lengua válida de comunicación por todo el Mediterráneo, en lo que luego será Imperio romano y, desde Alejandro Magno, también en las regiones que luego constituirán el Imperio parto, incluso en reinos como Sogdiana. Por su parte, el sánscrito sería lengua entendida por las élites del Imperio kushan y también por monjes budistas y algunos altos funcionarios del Imperio han en China.

El sogdiano, o, para ser más precisos, el protosogdiano, fue una lengua muy relevante en los primeros siglos de la Ruta de la Seda, pues la hablaban los mercaderes de la gran ruta comercial en Asia central, poniendo así en comunicación los protectorados chinos occidentales con el reino de Sogdiana y las regiones fronterizas de Partia.

Por fin, nos quedan las lenguas *intraimperiales* como el latín, propia del Imperio romano, y el parto, dentro de Partia y sus dominios.

Tamura precisaba conocer griego y sánscrito para su gran periplo y Druso necesitaba, al menos, un intérprete sogdiano. De este modo, junto con algunos otros personajes como Fan Chun, la comunicación entre hombres y mujeres de orígenes tan diversos es posible en *La legión perdida*.

Vuelta a Trajano

Siempre quedará abierto el debate de quién tenía razón: ¿Trajano o Adriano? El primero pensaba que la mejor defensa era un buen ataque y por eso su política de conquistas y anexiones, y el segundo consideraba que Roma no podía abarcar tanto. A favor de Trajano está la idea de que el flujo de riquezas que habría aportado el control de Partia y todas sus provincias, con la eliminación de los partos como incómodos intermediarios en el comercio de la Ruta de la Seda, habría sido de tal envergadura que habría permitido incrementar la capacidad no sólo económica sino también militar de Roma. Desde la perspectiva de Trajano controlar Oriente habría ayudado a tener más recursos para defender las fronteras del Danubio y el Rin en siglos posteriores. En contra de esta visión y a favor de la idea defensiva de Adriano está el que la extensión del Imperio habría sido tan enorme, con unas fronteras tan extensas, que la caída habría tenido lugar mucho antes. Es difícil saber quién tenía razón. Trajano pensaba siempre a lo grande, Adriano con prudencia o con egoísmo o, quizá, con ambas ideas en la mente.

Lo que es indiscutible es que Trajano tenía un sueño de expansión que fue mucho más allá de lo que sus contemporáneos romanos fueron capaces de asimilar o de entender, ya fuera por ser más sensatos que el emperador hispano o porque tenían grabado a fuego el eterno recuerdo de la legión perdida. Es muy posible que, como dice el personaje de Domicia Longina en la novela, Trajano fuera derrotado sólo por un enemigo, por un fantasma, por el fantasma de la legión perdida.

Diferentes emperadores intentaron luego resolver el problema de la frontera con Partia, pero pese a victorias parciales, ya era tarde para reavivar los planes de Trajano. La oportunidad de que el mundo desde Hispania y Britania hasta la India fuera romano, para bien o para mal, se había perdido.

Pero nos quedan textos, leyendas y teorías sobre aquel sueño de Trajano, imágenes y retazos de una historia casi olvidada que, sin embargo, en *La legión perdida*, cada vez que alguien pasee por sus páginas, vuelven a cobrar vida.

2

GLOSARIO DE TÉRMINOS LATINOS

ab urbe condita: «Desde la fundación de la ciudad.» Era la expresión que se usaba a la hora de citar un año, pues los romanos los contaban desde la fecha de la fundación de Roma, que corresponde tradicionalmente con 754 a.C. En la trilogía de Trajano se usa el calendario moderno con el nacimiento de Cristo como referencia, pero ocasionalmente se cita la fecha según el calendario romano para que el lector tenga una perspectiva de cómo sentían los romanos el devenir del tiempo y los acontecimientos con relación a su ciudad.

aerarium: Erario público del Estado romano que se nutría de los impuestos portuarios y otros tributos diversos de la actividad comercial. Frontino explica con detalle el funcionamiento de estos impuestos en el capítulo 33 de *Circo Máximo.*

Africa Nova: Provincia romana que se corresponde aproximadamente con la región de la antigua Numidia.

alae: Unidades de caballería auxiliar de una legión romana.

Alea jacta est: «La suerte está echada», frase que Julio César pronunció al cruzar el río Rubicón del norte de Italia con un ejército armado en su camino a Roma, una acción prohibida por las leyes de la época. La sentencia muestra que Julio César estaba convencido de que tras cruzar ese río ya no había vuelta atrás en su lucha por el poder absoluto en Roma. La frase parece tener su origen en el juego de los dados donde indicaría que «los dados (y la suerte de los mismos) están lanzados» una vez que uno los arroja al suelo durante el juego. Suetonio atribuye la frase a Julio César y Plutarco nos apunta que quizá César pudiera haberla tomado de una obra del escritor griego Menandro. A partir de la obra de Suetonio, se usaba en ocasiones de importancia para indicar que ya se había tomado una decisión y que todo quedaba en manos de la diosa Fortuna.

alimenta: Programa establecido por el emperador Nerva cuyo fin era distribuir alimentos entre los más necesitados de Roma, en particular entre los niños. Nerva apenas tendría tiempo de poner el programa en marcha, pero su sucesor Trajano lo desarrollaría durante su gobierno.

Amnis Traianus: También conocido como el canal o el río de Trajano. Se trataba de un canal que conectaba el mar Mediterráneo con la mar Eritrea, es decir, con el actual mar Rojo. El canal aprovechaba uno de los brazos del delta del Nilo y algunos lagos en una parte del recorrido, y podría ser que también usara parte de un canal que previamente construyeron los faraones. No sabemos con seguridad quién se hizo cargo de semejante obra, aunque sería muy posible que Apolodoro de Damasco, el gran arquitecto de Trajano, estuviera al cargo de la misma total o parcialmente.

andabata, andabatae: Gladiador condenado a luchar a ciegas con un casco que no tenía visión alguna; era una dura forma de condena en la Roma imperial. El pueblo se divertía intentando orientarlos o confundirlos aún más desde las gradas.

Anfiteatro Flavio: El anfiteatro más grande del mundo, construido en Roma durante el reinado de Vespasiano, inaugurado por Tito y ampliado posteriormente por Domiciano. Aunque en él se celebraban cacerías, ejecuciones en masa de condenados a muerte y quizá en algún momento alguna *naumaquia* o batalla naval, ha pasado a la historia por ser el lugar donde luchaban los gladiadores de Roma. En la trilogía de Trajano se describen su construcción y algunas de estas luchas de gladiadores.

annales: Archivos históricos de la antigua Roma en los que quedaban registrados los nombramientos anuales de los diferentes magistrados y cualquier otro suceso relevante.

annona: El trigo que se distribuía gratuitamente por el Estado entre los ciudadanos libres de Roma. Durante un largo período, Sicilia fue la región que más grano proporcionaba a la capital del Imperio, pero en la época de Trajano Egipto era ya el reino más importante como exportador de grano a Roma.

ante diem VI Kalendas Iulias: Seis días antes del primero de julio, y como los romanos contaban el día que se tomaba como referencia (en este caso *Kalendas*) y el día desde el que se comenzaba la cuenta, esta fecha equivalía al 26 de junio.

apodyterium: Vestuario de las termas donde uno se podía desvestir.

a posteriori: Expresión latina que significa «más tarde» o «después de».

ara: Altar.

Ara pudicitia: Altar levantado por orden del emperador Trajano en honor a la emperatriz Plotina. Apenas hay datos sobre el mismo.

arenari: Esclavos encargados de alisar la arena en el Anfiteatro Flavio después de un combate.

Argiletum: Avenida que partía del foro en dirección norte dejando el gran *Macellum* al este.

armamentorum: Lugar donde se almacenaban las armas dentro de un campamento legionario o en los *castra praetoria* de Roma.

armaria: Los grandes armarios donde se preservaban los numerosos rollos en las bibliotecas de la antigua Roma.

Armenia et Mesopotamia in potestatem P.R. redactae: Leyenda inscrita en una serie de monedas de época trajana para conmemorar la anexión de estos territorios al Imperio de Roma como nuevas provincias. En la actualidad hay muy pocas monedas con esta inscripción y su valor es incalculable. El texto significa que «Armenia y Mesopotamia han sido sometidas a la autoridad del pueblo romano».

atriense: El esclavo de mayor rango y confianza en una *domus* romana. Actuaba como capataz supervisando las actividades del resto de los esclavos y gozaba de gran autonomía en su trabajo.

Atrium Vestae: La casa donde residían las vírgenes vestales, las novicias en el sagrado sacerdocio y la Vestal Máxima. Estaba situada en el centro de Roma, en el mismo foro, al lado del Templo de Vesta.

attramentum: Nombre que recibía la tinta de color negro en la época descrita en *La legión perdida.*

augur: Sacerdote romano encargado de la toma de los auspicios y con capacidad de leer el futuro, sobre todo, en el vuelo de las aves. Plinio el Joven sería nombrado augur por el emperador Marco Ulpio Trajano.

augur publicus populi romani quiritium: Título completo de los augures públicos de Roma.

auguraculum: El espacio sagrado donde un augur realizaba los ritos para predecir el futuro.

augusto, augusta: Tratamiento que recibía el emperador y aquellos miembros de la familia imperial que el emperador designase. Era la máxima dignidad desde el punto de vista de la nobleza.

Aula Regia: El gran salón de audiencias del palacio imperial de Roma en un extremo de la *Domus Flavia*. Se cree que en el centro de esta gran sala Domiciano ordenó que se situara un imponente trono imperial desde el que se dirigía a sus súbditos.

aureus: Moneda de oro que equivalía, en época de Trajano, aproximadamente a cien sextercios.

aurum: Oro.

auspex: Augur familiar.

autoritas: Autoridad, poder.

Baetica: Provincia romana al sur de Hispania de la que fueron oriundos emperadores de Roma como Trajano o Adriano. Era una provincia profundamente romanizada.

ballistae: Catapulta o pieza de artillería romana utilizada en los asedios a fortalezas o ciudades enemigas amuralladas.

Balneum Surae: Termas construidas por orden de Trajano en recuerdo del senador hispano Sura, que tanto lo apoyó en su ascenso a emperador. Fueron destruidas y restauradas varias veces a lo largo de la convulsa historia de la Roma de los siglos IV y V. Se ubicaron en el Aventino pero hoy día no quedan restos arqueológicos relevantes.

basílica Emilia: Una basílica para impartir justicia construida en el año 179 a.C. por la familia Fulvia y Emilia, por lo que en un principio se denominó basílica Fulvia y Emilia, pero tras la reconstrucción de la misma por Emilio Lépido en 78 a.C. ya pasó a denominarse simplemente como basílica Emilia. Aún tuvo que ser reconstruida en varias ocasiones más, concretamente en 55 a.C. (las obras no terminaron hasta 34 a.C.) y en 14 a.C. Sus dimensiones no eran tan grandes como las de la basílica Julia, pero estaban en torno a los ochenta metros de longitud por treinta de ancho aproximadamente.

basílica Julia: Cerraba el foro por uno de sus extremos. Era de grandes dimensiones, con más de cien metros de longitud. Se levantó donde antes estaba la basílica Sempronia, que los Graco construyeron donde estaba la casa de Escipión el Africano. La basílica Julia tenía cuatro naves menores y una gran nave central. Julio César, de quien toma el nombre, inició el proyecto, pero sería el emperador Augusto quien la terminara.

bestiarius, bestiarii: Esclavo o liberto que se encargaba de cuidar las fieras de los anfiteatros. Carpophorus fue uno de los más famosos, a la par que terribles, *bestiarii* de todos los tiempos. Sus crueles «juegos» entre fieras y seres humanos indefensos encandilaron al pueblo romano durante años.

birreme: Barco, normalmente militar, de la armada romana o de otro imperio de la antigüedad (por ejemplo Cartago) que tenía remeros repartidos en dos niveles.

buccinator: Trompetero de las legiones.

bucellata: Galletas saladas que podían elaborarse de muchas formas diferentes, aunque con frecuencia contenían romero y olivas. Los legionarios y la caballería romana las llevaban como provisiones por su resistencia a los cambios medioambientales, su poco peso y elevado valor nutritivo. Se comían solas o mojadas en caldo.

bulla: Amuleto que comúnmente llevaban los niños pequeños en Roma. Tenía la función de alejar los malos espíritus.

calceus: Calzado romano tipo bota que se ataba con cordones o cintas.

caldarium: Sala con una piscina de agua caliente en unas termas romanas.

caligae: Sandalias militares.

calon, calones: Singular y plural del término usado para referirse al esclavo de un legionario. Normalmente no intervenían en las acciones de guerra.

canabae legionis: Conjunto de tiendas, comercios y almacenes de todo tipo que se erigían en cabañas ligeras fáciles de montar y desmontar y que se establecían al lado de los grandes campamentos legionarios romanos para satisfacer las necesidades de aprovisionamiento de las tropas. Con frecuencia, estos conjuntos de tiendas en vecindad con un campamento romano dieron lugar a poblaciones enteras.

capite velato: Con la cabeza cubierta con una capucha, un velo o alguna otra prenda similar. Algunos sacrificios requerían que los oficiantes se cubrieran la cabeza.

carcer: Compartimento o gran cajón desde el que salían las cuadrigas en un extremo del Circo Máximo para dar inicio a una carrera. Había doce, y los que estaban justo enfrente de la recta eran los más codiciados por los aurigas, ya que ofrecían una posición ventajosa en la salida en comparación con los que estaban en el extremo contrario.

cardo: Línea de norte a sur que trazaba una de las avenidas principales de un campamento romano o que un augur dibujaba en el aire para dividir el cielo en diferentes secciones a la hora de interpretar el vuelo de las aves.

carpe diem: Expresión latina que significa «goza del día presente», «disfruta de lo presente», tomada del poema *Odae se Carmina* (1, 11, 8) del poeta Horacio.

carpentum: Pequeño carro, normalmente de dos ruedas. Las vestales utilizaban con frecuencia este tipo de vehículo para sus desplazamientos por Roma o por los alrededores de la ciudad.

carroballistas: Carros en los que se montaban ballestas para arrojar largas lanzas contra los enemigos. Trajano los introdujo como una original novedad militar para atacar de forma directa a la temida caballería catafracta sármata y parta.

caseus: Queso.

cassis: Un casco coronado con un penacho adornado de plumas púrpura o negras.

Cástor: Junto con su hermano Pólux, uno de los dioscuros griegos asimilados por la religión romana. Su templo, el de los Cástores, o de Cástor y Pólux, servía de archivo a la orden de los *equites* o caballeros romanos. El nombre de ambos dioses era usado con frecuencia a modo de interjección.

castra praetoria: El campamento general fortificado de la guardia pretoriana construido por Sejano, jefe del pretorio del emperador Tiberio, al norte de Roma.

casus belli: Motivación para iniciar una guerra. Roma, desde tiempos de la República, buscaba siempre una justificación para encontrar en una nueva guerra y esta motivación la denominaba *casus belli*.

catafractos: Caballería acorazada propia de los ejércitos de Persia, Partia y otros imperios de Oriente y también de los pueblos sármatas al norte del Danubio. Este tipo de unidades se caracterizaba porque tanto el caballo como el jinete iban protegidos por fuertes corazas que los hacían prácticamente invulnerables al enemigo. Los romanos sufrieron numerosas derrotas frente a este tipo de caballería hasta que poco a poco fueron incorporando unidades catafractas a la propia caballería de las legiones. El precursor de esta renovación sería el emperador Trajano.

cathedra: Silla sin reposabrazos con respaldo ligeramente curvo. Al principio sólo la usaban las mujeres, por considerarla demasiado lujosa, pero pronto su uso se extendió también a los hombres. Fue usada luego por jueces para impartir justicia o por los profesores de retórica clásica. De ahí la expresión «hablar *ex cathedra*».

caveas: Gradas de los grandes edificios públicos de Roma, de los teatros, anfiteatros o circos.

centesima rerum venalium: Impuesto extraordinario que se activaba excepcionalmente con fines militares.

chirurgus: Médico cirujano.

circo Flaminio: Otro de los grandes circos, o pistas de carreras de Roma. Era menor que el Circo Máximo y en él se celebraban los juegos plebeyos.

Circo Máximo: El circo más grande del mundo antiguo. Sus gradas podían albergar, tras la gran ampliación que realizó Julio César, hasta 150.000 espectadores sentados. Éste era el recinto donde se celebraban las espectaculares carreras de carros. Estaba situado entre los montes Palatino y Aventino, donde se celebraban carreras y juegos desde tiempos inmemoriales. Con la ampliación, la pista tenía unos 600 metros de longitud y más de 200 metros de ancho.

cladivata: Barco mercante de la marina romana normalmente de dos mástiles. El origen de su nombre no está claro aunque se apunta que puede estar relacionado con el emperador Claudio.

Claudia: Sobrenombre de la legión VII, que a veces se denominaba legión VII *Claudia Pia Fidelis.* El nombre original era *Macedónica,* pero se ganó el sobrenombre de *Claudia* por su fidelidad al emperador Claudio durante las rebeliones del año 42 d.C.

codex: Códice en forma de libro formado a partir de pegar o coser varias hojas independientes de papiro o pergamino.

codo: Antigua unidad de medida de origen antropométrico que por lo general indicaba la longitud de un objeto tomando como referencia el espacio entre el codo y el final de la mano abierta. Esta unidad oscilaba de una civilización a otra aunque en la mayor parte del mundo helénico el codo equivalía, aproximadamente, a medio metro, 0,46 m para los griegos y 0,44 m para los romanos.

cognomen: Tercer elemento de un nombre romano que indicaba la familia específica a la que una persona pertenecía. Así, por ejemplo, Trajano era el *cognomen* del primer emperador hispano de la historia, cuya juventud se recrea en *Los asesinos del emperador.* Se considera que con frecuencia los *cognomen* deben su origen a alguna característica o anécdota de algún familiar destacado, pero no se sabe con certeza de dónde procede el *cognomen* Traianus.

cohortes sagitarii: Unidades de arqueros incorporadas a las legiones de Roma.

cohortes urbanae: Eran la continuación en época imperial del cuerpo republicano de las *legiones urbanae* o tropas que permanecían en la ciudad de Roma acantonadas como salvaguarda de la ciudad, y actuaban como milicia de seguridad y como tropas militares en caso de asedio o guerra.

cohortes vigilum o vigiles: Cuerpo de vigilancia nocturna creado por el emperador Augusto, especialmente dedicado a la lucha contra los frecuentes incendios que asolaban los diferentes barrios de Roma.

Columna Traiani: La columna de Trajano es la más famosa de todas las columnas triunfales levantadas por los emperadores romanos. Es un impresionante monumento de más de 30 metros de altura, unos 38 si incluimos el pedestal, que conmemora la victoria de Trajano sobre los dacios. Fue erigida en torno al año 113 d.C. bajo la supervisión de Apolodoro de Damasco, el gran arquitecto de Trajano. En sus relieves se reproducen con detalle los episodios centrales de las dos campañas militares de Trajano en la Dacia. El interior es hueco, con una larga escalinata en caracol que conduce a lo alto pero a la que no se permite acceder al público. La columna se empleó también como tumba de Trajano, donde se depositaron las cenizas del emperador tras su muerte. El hecho de que el monumento no esté en el centro del gran foro de Trajano, sino en su extremo oeste, podría ser para que la tumba quedara fuera del *pomerium* sagrado de Roma, una línea imaginaria que marcaba el centro de la urbe, en el que, en principio, no se podían hacer enterramientos. La columna estaba pintada en su momento con vivos colores rojos, amarillos, azules, etcétera, que se han perdido con el paso del tiempo. La nueva iluminación de los foros romanos, estrenada en abril de 2015, realza la columna de Trajano de forma llamativa.

comissatio: Larga sobremesa que solía tener lugar tras un gran banquete romano. Podía durar toda la noche.

Commentari de Bello Civili: O *Comentarios sobre la guerra civil* escritos por Julio César, donde el dictador narra sus enfrentamientos militares con Pompeyo y sus seguidores.

Commentari de Bello Gallico: O *Comentarios sobre la Guerra de las Galias*, donde Julio César describe con todo lujo de detalles su conquista de la Galia, Bélgica, Helvetia y parte de Germania.

confectores: Ejecutores armados con palos gruesos encargados de matar o rematar, según conviniera, a un gladiador herido o cobarde. Podían ser trabajadores del anfiteatro o esclavos.

congiarium: Donativo especial que el emperador ofrecía a los ciudadanos de Roma para celebrar un gran triunfo militar. Trajano fue particularmente generoso con estos donativos. En concreto, el que concedió tras la segunda guerra dácica fue el mayor hasta la fecha.

consilium o consilium augusti: Estado Mayor que aconsejaba al *legatus* o emperador en campaña, o consejo de asesores imperiales, normalmente libertos, que proporcionaban información al César para el mejor gobierno de Roma. También podían formar parte de este consejo senadores y diferentes altos funcionarios del Estado romano.

contubernium: La unidad mínima en una cohorte romana, compuesta por ocho legionarios que compartían tienda y rancho.

corvus: Gigantesco gancho asido a una poderosa soga que sostenía la pasarela que los romanos utilizaban para abordar barcos enemigos.

crassus: Craso, procedente del *cognomen* Craso de Marco Licinio Craso, el cónsul romano que condujo a las legiones de Roma a uno de sus mayores desastres en la famosa derrota de Carrhae. Craso ordenó cruzar el Éufrates, luego se alejó del río y decidió luchar contra la caballería parta en una llanura, donde fue rodeado y sus tropas fueron diezmadas por el enemigo. Los partos, además, hicieron más de diez mil prisioneros, el equivalente a una legión entera con tropas auxiliares incluidas. El destino de estos prisioneros es un enigma para el que los historiadores ofrecen diferentes teorías. *La legión perdida* recrea una de estas posibles teorías. Más allá de lo que ocurriera con la legión perdida en Asia central, el término *craso* viene recogido en el *Diccionario de la Real Academia* con la acepción de «indisculpable», es decir, algo que no tiene excusa alguna, en referencia al tremendo error que el cónsul cometió en Carrhae. Mucha gente emplea aún la expresión «craso error» para referirse, correctamente, a una falta indisculpable, pero no son muchos los que conocen con precisión el origen exacto de la frase.

crimen incesti: El peor crimen del que podía ser acusada una vestal: Si se consideraba que la sacerdotisa podía haber perdido su sagrada virginidad, se celebraba un juicio ante el Colegio de Pontífices bajo la presidencia del *Pontifex Maximus.* Si se encontraba a la vestal culpable de dicho crimen se la condenaba a ser enterrada viva.

cuadriga: Carro romano tirado por cuatro caballos.

cuatrirreme: Navío militar de cuatro hileras de remos. Variante de la *trirreme.*

cubiculum: Pequeño habitáculo para dormir.

cum imperio: Con mando sobre un ejército.

Curia o Curia Julia: Es el edificio del Senado que sustituía al más antiguo denominado *Curia Hostilia,* construido en el Comitium por orden de Tulio Hostilio, de donde deriva su nombre. En el año 52 a.C. la *Curia Hostilia* fue destruida por un incendio y reemplazada por una edificación mayor que recibió el nombre de la familia más poderosa del momento. Aunque el Senado podía reunirse en otros lugares, este edificio era el punto habitual para celebrar sus sesiones. La *Curia Julia* perduró durante todo el Imperio hasta que un nuevo incendio la arrasó en el reinado de Carino. Diocleciano la reconstruyó y la amplió. También puede usarse el término para referirse a la clase senatorial.

cursus honorum: Nombre que recibía la carrera política en Roma. Un ciudadano podía ir ascendiendo en su posición accediendo a diferentes cargos de género político y militar, desde una edilidad en la ciudad de Roma hasta los cargos de cuestor, pretor, censor, procónsul, cónsul o, en momentos excepcionales, dictador. Éstos eran electos, aunque el grado de transparencia de las elecciones fue evolucionando dependiendo de las turbulencias sociales a las que se vio sometida la República romana. En la época imperial, el progreso en el *cursus honorum* dependía sustancialmente de la buena relación que cada uno mantuviera con el emperador.

Dacicus: Título que recibió Trajano del Senado romano como reconocimiento a su conquista de la Dacia y su posterior sometimiento y anexión como provincia nueva del Imperio.

damnatio memoriae: O «maldición a la memoria» de una persona. Cuando un emperador moría el Senado solía deificarle, transformarlo en dios, excepto si había sido un César tiránico, en cuyo caso se reservaba el derecho de maldecir su memoria. Cuando ocurría esto se destruían todas las estatuas de dicho emperador y se borraba su nombre de todas las inscripciones públicas. Incluso se raspaba su efigie en todas las monedas para que no quedara rastro alguno sobre la existencia de aquel tirano. Durante el siglo I el Senado ordenó una *damnatio memoriae* para el emperador Calígula, otra para Nerón y, finalmente, otra más para Domiciano, como se ilustra en *Los asesinos del emperador*, la primera novela de la trilogía de Trajano.

De architectura: Tratado de Vitrubio sobre construcción que fue referencia máxima durante siglos para los arquitectos imperiales de Roma y, posteriormente, en el Renacimiento.

De facto: «De hecho» o «en realidad»; es una expresión latina que puede usarse en contraposición con *de iure*, es decir, «según la ley». Como todos sabemos, más de una vez los hechos y la ley, lamentablemente, no van de la mano.

De Vita Caesarum: La obra más conocida de Suetonio, donde nos relata la vida de los primeros Césares de Roma, desde Augusto hasta Nerva.

decumanus: Línea de este a oeste que trazaba una de las avenidas principales de un campamento romano o que un augur dibujaba en el aire para dividir el cielo en diferentes secciones a la hora de interpretar el vuelo de las aves.

devotio: Sacrificio supremo en el que un general, un oficial o un soldado entrega su propia vida en el campo de batalla o suicidándose posteriormente para salvar el honor del ejército.

domus: Típica vivienda romana de la clase más acomodada, normalmente compuesta de un vestíbulo de entrada a un gran atrio en cuyo centro se encontraba el *impluvium*. Alrededor del atrio se distribuían las estancias principales y al fondo se encontraba el *tablinum*, pequeño despacho o biblioteca de la casa. En el atrio había un pequeño altar para ofrecer sacrificios a los dioses *lares* y *penates* que velaban por el hogar. Las casas más ostentosas añadían un segundo atrio posterior, generalmente porticado y ajardinado, denominado peristilo.

Domus Aurea: El gran palacio que el emperador Nerón ordenó construir sobre terreno público expropiado en el centro de Roma tras el gran incendio que asoló la ciudad durante su reinado. Nerón culpó a los cristianos del incendio pero aprovechó para edificar en gran parte de la zona quemada un inmenso palacio con más de mil aposentos, techos ornamentales y decoraciones con mármol y piedras preciosas. Vespasiano vivió en la *Domus*

Aurea un tiempo a la espera de que se terminara el palacio imperial nuevo, la *Domus Flavia*, pero ordenó que los jardines recuperados de la *Domus Aurea* retornaran al pueblo y aprovechó su espacio para edificar allí el gigantesco Anfiteatro Flavio.

Domus Flavia: El gran palacio imperial levantado en el centro de Roma por orden de la dinastía Flavia. Domiciano fue su principal impulsor y quien se estableció allí por primera vez. En dicho palacio tuvieron lugar los hechos del 18 de septiembre del año 96 que se narran en *Los asesinos del emperador*. El *Aula Regia*, los grandes peristilos porticados, las cámaras imperiales y el hipódromo son las secciones más relevantes de este palacio, estancias que siguen apareciendo reflejadas en *Circo Máximo* y *La legión perdida*.

donativum: Paga especial que los emperadores abonaban a los pretorianos para celebrar su llegada al poder. Galba se negó a pagarlo, lo que facilitó la rebelión de la guardia pretoriana que apoyó a Otón, quien sí se comprometió a pagarlo. Domiciano fue particularmente generoso con los pretorianos con el fin de garantizarse su fidelidad absoluta.

duplicarius: Oficial romano que cobraba el doble del sueldo normal. Habitualmente se trataba de un premio por haber demostrado gran valor en el campo de batalla.

ego: Yo.

Eolo: Dios del viento.

equites singulares augusti: Cuerpo especial de caballería dedicado a la protección del emperador.

escorpión: Máquina lanzadora de piedras diseñada para ser usada en los grandes asedios.

et cetera: Expresión latina que significa «y otras cosas», «y lo restante», «y lo demás».

falera, falerae: Singular y plural de una condecoración militar en forma de placa o medalla que se colgaba del pecho.

flamen: Sacerdote.

flamen dialis: Era el sacerdote encargado del culto de Júpiter, uno de los más respetados e influyentes; sin embargo, este sacerdocio estaba sujeto a tantas restricciones públicas y privadas que en ocasiones era difícil encontrar a alguien que quisiera ocupar este puesto.

foro Boario: El mercado del ganado, situado junto al Tíber, al final del *Clivus Victoriae*.

foro holitorio: Mercado de fruta y verdura en Roma.

Foro o *forum Traiani:* El foro de Trajano, el más grande todos los foros imperiales, erigido por orden del gran emperador hispano con el diseño arquitectónico de Apolodoro de Damasco. Es una extensión del foro de Augusto hacia el noroeste pero de enormes dimensiones, entre la colina del Capitolio y la del Quirinal. Consistía en grandes plazas que se sucedían, con la gran basílica Ulpia, la *Columna Traiani* y las bibliotecas. No estaba construido en torno a un gran templo central, como era el caso de los foros anteriores.

Fortuna audaces iuvat: «La fortuna favorece a los audaces»; es una cita procedente del libro X de la *Eneida* de Virgilio, aunque la frase original es ligeramente diferente. Realmente el poeta escribió: *Audentes fortuna iuvat.* El significado, no obstante, es prácticamente el mismo.

frigidarium: Sala con una piscina de agua fría en unas termas romanas.

Galia Narbonensis: Provincia romana que incluía todo el sur de la Galia.

garum: Pesada pero jugosa salsa de pescado de origen ibero que los romanos incorporaron a su cocina.

Gemina: «Gemela». Era el término que los romanos empleaban para indicar una legión fruto de la fusión de dos o más legiones anteriores. Éste sería el caso de la legión VII *Hispana* o *Galbiana*, que recibió el nombre de Gemina al fusionarse con los legionarios de la legión I *Germánica*. Lo mismo ocurre con la legión XIV (o XIIII) que recibió el nombre de *Gemina* al absorber legionarios de otra legión sin identificar que, seguramente, participó en la batalla de Alesia. El sobrenombre de *Gemina* lo podemos encontrar en otras legiones fusionadas como la X o la XIII.

gens: El *nomen* de la familia o tribu de un clan romano.

Germánica: Legión I que luego será fusionada con la legión VII *Galbiana* para crear la legión VII *Gemina*, ubicada en León durante el reinado de Domiciano y bajo el mando de Marco Ulpio Trajano durante varios años.

Germanicus: Sobrenombre que los emperadores se otorgaban cuando conseguían una gran victoria sobre las tribus germánicas. El emperador Domiciano se otorgó a sí mismo este título tras su supuesta gran victoria sobre los catos.

gladio, gladius, gladii: Forma en español y singular y plural en latín de la espada de doble filo de origen ibérico que en el período de la segunda guerra púnica fue adoptada por las legiones romanas.

gladiatrix: Gladiadora, luchadora en la arena de los anfiteatros romanos. Hay numerosas fuentes clásicas que confirman la existencia de estas luchadoras (Estacio, Juvenal, Marcial o Suetonio entre otros); incluso hay una ley promulgada en la época del Bajo Imperio que prohibía la participación de más gladiadoras en los *munera*. El término como tal, no obstante, no aparece en las fuentes clásicas, sino que se habla de mujeres guerreras.

gymnasium: Edificio en el que se instruía a los hombres jóvenes (sólo a los hombres) en deportes, ciencia o arte.

Habet, hoc habet: Literalmente «lo tiene, lo tiene»; era una expresión comúnmente empleada por el público asistente a una lucha de gladiadores en el Anfiteatro Flavio para indicar que un contendiente estaba a punto de derrotar a su oponente.

Hades: El reino de los muertos.

Hércules: Es el equivalente al Heracles griego, hijo ilegítimo de Zeus concebido en su relación, bajo engaño, con la reina Alcmena. Por asimilación, Hércules era el hijo de Júpiter y Alcmena. Entre sus múltiples hazañas se encuentra su viaje de ida y vuelta al reino de los muertos, lo que le costó un severo castigo al dios Caronte. Su nombre se usa con frecuencia como una interjección.

Historia Naturalis: O *Naturalis Historia* es una impresionante enciclopedia escrita por Plinio el Viejo en treinta y siete volúmenes en la que describe conocimientos de la época romana sobre arte, historia, botánica, astronomía, geografía, zoología, medicina, magia, mineralogía, etc. Para esta magna obra, Plinio se documentó con más de dos mil libros diferentes, algo absolutamente impactante si consideramos que está escrita en el siglo I d.C.

hora prima: La primera hora del día romano, que se dividía en doce horas. Correspondía con el amanecer.

hora sexta: La sexta hora del día romano, que se dividía en doce horas; equivalía al mediodía. Ésta fue la hora marcada por los conjurados para intentar asesinar al emperador Domiciano. Del término sexta deriva la palabra española actual «siesta».

horreum, horrea: Singular y plural de los grandes almacenes que se levantaban junto a los muelles del puerto fluvial de Roma.

idus: De acuerdo con el calendario romano, las *idus* se correspondían con el día 13 de los meses de enero, febrero, abril, junio, agosto, septiembre, noviembre y diciembre y con el día 15 de los meses de marzo, mayo, julio y octubre. Las *idus* más famosas son, sin duda, aquellas que hacen referencia al mes de marzo del año 44 a.C., cuando Julio César fue asesinado. El género de este término es masculino según el *Diccionario de la Real Academia Española*, pero en las novelas de Trajano el término aparece en cursiva, es decir, en latín, y en lengua latina este vocablo es femenino.

impedimenta: Conjunto de pertrechos militares que los legionarios transportaban consigo durante una marcha.

imperator: General romano con mando efectivo sobre una, dos o más legiones. Normalmente un cónsul era *imperator* de un ejército consular de dos legiones. En época imperial el término evolucionó para referirse a la persona que tenía el mando sobre todas las legiones del Imperio, es decir, el César, con poder militar absoluto.

Imperator Caesar Augustus: Títulos que el Senado asignaba para el príncipe, es decir, para el emperador o César.

imperium: En sus orígenes era la plasmación de la proyección del poder divino de Júpiter en aquellos que, investidos como cónsules, de hecho ejercían el poder político y militar de la República durante su mandato. El *imperium* conllevaba el mando de un ejército consular compuesto de dos legiones completas más sus tropas auxiliares.

impluvium: Pequeña piscina o estanque que, en el centro del atrio, recogía el agua de la lluvia que después podía ser utilizada con fines domésticos.

indictiones: Impuestos específicos creados con una finalidad particular, por ejemplo financiar una obra pública concreta, como un puente o un acueducto.

in extremis: Expresión latina que significa «en el último momento». En algunos contextos puede equivaler *a in articulo mortis*, aunque no en esta novela.

in situ: «En el lugar» o «en el sitio».

In vino veritas: «En el vino está la verdad», frase que da a entender que quien ingiere vino termina siempre diciendo la verdad. La cita suele atribuirse a Plinio el Viejo, pero la idea es mucho más antigua. De hecho Heródoto ya indica que los persas pensaban que si se tomaba una decisión ebrio era conveniente revisarla sobrio. Este mismo concepto puede encontrarse en un poema de Alceo en griego, y en griego volvería insistir en esta idea Erasmo de Rotterdam en sus *Adagio* siglos después. Con frecuencia, la cita se complementa de la siguiente forma: *In vino veritas, in aqua sanitas*, es decir «con el vino la verdad y con el agua la salud», que parece tener mucho fundamento.

insula, insulae: Singular y plural de un edificio de apartamentos. En tiempo imperial alcanzaron los seis o siete pisos de altura. Su edificación, con frecuencia sin control alguno, daba lugar a construcciones de poca calidad que podían derrumbarse o incendiarse con facilidad, con los consiguientes desastres urbanos.

Interim: En español, según el *Diccionario de la Real Academia*, es «interin» sustituyendo la «m» del latín por una «n». Significa «entretanto».

io triumphe: Expresión de júbilo que el pueblo de Roma repetía a lo largo del desfile triunfal de uno de sus generales o emperadores victoriosos. Equivale a «Viva el triunfo».

ipso facto: Expresión latina que significa «en el mismo momento», «inmediatamente».

Iugera: Iugerum en singular; era una medida de extensión utilizada en la antigua Roma. Un *Iugerum* equivalía aproximadamente a 0,25 hectáreas.

Júpiter Óptimo Máximo: El dios supremo, asimilado al dios griego Zeus. Su *flamen*, el *dialis*, era el sacerdote más importante del colegio. En su origen, Júpiter era latino antes que romano, pero tras su incorporación a Roma protegía la ciudad y garantizaba el *imperium*, por ello el *triunfo* era siempre en su honor.

kalendae: El primer día de cada mes. Se correspondía con la luna nueva. En latín esta palabra es de género femenino.

lanista: El preparador de gladiadores de un colegio de lucha.

lardum: Bacon o grasa.

lares: Los dioses que velan por el hogar familiar.

legatus, legati: Legados, representantes o embajadores, con diferentes niveles de autoridad a lo largo de la dilatada historia de Roma. En la trilogía de Trajano el término hace referencia a quien ostentaba el mando de una legión. Cuando era designado directamente por el emperador y tenía bajo su mando varias legiones era frecuente que se usara el término *legatus augusti*.

legatus augusti: Legado nombrado directamente por el emperador con varias legiones bajo su mando.

legatus legionis: El legado o general al mando de una legión.

legio: Legión. El término también dio origen al nombre de la ciudad española de León.

lemures: Espíritus de los difuntos, generalmente malignos, adorados y temidos por los romanos.

lemuria: Fiestas en honor de los *lemures*, espíritus de los difuntos. Se celebraban los días 9, 11 y 13 de mayo.

lena: Meretriz, dueña o gestora de un prostíbulo.

libitinarii: Esclavos o trabajadores del Anfiteatro Flavio encargados de retirar y en ocasiones enterrar a los gladiadores muertos.

liburna: Nave pequeña y ligera empleada por los piratas del Mediterráneo que terminó siendo incorporada, por su buena maniobrabilidad, a las armadas romanas. Su nombre parece provenir de Liburnia, en la provincia de Dalmacia. Normalmente sólo había una línea de remos, pero las había de dos, tres y más niveles: así había *liburnae birremes*, *liburnae trirremes*, etc. Tuvieron un papel activo en la batalla de Actium, donde Augusto derrotó a Marco Antonio.

lictor: Funcionario público romano que servía en el ejército consular romano prestando el servicio especial de escolta del jefe supremo de la legión: el cónsul. Un cónsul tenía derecho a estar escoltado por doce *lictores*; y un dictador, por veinticuatro. Durante la República estos funcionarios escoltaban también a los diferentes magistrados de la ciudad. En época imperial, un *lictor* actuaba de representante de cada una de las centurias de los *comitia centuriata* (comicios por centurias), la más antigua asamblea de Roma.

limes: La frontera del Imperio romano. Con frecuencia amplios sectores del *limes* estaban fuertemente fortificados, como era el caso de la frontera de Germania y posteriormente en Britania con el Muro de Adriano.

lorica: Armadura de un legionario romano elaborada con cota, una malla hecha de anillas metálicas o, posteriormente, con escamas o láminas de metal. Esta última sería luego conocida como *lorica segmentata*.

ludi: Juegos. Podían ser de diferente tipo: *circenses*, es decir, celebrados en el Circo Máximo, donde destacaban las carreras de carros; *ludi scaenici*, celebrados en los grandes teatros de Roma, como el teatro Marcelo, donde se representaban obras cómicas o trágicas o espectáculos con mimos, muy populares en la época imperial. También estaban las *venationes* o cacerías y, finalmente, los más famosos, los *ludi gladiatorii,* donde luchaban los gladiadores en el anfiteatro.

Ludus latrunculorum: Juego de mesa y de estrategia al que jugaban con frecuencia los legionarios de Roma.

Ludus Magnus: El mayor colegio de gladiadores de Roma. Se levantó justo al lado del gran Anfiteatro Flavio, con el que se cree que estaba comunicado directamente por un largo túnel.

Macellum: Uno de los más grandes mercados de la Roma antigua, ubicado al norte del foro.

machinae tractoriae: El conjunto de máquinas construidas para la manipulación y elevación de sillares de piedra y otros materiales de gran tamaño.

magnis itineribus: Avance de las tropas legionarias a marchas forzadas.

manica: Protecciones de cuero o metal que usaban los gladiadores para protegerse los antebrazos durante un combate.

Mare Nostrum: O *Nostrum Mare* o *Internum Mare,* es decir, «Nuestro mar» o «mar interno» fueron sobrenombres que los romanos dieron al Mediterráneo durante la época imperial en la que controlaron esta agua con su poderosa flota.

Marte: Dios de la guerra y los sembrados. A él se consagraban las legiones en marzo, cuando se preparaban para una nueva campaña. Normalmente se le sacrificaba un carnero.

Mausoleum Augusti: La gran tumba del emperador Augusto, construida en 28 a.C. en forma de gran panteón circular.

medicus: Médico, profesión especialmente apreciada en Roma. De hecho, Julio César concedió la ciudadanía romana a todos aquellos que ejercían esta profesión.

memento mori: «Recuerda que vas a morir», palabras que un esclavo pronunciaba al oído de un cónsul o procónsul que celebraba un triunfo en la República de Roma; durante la época imperial eran los emperadores los que celebraban estos desfiles triunfales y, teóricamente, un esclavo debería pronunciar estas mismas palabras, aunque no es probable que algún César endiosado estuviera dispuesto a escucharlas.

milla: Los romanos medían las distancias en millas. Una milla romana equivalía a mil pasos y cada paso a 1,4 o 1,5 metros aproximadamente, de modo que una milla equivalía a entre 1.400 y 1.500 metros actuales, aunque hay controversia sobre el valor exacto de estas unidades de medida. En *La legión perdida* las he usado con los valores referidos anteriormente.

mirmillo: Gladiador que llevaba un gran casco con una cresta a modo de aleta dorsal de un pez inspirada en el mítico animal marino *mormyr.* Sólo usaba una gran espada recta como arma ofensiva y se protegía con un escudo rectangular curvo de grandes dimensiones.

missus: «Indultado». Gladiador al que se le perdonaba la vida aunque hubiera sido derrotado durante el combate.

mitte: Expresión que usaba el *editor* de los juegos o el público en general para pedir que se dejara ir al gladiador aunque hubiera sido derrotado.

mulsum: Bebida muy común y apreciada entre los romanos elaborada al mezclar el vino con miel.

munera, munera gladiatoria: Juegos donde combatían decenas de gladiadores, normalmente por parejas.

muralla serviana: Fortificación amurallada levantada por los romanos en los inicios de la República para protegerse de los ataques de las ciudades latinas con las que competía por conseguir la hegemonía en Lacio. Estas murallas protegieron durante siglos la ciudad hasta que, decenas de generaciones después, en el Imperio, se levantó la gran muralla aureliana. Un resto de la muralla serviana es aún visible junto a la estación de ferrocarril Termini en Roma.

Naturalis Historia: Véase *Historia Naturalis.*

naumachia: Batalla naval que tenía lugar o bien en un lago o en un gran estanque artificial construido al efecto. El emperador Claudio celebró naumaquias en lagos cercanos a Roma, mientras que Trajano construyó uno de estos grandes estanques, que por extensión también fueron llamados naumaquias.

nefasti: Días que no eran propicios para actos públicos o celebraciones.

Neptuno: En sus orígenes, dios del agua dulce. Luego, por asimilación con el dios griego Poseidón, será también el dios de las aguas saladas del mar. Domiciano concluirá que Neptuno le obedece cuando las aguas del Rin engullen al inmenso ejército de los catos.

nobilitas: Selecto grupo de la aristocracia romana republicana compuesto por todos aquellos que en algún momento de su *cursus honorum* habían ostentado el consulado, es decir, la máxima magistratura del Estado.

nomen: También conocido como *nomen gentile* o *nomen gentilicium,* indica la *gens* o tribu a la que una persona estaba adscrita. El protagonista de esta novela pertenecía a la tribu Ulpia, de ahí que su *nomen* sea Ulpio, Marco Ulpio Trajano.

nonae: El séptimo día en el calendario romano de los meses de marzo, mayo, julio y octubre, y el quinto día del resto de los meses. Es decir, el quinto día de los meses de menos de 31 días y el séptimo día de los meses de 31 días.

Nova Via: Avenida paralela a la *Via Sacra* junto al Templo de Júpiter Stator.

Nundinae: Días de mercado en el calendario romano.

Odeón: Del latín *Odeum*. Nombre que recibían edificios o espacios públicos destinados al canto, el teatro o la poesía y que, ocasionalmente, podían ser empleados para reuniones de carácter público. Selinus disponía de un pequeño edificio de este tipo.

Optimus Princeps: El mejor de los príncipes posibles o el mejor de los gobernantes; título que Trajano recibió del Senado por su excelente gobierno, sus admirables conquistas y su capacidad de gestionar el Imperio con audacia, templanza y justicia, aptitudes hoy muy escasas en los gobernantes del siglo XXI.

optio: Oficial de las legiones por debajo del centurión.

ovatio: Una celebración de victoria de menor rango que la del triunfo. Un cónsul o *legatus* romano podía recibir este honor cuando la victoria se conseguía contra enemigos serviles (esclavos que se hubieran rebelado) o cuando en la contienda no se había derramado mucha sangre. Una de las diferencias más destacadas con el triunfo es que en la *ovatio* no se entraba en la ciudad en una cuadriga tirada por cuatro caballos blancos, sino que se llegaba a pie.

paedagogus: Tutor casi siempre de origen griego que enseñaba oratoria, historia, literatura y otras disciplinas a jóvenes patricios romanos.

palla: Manto que las romanas se ponían sobre los hombros por encima de la túnica o toga.

palma lemniscata: Corona que se entregaba a un atleta o a un gladiador victorioso. Estaba adornada con lemniscos, cintas, con frecuencia de diferentes colores para hacerla más vistosa.

paludamentum: Prenda abierta, cerrada con una hebilla, similar al *sagum* de los oficiales, pero más larga y de color púrpura. Era como un gran manto que distinguía al general en jefe de un ejército romano.

panis militaris: Pan militar.

Parthicus: Título que recibió Trajano por parte del Senado de Roma hasta en dos ocasiones como reconocimiento por haber rendido y anexionado Partia al Imperio romano. Parece que la primera vez no lo aceptó, pero sí después cuando se le volvió a ofrecer. Sería un sobrenombre que el emperador hispano añadiría al de *Dacicus*, otorgado por el Senado en reconocimiento de su anterior conquista y anexión de la Dacia.

pater familias: El cabeza de familia tanto en las celebraciones religiosas como a todos los efectos jurídicos.

patres conscripti: Los padres de la patria; forma habitual de referirse a los senadores. Este término deriva del antiguo *patres et conscripti.*

patria potestas: El conjunto de derechos, pero también de obligaciones, que las leyes de la antigua Roma reconocían a los padres con relación a las vidas y bienes de sus hijos.

penates: Las deidades que velan por el hogar.

pilum, pila: Singular y plural del arma propia de los *hastati* y *príncipes.* Se componía de una larga asta de madera de hasta metro y medio que culminaba en un hierro de similar longitud. En tiempos del historiador Polibio —y probablemente en la época de esta novela— el hierro estaba incrustado en la madera hasta la mitad de su longitud mediante fuertes remaches. Posteriormente evolucionaría, para terminar sustituyendo uno de los remaches por una clavija que se partía cuando el arma era clavada en el escudo enemigo, dejando que el mango de madera quedara colgando del hierro ensartado en el escudo y trabando al rival. Éste, con frecuencia, se veía obligado a desprenderse de su ara defensiva. En la época de Julio César el mismo efecto se conseguía de forma distinta mediante una punta de hierro que resultaba imposible de extraer del escudo. El peso del *pilum* oscilaba entre 0,7 y 1,2 kilos y podía ser lanzado por los legionarios a una media de veinticinco metros de distancia, aunque los más expertos podían arrojar esta lanza hasta a cuarenta metros. En su caída podía atravesar hasta tres centímetros de madera o, incluso, una placa de metal.

Pólux: Junto con su hermano Cástor, uno de los dioscuros griegos asimilados por la religión romana. Su templo, el de los Cástores, o de Cástor y Pólux, servía de archivo a la orden de los *equites* o caballeros romanos. El nombre de ambos dioses era usado con frecuencia a modo de interjección.

pomerium: Era el centro de la antigua ciudad de Roma, cuyos límites nunca han estado bien documentados pero no llegaba a abarcar, al menos en un principio, ni las siete colinas. Estaba delimitado por una línea imaginaria marcada por piedras o mojones. Dentro del *pomerium* no se podían hacer enterramientos ni portar armas, aunque en época imperial estas normas fueron relajándose. También hubo diferentes modificaciones de la extensión del *pomerium*: primero el dictador Sila en tiempos republicanos lo amplió y después diferentes emperadores como Augusto, Nerón, Claudio o el propio Trajano extendieron el *pomerium* en diferentes momentos de la historia de Roma.

Pontifex Maximus: Máxima autoridad sacerdotal de la religión romana. Vivía en la *Regia* y tenía plena autoridad sobre las vestales, elaboraba el calendario (con sus días *fastos* o *nefastos*) y redactaba los anales de Roma. En época imperial era frecuente que el emperador asumiera el pontificado máximo durante todo su gobierno o durante parte del mismo. Domiciano hará uso de este título para juzgar y sentenciar a muerte a varias vestales. Presidía el Colegio de Pontífices.

Porta Capena: Una de las puertas de la muralla serviana de Roma próxima a la colina de Celio.

Porta sananivaria: La puerta por la que salían del anfiteatro los gladiadores victoriosos.

Porta Sanqualis: Puerta de las murallas de Roma en el sector occidental de la colina Quirinal.

Porta Triumphalis: Puerta de ubicación desconocida por la que el general victorioso entraba en la ciudad de Roma para celebrar un desfile triunfal.

Portus Traiani Felicis: El puerto marítimo de Roma ampliado por Trajano. El puerto de Roma en Ostia, pese a las obras de mejora del emperador Claudio, seguía siendo endeble ante las tormentas y tempestades, de forma que Trajano ordenó una ampliación del mismo excavando una gigantesca extensión de terreno en forma hexagonal, que se transformó en el corazón del puerto marino de la capital del Imperio. La construcción, como tantas otras de la época de Trajano, estuvo a cargo de Apolodoro de Damasco. El puerto hexagonal es ahora un lago que está bien conservado, visible desde el aire cuando se aterriza en el aeropuerto internacional de Roma en Fiumicino. De hecho, *Fiumici-*

no quiere decir «pequeño río» y hace referencia al canal que conectaba este nuevo puerto de Trajano con el río Tíber.

possum: Puedo.

post mortem: Después de la muerte.

potest: Puede.

potestas tribunicia: Poder tribunicio.

praefectus castrorum: Oficial en jefe de un campamento romano encargado de todo lo relacionado con el funcionamiento del mismo.

praenomen: Nombre particular de una persona, que luego era completado con su *nomen* o denominación de su tribu y su *cognomen* o nombre de su familia. En el caso de Trajano, su *praenomen* era Marco.

praetorium: Tienda o edificio del general en jefe de un ejército romano. Se levantaba en el centro del campamento, entre el *quaestorium* y el foro. El *legatus* o el propio emperador, si éste se había desplazado a dirigir la campaña, celebraba allí las reuniones de su Estado Mayor.

prima vigilia: La primera de las cuatro partes en las que se dividía la noche en la antigua Roma.

primus pilus: El primer centurión de una legión, generalmente un veterano que gozaba de gran confianza entre los tribunos y el cónsul o procónsul al mando de las legiones.

princeps senatus: El senador de mayor edad. Por su veteranía gozaba de numerosos privilegios, como el de hablar primero en una sesión. Durante la época imperial, el emperador adquiría esta condición independientemente de su edad.

procurator bibliothecae augusti: El bibliotecario imperial, encargado por el emperador de velar por la buena ordenación de las bibliotecas de Roma y por la conservación de todos los papiros que contenían aquellos antiguos centros de conocimiento. Aunque no está confirmado por completo, parece ser que Cayo Suetonio Tranquilo fue el bibliotecario imperial, al menos por un tiempo, durante la época de Trajano.

pronaos: Sección frontal de un templo clásico que sirve de antesala a la gran nave central.

pugio: Puñal o daga romana de unos 24 centímetros de largo por unos 6 centímetros de ancho en su base. Al estar dotada de un nervio central que la hacía más gruesa en esa zona, el arma resultaba muy resistente, capaz de atravesar una cota de malla.

pulvinar: El gran palco imperial en el Circo Máximo, situado en el centro de las gradas, a mitad de una de las grandes rectas de la arena de la pista, desde donde el emperador y su familia asistían a las competiciones de cuadrigas y otros eventos relevantes.

quaestor: Era el encargado de velar por los suministros y las provisiones de las tropas legionarias, supervisaba los gastos y se ocupaba de otras diversas tareas administrativas.

quaestor imperatoris: Cuestor imperial.

quaestorium: Gran tienda o edificación dentro de un campamento romano de la época republicana o imperial donde trabajaba el *quaestor.* Normalmente estaba ubicado junto al *praetorium* en el centro del campamento.

quarta vigilia: La última hora de la noche, justo antes del amanecer.

quinquerreme: Navío militar con cinco hileras de remos. Variante de la *trirreme.* Tanto *quinquerreme* como *trirreme* se pueden encontrar en la literatura sobre historia clásica en masculino o femenino, si bien el *Diccionario de la Real Academia Española* recomienda el masculino.

quis: Quién.

Respice post te! Hominem te ese memento: «¡Mira tras de ti! Recuerda que eres un hombre». Palabras que un esclavo pronunciaba a oídos del cónsul que celebraba un triunfo en Roma para recordarle que era mortal. Otra alternativa es que el esclavo en cuestión dijera: *memento mori.*

retiarius, retiarii: Singular y plural del gladiador que combatía con un tridente o fascina de 1,60 metros y una daga pequeña o *pugio.* También llevaban una red *(rete)* de 3 metros de diámetro. Si el *retiarius* la perdía sin que inmovilizara al oponente, era muy probable que perdiera el combate.

rictus: El *Diccionario de la Real Academia Española* define este término como «el aspecto fijo o transitorio del rostro al que se atribuye la manifestación de un determinado estado de ánimo». A la Academia le falta añadir que normalmente este vocablo comporta connotaciones negativas, de tal modo que rictus suele referirse a una mueca del rostro que refleja dolor o sufrimiento físico o mental, o, cuando menos, gran preocupación por un asunto.

rostra: En el año 338 a.C., tras el triunfo de Maenius sobre los Antiates, se llevaron a Roma seis espolones de las naves apresadas que se usaron para decorar una de las tribunas desde la que los oradores podían dirigirse al pueblo congregado en al gran explanada del foro. Estos espolones recibieron el sobrenombre de *ros-*

tra, pues *rostrum* en singular significa, en su acepción náutica, espolón.

rudis: Espada de madera que sólo se entregaba a un gladiador cuando el emperador le concedía la libertad.

sagittarius, sagittarii: Singular y plural de un gladiador especializado en el tiro con arco. Si dos de ellos se enfrentaban en combate se les ubicaba en extremos opuestos y lanzaban flechas el uno contra el otro hasta herirse mortalmente. Alguna flecha perdida podía caer en las gradas y herir al público.

sagum: Es una prenda militar abierta que suele ir cosida con una hebilla; algo más larga que una túnica y con una lana de mayor grosor. El general en jefe llevaba un *sagum* más largo y de color púrpura que recibía el nombre de *paludamentum*.

samnita: Gladiador que luchaba con una espada corta y pesada, protegido por un escudo de grandes dimensiones y con un casco con visor y cresta.

Saturnalia: Tremendas fiestas donde el desenfreno estaba a la orden del día. Se celebraban desde el 17 hasta el 23 de diciembre en honor del dios Saturno, el dios de las semillas enterradas en la tierra.

secunda mensa: Segundo plato en un banquete romano.

secunda vigilia: Segunda hora de las cuatro en las que se dividía la noche en la antigua Roma.

sella: El más sencillo de los asientos romanos. Equivale a un simple taburete.

sella curulis: Como la *sella*, carece de respaldo, pero es un asiento de gran lujo, con patas cruzadas y curvas de marfil que se podían plegar para facilitar el transporte, pues se trataba del asiento que acompañaba al cónsul en sus desplazamientos civiles o militares.

signifer: Portaestandarte de las legiones.

silphium: Planta procedente de Cirene, en el norte de África, muy apreciada en la época antigua como especia para sazonar alimentos y por sus efectos medicinales. Ya desde Hipócrates se empleaba para calmar la tos, estados febriles y otras dolencias similares. Pero su uso más importante parece ser el de eficaz abortivo, si tenemos en cuenta que Plinio el Viejo citaba esta planta como capaz de generar grandes menstruaciones que, muy probablemente, en el caso de un embarazo no deseado, terminaban con el proceso. La planta, quizá por sobreexplotación o por otros motivos desconocidos, terminó extinguiéndose.

singulares: Cuerpo especial de caballería dedicado a la protección del emperador o de un César.

solium: Asiento de madera con respaldo recto, sobrio y austero.

spatha: Espada militar romana más larga que un *gladio* legionario que normalmente portaban los oficiales o, con frecuencia, los jinetes de las unidades de caballería.

spina: El gran muro de piedra y ladrillo levantado en el centro del Circo Máximo y de otros grandes circos del Imperio. Solía estar decorado con estatuas y otros elementos impactantes. En el Circo Máximo destacaban los obeliscos llevados desde Egipto, así como los delfines de bronce y los huevos de piedra que indicaban cuántas vueltas quedaban para finalizar la carrera.

spolarium: Sala de un anfiteatro donde se descuartizaban los cadáveres de las bestias o los hombres y las mujeres que hubieran fallecido durante una jornada de juegos.

stans missus: «Indultado en pie», es decir, que se perdona la vida del gladiador o de los dos gladiadores porque ninguno ha llegado a caer al suelo durante la lucha; era casi equivalente a una victoria.

statu quo: Expresión latina que significa «en el estado o la situación actual». «*Status quo*» es la forma popular en que se suele usar esta expresión, pero es incorrecta, ya que no concuerda con la gramática latina, pues se rompe la concordancia de los casos declinados de cada una de las palabras.

stilus: Pequeño estilete empleado para escribir o bien sobre tablillas de cera grabando las letras o bien sobre papiro utilizando tinta negra o de color.

tabernae: Tabernas romanas normalmente ubicadas en la parte baja de las *insulae* o los edificios de varias plantas de cualquier ciudad del Imperio.

tablinum: Habitación situada en la pared del atrio en el lado opuesto a la entrada principal de la *domus*. Esta estancia estaba destinada al *pater familias*, haciendo las veces de despacho particular del dueño de la casa.

Tarraconensis: Provincia nororiental de Hispania con capital en Tarraco, aunque con una legión establecida en la remota Legio (León) para proteger las ricas minas de oro de aquella región.

Templo de Júpiter: Quizá el templo más importante de Roma, dedicado al dios supremo Júpiter, al que acompañaban las diosas Juno y Minerva, la tríada más tradicional del panteón romano. Con varias hileras de seis columnas corintias de mármol y el techo recubierto de oro, se levantaba magnífico e impresionante en lo alto de la colina Capitolina. En este templo concluían los grandes desfiles triunfales.

Templum Gentis Flaviae: Fue un templo de grandes dimensiones construido en época flavia, posiblemente por orden de Domiciano, para que sirviera de tumba para diferentes miembros de la familia imperial. No se respetó la norma de que dentro del *pomerium* no se podían hacer enterramientos, pero Domiciano, como se explica en la novela *Los asesinos del emperador*, no era hombre de respetar costumbres ni leyes. El monumento se ha perdido pero parece que pudo estar emplazado en la colina del Quirinal, próximo al lugar de nacimiento de Domiciano.

tepidarium: Sala con una piscina de agua templada en unas termas romanas.

tertia vigilia: La tercera de las cuatro horas en las que se dividía la noche en la antigua Roma.

testudo: Formación militar en la que los legionarios se protegen con los escudos marchando muy unidos, de forma que la unidad se asemeja a una tortuga o a las escamas de un pez. Esta particular formación militar es la que parece que presenció el general Tang en la batalla de Kangchú, tal y como refiere en sus memorias recogidas en el *Hou Han Shu*. En función de este comentario y otros similares, el profesor Dubs elaboró la teoría de que los mercenarios extranjeros que combatían junto a los hunos en aquella batalla podrían ser miembros de la legión perdida de Craso.

Traiana Fortis: «Fuerte trajana», sobrenombre de una de las nuevas legiones de Roma creada por Trajano.

Traianus: Cognomen de la familia hispana del que luego habría de ser el famoso emperador Marco Ulpio Trajano.

tribuno laticlavio: Alto oficial de una legión romana. Trajano empezó su carrera militar como *tribuno laticlavio* bajo el mando de su padre en Oriente.

triclinium, triclinia: Singular y plural de los divanes sobre los que los romanos se recostaban para comer, especialmente durante la cena. Lo más frecuente es que hubiera tres, pero podían añadirse más en caso de que fuera necesario ante la presencia de invitados.

triplex acies: Formación típica de ataque de una legión romana. Las diez cohortes se distribuían en forma de damero, de modo que unas quedaban en posición avanzada, otras en posición intermedia y las últimas, normalmente las que tenían los legionarios más experimentados, en reserva.

trirreme: Barco de uso militar del tipo galera. Su nombre romano *trirreme* hace referencia a las tres hileras de remos que, dispuestas a cada lado, impulsaban la nave.

triunfo: Desfile de gran boato y parafernalia que un general victorioso realizaba por las calles de Roma. Para ser merecedor de tal honor, la victoria por la que se solicitaba este premio debía haber sido conseguida durante el mandato como cónsul o procónsul de un ejército consular o proconsular. En la época imperial, normalmente sólo el César podía disfrutar de un *triunfo*.

triunviros: Legionarios que hacían las veces de policía en Roma o en ciudades conquistadas. Con frecuencia patrullaban por las noches y velaban por el mantenimiento del orden público.

tubicines: Trompeteros de las legiones que hacían sonar las grandes tubas con las que se daban órdenes para maniobrar las tropas.

turma, turmae: Singular y plural del término que describe un pequeño destacamento de caballería compuesto por tres *decurias* de diez jinetes cada una.

uenatio: Cacería.

Ulpia Victrix: «Vencedora Ulpia»; sobrenombre de la legión XXX de Roma creada por Trajano.

valetudinarium: Hospital militar dentro de un campamento legionario.

Velabrum: Barrio entre el *foro Boario* y la colina Capitolina. Antes de la construcción de la *Cloaca Máxima* fue un pantano.

velarium: Techo de tela extensible instalado en lo alto del Anfiteatro Flavio que se desplegaba para proteger al público del sol. Para manejarlo se recurría a los marineros de la flota imperial de Miseno.

venationes: Cacerías de fieras salvajes organizadas en un anfiteatro o en un circo de la antigua Roma.

vestal: Sacerdotisa perteneciente al colegio de las vestales dedicadas al culto de la diosa Vesta. En un principio sólo había cuatro, aunque posteriormente se amplió el número de vestales a seis y, finalmente, a siete. Se las escogía cuando tenían entre seis y diez años de familias cuyos padres estuvieran vivos. El período de sacerdocio era de treinta años. Al finalizar, las vestales eran libres para contraer matrimonio si así lo deseaban, pero durante su sacerdocio debían permanecer castas y velar por el fuego sagrado de la ciudad. Si faltaban a sus votos eran condenadas, sin remisión, a ser enterradas vivas. Si, por el contrario, mantenían sus votos, gozaban de gran prestigio social hasta el punto de que podían salvar a cualquier persona que, una vez condenada, fuera llevada para su ejecución. Vivían en una gran mansión próxima al Templo de Vesta. También estaban encargadas de elaborar la *mola salsa*, ungüento sagrado utilizado en muchos sacrificios. En la época de Domiciano se ejecutó a varias vestales, incluida la Vestal Máxima. Tras este suceso, dos legiones fueron aniquiladas por el enemigo, de modo que no parece que los dioses romanos consideraran aquellas ejecuciones como justas.

vexillatio, vexillationes: Singular y plural de una unidad de una legión, de composición variable, que era enviada por parte de una legión a otro lugar del Imperio por mandato del César con el fin de reforzar el ejército imperial en una campaña militar.

Via Appia: Calzada romana que parte desde la puerta Capena de Roma hacia el sur de Italia.

Via Labicana: Avenida que parte del centro de la ciudad y transcurre entre el monte Esquilino y el monte Viminal.

Via Lata: Avenida que parte de Roma hacia el norte para enlazar con la *Via Flaminia.*

Via Latina: Calzada romana que parte desde la *Via Appia* hacia el interior en dirección sureste.

Via Nomentana: Avenida que parte del centro de Roma en dirección norte hasta la *Porta Collina.*

via principalis: La calle principal en un campamento romano que pasa justo enfrente del *praetorium.*

Via Sacra: Avenida que conecta el foro de Roma con la *Via Tusculana.*

Via Triumphalis: Una gran avenida de la antigua Roma por donde discurría la procesión victoriosa de un triunfo en su camino hacia el circo Flaminio. En la actualidad se corresponde, aproximadamente, con la moderna Via dei Fori.

Vicesima hereditatum: Impuesto extraordinario que se activaba con fines militares.

vir eminentissimus: Fórmula de respeto con la que un inferior debía dirigirse a un jefe del pretorio.

3

GLOSARIO DE TÉRMINOS PARTOS Y DE VOCABLOS DE OTRAS LENGUAS HABLADAS EN EL IMPERIO PARTO

Los emperadores del Imperio parto promovieron el uso del griego como lengua de la corte y de comunicación por todos sus territorios. El arameo también era usado de forma amplia en muchas regiones como otra *lingua franca*. El idioma parto, una lengua de origen iranio, era empleado por la nobleza arsácida nativa de la región de Partia. Por eso los personajes partos aristocráticos de *La legión perdida* usan entre ellos el parto pero entienden perfectamente el griego, hasta el punto de poder leer la lengua de Homero o poder presenciar una representación de una obra de teatro griego y disfrutar de la misma.

Centrándonos en el parto, a continuación presento una pequeña recopilación de algunos términos que aparecen a lo largo de la novela. Este glosario no podría haber sido elaborado sin la ayuda de la catedrática Julita Juan Grau. De hecho, es sólo la punta del iceberg de un glosario mucho más extenso que la profesora Juan Grau elaboró para que dispusiera de una amplia variedad de términos para la novela. Esto me ha permitido dar pequeñas pinceladas de una lengua que fue el idioma nativo de una élite aristocrática que gobernó un gigantesco imperio y se enfrentó, una y otra vez, a Roma.

Bāmbišnān Bāmbišn: Reina de reinas.
Bānūg: Dama, joven mujer de la nobleza parta.
Hrōm: Roma. En pahlavi sasánida, no pahlavi arsácida, es decir parto. En parto sería *Frōm*. Lo más probable es que en la época de *La legión perdida* se usara la variante *Frōm*, pero como en *Circo Máximo* usé la variante sasánida he decidido mantenerla, si bien es oportuna la precisión.

Kārwān: Caravana.

Lāb: Súplica.

Mig: Nube, niebla.

Mry: Gobernador. No es parto, sino una variante aramea honorífica que significaba «mi señor», pero siendo el arameo lengua de uso común en diferentes regiones controladas por los partos, no sería extraño que en una ciudad como Hatra, por ejemplo, se usara dicho término, o que un rey de reyes lo empleara para referirse a alguien que actuara como gobernante principal de una ciudad, satrapía o región.

Mušḫuššu: Mítico animal, entre dragón y serpiente, que aparece recreado en los azulejos de las paredes de la puerta de Istar de Babilonia. No es un nombre parto, sino un vocablo de la lengua antigua de Babilonia, pero si ha llegado hasta nosotros es seguro que en la época arsácida de la novela sería de uso común, al menos, en esa ciudad.

Padistud: Palabra, promesa, voto.

Parwāngāh: Trono.

Šabestān: Gineceo, apartamentos privados. Por metonimia el vigilante del gineceo fue referido con el mismo nombre, de modo que también significa «eunuco», que es el uso que le hemos dado en la novela, eso sí en su forma derivada: Šābestān.

Šāhān šāh: Rey de reyes.

Šhar Bāmbišn: Reina consorte.

Spāhbod, Spāhbed: General del ejército parto, comandante, literalmente maestro *(bod)* de armas *(spāh)*.

Spandarmati: Último mes de calendario parto que equivale, no obstante, al mes de mayo de nuestro calendario.

A lo largo de *La legión perdida* he transcrito los términos partos siempre con alfabeto latino, usando diacríticos pero de forma que se pudiera leer por lectores no familiarizados con el alfabeto original. No obstante, incluyo aquí una muestra de cómo se escribirían en parto los siguientes términos: «trono» y «rey de reyes». Si alguien va a comprobar la reconstrucción letra por letra, recuerde que el parto se escribe de derecha a izquierda.

Parwāngāh: ơ⊦ﻝﻝﺯﻝﻝﺭﺭ/ﻝ

Šāhān šāh: ơ⊦ﻝﺕ ﻝﻝﻭ⊦ﻝﺕ

Y a continuación transcribo en una tabla de tres columnas el alfabeto original de lengua parta completo: en la primera columna tenemos el nombre del diacrítico o de la letra parta, en la segunda su correspondencia con el alfabeto latino y en la tercera la grafía real en lengua parta.

ALFABETO PARTO		
Aleph	'	
Ayin	'	
Aleph	A	
Beth	B	
Sadhe	C/Č	
Daleth	D	
Pe	F	
Gimel	G	
He	H	
Heth	Ħ	
Yodh	J	
Kaph	K	
Lamed	L	
Mem	M	
Nun	N	
Pe	P	
Qoph	Q	
Resh	R	
Samekh	S	
Shin	Š	
Sadhe	Ş	
Taw	T	
Teth	Ţ	
Waw	W	
Heth	X	
Yodh	Y	
Zayin	Z/Ž	

4

GLOSARIO DE SÁNSCRITO

El sánscrito es, esencialmente, una lengua por y para la religión. En la actualidad se emplea en los cantos del hinduismo, jainismo y budismo. En *La legión perdida* el sánscrito es utilizado para la transmisión del budismo a través de la Ruta de la Seda por todo el Imperio kushan y el Imperio han de China. En la época en la que tienen lugar los acontecimientos que se narran en la novela, el sánscrito no tenía un alfabeto propio, sino que cada región y cultura lo transcribía a su propio alfabeto. Con frecuencia se usaba el alfabeto pali, el prácrito y otros similares. También se utilizaba el alfabeto brahmi o el karosthi, que era común y muy extendido en la Ruta de la Seda. Sin embargo, a partir del año 1000 d.C. se utiliza el alfabeto devanagari, que es el que se usa desde entonces y el que consta en la Wikipedia si se busca una palabra sánscrita como *Dharmapada*. Pero el personaje de Tamura nunca podría haber visto esta palabra escrita en este alfabeto porque el devanagari es muy posterior. En la corte kushan del siglo II d.C. es razonable pensar que, si bien los monjes pudieron usar el pali u otro alfabeto, también emplearon el silabario kushana de la aristocracia gobernante. Ésta es la opción por la que he optado cuando he transcrito la palabra *Dharmapada* en el libro V con silabario kushana. Es cierto que Buda pidió que sus enseñanzas se transcribieran a lenguas más próximas al pueblo llano, pero con el tiempo también se tradujeron a lenguas de élite, como el sánscrito en sus diferentes versiones, y es a través de éste que, entre los siglos I y II de nuestra era, el budismo llega a China.

El sánscrito, en el período que abarca la novela, estaría en transición entre el sánscrito arcaico y el sánscrito clásico.

En todo caso, al igual que con el parto, he optado por transcribir casi siempre los términos sánscritos con el alfabeto latino moderno, de modo que los lectores puedan pronunciar las palabras y ver cómo sonaban. Además esta transcripción permite ver hasta qué punto muchas palabras del sánscrito comparten una misma raíz con lenguas europeas modernas. Esto es particularmente evidente en muchos números, como se puede comprobar en el pequeño listado de palabras que sigue:

Aśva: Caballo
Matṛ: Madre.
Jana: Gente.
Hṛd: Corazón.
Saptam: Siete
Navan: Nueve.
Catur: Cuatro.
Tri: Tres.

Otras palabras sánscritas pueden no verse reconocidas con facilidad en español, como corazón, pero sí en otras lenguas germánicas, como el inglés *(heart)*.

No explico aquí el significado de Adhīśvara āhvāyaka, ya que éste se desvela a lo largo de la novela y alguien puede estar leyendo este glosario antes o durante la lectura de la narración.

Lo que sí incluyo es el silabario kushana y ejemplos de algunas palabras sánscritas escritas con esos caracteres para que el lector visualice cómo era esa lengua. El silabario kushana se escribe, como en español y la mayoría de las lenguas occidentales, de izquierda a derecha.

SILABARIO KUSHANA					
a	ā	i	u	e	o
ㅋ	ㅋ	⊐	L	◁	𝟐
ka	kha	ga	gha		
╁	𝟚	�	৶		
ca	cha	ja	jha		
৶	♭	E	ᑭ		
ṭa	ṭha	ḍa	ḍha	ṇa	
⟨	o	⟨	𝟐ₒ	𝒳	
ta	tha	da	dha	na	
𝝠	O	⟨	◖	𝝠	
pa		ba	bha	ma	
𝟸		☐	�r⌐	𝗫	
ya	ra	la	va		
ϙ	❘	𝟸	◮		
śa	ṣa	sa	ha		
ॱ९	𝗬	₆	⊔		

Ejemplos de palabras sánscritas escritas en silabario kushana:

Aśva: ㅋ ९ ◮
Matṛ: 𝗫 𝝠 ❘ ⊐
Jana: E 𝝠
Dharmapada: ◖ ❘ 𝗫 𝟐 ⟨

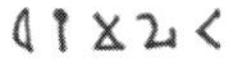

5

GLOSARIO DE CHINO CLÁSICO

La lengua china, como cualquier otro idioma, ha ido evolucionando. En la época de *La legión perdida* los personajes han de la novela, todos ellos altos funcionarios, ministros, militares de máximo rango y la familia imperial, emplean la variante conocida hoy día como 古文, *gǔwén*, es decir, chino clásico. De hecho, el término significa «texto antiguo». El chino clásico era la variante usada por las élites cultas de China desde aproximadamente el siglo V a.c. hasta el siglo II d.C., lo que coincide en gran medida con el dominio de las dinastías han del oeste y del este en China, que controlaron el gobierno desde el siglo III a.c. hasta principios del siglo III d.c.

A partir de la caída del Imperio han, el chino clásico desaparece en su uso oral, pero una variante muy similar permanece como chino literario y se seguirá empleando hasta bien entrado el siglo XX.

En su apogeo, el chino clásico llegó a ser utilizado no sólo en China, sino también en Corea, Japón o Vietnam, donde se lo conocía como «la lengua de los han».

Al igual que he hecho con el parto, la mayoría de las veces que aparece esta lengua en *La legión perdida* la he transcrito con caracteres del alfabeto latino, de modo que los lectores puedan, al menos, tener una idea de cómo sonaría cada término. Las formas de transcribir un vocablo —ya sea del chino clásico o incluso del moderno— a alfabeto latino son diversas y es frecuente que encontremos en fuentes distintas modos diferentes de transcribir un mismo término. A modo de ejemplo, la capital de la China moderna puede denominarse Pequín o Beijing.

Para la mayoría de los términos que aparecen en la novela he recurrido a su transcripción según *The Cambridge History of*

China (1978, volumen I). Ocasionalmente, en el glosario recojo otras transcripciones que se han hecho populares de algunos de los términos utilizados en la novela, aunque he seguido casi siempre la propuesta por los profesores Denis C. Twitchett y John F. Fairbank en el libro referido, que sigue siendo obra de culto entre los estudiosos de la China imperial.

Excepcionalmente he transcrito en caracteres de chino clásico (junto con su traducción al español) algunos párrafos, en particular cuando se hace mención a la relevancia de la caligrafía cuidadosa propia de esta variante idiomática. La ayuda de la profesora Li Joan Su, de Si Chuan Normal University, tal y como he comentado en los agradecimientos, ha sido esencial para asegurar que estos textos estén convenientemente transcritos y traducidos.

Para terminar, opté porque los nombres de los imperios, reinos y elementos geográficos de especial importancia en el relato fueran referidos por los personajes chinos precisamente en su lengua. Una de las constantes en mis novelas es, en la medida de lo posible, transmitir a quienes las leen los diferentes puntos de vista de cada personaje y ello conlleva la recreación, hasta cierto punto, de su forma de pensar, incluyendo, al menos de modo parcial, su lengua. Por eso el consejero Fa Chun, la emperatriz Deng en época de Trajano o el general Tang en época de Craso hablan de Da Qin cuando se refieren a Roma, de An-Shi cuando hablan de Partia o de Kangchú cuando se refieren a Sogdiana, etcétera.

An-shi: Partia o el Imperio parto.
Bu: Unidad de longitud que equivalía aproximadamente a 1,2 metros.
Chanyu: Jefe de todo su pueblo, normalmente referido al líder de los hunos al norte o al noroeste de la Gran Muralla.
Chiang-chün: General del ejército.
Chueh chang: Arquero especializado en el manejo de ballestas de enorme tamaño cuyo alcance era muy superior al de los arcos o ballestas convencionales. Normalmente eran guerreros de gran corpulencia y estatura, pues sólo los más fuertes podían cargar estas armas.
Dao: Espada o sable curvo de un solo filo elaborada con bronce al

principio, y de acero en la época del Imperio han. Constituía una de las cuatro armas básicas de las artes marciales, junto con la espada *jian* de doble filo, la lanza y el bastón. Se la considera precursora de la katana japonesa.

Da Qin: Roma o Imperio romano. En la novela lo he usado para referirme siempre a Roma, pero no está claro si con este término los chinos de la época han se referían al Imperio romano en su conjunto o la región de Oriente Próximo, concretamente Siria, que en aquel período ya estaba bajo la órbita de Roma. «Da» significaría «gran» y «Qin» hace referencia al primer emperador de China, con lo que se puede pensar que querían decir algo así como «gran imperio» o «gran emperador», añadiendo el matiz de que, quizá, desde la perspectiva China aquel gran imperio tenía origen en antepasados chinos. Como se ve, todos pensamos que somos el centro del mundo.

Dayuán: Antiguo reino de Fergana en Asia central que se corresponde con la parte suroriental del actual Uzbekistán. Era una región fértil, famosa por sus caballos y clave en la Ruta de la Seda.

Han Shu: Libro de la antigua dinastía han (del oeste) que narra los acontecimientos fundamentales de China desde finales del siglo III a.C. hasta principios del siglo I d.C. Fue compuesto por el historiador Fan Ye en torno al siglo V d.C.

Hou Han Shu: Libro de la dinastía han posterior o del este. Narra la continuación de la historia de China desde principios del siglo I d.C. hasta principios del siglo III d.C. Es atribuido al historiador chino Fan Ye, del siglo V d.C.

Houfeng didongyi: Forma en la que se denominaba al primer sismógrafo inventado por Zang Heng en la corte han; significa «instrumento para medir los vientos de las estaciones y los movimientos terrestres», aunque es más poética la traducción, usada ocasionalmente, de «la veleta de los temblores de tierra».

Hou-kuan: Compañía de un ejército del Imperio han.

Hsiao-wei: Coronel del ejército han.

Hsiung-nu o xiongnu: Los hunos que poblaban grandes regiones al norte y al noroeste de la Gran Muralla y principal motivo por el que los emperadores han reforzaron constantemente las fortificaciones defensivas de los límites septentrional y occidental de su imperio. Las conflictos bélicos fueron constantes entre los han y los hunos, siendo la guerra contra el líder huno Zhizhi uno de los enfrentamientos armados más importantes.

Jian: Espada de doble filo que en principio fue de bronce pero que en la época de *La legión perdida* ya se fabricaba de acero. Era un arma, normalmente, de mayor envergadura que el sable *dao;* las más largas debían blandirse con dos manos. Era mucho más mortífera, pero requería de mayor esgrima y, por tanto, más entrenamiento para resultar letal. También era mucho más cara, de modo que fue el arma propia de nobles, emperadores o militares de alto rango.

Kangchú: Denominación china del reino de Sogdiana, territorio de origen iranio aqueménida que se extendía al sur del mar Aral y el lago Balkash, en lo que hoy sería parte de Uzbekistán y Tayikistán, incluyendo ciudades legendarias como Samarkanda. Era una región clave en la Ruta de la Seda y paso obligado para las caravanas.

Li: Unidad de longitud que equivalía aproximadamente a 0,4 km. La equivalencia oscila según la época.

Pao chu: Pequeño pedazo de bambú fresco que se prendía sobre las tumbas o las cenizas de un antepasado para ahuyentar los malos espíritus.

Pu-Ku: Denominación china del lago Balkash.

Shang chiang-chün: General del ejército.

Shanyu: Ver chanyu.

Shendu: Denominación china de la antigua India.

Shou: Gobernador.

T'ai-tzu t'ai-fu: Tutor jefe.

Taixue: Academia imperial. Era el lugar donde se preparaba a los futuros funcionarios de más alto rango dentro de la estructura de gobierno del Imperio han. En ella se explicaban las enseñanzas de Confucio, literatura clásica china y otras disciplinas. Aunque en la entrada de la Wikipedia sobre la Taixue se dice que la incorporación al servicio funcionarial hasta el siglo x era más por recomendación que mediante méritos al superar un examen, ya en el siglo II d.C., el matemático y astrónomo Zhang Heng implantó un examen para disminuir las recomendaciones y la corrupción a la hora de acceder al funcionariado. Esto se hizo siempre con el apoyo de la emperatriz Deng, tal y como se ilustra en *La legión perdida.*

Tu-wei-fu: Regimientos militares.

Ying: División o regimiento militar de gran tamaño, parte de un ejército.

Yuegzhi o yuegzi: Denominación china de los kushan y su imperio, que se extendía por el norte de la actual India y amplias regiones de Afganistán.

Yu-shih chung-ch'eng: Un asistente personal del ministro de Obras Públicas. Era el encargado de gestionar las grandes obras públicas del Imperio han.

Wu-sun: Pueblo nómada de las estepas de Asia central que vivió entre el Imperio kushan, los hunos más al norte y el Imperio han al este. Con frecuencia estaba en conflicto con sus vecinos por cuestiones territoriales.

6

ÁRBOLES GENEALÓGICOS

Árbol genealógico de la dinastía Ulpio-Aelia o Antonina

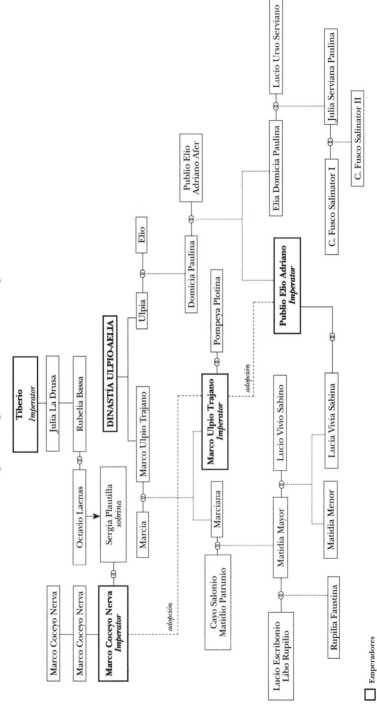

Árbol genealógico de la dinastía Arsácida parta (*)
(De 40 d.C. a 191 d.C.)

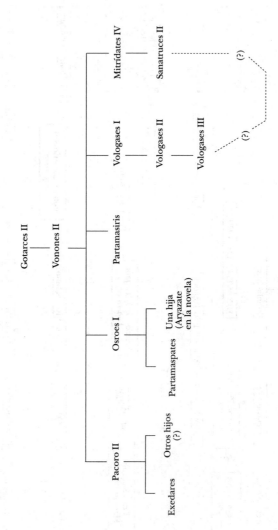

(*) La dinastía Arsácida parta era más numerosa. Presentamos una versión simplificada.

7

MAPAS

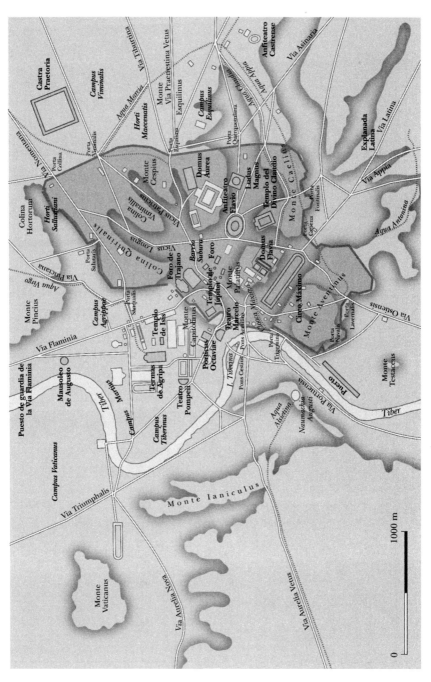

7.1. Plano de Roma a comienzos del siglo II d.C.

1117

7.2. Plano de Partia a comienzos del siglo II d.C.

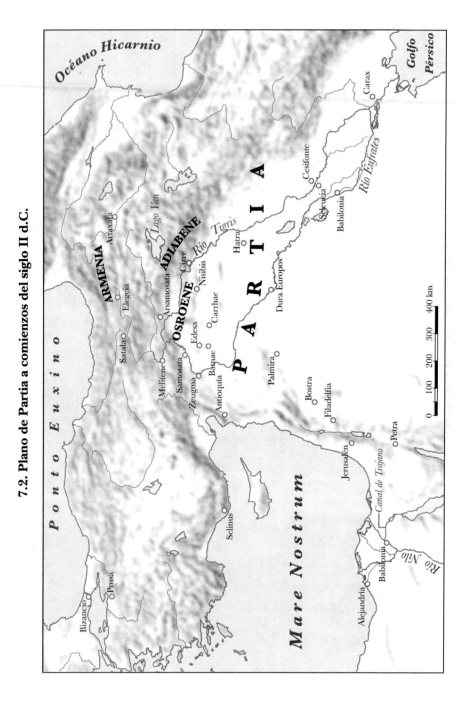

7.3. Batalla de Carrhae (fase I)

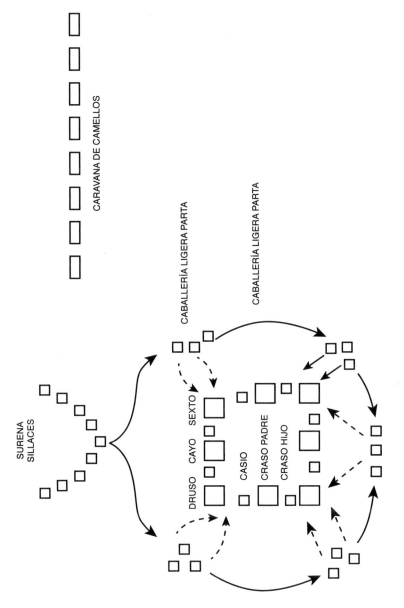

SURENA
SILLACES

CARAVANA DE CAMELLOS

CABALLERÍA LIGERA PARTA

CABALLERÍA LIGERA PARTA

DRUSO CAYO SEXTO

CASIO

CRASO PADRE

CRASO HIJO

7.4. Batalla de Carrhae (fase II)

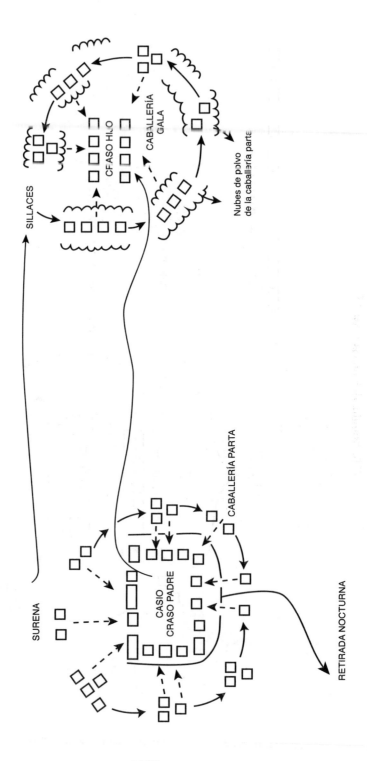

7.5. Batalla del Tigris (fase I)

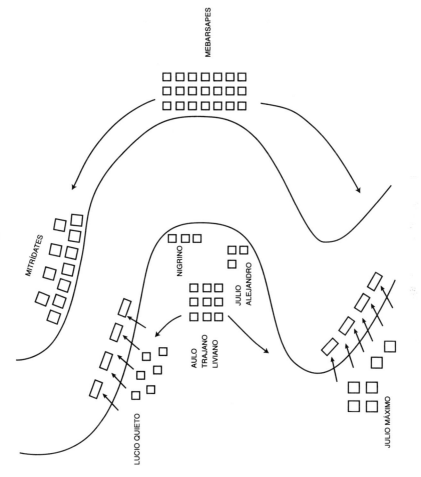

MEBARSAPES

MITRÍDATES

NIGRINO

JULIO ALEJANDRO

AULO TRAJANO LIVIANO

LUCIO QUIETO

JULIO MÁXIMO

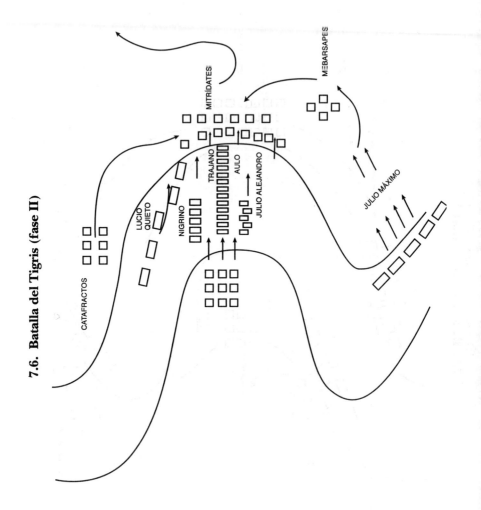

7.6. Batalla del Tigris (fase II)

CATAFRACTOS

LUCIO QUIETO

NIGRINO

TRAJANO

AULO

JULIO ALEJANDRO

MITRÍDATES

MEBARSAPES

JULIO MÁXIMO

7.7. Batalla de Kangchú (fase I)

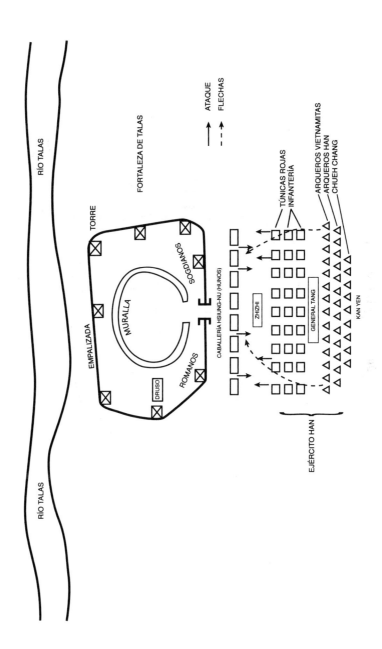

RÍO TALAS

RÍO TALAS

FORTALEZA DE TALAS

ATAQUE

FLECHAS

TORRE

EMPALIZADA

MURALLA

SOGDIANOS

DRUSO

ROMANOS

CABALLERÍA HSIUNG-NU (HUNOS)

TÚNICAS ROJAS
INFANTERÍA

ZHIZHI

GENERAL TANG

ARQUEROS VIETNAMITAS
ARQUEROS HAN
CHUEH CHANG

KAN YEN

EJÉRCITO HAN

1123

7.8. Batalla de Kangchú (fase II)

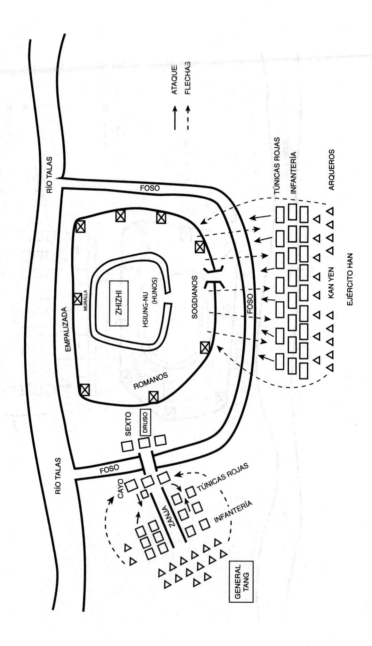

7.9. Batalla de Kangchú (fase III)

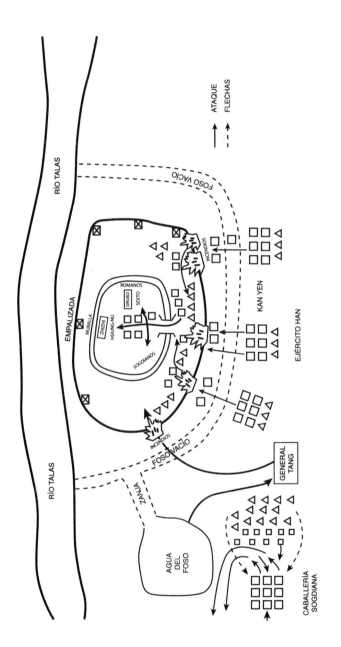

RÍO TALAS

RÍO TALAS

EMPALIZADA

FOSO VACÍO

MURALLA

ROMANOS

DRUSO

SEXTO

ZHIZHI

HSIUNG-NU

SOGDIANOS

INCENDIOS

KAN YEN

EJÉRCITO HAN

INCENDIOS

FOSO VACÍO

ZANJA

AGUA DEL FOSO

GENERAL TANG

CABALLERÍA SOGDIANA

ATAQUE

FLECHAS

8

ILUSTRACIONES DE DIFERENTES
GUERREROS Y LEGIONARIOS

A continuación se muestran diversas ilustraciones donde se pueden observar los uniformes, la indumentaria característica y el armamento de la caballería ligera parta y catafracta, de la caballería del Imperio han o de legionarios romanos.

Legionario romano del siglo II d. C.

Caballería romana de la guardia pretoriana del siglo II d. C.

Infantería del Imperio han.

Caballería del Imperio han.

Jinete de la caballería ligera parta y catafracto.

9

BIBLIOGRAFÍA

ADKINS, L. y ADKINS, R., *El Imperio romano: historia, cultura y arte*, Madrid, Edimat, 2005.

ALFARO, C., *El tejido en época romana*, Madrid, Arco Libros, 1997.

ALVAR, J. y BLÁZQUEZ, J. M. (eds.), *Trajano*, Madrid, Actas, 2003.

ÁLVAREZ MARTÍNEZ, J. M., et al., *Guía del Museo Nacional de Arte Romano*, Madrid, Ministerio de Cultura, 2008.

ANGELA, A., *Un día en la antigua Roma. Vida cotidiana, secretos y curiosidades*, Madrid, La Esfera de los Libros, 2009.

—, *The Reach of Rome: A Journey Through the Lands of the Ancient Empire Following a Coin*, Nueva York, Rizzoli ex libris, 2013.

ANGLIM, S.; JESTICE, P. G.; RICE, R. S.; RUSCH, S. M. y SERRATI, J., *Técnicas bélicas del mundo antiguo (3000 a.C.-500 d.C.). Equipamiento, técnicas y tácticas de combate*, Madrid, LIBSA, 2007.

ANÓNIMO, *The Voyage around the Erythraean Sea*, University of Washington, <https://depts.washington.edu/silkroad/texts/periplus/periplus.html>.

APIANO, *Historia de Roma I*, Madrid, Gredos, 1980.

ARKENBERG, J. S., *East Asian History Sourcebook: Chinese Accounts of Rome, Byzantium and the Midlle East, c. 91 B.C.E. - 1643 C.E.*, University of Washington, <http://depts.washington.edu/silkroad/texts/romchin1.html>.

ASIMOV, I., *El Cercano Oriente*, Madrid, Alianza Editorial, 2011.

BÁEZ, F., *Las maravillas perdidas del mundo: Breve historia de las grandes catástrofes de la civilización*, Océano, 2012.

BARREIRO RUBÍN, V., *La guerra en el mundo antiguo*, Madrid, Almena, 2004.

BASHAM, A. L., *El prodigio que fue la India*, Valencia, Pre-textos Índika, 2009.

BENNET, J., *Trajan. Optimus Princeps*, Bloomington e Indianápolis, Indiana University Press, 2001.

BIESTY, S., *Roma vista por dentro*, Barcelona, RBA, 2005.

BIRLEY, A., *Adriano: la biografía de un emperador que cambió el curso de la historia*, Madrid, Gredos, 2010.

BLÁZQUEZ, J. M., *Artesanado y comercio durante el Alto Imperio*, Madrid, Akal, 1990.

—, *Agricultura y minería romanas durante el Alto Imperio*, Madrid, Akal, 1991.

—, *Trajano*, Barcelona, Ariel, 2003.

—, *Adriano*, Barcelona, Ariel, 2008.

BOARDMAN, J.; GRIFFIN, J. y MURRIA, O., *The Oxford History of The Roman World*, Reading, Gran Bretaña, Oxford University Press, 2001.

BOWMAN, A. K., GARNSEY, P., y RATHBONE, D., *The Cambridge Ancient History, Second Edition, Volume XI: The High empire 70-192*, Cambridge, Cambridge University Press, 2008.

BRANCUS, G., *Cercetări asupra fondului tracodac al limbii române*, Bucarest, Editura Dacica, 2009.

BRAVO, G., *Historia de la Roma antigua*, Madrid, Alianza Editorial, 2001.

—, *Nueva historia de la España antigua*, Madrid, Alianza Editorial, 2011.

BROSIUS, M., «Women in pre-islamic Iran», *Encyclopaedia Iranica*, ed. de E. Yarshater <http://www.iranica.com/newsite/index.isc?>.

BURREL, G., *Historia universal comparada*, volumen II, Barcelona, Plaza & Janés, 1971.

BUSSAGLI, M., *Rome: Art and Architecture*, China, Ullmann Publishing, 2007.

BUSUIOCEANU, A., *Zalmoxis*, Bucarest, Editura Dacica, 2009.

CAMMANN, S. V., «Review of Homer H. Dubs, *A Roman City in Ancient China*», en *The Journal of Asian Studies*, vol. 21, nº. 3 (mayo 1962), págs. 380-382.

CAPO, S., *Trajan's Column*, Viterbo, Comosavona s.r.l., 2000.

CARRERAS MONFORT, C., «Aprovisionamiento del soldado romano en campaña: la figura del *praefectus vehiculorum*», en *Habis*, n.º 35, 2004.

CARY, M., «Maes, Qui et Titianus», *The Classical Quarterly*, New Series, 6.3/4 (julio-octubre 1956), págs. 130-134.

CASIO, D., *The Roman History: The Reign of Augustus*, Londres, Penguin, 1987.

CASSON, L., *Las bibliotecas del mundo antiguo*, Barcelona, Edicions Bellaterra, 2001.

CASTELLÓ, G., *Archienemigos de Roma*, Madrid, Book Sapiens, 2015.

CASTILLO, E., «Ostia, el principal puerto de Roma», en *Historia-National Geographic*, n.º 107.

CEINOS, P., *Historia breve de China*, Madrid, Sílex, 2006.

CHAURASIA, R. S., *History of Ancient India: Earliest Times to 1200 A.D.*, Delhi, Forward book Depot Educational Publishers, 1992.

CHIC GARCÍA, G., *El comercio y el Mediterráneo en la Antigüedad*, Madrid, Akal, 2009.

CLARKE, J. R., *Sexo en Roma. 100 a.C. 250 d.C.*, Barcelona, Océano, 2003.

CODOÑER, C. (ed.), *Historia de la literatura latina*, Madrid, Cátedra, 1997.

—, y FERNÁNDEZ CORTE, C., *Roma y su imperio*, Madrid, Anaya, 2004.

COMOTTI, G., *La música en la cultura griega y romana*, Madrid, Ediciones Turner, 1986.

CONNOLLY, P., *Tiberius Claudius Maximus: The Cavalry Man*, Oxford, Oxford University Press, 1988.

—, *Tiberius Claudius Maximus: The Legionary*, Oxford, Oxford University Press, 1988.

—, *Ancient Rome*, Oxford, Oxford University Press, 2001.

CORTÉS COPETE, J.M, «Trajano, el ultimo conquistador de Roma», en *Historia-National Geographic*, n.º 64.

CRAWFORD, M., *The Roman Republic*, Cambridge, Massachusetts, Harvard University Press, 1993.

DANDO-COLLINS, S., *Legiones de Roma: La historia definitiva de todas las legiones imperiales romanas*, Madrid, La Esfera de los Libros, 2012.

DOVAL, G., *Breve historia de la China milenaria*, Nowtilus, Madrid, 2010.

Dubs, H. H., «A Roman City in Ancient China», en *Greece and Rome*, Second Series, vol. 4, n.º 2 (octubre 1957), págs. 139-148.

—, «Respuesta a Cammann», en *The Journal of Asian Studies*, vol. 22, n.º 1 (noviembre 1962), págs. 135-136.

Dupuy, R. E.y and Dupuy, T. N., *The Harper Encyclopedia of Military History from 3500 B.C. to the Present*, Nueva York, Harper Collins Publishing, 1933.

Ebrey, P. B., *Historia de China*, Madrid, La Esfera de los Libros, 2009.

Embree, A. T. y Wilhelm, F., *India: Historia del subcontinente desde las culturas del Indo hasta el comienzo del dominio inglés*, Madrid, Siglo XXI de España Editores, 1967.

Enrique, C. y Segarra, M., *La civilización romana. Cuadernos de Estudio, 10. Serie Historia Universal*, Madrid, Editorial Cincel y Editorial Kapelusz, 1979.

Eliade, M. y Couliano, I. P., *Diccionario de las religiones*, Barcelona, Paidós, 2007.

Escarpa, A., *Historia de la ciencia y de la técnica: tecnología romana*, Madrid, Akal, 2000.

Espinós, J.; Masià, P.; Sánchez, D. y Vilar, M., *Así vivían los romanos*, Madrid, Anaya, 2003.

Espluga, X. y Miró i Vinaixa, M., *Vida religiosa en la antigua Roma*, Barcelona, Editorial UOC, 2003.

Fernández Algaba, M., *Vivir en Emérita Augusta*, Madrid, La Esfera de los Libros, 2009.

Fernández Vega, P. A., *La casa romana*, Madrid, Akal, 2003.

Fox, R. L., *El mundo clásico: La epopeya de Grecia y Roma*, Barcelona, Crítica, 2007.

Fundación CV y MARQ (eds.), *Señores del Cielo y de la Tierra: China en la dinastía han 206 a.C. - 220 d.C.*, Alcoy, Gráficas Alcoy, 2014.

Gallud Jardiel, E., *Historia breve de la India*, Madrid, Sílex, 2005.

Gallud Jardiel, E. (ed.), *Antología de literatura clásica de la India: Textos sánscritos*, Madrid, Miraguano SA Ediciones, 2000.

García Gual, C., *Historia, novela y tragedia*, Madrid, Alianza Editorial, 2006.

GARCÍA MENÉNDEZ, S. y GONZÁLES HUERTAS, J. R., *Historia de China: Día a día en la China milenaria*, Madrid, LIBSA, 2006.

GARDNER, J. F., *El pasado legendario. Mitos romanos*, Madrid, Akal, 2000.

GARGANTILLA, P., *Breve historia de la medicina: Del chamán a la gripe A*, Madrid, Nowtilus, 2011.

GARLAN, Y., *La guerra en la antigüedad*, Madrid, Aldebarán, 2003.

GASSET, C. (dir.), *El arte de comer en Roma: alimentos de hombres, manjares de dioses*, Mérida, Fundación de Estudios Romanos, 2004.

GIAVOTTO, C. (coord.), *Roma*, Barcelona, Electa Mondadori, 2006.

GOLDSWORTHY, A., *Grandes generales del ejército romano*, Barcelona, Ariel, 2003.

GOMÁ, D., «La Ruta de la Seda: El tráfico entre China y Roma», en *Historia y Vida*, n.º 481.

GÓMEZ PANTOJA, J., *Historia Antigua (Grecia y Roma)*, Barcelona, Ariel, 2003.

GONZÁLEZ BUENO, A., *Historia de la Ciencia y de la Técnica (Volumen 9): India y China*, Madrid, Akal, 1991.

GONZÁLEZ TASCÓN, I. (dir.), *Artifex: ingeniería romana en España*, Madrid, Ministerio de Cultura, 2002

GOODMAN, M., *The Roman World: 44BC-AD180*, Bristol, Routledge, 2009.

GRAETZ, H., *History of the Jews*, Philadelphia, Jewish Publication Society of America, 1891.

GRANT, M., *Atlas Akal de Historia Clásica del 1700 a.C. al 565 d.C.*, Madrid, Akal, 2009.

GRIMAL, P., *La vida en la Roma antigua*, Barcelona, Paidós, 1993.

—, *La civilización romana. Vida, costumbres, leyes, artes*, Barcelona, Paidós, 1999.

GUILLÉN, J., *Urbs Roma. Vida y costumbres de los romanos. I. La vida privada*, Salamanca, Ediciones Sígueme, 1994.

—, *Urbs Roma. Vida y costumbres de los romanos. II. La vida pública*, Salamanca, Ediciones Sígueme, 1994.

—, *Urbs Roma. Vida y costumbres de los romanos. III. Religión y ejército*, Salamanca, Ediciones Sígueme, 1994.

HACQUARD, G., *Guía de la Roma Antigua*, Madrid, Centro de Lingüística Aplicada ATENEA, 2003.

HADAS-LEBEL, M., *Flavio Josefo*, Herder, 1994.

HAMEY, L. A. y HAMEY, J. A., *Los ingenieros romunos*, Madrid, Akal, 2002.

HARMATTA, J., *Languages and Literature in the Kushan Empire*, UNESCO, 1996, <http://en.unesco.org/silkroad/sites/sil kroad/files/knowledge-bank-article/vol_II%20silk%20 road_languages%20and%20literature%20in%20the%20 kushan%20empire.pdf>.

HARRIS, R., *Pompeya*, Barcelona, Grijalbo, 2004.

HERRANZ MARTÍN, M., *Sabiduría china*, Madrid, Kailas Editorial S.L., 2012.

HERRERO LLORENTE, V. J., *Diccionario de expresiones y frases latinas*, Madrid, Gredos, 1992.

HITCHINS, K., *The Identity of Romania*, Bucarest, The Encyclopaedic Publishing House, 2009.

HUGLSTAD, A., *Alanya and Beyond: From Antalya to Anamur*, Alanya, Gunrzrapi, 2008.

Huβmann, S., «La guerra parta de Trajano», en *Desperta Ferro*, n.º 11.

JAMES, S., *Roma Antigua*, Madrid, Pearson Alhambra, 2004.

JOHNSTON, H. W., *The Private Life of the Romans*, <http://www.forumromanum.org/life/johnston.html>.

JUVENAL (ed. bilingüe de Rosario Cortés Tovar), *Sátiras*, Madrid, Cátedra, 2007.

KHEZRI, A. R., RODRÍGUEZ, J., BLÁZQUEZ, J. M. y ANTÓN, J. A., *Persia, cuna de civilización y cultura*, Madrid, Almuzara, 2011.

KNAPP, R. C., *Los olvidados de Roma: Prostitutas, forajidos, esclavos, gladiadores y gente corriente*, Barcelona, Ariel, 2011.

KÜNZL, E., *Ancient Rome*, Berlín, Tessloff Publishing, 1998.

LACEY, M. y DAVIDSON, S., *Gladiators*, China, Usborne, 2006.

LAGO, J. I. y GARCÍA PINTO, A., *Trajano: Las campañas de un emperador hispano*, Madrid, Almena, 2008.

LE BOHEC, Y., *El ejército romano*, Barcelona, Ariel, 2004.

LE GALL, J. y LE GLAY, M., *El Imperio romano: De Actium hasta la muerte de Severo Alejandro (31 a.C.-235 d.C.)*, Madrid, Akal, 1995.

LEONI, D., *Le monete di Roma - Trajano: Percorso storico-culturale svolto tra le immagini più significative delle monete battute durane il regno dei più importante imperatori romani*, Verona, Monete di Roma, 2009.

LEWIS, J. E. (ed.), *The Mammoth Book of Eyewitness. Ancient Rome: The History of the Rise and Fall of the Roman Empire in the words of Those Who Were There*, Nueva York, Carroll and Graf, 2006.

LIVIO, T., *Historia de Roma desde su fundación*, Madrid, Gredos, 1993.

LÓPEZ, A. y POCIÑA, A., *La comedia romana*, Madrid, Akal, 2007.

LUCIANO, D. y PRICHETT, G., «Criptology: From Caesar's Ciphers to PublicKey Cryptosystems», *The College Mathematics Journal*, vol. 18, 1: 217, enero de 1987.

MACDONALD, F., *100 Things You Should Know about Ancient Rome*, China, Miles Kelly Publishing, 2004.

MACAULAY, D., *City: A Story of Roman Planning and Construction*, Boston, Houghton Mifflin Company, 1974.

MALISSARD, A., *Los romanos y el agua: La cultura del agua en la Roma antigua*, Barcelona, Herder, 2001.

MANGAS, J., *Historia del mundo antiguo 48. Roma: Los julio-claudios y la crisis del 68*, Madrid, Akal, 1996.

—, *Historia del mundo antiguo 49. Roma: Los flavios*, Madrid, Akal, 1990.

—, *Historia del mundo antiguo 54. Roma: Agricultura y minería romanas durante el Alto Imperio*, Madrid, Akal, 1991.

—, *Historia del mundo antiguo 55. Roma: artesanado y comercio durante el Alto Imperio*, Madrid, Akal, 1990.

—, *Historia de España 3: De Aníbal al emperador Augusto. Hispania durante la República romana*, Madrid, Ediciones Temas de Hoy, 1995.

—, *Historia Universal. Edad Antigua. Roma*, Barcelona, Vicens Vives, 2004.

MANIX, D. P., *Breve historia de los gladiadores*, Madrid, Nowtilus, 2004.

MARCO SIMÓN, F., PINA POLO, F. y REMESAL RODRÍGUEZ, J. (eds), *Viajeros, peregrinos y aventureros en el mundo antiguo*, Barcelona, Publicacions i Edicions de la Universitat de Barcelona, 2010.

MARCHESI, M., *La novela sobre Roma*, Barcelona, Robinbook, 2009.

MARTÍN, R. F., *Los doce Césares: Del mito a la realidad*, Madrid, Aldebarán, 1998.

MATTESINI, S., *Gladiators*, Italia, Archeos, 2009.

MATYSZAK, P., *Los enemigos de Roma*, Madrid, OBERON Grupo Anaya, 2005.

—, *Legionario: El manual del legionario romano (no oficial)*, Madrid, Akal, 2010.

—, *La antigua Roma por cinco denarios al día*, Madrid, Akal, 2012.

MAUREEN, C., *Earthly Paradises: Ancient Gardens in History and Archaeology*, Londres, British Museum, 2003

MCKEOWN, J. C., *Gabinete de curiosidades romanas*, Barcelona, Crítica, 2011.

MELANI, Ch.; FONTANELLA, F. y CECCONI, G. A., *Atlas ilustrado de la Antigua Roma: De los orígenes a la caída del Imperio*, Madrid, Susaeta, 2005.

MENA SEGARRA, C. E., *La civilización romana*, Madrid, Cincel Kapelusz, 1982.

MENÉNDEZ ARGÜÍN, A. R., *Pretorianos: la guardia imperial de la antigua Roma*, Madrid, Almena, 2006.

MIELCZAREK, M., *Cataphracti and Clibanarii: Studies on the Heavy Armoured Calvalry of the Ancient World*, Polonia, Oficyna Naukowa, 1993.

MONTANELLI, I., *Historia de Roma*, Barcelona, De Bolsillo, 2002.

MOSTERÍN, J., *China: Historia del pensamiento*, Madrid, Alianza Editorial, 2007.

NANCARROW, P., *La antigua China y la Gran Muralla*, Madrid, Akal/Cambridge, 1990.

NAVARRO, F. (ed.), *Historia Universal. Atlas Histórico*, Madrid, Salvat El País, 2005.

NIETO, J., *Historia de Roma: Día a día en la Roma antigua*, Madrid, Libsa, 2006.

NOGALES BASARRATE, T., *Espectáculos en Augusta Emérita*, Badajoz, Ministerio de Educación, Cultura y Deporte Museo Romano de Mérida, 2000.

NOSSOV, K., *Gladiadores: El espectáculo más sanguinario de Roma*, Madrid, Libsa, 2011.

OLCINA DOMÉNECH, M. y PÉREZ JIMÉNEZ, R., *La ciudad ibero romana de Lucentum*, Alicante, MARQ y Diputación de Alicante, 2001.

PAPADOPOL-CALIMAH, A., *Scrieri vechi pierdute atingătoare de Dacia*, Bucarest, Editura Dacica, 2007.

PAYNE, R., *Ancient Rome*, Nueva York, Horizon, 2005.

PEERS, C., *Battles of Ancient China*, Barnsley, Pen and Sword Military, 2013.

PEER, J. C., *Imperial Chinese Armies (1): 200 BC - AD 589*, Oxford, Osprey, 2008.

PÉREZ MÍNGUEZ, R., *Los trabajos y los días de un ciudadano romano*, Valencia, Diputación provincial, 2008.

PERNOT, F., *La Ruta de la Seda: Desde Asia hasta Europa tras la huella de aventureros y comerciantes*, Bath, Parragon Books Ltd., 2001.

PIÑERO, A., *Guía para entender el Nuevo Testamento*, Madrid, Editorial Trotta, 2008.

PISA SÁNCHEZ, J., *Breve historia de Hispania*, Madrid, Nowtilus, 2009.

PITILLAS, E., *Los judíos de época romana, ss. I-II d.C.: análisis histórico de un contexto de enfrentamientos y tensiones*, Zaragoza, Libros Pórticos, 2010.

PLINIO EL JOVEN, *Epistolario (libros IX). Panegírico del emperador Trajano*, Madrid, Cátedra, 2007.

POLIBIO, *The Rise of the Roman Empire*, Londres, Penguin, 1979.

POMEROY, S., *Diosas, rameras, esposas y esclavas: Mujeres en la antigüedad clásica*, Madrid, Akal, 1999.

POSADAS, J. L., *Año 69: El año de los cuatro emperadores*, Madrid, Laberinto, 2009.

—, *Los emperadores romanos y el sexo*, Madrid, Sílex, 2011.

—, «Trajano, el emperador hispano», en *Historia-National Geographic*, n.º 81.

POTTER, D., *Emperors of Rome: The Story of Imperial Rome from Julius Caesar to the Last Emperor*, Londres, Quercus, 2011.

POTTER, L. G. (ed.), *The Persian Gulf in History*, Nueva York, Palgrave Macmillan, 2009.

QUESADA SANZ, F., *Armas de Grecia y Roma*, Madrid, La Esfera de los Libros, 2008.

RANKOV, B. y HOOK, R., *La guardia pretoriana*, Barcelona, RBA/ Osprey Publishing, 2009.

RAPSON, E. J. (eds.), *The Cambridge History of India, Volume I: Ancient India*, Cambridge, Cambridge University Press, 1922.

RAWDING, F. W., *Buda*, Madrid, Akal-Cambridge, 1991.

REU, D., *Pietrele dacilor socotesc / The Dacian Stones Can Count*, Bucarest, Editura Biblioteca Bucurestilor, 2011.

RODRÍGUEZ GUTIÉRREZ, O., *Hispania Arqueológica: Panorama de la cultura material de las provincias hispanorromanas*, Sevilla, Universidad de Sevilla-Secretariado de Publicaciones, 2011.

ROLDÁN, J. M., *El ejército de la república romana*, Madrid, Arco, 1996.

—, *Historia de la humanidad 10: Roma republicana*, Madrid, Arlanza ediciones, 2000.

ROSTOVTZEFF, M., *Historia social y económica del mundo helenístico, volumen I*, Madrid, Espasa Calpe, 1967.

—, *Historia social y económica del mundo helenístico*, vol. II, Madrid, Espasa Calpe, 1967.

SÁNCHEZ-HERNÁNDEZ, J. P., «Las dos caras del emperador Adriano», en *Historia-National Geographic*, n.º 75.

SANTOS YANGUAS, N., *Textos para la historia antigua de Roma*, Madrid, Cátedra, 1980.

SAQUETE, C., *Las vírgenes vestales. Un sacerdocio femenino en la religión pública romana*, Madrid, Consejo Superior de Investigaciones Científicas, 2000.

SCARBE, C., *Chronicle of the Roman Emperors*, Londres, Thames & Hudson, 2001.

SCARRE, C., *The Penguin Historical Atlas of Ancient Rome*, Londres, Penguin, 1995.

SCHEIDEL, W. (ed.), *Rome and China: Comparative Perspectives on Ancient World Empires*, Oxford, Oxford University Press, 2009.

SCHIROKAUER, C. y BROWN, M., *Breve historia de la civilización china*, Barcelona, Ediciones Bellaterra, 2006.

SEGURA MURGUÍA, S., *El teatro en Grecia y Roma*, Bilbao, Zidor Consulting, 2001.

SHAUGHNESSY, E., *La antigua China: Vida, mitología y arte*, Madrid, Ediciones Jaguar, 2005.

SKALMOWSKI, W. y VAN TONGERLOO, A., *Medioiranica: Proceedings of the International Colloquium Organized by the Katholieke Universiteit*, Leuven, Peeters Publishers, 1993.

SMITH, W., *A Dictionary of Greek and Roman Antiquities*, John Murray, London, 1875. También en: <http://penelope. uchicago.edu/Thayer/E/Roman/Texts/secondary/SMI GRA*/Flamen.html>.

SORA, S., *Fortarete dacice din muntii Orastiei*, Segovia, Artec Impresiones, 2009.

SPRAGUE, M., *Chinese Swords: The Evolution and Use of the Jian and Dao*, Amazon, Marston Gate, 2013.

SUETONIO, *La vida de los doce Césares*, Madrid, Austral, 2007.

TÁCITO, C., *Vida de Julio Agrícola. Diálogo de los oradores*, Madrid, Akal, 1999.

—, *Historias*, Madrid, Cátedra, 2006.

—, *Germania*, Buenos Aires, Losada, 2007.

TENTEA, O., *The Museum of Dacian and Roman Civilisation Deva*, Deva, The Centre for Roman Military Studies, Qual Media, 2009.

The Office of Chinese Language Council International y The Overseas Chinese Office of the State Council, *Conocimientos comunes de la historia china*, China, Sinolingua/China Photo Press, 2006.

THUBRON, C., *La sombra de la Ruta de la Seda*, Barcelona, Ediciones Península, 2006.

TONER, J., *Sesenta millones de romanos*, Barcelona, Crítica, 2012.

TURBULL, S., *The Great Wall of China 221 BC - Ad 1644*, Oxford, Osprey, 2007.

—, *Chinese Walled Cities 221 BC - Ad 1644*, Oxford, Osprey, 2009.

TWITCHETT, D. y FAIRBANK, J. K. (eds.), *The Cambridge History of China*, Cambridge Histories Online/Cambridge University Press, 2008.

TZU, S., *El arte de la guerra*, Madrid, Ediciones Martínez Roca, 1999.

—, *El arte de la guerra (edición bilingüe: chino-español)*, Madrid, Tikal Ediciones.

VALENTÍ FIOL, E., *Sintaxis latina*, Barcelona, Bosch, 1984.

VIDAL, G., Creation, Gran Bretaña, Abacus, 2011.

VILLAR GUAJARDO, R. I., *Los getodacios: homenaje al pueblo romano*, México, Senado de la República, 2004.

VV AA, *La Sagrada Biblia*, Madrid, Gaspar y Roig, editores, 1854.

VV. AA., *La Biblia interconfesional. Nuevo Testamento*, Madrid, Bac-Edicabi-Sbu, 1978.

VV. AA., «*El Imperio romano de Trajano a Marco Aurelio*» en *Desperta Ferro*, n.º 11.

VV. AA., «Historia de la prostitución» en Correas, S. (dir.), *Memoria de la Historia de cerca*, IX, 2006.

VV. AA., *Historia Augusta*, Madrid, Akal, 1989.

VV. AA., *The Museum of the Imperial Forums in Trajan's Market*, Milán, Mondadori Electa, 2013.

VV. AA., *Historia año por año: La guía visual definitiva de los hechos históricos que han conformado el mundo*, Madrid, Akal, 2012.

VV. AA., *Historia de los grandes imperios: El desarrollo de las civilizaciones de la antigüedad*, Madrid, Libsa, 2012.

WILKES, J., *El ejército romano*, Madrid, Akal, 2000.

WISDOM, S. y MCBRIDE, A., *Los gladiadores*, Madrid, RBA/Osprey Publishing, 2009.

WRIGHT, C. y Brainerd, J. A., *Historic Incidents and Life in India*, Chicago, Brainerd, 1866.

YIPING, Z., *The Opening of the Silk Road*, China, China Intercontinental Press, 2010.

YOSHIDA, Y., «Sogdian Personal Names in Chinese Sources», en *Enciclopedia Iránica*, Agosto, 2006.

YULE, H., *Cathay and the Way Thither*, Hakult Society, Londres (primera edición: 1866), 1915.

YUANXIANG, X., *Confucio: Un filósofo para la eternidad*, China, Chinese Intercontinental Press, 2010.

ÍNDICE

HISTORIA DE LA LEGIÓN PERDIDA
Tiempos de Julio César, Pompeyo y Craso, mediados del siglo I a.C.
LIBRO I

HISTORIA DE TRAJANO
Principios del siglo II d.C.
LIBRO I
Misiones secretas

HISTORIA DE LA LEGIÓN PERDIDA
Tiempos de Julio César, Pompeyo y Craso,
mediados del siglo I a.C.
LIBRO II

HISTORIA DE TRAJANO
Principios del siglo II d.C.
LIBRO II
Casus belli

HISTORIA DE LA LEGIÓN PERDIDA
Tiempos de Julio César, Pompeyo y Craso,
mediados del siglo I a.C.
LIBRO III

HISTORIA DE TRAJANO
Principios del siglo II d.C.
LIBRO III
Armenia

HISTORIA DE LA LEGIÓN PERDIDA
Tiempos de Julio César, Pompeyo y Craso,
mediados del siglo I a.C.
LIBRO IV

HISTORIA DE TRAJANO
Principios del siglo II d.C.
LIBRO IV
Mesopotamia

HISTORIA DE LA LEGIÓN PERDIDA
Tiempos de Julio César, Pompeyo y Craso,
mediados del siglo I a.C
LIBRO V

HISTORIA DE TRAJANO
Principios del siglo II d.C.
LIBRO V
La cólera de los dioses

HISTORIA DE TRAJANO
Principios del siglo II d.C.
LIBRO VII
La rebelión

HISTORIA DE LA LEGIÓN PERDIDA
Tiempos de Julio César, Pompeyo y Craso,
mediados del siglo I a.C.
LIBRO VIII

HISTORIA DE TRAJANO
Principios del siglo II d.C.
LIBRO VIII
El final de un sueño